ANNUAL REVIEW OF PSYCHOLOGY

ANNUAL REVIEW OF PSYCHOLOGY

MARK R. ROSENZWEIG, *Editor*
University of California, Berkeley

LYMAN W. PORTER, *Editor*
University of California, Irvine

VOLUME 26

1975

ANNUAL REVIEWS INC.   4139 EL CAMINO WAY   PALO ALTO, CALIFORNIA 94306

ANNUAL REVIEWS INC.
Palo Alto, California, USA

International Standard Book Number: 0–8243–0226–5
Library of Congress Catalog Card Number: 50–13143

Annual Reviews Inc. and the Editors of its
publications assume no responsibility for the
statements expressed by the contributors to this Review.

REPRINTS

The conspicuous number aligned in the margin with the title of each article in this
volume is a key for use in ordering reprints. Available reprints are priced at the
uniform rate of $1 each postpaid. Effective January 1, 1975, the minimum accep-
table reprint order is 10 reprints and/or $10.00, prepaid. A quantity discount is
available.

PRINTED AND BOUND IN THE UNITED STATES OF AMERICA

ANNUAL REVIEWS INC. is a nonprofit corporation established to promote the advancement of the sciences. Beginning in 1932 with the *Annual Review of Biochemistry*, the Company has pursued as its principal function the publication of high quality, reasonably priced Annual Review volumes. The volumes are organized by Editors and Editorial Committees who invite qualified authors to contribute critical articles reviewing significant developments within each major discipline.

Annual Reviews Inc. is administered by a Board of Directors whose members serve without compensation.

Annual Reviews are published in the following sciences: Anthropology, Astronomy and Astrophysics, Biochemistry, Biophysics and Bioengineering, Earth and Planetary Sciences, Ecology and Systematics, Entomology, Fluid Mechanics, Genetics, Materials Science, Medicine, Microbiology, Nuclear Science, Pharmacology, Physical Chemistry, Physiology, Phytopathology, Plant Physiology, Psychology, and Sociology (to begin publication in 1975). In addition, two special volumes have been published by Annual Reviews Inc.: *History of Entomology* (1973) and *The Excitement and Fascination of Science* (1965).

PREFACE

Chapters 1 and 3 of this volume represent an innovation. They review topics not on the Master Plan but of much current interest. They were also prepared more speedily than the other chapters so that they could reflect the most recent developments. We intend to include such special chapters in the forthcoming volumes and will welcome reactions to the chapters and to this policy.

The Master Plan serves as a guide but not as a rigid prescription for the allocation of subjects in the successive volumes. Furthermore the Plan is subject to review and modification at each of the annual meetings of the Editorial Committee. The current form of the Plan is given below, and comparison with the version in Volume 22, 1971, will show a number of important changes, both in the listing of topics and in the recommended frequencies of their occurrence.

Authors are asked to review selectively within the area assigned. They are not expected to review a whole domain but to choose the most significant and important developments within that domain. Nor are they required to restrict their treatment to work of the last few years. In some cases, as will be seen in this present volume, authors select a specialized subsection of the topic for intensive review. Each volume thus emphasizes some topics while slighting others, but over a span of a few years the selection of topics and of authors is intended to give a rounded portrayal of current developments of psychological research and theory. The Editorial Committee sees its main task as nominating highly qualified authors who are then given wide discretion, but limited space, for the preparation of their reviews.

Paul Mussen, as outgoing editor, shared the editorial duties of Volume 25 (1974); because of an error his name was not listed as an editor in that volume. It is a pleasure to have collaborated with Paul Mussen in the preparation of Volumes 20–25 and to be sharing these duties now with Lyman Porter.

M. R. R.

MASTER PLAN

* The numbers represent the intervals in years between successive chapters. The Xs indicate only occasional appearance.

CHAPTERS PLANNED FOR NEXT
ANNUAL REVIEW OF PSYCHOLOGY
VOLUME 27 (1976)

CONTENTS

THE PSYCHOLOGY OF WOMEN—SELECTED TOPICS

Martha T. Shuch Mednick[1]
Department of Psychology, Howard University, Washington, D.C. 20001
and Hilda J. Weissman
Washington School of Psychiatry, Washington, D.C. 20009

It is fitting that the first article on this topic in the *Annual Review of Psychology* be written in the inaugural year of the APA Division on the Psychology of Women. The Division has defined itself as dedicated to research on women; a charter membership of more than 800 must be viewed as one measure of current interest in this field. It is in practical terms too soon to look at the effect of the Division; we hope that the reviews that follow this mini-survey will reflect its catalyzing function and provide a more comprehensive view of the field than is now possible. The study of many aspects of the female experience is accelerating, and the problem areas and questions raised touch on every substantive, methodological, and practical domain of psychology.

This is a report on recent work in selected areas. It is limited by space, by the frank biases of the authors, and by topical popularity. We will turn first to the psychological study of sex roles, fundamental to most research concerning women. The second topic concerns a new look at achievement motivation in women. While some segments of society are rejecting the achievement ethic, there is a growth of interest in patterns and determinants of women's school performance and career development (4, 43, 54, 114, 134). The third topic concerns the impact of feminist thought and knowledge about female sexuality on the theories and practice of psychotherapy. The common thread throughout is a questioning of age-old assumptions about sex roles and sex identity.

There is and continues to be a great emphasis on spelling out differences in

[1] Weissman is responsible for the section on therapy and Mednick is responsible for choice of topics and the remainder of the review. The authors wish to express appreciation to Saundra R. Murray for her generous contribution of time, effort, and ideas, and to Leona W. Levine for editorial and other assistance in the preparation of the manuscript.

The literature survey is current, stressing 1972 and 1973; however, selected works published earlier than 1972 are mentioned, as are several appearing in early 1974 or still in press.

abilities and personality traits and their biosocial bases (123). Older and newer works set in the frame of infant and childhood development have provided us with cogent reviews and thorough analyses (80, 81, 124). The controversies are not resolved but they have been well defined, and certainly this will continue to be a "hot topic" generating emotion and political action as well as research. This is not the main concern of this review; the focus is on women more than girls and on intragroup variations and individuality more than on sex differences. Sex comparisons cannot be and are not ignored—in fact, we may in the end realize that understanding women has led us to a clearer understanding of men and of people in general (22).

Two recent texts on the psychology of women (6, 123) emphasized the biological approach as well as early socialization. The text by Sherman is a well-reasoned, analytical look at the empirical findings about females. More questions are asked than answered—an accurate reflection of the state of the art. Bardwick's text is personal, presenting a biosocial theory of feminine development whose basis has been questioned[2] (33). Bardwick has edited a book of readings (7) which also stresses biology and early socialization (10). Other collections have taken a social-psychological approach (89, 90, 138). A comprehensive annotated bibliography of the interdisciplinary as well as international literature on sex roles is available (3).

PSYCHOLOGICAL STUDY OF SEX ROLES

Research and writing about sex roles have moved from description and an acceptance of the givens (120) to a concern with the dynamics and implications of change (59, 60, 63, 76, 87). Compelling questions about the nature and mutability of social institutions such as marriage, the family, and even motherhood and fatherhood have been raised (14, 15, 56, 59, 116). Holter (60) presents an analysis of how social structures perpetuate even nonfunctional sex role distinctions, and spells out the requirements and consequences of role change. She is fully cognizant of the psychological factors which help maintain the status quo, such as the power of entrenched attitudes and behaviors and immutable self concepts. Similar points have been raised by Bem & Bem (13) in a social-psychological analysis of the influence and pervasiveness of sex role ideology. The implication of role change for men (135) and generally held conceptions of masculinity has received some attention (102), but little empirical work has appeared.

Sex role variation has been studied in numerous societies (16, 18, 50, 61, 87, 113, 116, 120). The comparisons help clarify the possibilities of change, but causal generalizations are problematic. It does seem clear that even in societies with conscious women's emancipation ideologies, role change is superficial (59, 88). Major social factors such as variation in birth rates, sex ratios, technological changes, economic conditions, and national crises (75) may be more potent (even

---

[2] See also review by E. E. Maccoby (1972) on The Meaning of Being Female in *Contemp. Psychol.* 17:369–72.

if temporary) effectors than ideology or legislation, and these must be included in any study of role variation over time and across cultures.

Sex Role Identity

Discussions of sex or gender identity emphasize models of early socialization and their implications for later personality functioning and malfunctioning (e.g. 65, 68, 93). Although critical of the content of Freudian thinking about the development of the feminine personality, Bardwick (6) adheres to classic psychodynamic assumptions regarding the significance of biology and early experience. Such assumptions (unleavened by considerations of environmental challenge) lead to pessimistic conclusions about the possibilities of sex role change, and their validity is being questioned.

Challenge is also directed at the definitions and measures of many overlapping sex role concepts. Indeed major integrative problems stem from the vagueness of the constructs and capricious variation in measurement. For instance, Constantinople (26) addressed part of this problem in a thorough review of the literature on masculinity-femininity (MF). She noted the definitional ambiguity which was not resolved by the operational recourse to "items which separate men from women." Major measures of MF confuse or merge the concepts of sex role identity, sex role preferences, and sex role adoption. Indeed MF measures are also called measures of sex-typing (17) and sex role standards (35, 130). Constantinople concludes that most MF instruments are multidimensional, including various affective and cognitive components, and moreover rejects the assumption that MF is a bipolar trait. Thus evidence suggests that masculinity and femininity are not opposites; each should be conceptualized and measured independently. This is consonant with Carlson's (22) view that characteristics viewed as masculine and those regarded as feminine may co-exist and interact. Helson's (e.g. 55) studies of the creative personality focus on such a conception and indicate that effective creative functioning in men and women may be best understood in these terms.

Other recent research is also addressed to the bipolarity controversy. J. H. Block (16, 17) presents a model of sex role conceptions and provides evidence, based on cross-national and longitudinal data, that the most effective functioning is a product of the incorporation of positive aspects of both the masculine and feminine sex roles. However, she found that the socialization process enhances this trait co-existence for men but not for women. Thus, "For males, socialization tends to enhance experiential options and to encourage more androgynous sex role definitions . . . for women the socialization process tends to reinforce the nurturant, docile submission and conservative aspects of . . . the role . . . discourage self assertiveness, achievement orientation and independence" (16, p. 525).

Similar results are reported by Spence and her colleagues (130), who found that for men and women the endorsement of both highly valued masculine traits and feminine traits correlated positively with ratings of self esteem. S. L. Bem (11, 12), who like Spence et al (129) is engaged in the development of a new instrument, found that androgynous individuals are more likely to behave adaptively, i.e. do what the situation rather than a rigid sex-role self-concept demands. She also noted a "behavioral deficit" in the most feminine females. That the female role is related to indicators of stress, conflict, and incompetence has been demonstrated in several other recent studies (48, 66, 105, 109, 147). It seems quite safe to predict that the *Zeitgeist* will combine with the stimulating force of new techniques and alternative theories to generate further empirical work on the redefinition and refinement of these concepts.

Stereotypes

An extensive series of studies conducted by Broverman and her colleagues has become standard reference in the research and in popular feminist literature. This work has even been referred to and inserted in hearings on sex discrimination before the Congress of the United States. In a review (20) of their own work, these investigators concluded that stereotypic thinking about sex role related personality traits is pervasive. Furthermore, a greater number of desirable traits are assigned to men than to women, the valued traits for men forming a competence cluster, while those for women form a warmth-expressiveness cluster.

Stereotypic thinking and adherence to traditional role expectations does appear to be pervasive. It is found in school settings (5, 36, 78, 79, 101, 115), in children's literature (143), in U.S. as well as Israeli communes (88, 92, 148), in widely used text books (8),[3] in the mass media (107), and in language styles (141). The occupational world is sex-typed (70, 100, 125); specific job-sex patterns vary across cultures, but prestige and economic value is always higher for those which are male occupied (59, 88, 116). Occupational prestige levels change when the other sex moves in; this has been recently verified in a laboratory setting (137). The perceptions of required and personal job characteristics or requirements also reflect sex role assumptions (119).

There is some work suggesting that stereotypic sex role attitudes held about others or the self are significant moderators or determinants of various classes of behaviors. These include occupational choice (72, 75), attraction (121), activism (118), and achievement (2, 77, 101, 136; also see section on achievement). Several studies indicate that sex role considerations may account for variations in helping behavior and that the nature of the situation interacts with biological sex and sex role in the elicitation of help. Men and women helpers are equally affected (47, 52, 139).

Ellis & Bentler (35) report that women but not men who perceive extreme sex differences endorse traditional role standards. Additionally, women who scored high on a measure of status seeking regarded themselves as nontraditional—that is, different from women in general. It is also of interest that women like women depicted in masculine but not feminine role activities, even when they are incompetent. This is most true for women with pro-feminist attitudes. Men on the

---

[3] A report on sex bias in psychology textbooks is available from the American Psychological Association, Office of Educational Affairs (unpublished manuscript, J. Birk et al).

other hand did not show this "pro-masculine bias" (128) and liked competent women regardless of the role enacted.

Women's views of men's opinions affect their behavior (53, 62), but there is some evidence that men don't think what women think they think (132). With regard to opposite sex attraction, women were attracted to "masculine" males, while men were equally attracted to "masculine" and "feminine" females (121). Males' response to women depicted in roles varying in degree of "liberatedness" was examined in a study by Dufresne (32). Liberated women aren't "liked," but they are assigned higher status jobs than the neutrally regarded traditionals. Equalitarian women fare the best; they are liked and given high status assignments. Studies of this type should be repeated with different role incumbents, since the actor's personal characteristics may influence judgments. Another question concerns the subject populations . . . will men (or women) actually doing the hiring respond as college sophomores do? Also critical is a look at the extent to which attitudinal statements and judgments about videotaped or otherwise simulated role incumbents relate to behavior. Such research is needed before we can conclude that women are totally misguided in their beliefs about "What Men Want." Finally, questions about the reactions of women to variations in male role behavior as well as *men's* concerns about what women think have yet to be explored.

ACHIEVEMENT TENDENCIES IN WOMEN— IS THERE A NEW LOOK?

In their article on personality in the 1971 *Annual Review of Psychology*, Sarason & Smith singled out the area of achievement motivation as one which has been based almost exclusively on the study of men. This practice was accurately attributed to the conclusion by McClelland and his colleagues that women need approval and men need success. It should be added that neither McClelland nor Atkinson nor their offspring chose to identify their work as the psychology of male achievement motivation. The message was left between the lines. Sarason & Smith noted, "In view of evolving changes in cultural conceptions of female roles and aspirations, greater contemporary research on achievement motivation in women seems warranted" (118a, p. 409). The view from early 1974 indicates that this is happening; the following reviews a portion of recent work.

Two review papers framed in different theoretical contexts focus on the affiliation-achievement conflict. Hoffman (57) asserts that females are inadequately socialized for independence and thus do not develop adequate mastery skills. She argues, too, that female achievement behavior is motivated by a drive to please rather than to succeed and that success and affiliation are in reality often incompatible. A specific prescription for mastery training for girls is suggested. However, Stein & Bailey (131) conclude that girls and women are achievement oriented but learn to value sex role appropriate social skills. The basis for learning is the same for boys and girls: social reinforcement, i.e. response to approval. They reject the hypothesis that the males and females are different in level of affiliative need, basing much of their argument on evidence that boys and girls are not differentially responsive to social approval or disapproval in a variety of social learning experiments. Stein & Bailey and Hoffman agree that certain kinds of achievement behaviors are incompatible with the typical feminine sex role training pattern, and that independence and mastery training must be facilitated (also 124).

Fear of Success

The fear of success (FOS)[4] was postulated by Horner (62) within the framework of Atkinson's expectancy-value theory to account for sex differences in achievement behavior. She developed a fantasy measure of the motive that accounted for performance decrements by high ability women in mixed-sex competitive achievement settings. The idea was that women were motivated to achieve but that fear is aroused by the anticipation of negative consequences of success. It is not a wish or need to fail. The latter concept, which one writer does introduce[5] and at least one study purported to examine (85), would imply an expectation of *positive* consequences from failure in achievement situations.

Recent studies of FOS have looked at variations in incidence of imagery and have generally attempted to explore the validity of the concept. Although Horner noted an increase in FOS in women from 1965 to 1971, others report lowered incidence or diminished sex differences for a variety of settings and age groups (21, 37, 58, 104, 112, 140). That social factors affect degree of FOS imagery is suggested by several studies of black women (87, 106, 145). Hoffman found no sex differences, but women did show as much FOS in 1971 as in 1965. Thematic analysis suggested that college women are as fearful as ever but that college men now seem to be downgrading success (58). A study of students in the fifth through eleventh grades reported similar thematic differences (21). On the other hand, Ward & Mausner (140) found that their high school students told few affiliative rejection stories. Monahan et al (94) found high FOS in women, but *both* men and women told FOS stories for successful women but not for men. They suggest that this supports a learned social role rather than motivational explanation for the concept. Horner and others (21, 58, 112) have attributed variations in both male and female imagery to sex differences in scoring, the changed social climate, subject characteristics, and stimulus properties. To date, however, the results are such that none of the explanations are consistently supported.

Other investigations have attempted to verify predictions about the effects of variations in FOS. The hypothesis that opposite sex competition leads to a performance decrement for women is supported by several studies (62, 86, 104, 144)

---

[4] Margaret Mead referred to women's fears of success in *Male and Female*, published in 1949. Klinger postulated the same concept in another context (69).

[5] J. E. Albino (unpublished manuscript, 1974) makes the provocative suggestion that this is analogous to the Freudian concept of feminine masochism, but also notes the absence of evidence for such a motive.

but not by others (21, 27, 127, 140). Sex role traditionality was found to moderate the expected relationship of FOS and performance (104) and was the only significant predictor in another (103); Sorrentino & Short (127) found that high FOS women performed *better* on a male sex-typed task than a "female" task. This is not only contrary to Horner's predictions, but also to other work (131) regarding sex-typing and achievement oriented behavior. The nature of the task was also explored by McGuinness (86) in the only study that varied difficulty level. A performance decrement due to mixed sex competition was related to FOS for both men and women, but only on a task of moderate difficulty. This suggests that the study of the effect of task variables is a fruitful direction for further research.

Horner's theory also predicts that high ability women are most likely to have FOS. The complexities of predicting actual achievement from individual differences in motivation, expectancy, or attributional measures have been thoroughly discussed in the achievement motivation literature (108, 142). Direct tests of the relationship between ability and FOS do not support the theory (71, 104), but several studies may be cited as showing indirect support (21, 99, 127).

Peplau's (104) study of dating couples appears to reject Horner's prediction that attitudes of and perceptions of supportiveness from a boyfriend is negatively related to FOS. A study of black women also rejected this hypothesis, but found that the degree of attachment to a man (e.g. dating vs engaged) moderated the relationship of FOS and attitudes about black militancy. Thus attached women who had militant attitudes had less FOS than their unattached counterparts (106).

Horner's construct has indeed stimulated an energetic "new look" in one direction, but it is clear that refinement of the measure[6] and the concept should be encouraged so that adequate testing and modification of the theory may proceed.

Expectancies and Causal Attribution

The general literature on achievement motivation has burgeoned with studies emphasizing cognitive factors as influencers of achievement behavior (38, 142). The research on sex differences in expectancies and causal attributions about success and failure has been summarized by Frieze (42; see also 131) and also suggests promising new directions for research on women and achievement. Many have argued that motivational research reinforces victim rather than institutional blame (112). However, it is also important to recognize that self blame is generated through certain types of misattributions. Gurin & Gurin (49) have suggested that the effect of social change on expectations about success and failure and behavioral change must be based on a complete understanding of the self-attributional process. They suggest that this process may provide a linkage of institutional change to individual response.

Recent reviews and new findings (29, 40, 42, 131) clearly document lower expectations for female than male performance on tasks involving intellectual mastery. We have already seen that tasks and traits typed as female are devalued.

---

[6] A new scoring system was demonstrated by Horner at the American Psychological Association, 1973.

Expectancies about one's own performance are also low; women generally expect to fail (42, 131).

There are also sex differences in causal attributions for success and failure (42). Men generally attribute their success to stable factors such as ability and failure to luck which is unstable. Women, on the other hand, tend to attribute failure to ability and success to effort. However, these relationships are moderated by individual differences in level of achievement motivation (42), fear of success (39), ability level, and the relationship of expected to actual outcomes (126). Using Weiner's (142) attributional analysis of achievement motivation as a conceptual framework, Frieze (42) derives practical implications for women's achievement efforts from these findings.

The importance of sex role considerations was shown in a study of causal attributions about others' performance (29). It was found that both men and women rated men as more successful than women on "masculine" as well as on "feminine" tasks. On masculine tasks good performance by a man was attributed to skill, while good performance by a woman was attributed to luck. Furthermore, performance on a masculine task was valued more highly than on the feminine task. In the same vein, Feldman & Kiesler (40) report that "those who are number two try harder." When evaluating peers, subjects attributed women's success to hard work and failure to lack of effort. This was not the case for the attributions about men's performance. In a second phase of the study they found that men and women were expected to be equally successful as pediatricians but not as surgeons. Again, woman's success was attributed to her hard work rather than her ability. As these authors note, other findings (38) indicate that stable factors such as ability are found to be attributed to expected outcomes, and since men are expected to be successful, such attributions are probable. In contrast, variable factors such as effort are used more often to explain unexpected outcomes—such as woman's success. Self attributions and attributions about others seem to go hand in hand, and both reflect expectations based on sex role assumptions.

WOMEN AND PSYCHOTHERAPY

Criticism of the Freudian theory of female psychosexual development has been simmering along since it was first presented. The theoretical issues and their consequences for women in "real life" as well as in psychotherapy surged to a full boil in the late 1960s. The assault on the validity of the theory and discussions of its influence on therapists and on the *Zeitgeist*, as well as its consequences for women in or out of emotional difficulties has continued to grow in both volume and intensity. However, as can be seen from the following summary, there is more speculation than empirical work.

Rice & Rice (111) write of the perplexity and lack of empathetic understanding of male therapists concerning their women patients' complaints and dissatisfactions. Explaining women's resulting hostility as transference has become less satisfactory.

The feminist issue in psychotherapy has been stated in extreme terms. It is

Chesler's (24) thesis that men (including men therapists) drive women crazy, in order to maintain a male sexist hegemony. The Brovermans (19) demonstrated that clinicians view "mentally healthy women" as passive, emotional, subjective, etc—characteristics they otherwise attribute to "mentally unhealthy adults." Does this pressure their patients into diminishing or even self-destructive roles? It seems that therapists support sex-role stereotypes and the status quo in general (1, 83).

There is strong feeling in counter-cultural and radical feminist circles that psychotherapy in general, and certainly the psychotherapy establishment, is destructive to the human potential of women. Various groups have established lists of accredited, feminist therapists, who are considered to be freer of exploitative bias toward women than establishment therapists, although the categories overlap. There has been a proliferation of therapy substitutes for women: 1. consciousness-raising groups originally developed by the National Organization for Women, but now burgeoning in various other institutions; 2. assertiveness-training groups, generally using behavior modification techniques such as modeling, role-playing, desensitization, etc; 3. continuing education programs at colleges and universities, which combine vocational and sensitivity training; 4. encounter and sensitivity training groups focusing on women; and 5. associations of para-professionals stressing supportive, assertive, and confrontational methods.

Polemic aside, what does the literature reveal of professional response to the issues raised? There is much theoretical discussion but little systematic development or research on theory or practice. A survey of the research literature on psychotherapy and mental illness relating to women, and female sexuality, reveals a heavy predominance of interest in two areas: abortion and frigidity. In a summary of medical and psychiatric attitudes about psychiatric indications for induced abortion, White (146) asserted that individual physicians held rabid opinions about criteria but were in total disagreement. He says, "Is it possible that the pregnant woman symbolizes the proof of male potency and that if we loosen our rule over women and grant them the right to dispose of that proof when *they* want to, we men then feel terribly threatened lest women can at will rob us of the proof of our potency and masculinity?"

Turning to the literature on frigidity, most articles deal with it as a dysfunctional symptom resulting from ignorance, fear, hostility, etc. With regard to treatment, several papers focus on the use of behavior modification (e.g. 34, 64), hypnosis with and without stag films (9),[7] and similar more or less mechanistic techniques (31). While the psychoanalysts do look at frigidity in relation to the woman's life history and pattern, it is still seen as a pathological symptom, never as a conflicted attempt to control her anatomical destiny. Fisher (41) has written a large book on *The Female Orgasm*, which has been criticized on this as well as other grounds by Money et al (95). An alternative way of looking at frigidity, similarly conjectural, is in terms of existential conflict rather than inconvenience or reproach to the male, or defect or failure in the female. Sherfey (122) has observed that "each orgasm

---

[7] Sales brochure for slides and tape presentation by Gilbert MacVaugh, Frigidity: Successful Treatment in One Hypnotic Imprint Session with the Oriental-Relaxation Technique.

tends to increase pelvic vasocongestion," hence readiness for further orgasms. Since most sexual partners could not meet the women's level of repeated readiness, her "frigidity" could be seen as the self-protective outcome of an approach-avoidance conflict, whereby she avoids chronic pelvic congestion—a condition which in fact does occur in many women (and which Freud considered the basis of anxiety neurosis). Even if a tireless partner were available, the prospect of reversion to an instinct-dominated existence, where every orgasm led to more until a state of physical exhaustion was reached, also conflicts realistically with a human range of goals.

Other popular topics are represented by the many clinical reports on contraceptives for women's use, on treatments with psychotropic drugs, and on the effects of gynecological surgery on women's sex life. The charge that therapists see women as functional or dysfunctional objects rather than as humans (see 25, pp. 47, 73, 75–82) seems to have some foundation in the selection of such topics for communication to one's peers about one's work with women patients. It is also true that there are increasing numbers of articles sensitive to women's emotional problems in realistic contexts (91).

The remainder of this article will deal with a few promising developments and more critical rhetoric in psychoanalytic thought, which still seems to be the most influential theoretical basis for treatment situations in clinics and private practice.

Of the numerous articles calling for the revision of psychoanalytic theory and practice, one by Kronsky (73) is outstanding: soundly based in psychoanalytic understanding, free from rhetoric, and specific in its recommendations to the therapist. Kronsky sees women as frequently suffering from a free-floating sense of guilt resulting from inconsistent super-ego prohibitions or a double bind. She urges that the therapist avoid interpretation or mirroring while the patient is venting her rage, her competitiveness, hatred, and envy of men, lest these techniques result in re-repression, with these feelings becoming ego-dystonic, and an inauthentic femininity covering all. Moulton (97) speaks in similar terms and amplifies these themes. Chasseguet-Smirgel (23) has collected a book of articles by French women analysts who regard fulfillment as covering a broader range than matehood and motherhood.

Some male analysts have also spoken out on various aspects of the weakness of orthodox analytic theory in dealing with women's development. Gelb (45) states, "I believe that many in the field of psychoanalysis have been guilty of contributing heavily to the coercive institutionalization of male and female roles which have little to do with sexual identity." While women and men have been struggling toward competence and relatedness, many psychoanalysts discourse about the glory of passivity to women and about "reestablishing masculine identity" to men—rather than moving toward full capacity as human beings. Chodoff (25) points out that the evidence that Freud got from his patients for his theory of infantile sexuality can be explained by the demand characteristics of the doctor-patient relationship. Chodoff states, "I submit that the role attributed to infantile sexuality in general and to penis envy in particular ... cannot be proved on biologic and other empirical grounds, no matter how widely and repetitiously they are given the status of unassailable truths in large segments of educated opinion in the United States." If the evidence for infantile sexuality is not convincing, Freud's theory of feminine psychology needs to be revised. Salzman (117) underlines the need to recognize that "the psychology of the female . . . is determined by her inherent biological potentiality in a changing cultural matrix." He stresses the importance of religious doctrines and technological limitations in presumptions about woman's natural role. Marmor (84) observes that the fallacy in the common argument that the male's aggressivity and the female's passivity are both "natural" lies in the confusion between what statistically describes the behavior of men and women and what motivates that behavior.

Miller (91) holds that psychoanalysis is now at a turning point, the old sexual theories having failed to solve people's problems in living. She points out that "the notions of renunciation and disengagement inherent in the 'masculine' growth model have meant limitations on full human development for men and women alike."

The onslaught against Freudian theory received its greatest recent impetus from implications of the work of Masters and Johnson and of Sherfey (122). The distinction between "clitoral" and "vaginal" orgasms had been a linchpin of the theory of feminine sexuality, which was supposed to develop in two stages. The first was an immature "phallic," "masculine" stage where the female's enjoyment of her clitoris reflected her penis envy and rebellion against her inferior sexual equipment and castrated state. This had to be given up for the attainment of the second stage, a stage of "feminine" orgastic experience based on the passivity of the vagina and acceptance of her castrated state. Masters' and Johnson's studies have been accepted as demolishing the Freudian distinction between "clitoral" and "vaginal" orgasms in women, while Sherfey's integration of major contributions from embryology, biology, and gynecology has cast doubt on Freud's depiction of female sexuality as a pallid counterpart of the male's, and only perilously achieved at that. She started with the previously overlooked finding by embryologists that all mammalian embryos are now known to be anatomically female in the early stages of life—until the sixth week of fetal life in the human— when, in the presence of the Y chromosome, fetal androgens bring about the differentiation of the male from the female anlage. She then went on to theorize on the basis of endocrinological research that early human females developed an inordinate cyclic sexual capacity which must have been a major barrier to the evolution of modern man, to the extent that it interfered with maternal care. Feminine hypersexuality therefore had to be suppressed, first in the interest of longer and more richly developmental human childhood, and then in the interest of property rights and ascertainable lines of descent after settled agricultural economies came into being. Although the race needed the suppression of female hypersexuality, one might guess that the individual male suffered from the comparison with this female, especially before the knowledge of paternity. The uneasy attainment of this giant step for mankind may have had to be buttressed by the development of the compensatory hypermasculinity which has characterized so many human societies.

Freud postulated that the development to psychosexual maturity was more difficult and uncertain for women, since their first love object was of the same sex, whereas males have heterosexual objects from the beginning. With the male, heterosexuality was supposed to be primary, while for the female it is only achieved after tortuous changes. Stoller (133) offers other observations and thoughts in connection with Freud's postulation. Before the mother becomes the male infant's love object, there is a stage of symbiosis when he has not yet separated from his mother and distinguished his body and psyche as different from hers—and "*she is female with a feminine gender identity.*" Therefore, heterosexuality is *not* a given for males, but an achievement, whereas femininity for females *is* given by the earliest identification, not tortuously arrived at through castration, humiliation, renunciation as Freud said. Symbiosis anxiety is seen as an important motive force in the development of masculinity.

Gadpaille (44), in a review of physiological and other research, wrote in 1972:

Perhaps even male chauvinism and the worldwide predominance of male domination ... (is) intensely motivated as a denial of an unconscious awareness by man of his greater fragility and vulnerability, both physically and psychosexually, compared to women. ... The male is more vulnerable in virtually every way with the exception of physical prowess: there is greater difficulty in achieving maleness and masculinity, coupled with an increased vulnerability of males to disruption of sexual function and to physical and psychosexual disorders.

In confirmation, there is the 1972 publication by Ginsberg, Frosch & Shapiro (46) observing that the obsolescence of the virginity taboo has disrupted the former ecological balance in society resulting in disequilibrium for males, and the rise of what they call "the new impotence."

Madigan (82) found sex mortality differentials to be biologically caused, not the result of social conditions. He found that both sexes equally lack resistance to infectious and contagious diseases, but that women have greater constitutional resistance to degenerative diseases.

Paralleling the critique of Freudian theory regarding female development and malfunctioning is a revival or shift of interest to Jungian psychology with its stress on the existence of both masculine and feminine polarities in each individual (30, 51). The research referred to in the earlier section on sex role definitions is also germane.

Various streams of thought have been flowing together in the last few years which suggest a need for far-ranging reorientation of the androcentric epistemology of our culture if a psychological understanding of women and men is to be developed which can bear reality testing. Morgan (96) offers a sparkling alternative to the androcentric evolutionist theories. She says:

I believe the deeply rooted semantic confusion between 'man' as a male and 'man' as a species has been fed back into and vitiated a great deal of the speculation that goes on about the origins, development, and nature of the human race. ... A very high proportion of the thinking on these topics is androcentric ... in the same way as pre-Copernican thinking was geocentric. . . . One of these days an evolutionist is going to strike a palm against his large-domed head and cry: 'Of course! We assumed the first human being was a man!'

Daly (28) proclaims the need for a counteraction to patriarchy's naming of reality and morality as in the story of the Fall of Adam and Eve, whereby the "male's viewpoint is metamorphosed into God's viewpoint" (28, p. 47). According to myths, women are weak and evil (98). Theodor Reik (110) discusses the myth of the Creation as a denial of the reality that man is born of woman, not vice versa, and also in terms of what Stoller called symbiosis anxiety. Lederer (74) also goes into prehistory and paleoanthropology to decipher the counterphobic denigration of women in patriarchal society. There has been renewed interest in what can be learned of the genesis of androcentric psychoanalytic theories from the sociology of knowledge (67). We are clearly at a point where psychoanalytic theories of feminine development can thrive only with a transfusion from other disciplines: biological, historical, economic, and sociological.

CONCLUDING COMMENTS

This selective review on the psychology of women has, as we predicted at the outset, raised many questions. It is perhaps banal, but nevertheless necessary, to stress that there are unresolved conceptual and methodological issues within each area which will have to be raised again and reevaluated as the field develops. The different styles of the two authors probably reflect the differing state of the art in their fields. Still, if a major theme can be discerned, it is that of the sexual division of personality characteristics based on the male thinker's view of reality. To the extent this division is accepted, individual women, and men to a lesser degree, are constricted in their personal fulfillment, and society is hobbled in both competence and relatedness.

Literature Cited

1. Abramowitz, S. I., Abramowitz, C. V., Jackson, C., Gomes, B. 1973. The politics of clinical judgment. *J. Consult. Clin. Psychol.* 41:385–91
2. Alper, T. G. 1973. The relationship between role orientation and achievement motivation in college women. *J. Pers.* 41:9–31
3. Astin, H. S., Parelman, A., Fisher, A. 1974. *Annotated Bibliography of Sex Roles.* NIMH–USPHS, ADM 75–166
4. Astin, H. S., Suniewick, N., Dweck, S. 1971. *Women, A Bibliography on Their Education and Careers.* Washington, D.C.: Human Service Press
5. Babladelis, G. 1973. Sex-stereotyping: students' perceptions of college professors. *Percept. Mot. Skills* 37:47–50
6. Bardwick, J. M. 1971. *Psychology of Women.* New York: Harper & Row
7. Bardwick, J. M., Ed. 1972. *Readings on the Psychology of Women.* New York: Harper & Row
8. Bart, P. 1973. A funny thing happened on the way to the orifice: women in gynecology textbooks. See Ref. 63, 283–88
9. Beigel, H. 1972. The use of hypnosis in female sexual anaesthesia. *J. Am. Soc. Psychosom. Dent. Med.* 19:4–14
10. Bem, S. L. 1973. But what can woman

become? *Contemp. Psychol.* 18:450
11. Bem, S. L. 1974. The measurement of psychological androgyny. *J. Consult. Clin. Psychol.* 42:165–72
12. Bem, S. L. 1975. Sex-role adaptability: one consequence of psychological androgyny. *J. Pers. Soc. Psychol.* In press
13. Bem, S. L., Bem, D. J. 1971. Training the woman to know her place: the power of a non-conscious ideology. In *Roles Women Play: Readings Towards Women's Liberation*, ed. M. H. Garskoff. Belmont, Calif.: Brooks/Cole
14. Bernard, J. 1972. *Future of Marriage*. New York: World Publ.
15. Bernard, J. 1974. *Future of Motherhood*. New York: Dial Press
16. Block, J. H. 1973. Conceptions of sex roles. *Am. Psychol.* 28:512–26
17. Block, J., von der Lippe, A., Block, J. H. 1973. Sex role and socialization patterns: some personality concomitants and environmental antecedents. *J. Consult. Clin. Psychol.* 41:321–41
18. Boserup, E. 1970. *Woman's Role in Economic Development*. New York: St. Martin's
19. Broverman, I. K., Broverman, D. M., Clarkson, F. E., Rosenkrantz, P. S., Vogel, S. R. 1970. Sex-role stereotypes and clinical judgments of mental health. *J. Consult. Clin. Psychol.* 34:1–7
20. Broverman, I. K., Vogel, S. R., Broverman, D. M., Clarkson, F. E., Rosenkrantz, P. S. 1972. Sex role stereotypes: a current appraisal. *J. Soc. Issues* 28:59–78
21. Burghardt, N. R. 1973. *The Motive to Avoid Success in School Aged Males and Females*. Presented at Am. Psychol. Assoc. Meet. Montreal
22. Carlson, R. 1972. Understanding women: implications for personality theory and research. *J. Soc. Issues* 28: 17–32
23. Chasseguet-Smirgel, J. 1970. *Female Sexuality: New Psychoanalytic Views*. Ann Arbor: Univ. Michigan Press
24. Chesler, P. 1972. *Women and Madness*. Garden City, N. Y.: Doubleday
25. Chodoff, P. 1973. Feminine psychology and infantile sexuality. See Ref. 91, 183–200
26. Constantinople, A. 1973. Masculinity-

femininity: an exception to a famous dictum? *Psychol. Bull.* 80:389–407
27. Crummer, M. L. 1972. *Sex-role identification, "motive to avoid success" and competitive performance in college women.* PhD thesis. Univ. Florida, Gainesville. 89 pp.
28. Daly, M. 1973. *Beyond God the Father: Toward a Philosophy of Women's Liberation.* Boston: Beacon
29. Deaux, K., Emswiller, T. 1974. Explanations of successful performance on sex-linked tasks: what is skill for the male is luck for the female. *J. Pers. Soc. Psychol.* 29:80–85
30. de Castillejo, I. C. 1973. *Knowing Woman.* New York: Harper & Row
31. DeMoor, W. 1972. Vaginismus: etiology and treatment. *Am. J. Psychother.* 26:207–15
32. Dufresne, J. M. M. 1971. *Differential reactions of males to three different female sex roles.* PhD thesis. Univ. Connecticut, Storrs. 199 pp.
33. Ehrlich, C. 1973. The woman book industry. See Ref. 63, 268–82
34. Eicher, W. 1973. Psychogenesis and treatment of female functional sexual disorders. *Med. Welt* 24:1270–72
35. Ellis, L. J., Bentler, P. M. 1973. Traditional sex-determined role standards and sex stereotypes. *J. Pers. Soc. Psychol.* 24:28–34
36. Entwisle, D. R., Greenberger, E. 1972. Adolescents' views of women's work role. *Am. J. Orthopsychiat.* 42:648–56
37. Feather, N. T., Raphelson, A. C. 1974. Fear of success in Australian and American student groups: motive or sex-role stereotype? *J. Pers.* 42: 190–201
38. Feather, N. T., Simon, J. G. 1971. Attribution of responsibility and valence of outcome in relation to expectations of success based upon selective or manipulative control. *J. Pers. Soc. Psychol.* 18:173–88
39. Feather, N. T., Simon, J. G. 1973. Fear of success and causal attribution for outcome. *J. Pers.* 41:525–42
40. Feldman, S. A., Kiesler, S. B. 1975. Those who are number two try harder: the effect of sex on attributions of causality. *J. Pers. Soc. Psychol.* In press
41. Fisher, S. 1973. *The Female Orgasm:*

Psychology, Physiology, Fantasy. New York: Basic Books

42. Frieze, I. H. 1975. Women's expectations for and causal attributions of success and failure. See Ref. 90

43. Furniss, W. T., Graham, P. A. 1974. *Women in Higher Education.* Washington, D. C.: Am. Counc. Educ.

44. Gadpaille, W. J. 1972. Research into the physiology of maleness and femaleness. *Arch. Gen. Psychiat.* 26: 193–206

45. Gelb, L. 1973. Masculinity-femininity: a study in imposed inequality. See Ref. 91, 363–406

46. Ginsberg, G. L., Frosch, W. A., Shapiro, T. 1972. The new impotence. *Arch. Gen. Psychiat.* 26:218–20

47. Gruder, C. L., Cook, T. D. 1971. Sex, dependency and helping. *J. Pers. Soc. Psychol.* 19:290–94

48. Gump, J. P. 1972. Sex-role attitudes and psychological well-being. *J. Soc. Issues* 28:79–92

49. Gurin, G., Gurin, P. 1970. Expectancy theory in the study of poverty. *J. Soc. Issues* 26:83–104

50. Haavio-Mannila, E. 1971. Convergences between East and West: tradition and modernity in sex roles in Sweden, Finland and the Soviet Union. *Acta Sociol.* 14:114–25

51. Harding, M. E. 1970. *The Way of All Women.* New York: Putnam

52. Harris, M. B., Bays, G. 1973. Altruism and sex roles. *Psychol. Rep.* 32:1002

53. Hawley, P. 1971. What women think men think: does it affect their career choice? *J. Couns. Psychol.* 18:193–99

54. Helson, R. 1972. The changing image of the career woman. *J. Soc. Issues* 28:33–46

55. Helson, R. 1973. Heroic and tender modes in women authors of fantasy. *J. Pers.* 41:493–512

56. Hochschild, A. R. 1973. A review of sex role research. See Ref. 63, 249–67

57. Hoffman, L. W. 1972. Early childhood experiences and women's achievement motives. *J. Soc. Issues* 28:157–76

58. Hoffman, L. W. 1974. Fear of success in males and females: 1965 and 1972. *J. Consult. Clin. Psychol.* 42:353–58

59. Holter, H. 1970. *Sex Roles and Social Structure.* Oslo: Universitetsforlaget

60. Holter, H. 1971. Sex roles and social change. *Acta Sociol.* 14:2–12

61. Holmstrom, E. I. 1973. Changing sex roles in a developing country. *J. Marriage Fam.* 35:546–53

62. Horner, M. S. 1972. Toward an understanding of achievement-related conflicts in women. *J. Soc. Issues* 28: 157–75

63. Huber, J. 1973. *Changing Women in a Changing Society.* Univ. Chicago

64. Husted, J. R. 1972. The effect of method of systematic desensitization and presence of sexual communication in the treatment of female sexual anxiety by counter-conditioning. *Diss. Abstr. Int.* 33:441

65. Kagan, J. 1964. Acquisition and significance of sex typing and sex role identity. In *Review of Child Development Research,* ed. M. L. Hoffman, L. W. Hoffman. New York: Russell Sage Found.

66. Kando, T. M. 1972. Role strain: comparison of males, females, and transsexuals. *J. Marriage Fam.* 34:459–64

67. Klein, V. 1946. *The Feminine Character, History of an Ideology.* London: Kegan Paul

68. Kohlberg, L. 1966. A cognitive-developmental analysis of children's sex-role concepts and attitudes. See Ref. 80, 82–173

69. Klinger, E. 1969. Fantasy need achievement and performance: a role analysis. *Psychol. Rev.* 76:574–91

70. Kreps, J. 1971. *Sex in the Marketplace: American Women at Work.* Baltimore: Johns Hopkins

71. Kresojevich, I. Z. 1972. *Motivation to avoid success in women as related to year in school, academic achievement and success context.* PhD thesis. Michigan State Univ., Lansing. 92 pp.

72. Kriger, S. F. 1972. Nach and perceived parental childrearing attitudes of career women and homemakers. *J. Vocat. Behav.* 2:419–32

73. Kronsky, B. J. 1971. Feminism and psychotherapy. *J. Contemp. Psychother.* 2:89–98

74. Lederer, W. 1968. *The Fear of Women.* New York: Harcourt Brace Jovanovich

75. Lipman-Blumen, J. 1972. How ideol-

ogy shapes women's lives. *Sci. Am.* 226:34-42

76. Lipman-Blumen, J. 1973. Role de-differentiation as a system response to crisis: occupational and political roles of women. *Sociol. Inq.* 43:105-29

77. Lirtzman, S. I., Wahba, M. A. 1972. Determinants of coalitional behavior of men and women: sex roles or situational requirements? *J. Appl. Psychol.* 56:406-11

78. Looft, W. R. 1971. Vocational aspirations of second-grade girls. *Psychol. Rep.* 28:241-42

79. Looft, W. R. 1971. Sex differences in the expression of vocational aspiration by elementary school children. *Develop. Psychol.* 5:366

80. Maccoby, E. E., Ed. 1966. *The Development of Sex Differences.* Stanford Univ. Press

81. Maccoby, E. E., Jacklin, C. N. 1973. Sex differences in intellectual functioning. *Proc. 1972 Invitational Conf. Test. Probl.* Princeton: Educ. Test. Serv.

82. Madigan, F. C. 1957. Are sex mortality differentials biologically caused? *Milbank Mem. Fund Quart.* 35:202-23

83. Maracek, J. 1974. *When Stereotypes Hurt: Responses to Dependent and Aggressive Communications.* Presented at East. Psychol. Assoc. Meet. Philadelphia

84. Marmor, J. 1968. Changing patterns of femininity. In *The Marriage Relationship,* ed. S. Rosenbaum, I. Alger. New York: Basic Books

85. Maxwell, P. G., Gonzalez, A. E. 1972. Traditional and nontraditional role choice and need for failure among college women. *Psychol. Rep.* 31:545-46

86. McGuinness, E. L. 1974. *Success avoidance and competitive performance.* MS thesis. Rutgers Univ., New Brunswick, N.J. 109 pp.

87. Mednick, M. T. S. 1973. Motivational and personality factors related to career goals of black college women. Report to Manpower Admin., U.S. Dep. Labor, Publ. No. 218969. Springfield, Va.: NTIS

88. Mednick, M. T. S. 1975. Social change and sex role inertia: the case of the kibbutz. See Ref. 90

89. Mednick, M. T. S., Tangri, S. S. 1972. New perspectives on women. *J. Soc. Issues* 28(2):1-250

90. Mednick, M. T. S., Tangri, S. S., Hoffman, L. W., Eds. 1975. *Women: Social Psychological Perspectives on Achievement.* New York: Holt, Rinehart & Winston. In press

91. Miller, J. B. 1973. *Psychoanalysis and Women.* Baltimore: Penguin Books

92. Minturn, L. 1973. *Sex Role Differentiation in Contemporary Communes.* Presented at Am. Psychol. Assoc. Meet. Montreal

93. Mischel, W. 1966. A social-learning view of sex differences in behavior. See Ref. 80, 56-81

94. Monahan, L., Kuhn, D., Shaver, P. 1974. Intrapsychic versus cultural explanations of the "fear of success" motive. *J. Pers. Soc. Psychol.* 29:60-64

95. Money, J., Walker, P. A., Higham, E. 1974. My orgasm belongs to daddy. *Contemp. Psychol.* 19:399-400

96. Morgan, E. 1972. *The Descent of Woman.* New York: Bantam Books

97. Moulton, R. 1970. A survey and re-evaluation of the concept of penis envy. *Contemp. Psychoanal.* 7:84-104

98. Moulton, R. 1973. The myth of femininity: a panel. *Am. J. Psychoanal.* 33:45-49

99. Nowicki, S. 1973. *Predicting Academic Achievement of Females from a Locus of Control Orientation: Some Problems and Some Solutions.* Presented at Am. Psychol. Assoc. Meet. Montreal

100. Oppenheimer, V. 1975. Woman's occupations. See Ref. 90

101. Orzeck, L. A. 1972. *Stereotypes and expectations: how people react to female and male competitors and cooperators.* PhD thesis. Univ. Colorado, Boulder. 180 pp.

102. Palme, O. 1972. The emancipation of man. *J. Soc. Issues* 28:237-46

103. Parker, V. J. 1971. *Fear of success, sex-role orientation of the task and competition condition as factors affecting women's performance in achievement-oriented situations.* PhD thesis. Ohio State Univ., Columbus. 135 pp.

104. Peplau, L. A. 1973. *The impact of fear of success, sex-role attitudes and opposite-sex relationships on women's*

intellectual performance: an experimental study of competition in dating couples. PhD thesis. Harvard Univ., Cambridge

105. Putnam, B. A., Hansen, J. C. 1972. Relationship of self-concept and feminine role concept to vocational maturity in young women. *J. Couns. Psychol.* 19:436-40

106. Puryear, G. R., Mednick, M. S. 1974. Black militancy, affective attachment, and the fear of success in black college women. *J. Consult. Clin. Psychol.* 42:263-66

107. Ray, L. 1972. The woman's magazine short-story heroine in 1957 and 1967. See Ref. 116, 41-62

108. Raynor, J. O. 1970. Relationships between achievement-related motives, future orientation, and academic performance. *J. Pers. Soc. Psychol.* 15:28-33

109. Recely, N. L. C. 1972. *Level of self-esteem and conformity to sex-role stereotypes.* PhD thesis. Univ. Colorado, Boulder. 162 pp.

110. Reik, T. 1960. *The Creation of Woman.* New York: Braziller

111. Rice, J. K., Rice, D. G. 1973. Implications of the women's liberation movement for psychotherapy. *Am. J. Psychiat.* 130:191-96

112. Robbins, L., Robbins, E. 1973. Comment on: toward an understanding of achievement related conflicts in women. *J. Soc. Issues* 29:133-37

113. Rosaldo, M. Z., Lamphere, L. 1974. *Woman, Culture and Society.* Stanford Univ. Press

114. Rossi, A. S., Calderwood, A. 1973. *Academic Women on the Move.* New York: Russell Sage Found.

115. Saario, T., Jacklin, C., Tittle, C. 1973. Sex-role stereotyping in public schools. *Harvard Educ. Rev.* 43:386-416

116. Safilios-Rothschild, C. 1972. *Toward a Sociology of Women.* Lexington, Mass.: Xerox Corp.

117. Salzman, L. 1967. Psychology of the female: a new look. *Arch. Gen. Psychiat.* 17:195-203

118. Sanger, S. P., Alker, H. A. 1972. Dimensions of internal-external locus of control and the women's liberation movement. *J. Soc. Issues* 28:115-29

118a. Sarason, I. G., Smith, R. E. 1971. Personality. *Ann. Rev. Psychol.* 22:393-446

119. Schein, V. E. 1973. The relationship between sex-role stereotypes and requisite management characteristics. *J. Appl. Psychol.* 57:95-100

120. Seward, G. H., Williamson, R. C., Eds. 1970. *Sex Roles in Changing Society.* New York: Random House

121. Seyfried, B. A., Hendrick, C. 1973. When do opposites attract? When they are opposite in sex and sex-role attitudes. *J. Pers. Soc. Psychol.* 25:15-20

122. Sherfey, M. J. 1972. *The Nature and Evolution of Female Sexuality.* New York: Random House

123. Sherman, J. A. 1971. *On the Psychology of Women.* Springfield, Ill.: Thomas

124. Sherman, J. A. 1972. *Social Values, Femininity and the Development of Female Competence.* Presented at Meet. Am. Assoc. Advan. Sci., Washington, D.C.

125. Sherman, L. J. 1973. A psychological view of women in policing. *J. Police Sci. Admin.* 1:383-93

126. Simon, J. G., Feather, N. T. 1973. Causal attributions for success and failure at university examinations. *J. Educ. Psychol.* 64:46-56

127. Sorrentino, R. M., Short, J. A. 1974. Effects of fear of success on women's performance at masculine versus feminine tasks. *J. Res. Pers.* In press

128. Spence, J. T., Helmreich, R. 1972. Who likes competent women? Competence, sex role congruence of interests, and subjects' attitudes toward women as determinants of interpersonal attraction. *J. Appl. Soc. Psychol.* 2:197-213

129. Spence, J. T., Helmreich, R., Stapp, J. 1973. A short version of the Attitudes towards Women Scale (AWS). *Bull. Psychon. Soc.* 2:219-20

130. Spence, J. T., Helmreich, R., Stapp, J. 1975. Ratings of self and peers on sex-role attributes and their relation to self-esteem. *J. Pers. Soc. Psychol.* In press

131. Stein, A. H., Bailey, M. M. 1973. The socialization of achievement orientation in females. *Psychol. Bull.* 80:345-66

132. Steinmann, A., Fox, D. J. 1970. Atti-

tudes towards women's family role among black and white undergraduates. *Fam. Coord.* 19:363–68

133. Stoller, R. J. 1974. Symbiosis anxiety and the development of masculinity. *Arch. Gen. Psychiat.* 30:164

134. Tangri, S. S. 1972. Determinants of occupational role innovation among college women. *J. Soc. Issues* 28: 177–200

135. Tavris, C. 1973. Who likes women's liberation—and why: the case of the unliberated liberals. *J. Soc. Issues* 29:175–92

136. Thurber, S. 1972. Defensive externality and academic achievement by women. *Psychol. Rep.* 30:454

137. Touhey, J. C. 1974. Effects of additional women professionals on ratings of occupational prestige and desirability. *J. Pers. Soc. Psychol.* 29:86–90

138. Unger, R. K., Denmark, F. L. 1974. *Woman: Dependent or Independent Variable.* New York: Psychol. Dimensions

139. Unger, R. K., Raymond, B. J., Levine, S. M. 1974. Are women a "minority" group? Sometimes! *Int. J. Group Tensions* 4:71–81

140. Ward, S. W., Mausner, B. 1973. Behavioral and fantasied indicators of avoidance of success in men and women. *J. Pers.* 41:457–470

141. Warshay, D. W. 1972. Sex differences in language style. See Ref. 116, 3–9

142. Weiner, B. 1972. *Theories of Motivation.* Chicago: Markham

143. Weitzmann, L. J., Eifler, D., Hokada, E., Ross, C. 1972. Sex-role socialization in picture books for children. *Am. J. Sociol.* 77:1125–49

144. Wellens, G. J. 1972. *The motive to avoid success in high school seniors: Nach shifts and psychological correlates.* PhD thesis. Illinois Inst. Technol., Chicago. 217 pp.

145. Weston, P., Mednick, M. T. S. 1970. Race, social class and the motive to avoid success in women. *J. Cross-Cult. Psychol.* 1:284–91

146. White, R. B. 1966. Induced abortions: a survey of their psychiatric implications, complications, and indications. *Texas Rep. Biol. Med.* 24:531–58

147. Williams, J. H. 1973. Sexual role identification and personality functioning in girls: a theory revisited. *J. Pers.* 41:1–9

148. Wolf, C., Gunderson, D. 1973. Sex roles in mountain communes: Utopia lost. *Impact* 2:52–60

HYPNOSIS[1]

Ernest R. Hilgard[2]

Department of Psychology, Stanford University
Stanford, California 94305

Five trends in hypnosis research, theory, and practice are notable since the previous review of 10 years ago (85). They are listed briefly here, and the documentation given in the body of the review.

First, the controversy over the utility of the concept of "trance" or "hypnotic state" is kept alive by those who oppose the concept, but the issue has not proved to be a fruitful one. Only the nontrance advocates believe that they have introduced a new paradigm; those who seem to them to be committed to the trance concept commonly use the term in a phenomenal or descriptive way, without giving it the centrality that the opponents expect of the proponents. The residual arguments are in fact commonly over problems of experimental design and data analysis, having nothing to do with the trance concept as such; the differences are not paradigmatic but methodological. The recent introduction of neodissociation theory now offers an interpretation in terms of multiple cognitive controls whose hierarchical relationships may be modified by hypnotic procedures. Because these control systems can be fractionated in various ways, and are not as pervasive as a general "hypnotic state," the neodissociation interpretation may substitute in some respects for the trance concept, while recognizing that the hyponotized subject is indeed in some way altered.

Second, there is a convergence of all investigators upon the role played by the subject's imaginative and fantasy productions. This is reflected in the supplementation of objective indices of responsiveness to suggestions by subjective measures derived from questioning the subject, and by a reduction in the emphasis given to conclusions based on superficial performances that are readily modified by situational variables.

---

[1] The survey of literature pertinent to this review was concluded in February 1974. Because this review deals with the literature of 10 years, covering material since the preceding review (85), it has been necessary to be highly selective. I estimate that 200 relevant journal articles and books now appear in the scientific literature each year, so that limiting the reference list to 200 titles means that only 1 in 10 can be cited.

[2] The review was aided by Grant MH-3859 from the NIMH.

Third, the increasing emphasis upon imaginative involvements and absorption calls attention to enduring individual differences in these abilities. The relative persistence of a subject's level of hypnotic responsiveness through time and over the varying demands made of him in experimental contexts can now be interpreted according to the roots of these fantasy involvements: influences upon him originating in childhood, and possibly a contribution through hereditary potential. Because the major source of variance in hypnotic responsiveness lies in these persistent individual differences, appropriate experimental designs are now taking them into account.

Fourth, recent advances in brain psychophysiology give added support to the above basis for individual differences. Studies of hemispheric laterality of function now indicate that hypnotic responsiveness is associated with a preference for right hemisphere function in well lateralized right-handed subjects. This finding is coherent with the role of the right hemisphere in imagination.

Fifth, the clinical applications of hypnosis in pain reduction and in psychotherapy have become more sophisticated, and hypnosis is now used either alone or in conjunction with other types of behavior modification. The clinical findings have a feedback relationship with laboratory findings, and serve to correct exaggerated claims for or against the efficacy of hypnosis.

THE TRANCE CONTROVERSY

The puzzling problem of the existence and nature of one or more hypnotic states has been magnified into a controversy by those who describe themselves as nonstate theorists and believe that by rejecting the state or trance concept they have introduced a new paradigm into the investigation of hypnotic-like behavior (e.g. Barber 10, 12; Sarbin & Coe 164). Such a polarization of standpoints has both its positive and its negative aspects: positive in that it requires all parties to clarify their concepts, negative in that it leads to defending a priori viewpoints rather than in engaging in a more open inquiry regarding the answers to perplexing problems.

Three Issues Intertwined

The arguments over state and nonstate center around three polar concepts that are not clearly distinguished in much of the controversial discussion. The first pair of concepts can be designated the *trait* vs *state* distinction, that is, whether hypnotic responsiveness is more a matter of the characteristics of the subject than of the state produced by hypnotic induction. This is subject to empirical answer, and the bulk of the evidence, so far as this issue is concerned, favors trait over state. The second of the polarities has to do with the relative importance of *traits* vs *situational factors*. While the question of state is not at issue here, a preference for the influence of situational factors is evidenced by those who object to the state concept, reflecting similar controversies in contemporary social psychology (27). Here again the empirical evidence favors trait over situation, in that baseline responses to hypnotic suggestions contribute more to the variance of hypnotic responses than to modifications in the experimental manipulations (181). The third dichotomy is that between *state* and *situation*. Granted that an experimental and control group are equated for their individual differences by random selection, hence alike in "traits," does hypnotic induction (presumably producing a "state" according to state theorists) succeed any better than nonhypnotic manipulations in producing hypnotic-like responses? The evidence increasingly favors some enhancement of hypnotic-like behavior as a consequence of induction, but the enhancement is not great and the theoretical problems are not simple, so that this is the least resolved of the three issues.

Original Task Motivation Instructions (OTMI), with False Reference Standards, in Support of the Nonstate Position

The thread that more than any other runs through the studies in Barber's laboratory from 1962 to about 1972 is the demonstration that task-motivation instructions, administered without hypnotic induction, yield essentially the same results in responsiveness as a standard hypnotic induction as measured by the Barber Suggestibility Scale (BSS), hence opposing the need for a concept of hypnotic state. In order to examine this claim on empirical grounds, it is necessary first of all to clarify what is meant by these task-motivation instructions. In their original form they do more than exhort the subject to do his best; instead they provide false reference information through statements such as *"everyone* can do this if they really try. I myself can do it quite easily and *all* the previous subjects that participated in the experiment were able to do it"* (Barber & Calverley 13, emphasis supplied). Because *all* subjects have never done the things suggested, this is false information, and strongly invites the subject to comply lest he feel himself to be a deviant or a failure.

Bowers (24) surmised that subjects confronted by such extreme compliance demands might report experiences about which they felt unsure in order to avoid acknowledging that they were deviant or uncooperative. He tested this conjecture by having subjects interviewed by a different experimenter after visual and auditory hallucinations were requested following the original task-motivation instructions (OTMI). The new experimenter used "honesty instructions," explaining to the subjects that science would be served by their being absolutely honest in reporting what they had experienced. He found what he had anticipated—that many subjects corrected their reports of hallucinations downward, denying that they had experienced them as vividly as reported. Spanos & Barber (181) supplemented Bowers' experiment by determining whether or not similar corrections would be made if "honesty instructions" followed hypnotic induction. They confirmed Bowers' findings for visual hallucinations, showing not only that corrections were made following OTMI procedures, but that they were significantly more extreme than those following hypnotic induction. In other words, hypnotic induction in its standard form does not place as much pressure for compliance on the subjects as OTMI procedures do. The findings with auditory hallucinations were more ambiguous. As a consequence of these studies, it turns out that hypnotic induction and OTMI are not alike in their consequences, and all the earlier studies in which they are compared on the basis of BSS scores, uncorrected for honesty, are to that extent less convincing. Barber's laboratory has now adopted revised task motivation instructions (RTMI), in which the misinformation has been deleted. The new RTMI may take the form: "Other students were able to think of their hand in this way (as insensitive to pain) and it isn't as hard as it seems" (Spanos, Barber & Lang 184). With these RTMI the "honesty correction" is no longer significant, but of course the results cannot be used to justify assertions based on the OTMI procedure.

The Real-Simulator Design in Support of a Trance Concept

At a descriptive level, subjects behave differently when hypnotized and when not hypnotized (153), and they report changes in the way 'they feel (198, 198a). This is sufficient reality to permit the experimenter to do his research and the clinician to use hypnotic procedures without their becoming embroiled in the state issue.

One investigator in particular has attempted to delineate the changes in behavior that the hypnotic state is responsible for. Orne, in a series of papers, has proposed for this purpose the real-simulator design (136, 137). The responses of highly hypnotizable subjects ("reals") are compared with those of insusceptible subjects who try to act as they believe highly hypnotizable subjects would ("simulators"). Even if real and simulator perform alike it does not disprove a state concept, but it leaves the matter open for other evidence. What Orne hopes to find, however, are some differences that go beyond the obvious or implied demands of the hypnotist, something that hypnosis *adds to* these demands, not shown by the simulators.

Occasionally significant differences are found between reals and simulators (51, 138, 140), but the method is not universally successful in finding such differences (41, 135). Sometimes simulators overreact, as by having too much posthypnotic amnesia when that has been suggested (212).

The real-simulator design has been subjected to a number of criticisms: the reals and simulators come from different populations, and perhaps the differences reflect "traits" rather than "states" (10); the groups receive different instructions, and hence are playing different roles (164); in its very effort at objectivity, the method falls into some of the traps of the nonstate theorists (23, 26). It is avowedly a design with severe limitations, which Orne recognizes, but when properly used tells us a good deal about hypnosis (172).

THEORIES OF HYPNOSIS

The arguments over trance are only indirectly related to theories of hypnosis because hypnotic-like behavior has to be explained in detail regardless of how it is conceptualized in general.

Conditioning Theories

Explanations in terms of learning have been favored in psychology for many years, encouraged by the conditioning explanations of Pavlov, Watson, Hull, Skinner, and many others. Although earlier applications to hypnosis were made by Pavlov and later by Hull, Edmonston has been a more recent spokesman for the conditioned response interpretation (47). Another effort to use conditioning concepts consistently has been made by Barrios (16) to explain responses to posthypnotic suggestion as higher-order conditioning. A total theory, with more than plausible analogies with conditioning, has not been developed.

Input-Output ("Operational") Theory

Stimulus-response concepts were originally derived from the reflex arc and elaborated in conditioning theories. Broadened out by functionalists into a conception of antecedent and consequent variables, the contemporary derivative of these early positions has become an input-output logic that can be applied to various forms of information processing or situation-behavior sequences. Barber (10) has adopted this general logic for the interpretation of hypnotic behavior, seeking to find those antecedent variables (task-attitude, task-expectancy, task-motivation, toning and wording of suggestions, and tone and wording of inquiry) that determine the responses that are recorded. His omission of individual differences in base rates seems to arise because these are hard to conceive as antecedent variables; base rates have to be measured as consequents. In a formal sense, Barber's theory is a set of experimental procedures for assuring reproducibility of results. He does not order the data according to any explanatory principles because, in effect, he believes that there is nothing unusual about hypnosis to require explanation. More recently, as goal-directed fantasy has come to play a larger part in his experiments, especially those with Spanos, fantasy evocation tends to become more nearly an explanatory variable (180, 182, 183).

Role Theory

An exposition of book length now supplements Sarbin's earlier expositions of his role theory (163). The current theory of Sarbin & Coe (164) is elaborated as a social communication interpretation, one in which a person adopts a role suited to the other and behaves accordingly. He may become very deeply engrossed in the role (that is, he may show organismic involvement in it) even to the degree that it becomes irreversible. Because such organismic involvement is accepted, there is little difference to be detected between this position and the state-theories to which it is set as alternative. However, it provides a convenient frame of reference and a consistent alternative vocabulary for discussing hypnotic phenomena. Unfortunately, it gives the impression that there is less remaining to be explained than is actually the case.

Psychoanalytic Theory

The Gill & Brenman (64, 65) interpretation of hypnosis as adaptive regression continues to be one focus of discussion. The position has been criticized from a nonstate position (154) and from an alternative ego-psychoanalytic standpoint (204). It has been supported by Gruenewald, Fromm & Oberlander (76), who find experimentally more primary process intrusions in Rorschach responses when subjects are hypnotized than when the same subjects are not hypnotized, and by

Gur (79) in his study of creativity. Lavoie et al (113) have reported that hypnotic susceptibility among schizophrenics correlates negatively with primary regression and positively with adaptive regression, again using Rorschach signs. Like role-theory, psychoanalysis provides a ready-made vocabulary and an imbeddedness of hypnosis within a theory of larger scope.

Multiple-Aspect Theories

The desire for parsimony is an esthetic feature of most scientific theories, but a parsimonious explanation can be overdone when knowledge is uncertain, as, for example, if hypnosis is described as *only* adaptive regression, or *nothing but* role enactment. As an illustration of a theory of more dimensions, we may consider Shor's (174), that has three dimensions or factors: hypnotic role-taking involvements, trance depth, and archaic involvement. The first of these recognizes the merits of Sarbin's position in its organismic involvement aspect; the second equates hypnosis with other altered states of consciousness; and the third derives from psychoanalytic theory. Trance depth refers to the fading of generalized reality orientation, and archaic involvement is similar to what psychoanalysts call regressive transference.

Neodissociation Theory

Dissociation theory was prevalent in the 19th century and early in the 20th century as a description of what happened in hypnosis, but it went out of favor. I have only recently revived it in an altered form that I call *neodissociation theory* (89–91, 107). The theory postulates a hierarchy of control systems operating at any one time in a given individual, and sees hypnosis as modifying the hierarchical arrangement of these controls, so that some become segregated (dissociated) from others. The theory is designated by a new name in order to disclaim some of the features commonly attributed to dissociation. For example, it has often been supposed that if a dissociation occurs, there should be less interference between simultaneous tasks, so that if one of them is performed out of awareness, it should not affect a task performed with full awareness. This is not the case; it can be shown experimentally that when a task is performed out of awareness through hypnotic suggestion (or as a result of posthypnotic suggestion), there will be *more* interference between the tasks than when both are performed with full awareness (106, 190). The reason is simply that we are dealing with multiple cognitive controls operating simultaneously or intermittently, and there are added burdens on the control systems when a task has to be kept out of awareness while it is being performed; in other words, it costs some cognitive effort to deploy attention away from a task that is at all difficult to do.

The neodissociation theory received support from experiments on pain reduction within hypnosis when it was found through automatic writing or automatic talking that some cognitive system within the person (called metaphorically "the hidden observer") reported awareness of the pain even though neither pain nor suffering was reported in the hypnotic analgesic state (107). While the dissociation in this case has some resemblance to amnesia, it differs from ordinary posthypnotic amnesia in that the pain reported by "the hidden observer" was deflected from full awareness before it had ever become conscious. Once one has been alerted to the possibilities uncovered in these experiments, attention becomes drawn to a number of observations made over the years, especially by clinicians, that bear upon such dissociations (e.g. 167).

If hypnosis is interpreted as but one method by which to reorder the hierarchies among multiple cognitive control systems, the interpretation has some advantage over a more general state theory. The neodissociation theory recognizes that control systems can be altered in various ways other than by hypnotic procedures. Some partial effects found within hypnotic practice are difficult to square with a theory requiring a highly pervasive hypnotic state. For example, an arm contracture, suggested to persist after termination of hypnosis, may in fact persist after hypnosis is formally ended. The neodissociation interpretation permits the contracture to be referred to a partially dissociated control system affecting the muscles of an arm, without involving the whole of the person's cognitive activities. Such an interpretation may very well temper the debates over state theory in that it satisfies the state theorist by recognizing some obvious changes in the control systems of the subject brought about by the hypnotic procedures, without offering an explanation for the specific changes on the basis of some characteristic that separates every instance of hypnosis from other alterations of cognitive controls.

THE HYPNOTIZABLE PERSON

Large individual differences in hypnotic responsiveness have long been recognized; more recently many efforts have been made to quantify these differences, to determine their stability and modifiability, to find personality and situational correlates of them, and to design experiments that take full account of their existence.

Hypnotic Responsiveness Scales

The scales for measuring hypnotic responsiveness go by various names such as depth scales, suggestibility scales, or susceptibility scales, but these names do not specify any important differentiating characteristics; each provides a sample of hypnotic-like behavior, scored according to the number of items "passed." Fuller reports have appeared on scales that were earlier standardized (8, 86, 121), and a formal revision of an earlier scale has appeared (209). Scales that have been translated into other languages and tested in other cultures, e.g. German (80a) and Japanese (203a), have shown very similar distributions of hypnotic responsiveness. A newcomer, a short scale standardized on a large clinical population, is that of Spiegel, yielding a hypnotic induction profile score of 1 to 5 (not to be confused with the earlier Stanford profile scales), and giving prominence to his eye-roll sign (188, 189). The characteristics of his scale do not seem much different from the other available scales, and his scores correlate positively with them. The Stanford

Hypnotic Susceptibility Scale, Form A (SHSS-A) has been compared experimentally with the Barber Suggestibility Scale (BSS), and they have been found to have much in common, particularly if the subjective correction of the objective scores on the BSS has been made (158).

Among the variants of these scales is a group alert scale that moves away from the association of hypnosis with sleep but still correlates with more familiar scales (205).

Supplements to Standardized Scales

Barber (10) introduced a subjective correction to the objective scores of the BSS, at first merely correcting downward those "objectively passed" items that seemed unconvincing to the subject. A separate subjective score was later introduced, in which the subjective convincingness of each item was scaled whether or not the item was objectively passed. With the new subjective scores, the correlation between objective and subjective scores that was spuriously high with the old method (158) fell to .44, showing that the two scores have much less in common than originally supposed (185).

Another supplement to the standardized scales is provided by clinical observations and estimates, as used by Orne, Shor, and their associates in defining "plateau responsiveness," that is, when the subject has reached a plateau after repeated hypnotic experiences (139, 175, 177).

Stability of Measured Differences

Some measure of consistency in human characteristics is congruent with the possibility of change; the question of relative stability has to be answered empirically. Some stability is shown by retest reliabilities with alternate forms of responsiveness scales, commonly in the upper .80s or lower .90s. In a longterm retest with SHSS-A, subjects tested while they were students in a university were retested again at an average of 10 years later, and yielded a retest correlation of .60, despite the changes in living and working arrangements and the responsibilities of young adult life outside the university (130).

A second evidence of stability comes from a possible hereditary component in hypnotic responsiveness, as derived from a study of twins and their families. Monozygous twins, separately tested at the same time, produced scores of the SHSS-A correlating .56, while dizygous twins correlated only .18, with their low correlations supported by those between other family members. The computed index of heritability (h^2) of .62 was highly significant, and leaves open the possibility of some genetic factor (129).

A third line of evidence derives from the continuity between experiences in early childhood and those of adult life that are related to hypnotizability, especially forms of imaginative involvement often encouraged in association with parents; some later influences of childhood discipline are also found (96). In other words, continuities can be provided by significant social-environmental influences as well as by hereditary ones.

Modification of Susceptibility

A review of efforts to change hypnotic responsiveness in the laboratory lists some 175 references, but not over one tenth of these have anything to do with persistent changes (45).

Among the interventions that have been tried are clinical reassurances to relieve anxiety and create a more favorable attitude (38, 175); participation in "consciousness-expanding" or encounter group sessions (170, 197); methods resembling operant conditioning or behavior modification (161); various kinds of modeling or imitative behavior (43, 44, 105); sensory deprivation (162, 210); muscular relaxation induced by EMG feedback (211); special demonstrations and communications about hypnosis (44, 75); and requiring close attention to the hypnotist's words by giving electric shocks for evidence of inattention (78).

The most common finding of the studies has been that the scores show a mean gain of a few points over a control group, and that these gains are either fairly uniform across the board, or are greater for those with initial scores in the middle range. The final scores usually correlate substantially with the initial scores. The hope of producing hypnotic virtuosos out of originally low scorers has not been fulfilled.

Personality Correlates of Hypnotic Responsiveness

The most interesting relationships fall into four areas: imagery, imaginative involvements (absorption), creativity, and cerebral function (especially hemispheric laterality). Cerebral function will be considered later (p. 28).

Despite some conflicting evidence, the residual result from relating imagery to hypnosis seems to be a low but positive relationship (96, 141, 145, 186, 193).

The relationships between imaginative involvements and hypnosis that turned up conspicuously in the clinical studies of J. R. Hilgard (96, 97) have now been incorporated in a pencil-and-paper test that correlates positively with hypnotic susceptibility. Tellegen & Atkinson (199) added appropriate imaginative involvement or absorption items to others selected from the MMPI as most representative of the two commonly reported MMPI factors: a stability-neuroticism factor and an intraversion-extraversion factor. Subsequent factor analysis revealed three factors, two of them corresponding to the familiar MMPI factors, and one corresponding to the new absorption scale. Only absorption consistently correlated with hypnotizability in two replications with large samples.

Creativity, which must bear some relationship to free fantasy, has also produced some interesting if baffling relationships to hypnotic responsiveness (Bowers & Bowers 28, Bowers 29). Both sex and level of susceptibility have to be taken into consideration as moderating variables (Bowers 25). The correlations between creativity tests and hypnosis are usually found only for female subjects, and correlations vary within subject groups stratified according to levels of hypnotic ability. Others have also reported higher correlations for women than for men between hypnotic scores and creativity on a variety of tests (147).

Improving creativity through hypnosis is another matter from finding a correlation between hypnotizability and creativity scores. Recently R. C. Gur (79) has been able to show a relationship whereby male subjects selected as high in hypnotizability score higher in creativity under hypnosis than in the nonhypnotic condition, particularly in figural creativity on a picture construction test.

It should be noted that many "plausible" relationships between personality characteristics and hypnotic susceptibility are not confirmed empirically. Among these are various components of cognitive styles such as tests of repression-sensitization, leveling-sharpening, or field dependence and independence. Some positive correlations commonly emerge when a number of tests are used, but sometimes the signs are reversed from one study to another (66, 178).

PSYCHOPHYSIOLOGICAL CORRELATES OF HYPNOTIC RESPONSIVENESS AND OF THE HYPNOTIC CONDITION

Numerous reviewers have come to the conclusion that no physiological indicator has been found to tell when a person is hypnotized (9, 165), but the search continues.

EEG Correlates of Hypnotic Responsiveness

A person who is highly responsive to hypnotic procedures tends to have a high resting EEG-alpha, in the range of 7 to 13 Hz. That is, not hypnotized, and sitting with eyes closed in a semi-darkened room, the more highly susceptible subject is more likely to produce alpha waves of higher voltage and for longer overall duration (7, 122, 134). These studies have been criticized (52, 143), but more recent findings continue to support the relationship (131). Some studies, to be sure, show technical and statistical problems that make their results difficult to interpret (60, 202). The intriguing possibility has been put forward, with moderate experimental support, that hypnotic responsiveness can be enhanced by feedback training in the production of alpha (50).

Other electrical measures of brain activity, such as evoked potentials, have usually given negative results, although one study shows that under conditions of selective attention more highly hypnotizable subjects increased their sensory evoked responses more than the less highly susceptible (59).

Laterality of Function

By now it is well known that some specialization of function (not mere lateral dominance) characterizes the activities of the two cerebral hemispheres in man. These findings have led to efforts to relate laterality to hypnotic responsiveness.

When a subject is asked to solve a mental problem by an experimenter seated before him and looking him in the eyes, the subject tends to divert his eyes in a characteristic manner, either to the right or to the left. These conjugate lateral eye movements are activated by the opposite hemisphere, so that they can serve in part as an indicator of activity in that hemisphere. Bakan (5), the first to note a possible relationship to hypnosis, found a significant positive correlation between the tendency to move the eyes to the left and hypnotic susceptibility, leading to the conjecture that the highly responsive subject tends to favor the right hemisphere. The results were subsequently confirmed, but in one case weakly (131a) and in another case somewhat indirectly (80). A subsequent experiment by R. C. Gur and R. E. Gur (in preparation) confirmed Bakan's results strongly through the use of appropriate moderating variables (sex, handedness, and eyedness). Coherent with other reports, they found indications that right-handed males were more completely lateralized than the right-handed females, and conversely, that left-handed females were more completely lateralized than left-handed males. The consequence was that eye movements predominantly to the right correlated negatively with hypnosis for right-handed males, and positively for left-handed females. These results are coherent with the interpretation of hypnosis as a right hemisphere function for those who are strongly right-handed, and a left hemisphere function for those who are strongly left-handed. Although there was some relationship between degree of left-handedness and hypnotizability in males, Bakan's (6) finding of a greater variability of hypnotic scores among the left-handed was not confirmed.

Neutral Hypnosis

The hope of finding a specific physiological correlate of the established hypnotic state requires some sort of definition of "neutral hypnosis," because it is well known that the hypnotized subject can do anything from dancing a jig to lying in a stupor. Defining neutral hypnosis is a dubious procedure because the definition itself will bias the findings. Hypnosis cannot be defined as extreme relaxation because it can equally well be described as a hyperalert state (119, 205). The possibility of finding some physiological sign that will persist against the various backgrounds of hypnotic behavior is remote but the search goes on, for example, with respect to electromagnetic fields (151), electrodermal responses (48, 148), or eye movements distinguishing between the more and less susceptible subjects (207).

Psychophysiological Correlates of Pain Reduction
or Production within Hypnosis

The behavioral successes of pain reduction in the laboratory through hypnosis have been demonstrated repeatedly (15, 55a, 87, 88, 93, 184). The studies agree that the amount of pain reduction is correlated with measured hypnotic responsiveness, usually in the range of .40 to .50. It does not matter very much whether the suggestions for pain reduction are given in the nonhypnotic state or after hypnotic induction, so that the results are more attributable to individual differences in responsiveness to suggestions than to hypnosis as such. The responsiveness to suggestions of the hypnotic type can be distinguished, however, from placebo response (123). On the psychophysiological side, the usual finding is that the changes in either heart rate or blood pressure tend to be minimally affected by the reduction in pain through suggestion. Sachs (160) has shown some difference between the blood pressure rise when the pain is felt and when it is reduced by suggestion, but the blood pressure still responded to the stress of ice water even though the subject reported no pain whatever. In ischemic pain produced by a tourniquet followed by exercise, Lenox (116) reported differential effects as between the nonhypnotic condition and hypnotic analgesia, with a leveling of both blood pressure and heart rate when the pain was not being felt. Attempts to replicate his results in the same laboratory (unpublished) have met with only partial successs.

Pain can also be produced in hypnosis through suggestion, to serve as a control for the condition in which there is actual physical stress. Results are somewhat complex, but they do not generally parallel very closely the changes when the actual stress occurs (46, 88).

The burden of the findings is that hypnotic analgesia does not have very profound effects on the usual physiological indicators, a result consonant with the presence of pain reports by "the hidden observer" in the automatic talking experiments. The evidence is reviewed in greater detail in Hilgard & Hilgard (94).

Unilateral Control of Skin Temperature

Voluntary control of temperature differences between the hands has been reported (125, 155), but the separate effects of feedback and hypnosis still have to be clarified. Temperature changes are often noted, for example, in autogenic training (82a). In one study of heartrate modification in which autogenic training and feedback were used, some highly hypnotizable subjects appeared to be less responsive to feedback than less highly hypnotizable ones, possibly because of a distorted awareness of their own bodily processes (39).

SPECIMEN HYPNOTIC PHENOMENA: AMNESIA, ILLUSIONS, HALLUCINATIONS, AND DREAMS

Limitations of space forbid a thorough review of the various hypnotic phenomena that are subject to laboratory investigation. To avoid a too telegraphic summary, a few phenomena illustrative of cognitive distortion or imaginative production have been selected for review.

Amnesia

Posthypnotic amnesia fits the pattern of dissociation because something which the subject once was able to recall (and will recall again) is temporarily inhibited and thus is lower in the hierarchy of available cognitive information. The studies have been reviewed by Cooper (37). Three issues are prominently under discussion: 1. the degree to which amnesia is spontaneous following hypnosis, with the indications that it is rarely present unless it is suggested or expected by the subject (36, 92); 2. source amnesia, in which the content that is learned under hypnosis is recalled although the subject has forgotten that it was learned under hypnosis (36, 51, 62); and 3. the relative importance of hypnotic induction before response to amnesia suggestions (14, 185, 200). Induction turns out to be less important than might be expected.

Cooper (37) showed that the bimodality in distribution of posthypnotic amnesia is attributable to two underlying distributions: (*a*) ordinary forgetting of incidental learning, not recoverable; (*b*) truly suggested amnesia, in which the forgotten material is remembered again when a release signal is given. As a technical matter, in scoring hypnotic scales recoverable amnesia should be used in a refined scoring of susceptibility to amnesia, a point also made by others (104, 133). The bimodality of amnesia scores occurs at all levels of scoring of hypnotic susceptibility (104); children's amnesia scores are heavily influenced by ordinary forgetting.

More highly hypnotizable subjects, when reporting a few items remembered from among a larger number because of amnesia suggestions, tend to report these items in a random order, while less susceptible subjects, reporting the same number of items, tend to give them in the order in which they occurred (54). It appears that amnesia suggestions in the more hypnotizable disrupt ordinary retrieval processes.

Memories dissociated in amnesia still interact with other cognitive processes, as neodissociation theory would predict. For example, interpolated learning in a retroactive paradigm interferes with the recall of prior learned material even though the subject is amnesic for the interpolated material (74).

Visual Illusions and Hallucinations

Parrish, Lundy & Leibowitz (142) showed that in hypnotically induced age regression two illusions changed in their frequency of effects in accordance with known age changes. Unfortunately, efforts to replicate the finding have been unsuccessful (4, 146). Ablating the background through negative hallucination failed to cancel the Ponzo illusion (128). A comparable finding was earlier reported for delayed auditory feedback; a more recent experiment has again reported that speech disruption through such feedback continues even though the subject is hypnotically deaf to his own voice (166).

These largely negative results are countered by one positive finding with visual hallucinations. Graham (71), using a conditioned hallucination paradigm, found that the positive hallucination of a dark background on a white card produced the contrast hallucination, a gray circle appearing lighter against this background than against a white background. Simulating subjects failed to produce the effect.

Eye movements to the hallucination of a moving object appear grossly similar to the movements that would occur if the object were physically there and moving (30, 55), but more exact measures show that the movements differ in detail from those in the presence of the physical object, whether it be the nystagmus movements of following horizontal movements of separated bars, or the regular pursuit movements in watching a swinging pendulum (72, 73, 117).

Not classifying strictly as a study of either illusion or hallucination, but related in that there is a modification of visual stimulus processing, is a report by Graham & Leibowitz (70) on the modification of visual acuity. Myopic subjects improved their visual acuity both in the laboratory and in the outside world following hypnotic suggestions. The puzzling finding was that the change in acuity took place without any physical change in eye refraction as measured through a laser technique that permitted simultaneous measurement of refraction and acuity. It appears that whatever change in acuity took place must have been owing to some change in processing of retinal information at higher levels.

Sleep and Dreams

Although hypnosis does not show the EEG characteristics of sleep, the interaction between sleep and hypnosis continues to be of interest. Kratochvil & Macdonald (109) appeared to show that a hypnotic condition induced prior to sleep could continue after genuine sleep intervened, but the possibility of a rapid reinstatement cannot be ruled out.

Some subjects can respond to suggestions while EEG criteria indicate that they are asleep. For example, a suggestion such as "Whenever I say the word 'pillow' your pillow will feel uncomfortable and you will move it" can be given in stage REM sleep, with the appropriate response elicited during a later REM period (53).

Dreams within hypnosis and night dreams may have some modal differences, but their phenomenal contents clearly overlap (95, 196). The hypnotic dreams of the more highly susceptible subjects are more like their night dreams (196). Tart has reviewed the literature on hypnotic dreams and on attempts to control night dreams through hypnosis (194, 195). Books by Moss (132) and Sacerdote (159) consider hypnotic dreams in wider contexts.

An interesting possibility was opened up by Arkin, Hastey & Reiser (3) when they employed posthypnotic suggestion to produce sleep-talking while the subject was dreaming, providing a description of dream content while the dream was occurring. The method is apparently limited to those who have a history of sleep-talking, but it is still fascinating (2).

CLINICAL APPLICATIONS

A number of books have appeared on clinical approaches within the period of this review, but apart from the large book by Granone (69) in Italian, with a Spanish translation, there is no general survey of the clinical literature. Mention may be made, however, of books designed largely for the practitioner (32, 84, 203). Collections of the clinical papers of Milton Erickson have appeared in two volumes (81, 82), and a summary of his methods is available in a journal article (17). Because of Erickson's ingenuity and inventiveness, his techniques are worth studying for the manner in which they free the reader from stereotyped ideas about hypnotic procedures.

Relation to Behavior Modification

Because hypnosis and behavior modification are both psychological, they readily suggest comparison. Several of the reports show that they may be combined in the practice of the individual investigator (42, 115, 208). Many unsolved problems remain, with answers lacking on how to decide which is the method of choice for a given person with a given complaint.

Relation to Acupuncture

The current interest in acupuncture has led to numerous discussions of the relationship between hypnotic pain reduction and pain reduction by way of inserted needles. The successes of acupuncture in major surgery can be matched by equal successes of operations performed with the help of hypnosis. Pain reduction in animals, claimed for acupuncture, has not been demonstrated with hypnosis, though forms of animal hypnosis (animal catalepsy) have long been studied (150). The research evidence is not yet firm, but it appears that there are elements of suggestion in acupuncture processes, in addition to whatever physiological effects the needles or electrical stimulation may add to the control of pain (110, 173, 206a).

Symptom Control in Clinical Practice

The relation between smoking and lung cancer has led many habitual smokers to seek to break the habit, and many have sought the help of hypnosis (102). Treatment varies from a number of sessions to a single session. Success in a single session has been reported by Spiegel (187), who begins with his hypnotic induction profile (189) and then has the subject commit himself to a standard set of self-suggestions, and to reinforce his resolve to give up smoking by an inconspicuous self-hypnotic procedure that can be practiced in public. He finds from records of hundreds of cases that the more hypnotically responsive the subject is, the more likely he is to give up smoking in the short run, but after a year only about 20% will still not be smoking, and this residual group does not appear to be weighted with the more highly hypnotizable. It is commendable to have his reports on a large number of cases, with sufficient follow-up so that both the successes and failures can be known.

Migraine headache is a debilitating symptom normally recalcitrant to treatment, yet it has been successfully treated in a large number of cases through hypnosis, especially by Harding (83). Careful follow-ups of 90 cases showed 34 with complete relief for periods up to 8 years, another 29 with substantial reduction in frequency, duration, or intensity of the migraine periods, and the remaining 27 either failures or lost to follow-up.

Another troubling set of symptoms arises when a limb has been amputated and the patient has a "phantom limb" replacing the lost member, often registering pain. A series of 37 of these cases have been reported as treated hypnotically by Cedercreutz & Uusitalo (31) with considerable success, 20 of 37 being symptom-free after treatment, with 10 improved. A year later 8 remained symptom-free and 10 improved.

There is a large literature on the hypnotic control of other pains in surgery and in the clinic, pain from labor in childbirth, broken bones, dental extractions, back pains, burns, terminal cancer. The reviews by Barber (11, 12), because they emphasize limiting conditions, give the erroneous impression that there are few clinical successes and contradict his own success in the relief of laboratory pain.

Other reviews of hypnosis in the clinic give evidence of success, e.g. Scott (169), Crasilneck & Hall (40), and Marmer (124).

Psychosomatic Problems

Hypnosis has been tried with some success in a number of psychosomatic complaints (101, 144, 149).

Warts have long been a topic for speculation (and superstition). Success in removing warts by suggestion has been reported (35, 192), but there have also been reported failures (199a). Confusing findings are also found for other skin eruptions. Purpuric lesions (skin spots owing to slight hemorrhages) were produced as a result of suggested emotions (1). Black (20) reported success in altering an atopic skin inflammation, but an attempted replication failed (18). It appears that suggestion may succeed in subjects who meet two criteria: (a) they have a history of psychosomatic reactions in the system being studied; and (b) they are highly responsive to hypnotic suggestions. Negative results apparently occur when these conditions are not met; whether the conditions are sufficient to guarantee positive results is not known.

Various symptoms

To give some idea of the variety of uses that have been made of hypnosis in clinical practice, an arbitrary selection of topics is listed here with a single specimen citation of each: hiccups (157), insomnia (22), phobias (99), psoriasis (56), seizure states [adult (120), child (61)], heart and stress (213), stuttering (126).

Patients Showing Psychotic Behavior

Psychotherapy of patients with mild behavior disorders ("neurotic symptoms") is commonplace in hypnotic practice, but it has often been assumed that psychotics could not be hypnotized. Recent evidence shows that schizophrenic patients, if they are in contact at all, show much the same distribution of hypnotic responsiveness as other subjects (114, 206). They are also candidates for psychotherapy by way of hypnotic procedures (19).

HYPNOSIS AS A TOOL IN PSYCHOLOGICAL INVESTIGATIONS NOT CONCERNED PRIMARILY WITH HYPNOSIS

Any orderly phenomena become interesting in themselves but also have the potential of usefulness in experiments whose substantive interest lies elsewhere. Hypnosis has been used to control conditions in other experiments in a variety of contexts (21, 68, 118, 152).

Learning, Memory, and Skilled Performances

What can we learn about processes of acquisition, retention, and retrieval that are of general psychological significance by using hypnosis to control attention, emotional arousal, or other background aspects of learning and memory? The experiments of Blum and his associates provide good illustrations recently summarized by him (21). Using a few highly trained subjects he is able to control anxiety level, cognitive arousal, or pleasure, and determine the consequences for learning of these conditions as parameters of learning and performance.

Social Motivation and Behavior

An ingenious earlier study by Rosenberg (156) showed how hypnosis could be used to control attitudes to then current social problems and result in a cognitive reorganization according to a theory not itself based on hypnosis. Later, Zimbardo and his associates (214) tested the theory of cognitive dissonance by studying changes in the interference with a learned performance by evoked pain. A manipulation by cognitive dissonance reduced the amount of interference by the pain, and could be compared with the pain reduction when the interference was reduced by hypnosis. In a related experiment, hypnosis was used instead of epinephrine to produce an aroused state to test the effect of the social situation on perceived emotion (215).

Psychopathology and Psychotherapy

According to Levitt & Chapman (118), the most frequent use of hypnosis as a research supplement has been in the artificial induction of emotional and psychopathological states in order to allow investigation of their underlying dynamics (e.g. 171, 179, 191).

Monitoring and Controlling Subjective States and Their Physiological Correlates

Hypnosis permits the maintenance of a subject's state of arousal at a remarkably uniform level, if that is desired. It may be that the successes in unilateral control of hand temperature (125, 159), in which hypnosis is combined with biofeedback, have relied on a kind of "verbal curare" to maintain some of the uniformities that Miller and his associates have produced by curarizing their rats in order to condition such unilateral vasomotor responses (127).

Cautions in the Use of Hypnosis

The hazards of hypnosis to the subject are minimal (98), but the experimenter may risk experimental failure by expecting too much from hypnosis. While important effects can be produced through hypnotic-like suggestions, the effects have to be studied for themselves in pilot studies and cannot be assumed to have the status of adequate controls until they have been tested; fortunately, many of them will pass the test.

CONTEMPORARY HISTORY

The years since the earlier review have witnessed a substantial increase in hypnotic interest and activity, including the establishment of Division 30 within the APA, with a membership of 433 in 1973, and a revitalized International Society of Hypnosis, bringing together those from around the world who are interested in the scientific and clinical aspects of hypnosis.

The boundaries of hypnosis, especially in its clinical applications, are confused by two related developments. The first is *autogenic* training, a somewhat ritualized relaxation technique developed by Schultz in Germany, now widely used throughout the world, especially in Germany and Japan (168). Its practitioners recognize a close relationship to hypnosis (especially autohypnosis) and commonly take leadership in hypnotic societies (Gheorghiu, Langen & Velden 63). The second is *sophrology*, a form of psychotherapy founded by Caycedo in Spain and Gubel in Argentina, and now widely adopted throughout Mexico and South America. Although some of its adherents distinguish between it and hypnosis (on the grounds that it is somewhat broader) others seem to make no distinction (77).

Books Offering Major Reviews of the Research Literature

Several recent books in English provide a wide coverage of the experimental literature (10, 33, 58, 67, 86, 164). Three books provide collections of reports from international congresses or other international seminars (34, 111, 112). Major books continue to appear in other languages (33, 69, 103, 108). More specialized books have been referred to under appropriate topics.

Historical Reviews

A number of original documents important in the early history of mesmerism and hypnosis have been republished in the collections edited by Shor & Orne (176) and Tinterow (201). Ellenberger's book (49) deserves special mention because from its title it would not be inferred that it is the best history of hypnosis now available.

A LOOK TO THE FUTURE

Hull (100), ready to leave the field after his book was written, bequeathed 102 experimentable problems for the future investigator. Many of his questions remain unanswered. Fromm's (57) anticipations for future research will be interesting to review after more years have passed. The gratifying advances in experimental studies need to be supplemented by multivariate approaches to bring order out of the countless variables with minor effects. The anecdotal clinical literature, valuable as it is, needs more systematic studies to determine who can profit by what kind of treatment, with attention to measurable individual differences as well as the influences of the patient's personal history.

Literature Cited

1. Agle, D. P., Ratnoff, O. D., Wasman, M. 1967. Studies in autoerythrocyte sensitization: The induction of purpuric lesions by hypnotic suggestion. *Psychosom. Med.* 29:491–503
2. Arkin, A. M., Antrobus, J. S., Toth, M. F., Baker, J., Jackler, F. 1972. A comparison of the content of mentation reports elicited after nonrapid eye movement (NREM) associated sleep utterance and NREM "silent" sleep. *J. Nerv. Ment. Dis.* 155:427–35
3. Arkin, A. M., Hastey, J. M., Reiser, M. F. 1966. Post-hypnotically stimulated sleep-talking. *J. Nerv. Ment. Dis.* 142:293–309
4. Ascher, L. M., Barber, T. X., Spanos, N. P. 1972. Two attempts to replicate the Parrish-Lundy-Leibowitz experiment on hypnotic age regression. *Am. J. Clin. Hypn.* 14:178–85
5. Bakan, P. 1969. Hypnotizability, laterality of eye movements, and functional brain asymmetry. *Percept. Mot. Skills* 28:927–32
6. Bakan, P. 1970. Handedness and hypnotizability. *Int. J. Clin. Exp. Hypn.* 18:99–104
7. Bakan, P., Svorad, D. 1969. Resting EEG alpha and asymmetry of reflective lateral eye movements. *Nature* 223:975–76
8. Barber, T. X. 1965. Measuring "hypnotic-like" suggestibility with and without "hypnotic induction"; psychometric norms, and variables influencing response to the Barber Suggestibility Scale (BSS). *Psychol. Rep.* 16:809–44
9. Barber, T. X. 1965. Physiological effects of "hypnotic suggestions": A critical review of recent research (1960–64). *Psychol. Bull.* 63:201–22
10. Barber, T. X. 1969. *Hypnosis: A Scientific Approach.* New York: Van Nostrand-Reinhold. 282 pp.
11. Barber, T. X. 1970. *LSD, Marihuana, Yoga, and Hypnosis.* Chicago: Aldine
12. Barber, T. X. 1972. Suggested "hypnotic" behavior: The trance paradigm versus an alternative paradigm. See Ref. 58, 115–82
13. Barber, T. X., Calverley, D. S. 1964. Toward a theory of hypnotic behavior: Effects on suggestibility of defining the situation as hypnosis and defining response to suggestions as easy. *J. Abnorm. Soc. Psychol.* 68:585–92
14. Barber, T. X., Calverley, D. S. 1966. Toward a theory of "hypnotic" behavior: Experimental analyses of suggested amnesia. *J. Abnorm. Psychol.* 71:95–107
15. Barber, T. X., Cooper, B. J. 1972. Effects on pain of experimentally induced and spontaneous distraction. *Psychol. Rep.* 31:647–51
16. Barrios, A. A. 1973. Posthypnotic suggestion as higher-order conditioning—methodological and experimental analysis. *Int. J. Clin. Exp. Hypn.* 21:32–50
17. Beahrs, J. O. 1971. The hypnotic psychotherapy of Milton H. Erickson. *Am. J. Clin. Hypn.* 14:73–90
18. Beahrs, J. O., Harris, D. R., Hilgard, E. R. 1970. Failure to alter skin inflammation by hypnotic suggestion in five subjects with normal skin reactivity. *Psychosom. Med.* 32:627–32
19. Biddle, W. E. 1967. *Hypnosis in the Psychoses.* Springfield: Thomas. 139 pp.
20. Black, S. 1963. Inhibition of immediate-type hypersensitivity response by direct suggestion under hypnosis. *Brit. Med. J.* 1:925–29
21. Blum, G. S. 1972. Hypnotic programming techniques in psychological experiments. See Ref. 58, 359–85
22. Borkovec, T. D., Fowles, D. C. 1973. Controlled investigation of the effects of progressive and hypnotic relaxation on insomnia. *J. Abnorm. Psychol.* 82:153–58
23. Bowers, K. S. 1966. Hypnotic behavior: The differentiation of trance and demand characteristic variables. *J. Abnorm. Psychol.* 71:42–51
24. Bowers, K. S. 1967. The effect of demands for honesty on reports of visual and auditory hallucinations. *Int. J. Clin. Exp. Hypn.* 15:31–36
25. Bowers, K. S. 1971. Sex and susceptibility as moderator variables in the relationship of creativity and hyp-

notic susceptibility. *J. Abnorm. Psychol.* 78:93–100

26. Bowers, K. S. 1973. Hypnosis, attribution, and demand characteristics. *Int. J. Clin. Exp. Hypn.* 21:226–38
27. Bowers, K. S. 1973. Situationism in psychology: An analysis and a critique. *Psychol. Rev.* 80:307–36
28. Bowers, K. S., Bowers, P. G. 1972. Hypnosis and creativity: A theoretical and empirical rapprochement. See Ref. 58, 255–91
29. Bowers, P. G. 1967. Effect of hypnosis and suggestions of reduced defensiveness on creativity test performance. *J. Pers.* 35:311–22
30. Brady, J. P., Levitt, E. E. 1966. Hypnotically induced visual hallucinations. *Psychosom. Med.* 28:351–63
31. Cedercreutz, C., Uusitalo, E. 1967. Hypnotic treatment of phantom sensations in 37 amputees. See Ref. 112, 65–66
32. Cheek, D. B., LeCron, L. M. 1968. *Clinical Hypnotherapy.* New York: Grune & Stratton. 245 pp.
33. Chertok, L. 1966. *Hypnosis.* New York: Pergamon. 176 pp. Transl. from *L'Hypnose* 1963. Paris: Masson. 224 pp. 3rd ed.
34. Chertok, L., Ed. 1969. *Psychophysiological Mechanisms of Hypnosis.* New York: Springer-Verlag. 207 pp.
35. Clarke, G. H. V. 1965. The charming of warts. *J. Invest. Dermatol.* 45:15–21
36. Cooper, L. M. 1966. Spontaneous and suggested posthypnotic source amnesia. *Int. J. Clin. Exp. Hypn.* 14:180–93
37. Cooper, L. M. 1972. Hypnotic amnesia. See Ref. 58, 217–52
38. Cooper, L. M., Banford, S. A., Schubot, E., Tart, C. T. 1967. A further attempt to modify hypnotic susceptibility through repeated individualized experience. *Int. J. Clin. Exp. Hypn.* 3:118–24
39. Cowings, P. S. 1973. *Combined use of autogenic training and biofeedback in conditioned autoregulation of autonomic responses in humans.* PhD thesis. Univ. California, Davis
40. Crasilneck, H. B., Hall, J. A. 1973. Clinical hypnosis in problems of pain. *Am. J. Clin. Hypn.* 15:153–61
41. Damaser, E. C., Shor, R. E., Orne, M. T. 1963. Physiological effects during hypnotically requested emotions. *Psychosom. Med.* 25:334–43
42. Dengrove, E. 1973. Uses of hypnosis in behavior therapy. *Int. J. Clin. Exp. Hypn.* 21:13–17
43. DeVoge, J. T., Sachs, L. B. 1973. Modification of hypnotic susceptibility through imitative behavior. *Int. J. Clin. Exp. Hypn.* 21:70–77
44. Diamond, M. J. 1972. The use of observationally presented information to modify hypnotic susceptibility. *J. Abnorm. Psychol.* 79:174–80
45. Diamond, M. J. 1974. The modification of hypnotizability: A review. *Psychol. Bull.* 81:180–98
46. Dudley, D. L., Holmes, T. H., Ripley, H. S. 1967. Hypnotically induced and suggested facsimile of head pain. *J. Nerv. Ment. Dis.* 144:258–65
47. Edmonston, W. E. Jr. 1967. Stimulus-response theory of hypnosis. See Ref. 67, 345–87
48. Edmonston, W. E. Jr. 1968. Hypnosis and electrodermal responses. *Am. J. Clin. Hypn.* 11:16–25
49. Ellenberger, H. F. 1970. *The Discovery of the Unconscious: The History and Evolution of Dynamic Psychiatry.* New York: Basic Books. 932 pp.
50. Engstrom, D. R., London, P., Hart, J. L. 1970. Hypnotic susceptibility increased by EEG alpha training. *Nature* 227:1261–62
51. Evans, F. J. 1971. *Contextual Forgetting: A Study of Source Amnesia.* Presented at meet. East. Psychol. Assoc. New York
52. Evans, F. J. 1972. Hypnosis and sleep: Techniques for exploring cognitive activity during sleep. See Ref. 58, 43–83
53. Evans, F. J., Gustafson, L. A., O'Connell, D. N., Orne, M. T., Shor, R. E. 1970. Verbally induced behavioral responses during sleep. *J. Nerv. Ment. Dis.* 150:171–87
54. Evans, F. J., Kihlstrom, J. F. 1973. Posthypnotic amnesia as disrupted retrieval. *J. Abnorm. Psychol.* 82:317–23
55. Evans, F. J., Reich, L. H., Orne, M. T. 1972. Optokinetic nystagmus, eye movements, and hypnotically induced hallucinations. *J. Nerv. Ment. Dis.* 152: 419–31

55a. Evans, M. B., Paul, G. L. 1970. Effects of hypnotically suggested analgesia on physiological and subjective responses to cold stress. *J. Consult. Clin. Psychol.* 35:362–71

56. Frankel, F. H., Misch, R. C. 1973. Hypnosis in a case of long-standing psoriasis in a person with character problems. *Int. J. Clin. Exp. Hypn.* 21:121–30

57. Fromm, E. 1972. Quo vadis hypnosis? Predictions of future trends in hypnosis research. See Ref. 58, 575–86

58. Fromm, E., Shor, R., Eds. 1972. *Hypnosis: Research developments and Perspectives.* Chicago: Aldine-Atherton. 656 pp.

59. Galbraith, G. C., Cooper, L. M., London, P. 1972. Hypnotic susceptibility and the sensory evoked response. *J. Comp. Physiol. Psychol.* 80:509–14

60. Galbraith, G. C., London, P., Leibovitz, M. P., Cooper, L. M., Hart, J. T. 1970. EEG and hypnotic susceptibility. *J. Comp. Physiol. Psychol.* 72:125–31

61. Gardner, G. G. 1973. Use of hypnosis for psychogenic epilepsy in a child. *Am. J. Clin. Hypn.* 15:166–69

62. Gheorghiu, V. A. 1973. *Hypnose und Gedächtnis.* Munich: Goldmann. 133 pp.

63. Gheorghiu, V. A., Langen, D., Velden, M. 1971. Die Einstellung zu autogenem Training oder Hypnose. *Z. Psychosom. Med. Psychoanal.* 21:129–37

64. Gill, M. M. 1972. Hypnosis as an altered and regressed state. *Int. J. Clin. Exp. Hypn.* 20:224–37

65. Gill, M. M., Brenman, M. 1959. *Hypnosis and Related States: Psychoanalytic Studies in Regression.* New York: Int. Univ. Press. 405 pp.

66. Goldberger, N. I., Wachtel, P. L. 1973. Hypnotizability and cognitive controls. *Int. J. Clin. Exp. Hypn.* 21:298–304

67. Gordon, J. E., Ed. 1967. *Handbook of Clinical and Experimental Hypnosis.* New York: Macmillan. 653 pp.

68. Ibid. Hypnosis in research on psychotherapy, 148–202

69. Granone, F. 1972. *Trattato di ipnosi (sofrologia).* Torino: Boringhieri. 1081 pp. 2nd ed.

70. Graham, C., Leibowitz, H. W. 1972. Effect of suggestion on visual acuity. *Int. J. Clin. Exp. Hypn.* 20:169–86

71. Graham, K. R. 1969. Brightness contrast by hypnotic hallucination. *Int. J. Clin. Exp. Hypn.* 17:62–73

72. Graham, K. R. 1970. Optokinetic nystagmus as a criterion of visual imagery. *J. Nerv. Ment. Dis.* 151:411–14

73. Graham, K. R. 1970. Eye movements during waking imagery and hypnotic hallucinations. *Diss. Abstr. Int.* 30(8-B):3887–88

74. Graham, K. R., Patton, A. 1968. Retroactive inhibition, hypnosis and hypnotic amnesia. *Int. J. Clin. Exp. Hypn.* 16:68–74

75. Gregory, J., Diamond, M. J. 1973. Increasing hypnotic susceptibility by means of positive expectancies and written instructions. *J. Abnorm. Psychol.* 82:363–67

76. Gruenewald, D., Fromm, E., Oberlander, M. I. 1972. Hypnosis and adaptive regression: An ego-psychological inquiry. See Ref. 58, 495–509

77. Gubel, I. 1973. From hypnosis to sophrology: Eleven years of teaching. *Am. J. Clin. Hypn.* 15:258–62

78. Gur, R. C. 1973. *An experimental investigation of a new procedure for enhancing hypnotic susceptibility.* Unpublished PhD thesis. Michigan State Univ., East Lansing

79. Gur, R. C. 1971. *The enhancement of creativity via free imagery and hypnosis.* Unpublished MA thesis. Michigan State Univ., East Lansing

80. Gur, R. E., Reyher, J. 1973. Relationship between style of hypnotic induction and direction of lateral eye movement. *J. Abnorm. Psychol.* 82:499–505

80a. Halder, P., Junkers, G., Latke, H. 1972. Die Stanford-Skala zur Erfassung der hypnotische Suszetibilität. *Diagnostica* 18:141–49

81. Haley, J., Ed. 1967. *Advanced Techniques of Hypnosis and Therapy: Selected Papers of Milton H. Erickson, M. D.* New York: Grune & Stratton. 557 pp.

82. Haley, J. 1973. *Uncommon Therapy: The Psychiatric Techniques of Milton H. Erickson, M. D.* New York: Norton. 315 pp.

82a. Harano, K., Ogawa, K., Naruse, G. 1965. A study of plethysmography and skin temperature during active concentration and autogenic exercise. In *Autogenes Training: Correlationes Psychosomaticae*, ed. W. Luthe, 55–58. Stuttgart: Verlag. 325 pp.

83. Harding, H. C. 1967. Hypnosis in the treatment of migraine. See Ref. 112, 131–34

84. Hartland, J. 1971. *Medical and Dental Hypnosis*. Baltimore: Williams & Wilkins. 389 pp. 2nd ed.

85. Hilgard, E. R. 1965. Hypnosis. *Ann. Rev. Psychol.* 16:157–80

86. Hilgard, E. R. 1965. *Hypnotic Susceptibility*. New York: Harcourt, Brace & World. 434 pp.

87. Hilgard, E. R. 1969. Pain as a puzzle for psychology and physiology. *Am. Psychol.* 24:103–13

88. Hilgard, E. R. 1971. Pain: Its reduction and production under hypnosis. *Proc. Am. Phil. Soc.* 115:470–76

89. Hilgard, E. R. 1973. Dissociation revisited. In *Historical Conceptions of Psychology*, ed. M. Henle, J. Jaynes, J. J. Sullivan, 205–19. New York: Springer. 323 pp.

90. Hilgard, E. R. 1973. A neodissociation theory of pain reduction in hypnosis. *Psychol. Rev.* 80:396–411

91. Hilgard, E. R. 1974. Toward a neodissociation theory: Multiple cognitive controls in human functioning. *Perspect. Biol. Med.* 17:301–16

92. Hilgard, E. R., Cooper, L. M. 1965. Spontaneous and suggested posthypnotic amnesia. *Int. J. Clin. Exp. Hypn.* 13:261–73

93. Hilgard, E. R. et al 1974. The psychophysics of cold pressor pain and its modification through hypnotic suggestion. *Am. J. Psychol.* In press

94. Hilgard, E. R., Hilgard, J. R. 1975. *Pain Control Through Hypnosis and Suggestion*. Los Altos, Calif.: Kaufmann. In press

95. Hilgard, E. R., Nowlis, D. P. 1972. The contents of hypnotic dreams and night dreams: An exercise in method. See Ref. 58, 511–24

96. Hilgard, J. R. 1970. *Personality and Hypnosis: A Study of Imaginative Involvement*. Univ. Chicago Press. 304 pp.

97. Hilgard, J. R. 1974. Imaginative involvement: Some characteristics of the highly hypnotizable and nonhypnotizable. *Int. J. Clin. Exp. Hypn.* 22: 138–56

98. Ibid. Sequelae to hypnosis. In press

99. Horowitz, S. L. 1970. Strategies within hypnosis for reducing phobic behavior. *J. Abnorm. Psychol.* 75:104–12

100. Hull, C. L. 1930–31. Quantitative methods of investigating hypnotic suggestion. *J. Abnorm. Soc. Psychol.* 25:200–23, 390–417

101. Ikemi, Y. 1967. Psychological desensitization in allergic disorders. See Ref. 112, 160–65

102. Johnston, E., Donoghue, J. R. 1971. Hypnosis and smoking: A review of the literature. *Am. J. Clin. Hypn.* 13: 265–72

103. Katzenstein, A., Ed. 1971. *Hypnose: Aktuelle Probleme in Theorie, Experiment und Klinik*. Jena: Fischer. 327 pp.

104. Kihlstrom, J. F., Evans, F. J. 1973. *Forgetting to count reversibility: What constitutes posthypnotic amnesia?* Presented at meet. Soc. Clin. Exp. Hypn. Newport Beach, Calif.

105. Klinger, B. I. 1970. Effect of peer model responsiveness and length of induction procedure on hypnotic responsiveness. *J. Abnorm. Psychol.* 75:15–18

106. Knox, V. J., Crutchfield, L., Hilgard, E. R. 1973. *The nature of task interference in hypnotic dissociation*. Presented at meet. Soc. Clin. Exp. Hypn. Newport Beach, Calif.

107. Knox, V. J., Morgan, A. H., Hilgard, E. R. 1974. Pain and suffering in ischemia: The paradox of hypnotically suggested anesthesia as contradicted by reports from "the hidden observer." *Arch. Gen. Psychiat.* 30:840–47

108. Kratochvil, S. 1972. *Podstata Hypnózy a Spanek* (The nature of hypnosis and its relationship to sleep). Prague: Academia. 217 pp.

109. Kratochvil, S., Macdonald, H. 1972. Sleep in hypnosis: A pilot EEG study. *Am. J. Clin. Hypn.* 15:29–37

110. Kroger, W. S. 1972. Hypnotism and acupuncture. *J. Am. Med. Assoc.* 200:1012–13

111. Langen, D., Ed. 1972. *Hypnose und Psychosomatische Medizin*. Stuttgart:

Hippokrates. 276 pp.

112. Lassner, J., Ed. 1967. *Hypnosis and Psychosomatic Medicine*. New York: Springer-Verlag. 329 pp.

113. Lavoie, G., Sabourin, M., Ally, G., Langlios, J. 1973. *Hypnotizability as a function of adaptive regression and drive representations in chronic schizophrenia*. Presented at meet. Soc. Clin. Exp. Hypn. Newport Beach, Calif.

114. Lavoie, G., Sabourin, M., Langlois, J. 1973. Hypnotic susceptibility, amnesia, and IQ in chronic schizophrenia. *Int. J. Clin. Exp. Hypn.* 21:157–67

115. Lazarus, A. A. 1973. "Hypnosis" as a facilitator in behavior therapy. *Int. J. Clin. Exp. Hypn.* 21:25–31

116. Lenox, J. R. 1970. Effect of hypnotic analgesia on verbal report and cardiovascular responses to ischemic pain. *J. Abnorm. Psychol.* 75:199–206

117. Lenox, J. R., Lange, A. F., Graham, K. R. 1970. Eye movement amplitudes in imagined pursuit of a pendulum with eyes closed. *Psychophysiology* 6:773–77

118. Levitt, E. E., Chapman, R. H. 1972. Hypnosis as a research method. See Ref. 58, 85–113

119. Liebert, R. M., Rubin, N., Hilgard, E. R. 1965. The effects of suggestions of alertness in hypnosis on paired-associate learning. *J. Pers.* 33:605–12

120. Lindner, H. 1973. Psychogenic seizure states: A psychodynamic study. *Int. J. Clin. Exp. Hypn.* 21:261–71

121. London, P., Cooper, L. M. 1969. Norms of hypnotic susceptibility in children. *Develop. Psychol.* 1:113–24

122. London, P., Hart, J. T., Leibovitz, M. P. 1968. EEG alpha rhythms and susceptibility to hypnosis. *Nature* 219: 71–72

123. McGlashan, T. H., Evans, F. J., Orne, M. T. 1969. The nature of hypnotic analgesia and placebo response to experimental pain. *Psychosom. Med.* 31:227–46

124. Marmer, M. J. 1969. Unusual applications of hypnosis in anesthesiology. *Int. J. Clin. Exp. Hypn.* 17:199–208

125. Maslach, C., Marshall, G., Zimbardo, P. 1972. Hypnotic control of peripheral skin temperature: A case report. *Psychophysiology* 9:600–5

126. Masson, L. I., Kovitz, D. M., Muir, L.

M. 1972. Comparative study of the treatment of stuttering by three relaxing methods. *Brit. J. Clin. Hypn.* 3:34–39

127. Miller, N. E. 1969a. Learning of visceral and glandular responses. *Science* 163:434–45

128. Miller, R. J., Hennessy, R. T., Leibowitz, H. W. 1973. The effect of hypnotic ablation of the background on the magnitude of the Ponzo perspective illusion. *Int. J. Clin. Exp. Hypn.* 21:180–91

129. Morgan, A. H. 1973. The heritability of hypnotic susceptibility in twins. *J. Abnorm. Psychol.* 82:55–61

130. Morgan, A. H., Johnson, D. L., Hilgard, E. R. 1974. The stability of hypnotic susceptibility: A longitudinal study. *Int. J. Clin. Exp. Hypn.* 22:249–57

131. Morgan, A. H., Macdonald, H., Hilgard, E. R. 1974. EEG alpha: Lateral asymmetry related to task and hypnotizability. *Psychophysiology*. In press

131a. Morgan, A. H., McDonald, P. J., Macdonald, H. 1971. Differences in bilateral alpha activity as a function of experimental task with a note on lateral eye movements and hypnotizability. *Neuropsychologia* 9:459–69

132. Moss, C. S. 1967. *The Hypnotic Investigation of Dreams*. New York: Wiley. 290 pp.

133. Nace, E. P., Orne, M. T., Hammer, A. G. 1974. The reversibility of amnesia. *Arch. Gen. Psychiat.* In press

134. Nowlis, D. P., Rhead, J. C. 1968. Relation of eyes-closed resting EEG alpha activity to hypnotic susceptibility. *Percept. Mot. Skills* 27:1047–50

135. O'Connell, D. N., Shor, R. E., Orne, M. T. 1970. Hypnotic age regression: An empirical and methodological analysis. *J. Abnorm. Psychol. Monogr.* 76 (3, Pt. 2)

136. Orne, M. T. 1971. The simulation of hypnosis: Why, how, and what it means. *Int. J. Clin. Exp. Hypn.* 19:183–210

137. Orne, M. T. 1972. On the simulating subject as a quasi-control group in hypnosis research: What, why, and how. See Ref. 58, 339–443

138. Orne, M. T., Evans, F. J. 1966. Inadvertent termination of hypnosis with

hypnotized and simulating subjects. *Int. J. Clin. Exp. Hypn.* 14:61–78

139. Orne, M. T., O'Connell, D. N. 1967. Diagnostic ratings of hypnotizability. *Int. J. Clin. Exp. Hypn.* 15:125–33

140. Orne, M. T., Sheehan, P. W., Evans, F. J. 1968. Occurrence of posthypnotic behavior outside the experimental setting. *J. Pers. Soc. Psychol.* 9:189–96

141. Palmer, R. D., Field, P. B. 1968. Visual imagery and susceptibility to hypnosis. *J. Consult. Clin. Psychol.* 32:456–61

142. Parrish, M., Lundy, R. M., Leibowitz, H. W. 1969. Effect of hypnotic age regression on the magnitude of the Ponzo and Poggendorff illusions. *J. Abnorm. Psychol.* 74:693–98

143. Paskewitz, D. A., Orne, M. T. 1973. Visual effects on alpha feedback training. *Science* 181:360–63

144. Perloff, M., Spiegelman, J. 1973. Hypnosis in the treatment of a child's allergy to dogs. *Am. J. Clin. Hypn.* 15:269–72

145. Perry, C. 1973. Imagery, fantasy and hypnotic susceptibility: A multidimensional approach. *J. Pers. Soc. Psychol.* 26:208–16

146. Perry, C., Chisholm, W. 1973. Hypnotic age regression and the Ponzo and Poggendorf illusions. *Int. J. Clin. Exp. Hypn.* 21:192–204

147. Perry, C., Wilder, S., Appignanesi, A. 1973. Hypnotic susceptibility and performance on a battery of creativity measures. *Am. J. Clin. Hypn.* 15:170–80

148. Pessin, M., Plapp, J. N., Stern, J. A. 1968. Effects of hypnosis induction and attention direction on electrodermal responses. *Am. J. Clin. Hypn.* 10:198–206

149. Philipp, R. L., Wilde, G. J. S., Day, J. H. 1972. Suggestion and relaxation in asthmatics. *J. Psychosom. Res.* 16:193–204

150. Ratner, S. C. 1967. Comparative aspects of hypnosis. See Ref. 67, 550–87

151. Ravitz, L. J. 1970. Electromagnetic field monitoring of changing state-function, including hypnotic states. *J. Am. Soc. Psychosom. Dent. Med.* 17:119–27

152. Reyher, J. 1967. Hypnosis in research

on psychopathology. See Ref. 67, 110–47

153. Reyher, J. 1973. Can hypnotized subjects simulate waking behavior? *Am. J. Clin. Hypn.* 16:31–36

154. Richman, D. N. 1965. A critique of two recent theories of hypnosis: The psychoanalytic theory of Gill and Brenman contrasted with the behavioral theory of Barber. *Psychiat. Quart.* 39:278–92

155. Roberts, A. H., Kewman, D. G., Macdonald, H. 1973. Voluntary control of skin temperature: Unilateral changes using hypnosis and feedback. *J. Abnorm. Psychol.* 82:163–68

156. Rosenberg, M. J. 1960. Cognitive reorganization in response to the hypnotic reversal of attitudinal affect. *J. Pers.* 28:39–63

157. Rubin, R. B. 1972. The hypnotherapeutic management of intractable hiccups. *Brit. J. Clin. Hypn.* 3:82–87

158. Ruch, J. C., Morgan, A. H., Hilgard, E. R. 1973. Behavioral predictions from hypnotic responsiveness scores with and without prior induction procedures. *J. Abnorm. Psychol.* 82:543–46

159. Sacerdote, P. 1967. *Induced Dreams.* New York: Vantage. 174 pp.

160. Sachs, L. B. 1970. Comparison of hypnotic analgesia and hypnotic relaxation during stimulation by a continuous pain source. *J. Abnorm. Psychol.* 76:206–10

161. Sachs, L. B., Anderson, W. L. 1967. Modification of hypnotic susceptibility. *Int. J. Clin. Exp. Hypn.* 15:172–80

162. Sanders, R. S., Reyher, J. 1969. Sensory deprivation and the enhancement of hypnotic susceptibility. *J. Abnorm. Psychol.* 74:375–81

163. Sarbin, T. R., Andersen, M. L. 1967. Role-theoretical analysis of hypnotic behavior. See Ref. 67, 319–44

164. Sarbin, T. R., Coe, W. C. 1972. *Hypnosis: A Social Psychological Analysis of Influence Communication.* New York: Holt, Rinehart & Winston. 279 pp.

165. Sarbin, T. R., Slagle, R. W. 1972. Hypnosis and psychophysiological outcomes. See Ref. 58, 185–214

166. Scheibe, K. E., Gray, A. L., Keim, C. S.

1968. Hypnotically induced deafness and delayed auditory feedback: A comparison of real and simulating subjects. *Int. J. Clin. Exp. Hypn.* 16:158–64

167. Schilder, P. F. 1956. *The Nature of Hypnosis.* New York: Int. Univ. Press. 204 pp.

168. Schultz, J. H., Luthe, W. 1969. *Autogenic Methods.* New York: Grune & Stratton. 255 pp.

169. Scott, D. L. 1973. Hypnoanalgesia for major surgery: A psychodynamic process. *Am. J. Clin. Hypn.* 16:84–91

170. Shapiro, J. L., Diamond, M. J. 1972. Increases in hypnotizability as a function of encounter group training: Some confirming evidence. *J. Abnorm. Psychol.* 79:112–15

171. Sheehan, P. W. 1969. Artificial induction of posthypnotic conflict. *J. Abnorm. Psychol.* 74:16–25

172. Sheehan, P. W. 1973. Escape from the ambiguous: Artifact and methodologies of hypnosis. *Am. Psychol.* 28:983–93

173. Shibutani, K. 1973. Evaluation of the therapeutic effect of acupuncture. *Proc. NIH Acupuncture Res. Conf. Feb. 28–Mar. 1, 1973.* Bethesda, Md.: DHEW Publ. No. (NIH) 74–165, 28–31

174. Shor, R. E. 1970. The three-factor theory of hypnosis as applied to the book-reading fantasy and to the concept of suggestion. *Int. J. Clin. Exp. Hypn.* 18:89–98

175. Shor, R. E., Cobb, J. C. 1968. An exploratory study of hypnotic training using the concept of plateau hypnotizability as a referent. *Am. J. Clin. Hypn.* 10:178–97

176. Shor, R. E., Orne, M. T., Eds. 1965. *The Nature of Hypnosis: Selected Basic Readings.* New York: Holt, Rinehart & Winston. 504 pp.

177. Shor, R. E., Orne, M. T., O'Connell, D. N. 1966. Psychological correlates of plateau hypnotizability in a special volunteer sample. *J. Pers. Soc. Psychol.* 3:80–95

178. Silber, M. J. 1973. Hypnotizability as related to repression-sensitization and mood. *Am. J. Clin. Hypn.* 15:245–49

179. Sommerschield, H., Reyher, J. 1973. Posthypnotic conflict, repression, and psychopathology. *J. Abnorm. Psychol.* 82:278–90

180. Spanos, N. P. 1971. Goal-directed fantasy and the performance of hypnotic test suggestions. *Psychiatry* 34:86–96

181. Spanos, N. P., Barber, T. X. 1968. "Hypnotic" experiences as inferred from subjective reports: Auditory and visual hallucinations. *J. Exp. Res. Pers.* 3:136–50

182. Spanos, N. P., Barber, T. X. 1972. Cognitive activity during "hypnotic" suggestibility: Goal directed fantasy and the experience of nonvolition. *J. Pers.* 40:510–24

183. Spanos, N. P., Barber, T. X. 1974. Toward a convergence in hypnosis research. *Am. Psychol.* 29:500–11

184. Spanos, N. P., Barber, T. X., Lang, G. 1974. Cognition and self-control: Cognitive control of painful sensory input. In *Cognitive Alterations of Feeling States,* ed. H. London, R. Nisbett. Chicago: Aldine. In press

185. Spanos, N. P., Ham, M. L. 1973. Cognitive activity in response to hypnotic suggestion: Goal directed fantasy and selective amnesia. *Am. J. Clin. Hypn.* 15:191–98

186. Spanos, N. P., Valois, R., Ham, M. W., Ham, M. L. 1973. Suggestibility and vividness and control of imagery. *Int. J. Clin. Exp. Hypn.* 21:305–11

187. Spiegel, H. 1970. A single-treatment method to stop smoking using ancillary self-hypnosis. *Int. J. Clin. Hypn.* 18:235–50

188. Spiegel, H. 1972. An eye-roll test for hypnotizability. *Am. J. Clin. Hypn.* 15:25–28

189. Spiegel, H. 1973. Hypnotic induction profile as a quick diagnostic guide. *Am. J. Orthopsychiat.* 43:270–71

190. Stevenson, J. H. 1972. *The effect of hypnotic and posthypnotic dissociation on the performance of interfering tasks.* Unpublished PhD thesis. Stanford Univ., Stanford, Calif.

191. Stross, L., Shevrin, H. 1969. Hypnosis as a method for investigating unconscious thought process: A review of research. *J. Am. Psychoanal. Assoc.* 17:100–35

192. Surman, O. S., Gottlieb, S. K., Hackett, T. P., Silverbe, E. L. 1973. Hypnosis in treatment of warts. *Arch. Gen. Psychiat.* 27:439–41

193. Sutcliffe, J. P., Perry, C. W., Sheehan, P. W. 1970. The relation of some aspects of imagery and fantasy to hypnotizability. *J. Abnorm. Psychol.* 76:279–87

194. Tart, C. T. 1965. The hypnotic dream: Methodological problems and a review of the literature. *Psychol. Bull.* 63:87–99

195. Ibid. Toward the experimental control of dreaming: A review of the literature. 64:81–91

196. Tart, C. T. 1966. Types of hypnotic dreams and their relation to hypnotic depth. *J. Abnorm. Psychol.* 71:377–82

197. Ibid 1970. Increases in hypnotizability resulting from a prolonged program for enhancing personal growth. 75:260–66

198. Tart, C. T. 1970. Self-report scales of hypnotic depth. *Int. J. Clin. Exp. Hypn.* 18:105–25

198a. Tart, C. T. 1972. States of consciousness and state-specific sciences. *Science* 176:1203–10

199. Tellegen, A., Atkinson, G. 1974. Openness to absorbing and self-altering experiences ("absorption"), a trait related to hypnotic susceptibility. *J. Abnorm. Psychol.* 83:268–77

199a. Tenzel, J. H., Taylor, R. L. 1969. An evaluation of hypnosis and suggestions as treatment for warts. *Psychosomatics* 10:252–57

200. Thorne, D. E. 1969. Amnesia and hypnosis. *Int. J. Clin. Exp. Hypn.* 17:225–41

201. Tinterow, M. M., Ed. 1970. *Foundations of Hypnosis: From Mesmer to Freud.* Springfield, Ill.: Thomas. 606 pp.

202. Ulett, G. A., Akpinar, S., Itil, T. M. 1972. Quantitative EEG analysis during hypnosis. *Electroencephalogr. Clin. Neurophysiol.* 33:361–68

203. Ulett, G. A., Peterson, D. B. 1965. *Applied Hypnosis and Positive Suggestion.* St. Louis: Mosby. 134 pp.

203a. Umemoto, T., Saito, T., Osawa, H. 1963. Standardization of Stanford Hypnotic Susceptibility Scale for Japanese sample (in Japanese). In *Yearbook of Hypnotic Studies* (Japanese), ed. G. Naruse, 8:35–44. Tokyo: Seishinshobo

204. Van der Walde, P. H. 1965. Interpretation of hypnosis in terms of ego psychology. *Arch. Gen. Psychiat.* 12:438–47

205. Vingoe, F. J. 1973. Comparison of the Harvard group scale of hypnotic susceptibility, Form A and the group alert trance scale in a university population. *Int. J. Clin. Exp. Hypn.* 21:169–78

206. Vingoe, F. J., Kramer, E. F. 1966. Hypnotic susceptibility of hospitalized psychotic patients: A pilot study. *Int. J. Clin. Exp. Hypn.* 14:47–54

206a. Wall, P. 1972. An eye on the needle. *New Sci.* July 20, 129–31

207. Weitzenhoffer, A. M. 1969. Hypnosis and eye movements. I. Preliminary report on a possible slow eye movement correlate of hypnosis. *Am. J. Clin. Hypn.* 11:221–27

208. Ibid 1972. Behavior therapeutic techniques and hypnotherapeutic methods. 15:71–82

209. Weitzenhoffer, A. M., Hilgard, E. R. 1967. *Revised Stanford Profile Scales of Hypnotic Susceptibility, Forms I and II.* Palo Alto, Calif.: Consult. Psychol. Press

210. Wickramasekera, I. 1970. Effects of sensory restriction on susceptibility to hypnosis: A hypothesis and more preliminary data. *J. Abnorm. Psychol.* 76:69–75

211. Ibid 1973. Effects of electromyographic feedback on hypnotic susceptibility: More preliminary data. 82:74–77

212. Williamsen, J. A., Johnson, H. J., Eriksen, C. W. 1965. Some characteristics of posthypnotic amnesia. *J. Abnorm. Psychol.* 70:123–31

213. Yanovski, A., Curtis, G. C. 1968. Hypnosis and stress. *Am. J. Clin. Hypn.* 10:149–56

214. Zimbardo, P. G., Rapaport, C., Baron, J. 1969. Pain control by hypnotic induction of motivational states. In *Cognitive Control of Motivation*, ed. P. G. Zimbardo, 136–52. Chicago: Scott, Foresman. 300 pp.

215. Zimbardo, P. G., Maslach, C., Marshall, G. 1972. Hypnosis and the psychology of cognitive and behavioral control. See Ref. 58, 539–71

DRUG USE AND ABUSE § 227

William H. McGlothlin[1]

Department of Psychology, University of California at Los Angeles
Los Angeles, California 90024

In recent years, public concern about nonmedical drug use has stimulated a generous allocation of research funds, and this has resulted in a very large body of literature over a wide range of disciplines. The present brief review is necessarily highly selective, both in terms of the areas covered and the literature cited within specific fields. Some areas have been arbitrarily excluded because of the limits of space; others such as pharmacology and animal experimentation have been omitted because of the author's lack of familiarity with the literature. Alcohol and tobacco are not considered, although the aggregate individual and social costs resulting from their use is clearly much larger than that for other drugs. I have attempted to anticipate the topics of general reader interest—emphasizing such areas as current trends in the heroin epidemic, the individual and social impact of marijuana use, evaluations and new developments in treatment and the effectiveness of prevention efforts. Special attention has been given to the epidemiological and behavioral research which describe the dimensions, significance, and trends of current nonmedical drug use.

Probably the best general reviews of nonmedical drug use are contained in the recent reports of the U.S. and Canadian drug commissions. Both commissions issued separate reports on marijuana (23, 80), followed by documents on the overall subject of drug abuse and social policy (24, 79). Reviews of current marijuana research are provided by the annual *Marihuana and Health reports* to Congress (90). The *Federal Strategy for Drug Abuse and Drug Traffic Prevention* reports (1973 and 1974) describe the overall Federal activities and goals, and are a good source of current statistics related to drug use, treatment, and prevention (99, 100).

[1] Preparation of this chapter was supported by Research Scientist Award No. KO5–DA–70182 from the National Institute of Mental Health.

45

THE RECENT EPIDEMIC

Before examining the current prevalence and patterns of drug use, it is of interest to note some of the unique characteristics of the recent drug epidemic among middle class youth. Its initiation in the early 1960s was largely unrelated to the then existing population of users among lower class minority groups. Only opiates, marijuana, and cocaine were proscribed at that time, and the limited nonmedical use of amphetamines and barbiturates was not viewed as a significant problem. Hallucinogen use was almost entirely limited to the ritual consumption of peyote by the Indians. The introduction of marijuana and hallucinogens to the middle class was closely related to the hippie movement and the popularization of LSD which preceded this phenomenon (70). LSD was probably crucial to the formation of the hippie or psychedelic movement, but the ideological and life-style features extended far beyond the associated drug use. Its spread was facilitated by the mass media, popular music, and the introduction of the underground press. In the opinion of the reviewer, the hippie movement of the 1960s was quite a significant social phenomenon. While it did not fully involve more than a small proportion of the total youth population, it influenced the philosophy, music, dress, attitudes, values, and drug-using behavior of a much larger group (69). Much of the widespread adoption of marijuana and other drug use can be viewed as marginal participation of the masses in the styles set by the hippie movement.

With the popularizing of the hippie movement, the original significance of LSD and other drugs was largely dissipated, and ideological factors are not regarded as a major motivation for use at present. Nevertheless, the explanation for many aspects of current drug usage can be traced to the manner of introduction into the culture. First, usage continues to be heavily concentrated among the young—that segment of the population most susceptible to fads and styles. Second, whereas illicit drug use had been largely limited to lower class minority groups in the past, the new phenomena were predominantly among middle class whites. For obvious reasons, the former groups were not responsive to a movement advocating dropping out of an overmaterialistic society. Third, normal curiosity and rebelliousness are more often factors in initiation than are personality defects or poor family backgrounds. Also, the ratio of female to male users is higher than for previous illicit drug usage, probably because of the higher acceptability of the behavior within the peer group. Fourth, the predominant pattern of infrequent usage of small quantities reflects the fact that most individuals are participating in a fad or style rather than being primarily attracted by the pharmacological properties of the drug. Finally, the rapid spread of drug use among secondary and college students throughout most countries of the world is clearly a copying of a style initiated in the United States. Some of these countries such as India have had lower class cannabis-using populations for centuries, but current student usage is an adoption of Western styles rather than a diffusion from indigenous sources. With the peak of the hippie movement now several years past, some of the above relationships are beginning to become less relevant; however, they still need to be considered in interpreting the present status of nonmedical drug use.

PREVALENCE AND TRENDS

Opiates

The available data permit only a rough estimate of the number of narcotics addicts currently in the United States. Since the population is not sufficiently accessible to household and student surveys (16), various other methods have been employed. Until recently the only estimates were based on case registers. The Bureau of Narcotics and Dangerous Drugs maintained a register based on state and federal arrest reports, and a New York City register included both arrest and health agency data (5). Attempts to estimate the proportion of the overall population contained in registers have been based on the percentage of narcotics deaths (5, 85) or new arrests (39) which are contained in the registers. Other estimates have been based on the incidence of reported serum hepatitis cases (a disease often spread through unsterile self-injection procedures) and a compilation of estimates from state health agencies (20). The estimated addict population adopted by the Federal Strategy report in 1973 was 500 to 600 thousand (99). In 1974, DuPont (30) estimated a population of 630,000 in the following categories: treatment—130,000; incarcerated—100,000; currently abstinent—200,000; and active addicts—200,000. This points up another difficulty in terms of the definition of an addict—whether persons temporarily abstinent for various reasons are to be included in the estimated addict population. There is also apparently a large number of persons who have used heroin to some extent but have not become addicted. In the 1972 household survey conducted for the U.S. Marihuana Commission, 0.6% of those age 12–17 and 1.3% of those 18 and over reported one or more experiences with heroin (approximately 1.8 million) (79). As mentioned earlier, such surveys typically miss the majority of the street addict population.

Of more importance than the crude prevalence estimates are the data on incidence and trends that have recently become available. With the large number of heroin addicts currently in treatment, it is possible to determine in retrospect that a large heroin epidemic began in the mid-1960s and peaked around 1967–69. Data from New York show the incidence of first use peaked in 1967 and then declined sharply (43). These findings were replicated for persons entering treatment for each year from 1969 to 1973, so the results are apparently not an artifact of the interval between initiation of use and treatment entry. DuPont & Greene (31) found a similar peak in 1969 for incidence of first use in Washington, and Newmeyer (82) reports the same results for San Francisco. Evidence also points to a decline in the number of active addicts. Death rates attributed to narcotics have declined, as have the number of cases of hepatitis (31, 43). In Washington, D.C., positive urine tests among arrestees in 1973 showed a significant decline over that for 1972 (31). Finally, the recent decrease in property-related crime has been related to the downturn in the prevalence of active heroin addiction (31, 43).

While it now seems reasonably well established that an epidemic in the initiation of heroin addiction occurred in the late 1960s, and that the indices of active addiction have also now declined, the reasons for these events are less clear. Some of the increase in heroin addiction was clearly a spillover from the middle class

Table 1 Percentage reporting nonmedical drug use in various surveys

Drug	Source	Population	Frequency of use	67	68	69	70	71	72	73	74
								Year of survey			
Marijuana	Gallup (35)	National, ≥ 18	ever used	5		4			11	12	
Marijuana	Gallup (34, 35a)	National, College	ever used			22	42	51			55
Marijuana	Marijuana Comm. (79)	National, 12–17	ever used					14	14		
		National, ≥ 18	ever used					15	16		
Marijuana	Blackford (11)	Ca. H. S. seniors	≥ 1 time[a]		38	44	50	53	57	59	60
			≥ 10 times[a]		22	28	29	37	40	42	43
			≥ 50 times[a]				19	25	26	26	28
Any hallucinogen	Gallup (34)	National, College	ever used	1		4	14	18			
Any hallucinogen	Marijuana Comm. (79)	National, 12–17	ever used						5		
		National, ≥ 18	ever used						5		
LSD	Blackford (11)	Ca. H. S. seniors	≥ 1 time[a]		13	17	15	16	17	17	18
			≥ 10 times[a]		5	7	5	5	5	5	4
			≥ 50 times[a]				2	2	2	2	1
Amphetamines	Gallup (34)	National, College	ever used				16	22			
Ethical stimulants	Marijuana Comm. (79)	National, 12–17	ever used						4		
		National, ≥ 18	ever used						5		
Amphetamines	Blackford (11)	Ca. H. S. seniors	≥ 1 time[a]		18	23	20	25	25	21	23
			≥ 10 times[a]		8	10	8	10	11	9	9
			≥ 50 times[a]				3	5	5	4	4
Barbiturates	Gallup (34)	National, College	ever used			10	15	15			
Ethical sedatives	Marijuana Comm. (79)	National, 12–17	ever used						3		
		National, ≥ 18	ever used						4		
Barbiturates	Blackford (11)	Ca. H. S. seniors	≥ 1 time[a]		14		14	17	15	13	15
			≥ 10 times[a]		5		5	6	5	5	4
			≥ 50 times[a]		2		2	3	2	2	1

[a] San Mateo County high school seniors; times used during past 12 months.

marijuana-hallucinogen epidemic discussed in the previous section. Sheppard, Gay & Smith (91) report that 40% of those addicted to heroin since 1967 in the Haight-Ashbury drug subculture of San Francisco were heavy users of psychedelic drugs prior to using heroin. However, there was also a marked parallel increase in the incidence of addiction among the lower class minority groups, which have traditionally been involved in heroin use. In what manner this may have been related to the middle class epidemic is unknown. It peaked considerably sooner than the incidence of marijuana and hallucinogen use among the middle class (see Table 1), although it did parallel the vital phase of the hippie movement (1966–69) fairly closely.

The large increase in the availability of addiction treatment facilities in the past few years is undoubtedly the source of some of the decline in the indices of current active addiction. The number in methadone maintenance treatment alone has increased from 4000 in 1969 (109) to approximately 80,000 in 1974 (30). Another factor is the success of law enforcement in limiting the availability of heroin. Substantial increases in the retail price of heroin have resulted, with an accompanying decline in the average amount consumed (13, 31). The decline in the indices of addiction prevalence may also be related to the natural decline of an epidemic. DuPont & Greene (31), as well as others, have noted the development of an anti-heroin attitude within the community.

Marijuana

Whereas there have been no satisfactory surveys of narcotics addiction in the United States, there is an abundance of surveys of marijuana and other drug use, mostly among student populations. The Marihuana Commission compiled a file of over 200 such surveys, involving more than 900,000 students (79). Table 1 presents survey results for the period 1967–73. The Gallup national poll of college students indicates the prevalence of any use of marijuana increased from 5% in 1967 to 51% in 1971, and the 1971 and 1972 Marihuana Commission surveys found approximately 15% of both youth (age 12–17) and adults had used the drug. The annual high school survey of San Mateo County, California, is of particular interest, since it has employed a standard instrument over the past 7 years and bases its statistics on use during the preceding year rather than in terms of ever having used. The data in Table 1 are based on responses from approximately 5000 high school seniors per year. San Mateo County is adjacent to San Francisco, and thus had an earlier and more pronounced exposure to the hippie movement than did most other areas. The drug usage rates are substantially higher than for most other parts of the country, and probably serve as good indicators of the maximum level of acceptance for the various drugs. It will be noted that marijuana, which is widely regarded as a relatively harmless drug, has continued to increase in popularity, whereas use of the other drugs has been essentially stable over the past few years.

Hallucinogens

The opinion is often expressed that the use of LSD and other hallucinogens has declined sharply over the past few years. Certainly the aggressive propagandizing of hallucinogen use has largely disappeared, along with the accompanying mass media publicity. Also, the incidence of hospitalizations for bad trips is markedly reduced. However, the available survey data does not show a corresponding decline in use. The rate of LSD use for San Mateo County high school seniors (Table 1) has been stable at about 17% for the past 6 years. Because LSD has often been sold under the name of mescaline in recent years, the actual usage of LSD may have increased.[2]

Stimulants and Depressants

Only a portion of nonmedical stimulant and sedative use is detectable through household and student surveys. The intravenous methamphetamine (speed) using population is generally not accessible, and the same is true for sedative and stimulant use by narcotic addicts, alcoholics, and other members of the street drug subculture. One Canadian study of a large sample of hospitalized alcoholics found 10% were barbiturate abusers and one-third of these either were or had been addicted (28). In addition, two studies of heroin addicts admitted to the Lexington hospital in the mid-1960s found the incidence of barbiturate-sedative addiction to be 23% and 35% (17, 42). In 1971 Eckerman et al (32) examined urine specimens collected from random samples of arrestees in six major U.S. cities. The percentage positive for barbiturates ranged from 1% in New York City to 14% for nondrug arrests in Los Angeles. In the three cities for which amphetamine screening was performed, the percentage of positive returns was approximately 3%.

While there are no reliable estimates of the prevalence of intravenous methamphetamine use, there is considerable evidence that usage is down from the peak level reached in the late 1960s. Illicit manufacture has apparently declined, and monthly monitoring of the illicit market by the Bureau of Narcotics and Dangerous Drugs reveals that in most cities the drug is no longer available in large lots (67). Apparently, the high-dose intravenous use observed in the late 1960s has proved to be self-limiting, and most of the concentrated enclaves of users have disappeared (95).

Recent reports by the U.S. and Canadian drug commissions warned of an increasing prevalence in nonmedical use of barbiturates and other sedatives (24, 79). In particular, the nonbarbiturate sedative methaqualone has become popular on the illicit market (37). This reported increase in sedative use is not reflected in the available survey data (Table 1), but may exist among users not accessible to this approach. Certain locales, such as Southern California, are known to have a heavy concentration of sedative abusers. The U.S. Drug Commission also called

---

[2] LSD, phencyclidine (PCP), and MDA (3, 4-methylene-dioxyamphetamine) are the only hallucinogens available on the illicit market with any regularity at the present time. Of those hallucinogens analyzed by the Federal Bureau of Narcotics and Dangerous Drugs in fiscal year 1971, 80% were LSD and another 10% were LSD and phencyclidine in combination (67). However, illicit hallucinogens are now so frequently alleged to be mescaline that some recent student surveys show the use of mescaline or other non-LSD hallucinogens to be reported more frequently than LSD (9).

attention to the overuse of barbiturates via prescription, calling it "America's hidden drug problem, comparable perhaps to the scope of hidden opiate dependence around the turn of the century" (79). In addition, the Federal government recently acted to sharply curtail the availability of prescription amphetamines, about 85% of which had been used for weight control (67). On the other hand, the authors of the only systematic national survey (1970–71) on the medical use of psychotropic drugs arrived at essentially the opposite conclusion—that usage was comparable to that for other Western industrialized nations, with only minimal excessive use (83).

Cocaine has recently reappeared on the illicit market after an absense of many years. Since this is a relatively new phenomenon, there is little data on incidence and prevalence (107). The 1972 U.S. Drug Commission survey did find 1.5% of youth and 3.2% of adults reporting some usage—more than double the corresponding percentages for any use of heroin (79).

While alcohol use is not included in this review, it should be noted that the rate of increase in illicit use of alcohol by minors during the past 2 or 3 years has probably exceeded that for marijuana or any of the other drugs discussed here (11, 24, 79).

PATTERNS OF USE: FREQUENCY, AMOUNT, AND DURATION

Opiates

The available survey data indicate that the number of persons who have had some experience with heroin is probably three to four times the current addict population (79). Some portion of these occasional users will eventually become addicted, but it does appear that addiction is not as inevitable as was previously believed. One of the probable reasons for the lower addiction potential among today's users is the typical pattern of multidrug use—heroin may simply be one of several drugs employed on an intermittent basis. Another likely factor is the small amounts of heroin currently consumed. DuPont & Greene (31) cite data for Washington, D.C. showing the average heroin content of the consumer package dropping from 7% in 1970 to 2% in 1973. In 1973, the average amount of heroin per package was only 5 mg. At this level, the typical addict would consume only about 20 mg of heroin per day in comparison to around 60 mg a few years earlier, or a maintenance dose of 135 mg for an English addict in 1969 (98). As a result of the low quality and high prices, most treatment programs report that current addicts evidence only minimal withdrawal signs when deprived of the drug.

One of the most significant recent studies in drug addiction concerns the subsequent drug-using behavior of U.S. military personnel addicted to opiates in Vietnam (86). Of a random sample of 451 army enlisted men who were returned to the United States in September 1971, 44% indicated they had used opiates in Vietnam and 20% felt they were addicted. Eight to 12 months after their return, 10% reported some use of narcotics, 2% indicated current use, and 0.7% addiction.

Urinalysis tests showed 0.7% positive for narcotics. Only 5% of the sample received treatment after return to the United States, and almost all of this was brief and occurred prior to discharge. This natural experiment demonstrates that a drug-using behavior which had been considered highly resistive to change may be strongly dependent on environmental conditions. In Vietnam, pure heroin was available for $2.50 per 250 mg (43); the mode of administration (heroin smoking) was one not generally associated with addiction, and those affected were subjected to the stress, boredom, and low morale associated with restricted environmental conditions and combat in an unpopular war. Upon return to the United States, continued use of regular narcotics required the expenditure of large sums of money for low-quality heroin, which in turn required intravenous administration to produce significant effects; family and associates were disapproving of narcotics use; and the environmental conditions and opportunities for nondrug activities were greatly improved.

Marijuana

In assessing the significance of current marijuana usage in the United States, it is instructive to compare the patterns of use with those for cultures with a long history of cannabis use. First, with respect to frequency of use, the ratio of daily to occasional cannabis use is very much higher in those cultures than that currently observed in the United States. The Indian Hemp Commission (47) concluded that the more potent preparations (ganja and charas) were seldom used except as a daily habit; and a recent study of the extensive use in Jamaica estimated 40 to 50 percent of the male population used on a daily basis (*Marihuana and Health*, 1972) (90). Other studies in North Africa have estimated that daily use represents one-third or less of the total population of users (87, 96). In any event, less-than-daily use in these cultures is generally ignored as having little significance. In contrast, the 1971 Marihuana Commission survey (1), which found 15% of the population had used marijuana, reported only 0.6% of youth and 0.5% of adults used marijuana one or more times per day. However, the more frequent patterns of use are apparently increasing. The 1972 Marihuana Commission survey found little change in overall prevalence of use, but the rate of daily or more frequent use more than doubled: 1.3% for youth and 1.4% for adults. Similarly, the 1971 results for one or more uses per week were 2.5% for youth and 1.9% for adults, compared to 4.0% and 4.1% respectively in 1972.

The same situation exists with regard to the amount of drug consumed. The typical occasional user in the United States smokes about one 0.5 gram marijuana cigarette per occasion (68). Daily users average around three cigarettes per day with a maximum of about 10. Since most marijuana consumed in the United States averages no more than 1% of the active ingredient—tetrahydracannabinol (THC)[3]—the casual user is estimated to consume about 5 mg THC per occasion.

---

[3] Analyses of 40 large seizures (100–2000 pounds each) made by U.S. Customs at the Mexican border in 1971 showed only 25% exceeded 1% in THC content (range 0.07 to 2.87 percent) (14).

Daily users average around 15 mg per day, with very heavy users taking 50 mg. By comparison, moderate daily users in Egypt, Morocco, and India are estimated to consume around 40–60 mg THC per day, with heavy users averaging about 200 mg (69). A recent study in Jamaica estimated heavy usage at around 400 mg THC per day (81), and 100 mg experimental doses are routinely administered to heavy hashish-using subjects in Greece (75). One *ad libitum* experiment in Greece found chronic hashish users averaged 3 to 7 grams of hashish (est. 150–350 mg THC) per day for 30 days (76).

American users are quite capable of consuming larger amounts. A recent 21-day *ad libitum* study found subjects who were previously casual users averaged 60 mg THC per day during the experiment, while subjects who used marijuana daily prior to the experiment averaged 100 mg (81). Similarly, a sample of U.S. military users in Germany was reported to average 3 grams of hashish per day (est. 150 mg THC) (103). However, it may be concluded that under normal conditions, the average amount of marijuana consumed by the U.S. user represents only a small percent of that for other cultures with well-established cannabis-using populations.

The low frequency of marijuana use and small amounts consumed fit the thesis advanced at the beginning of this review—namely, that the recent middle class drug epidemic is more the adoption of a popular style rather than an attraction to the pharmacological properties of the drug. If this thesis is valid, it would be expected that a high proportion of current users would likely discontinue the practice after a few years. For instance, students primarily responding to peer influence might be expected to terminate usage after leaving school. Data on this issue are rather sparse at present. The 1972 Marihuana Commission survey found that, of those 18 and over who had ever used, one-half had now stopped (79). Longitudinal studies of individual users are now in progress, but to the reviewer's knowledge there are no significant published results as yet. Studies of cannabis use in other cultures show initiation is also most common in adolescence and may be discontinued in adulthood. However, usage frequently persists for long periods; and persons using for 20–40 years are not uncommon. At least under conditions of cultural acceptance, cannabis usage appears to have a longevity comparable to that for alcohol and the opiates.

Hallucinogens

Unlike other psychoactive drugs, hallucinogens are rarely used on a daily basis. Tolerance to LSD occurs very rapidly, such that the effects are diminished on the second successive day of use and are largely absent after three daily administrations (19, 106). The same rapid tolerance exists for mescaline, psilocybin, and for some of the other hallucinogens. Thus, for practical purposes, these drugs cannot be used more than once or twice a week without losing much of their impact. Another reason for their relatively infrequent use is their lack of predictable effects. Habitual drug users generally seek to satisfy particular needs—escape, euphoria, anxiety relief, feelings of adequacy, etc. Since hallucinogens are quite inconsistent in terms of mood alteration, they do not meet this requirement.

Survey data support the expectation of infrequent use. Only about 25% of college students reporting having taken hallucinogens indicate usage within the past month (70). High school students tend toward more frequent use, with about 15% of those having used indicating one or more times per week (11, 16). The 1972 Marihuana Commission found similar results; of those having taken hallucinogens, 30% of youth and 15% of adults indicated use within the past month (1).

The amount of LSD taken per occasion is also relatively low. While the alleged potency of LSD dosage units on the illicit market is typically 200–250 mcg, quantitative evaluation of some 1000 samples in fiscal year 1971 found the median content to be 83 mcg (70). LSD dosages used for experimental and psychotherapeutic purposes are generally in the 50–200 mcg range.

The hallucinogens also tend to be self-limiting in terms of duration of use. Most users have been found to either discontinue usage or use very infrequently after a period of 2 or 3 years (8, 71, 88). The reason for this pattern is related to the drug effects. In addition to not being a reliable mood modifier, the hallucinogen experience tends to become less attractive with continued use. The major utility of these drugs is the uniqueness of the experience. As it is repeated many times, what was initially unique becomes more commonplace and there is a process of diminishing returns. The effect of hallucinogens is indeed "a trip" and trips tend to lose their appeal when repeated too often.

Stimulants and Depressants

The pattern of nonmedical stimulant use will vary with the motivation of the user. Students studying for examinations, truck drivers, and other persons attempting to temporarily combat fatigue will take them on an as-needed basis. Occasional usage also seems to be the pattern for oral consumption of stimulants by young persons for euphoriant purposes. Similar usage occurs for barbiturates and other sedatives, often in combination with alcohol or marijuana. When used in this manner the typical dosages are around 20–30 mg for amphetamines and 300 mg for secobarbital or other short- or intermediate-acting barbiturates (67).

An unknown number of persons use oral amphetamines nonmedically on a daily basis and acquire a high level of tolerance. Typical daily dosages for this group range from 200 to 700 mg per day (40, 53).

In addition to the occasional use of sedatives by youths using many drugs, there is also substantial consumption among alcoholics, heroin addicts, methadone patients, and others. Usage may be intermittent or chronic. Tolerance to barbiturates does not develop to the same extent as for amphetamines, and the ratio of lethal to therapeutic dose is also much smaller. The typical daily dosage reported for chronic nonmedical users is around 800–1500 mg (28), although daily dosages averaging 2400 mg have been observed among barbiturate-using heroin addicts (25). Daily dosages above the 500–800 mg level generally produce physical addiction (48).

The pattern of intravenous methamphetamine use in the late 1960s was in "runs" lasting several days, with only a few days between runs. The drug was injected several times per day, and the typical daily dosages were of the order of

800–2400 mg (58). As mentioned earlier, this type of high-dose intravenous use appears to have sharply declined, although some observers indicate that there is now a more moderate pattern of intravenous use on a more episodic basis (24, 95).

Relatively little is known about the current patterns of cocaine use other than from anecdotal reports. It is quite expensive, is considered to be a high-status drug, and is used mostly by the middle class marijuana-psychedelic group (107). The usual mode of administration is sniffing rather than the intravenous route employed by heroin addicts during an earlier period. Partly because of the high cost, most current usage is thought to be intermittent and in small amounts.

ETIOLOGY AND METHODS OF SPREAD

The limited scope of this review does not permit a review of the demographic, behavioral, and personality variables related to opiate addiction. Books by Chien and associates (18) and Ball & Chambers (7) provide good descriptions for the pre-1960 era. Robins (86) describes the military Vietnam opiate user as follows: "The man most likely to be detected positive in Vietnam was a young, single, black, low-ranking member of the Regular Army who had little education, came from a broken home, had an arrest history before Service, and had used drugs before Service."

The spread of heroin use has recently been investigated in terms of the contagious disease model (45, 46, 60), an approach first utilized by de Alarcon in England (26). The method shows considerable promise for identifying users in the early stages of an epidemic, especially when it occurs in a fairly well defined community. This, in turn, permits the early application of intervention approaches.

The characteristics of the current young middle class drug user have been described in dozens of studies—mostly for college populations. The early studies typically compared users and nonusers of marijuana. As the latter category receded to a minority status in some schools, populations were generally categorized in terms of frequent, occasional, and nonuse. Users are more likely than nonusers to come from urban professional families with above average education and income (12, 21, 38). Especially during the early phases of the epidemic, use was much higher for white as opposed to minority groups (12, 84). Males outnumber females, especially in the more frequent-use categories (68). Users are somewhat more likely to come from broken homes (12, 92), or to describe their parents' relationship as poor (6), and to have liberal parents (44). They are more likely to have fathers who use alcohol and tobacco and mothers who use tranquilizers (44, 92). However, Kandel (54) recently employed data obtained from triads—parents, adolescent and best school friend—to establish that, while parent's drug usage was positively related to adolescent use, peer group influence was much greater.

Haagen (41) has conducted one of the more interesting studies of the social and psychological correlates of marijuana use. He collected extensive biographical and test data at the time of college admission (1965), when virtually none of the sample had used marijuana, and again following the third year of college when

59% reported some use. At the time of admission, those who subsequently became occasional or frequent marijuana users scored slightly higher than the nonuser group on aptitude and achievement tests. On the other hand, the group that later used frequently had poorer study habits in high school, worked less hard, were more dissatisfied with school, and made lower grades than did the nonuser group. The frequent-using group were much more undecided as to their intended major at the time of admission, and continued to be uncertain about plans subsequent to college. They were more interested in social life, more accepting of nonconformist philosophy, and moved more in this direction during college. Another longitudinal study by Johnson (51a) followed 2200 males from the 10th grade in 1966 to one year past high school (1970). The findings are generally the same as those found by Haagen, but more limited in scope.

Smith (93, 94) has also conducted a prospective study of high school students, finding self and peer ratings of rebelliousness to be among the best predictors of those who subsequently became users of marijuana and other drugs. Jessor et al (50) have also reported some success in predicting, on the basis of various personality, belief, and attitude scores, which high school nonusers would subsequently initiate marijuana use. In addition, they found that those beginning use showed greater changes on these variables than did the continuing nonusers. None of these results occurred in the college sample.

As would be expected, users are more likely to consume alcohol and tobacco. In general, they exhibit a more unstable life style with respect to residence, work, school, and goals (44). They receive more traffic violations (44, 51), are more likely to have sought psychiatric counseling (51), are less religious, belong to fewer organizations, and participate less in athletics (41, 44). Users have sexual relations at an earlier age, more frequently, and with more partners (44, 51). They exhibit more liberal and leftist political views, see themselves as outside the larger society, have less respect for authority, and are more likely to be activists (12, 38, 44).

EFFECTS OF MARIJUANA AND HALLUCINOGEN USE

Again, space does not permit more than a cursory examination of the literature in this area. At present the only clearly established physical complication resulting from heavy marijuana or hashish use is bronchitis (103). Two widely publicized preliminary studies have suggested possible serious physical damage from heavy marijuana use. One found evidence of cerebral atrophy among a sample of ten hospitalized patients with a history of marijuana and other drug use (15). The second reported a significantly lower level of cellular mediated immunity among marijuana users as compared to nonusers (77). Neither of these findings has been replicated. One recent study reported a depression of testosterone levels among a sample using marijuana four or more times per week (mean of 9 cigarettes per week) (56a). Soueif found a sample of 850 imprisoned for hashish use in Egypt tended to score lower than nonusers on various psychomotor and simple cognitive tests; however, adequate controls for age and education were not maintained (97).

Several authors have attributed various adverse behavioral and personality problems to the frequent use of marijuana, especially that by adolescents (55–57). Others have criticized these conclusions on methodological grounds, showing that the same results can be predicted equally well by other associated forms of deviance such as premarital sex and high school truancy (4, 51). Regardless of the extent to which the relationship is causal or associational, there is clear evidence that heavy marijuana and hallucinogen users do consistently exhibit high rates of unemployment and general underachievement (8, 10, 88).

Two recent experimental studies have explored the effect of marijuana on productivity. In one study subjects were engaged in a microeconomy system in which they were paid on a piecework basis for making wooden stools or weaving woolen belts over a period of 3 to 4 months (23). The results showed dose-dependent decrements in productivity, and discontinuation of marijuana was followed by an increase in productivity. The second study collected detailed data on the work output of Jamaican laborers before and after smoking marijuana (89). The results showed marijuana intake caused decreased productivity per unit of time, an increase in calories consumed per unit of work, and less organization in work movements, greater repetition, and greater variability as measured in a videotape analysis.

With regard to hallucinogen effects, the long-term psychological effects of LSD have been reviewed recently by McWilliams & Tuttle (74). While the long-standing controversy over LSD and chromosomal alterations is not completely resolved, recent reviews suggest that it does not cause lasting chromosome breaks in vivo (29, 61). Four studies have employed at least a portion of the Halstead-Reitan test battery in an attempt to measure any LSD-related organicity. Three of these (3, 22, 72) found that the LSD group scored worse than the comparison group on some of the tests, but the results were not consistent across the three studies. The other study found no effect (108). None was able to control for possible predrug differences in the LSD and comparison groups. Furthermore, those test differences found were generally not correlated with the number of reported LSD ingestions.

PREVENTION

Public concern over the recent drug epidemic has stimulated a large increase in prevention efforts in the past few years. Those directed at limiting the supply have been relatively successful with regard to heroin (13, 31). However, the overall impact of drug education efforts are regarded as highly uncertain.[4] This sentiment is reflected by a 1973 moratorium on the Federal production and support of new educational and mass media materials related to drug abuse (99). Also, in 1973 the National Marihuana Commission (79) concluded that no drug education program in the United States or elsewhere had been proved sufficiently successful to warrant its recommendation, and therefore suggested a moratorium on all drug

---

[4] Good reviews of drug education and other prevention efforts are contained in Wald & Abrams (105) and Abrams, Garfield & Swisher (2).

education programs in the schools and the repeal of legislative requirements for such courses in the school curriculum. These rather drastic recommendations resulted from the inability to demonstrate that drug education programs were effective in reducing drug-using behavior, and in some instances the programs may well have been counterproductive (101, 102). Mass media drug prevention efforts were similarly unevaluated (78).

Part of the drug education problem stemmed from the uniqueness of the middle class drug epidemic discussed at the beginning of this review. Previously, drug education stressed the health hazards of alcohol and tobacco and, while the warnings might be ignored, there was no active opposition to the material being presented. With the advent of the new drug epidemic, teachers were at a disadvantage with respect to the students because of the lack of first-hand experience with the drugs being discussed. They were also faced with the problem of how to deal with drug use closely associated with an antiestablishment movement. Whereas student use of alcohol and tobacco had long been associated with rebellion against authority, there was previously no associated prodrug philosophy which claimed beneficial effects from the drug use per se. Finally, the teacher was forced to advocate complete abstinence with regard to illicit drugs, a stance that was likely to be rejected outright by the casual marijuana user.

In the face of these difficulties, there has been a tendency to de-emphasize the drug issue by integrating the educational material with other relevant courses, and to utilize "affective training" techniques aimed at developing overall responsible behavior. Problem solutions, peer group pressure, and value clarification are explored by methods ranging from casual rap sessions to intensive encounter groups. Without questioning the potential value of these approaches, many do see a danger of overgeneralizing, i.e. dismissing cognitive drug education on the basis of experience obtained in the recent highly atypical drug epidemic. Drug use is not normally encountered as an integral part of an ideological movement replete with advocates, a supportive underground press, and an accompanying art and music form.

Most of the secondary prevention techniques which have been employed have not come under the criticism leveled at drug education efforts. These include school counseling, "hot lines," crisis centers, free clinics, and street drug analysis services. Such intervention approaches usually aim at preventing the young drug user from drifting into more destructive drug using or other behavior. They are typically more oriented toward encouraging moderation and good judgment than total abstinence, and serve a useful function in helping prevent further social isolation and alienation of a group that is not especially deviant in other respects.

TREATMENT

Treatment emphasis has been largely limited to narcotics addiction, and methadone maintenance is currently the major modality. DuPont (30) estimated there were around 80,000 methadone maintenance patients in 1974, and that the number had been stable for the preceding year. With the exception of a few localities, there are currently no waiting lists for methadone or other forms of treatment. The other well-defined volunteer modality is the therapeutic community, with a probable population of 10–15 thousand. Civil commitment accounts for an additional 18,000 (not including those also on methadone maintenance) in the Federal, California, and New York programs (73). An unknown additional number receive treatment at various detoxification and other centers—primarily on an outpatient basis. DuPont (30) estimated a total treatment population of 130,000 in 1974. Since treatment capacity is no longer a limiting factor, Federal efforts are being made to increase the treatment population through an informal system of diversion from the criminal justice system (TASC—Treatment Alternatives to Street Crime) (99).

It is probably fair to conclude that methadone maintenance has passed the honeymoon stage. The criticism of substituting one narcotic for another has continued, and as yet there is little evidence that a significant portion of methadone patients are eventually able to withdraw and remain abstinent. As this form of treatment has expanded and incorporated a less select population of addicts, the early one-year retention rates of 85%, found by Dole (36), have tended to drop closer to 40 to 50 percent (65). Some authors have also challenged the highly optimistic early reports of improved socialization in terms of employment and reduced crime (62). Nevertheless, methadone maintenance has been able to attract and retain a much higher number of narcotics addicts than any other form of volunteer treatment. There is little doubt that it has substantially reduced both the individual and social costs of addiction. Therapeutic communities (27) achieve excellent results for some addicts at relatively low cost; however, only a fraction of the addict population is attracted to this mode of treatment, and only about 10% of these remain (33, 63). Civil commitment, as it is now employed, is generally considered too coercive for the individual benefits achieved (59, 64); although for perhaps two-thirds of the addict population, some level of compulsion is probably necessary to limit the associated criminal costs of addiction (73).

Experimental heroin maintenance programs have been proposed in both the United States and Canada as a means of attracting larger numbers of addicts into treatment (24, 104). This approach has been relatively successful in England,[5] but the differences in the history, size, and nature of the problem makes it unlikely that it will be adopted in the United States in the near future.

A great deal of research has been directed toward developing a satisfactory opiate antagonist in the past few years. Cyclazocine has been in experimental use for several years, and oral doses effectively block opiate effects for 24 hours. However, it frequently produces undesirable side effects. Naloxone is an effective antagonist with little or no agonist activity; however, it is short acting, requires large doses, and is expensive. The most promising antagonist currently in the clinical testing phase is naltrexone. It is effective for 24 hours in moderate oral doses and has little agonist activity (66). While this represents a considerable

---

[5] In actuality, most maintenance patients in England now receive methadone rather than heroin, although it is typically injected rather than taken orally (52).

advance in the search for effective narcotic antagonists, it does not solve the problem of treatment motivation on the part of the patient. Many observers believe that a means of producing a narcotic blockade for several days or weeks is necessary before this approach will have wide applicability. Research is also continuing on the long-acting methadone congeners (49).

Treatment and preventive directions which are to be emphasized in current Federal plans include: expanded treatment for polydrug abuse; further attempts to provide job opportunities for the ex-drug addict; efforts to enlarge the treatment population through cooperation between therapeutic agencies and the criminal justice systems; school-based early intervention programs; and increased law enforcement efforts against illicit drug traffic (100).

Literature Cited

1. Abelson, H., Cohen, R., Schrayer, D., Rappeport, M. 1973. Drug experience, attitudes and related behavior among adolescents and adults. In *Drug Use in America: Problem in Perspective.* Appendix, Nat. Comm. Marihuana and Drug Abuse, 1:489–867. Washington, D.C.: GPO. 1243 pp.
2. Abrams, L. A., Garfield, E. F., Swisher, J. D., Eds. 1973. *Accountability in Drug Education.* Washington, D.C.: Drug Abuse Council. 168 pp.
3. Accord, L. D., Barker, D. D. 1973. Hallucinogenic drugs and cerebral deficit. *J. Nerv. Ment. Dis.* 156:281–83
4. Altman, H., Evenson, R. C. 1973. Marijuana use and subsequent psychiatric symptoms: A replication. *Comp. Psychiat.* 14:415–20
5. Andima, H., Krug, D., Bergner, L., Patrick, S., Whitman, S. 1973. A prevalence estimation model of narcotics addiction in New York City. *Am. J. Epidemiol.* 98:56–62
6. Anker, J. L., Milman, D. H., Kahan, S. A., Valenti, C. 1971. Drug usage and related patterns of behavior in university students: 1. General survey and marihuana use. *J. Am. Coll. Health Assoc.* 19:178–86
7. Ball, J. C., Chambers, C. D., Eds. 1970. *The Epidemiology of Opiate Addiction in the United States.* Springfield, Ill.: Thomas. 337 pp.
8. Barron, S. P., Lowinger, P., Ebner, E. 1970. A clinical examination of chronic LSD use in the community. *Comp. Psychiat.* 11:69–79
9. Berg, D. F., Broecker, L. P. 1972. *Illicit Use of Dangerous Drugs in the United States: A Compilation of Studies, Surveys, and Polls.* BNDD
10. Blacker, K. H., Jones, R. T., Stone, G. C., Pfefferbaum, D. 1968. Chronic users of LSD: The "Acidheads." *Am. J. Psychiat.* 125:341–51
11. Blackford, L. 1974. *Student Drug Use Surveys, San Mateo County, California.* Prelim. Rep., County Dep. Health and Welfare, San Mateo
12. Blum, R. H. & Associates 1969. *Drugs II, Students and Drugs.* San Francisco: Jossey-Bass. 399 pp.
13. Brown, G. F. Jr., Silverman, L. R. 1973. *The Retail Price of Heroin: Estimation and Applications.* Washington, D.C.: Drug Abuse Council. 56 pp.
14. Bureau of Narcotics and Dangerous Drugs 1972. *Microgram* 5(10)
15. Campbell, A. M. G., Evans, M., Thomson, J. L. G., Williams, M. J. 1971. *Lancet* 2 & Index:1219–24
16. Chambers, C. D. 1971. *An Assessment of Drug Use in the General Population: Drug Use in New York State.* Narcotic Addict. Contr. Comm. Spec. Rep. No. 1
17. Chambers, C. D. 1969. Barbiturate-sedative abuse: A study of prevalence among narcotic abusers. *Int. J. Addict.* 4:45–57
18. Chein, I., Gerard, D. L., Lee, R. S., Rosenfeld, E. 1964. *The Road to H: Narcotics, Delinquency, and Social Policy.* New York: Basic Books. 482 pp.
19. Cholden, L. W., Kurland, A., Savage, C. 1955. Clinical reactions and tolerance to LSD in chronic schizophrenia.

J. Nerv. Ment. Dis. 122:211-21
20. Cimino, J. A., Doud, R. M., Andima, H. S., West, S. A. 1973. Narcotic addiction in the United States: A nationwide survey. *Contemp. Drug Probl.* 2:401-15
21. Cohen, H. 1970. Principal conclusions from the report: "Psychology, social-psychology and sociology of illicit drug use." *Brit. J. Addict.* 65:39-44
22. Cohen, S., Edwards, A. E. 1969. LSD and organic brain damage. *Drug Dependence* 5:1-4
23. Commission (Canadian) of Inquiry into the Non-Medical Use of Drugs 1972. *Cannabis.* Ottawa: Inform. Can. 426 pp.
24. Commission (Canadian) of Inquiry into the Non-Medical Use of Drugs 1973. *Final Report.* Ottawa: Inform. Can. 1148 pp.
25. Cumberlidge, M. C. 1968. The abuse of barbiturates by heroin addicts. *Can. Med. Assoc. J.* 98:1045-49
26. de Alarcon, R. 1969. The spread of heroin abuse in a community. *Bull. Narc.* 21:17-22
27. Deitch, D. A. 1973. Treatment of drug abuse in the therapeutic community: Historical influences, current considerations and future outlook. In *Drug Use in America: Problem in Perspective.* Appendix, Nat. Comm. Marihuana and Drug Abuse 4:158-75. Washington, D.C.: GPO. 863 pp.
28. Devenyl, P., Wilson, M. 1971. Abuse of barbiturates in an alcoholic population. *Can. Med. Assoc. J.* 104:219-21
29. Dishotsky, N. I., Loughman, W. D., Mogar, R. E., Lipscomb, W. R. 1971. LSD and genetic damage. *Science* 172:431-40
30. DuPont, R. L. 1974. *The Future of the Federal Drug Abuse Program.* Presented at 36th Ann. Sci. Meet. Comm. Probl. Drug Dependence, Mexico City
31. DuPont, R. L., Greene, M. H. 1973. The dynamics of a heroin addiction epidemic. *Science* 181:716-22
32. Eckerman, W. C., Bates, J. D., Rachel, J. V., Poole, W. K. 1971. *Drug Usage and Arrest Charges.* BNDD
33. Freedman, D. X., Senay, E. C. 1973. Methadone treatment of heroin addiction. *Ann. Rev. Med.* 24:153-64

34. *Gallup Opinion Index* 1972. 80:17-29. New Jersey: Princeton Opinion Press
35. Ibid 1973. 93:24-26
35a. Gallup Opinion Poll 1974. *New York Times* May 14
36. Gearing, F. R. 1970. Evaluation of methadone maintenance treatment program. *Int. J. Addict.* 5:517-43
37. Gerald, M. C., Schwirian, P. M. 1973. Nonmedical use of methaqualone. *Arch. Gen. Psychiat.* 28:627-31
38. Goode, E. 1970. *The Marijuana Smokers.* New York: Basic Books. 340 pp.
39. Greenwood, J. A. 1971. *Estimating Number of Narcotic Addicts.* BNDD. SCID-TR-3
40. Griffith, J. 1966. A study of illicit amphetamine drug traffic in Oklahoma City. *Am. J. Psychiat.* 123:560-69
41. Haagen, C. H. 1970. *Social and psychological characteristics associated with the use of marijuana by college men.* Middletown, Conn.: Wesleyan Univ.
42. Hamburger, E. 1964. Barbiturate use in narcotic addicts. *J. Am. Med. Assoc.* 189:366-68
43. Harris, T. G. 1973. "As far as heroin is concerned, the worst is over." *Psychol. Today* 7:68-79, 85
44. Hochman, J. L., Brill, N. Q. 1971. *Marijuana Use and Psychosocial Adaptation.* Presented at Meet. Am. Psychiat. Assoc. Washington, D.C.
45. Hughes, P. H., Crawford, G. A. 1972. A contagious disease model for researching and intervening in heroin epidemics. *Arch. Gen. Psychiat.* 27:149-55
46. Hunt, L. G. 1973. *Heroin Epidemics: A Quantitative Study of Current Empirical Data.* Washington, D.C.: Drug Abuse Council. 45 pp.
47. *Indian Hemp Drugs Commission Report, 1893-1894, Marijuana.* 1969. Introduction by J. Kaplan. Silver Spring, Md.: Jefferson
48. Jaffe, J. H. 1970. Drug addiction and drug abuse. In *The Pharmacological Basis of Therapeutics,* ed. L. S. Goodman, A. Gilman. New York: MacMillan. 4th ed.
49. Jaffe, J. H., Schuster, C. R., Smith, B. R., Blachley, P. H. 1970. Comparison of acetylmethadol and methadone in

the treatment of long-term heroin users. *J. Am. Med. Assoc.* 211:1834–36

50. Jessor, R., Jessor, S. L., Finney, J. 1973. A social psychology of marijuana use: Longitudinal studies of high school and college youth *J. Pers. Soc. Psychol.* 26:1–15

51. Johnson, B. D. 1973. *Marihuana Users and Drug Subcultures.* New York: Wiley. 290 pp.

51a. Johnson, L. 1973. *Drugs and American Youth.* Ann Arbor: Univ. Michigan. 273 pp.

52. Josephson, E. 1973. The British response to drug abuse. See Ref. 27, 4:176–97

53. Kalant, O. J. 1966. *The Amphetamines: Toxicity and Addiction.* Springfield, Ill.: Thomas

54. Kandel, D. 1973. Adolescent marihuana use: Role of parents and peers. *Science* 181:1067–70

55. Kolansky, H., Moore, W. T. 1971. Effects of marihuana on adolescents and young adults. *J. Am. Med. Assoc.* 216:486–92

56. Ibid 1972. Toxic effects of chronic marihuana use. 222:35–41

56a. Kolodny, R. C., Masters, W. H., Kolodner, R. M., Toro, G. 1974. Depression of plasma testosterone levels after chronic intensive marihuana use. *N. Engl. Med. J.* 290:872–74

57. Kornhaber, A. 1971. Marihuana in an adolescent psychiatric outpatient population. *J. Am. Med. Assoc.* 215:1988

58. Kramer, J. C., Fischman, V. S., Littlefield, D. C. 1967. Amphetamine abuse: Pattern and effects of high doses taken intravenously. *J. Am. Med. Assoc.* 201:305–9

59. Kramer, J. C. 1970. The state versus the addict: Uncivil commitment. *Boston Univ. Law Rev.* 50:1–22

60. Levengood, R., Lowinger, P., Schooff, K. 1973. Heroin addiction in the suburbs—an epidemiologic study. *Am. J. Public Health* 63:209–14

61. Long, S. Y. 1972. Does LSD induce chromosomal damage and malformations? A review of the literature. *Teratology* 6:75–90

62. Lukoff, I. *Issues in the Evaluation of Heroin Treatment, Epidemiology of Hallucinogens.* In press

63. Mandell, A. 1972. The sociology of a multimodality strategy in the treatment of narcotic addicts. In *Progress in Drug Abuse,* ed. P. Blachley, 122–33. Springfield, Ill.: Thomas. 321 pp.

64. Mandell, W., Amsel, Z. 1973. *Status of Addicts Treated Under the NARA Program.* Dep. Ment. Hyg., Sch. Hyg. and Public Health, Johns Hopkins Univ., Baltimore

65. Mandell, W., Goldschmidt, P. G., Grover, P. 1973. *An Evaluation of Treatment Programs for Drug Abusers,* Vol. 2, Summary. Sch. Hyg. and Public Health, Johns Hopkins Univ., Baltimore

66. Martin, W. R., Jasinski, D. R., Mansky, P. A. 1973. Naltrexone, an antagonist for the treatment of heroin dependence. *Arch. Gen. Psychiat.* 28:784–91

67. McGlothlin, W. H. 1973. *Amphetamines, Barbiturates and Hallucinogens: An Analysis of Use, Distribution and Control.* BNDD. SCID-TR-9. 103 pp.

68. McGlothlin, W. H. 1972. Marijuana: An analysis of use, distribution and control. *Contemp. Drug Probl.* 1:467–500

69. McGlothlin, W. H. Sociocultural factors in marijuana use in the United States. To appear in *Cross-Cultural Perspectives on Cannabis,* ed. V. Rubin. In press

70. McGlothlin, W. H. The epidemiology of hallucinogenic drug use. To appear in *Epidemiology of Drug Use,* ed. E. Josephson, 277–301. Washington, D.C.: Winston. In press

71. McGlothlin, W. H., Arnold, D. O. 1971. LSD revisited: A ten-year follow-up of medical LSD use. *Arch. Gen. Psychiat.* 24:35–49

72. McGlothlin, W. H., Arnold, D. O., Freedman, D. X. 1969. Organicity measures following repeated LSD ingestion. *Arch. Gen. Psychiat.* 21:704–9

73. McGlothlin, W. H., Tabbush, V. C. 1974. Costs, benefits, and potential for alternative approaches to opiate addiction control. In *Drugs and the Criminal Justice System,* ed. J. A. Inciardi, C. D. Chambers, 2:77–124. Beverly Hills: Sage. 249 pp.

74. McWilliams, S., Tuttle, R. J. 1973. Long-term psychological effects of

LSD. *Psychol. Bull.* 79:341–51
75. Miras, C. J., Coutselinis, A. 1970. *The Distribution of Tetrahydrocannabinol-^{14}C in Humans.* Rep. No. 24, UN Secretariat publ. ST/SOA/SER.S/24
76. Miras, C. J., Coutselinis, A. 1970. *The Presence of Cannabinols in the Urine of Hashish Smokers.* Rep. No. 25, UN Secretariat publ. ST/SOA/SER.S/25
77. Nahas, G. G., Suciu-Foca, N., Armand, J., Morishima, A. 1974. Inhibition of cellular mediated immunity in marihuana smokers. *Science* 183: 419–20
78. National Academy of Science 1972. *Panel on the Impact of Information and Drug Use and Misuse.* Phase I. Washington, D.C.
79. National Commission on Marihuana and Drug Abuse 1973. *Drug Use in America: Problem in Perspective.* Washington, D.C.: GPO. 481 pp.
80. National Commission on Marihuana and Drug Abuse. 1972. *Marihuana: A Signal of Misunderstanding.* Washington, D.C.: GPO. 184 pp.
81. Ibid 1972. Appendix, Vol. I, 608 pp.
82. Newmeyer, J. A. 1973. *The End of the Heroin Epidemic of the San Francisco Bay Area.* Presented at 35th Ann. Sci. Meet. Comm. Probl. Drug Dependence, Chapel Hill
83. Parry, H. J., Balter, M. B., Mellinger, G. D., Cisin, I. H., Manheimer, D. I. 1973. National patterns of psychotherapeutic drug use. *Arch. Gen. Psychiat.* 28: 769–83
84. Preston, J. D. 1970. *A Survey of Drug Use Among High School Students in Houston.* Texas Agr. Exp. Sta., Dep. Inform. Rep. No. 70–9
85. Richards, L. G., Carroll, E. E. 1970. Illicit drug use and addiction in the United States. *Public Health Rep.* 85:1035–41
86. Robins, L. N. 1973. A follow-up of Vietnam drug users. *Spec. Action Office Monogr.* Ser. A:1–23
87. Roland, J. L., Teste, M. 1958. Le cannabisme au Maroc. *Maroc-Méd.* 387: 694–703
88. Salzman, C., Lieff, J., Kochansky, G. E., Shader, R. I. 1972. The psychology of hallucinogenic drug discontinuers. *Am. J. Psychiat.* 129:755–61

89. Schaeffer. J. H. 1973. Cannabis sativa and agricultural work in a Jamaican hill community. In *Effects of Chronic Smoking of Cannabis in Jamaica,* ed. V. Rubin, L. Comitas. New York: Res. Inst. Study of Man
90. Secretary of Health, Education, and Welfare 1971, 1972, 1973. *Marihuana and Health.* 1st, 2nd, and 3rd Ann. Rep. Congr.
91. Sheppard, C. W., Gay, G. R., Smith, D. E. 1971. The changing patterns of heroin addiction in the Haight-Ashbury subculture. *J. Psychedelic Drugs* 3: 22–30
92. Smart, R. G., Fejer, D. 1971. Recent trends in illicit drug use among adolescents. *Can. Ment. Health* Suppl. 68
93. Smith, G. E. 1973. *Antecedents of Teenage Drug Use.* Presented at 35th Ann. Sci. Meet. Comm. Probl. Drug Dependence, Chapel Hill
94. Smith, G. E. 1974. *Early Precursors of Teenage Drug Use.* Presented at 36th Ann. Sci. Meet. Comm. Probl. Drug Dependence, Mexico City
95. Smith, R. C. 1972. Observations on the illicit marketplace of psychedelics, amphetamines, and barbiturates. See Ref. 67, Appendix B
96. Soueif, M. I. 1967. Hashish consumption in Egypt, with special reference to psychosocial aspects. *Bull. Narc.* 19: 1–12
97. Ibid 1971. The use of cannabis in Egypt: A behavioral study. 23:17–28
98. Stimson, G. V., Ogborne, A. C. 1970. A survey of a representative sample of addicts prescribed heroin at London clinics. *Bull. Narc.* 22:13–22
99. Strategy Council on Drug Abuse 1973. *Federal Strategy for Drug Abuse and Drug Traffic Prevention.* Washington, D.C.
100. Ibid 1974
101. Stuart, R. B. Teaching facts about drugs: Pushing or preventing. *J. Educ. Psychol.* In press
102. Swisher, J. D., Crawford, J. R. Jr. 1971. An evaluation of a short-term drug education program. *Sch. Couns.* 18: 265–72
103. Tennant, F. S., Preble, M., Prendergast, T. J., Ventry, P. 1971. Med-

ical manifestations associated with hashish. *J. Am. Med. Assoc.* 216: 1965–69

104. Vera Institute of Justice, N.Y.C. 1971. *Heroin Research and Rehabilitation Program.* Discussion proposal

105. Wald, P. M., Abrams, A. 1972. Drug education. In *Dealing with Drug Abuse.* New York: Praeger

106. Wolbach, A. B. Jr., Isbell, H., Miner, E. J. 1962. Cross tolerance between mescaline and LSD-25 with and comparison of the mescaline and LSD reactions. *Psychopharmacology* 3:1–14

107. Woods, J. H., Downs, D. A. 1973. The psychopharmacology of cocaine. See Ref. 1, 1:116–39

108. Wright, M., Hogan, T. P. 1972. Repeated LSD ingestion and performance on neuropsychological tests. *J. Nerv. Ment. Dis.* 154:432–38

109. Zitrin, A. 1970. Press conference. *Int. J. Addict.* 5:563–80

ADULT DEVELOPMENT AND AGING[1]

K. Warner Schaie[2] and Kathy Gribbin
Ethel Percy Andrus Gerontology Center, University of Southern California
Los Angeles, California 90007

The psychology of aging appears to have matured markedly during the 5 years recorded in this chapter. While the careful mapping of differences in performance and behavior characteristics of young and old organisms is continuing, there has been a significant shift of interest towards the direct explication of age changes by means of descriptive as well as experimental strategies. Psychologists interested in aging have established more contact with those engaged in the study of earlier developmental stages than has been the case previously, and in turn, have made significant methodological contributions to developmental psychology in general. Indeed, perhaps the most noteworthy change has been an increasing interest in life-span developmental psychology on the part of gerontologists who are now willing to give more than lip service to the fact that organisms are not born old [but see Baltes (16)]. As evidence of this change, note, for example, the change in name of Division 20 from a "Division on Maturity and Old Age" to a "Division of Adult Development and Aging." Equally important has been the recognition that the implicit decrement model of aging is unduly pessimistic and not necessarily isomorphic with empirical fact. The introduction of more sophisticated methodologies has highlighted the fact that much of our knowledge of adult development is based on the comparison of different cohorts, and consequently, for all we know, in the past we might have collected data for a psychology of generational differences rather than for a psychology of aging. These issues have received

---

[1] See NAPS document No. 02431 for 68 pages of supplementary material. Order from ASIS/NAPS c/o Microfiche Publications, 305 E. 46th Street, New York, NY 10017. Remit in advance for each NAPS accession number. Make checks payable to Microfiche Publications. Microfiche are $1.50, and photocopies are $10.70. Outside of the U.S. or Canada, postage is $.50 for a fiche or $2.00 for a photocopy.

[2] Preparation of this chapter was facilitated in part by a research grant HD 8458–01 from the National Institute of Child Health and Human Development. We are grateful to Margaret Skitarelic and Maureen Wade, who assisted greatly by prescreening more than a thousand papers initially reviewed for this chapter.

considerable attention, as have the consideration of change or stability in social roles and the determination of psychophysiological correlates of age changes in behavior. The viability of the field is further demonstrated by APA's significant participation in the 1971 White House Conference on Aging, which included a major task force report (96) and the appearance of a number of books on aging and life-span developmental psychology at a markedly incremental level of sophistication.

Because of the huge number of publications which have appeared in this area since Botwinick's chapter on Geropsychology in the 1970 *Annual Review of Psychology* (45a), some exclusions had to be made. First, we decided to review primarily literature on human development and to neglect work with animals. This decision was quite arbitrary and made simply because of the impossibility of covering everything. The second exclusion was quite purposive. That is, since the senior author has consistently argued that the pathology of old age is corollary but not causal to aging (287, 288), it was felt that the literature on psychopathology and physiological deficit in the aged would more properly be reviewed in chapters devoted to the substantive issues of pathology and deficit.

The plan of this chapter is to discuss first some of the major methodological issues; next to review briefly books primarily concerned with adult development; and then to proceed with a review of the most noteworthy substantive contributions in the research literature.

As in previous reviews, no attempt has been made at comprehensiveness. Our effort has been directed towards indicating the more significant research avenues, methodological innovations, and attempts at systematization. Covered in this chapter is the literature from the latter part of 1968 through the end of 1973, with some inclusion of papers appearing in early 1974.

METHODOLOGICAL ISSUES

We will first consider the question of how one should look at adult development; next, the implications ensuing from the debate concerning the relationship of data obtained from studies employing the cross-sectional or longitudinal method and the proposals for more sophisticated mixed strategies will be reviewed. Attention will also be given to multivariate methods particularly relevant to the study of adult development, the debate about the assessment of functional age, the issues concerning the prediction of life-span, and the beginning interest in manipulation of the age variable.

How Should One Look at Adult Development?

The developmentalist interested in childhood and adolescence has no problem in making credible a basic developmental model whose best fit would be a Gompertz type function involving decelerating rate of growth.[3] No such simple solution is

---

[3] This attitude has been challenged recently by the proposal to substitute behavior modification paradigms for organismic models of development (cf 223).

readily available for the study of adult development. Most investigations in the past have implicitly accepted the validity of an irreversible decrement model and consequently have assumed that age differences in a given behavior between young and old (which most often yields differences in favor of the young) can indeed be interpreted as evidence of ontogenetic age decrement. However, as early as 1940 and again more recently, Kuhlen (182) has pointed out to us that much of what appears as age differences to the casual observer might indeed more properly be identified as the effect of sociocultural change. More recently, and quite independently, this issue has been formalized in the sociological literature by Ryder (276) and in the psychological literature by Schaie (281), by considering the relationship between cross-sectional and longitudinal data.

Such analyses reveal the plausibility of alternative models. Indeed, for the period of adulthood, a stability model seems plausible for many variables of interest to the psychologist [notably the crystallized mental abilities (145) and many personality variables (228)]. Another alternative is a decrement-with-compensation model, which would permit both ontogenetic decrement as well as compensation by successively more favorable environmental life support systems. It is assumed here that many of the difficulties of the aged could be remedied by alternative modifications of the young and middle aged vis-à-vis the old (287, 315). A more radical alternative has been proposed by Wohlwill (346), who suggests that age in developmental studies ought to be treated as a dependent rather than an independent variable.

Within the alternative models for adult age functions, there has been an increasing interest in trying to determine the relative contribution of heritability and environment in the maintenance of behavior in old age, an issue which clearly relates to public policy regarding retirement and rehabilitation and may well become as controversial as that over the role of compensatory education in childhood. Most pertinent methodological contributions to this issue have been provided by Cattell (69, 70), Buss (58), and by Schaie, Baltes & Nesselroade (289). Relevant discussions of the relation of possible age-related defects in chromosome structure are given by Jarvik & Kato (161).

Studies concerned with the total life-span are faced with the problem that prospective investigations will frequently extend beyond the life expectancy of the investigator. Greater emphasis has therefore been placed upon retrospective accounts, and particularly the use of life-history analyses. Problems here concern the reliability of such information, the intrusion of contemporary stereotypes, and generalized differences in perceived social desirability (62, 157, 196, 300, 326). Back & Bourque (13) introduced an interesting life-graph approach which at one point in time collects subjective judgments for prospective and retrospective data on members of different cohorts over their anticipated life-span.

Considerable attention has been given to the issue of sampling. Although continued demand is made for more representative samples, it has become evident that in a longitudinal study a sample which is representative of a given population at the study's inception will become successively less representative due to the effects of nonrandom experimental mortality (sample attrition). If the sample is maintained in its entirety throughout the life of the study, it will cease to be representative because of changes in the parent population. Studies of specific processes, therefore, might best be conducted with carefully selected non-representative samples which define the limits of the behavior of interest (see 288, 295 for more detailed discussions of this issue). The effects of selective dropout of subjects have been documented in a number of studies which invariably show that residual samples score higher on tests of ability and are rated more in the socially desirable direction than is true for the initial sample (9, 24, 43, 260, 291).

Age Changes Vs Age Differences Vs Sociocultural Change

Much recent controversy in the psychology of aging regarding the interpretability of data has centered around the conflicting data obtained from cross-sectional and longitudinal studies, particularly upon the topic of age decrement in intelligence (cf 23).

Schaie was able to show that both cross-sectional and longitudinal methods are special cases deducible from a general developmental model (281, 282). A third possible approach is the time-lag method, which compares samples of the same age at different points in time. These three methods represent confoundings, two at a time, of the three components of age, time of measurement, and cohort (time of birth). Results from any two methods of descriptive analysis can therefore agree only under rather unusual circumstances. Since neither cross-sectional nor longitudinal methods can yield unambiguous measures of age differences (cross-sectional) or age changes (longitudinal), it was recommended that new mixed strategies involving the replication of either cross-sectional or longitudinal studies be considered to permit the segregation of variance due to chronological age from that attributable to cohort differences in cross-sectional studies and from non-age related environmental effects of longitudinal studies [see (286) for an heuristic example]. As a consequence, it was proposed that many age differences reported in the literature should more parsimoniously be interpreted as generational differences (284) and that results from single-cohort longitudinal studies were probably uninterpretable for most psychological variables (285). It was further suggested that studies hypothesizing the age decrement model required data analyzed via the cohort-sequential method (two or more cohorts tested at two or more common ages), that studies assessing the stability model required the cross-sequential method (two or more cohorts tested at two or more common times of measurement), and that the assumption of a decrement-with-compensation model requires analysis via the time-sequential method (two or more ages examined at two or more common times of measurement) (288).

Baltes (15) examined the general developmental model, and in addition to suggesting caution in its interpretation, concluded that since two of the three components of developmental change are of necessity confounded, it would suffice to utilize only two sequential strategies termed cross-sectional and longitudinal sequences (cf 19). This argument has been examined by Buss (58), who agrees with Baltes, and by Wohlwill (347), who agrees with Schaie.[4]

Discussion of the general developmental model and the empirical studies employing sequential strategies which have been stimulated thereby suggests that researchers on adult development are concerned with at least three distinct issues: age changes, age differences, and sociocultural change.

The researcher interested in age changes wishes to find lawful relationships that describe ontogenetic change across the life course of a species; these relationships either generalize across cohorts or yield functions that vary for successive cohorts in a predictable fashion. In this instance, the conventional longitudinal method will provide insights only for the specific cohort under study unless we subscribe to the irreversible-decrement model. Otherwise, either the cross-sequential or the cohort-sequential method would be required before generalization is possible.

The investigator concerned with age differences wishes to determine in what manner individuals of different ages differ in behavior at one point in time. If it does not matter whether such difference is due to age or generational differences, then the cross-sectional method is perfectly applicable. However, if we wish to consider either the stability or the decrement with compensation model in explaining age differences, it then becomes necessary to employ the cross-sequential or time-sequential methods.

But many investigators in the psychology of aging are not really interested in aging per se. Rather, they wish to determine whether there are generational differences which explain differential behaviors of the young and old at some point in time. These investigators are really concerned with the effect of sociocultural change, which in the absence of age changes can best be studied by the cross-sectional method, or in their presence by the time-sequential method.

Studies of adult development which have applied the new sequential strategies in the area of intelligence include (199, 224, 290, 292, 296, 297); in the area of visual illusions (101); and in the social-personality domain (259, 294, 350). But several major ongoing studies (e.g. the Boston Normative Aging Studies, Duke Longitudinal Studies, NIH Intramural Longitudinal Study) have been redesigned to permit sequential analyses, and the next few years will see the publication of findings based on firmer ground than the data thus far at hand.

Cohort analysis has also received much stimulation by recent advances in the sociological literature (261), and has begun to affect the social-psychological literature in conjunction with the above-described considerations in developmental psychology. Methodologically sophisticated treatments of intergeneration differences are presented by Bengtson & Black (30), Bengston and Kuypers (31),

---

[4] A further analysis of the general developmental model and the "Baltes-Schaie controversy" is provided by Botwinick (48). Baltes and Schaie have recently concluded that their apparent controversy represents an incomplete explication of the model. They agree that the several data matrices suggested in the original paper (281) are useful, but that a number of different extensions of the model may make it more powerful (289).

Klecka (175), Edwards (94), and Palmore & Whittington (235). Methodologically less satisfactory attempts (because they essentially disregard the confounding of age and generations) dealing with the psychological aspects of intergenerational problems are reported by Garsee (120), Kalish & Johnson (166), Wake & Sporakowski (335), and equally limited analyses of the "generation gap" are provided by Cameron (65) and by Fengler & Wood (110).

Statistical Procedures for the Analysis of Aging Data

A number of recent advances in the application of multivariate procedures to data involving change over age and/or time are of interest to gerontologists. Cattell (68) has extended his data box to provide for analyses across ages and cultures. Detailed treatments of longitudinal factor analyses are provided by Bentler (33) and by Corballis & Traub (78). Criteria for matching factors over occasions are examined by Nesselroade & Baltes (222). The latter authors (20) also provide a detailed account of procedures and problems in the developmental analysis of individual differences on multiple measures, and Buss (59) has investigated an extension of Cattell's data box to age changes and differences. The problem of regression to the mean has been investigated conceptually by Furby (118) and empirically by Nesselroade, Schaie & Baltes (224). An extension of latent structure analysis to developmental data is advocated by Murray, Wiley & Wolfe (216). Finally, much useful material may be found in Wohlwill's chapter on correlational methods in the study of developmental change (347, pp. 248–88).

Functional Age

Dissatisfaction with chronological age as the independent variable in gerontological studies has led to an examination of the concept of functional age. First discussed by Birren (38), this concept suggests that individuals age at different rates along different dimensions, and that one might estimate an individual's functional age very much along the lines of the old mental age concept. Functional age would be a convenient method to apply to problems of variable retirement. However, studies of the concept in an industrial context reveal that few individuals are significantly ahead or behind their calendar age on a variety of measures (89, 90). The functional age strategy has been most recently revived by Nuttall (230). Data based upon application of the functional age concept to psychological variables have recently been presented for the measurement of social age (267), abilities and personality (116), and for interpersonal and self-concept variables (168). It should be noted that the functional age concept requires assumption of the decrement model of aging and consequently may be inappropriate for many psychological variables over the major portion of the adult life-span.

Prediction of Death

More compatible with an adult stability model are the discussions of terminal drop and the prediction of death from changes in cognitive function. Here it is argued that changes in performance and personal adjustment within individuals occur as precursors of death. Because of the complexity of psychological processes, the first indications of systemic breakdown might therefore be detected long before severe physiological decrement leading to a death trajectory can be reliably detected. This argument has been most clearly advanced by Riegel & Riegel (258). Data from retrospective analyses suggesting that such terminal drop might indeed occur anywhere between 1 and 5 years prior to death are presented by Lieberman & Caplan (195), Riegel (256), Blum & Jarvik (42) and by Reimanis & Green (255). Other discussions of the differential characteristics of survivors in longitudinal studies and the psychological concomitants of longevity may be found in Eisdorfer & Wilkie (98), Powers & Bultena (251), Hall et al (132), Bartko et al (26), Jarvik & Blum (158), Pfeiffer (242), Rose (266) and Savage (280). See also the methodologically oriented volume by Rose & Bell (268).

Experimental Manipulation of the Aging Variable

Although much gerontological research requires quasi-experimental designs, there is an increasing attempt to bring aging phenomena under laboratory control by means of behavior modification strategies (149, 185, 263). These studies suggest that there may be reversibility for many phenomena considered in the past to be irreversible and overdetermined developmental trends, and thus would seem to reopen many issues regarding possible roles of the old in society (also cf 287). A related trend is the cautious investigation of age simulation studies (17, 20). Finally, there have been a number of reviews of strategies to be applied to the experimental study of aging variables (22, 39, 126, 142).

BOOKS

Numerous books covering a wide variety of material have recently been published. These may be divided into those dealing with general life-span issues (72, 81, 127); specific topic approaches covering the life-span (22, 153, 202, 223), those dealing with adulthood and aging in general (12, 25, 40, 48, 60, 61, 74, 96, 171, 181, 233); and those on specific topics of aging (29, 54, 138, 160, 234, 268, 283, 341). Of specific interest to those concerned with methodological issues are books by Goulet & Baltes (127) and Nesselroade & Reese (223). The series on issues in developmental psychology (22, 127, 223) promises to be most useful for those interested in life-span approaches, while the product of the APA Task Force on Aging (96), which represents an effort to include all the major fields of the psychology of aging, should be of interest to those desiring broad general coverage on this area.

COGNITIVE PROCESSES

The past 5 years hopefully have seen the last accumulation of cross-sectional studies of intellectual function which by use of inadequate samples and the inappropriate comparison of young and old samples with very different characteristics report data on decrement which, as indicated earlier in this chapter, ought at best to be considered evidence for generational age differences. Detailed discussions of these issues may be found in Baltes & Labouvie (18) and Botwinick (48). For a brief nontechnical summary, see Baltes & Schaie (23).

From the evidence now accumulating, it appears that the earlier notion of an irreversible decrement model for intelligence can no longer be upheld. Indeed, there is reason to believe that given a suitably favorable environment there may be gain in certain intellectual functions into very old age. Apparent decrement in the longitudinal studies appears to relate to substantial population differences in environmental aspects correlated with intelligence, which have either become more favorable for younger cohorts, or which are amenable to compensatory intervention.

In this section some of the recent findings on confoundings which have led to earlier misleading interpretations of the status of intellectual development in adulthood will be considered. For the record, we will then mention a few of the more interesting follow-up studies, where we must note that their results may be cohort specific. In addition, we will consider some novel studies on age differences in intelligence, noting that they most likely have little or nothing to say with regard to aging within individuals.

Differential Pattern of Adult Development

Studies of adult development with global IQ estimators such as the Army Alpha and the Wechsler scales (cf 209) conceal patterns of change because they provide averages of functions which may have different slopes or are of questionable factorial complexity. Formal models of differential development have therefore been conceptualized primarily in the context of the fluid versus crystallized intelligence model (144-146). It appears that the life course of the acculturated crystallized intelligence factors does not show any decrement whatsoever, while fluid dimensions which depend upon species-specific and probably biologically mediated functions tend to decline as a corollary of decrement in speed of capacity of response (83, 145, 284). Moreover, evidence is beginning to emerge which suggests that the pattern of adult intelligence may emerge prior to early adolescence (113).

Far less certain are differential findings for the verbal and performance parts of the Wechsler, since we do not know whether the discrepancy in older subjects is due to differential decline or differential initial performance levels in successive generations.

Ontogenetic Versus Generational Change

A number of studies with the Primary Mental Abilities have now conclusively demonstrated that actual decrement for Verbal Meaning, Space, Reasoning, and Number does not occur until the late sixties, and that the point of decline is shifting upwards with increasing asymptotic level for successive generations. This information is provided in short-term longitudinal studies over 7 and 14 year periods within cohorts (290, 296). It has also been verified in studies with independent random samples which control for the effect of repeated testing and loss of representativeness in a longitudinal study (292, 297). These results are maintained also when appropriate controls are introduced for the effects of subject attrition (24, 291). Factor analysis and cross-occasion factor matching designs for separating ontogenetic and generational change have also been used to show that the life course for the second order factors of crystallized intelligence, cognitive flexibility, and visualization is stable or incremental throughout adulthood, while the life course for visuo-motor flexibility suggests age decrement in early adulthood, decelerating in rate in old age (224). Similar findings occur when differential life courses are charted for individuals differentiated by initial level or performance, with past reports of differential change being attributed to regression effects (21).

It should be noted that the story is far less clear for Word Fluency for which previous studies have noted significant within-generation decrement (284). Most recent findings here suggest that there are significant secular trends which indicate systematic decrements or increments not depending upon the subject's age, but rather upon the time period which is being monitored (290, 292).

Comparability of Factor Structure

A most frustrating problem remaining to be solved is the question of stability in factor structure. Only a beginning has been made to consider the possibility that the organization of abilities in old age might differ from that of the young (135, 224, 247). Whether or not this will lead to the construction of alternate test forms for individuals of advanced age remains to be seen.

Factors Influencing Intellectual Performance

In addition to the discovery of generational differences, there has been a concerted effort to identify parameters which account for the fact that under certain conditions the elderly can show better performance than is generally expected. The effect of cautiousness and other motivational ability-extraneous factors upon intelligence-test performance has been investigated by Botwinick (45) and by Furry & Baltes (119), who show that situational factors and instructional set may indeed markedly affect intellectual performance (also see 112, 186). Favorable performance differentials in intelligence test performance for measures of fluid ability were noted for adults engaging in physical fitness exercises (250). Similarly, favorable performance on WAIS measures were noted for individuals with relatively low blood pressure (343), those with a lesser incidence of systemic disease (344), and fewer negative neurophysiological indicators (337). The effect of physiological systems on intellectual performance is discussed in more detail by Eisdorfer (95) and Jarvik & Cohen (159). But when short-term longitudinal studies are conducted for reasonably heterogeneous groups, it is again clear that sociocultural differences rather than age seem most important (274).

Follow-up Studies

A number of single cohort studies have again been reported upon during this period. In general they show little or no age decrement except for the period of very advanced age or during the terminal period shortly before subject's death where that variable has been controlled for. Worth mentioning in this group is a further follow-up on the Berkeley Guidance study at midlife (27, 141); further reports on the survivors of the Kallman-Jarvik twin study (41, 43); and a historically interesting follow-up of one of the early age-difference studies with the Babcock-Levy test (121).

Cross-Sectional Studies

A few cross-sectional studies are mentioned here because they investigate age differences with instruments not previously applied to aged populations. This group of studies investigated a Spanish version of the WAIS (130); the General Aptitude Test battery (117); the Draw-a-Man test (299); the Quick test (193); the Stroop Color Word Test (36); and Stein's Symbol Gestalt and the Wechsler Memory Test (295). Witkins' field dependence-independence measures finally have been investigated in relation to intelligence by Erlemeier, Schreiner & Schnurer (107).

Concept Attainment and Problem Solving

Research on concept attainment has recently taken a different turn because of a new focus of interest on the performance of older persons on Piagetian tasks. Although Piaget (114) postulates that the last stage of intellectual growth, formal operations, is reached at about the age of 12, several investigators have found consistent and reliable differences in the stage of conceptual development of young, young adult, and older subjects (237, 273, 313, 329). These studies seem to support the proposition that with age there is a curvilinear development on Piagetian tasks (143, 200, 273). It should be remembered, however, that although these investigators are postulating a developmental change, their evidence is based on age differences.

In attempts to find other factors which might account for age differences on Piagetian tasks, several variables have been investigated. Sex differences are not significant (273, 313) and neither is vocabulary (313). The effect of years of education is unclear since one study found a strong relationship (238) and the other did not (273). In a critical analysis, Riegel (257) contends that Piaget's theory does not adequately represent the thoughts and emotions of mature and creative persons and therefore is inappropriate for describing them. He feels that use of the dialectic approach is more appropriate than Piaget's schema to interpret qualitative aging phenomena.

Problem solving has not received much attention recently. Older people normally perform more poorly than do younger (87, 88, 219, 262, 353). Denney & Denney (87) suggest this may be the result of the failure of older people to base their questioning strategies upon any classification system. Strategies have also been observed on tasks requiring guessing future events. Sanford & Maule (279) found on two experiments that neither young nor old subjects adopted the best strategy, but the old performed more poorly than the young; yet Sanford, Griew & O'Donnell (278) found no age difference in performance on prediction tasks offering two or three alternatives.

Learning

Studies of learning and memory normally employ cross-sectional designs which, as stated above, seriously limit our understanding of the changes with age which occur in these processes. Since cohort differences have not been investigated, the particular contribution of this effect is presently unknown. Description is, therefore, limited to age differences.

Relatively few recent studies have been devoted to age differences in learning. Although learning ability had long been felt to decline with age, the current viewpoint holds that observed deficits in learning may be the result of performance differences rather than as a function of a decreased ability to learn. One such performance factor was reported by Eisdorfer, Nowlin & Wilkie (97), who found that the learning of older subjects was improved by the administration of propranolol. The results were interpreted as supporting the hypothesis that the observed learning deficit in the aged is the result of heightened arousal of the autonomic nervous system. A more behavioral approach related to this hypothesis demonstrated that reinforcement was effective in decreasing omission errors and the number of trials to criterion (190), and that both social and objective rewards improve performance (154).

Another factor often used to determine age differences in performance is stimulus pacing (cf 48). In general, the faster the stimulus pacing, the poorer the performance of older relative to younger persons. One study which held the anticipation interval constant and looked at the total time available for learning rather than at the number of trials to criterion did not find a significant pacing effect (173). When the anticipation interval is varied, differential age differences did emerge (212). When interference effects were also manipulated, however, the anticipation interval was no longer important (331), but interference effects impaired the performance of older people (187, 331). Biofeedback conditioning, a task which may equate age groups in terms of interference effects since it is novel to both, was learned as well by old subjects as by young (349). Older subjects learn concrete items better than abstract items, and the strategies they use to learn them differ from those employed by young subjects (272). An inefficient learning set has been hypothesized to account for some of the differences (211). In addition, older subjects perform poorly on tasks requiring conceptual shifts (220, 221), although there are conflicting results (77).

Memory

Although conceptually different, learning and memory are inextricably linked—how can one remember something which has never been learned? As has been found with learning performance, the ability to remember seems to decline with age, although not under all conditions. Consequently, investigations have been undertaken to ascertain where the differences exist, and, perhaps more importantly, to try to identify what factors may account for the observed decrement (cf 8).

Age deficits are normally found on paced tasks (172, 318), tasks which demand a constant switching of attention (80), tasks which require a change of set (332), and tasks which require free recall rather than recognition (133). Since several studies have found that the search through memory seems to be much slower in older people (6, 7, 106), Anders, Fozard & Lillyquist (7) postulate that the less rapid access to memorized information handicaps the performance of older people and may be a factor in the observed decrements.

Another approach to identify underlying mechanisms which may affect memory processes as one ages involves perceptual processing. Harwood & Naylor (134) assessed the maximum rate of information acceptance of young and old subjects on three tasks of graded difficulty and found it to be lower in the elderly than in the young. Surwillo (314), investigating simple and choice reaction time, concluded that old age is accompanied by a slowing of information processing. Similarly, studies of dichotic listening show that with age there is a decrease in performance (302). Clark & Knowles (76) found an age-related decrease for both written and vocal recall and for the digits reported either first or second in sequence. This deficit was found predominantly in the material which had been presented to the left ear, but was not a function of a selective left-ear hearing loss, and may decrease the amount of information that reaches the short-term store and is thus available at output.

Several studies have confirmed that the modality in which the stimulus is presented has a significant effect on observed memory deficits. Older people seem to be disproportionately impaired on visual as opposed to auditory recall tasks (108, 318). In an investigation also concerned with auditory storage, Laurence & Trotter (188) studied the effect of homophones, acoustically similar words, acoustically unrelated words, and blocked vs random listing of the items in a free recall test. Homophones were recalled best and acoustically similar words were recalled least by both young and old. Surprisingly, the elderly seemed to recall more words under the random list structure than under the blocked. These findings were interpreted to support the proposition that the elderly cannot make as efficient use of structural redundancy as can the young.

One group of studies investigated the opportunity of organizing the material to be remembered. The position taken is that the observed age differences may be the result of inefficient organizational procedures by the elderly (124, 150–152). The role the nature of the task plays in influencing retention is still uncertain. Studies report differential age effects with a retroactive inhibition paradigm (332) and transfer tasks (330), although the latter study attributes this to better performance by the young subjects rather than poorer performance by the old. In another report, bright older people were subject to forgetting because of interference from contextual associations (51). Other studies found no differential interference effects as a function of age when subjects were matched for intelligence (169) and learning performance (210), although one study found no differential effect in two experiments until subjects were equated by a control criterion (321). Goulet (125) discussed the various methodological and theoretical issues involved.

Meaningfulness of the material may result in age differences in memory. But

Kinsbourne (172) did not find that the old performed differently from the young when the task was to recall items which varied in the sequential dependencies between successive letters. The performance of both age groups improved as the items more closely approximated written English. On the other hand, older subjects seemed to perform better as the meaning and familiarity of the stimulus increased (134, 147, 148). Taub (317) found both young and old subjects performed more poorly as the complexity of the stimulus arrangement increased, but that the decreases were similar for both, while Howell (147) found the older subjects performed differentially worse than young on more complex tasks. Repeated testing or practice may improve the memory of older people (240), but there is no evidence that it aids the elderly any more than the young (319, 320). Attempts to improve learning (53) and memory (85) by manipulating biological mediators through the administration of yeast RNA have not been successful. However, the administration of pentylenetetrazol was found to lead to improvement (189); nevertheless, administration of drugs may have a placebo effect (218). Also, hyperoxygenation seems to lead to improvements (155, 156), while alcohol has differential age effects (both decremental and incremental) on a variety of tasks (345).

PERCEPTION AND PSYCHOPHYSIOLOGY

Sensation and Illusions

It has long been known that hearing decreases with age (cf 79), although the effect is much smaller in certain cultures (268a). Recent research on hearing and aging is concerned with related processing abilities. Much of this research involves work with speech distortion. The aging auditory mechanism has decreased capacities in integrating and understanding distorted messages even in persons who have relatively normal hearing audiometrically (34, 207, 253, 342). Bergman (35) suggests this may be due to problems in time-related processing abilities. Another approach to comparing speech perceptions involves the use of the verbal transformation effect (illusory changes which occur while listening to recordings of repeated words). With age there is a loss of susceptibility to this effect (338), which is even less noticeable in deteriorated older people (232). Rees & Botwinick (254) measured the sensory and decision processes in an auditory signal detection task. They concluded that the magnitude of auditory deficits in old age may be overestimated due to the greater cautiousness of the elderly, since the aged had higher criterion scores than the young, while the differences in detectability were not significant. The risk avoidance or greater cautiousness of the elderly has been found elsewhere (45) and may play a part in much of the observed performance decrements of older people.

That visual function declines with age has also long been established (cf 79). Temporal characteristics seem to be a factor in visual perception since older people require longer exposure duration to identify forms even when matched with younger subjects on standard measures of visual acuity, and they have a longer critical duration over which time-intensity reciprocity holds for form identification (105). A somewhat different approach to looking at temporal factors is described by Storandt (312), who tested recognition across visual fields. Finding that stimuli presented in the same visual field in both training and recognition were recalled faster than those presented in the opposite field for recognition, she concluded there is a less than perfect connection via the corpus callosum; however, the difference is the same for both young and old subjects.

The other modalities have not received much recent attention. Contrary to popular opinion, elderly subjects did not differ from young or middle-aged adults in the perception of comfortable temperature (265). In a study of the aging voice, it was found that with age there is an increase in the mean vocal intensity for reading and speaking and a decrease in the overall reading rate and mean sentence reading rate (275). It was also found that age can be systematically identified from voice samples (309).

Most recent research on visual illusions involved attempts to identify factors which may account for the observed age differences. These included cohort and time of measurement differences (101), inaccurate perceptions (99), verbal intelligence (100), and sensory deprivation (122).

Central Nervous System

The slowing of alpha rhythm has been frequently reported as a function of age (325, 336, 348). Studies of behavioral correlates of temporal lobe activity have conflicting results. Significant relationships are found on verbal-performance discrepancies of relatively healthy subjects (91, 337), but not when subjects are matched on such variables as age, socioeconomic status or education (337). On a conditioning task, measures of EEG have shown greater reactivity for the old than the young (310), although in cases of severe senile deterioration, diffuse slowing has been observed (231). The effects of EEG activity during sleep are much greater than any other age-related EEG characteristic (109). The percentage of rapid eye movement (REM) sleep remains stable among adults until around age 80, where it drops markedly (109) for both males and females (165). Correlations between cognitive and drive functioning on amounts of REM sleep in the aged were found (164). Such results suggest changes in CNS functioning are involved (109, 164).

Average evoked response from scalp recordings following the presentation of a stimulus show that the amplitudes of various portions of the wave form tend to change differentially with age for visual, somatosensory, and auditory stimulation (92, 203, 298). In a thorough review of this area, Thompson & Marsh (325) are led to the conclusion that individual differences such as intelligence, personality, and sex should be considered in research on evoked responses. The little available information on the effects of age on contingent negative variation show no age differences in males (206).

Autonomic Nervous System

Few recent studies have been devoted to behavioral correlates and the aging autonomic nervous system. In general, the aged show less responsivity than the young, as measured by the galvanic skin response (215, 310) and cardiovascular responsivity (214, 310, 325), and greater reactivity as measured by free fatty acid mobilization (97). With one exception (186), most investigations of the arousal hypothesis using behavioral manipulations of levels of arousal in young and old subjects have not been successful in establishing differential age effects (37, 131, 162).

Reaction Time

As with many other abilities, the slowing with age of response speed has long been recognized (cf 48). Proposing that perceptual deprivation would facilitate reaction time (RT) in old subjects by making them more responsive to sensory stimulation, Kemp (170) tested both young and old age groups but found no difference between experimental and control groups. On a task involving stimulus repetition on two-choice RT, examination of the frequency distributions led Waugh and associates (339) to conclude that the long latencies of the aged were a function of impaired psychomotor rather than decision-making efficiency. Studies designed to test the proposition that this loss is due mainly to sensory ability differences between the old and the young (46, 47, 49) suggest that the slowing is not attributable to sensory factors. Since previous results suggested motor factors were not important, Botwinick (47) concluded that central mechanisms underlie the slowing with age. Along this line, testing the hypothesis that EEG alpha rhythm is the master timing mechanism for behavior, Woodruff (348) used the biofeedback technique with both young and old subjects to manipulate brain wave frequency. She found that the slowing of the EEG alpha rhythm could not completely account for the slowing of RT with age (cf 324).

Studies testing whether variations in heart rate could account for age-related slowing have found no relationship (50, 214, 325). But subjects with a personality type predisposing them to coronary heart disease had longer response latencies for both simple and choice RT than did subjects of a different personality type (1). Studies which show few age differences in response speed are quite infrequent, although among nonathletes, RT age differences are not observed (50). In addition, age differences in RT disappear as a result of extensive practice, and this practice effect may show positive transfer to performance on ability tests (149).

PERSONALITY

The last few years have been particularly rich in reviews concerning our knowledge of adult personality development and have shown some progress in theory development, but they have been poverty stricken in contributions to our data base. Just as in the area of intelligence, we are discovering that much of the older literature suffers from fatal methodological flaws, that whole theories such as disengagement may have been built on methodological artifacts, but that the evidence which might help us build new models is accumulating very slowly.

Reviews

In her 1968 review of personality and aging, Chown (73) concluded that there is evidence for disengagement, but that it does not seem to occur voluntarily. She described conflicting evidence, some for stability and some for change, for many of the popular personality questionnaires and rating methods, but she deplored the absence of longitudinal studies which might help clarify issues. Much the same tale is told by Schaie & Marquette (293), who consider multivariate studies of personality in adulthood and have to conclude that there is as yet little understanding of personality structure beyond the college age period. Neugarten (226–228) is somewhat more optimistic, but would like to see a trend towards expanding our network of naturalistic observations (see also Neugarten 225). She is particularly impressed with our lack of understanding of how some people age successfully, and concludes that while disengagement theory may indeed describe real phenomena, this theory seems inadequate in handling the behavior of successfully aging individuals. Other more limited reviews in the personality area have been provided from a life-span perspective for socialization and sex-role development (104), creativity and cognitive style (178), person perception research (217), continuity models of personality (198), and the social learning approach to personality development (4).

Theory Development

There is continuing discussion on the utility of the disengagement as against an activity model. Of particular interest here is evidence in cross-national studies that a positive relation between activity level and life satisfaction can be demonstrated in different urban centers (138). Similar findings are presented by Hess & Bradshaw (140) for a heterogeneous group of subjects from high school to retirement age. On the other hand, there is some support for disengagement in the study of a VA domiciliary population (305). Another study suggests differentiating between psychological and physical disengagement (11). An attempt at incorporating certain aspects of the disengagement model into a cognitive theory of personality is provided by Thomae (322), and at least one empirical study tries to relate disengagement to field-dependence (340).

Of considerable interest is Kohlberg's recent attempt to extend his theory of moral development into adulthood (179). This is the first systematic attempt since Erikson to extend personality theory beyond adolescence, and while the evidence thus far presented for the development of adult moral stages is slim (180, 183), it is likely that this forward thrust may lead to other ventures in the extension of theoretical models which in the past were not explicated beyond adolescence.

Sequential Studies

Methodologically more sophisticated studies are beginning to appear in the personality literature. Woodruff & Birren (350) applied sequential methods to a follow-up of the California Personality Inventory first administered in 1944. They asked subjects to describe themselves in 1970 as they thought they were like in 1944 and as they were like now. Their findings indicate that there were few objective changes over the 26 year period, but that subjects differed significantly in their subjective description of their personality at the earlier age. Further comparison with a young control group in 1970 revealed substantial generation differences. Sequential methods have also been applied to a 14-year study of the trait of social responsibility (294) with apparent secular trends but no age trends, and to personality perceptual rigidity with similar results (290).

Longitudinal Studies

A number of personality variables have also been studied longitudinally in conjunction with studies already referred to in the section on intelligence. Much of the evidence from studies such as the Berkeley guidance study (cf 198) support a continuity model. Much of this evidence, however, as yet reaches only into the middle years. A longitudinal study specifically oriented to uncover changes over the decade from 70 to 80 in a group of community elderly in rural Pennsylvania is reported in a monograph by Britton & Britton (54). These findings are frustrating because they do not show any clear trends, but rather suggest that over this age period at least, individual situational variables may be most important. On the matter of survival, it appears that there were no systematic relations with personality measures for men, but that the female survivors scored higher on measures reflecting activity; another blow to disengagement. Samples were quite small and measures many, so that this study must be viewed as generating research hypotheses rather than providing definitive answers to the question of whether or not continuity of personality extends into very old age.

Personality Structure

Several factor-analytic studies have examined adult personality structure in the aged, unfortunately most often with samples too small to permit sound conclusions. In this group are studies of personality and cognitive style (304) and of the MMPI (56).

A somewhat different approach is taken by Goodwin & Schaie (123), who identified 13 personality factors analogous to those found by Cattell in a personality questionnaire administered previously to 991 subjects aged 21 to 75. Estimates of cross-sectional personality differences result in findings of stability for factors C, F, G, I, and M with unsystematic age trends for the remaining factors. A study of the Cattell 16 PF profiles of women psychologists belonging to three different generations showed profiles that were consistently more like men than women from the general population. There were some generational differences, with the younger cohort scoring higher in drive and self-reliance as well as being more impulsive (14). The relationship of anomie and cognitive structure (86) and of antecedent life styles and old age (103, 197, 328) have also been examined with inconclusive results.

Personality attributes and values of women past 35 years of age who were resuming their education were compared with women who were in the educational process at the "normal" age. The older women were less identified with the feminist movement but more dominant than women currently in college (354) [cf also changes in timing of social roles as discussed by Neugarten & Datan (229)].

Miscellaneous Cross-Sectional Studies

A number of cross-sectional studies which report age differences are mentioned for the record, even though again it is unclear whether their results should not more parsimoniously be interpreted as evidence of generational differences. Grant (129) examined age differences with the Tennessee self-sort across five age levels from 20 to 70 and found a curvilinear trend in positive self attribution. A study of achievement motivation on the TAT found no systematic age differences, while Klein (176) found old subjects conform more than young, unless they perceived themselves as competent in the task (177). A study of gambling and aging showed old people expected to lose while young expected to win, the interpretation of which was based upon locus of control (311). Two studies of time-perspective in the elderly found situational and specific personality-related variables to be more important than the subject's age (204, 303).

Other topics for which age differences between young and old adults have been explored during this period include the relation of egocentrism and social interaction (201), hypnotic susceptibility (213), the relationship between self-concept and reminiscence (137, 194), factors which affect life satisfaction and morale such as health (84, 115, 327), socioeconomic status (44, 84, 115, 327), age integrated communities (249), informal social interactions with friends (93, 192, 246, 316), future commitments (301), and personality variables (128, 191). Many of these studies found that these factors are more predictive of satisfaction than is age change per se. In an article discussing such criteria to predict adjustment and disengagement, Carp (67) argues against a simple composite measure of adjustment and suggests mapping the dimensions. Maddox (205) takes this argument a step further, arguing that the search for a single mode of adaptation to aging is both empirically and theoretically unjustified. Others suggest alternatives to the current theoretical models (184, 351).

ATTITUDES

Theoretical discussions of behavior changes in old age often suggest that such change—and in particular the withdrawal and disengagement phenomena—might be accounted for by negative changes in the self-concept of the aged, which in turn might be mediated by effects of societal stereotypes about the aged (cf 32). These issues have been investigated most intensively in the context of attitudes and perceptions of individuals across generations (cf 333). Britton & Britton (55) compared second, fourth, and sixth graders on their ability to distinguish between pictures of young, middle-aged and old. This discrimination was successful by fourth graders, and while younger stimuli were consistently seen as better-looking, older stimuli were seen as competent and understanding. Perception of grandparents has also been related to age of child, the older the child the more distant is the grandparent seen (163). Attitudes of the old towards themselves and the young in turn seem to be related to the positiveness of life satisfaction for the elderly subject (82, 167). Studies in which older and younger subjects rate themselves and others tend to produce inferred age differences which are not congruent with descriptions of attitudes by the separate age samples of themselves, supporting the notion that societal attitudes may indeed be mediated by erroneous stereotypes (3, 28, 52, 64, 236, 269). But these stereotypes may be in the process of change, since value orientations have been found to shift across generations (166, 239, 307) and differ in rural and urban areas (352). Objective versus perceived age differences in personality were compared for adolescents, middle-aged, and old subjects. The middle-aged were always correctly perceived but tended to misperceive the other two age groups (5) [also cf review of the person-perception literature (217)].

There is a limited amount of information upon the effects of attempting attitude modification in the young towards the aging. The use of imagery has been reported with positive results (71), while didactic lectures did not effect positive change in medical students (75).

Most older people are willing to talk freely on the topic of death and express no fear about it (174, 264). Since it has been found that people think about death throughout the life span more frequently than they estimate they do, death would, nevertheless, still appear to be a "taboo" topic (66). While euthanasia has received much attention in the popular press, only one study reported the attitudes of older people on this topic. In general, the aged reject euthanasia, although some do favor omitting life-sustaining measures which merely prolong the timing of death (252).

Sexuality

Although with younger subjects there is now relative freedom to inquire about sexual relations, it is still fairly difficult to obtain such information from the aged (241). Nevertheless, some information about the sexual thoughts and activities of older people is available. In general, while there is a decline in sexual activity (245), and a reduction in thoughts involved with sexual matters (63), sex continues to play an important role in the lives of most older people (244), at least until age 75 (334). Men report greater interest and activity than do women (244, 245), although for the women, this may be due to lack of a socially sanctioned partner (243). In addition, health probably plays a significant role (243, 334).

Retirement

Most of the literature on retirement is based upon factors influencing adjustment. Among the factors found to lead to better adjustment to retirement are good health (2, 102, 139, 323), adequate income (139, 248, 323), higher level of education (139), preretirement planning (139), and part-time work (139, 277).

Contrary to general opinion, health generally improves in retirement (308). Several studies reported that those living in retirement communities had a higher morale than those living in age-integrated communities (57, 208, 306).

It was suggested that only when work holds a central organizing position in a person's life should attitudes toward work influence retirement attitudes (111). This seems particularly pertinent for academicians who were found to continue their professional involvements long after retirement (2, 270, 271) and for teachers, although to a lesser degree (10, 136).

Literature Cited

1. Abrahams, J. P., Birren, J. E. 1973. Reaction time as a function of age and behavioral predisposition to coronary heart disease. *J. Gerontol.* 28:471–78
2. Acuff, G., Allen, D. 1970. Hiatus in "meaning": Disengagement for retired professors. *J. Gerontol.* 25: 126–28
3. Ahammer, I. M. 1971. Actual versus perceived age differences and changes: Young adults and older people view themselves and each other. *Proc. Ann. Conv. APA* 6:593–94
4. Ahammer, I. M. 1973. Social learning theory as a framework for the study of adult personality development. See Ref. 22, 253–84
5. Ahammer, I. M., Baltes, P. B. 1972. Objective versus perceived age differences in personality: How do adolescents, adults, and older people view themselves and each other? *J. Gerontol.* 27:46–51
6. Anders, T. R., Fozard, J. L. 1973. Effects of age upon retrieval from primary and secondary memory. *Develop. Psychol.* 9:411–15
7. Anders, T. R., Fozard, J. L., Lillyquist, T. D. 1972. Effects of age upon retrieval from short-term memory. *Develop. Psychol.* 6:214–17
8. Arenberg, D. 1973. Cognition and aging: Verbal learning, memory, problem solving, and aging. See Ref. 96, 74–97
9. Atchley, R. C. 1969. Respondents versus refusers in an interview study of retired women: An analysis of selected characteristics. *J. Gerontol.* 24:42–7
10. Atchley, R. C. 1971. Retirement and work orientation. *Gerontologist* 11: 29–32
11. Atchley, R. C. 1971. Disengagement among professors. *J. Gerontol.* 26: 476–80
12. Atchley, R. C. 1972. *The Social Forces in Later Life: An Introduction to Social Gerontology.* Belmont, Ca.: Wadsworth
13. Back, K. W., Bourque, L. B. 1970. Life graphs: Aging and cohort effects. *J. Gerontol.* 25:249–55
14. Bachtold, L. M., Weiner, E. E. 1971. Personality profiles of women psychologists: Three generations. *Develop. Psychol.* 5:273–78
15. Baltes, P. B. 1968. Longitudinal and cross-sectional sequences in the study of age and generation effects. *Hum. Develop.* 11:145–71
16. Baltes, P. B., Ed. 1973. Life-span models of psychological aging: A white elephant? *Gerontologist* 13:458–92
17. Baltes, P. B., Goulet, L. R. 1971. Exploration of developmental variables by manipulation and simulation of age differences in behavior. *Hum. Develop.* 14:149–70
18. Baltes, P. B., Labouvie, G. V. 1973. Adult development of intellectual performance: Description, explanation and modification. See Ref. 96, 157–219
19. Baltes, P. B., Nesselroade, J. R. 1970. Multivariate longitudinal and cross-sectional sequences for analyzing generational change: A methodological note. *Develop. Psychol.* 2:163–68
20. Baltes, P. B., Nesselroade, J. R. 1973. The developmental analysis of individual differences on multiple measures. See Ref. 223, 219–51
21. Baltes, P. B., Nesselroade, J. R., Schaie, K. W., Labouvie, E. W. 1972. On the dilemma of regression effects in examining ability level-related differentials in ontogenetic patterns of adult intelligence. *Develop. Psychol.* 6:78–84
22. Baltes, P. B., Schaie, K. W., Eds. 1973. *Life-Span Developmental Psychology: Personality and Socialization.* New York: Academic
23. Baltes, P. B., Schaie, K. W. 1974. Aging and IQ: The myth of twilight years. *Psychol. Today* 7:35–40
24. Baltes, P. B., Schaie, K. W., Nardi, A. H. 1971. Age and experimental mortality in a seven-year longitudinal study of cognitive behavior. *Develop. Psychol.* 5:18–26
25. Barrett, J. H. 1972. *Gerontological Psychology.* Springfield, Ill.: Thomas
26. Bartko, J. J., Patterson, R. D., Butler, R. N. 1971. Biomedical and behavioral predictors of survival among normal aged men: A multivariate analysis. See Ref. 234
27. Bayley, N. 1968. Cognition and aging. See Ref. 283, 97–119
28. Bell, B. D., Stanfield, G. G. 1973.

Chronological age in relation to attitudinal judgments: An experimental analysis. *J. Gerontol.* 28:491–96

29. Bengtson, V. L. 1973. *The Social Psychology of Aging.* New York: Bobbs-Merrill

30. Bengtson, V. L., Black, K. D. 1973. Intergenerational relations and continuities in socialization. See Ref. 22, 208–34

31. Bengtson, V. L., Kuypers, J. A. 1971. Generational differences and the developmental stake. *Aging & Hum. Develop.* 2:249–60

32. Bennett, R., Eckman, J. 1973. Attitudes toward aging: A critical examination of recent literature and implications for future research. See Ref. 96, 575–94

33. Bentler, P. M. 1973. Assessment of developmental factor change at the individual and group level. See Ref. 223, 145–74

34. Bergman, M. 1971. Changes in hearing with age. *Gerontologist* 11:148–51

35. Bergman, M. 1971. Hearing and aging: Implications of recent research findings. *Audiology* 10:164–71

36. Bettner, L. B., Jarvik, L. F., Blum, J. E. 1971. Stroop color-word test, non-psychotic organic brain syndrome and chromosome loss in aged twins. *J. Gerontol.* 26:458–69

37. Bicknell, A. T. 1970. *Aging, arousal, and vigilance.* Unpublished PhD thesis. Texas Tech. Univ., Lubbock

38. Birren, J. E., Ed. 1959. Principles of research on aging. In *Handbook of Aging and the Individual,* 3–42. Univ. Chicago Press

39. Birren, J. E. 1970. Toward an experimental psychology of aging. *Am. Psychol.* 25:124–35

40. Bischof, L. J. 1969. *Adult Psychology.* New York: Harper & Row

41. Blum, J. E., Fossage, J. J., Jarvik, L. F. 1972. The intellectual changes and sex differences in octogenarians: A twenty-year longitudinal study of aging. *Develop. Psychol.* 7:178–87

42. Blum, J. E., Jarvik, L. F. 1969. Variations in intellectual decline as indictors of pathology: A longitudinal twin study. *Proc. 77th Ann. Conv. APA* 4:743–44

43. Blum, J. E., Jarvik, L. F., Clark, E. T. 1970. Rate of change on selective tests

of intelligence: A twenty-year longitudinal study of aging. *J. Gerontol.* 25:171–76

44. Bortner, R. W., Hultsch, D. F. 1970. A multivariate analysis of correlates of life satisfaction in adulthood. *J. Gerontol.* 25:41–47

45. Botwinick, J. 1969. Disinclination to venture response versus cautiousness in responding: Age differences. *J. Genet. Psychol.* 119:241–49

45a. Botwinick, J. 1970. Geropsychology. *Ann. Rev. Psychol.* 21:239–72

46. Botwinick, J. 1971. Sensory-set factors in age differences in reaction time. *J. Genet. Psychol.* 119:241–49

47. Ibid 1972. Sensory perceptual factors in reaction time in relation to age. 121:173–77

48. Botwinick, J. 1973. *Aging and behavior.* New York: Springer

49. Botwinick, J., Storandt, M. 1972. Sensation and set in reaction time. *Percept. Mot. Skills* 34:103–6

50. Botwinick, J., Thompson, L. W. 1971. Cardiac functioning and reaction time in relation to age. *J. Genet. Psychol.* 119:127–32

51. Boyarsky, R. E., Eisdorfer, C. 1972. Forgetting in older persons. *J. Gerontol.* 27:254–58

52. Braun, P. H. 1973. Finding optimal age groups for investigating age-related variables. *Hum. Develop.* 16:293–303

53. Britton, A. et al 1972. Failure of ingestion of RNA to enhance human learning. *J. Gerontol.* 27:478–81

54. Britton, J. H., Britton, J. O. 1972. *Personality Changes in Aging.* New York: Springer. 221 pp.

55. Britton, J. O., Britton, J. H. 1969. Discrimination of age by preschool children. *J. Gerontol.* 24:457–60

56. Britton, P. G., Savage, R. D. 1969. The factorial structure of the Minnesota Multiphasic Personality Inventory from an aged sample. *J. Genet. Psychol.* 114:13–17

57. Bultena, G. L., Wood, V. 1969. The American retirement community: Bane or blessing. *J. Gerontol.* 24:209–17

58. Buss, A. R. 1973. An extension of developmental models that separate ontogenetic changes and cohort differences. *Psychol. Bull.* 80:466–79

59. Buss, A. R. 1974. A general develop-

mental model for interindividual differences, intraindividual differences and intraindividual changes. *Develop. Psychol.* 10:70–78

60. Busse, E. W., Jeffers, F. C., Eds. 1969. *Proceedings of Seminars 1965–69: Duke University Council on Aging and Human Development.* Durham, N. C.: Duke Univ.

61. Busse, E. W., Pfeiffer, E., Eds. 1969. *Behavior and Adaptation in Late Life.* Boston: Little, Brown

62. Butler, R. N. 1971. Age: The life review. *Psychol. Today* 5:49–51

63. Cameron, P. 1969. The "life-force" and age. *J. Gerontol.* 24:199–200

64. Cameron, P. 1970. The generation gap: Which generation is believed powerful as generational members' self-appraisals of power. *Develop. Psychol.* 3:403–4

65. Cameron, P. 1972. Pre-medicare beliefs about the generations regarding medicine and health. *J. Gerontol.* 27:536–39

66. Cameron, P., Stewart, L., Biber, H. 1973. Consciousness of death across the life-span. *J. Gerontol.* 28:92–95

67. Carp, F. M. 1969. Compound criteria in gerontological research. *J. Gerontol.* 24:341–47

68. Cattell, R. B. 1969. Comparing factor trait and state scores across ages and cultures. *J. Gerontol.* 24:348–60

69. Cattell, R. B. 1970. Separating endogenous, exogenous, ecogenic and epogenic component curves in developmental data. *Develop. Psychol.* 3:151–62

70. Cattell, R. B. 1973. Unraveling maturational and learning development by the comparative MAVA and structured learning approaches. See Ref. 223, 111–44

71. Cautela, J. R., Wisocki, P. A. 1969. The use of imagery in the modification of attitudes toward the elderly: A preliminary report. *J. Psychol.* 73:193–99

72. Charles, D. C., Looft, W., Eds. 1973. *Readings in Psychological Development Through Life.* New York: Holt, Rinehart & Winston

73. Chown, S. M. 1968. Personality and aging. See Ref. 283, 134–57

74. Chown, S. M. 1973. *Human Aging: Selected Readings.* Baltimore: Penguin. 397 pp.

75. Cicchetti, D. V., Fletcher, C. R., Lerner, E., Coleman, J. V. 1973. Effects of a social medicine course on the attitudes of medical students toward the elderly: A controlled study. *J. Gerontol.* 28:370–73

76. Clark, L. E., Knowles, J. B. 1973. Age differences in dichotic listening performance. *J. Gerontol.* 28:173–78

77. Coppinger, N. W., Nehrke, M. F. 1972. Discrimination learning and transfer of training in the aged. *J. Genet. Psychol.* 120:93–102

78. Corballis, M. C., Traub, R. E. 1970. Longitudinal factor analysis. *Psychometrika* 35:79–98

79. Corso, J. F. 1971. Sensory processes and age effects in normal·adults. *J. Gerontol.* 26:90–105

80. Craik, F. I. 1971. Age differences in recognition memory. *Quart. J. Exp. Psychol.* 23:316–23

81. Crow, L. D., Graham, T. F. 1973. *Human Development and Adjustment.* Toronto, N. J.: Littlefield, Adams

82. Cryns, A. G., Monk, A. 1972. Attitudes of the aged towards the young. A multivariate study in intergenerational perception. *J. Gerontol.* 27:107–112

83. Cunningham, W. R., Clayton, V. 1973. "Fluid" and "crystallized" intelligence in the elderly. *Proc. 81st Ann. Conv. APA*

84. Cutler, S. J. 1972. The availability of personal transportation, residential location, and life satisfaction among the aged. *J. Gerontol.* 27:384–89

85. Dalderup, L. M. et al 1970. An attempt to change memory and serum composition in old people by a daily supplement of dried baker's yeast: *J. Gerontol.* 25:320–24

86. Davol, S. H., Reimanis, G. 1969. Anomie and cognitive structure in a geriatric sample. *J. Genet. Psychol.* 115:133–41

87. Denney, D. R., Denney, N. W. 1973. The use of classification for problem solving: A comparison of middle and old age. *Develop. Psychol.* 9:275–78

88. Denney, N. W., Lennon, M. L.

1972. Classification: A comparison of middle and old age. *Develop. Psychol.* 7:210–13

89. Dirken, J. M. 1968. A tentative judgment about the "yard stick" for functional age. *Mens En Ondernem.* 22:342–51

90. Ibid. The functional age of industrial workers: The development of a method of measurement, 226–73

91. Drachman, D. A., Hughes, J. R. 1971. Memory and the hippocampal complexes: III. Aging and temporal EEG abnormalities. *Neurology* 21:1–14

92. Dustman, R. E., Beck, E. C. 1969. The effects of maturation and aging on the wave form of visually evoked potentials. *Electroencephalogr. Clin. Neurophysiol.* 26:2–11

93. Edward, J. N., Klemmack, D. L. 1973. Correlates of life satisfaction: Pre-examination. *J. Gerontol.* 28:497–502

94. Edwards, O. L. 1972. Intergenerational variation in racial attitudes. *Sociol. Soc. Res.* 57:22–31

95. Eisdorfer, C. 1969. Intellectual and cognitive changes in the aged. See Ref. 61, 237–47

96. Eisdorfer, C., Lawton, M. P. 1973. *The Psychology of Adult Development and Aging.* Washington, D.C.: APA

97. Eisdorfer, C., Nowlin, J., Wilkie, F. 1970. Improvement of learning in the aged by modification of autonomic nervous system activity. *Science* 170:1327–29

98. Eisdorfer, C., Wilkie, F. 1973. Intellectual changes with advancing age. See Ref. 160, 21–29

99. Eisner, D. A. 1972. Life-span age differences in visual perception. *Percept. Mot. Skills* 34:857–858

100. Eisner, D. A., Apfeldorf, M. 1971. Verbal intelligence and susceptibility to visual illusions. *Percept. Mot. Skills* 33:1298

101. Eisner, D. A., Schaie, K. W. 1971. Age changes in response to visual illusions from middle to old age. *J. Gerontol.* 26:146–50

102. Ellison, D. L. 1969. Alienation and the will to live. *J. Gerontol.* 24:361–67

103. Elmore, J. L. 1970. Adaptation to aging. *Gerontologist* 10:50–53

104. Emmerich, W. 1973. Socialization and sex role development. See Ref. 22, 123–44

105. Eriksen, C. W., Hamlin, R. M., Breitmeyer, R. G. 1970. Temporal factors in visual perception as related to aging. *Percept. Psychophys.* 7:354–56

106. Eriksen, C. W., Hamlin, R. M., Daye, C. 1973. Aging adults and rate of memory scan. *Bull. Psychon. Soc.* 1:259–60

107. Erlemeier, N., Schreiner, M., Schnurer, H. 1972. Relationships between intelligence and cognitive style (Witkins) in older ages. *Z. Entwickl. Psychol. Padagog.* 4:183–93

108. Farrimond, T. 1969. Age differences in speed of retrieval from memory store. *Aust. J. Psychol.* 21:79–83

109. Feinberg, I. 1969. Effects of age on human sleep patterns. In *Sleep Physiology and Pathology*, ed. A. Kales. Philadelphia: Lippincott

110. Fengler, A. P., Wood, V. 1972. The generation gap: An analysis of attitudes on contemporary issues. *Gerontologist* 12:124–28

111. Fillenbaum, G. G. 1971. On the relation between attitude to work and attitude to retirement. *J. Gerontol.* 26:244–48

112. Fisher, J. 1973. Competence, effectiveness, intellectual functioning, and aging. *Gerontologist* 13:62–68

113. Fitzgerald, J. M., Nesselroade, J. R., Baltes, P. B. 1973. Emergence of adult intellectual structure: Prior to or during adolescence? *Develop. Psychol.* 9:114–19

114. Flavell, J. H. 1963. *The Developmental Psychology of Jean Piaget.* New York: Van Nostrand

115. Fowler, F. J. Jr., McCalla, M. E. 1969. Correlates of morale among aged in greater Boston. *Proc. 77th Ann. Conv. APA* 4:733–34

116. Fozard, J. L. 1972. Predicting age in the adult years from psychological assessments of abilities and personality. *Aging & Hum. Develop.* 3:175–82

117. Fozard, J. L., Nuttall, R. L. 1971. General aptitude test battery scores for men differing in age and socioeconomic status. *J. Appl. Psychol.* 55:372–79

118. Furby, L. 1973. Interpreting regression toward the mean in developmental research. *Develop. Psychol.* 8:172–79

119. Furry, C. A., Baltes, P. B. 1973. The effect of age differences in ability-extraneous performance variables on the assessment of intelligence in children, adults and the elderly. *J. Gerontol.* 28:73–80

120. Garsee, J. W. 1972. Some developmental correlates of individually perceived generation differences in value role-taking. *Diss. Abstr.* 33:1816

121. Gilbert, J. G. 1973. Thirty-five year follow-up of intellectual functioning. *J. Gerontol.* 28:68–72

122. Girotti, G., Beretta, A. 1969. Apparent vertically following short-term sensory deprivation: Differential performances in young and old men. *Cortex* 5:74–86

123. Goodwin, K. S., Schaie, K. W. 1969. Age differences in personality structure. *Proc. 77th Ann. Conv. APA* 4(pt. 2):713–14

124. Gordon, S. K., Clark, N. E. 1973. Adult age differences in recent and delayed prose retention and word recognition memory. *Proc. 81st Ann. Conv. APA* 8:771–72

125. Goulet, L. R. 1972. New directions for research on aging and retention. *J. Gerontol.* 27:52–60

126. Goulet, L. R. 1973. The interfaces of acquisition: Models and methods for studying the active, developing organism. See Ref. 223

127. Goulet, L. R., Baltes, P. B. 1970. *Life-Span Developmental Psychology: Research and Theory.* New York: Academic

128. Granick, S. 1973. Morale measures as related to personality, cognitive, and medical functioning of the aged. *Proc. 81st Ann. Conv. APA* 8:785–86

129. Grant, C. H. 1969. Age differences in self-concept from early adulthood through old age. *Proc. 77th Ann. Conv. APA* 4:717–18

130. Green, R. F. 1969. Age-intelligence relationships between ages sixteen and sixty-four. A rising trend. *Develop. Psychol.* 1:618–27

131. Gribbin, K., Birren, J. E. 1973. Audience effect and task complexity: Differential factors with age? *Proc. 81st Ann. Conv. APA* 8:767–68

132. Hall, E. H., Savage, R. D., Bolton, N., Pidwell, D. M., Blessed, G. 1972. Intellect, mental illness, and survival in the aged: A longitudinal investigation. *J. Gerontol.* 27:237–44

133. Harwood, E., Naylor, G. F. K. 1969. Recall and recognition in elderly and young subjects. *Aust. J. Psychol.* 21:251–57

134. Ibid. Rates of information-transfer in elderly subjects, 127–36

135. Ibid 1971. Changes in the constitution of the WAIS intelligence pattern with advancing age. 23:297–303

136. Havighurst, R. J., Devries, A. 1969. Life styles and free time activities of retired men. *Hum. Develop.* 12:34–54

137. Havighurst, R. J., Glasser, R. 1972. An exploratory study of reminiscence. *J. Gerontol.* 27:245–53

138. Havighurst, R. J., Munnichs, J., Neugarten, B. 1969. *Adjustment to Retirement: A Cross-National Study.* Assen, The Netherlands: Van Gorcum

139. Heidbreder, E. M. 1972. Factors in retirement adjustment: White-collar/blue-collar experience. *Ind. Gerontol.* 12:69–79

140. Hess, A. L., Bradshaw, H. L. 1970. Positiveness of self-concept and ideal self as a function of age. *J. Genet. Psychol.* 117:57–67

141. Honzik, M. P., MacFarlane, J. W. 1973. Personality development and intellectual functioning from 21 months to 40 years. See Ref. 160, 45–58

142. Hooper, F. H. 1973. Cognitive assessment across the life-span: Methodological implications of the organismic approach. See Ref. 223, 299–316

143. Hooper, F. H., Fitzgerald, J., Papalia, D. 1971. Piagetian theory and the aging process: Extensions and speculations. *Aging & Hum. Develop.* 2:3–20

144. Horn, J. L. 1968. Organization of abilities and the development of intelligence. *Psychol. Rev.* 75:242–59

145. Horn, J. L 1970. Organization of data on life-span development of human abilities. See Ref. 126, 424–66

146. Horn, J. L. 1972. Intelligence: Why it grows, why it declines. See Ref. 153

147. Howell, S. C. 1972. Age, familiarity and complexity as recognition variables. *Percept. Mot. Skills* 34:732-34
148. Howell, S. C. 1972. Familiarity and complexity in perceptual recognition. *J. Gerontol.* 27:364-71
149. Hoyer, W. J., Labouvie, G. V., Baltes, P. B. 1973. Modifications of response speed deficits and intellectual performance in the elderly. *Hum. Develop.* 16:233-42
150. Hultsch, D. F. 1969. Adult age differences in the organization of free recall. *Develop. Psychol.* 1:673-78
151. Hultsch, D. F. 1971. Organization and memory in adulthood. *Hum. Develop.* 14:16-29
152. Hultsch, D. F. 1971. Adult age differences in free classification and free recall. *Develop. Psychol.* 4:338-42
153. Hunt, J. M., Ed. 1972. *Human Intelligence*. New Brunswick, N.J.: Transaction Books
154. Jackson, M. A. 1970. The effect of social and objective reward upon verbal learning in a disengaged and engaged population. *Diss. Abstr.* 31:2283
155. Jacobs, E. A., Winter, P. M., Alvis, H. J. 1969. Hyperoxygenation effect on cognitive functioning in the aged. *Proc. 77th Ann. Conv. APA* 4:721-22
156. Jacobs, E. A., Winter, P. M., Alvis, H. J. 1969. Hyperoxygenation effect on cognitive functioning in the aged. *New Engl. J. Med.* 28:753-57
157. Jarvik, L. F., Bennett, R., Blummer, B. 1973. Design of a comprehensive life history interview schedule. See Ref. 160, 127-36
158. Jarvik, L. F., Blum, J. E. 1971. Cognitive declines as predictors of mortality in twin pairs: A twenty year longitudinal study of aging. See Ref. 234, 199-209
159. Jarvik, L. F., Cohen, D. 1973. A biobehavioral approach to intellectual changes with aging. See Ref. 96, 220-80
160. Jarvik, L. F., Eisdorfer, C., Blum, J. E., Eds. 1973. *Intellectual Functioning in Adults*. New York: Springer
161. Jarvik, L. F., Kato, T. 1969. Chromosomes and mental changes in octogenarians: Preliminary findings. *Brit. J.*

162. Jeffrey, D. W. 1970. Age differences in serial reaction time as a function of stimulus complexity under conditions of noise and muscular tension. *Diss. Abstr.* 30:5258
163. Kahana, B., Kahana, E. 1970. Grandparenthood from the perspective of the developing grandchild. *Develop. Psychol.* 3:98-105
164. Kahn, E., Fisher, C. 1969. The sleep characteristics of the normal aged male. *J. Nerv. Ment. Dis.* 148:477-94
165. Kahn, E., Fisher, C., Lieberman, L. 1970. Sleep characteristics of the human aged female. *Comp. Psychiat.* 11:274-78
166. Kalish, R. A., Johnson, A. E. 1972. Value similarities and differences in three generations of women. *J. Marriage Fam.* 34:49-54
167. Kaplan, H. B., Pokorny, A. D. 1970. Aging and self-attitude: A conditional relationship. *Aging & Hum. Develop.* 1:241-50
168. Kastenbaum, R., Derbin, V., Sabatini, P., Artt, S. 1972. "The ages of me": Toward personal and interpersonal definitions of functional aging. *Aging & Hum. Develop.* 3:197-212
169. Keevil-Rogers, P., Schnore, M. M. 1969. Short-term memory as a function of age in persons of above average intelligence. *J. Gerontol.* 24:184-88
170. Kemp, B. J. 1973. Reaction time of young and elderly subjects in relation to perceptual deprivation and signal-on versus signal-off conditions. *Develop. Psychol.* 8:268-72
171. Kimmel, D. C. 1973. *Adulthood and Aging*. New York: Wiley
172. Kinsbourne, M. 1973. Age effects on letter span related to rate and sequential dependency. *J. Gerontol.* 28:317-19
173. Kinsbourne, M., Berryhill, J. L. 1972. The nature of the interaction between pacing and the age decrement in learning. *J. Gerontol.* 27:471-77
174. Kinsey, L. R., Roberts, J. L., Logan, D. L. 1972. Death, dying, and denial in the aged. *Am. J. Psychiat.* 129:161-66
175. Klecka, W. R. 1971. Applying political generations to the study of political

Psychiat. 115:1193-94

behavior: A cohort analysis. *Public Opin. Quart.* (Fall) 35:358–73
176. Klein, R. L. 1972. Age, sex, and task difficulty as predictors of social conformity. *J. Gerontol.* 27:229–36
177. Klein, R. L., Birren, J. E. 1973. Age, perceived self-competence and conformity: A partial explanation. *Proc. 81st Ann. Conv. APA* 8:799–80
178. Kogan, N. 1973. Creativity and cognitive style: A life-span perspective. See Ref. 22, 146–78
179. Kohlberg, L. 1973. Continuities in childhood and moral development revisited. See Ref. 22, 180–204
180. Kohlberg, L., Kramer, R. 1969. Continuities and discontinuities in childhood and adult moral development. *Hum. Develop.* 12:93–120
181. Koller, M. L. 1968. *Social Gerontology.* New York: Random House
182. Kuhlen, R. G. 1963. Age and intelligence: The significance of cultural change in longitudinal vs. cross-sectional findings. *Vita Hum.* 6:113–24
183. Kuhn, D., Langer, J., Kohlberg, L., Haan, N. 1974. The development of formal operations in logical and moral judgment. *Genet. Psychol. Monogr.* In press
184. Kuypers, J. A., Bengtson, V. L. 1973. Social breakdown and competence: A model of normal aging. *Hum. Develop.* 16:181–201
185. Labouvie, G. V., Hoyer, W. J., Baltes, M. M., Baltes, P. B. 1974. Operant analysis of intellectual behavior in old age. *Hum. Develop.* In press
186. Lair, C. V., Moon, W. H. 1972. The effects of praise and reproof on the performance of middle aged and older subjects. *Aging & Hum. Develop.* 3:279–84
187. Lair, C. V., Moon, W. H., Kausler, D. H. 1969. Associative interference in the paired associate learning of middle-aged and old subjects. *Develop. Psychol.* 9:548–52
188. Laurence, M. W., Trotter, M. 1971. Effect of acoustic factors and list organization in multitrial free recall learning of college age and elderly adults. *Develop. Psychol.* 5:202–10
189. Leckman, J., Ananth, J. V., Ban, T. A., Lehmann, H. E. 1971. Pentylenetetra-

zol in the treatment of geriatric patients with disturbed memory function. *J. Clin. Pharmacol. New Drugs* 11:301–3
190. Leech, S., Witte, K. L. 1971. Paired-associate learning in elderly adults as related to pacing and incentive conditions. *Develop. Psychol.* 5:180
191. Lehr, U., Rudinger, G. 1969. Consistency and change of social participation in old age. *Hum. Develop.* 12:255–67
192. Lemon, B. W., Bengtson, V., Peterson, J. A. 1972. An exploration of the activity theory of aging: Activity types and life satisfaction among in-movers to a retirement community. *J. Gerontol.* 27:511–23
193. Levine, N. R. 1971. Validation of the quick test for intelligence screening of the elderly. *Psychol. Rep.* 29:167–72
194. Lewis, C. N. 1971. Reminiscing and self-concept in old age. *J. Gerontol.* 26:240–43
195. Lieberman, M. A., Coplan, A. S. 1970. Distance from death as a variable in the study of aging. *Develop. Psychol.* 2:71–84
196. Lieberman, M. A., Falk, J. M. 1971. The remembered past as a source of data for research on the life cycle. *Hum. Develop.* 14:132–41
197. Linn, M. W. 1973. Perceptions of childhood: Present functioning and past events. *J. Gerontol.* 28:202–6
198. Livson, N. 1973. Developmental dimensions of personality: A life-span formulation. See Ref. 22, 98–122
199. Looft, W. R. 1970. Note on WAIS vocabulary performance by young and old adults. *Psychol. Rep.* 16:943–46
200. Looft, W. R. 1972. Egocentrism and social interaction across the life span. *Psychol. Bull.* 78:73–92
201. Looft, W. R., Charles, D. C. 1971. Egocentrism and social interaction in young and old adults. *Aging & Hum. Develop.* 2:21–28
202. Lowe, G. R. 1972. *The Growth of Personality: From Infancy to Old Age.* Harmondsworth, England
203. Luders, H. 1970. The effects of aging on the wave form of the somatosensory cortical evoked potential. *Electroencephalogr. Clin. Neurophysiol.* 29:450–60

204. Lynch, D. J. 1971. Future time perspective and impulsivity in old age. *J. Genet. Psychol.* 118:245–52
205. Maddox, G. L. 1970. Adaptation to retirement. *Gerontologist* 10:14–18
206. Marsh, G. R., Thompson, L. W. 1973. Effects of age on the contingent negative variation in a pitch discrimination task. *J. Gerontol.* 28:56–62
207. Marston, L. E., Goetzinger, C. P. 1972. A comparison of sensitized words and sentences for distinguishing nonperipheral auditory changes as a function of aging. *Cortex* 8:213–23
208. Martin, W. C. 1973. Activity and disengagement: Life satisfaction of in-movers into a retirement community. *Gerontologist* 13:224–27
209. Matarazzo, J. D. 1972. *Wechsler's Measurement and Appraisal of Adult Intelligence.* Baltimore: Williams & Wilkins
210. Moenster, P. A. 1972. Learning and memory in relation to age. *J. Gerontol.* 27:361–63
211. Monge, R. H. 1969. Learning in the adult years set or rigidity. *Hum. Develop.* 12:121–40
212. Monge, R. H., Hultsch, D. F. 1971. Paired association learning as a function of adult age and the length of the anticipation and inspection intervals. *J. Gerontol.* 26:157–62
213. Morgan, A. H., Hilgard, E. R. 1973. Age differences in susceptibility to hypnosis. *Int. J. Clin. Exp. Hypn.* 21:78–85
214. Morris, J. D., Thompson, L. W. 1969. Heart rate changes in a reaction time experiment with young and aged subjects. *J. Gerontol.* 24:269–75
215. Morrow, M. C., Boring, F. W., Keough, T. E. III, Haesly, R. R. 1969. Differential GSR conditioning as a function of age. *Develop. Psychol.* 1:299–302
216. Murray, J. R., Wiley, D. E., Wolfe, R. G. 1971. New statistical techniques for evaluating longitudinal models. *Hum. Develop.* 14:142–48
217. Nardi, A. H. 1973. Person-perception research and the perception of lifespan development. See Ref. 22, 285–301
218. Nash, M. M., Zimring, F. M. 1969. Prediction of reaction to placebo. *J. Abnorm. Psychol.* 74:568–73
219. Nehrke, M. F. 1972. Age, sex, and education difference in syllogistic reasoning. *J. Gerontol.* 27:466–70
220. Ibid 1973. Age and sex differences in discrimination learning and transfer of training. 28:320–27
221. Nehrke, M. F., Coppinger, N. W. 1971. The effect of task dimensionality on discrimination learning and transfer of training in the aged. *J. Gerontol.* 26:151–56
222. Nesselroade, J. R., Baltes, P. B. 1970. On a dilemma of comparative factor analyses: A study of factor matching based on random data. *Educ. Psychol. Meas.* 30:935–48
223. Nesselroade, J. R., Reese, H. W., Eds. 1973. *Life-Span Developmental Psychology: Methodological Issues.* New York: Academic
224. Nesselroade, J. R., Schaie, K. W., Baltes, P. B. 1972. Ontogenetic and generational components of structural and quantitative change in adult cognitive behavior. *J. Gerontol.* 27:222–28
225. Neugarten, B. L. 1969. Continuities and discontinuities of psychological issues into adult life. *Hum. Develop.* 12:121–30
226. Neugarten, B. L. 1971. Grow old along with me! The best is yet to be. *Psychol. Today* 5:45–48
227. Neugarten, B. 1972. Personality and the aging process. *Gerontologist* 12:9–15
228. Neugarten, B. L. 1973. Personality change in late life: A developmental perspective. See Ref. 96, 311–31
229. Neugarten, B. L., Datan, N. 1973. Sociological perspectives on the life cycle. See Ref. 22, 53–69
230. Nuttall, R. L. 1972. The strategy of functional age research. *Aging & Hum. Develop.* 3:149–52
231. Obrist, W. D., Chivian, E., Cronqvist, S., Ingvar, D. H. 1970. Regional cerebral blood flow in senile and presenile dementia. *Neurology* 20:315–22
232. Obusek, C. J., Warren, R. M. 1973. A comparison of speech perception in senile and well-preserved aged by means of the verbal transformation effect. *J. Gerontol.* 28:184–88

233. Palmore, E., Ed. 1970. *Normal Aging.* Durham, N. C.: Duke Univ. Press. 431 pp.
234. Palmore, E., Jeffers, F. C., Eds. 1971. *Prediction of Life-Span.* Lexington, Mass.: Heath
235. Palmore, E. B., Whittington, F. 1971. Trends in the relative status of the aged. *Soc. Forces* 50:84–91
236. Palmore, E. B. 1973. Ageism compared to racism and sexism. *J. Gerontol.* 28:362–69
237. Papalia, D. E. 1972. The status of several conservative abilities across the life-span. *Hum. Develop.* 15:229–43
238. Papalia, D. E., Kennedy, E., Sheehan, N. 1973. Conservation of space in noninstitutionalized old people. *J. Psychol.* 84:75–79
239. Payne, S., Summers, D. A., Steward, T. R. 1973. Value differences across three generations. *Sociometry* 36:20–30
239. Peak, D. T. 1970. A replication study of changes in short-term memory in a group of aging community residents. *J. Gerontol.* 25:316–19
241. Pfeiffer, E. 1969. Sexual behavior in old age. In *Behavior and Adaptation in Late Life*, ed. E. Pfeiffer, E. W. Busse. Boston: Little, Brown
242. Pfeiffer, E. 1971. Physical, psychological and social correlates of survival in old age. See Ref. 234, 223–35
243. Pfeiffer, E., Davis, G. C. 1972. Determinants of sexual behavior in middle and old age. *J. Am. Geriat. Soc.* 20:151–58
244. Pfeiffer, E., Verwoerdt, A., Davis, G. C. 1972. Sexual behavior in middle life. *Am. J. Psychiat.* 128:1262–67
245. Pfeiffer, E., Verwoerdt, A., Wang, H. 1969. The natural history of sexual behavior in a biologically advantaged group of aged individuals. *J. Gerontol.* 24:193–98
246. Pihlbad, C. T., Adams, D. L. 1972. Widowhood, social participation and life satisfaction. *Aging & Hum. Develop.* 3:323–30
247. Poitrenaud, J. 1971. (A general review of factorial studies concerning the variations in intellectual structure during the period of geriatric degeneration.) *Rev. Psychol. Appl.* 21:145–87

248. Pollman, A. W. 1971. Early retirement: A comparison of poor health to other retirement factors. *J. Gerontol.* 26:41–45
249. Poorkaj, H. 1972. Social-psychological factors and successful aging. *Sociol. Soc. Res.* 56:289–300
250. Powell, R. R., Pohndorf, R. H. 1971. Comparison of adult exercisers and nonexercisers on fluid intelligence and selected physiological variables. *Res. Quart.* 42:70–77
251. Powers, E. A., Bultena, G. L. 1972. Characteristics of deceased dropouts in longitudinal research. *J. Gerontol.* 27:530–35
252. Preston, C. E., Williams, R. H. 1971. View of the aged on the timing of death. *Gerontologist* 11:300–4
253. Punch, K. L., McConnell, F. 1969. The speech discrimination function of elderly adults. *J. Aud. Res.* 9:159–66
254. Rees, J. N., Botwinick, J. 1971. Detection and decision factors in auditory behavior of the elderly. *J. Gerontol.* 26:133–36
255. Reimanis, G., Green, R. F. 1971. Imminence of death and intellectual decrement in the aging. *Develop. Psychol.* 5:270–72
256. Riegel, K. F. 1971. The prediction of death and longevity in longitudinal research. See Ref. 234, 139–47
257. Riegel, K. F. 1973. Dialectic operations: The final period of cognitive development. *Hum. Develop.* 16:346–70
258. Riegel, K. F., Riegel, R. M. 1972. Development, drop, and death. *Develop. Psychol.* 6:306–19
259. Riegel, K. F., Riegel, R. M., Meyer, G. 1967. Sociopsychological factors of aging: A cohort-sequential analysis. *Hum. Develop.* 10:27–56
260. Riegel, K. F., Riegel, R. M., Meyer, G. 1968. The prediction of retest resisters in research on aging. *J. Gerontol.* 23:370–74
261. Riley, M. W., Johnson, M., Foner, A. 1972. *Aging and Society: A Sociology of Age Stratification.* New York: Russell Sage Found.
262. Rimoldi, H. J., Vander Woude, J. W. 1969. Aging and problem solving. *Arch. Gen. Psychiat.* 20:215–25

263. Risley, T. R., Wold, M. M. 1973. Strategies for analyzing behavioral change over time. See Ref. 223, 177–83

264. Roberts, J. L., Kimsey, L. R., Logan, D. L. 1970. How aged in nursing homes view dying and death. *Geriatrics* 25:115–19

165. Rohles, F. H. Jr. 1969. Preference for the thermal environment by the elderly. *Hum. Factors* 11:37–41

266. Rose, C. L. 1971. Critique of longevity studies. See Ref. 234

267. Rose, C. L. 1972. Measurement of social age. *Aging & Hum. Develop.* 3:153

268. Rose, C. L., Bell, B. 1971. *Predicting Longevity: Methodology and Critique.* Lexington, Mass.: Heath

268a. Rosen, S., Olin, P., Rosen, H. V. 1970. Dietary prevention of hearing loss. *Acta Otolaryngol.* 70:242–47

269. Rosencranz, H. A., McNevin, T. E. 1969. A factor analysis of attitudes toward the aged. *Gerontologist* 9:55–59

270. Rowe, A. R. 1972. The retirement of academic scientists. *J. Gerontol.* 27:113–18

271. Ibid 1973. Scientists in retirement. 18:345–50

272. Rowe, E. J., Schnore, M. M. 1971. Item concreteness and reported strategies in paired-associate learning as a function of age. *J. Gerontol.* 470–75

273. Rubin, K. H., Attewell, P. W., Tierney, M. C., Tumolo, P. 1973. Development of spatial egocentrism and conservation across the life span. *Develop. Psychol.* 9:432

274. Rudinger, C. 1972. (Determinants of intellectual performance: Results from the Bonn Gerontological Longitudinal Study.) *Arch. Psychol.* 125:23–38

275. Ryan, W. J. 1972. Acoustic aspects of the aging voice. *J. Gerontol.* 27:265–68

276. Ryder, N. B. 1965. The cohort as a concept in the study of social changes. *Am. Sociol. Rev.* 30:843–61

277. Saltz, R. 1971. Aging persons as child-care workers in a Foster Grandparent Program: Psycho-social effects and work performance. *Aging & Hum. Develop.* 2:314–40

278. Sanford, A., Griew, S., O'Donnell, L. 1972. Age effects in simple prediction behavior. *J. Gerontol.* 27:259–64

279. Sanford, A. J., Maule, A. J. 1973. The concept of general experience: Age and strategies in guessing future events. *J. Gerontol.* 28:81–88

280. Savage, R. D. et al 1972. A developmental investigation of intellectual functioning in the community aged. *J. Genet. Psychol.* 121:163–67

281. Schaie, K. W. 1965. A general model for the study of developmental problems. *Psychol. Bull.* 64:92–107

282. Schaie, K. W. 1967. Age changes and age differences. *Gerontologist* 7:128–32

283. Schaie, K. W., Ed. 1968. *Theories and Methods of Research in Aging.* Morgantown: West Virginia Univ. Library

284. Schaie, K. W. 1970. A reinterpretation of age-related changes in cognitive structure and functioning. See Ref. 126, 485–507

285. Schaie, K. W. 1972. Can the longitudinal method be applied to psychological studies on human development? In *Determinants of Human Behavior,* ed. F. Z. Moenks, W. W. Hartup, J. deWit, 3–22. New York: Academic

286. Schaie, K. W. 1972. Limitations on the generalizability of growth curves of intelligence. *Hum. Develop.* 15:141–52

287. Schaie, K. W. 1973. Reflections on papers by Looft, Peterson and Sparks: Towards an ageless society? *Gerontologist* 13:31–35

288. Schaie, K. W. 1973. Methodological problems in descriptive developmental research on adulthood and aging. See Ref. 223, 253–80

289. Schaie, K. W., Baltes, P. B., Nesselroade, J. R. 1974. Further thoughts on this interpretation of a general model for the study of developmental problems. Unpublished manuscript. Univ. Southern California

290. Schaie, K. W., Labouvie-Vief, G. 1974. Generational versus ontogenetic components of change in adult cognitive behavior: A fourteen year cross-sequential study. *Develop. Psychol.* 10:305–20

291. Schaie, K. W., Labouvie, G. V., Barrett, T. J. 1973. Selective attrition effects in a fourteen-year study of adult intelligence. *J. Gerontol.* 28:328–34

292. Schaie, K. W., Labouvie, G. V., Buech,

B. U. 1973. Generational and cohort-specific differences in adult cognitive functioning: A fourteen-year study of independent samples. *Develop. Psychol.* 9:151–66

293. Schaie, K. W., Marquette, B. 1972. Personality in maturity and old age. In *Multivariate Personality: Contributions to the Understanding of Personality in Honor of Raymond B. Cattell*, ed. R. M. Dreger, 612–32. Baton Rouge, La.: Claitor

294. Schaie, K. W., Parham, I. A. 1974. Social responsibility in adulthood: Ontogenetic and socio-cultural change. *J. Pers. Soc. Psychol.* In press

295. Schaie, K. W., Strother, C. R. 1968. Cognitive and personality variables in college graduates of advanced age. In *Human Behavior and Aging: Recent Advances in Research and Theory*, ed. G. A. Talland, 281–308. New York: Academic

296. Schaie, K. W., Strother, C. R. 1968. The cross-sequential study of age changes in cognitive behavior. *Psychol. Bull.* 70:671–80

297. Schaie, K. W., Strother, C. R. 1968. The effects of time and cohort differences on the interpretation of age changes in cognitive behavior. *Multivar. Behav. Res.* 3:259–93

298. Schenkenberg, T. 1970. *Visual, auditory, and somatosensory evoked responses of normal subjects from childhood to senescence.* Unpublished PhD thesis. Univ. Utah, Salt Lake City

299. Schmitz-Scherzer, R., Rudinger, G. 1970. The draw-a-man test (DAM) in gerontological research: A pilot study. *Z. Entwpsychol. Paediat. Psychol.* 2: 60–68

300. Schoenfeldt, L. F. 1973. Life history subgroups as moderators in the prediction of intellectual change. See Ref. 160, 31–44

301. Schonfield, D. 1973. Future commitments and successful aging: I. The random sample. *J. Gerontol.* 28:189–96

302. Schonfield, D., Trueman, V., Kline, D. 1972. Recognition test of dichotic listening and the age variable. *J. Gerontol.* 27:487–93

303. Schreiner, M. 1970. On the future-oriented time perspective of elderly people. *Z. Entwpsychol. Paediat. Psychol.* 2:28–46

304. Schreiner, M., Erlemeier, N., Glasmacher, J. 1973. [Personality and cognitive style (Witkin) in old age.] *Z. Entwpsychol. Paediat. Psychol.* 5:29–41

305. Schwartz, A. N., Proppe, H. G. 1969. Perception of privacy among institutionalized aged. *Proc. 77th Ann. Conv. APA* 4:727–28

306. Seguin, M. M. 1973. Opportunity for peer socialization in a retirement community. *Gerontologist* 13:208–14

307. Seltzer, M. M., Atchley, R. C. 1971. The concept of old: Changing attitudes and stereotypes. *Gerontologist* 11: 226–30

308. Shanas, E. 1970. Health and adjustment in retirement. *J. Gerontol.* 10: 19–21

309. Shipp, T., Hollien, H. 1969. Perception of the aging male voice. *J. Speech Hear. Res.* 12:703–10

310. Shmavonian, B. M., Miller, L. H., Cohen, S. E. 1970. Differences among age and sex groups with respect to cardiovascular conditioning and reactivity. *J. Gerontol.* 25:87–94

311. Stone, K., Kalish, R. 1973. Of poker, roles and aging: Description, discussion, and data. *Aging & Hum. Develop.* 4:1–13

312. Storandt, M. 1972. Recognition across visual fields and age. *J. Gerontol.* 27:482–86

313. Storck, P. A., Looft, W. R., Hooper, F. H. 1972. Interrelationships among Piagetian tasks and traditional measures of cognitive abilities in mature and aged adults. *J. Gerontol.* 27:461–65

314. Surwillo, W. W. 1973. Choice reaction time and speed of information processing in old age. *Percept. Mot. Skills* 36:321–22

315. Swenson, W. M. 1972. Psychological aspects of aging in the American culture. *Psychiat. Ann.* 2:28–35

316. Tallmer, M., Kutner, B. 1969. Disengagement and the stress of aging. *J. Gerontol.* 24:70–75

317. Taub, H. A. 1972. A further study of aging, short-term memory, and complexity of stimulus organization. *J.*

Genet. Psychol. 120:163–64

318. Taub, H. A. 1972. A comparison of young adult and old groups on various digit span tasks. *Develop. Psychol.* 6:60–65

319. Taub, H. A. 1973. Memory span, practice and aging. *J. Gerontol.* 28:335–38

320. Taub, H. A., Long, M. K. 1972. The effects of practice on short-term memory of young and old subjects. *J. Gerontol.* 27:494–99

321. Taub, H. A., Walker, J. B. 1970. Short-term memory as a function of age and response interference. *J. Gerontol.* 25:177–83

322. Thomae, H. 1970. Theory of aging and cognitive theory of personality. *Hum. Develop.* 13:1–16

323. Thompson, G. B. 1973. Work versus leisure roles: An investigation of morale amoung employed and retired men. *J. Gerontol.* 28:339–44

324. Thompson, L. W., Botwinick, J. 1968. Age differences in the relationship between EEG arousal and reaction time. *J. Psychol.* 68:167–72

325. Thompson, L. W., Marsh, G. R. 1973. Psychophysiological studies of aging. See Ref. 96, 112–48

326. Tismer, K. G. 1971. (Old age in relation to past life history.) *Z. Entwpsychol. Paed. Psychol.* 3:14–24

327. Tissue, T. 1971. Disengagement potential: Replication and use as an explanatory variable. *J. Gerontol.* 26:76–80

328. Tissue, T., Wells, L. 1971. Antecedent lifestyles and old age. *Psychol. Rep.* 29:1100

329. Tomlinson-Keasey, C. 1972. Formal operations in females from eleven to fifty-four years of age. *Develop. Psychol.* 6:364

330. Traxler, A. 1971. Age differences in interference effects in R-S recall as a function of transfer paradigm. *Proc. 79th Ann. Conv. APA* 6:607–8

331. Traxler, A. J. 1972. Negative transfer effects in paired associate learning in young and elderly adults. *Proc. 80th Ann. Conv. APA* 7:655–56

332. Traxler, A. J., Britton, J. H. 1970. Age differences in retroaction as a function of anticipation interval and transfer

paradigm. *Proc. 78th Ann. Conv. APA* 5:683–84

333. Troll, L. 1970. Issues in the study of generations. *Aging & Hum. Develop.* 1:199–218

334. Verwoerdt, A., Pfeiffer, E., Wang, H. S. 1969. Sexual behavior in senescence. II. Patterns of sexual activity and interest. *Geriatrics* 24:137–54

335. Wake, M. J., Sporakowski, M. J. 1972. Intergenerational comparison of attitudes toward supporting aged parents. *J. Marriage Fam.* 34:42–48

336. Wang, H. S., Busse, E. W. 1969. EGG of healthy old persons—A longitudinal study: I. Dominant background activity and occipital rhythm. *J. Gerontol.* 24:419–26

337. Wang, H. S., Obrist, W. D., Busse, E. W. 1970. Neurophysiological correlates of the intellectual function of elderly persons living in the community. *Am. J. Psychiat.* 126:1205–12

338. Warren, R. M., Warren, R. P. 1971. Some age differences in auditory perception. *Bull. NY Acad. Med.* 47:1365–77

339. Waugh, N. C., Fozard, J. L., Talland, G. A., Ervin, D. E. 1973. Effects of age and stimulus repetition on two-choice reaction times. *J. Gerontol.* 28:467–70

340. Weinbaum, L. 1969. A study of Cumming's extension of the disengagement theory using Block's rationale on the MMPI with predictions on a measure of field-dependence for two disengaged samples. *Diss. Abstr.* 30:1033–34

341. Welford, A. T., Birren, J. E. 1969. *Interdisciplinary Topics in Gerontology: Decision Making and Age.* New York: Karger

342. Welsh, O. L., Luterman, D. M., Bell, B. 1969. The effects of aging on responses to filtered speech. *J. Gerontol.* 24:189–92

343. Wilkie, F. L., Eisdorfer, C. 1971. Intelligence and blood pressure in the aged. *Science* 172:959–62

344. Wilkie, F. L., Eisdorfer, C. 1973. Systemic disease and behavioral correlates. See Ref. 160

345. Wilson, A. S., Barboriak, J. J., Kass, W. A. 1970. Effects of alcoholic beverages and congeners on psychomotor skills in

old and young subjects. *Quart. J. Stud. Alc. Suppl.* No. 5:115–29

346. Wohlwill, J. F. 1970. The age variable in psychological research. *Psychol. Rev.* 77:49–64

347. Wohlwill, J. F. 1973. *The Study of Behavioral Development.* New York: Academic

348. Woodruff, D. S. 1972. *Biofeedback control of the EEG alpha rhythm and its effects on reaction time in the young and old.* Unpublished PhD thesis. Univ. Southern California

349. Woodruff, D. S., Birren, J. E. 1972. Biofeedback conditioning of the EEG alpha rhythm in young and old subjects. *Proc. 80th Ann. Conv. APA* 7(pt. 2):673–74

350. Woodruff, D. S., Birren, J. E. 1972. Age changes and cohort differences in personality. *Develop. Psychol.* 6:252–59

351. Youmans, E. G. 1969. Some perspectives on disengagement theory. *Gerontologist* 9:254–58

352. Youmans, E. G. 1973. Age stratification and value orientations. *Aging & Hum. Develop.* 4:54–65

353. Young, M. L. 1971. Age and sex differences in problem solving. *J. Gerontol.* 26:330–36

354. Zatlin, C. E., Storandt, M., Botwinick, J. 1973. Personality and values of women continuing their education after thirty-five years of age. *J. Gerontol.* 28:216–21

DEVELOPMENTAL PSYCHOLOGY §229

E. Mavis Hetherington and Curtis W. McIntyre
Department of Psychology, University of Virginia
Charlottesville, Virginia 22901

INTRODUCTION

In this chapter the literature from June 1972 to June 1973 was to have been reviewed; however, the chapter on developmental psychology by Baer & Wright in the 1974 *Annual Review of Psychology* encompassed much of the research in the last half of 1972. In order to avoid redundancy, 1972 studies are reviewed here only when they are necessary to make a theoretical or methodological point, or are part of an ongoing controversy or series of studies, or were omitted from the previous chapter. Therefore, this is mainly a review of the literature in the first half of 1973, and because there were so few related papers on certain topics in that period, many of the areas traditionally covered have been omitted or given only cursory treatment.

Space limitations also led to restrictions in the range of topics and in the inclusion of articles within topics. No attempt was made to review the work in the burgeoning fields of deviant behavior in children, mental retardation, gerontology, and behavior modification or intervention studies. In general, a preference was given to problems where considerable research activity had been engendered because of theoretical controversies or relevance to social issues. In addition, the authors tended to focus on areas in which they have particular interest and expertise and to neglect fields in which they felt less able to do a cogent review. This has led to the omission of entire topics which many developmental psychologists would regard as important, to the reporting of only the most outstanding studies within a field, and sometimes to the exclusion of an interesting paper because it did not fit into the organization of the chapter.

LEARNING, LANGUAGE, AND COGNITION

Learning, language, and cognition are grouped within the same major section because many of the questions, theoretical concerns, and research strategies discussed are common to all three. In many cases the assignment of studies to these three content areas appears arbitrary, since many studies labeled learning could equally as well have been labeled language or cognition and vice versa.

Learning

Three basic trends are found in the learning literature: first, a shift away from the traditional learning-conditioning orientation with its focus on demonstrations of the applicability of learning paradigms and explanations to new situations; second, a move toward closer examination of the influences of both the child's capacities and the demand characteristics of the tasks themselves on learning; and third, an increasing interest in both rule learning and the child's cognitive structures which has resulted in a convergence of issues from learning, language development, and cognition.

The shift away from the traditional learning/conditioning orientation can be seen both in Stevenson's (255) critical analysis of theory and research in children's learning and in the current experimental reports. It is clear that three of Stevenson's departures from the traditional learning orientation—focusing on the informational value of reinforcement, emphasizing the importance of attention and perception for learning, and critically reexamining the mediation literature—are paralleled in recent research activity.

The informational value of reinforcers and changes in their functional relationships with age are demonstrated in Spear & Spear's (253) examination of the different effects of evaluative comments on younger and older children. They argued that evaluative comments directed younger children's attention to the task at hand, while the older children's increased ability to regulate their own performance allowed them to use evaluative comments to guide their behavior. Moreover, Feldstein (68) showed that uncertainty reduction has an incentive value of its own which is independent of tangible rewards. Along a somewhat different line, Masters & Mokros (177) examined the distracting and satiating effects of high and low magnitude incentives for children. Low magnitude incentives produced both more rapid acquisition and greater continued utilization of the acquired response. In general, their results suggested that distraction plays an important role in determining acquisition rate, while satiation plays an important role in determining the continued utilization of the acquired response.

The importance of attention and perception in children's learning is revealed in two studies in which the impact of the spatial separation of stimulus components upon central and incidental learning was examined. Wheeler & Dusek (270) found that the spatial separation of components resulted in central learning increasing with age, between kindergarten and fifth grade, while incidental learning remained constant. Similarly, Hale & Piper (106) found differences in incidental learning between stimuli having integrated or spatially separated components. Incidental learning increased with age, between 8 and 12 years, when the stimulus components were integrated, but remained constant when the stimulus components were separated spatially.

The widespread critical reexamination of the mediational literature is exemplified by Cole & Medin's (53) challenge of its basic focus. They questioned the need for additional demonstrations of the existence of mediation in children, urging instead that the future focus of mediation studies involve a more careful consideration of the conditions necessary for its occurrence. Although they agreed in general with Cole & Medin, Brown & Campione (36) differed in their assessment of the important problems in the area. In addition, they raised the issue of whether shift paradigms involved mediated learning or mediated transfer.

Closer examination of the influences of both the child's capacities and the demand characteristics of the tasks themselves on learning is reflected in the paired-associate learning literature. For example, Mallory (170) classified kindergarteners and second graders as "visualizers" or "verbalizers" and found superior paired-associate performance for the former under visual-elaboration conditions and for the latter under verbal-elaboration conditions. Similarly, a comparison of subject-provided and experimenter-provided imagery revealed superior paired-associate performance by both fourth and sixth graders when they provided their own imagery (51). The significant impact of the demand characteristics of the memory tasks themselves on children's paired-associate performance was demonstrated by Homzie, Noyes & Lovelace (120), who found different patterns of results for picture pairs and picture-word pairs, depending upon whether recall or recognition tests were used. In general, these studies indicate that a child's performance on a specific learning task can be altered radically by simple variations in instructions or in the task itself.

An increasing interest in both rule learning and the child's cognitive structures has resulted in several learning oriented studies of the effects of language on cognition. Since many of these studies were discussed in detail in the previous review by Baer & Wright (12), they are only listed here. These studies involved imitation and language behavior (45, 111, 271); training and conservation (57, 191, 236, 245); and training and classification (46, 151, 199, 211, 243).

Language

The infant's receptive language abilities, social class and ethnic influences on children's language, and the relationship between language and cognition continue to be topics of interest for many investigators.

Most of the studies of infants' receptive language abilities involved the effects of either acoustic or social stimuli on the infant's discriminatory or vocalitory abilities. Using a sucking and habituation technique, Morse (198) demonstrated that 40–54 day old infants were able to discriminate intonation and place of articulation cues. Focusing more on social cues, Barrett-Goldfarb & Whitehurst (14) found that stimulation with either father's or mother's voice suppressed the 1-year-old's spontaneous vocalizations, with greater suppression being obtained with the voice most preferred by the infant. Comparing social class differences, Tulkin (261) found greater differential responding to mother's and stranger's voices by middle class rather than working class 10-month-olds.

Concern with social class and ethnic influences on children's language was evident in this year's literature as developmental psycholinguists continued widening their domain to include children from a wide range of socioeconomic and cultural backgrounds. Some of the original interests in so-called "disadvantaged" children arose from a suggestion that their language was in some sense linguistically deficient and that this linguistic deficiency subsequently led to cognitive deficits. However, little support for this suggestion of linguistic deficiency has been found. For example, in a comparison of elementary school children from four subcultures, Hall, Turner & Russell (107) failed to find any evidence of black dialect interference with the comprehension of standard English. More recently, this original focus on linguistic deficits has been replaced by an interest in cultural and language differences between various social and ethnic groups. As Ginsburg (90) has noted, the failure of disadvantaged children in white, middle class school systems may be due to cultural and language differences rather than to deficiencies. The importance of the situation and demands of the task in the study of cultural differences in language can be seen in a study by Jones & McMillan (135), in which the speech of lower and middle class children in structured and natural settings was compared. Numerous differences were found. The greatest was in a structured setting when the children were asked to describe abstract events; the lower class children used shorter sentences and were more context bound.

The concern about the relationship between language and cognition is also found in the study of the role of linguistic deficits in deaf children and their intellectual performance. Bornstein & Roy (28) criticized Furth's (79) earlier conclusion that although deaf children are linguistically deficient, their thought processes are similar to those of hearing children, and therefore cognitive functioning must be explained without recourse to verbal processes. In essence, Bornstein & Roy rejected Furth's basic assumption of linguistic deficiency in deaf children. In rebuttal, Furth (80) reaffirmed his conclusion and argued that deaf children are limited in their ability to handle linguistic rules. In an independent review, Bonvillian, Charrow & Nelson (25) found no evidence of intellectual deficiency in the deaf and argued that similar linguistic abilities underly sign language and spoken language. In conclusion, they appealed for greater use of sign language in the education of the deaf. Some empirical support for the effective use of sign and total communication in preschool programs for hearing-impaired children is contained in the preliminary reports of a longitudinal study by Moores and his associates (195, 196).

A more purely psycholinguistic orientation to the relationship between language and cognition was evident in the work of R. Brown and his students (37) and of Slobin (250). Here the focus is on the importance of the child's stage of cognitive development and real world environment on his language development. This has led to a shift away from purely syntactic analyses of children's early speech to an increasing interest in the child's intended meaning or semantic content. This is also reflected in Brown's use of case grammars in interpreting children's language. In addition, both Brown and Slobin are concerned with the identification of linguistic universals in language development.

In a study of the word acquisition of one- to two-year-olds, which clearly reflects the shift in interest from syntax to semantics, Nelson (202) found that the names of objects which show salient features of change (e.g. ball or car) are often learned first. She also found that children classified as referential or object-oriented speakers built larger vocabularies more quickly than children classified as expressive or self-oriented speakers. She interpreted her results in the context of an interaction model which interrelates the child's preverbal concepts, his acquisition strategies, and parental-acceptance patterns. In an unrelated study, Wolff & Wolff (277) correlated speech and motor activity in 4- to 5-year-old children; the quality of speech output was correlated with gross motor activity, while the sophistication of verbal output was correlated with fine manipulative activity. These results are consistent with Luria's (165, 166) earlier suggestions that after 4½ years of age the child is able to use internalized verbalizations to organize sequences of motor activity.

Cognition

The work on both traditional concept formation and Piagetian tasks continues to flourish. A substantial number of the concept formation studies were fairly traditional in orientation, involving closer examinations of the effects of reward (66, 99); perceptual salience (105, 186, 192); and negative instances (122, 143).

Interest continued in the Piagetian literature in the relationship between compensation and conservation (57, 89, 96) and the order of emergence of various types of conservation (31, 32, 142). Since many of the compensation studies have been discussed by Baer & Wright (12), only a select few of the order of emergence studies are mentioned briefly here. Two of these studies (32, 140) supported Piaget's previous findings. However, significant inconsistencies were reported by Brainerd (31), who found that transitivity emerges before conservation which, in turn, emerges before class inclusion. He uses these results to challenge Piaget's analysis of seriation.

In an innovative variation of the basic conservation task, Singer & Kornfield (246) asked 5-year-olds, 7-year-olds, and young adults to make verbal judgments of conservation as well as to choose which container of juice (or candy) they would like to consume. When the verbal index was used, only the 5-year-olds failed to conserve. However, with the consummatory index all three groups failed to conserve; they chose the container which looked bigger. Along a somewhat different line, Fein (67) studied children's judgments of causality and found that "mature" judgments of social causality appeared earlier than similar judgments for physical causality. Clearly, closer consideration should be given to the importance of so-called social stimuli for perceptual development, e.g. mother, a social stimulus, may be the first object to show permanence in the infant's perceptual world.

INDIVIDUAL DIFFERENCES IN INTELLECTUAL DEVELOPMENT AND ACHIEVEMENT

Race, Social Class, and Intelligence

It is now 5 years since Arthur Jensen wrote his controversial paper on the heritability and possible racial differences in IQ in the 1969 *Harvard Educational Review*.

This led to a reactivation of the nature-nurture issue, attacks and counterattacks which were often scholarly, but sometimes emotional polemics, and an attempt to discredit or eliminate intelligence tests. In addition, behavior genetics became popular in the mass media, and the complex issues involved in the heritability and assessment of intelligence were simplified, sometimes in a misleading manner, for presentation to the public. That this controversy has had considerable impact is apparent in the number of schools ceasing to use intelligence tests and the legal and senatorial disputes about the acceptability of using test batteries as educational or occupational screening devices, particularly in situations involving minority groups.

The conflict rather than abating is accelerating. At least 15 books and collections of readings dealing with the issue have been published in the past year. In addition, a vast array of papers appeared, dealing with the predictive validity of IQ tests, factors affecting racial and social class differences in IQ, and social, philosophical, and educational influences that have led to the concepts of intellectual functioning held and valued by Americans and much of Western society.

In two volumes, *Genetics and Education* (132) and *Educability and Group Differences* (133), Jensen again presents his arguments that there are two qualitatively different types of abilities, Level I or associative ability and Level II or cognitive ability. Level I ability is equally distributed across social classes and racial groups. He proposes that Level II ability, which is highly correlated with intelligence test performance and academic achievement, is differentially distributed and found less in lower class individuals and blacks. Thus Jensen avers that IQ differences between low and middle socioeconomic status children are not primarily due to cultural bias on tests or experiential factors but reflect genetically based differences in Level II intelligence, which involves abstract reasoning and mental transformations and manipulations rather than the simple reproduction of stimulus input. *Genetics and Education* is largely comprised of earlier published papers including the *Harvard Educational Review* paper; however, Jensen also reports some new research dealing with the relationship between Level I and Level II ability in what he calls primary and secondary retardation. He says it is important to distinguish between primary retardation, which involves a deficiency in both Levels I and II abilities, and secondary retardation, in which only Level II deficits are manifested. When retardation occurs in middle class children it is usually primary, whereas in lower class and black children secondary retardation is more frequent. Jensen goes on to say that IQ tests should be devised to test both Level I and II abilities so that secondary retardates who have difficulty in achieving in school, but who may later function adequately socially and economically, can be distinguished from primary retardates who appear inadequate in most realms. Once identified, educational programs utilizing Level I abilities might be developed for the secondary retardates.

An example of the frequently found differences in interpretation of the same data in this area is exhibited by contrasting views of Jensen and Mercer (187, 188) in discussing the fact that traditional IQ tests do not predict economic, vocational, and social competence for members of the lower class, but do for the middle class.

Whereas Jensen cites this as evidence for the differential distribution of Level II abilities across classes and races, Mercer presents it as evidence of cultural bias in standard intelligence tests.

In *Educability and Group Differences* Jensen extends his genetic argument and reviews findings which he believes eliminate environmental, educational, economic, motivational, and language factors, or cultural bias in tests, as adequate to explain the lower IQs and achievement of blacks. He notes that American Indians and Mexican Americans, who on many environmental factors are more disadvantaged than blacks, perform better on nonverbal IQ tests and in academic achievement. He also adds that the differences between blacks and whites in IQ increase rather than decrease with rising socioeconomic level.

Herrnstein, in his new book, *IQ in the Meritocracy* (115), reviews much of the same literature on social class differences in IQ as Jensen did, and arrives at a theory which differs from, but is compatible with, that of Jensen. He speculates that IQ, education, occupational success, and social mobility are correlated. Since the brighter, more successful individuals tend to be upwardly mobile and people usually intermarry within their own class, a genetically based meritocracy is being formed. He believes that with great social mobility where people can find their natural level, the upper classes will have an increasingly greater genetically based intellectual capacity than the lower classes.

A third very disparate point of view is presented by Jencks in his book, *Inequality* (131). Jencks says educational opportunities, cognitive skills, educational credentials, occupational status, income, and vocational satisfaction are unequally distributed. Both genetic and environmental factors play a role in the development of cognitive inequality, but cognitive differences as measured by IQ tests do not seem to be as strongly related to educational success as is family background. In addition, although educational attainment is related to occupational status, it has little effect on earnings within any given occupation. On the basis of this correlational data, Jencks somehow reaches the rather pessimistic and questionable conclusion that educational innovations or reform will have little effect on inequality; that equal access to education will have little effect since black and lower status individuals are less likely to take advantage of educational opportunities; and finally that economic equality is the only solution to the problem, but that this is unlikely to occur in the near future.

Other contributors to this discourse maintain that blacks and lower status individuals will not improve their situation until qualitative rather than quantitative views of the disparate forms that abilities, competencies, and personal worth can assume are accepted by society (70, 163). Looft (163) argues that the schools are largely responsible for transmitting and maintaining narrow cultural attitudes toward competence and achievement, and that educational institutions must foster a pluralistic attitude and programs that encourage and value a heterogeneous group of abilities and life styles.

Research evidence continues to accumulate that many environmental, motivational, and personality factors may affect class and race differences in performance, including differential expectations and treatment of black and white

children by teachers (229), greater assumption of personal responsibility following failure by white than black children (78, 81), and high situational test anxiety
in disadvantaged children (283). The results of effects of race of examiner on test
performance of black and white children continue to be inconsistent. France (75)
and Solkoff (251) found that a white examiner did not depress performance by
black children; however, France but not Solkoff found a black examiner led to
lower IQ scores in white children.

The issue of the relative contribution of heredity and environment to race and
social status differences in IQ is unlikely to be resolved with the restrictions
necessary in human research and the limitations of currently available research
methodology. We cannot take samples of black and white twins and rear them in
controlled experimental conditions. As long as any methodologically feasible
studies have partially flawed designs, the testing of alternate models to explain
race and social status differences in intellectual performance will be inconclusive
and the furor will continue.

Sex Differences in Intellectual Development, Creativity and Achievement

The study of sex differences shares some of the problems of the investigation of
social class or racial differences in development. The topics are emotionally loaded
and socially significant, and the research findings are open to alternative interpretations. The results of research on sex differences are even less consistent than
those on race and social class. A popular subject this year has been sex differences
in intellectual development, creativity, and achievement. Sex differences are
found in cognitive functioning and in correlates of intellectual performance on a
wide variety of tasks.

On creativity tests males between the ages of 7 and 10 were found to make a
larger proportion of original or unique responses, although girls gave a larger
number of overall responses on any item (22, 125). In correlates of creativity boys
and girls also were found to differ. In a study of the stability of creative ability
between the fifth and tenth grade it was found that consistency for males was
obtained only under conditions of group test administration and for females under
a more personal, supportive, individual testing procedure (146). In addition, no
correlation between IQ and creativity was obtained for girls at either age, but for
boys by grade ten, IQ and creativity correlated. Schubert (238) also reported a
correlation between intelligence and creativity in adult males, but this was most
marked in the range of low intelligence test scores. However, in a study of
kindergarten children no relationship between IQ and ideational creativity were
found for either boys or girls (247). These findings suggest an increasing convergence with age between IQ and creativity for boys but not for girls.

In addition to sex differences in changing patterns of relationships for IQ and
creativity over age, the personality attributes associated with creativity differ for
boys and girls (247). Highly creative kindergarten boys are more open, expressive,
exploratory, and playful. In contrast, both high creative-high IQ and low
creative-low IQ girls are inhibited, lacking in self confidence, and less effective with
peers.

McCall, Hogarty & Hurlburt (180), in a reanalysis of the longitudinal Fels Institute data, reported sex differences in correlates of IQ with age. Girls' infant test scores, in contrast to those of boys, show higher correlations with later IQ. In addition, infant vocalization predicts later mental performance for girls but not for boys, whereas frolicsome social activity in male but not in female infants is negatively related to later IQ scores. These results seem to support earlier findings of Bell, Weller & Waldrop (19) that low intensity, low reactive behavior in male neonates is related to advanced cognitive development at 2½ years of age.

In another analysis of older children drawn from the Fels longitudinal study it was reported that in school-aged children, activity was negatively associated with achievement striving in boys and positively in girls (15). There is considerable evidence from twin studies that social responsiveness and activity level may have a substantial heritable component (234, 273). Thus these genetically determined temperamental characteristics may be directly associated with poor intellectual performance and achievement striving in boys, or may elicit social feedback which leads to the development of these behaviors. Battle & Lacey (15) found that from the earliest years mothers responded negatively to the hyperactive behavior of their sons but not their daughters, and that their negative feelings were particularly related to critical evaluations of their cognitive development and achievement. This was reflected in the self-doubt, anxiety, and feelings of incompetence in achievement reported by adolescent and adult males who had been hyperactive children. Thus hyperactivity in males seems to elicit negative feedback from mothers, which may mediate the development of attitudes and behaviors related to poor achievement and cognitive performance in sons.

In addition to sex differences in correlates of early precursors of achievement and intellectual development, sex differences appear in relationships between motivation, attitudes, and achievement in the nursey school and later school years. The early difficulties boys experience in school are frequently attributed to disparities between cultural forces toward masculine sex role typing and the sex typed characteristics of the school and teachers. The lack of male teachers to serve as role models and the encouragement by female teachers of conforming, unassertive behavior which is incongruous with the masculine sex role are said to result in boys experiencing stress and conflict in the early school years and coming to regard academic activities and objects as feminine.

Primary teachers report that they approve of dependent behavior more than aggressive behavior in both boys and girls (159). Does this mean that they treat boys and girls differently because boys are more likely to show aggressive behavior? Biber, Miller & Dyer (23) find that female teachers are more likely to make instructional contacts to girls, but that about the same proportion of instructional contacts with boys and girls involves positive reinforcement. This still means, in terms of absolute frequency of positive reinforcements, boys have fewer positive transactions with their female teachers than do girls. This finding is supported by a study of interactions of male and female teachers with preschool boys and girls (157) in which boys were found to receive more disapproval than girls from both male and female teachers. However, male teachers were much more approving of boys than were female teachers, and were more likely to assign boys leadership positions. Boys in turn were more likely to affiliate themselves with male teachers and view themselves as being preferred to girls by male teachers, whereas girls saw themselves being preferred by all teachers. The authors conclude that male teachers in contrast to female teachers create classroom conditions which are more congenial to young boys and that except for reduced leadership positions this did not seem to be done at serious cost to the welfare of young girls.

Peer influences also seem to play a role in boys' attitudes toward school. Even with female teachers, boys who attend all-male classes are more likely to judge school-related reading items as a male activity than are boys who are in coeducational classes (182).

Although the school setting appears to have adverse effects for boys, it is by no means a constructive and stimulating one for girls. During the elementary and high school years the encouragement of sex typed behaviors in women begins to be manifested in attitudes and behavior which interfere with achievement. Negative attitudes toward their own abilities and the development of passive behaviors which are incompatible with high achievement are inculcated in girls. Fifth grade girls underestimate the probability of their success (91) and are less likely than boys to persist in the face of sustained failure and to emphasize the role of effort in determining the outcome of their behavior (63). Girls appear to be characterized by learned helplessness. Although internality and acceptance of responsibility tend to be related to academic success for both boys and girls (52), boys who accept responsibility for their academic successes and girls who accept blame for their failures are most likely to be higher achievers. The relationship between internality and academic performance is higher for boys than for girls, and the relationship between IQ and achievement is higher for girls than for boys (52).

It is apparent that there are many sex differences in correlates of intellectual development and achievement throughout the course of development. These appear to be the result of complex transactions between genetic and constitutional factors, cultural forces involved in sex role typing, and differential responses by parents, teachers, and peers to the same characteristics in boys and girls (15, 23, 157, 159).

Cognitive Style

Many of the studies on cognitive style which have appeared recently deal with problem solving strategies in children having different cognitive styles. Reflective in contrast to impulsive children show more mature problem solving strategies (3, 10) and are more likely to consider several alternative hypotheses in problem solving and to use more efficient testing strategies (185). In addition, reflectives show different deployment of attention than impulsives. Although both reflectives and impulsives on the matching familiar figures (MFF) test use the same basic strategy of making comparisons between the standard and the variants, reflectives are more systematic and make a larger proportion of these comparisons (11). More selective attention in focusing on relevant aspects of a problem also is manifested by reflectives (108, 203).

Some similarities in deployment of attention between reflective and field independent children have been found. Field independent in contrast to field dependent children are less distracted by external cues in problem solving (174), and are more able to attend to relevant cues in conservation tasks (73). They also attend relatively more to cues within the task rather than to social cues emitted by the experimenter, such as the experimenter looking at or leaning toward the correct stimuli in a discrimination learning task (228).

Attempts to relate other individual difference variables to cognitive style have not been entirely consistent. Mann (171) found that reflectives were more cautious in decision making than impulsives, but this was not supported in a study of risk taking by Kopfstein (147).

Campbell (43) offers some evidence for an interaction between cognitive style in children and maternal behavior. Mothers of impulsive children have lower academic expectations for their children and do not intervene or structure learning situations as much as do mothers of either reflective or clinically diagnosed hyperactive children. Hyperactive children share some common characteristics with impulsive children, such as short attention spans, greater field dependency, and an inability to inhibit motor movement (44, 112). It might thus be expected that the mother-child interactions of hyperactive and impulsive children would be similar. However, this is not the case. Mothers of hyperactive children in contrast to those of impulsive children provide more direct help, encouragement, and impulse control suggestions during difficult tasks and are more similar in their behaviors to mothers of reflective children (43).

MEMORY

The current year was very exciting for investigators of children's memory. Only a few studies were directed primarily at demonstrating the correlation of children's memory capacity with their age—an already well-established fact. Most of the studies reported were directed toward a clearer specification of the impact of children's cognitive skills on their memory capabilities (which almost caused the authors to label this section "Applied Cognition" rather than "Memory"). Most of these studies can be classified into three groups which involve either children's acquisition strategies, experimenter interventions, or semantic integration. The first two groups are closely related to Flavell's (71) suggestions about the importance of production deficiencies for children's memory defects, while the third reflects an increasing interest in the influence of semantic integration, a cognitive phenomenon first described by Bransford & Franks (33), upon children's recognition memory.

Children's Acquisition Strategies

The importance of children's use or nonuse of acquisition strategies for their subsequent memory performance was investigated by Flavell and his students. They examined children's abilities to use the cognitive skills necessary for directing or monitoring their own memory behavior as well as their use of both study and retrieval strategies. In one study, Appel et al (8) found no difference in subsequent memory between groups of preschoolers who were told either to look at or to memorize a set of items. They concluded that the very young child is not aware of any difference between perceiving and remembering, and memorization itself is a cognitive skill which develops in children. The knowledge which an elementary school child possesses about his own memory abilities was assessed by Moynahan (200) with a task which required children to predict the relative ease with which sets of categorized or noncategorized items would be remembered. Such knowledge, termed metamemory by Tulving & Madigan (262), was evidenced by third graders.

In a study directed specifically at the development of study strategies, Masur, McIntyre & Flavell (178) investigated the age at which children begin to use the simple strategy of selecting missed items for study. They found that this simple strategy was not used spontaneously by first graders but was used by third graders. Similarly, in another study directed at the development of the use of indirect retrieval cues, Ritter et al (225) found that such cues were not used spontaneously by 3½-year-olds but were used by 6½-year-olds. Evidently it cannot be assumed that even the simplest study or retrieval strategies are possessed by very young children.

Experimenter Interventions

The impact of experimenter interventions upon children's memory performance was examined by numerous researchers. Typically, these studies involved demonstrations of increments in memory performance due to rehearsal suggestions (104, 230, 272), clustering cues (144, 145, 161, 244), or other organizational cues (110).

Semantic Integration

A high degree of accuracy in young children's recognition memory for pictures was demonstrated by Entwisle & Huggins (65) and Scott (240). However, a substantial reduction in the recognition accuracy of elementary school children after they spontaneously integrated the relationships contained within semantically related pictures was demonstrated by Paris (212) and Peterson & Danner (215). Evidently the children did not retain information about individual pictures; instead, they based their recognition judgments on agreement with "semantic integrations." The importance of this semantic integration for memory, especially if memory has a reconstructive basis, is aptly reflected in Paris' conclusion that the "... comprehension of the way events are related, to a large degree, underlies memory" (212, p. 5).

PERCEPTUAL-MOTOR DEVELOPMENT

A large number of studies were directed toward attentional processes in infants. Most of these studies reflected methodological focuses as psychologists investigating infants continued to refine their techniques. Methodological improvements were suggested for the corneal reflection (231, 248, 249), visual preference (121), habituation (179), and cardiac deceleration techniques (239).

The rest of the perceptual-motor development literature reflected a predominant interest in more traditional topics, e.g. depth perception (282); shape perception (1, 56, 129, 264); selective attention (61); and illusions (158, 220, 269). However, in two other topics, motoric-graphic skills and spatial reference systems, an increasing interest in cognitive influences on perceptual-motor development was manifested.

Motoric-Graphic Skills

A number of studies involving skilled motor activity and children's graphic abilities were reported. Bruner (38) and Koslowski & Bruner (149) traced the acquisition of early skilled motor actions. Bruner (38) suggested that the arousal of motoric intention calls into play minimally organized actions which are reshaped by feedback into skilled actions that require only a minimum of attention. Koslowski & Bruner (149) observed five successive age-related strategies used by 12- to 24-month-olds as they learned to use a lever. The strategies involved recombining and "modularizing" already existing acts.

Just as Bruner suggested skilled actions are made up of component acts which are organized into a rule-governed serial order, Goodnow & Levine (98) proposed treating graphic behavior as syntactic behavior and interpreting age changes in children's drawing abilities in terms of shifting hierarchies of rules.

Several other studies of children's graphic skills were reported (64, 76, 95, 97, 222, 258). In one of these studies, Freeman & Janikoun supported Piaget's notions of mental image domination of young children's drawings when they observed that young children draw what they know rather than what they see. Their results indicated a shift from this intellectual realism to a visual realism at about 7–8 years of age.

Spatial Reference Systems

Studies of the development of children's spatial reference systems received considerable attention during the current year. Most noteworthy among these was a series of investigations by Pick and his associates. In an overview paper presented at the 1972 APA meetings, Pick (216) discussed three concepts—space, cognitive maps, and frames of reference—which are intimately related to the development of spatial reference systems, and suggested several innovative techniques for their exploration. Two of these techniques were developed more fully in later papers presented at the 1973 SRCD meetings. In one of these (217), 4- and 5-year-olds were asked a series of specific questions about the spatial layout of their rooms (e.g. Where is the bed located?) and their homes (e.g. What room is behind this wall?). The differences in performance observed between 4- and 5-year-olds were related to differences in the frames of reference which were characteristic of their spatial reference systems. In the other study (2), the incidental and intentional memory of 3–5 and 7–8 year olds for specific environmental locations were compared. The results indicated that the older children spontaneously tagged events with their environmental locations and made use of a frame of reference which was relatively independent of the location of specific objects. In slightly tangential but related papers presented at the same SRCD meetings, Warren (267) discussed the role played by early vision and blindness in the development of spatial reference systems, and Yonas (281) discussed the relationship between shading cues for depth and the development of spatial reference systems.

ROLE-TAKING AND COMMUNICATION SKILLS

The current year was highlighted by several theoretical and methodological advances in role-taking research.

Theoretical Advances

In view of the recent debate between Chandler & Greenspan (47) and Borke (27) concerning the role-taking abilities of young children, the work of Flavell and his students is of particular interest. Recall that Chandler & Greenspan argued, in support of Piaget, that young children are primarily egocentric and that role-taking abilities do not emerge until early adolescence. Moreover, they suggested that Borke's (26) report of emotional role-taking abilities in young children represents "ersatz egocentrism" (i.e. it results from predictions based upon projection, identification, and stereotyping). To the contrary, Borke (27) argued that children as young as 3 years of age possess emotional role-taking abilities and that previous failures to find evidence supporting her position were due to the limited response capacities of very young children. Moreover, she suggested that emotional role-taking (empathetic awareness) originates in infancy and develops in a hierarchical stage-like fashion.

Independent support for Borke's position appeared in Flavell's (72) important paper which contained two major theoretical contributions: a general sequential model for interpersonal inference, and a more specific sequential model for the development of perceptual role-taking abilities during early childhood. The interpersonal inference model contained four sequential subcomponents: existence—the basic knowledge that others possess covert psychological processes; need—an understanding that the present situation requires inferences about others' psychological processes; inference—the actual inferential or computational activity itself involved in generating estimates of other's psychological processes; and application—the behavior which follows as a consequence of the inferential activity. The model for the development of perceptual role-taking abilities in early childhood involved four stage-like levels: Level 0—the child has no representational (symbolic) knowledge that others have visual experiences; Level 1—the child can represent that others see objects; Level 2—the child can represent qualitatively the various perspectives of objects seen by others; Level 3—the child can represent quantitatively the retinal image another has of a visual array. Empirical support for the existence of these levels was reported by Masangkay et al (172) and McIntyre et al (184), who used very simple role-taking tasks to demonstrate Level 1 abilities in 3-year-olds and Level 2 abilities in 5-year-olds.

Early role-taking ability was also found by Shatz & Gelman (242), who report that 4-year-olds, who perform poorly on egocentrism tests, are capable of adjusting their speech for different listeners. In general, the speech which 4-year-olds directed toward 2-year-olds was simpler, shorter, and contained more attentional utterances than the speech they directed toward adults. Along similar lines, Gleason (92) looked at how children and adults change the style of their communications to fit listeners of various ages. Typically, the style changes of very young children involve jabbering at siblings and parents, whining at parents or parental figures, and falling silent in the presence of adults. However, 4- to 8-year-olds use four basic communicative styles: baby-talk, directed toward babies; peer-group colloquial, directed toward siblings and friends; formal, directed toward adults and strangers; and socialization language, directed toward somewhat younger children. Both the amount and the quality of children's style switching increases with age.

In general, the evidence obtained from both role-taking and communication studies indicated that some rudimentary role-taking skills are possessed by very young children. Evidently Piaget's conclusion that young children are basically egocentric and role-taking skills do not develop until late middle childhood or early adolescence was influenced by the complexity of the tasks he used. It is clear from the recent work with much simpler tasks that his view needs to be questioned. Moreover, it is also apparent that his conception of the relationship between role-taking and communication skills needs to be reconsidered. However, this is only one part of a more general need to examine closely the interrelationships between the various role-taking, communication, and cognitive skills of young children to determine whether they are reflections of a change of an underlying cognitive competency (e.g. egocentrism), as Piaget would suggest, or whether each has an ontogenetic history of its own. Rubin (227) examined this general question by intercorrelating the performances of elementary school children on spatial, cognitive, recursive thinking, and communicative role-taking tasks. Three of the role-taking tasks—spatial, recursive thinking, and communicative—were significantly intercorrelated and factor analysis revealed a general egocentrism factor. In another investigation of this same question, Van Lieshout et al (266) found similar results using younger children (3–5 year olds) and different role-taking tasks. Although both of these studies suggest that there is a cognitive factor of egocentrism associated with a number of role-taking tasks, they cannot be regarded as conclusive given the lack of supporting studies and the general lack of knowledge about the difficulty and reliability of the role-taking tasks themselves. More studies of this question are definitely needed.

In contrast to the predominant focus on the role-taking abilities of young children, Looft (164) suggested that more attention should be given to egocentrism across the entire life-span. He suggested that many of the characteristics commonly associated with aging (e.g. rigidity, regression, and psychosocial disengagement) are manifestations of or contributions to an increase in egocentrism in later life.

Methodological Advances

The separation of perceptual role-taking tasks into rotation, perspective, and perspective-move tasks was suggested by Huttenlocher & Presson (127). Rotation tasks require the child to predict the future appearance of an array of objects that will be rotated, whereas perspective and perspective-move tasks require the child to predict the appearance of a fixed array of objects after either someone else (perspective) or the child himself (perspective-move) moves with respect to it. Huttenlocher & Presson found the perspective task to be much more difficult than either the rotation or the perspective-move task. They interpreted their results in terms of psychological restrictions on imagination, i.e. the child's present spatial position makes it difficult for him to imagine himself at another position but it does not hinder his ability to imagine the array in other positions.

Several other intriguing tasks were reported during the year. Overton & Jackson (208) asked 3-, 4-, 6-, and 8-year-olds to perform fairly commonplace actions with imagined objects (e.g. pretend you are combing your hair, drinking from a cup, etc). A clear developmental pattern indicating the importance of motor activity for younger children's imagination emerged: younger children evidenced difficulty with the task; somewhat older children completed the task by substituting part of their body for the imagined object; and older children performed the actions with imagined objects without difficulty. Another developmental pattern emerged when Wolman, Lewis & King (278) asked elementary school children to describe their emotions. They found that the older children tended to refer to their emotions as being more toward the interior of their bodies and more localized in specific regions, especially the head-brain region.

SOCIAL AND PERSONALITY DEVELOPMENT

Several trends in the study of personality and social development can be detected. First, the impact of cognitive psychology is apparent. The interaction of cognitive skills, perception, attention, and judgments with social behavior are the focus of many studies. Second, there is an emphasis on the cultural relativism of behavior. Investigators are less prone to label divergent behaviors among groups as deficits and more likely to regard them as differences. Third, studies of the family, particularly of parent-child interaction, are proliferating. Finally, concern with social relevance has led to a modest movement toward the use of more naturalistic methods and an uneasy questioning of the ecological validity of the results of that most cherished cornerstone of psychology, the laboratory experiment.

Modeling

The topic in social development which continues to be the focus of the most research is that of modeling. Over 40 modeling studies were published in the last year.

A well-known behavior modifier once said it was time research on the application of operant methods passed beyond atheoretical "Whoopee!" studies where with each new behavior conditioned the investigator yelled, "Whoopee! We can condition _____!" It now seems clear that under the right circumstances children will imitate almost anything. Whoopee! Children will imitate moral judgments (140, 219, 263). Whoopee! Children will imitate altruistic behavior (189, 197, 280). Whoopee! Children will imitate resistance and yielding to temptation (226, 275, 276). Whoopee! Children will imitate aggressive behavior (54, 58, 102, 204) and self-reward (152), and social interactions (205), and perceptual judgments (59), and vocal and linguistic responses (111, 123), and concept formation (284, 285), and facial expressions (109), and commodity preferences (254), and teachers' preferences and behaviors (69, 218), and picture preferences (130), and button pressing (260), and cognitive style, and Whoopee! Almost anything!

It would be unfair to say that all of the above studies were just "Whoopee!" studies; some are well-designed studies that deal with important issues. However, it is unfortunate that few are developmental studies which look at age-related determinants and changes in imitation, and few are part of a larger programmatic series designed to clarify theoretical issues.

Three issues appear to be the focus of much of the current research on imitation: the role of cognitive and motivational factors in imitation; the relative efficacy and interactions of imitation and reinforcement in modifying behavior (123, 205); and the generalization of imitative responses across situations and from verbal to behavioral responses. Only a few representative studies which seem the best within each topic will be presented. The research on generalization will be discussed later under the topics of moral development and aggression which have been the behaviors of interest in most of these studies.

Several of the more interesting studies deal with the role of informational cues in mediating imitative behavior. The presence of a common dimension (254) and provision of a response rule (285) increase imitative concept learning. Bandura (13) and Liebert & Fernandez (162) have proposed that vicarious reinforcement can be regarded as a type of informational cue and that it increases imitation because it informs subjects of consequences of behaving similarly to a model. Thelen et al (260) support this position by demonstrating that vicarious reinforcement enhances imitation when subjects expect to perform the model's behavior but does not when there is no expectancy to perform.

Zigler & Yando (284) stress the interaction of cognitive and motivational factors in imitation in an excellent study of younger and older institutionalized and noninstitutionalized children. The investigators propose that as children develop and become more cognitively proficient, their effectance motivation leads them to rely more on their own cognitive processes and less on cues from others in problem solving. However, although imitation will decrease with age under most circumstances, ambiguous situations or problems beyond their cognitive ability will motivate children to increase imitative responses.

Studies of the effects of a model's nurturance on directing attention toward characteristics of the model and motivating the child to imitate continue to yield inconsistent results, although two well-designed studies by Yarrow and her colleagues make major contributions to clarifying the conditions under which nurturance may facilitate imitation (279, 280). These studies differ from most previous laboratory studies of the effects of the model's nurturance on imitation by having the children interact with nurturant or non-nurturant models playing the role of teachers in a nursery school setting over a period of several weeks. Thus the contact is more sustained and the setting and relationship with the child is more naturalistic than in most experimental studies. Under these conditions it was found that nurturant models were more likely to facilitate the imitation of nurturant but not of non-nurturant behaviors by children, whereas non-nurturant models facilitated the imitation of aggressive behaviors (279). These studies make it clear that imitation is selective and that different characteristics of a model facilitate the imitation by children of different behaviors exhibited by the model. In addition, the models' nurturance increased delayed imitation (279) and imitation of the models' helping behavior in a new situation outside of the nursery school (280). These results in conjunction with those of previous studies using parents as models where warm parents were found to increase imitation of incidental behaviors in children, especially in daughters (117, 201), or studies involving extended nurturant interactions (113) by peers, suggest that sustained warm relationships such as those with parents, caretakers, or peers do enhance imitative behavior in children. In contrast, short-term laboratory warmth manipulations with strange experimenters, preceding a modeling task, often fail to do so. Such disparities are leading investigators to question the generalizability of such laboratory studies of imitation and to ask whether these studies show what children can do rather than what they actually do in more naturalistic situations.

Although in laboratory studies nurturance of the model may not increase imitative responses, there is evidence that non-nurturance may **actually** suppress imitative behavior. In accord with earlier findings of Patterson, **Littman & Brown** (213), a recent study by Jeffrey, Hartmann & Gelfand (130) found that second and third grade children significantly mismatched their responses on a picture preference test with those of a nonresponsive model. This problem of negative imitation is one with great practical and theoretical significance and on which there is little research.

Moral Development and Self-Control

Over the past decade two marked changes in the study of moral development have occurred. First, there has been some convergence of the approaches of social learning theorists and cognitive psychologists. Rather than the former focusing on moral behavior and the latter on judgments of morality, a current interest in the interaction between ethical behavior and reasoning is apparent. Second, there is increasing interest in studies on prosocial behavior and a waning of interest in studies on negative aspects of behavior. There are few studies of aggression, and many of helping, sharing, and cooperating. This seems to be part of a general trend toward viewing the child positively in terms of his competencies rather than negatively in terms of his deficiencies.

MORAL JUDGMENTS   Studies of children's judgments of moral dilemmas have focused on methodological issues, modification of ethical judgments, and the relationship of judgments to behavior.

Methodological controversies are pervasive in this area. It has been found that both the type and content of moral dilemmas (41, 55, 133a, 134) and mode of presentation of the dilemmas (48) influence the ethical judgments of children.

The use of stories involving positive intentions, causal information about a wrongdoing and subsequent misfortune, and the videotaped rather than traditional verbal presentation of moral dilemmas result in more intentionality responses, and in intentionality being expressed at a younger age than 8 or 9 when it is usually first found by investigators using variations of Piaget's original methodology. These findings suggest that in evaluating or comparing the results of studies of moral judgments and reasoning, both the content and mode of presentation of dilemmas must be considered.

The second large group of studies in moral judgments deals with the effectiveness of models in altering the ethical judgments of children. In the 1971 *Annual Review of Psychology*, Hartup & Yonas concluded that in spite of the many arguments advanced by cognitively oriented psychologists against the effectiveness of modeling in altering moral judgments, the facts indicate that "modeling is implicated as a *process* in the development of children's moral thinking even though the *extent* to which modeling is involved in the development of moral judgments and the nature of its interaction with other aspects of the child's cognitive functioning are less clear" (114, p. 374).

Little new evidence has been garnered to alter that conclusion. Some of the conflicting findings in this area appear to be due to the wide variations in the modeling procedures used, the particular aspect of moral thinking or behavior studied, and the interval between the modeling procedure and assessment of change.

In most studies children are asked to judge the seriousness of moral dilemmas and to give reasons for their judgments. Keasey (140) suggests that part of the confusion in findings results from not distinguishing between shifts in the moral level of the opinions stated and that of the reasons offered to justify the opinions. In a study using three modeling conditions, varying opinions with or without reasoning at the subjects' own level of moral development or one stage above, the effects of the model's opinions and reasoning varied over time, and changes in moral opinions and in reasoning by the subjects were found to be unrelated.

Brainerd (30) argued that judgments on Piagetian tasks are more appropriate than explanations as bases for inferences about cognitive structures since they are less vulnerable to Type II errors. Reese & Schack (224) responded that "a more reasonable conclusion is that explanations may yield more Type II errors, but judgments yield more Type I errors; hence a choice between them depends upon which type of error is considered more serious. It is recommended that both be used, and their interrelationship studied" (224, p. 67).

Two investigations appeared of the generalizability to behavior of the effects of being exposed to the ethical judgments and reasoning of the models. Turiel &

Rothman (263) found that the model's level of reasoning had little effect on the subject's subsequent reasoning, and generalizability from the model's reasoning to the subject's decision to continue punishing another person in a Milgrim-type obedience situation showed only stage restricted changes. The model's reasoning at the stage above led to an upward shift in behavioral choice for stage 4 but not stage 2 and 3 subjects. Prentice (219) found that live and symbolic modeling of intentionality was effective in increasing intentionality responses in delinquent males but that the effects did not generalize to a nonmanipulated aspect of moral judgment, moral relativism, or to delinquent behavior during the following 9 months.

In view of the continuing findings of no (252) or extremely modest relationships (60) between verbally stated values and behavior, and of the stage specificity of such relationships (232, 263), it seems unduly optimistic to expect the brief modeling of verbalized standards to lead to marked or enduring changes in behavior. The lack of effectiveness of verbalized standards of a model in changing children's ethical behavior is consistent with the results of laboratory studies of the effects of models on the self-reward or sharing and helping behavior of children, which will be reported in the next section. The actions but not the verbalizations of the model are usually found to be effective in altering children's prosocial behavior.

PROSOCIAL BEHAVIOR   The accelerating interest in prosocial behavior is indicated by the devotion of an entire issue of the *Journal of Social Issues* (274) to positive forms of social behavior. Most of the research in this area has focused on sharing, helping and cooperative behavior.

In studies involving subject characteristics it has been shown that older children are more likely to share than younger children, and that normal children are more likely to cooperate than retarded children (169). In addition, cultural factors affect prosocial behavior. Middle class boys are more likely to share on the basis of reciprocity than are lower class boys who tend to share on the basis of a social responsibility norm (62). Urban Canadian children cooperate less than rural Blackfoot Indians (190). Anglo-American children are more rivalrous than Mexican-American children, and this cultural difference increases with age for boys but not for girls (136). The great emphasis on achievement and independent striving, particularly for boys, in middle class, urban, Anglo cultures interferes with cooperative relations with others.

Affect is assumed to play an important role in altruistic behavior (9). When affect was directly manipulated by having 7- to 8-year-old children think sad or happy thoughts, positive affect was found to increase and negative affect to decrease sharing (194). Investigators have attributed an increase in both altruistic and self-rewarding behavior following success to the positive affect associated with the success experience (40, 150). However, the proposal by Underwood, Moore & Rosenhan (265) that self-gratification and other gratification are positively correlated is difficult to support with their finding that thinking sad thoughts decreased altruism but increased self-gratification.

In addition, in preschool children self-reward (176) and sharing with others (153) is apparently unrelated to the child's perception of the adequacy of his performance on a task. By age 7, however, self-reward is more likely to follow a success than a failure experience (175).

In a review of the literature on prosocial behavior in children, Bryan (39) concludes that symbolic modeling and verbalization of altruistic standards are most likely to increase prosocial verbalizations, whereas altruistic behavior in models increases prosocial behavior. In the rare cases where verbalization has been shown to have some effect on behaviors, such as resistance to deviation in children, it has been much less effective and enduring than that of behavioral models (276). However, even behavioral models are more effective in eliciting deviations and disinhibitory effects than in increasing self-control or altruism (39, 118, 226, 275).

Three naturalistic studies show the effects of modeling on prosocial behaviors (77, 279, 280). In the previously cited studies conducted in a nursery school setting, Yarrow and her colleagues (279, 280) found that nurturant behavior in contrast to symbolic modeling of nurturance was most effective in eliciting "live" altruism in preschool children. Only children with nurturant caretakers, who had demonstrated helping in both symbolic and actual distress situations, facilitated long-term altruistic behavior in children. The Yarrow, Scott & Waxler study (280) is particularly impressive since the situational generalization of modeling was assessed in an unfamiliar home setting which differed completely from the training situation in the school.

In a third naturalistic study (77) in which lower and middle class nursery school children were shown aggressive, prosocial, or neutral films over a 9-week period, aggressive films increased disobedience and the inability to tolerate delay, and increased aggressive behavior in children who were already above the mean on aggression. Whereas prosocial films increased altruistic behavior only in low socioeconomic status children, it improved task persistence, rule obedience, and tolerance for delay of gratifications for both lower and middle class children. In this study both behavioral modeling and verbalization of standards were present in the films, and the relative effectiveness of the two cannot be separated.

Many studies have demonstrated that in addition to the models' behavior the consequences of the models' actions influence self and other reward by the viewer (39). Sharing is facilitated not only by seeing a model punished for a refusal to share, but also by viewing noncontingent vicarious punishment of the model which has a generalized inhibitory effect on antisocial behaviors of the viewer (197).

AGGRESSION   The scattered studies of childhood aggression seem to show no particular focus or theoretical concerns. One wonders if the dearth of significant studies on this problem is attributable to a feeling by many investigators that the important questions about aggression have already been answered.

As might be expected, studies on the imitation of aggression continue to appear. Evaluations of the models' behavior by co-observers affected the aggressive responses of 10-year-old children more than 5-year-old children when they were alone (102). In addition, for younger but not older subjects, temporal separation occurring between an aggressive act and punishment of the model obscures the message that aggression is negatively motivated and leads to unpleasant consequences (54). Hence the delayed punishment of the model was not effective in inhibiting the imitation of aggressive responses by the younger children. Children's destructive play increases and constructive play decreases following realistically but not stylistically filmed aggression (204). The importance of sex of model and sex appropriateness of behavior is again demonstrated in a study of emotionally disturbed boys by Davids (58). Male aggressive models were more influential in increasing the boys' aggressive behavior, but female nonaggressive models were most effective in increasing nonaggressive behaviors. Female models were most effective in modifying verbalizations, with the nonaggressive female model increasing nonaggressive verbalization, and the aggressive female decreasing nonaggressive verbalizations.

In a study of 7-, 9-, and 12-year-old children, Shantz & Voydanoff (241) found that the tendency to respond with less retaliatory aggression to accidental than intentional provocation, and to verbal in contrast to physical provocations, increased with age.

An unusual study of aggression was one dealing with "mobbing" behavior in Swedish school boys in which one or several boys systematically harass and use violence against another (206). Great stability in the behaviors of the bullies and the whipping boys (scapegoats) were found over a one-year period. Bullies were physically strong, verbally and physically aggressive, and had poor self-control; however, they were popular with their peers, particularly with girls. This correlation between externalizing aggression and popularity in boys was also found in a study of Guatemalan children (4), and has previously been reported in studies of lower class American boys. In contrast, whipping boys tended to be physically weak, fearful, unpopular, and have low self-esteem. Both bullies and whipping boys seemed to have more deviant parental relationships than did well-adjusted boys. Bullies were alienated from their fathers and felt their parents were lacking in affection. Whipping boys had close relationships with their parents, but the parents were reported to be indulgent, overprotective, and overanxious with their sons.

PUNISHMENT AND SELF-CONTROL   It is difficult to draw any general conclusions from these investigations of punishment since they study different forms of punishment on a variety of children's responses with subjects of varying ages. A high intensity buzzer appears to be the most popular form of punishment used in laboratory studies with children, and three studies involving noxious noise are reviewed below.

Consistent punishment by a noxious noise results in faster inhibition of the response of hitting a Bobo doll by 8- to 10-year-old boys than does inconsistent punishment (210), and punishment suppressed this response more rapidly than a no-punishment extinction procedure.

In contrast, Grusec & Ezrin (103) found that reinforcement for self-criticism increased self-critical responses, whereas the technique of punishment, either love withdrawal or withdrawal of material resources in combination with a buzzer, had no effect. The difference in results in these two studies may be attributable to the differences in the dependent behaviors studied.

LaVoie (154), using mothers and fathers as punitive agents, found that both a buzzer and a rationale were effective in increasing resistance to deviation in adolescent boys, although a rationale was more effective. The use of a rationale appears to be more effective in reducing deviant behavior in adolescents than with the younger children used in previous studies (49, 50, 155, 209). LaVoie (155) agrees with earlier reports by Hoffman & Saltzstein (119) in finding that mothers were more effective as punitive agents than were fathers and that mothers may play a more important role than fathers in the acquisition of self-control. He suggests that this may be because after the adolescent has transgressed, the mother is more likely than the father to let the child explain his transgression and to modify her discipline in response to his explanation. The punishment from the mother therefore might be more justifiable from the son's point of view than punishment from the less responsive and less communicative father. This finding differs from that of a laboratory analog study of discipline which used a very similar resistance to temptation task and found that latency until deviation in second and third grade children was more affected by the commands of a dominant male than female agent. No other effects of sex or nurturance of agent were obtained, but dominant adults giving either permissive or prohibitive commands were more effective than nondominant agents in shaping self-control (257). This disparity in the effectiveness of male and female agents may be attributable to age differences in the subjects (perhaps mothers and females become more important with age) or to the fact that the situation in the laboratory analog studies with strange adults is not analogous to responses to real parents, even within the laboratory. Generalizations from laboratory analog studies of buzzer punishment and M&M rewards administered by strange adults compared to the effectiveness of parental discipline practices within the home seem to be even more precarious. Although even within the unfamiliar and contrived laboratory setting administration of buzzer punishment may convey information about the demands of the experimental task, and rationales may convey even more information, neither involve the sustained, intense affective component of parental discipline within the home.

Racial Awareness and Attitudes

Although the recent literature is deluged with articles on racial differences, only a few studies on racial awareness and attitudes have appeared. Masangkay et al (173), in a cross-sectional study of 10- and 15-year-old children, show that generalized attitudes involving positive and negative evaluations of ethnic groups occur at an earlier age than does the attribution of specific traits associated with the ethnic stereotype. Traits attributed to the child's ingroup were learned before those of outgroup stereotypes.

That this later differentiation of traits in outgroup members is at least partly attributable to problems in perceptual discrimination of members of other races is found in some of the studies from the ongoing research program of Katz (138, 139). Katz (138) finds that young children experience more difficulty in learning to discriminate faces of another race. She proposes that the labeling of racial groups with distinctive racial names may lead to a lack of differentiation among individual members of the group and result in evaluative statements being more readily generalized to all group members. Through labeling and perceptual training techniques she was able to increase the perceptual differentiation of the other-group faces, and as perceptual differentiation improved, prejudice scores decreased (139).

Sex Differences in Social Development

Several major reviews of the literature on sex differences and gender identity have appeared recently. In her book, *Male and Female* (126), and in a provocative review in *Human Development* (125), Hutt emphasized the role of biological and morphological factors in the development of sex differences. In contrast, in their book, *Man and Woman, Boy and Girl* (193), Money & Ehrhardt reviewed biological factors in sexual differentiation and gender identity, but presented a more balanced interpretation of sex differences as being based on transactions between biological and experiential factors.

Hutt (124, 126) places great emphasis on the relatively greater docility, and lack of aggressiveness, curiosity, exploration, and creativity in females. In addition, she reports that females are less active and aggressive, show more proximity-seeking behavior toward the mother, are more interested in toys with faces, and are more nurturant than males. She suggests that boys are more interested in objects or things and girls in people.

Maccoby and her colleagues (128, 168), in reviewing the literature and in investigating sex differences in toy preferences, behavior at a barrier, activity, and seeking proximity to the mother, arrive at very different conclusions. They report that the majority of studies find no sex differences in proximity seeking or stable sex differences in activity level in young children, and that activity level is not a stable individual characteristic over time (167). Their own results tend to support these findings. In only one subexperiment were one-year-old boys found to be more active than girls. In addition, no sex differences in seeking to be near the mother were found (167). In contrast to the frequently cited findings of Goldberg & Lewis (94), when year-old children were confined behind a barrier, there were no sex differences in position behind the barrier or manipulation of the barrier, although under conditions of moderate stress girls cried more at the barrier. Sex differences in preferences for toys with faces were not found. In fact, boys showed a marked preference for a robot with a face (128). However, there is some evidence reported that girls may be more responsive to social stimuli than are boys. In a visual recognition task, 5- to 6-month-old infant girls could more readily discriminate among upright faces than could boys (66). In a study of communication in grade school children, girls were more likely than boys to adapt their communications in accord with the characteristics of the listeners (7).

One of the social behaviors in which there is relatively consistent evidence of sex differences is in aggressive behavior. Brindley et al (35) found that two-thirds of all aggressive acts in nursery school were displayed by boys, and that the boys elicited more aggression than did girls. Girls, as is frequently reported, were more likely to use verbal aggression. These results are corroborated in a study by McGurk & Lewis (183) in which nursery school boys were found to be more aggressive and independently active and girls more help-seeking and obedient.

Family Interaction

Two trends in the study of parent-child relations can be seen. First, the missing parent, the father, has begun to appear in family studies. In the past, investigators seem to have focused more on the effects of father absence than on the role of the present father in child development. Second, investigators of family interaction have moved away from a reliance on parental reports of attitudes and child rearing practices to direct observation of parent-child interactions.

STUDIES OF PARENT-INFANT INTERACTIONS   These studies focused on two topics: investigations of cultural differences and studies of attachment.

Although the precocity of African infants at birth is frequently reported, Warren (268), in a careful review of the literature, concludes that because of methodological deficits in such studies no such conclusion can validly be drawn. He is particularly critical of the measurement problems and confusion in the reporting of data in the frequently cited studies by Geber and Dean (82-88). He proposes that the most fruitful approach to this topic is to study not racial differences but differences in the social level or specific aspects of the cultural milieu and their effects on the development of the child.

In papers reported in a symposia on Cross-Cultural Studies of Mother-Infant Interaction, many of the investigators appear to be utilizing the strategy recommended by Warren. Brazelton (34), in his study of Zinacanteco Indian infants of Southeastern Mexico, and Rebelsky (223), in her study of Dutch infants, both propose that although the child rearing practices utilized within these groups differ from those in the United States, they are appropriate for training the kind of people considered desirable in the culture. Although the restrictive, nurturant patterns of Zinacanteco mothers in caring for their infants is associated with imitative, nonexploratory behavior, this is adaptive in a culture in which conformity and acceptance of highly structured roles necessary for survival are valued, in contrast to the emphasis on individuality and independence in children in the United States.

Certain cultural variations in parental stimulation of the infant may lead to differential development of abilities in children (100). Goldberg (93) proposes that accelerated development of Zambian infants on spatial ability in contrast to object ability, compared in American norms, may be attributable to Zambian infants getting varied stimulation and constant contact by being carried in a sling by the mother, accompanied by little access to objects or toys for play. Lewis & Wilson (160) report striking social class differences in American mothers' interactions with their 12-week-old infants; although the amount of overall stimulation and the amount of contingent stimulation did not differ, the type of stimulation did vary. Middle class mothers tended to respond to infant vocalizations by vocalizing, and to fretting by holding and touching; the reverse was true for lower class mothers. Greenfield (100) argues that it is the appropriateness of the mother's contingent response that is important in the development of the child, and that whereas vocalizing to a child's vocal responses should lead to increased imitative vocalization in the child, vocalization in contrast to physical contact is an inappropriate response to fretting.

The number of studies of attachment have diminished lately, but in a study by Beckwith (17), evidence continues to accumulate that infants are most attached and socially responsive to mothers who are attentive and respond rapidly to the babies' signals, and who are permissive in permitting the infant to express his impulses and explore. These findings are in agreement with those in previous studies of attachment which emphasize qualitative differences in maternal responsiveness as a determinant of infant social behavior (5, 235). Reinforcement theorists would predict that such rapid maternal responding to an infant's cries might increase attachment but should also reinforce crying. However, Bell & Ainsworth (20) found that consistency and promptness of maternal response was associated not only with an increase in attachment but also a decline in frequency and duration of infant crying over the course of the first year of life.

Although Bell & Ainsworth (20) report that close physical contact is the most effective means of terminating crying, other investigators suggest that it may be the vestibular-proprioceptive stimulation involved in picking up and holding the infant rather than contact per se which is the most important factor in soothing (148, 214, 259).

PARENT-CHILD INTERACTION WITH OLDER CHILDREN   The most frequently investigated behaviors of children in current family interaction studies involving children beyond infancy are intellectual development, self-control, and moral development.

Interest in the relation of social class and ethnicity and family interaction styles has generated several studies. Two which used both mothers and fathers studied the relation of socioeconomic factors and parent-son interaction. Busse & Busse (42) found more highly educated black fathers and mothers talked more to their 11-year-old sons that did less educated parents. In addition, more educated mothers showed greater encouragement of autonomy than less educated mothers, and more educated fathers were more overtly affectionate than less educated fathers.

Radin (221) studied the correlates of paternal behavior and 5-year-old sons' IQ in lower and middle class white families. She found that in lower class families paternal restrictiveness and high expectations of grades were negatively related to their IQ scores, whereas in middle class families paternal nurturance, particularly in the form of asking information of the child, was associated with higher IQs in their sons.

In contrast to these two studies which emphasized social class differences in correlates and patterns of parent-child interaction, Steward & Steward (256) found that maternal differences in styles of teaching their 3-year-old sons were more closely related to ethnicity than to social class.

Lack of self-control and deviant behavior in children has been associated with the inability of fathers to assert their authority (6), and lack of control (101), low communication (154), and low achievement standards (74) in mothers. Mothers seem to play a more important role in their sons' acquisition of self-control than do fathers. This has been attributed to the greater availability and involvement of the mother in discipline during the day when the father is at work, and to the greater communicativeness of the mother (155, 156). In a laboratory resistance to temptation task with adolescent sons, fathers were found to be more likely to intervene or punish with no opportunity for explanation from the son following transgressions. Mothers were more likely to encourage the child to explain his acts, discuss the implications of the transgression, and the reasons for her responses preceding discipline. These are the kinds of behaviors that previously have been found to be associated with greater self-control in children (9, 16, 119).

The greater communication between mother and child is also found in a laboratory study of teaching styles of mothers and fathers with their daughters (207). In spite of the great theoretical impact that Bell's paper (18) on the role of the child in shaping the behavior of parents has had, only a handful of studies have directly investigated this issue. The Osofsky study is an excellent example of the mutual shaping of parent and child responses. Parents interact more and are more controlling in teaching their preschool daughters how to do puzzles when the daughters are dependent than when they are independent. However, fathers are more likely to help the child physically or become more detached, whereas the mother more frequently encourages independence and explains, questions, and comments to her daughter. In turn, the girls are more likely to demonstrate task-oriented behaviors with their fathers and demands for support and attention with their mothers.

Family Structure

The two aspects of family structure which continue to receive the most attention are father absence and birth order.

FATHERLESS FAMILIES Studies of the effects of father absence on child development have frequently involved simple-minded comparisons of the differences between children reared in homes with or without fathers. Usually little attention is paid to such factors as the time and cause of separation from the father, the age of the child at the time of testing, and stresses and variations in family functioning that might mediate any differences found in children from intact or fatherless families. Two recent studies of father absence consider some of these problems

(116, 233). Both studies found diverse effects of father absence on children according to whether separation had been caused by the father's death or by divorce or desertion. Santrock (233) found that the adverse effects on cognitive development and achievement of father absence due to divorce or desertion is greatest if it has occurred in the first 2 years of life for boys and girls, and death of the father is most detrimental if it occurs in ages 6 to 9 for boys. Boys with absent fathers showed lower IQ and achievement than boys from intact homes or girls with absent fathers.

In one of the few studies in which the effects of father absence on the social and emotional development of adolescent girls were systematically investigated, few deviations in traditional measures of sex role typing and in relations with female peers and adults were found (116). This is congruent with the findings on younger girls from homes with absent fathers. Although relations with other females were normal, disruptions in interactions with males by girls with absent fathers occurred. Both girls who had lost their fathers due to divorce or due to death reported being tense and anxious around males, but they showed different methods of coping with their anxiety. In contrast to girls from intact families, daughters of divorcees manifested more proximity and attention seeking from males, earlier heterosexual behavior, and various forms of nonverbal communication with males associated with receptiveness. However, the daughters of widows showed inhibition, rigidity, avoidance, and restraint around males. It was proposed that experience in interacting with a warm, appreciative father helps daughters acquire appropriate interpersonal skills and a sense of confidence and competence in subsequent relationships with males. The diverse responses of daughters of divorcees and widows were associated with the aggrandized image of the dead father held by widows and their daughters, the negative attitudes toward the father of divorcees and their daughters, and the variations in the characteristics of the divorcees and widows and their home situation.

BIRTH ORDER   The investigation of sibling influences and the effects of birth order frequently have yielded contradictory results. In two apparently well-designed studies on birth order, family size, and intelligence, one conducted in the United States (181) and one in the Netherlands (21), completely antithetical results were obtained. In the former study, no associations between IQ, family size, and birth order were found, whereas in the latter study, performance on the Raven Progressive Matrices decreased as family size and birth order increased. Although the age and nationality of the subjects and the tests used in the two studies differs, in both studies the confounding effects of social class and birth order with family size were carefully controlled. It is difficult to explain such gross discrepancies in results.

In a third study of Catholic families in Ireland (141), where it is assumed that family size is less likely to be confounded with social status, a measure of modified ordinal position was obtained by dividing each child's ordinal position by the number of children in the family. This reduced but did not eliminate the association between family size and ordinal position. A multiple regression coefficient indicated that social status, family size, and modified ordinal position were related to verbal reasoning ability. However, as is true with most studies in this area in which statistically significant results are obtained, the effects of ordinal position account for only a small portion of the variance in intellectual performance, and the practical significance of these findings must be questioned.

A fairly consistent finding that sex role typing in younger boys is influenced by the sex of the older sibling is supported by two studies. Bigner (24) found that preschool children showed sex role preferences which accorded with the sex of their older sibling. In a second study of college students, males with an older sister reported themselves to have homosexual inclinations, sexual repugnance, and avoidance of sexual relationships (137).

It has been reported that firstborn children employ more high-power persuasive techniques on their younger siblings, while laterborns employ more low-power persuasive techniques on their elder siblings. In a well conceptualized study Bragg, Ostrowski & Finley (29) show that in previous studies, birth order and age of the target are confounded. When these effects are varied, the major differences in persuasive techniques are found to be attributable to the age of the target and not the birth order of the subject.

Finally, in a critical review of birth order effects, Schooler (237) concludes that if one allows for the fluctuations over time in population statistics, there is almost no reliable evidence for birth order effects among males. Although her argument is convincing, and biases in long-term population trends can explain many of the birth order findings, the studies used in her review are highly selected. In her section on differences in parental approaches to children of different birth ranks, she cites only three studies of parental reports of their treatment of their children and covers none of the recent laboratory or observational studies of parents interacting with their neonates or older children in which marked birth order effects have been obtained. In addition, the extensive work of Sutton-Smith and Rosenberg is never mentioned.

FINAL COMMENT

Perhaps the most marked feature in the field of developmental psychology is the lack of satisfactory theories of child development. Many investigators seem to have coped with this problem by doing completely atheoretical research; others are busy patching, mending, and modifying old theories; and some are building mini-theories that deal with very restricted areas of behavior. Although some modest theoretical convergence between areas is occurring, notably in the increased awareness of the role of cognitive factors in a variety of behaviors, one comes away from a review of the literature feeling that developmental psychologists working in different areas don't talk to each other. Little systematic theoretical research is being done; more concern is focused on methodological than theoretical refinements; few attempts are being made to organize and integrate the morass of findings on child psychology that we now have. The literature is replete with highly redundant, often trivial research or "single shot" studies that add little to our understanding of developmental processes. It seems to be an inefficient approach to the study of children's behavior. Although the familiar cry "to get it all together" seems to be asking an impossibility, the time is ripe to get some of it together. The current need is for a careful analysis, synthesis, and evaluation of the information we now have and an attempt to evolve theories which will result in more systematic and fruitful strategies of research.

Literature Cited

1. Abravanel, E. 1972. How children combine vision and touch when perceiving the shape of objects. *Percept. Psychophys.* 2:171–75
2. Acredolo, L. P., Pick, H. L. 1973. *Incidental versus intentional memory for spatial location.* Presented at Meet. Soc. Res. Child. Develop., Philadelphia
3. Adams, W. V. 1972. Strategy differences between reflective and impulsive children. *Child Develop.* 43:1076–80
4. Adinolfi, A. A., Watson, R. I. Jr., Klein, R. E. 1973. Aggressive reactions to frustrations in urban Guatemalan children: The effects of sex and social class. *J. Pers. Soc. Psychol.* 25:227–33
5. Ainsworth, M. D. S. 1969. Object relations, dependency, and attachment: A theoretical review of the infant-mother relationship. *Child Develop.* 40:969–1025
6. Alkire, A. A. 1972. Enactment of social power and role behavior in families of disturbed and nondisturbed preadolescents. *Develop. Psychol.* 7:270–76
7. Alvy, K. T. 1973. The development of listener adapted communications in grade-school children from different social-class backgrounds. *Genet. Psychol. Monogr.* 87:33–104
8. Appel, L. F. et al 1972. The development of the distinction between perceiving and memorizing. *Child Develop.* 43:1365–81
9. Aronfreed, J. 1968. *Conduct and Conscience: The Socialization of Internalized Control over Behavior.* New York: Academic. 405 pp.
10. Ault, R. L. 1973. Problem-solving strategies of reflective, impulsive, fast-accurate, and slow-inaccurate children. *Child Develop.* 44:259–66
11. Ault, R. L., Crawford, D. E., Jeffrey, W. E. 1972. Visual scanning strategies of reflective, impulsive, fast-accurate, and slow-inaccurate children on the matching familiar figures test. *Child Develop.* 43:1412–17
12. Baer, D. M., Wright, J. C. 1974. Developmental psychology. *Ann. Rev. Psychol.* 25:1–82
13. Bandura, A. 1965. Vicarious processes: A case of no-trial learning. In *Advances in Experimental Social Psychology*, ed. L. Berkowitz, 2:3–55. New York: Academic. 348 pp.
14. Barrett-Goldfarb, M. S., Whitehurst, G. J. 1973. Infant vocalization as a function of parental voice selection. *Develop. Psychol.* 8:273–76
15. Battle, E. S., Lacey, B. 1972. A context for hyperactivity in children, over time. *Child Develop.* 43:757–73
16. Baumrind, D., Black, A. 1967. Socialization practices associated with dimensions of competence in preschool boys and girls. *Child Develop.* 38: 291–327
17. Beckwith, L. 1972. Relationships between infants' social behavior and their mothers' behavior. *Child Develop.* 43:397–411
18. Bell, R. Q. 1968. A reinterpretation of the direction of effects in studies of socialization. *Psychol. Rev.* 75:81–95
19. Bell, R. Q., Weller, G. M., Waldrop, M. F. 1971. Newborn and preschooler: Organization of behavior and relations between periods. *Monogr. Soc. Res. Child Develop.* 36(142):1–145.
20. Bell, S. M., Ainsworth, M. D. S. 1972. Infant crying and maternal respon-

siveness. *Child Develop.* 43:1171–90
21. Belmont, L., Marolla, F. A. 1973. Birth order, family size and intelligence. *Science* 182:1096–1101
22. Bhavnani, R., Hutt, C. 1972. Divergent thinking in boys and girls. *J. Child Psychol. Psychiat.* 13:121–27
23. Biber, H., Miller, L. B. Dyer, J. L. 1972. Feminization in preschool. *Develop. Psychol.* 7:86
24. Bigner, J. J. 1972. Sibling influence on sex-role preference of young children. *J. Genet. Psychol.* 121:271–82
25. Bonvillian, J. D., Charrow, V. R., Nelson, K. E. 1973. Psycholinguistic and educational implications of deafness. *Hum. Develop.* 16:321–45
26. Borke, H. 1971. Interpersonal perception of young children. *Develop. Psychol.* 5:263–69
27. Ibid 1972. Chandler & Greenspan's Ersatz Egocentrism: A rejoinder. 7:107–9
28. Bornstein, H., Roy, H. L. 1973. Comment on Linguistic Deficiency and Thinking: Research with Deaf Subjects 1964–1969. *Psychol. Bull.* 79:211–14
29. Bragg, B. W. E., Ostrowski, M. V., Finley, G. E. 1973. The effects of birth order and age of target on use of persuasive techniques. *Child Develop.* 44:351–54
30. Brainerd, C. J. 1973. Judgment and explanations as criteria for the presence of cognitive structures. *Psychol. Bull.* 79:172–79
31. Brainerd, C. J. 1973. Order of acquisition of transitivity, conservation, and class inclusion of length and weight. *Develop. Psychol.* 8:105–16
32. Brainerd, C. J., Brainerd, S. H. 1972. Order of acquisition of number and quantity conservation. *Child Develop.* 43:1401–6
33. Bransford, J. D., Franks, J. J. 1971. The abstraction of linguistic ideas. *Cogn. Psychol.* 2:331–50
34. Brazelton, T. B. 1972. Implications of infant development among the Mayan Indians of Mexico. *Hum. Develop.* 15:90–111
35. Brindley, C., Clarke, P., Hutt, C., Robinson, I., Wethli, E. 1972. Sex differences in the activities and social interactions of nursery school children. In *Comparative Ecology and Behavior of Primates*, ed. R. P. Michael, J. H. Crook. London: Academic
36. Brown, A. L., Campione, J. C. 1973. Mediation in discrimination transfers: A reply to Cole and Medin. *J. Exp. Child Psychol.* 15:356–59
37. Brown, R. 1972. *A First Language/The Early Stages.* Cambridge: Harvard Univ. Press. 437 pp.
38. Bruner, J. S. 1973. Organization of early skilled action. *Child Develop.* 44:1–11
39. Bryan, J. H. 1972. Why children help: A review. *J. Soc. Issues* 28:87–104
40. Bryan, J. H., London, P. 1970. Altruistic behavior by children. *Psychol. Bull.* 73:200–11
41. Buchanan, J. P., Thompson, S. K. 1973. A quantitative methodology to examine the development of moral judgment. *Child Develop.* 44:186–89
42. Busse, T. V., Busse, P. 1972. Negro parental behavior and social class variables. *J. Genet. Psychol.* 120:287–94
43. Campbell, S. B. 1973. Mother-child interaction in reflective, impulsive, and hyperactive children. *Develop. Psychol.* 8:341–49
44. Campbell, S. B., Douglas, V. I., Morgenstern, G. 1971. Cognitive styles in hyperactive children and the effect of methylphenidate. *J. Child Psychol. Psychiat.* 12:55–67
45. Carroll, W. R., Rosenthal, T. L., Brysh, C. G. 1972. Social transmission of grammatical parameters. *J. Educ. Psychol.* 63:589–96
46. Caruso, J. L., Resnick, L. B. 1972. Task structure and transfer in children's learning of double classification skills. *Child Develop.* 43:1297–1308
47. Chandler, M. J., Greenspan, S. 1972. Ersatz egocentrism: A reply to H. Borke. *Develop. Psychol.* 7:104–6
48. Chandler, M. J., Greenspan, S., Barenboim, D. 1973. Judgments of intentionality in response to videotaped and verbally presented moral dilemmas: The medium is the message. *Child Develop.* 44:315–20

49. Cheyne, J. A. 1969. *Punishment and reasoning in the development of self control.* Presented at Bien. Meet. Soc. Res. Child Develop. Santa Monica, Calif.

50. Cheyne, J. A., Walters, R. H. 1969. Intensity of punishment, timing of punishment, and cognitive structure as determinants of response inhibition. *J. Exp. Child Psychol.* 7:231–44

51. Clarkson, T. A., Haggith, P. A., Tierney, M. C., Kobasigawa, A. 1973. Relative effectiveness of imagery instructions and pictorial interactions on children's paired-associate learning. *Child Develop.* 44:179–81

52. Clifford, M. M., Cleary, T. A. 1972. The relationship between children's academic performance and achievement accountability. *Child Develop.* 43:647–55

53. Cole, M., Medin, D. 1973. Critical notes and letters on the existence and occurrence of mediation in discrimination transfer: A critical note. *J. Exp. Child Psychol.* 15:352–55

54. Collins, W. A. 1973. Effect of temporal separation between motivation, aggression, and consequences: A developmental study. *Develop. Psychol.* 8:215–21

55. Costanzo, P. R., Coie, J. D., Grumet, J. F., Farnill, D. 1973. A reexamination of the effects of intent and consequence on children's moral judgments. *Child Develop.* 44:154–61

56. Cronin, V. 1973. Cross-modal and intramodal visual and tactual matching in young children. *Develop. Psychol.* 8:336–40

57. Curcio, F., Kattef, E., Levine, D., Robbins, O. 1972. Compensation and susceptibility to conservation training. *Develop. Psychol.* 7:259–65

58. Davids, A. 1972. Effects of aggressive and nonaggressive male and female models on the behavior of emotionally disturbed boys. *Child Develop.* 43:1443–48

59. Davidson, E. S., Liebert, R. M. 1972. Effects of prior commitment on children's evaluation and imitation of a peer model's perceptual judgments. *Percept. Mot. Skills* 35:825–26

60. Dlugokinski, E., Firestone, I. J. 1973. Congruence among four methods of measuring other-centeredness. *Child Develop.* 44:304–8

61. Doyle, A. 1973. Listening to distraction: A developmental study of selective attention. *J. Exp. Child Psychol.* 15:100–15

62. Dreman, S. B., Greenbaum, C. W. 1973. Altruism or reciprocity: Sharing behavior in Israeli kindergarten children. *Child Develop.* 44:61–68

63. Dweck, C. S., Repucci, N. D. 1973. Learned helplessness and reinforcement responsibility in children. *J. Pers. Soc. Psychol.* 25:109–16

64. Eldred, C. A. 1973. Judgments of right side up and figure rotation by young children. *Child Develop.* 44:395–99

65. Entwisle, D. R., Huggins, W. H. 1973. Iconic memory in children. *Child Develop.* 44:392–94

66. Fagan, J. F. 1972. Infants' recognition memory for faces. *J. Exp. Child Psychol.* 14:453–76

67. Fein, D. A. 1973. Judgments of causality to physical and social picture sequences. *Develop. Psychol.* 8:147

68. Feldstein, J. H. 1973. Effects of uncertainty reduction, material rewards, and variety on children's choice behavior. *J. Exp. Child Psychol.* 15:125–36

69. Feshbach, N. D., Feshbach, S. 1972. Imitation of teacher preferences in a field setting. *Develop. Psychol.* 7:84

70. Fischer, C. T. 1973. Intelligence contra IQ. *Hum. Develop.* 16:8–20

71. Flavell, J. H. 1970. Developmental studies of mediated memory. In *Advances in Child Development,* ed. H. W. Reese, L. P. Lipsitt, 5:182–211. New York: Academic. 265 pp.

72. Flavell, J. H. 1973. The development of inferences about others. In *Understanding Other Persons,* ed. T. Mischel, 66–116. London: Blackwell

73. Fleck, J. R. 1972. Cognitive styles in children and performance on Piagetian conservation tasks. *Percept. Mot. Skills* 35:747–56

74. Fodor, E. M. 1973. Moral development and parent behavior antecedents in adolescent psychopaths. *J. Genet. Psychol.* 122:37–43

75. France, K. 1973. Effects of "white" and of "black" examiner voices on IQ scores of children. *Develop. Psychol.* 8:144

76. Freeman, N. H., Janikoun, R. 1972. Intellectual realism in children's drawings of a familiar object with distinctive features. *Child Develop.* 43:1116–21

77. Friedrich, L. K., Stein, A. H. 1973. Aggressive and prosocial television programs and the natural behavior of preschool children. *Monogr. Soc. Res. Child Develop.* 38, No. 4

78. Friend, R. M., Neale, J. M. 1972. Children's perceptions of success and failure: An attributional analysis of the effects of race and social class. *Develop. Psychol.* 7:124–28

79. Furth, H. G. 1971. Linguistic deficiency and thinking: Research with deaf subjects 1964–1969. *Psychol. Bull.* 76:58–72

80. Ibid 1973. Further thoughts on thinking and language. 79:215–16

81. Garrett, A. M., Willoughby, R. H. 1972. Personal orientation and reactions to success and failure in urban black children. *Develop. Psychol.* 7:92

82. Geber, M. 1958. The psychomotor development of African children in the first year and the influence of maternal behavior. *J. Soc. Psychol.* 47:185–95

83. Geber, M. 1958. L'enfant Africain occidentalise et de niveau social superieur en Ouganda. *Courrier* 8:517–23

84. Geber, M. 1960. Problemes poses par le developpement du jeune enfant Africain en fonction de son milieu social. *Travail Humain* 12:97–111

85. Geber, M. 1962. Longitudinal study and psychomotor development among Baganda children. *Proc. 14th Int. Congr. Appl. Psychol.* Copenhagen

86. Geber, M., Dean, R. F. A. 1957. Gesell tests on African children. *Pediatrics* 20:1055–65

87. Geber, M., Dean, R. F. A. 1957. The state of development of newborn African children. *Lancet* 1:1216–19

88. Geber, M., Dean, R. F. A. 1964. Le developpement psychomoteur et somatique des jeunes enfants Africains en Ouganda. *Courrier* 15:425–37

89. Gelman, R., Weinberg, D. H. 1972. The relationship between liquid conservation and compensation. *Child Develop.* 43:371–83

90. Ginsburg, H. 1972. *The Myth of the Deprived Child; Poor Children's Intellect and Education.* Englewood Cliffs, N.J.: Prentice Hall. 252 pp.

91. Gjesme, T. 1973. Achievement-related motives and school performance for girls. *J. Pers. Soc. Psychol.* 26:131–36

92. Gleason, J. B. 1973. Code switching in children's language. In *Cognitive Development and the Acquisition of Language,* ed. T. E. Moore, 159–67. New York: Academic. 308 pp.

93. Goldberg, S. 1972. Infant care and growth in urban Zambia. *Hum. Develop.* 15:77–89

94. Goldberg, S., Lewis, M. 1969. Play behavior in the year-old infant: Early sex differences. *Child Develop.* 40:21–31

95. Goldstein, D. M., Wicklund, D. A. 1973. The acquisition of the diagonal concept. *Child Develop.* 44:210–13

96. Goodnow, J. J. 1973. Compensation arguments on conservation tasks. *Develop. Psychol.* 8:140

97. Goodnow, J. J., Friedman, S. 1972. Orientation in children's human figure drawings: An aspect of graphic language. *Develop. Psychol.* 7:10–16

98. Goodnow, J. J., Levine, R. A. 1973. "The grammar of action": Sequence and syntax in children's copying. *Cogn. Psychol.* 4:82–98

99. Greenbaum, C. W., Weiss, L. R., Landau, R. 1972. Type of reward, social class, and concept switching in preschool children. *J. Genet. Psychol.* 121:91–106

100. Greenfield, P. M. 1972. Cross-cultural studies of mother-infant interaction: Towards a structural-functional approach. *Hum. Develop.* 15:131–38

101. Greenglass, E. R. 1972. A cross-cultural study of the relationship between resistance to temptation and maternal communication. *Genet. Psychol. Monogr.* 86:119–39

102. Grusec, J. E. 1973. Effects of co-observer evaluations on imitation: A developmental study. *Develop. Psychol.* 8:141

103. Grusec, J. E., Ezrin, S. A. 1972. Tech-

niques of punishment and the development of self-criticism. *Child Develop.* 43:1273-88

104. Hagen, J. W., Hargrave, S., Ross, W. 1973. Prompting and rehearsal in short-term memory. *Child Develop.* 44:201-4

105. Hale, G. A., Morgan, J. S. 1973. Developmental trend in children's component selection. *J. Exp. Child Psychol.* 15:302-14

106. Hale, G. A., Piper, R. A. 1973. Developmental trends in children's incidental learning: Some critical stimulus differences. *Develop. Psychol.* 8:327-35

107. Hall, V. C., Turner, R. R., Russell, W. 1973. Ability of children from four subcultures and two grade levels to imitate and comprehend crucial aspects of standard English: A test of the different language explanation. *J. Educ. Psychol.* 64:147-58

108. Hallahan, D. P., Kauffman, J. M., Ball, D. W. 1973. Selective attention and cognitive tempo of low achieving and high achieving sixth grade males. *Percept. Mot. Skills* 36:579-83

109. Hamilton, M. L. 1973. Imitative behavior and expressive ability in facial expression of emotion. *Develop. Psychol.* 8:138

110. Harris, G. J., Burke, D. 1972. The effects of grouping on short-term serial recall of digits by children: Developmental trends. *Child Develop.* 43:710-16

111. Harris, M. B., Hassemer, W. G. 1972. Some factors affecting the complexity of children's sentences: The effects of modeling, age, sex, and bilingualism. *J. Exp. Child Psychol.* 13:447-55

112. Harrison, A., Nadelman, L. 1972. Conceptual tempo and inhibition of movement in black preschool children. *Child Develop.* 43:657-68

113. Hartrup, W. W., Coates, B. 1967. Imitation of a peer as a function of reinforcement from the peer group and rewardiness of the model. *Child Develop.* 38:1003-16

114. Hartup, W. W., Yonas, A. 1971. Developmental psychology. *Ann. Rev. Psychol.* 22:337-92

115. Herrnstein, R. J. 1973. *IQ in the Meritocracy.* Boston: Little, Brown. 235 pp.

116. Hetherington, E. M. 1972. Effects of father absence on personality development in adolescent daughters. *Develop. Psychol.* 7:313-26

117. Hetherington, E. M., Frankie, G. 1967. Effects of parental dominance, warmth and conflict on imitation in children. *J. Pers. Soc. Psychol.* 6:119-25

118. Hoffman, M. L. 1970. Moral development. In *Carmichael's Manual of Child Psychology,* ed. P. H. Mussen, 2:261-360. New York: Wiley. 872 pp.

119. Hoffman, M., Saltzstein, H. 1967. Parent discipline and the child's moral development. *J. Pers. Soc. Psychol.* 5:45-57

120. Homzie, M. J., Noyes, E. J., Lovelace, E. A. 1973. Children's memory for picture vs. word responses in paired associates: Recall and recognition tests. *Am. J. Psychol.* 86(3):567-77

121. Horowitz, F. D., Paden, L., Bhana, K., Self, P. 1972. An infant-control procedure for studying infant visual fixations. *Develop. Psychol.* 7:90

122. Houtz, J. C., Moore, J. W., Davis, J. K. 1973. Effects of different types of positive and negative instances in learning "nondimensioned" concepts. *J. Educ. Psychol.* 64:206-11

123. Hursh, D. E., Sherman, J. A. 1973. The effects of parent-presented models and praise on the vocal behavior of their children. *J. Exp. Child Psychol.* 15:328-39

124. Hutt, C. 1972. Neuroendocrinological, behavioral and intellectual aspects of sexual differentiation in human development. In *Gender Differences—Their Ontogeny and Significance,* ed. Ounstead, Taylor. London: Churchill

125. Hutt, C. 1972. Sex differences in human development. *Hum. Develop.* 15:153-70

126. Hutt, C. 1973. *Males and Females.* Baltimore: Penguin. 158 pp.

127. Huttenlocher, J., Presson, C. C. 1973. Mental rotation and the perspective problem. *Cogn. Psychol.* 4:277-99

128. Jacklin, C. N., Maccoby, E. E., Dick, A. E. 1973. Barrier behavior and toy preference: Sex differences (and their absence) in the year-old child. *Child Develop.* 44:196-200

129. Jackson, J. P. 1973. Development of

visual and tactual processing of sequentially presented shapes. *Develop. Psychol.* 8:46–50

130. Jeffrey, D. B., Hartmann, D. P., Gelfand, D. M. 1972. A comparison of the effects of contingent reinforcement, nurturance, and nonreinforcement on imitative learning. *Child Develop.* 43:1053–59

131. Jencks, C. 1972. *Inequality.* New York: Basic Books. 399 pp.

132. Jensen, A. R. 1972. *Genetics and Education.* New York: Harper & Row. 378 pp.

133. Jensen, A. R. 1973. *Educability and Group Differences.* New York: Harper & Row. 407 pp.

133a. Jensen, L. C., Hughston, K. 1973. The relationship between type of sanction, story content, and children's judgments which are independent of sanction. *J. Genet. Psychol.* 122:49–54

134. Jensen, L. C., Rytting, M. 1972. Effects of information and relatedness on children's belief in immanent justice. *Develop. Psychol.* 7:93–97

135. Jones, P. A., McMillan, W. B. 1973. Speech characteristics as a function of social class and situational factors. *Child Develop.* 44:117–21

136. Kagan, S., Madsen, M. C. 1972. Rivalry in Anglo-American and Mexican children of two ages. *J. Pers. Soc. Psychol.* 24:214–20

137. Kahn, M. H., Mahrer, A. R., Bornstein, R. 1972. Male psychosexual development: Role of sibling sex and ordinal position. *J. Genet. Psychol.* 121:187–96

138. Katz, P. A. 1973. Perception of racial cues in preschool children: A new look. *Develop. Psychol.* 8:295–99

139. Katz, P. A. 1973. Stimulus predifferentiation and modification of children's racial attitudes. *Child Develop.* 44:232–37

140. Keasey, C. B. 1973. Experimentally induced changes in moral opinions and reasoning. *J. Pers. Soc. Psychol.* 26:30–38

141. Kellaghan, T., MacNamara, J. 1972. Family correlates of verbal reasoning ability. *Develop. Psychol.* 7:49–53

142. Keller, H. R., Hunter, M. L. 1973. Task differences on conservation and transitivity problems. *J. Exp. Child Psychol.* 15:287–301

143. Knight, C. A., Scholnick, E. K. 1973. Training comparison of the subset and the whole set: Effects on inferences from negative instances. *Child Develop.* 44:162–65

144. Kobasigawa, A., Middleton, D. B. 1972. Free recall of categorized items by children at three grade levels. *Child Develop.* 43:1067–72

145. Kobasigawa, A., Orr, R. R. 1973. Free recall and retrieval speed of categorized items by kindergarten children. *J. Exp. Child Psychol.* 15:187–92

146. Kogan, N., Pankove, E. 1972. Creative ability over a five-year span. *Child Develop.* 43:427–42

147. Kopfstein, D. 1973. Risk-taking behavior and cognitive style. *Child Develop.* 44:190–92

148. Korner, A. F., Thoman, E. B. 1972. The relative efficacy of contact and vestibular-proprioceptive stimulation in soothing neonates. *Child Develop.* 43:443–53

149. Koslowski, B., Bruner, J. S. 1972. Learning to use a lever. *Child Develop.* 43:790–99

150. Krebs, D. 1970. Altruism: An examination of the concept and a review of the literature. *Psychol. Bull.* 73:258–302

151. Kuhn, D. 1972. Mechanisms of change in the development of cognitive structures. *Child Develop.* 43:833–44

152. Kunce, J. T., Thelen, M. H. 1972. Modeled standards of self-reward and observer performance. *Develop. Psychol.* 7:153–56

153. Lane, I. M., Coon, R. C. 1972. Reward allocation in preschool children. *Child Develop.* 43:1382–89

154. LaVoie, J. C. 1973. Punishment and adolescent self-control. *Develop. Psychol.* 8:16–24

155. LaVoie, J. C. 1973. The effects of an aversive stimulus, a rationale, and sex of child on punishment effectiveness and generalization. *Child Develop.* 44:505–10

156. LaVoie, J. C., Looft, W. R. 1973. Parental antecedents of resistance-to-temptation behavior in adolescent males. *Merrill-Palmer Quart.* 19

157. Lee, P. C., Wolinsky, A. L. 1973. Male

teachers of young children: A preliminary empirical study. *Young Children* 28:342-52

158. Leibowitz, H. W., Pick, H. L. Jr. 1972. Cross-cultural and educational aspects of the Ponzo perspective illusion. *Percept. Psychophys.* 12:430-32

159. Levitin, T. E., Chananie, J. D. 1972. Responses of female primary school teachers to sex-typed behaviors in male and female children. *Child Develop.* 43:1309-16

160. Lewis, M., Wilson, C. D. 1972. Infant development in lower-class American families. *Hum. Develop.* 15:112-27

161. Liberty, C., Ornstein, P. A. 1973. Age differences in organization and recall: The effects of training in categorization. *J. Exp. Child Psychol.* 15:169-86

162. Liebert, R. M., Fernandez, L. E. 1970. Effects of vicarious consequences on imitative performance. *Child Develop.* 41:847-52

163. Looft, W. R. 1973. Conceptions of human nature, educational practice, and individual development. *Hum. Develop.* 16:21-32

164. Looft, W. R. 1972. Egocentrism and social interaction across the life span. *Psychol. Bull.* 78:73-92

165. Luria, A. R. 1961. *The Role of Speech in the Regulation of Normal and Abnormal Behavior*. New York: Pergamon. 148 pp.

166. Luria, A. R., Yudovich, F. A. 1959. *Speech and the Development of the Mental Processes of the Child*. London: Staples

167. Maccoby, E. E., Feldman, S. S. 1972. Mother attachment and stranger reactions in the third year of life. I. A short-term longitudinal study of American children. II. A cross-cultural comparison in Israel. *Monogr. Soc. Res. Child Develop.* 146 (Whole No. 1)

168. Maccoby, E. E., Jacklin, C. N. 1973. Stress, activity, and proximity seeking: Sex differences in the year-old child. *Child Develop.* 44:34-42

169. Madsen, M. C., Connor, C. 1973. Cooperative and competitive behavior of retarded and nonretarded children at two ages. *Child Develop.* 44:175-78

170. Mallory, W. A. 1972. Abilities and developmental changes in elaborative strategies in paired-associate learning of young children. *J. Educ. Psychol.* 63:202-17

171. Mann, L. 1973. Differences between reflective and impulsive children in tempo and quality of decision making. *Child Develop.* 44:274-79

172. Masangkay, Z. S., McCluskey, K. A., McIntyre, C. W., Sims-Knight, J., Vaughn, B. E., Flavell, J. H. The early development of inferences about the visual percepts of others. *Child Develop.* 45:357-66

173. Masangkay, Z. S., Villorente, F. F., Somcio, R. S., Reyes, E. S., Taylor, D. M. 1972. The development of ethnic group perceptions. *J. Genet. Psychol.* 121:263-70

174. Massari, D. J., Mansfield, R. S. 1973. Field dependence and outer-directedness in the problem solving of retardates and normal children. *Child Develop.* 44:346-50

175. Masters, J. C. 1972. Effects of success, failure, and reward outcome upon contingent and noncontingent self-reinforcement. *Develop. Psychol.* 7:110-18

176. Masters, J. C. 1973. Effects of age and social comparison upon children's noncontingent self-reinforcement and the value of a reinforcer. *Child Develop.* 44:111-16

177. Masters, J. C., Mokros, J. R. 1973 Effects of incentive magnitude on discriminative learning and choice preference in young children. *Child Develop.* 44:225-31

178. Masur, E. F., McIntyre, C. W., Flavell, J. H. 1973. Developmental changes in apportionment of study time among items in a multitrial free recall task. *J. Exp. Child Psychol.* 15:237-46

179. McCall, R. B., Hogarty, P. S., Hamilton, J. S., Vincent, J. H. 1973. Habituation rate and the infant's response to visual discrepancies. *Child Develop.* 44:280-87

180. McCall, R. B., Hogarty, P. S., Hurlburt, N. 1972. Transitions in infant sensorimotor development and the prediction of childhood IQ. *Am. Psychol.* 27:728-48

181. McCall, J. N., Johnson, O. G. 1972.

The independence of intelligence from family size and birth order. *J. Genet. Psychol.* 121:207–13

182. McCracken, J. H. 1973. Sex typing of reading by boys attending all male classes. *Develop. Psychol.* 8:148

183. McGurk, H., Lewis, M. 1972. Birth order: A phenomenon in search of an explanation. *Develop. Psychol.* 7:366

184. McIntyre, C. W., Vaughn, B. E., Flavell, J. H. 1973. Early developmental changes in the ability to infer the visual percepts of others. *Proc. 81st Ann. Conv. APA* 8:99–100

185. McKinney, J. D. 1973. Problem-solving strategies in impulsive and reflective second graders. *Develop. Psychol.* 8:145

186. Medin, D. L. 1973. Measuring and training dimensional preferences. *Child Develop.* 44:359–62

187. Mercer, J. R. 1971. Sociocultural factors in labeling mental retardates. *Peabody J. Educ.* 48:188–203

188. Mercer, J. R. 1972. IQ: The lethal label. *Psychol. Today* 6:44

189. Midlarsky, E., Bryan, J. H., Brickman, P. 1973. Aversive approval: Interactive effects of modeling and reinforcement on altruistic behavior. *Child Develop.* 44:321–28

190. Miller, A. G., Thomas, R. 1972. Cooperation and competition among Blackfoot indian and urban Canadian children. *Child Develop.* 43:1104–10

191. Miller, S. A., Schwartz, L. C., Stewart, C. 1973. An attempt to extinguish conservation of weight in college students. *Develop. Psychol.* 8:316

192. Modreski, R. A., Goss, A. E. 1972. Young children's names for and matches to form-color stimuli. *J. Genet. Psychol.* 121:283–93

193. Money, J., Ehrhardt, A. A. 1972. *Man and Woman, Boy and Girl.* Baltimore: Johns Hopkins Univ. Press. 311 pp.

194. Moore, B. S., Underwood, B., Rosenhan, D. L. 1973. Affect and altruism. *Develop. Psychol.* 8:99–104

195. Moores, D., McIntyre, C. 1971. *Evaluation of programs for hearing impaired children: Progress report 1970–71.* Univ. Minnesota Res., Develop. Demon. Center Res. Rep. 27

196. Moores, D., McIntyre, C., Weiss, K.

1972. *Evaluation of programs for hearing impaired children: Progress report 1971–72.* Univ. Minnesota Res. Develop. Demon. Center Res. Rep. 39

197. Morris, W. M., Marshall, H. M., Miller, R. S. 1973. The effect of vicarious punishment on prosocial behavior in children. *J. Exp. Child Psychol.* 15:222–36

198. Morse, P. A. 1972. The discrimination of speech and nonspeech stimuli in early infancy. *J. Exp. Child Psychol.* 14:477–92

199. Mouw, J. T., Hecht, J. T. 1973. Transfer of the "concept" of class inclusion. *J. Educ. Psychol.* 64:57–62

200. Moynahan, E. D. 1973. The development of knowledge concerning the effect of categorization upon free recall. *Child Psychol.* 44:238–46

201. Mussen, P. H., Parker, A. L. 1965. Mother nurturance and girls' incidental imitative learning. *J. Pers. Soc. Psychol.* 2:94–97

202. Nelson, K. 1973. Structure and strategy in learning to talk. *Monogr. Soc. Res. Child Develop.* 38 (No. 1–2, Serial No. 149)

203. Neussle, W. 1972. Reflectivity as an influence on focusing behavior of children. *J. Exp. Child Psychol.* 14:265–76

204. Noble, G. 1973. Effects of different forms of filmed aggression on children's constructive and destructive play. *J. Pers. Soc. Psychol.* 26:54–59

205. O'Connor, R. D. 1972. Relative efficacy of modeling, shaping, and the combined procedures for modification of social withdrawal. *J. Abnorm. Psychol.* 79:327–34

206. Olweus, D. 1973. Personality factors and aggression with special reference to violence within the peer group. *Rep. Inst. Psychol. Univ. Bergen, Norway,* No. 4

207. Osofsky, J. D., O'Connell, E. J. 1972. Parent-child interaction: Daughters' effects upon mothers' and fathers' behaviors. *Develop. Psychol.* 7:157–68

208. Overton, W. F., Jackson, J. P. 1973. The representation of imagined objects in action sequences: A developmental study. *Child Develop.* 44:309–14

209. Parke, R. D. 1969. Effectiveness of punishment as an interaction of inten-

sity timing, agent nurturance and cognitive structuring. *Child Develop.* 40: 213-35

210. Parke, R. D., Deur, J. L. 1972. Schedule of punishment and inhibition of aggression in children. *Develop. Psychol.* 7:266-69

211. Parker, R. K., Sperr, S. J., Rieff, M. L. 1972. Multiple classification: A training approach. *Develop. Psychol.* 7: 188-94

212. Paris, S. G. 1972. *Children's constructive memory.* Presented at Meet. Soc. Res. Child Develop. Philadelphia

213. Patterson, G. R., Littman, I., Brown, T. R. 1968. Negative set and social learning. *J. Pers. Soc. Psychol.* 8:109-16

214. Pederson, D. R., Ter Vrugt, D. 1973. The influence of amplitude and frequency of vestibular stimulation on the activity of two-month-old infants. *Child Develop.* 44:122-28

215. Peterson, R. G., Danner, F. W. 1973. *The development of recognition memory as applied cognition.* Presented at Meet. Soc. Res. Child Develop. Philadelphia

216. Pick, H. L. 1972. *Mapping children—mapping space.* Presented at Ann. Meet. APA Honolulu

217. Pick, H. L., Acredolo, L. P., Gronseth, M. 1973. *Children's knowledge of the spatial layout of their homes.* Presented at Meet. Soc. Res. Child Develop. Philadelphia

218. Portuges, S. H., Feshbach, N. D. 1972. The influence of sex and socioethnic factors upon imitation of teachers by elementary school children. *Child. Develop.* 43:981-89

219. Prentice, N. M. 1972. The influence of live and symbolic modeling on promoting moral judgment of adolescent delinquents. *J. Abnorm. Psychol.* 80: 157-61

220. Quina, K., Pollack, R. H. 1972. Effects of test line position and age on the magnitude of the Ponzo illusion. *Percept. Psychophys.* 12:253-56

221. Radin, N. 1973. Observed paternal behaviors as antecedents of intellectual functioning in young boys. *Develop. Psychol.* 8:369-76

222. Rand, C. W. 1973. Copying in drawing: The importance of adequate visual analysis versus the ability to utilize drawing rules. *Child Develop.* 44:47-53

223. Rebelsky, F. 1972. First discussant's comments: Cross-cultural studies of mother-infant interaction. *Hum. Develop.* 15:128-30

224. Reese, H. W., Schack, M. L. 1974. Comment on Brainerd's criteria for cognitive structures. *Psychol. Bull.* 81:67-69

225. Ritter, K., Kaprove, B. H., Fitch, J. P., Flavell, J. H. 1973. The development of retrieval strategies in young children. *Cogn. Psychol.* 5:310-21

226. Rosenkoetter, L. I. 1973. Resistance to temptation: Inhibitory and disinhibitory effects of models. *Develop. Psychol.* 8:80-84

227. Rubin, K. H. 1973. Egocentrism in childhood: A unitary construct? *Child Develop.* 44:102-10

228. Ruble, D. N., Nakamura, C. Y. 1972. Task orientation versus social orientation in young children and their attention to relevant social cues. *Child Develop.* 43:471-80

229. Rubovits, P. C., Maehr, M. L. 1973. Pygmalion black and white. *J. Pers. Soc. Psychol.* 25:210-18

230. Sabo, R. A., Hagen, J. W. 1973. Color cues and rehearsal in short-term memory. *Child Develop.* 44:77-82

231. Salapatek, P., Haith, M., Maurer, D., Kessen, W. 1972. Error in the corneal-reflection technique: A note on Slater and Findlay. *J. Exp. Child Psychol.* 14:493-97

232. Saltzstein, H. D., Diamond, R. M., Belenky, M. 1972. Moral judgment level and conformity behavior. *Develop. Psychol.* 7:327-36

233. Santrock, J. W. 1972. Relation of type and onset of father absence to cognitive development. *Child Develop.* 43: 455-69

234. Scarr, S. 1966. Genetic factors in activity motivation. *Child Develop.* 37: 663-73

235. Schaffer, H. R., Emerson, P. E. 1964. The development of social attachments in infancy. *Monogr. Soc. Res. Child Develop.* 29 (No. 3, Serial No. 94)

236. Schnall, M., Alter, E., Swanlund, T., Schweitzer, T. 1972. A sensory-motor context affecting performance in a conservation task: A closer analogue of reversibility than empirical return. *Child Develop.* 43:1012-23

237. Schooler, C. 1972. Birth order effects: Not here, not now! *Psychol. Bull.* 78:161

238. Schubert, D. S. P. 1973. Intelligence as necessary but not sufficient for creativity. *J. Genet. Psychol.* 122:45–47

239. Schwartz, A. N., Campos, J. J., Baisel, E. J. Jr. 1973. The visual cliff: Cardiac and behavioral responses on the deep and shallow sides at five and nine months of age. *J. Exp. Child Psychol.* 15:86–99

240. Scott, M. S. 1973. The absence of interference effects in preschool children's picture recognition. *J. Genet. Psychol.* 122:121–26

241. Shantz, D. W., Voydanoff, D. A. 1973. Situational effects on relatiatory aggression at three age levels. *Child Develop.* 44:149–53

242. Shatz, M., Gelman, R. 1973. The development of communication skills: Modifications in the speech of young children as a function of listener. *Monogr. Soc. Res. Child Develop.* 38 (5, Serial No. 152)

243. Sheppard, J. L. 1973. Conservation as part and whole in the acquisition of class inclusion. *Child Develop.* 44: 380–83

244. Shultz, T. R., Charness, M., Berman, S. 1973. Effects of age, social class, and suggestion to cluster on free recall. *Develop. Psychol.* 8:57–61

245. Siegler, R. S., Liebert, R. M. 1972. Effects of presenting relevant rules and complete feedback on the conservation of liquid quantity task. *Develop. Psychol.* 7:133–38

246. Singer, D. G., Kornfield, B. 1973. Conserving and consuming: A developmental study of abstract and action choices. *Develop. Psychol.* 8:314

247. Singer, D. L., Rummo, J. 1973. Ideational creativity and behavioral style in kindergarten-age children. *Develop. Psychol.* 8:154–61

248. Slater, A. M., Findlay, J. M. 1972. The measurement of fixation position in the newborn baby. *J. Exp. Child Psychol.* 14:349–64

249. Ibid. The corneal-reflection technique: A reply to Salapatek, Haith, Maurer & Kessen, 497–99

250. Slobin, D. I. 1973. Cognitive prerequisites for the development of gram-

mar. In *Studies in Child Language Development*, ed. C. A. Ferguson, D. I. Slobin. New York: Holt, Rinehart & Winston

251. Solkoff, N. 1972. Race of experimenter as a variable in research with children. *Develop. Psychol.* 7:70–75

252. Solomon, D., Faizunisa, A., Kfir, A. D., Houlihan, K. A., Yaeger, J. 1972. The development of democratic values and behavior among Mexican-American children. *Child Develop.* 43:625–38

253. Spear, P. S., Spear, S. A. 1972. Reinforcement, discrimination learning, and retention in children. *Develop. Psychol.* 7:220

254. Spiegler, M. D., Liebert, R. M. 1973. Imitation as a function of response commonality, serial order, and vicarious punishment. *J. Exp. Child Psychol.* 15:116–24

255. Stevenson, H. W. 1972. *Children's Learning.* New York: Appleton-Century-Crofts. 338 pp.

256. Steward, M., Steward, D. 1973. The observation of Anglo-, Mexican-, and Chinese-American mothers teaching their young sons. *Child Develop.* 44:329–37

257. Stouwie, R. J. 1972. An experimental study of adult dominance and warmth, conflicting verbal instructions, and children's moral behavior. *Child Develop.* 43:959–71

258. Strayer, J., Ames, E. W. 1972. Stimulus orientation and the apparent developmental lag between perception and performance. *Child Develop.* 43: 1345–54

259. Ter Vrugt, D., Pederson, D. R. 1973. The effects of vertical rocking frequencies on the arousal level in two-month-old infants. *Child Develop.* 44:205–9

260. Thelen, M. H., Rennie, D. L., Fryrear, J. L., McGuire, D. 1972. Expectancy to perform and vicarious reward: Their effects upon limitation. *Child Develop.* 43:699–703

261. Tulkin, S. R. 1973. Social class differences in infants' reactions to mother's and stranger's voices. *Develop. Psychol.* 8:137

262. Tulving, E., Madigan, S. A. 1970. Memory and verbal learning. *Ann. Rev. Psychol.* 21:437–84

263. Turiel, E., Rothman, G. R. 1972. The influence of reasoning on behavioral choices at different stages of moral development. *Child Develop.* 43:741–56
264. Turnure, C. 1972. Perceptual learning in young children: Varied context and stimulus labels. *Am. J. Psychol.* 85:339–50
265. Underwood, B., Moore, B. S., Rosenhan, D. L. 1973. Affect and self-gratification. *Develop. Psychol.* 8:209–14
266. Van Lieshout, C. F. M., Leckie, G., Smits-Van Sonsbeek, B. 1973. *The effects of a social perspective-taking training on empathy and role-taking ability of preschool children.* Presented at Meet. Int. Soc. Study Behav. Develop., Ann Arbor, Mich.
267. Warren, D. H. 1973. *Early versus late blindness: The role of early vision in spatial reference systems.* Presented at Meet. Soc. Res. Child Develop. Philadelphia
268. Warren, N. 1972. African infant precocity. *Psychol. Bull.* 78:353–67
269. Weintraub, D. J., Tong, L., Smith, A. L. 1973. Muller-Lyer versus size/reflectance-contrast illusion: Is the age-related decrement caused by a declining sensitivity to brightness contours? *Develop. Psychol.* 8:6–15
270. Wheeler, R. J., Dusek, J. B. 1973. The effects of attentional and cognitive factors on children's incidental learning. *Child Develop.* 44:253–58
271. Whitehurst, G. J. 1972. Production of novel and grammatical utterances by young children. *J. Exp. Child Psychol.* 13:502–15
272. Wilder, L., Levin, J. R. 1973. A developmental study of pronouncing responses in the discrimination learning of words and pictures. *J. Exp. Child Psychol.* 15:278–86
273. Willerman, L. 1973. Activity level and hyperactivity in twins. *Child Develop.* 44:288–93
274. Wispe, L. G., Ed. 1972. Positive forms of social behavior. *J. Soc. Issues* 28 (entire)
275. Wolf, T. M. 1973. Effects of televised modeled verbalizations and behavior on resistance to deviation. *Develop. Psychol.* 8:51–56
276. Wolf, T. M., Cheyne, J. A. 1972. Persistence of effects of live behavioral, televised behavioral, and live verbal models on resistance to deviation. *Child Develop.* 43:1429–36
277. Wolff, P., Wolff, E. A. 1972. Correlational analysis of motor and verbal activity in young children. *Child Develop.* 43:1407–11
278. Wolman, R. N., Lewis, W. C., King, M. 1972. The development of the language of emotions: IV. Bodily referents and the experience of affect. *J. Genet. Psychol.* 121:65–81
279. Yarrow, M. R., Scott, P. M. 1972. Imitation of nurturant and nonnurturant models. *J. Pers. Soc. Psychol.* 23:259–70
280. Yarrow, M. R., Scott, P. M., Waxler, C. Z. 1973. Learning concern for others. *Develop. Psychol.* 8:240–60
281. Yonas, A. 1973. *The development of spatial reference systems in the perception of shading information for depth.* Presented at Meet. Soc. Res. Child Develop. Philadelphia
282. Yonas, A., Hagen, M. 1973. Effects of static and motion parallax depth information on perception of size in children and adults. *J. Exp. Child Psychol.* 15:254–65
283. Zigler, E., Abelson, W. D., Seitz, V. 1973. Motivational factors in the performance of economically disadvantaged children on the Peabody Picture Vocabulary Test. *Child Develop.* 44:294–303
284. Zigler, E., Yando, R. 1972. Outerdirectedness and imitative behavior of institutionalized and noninstitutionalized younger and older children. *Child Develop.* 43:413–25
285. Zimmerman, B. J., Rosenthal, T. L. 1972. Concept attainment, transfer, and retention through observation and rule-provision. *J. Exp. Child Psychol.* 13:139–59

BIOLOGICAL RHYTHMS AND ANIMAL BEHAVIOR[1]

§230

Benjamin Rusak[2] *and Irving Zucker*[3]
Department of Psychology, University of California
Berkeley, California 94720

> He appointed the moon for seasons: the sun knoweth his going down. Thou makest darkness, and it is night: wherein all the beasts of the forest do creep forth. The young lions roar after their prey, and seek their meat from God. The sun ariseth, they gather themselves together, and lay them down in their dens. Man goeth forth unto his work and to his labor until the evening.
>
> Psalm 104: 19–23

INTRODUCTION

The rhythmic or cyclic nature of animal behavior has been appreciated by man since early in recorded history (158). Formerly, attempts to understand daily cycles of activity, annual reproductive rhythms, and the seasonal occurrence of migration and hibernation emphasized changes in the external environment as the causative or driving forces underlying periodicity. This view predominated well into the present century and assigned a more or less passive role to the organism displaying the rhythm; only within the last quarter century have biological clocks within living organisms been widely recognized as major determinants of behavioral and physiological rhythms. The potential adaptive significance of these

[1] Investigations by the authors and preparation of the manuscript were supported by research grant HD–02982 from the National Institute of Child Health and Human Development and by the Committee on Research of the University of California. We are grateful to Darlene Frost for bibliographic assistance and to Deedra McClearn for typing the manuscript.
[2] Supported by an Abraham Rosenberg Fellowship from the University of California.
[3] Supported by a USPHS Career Development Award K4–HD–42413.

137

rhythms and their probable mode of evolution have been considered in several reviews (69, 124, 150).

Psychologists have long been interested in the timing of behavior and have struggled with behavioral periodicity in their theories of motivation. At issue here is why a given animal is active at one time and quiet at another; why it eats, copulates, sleeps, or fights at one time of day and not at another. In general, animal behaviorists within the American psychological tradition have not given adequate weight to the role of biological clocks in their answers to these questions. Thus, one of our main goals in this article is to emphasize the importance of biological clocks for the general understanding of behavior and more particularly in the design and interpretation of studies concerned with behavioral phenomena. We have dealt primarily with vertebrate and especially mammalian behavior, but have not attempted to cite all the relevant recent literature. Limitations of space have often forced us to cite a single review article rather than several original research reports. We have emphasized daily and seasonal cycles in behavior and physiology and have not considered rhythmic components of human performance, nor the involvement of biological clocks in periodic illness.

A number of books on biological rhythms are of special interest to students of animal behavior. Broadest in scope are the volumes edited by Aschoff (9) and by Menaker (125), and the reviews by Cloudsley-Thompson (42), Luce (113), and Bünning (37). The most recently published volume of *The Neurosciences* contains several articles of interest and provides an excellent introduction to biological rhythm research (127, 152, 189). Several more specialized monographs describe human circadian rhythms (43, 46) or individual research programs (170). Articles on biological rhythms are found in scores of scientific periodicals; two recently founded journals, *Journal of Interdisciplinary Cycle Research* and *Chronobiologia* are devoted to reports on biological periodicity.

Definition of Terms Used

The novice is frequently intimidated by the unfamiliar mathematical symbols used to describe parameters of rhythmic behavior. The analogy between biological clocks and physical oscillators has prompted the wholesale adoption of a complex terminology and methods of data analysis (148); these are useful but not essential to an understanding of basic principles. The main concepts and symbols encountered are listed below; this brief description is based on a report by Aschoff et al (16). *LD cycle*: Alternating periods of light and darkness (or brighter and dimmer phases) whose durations are given as in LD 14:10. This designates a cycle of 14 hr of light, alternating with 10 hr of no measurable light (darkness). The intensity of illumination during the respective phases is often indicated.

LL, DD: Respectively, continuous illumination and continuous darkness.

Zeitgeber: A periodic environmental factor that entrains a biological rhythm; the LD cycle is the paramount example of a zeitgeber.

Endogenous rhythm: One requiring no periodic environmental input to maintain its periodicity; a self-sustaining oscillation.

Entrainment: The coupling of an endogenous rhythm to a zeitgeber such that both display the same period (synchronization).

Period: The duration of a single cycle; i.e. the time between successive recurrences of a specified phase of a cycle. Designated as τ for the biological rhythm and T for the zeitgeber.

Frequency: The reciprocal of the period; i.e. if τ = 0.5 hr then the frequency is 2 cycles per hr.

Phase: The instantaneous state of an oscillation. Any point within a cycle.

Phase angle: The value on the abscissa corresponding to a particular phase of a cycle; this is given as some fraction of the total cycle (hours, degrees, radians) and is represented by ϕ for a biological rhythm and Φ for a zeitgeber.

Phase angle difference: The difference between corresponding phase angles of two coupled oscillators.

Phase shift: A displacement of an oscillation along the time axis, designated $\Delta\phi$ and $\Delta\Phi$ for biological rhythms and zeitgebers, respectively. A shortening of the period is a phase advance while a lengthening is a phase delay.

Free-running rhythm: A self-sustaining rhythm not entrained to any zeitgeber and therefore displaying its spontaneous period, usually under constant conditions.

Circadian rhythm: An endogenous rhythm with a period of approximately 24 hr. The range of deviation permitted for classification as a circadian rhythm is undefined, but limits between 21 and 27 hr are usually suggested.

CIRCADIAN RHYTHMS

General Considerations

The analogy between circadian clocks and physical oscillators has been fruitful both in generating empirical research and in providing a theoretical framework for biochronometry (9, 152, 200). The basic principle of this analogy is that rhythmic behavioral and physiological functions can be analyzed in terms of the known properties of linear (pendulum-like) and nonlinear (capacitor-like) physical oscillators (201). There is now abundant evidence that multicellular organisms contain many oscillators, each of which may have different characteristics and periods. A human subject under constant environmental conditions may simultaneously display free-running periodicities of 33 hr duration for the sleep-wakefulness cycle and of 25 hr duration for the rhythm in body temperature (12).

A single rhythmic function (e.g. locomotor activity) may reflect the operation of two or more independent oscillators that normally are strongly coupled but may in fact show different natural frequencies and different sensitivities to light (152). One oscillator can only be phase-advanced by light and the other only phase-delayed. Together these oscillators can account for effects that have hitherto been interpreted in terms of a single oscillator with differentially sensitive phases. The dual-oscillator model is supported by the "splitting" of an apparently uniform rhythm into two independent components. Under special constant conditions, viz.

very dim illumination for tree shrews (*Tupaia belangeri*) (90) or very bright light for hamsters (*Mesocricetus auratus*) (152) or after hypothalamic lesions in the latter species (see 206a) these oscillators may become dissociated and free-run relative to each other. Starlings (*Sturnus vulgaris*) may show similar splitting of their activity rhythms when injected with testosterone (75a). Other evidence supporting this model includes the effects of contracting "skeleton" photoperiods (152) and the ubiquity of bimodal activity patterns throughout the animal kingdom (11).

The gross behavioral measures commonly used and the strong tendency for oscillators to remain coupled have prevented the more frequent detection of multiple oscillators for each measurable rhythmic function. The integrated cyclic behavior of multicellular organisms can be conceived as resulting from a complex interaction among oscillators possessing circadian and noncircadian frequencies; the neurophysiological basis for the interaction within and between oscillatory constituents remains unexplored (152).

Much of what is known about circadian clocks has been learned from observing the effects of light on rhythmic behaviors. Some of these relations have been summarized by Aschoff (9). His *Circadian Rule* states that as the intensity of constant illumination increases, the frequency of the free-running rhythm increases for day-active species and decreases for night-active animals. These effects predict the behavior of oscillators under entrained conditions as well; thus any manipulation that increases the frequency of the circadian clock relative to that of the zeitgeber will cause the animal's oscillator to phase lead the zeitgeber by increasing amounts [e.g. this will occur in L-active animals when light intensity is increased (10)]. These principles have been confirmed in many species and disconfirmed in several others (88).

The Circadian Rule is useful in interpreting the effects of various experimental manipulations. For example, a treatment which "decreases nocturnality" in a LD cycle may in fact decrease the τ of the underlying activity rhythm and thereby cause a phase advance relative to the LD cycle. Alternatively, the treatment could increase or decrease sensitivity to light in the entrainment pathway, and thereby alter the phase angle of activity onset without effecting a reduction in rhythm amplitude per se.

Kavanau (101) has suggested that species are physiologically adapted to be active at a particular "optimum level" of illumination; intensities above or below this level will decrease activity, so the linearity implied by the Circadian Rule may apply only in the middle range of illumination intensity (101). Both laboratory and field observations support Kavanau's position in demonstrating that many species are most active at moderate illumination intensities (twilight) rather than during the brightest or darkest part of the day-night cycle (42). Kavanau's somewhat untraditional methods of data analysis, his measurement of activity over rather limited time spans, and the lack of uniformity between his analyses and those used in establishing the Circadian Rule weaken his criticisms of the latter (101). Nevertheless, his testing of animals over a broad range of light intensities, use of controlled twilight transitions, and investigation of a diverse array of species are all features that recommend his work (102); the prediction of an optimum species-specific illumination intensity, frequently in an intermediate range, is worthy of rigorous testing.

Functional Significance

Biological clocks may have evolved to time behavior in relation to the external environment. For example, the initiation of eclosion activity several hours prior to dawn is such that the emergence of adult *Drosophila* from pupae coincides with the optimal humidity level (150). Certain circadian timers can also function as true clocks, that is, they can be consulted at any time. The sun-compass orientation of birds (89) and bees (197) allows animals to modify their flight direction relative to the sun's position, exactly as if they had access to time of day information; thus they respond to where the sun "should" be at a given time. Such information may be crucial for navigation during migration. Circadian clocks are used by some species to measure daylength and thus are useful in timing seasonal events (see *Seasonal Rhythms*).

Timing is also crucial in relation to other organisms; predators hunt when prey are most active, and related species that feed on similar diets can avoid certain types of competition by foraging at different times of day (cf 145; 194, p. 343). Ostriches (*Struthio* sp.) provide an example of the function of daily rhythms in relation to camouflage. In their usual desert habitat the black-plumed male sits on the nest at night while the pale brown female incubates the eggs by day (119a). Ringdoves (*Streptopelia risoria*) show a similar temporal division of labor (Whitman, cited in 107a).

The internal milieu is a temporally integrated system whose continuity depends on biological clocks and their coupling as well as on feedback relations. In *Drosophila* longevity is considerably decreased on 21 or 27 hr LD cycles. Presumably cycles that differ from 24 hr cause dysfunctional internal phase relations among various rhythms (156). The synchronization of enzymatic activity in various organs and the synergistic actions of hormones that depend on precise temporal patterns of secretion are but a few examples of the need for synchronization of internal processes.

Menaker (124) notes that very little is known concerning the adaptive significance of particular rhythms in particular organisms, but concludes that "rhythms will eventually be shown to confer many different kinds of selective advantage on organisms which possess them."

Physiological Basis for Entrainment by Light

RECEPTORS   The existence and functional significance of extraocular photoreceptors in nonmammalian vertebrates is well established (127), but none of the adult mammals studied to date show signs of entrainment by light after removal of the eyes. Since only nocturnal species have been studied systematically, it remains possible that direct penetration of light through the skull (70, 208) and extraocular photoreceptors could entrain rhythmic functions in diurnal mammals (cf 126). On the basis of current information it is most likely that ocular receptors are the principal, if not the exclusive, mediators of light entrainment in mammals.

The specific retinal elements involved in entrainment are unknown; whether unique classes of receptors underlie visual perception and entrainment by light also remains to be established; hitherto unsuspected receptors are apparently involved in both processes. Excellent light-dark discrimination has been demonstrated in albino rats (*Rattus norvegicus*) after complete destruction of the retinal receptor layer by exposure to LL (5), although in one study 50% of the LL rats did not consistently perform above chance levels and the remaining animals required more trials to reach criterion than controls (22). Degeneration of photoreceptors induced by exposure to constant illumination of moderate intensity is usually complete after one month (5), and is not reversed when rats are returned to a LD cycle (55). The optic tract and lateral geniculate nucleus of most of these animals show no response to photic stimulation (143).

Nevertheless, these animals can entrain their corticosterone rhythms to the LD cycle (55) and show light-dependent reproductive and pineal responses (167). It is not known whether these functions are performed by a few residual rods or by an entirely different kind of receptor (e.g. bipolar or ganglion cells). The harderian glands, located within the orbital cavity directly behind the eye, do not appear to be the photoreceptors involved in these processes (166). Reiter has speculated that some cellular element within the eye other than the classical photoreceptors transmits information to the hypothalamus and that a humoral agent secreted by the eye also may be involved (166, 167).

According to Caley et al (39), mice (*Mus musculus*) with retinas devoid of classical photoreceptors manifest circadian rhythms in feeding that differ from those of control animals; the latter show the usual nocturnal feeding cycles whereas the rodless animals reportedly have a "freely running rhythm" relative to day and night (39). This observation, if confirmed, would imply that entrainment of feeding by the illumination cycle is mediated by the rods. Unfortunately, the only published records of feeding rhythms in CBA/Ki mice (110) do not support the conclusions of Caley et al: the feeding patterns of these animals (110, Fig. 6) appear to be well within the normal range for nocturnality. The existence of free-running rhythms would be difficult to prove given the frequency with which feeding was recorded. Mouse strains with various ocular abnormalities (180) provide an excellent and to date unexploited opportunity for the analysis of receptor mechanisms underlying entrainment, photoperiodicity, and visual perception.

PHOTOPIGMENTS   The photopigments involved in entrainment are unknown; systematic studies of action spectra and thresholds for entrainment are almost completely lacking (127). Green light is most effective as a zeitgeber for the rat's circadian body temperature rhythm, with red and ultraviolet wavelengths relatively ineffective (119). Short wavelengths are most effective for phase-shifting the daily rhythm of torpor in pocket mice (*Perognathus penicillatus*) (71). The correspondence between the rhodopsin sensitivity curve and the efficacy of various wavelengths for entrainment (119) suggests that rhodopsin may be involved in the latter process. It would be useful to test this hypothesis on rats deprived of photoreceptors by prior exposure to constant light.

Wavelengths corresponding to blue and green light most effectively influence locomotor activity of mice (183) and also constitute the components of white light mainly responsible for the degenerative changes induced by constant illumination (4). The possibility that a given wavelength range is maximally effective for entraining all rhythmic functions in a given organism is intriguing and worthy of experimental verification. This seems to be the case in the moth *Pectinophora gossypiella* in which effective spectral components for phasing several behaviors are similar but different from those involved in photoperiodic time measurement (155). The wavelengths most effective in mammals with good photopic vision are completely unknown.

Photopigments involved in entrainment may be distinct from those that mediate other light-dependent functions (e.g. the visual perception of objects). Thus carotenoid depleted *Drosophila* have retinules grossly deficient in rhodopsin and their visual receptors show a 3 log-unit reduction in light sensitivity; nevertheless, the sensitivity of their circadian emergence rhythm to the phase-shifting effect of light flashes appears to be normal (205).

CENTRAL VISUAL PROJECTIONS   Light impinging on the mammalian eye almost certainly acts via the established visual projections to entrain the central oscillators underlying rhythmicity. A neurohumoral mechanism for entrainment seems at best a remote possibility.

The central visual projections have been most extensively studied in the albino rat; information on this species is summarized by Moore (131). He notes that all visual input from the eye enters the optic chiasm via the optic nerve. Of the three pathways leaving the chiasm the largest is the primary optic tract (POT) which consists of uncrossed and decussating retinal components that terminate in the superior colliculus, pretectum, and lateral geniculate. The superior accessory optic tract (SAOT) runs within the POT and terminates in the midbrain tegmentum. A third visual pathway that leaves the chiasm, the inferior accessory optic tract (IAOT), consists entirely of crossed retinal fibers; after leaving the chiasm it runs in the ventral part of the brain along with fibers of the medial forebrain bundle and eventually terminates in the medial terminal nucleus of the midbrain tegmentum (81). The IAOT has been traced in a number of mammalian species but apparently is not present in the golden hamster (56).

A fourth visual pathway, the retinohypothalamic tract (RHT) provides a direct connection between the retina and the suprachiasmatic nuclei of the hypothalamus. This projection is bilateral even in rodent strains in which all other components of the retinal projection are crossed (83). Input to the contralateral suprachiasmatic nucleus (SCN) is about twice as heavy as to the ipsilateral side; most retinal fibers terminate in the ventral part of the SCN where they form asymmetric synapses either on small dendritic branches or on dendritic spines (83). The distribution, receptive fields, and discharge properties of the retinal ganglion cells that project to the SCN are unknown (83). Although a retinohypothalamic pathway had previously been described (137), the definitive proof of its existence in mammals required the use of autoradiographic tracing techniques and was accomplished only within the past 4 years (83, 130, 131). The RHT remains difficult to detect with conventional tracing procedures such as silver impregnation (111); a thoughtful discussion of problems involved in this analysis is contained in (83). To date the RHT has been described in mammals representing several orders, including rodents, carnivores, marsupials, and primates (130). It also exists in birds (123) and other nonmammalian vertebrates (137).

There is no firm evidence that pathways other than the retinohypothalamic tract are essential for entrainment of mammalian circadian rhythms. Lesions that bilaterally interrupt the primary and/or accessory optic tracts do not eliminate steady state nocturnal drinking rhythms of albino rats maintained on a LD 12:12 cycle (187) or locomotor rhythms of pigmented rats (3). It was also reported that POT transection did not affect the phase-shifting of the drinking rhythm after a 12 hr shift in the illumination cycle (187). Subsequent observations show that lesions aimed at the lateral geniculate nuclei to interrupt the primary optic tracts retard the rate of phase-shifting of the hamster wheel running rhythm; re-entrainment requires 3 times as long as for controls (206a). Final steady state entrainment is comparable to that of unlesioned hamsters. Failure to observe similar changes with respect to the rat's drinking rhythm may be due to procedural differences between the studies.

Interruption of the primary and accessory optic tracts also does not interfere with steady state adrenal corticosterone rhythms or with the pineal rhythm of N-acetyltransferase (131). Entrainment of these rhythms as well as the circadian locomotor rhythm of rats (186) and the locomotor and drinking rhythms of hamsters (see 206a) is disrupted by lesions that destroy the retinohypothalamic projection. Knife cuts posterior to the SCN also disrupt entrainment of the adrenal corticosterone and the pineal N-acetyltransferase rhythms (131, 132), perhaps by interrupting efferents from the SCN. Although this pathway has not been adequately described, Krieg (105) suggests that SCN axons course dorsally and then caudally in the periventricular system.

The retinohypothalamic projection is probably necessary and sufficient for photic entrainment of mammalian circadian rhythms, and the primary optic tracts may influence these processes by virtue of their indirect connections with the suprachiasmatic nuclei (190).

Zeitgebers Other than Light

Light is the acknowledged dominant zeitgeber for mammalian rhythms. In our own species, however, social factors may synchronize free-running rhythms (13) and experimental instructions can override illumination effects (142). In social isolation some human rhythms may free-run in the presence of "adequate" LD cycles to which other animals would entrain (13). Social stimuli may be more important synchronizers of human rhythms because we control our environment to a greater extent than do other mammals; this could have reduced the biological significance of the illumination cycle. Caution should be exercised in drawing such a conclusion because animal subjects are rarely tested in social situations and the effectiveness of social cues in entraining their rhythms is largely unknown. The likely efficacy of social stimuli is indicated by the observation that nondominant rats in a seminatural setting modify their eating and activity rhythms to avoid conflict with dominant animals (40). The changes observed in animal activity rhythms after human disruption of their environments (101) also suggest an important role for nonlight factors in modifying mammalian rhythms.

A sparrow housed in constant dim illumination has been entrained to the sight and/or sound of a conspecific; recorded bird song can also entrain the activity rhythms of some sparrows, but this zeitgeber is far weaker than an illumination cycle (128). The cycle of maternal behavior has been proposed as a social stimulus that may contribute to the development of rhythmicity in the young (1). However, rat pups reared with constant access to maternal care, supplied by mothers on opposite LD cycles, show the normal development of rhythmicity (69).

Perhaps the most extensively documented social influences are connected with reproductive rhythms. In some species synchronization of estrus can be effected by the presence of males; female mice exposed to the odor of males tend to come into heat and to ovulate on the same day of the estrous cycle (34). Pheromonal mechanisms may also be involved in the reported synchronization of menstruation in women who live together in college dormitories (118). There has been virtually no experimental exploration of the influence of conspecifics on daily rhythms of mammalian behavior.

Other weak zeitgebers include electrical fields (202) and cyclic pressure changes (80). Some stimuli may affect specific rhythms without necessarily acting as classical zeitgebers; e.g. limited daily temporal access to food or water rephases rhythms of locomotor activity (29), adrenal corticosterone secretion (98), sleep (134), and metabolic cycles (28). Handling of animals at the same time each day may induce gonadal degeneration or growth, depending on when it occurs relative to the animal's day-night cycle (122). The neural mechanisms by which environmental stimuli other than light gain access to biological clocks that govern rhythmic behavior have not been delineated.

Temperature cycles, although effective as zeitgebers for poikilotherms, are ineffective for mammals (161). Mammals, in common with other animals, show excellent temperature compensation in preserving periodicity within narrow limits. Although the biological clock is presumably chemical in nature, the rate of change of τ as temperature changes (Q_{10}) is extremely small compared to that of other chemical reactions (161).

Neural Control

Although circadian rhythms can occur in plants and in protozoa lacking nervous systems, the generation of these rhythms in metazoa probably is accomplished primarily via nervous mechanisms. Even among mammals, however, the adrenal gland (6) and the intestine (37) can display endogenous daily rhythms of secretion and contraction, respectively, in complete isolation from neural influences. In the intact organism phasing of these rhythms is subject to control by central neural pacemakers.

NONMAMMALIAN SPECIES   Neural control of rhythms has been studied mainly in nonmammalian species, and the perspective gained from this work is useful in evaluating and guiding research with mammals. The optic lobes of insect brains have been implicated in the generation of activity rhythms and other circadian cycles (32, 112). The early view that a neurohumoral agent was involved in rhythm generation has been vigorously challenged (32) but has also received renewed support from the demonstration of interanimal transfer of rhythmicity in parabiotic cockroaches (48). The distinctive circadian rhythm of cocoon emergence (ecdysis) can also be transferred by brain transplants between two closely related moth species (192). Truman's elegant studies showed that the timing but not the motor pattern of ecdysis was affected by brain transfer; this effect was accomplished even when the brain was implanted in the abdomen of the pupa and therefore in the absence of normal neural connections. Although this suggests neurohumoral mediation of rhythmicity, it is important to distinguish between nonhumoral clock mechanisms and humoral linkage of the neural clock to motor systems that express rhythmical behavior.

Circadian rhythms of neural activity have been demonstrated in a single neuron of the *Aplysia* parietovisceral ganglion (189) and in the optic nerve discharge of the excised *Aplysia* eye (94). Jacklet & Geronimo (95) cut away portions of the eye in vitro and observed normal circadian rhythmicity in optic nerve activity when only 20% of the eye was left intact. When a larger portion of the eye was destroyed, the period of the rhythm decreased; with 2% of the eye remaining, only ultradian ($\ll$ 24 hr) frequencies of electrical discharge were expressed. One interpretation of these findings is that the cells whose fibers form the optic nerve are themselves pacemakers independently generating ultradian rhythms and that a minimal number of such mutually coupled oscillators interact to produce a circadian rhythm of spike discharge (95). This view emphasizes circadian rhythmicity as an emergent property of the interaction among oscillators. The alternative proposal is that the reduction in the period of the *Aplysia* optic nerve rhythm involved the fortuitous destruction of crucial circadian pacemaker cells within the eye which synapse chemically onto optic nerve neurons (189). The issue is unresolved, but there is strong evidence indicating that chemical synapses are not involved and that oscillators in this preparation are electrotonically coupled (94).

The avian pineal may possibly be a clock for generating activity and body temperature rhythms (127). Pinealectomized (pinx) sparrows display a normal rhythm of body temperature and perch-hopping activity when exposed to a LD cycle; however, in DD where normal birds generate clearcut free-running circadian rhythms, pinx birds are hyperthermic and continuously active and show no signs of circadian rhythmicity in these functions (26, 27). The pineal may be a master oscillator that hierarchically entrains other oscillators, each of which is responsible for circadian rhythmicity in a particular function (127); alternatively the pineal may be a coupling device between a master driving oscillator located elsewhere and other light-sensitive damped oscillators that in turn drive overt circadian rhythms (127).

MAMMALS   The effect of selective lesions of the mammalian nervous system on rhythmicity has most often been studied only under entrained conditions. Any alteration in the temporal pattern of a single physiological or behavioral parameter studied in a LD cycle is subject to a variety of interpretations and cannot be used to localize a clock within the destroyed brain region. The changes that have been described after brain lesions include a temporary reversal in the phasing of the peak in corticosterone release in dogs without olfactory bulbs (7), temporary elimination of the rat's corticosterone rhythm after transection of the fornix (109), and elimination of this rhythm after basal hypothalamic isolation (74). Lesions of the ventromedial or dorsomedial hypothalamus reduce the normal day-night differences in feeding (18, 23), while lesions of the lateral hypothalamus accentuate the nocturnal feeding rhythms of rats (99); medial septal lesions exaggerate the apparent nocturnality of activity rhythms of hamsters (87) and the drinking rhythms of rats, and increase the rate at which rat drinking rhythms phase shift after a change in the LD cycle (Rusak & Zucker, unpublished observations, 1972). Superior cervical ganglionectomy retards the rate of entrainment of feeding behavior in rats (20), and lesions interrupting the primary optic tracts of hamsters slow the phase shifting of the locomotor activity rhythm (206a).

The problems inherent in such studies are exemplified by one performed in our laboratory (see 206a); lesions of the raphe nuclei of rats increased overall wheel running activity and greatly reduced the nocturnality of this rhythm. However, when tested in constant dim light these rats generated normal free-running rhythms with τs of approximately 25 hours, as shown by power spectral analysis. Raphe lesions clearly increased the level of activity but did not eliminate the endogenous rhythmic fluctuations around the higher mean level. Such results emphasize the need for sufficient time series (24, 25) and adequate statistical analysis of data obtained under proper experimental conditions before one may conclude that any neural, chemical, or other manipulation has "eliminated" the rhythmicity of a behavioral system. It should be emphasized that it is far easier to affect motor systems involved in expression of rhythmicity than the clock mechanism itself.

Richter has reported a complete and convincing loss of circadian rhythmicity of eating, drinking, and wheel running activity in blinded rats with hypothalamic lesions of unspecified size and location (171). More recently, suprachiasmatic (SCN) lesions have been reported to eliminate rhythmicity in pooled mean levels of plasma corticosterone sampled at different times during a LD cycle (132). Individual records of wheel running activity and drinking recorded in LD cycles and in constant light showed an elimination of circadian rhythmicity after SCN lesions (186). Our recent studies of hamsters with SCN lesions suggest a complex role for this brain region in the production, coordination, and entrainment of behavioral rhythms (see 206a). Critchlow (47) had earlier implicated the SCN in the control of estrous cyclicity; his observations have been extended in more recent work which also suggests that the SCN is involved in the control of daily surges in luteinizing hormone and in the timing of ovulation in several species (38, 76). Whether the SCN serves as a master clock, a central coupler of rhythms, or as one complex oscillator in a multioscillator system is unknown. The adjacent medial preoptic area (97) and the lateral hypothalamus (176) both show regular changes in spontaneous electrical activity during lengthy recording sessions; it has not been established that these cycles represent true circadian rhythmicity nor that the rhythmic activity originates independently at each recording site.

The importance of the hypothalamus in the regulation of rhythmicity is supported by human clinical data; patients with hypothalamic damage show a reversal of normal patterns of electrolyte excretion (107). Another report (146) cites a loss of normal body temperature rhythms after an increase in third ventricular pressure which presumably interferes with the function of midline hypothalamic nuclei.

Chemical Control

CHEMICAL BASIS OF CLOCKS   In multicellular organisms the output of a circadian oscillator may be the product of interactions among a large population of cells. Other cells may couple the oscillator to the external environment or to effectors that express the observable circadian rhythm. Chemicals may operate at any or all of these levels of organization. As a consequence, pharmacological or chemical modification of circadian rhythmicity does not necessarily imply that the oscillator itself has been affected.

The period (τ) of biological clocks reflects the basic process involved in time measurement and is remarkably intractable to a wide range of pharmacological agents, including inhibitors of macromolecular synthesis, anesthetics, hallucinogens, poisons, and other drugs traditionally used in pharmacological research (49, 140, 154, 170). The few agents that have affected τ have done so only within narrow limits, and these successes have not led to a clear understanding of the chemical nature of biological clocks.

Dilute solutions of ethyl alcohol (ETOH) lengthen the endogenous tidal rhythm of the isopod *Excirolana chiltoni* (58); 0.5% ETOH increases τ by an average of approximately one hour and dosage dependence is apparently linear up to 1%. Reliable but considerably smaller lengthening of τ of the hamster locomotor rhythm occurs when blind animals are chronically ingesting 20% ETOH (206a).

Deuterium oxide (D_2O), also known as heavy water, is the only chemical agent that consistently affects the period of many free-running circadian oscillators. It lengthens τ in plants and in a variety of unicellular and multicellular animals (154). In the mouse τ of the locomotor rhythm is increased in proportion to the concentration of D_2O in the water supply; a maximum increase of 7.4% was obtained with a 30% solution. In a LD cycle phase lags of entrainment are frequently recorded, and in some cases the activity rhythm "breaks away" from the illumination cycle and free-runs (54). Pittendrigh et al (154) have summarized some of the effects of D_2O on biological systems. Partial deuteration slows virtually every biological process and rate depression is explainable by many different potential causes; they postulate that D_2O produces its effects on circadian rhythms by diminishing effective cell temperature. Some preliminary evidence obtained with the *Drosophila* emergence rhythm supports this view.

Chemical manipulation of unicellular and in vitro systems will not be reviewed here except to cite the frequently stated generalization that the intracellular production of a circadian periodicity may depend on the transmembrane potential and on the permeability of specific ionic channels (59, 140, 189). Alcohol, D_2O, and other chemicals (e.g. lithium) which lengthen the periods of various clocks have all been described as increasing the stability of biological membranes. A recently developed membrane model of the circadian clock (140) suggests that timing is the result of a feedback system involving transmembrane ion gradients and protein-dependent ion transport channels. This model accounts for temperature compensation of τ on the basis of the temperature adaptation of the membrane lipid bilayer. The rate of ion diffusion and of horizontal movement of the proteins responsible for ion transport would both be compensated for temperature change by this mechanism. The fact that K^+ pulses (59) and valinomycin, which causes an accumulation of K^+ (37), can produce phase shifts similar to those produced by L pulses suggests a crucial role for K^+ in the production of circadian rhythmicity and its entrainment by light (140).

The existence of a general homeostasis of τ in the face of all potential perturbations occurring within cells (153) might account for the transitory nature and small magnitude of drug induced changes in circadian systems. The variation in τ effected by all changes in light, temperature, and chemical stimulation is small, usually of the order of 5% and very rarely exceeding 10% (152). As noted by Pittendrigh (152, 153), the apparent homeostasis of τ is a major barrier to evaluating the quantitative effects of any agent used to disturb the circadian oscillator and complicates assessment of the chemical nature of biological clocks.

CHEMICAL INFLUENCES ON RHYTHM AMPLITUDE   The degree to which rhythms in brain chemistry affect amplitude of behavioral rhythms remains to be established. Discrete portions of the mammalian nervous system and the brain as a whole display circadian fluctuations in 5-hydroxytryptamine (5-HT), norepinephrine (NE), and possibly in dopamine (DA). The amplitude of these rhythms and their phase relations to the illumination cycle are species-specific (85, 133).

Depletion of 5-HT which is produced by injecting parachlorophenylalanine temporarily reduces the nocturnal feeding, drinking, and activity rhythms of rats; the amplitude of these rhythms recovers to control levels within one week (31, 66, 206a). Similar effects are observed after 6-OH DA treatments that markedly reduce brain NE; the nocturnal activity rhythm is attenuated but not entirely eliminated two to three weeks after treatment (85) and normal three to four weeks later (182). The effects of these drugs on the free-running periods of these behaviors were not reported.

Noradrenergic mechanisms appear to link endogenous rhythms with the cycle of environmental illumination. The β-adrenergic blocking agent 1-propanalol prevents the dark-triggered increase in rat pineal enzyme activity (53); NE depletion also interferes with entrainment of body temperature in a monkey (*Cebus albifrons*) (203).

The 24 hr periodicity of eating behavior observed in rats maintained in LD 10:14 disappeared when amphetamine was added to the water supply (30). In a similar study rats ingesting amphetamine equivalent to 20 mg/kg of body weight increased their wheel running activity throughout the 24 hr period so that entrainment to the LD cycle seemed to disappear (49). The hyperactivity produced by amphetamine also obscured the free-running rhythm of rats maintained in constant light. The authors conclude that amphetamine disrupted the circadian activity rhythm, but they provide no quantitative estimate of τ; from visual inspection of their records we conclude that circadian rhythmicity may have persisted under the drug condition.

Removal of endocrine organs reduces the amplitude of various rhythms including those of body temperature (65), locomotor activity (170), and food and water intake (187, 188). The effects are presumably dependent on chemical-hormonal changes consequent to gland extirpation. None of these procedures appears to affect the periodicity of the underlying behavioral rhythms (160, 170), but see (37, p. 57) for a discussion of adrenal effects on physiological periodicities.

This brief survey illustrates that it is far easier to alter the amplitude of biological rhythms than to affect their periodicity. The specific chemical substrates underlying zeitgeber perception or coupling of oscillators to effector systems are unknown, and the possibility exists that coupling within the mammalian neural clock and between it and other systems may be electrotonic rather than chemical (cf 95). Electrotonic coupling has been described in several mammalian neural structures, including the visual system (22a).

DRUG EFFECTS ON BEHAVIOR   Responsiveness to drugs fluctuates with the phase of the organism's circadian cycle; the timing of crests and troughs of susceptibility can also vary from one drug to the next and depends on the function and species studied.

Mortality of rats after a single injection of amphetamine at different times of day reached a peak of 78% at 0600 hr and a trough of 7% at 0300 hr; these animals were maintained on a LD 12:12 cycle with light onset at 0600 hr (175). Fluctuations of a similar nature have been noted for a wide array of physiological parameters and for various classes of drugs. These findings are of importance in chemical therapeutics where it has often been tacitly assumed that animals are steady state systems whose sensitivity to drugs is invariant across time of day.

An exhaustive review of research in this area (162) and our subsequent literature search indicate that biological time of day has been manipulated as an independent variable in but a few psychopharmacological studies. This is unfortunate since drug effects on behavior are almost certainly as subject to modification by endogenous rhythms as the more traditionally investigated physiological parameters. Insufficient recognition of this point may account for seemingly discrepant findings (cf 117, 173). Biological time of day is a decisive determinant of the effects of *l*-NE on food intake; when applied directly to the lateral hypothalamus of rats during the L phase of a LD 12:12 cycle, NE increases food intake; in the dark phase NE depresses food consumption (117). This effect may depend on circadian fluctuations in the activity and sensitivity of lateral hypothalamic neurons (176).

The dose-response curve for increasing locomotor activity with amphetamine is steeper in the L than the D part of the illumination cycle (60); sleeping time of rats on a LD 12:12 cycle is a function of the hour of barbiturate administration (162). These findings suggest the importance of controlling for or better yet manipulating biological time of day as a variable in psychopharmacological research. The meager data currently available suggest that the new findings and perspectives gained from such an analysis will be well worth the effort.

SEASONAL RHYTHMS

Photoperiodism

Homeothermic species in temperate and arctic climates must adapt to seasonal changes in temperature, predator pressure, and the availability of food and protective cover. In doing so they undergo hibernation (135), estivation, migration, seasonal and opportunistic breeding, and delayed uterine implantation (174, 194). Social reorganization, daily torpor, and changes in fur quality and coloration are also among the adaptations observed in mammals on a seasonal basis (96, 184, 185).

Physiological and behavioral responses must often be initiated well in advance of the seasonal conditions they are designed to meet. Hibernating mammals store food or body fat long before snow cover and cold make feeding impossible and hibernation essential for survival (194, p. 378). Birds show precise timing of premigratory fattening and development of functional reproductive organs in advance of their arrival at distant breeding grounds (62). Mechanisms that rely exclusively on simple responsiveness to current conditions are inadequate to account for these phenomena; animals clearly use information about time of year to anticipate critical conditions. Most species use the stable and regular annual cycle of change in daylength (photoperiod) to time seasonal events. Photoperiodic time measurement (PTM) is evident in the initiation of seasonal reproduction, but it also mediates other seasonal cycles. An understanding of the formal models proposed to account for PTM is essential to any consideration of research on seasonal rhythms.

MODELS OF PHOTOPERIODIC TIME MEASUREMENT (PTM)

(a) *The hourglass model*   The mechanism whereby an organism may directly measure the duration of a L or D period by accumulating some endproduct during one phase and not the other has been compared to an hourglass. This type of mechanism has been confirmed in a few insects (155) but apparently is not applicable to mammalian PTM.

(b) *Bünning's hypothesis*   This states that an endogenous circadian oscillator mediates PTM. In its role as zeitgeber light first entrains a circadian photosensitivity rhythm; the second function of light is induction of the photoperiodic response. This occurs if and only if light extends into the photoinducible (sensitive) phase of the circadian cycle. If it is assumed that dawn sets a photosensitive phase to occur 14 to 15 hr later, then light will fall in the inducible phase only when days are long (in excess of 14 hr). In this way a short period of light coinciding with a critical photosensitive phase can induce the seasonal changes associated with long days; otherwise the animal will behave as if under short-day conditions. Animals need not experience light continuously for effective PTM; this is an attractive feature in accounting for the excellent PTM observed in fossorial animals who may be exposed to daylight only near dawn and dusk each day (37).

Photoperiods of any given duration occur twice each year and PTM depends on the animal distinguishing 14 hr of light in the spring from 14 hr of light in the fall; many animals show a photorefractory period such that photoinduction by long days (spring) takes place only if these days are preceded by an extended period of short days (winter) (37). The specific form of Bünning's hypothesis described above relies on the coincidence of an internal state (photosensitivity) with an external condition (light) and has been called an *external coincidence model* (151).

(c) *The internal coincidence model* (151)   This assumes that the sole function of light is to entrain various circadian oscillators such that they bear different phase relation to each other under different photoperiods. PTM and induction depend on a seasonally unique phase relation of these oscillators and no direct inductive role is ascribed to light. Two oscillators entrained respectively to dawn and dusk could serve this function (152). A corollary of this model is that entrainment by nonlight zeitgebers could achieve the proper internal relations among oscillators and thereby effectively mediate "photoperiodic" time measurement in the absence of light (151). Such studies are currently in progress with temperature zeitgebers, but the predicted effect has yet to be demonstrated (152).

(d) *The resonance effect*   Since laboratory tests of PTM frequently use exotic lighting schedules, one cannot conclude that the circadian system is actually involved in PTM merely because the schedules in which L recurs at modulo 24 hr intervals are most effective for induction (152). A noncircadian mechanism might measure light duration but produce maximum induction only when the animal's physiological mechanisms are synchronized by a cycle approximating the natural frequency. In general an organism is assumed to function most efficiently when its internal oscillators have the proper phase relations and this occurs only when entrained to 24 hr cycles.

TESTS OF THE MODELS   Tests of Bünning's hypothesis typically involve noninductive entraining light periods followed by brief "flashes" of light at various intervals during the succeeding dark periods. The pitfalls inherent in interpreting such studies derive from the difficulty in distinguishing entraining from inductive effects of light (152). Elliott et al (57) recently attempted to circumvent this problem by concurrently recording locomotor activity and testicular development of hamsters exposed to such LD sequences. When the hamsters' activity cycles were stably entrained to the illumination cycles their testes showed unique daily phases of sensitivity to the inductive effects of light; these phases recurred at 24 hr intervals in accord with Bünning's hypothesis. However, these results may also be amenable to an explanation in terms of light entraining a dawn oscillator one day and a dusk oscillator on another in such a way as to maintain an inductive internal phase relationship, i.e. an internal coincidence model involving only entraining and not inductive actions of light is still not ruled out (57).

Results obtained with the moth *Pectinophora gossypiella* do not support Bünning's hypothesis. In this species, where it is possible to separate the inductive and entraining properties of light, no circadian involvement in PTM was observed (155). Replication of this experiment in mammalian species in which circadian systems seem to be implicated awaits the discovery of light wavelengths and intensities consistent with induction but not with entrainment.

The importance of photoperiodic time measurement and the intricate interaction among biological clocks, hormones, and behavior are most clearly illustrated by Meier's elegant studies on sparrows (120, 121). Injections of corticosterone and prolactin induce premigratory fattening, gonadal development, and *zugunruhe* (directed migratory restlessness) only when they bear a particular phase relation to each other. Prolactin injected 12 hr after corticosterone produces all these effects and the *zugunruhe* is directed northward (spring mode); if prolactin is given 4 hr after corticosterone, only fattening occurs and *zugunruhe* is directed southward (fall mode). Prolactin injections bearing other phase relations to corticosterone are ineffective.

Meier's evidence suggests that the peak in endogenous corticosterone secretion is followed 4 to 8 hr later by a photoinducible phase during which light can trigger release of luteinizing hormone (LH). A second photoinducible phase 16–22 hr after the corticosterone peak permits light to stimulate release of follicle stimulating hormone (FSH). The maintenance of photosensitivity at these phases depends on entrainment of the prolactin rhythm at an appropriate phase relative to the peak in corticosterone secretion (121). These data are consistent with the following hypotheses: light entrains the circadian rhythms of corticosterone and prolactin release, with daylength determining the internal phase relations between these rhythms; when the proper phase relation occurs, it in turn entrains a circadian rhythm of photosensitivity during which light may act to influence pituitary release of LH and FSH. This results in spermiogenesis, testis growth, and other signs of spring migration, or in the fattening and *zugunruhe* typical of autumn migration. Stress produced by handling sparrows and pricking them with a needle at appropriate times of day can also phase the corticosterone rise so that photoinduction can take place (122).

Careful tests of entrainment of the circadian system with nonlight cues are needed to improve our understanding of the control of seasonal breeding and migration. Such experiments could provide valuable information about the relative importance of the internal and external coincidence systems already impli-cated by Meier's findings. They could also provide insights into the physiological mechanisms whereby many internal oscillators can be entrained and phase shifted relative to each other and to environmental cycles.

Circannual Rhythms

Endogenous annual oscillations (circannual rhythms) provide a second mechan-ism, independent of photoperiodic time measurement, for timing of seasonal events. To qualify as endogenous, a circannual rhythm must persist under constant environmental conditions and occur year after year with a free-running period of approximately one year. It is hardly surprising that few studies have adequately satisfied this demanding criterion.

The existence of such endogenous annual oscillations has also been controver-sial because closely related species differ strikingly with respect to the existence and general form of these rhythms. Unlike daily rhythms, annual cycles are a new evolutionary development of adaptive significance only to relatively long-lived species (63). If, as seems likely, a great diversity of mechanisms evolved indepen-dently to mediate annual cyclicity, then the search for unitary mechanisms and models based exclusively on a circadian paradigm may be inappropriate (77).

Among the most convincing examples of circannual rhythms is the hibernation rhythm of blinded ground squirrels (*Citellus lateralis*) maintained for years in a constant environment at 3° C. In one individual the intervals between successive entries into hibernation were 313, 314, and 310 days, respectively (149). Heller & Poulson, studying other ground squirrels (*Spermophilus*), maintain that "regard-less of the experimental manipulations we imposed upon the animals, the free-running period length measured from terminal arousal to terminal arousal is generally only slightly less than a year and shows remarkably little variation" (82). In yet another species of ground squirrel the hibernation-weight gain rhythm damps out after one year and few subjects show a second cycle (136). Endogenous annual rhythms may also regulate antler growth in pika deer (*Cervus nippon*) (73), fat deposits in woodchucks (*Marmota monax*) (51), water intake and body weight in ground squirrels (149), and hibernation in chipmunks (*Eutamias*) (82). The evidence that these rhythms are truly endogenous is far less compelling than for circadian rhythms. For example, the detection of circannual rhythms is strongly dependent on the maintenance of a particular daily LD cycle. Some species require a LD 12:12 cycle, while others need a LD 11:13 cycle to express their annual rhythms (77); the annual cycle of antler growth in the pika deer occurs on LD 16:8 or LD 8:16 but not on a LD 12:12 cycle (73).

The peculiarities and advantages of the endogenous timers of different species that have such stringent and divergent requirements remain unknown. A number of annual rhythms may be subject to separate endogenous and exogenous con-trols. Part of the cycle is entirely independent of external input (*endogenous component*) and a second part requires a particular LD cycle or temperature to trigger or terminate some crucial event. If this *exogenous component* is provided, the annual rhythm is expressed; in its absence the endogenous process is arrested at the blocked phase.

The interaction of endogenous and exogenous controls in seasonal rhythms is clearly illustrated by Reiter's work with golden hamsters. In these animals short photoperiods initiate testicular regression, culminating within 8 weeks in reproductive quiescence. After 25 weeks of continual exposure to the short photoperiod, the gonads undergo spontaneous recrudescence and become functionally mature (164). Testicular development and recrudescence proceed independently of any need for the long photoperiods (168) otherwise required to maintain testicular function, and thus appear to be endogenously controlled. However, a second cycle of testicular regression in short photoperiod conditions will *not* occur unless the animals first experience many weeks of long-day conditions (164).

These findings are in good accord with field observations cited by Reiter (163). Short laboratory photoperiods may simulate the conditions hamsters are exposed to in the late fall when they enter underground burrows and hibernate in the absence of light until the following spring. The 20-week period of sexual dormancy induced by the short photoperiod prevents delivery of young during the disadvantageous fall and winter seasons; the subsequent testicular recrudescence, independent of light, insures that sexual competence coincides with spring emergence and that young are born during the season optimal for survival (165). The pineal gland has been implicated in these and other seasonal reproductive events, and its contributions are ably documented by Reiter (164).

Seasonal Influences on Behavior

In addition to prominent annual rhythms in hibernation and reproduction, there are more subtle but nevertheless important seasonal influences on physiology and behavior (cf 35). One direct seasonal influence is due to the changing availability of foodstuffs. Rodents feeding on the protein-rich spring and summer herbage grow faster and reach sexual maturity earlier than those ingesting the starchy foods available in the autumn (78). Certain opportunistic breeders living in arid regions reproduce only after favorable and unpredictable events such as rainfall (174).

Other seasonal influences are less direct. Goldfish perform better in learning tasks and are more active in winter than during the summer spawning season. Reducing the amount of light to which they are exposed improves summer performances (179). Under natural lighting conditions the occurrence of estrus in pocket mice (*Perognathus penicillatus*) is little influenced by the presence of males; it has a high incidence in spring and summer and low in autumn and winter. However, under constant long or short photoperiods the annual cycle is disrupted and the presence or absence of males becomes an important variable (144). Snowshoe hares (*Lepus americanus*) gonadectomized during their breeding season increase LH and FSH synthesis and release; no such increases in hormone secretion are detected when gonadectomy is performed out of the breeding season (52). Male *Microtus* are more aggressive in paired encounters when captured in their breeding season than at other times of year (193).

The pattern of daily activity often changes with the seasons (194, p. 345). Three species of voles showed a single nocturnal activity peak during summer, but all gradually became diurnal with one or more activity peaks during winter (75). In spring, arctic deer mice (*Peromyscus maniculatus*) have a pronounced daily activity rhythm which may be related to effective foraging and mating; in winter, they undergo daily torpor and are weakly nocturnal (184). Woodchucks emerging from hibernation in late winter show scattered daily activity; by spring they have a strong afternoon activity peak, in summer a bimodal pattern, and in the fall scattered activity culminating in winter hibernation (33).

Little is known about whether these seasonal cycles persist under constant laboratory conditions, but there is a suggestion that hamsters breed more readily in spring than in winter, even under unchanging light and temperature conditions (164).

The particular conditions of illumination, ambient temperature, and availability and quality of food in laboratory studies may mimic those of a given season; the effects of subsequent experimental manipulations may therefore be affected by the induction or blockade of seasonal phenomena. To select appropriate laboratory conditions, one must be familiar with the ecology of the species being studied; such knowledge has often been lacking or ignored in psychobiological research.

RHYTHMS AND BEHAVIORAL FUNCTIONS

The final sections of this review are concerned with the rhythmic aspects of specific behavioral phenomena. Psychologists and physiologists appreciated that behaviors associated with sleep, activity, food ingestion, and reproduction had an intrinsic cyclicity long before they suspected that other behaviors might be similarly organized. As a consequence, the evidence is far more satisfactory for the former behaviors than for the processes involved in sensation, perception, and learning.

Eating and Drinking

The frequency and periodicity of mammalian eating behavior depend on the nature and availability of the diet eaten and may be characteristically quite different for carnivores, herbivores, omnivores, etc. Size and metabolic rate, type of digestive system, endogenous activity rhythms, and numerous environmental factors, viz. temperature, illumination, humidity, presence of conspecifics and predators, and reproductive status, also may dictate the distribution and quantity of food consumed. The feeding frequency of smaller nocturnal mammals will also depend on the availability of an insulated nest that reduces metabolic demands imposed by changes in environmental temperature and humidity, and that provides a dark retreat during daytime.

The survival of mammals and the maintenance of energy balance depend on foraging, hunting, and often returning with food to nests or storage areas. Much of the observable spontaneous activity of mammals in the wild is related to feeding, and it probably is inappropriate to analyze one without considering the other. Eliminating the necessity to search for food may well be a critical factor influencing periodicity of intake; e.g. in nature the activity cycle and feeding behavior of an insectivorous rodent may be linked to that of the invertebrates that form part of its diet and which themselves show marked fluctuations in daily activity (17).

In typical laboratory studies of eating behavior the periodicity of intake is established while excess food is freely available at all times. A dark nest box is rarely provided, so the nocturnal animal must experience long periods of light or modify its behavior to minimize light exposure (e.g. increased sleeping during the L phase). The addition of a dark place in the cage stimulated a South American rodent (*Oxymycterus rutilans*) to eat a greater proportion of its food during the L portion of the illumination cycle (196). Albino rats given access to a constantly dark tunnel and burrow in addition to an open field where food and water were available under a LD 12:12 cycle altered the temporal pattern of their eating and drinking (Rusak & Block, unpublished observations, 1973).

The study of the effects of food restriction on subsequent eating is complicated by the variety of feeding styles adopted by mammals. Large predatory mammals obtain substantial quantities of easily digestible food at irregular intervals and may gorge themselves during one relatively brief feeding; they are adapted to fare quite well without further food for days. Other mammals, such as those eating diets of low caloric density and high cellulose content, may be compelled to eat relatively continuously throughout the day and night. This would appear to be true of the larger herbivores, including some of the ruminants (17). Some herbivorous animals have very limited abilities to compensate for periods of food deprivation and only slowly regain weight loss during starvation (Silverman & Zucker, unpublished observations, 1973). The degree of depletion induced by starvation and in fact the survival of rodents may depend on the time of day during which food deprivation occurs (138).

ENTRAINMENT   Rats with ad lib access to food and water in a bare laboratory cage are nocturnal feeders and drinkers. In a LD 12:12 cycle they eat 75% of their food and drink 85% of their water during the dark phase (206). In LD 14:10 a peak of eating occurs with the onset of darkness and a second peak about 6 hours later (191). The nocturnal drinking rhythm may be partially independent of the nocturnal feeding rhythm (141), and relations between food and water intake may differ fundamentally in the different phases of the illumination cycle (206, 207).

In hamsters drinking is 85% nocturnal on a LD 12:12 cycle, but only 58% of feeding occurs during the dark phase (207). In guinea pigs there is no obvious nocturnal, diurnal, or crepuscular cycle, and the animals appear to eat and drink at regular intervals throughout the day and night (86). Some primates appear to be exclusively diurnal feeders, and observations of monkeys (*Macaca mulatta*) in seminatural conditions suggest that they withdraw to trees and do very little eating between dusk and dawn (195).

SHORT-TERM CYCLES   There is a significant positive correlation between the rat's meal size and the interval to the next meal (108). This relation does not appear to be a general description of the rat's feeding behavior; according to Panksepp (147), it holds during specific metabolic states and is a consequence of statistical procedures of questionable validity. He proposes instead that the "free-feeding pattern of rats is generated by an internal signal of body nutrient depletion-repletion which varies in a circadian fashion" and that the satiating capacity of ingested food and the depriving capacity of intermeal intervals vary across the day.

This concept is supported by other findings; e.g. the effectiveness of the suppression of oral intake by intragastric loading of nutrients depends not only on the number of calories infused but also on the temporal distribution of infusions relative to the normal time of feeding (159). Factors other than total caloric intake thus play a role in determining satiety. Some circadian rhythms in blood amino acids are not directly related to ingestion of dietary proteins and are evident on the day of birth in human infants (64). These rhythms could be manifestations of a neural system that generates a circadian depletion-repletion cycle.

Failure to simulate environmental conditions more representative of those experienced by animals in nature may lead one to generate reliable but invalid laboratory data on feeding patterns. Extrapolation from results obtained with a particular species, tested under a limited set of conditions, to mammalian feeding in general glosses over a wealth of information about species specificities that range from radical differences in intestinal and gastric morphology (41) to elaborate food storage techniques practiced by certain mammals (194, p. 323–24). Consider for example that albino rats, often studied as models of human feeding, reingest approximately 40% of the feces they produce when studied under laboratory conditions. This coprophagy shows a pronounced daily rhythm (114) that permits the recovery of valuable nutrients (19). The influence of this cycle of coprophagy on meal patterns and on the rat's adjustment to alterations in food availability and in diet quality deserves experimental attention.

Sleep and Activity

Animal rest and activity cycles have been investigated more thoroughly than any other rhythmic function. Such cycles seem to be fundamental to the temporal organization of all animal behavior and are found both in the simplest and most complex organisms. The relative ease with which activity can be continuously monitored over long intervals recommends it to the student of biological rhythmicity. However, measurement of activity in laboratory settings is subject to many of the same problems as were enumerated in the preceding section. The availability and quality of food, the presence of burrows, and the use of gradual light-dark transitions may alter the timing of activity (17, 100, 101; Rusak & Block, unpublished observations, 1973). The distribution of activity as recorded in the laboratory may differ from that in the field (102), particularly if seasonal variations occur.

The methods used for monitoring activity (stabilimeter, activity wheel, photocell, etc) influence the nature of the results obtained (14, 67, 169). Nevertheless, measures as diverse as chewing, drinking, eating, and wheel running may yield quite similar nocturnal patterns when studied in a single species (171). If one is concerned with the temporal distribution of these behaviors rather than with the function or topography of the response being measured, then one may be justified in studying one endpoint (e.g. wheel running) as an index of the animal's temporal organization. However, since a given manipulation (e.g. a brain lesion or a drug) can have different effects depending on the type of device used to measure activity (cf 115), it is important to determine the generality of treatment effects by studying a number of different responses. This is obviously necessary where one suspects a multiplicity of clocks for different functions.

Researchers have recognized the importance of circadian and ultradian rhythms in the control of sleep. Kleitman (104) proposed that the arousal level of an individual varies throughout the day and is a function of an ultradian species-specific, rest-activity cycle that persists through the sleep and waking states. The proportion of the various sleep stages recorded depends on when in relation to their circadian cycle individuals first fall asleep (199).

The function of sleep has interested many writers and may be, as some have suggested (181, 199), to prevent wasteful and dangerous expenditure of energy at nonoptimal times of day; the rest-activity cycle would thus ensure that each species is active only when its activity has the greatest potential survival value. The idea that sleep serves primarily this function rather than one of metabolic recovery is supported by data obtained on human (15) and hamster subjects (129); under free-running conditions sleep time is *inversely* proportional to the length of the preceding period of spontaneous wakefulness. This relation is predicted by a circadian organization of the sleep-wakefulness cycle since the total of rest and active periods must equal a stable τ value. The opposite is predicted by any theory that emphasizes the recovery function of sleep. The development of a sleep "need" after periods of sleep deprivation (202a) does suggest that some recovery occurs during sleep; this may be a more recently evolved function superimposed on the basic timing process of the sleep-wakefulness cycle.

Exposing burrow-dwelling rodents to obligatory LD cycles may restrict the amount and distribution of the various sleep stages (68, 134). In constant darkness or when given access to a darkened retreat, rats may make up a chronic sleep "debt" incurred under standard laboratory conditions (68). These findings require further study and confirmation, but they emphasize the need for consideration of species' ecology, particularly in relation to light exposure.

Reproduction

The reproductive physiology and behavior of many mammals has an intrinsic rhythmicity. The ovaries of polyestrous spontaneous ovulators pass through follicular and luteal phases of relatively fixed duration, and the cycle is repeated unless interrupted by copulation or pregnancy. The limited life span of ovulated ova makes it essential that mating behavior and insemination be temporally synchronized with the period during which fertilization is most likely to occur. In many mammals the coupling of sexual receptivity and ovulation to the same fixed sequence of hormonal events assures this outcome. Synchronization of ovulation and sexual behavior is mediated in female rats by neural control of the pituitary (61, 72, 204) and may possibly involve adrenal participation (116).

The endogenous nature of the biological clock controlling the hamster estrous cycle has been definitively established (2); in constant illumination behavioral estrous cycles free-run with a period greater than 4 days (a circaquadridian rhythm). The timer that mediates this cycle probably functions with a circadian rather than a circaquadridian periodicity (2). Neural pathways that promote preovulatory LH release do so at 24 hr intervals (103, 139), but ovulation occurs only on the day of the cycle that coincides with high plasma estrogen levels (139). Spontaneous or pharmacologically induced blockade of ovulation extends the cycle by 24 hr rather than by an entire cycle length (2), further supporting a circadian organization of estrous cyclicity. Failure to establish free-running estrous cyclicity in rats housed in constant light does not argue against the endogenous nature of this rhythm. The albino rats used in these studies are abnormally sensitive to the disruptive effects of constant light (36), and the cessation of ovulation and onset of persistent estrus in LL speak to a desynchronization or damping of the various hormone rhythms that contribute to the ovulation cycle (cf 178).

One unresolved major question, as noted by Everett (61), is whether the clock for cyclic LH release and ovulation exists in both sexes. According to one view (72, p. 240), the inherently cyclic preoptic area regulates cyclic release of gonadotropins in female rats; in males cyclicity of this neural substrate is thought to be suppressed during perinatal sexual differentiation. The result is that the adult male or the adult female exposed to androgens during the critical period of sexual differentiation is acyclic. An alternative hypothesis is that the clock for cyclic LH release, ovulation, and cyclic behavioral receptivity is present in adults of both sexes; females may differ from males in the coupling of the clock to the hypophysiotropic apparatus for gonadotropin secretion (cf 61) and in the feedback effects of steroids on the hypothalamic-pituitary axis. We propose that hormonally mediated changes in these functions, rather than in the clock mechanism per se, are responsible for the lack of cyclicity in adult male rats. This conclusion is based on the observations that the clock for ovulation is present on the day of birth in rats of both sexes (79) and on the general ineffectiveness of all chemical agents in changing the basic periodicity of biological clocks.

The induction of sexual receptivity in many rodents ordinarily depends on the synergistic action of estrogens and progesterone (157, 204); these hormones act on a neural substrate to promote lordosis and other species-specific components of behavioral receptivity. The extent to which circadian fluctuations in the number of central binding sites for estrogens and progesterone contribute to the time of onset of receptivity is unknown. Binding capacity may remain constant on each day of the cycle and within any given day. Significant diurnal variation in the secretion of hormones could be principally responsible for the behavioral rhythm. The rhythmicity of estrogen secretion is difficult to assess from the published records (93); however, the steady and seemingly continuous rise in estrogen secretion between vaginal diestrus and proestrus reduces the probable functional significance of any such rhythm. The dirunal variation in peripheral plasma progesterone concentrations on each day of the estrous cycle is of adrenal rather than ovarian origin

(116), and is probably of some significance in determining the onset of behavioral receptivity (178).

The data referred to above are derived mainly from studies of rats and hamsters, two spontaneously ovulating species. According to Conoway (45), this type of ovarian cycle is of restricted occurrence among mammals; induced ovulation is the more widespread phenomenon. In the reflex ovulator, ovulation is induced by copulation and occurs a fixed number of hours after mating; this could diminish the significance of photoperiodic synchronization of ovulation.

Comparatively little has been written about the synchronizing influence of illumination on daily cycles of copulation in male mammals. Beach & Levinson (21) report that male rats tested during the dark portion of a LD 12:12 cycle ejaculate much more frequently than when tested during the L phase. The peak in the male's copulation in this species coincides with the peak in the female's receptivity. Blind female rats cohabiting with blind males are not impregnated except when the female's free-running period of sexual receptivity overlaps the active phase of the male's free-running rest-activity cycle (171a).

Sadleir (174, p. 160) notes that the modal arrangement among mammals is that the male has a breeding season which overlaps that of the female; in other mammals males are fertile and capable of mating throughout the year and their female counterparts may breed continuously or have discrete breeding seasons. The significance of the males of certain species maintaining breeding capacity during the female's period of reproductive quiescence may relate to other functions of testicular hormones, as for example, in influencing aggressive behavior or population dynamics (174). For an extensive discussion of the role of environmental stimuli in establishing readiness to breed in mammals, the interested reader should consult the excellent monograph by Sadleir (174).

Sensation

What little information currently is available suggests that sensory systems undergo circadian fluctuations in sensitivity. In the crayfish (*Procambarus*) the responses of retinal photoreceptors and of central visual interneurons to repeated light flashes vary across a circadian cycle that depends on the hormonally controlled, endogenously timed migration of retinal pigments (8). Mechanoreceptors of this species also show a daily cycle of sensitivity to stimulation.

The responsiveness of the toad (*Bufo bufo*) to stimuli which mimic natural prey objects fluctuates seasonally. In summer toads emit more prey-catching responses to a light object moving against a dark background than to a dark object on a white background; in winter responsiveness to the light object is greatly reduced. Firing rates of retinal ganglion cells show parallel seasonal changes in sensitivity to these stimuli. This effect is apparently achieved by centrifugal control of the retina and accomplishes at the sensory level the behavioral changes essential to the toad's annual cycle of feeding and hibernation. The decline in responsiveness to fly-like objects as winter approaches coincides with the cessation of feeding and the animal's preparation for hibernation (61a).

Circulating levels of adrenal corticoids modify sensory thresholds of audition, taste, and vision in several mammalian species (44, 84). The well-established daily fluctuations in adrenal corticoid secretion (cf 106) encompass a sufficiently large range to measurably affect sensory thresholds in human subjects (84). Increased nocturnal sensitivity to stimuli may also account in part for the greater incidence of stimulation-induced seizures in mice (177) and rats (198) during the dark phase of the illumination cycle.

Learning and Memory

The discovery of a time-sense in bees was one of the first demonstrations of a circadian organization of learning and memory (197). Bees can be trained to return to a particular site at a specific time of day; once trained they return to the food site at approximately 24 hr intervals. They can learn to fly to several different sites to selectively obtain food at different times of day but cannot be trained to return to a given location at long intervals that differ substantially from 24 hr (37, p. 160). Such temporal constraints on learning are also evident in rats restricted to feeding for one hour per day. When maintained on a 24 hr illumination cycle (LD 12:12) these animals increase their activity in anticipation of the daily feeding (29); they do not show activity in anticipation of feedings given at 19 hr or 29 hr intervals, even if raised from birth on 19 and 29 hr illumination cycles (29).

A starling was trained at a fixed time of day to obtain food in a circular arena from the one feeding dish among 12 that lay in the direction of the sun. When tested at other times of day the bird did not simply fly towards a feeder in the direction of the sun, but compensated for the sun's movement and flew to a feeder in the same compass direction to which it had been trained. Thus the starling did not readily learn a simple assocation of food with a salient environmental stimulus (the sun), but rather learned a complex rule about the direction of food availability relative to the sun's position and its own internal clock (89, 104a).

Rats acquire and retain passive avoidance tasks more readily at some times of day than at others (50). Regardless of the actual clock time of training, performance of active and passive avoidance behaviors is best 24 hr after training and at multiples of 24 hr (48 and 72 hr). Retention is also fairly good at 12 hr multiples after training and very poor at intermediate times (91, 92). These effects are independent of the actual time of day at which original training takes place. Apparently, rats tested in passive and active avoidance tasks learn not only a spatial relation, i.e. that a particular area is safe or dangerous for them, but also when the area has these properties. The apparent temporal coding of such learning has only become evident within the past few years and adds an entirely new dimension to the interpretation of learning phenomena (cf 91, 92).

The circadian involvement in learning is advantageous in that it permits bees to visit flowers only during the limited periods each day when the latter secrete nectar. For rats the temporal modulation of what is learned may serve to increase the plasticity of behavior. An animal need not universally avoid the place where it was frightened or driven off by a competitor; it can return regularly at another time of day when the competitor is absent and feed unmolested (cf 40).

CONCLUSIONS

The importance of the temporal organization of behavior is difficult to overestimate. In nature a premium is placed on animals performing responses at appropriate times of the day and seasons of the year. We have tried to indicate the central role of biological clocks in the integration of the animal's internal milieu and in the synchronization of these functions and of behavior to environmental periodicities.

Biological clocks are inherited (69, 172), manifested in the adult animal independently of specific postnatal "learning" experiences (150), and provide the substrate for the inherent rhythmicity of most animal behavior. The treatment of living animals and their behavior as steady state systems invariant across time of day has been common in many branches of psychology and biology but can no longer be justified (162). As a research strategy, ignoring biorhythmicity may confound the effects of other independent variables, or at least increase the variance associated with any given experimental procedure.

Biochronometry has much to offer psychologists in understanding behavior as a cyclic phenomenon whose periodicity serves important functions. By providing methods of analysis and a theoretical framework it gives us the tools to deal with and understand the temporal organization of behavior.

Literature Cited

1. Ader, R., Grota, L. J. 1970. Rhythmicity in the maternal behaviour of *Rattus norvegicus. Anim. Behav.* 18:144–50
2. Alleva, J. J., Waleski, M. V., Alleva, F. R. 1971. A biological clock controlling the estrous cycle of the hamster. *Endocrinology* 88:1368–79
3. Altman, J. 1962. Diurnal activity rhythms of rats with lesions of superior colliculus and visual cortex. *Am. J. Physiol.* 202:1205–7
4. Anderson, K. V., Coyle, F. P., O'Steen, W. K. 1971. Retinal degeneration produced by low intensity colored light. *Exp. Neurol.* 35:233–38
5. Anderson, K. V., O'Steen, W. K. 1972. Black-white and pattern discrimination in rats without photoreceptors. *Exp. Neurol.* 34:446–54
6. Andrews, R. V. 1969. Temporal relationships of puromycin and ACTH effects on cultured hamster adrenal glands. *Comp. Biochem. Physiol.* 30:123–28
7. Arcangeli, P., Digiesi, V., Madeddu, G., Toccafondi, R. 1973. Temporary

displacement of plasma corticoid circadian peak induced by ablation of olfactory bulbs in dog. *Experientia* 29:358–59
8. Aréchiga, H. 1974. Circadian rhythm of sensory input in the crayfish. In *The Neurosciences, Third Study Program,* ed. F. O. Schmitt, F. G. Worden, 517–23. Cambridge: MIT Press. 1107 pp.
9. Aschoff, J. 1960. Exogenous and endogenous components in circadian rhythms. *Symp. Quant. Biol.* 25:11–28
10. Aschoff, J. 1965. The phase-angle difference in circadian periodicity. In *Circadian Clocks,* ed. J. Aschoff, 262–76. Amsterdam: North-Holland. 479 pp.
11. Aschoff, J. 1966. Circadian activity pattern with two peaks. *Ecology* 47:657–62
12. Aschoff, J. 1969. Desynchronization and resynchronization of human circadian rhythms. *Aerosp. Med.* 40:844–49
13. Aschoff, J., Fatranska, M., Giedke, H.

1971. Human circadian rhythms in continuous darkness: Entrainment by social cues. *Science* 171:213–15
14. Aschoff, J., Figala, J., Poppel, E. 1973. Circadian rhythms of locomotor activity in the golden hamster (*Mesocricetus auratus*) measured with two different techniques. *J. Comp. Physiol. Psychol.* 85:20–28
15. Aschoff, J. et al 1971. Interdependent parameters of circadian activity rhythms in birds and man. See Ref. 125, 3–29
16. Aschoff, J., Klotter, K., Wever, R. 1965. Circadian vocabulary. See Ref. 10, x–xix
17. Ashby, K. R. 1972. Patterns of daily activity in mammals. *Mammal Rev.* 1:171–85
18. Balagura, S., Devenport, L. D. 1970. Feeding patterns of normal and ventromedial hypothalamic lesioned male and female rats. *J. Comp. Physiol Psychol.* 71:357–64
19. Barnes, R. H. 1957. Prevention of coprophagy in the rat. *J. Nutr.* 63:489–98
20. Baum, M. J. 1970. Light-synchronization of rat feeding rhythms following sympathectomy or pinealectomy. *Physiol. Behav.* 5:325–29
21. Beach, F. A., Levinson, G. 1949. Diurnal variation in the mating behavior of male rats. *Proc. Soc. Exp. Biol. Med.* 72:78–80
22. Bennett, M. H., Dyer, R. F., Dunn, J. D. 1973. Visual dysfunction after long-term continuous light exposure. *Exp. Neurol.* 40:652–60
22a. Bennett, M. V. L. 1972. A comparison of chemically and electrically mediated transmission. In *Structure and Function of Synapses*, ed. G. D. Pappas, D. P. Purpura, 221–56. New York: Raven. 308 pp.
23. Bernardis, L. L. 1973. Disruption of diurnal feeding and weight gain cycles in weanling rats by ventromedial and dorsomedial hypothalamic lesions. *Physiol. Behav.* 10:855–61
24. Binkley, S. 1973. Rhythm analysis of clipped data: Examples using circadian data. *J. Comp. Physiol.* 85:141–46
25. Binkley, S., Adler, K., Taylor, D. H. 1973. Two methods for using period length to study rhythmic phenomena. *J. Comp. Physiol.* 83:63–71

26. Binkley, S., Kluth, E., Menaker, M. 1971. Pineal function in sparrows: Circadian rhythms and body temperature. *Science* 174:311–14
27. Binkley, S., Kluth, E., Menaker, M. 1972. Pineal and locomotor activity. *J. Comp. Physiol.* 77:163–69
28. Bobillier, P., Mouret, J. R. 1971. The alterations of the diurnal variations of brain tryptophan, biogenic amines and 5-hydroxyindole acetic acid in the rat under limited time feeding. *Int. J. Neurosci.* 2:271–82
29. Bolles, R. C., Stokes, L. W. 1965. Rat's anticipation of diurnal and a-diurnal feeding. *J. Comp. Physiol. Psychol.* 60:290–94
30. Borbély, A. A. 1966. The influence of amphetamine on the periodic feeding behavior of the albino rat. *Brain Res.* 1:395–402
31. Borbély, A. A., Houston, J. P., Waser, P. G. 1973. Physiological and behavioral effects of parachlorophenylalanine in the rat. *Psychopharmacologia* 31:131–42
32. Brady, J. 1971. The search for an insect clock. See Ref. 125, 517–24
33. Bronson, F. H. 1962. Daily and seasonal activity patterns in woodchucks. *J. Mammal.* 43:425–27
34. Bronson, F. H. 1971. Rodent pheromones. *Biol. Reprod.* 4:344–57
35. Brown, E. B. III 1973. Changes in patterns of seasonal growth of *Microtus pennsylvanicus*. *Ecology* 54:1103–10
36. Brown-Grant, K., Davidson, J. M., Greig, F. 1973. Induced ovulation in albino rats exposed to constant light. *J. Endocrinol.* 57:7–22
37. Bünning, E. 1973. *The Physiological Clock*. New York: Springer. 258 pp.
38. Butler, J. E. M., Donovan, B. T. 1971. The effect of surgical isolation of the hypothalamus upon reproductive function in the guinea pig. *J. Endocrinol.* 50:507–14
39. Caley, D. W., Johnson, C., Liebelt, R. A. 1972. The postnatal development of the retina in the normal and rodless CBA mouse: A light and electronmicroscopic study. *Am. J. Anat.* 133:179–211
40. Calhoun, J. B. 1962. *The Ecology and Sociology of the Norway Rat*. Bethesda: USPHS. 288 pp.

41. Carleton, M. D. 1973. A survey of gross stomach morphology in New World Cricetinae (Rodentia, Muroidea), with comments on functional interpretations. *Misc. Publ. Mus. Zool. Univ. Mich.* 146:1–43

42. Cloudsley-Thompson, J. L. 1961. *Rhythmic Activity in Animal Physiology and Behaviour.* New York: Academic. 236 pp.

43. Colquhoun, W. P., Ed. 1971. *Biological Rhythms and Human Performance.* New York: Academic. 283 pp.

44. Conn, F. W., Mast, T. E. 1973. Adrenal insufficiency and electrophysiological measures of auditory sensitivity. *Am. J. Physiol.* 225:1430–36

45. Conoway, C. H. 1971. Ecological adaptation and mammalian reproduction. *Biol. Reprod.* 4:239–47

46. Conroy, R. T. W. L., Mills, J. N. 1970. *Human Circadian Rhythms.* London: Churchill. 236 pp.

47. Critchlow, V. 1963. The role of light in the neuroendocrine system. In *Advances in Neuroendocrinology,* ed. A. V. Nalbandov, 377–402. Urbana: Univ. Illinois Press

48. Cymborowski, B., Brady, J. 1972. Insect circadian rhythms transmitted by parabiosis—a re-examination. *Nature New Biol.* 236:221–22

49. Davies, J. A., Ancill, R. J., Redfern P. H. 1973. Hallucinogenic drugs and circadian rhythms. In *Biochemical and Pharmacological Mechanisms Underlying Behavior. Progr. Brain Res.* 36: 79–95

50. Davies, J. A., Navaratnam, V., Redfern, P. H. 1973. A 24-hour rhythm in passive-avoidance behaviour in rats. *Psychopharmacologia* 32:211–24

51. Davis, D. E. 1967. The annual rhythm of fat deposition in woodchucks (*Marmota monax*). *Physiol. Zool.* 40: 391–402

52. Davis, G. J., Meyer, R. K. 1973. Seasonal variation in LH and FSH of bilaterally castrated snowshoe hares. *Gen. Comp. Endocrinol.* 20:61–68

53. Deguchi, T., Axelrod, J. 1972. Control of circadian change of serotonin N-acetyltransferase activity in the pineal organ by the β-adrenergic receptor. *Proc. Nat. Acad. Sci.* 69:2547–50

54. Dowse, H. B., Palmer, J. D. 1972. The chronomutagenic effect of deuterium oxide on the period and entrainment of a biological rhythm. *Biol. Bull.* 143: 513–24

55. Dunn, J., Dyer, R., Bennett, M. 1972. Diurnal variation in plasma corticosterone following long-term exposure to continuous illumination. *Endocrinology* 90:1660–63

56. Eichler, V. B., Moore, R. Y. 1974. The primary and accessory optic systems in the golden hamster, *Mesocricetus auratus. Acta Anat.* In press

57. Elliott, J. A., Stetson, M. H., Menaker, M. 1972. Regulation of testis function in golden hamsters: A circadian clock measures photoperiodic time. *Science* 178:771–73

58. Enright, J. T. 1971. The internal clock of drunken isopods. *Z. Vergl. Physiol.* 75:332–46

59. Eskin, A. 1974. Circadian rhythmicity in the isolated eye of *Aplysia*: Mechanisms of entrainment. See Ref. 8, 531–35

60. Evans, H. L., Ghiselli, W. B., Patton, R. A. 1973. Diurnal rhythm in behavioral effects of methamphetamine, p-chloromethamphetamine and scopolamine. *J. Pharmacol. Exp. Ther.* 186:10–17

61. Everett, J. W. 1972. Brain, pituitary gland, and the ovarian cycle. *Biol. Reprod.* 6:3–12

61a. Ewert, J.-P., Siefert, G. 1974. Neuronal correlates of seasonal changes in contrast-detection of prey catching behaviour in toads (*Bufo bufo* L.). *Vision Res.* 14:431–32

62. Farner, D. S. 1970. Predictive functions in the control of annual cycles. *Environ. Res.* 3:119–31

63. Farner, D. S. 1971. Discussion. See Ref. 125, 426–27

64. Feigen, R. D., Beisel, W. R., Wannemacher, R. W. 1971. Rhythmicity of plasma amino acids and relation to dietary intake. *Am. J. Clin. Nutr.* 24:329–41

65. Ferguson, D. J., Visscher, M. B., Halberg, F., Levy, L. M. 1957. Effects of hypophysectomy on daily temperature variation in C_3H mice. *Am. J. Physiol.* 190:235–38

66. Fibiger, H. C., Campbell, B. A. 1971. The effect of para-chlorophenylalanine on spontaneous locomotor activ-

ity in the rat. *Neuropharmacology* 10: 25–32

67. Finger, F. W. 1969. Estrus and general activity in the rat. *J. Comp. Physiol. Psychol.* 68:461–66

68. Fishman, R., Roffwarg, H. P. 1971. REM sleep inhibition by light in the albino rat. *Exp. Neurol.* 36:166–78

69. Folk, G. E. Jr. 1966. *Introduction to Environmental Physiology.* Philadelphia: Lea & Febiger. 321 pp.

70. Ganong, W. F., Shepard, M. D., Wall, J. R., Van Brunt, E. E., Clegg, M. T. 1963. Penetration of light into the brain of mammals. *Endocrinology* 72: 962–63

71. Gordon, S. A., Brown, G. A. 1971. Circadian temperature rhythms in *Perognathus penicillatus.* See Ref. 125, 363–71

72. Gorski, R. A. 1971. Gonadal hormones and the perinatal development of neuroendocrine function. In *Frontiers of Neuroendocrinology*, ed. L. Martini, W. F. Ganong, 237–90. New York: Oxford Univ. Press. 419 pp.

73. Goss, R. J. 1969. Photoperiodic control of antler cycles in deer. II. Alterations in amplitude. *J. Exp. Zool.* 171:223–34

74. Greer, M. A., Panton, P., Allen, C. F. 1972. Relationship of nycthemeral cycles of running activity and plasma corticosterone concentration following basal hypothalamic isolation. *Horm. Behav.* 3:289–95

75. Grodziński, W. 1963. Seasonal changes in the circadian activity of small rodents. *Ekol. Polska* B9:3–17

75a. Gwinner, E. 1974. Testosterone induced "splitting" of circadian locomotor activity rhythms in birds. *Science* 185:72–74

76. Halász, B. 1969. The endocrine effects of isolation of the hypothalamus from the rest of the brain. See Ref. 72, 307–42

77. Hamner, W. M. 1971. On seeking an alternative to the endogenous reproductive rhythm hypothesis in birds. See Ref. 125, 448–61

78. Hansson, L. 1972. Seasonal changes in physiology and nutrition of herbivorous small rodents. *Aquilo Ser. Zool.* 13:53–55

79. Harris, G. W. 1964. Sex hormones,

brain development and brain function. *Endocrinology* 75:627–48

80. Hayden, P., Lindberg, R. G. 1969. Circadian rhythm in mammalian body temperature entrained by cyclic pressure changes. *Science* 165:1288–89

81. Hayhow, W. H., Sefton, A., Webb, C. 1962. Primary optic centers of the rat in relation to the terminal distribution of the crossed and uncrossed optic fibers. *J. Comp. Neurol.* 118:295–322

82. Heller, H. C., Poulson, T. L. 1970. Circannian rhythms. II. Endogenous and exogenous factors controlling reproduction and hibernation in chipmunks (*Eutamias*) and ground squirrels (*Spermophilus*). *Comp. Biochem. Physiol.* 33:357–83

83. Hendrickson, A. E., Wagoner, N., Cowan, W. M. 1972. An autoradiographic and electron microscopic study of retino-hypothalmic connections. *Z. Zellforsch.* 135:1–26

84. Henkin, R. I. 1970. The effect of corticosteroids and ACTH on sensory systems. In *Pituitary, Adrenal and the Brain*, ed. D. DeWied, J. A. W. M. Weijnen, 270–94. Amsterdam: Elsevier, 357 pp.

85. Héry, F., Rouer, E., Glowinski, J. 1973. Effect of 6-hydroxydopamine on daily variations of 5-HT synthesis in the hypothalamus of the rat. *Brain Res.* 58:135–46

86. Hirsch, E. 1973. Some determinants of intake and patterns of feeding in the guinea pig. *Physiol. Behav.* 11: 687–704

87. Hobbs, S. H., Miller, C. R., Bunnell, B. N., Peacock, L. J. 1972. General activity in hamsters with septal lesions. *Physiol. Behav.* 9:349–52

88. Hoffmann, K. 1965. Overt circadian frequencies and circadian rule. See Ref. 10, 87–94

89. Ibid. Clock mechanisms in celestial orientation of animals, 426–41

90. Hoffmann, K. 1971. Splitting of the circadian rhythm as a function of light intensity. See Ref. 125, 134–46

91. Holloway, F. A., Wansley, R. A. 1973. Multiphasic retention deficits at periodic intervals after passive avoidance learning. *Science* 180:208–10

92. Holloway, F. A., Wansley, R. A. 1973.

Multiple retention deficits at periodic intervals after active and passive avoidance learning. *Behav. Biol.* 9: 1-14

93. Hori, T., Ide, M., Miyake, T. 1968. Ovarian estrogen secretion during the estrous cycle and under the influence of exogenous gonadotropins in rats. *Endocrinol. Jap.* 15:215-22

94. Jacklet, J. W. 1973. The circadian rhythm in the eye of *Aplysia. J. Comp. Physio.* 87:329-38

95. Jacklet, J. W., Geronimo, J. 1971. Circadian rhythm: Population of interacting neurons. *Science* 174:299-302

96. Johnson, E. 1972. Moulting cycles. *Mammal. Rev.* 1:198-208

97. Johnson, J. H., Terkel, J., Whitmoyer, D. I., Sawyer, C. H. 1971. A circadian rhythm in the multipleunit activity (MUA) of preoptic neurons in the female rat. *Anat. Rec.* 169:348

98. Johnson, J. T., Levine, S. 1973. Influence of water deprivation on adrenocortical rhythms. *Neuroendocrinology* 11:268-73

99. Kakolewski, J. W., Deaux, E., Christensen, J., Case, B. 1971. Diurnal patterns in water and food intake and body weight changes in rats with hypothalamic lesions. *Am. J. Physiol.* 221:711-18

100. Kavanau, J. L. 1968. Activity and orientational responses of white-footed mice to light. *Nature* 218:245-52

101. Kavanau, J. L. 1969. Influences of light on activity of small mammals. *Ecology* 50:548-57

102. Kavanau, J. L., Ramos, J., Havenhill, R. M. 1973. Compulsory regime and control of environment in animal behaviour. II. Light level preference of carnivores. *Behaviour* 46:279-99

103. Kawakami, M., Terasawa, E., Ibuki, T. 1970. Changes in multiple unit activity of the brain during the estrous cycle. *Neuroendocrinology* 6:30-48

104. Kleitman, N. 1963. *Sleep and Wakefulness.* Chicago: Univ. Chicago Press

104a. Kramer, C. 1952. Experiments on bird orientation. *Ibis* 94:265-85

105. Krieg, W. J. S. 1932. The hypothalamus of the albino rat. *J. Comp. Neurol.* 55:19-89

106. Krieger, D. T. 1973. Effect of ocular enucleation and altered lighting regimes at various ages on the circadian periodicity of plasma corticosteroid levels in the rat. *Endocrinology* 93: 1077-91

107. Krieger, D. T., Krieger, H. P. 1967. Circadian patterns of urinary electrolyte excretion in central nervous system disease. *Metabolism* 16:815-23

107a. Lehrman, D. S. 1961. Hormonal regulation of parental behavior in birds and infrahuman mammals. See Ref. 204, 1268-1382

108. LeMagnen, J., Devos, M. 1970. Metabolic correlates of the meal onset in the free food intake of rats. *Physiol. Behav.* 5:805-14

109. Lengvári, I., Halász, B. 1973. Evidence for a diurnal fluctuation in plasma corticosterone after fornix transection in the rat. *Neuroendocrinology* 11: 191-96

110. Liebelt, R. A., Perry, J. 1967. Action of goldthioglucose on the central nervous system. In *Handbook of Physiology*, sect. 6, *Alimentary Canal* 1:271-86

111. Lin, H., Ingram, W. R. 1972. Probable absence of connections between the retina and the hypothalamus in the cat. *Exp. Neurol.* 37:23-36

112. Loher, W. 1972. Circadian control of stridulation in the cricket *Teleogryllus commodus* Walker. *J. Comp. Physiol.* 79:173-90

113. Luce, G. G. 1970. *Biological Rhythms in Psychiatry and Medicine.* Chevy Chase: NIMH

114. Lutton, C. L., Chevallier, F. 1973. Coprophagie chez le rat blanc. *J. Physiol.* (Paris) 66:219-28

115. Lynch, G. S. 1970. Separable forebrain systems controlling different manifestations of spontaneous activity. *J. Comp. Physiol. Psychol.* 70:48-59

116. Mann, D. R., Barraclough, C. A. 1973. Changes in peripheral plasma progesterone during the rat 4-day estrous cycle: An adrenal diurnal rhythm. *Proc. Soc. Exp. Biol. Med.* 142:1226-29

117. Margules, D. L., Lewis, M. J., Dragovich, J. A., Margules, A. S. 1972. Hypothalamic norepinephrine: Circadian rhythms and the control of feeding behavior. *Science* 178:640-42

118. McClintock, M. K. 1971. Menstrual

synchrony and suppression. *Nature* 229:244-45

119. McGuire, R. A., Rand, W. M., Wurtman, R. J. 1973. Entrainment of the body temperature rhythm in rats: Effect of color and intensity of environmental light. *Science* 181:956-57

119a. McLaughlin, G. R., Liversidge, R. 1958. *Roberts Birds of South Africa.* Cape Town: Cape Times Ltd. 504 pp.

120. Meier, A. H. 1973. Daily hormone rhythms in the white-throated sparrow. *Am. Sci.* 61:184-87

121. Meier, A. H., Dusseau, J. W. 1973. Daily entrainment of the photoinducible phases for photostimulation of the reproductive system in the sparrows, *Zonotrichia albicollis* and *Passer domesticus. Biol. Reprod.* 8:400-10

122. Meier, A. H. et al 1973. Daily variations in the effects of handling on fat storage and testicular weights in several vertebrates. *J. Exp. Zool.* 184:281-88

123. Meier, R. E. 1973. Autoradiographic evidence for a direct retino-hypothalamic projection in the avian brain. *Brain Res.* 53:417-21

124. Menaker, M. 1969. Biological clocks. *Bioscience* 19:681-92

125. Menaker, M., Ed. 1971. *Biochronometry.* Washington: Nat. Acad. Sci. 662 pp.

126. Menaker, M. 1971. Rhythms, reproduction and photoreception. *Biol. Reprod.* 4:295-308

127. Menaker, M. 1974. Aspects of the physiology of circadian rhythmicity in the vertebrate nervous system. See Ref. 8, 479-89

128. Menaker, M., Eskin, A. 1966. Entrainment of circadian rhythms by sound in *Passer domesticus. Science* 154:1579-81

129. Mitler, M. M., Sokolove, P. G., Pittendrigh, C. S., Dement, W. C. 1973. Activity-inactivity and wakefulness-sleep rhythms in the hamster under three lighting conditions. *Sleep Res.* 2:189

130. Moore, R. Y. 1973. Retinohypothalamic projection in mammals: A comparative study. *Brain Res.* 49:403-9

131. Moore, R. Y. 1974. Visual pathways and the central neural control of diurnal rhythms. See Ref. 8, 537-42

132. Moore, R. Y., Eichler, V. B. 1972. Loss of a circadian adrenal corticosterone rhythm following suprachiasmatic lesions in the rat. *Brain Res.* 42:201-6

133. Morgan, W. W., McFadin, L. S., Harvey, C. Y. 1973. A daily rhythm in norepinephrine content in regions of the hamster brain. *Comp. Gen. Pharmacol.* 4:47-52

134. Mouret, J. R., Bobillier, P. 1971. Diurnal rhythms of sleep in the rat: Augmentation of paradoxical sleep following alterations of the feeding schedule. *Int. J. Neurosci.* 2:265-70

135. Mrosovsky, N. 1971. *Hibernation and the Hypothalamus.* New York: Appleton-Century-Crofts. 287 pp.

136. Mrosovsky, N., Lang, K. 1971. Disturbances in the annual weight and hibernation cycles of thirteen-lined ground squirrels kept in constant conditions and the effects of temperature changes. *J. Interdisciplinary Cycle Res.* 2:79-90

137. Nauta, W. J. H., Haymaker, W. 1969. Hypothalamic nuclei and fiber connections. In *The Hypothalamus,* ed. W. Haymaker, E. Anderson, W. J. H. Nauta, 136-209. Springfield: Thomas

138. Nelson, W., Cadotte, L., Halberg, F. 1973. Circadian timing of single daily "meal" affects survival of mice. *Proc. Soc. Exp. Biol. Med.* 144:766-69

139. Norman, R. L., Blake, C. A., Sawyer, C. H. 1973. Estrogen-dependent twenty-four hour periodicity in pituitary LH release in the female hamster. *Endocrinology* 93:965-70

140. Njus, D., Sulzman, F. M., Hastings, J. W. 1974. Membrane model for the circadian clock. *Nature* 248:116-20

141. Oatley, K. 1971. Dissociation of the circadian drinking pattern from eating. *Nature* 229:494-96

142. Orth, D. N., Island, D. P. 1969. Light synchronization of the circadian rhythm in plasma cortisol (17-OHCS) concentration in man. *J. Clin. Endocrinol. Metab.* 29:479-86

143. O'Steen, W. K., Anderson, K. V. 1971. Photically evoked responses in the visual system of rats exposed to continuous light. *Exp. Neurol.* 30:525-34

144. Ostwald, R. et al 1972. Influence of

photoperiod and partial contact on estrus in the desert pocket mouse, *Perognathus penicillatus*. *Biol. Reprod.* 7:1–8

145. Owings, D. H., Lockard, R. B. 1971. Different nocturnal activity patterns of *Peromyscus californicus* and *Peromyscus eremicus* in lunar lighting. *Psychon. Sci.* 22:63–64

146. Page, R. B., Galicich, J. H., Grunt, J. A. 1973. Alteration of circadian temperature rhythm with third ventricular obstruction. *J. Neurosurg.* 38:309–19

147. Panksepp, J. 1973. Reanalysis of feeding patterns in the rat. *J. Comp. Physiol. Psychol.* 82:78–94

148. Pavlidis, T. 1973. *Biological Oscillators: Their Mathematical Analysis.* New York: Academic. 207 pp.

149. Pengelley, E. T., Asmundson, S. J. 1972. An analysis of the mechanisms by which mammalian hibernators synchronize their behavioral physiology with the environment. In *Hibernation and Hypothermia, Perspectives and Challenges*, ed. F. E. South, J. P. Hannon, J. R. Willis, E. T. Pengelley, N. R. Alpert, 637–61. Amsterdam: Elsevier

150. Pittendrigh, C. S. 1960–61. On temporal organization in living systems. *Harvey Lect. Ser.* 56:93–125

151. Pittendrigh, C. S. 1972. Circadian surfaces and the diversity of possible roles of circadian organization in photoperiodic induction. *Proc. Nat. Acad. Sci.* 69:2734–37

152. Pittendrigh, C. S. 1974. Circadian oscillations in cells and the circadian organization of multicellular systems. See Ref. 8, 437–58

153. Pittendrigh, C. S., Caldarola, P. C. 1973. General homeostasis of the frequency of circadian oscillations. *Proc. Nat. Acad. Sci.* 70:2697–2701

154. Pittendrigh, C. S., Caldarola, P. C., Cosbey, E. S. 1973. A differential effect of heavy water on temperature-dependent and temperature-independent aspects of the circadian system of *Drosophila pseudoobscura*. *Proc. Nat. Acad. Sci.* 70:2037–41

155. Pittendrigh, C. S., Eichhorn, J. H., Minis, D. H., Bruce, V. G. 1970. Circadian systems. VI. Photoperiodic time mea-surement in *Pectinophora gossypiella*. *Proc. Nat. Acad. Sci.* 66:758–64

156. Pittendrigh, C. S., Minis, D. H. 1972. Circadian systems: Longevity as a function of circadian resonance in *Drosophila melanogaster*. *Proc. Nat. Acad. Sci.* 69:1537–39

157. Powers, J. B. 1970. Hormonal control of sexual receptivity during the estrous cycle of the rat. *Physiol. Behav.* 5:831–35

158. Psalm 104:19–23

159. Quartermain, D., Kissileff, H., Shapiro, R., Miller, N. E. 1971. Suppression of food intake with intragastric loading: Relation to natural feeding cycle. *Science* 173:941–43

160. Quay, W. B. 1970. Precocious entrainment and associated characteristics of activity patterns following pinealectomy and reversal of photoperiod. *Physiol. Behav.* 5:1281–90

161. Rawson, K. S. 1960. Effects of tissue temperature on mammalian activity rhythms. *Symp. Quant. Biol.* 25:105–13

162. Reinberg, A., Halberg, F. 1971. Circadian chronopharmacology. *Ann. Rev. Pharmacol.* 11:455–92

163. Reiter, R. J. 1972. Evidence for refractoriness of the pituitary-gonadal axis to the pineal gland in golden hamsters and its possible implications in annual reproductive rhythms. *Anat. Rec.* 173:365–72

164. Reiter, R. J. 1973. Comparative physiology: Pineal gland. *Ann. Rev. Physiol.* 35:305–28

165. Reiter, R. J. 1973. Pineal control of a seasonal reproductive rhythm in male golden hamsters exposed to natural daylight and temperature. *Endocrinology* 92:423–30

166. Reiter, R. J. 1973. Comparative effects of continual lighting and pinealectomy on the eyes, the harderian glands and reproduction in pigmented and albino rats. *Comp. Biochem. Physiol.* 44A:503–9

167. Reiter, R. J., Klein, D. C. 1971. Observations on the pineal gland, the harderian glands, the retina, and the reproductive organs of adult female rats exposed to continuous light. *J. Endocrinol.* 51:117–25

168. Reiter, R. J., Sorrentino, S., Hoffman,

R. A. 1970. Early photoperiodic conditions and pineal antigonadal function in male hamsters. *Int. J. Fertil.* 15:163-70

169. Richards, M. P. M. 1966. Activity measured by running wheels and observations during the oestrous cycle, pregnancy and pseudopregnancy in the golden hamster. *Anim. Behav.* 14:450-58

170. Richter, C. P. 1965. *Biological Clocks in Medicine and Psychiatry.* Springfield: Thomas. 108 pp.

171. Richter, C. P. 1967. Sleep and activity: Their relation to the 24-hour clock. *Proc. Assoc. Res. Nerv. Ment. Dis.* 45:8-27

171a. Richter, C. P. 1970. Dependence of successful mating in rats on functioning of the 24-hour clocks of the male and female. *Comm. Behav. Biol.* (A) 5:1-5

172. Richter, C. P. 1971. Inborn nature of the rat's 24-hour clock. *J. Comp. Physiol. Psychol.* 75:1-4

173. Rusak, B., Zucker, I. 1974. Fluid intake of rats in constant light and during feeding restricted to the light or dark portion of the illumination cycle. *Physiol. Behav.* 13:91-100

174. Sadleir, R. M. F. S. 1969. *The Ecology of Reproduction in Wild and Domestic Mammals.* London: Methuen. 321 pp.

175. Scheving, L. E., Vedral, D. F., Pauly, J. E. 1968. Daily circadian rhythm in rats to *D*-amphetamine sulphate: Effect of blinding and continuous illumination on the rhythm. *Nature* 219:621-22

176. Schmitt, M. 1973. Circadian rhythmicity in responses of cells in the lateral hypothalamus. *Am. J. Physiol.* 225:1096-1101

177. Schreiber, R. A., Schlesinger, K. 1972. Circadian rhythms and seizure susceptibility: Effects of manipulations of light cycles on susceptibility to audiogenic seizures and on levels of 5-hydroxytryptamine and norepinephrine in brain. *Physiol. Behav.* 8:699-703

178. Schwartz, N. B. 1969. A model for the regulation of ovulation in the rat. *Recent Progr. Horm. Res.* 25:1-55

179. Shashoua, W. E. 1973. Seasonal changes in the learning and activity

patterns of goldfish. *Science* 181:572-74

180. Sidman, R. L., Green, M. C., Appel, S. H. 1965. *Catalog of the Neurological Mutants of the Mouse.* Cambridge: Harvard Univ. Press. 82 pp.

181. Snyder, F. 1969. Sleep and REM as biological enigmas. In *Sleep, Physiology and Pathology*, ed. A. Kales, 266-80. Philadelphia: Lippincott

182. Sorenson, C. A., Ellison, G. D. 1973. Nonlinear changes in activity and emotional reactivity scores following central noradrenergic lesions in rats. *Psychopharmacologia* 32:313-25

183. Spalding, J. F., Holland, L. M., Tietjen, G. L. 1969. Influence of the visible color spectrum on activity in mice. *Lab. Anim. Care* 19:50-54

184. Stebbins, L. L. 1971. Seasonal variations in circadian rhythms of deer mice in northwestern Canada. *Arctic* 24:124-31

185. Ibid 1972. Seasonal and latitudinal variations in circadian rhythms of red-backed vole. 25:216-24

186. Stephan, F. K., Zucker, I. 1972. Circadian rhythms in drinking behavior and locomotor activity of rats are eliminated by hypothalamic lesions. *Proc. Nat. Acad. Sci.* 69:1583-86

187. Stephan, F. K., Zucker, I. 1972. Rat drinking rhythms: Central visual pathways and endocrine factors mediating responsiveness to environmental illumination. *Physiol. Behav.* 8:315-26

188. Stephan, F. K., Zucker, I. 1974. Endocrine and neural mediation of the effects of constant light on water intake of rats. *Neuroendocrinology* 14:44-60

189. Strumwasser, F. 1974. Neuronal principles organizing periodic behaviors. See Ref. 8, 459-78

190. Swanson, L. W., Cowan, W. M., Jones, E. G. 1974. An autoradiographic study of the efferent connections of the ventral lateral geniculate nucleus in the albino rat and the cat. *J. Comp. Neurol.* 156:143-64

191. ter Haar, M. B. 1972. Circadian and estrual rhythms in food intake in the rat. *Horm. Behav.* 3:213-19

192. Truman, J. W. 1971. The role of the brain in the ecdysis rhythm of silkmoths: Comparison with the photo-

periodic termination of diapause. See Ref. 125, 483–501

193. Turner, B. N., Iverson, S. L. 1973. The annual cycle of aggression in *Microtus pennsylvanicus*, and its relation to population parameters. *Ecology* 54: 967–81

194. Vaughan, T. A. 1972. *Mammalogy*. Philadelphia: Saunders. 463 pp.

195. Vessey, S. H. 1973. Night observations of free-ranging rhesus monkeys. *Am. J. Phys. Anthropol.* 38:613–20

196. Vilchez, C. A., Echave Llanos, J. M. 1971. Circadian rhythm in the feeding activity of *Oxymycterus rutilans*: Role played by light and food availability. *J. Interdisciplinary Cycle Res.* 2:73–77

197. von Frisch, K. 1971. *Bees*. Ithaca: Cornell Univ. Press. 157 pp.

198. Wada, J. A., Asakura, T. 1970. Circadian alteration of audiogenic seizure susceptibility in rats. *Exp. Neurol.* 29:211–14

199. Webb, W. B. 1971. Sleep behaviour as a biorhythm. See Ref. 43, 149–77

200. Wever, R. 1965. A mathematical model for circadian rhythms. See Ref. 10, 47–63

201. Ibid. Pendulum versus relaxation oscillation, 74–83

202. Wever, R. 1971. Influence of electric fields on some parameters of circadian rhythms in man. See Ref. 125, 117–32

202a. Williams, H. L., Holloway, F. A.,

Griffiths, W. J. 1973. Physiological psychology: Sleep. *Ann. Rev. Psychol.* 24:279–316

203. Winget, C. M., Vernikos-Danellis, J., Sakellaris, P. C. 1973. Noradrenergic control of circadian rhythms in *Cebus albifrons*. *Am. J. Phys. Anthropol.* 38:331–38

204. Young, W. C. 1961. The hormones and mating behaviour. In *Sex and Internal Secretions*, ed. W. C. Young, 1173–1239. Baltimore: Williams & Wilkins

205. Zimmerman, W. F., Goldsmith, T. H. 1971. Photosensitivity of the circadian rhythm and of visual receptors in carotenoid-depleted *Drosophila*. *Science* 171:1167–69

206. Zucker, I. 1971. Light-dark rhythms in rat eating and drinking behavior. *Physiol. Behav.* 6:115–26

206a. Zucker, I., Rusak, B., King, R. G. Jr. 1975. Neural bases for circadian rhythms in rodent behavior. In *Advances in Psychobiology*, ed. G. Newton, A. H. Riesen. New York: Wiley

207. Zucker, I., Stephan, F. K. 1973. Light-dark rhythms in hamster eating, drinking, and locomotor behaviors. *Physiol. Behav.* 11:239–50

208. Zweig, M., Snyder, S. H., Axelrod, J. 1966. Evidence for a nonretinal pathway of light to the pineal gland of newborn rats. *Proc. Nat. Acad. Sci.* 56:515–19

THINKING AND CONCEPT ATTAINMENT

§231

Edith D. Neimark[1] and John L. Santa

Douglass College, Rutgers University
New Brunswick, New Jersey 08903

INTRODUCTION

This review draws upon available work in English published during the period 1970 through 1973. The reference list was derived from two computer searches (Medline and Compfile), *Psychological Abstracts*, and the contents of relevant major journals for the 4 year period. The resulting yield was much too large to be included in this review. A more compelling argument for selectivity and evaluation stems from the state of the field itself: it is diffuse, parochially compartmentalized, and lacking in comprehensive theorizing.

There is little doubt that the mind is back in style. The words "cognition" and "cognitive" occur in current literature with high frequency in such disparate areas as memory, perception, and even conditioning. The period of review has seen the appearance of three new journals: *Cognitive Psychology*, *Cognition*, and *Memory and Cognition*. But the wide currency of the term has not been free of a certain amount of devaluation; "cognition" has so many variant meanings and connotations that the remaining common core seems to be "any activity involving CNS activity between its initiation and completion." With so broad a definition there is little, save spinal-level reflex, excluded from the class. This will not, therefore, be a review of "cognition." Rather, it is a review of "thinking" in the old-fashioned sense, where "thinking" is defined as "mental transformations employing symbolic surrogates of events, objects, and processes, or properties and relations thereof."

The theoretical framework underlying research on thinking has shifted over the years. There is now very little work explicitly inspired by Gestalt theory or by

[1] This review was prepared with support from Grant No. HD–01725 from the division of Child Health and Human Development. We are grateful to A. Tallau and P. Piermatti and the reference staff of the Rutgers Library of Science and Medicine for their assistance in obtaining materials.

173

muscle-twitch behaviorism. Even work with an S-R learning orientation has declined except in the study of concept attainment, and even here the theories are becoming considerably looser. Work employing computer analog models, on the other hand, has grown considerably. Of course, the term "computer analog" covers a great deal of territory from analysis of essentially perceptual aspects of information processing to writing out specific programs for some thinking task, to a general theory of production systems. Furthermore, the jargon of information processing is widely used throughout psychology, and probably comes as close to a universal language as any currently available, although it is often invoked meta-phorically rather than used in a meaningful sense.

Although there are still a number of investigators working on the traditional problems or with the traditional techniques of problem solving and concept attainment, most recent work takes its theoretical impetus from developments outside the traditional rubric. One major influence derives from the genetic epistemology of J. Piaget (187) which, while it does provide a comprehensive general framework for the study of all aspects of thought, tends to be compart-mentalized for most English-speaking psychologists into developmental psychol-ogy. Another major source of problems and theory stems from the area of psycholinguistics. Finally, there is a good deal of relevant input from the field of psychological testing (which space limitations do not permit us to cover). Although workers within each of these specialized frameworks are often engaged in similar research, they seem unaware of each others' efforts. One hesitates to invoke the tired analogy of the blind men and the elephant but it is certainly apt. In the interest of advancement of clear-sighted elephant exploration, the review which follows will be organized in terms of content area rather than theoretical orienta-tion.

MONOGRAPHS AND GENERAL SURVEYS

One indication of sustained interest in the area of thinking is the recent appear-ance of a number of textbook surveys which vary in breadth and depth of coverage and in relative weighting of theory or data. The most extensive of these in terms of coverage of the research literature is Johnson's (114) restructured and updated revision of his popular text. Manis (153) and Gardiner (77) each range widely in a broad and readable overview of disparate areas. Bolton (14) also offers an eclectic survey, organized with respect to theory rather than with respect to research content. Pollio (191) focuses more narrowly upon what he calls "symbolic activi-ty," while Bourne, Ekstrand & Dominowski (18) concentrate upon problem solv-ing, concept attainment, verbal learning, and language.

A number of monographs, some of which will be discussed in later sections of this review, have appeared. Foremost among these is the long-awaited book by Newell & Simon (176) on human problem solving. Other works on problem solving with a much more applied practical focus are a series of exercises to develop visual thinking (157), a review of educational and industrial applications (44), and a computer simulation of selected aspects of thought (42). In a class by itself is Razran's (197) heroic attempt to fit thought into an evolutionary perspective.

Three volumes which bring together scattered works have appeared: notes from Wertheimer's seminars (149), Maier's (151) collection of his own research papers, and a monograph in which Wason & Johnson-Laird (259) review and integrate a number of research studies conducted by them with their colleagues and students over the years. Finally, a translation of A. N. Sokolov's book on internal speech and thought (240) has appeared.

PROBLEM SOLVING

Interest in this area appears to be declining. Much of the research on problem solving proceeds at a deadening low level of empiricism: choose a problem, any problem, and see what variables affect it, in what way. Traditional problems seem to be chosen for the same reason that mountains are climbed, because they are there. Except possibly among test constructors, there is almost no prior analysis of what aspects of problem solving are to be isolated for scrutiny, why they are of special interest, or how best to analyze their role in relation to that of other behaviors. There is insufficient concern with validity of tasks, generality of findings, or whether independent variables affect the thought process rather than the context of performance. Admittedly some of these judgments presuppose the existence of a theory, and good general theories of problem solving are not in abundant supply; even a serviceable taxonomy of problems is lacking.

Insight Problems

The insight problem, cherished by Gestalt theory, emphasizes the role of perceptual restructuring in problem solving. Typical examples are Maier's two-string or coat rack problems, Duncker's candlestick problem, and the problems used by Köhler with his apes. Beck (7) reports on cooperative tool use in hamadryas baboon. Food placed outside the cage and out of reach could be obtained by use of an L-shaped stick not directly accessible to a large male who had demonstrated tool use prior to the start of the study. He could get the tool only through help of another smaller animal. After the first few trials the tool was fetched by a cooperative female, who, interestingly enough, never directly used the tool herself. Nor did any other animals in the cages appear to learn from imitation. Among chimpanzees, on the other hand, Menzel (159) reports that discovery that a pole could serve as a ladder was not only imitated but also widely generalized on a variety of occasions.

Work with human Ss has been concerned with factors promoting solution. Three studies examined the role of incubation. Murray & Denny (166) speculated that the facilatory effect of time away from the task would be a function of problem difficulty and/or the subject's ability (facilitation from a 5 minute break should occur for harder problems and low ability Ss). They found that more low ability Ss solved with a 5 minute interruption followed by 15 minutes on problem than solved on 20 minutes of continuous effort; for high ability the reverse was true. It was suggested that interruption facilitated by weakening interference, but protocols were not analyzed for direct evidence of this. Dominowski & Jenrick (50) repeated the experiment with an additional independent variable (hint as to solution) and a different problem but did not replicate the finding. However, the meaning of incubation was a bit ambiguous since S was not forewarned that he would return to work on the problem. Fulgosi & Guilford (70) varied both duration of interruption and presence or absence of forewarning; the latter had no effect upon solutions to a divergent thinking task whereas the former did. A longer interruption led to more, but not necessarily better, solutions.

Other research on insight problems has been concerned with sources of difficulty (152), effect of hints (25), relative availability of potential solutions (11, 96, 261) and transfer from various types of training (245). Each study demonstrated effectiveness of the independent variables investigated except the first, which used 2 different orders of each of 6 insight problems on a total of 544 subjects. The authors attribute their finding to differences among individuals as to what constitutes a source of difficulty for a given problem.

Anagram and Other Word Problems

As might be expected in an area as old and well established as anagram problem solving, there are no startling new developments. Most research is concerned with clarifying interactions among established variables (52, 80, 231, 257), refining indexes of performance (215), or for prediction thereof (80, 231); or proposing possible new independent variables associated with the task (113, 139, 241) or with the subject (138, 144, 158). Norms for solution frequency for multisolution five-letter anagrams with three to seven solutions have been reported (101).

One interesting and promising line of investigation takes variables such as priming or word imagery, whose effect has been explored in a verbal learning context, to search for similar effects on the anagram task; Jablonski & Mueller (113) found remarkably little effect of both these variables. A similar approach has been employed in exploring the effect of associationist variables upon related word problems such as predicting a hierarchy (51), filling in blanks (246), and analogy problems (82, 194) with predicted effects observed.

Mathematical Problem Solving

Use of mathematics problems as a vehicle for study of problem solving is quite common in East European literature which, with few exceptions (9, 10) is unavailable in English. Work under this general rubric ranges from studies possessing some direct application to education (35, 54, 146, 192, 242) to models for limited aspects of basic operations (1, 12, 93, 94, 180, 181, 185, 200) to theoretically oriented consideration of the foundations of number (21, 81), rules (218), and functions (103). The models for basic computational operations attempt to predict the time required for S to perform addition (92), subtraction (94), or multiplication (180) of single digit quantities m and n as a function of the relative magnitudes of the two quantities. Although research designed to test these models is well conceived and executed, it does not provide resounding support of the model; nor is it clear how the model would be extended to more complex problems. An alternative analog model for addition proposed by Restle (200), which is not limited to single digit value and sums, was not supported by the findings of Aiken (1). It is not clear why one should expect a computer analog model for these simple, highly overlearned operations to apply; such models might be more appropriately applied to mental calculation of more complex quantitites (even by lightning calculators).

In attempting to describe the ontogenesis of number concepts, Brainerd (21) and Gelman (81), working from different orientations and different reviews of the literature, independently reached the same conclusion that ordination is the first step.

Work with Other Kinds of Problems

Although there are a number of well-known problems whose structure has been analyzed and which would seem to be strong possibilities for more intensive investigation, there turns out to be relatively little work done with most of them, e.g. the tower of Hanoi. Greeno (91) has begun some systematic effort with a version of the missionaries and cannibal problem, and Markóva (154) offers a nice analysis of the effect of task complexity upon choice of strategy in the game of NIM. A similar analysis of *Mills*, a higher order tic-tac-toe, has been done by Schiopu (219). There is also an analysis of the structure of several games along with introduction of a new one, *HALMA* (55).

Models of Problem Solving Processes

The diagnostic problem solving paradigm, by virtue of its simple structure and seeming wide generality, would seem to offer a natural starting point for construction of a descriptive model of problem solving. Moreover, there exist many computer programs for this function, e.g. medical diagnosis, which could provide a prescriptive model for comparison against human practitioners. Nevertheless, only one model for diagnostic problem solving has appeared since 1970 (131).

Unquestionably the major contribution to a general theory of problem solving is the book by Newell & Simon (176), which deals in detail with three classes of problems: cryptarithmetic (solving for a code which substitutes for letters a unique digit equivalent), developing proofs in symbolic logic through application of appropriate rules, and choosing moves in chess. Each class of problems is subjected to a task analysis, the program is introduced and data for select subjects are presented and analyzed [as Johnson (114a) has noted, with something like Freudian thoroughness] in relation to the program. All subjects are educated, articulate, skilled adults who are instructed to think aloud while solving; their protocols, supplemented in some instances by eye-camera data, constitute the major data. The essence of the theoretical treatment is that human problem solving is to be understood through a description of three major determinant classes: (*a*) the task environment in which it takes place; (*b*) the space the solver uses to represent the environment, the task, and his accumulating knowledge about it; and (*c*) the program assembled for solution. Four propositions determine the relation among the three components: 1. Only a few gross characteristics of the information processing system are invariant over task and solver. 2. These characteristics are sufficient to determine that a task environment is represented as a problem space and that solution behavior occurs there. 3. The structure of the task environment determines the possible structures of the problem space. 4. The structure of the problem space determines the possible programs that can be used for problem solving.

The Role of Memory in Problem Solving

Memory has assumed such a prominent role in theories of problem solving (91, 105), concept attainment, and thinking in general, that it is well to consider the subject in a bit more detail. Most theories assume that thought-in-process takes place in an informationally limited processing space such as short-term memory (STM) or William James' "footlights of consciousness." Other relevant information, knowledge, skills, etc are stored in a more capacious accessory, generally called long-term memory (LTM), which is in constant communication with its short-term counterpart for purposes of information transfer in either direction.

The central property of many types of problems, which causes them to be problems, is the need to order large amounts of information so they can be dealt with in a manageable way. This may be achieved by development of more efficient processing strategies, codes, chunks, or external aids; i.e. it is not clear whether one is dealing with S's memory as a knowledge state, his repertoire of solution programs, some feature of task structure, or a combination of some or all of these. Consider, for example, the problem of uniquely assigning one element from each of several property classes to a coinciding category, as in the problem posed by Fisher (67) to introduce his treatment of Latin Square. Such problems are considerably simplified, if not trivialized, by resort to a recording and ordering algorithm such as the Latin or Graeco-Latin square, as has been demonstrated by Schwartz (221, 222). Similarly, there is an accumulating body of evidence that children's utilization of information improves considerably when they are provided with an external memory aid (53, 213).

In contrast to the essentially task-property aspects of memory noted above are the subject-related aspects which differentiate the novice from the pro. These have to do with the quality of the memory code and/or the resultant chunk (but most probably the former); relevant data come from developmental studies of memory and from analysis of skilled chess players. Among the developmental evidence (136, 164, 175) the Lehman & Goodnow (136) study provides especially convincing evidence for a shift in the nature of the code for patterned pencil taps from an iconic reproduction to a more abstract digit series. Still more abstract characterizations exist among adults in dealing with serial patterns (92, 201, 202, 232). There is even some evidence (239) that systematic training improves memory skills to a limited extent. Simon and his associates (28, 233–235) have studied the memory of chess players for meaningful—as contrasted with random—positions of pieces and find very superior memory among skilled players, which is explained in terms of chunking and adequately stimulated (235) by a new program combining perceptual and learning components.

CONCEPT IDENTIFICATION

Space limitations prevent review of the background to recent work in concept identification (CI); the interested reader can consult several sources (18, 69).

Mathematical Models of CI

Bower & Trabasso's (20, 252) extension of Restle's (199) CI models provided the focal thrust of stochastic modeling in the 1960s. The initial Bower-Trabasso model (20) conceives of CI (in the single attribute paradigm) as a process of hypothesis testing. The S learns a concept by sampling a single hypothesis randomly from the set of possible attribute-value hypotheses. The hypothesis is maintained as long as it is successful and discarded following an error. After an error, S resamples from the total set of possible hypotheses (i.e. an error is a recurrent event). The model is simple and powerful but so implausible that it has generated a large research effort to modify or refute it.

First, the memory assumptions were relaxed to assume limited memory constraints on the resampling process (e.g. 252). A number of investigators (2, 41, 61) have shown that Ss exhibit some degree of local consistency, i.e. the probability of repeating the same response on a sequence of adjacent success trials is a monotonic function of the number of stimulus values preserved across adjacent trials. Such sequential effects can be predicted by a simple extension of the Bower-Trabasso model (41), but the prediction is improved by assuming one- or two-trial memory.

Next, the single hypothesis assumption was eliminated, and Ss were assumed to sample a set of working hypotheses. This set of working hypotheses was allowed to change during sequences of successes by assuming that Ss temporarily eliminated hypotheses inconsistent with the reinforcement (30, 252). This assumption of focusing on successive positive trials was dictated by data (140) suggesting an increase in probability of correct response preceding the last error, a finding at odds with the all-or-none learning axiom of Bower & Trabasso's original model. In addition, several investigators noted a decrease in latency during runs of success trials both before and after the trial of last error (TLE) (57, 61). An interesting extension of these data was provided by Fink (66), who manipulated the number of attribute values available to Ss and found a decrease in latency beyond the TLE, but only for conditions with multiple dimensions available. Fink also asked Ss to identify the point at which they felt they had solved the problem. Latencies were constant from that point on for all conditions. Perhaps Ss can be trusted to know what they are doing in CI experiments, a point with interesting implications to be considered later.

Assumptions of focusing during runs of success trials have also been supported by the analysis of several dependent measures other than latency. Coltheart (38) and Falmagne (64) both found that S's confidence in hypotheses increased as a function of successive confirmations and decreased sharply after a disconfirmation. These data can be interpreted to support the Trabasso & Bower (252) assumption of focusing on positive trials (38). Another measure which suggests focusing during success runs was obtained by counting the number of attributes Ss choose to examine while solving a CI problem. Chatfield & Janek (29) and Millward & Spoehr (161) developed ingenious techniques which allow Ss to select only those attributes of interest on a particular trial. They find that the number of selected attributes (a) decreases following success trials, both before and after TLE; and (b) increases following error trials (29). Another source of evidence in favor of multiple hypothesis processing is the effect of intertrial interval (ITI) upon performance: longer intervals (up to an optimal level) improve performance (31, 62). These data are consistent with the Trabasso-Bower multiple hypothesis model, and can be explained by assuming that longer ITIs allow S to sort out his hypotheses with respect to trial outcome information.

Several extensions of the multiple hypothesis approach involve wholist strategies in which S checks all possible hypotheses simultaneously (31, 264). Both models assume that S entertains a set of active hypotheses on each trial, but neither assumes that an error is a recurrent event. Chumbley (31) assumes that on each trial S partitions his functional hypotheses into two subsets consistent with the two possible responses, e.g. those leading to response A and those leading to response B. If S is successful on the current trial, his active hypothesis set is reduced to the consistent subset on which his choice was based. On the other hand, if S is incorrect, he will attempt to recover the *other* subset and use it to continue focusing. Subjects resample a new set of active hypotheses only when they fail to recover the consistent subset, or when the consistent subset is reduced to zero. The subset sampling axiom is supported by Levine's recent finding that Ss seldom consider the solution dimensions prior to solving (86, 95, 141). He notes that S's presolution performance on solvable problems is similar to behavior of Ss working on insoluble problems. Failure to learn solvable problems is ascribed to subset sampling, excluding the solution dimension.

An attribute elimination model proposed by Wickens & Millward (264) assumes S samples an active set of hypotheses, checks the consistency of all hypotheses on each feedback trial, and resamples to form a new active subset when the current active set is reduced to zero. The process does not distinguish between errors and success, and S is assumed to eliminate all inconsistent hypotheses on every feedback trial. Such a model is considerably more efficient than those previously proposed and probably applies only to sophisticated Ss. In fact, Wickens & Millward (264) gave Ss a large number of successive CI problems and found that the Trabasso-Bower model predicted performance on the first or second problem, but Ss solved subsequent problems much more quickly than could be predicted by models which assume that errors are recurrent events.

Falmagne (61) noted that the Trabasso-Bower model can account for a general decrease in latency during a run of success trials, but the decrease should be the same during a run of successes regardless of where the success run begins. She found a greater decrease in latency on success runs prior to last error than on the success run following the TLE. This finding led her to postulate a single hypothesis strength model of CI. On each trial S either makes an hypothesis or fails to do so, in which case S can be considered to be in a passive state. Confirmations and disconfirmations influence the strength of hypotheses such that, in general, confirmation leads to an increase in the strength (or sampling weight) of all confirmed hypotheses. Similarly, disconfirmation leads to a reduction in the strength of all hypotheses consistent with the negative outcome.

The notion of a passive state emphasizes a separation of learning and responding. On some trials S fails to form an active hypothesis and simply guesses, but this has no influence on learning since conditioning occurs with every reinforcement independently of hypothesis behavior. On every trial there is some probability that Ss will resample an active hypothesis, although the probability of resampling following a success trial is much lower than following an error.

Falmagne (61) is able to predict the discrepancy in latency for success runs before and after last error and to explain a variety of confidence rating data as well as provide some predictions of sequential statistics (2, 38, 61, 63, 64). However, these data can be predicted as well by a variety of multiple hypothesis models (31, 252, 264).

In summary, the stochastic models of CI began as simplistic hypothesis testing models (20) and evolved to include greater memory of hypotheses, more sophisticated manipulation of hypothesis sets, and the possibility of learning from both success and error outcomes. These modifications have clearly made the stochastic models more plausible explanations of CI. However, the expanded models still have a number of serious limitations. First, while memory for hypotheses is now assumed, memory of instances is not, despite relatively strong evidence that Ss display memory of at least some prior instances (18, 104). These data suggest that Ss remember instances other than those in the immediate vicinity of the current trial. The failure to consider memory of instances (other than assumptions of local consistency) is probably not particularly important within the constraints of the experimental paradigms for single attribute CI. However, if the models are to be extended to more complex problem domains, it is apparent that instance memory must be acknowledged.

A related problem of stochastic models is their application to a very limited class of CI problems; single attribute classification is hardly representative of the set of possible classification schemes. Although stochastic models have been extended to more complicated problems, the stimuli employed are easily analyzed into a small number of dimensions. Such stimuli and concepts are indeed rare in the real world.

Finally, the goal of the various stochastic models has been to encapsulate *the* strategy of concept identification. Each model formulates axioms for a particular strategy or way of approaching the CI task. This approach persists in spite of the overwhelming data suggesting strategy variability both between and within people (23, 115, 161). In light of this variability, existing stochastic models could, at best, describe some sort of central tendency or the approach to a concept problem of some nonexistent average man. It is also instructive to note that the general class of Markov models typically used assume underlying distributions, such as the geometric, which build an extremely large variance into the models. Indow & Suzuki (111, 112) demonstrated the impact of large variance by showing that the Bower-Trabasso model was able to provide an excellent fit to their data, although they clearly identified three subsets of *S*s who used wholist focusing strategies, single hypothesis strategies, or unidentifiable strategies.

Models of Complex Attribute Identification

Trabasso & Bower treat conjunctive problems as two independent subproblems, each solved in the same hypothesis sampling fashion as outlined in their previous model (20). Nahinsky (167) extended the hypothesis approach in a manner that parallels the modifications of single attribute models. He assumed that *S*s solve a conjunctive problem by sampling a focus set of conjunctive hypotheses from the initial positive instance. On subsequent positive instances, if a value of an active hypothesis changes, then that hypothesis is deleted from the focus. On error trials, *S* is assumed to delete from the active set all hypotheses whose values remain the same. The *S* resamples a new focus set of hypotheses when the set of active hypotheses is reduced to zero. Resampling takes place from the complement of those hypotheses active on the trial of sampling.

A somewhat different model of conjunctive attribute identification is provided by Williams (265) in an extension of the computer oriented models of Hunt and associates (106). Williams assumes that *S* selects a focus sample of stimulus attribute values and stores them in a short-term memory, together with the trial outcome. Attention is focused primarily on those aspects of the stimulus that relate to the current hypothesis, and storage is dependent on the strength or salience of the attribute. A disconfirmation generally reduces the strength of a dimension, except when *S* forgets about the irrelevance of an attribute, in which case its strength increases over successive trials. New hypothesis selection derives from a search through the focus sample in STM for the most frequently occurring attribute which partitions positive and negative instances. A second dimension consistent with the first part of the hypothesis is then selected in the same fashion. Hunt's (106) work on CI simulation demonstrates that Williams' basic approach can be used to account for a wide range of complex problems. Nahinsky's model, on the other hand, seems implausible for problems with more than two relevant dimensions because the number of potential hypotheses becomes exceedingly large.

EMPIRICAL RESEARCH ON ATTRIBUTE IDENTIFICATION   For purposes of exposition, recent research efforts may be roughly classified as follows:

1. Strategies (23, 83, 84, 115, 133, 134, 160, 161, 262, 263).

2. Stimulus variables: intradimensional variability, irrelevant dimensions, relevant redundancy, concreteness (32, 98, 120, 133, 147, 167, 168, 177, 212, 220).

3. Trial outcome (blank, positive, negative) and number of response categories (2, 17, 37, 49, 100, 122, 132, 135, 142, 206, 238, 251).

4. Transfer of concepts; reversal and nonreversal shift paradigms (3, 56, 124, 126–128, 148, 162, 163, 205, 230, 255).

STRATEGIES   There has been some recent interest in distinguishing hypothesis vs associative strategies of CI. White (262, 263) obtained limited evidence suggesting that it is possible to train *S*s to use an hypothesis-oriented strategy in a conjunctive problem. Subjects given unsystematic pretraining with an arbitrary paired-associate task evidenced incremental learning, whereas Ss trained on a rule-governed problem showed a stationarity of presolution responses, suggestive of an all-or-none, hypothesis-oriented strategy. Millward & Spoehr (161) also present evidence that Ss learn a variety of systematic strategies over a sequence of CI problems.

Bruner and his associates (23) identified Ss who solve CI problems by attending to stimulus attributes (focusers) and those who test hypotheses (scanners). Within each of these classes two extremes have been identified as follows: 1. Focusers: (a) conservative (varying one attribute at a time; (b) gamblers (varying more than one attribute). 2. Scanners: (a) successive (one hypothesis at a time); (b) simultaneous (checking multiple hypotheses). Johnson (115) employed an interesting modification of the selection paradigm, which he calls the minimum information feedback procedure, in an attempt at more objective identification of concept strategies. A dialogue between S and a computer was established such that S could select instances and request instance names or check hypotheses. There was no a priori solution to the problem, but feedback was provided in a way that minimized the elimination of potential solutions. With this procedure, Johnson found it possible to distinguish three basic types of solution: conservative focus, successive scanning, and a generalized tactical approach. The "tacticians" were characterized by a deliberate but unsystematic approach to the problem which typically led to a quick solution. Johnson was able to obtain several independent identifications of these three strategies by employing various multivariate clustering techniques.

Several investigators have objected to attempts at specifying a small number of strategies (133, 134, 160). They note that it is possible to view the various strategies as a single continuum, and point out certain ambiguities associated with the dichotomy of focus and scanning strategies. On a problem with two values per dimension, for example, perfect focusing, varying one attribute at a time, is logically equivalent to simultaneous scanning (all possible hypotheses are partitioned into tenable and untenable sets). Focus gambling and simultaneous scanning can be mapped similarly onto each other. These apparent ambiguities led both Miller and Laughlin to a detailed analysis of the characteristics of perfect solutions under various strategies. In general, they find that in spite of the logical ambiguities, various strategies do lead to different efficiency of solution both in theory and practice, with the conservative focus being most efficient.

Laughlin (134) created a continuous measure of solution efficiency and focusing which can be applied to a variety of tasks and strategies. In a recent experiment (133) he found solution efficiency to be a direct function of the degree of induced focusing. Laughlin (135) has also extended his analysis to predict the relative difficulty of attribute identification under various logical rules, e.g. conjunctive, disjunctive, conditional, etc. On the basis of an analysis of the difficulty or "strain" required to use the focus strategy, he was able to predict correctly the ordering of difficulty for eight rule types. Giambra (84, 85) has replicated the predicted ordering with minor exceptions, but failed to find the correct order of difficulty when Ss were given nonexemplar start cards.

Laughlin (134) treats all strategies as a continuum representing various degrees of focusing. Bourne (17a) points out that it is not clear that Laughlin's index truly measures a focusing strategy, and in any case, the index is indistinguishable from problem solving efficiency. In other words, the existence of a scale which orders strategies does not lead directly to the conclusion that all strategies are variants of the same process. In fact, Johnson's (115) ability to identify distinct groups of strategies with multivariate clustering techniques seems to suggest that the various strategies are not simply approximations to pure focusing.

STIMULUS AND ENCODING VARIABLES   Haygood, Harbert & Omlor (98) reported a somewhat counterintuitive finding that Ss were able to solve both uni- and bi-dimensional problems faster as the number of levels/dimension was increased. These data can be interpreted on the basis of a positive focus strategy. With such a strategy S attends only to the positive instance—attributes which have not changed value. As the number of values/dimension increases, so also does the rate of change on irrelevant dimensions. However, an alternative explanation is possible. Since the paradigm of Haygood et al employed 50% positive instances, an increase in the number of values also changes the relative saliance of the positive value. The solution value must appear, on the average, on every other trial (50% positive ratio), but with six levels an irrelevant value would appear on only one-sixth of the trials. Recent experiments have failed to resolve this controversy (32, 133, 177, 220).

A few studies examined the effects of relevant redundant cues which typically lead to faster learning (147, 212). Rollings, Bethel & Deffenbacher (212) noted that the separation of redundant cues is an important variable in a problem which involves a verbalized string of dimension values, e.g. large, red, triangle. Subjects solved faster when the redundant cues were separated, and showed more two-cue solutions when the cues were adjacent. Solutions were fastest when the encoding order was grammatical, e.g. large, red triangle as opposed to triangle, red, large.

Despite the overriding emphasis on dimensional analysis of stimuli, there has been work on effects of exemplar representation and encoding. Nahinsky (167, 168) showed that with geometric drawings or concrete word problems Ss sample sets of values as mutually interacting parts, whereas with abstract word problems they sample dimensions independently.

TRIAL OUTCOMES AND RESPONSE CATEGORIES   Levine's (140) blank trials procedure for hypothesis identification has been widely employed (2, 122, 142, 206, 238). In the blank trials procedure blocks of nonfeedback trials are inserted into the CI sequence. The procedure is useful only if it does not disrupt normal CI processing, and several studies (2, 140) have shown no effect of nonreinforced trials upon number of errors to solution in single attribute problems. However, analyses of local consistency reflect clear differences between reinforced and non-reinforced trials (2). Levison & Restle (142) have also shown that nonreinforced trials reduce the number of multiple cue solutions, but not number of errors, in problems with relevant redundant cues.

An interesting postcript to the blank trials procedure is a demonstration by

Karpf & Levine (122) that hypothesis identification with the blank trials procedure coincides with S's own description of his current hypothesis. These data suggest little need for the blank trials procedure in single attribute tasks, but overt hypothesis statement can reduce errors with more complex problems (49).

Laughlin (132) demonstrated that the completeness of feedback influences ease of attribute identification in a wide variety of multiattribute problems. Subjects solve a conjunctive problem more quickly when they are told if the stimulus contains both critical values (TT), only one (TF, FT), or neither (FF). They are fastest when provided with a full truth table specification of the stimulus. More recently, Bourne (17) demonstrated that the availability of positive and negative classification information improves performance even when full truth table information is provided.

TRANSFER PARADIGMS   Interest continues in the special transfer problems created by dimensional shifts (125, 128). Explanations of the shift phenomenon fall into two broad classes: mediational and attentional. Anderson, Kemler & Shepp (3) identify four subclasses of attentional theories which derive from independent assumptions about selective attention (responding to a subset of the stimulus) and dimensional learning. They argue that the transfer shift data can be explained on the basis of either selective attention or simply dimensional learning. The latter explanation is supported (124) by evidence that Ss learn about both relevant and irrelevant dimensions.

These extensions of attentional theory make it almost indiscriminable from a mediational point of view. However, attempts continue to contrast mediational and attentional theories of the overlearning reversal effect (148, 205, 255), the optional, and the intra- and extradimensional shift paradigms (126, 127, 230). These data provide little advancement in our understanding of human conceptual behavior, but appear as the remnants of a waning controversy.

Modigliani (162, 163) has explored a different set of transfer problems and finds that Ss are quite sensitive to both irrelevant dimensions and added values on the relevant dimension in CI transfer situations. He notes that one must be careful in concept transfer tasks because it is quite possible for Ss to restrict the generality of their learning to a specific set of stimuli. Furthermore, his work adds support to the notion that Ss learn about stimulus configurations in addition to relevant dimensions.

COMPLETE AND RULE LEARNING PARADIGMS   In a rule learning task, S is provided with the relevant stimulus attributes and asked to discover the logical rule that the experimenter used to partition the stimulus domain. Considerable attention has been focused on the relative difficulty of rules based on the various logical connectives. There has been broad agreement that the rules can be ranked by difficulty in this order—affirmation, conjunction, inclusive disjunction, and conditional (19). The biconditional is sometimes easier, but usually more difficult than the conditional (85, 217). Peters & Denny (184) suggest that the conditional might be easier learned than the biconditional because it contains a smaller and more homogeneous nonexemplar class, i. e. in terms of a truth table classification the conditional treats TT, FF, and FT as positives and TF as negative; for the biconditional TT and FF are positive and TF and FT are negative. They suggest that the conditional might be easier because S can focus on the negative class and simply learn TF is negative. These data support such a contention by showing that the biconditional is easier than the conditional when Ss are induced to focus on the positive exemplars by the use of response labels. Gottwald (89) has shown a similar effect of labels in directing focus on positive or negative instances. Haygood & Bourne (97) proposed a multistage model of complete learning based on a relatively efficient truth table analysis of the problem. They conceive of S as going through successive stages of attribute identification, assignment of instances to a 2×2 truth table, and finally inferring the rule from the outcomes assigned to each truth table classification. Chumbley (31) presented a similar two-stage model for conjunctive problems. These approaches are supported by data suggesting (*a*) spontaneous acquisition of the truth table strategy over successive problems (16), and (*b*) improved performance after instructions on the truth table method (17, 48). Chumbley's two-stage version of this type of model has also received some support (196, 249).

The assumption of a truth table strategy as a model of CI produces at least a small credibility gap. Perhaps Ss are capable of such an effort, and they may even be induced to use the strategy, but it is certainly not typical of the untrained S. In general, the truth table might be more descriptive of E generating stimuli than of S solving a CI problem.

The most plausible and comprehensive models of the complete CI task are those of Hunt (106) and Ruskin (215a). Hunt uses a simulation approach with memory of prior stimuli to determine potentially relevant attributes, and then computes a concept by creating a decision tree based on attribute-value tests. Ruskin (215a) uses a more associative approach to derive a class of stochastic adaptation models. He assumes that Ss condition and remember stimulus-response information and eliminate responses based on adapted dimensions.

Critique of the CI Literature

The recent research and theory on CI provide some useful information about attention, discrimination, and logical rule usage, but unfortunately they have little to say about the identification, use, or formation of natural concepts. There has been only a limited effort to expand the horizons of CI to explore natural language concepts (172, 216) or such domains as color and form (99, 214). But, in general, existent CI models fail to capture the richness inherent in human conceptual behavior. As Wittgenstein (266) pointed out, natural concepts such as "dog" or "game" cannot be formed or identified on the basis of a partitioning rule because they do not necessarily share a set of common attributes.

A large part of contemporary CI research goes astray simply by choice of stimuli. Sampling of rules and dimension hypotheses is only likely with analyzable stimuli of low dimensionality. Furthermore, the dimensions in CI stimuli are usually uncorrelated and provide no basis for classification except as determined arbitrarily by the experimenter. Natural concepts, on the other hand, are usually based on a correlation of dimensions and a consequent clustering of exemplars.

Again, as Wittgenstein noted, the natural concept is determined not by rule but by similarities which are often vague and perhaps best thought of as "family resemblances." Phrased in this fashion the CI problem becomes one of judging relative similarity rather than identifying exemplars by rule. Work on pattern recognition, therefore, may be more relevant to naturalistic human conceptual behavior than traditional literature on CI. Of particular interest is recent work suggesting that Ss often react to complex stimuli as integrated entities prior to the full dimensional analysis proposed by conventional CI models (79, 145, 226).

Even more pertinent to understanding CI is work on classification of patterns based on knowledge of prototype (102, 198). Reed (198) provided an excellent demonstration that Ss learn to classify schematic faces on the basis of proximity to class prototypes. His Ss seemed to abstract a prototype from the known exemplars of a category, and then judged subsequent membership on the basis of similarity to this prototype. Reed's approach uses stimuli which are dimensional yet more natural than those typical of CI experiments, and he appears to capture at least the spirit of Wittgenstein's notion of "family resemblance." The idea of a prototype at the center of a loosely bounded concept provides a reasonable approach to the CI problem, but leaves unanswered questions of how the concept and prototype are formed.

LOGIC AND THOUGHT

Logical reasoning, e.g. within the framework of the classical syllogism, became a subject for investigation early in research in thought. At that time it was well established that logical rules do not describe psychological behavior of adult thinkers. Recently there has been a great increase in the study of logical thought as narrowly defined in relation to formal logic. Motivation for this research varies widely from theoretically based research to concern with empirical questions such as how language affects logical reasoning, how people interpret logical language, and the psychologic of reasoning from there; some research has even been interpreted as evidence that any child is capable of formal logic—or that no adult is.

Transitive Inference

The term refers to a logical filling in of gaps in information concerning pairs of elements A x B · B x C sharing a common relation, x. Where x is a relation defined on a polar continuum (e.g. fat-thin, fast-slow) the inference A x C is always valid (for noncontinuum relations such as, "is the nephew of," the conclusion is not necessarily valid). This is a logical operation of great power and generality which has been identified as a process of central importance for a number of theoretical view points.

Hunter (107), in a developmental study, established that some forms of presentation (of what he and others have called the *three-term series problem*) are much easier to solve than others. A linear ordering of elements and relations, as in the canonical form above, is easy; variations such as B $<$ A $\cdot$ B $>$ C are more difficult, in Hunter's view, because they require transformation to the canonical form by (a) conversion of the polarity of the relation, or (b) reordering of premises. If these assumptions are correct, then solution time should increase with an increase in the number of required transformations. This is what Hunter found, along with a suggestion that conversion is a simpler transformation than reordering. De Soto and his associates (45) suggested that one solves problems of this form by constructing a concrete spatial representation, "spatial paralogic," of the premises which orders the terms from most to least x. Huttenlocher (108) elaborated that position by adding a consideration of grammatical transformations involved in processing the sentences; in essence, she combined features of Hunter, who focused on translation of information as presented, and DeSoto et al, who focused on the representation of that information. When Ss are provided with paper and pencil and allowed to write the names of the elements as the premises are given, they do write names in a spatial order (118, 193). The Huttenlocher explanation was challenged by Clark (33), who proposed a linguistic interpretation incorporating a new variable, lexical marking, which assumes that the unmarked form of a polar continuum is simpler, thereby creating an asymmetry in the continuum. His alternative model leads to the same predictions of change in reaction time for various arrangements of the elements and premises as do the spatial models, except for one form never used in previous research—the *negative equative* (A is not as x as B). There has been some subsequent heated interchange (34, 109) as well as some relevant evidence (123) interpreted by its authors as support for Clark, but no additional light appears to have been shed on the nature of transitive inference. Johnson-Laird (117) proposes a classification of three-term series problem explanations into *operational* (107), *image* (45), and *linguistic* (33), and suggests that which strategy S uses is a function of his stage of experience with the problem; with experience one shifts from flexible general procedures to more specialized heuristics: from image to linguistic processing (no evidence is cited in support of this view).

Because transitive inference is a keystone in the development of concrete operations structures according to Piagetian theory, the age at which it is first clearly evidenced has become subject to scrutiny. Results of two experiments suggest that young children fail to reach a conclusion, not because they are incapable of inference, but because premise information is not stored in memory; when information availability is assured by providing an external memory aid (213) or by having the child overlearn component relations (24), performance is considerably improved. However, in light of a variety of recent evidence (253, 254, 267–269), much more limited conclusions appear to be in order: (a) children do not necessarily use logical inference if there is another, simpler, route to solution available (254); (b) preoperational children do not use inferential logic; (c) a number of procedural variables have a significant effect upon performance. Among the relevant variables are: ordering of elements and nature of relations included in the premises (254, 269), availability of consistent labels for the endpoints of the continuum (253), form of the questions and the nature of feedback (254, 267). The effect of some of these variables could have been predicted from the three-term series literature, and, in fact, there is evidence (254) that spatial representation is used and that response time is an inverse function of element separation.

Syllogistic Reasoning

As might be expected in a well-established research area, most recent work examines fine details in relation to earlier formulations (8, 207, 210, 211); examines effects of some individual difference variables (169), or, in the new psycholinguistic mode, the effect of surface structure on processing time (143); and, most interesting of the lot, the logic of logical errors (27). There are few surprises in the results: negation, passive voice, and other relatively standard grammatical transforms do slow processing (143) without necessarily introducing error (211); older and more poorly educated Ss show more errors of reasoning, especially with emotionally toned meaningful content (169). In syllogistic reasoning one must attend to form rather than content of the premises, and bright subjects do (4, 211). Where content changes produce big changes in interpretation, it may mean that S is poorly instructed or ignorant of logical conventions such as the status of amphigory (244). Ceraso & Provitera (27, p. 400) assert that "errors in reasoning are not the result of illogical or alogical processes, but are the result of an incomplete analysis of the logical structure of the syllogism," an argument they support by comparing performance on traditional and modified forms of the same syllogism. Additional support for this view is provided by evidence on interpretation of quantifiers (173).

Comprehension of Logical Symbols and Terms

Much of the research on logical thought focuses upon specific structural features and terms. Two important classes of terms are *quantifiers* (modifying terms such as "all," "some," "no," etc) and *connectives* (terms describing the relation among major terms such as "and," "or," "but not," "if then").

Work on quantifiers has addressed a variety of issues not readily amenable to integration and summary: the derivation of quantity from identity (90); processing-time differences (119); effect of lexical context of quantifiers upon their interpretation (116, 203, 204); and analysis of the errors in interpretation of "pure" (i.e. content-free) A, E, I, and O propositions and their compounds by identifying Venn diagram alternatives described by each statement (173). The last study, which included subjects from grade 6 through college, showed that "some" is too narrowly interpreted at all ages. Although interpretation broadens with age, even adults interpret "some" to exclude the possibility of "all"—an error which would not be corrected by the definition of "some" (e.g. "at least one") provided at the outset of studies of syllogistic reasoning.

There is only one study of understanding of logical symbols (75), but it is a major one which tested 300 children in grades 1 to 6 after 5 consecutive days of prior training on matching of instance and a symbolic expression. They also studied the effect of negated connectives (which was too difficult for most children in grades 5 and 6) and form of material. Element negation and form of connective were not sources of differential difficulty. Three clear ability levels emerged with matching of truth value, regardless of connective, characterizing the lowest level. This form of "matching" has also been reported elsewhere (60, 179).

Although the preceding study found no evidence that "or" is more difficult than "and," it is undoubtedly because S was to test one instance against a symbolic expression; other research with a similar procedure (179) or a more demanding response measure (174) shows clearly that "and" is the easiest connective. The first study (179) examined four conjunctives (and, both-and, but, neither-nor), two disjunctives (or, either-or), the conditional (if-then), and the biconditional (if and only if), in a test where subjects from grade 2–college were to indicate whether a statement characterized the presented instance picture. As in (75) the youngest Ss responded solely on the basis of match or mismatch, with little apparent attention to the form of the connective. Disjunctives are harder than conjunctives, while conditional and biconditional are not clearly differentiated from each other. In a partial replication (174) of an extensive Japanese study, subjects in grades 3–college were to respond to 16 descriptive statements by encircling *all* instances described; verbal or pictorial instances were provided. While even young children correctly interpret "and," "or" is incompletely interpreted until late adolescence. A follow-up (171) to identify sources of difficulty in comprehending the disjunctive revealed that "or" is rarely employed in spontaneous description but that set union is described in terms of conjunctions of intersects. Still another use of the connectives "and" and "or" arises in the pseudoimperative, comprehension of which has been examined by Springston & Clark (243).

Conditional Reasoning

The general structure of the conditional reasoning problem is a major premise, if p then q, followed by a premise posing one of the quantities or its negation (p, p̄, q, q̄) and a conclusion to be drawn or tested (q, q̄, p, p̄). The first (affirming the antecedent or *modus ponens*) and the last (denying the consequent or *modus tollens*) of the four possible arrangements are valid inferences whereas the middle two are invalid. Several experimenters (208, 209, 247) have presented 8 or 12 versions of these four basic forms to college students to judge the correctness of the conclusion and (in one case, 247) to rate confidence in the judgment. Although the relative difficulty of the four forms obtained on the two studies do not coincide, both find *modus ponens* to be easy for the majority of students. A later experiment (248) designed to determine the truth table for Ss who judged consistently showed that only 3% of 73 Ss concurred with logicians, while 64% treated the conditional as a biconditional; however, a change in the nature of response required of the subjects produced a substantial lowering of that value. A developmental study (248a) of children in grades 3–12 showed a consistent broadening of interpretation with age among children who interpreted the conditional in a consistent fashion: at first there was simple matching and interpretation as conjunction, later as biconditional, and finally as a conditional according to the rules of logic.

Evans (58, 60) varied the values of p and q in the first premise, "if p then q" (which in his studies were expressed as arrangements of colored forms of pairings of letters and numbers). In one study (60), for each rule S was to provide all instance combinations which would verify the rule and all which would refute it.

In another (58), S was to judge the validity of the antecedent (or its denial) when the consequent was (a) denied and (b) affirmed. In the second study, rule form had a marked effect: rules giving the antecedent in negative form, "if not p then . . . ," were much more productive of erroneous inference. The negative antecedent rule form was also more productive of incorrect initial selection of an infirming instance than was the positive antecedent form, but it had no effect upon selection of initial confirming instance (which was universally a choice of TT instance—e.g. pq̄ as verification of "if p then not q"; unfortunately, the proportion of Ss supplying all 3 noninfirming instances as verification was not reported).

Undoubtedly the most dramatic evidence on the vicissitudes of conditional reasoning stems from a task designed to be an analog of practical hypothesis testing: Wason's (258) four-card problem. To test a hypothesized causal relation of the form "p implies q," one looks for the only combination of p and q which can disprove the implication, i.e. p·q̄. In Wason's (258) experimental analog, S is given four cards marked E, K, 4, 7, and told that each card has a letter on one side and a number on the other. His task is to name those cards, and only those cards, which need to be turned over in order to determine whether the following rule is true or false: *If a card has a vowel on one side, then it has an even number on the other side.* The correct answer is to choose E and 7 (pq̄). In four replications of the experiment only 5 of 128 subjects gave this response; the majority chose E and 4, or even E alone. Because of reviewed data on efficient use of disconfirmatory evidence (64) and accurate reasoning with *modus tollens* for most adults, this is a puzzling finding. A number of studies have been run to clarify the causes of this strange behavior (150, 224, 259) or to offer an explanation for it (59); most of this research is summarized in Wason & Johnson-Laird (259). Seemingly small changes in material have large effects upon performance, with "realistic" material productive of many more correct solutions.

Formal Operations

The final stage of human intellectual development, which Piaget calls *formal operations*, is characterized by the capacity for formal logical reasoning in the form of hypothetico-deductive thought. Assertions that logical inference occurs well before adolescence—possibly among preschoolers—have been pretty well demolished (e.g. 225), and there is considerable evidence that adults do not display logical inference under a variety of conditions. There is even a reanalysis (26) of one of the Inhelder & Piaget protocols which found only 8 of the 16 binary operations. Piaget (188) has acknowledged the weight of evidence in a reevaluation of formal operations which proposes three alternative views, of which he prefers the last: that all normal adults eventually attain this stage but with individual variation dependent upon such factors as aptitudes and professional specialization. Two weaker formulations of formal operations have been proposed which do not emphasize logic (87, 170).

Generalization and Abstraction

Peel (182) makes the provocative suggestion that the qualitative shift in conceptualization which takes place in adolescence should be described in terms of two separable processes: generalization (on a continuum from particular to general) and abstraction (on a continuum from concrete to abstract), which can be independently assessed (183). He further notes "large degrees of generalization can be reached without recourse to abstraction, but high levels of abstraction can only be attained through the medium of increasing degrees of generalization" (182, p. 21). The distinction serves to focus a number of issues for research in thinking. First, although early concept studies (103a) were primarily concerned with understanding the processes of generalization and abstraction—and clinical applications (86a) still are—recent work has tended to lose sight of this central issue and to treat concept identification as a special case of discrimination. Second, there is considerable sloppiness in the use of the two terms which makes for needless confusion. For example, many stimulus materials described as "abstract" in no way reflect a distilling of some central essence of a conceptual class—rather, they are *arbitrary* and either content-free or artificially divorced from meaning. The Wason four-card problem is a convenient example which, in fact, serves to induce neither abstraction nor generalization (although there are probably individual differences in fixing a cut-off on the particular-to-general continuum, it is likely that N = 4 instances is well below any adult's threshold for generalization). On the other hand, generality and abstraction can serve as very productive continua for the manipulation of independent variables, as Collis (35, 36) has shown in his studies of mathematical reasoning.

Finally, there is a large body of cross-cultural evidence suggesting that the difficulties primitive peoples experience with "standard" laboratory tasks focus around just these issues. Scribner & Cole (223) note that the reasoning of unschooled individuals may well be sound, but it is particularistic in comparison with the reasoning of schooled groups. If one encounters only a limited number of instances, perhaps there is no need for summarizing generalizations; on the other hand, what characterizes the "expert" is experience of many instances. Further, in comparing characteristics of formal schooling as contrasted with informal education, they note that informal training occurs in its appropriate daily-life context whereas school learning is detached from the context of appropriate occurrence. Perhaps a certain degree of detachment is prerequisite for abstraction. In any event, abstract thinking may well be a product of formal education. As educational techniques for developing abstracting skills are perfected and institutionalized, therefore, one might expect not only to develop "corrective" training for special subgroups, but also to observe a long-term secular trend toward better performance on standard tests (130, 250).

LANGUAGE AND THOUGHT

There are many interrelated controversies associated with the question of the relation of language to thought. Most of these issues require a good deal of clarification before they can be subjected to experimental investigation; none of them is resolved by the very selective sampling reviewed in this section. That the whole subject is still very much alive is indicated by the volume of research which has appeared: the *International Journal of Psychology* devoted the entire first issue of 1971 to the subject with seven essays covering a broad range of topics.

Early behaviorists held that thought was nothing more than speech at a covert level and sought physiological evidence of muscular activity accompanying thought and, presumably, serving as the physiological vehicle for it. Most theorists today accept thought and language as separate and separable processes: there is language without thought and thought without language. Concern now tends to focus more on the ontogeny of the two processes or on the relative influence of the two processes upon each other.

Inner Speech

Early believers that thought is a covert process of talking to oneself recorded activity of the speech musculature during thinking and control activity for evidence in support of the assumption. McGuigan (155, 156) is perhaps the most articulate supporter of the conclusion that muscular accompaniments of thought have "some internal communication function, that they serve in the transmission of information."

Extensive experimental support for the position is provided by the work of A. N. Sokolov (240), who cites two types of evidence: (a) recording of EMG activity of the tongue and lower lip during mental arithmetic and silent reading; the phasic bursts assumed to reflect implicit articulation of words are intensified with increase in problem difficulty and oral presentation; (b) interference with understanding of text or taped material by concomitant performance of reciting a poem, counting to oneself, or even biting one's tongue. All these activities are assumed to interfere with comprehension through prevention of, or interference with, implicit speech; central interference (counting) is more inhibiting than peripheral (tongue-biting), and the effect of both diminishes over repetition of the task.

Private Speech

Vygotsky has proposed that talking to oneself assumes a function in promoting thought during the preschool years, at which age the child frequently speaks aloud when a difficult problem is encountered. With advancing age and socialization this dialogue with the self becomes interiorized. Empirical support for that position is now provided by several studies of Beaudichon (5, 6) with 300 5-10 year olds, 90 5-9 year olds, and 34 5-7 year olds performing a variety of tasks. Her evidence shows that although total spontaneous verbalization decreases with age, the proportion of all child verbalization serving a regulatory function increases with age. Amount of such private speech increases with task difficulty (and failure, 46) especially among 5-year-old children. Among younger children enforced silence is associated with poor performance, while required thinking aloud improves performance.

Conrad (40) provides a most elegant demonstration of increasing use of private speech—in this instance, as a verbal code to facilitate memorization—over the MA range 3–11 years. A short-term memory task requiring matching of a picture series was used with two sets of pictures: (a) objects whose names sound alike, e.g. *rat, cat, bat, bag*; (b) different-named objects, e.g. *girl, spoon, train*. Earlier work with adults had shown much poorer short-term recall for homophones, presumably because of interference generated during rehearsal. Below age 5 performance with the two sets was equivalent, thereafter there was increasing superiority for the nonhomophone deck.

Verbal Mediation

Consistent evidence from the studies above, showing that after age 5 the child begins to generate language in the service of thought, augments earlier findings of Kendler & Kendler (129) on the appearance of verbal mediators at about that age. In recent work the Kendlers use a 3-phase paradigm with an optional shift and test for the determinants thereof. Pooling the data of a number of studies shows consistent increase in optional reversal shift with increasing age. A parallel ontogeny has also been demonstrated (126) for optional intradimensional shift (which is assumed to reflect verbal mediation) as contrasted with extradimensional shift (which does not); ID shift increases sharply in relative frequency of occurrence from age 4½-8. Moreover, Ss choosing ID shifts learned the initial discrimination faster and were brighter than their age-mates choosing ED shifts. Similar evidence that brighter children choose the verbally mediated shift was reported for reversal shift for children in kindergarten but not second grade (22). Unlike most investigations in this area, this one used two tasks, involving different stimulus dimensions, administered a week apart to determine reliability of shift behavior (50% of grade k and 59% of grade 2 children were consistent). Kajita (121) proposes an alternative explanation of the ontogeny of reversal shift in terms of logic underlying the discrimination rather than use of language labels. Blank (13) offers perhaps the strongest evidence that most investigators have failed to find evidence for verbal mediation because they have used the wrong stimulus material: spatial rather than temporal. On the other hand, Olson (176a) offers the provocative suggestion that S's language can't affect his thought: what can S say to himself that he doesn't already know?

Flavell (68) has proposed two explanations for why a child may fail to display verbally mediated behavior: he fails to produce the mediator—production deficiency—or he produces a mediator but it exerts no control over his behavior—control deficiency. T. S. Kendler (128) attempted to tease the two processes apart and to demonstrate the ontogeny of each: her results show a rapid decline of control deficiency during the early school years and a more gradual decline of production deficiency, with decrease not beginning much before grade 4.

A popular strategy in evaluating the role of language upon thought has been to employ subjects lacking traditional form of language—e.g. the deaf. Work with the deaf continues (e.g. 13, 39, 73, 256), but not without question as to its interpretation (15, 74). Now that chimpanzees have been trained in the use of a symbol system for communication, new and untapped resources for investigation of the relation of language and thought are opened. The Gardners' (78) observation that their chimpanzee Washoe would on occasion climb into a tree and sit signing to herself is suggestive evidence in this regard.

Imagery

The Piagetian treatment of thought, through its distinction between figurative and operative features, tends to de-emphasize the role of language in the development of thought on two counts: (*a*) there are other figurative or representational systems besides language; and (*b*) the basic structure of thought is described in terms of operative properties whose development is relatively independent of figurative detail. Furth (71, 72) provides an illuminating discussion of the figurative-operative distinction.

After having devoted a lifetime of study to the ontogeny of operative thought, Piaget has turned to closer scrutiny of perception (186) and, in collaboration with Inhelder, of mental images (189) and memory (190) for additional light on the ontogeny and function of these figurative systems. The results in both the latter volumes are interpreted as supporting the conclusion that operational developments precede and determine figurative ones rather than the reverse [thus, by implication, . . . "it is not language which will explain the operations of the human mind, but cognitive operations that will provide the basis for explaining language" (65, p. 39)]. Space does not permit a review of all the evidence relevant to this issue; the remainder of this section will be devoted to a consideration of the major representational alternative to language—imagery.

Although "imagery" is returning to popularity in psychology (195), it is clear that the referents of the term are as many and varied as the users. Attempts to converge on imagery through the identification of a factor or factors from a battery of mental tests range from total failure (47, 237) to only moderate success (137, 178). An approach analogous with the behavioristic attempt to relate covert speech to thought has been somewhat more successful: pupillary dilation and EMG correlates (236) as well as alpha suppression in EEG (76) have been related to performance on an imagery task. Dale (43) reports interference with short-term retention of position information from tasks requiring vision presented during delay.

By far the most compelling evidence of mental transformation of a visual image or images comes from the work of Shepard and his associates (227–229). Two studies show a very orderly linear function relating reaction time required for performing an instructed transformation and the number of rotations or foldings required for (*a*) matching a variable with a standard figure (229); (*b*) determining whether arrows on two sides will meet when a flat six-sided figure is folded into a cube (228). Questioning of subjects in the second study showed that all of them use visual or kinesthetic imagery in performance of the task. An inverse relation of reaction time in judgment of "larger" and log estimated difference in size was obtained for judging the larger of two animals when presented with their names (165). Weber & Castleman (260) made another attempt at measuring the time to imagine.

Huttenlocher & Presson (110) distinguish two classes of mental rotation problem: *perspective problems* (e.g. Piaget's mountain problem), where the array is stationary and the observer moves with respect to it; and *rotation problems*, where the observer is fixed and must move the array with respect to himself. Perspective problems are considerably more difficult than rotation problems because, the authors suggest, they involve an additional element of relating the self to the coordination of observer and array. This reasoning suggests that perspective problems should be less difficult if the child is allowed to move, and that is true.

With respect to cognitive maps of real space, a study (159a) of food retrieval by 5–7 year old chimps of 5–18 food items scattered randomly while the animal was carried behind E, or penned in a detention cage, shows that animals (*a*) start on the side with more food, (*b*) choose a least distance path, and (*c*) rarely return to spots emptied earlier.

Literature Cited

1. Aiken, L. R. 1971. Mental mechanisms in performing elementary numerical operations. *Percept. Mot. Skills* 33:463–65.
2. Aiken, L. S., Santa, J. L., Ruskin, A. B. 1972. Nonreinforced trials in concept identification: Presolution statistics and local consistency. *J. Exp. Psychol.* 93:100–4
3. Anderson, D. R., Kemler, D. G., Shepp, B. E. 1973. Selective attention and dimensional learning: A logical analysis of two-stage attention theories. *Bull. Psychon. Soc.* 2:273–75
4. Bart, W. M. 1972. A comparison of premise types in hypothetico-deductive thinking at the stage of formal opertions. *J. Psychol.* 81:45–51
5. Beaudichon, J. 1973. Nature and instrumental function of private speech in problem solving situations. *Merrill-Palmer Quart.* 19:117–35
6. Beaudichon, J., Melot, A. M. 1971. Language and problem-solving. *Cesk. Psychol.* 15:579–83
7. Beck, B. B. 1973. Cooperative tool use by captive hamadryas baboons. *Science* 182:594–97
8. Begg, I., Denny, J. P. 1969. Empirical reconciliation of atmosphere and conversion interpretations of syllogistic reasoning errors. *J. Exp. Psychol.* 81:351–54
9. Bejat, M. 1970. Conceptual and imaginal thinking in problem solving. *Rev. Roum. Sci. Soc. Ser. Psychol.* 14:65–77
10. Ibid 1972. The role of the image in problem-solving. 16:169–80
11. Benjafield, J. 1971. Evidence for a two-process theory of problem-solving. *Psychon. Sci.* 23:397–99
12. Biederman, I. 1973. Mental set and mental arithmetic. *Mem. & Cogn.* 1:383–86
13. Blank, M. 1974. Cognitive functions of language in the preschool years. *Develop. Psychol.* 10:229–45
14. Bolton, N. 1972. *The Psychology of Thinking.* London:Methuen
15. Bornstein, H., Roy, H. L. 1973. Comment on linguistic deficiency and thinking: Research with deaf subjects 1964–1969. *Psychol. Bull.* 79:211–14
16. Bourne, L. E. 1970. Knowing and using concepts. *Psychol. Rev.* 77:546–56
17. Bourne, L. E. 1973. Effects of rule, memory, and truth-table information on attribute identification. *J. Exp. Psychol.* 101:283–88
17a. Bourne, L. E. 1973. Some forms of cognition: A critical analysis of several papers. In *Contemporary Issues in Cognitive Psychology: The Loyola Symposium*, ed. R. Solso, 313–24. Washington, D. C.: Winston/Wiley
18. Bourne, L. E., Ekstrand, B. R., Dominowski, R. L. 1971. *The Psychology of Thinking.* Englewood Cliffs, N.J.: Prentice-Hall
19. Bourne, L. E. Jr., Guy, D. E. 1968. Learning conceptual rules : I. Some inter-rule transfer effects. *J. Exp. Psychol.* 76:423–29
20. Bower, G. H., Trabasso, T. 1964. Concept identification. In *Studies in Mathematical Psychology*, ed. R. C. Atkinson, 32–94. Stanford Univ. Press
21. Brainerd, C. J. 1973. Mathematical and behavioral foundations of number. *J. Gen. Psychol.* 88:221–81
22. Brier, N., Jacobs, P. I. 1972. Reversal shifting: Its stability and relation to intelligence at two developmental levels. *Child Develop.* 43:1230–41
23. Bruner, J. S., Goodnow, J. J., Austin, G. A. 1956. *A Study of Thinking.* New York: Wiley
24. Bryant, P. E., Trabasso, T. 1971. Transitive inference and memory in young children. *Nature* 232:456–58
25. Burke, R. J. 1972. What do we know about hints in individual problem solving? Some conclusions. *J. Gen. Psychol.* 86:253–65

26. Bynum, T. W., Thomas, J. A., Weitz, L. J. 1972. Truth functional logic in formal operational thinking: Inhelder and Piaget's evidence. *Develop. Psychol.* 7:129–32

27. Ceraso, J., Provitera, A. 1971. Sources of error in syllogistic reasoning. *Cogn. Psychol.* 2:400–10

28. Chase, W. G., Simon, H. A. 1973. Perception in chess. *Cogn. Psychol.* 4:55–81

29. Chatfield, D. C., Janek, E. S. 1972. Attribute selection in concept identification. *J. Exp. Psychol.* 95:97–101

30. Chumbley, J. 1969. Hypothesis memory in concept learning. *J. Math. Psychol.* 6:528–40

31. Ibid 1972. A duo-process theory of concept learning. 9:17–35

32. Chumbley, J., Lau, P., Rog, D., Haile, G. 1971. Concept identification as a function of intradimensional variability, availability of previously presented material, and relative frequency of relevant attributes. *J. Exp. Psychol.* 90:163–65

33. Clark, H. H. 1969. Linguistic processes in deductive reasoning. *Psychol. Rev.* 76:387–404

34. Ibid 1972. On the evidence concerning J. Huttenlocher and E. T. Higgins' theory of reasoning: A second reply. 79:428–32

35. Collis, K. F. 1971. A study of concrete and formal reasoning in school mathematics. *Aust. J. Psychol.* 23:289–96

36. Ibid 1973. A study of children's ability to work with elementary mathematical systems. 25:121–30

37. Coltheart, V. 1973. Concept identification with and without blank trials. *Quart. J. Exp. Psychol.* 25:1–9

38. Coltheart, V. 1973. Confidence ratings as a response index in concept identification. *J. Exp. Psychol.* 97:46–50

39. Conrad, R. 1970. Short-term memory processes in the deaf. *Brit. J. Psychol.* 61:179–95

40. Conrad, R. 1971. The chronology of the development of covert speech in children. *Develop. Psychol.* 5:398–405

41. Cotton, J. W. 1971. A sequence-specific concept identification model: Infra structure for the Bower and Trabasso theory. *J. Math. Psychol.* 8:333–69

42. Crovitz, H. F. 1970. *Galton's Walk.*

New York: Harper & Row

43. Dale, H. C. A. 1973. Short-term memory for visual information, *Brit. J. Psychol.* 64:1–8

44. Davis, G. A. 1973. *Psychology of Problem Solving.* New York: Basic Books

45. DeSoto, C. B., London, M., Handel, S. 1965. Social reasoning and spatial paralogic. *J. Pers. Soc. Psychol.* 2:513–21

46. Deutsch, F., Stein, A. H. 1972. The effects of personal responsibility and task interruption on the private speech of preschoolers. *Hum. Develop.* 15:310–24

47. DiVesta, F. J., Ingersoll, G., Sunshine, P. 1971, A factor analysis of imagery tests. *J. Verb. Learn. Verb. Behav.* 10:471–79

48. Dodd, D. H., Kinsman, R. A., Klipp, R. D., Bourne, L. E. Jr. 1971. Effects of logic pretraining on conceptual rule learning. *J. Exp. Psychol.* 88:119–22

49. Dominowski, R. L. 1973. Requiring hypotheses and the identification of unidimensional, conjunctive and disjunctive concepts. *J. Exp. Psychol.* 100:387–94

50. Dominowski, R. L., Jenrick, R. 1972. Effect of hints and interpolated activity on solution of an insight problem. *Psychon. Sci.* 26:335–38

51. Duncan, C. P. 1970. The effect of the shape of the distribution of response strength and guessing errors in problem solving. *Am. J. Psychol.* 83:535–43

52. Edmonds, E. M., Mueller, M. R. 1969. Effect of word frequency restriction on anagram solution. *J. Exp. Psychol.* 79:545–46

53. Eimas, P. D. 1970. Effects of memory aids on hypothesis behavior and focusing in young children and adults. *J. Exp. Child Psychol.* 40:319–36

54. Egan, D. E., Greeno, J. G. 1973. Acquiring cognitive structure by discovery and rule learning. *J. Educ. Psychol.* 64:85–97

55. Elithorn, S., Telford, A. 1970. Game and problem structure in relation to the study of human and artificial intelligence. *Nature* 227:1205–10

56. Erickson, J. R. 1971. Problem shifts and hypothesis behavior in concept identification. *Am. J. Psychol.* 84:100–11

57. Erickson, J. R., Zakowski, M. M., Eh-

mann, E. D. 1966. All-or-none assumption in concept identification: Analysis of latency data. *J. Exp. Psychol.* 72:690–97

58. Evans, J. St. B. T. 1972. Reasoning with negatives. *Brit. J. Psychol.* 63:213–19

59. Evans, J. St. B. T. 1972. On the problems of interpreting reasoning data: logical and psychological approaches. *Cognition* 1:373–84

60. Evans, J. St. B. T. 1972. Interpretation and matching bias in a reasoning task. *Quart. J. Exp. Psychol.* 24:193–99

61. Falmagne, R. 1970. Construction of a hypothesis model for concept identification. *J. Math. Psychol.* 7:60–96

62. Ibid 1971. Concept identification: Effect of the intertrial interval on the efficacy and consistency of information processing. 8:240–47

63. Falmagne, R. 1971. Conjoint analysis of two concept identification tasks. *Acta Psychol.* 35:286–97

64. Falmagne, R. 1972. Memory process in concept identification. *J. Exp. Psychol.* 92:33–42

65. Ferreiro, E., Sinclair, H. 1971. Temporal relationships in language. *Int. J. Psychol.* 6:39–47

66. Fink, R. T. 1972. Response latency as a function of hypothesis-testing strategies in concept identification. *J. Exp. Psychol.* 95:337–42

67. Fisher, R. A. 1951. *The Design of Experiments*, p. 89. New York: Hafner. 6th ed.

68. Flavell, J. H. 1970 Developmental studies of mediated memory. In *Advances in Child Development and Behavior*, ed. H. W. Reese, L. P. Lipsitt, 5:182–211: New York: Academic

69. Flavell, J. H. 1970. Concept development. In *Carmichael's Manual of Child Psychology*, ed. P. H. Mussen, 1:983–1059. New York: Wiley

70. Fulgosi, A., Guilford, J. P. 1968. Short-term incubation in divergent production. *Am. J. Psychol.* 81:241–46

71. Furth, H. G. 1969. *Piaget and Knowledge*. Englewood Cliffs, N.J.: Prentice-Hall

72. Furth, H. G. 1970. On language and knowing in Piaget's developmental theory. *Hum. Develop.* 13:241–57

73. Furth, H. G. 1971. Linguistic deficiency and thinking: Research with deaf subjects. 1964–1969. *Psychol. Bull.* 76:58–72

74. Ibid 1973. Further thoughts on thinking and language. 79:215–16

75. Furth, H. G., Youniss, J., Ross, B. M. 1970. Children's utilization of logical symbols. *Develop. Psychol.* 3:36–57

76. Gale, A., Morris, P. E., Lucas, B., Richardson, A. 1972. Types of imagery and imagery types: An EEG study. *Brit. J. Psychol.* 63:523–31

77. Gardiner, W. L. 1973. *An Invitation to Cognitive Psychology*. Monterey, Calif.: Brooks/Cole

78. Gardner, B. T., Gardner, R. A. 1974. Comparing the early utterances of child and chimpanzee. In *Minnesota Symposium in Child Psychology*, Vol. 8, ed. A. Pick. Minneapolis: Univ. Minnesota Press. In press

79. Garner, W. R., Felfoldy, G. L. 1970. Integrality of stimulus dimensions in various types of information processing. *Cogn. Psychol.* 225–42

80. Gavurin, E. I., DeVito, C. 1973. Correlation of anagram solving to transition probability and word frequency. *J. Gen. Psychol.* 88:135–40

81. Gelman, R. 1972. The nature and development of early number concepts. In *Advances in Child Development and Behavior*, ed. H. Reese, 7:115–67. New York: Academic

82. Gentile, J., Kessler, D. K., Gentile, P. K. 1969. Process of solving analogy items. *J. Educ. Psychol.* 60:494–502

83. Giambra, L. M. 1971. Selection strategies for eight concept rules with nonexemplar start cards. *J. Exp. Psychol.* 87:78–92

84. Ibid. Selection strategies for eight concept rules with exemplar and nonexemplar start cards, 143–45

85. Ibid 1973. An interactive effect of the criterion in concept identification: Conditional and biconditional rule difficulty. 97:310–16

86. Glassman, W. E., Levine, M. 1972. Unsolved and insoluble problem behavior. *J. Exp. Psychol.* 92:146–48

86a. Goldstein, K., Scheerer, M. 1941. Abstract and concrete behavior: An experimental study with special tests. *Psychol. Monogr.* 53 No. 2 (Whole No. 239)

87. Goodnow, J. J. 1972. Rules and reper-

toires, rituals and tricks of the trade: Social and informational aspects to cognitive and representational development. In *Information Processing in Children*, ed. S. Farnham-Diggory, 83–102. New York: Academic

88. Goss, A. E. 1961. Verbal mediating responses and concept formation. *Psychol. Rev.* 68:248–74

89. Gottwald, R. L. 1971. Effects of response labels in concept attainment. *J. Exp. Psychol.* 91:30–33

90. Green, R. T., Laxon, V. J. 1970. The conservation of number, mother, water and a fried egg chez l'enfant. *Acta Psychol.* 32:1–30

91. Greeno, J. G. 1973. The structure of memory and the process of solving problems. See Ref. 17a, 4:103–33

92. Greeno, J. G., Simon, H. A. 1974. Processes for sequence production. *Psychol. Rev.* In press

93. Groen, G. J., Parkman, J. M. 1972. A chronometric analysis of simple addition. *Psychol. Rev.* 79:329–43

94. Groen, G. J., Poll, M. 1973. Subtraction and the solution of open sentence problems. *J. Exp. Child Psychol.* 16:292–302

95. Gumer, E., Levine, M. 1971. The missing dimension in concept learning: Dimensionality or local consistency. *J. Exp. Psychol.* 90:39–44

96. Guthrie, J. T. 1971. The effect of two types of verbal hierarchy on problem solving. *J. Gen. Psychol.* 84:213–18

97. Haygood, R. C., Bourne, L. E. 1965. Attribute- and rule-learning aspects of conceptual behavior. *Psychol. Rev.* 72:175–95

98. Haygood, R. C., Harbert, T. L., Omlor, J. 1970. Intradimensional variability and concept identification. *J. Exp. Psychol.* 83:216–19

99. Heider, E. R., Olivier, D. C. 1972. The structure of the color space in naming and memory for two languages. *Cogn. Psychol.* 3:337–54

100. Heim, S. V., Scholnick, E. K. 1972. Some hypotheses about negative instances in single-attribute concept attainment. *J. Exp. Psychol.* 93:130–37

101. Hicks, R. A., Hicks, M. J., Mansfield, H. 1969. A multi-solution anagram task. *Psychol. Rep.* 24:671–74

102. Homa, D., Cross, J., Cornell, D.,

Goldman, D., Schwartz, S. 1973. Prototype abstraction and classification of new instances as a function of number of instances defining the prototype. *J. Exp. Psychol.* 101:116–22

103. Huesmann, L. R., Cheng, C. M. 1973. A theory for the induction of mathematical functions. *Psychol. Rev.* 80:126–38

103a. Hull, C. L. 1920. Quantitative aspects of the evolution of concepts. *Psychol. Monogr.* 28 No. 1 (Whole No. 123)

104. Hunt, E. B. 1961. Memory effects in concept learning. *J. Exp. Psychol.* 62:598–609

105. Hunt, E. B. 1971. What kind of computer is man? *Cogn. Psychol.* 2:57–98

106. Hunt, E. B., Marin, J., Stone, P. J. 1966. *Experiments in Induction.* New York: Academic

107. Hunter, I. M. L. 1957. The solving of 3 term series problems. *Brit. J. Psychol.* 48:286–98

108. Huttenlocher, J. 1968. Constructing spatial images: A strategy in reasoning. *Psychol. Rev.* 75:550–60

109. Huttenlocher, J., Higgins, E. T. 1972. On reasoning, congruence, and other matters. *Psychol. Rev.* 79:420–27

110. Huttenlocher, J., Presson, C. C. 1973. Mental rotation and the perspective problem. *Cogn. Psychol.* 4:277–99

111. Indow, T., Suzuki, S. 1972. Strategies in concept identification: Stochastic model and computer simulation I. *Jap. Psychol. Res.* 14:168–75

112. Ibid 1973. Strategies in concept identification: Stochastic model and computer simulation II. 15:1–9

113. Jablonski, E. M., Mueller, J. H. 1972. Anagram solution as a function of instructions, priming, and imagery. *J. Exp. Psychol.* 94:84–89

114. Johnson, D. M. 1972. *Systematic Introduction to the Psychology of Thinking.* New York: Harper & Row

114a. Johnson, D. M. 1973. Review of Human Problem Solving, by A. Newell and H. A. Simon. *Am. J. Psychol.* 86:449–55

115. Johnson, E. S. 1971. Objective identification of strategy on a selection concept learning task. *J. Exp. Psychol. Monogr.* 90:167–96

116. Johnson-Laird, P. N. 1970. The interpretation of quantified sentences. In

Advances in Psycholinguistics, ed. G. B. Flores d'Arcais, W. J. M. Levelt, 347-72. Amsterdam: North-Holland

117. Johnson-Laird, P. N. 1972. The three term series problem. *Cogn. Psychol.* 1:57-82

118. Jones, S. 1970. Visual and verbal processes in problem solving. *Cogn. Psychol.* 1:201-14

119. Just, M. A., Carpenter, P. A. 1971. Comprehension of negation with quantifications. *J. Verb. Learn. Verb. Behav.* 10:244-53

120. Kahrs, C. R., Haygood, R. C. 1973. Relevant redundancy in disjunctive concept learning. *Bull. Psychon. Soc.* 1:335-36

121. Kajita, M. 1972. Mediational models in reversal and non-reversal shift learning. *Jap. Psychol. Res.* 14:1-7

122. Karpf, D., Levine, M. 1971. Blank-trial probes and introtacts in human discrimination learning. *J. Exp. Psychol.* 90:51-55

123. Keeney, T. J., Gaudino, D. L. 1973. Solution of comparative and negative equative three term series problems. *J. Exp. Psychol.* 101:193-96

124. Kemler, D. G., Shepp, B. E. 1971. Learning and transfer of dimensional relevance and irrelevance in children. *J. Exp. Psychol.* 90:120-27

125. Kendler, H. H., Kendler, T. S. 1962. Vertical and horizontal processes in problem solving. *Psychol. Rev.* 69:1-16

126. Kendler, H. H., Kendler, T. S., Ward, J. W. 1972. An ontogenetic analysis of optional intradimensional shifts. *J. Exp. Psychol.* 95:102-9

127. Kendler, H. H., Ward, J. W. 1971. Memory loss following discrimination of conceptually related material. *J. Exp. Psychol.* 88:435-36

128. Kendler, T. S. 1972. An ontogeny of mediational deficiency. *Child Develop.* 43:1-17

129. Kendler, T. S., Kendler, H. H. 1970. An ontogeny of optional shift behavior. *Child Develop.* 41:1-27

130. Koppen-Thulesius, L. K., Teichmann, H. 1972. Accelerative trends in intellectual development. *Brit. J. Soc. Clin. Psychol.* 11:284-94

131. Kozielecki, J. 1972. A model for diagnostic problem solving. *Acta Psychol.* 36:370-80

132. Laughlin, P. R. 1971. Concept attainment as a function of information specification and concept complexity. *J. Exp. Psychol.* 90:334-43

133. Ibid 1973. Focusing strategy in concept attainment as a function of instructions and task complexity. 98:320-27

134. Laughlin, P. R. 1973. Selection strategies in concept attainment. See Ref. 17a, 277-311

135. Laughlin, P. R., Kalowski, C. A., Metzler, M. E., Ostap, K. M., Venclouas, S. M. 1968. Concept identification as a function of sensory modality, information, and number of persons. *J. Exp. Psychol.* 77:335-40

136. Lehman, E. B., Goodnow, J. J. 1972. Memory for rhythmic series: age changes in accuracy and number coding. *Develop. Psychol.* 6:363

137. Leibovitz, M. P., London, P., Cooper, S. M., Hart, J. T. 1972. Dominance in mental imagery. *Educ. Psychol. Meas.* 32:679-703

138. LeMay, E. H. 1972. Anagram solutions as a function of task variables and solution word models. *J. Exp. Psychol.* 92:65-68

139. Ibid 1972. Stimulus generalization variables in anagram-problem solving. 93:349-53

140. Levine, M. 1966. Hypothesis behavior by humans during discrimination learning. *J. Exp. Psychol.* 71:331-36

141. Levine, M. 1971. Hypothesis theory and nonlearning despite ideal S-R-reinforcement contingencies. *Psychol. Rev.* 78:130-40

142. Levison, M. J., Restle, F. 1973. Effects of blank-trial probes on concept-identification problems with redundant relevant cue solutions. *J. Exp. Psychol.* 98:368-74

143. Lippman, M. Z. 1972. The influence of grammatical transform in a syllogistic reasoning task. *J. Verb. Learn. Verb. Behav.* 11:424-30

144. Lipton, C., Overton, W. F. 1971. Anticipatory imagery and modified anagram solutions: A developmental study. *Child Develop.* 42:615-23

145. Lockhead, G. R. 1972. Processing dimensional stimuli: A note. *Psychol. Rev.* 79:410-19

146. Loftus, E. F., Suppes, P. 1972. Structural variables that determine problem

solving difficulty in computer-assisted instruction. *J. Educ. Psychol.* 63: 531–42

147. Low, L. A., Fortier, J., Mickalide, W., Page, D., Troumpalos, D. 1973. Role of relevant, irrelevant, and redundant information in simple concept transfer. *Bull. Psychon. Sci.* 1:267–68

148. Lowenkron, B., Driessen, E. C. 1971. Solution mode in concept-identification problems and magnitude of the overlearning reversal effect. *J. Exp. Psychol.* 89:85–91

149. Luchins, A., Luchins, E. H. 1970. *Wertheimer's Seminars Revisited:* Problem solving and thinking, I, II, III. Albany, N.Y.: SUNY Faculty Student Assoc.

150. Lunzer, E. A., Harrison, C., Davey, M. 1972. The four-card problem and the generality of formal reasoning. *Quart. J. Exp. Psychol.* 24:326–39

151. Maier, N. R. F. 1970. *Problem Solving and Creativity in Individuals and Groups.* Belmont, Calif.: Brooks/Cole

152. Maier, N. R. F., Casselman, G. G. 1970. Locating the difficulty in insight problems: Individual and sex differences. *Psychol. Rep.* 26:103–17

153. Manis, M. 1971. *An Introduction to Cognitive Psychology.* Belmont, Calif.: Brooks/Cole

154. Markóva, I. 1969. Hypothesis formation and problem complexity. *Quart. J. Exp. Psychol.* 21:29–38

155. McGuigan, F. J. 1970. Covert oral behavior during the silent performance of language tasks. *Psychol. Bull.* 74: 309–26

156. McGuigan, F. J., Schoonover, R. A., Eds. 1973. *The Psychophysiology of Thinking.* New York: Academic

157. McKim, R. N. 1972. *Experiences in Visual Thinking.* Belmont, Calif.: Brooks/Cole

158. Mendelsohn, G. A., Covington, M. V. 1972. Internal processes and perceptual factors in verbal problem solving: A study of sex and individual differences in cognition. *J. Pers.* 40:451–71

159. Menzel, E. W. 1970. Menzel reporting on spontaneous use of poles as ladders. *Delta Primate Rep.*

159a. Menzel, E. W. 1973. Chimpanzee memory organization. *Science* 182: 943–45

160. Miller, L. A. 1971. Hypothesis analysis of conjunctive concept-learning situations. *Psychol. Rev.* 78:262–71

161. Millward, R. B., Spoehr, K. T. 1973. The direct measurement of hypothesis sampling strategies. *Cogn. Psychol.* 4:1–38

162. Modigliani, V. 1971. On the conservation of simple concepts: Generality of the affirmation rule. *J. Exp. Psychol.* 87:234–40

163. Modigliani, V., Rizza, J. P. 1971. Conservation of simple concepts as a function of deletion of irrelevant attributes. *J. Exp. Psychol.* 90:280–86

164. Moely, B. M., Olson, F. A., Halwes, T. G., Flavell, J. H. 1969. Production deficiency in young children's clustered recall. *Develop. Psychol.* 1:26–34

165. Moyer, R. S. 1973. Comparing objects in memory: Evidence suggesting an internal psychophysics. *Percept. Psychophys.* 13:180

166. Murray, H. G., Denny, J. P. 1969. Interaction of ability level and interpolated activity (opportunity for incubation) in human problem solving. *Psychol. Rep.* 24:271–76

167. Nahinsky, I. D. 1970. A hypothesis sampling model for conjunctive concept identification. *J. Math. Psychol.* 7:293–316

168. Nahinsky, I. D., Slaymaker, F. L., Aamiry, A., O'Brien, C. J. 1973. The concreteness of attributes in concept learning strategies. *Mem. & Cogn.* 1:307–18

169. Nehrke, M. F. 1972. Age, sex, and educational differences in syllogistic reasoning. *J. Gerontol.* 27:966–70

170. Neimark, E. D. 1970. Model for a thinking machine: An information processing framework for the study of cognitive development. *Merrill-Palmer Quart.* 16:345–68

171. Neimark, E. D. 1970. Development of comprehension of logical connectives: Understanding of "or." *Psychon. Sci.* 21:217–19

172. Neimark, E. D. 1974. Natural language concepts: Additional evidence. *Child Develop.* 45:508–11

173. Neimark, E. D., Chapman, R. H. 1974. Development of comprehension of logical quantifiers. In *Psychological Studies of Logic and its Development,*

ed. R. Falmagne. New York: Erlbaum. In press

174. Neimark, E. D., Slotnick, N. S. 1970. Development of the understanding of logical connectives. *J. Educ. Psychol.* 61:451–60

175. Neimark, E. D., Slotnick, N. S., Ulrich, T. 1971. Development of memorization strategies. *Develop. Psychol.* 5: 427–32

176. Newell, A., Simon, H. A. 1972. *Human Problem Solving.* Englewood Cliffs, N.J.: Prentice-Hall

176a. Olson, D. R. 1970. Language and thought: Aspects of a cognitive theory of semantics. *Psychol. Rev.* 77:257–73

177. Overstreet, J. D., Dunham, J. L. 1969. Effect of number of values and irrelevant dimension on dimension selection and associative learning in a multiple-concept problem. *J. Exp. Psychol.* 79:265–68

178. Paivio, A. 1971. *Imagery and Verbal Processes.* New York: Holt, Rinehart & Winston

179. Paris, S. G. 1973. Comprehension of language connectives and propositional logical relationships. *J. Exp. Child Psychol.* 16:278–91

180. Parkman, J. M. 1972. Temporal aspects of simple multiplication and comparison. *J. Exp. Psychol.* 95:437–44

181. Parkman, J. M., Groen, G. J. 1971. Temporal aspects of simple addition and comparison. *J. Exp. Psychol.* 89:333–42

182. Peel, E. A. 1971. Adolescent concept formation. In *Interdisciplinary Approaches to Language*, 6:21–29. London: Center for Information on Language Teaching and Research Reports and Papers

183. Peel, E. A. 1971. Generalizing and abstracting. *Nature* 230:600

184. Peters, K. G., Denny, J. P. 1971. Labeling and memory effects on categorizing and hypothesizing behavior for biconditional and conditional conceptual rules. *J. Exp. Psychol.* 87: 229–33

185. Peterson, M. J., Aller, S. 1971. Arithmetic problem solving. *J. Exp. Psychol.* 91:193–97

186. Piaget, J. 1969. *The Mechanisms of Perception.* New York: Basic Books

187. Piaget, J. 1970. Piaget's theory. See Ref. 69, 1:703–32

188. Piaget, J. 1972. Intellectual evolution from adolescence to adulthood. *Hum. Develop.* 15:1–12

189. Piaget, J., Inhelder, B. 1971. *Mental Imagery in the Child.* New York: Basic Books

190. Piaget, J., Inhelder, B. 1973. *Memory and Intelligence.* New York: Basic Books

191. Pollio, H. R. 1974. *The Psychology of Symbolic Activity.* Reading, Mass.: Addison-Wesley

192. Pollio, H. R., Rinehart, D. 1970. Rules and counting behavior. *Cogn. Psychol.* 1:388–402

193. Potts, G. R. 1972. Information processing strategies used in the encoding of linear ordering. *J. Verb. Learn. Verb. Behav.* 11:727–40

194. Powell, A., Vega, M. 1971. Word association and verbal analogy problems. *Psychon. Sci.* 22:103–4

195. Pylyshyn, Z. W. 1973. What the mind's eye tells the mind's brain: A critique of mental imagery. *Psychol. Bull.* 80:1–24

196. Raney, J. L., Thomson, W. J. 1973. Conjunctive, inclusive disjunctive, and conditional concept identification with binary dimensions. *J. Exp. Psychol.* 99:146–47

197. Razran, G. 1971. *Mind in Evolution.* Boston: Houghton-Mifflin

198. Reed, S. K. 1972. Pattern recognition and categorization. *Cogn. Psychol.* 3:382–407

199. Restle, F. 1962. The selection of strategies in cue learning. *Psychol. Rev.* 69:329–43

200. Restle, F. 1970. Speed of adding and comparing numbers. *J. Exp. Psychol.* 83:274–78

201. Restle, F. 1970. Theory of serial pattern learning: Structural trees. *Psychol. Rev.* 77:481–95

202. Restle, F. 1973. Serial pattern learning: Higher order transactions. *J. Exp. Psychol.* 99:61–69

203. Revlis, R., Hayes, J. R. 1972. The primacy of generalities in hypothetical reasoning. *Cogn. Psychol.* 3:268–90

204. Revlis, R., Lipkin, S. G., Hayes, J. R. 1971. The importance of universal quantifiers in a hypothetical reasoning

task. *J. Verb. Learn. Verb. Behav.* 10:86–91
205. Richman, C. L. 1973. Role of overtraining in reversal and conceptual shift behavior. *J. Exp. Psychol.* 99:285–87
206. Rimm, D., Roesch, R., Perry, R., Peebles, C. 1971. Effects of blank versus noninformative feedback and "right" and "wrong" on response repetition in paired-associate learning. *J. Exp. Psychol.* 88:26–30
207. Roberge, J. J. 1970. A reexamination of the interpretations of errors in formal syllogistic reasoning. *Psychon. Sci.* 19:331–33
208. Ibid 1971. An analysis of response patterns for conditional reasoning schemes. 22:338–39
209. Roberge, J. J. 1971. Some effects of negation on adults' conditional reasoning abilities. *Psychol. Rep.* 29: 839–44
210. Roberge, J. J. 1971. Further examination of mediated associations in deductive reasoning. *J. Exp. Psychol.* 87:127–29
211. Roberge, J. J. 1972. Effects of structure and semantics on the solution of pure hypothetical syllogisms. *J. Gen. Psychol.* 87:161–67
212. Rollings, H., Bethel, B., Deffenbacher, K. 1971. Relevant cue placement effects in concept identification tasks. *J. Exp. Psychol.* 87:9–12
213. Roodin, M. L., Gruen, G. E. 1970. The role of memory in making transitive judgments. *J. Exp. Child Psychol.* 10:264–75
214. Rosch, E. H. 1973. Natural categories. *Cogn. Psychol.* 4:328–50
215. Rosen, S. M. 1971. Solution difficulty and perseveration as functions of anagram type. *Psychol. Rec.* 21:401–8
215a. Ruskin, A. R. 1971. *A theory of complex concept learning.* PhD thesis. Stanford Univ., Stanford, Calif.
216. Saltz, E., Soller, E., Sigel, I. E. 1972. The development of natural language concepts. *Child Develop.* 43:1191–1202
217. Sawyer, C. R., Johnson, P. J. 1971. Conditional and biconditional rule difficulty under selection and reception conditions. *J. Exp. Psychol.* 89:424–26
218. Scandura, J. M. 1970. Role of rules in

behaviour: Toward an operational definition of what (rule) is learned. *Psychol. Rev.* 77:516–33
219. Schiopu, U. 1970. Thinking strategies in positional games by young children. *Rev. Roum. Sci. Soc. Ser. Psychol.* 14:3–15
220. Schultz, R. F., Dodd, D. H. 1972. Intradimensional variability in concept identification: A replication, extension, and partial clarification of the Haygood, Harbert, and Omlor findings. *J. Exp. Psychol.* 94:321–25
221. Schwartz, S. H. 1971. Modes of representation and problem solving: Well evolved is half solved. *J. Exp. Psychol.* 91:347–50
222. Schwartz, S. H., Fattaleh, D. L. 1972. Representation in deductive problem-solving: The matrix. *J. Exp. Psychol.* 95:343–48
223. Scribner, S., Cole, M. 1973. Cognitive consequences of formal and informal education. *Science* 182:553–59
224. Seggie, J. L. 1970. Variables involved in confirming the consistency of a learned concept. *Aust. J. Psychol.* 22:225–35
225. Shapiro, B. J., O'Brien, T. C. 1970. Logical thinking in children ages six through thirteen. *Child Develop.* 41:823–29
226. Shepard, R. N., Cermak, G. W. 1973. Perceptual-cognitive explanations of a toroidal set of free form stimuli. *Cogn. Psychol.* 4:351–77
227. Shepard, R. N., Chipman, S. 1970. Second order isomorphism of internal representations: Shape of states. *Cogn. Psychol.* 1:1–17
228. Shepard, R. N., Feng, C. 1972. A chronometric study of mental paper folding. *Cogn. Psychol.* 3:228–43
229. Shepard, R. N., Metzler, J. 1971. Mental rotation of three-dimensional objects. *Science* 171:701–3
230. Shepp, B. E., Adams, M. J. 1973. Effects of amount of training on type of solution and breadth of learning in optional shifts. *J. Exp. Psychol.* 101:63–69
231. Silvestri, P. J., Gavurin, E. I. 1972. Anagram solving and relative solution-word transition probability. *Percept. Mot. Skills* 35:338

232. Simon, H. A. 1972. Complexity and the representation of patterned sequences of symbols. *Psychol. Rev.* 79:369–82
233. Simon, H. A., Barenfeld, M. 1969. Information processing analysis of perceptual processes in problem solving. *Psychol. Rev.* 76:473–83
234. Simon, H. A., Chase, W. G. 1973. Skill in chess. *Am. Sci.* 61:394–403
235. Simon, H. A., Gilmartin, K. 1973. A simulation of memory for chess positions. *Cogn. Psychol.* 5:29–46
236. Simpson, H. M., Climan, M. H. 1971. Pupillary and electromyographic changes during an imagery task. *Psychophysiology* 8:483–90
237. Simpson, W. E., Vaught, G. M., Ham, M. L. 1971. Intercorrelations among imagery tasks. *Percept. Mot. Skills* 32:249–50
238. Slaymaker, F. 1972. Blank trial effects in concept identification. *J. Exp. Psychol.* 92:49–52
239. Smirnov, A. A., Istomina, F. M., Maltseva, K. P., Samokhvalova, V. I. 1971–72. The development of logical memorization techniques in the preschool and young school child. *Soviet Psychol.* 10:178–96
240. Sokolov, A. N. 1972. *Inner Speech and Thought.* London: Plenum
241. Solso, R. L., Topper, G. E., Macey, W. H. 1973. Anagram solution as a function of bigram versatility. *J. Exp. Psychol.* 100:259–62
242. Spears, W. C., Dodwell, P. C. 1970. An investigation of different instructional methods on number concept understanding and arithmetic learning. *Can. J. Behav. Sci.* 2:136–47
243. Springston, F. J., Clark, H. H. 1973. *All* and *or*, or the comprehension of pseudo imperatives. *J. Verb. Learn. Verb. Behav.* 12:258–72
244. Steinberg, D. D. 1972. Truth, amphigory, and the semantic interpretation of sentences. *J. Exp. Psychol.* 93:217–19
245. Stinessen, L. 1973. Effect of different training on solution of Katona's match-stick problems. *Scand. J. Psychol.* 14:106–10
246. Stratton, R. P., Wathen, K. E. 1972. Thinking of a word under instructional constraints. *Psychon. Sci.* 28:97–99
247. Taplin, J. E. 1971. Reasoning with conditional sentences. *J. Verb. Learn. Verb. Behav.* 10:219–25
248. Taplin, J. E., Staudenmayer, H. 1973. Interpretation of abstract conditional sentences in deductive reasoning.
248a. Taplin, J. E., Staudenmayer, H., Taddonio, J. L. 1974. Developmental changes in conditional reasoning: Linguistic or logical? *J. Exp. Child Psychol.* 17:360–73
249. Thomson, W. J. 1972. Effect of number of response categories on dimension selection, paired-associate learning, and complete learning in a conjunctive concept identification task. *J. Exp. Psychol.* 93:95–99
250. Tomlinson-Keasey, C., Keasey, C. B. 1972. Long-term cultural change in cognitive development. *Percept. Mot. Skills* 35:135–39
251. Toppino, T. C., Johnson, P. J. 1973. Effects of category composition and response label on attribute identification concept performance. *J. Exp. Psychol.* 101:289–95
252. Trabasso, T., Bower, G. H. 1968. *Attention in Learning.* New York: Wiley
253. Trabasso, T., Riley, C. A. 1973. *An information processing analysis of transitive inferences.* Presented at East. Psychol. Assoc., May 1973
254. Trabasso, T., Riley, C. A., Wilson, E. 1974. Spatial strategies in reasoning: A developmental study. See Ref. 173
255. Turrisi, F. 1973. Evidence for an attentional exploration of the overtraining reversal effect. *J. Exp. Psychol.* 101:246–57
256. Wallace, O., Corballis, M. C. 1973. Short-term memory and coding strategies in the deaf. *J. Exp. Psychol.* 99:334–48
257. Warren, M. W., Thomson, W. J. 1969. Anagram solution as a function of transition probabilities and solution word frequency. *Psychon. Sci.* 17:333–34
258. Wason, P. C. 1968. Reasoning about a rule. *Quart. J. Exp. Psychol.* 20:273–81
259. Wason, P. C., Johnson-Laird, P. N. 1972. *Psychology of Reasoning: Structure and Content.* Cambridge: Harvard Univ. Press
260. Weber, R. J., Castleman, J. 1970. The

time it takes to imagine. *Percept. Psychophys.* 8:165–68

261. Weisberg, R., Suls, J. M. 1973. An information-processing model of Duncker's candle problem. *Cogn. Psychol.* 4:255–76

262. White, R. M. 1972. Relationship of performance in concept identification problems to type of pretraining problem and response-contingent postfeedback intervals. *J. Exp. Psychol.* 94:132–40

263. Ibid. Effects of some pretraining variables on concept identification, 198–205

264. Wickens, T. D., Millward, R. B. 1971. Attribute elimination strategies for concept identification with practical subjects. *J. Math. Psychol.* 8:453–80

265. Williams, G. F. 1971. A model of memory in concept learning. *Cogn. Psychol.* 2:158–84

266. Wittgenstein, L. 1953. *Philosophical Investigations.* New York: Macmillan

267. Youniss, J. 1974. Inference as a developmental construction. See Ref. 173

268. Youniss, J., Dennison, A. 1971. Figurative and operative aspects of children's inference. *Child Develop.* 42:1837–47

269. Youniss, J., Murray, J. P. 1970. Transitive inference with nontransitive solutions controlled. *Develop. Psychol.* 2:169–75

AUDITORY PSYCHOPHYSICS[1] §232

Reinier Plomp
Institute for Perception TNO, Soesterberg, The Netherlands
and Faculty of Medicine, Free University, Amsterdam

In this contribution, I have tried to evade the Scylla of a critical but too specific review and the Charybdis of a general but too uncritical review by partly giving way to both dangers. The first half of the allocated space is used for a critical discussion on the origin of the low pitch of complex sounds. Referring to the proceedings of the 1969 Driebergen symposium (162), largely devoted to that question, Harris (87) wrote in his 1972 review on audition that "probably at least 3 years more should elapse before another review would be useful." Even though this period has barely expired, the present reviewer nonetheless feels that there is an urgent need for a reconsideration of the pitch problem in the light of recent experimental evidence. If von Békésy (246) was right in stating that, to some extent, our so-called theories of hearing are actually only theories of pitch perception, this may be a sufficient argument to devote half of this review to it. The second half is used for a general survey of other major topics of auditory psychophysics.

THE LOW PITCH OF COMPLEX SOUNDS

Complex sounds as produced by musical instruments and the vocal cords are characterized by a pitch equal to the pitch of the fundamental. According to their experimental conditions, or their preferred explanations, authors have referred to this pitch as residue pitch, periodicity pitch, time-separation pitch, repetition pitch, virtual pitch, etc. I will adopt in this review the term *low pitch* as a more neutral denotation for the pitch of complex sounds.

---

[1] With a few exceptions, only papers published in the years 1970 through 1973 are considered in this review. Articles not directly referring to the low pitch of complex sounds but related to subjects brought up in the discussion on the origin of low pitch are included in that part of the review. Limited space obliged me to leave out such subjects as speech perception, auditory memory, signal detection theory, temporal threshold shifts, and studies on animals. For the same reason, papers published in the *Proceedings of the Seventh International Congress on Acoustics*, Budapest 1971, were excluded.

Temporal Versus Spectral Base of Low Pitch

It is now well accepted that the low pitch of complex sounds is not derived from the fundamental. Von Békésy's (247) arguments in favor of the fundamental were answered many years ago by the undeniable demonstration that the low pitch does not disappear if the fundamental is completely masked by a band of noise. Apparently the harmonics are significant in one way or another. Experiments with amplitude-modulated signals (44, 196) demonstrated that for a constant modulation frequency, the low pitch depends upon the frequency of the carrier. This proves that the low pitch is based neither on the difference tone as a distortion product nor on the envelope of the waveform. De Boer (44) showed that the low-pitch behavior of these inharmonic tone complexes is in line with two alternative hypotheses: (a) low pitch is derived from the *time intervals* between peaks in the fine structure near successive crests of the waveform at some place along the cochlear partition; (b) low pitch is derived from the *power spectrum* and corresponds to the best estimate of the common divisor of the frequencies of the partials. A prerequisite of the first hypothesis is that the relevant harmonics are not resolved by the ear's frequency-analyzing mechanism; a prerequisite of the second is that they are resolved. The first hypothesis assumes that low pitch is based on *temporal* peripheral cues, the second that it is based on *spectral* peripheral cues.

De Boer considered the time intervals in the fine structure as the most probable basis of low pitch, and many investigators shared this view, explaining their experimental data almost exclusively in terms of temporal cues (see 162 and also chapters by A. M. Small and J. O. Nordmark in 236). De Boer did not exclude the possibility that the alternative hypothesis may hold as a complementary mechanism for widely separated partials, but for some time no one followed him in this respect. It was only recently that a few authors have suggested comparable views. We shall see in the following sections that in the light of recent experimental evidence the neglected rather than the favored hypothesis should get most of our attention.

Effects of Phase on Low Pitch

If pitch is related to the fine structure of the compound waveform of two or more harmonics, one would expect pitch to be sensitive to the phase relation among these harmonics. Ritsma & Engel's (178) experiments with quasi frequency-modulated signals supported this supposition. Wightman (268), using identical stimuli, could not confirm this result. On the contrary, he found that the low pitch was virtually invariant for shifting the phase relation from quasi frequency modulation to amplitude modulation. Patterson (148) came to the same conclusion by investigating the low pitch of inharmonic tone complexes, consisting of 6 or 12 partials, both for cosine and random phase conditions. This result was also verified by Wightman (268). The conclusion that the low pitch of complex sounds does not depend upon the phase relations among the harmonics is just what we should expect in the light of room acoustics, because the phase relations are completely random in reverberant sound fields (163).

Harmonics Dominant in Low-Pitch Extraction

In 1967, both Plomp and Ritsma published data relevant for deciding which harmonics are most effective in the extraction of low pitch. Ritsma (176) found that for fundamental frequencies between 100 and 400 Hz, pitch is based on the frequency region corresponding to the 3rd, 4th, and 5th harmonics. Reconsidering Plomp's (161) data, we can determine that the rank numbers of the most effective harmonics gradually decrease for higher fundamental frequencies, with the result that beyond ca 1400 Hz, pitch is determined by the fundamental itself. Bilsen (12), presenting his subjects with series of 2 or 3 simultaneous harmonics of an (absent) fundamental of 50–400 Hz against a background of white noise, found that the noise level needed to mask a low-pitch jump had a maximum for tone complexes around the 4th harmonic. Apparently this level is an appropriate measure of pitch perceptibility. For harmonics around the 8th and higher, the noise level required to mask the low pitch of the 3-component stimuli was influenced by their phases. A subsequent study (29a) showed that this phase effect is caused by the occurrence of strong combination tones of the type $f_1 - k(f_2 - f_1)$, to be discussed below.

The finding that the low harmonics up to the 5th are most effective in the sensation of low pitch suggests that frequency analysis may be essential for its origin. Soderquist (203) corroborated earlier observations (160) that subjects are able to hear the individual partials of a complex of tones if their frequency separation roughly exceeds critical bandwidth. This means that the first 5 to 8 harmonics of a complex tone are resolved. By means of masking experiments, Zwicker & Fastl (283) verified that the critical band does not develop in time but reflects a constant filter property of the ear (see also 208). Duifhuis (47–49) studied an interesting consequence of the limited resolving power of the hearing organ by using periodic pulses with spectra of which a single harmonic was eliminated. He found (47) that for up to 100 pulses per sec, this *absent* harmonic is audible as a pure tone if its rank number is above about 25. This seeming paradox could be explained by the transient type response of the basilar membrane to short pulses implied by limited frequency resolution. This response was scanned with a train of sine wave bursts following the individual pulses, of which the threshold as a function of time delay was measured (48). The resulting estimate of the quality factor Q of the auditory filter was $Q > 7$, to be compared with $Q \approx 6$ on the basis of critical bandwidth data.

The hypothesis that low pitch is based upon peaks in the power spectrum implies that a complex sound consisting exclusively of high harmonics not resolved by the ear should not have a low pitch. Terhardt (227) noted that the maximal center frequency of 3 harmonics for which low pitch can be observed [Ritsma's "existence region" (175)] is approximately equal to the minimal frequency separation of two tones required to distinguish their individual pitches. Using the same subjects for the investigation of both limits, Moore (128) checked this statement. Even at very low sensation levels, applied in order to avoid any effect of combination tones, he found that under some conditions the tone complex had a well-defined low pitch when none of the individual harmonics was separately audible. He considered this to be positive evidence that the time intervals in the fine structure do play an essential role in pitch perception. Moore observed also that the introduction of noise in the frequency range below two-tone complexes reduced the rank number of the highest harmonic that can be distinguished from the 10th to approximately the 7th as found earlier for multitone stimuli (160).

Role of Combination Tones

Even at low sound-pressure levels, two pure tones with frequencies f_1 and f_2 may give rise to aural combination tones with frequencies $f_1-k(f_2-f_1)$. Before discussing their significance for low-pitch perception, I first consider recent research on general properties of combination tones. Helle (93) and Smoorenburg (202) investigated the level and phase of the cubic combination tone $2f_1-f_2$ ($k = 1$) as a function of the levels of the primary tones, presenting additional evidence that the combination tone cannot be explained by a nonlinear frequency-independent term in the transfer function; combination tones with frequencies $f_1-k(f_2-f_1)$ are much more intense for small than for large values of f_2-f_1. Smoorenburg (201) found that the lower limit of the audibility region of $2f_1-f_2$ depends primarily on the level of the lower partial. This limit appeared to be nearly the same for $k = 1$, 2, ..., 6. He demonstrated also that these combination tones may play a misleading part in masking experiments. This question was explored very extensively by Greenwood (75). He was able to explain the notch in the masking audiograms of pure tones or narrow bands of noise, appearing on the high-frequency side of the masker, by the detection of cubic combination tones. The same process that creates combination tones also creates combination bands. This similarity was confirmed by further data (76–78) from which the levels of combination bands, given by $2f_1-f_2$, f_2-f_1, and $2(f_2-f_1)$, were estimated on the basis of the masked thresholds. Combination bands generated by mixtures of pure tones and narrow noise bands appeared to vary in level as a function of stimulus parameters in a way very similar to the variations in the level of combination tones produced by two pure tones, as measured by cancellation techniques. Zwicker & Fastl (284) presented additional experimental evidence for the equivalence of the two methods. Hall (83) compared the behavior of $2f_1-f_2$ and f_2-f_1 and found that both the amplitude and phase angle of the f_2-f_1 cancellation tone decrease with an increase of f_1 or f_2/f_1. For $f_1 : f_2 = 2 : 3$, the two combination tones coincide in frequency ($= \frac{1}{2}f_1$), and their interference manifests itself in a phase effect (84).

Another much disputed product of the ear's nonlinearity is the aural harmonic. By measuring the phase dependence of the threshold of a 2000-Hz probe tone presented simultaneously with a 1000-Hz tone, Clack, Erdreich & Knighton (36; see also 55) estimated the level of the aural harmonic at 2000 Hz. Their results indicate that its level is more than 50 dB below the level of the 1000-Hz tone for sound-pressure levels of this stimulus up to ca 65 dB. This low level supports the view that the aural harmonic is insufficient to explain the monaural phase effects for octave complexes with comparable levels of the two partials (86, 137, 172).

The origin of strong combination tones given by $f_1-k(f_2-f_1)$ remains a difficult question. All psychophysical evidence points to the cochlea as the source of the nonlinearity (75, 202). Since combination tones behave completely like tones presented to the ear, it seems inevitable that the nonlinear element is coupled back to the basilar membrane [but Wilson & Johnstone (273) were not able to observe corresponding basilar-membrane vibrations in guinea pig]. Crane (37) considered the mechanical impact between the hair cells and the tectorial membrane as a possible source of combination tones. Pfeiffer (158) and Smoorenburg (202) considered a signal-compressing type of nonlinearity to account for both combination tones and suppression effects (to be discussed below). Further research may reveal how essential the effect is for understanding the cochlear processes.

Returning to our pitch problem, some experiments by Smoorenburg (200) are highly relevant. He investigated the low pitch of two-tone complexes when, starting from the harmonic relation, both partials were shifted equidistantly ($\Delta f = 200$ Hz) in frequency (also studied by Sutton & Williams 221). For harmonics beyond the 5th, the low pitch changed more than could be explained by the partials alone (either by temporal or spectral cues). Essentially this behavior was an extreme form of what had been described earlier as "the second effect of pitch shift" (196). Recent data by Patterson (148) on the low pitch of inharmonic tone complexes consisting of 6 or 12 partials, with a frequency spacing of 200 Hz, and experiments by Greenhough, Williams & Wright (74) on 3-tone complexes show also this effect. Smoorenburg demonstrated that combination tones taking over the role of lower partials absent in the stimulus, rather than the presented partials themselves, were responsible for the low pitch. This explanation is supported by experiments of van den Brink (242). His finding that "the second effect of pitch shift" disappears at very low sensation levels of inharmonic 3-tone stimuli becomes clear by considering that the combination tones also disappear. All available data on the pitch of inharmonic tone complexes are in accord with the existence of a dominant frequency region as discussed above: the pitch extractor uses the available partials closest to this region, irrespective of whether these partials are present in the stimulus or created in the ear as combination tones.

Dichotic Versus Monotic Presentation of Harmonics

Perhaps the most significant recent study on the low pitch of complex sounds was carried out by Houtsma & Goldstein (101). Two-tone stimuli were presented either monotically (both harmonics to one ear) or dichotically (one harmonic to each ear). Subjects with extensive musical training and experience listened to pairs of these stimuli for which the low pitch (if heard) had equal a priori chances to jump according to 8 different musical intervals. In order to be sure that the subjects had used the low pitch of the stimulus as a whole rather than the individual pitches of the partials as a criterion for deciding which interval had been presented, the two harmonics of each stimulus were randomly chosen out of the three pairs (n-1, n), (n, n + 1), and (n + 1, n + 2). The most important finding was that at low sensation levels the subjects could recognize the musical intervals equally well for the monotic and dichotic conditions. In both cases, the percentage of correct responses increased for decreasing rank number of the harmonics. Apparently the presence of the peripheral compound waveform for the monotic condition—or its absence for the dichotic condition—is irrelevant for low pitch. The authors' inevitable conclusion was that the low pitch of the complex stimuli involved is mediated by a central processor operating on neural signals derived from those effective stimulus harmonics that are tonotopically resolved. Bilsen's (12) finding that the level of a white noise required to mask the low pitch of two simultaneous harmonics was equal for monotic and dichotic presentations up to $n \approx 8$, with a maximum for $n \approx 4$, confirms the previous results.

Relation between Low Pitch and the Pitches of the Harmonics

The theoretical implications of the remarkably high sensitivity of the auditory system to frequency shifts of pure tones already have engaged many investigators. From measurements on the frequency-difference limen for a tone burst, performed over a wide range of frequencies and durations, Moore (125, 126) concluded that the data are consistent with the operation of a time-measuring mechanism for frequencies below 5 kHz, and with a spectral or place mechanism for frequencies above this. Experimental data for narrow bands of noise were interpreted similarly (127). Discrimination experiments by Feth (59) with combinations of amplitude and frequency differences did not support the hypothesis that both parameters are encoded by a single mechanism. Tsumura, Sone & Nimura (241) investigated the detectability of frequency transitions for tone pulses of various durations. Ronken (187) found that equal effective bandwidth does not make short tone bursts with different envelopes equally discriminable. The frequency discrimination of a brief tonal signal seems to be rather independent of the addition of an interfering tone (113, 188). Nábělek, Nábělek & Hirsh (134, 135) performed extensive measurements on the pitch of tone bursts of changing frequency. For a comparison of the pitch behavior of pure tones and the low pitch of three-tone complexes, both of short duration, see Metters & Williams (123).

Kay & Matthews (107) published experimental evidence strongly suggesting that the human auditory pathways contain specific channels for frequency modulation. This highly interesting conclusion was drawn from experiments demonstrating that the ear's sensitivity for detecting frequency modulation is selectively diminished after exposure to a conditioning tone more deeply frequency modulated at almost the same rate.

The pitch of a pure tone does not depend exclusively upon its frequency but, to a small extent, also on other parameters such as a superimposed tone or noise (232). What are the consequences for the behavior of low pitch? Walliser (251) found that both as a function of sound-pressure level and of the level of superimposed noise, the shift of the low pitch of a group of harmonics is correlated with the shift of a pure tone coinciding with the lowest harmonic, but not with a pure tone coinciding with the (absent) fundamental. In a subsequent article (252), he showed that the frequency-difference limen for a complex tone is determined by the harmonic with the smallest frequency-difference limen rather than by the fundamental. Terhardt (226) observed that the subjective octave interval for pure tones, corresponding to a frequency ratio slightly larger than 1 : 2, can be related to the upward shift of the pitch of a pure tone if a lower tone is added. Furthermore, he found (228) that the low pitch of a series of harmonics is generally somewhat lower than the pitch of their fundamental. The subjective octave interval for complex tones could be predicted from these two effects (compare 220).

Another related approach was applied by van den Brink. Some preliminary observations (242) with stimuli consisting of three harmonics had indicated that the *binaural diplacusis* (here defined as the $\Delta f/f$ required to observe the same pitch if two comparable sounds are presented alternately to the two ears) for the low pitch of these stimuli approximates the average diplacusis of the spectral components individually rather than of the (absent) fundamental. More extensive experiments (to be published in *Acustica*) confirmed this result for harmonics up to the 8th. In a subsequent experiment, van den Brink (also to be published in *Acustica*) included dichotic stimuli consisting of two out of the three harmonics presented to one ear, coinciding in frequency with the corresponding harmonics of the monotic stimulus, and one partial presented to the opposite ear. The deviation of the latter partial from its harmonic value, required for equal low pitches of the monotic and dichotic stimuli, agreed excellently with the binaural diplacusis for that frequency. These are only two out of a large number of experiments consistently demonstrating that the low pitch of a complex tone is tightly coupled to the individual pitches of the harmonics from which the low pitch is derived. It seems very difficult to reconcile the results presented in this paragraph with any theory in which the compound waveform of two or more harmonics is considered to carry any pitch information.

Discussion

In summarizing the experimental results presented above, we may conclude that there are five consistent and powerful arguments against the hypothesis that the low pitch of complex sounds is derived from the time intervals between peaks in the fine structure of unresolved harmonics: (*a*) the irrelevance of phase; (*b*) the dominance of low-order harmonics; accentuated by (*c*) the role of combination tones; (*d*) the similar results for monotic and dichotic presentations; and (*e*) the correlation with the pitches of individual harmonics. On the contrary, the recent data present strong evidence in favor of the hypothesis that *frequency resolution* is a prerequisite of hearing low pitch. De Boer's (44) alternative, and neglected, hypothesis that low pitch is based on spectral cues should be accepted rather than the hypothesis that low pitch is based on temporal cues.

This conclusion implies that peaks in the stimulation pattern along the cochlear partition, as a result of the frequency-analyzing capacity of the cochlea, are essential as a basis for low pitch extraction. This suggests that as a modification of the classic "place theory," a central processor derives low pitch from the locations of the peaks of the stimulation pattern. Since for these peaks the nerve discharges are synchronized with the frequencies of the harmonics (up to ca 4000 Hz), we should not exclude the possibility that for the individual frequency components, temporal rather than spatial information is used as the neural code for their frequencies. It will be obvious that in this concept time plays a quite different role than in the criticized view that low pitch is based on the time intervals between peaks in the fine structure near successive crests of the compound waveform at some place along the cochlear partition. Available experimental data (e.g. 42, 126, 127) do not give conclusive evidence for excluding either topical or temporal information as possible codes for the frequencies of the harmonics. Similarly, the observed relation between low pitch and the pitches of the harmonics is not decisive. This relation only implies that both pitch modes are based upon the same neural information. If the effect of secondary parameters on pitch and the phenomenon of binaural diplacusis are related to the locations of the peaks of the stimulation pattern along the cochlear partition, this would speak well for the tonotopical code. There is, however, no compelling reason to exclude the possibility that the pitch variations have their origin in an imperfect transformation of the temporal code at some postcochlear center of the auditory pathway. Additionally, there is no reason to assume that the central pitch processor extracts low pitch from the *pitches* of the harmonics rather than that both pitch modes are extracted from the *same* neural information. The latter view can explain Moore's (128) finding, referred to above, that the audibility of the pitches of the individual harmonics is not a necessary condition for hearing low pitch.

Investigations on the production of a faint but distinct pitch when subjects are presented with stimuli consisting of a signal plus its time-delayed replica have in the past been interpreted as demonstrating that the time pattern of the nerve discharges does play a role in the sensation of low pitch. If these stimuli are presented monotically, the results can be interpreted satisfactorily in terms of spectral analysis. For instance, the superposition of white noise and its time-delayed replica, with a delay of τ seconds, results in a sound spectrum with periodic peaks for n/τ Hz, explaining why a "repetition pitch" corresponding to $1/\tau$ is observed. Continuing earlier experiments, Bilsen & Ritsma (15, 16, 177) were able to show that the concept of a dominance region also holds for repetition pitch. More intriguing was the finding by Bilsen & Goldstein (13; see also 61) that under favorable conditions this pitch does not disappear if white noise is presented to one ear and the delayed version to the other. In this case, no spectral cues are available at the peripheral level. The authors conclude that "known binaural and monaural phenomena on pitch of complex sounds appear to be compatible with a generalized place theory of pitch in which a central pitch mechanism reads across the characteristic frequency dimension of a centrally presented spectrum" in which interaural differences in timing are reflected.

What central processes are involved in extracting low pitch remains an open question. No available physiological data can help us. The models proposed in recent years are, therefore, rather speculative. Whitfield (266) suggested that low pitch may be the result of some sort of pattern recognition. Walliser (251, 253; see also 227) explained his experiments by a model in which the pitch of complex sounds corresponds to that subharmonic of the lowest present harmonic which is nearest to the frequency of the envelope of the signal's waveform. This model was modified and detailed by Terhardt (229–231), who considered low pitch to be based upon the pitches of the harmonics as the product of a process of auditory "Gestalt" perception in which a "learning process" is included. Wightman (269) presented a formalized model in which the pattern of the peripheral neural activity, reflecting the power spectrum of the stimulus, is assumed to be Fourier transformed into another pattern of which the positions of maximal activity determine the low pitch. Goldstein (71) proposed a statistical theory in which low pitch is the result of the following successive steps: perfect spectral analysis, noisy projection of the spectral components, optimal matching to a harmonic pattern, estimate of the rank numbers of the harmonics and the fundamental. It seems clear that there is an urgent need for physiological data on the processes involved in the extraction of low pitch from a complex sound.

FURTHER MONAURAL FUNCTIONS

Loudness

Just as for the low pitch of complex tones, rather established views on loudness have been challenged in recent years. Warren (256) presented experimental evidence suggesting that the generally accepted *sone* scale reflects the influence of experimentally induced biases. Free from known biasing factors, judgments of half-loudness correspond to ca 6 dB attenuation for tones. [For the effect of procedure on loudness functions, see also Ward (254, 255) and Schneider et al (194), and for interindividual differences see de Barbenza et al (43).] A similar approach for speech under reverberation (258) seems to support the hypothesis that half-loudness judgments are equivalent to estimates of the effect of doubling distance from listener to sound source. If this is true, traditional procedures for calculating loudness (102, 149, 214, 215; see also 8) should be reconsidered.

In addition, the use of simultaneous dichotic loudness balance procedures (as in 263 and 280) for investigating per-stimulatory loudness adaptation has been criticized by Fraser, Petty & Elliott (62, 157). They showed that the adaptation effect disappears if binaural interactions are reduced or eliminated. Further investigations (216–219; but see also 24, 92, 130, 271) supported this conclusion.

Other investigators studied the effect of various parameters on loudness. Scharf & Fishken (193) found that the ratio of binaural to monaural loudness for tone and noise is lower than the traditionally accepted value of 2.0. Levelt, Riemersma & Bunt (115) concluded from their experiments that binaural additivity of loudness holds for nonzero stimulation of the ears. Contralateral noise reduces the loudness of a 1000-Hz tone at low levels, but increases the loudness at moderate levels (190). The apparent loudness of a tone pip can be increased by 15 dB or more if it is preceded by a tone burst to the contralateral ear (63). Boone (22) provided evidence that the time constant governing the build-up of loudness of periodic tone bursts is of the order of 100 msec. The monaural loudness level of a 250-msec tone burst is only 1 phon below the level for durations of 2 sec or longer (57), whereas a fast onset seems to contribute to the loudness (69). This onset effect holds also for periodic acoustic transients (32; see also 33). Pure-tone equal-loudness contours appear to depend upon the frequency of the standard tone (124). In another study (194), these contours were derived from magnitude estimates. The most comfortable loudness levels of various sounds, extensively explored as a function of several parameters (243; see also 245), appear to scatter around 50 dB sound-pressure level, but are significantly lower for ascending than for descending tones (275). Stephens & Anderson (210, 213) found values around 100 dB SPL for the uncomfortable loudness level of a 1000-Hz tone (further loudness studies include 34, 103, 108, 136).

Timbre of Steady-State Complex Sounds

Von Bismarck (248–250) studied the timbre dissimilarities of various complex stimuli by means of semantic scales. Factor analysis applied on the scores of 35 sounds along 30 different scales resulted in "dull-bright" as the main factor (249). Further experiments showed that brightness (or sharpness) is primarily determined by the absolute frequency region of the loudest spectral components (250). Plomp & Steeneken (163) investigated the extent to which characteristic timbres are blurred by reverberation in a large hall.

The "Continuity Effect" and Lateral Suppression

As early as 1957, Thurlow (233) reported that under certain conditions the less intense component of a pair of alternating tones is heard as sounding continuously. This "continuity effect" appears to represent a general property of the hearing system; if an extraneous sound such as a cough or a tone burst completely replaces a speech sound in a recorded sentence, listeners believe they hear the missing sound (11, 257, 259, 261). The maximum sound-pressure level at which the continuity effect still holds resembles, as a function of frequency, the masked-threshold curve (52, 260), depending also slightly on the angular separation of the two tone sources (52). All experimental evidence supports the view (97–99) that the continuity (or pulsation) threshold of a certain sound stimulus, measured as a function of frequency, reflects the neural activity pattern induced by that sound along the cochlear partition.

Houtgast (97–100) adopted this effect as a psychophysical procedure for investigating lateral suppression (or inhibition) in hearing, already known neurophysiologically. He demonstrated (97, 99) that a noise with a steep positive or negative slope at a particular frequency shows significant edge effects, comparable to Mach bands in vision, if the noise and the probe tone are presented nonsimultaneously. This effect might be essential in explaining the observed pitches corresponding to the edges of a noise band (58, 70), as well as the phenomenon known as Zwicker's "negative afterimage" (117). The absence of lateral suppression in simultaneous masking (confirmed by Rainbolt & Small 173) can be understood by assuming that for that condition both the masker and the probe tone are subjected to the same suppression mechanism. Houtgast (98, 99) showed that a strong tone may reduce the level of a weaker tone of ca 20% lower frequency by more than 15 dB. The extent to which a tone is suppressed by simultaneous wide-band noise (99, 100) agrees quantitatively with the loudness reduction of a tone when noise is added.

Hellman's (94) finding that the loudness of a 1000-Hz tone tends to grow more rapidly in the presence of a narrow-band noise than of a wide-band noise can be explained by lateral suppression. Experiments with rippled-spectrum noise indicated (99) that the effective bandwidth of the ear's frequency-analyzing mechanism in nonsimultaneous masking is about half the critical bandwidth as found in simultaneous masking, which demonstrates quantitatively the sharpening or enhancement effect of the lateral suppression mechanism.

Origin of Tonal Consonance and Dissonance

The perceptual singularity of musical intervals consisting of two simultaneous tones with a simple frequency ratio was studied by means of identification tests of briefly presented chords (164). The results showed clearly that the chords were confused in terms of their width rather than their frequency ratio simplicity. This confirms the view that tonal consonance is related to interval width for pure tones. Chords consisting of tones of which the frequencies of the harmonics were compressed gave sensations consistent with Helmholtz's criterion for dissonance (198).

Detection of Sounds

Under this heading, I will report on a number of investigations in which the detection of a stimulus, whether or not superimposed on another sound, is involved.

Watson, Franks & Hood (262) found the sound-pressure level of 150-msec tone bursts required for 76% correct detection in a two-alternative forced-choice procedure to be in good agreement with the ISO audiometric-zero standard. On the basis of additional data, extension of this standard's present limit of 8,000 Hz up to 18,000 Hz was proposed (89, 140). The dependence of hearing threshold on the time the subject has been in quiet seems to be negligible (209). Anderson & Whittle (4; see also 25, 132, 205) provided evidence that the old "missing 6 dB" effect (discrepancy in threshold between free-field and earphone listening conditions) is caused by the physiological noise produced under a supra-aural earcap. Further evidence showed that under quite different conditions the ear's sensitivity is slightly enhanced by a preceding or succeeding stimulus (129, 138, 139). The interaction of the auditory and visual systems in signal detection was studied by Fidell (60). Karlovich et al (106) verified that the absence of temporal integration when the duration of a 125-Hz tone burst is varied between 200 and 5 msec is due to the spread of energy toward the higher, more sensitive frequency region. If this spread was checked by means of a low-pass filter, threshold behavior agreed with the integration curves as studied by many investigators (66, 150, 211, 212, 225). The role of energy spread if a tone burst is superimposed on a tone of the same frequency was demonstrated by Leshowitz & Wightman (114).

Many studies were devoted to the masked threshold of a brief probe sound as a function of various parameters (for recent reviews see 51, 54, 192, 286). Mulligan & Elrod (133) studied the detection of tones in noise in terms of signal-detection theory, whereas Reed & Bilger (174) considered the masked thresholds in relation to the various estimates of the critical bandwidth. Ahumada & Lovell (3) concluded that the detection of a tone burst in noise is determined by more than one feature. The deletion of a tone appears to be much harder to detect than the insertion of the same tone (197). Canahl (31) observed that four equally spaced tones mask a central (1000 Hz) signal much more than would be predicted from two tones. In comparing two with one masking tones, Chocholle (35) found a similar effect. Patterson (145) noted that the amount of masking is related to the short-term spectrum of brief maskers. Even for narrow noise bands, the noise masks a pure tone more effectively than the reverse (95). Leshowitz & Cudahy (112) investigated the amount of masking of a 5-msec probe tone at various delays after the onset of a 500-msec tonal masker of constant frequency. Masking appeared to be largest at the moments when the gradients of the maskers were steepest. Analogous to critical bandwidth, a critical masking interval of 10 to 14 msec has been proposed (151; see also 189). Zwicker & Schütte (285) studied, also by means of a probe signal shifted in time, the extent to which the ear is able to follow the random temporal changes of the sound level of narrow bands of noise and found that this ability is limited to bandwidths below ca 100 Hz.

The threshold for clicks in simultaneous masking as well as in forward and backward masking of 500-msec noise bursts was investigated by Wilson & Carhart (274). Presenting the click between two bursts resulted in threshold shifts greater than either forward or backward masking would have produced if operating alone. This condition compares with Duifhuis (48), who measured the threshold for brief probe tones presented with variable time delay with respect to the pulses of a pulse train. The nonadditivity of forward and backward masking was also observed by Patterson (144). Robinson & Pollack (180; see also 169) interpreted this effect in terms of a temporal integrating period. For noise bursts shorter than 200 msec, the amount of forward masking appears to depend primarily upon the product of duration and intensity of the masker (282). The effect of forward and backward masking on speech intelligibility was studied by Dirks & Bower (45). Zwislocki (287) published a quantitative psychophysiological theory of central masking which appeared to predict accurately single-unit characteristics of the auditory nerve and of primary-like populations in the cochlear nuclei and the superior olive.

Since experiments on intensity discrimination can be interpreted as detection experiments, some are included here. Viemeister (244) concluded that Weber's law holds also for a pure tone of 950 Hz if frequency regions at and above the second harmonic of the signal are masked by filtered noise. The generality of this conclusion was criticized by Schacknow & Raab (191). Intensity discrimination data on broad-band and high-pass filtered clicks were also consistent with Weber's law (152). Rochester (184) found that although the processes of the detection and of the discrimination of a change in duration seem to be very similar for weak signals presented in a background of continuous noise, corresponding experimental procedures gave different results. Luce & Green (116) presented a psychophysical theory which could account for Weber's law and other auditory functions. Using sinusoidally modulated noise, Rodenburg (185) studied the just-noticeable modulation depth of noise as a function of modulation frequency and found that the resulting temporal transfer function has a cutoff frequency of

40–80 Hz and an asymptotic slope of 6 dB per octave for higher modulation frequencies. Finally, I refer to three studies on the intensity perception of tone pulses (10, 23, 171).

Temporal Acuity

A number of papers have been published recently dealing with the interesting question of the shortest time interval within which the ear can discriminate the order of auditory events. Patterson & Green (146, 147; see also 72) presented subjects with pairs of very brief transient signals having identical energy spectra but different phase spectra. The results of these experiments suggested that the ear can discriminate differences in temporal order as small as 2.5 msec. Further research (73) indicated that this value is largely independent of frequency. Babkoff & Sutton (5; see also 186) used pairs of clicks of unequal intensity. Stimuli with different order of the two clicks could be discriminated if the interpulse interval exceeded ca 2 msec; the score of correct responses had a second minimum for intervals of 12–15 msec, whereas the perception of temporal order itself is a dominant cue only for longer intervals. The minimum detectable gap between successive tonal pulses, being as small as 2.5 msec for 3-msec pulses, appears to increase as a direct function of both the pulse duration and the frequency disparity between successive pulses (272). (Further related studies include 85, 111, 166–168, 179.)

Subjective Duration of Sounds

Zwicker (281) found that subjects are able to adjust the duration of a sound burst, a silent gap, or a time interval between two short pulses with an accuracy of ca 10% to the duration of a standard. For equal physical durations, the sensation of a gap or a time interval seems to be about half as long as of a burst. These experiments were continued by Burghardt (26–29). Below 400 msec, asymmetries between the subjective durations of a burst and a gap up to a factor of 5 were observed (29). This effect disappeared for durations above 1 sec. Below ca 3000 Hz, a short high-frequency sound burst has a substantially longer subjective duration than a low-frequency burst of the same physical duration; this trend is reversed above that frequency (28). Related investigations were carried out by Abel (1, 2). For durations above 50 msec, the Weber fraction for the discrimination of the duration of sound bursts is ca 0.1, in agreement with Zwicker's (281) results, whereas the discrimination for shorter durations is more in accord with a square-root relation (1). The Weber fraction for the discrimination of temporal gaps showed a local minimum at ca 2.5 msec and a maximum at 10 msec (2).

BINAURAL FUNCTIONS

Reviews on research on binaural hearing up to about 1966 by A. W. Mills, L. A. Jeffress, N. I. Durlach, and J. V. Tobias can be found in Volume II of *Foundations of Modern Auditory Theory* (237). A very extensive review (522 references) on spatial localization of sounds, including animals, was given by Erulkar (56).

Localization of Sounds

Harris (88) repeated and extended classic experiments on the minimum audible angles for tone sources in a free-field situation. Low values of 1°–2° over the frequency range from 125 through 6400 Hz were obtained. The data suggest that eliminating either the interaural time cue or the interaural intensity cue has only slight effects on the minimum audible angles (compare 91). When the two cues were rendered noncongruent, the difference in arrival time appeared to be prepotent over a difference of intensity up to ca 7 dB. In a separate paper (90), results for monaural and binaural localization were compared (see also 53). Stimulus durations of more than ca 2 sec are required to make good use of head movements for localization (235). For sources located in the median plane, localization is influenced primarily by the irregularities of the pinna (64). Toole (238) concluded that small head movements are not the main factor underlying the "externalization" of sounds.

Several of these questions have been studied extensively in some German laboratories in their search for stereophonic sound reproduction systems with a high degree of naturalness. An extensive review can be found in Blauert (20a). The same author (17) investigated the role of the outer ear in sound localization in the median plane. For time delays exceeding ca 0.5 msec at the ears, the precedence effect seems to be valid also in this plane (19; but see also 109). For high-frequency signals, even vertical shifts of sound sources corresponding to less than 4° were discriminated (264). It has been demonstrated (39, 41; see also 38, 40) that the acoustical crosstalk resulting from sound diffraction at the head when stereophonic signals are reproduced with two loudspeakers can be compensated for by special filters. Listening tests showed that in this way, even with two loudspeakers, nearly ideal localization for the entire horizontal plane including front-back discrimination can be obtained. The typical disadvantage of headphones for stereophonic listening, namely that the sound images are localized in the head (see 159 for a theory of this effect), has been conquered successfully by means of electrical circuits simulating loudspeaker-listening conditions (110, with 77 references; 21; see also 265).

Lateralization of Sounds

The fact that with headphones sounds are lateralized rather than localized is no problem for those investigators studying the lateralization of binaural signals. Yost, Wightman & Green (279) presented the ears of subjects with identical band-pass filtered clicks and found that the discrimination of lateral position of the sound image, induced by delays between the times of arrival at the ears, depends primarily on the low-frequency contents of the clicks. This holds also for localization (7). Using antiphasic clicks, Bilsen & Raatgever (14) were able to show that lateralization is derived from a dominant frequency region around ca 650 Hz. It is of interest that the same frequency region dominates dichotic repetition pitch (13). Thurlow & Jack (234) presented evidence that the lateralization of a noise stimulus is affected by a preceding adapting noise stimulus with a time-delay difference at the two ears. Perrott & co-workers (153–156) studied the limits of binaural fusion as a function of interaural frequency and signal duration. Pollack (165) studied the interaural correlation-discrimination threshold for pulse trains, and Dunn (50) investigated the effect of unilateral masking on the lateralization of binaural pulses.

Lateralization of a sound image can be achieved by introducing a time difference or an intensity difference between the signals presented to the ears. Traditionally the interaction of time and intensity has been studied in terms of a binaural "trading ratio" as if the effect of one of these parameters can be compensated for by the effect of the other. Recent research has brought forward further evidence that this view is not correct. Blauert (18, 20) found that oscillations of a sound image between the ears are detectable up to a slightly but significantly higher rate if the oscillations are based on interaural intensity differences rather than on interaural time differences. Hafter & Carrier (81) requested subjects to detect the difference between low-frequency tonal signals, leading in time to one ear but more intense to the other, and signals without any difference at the ears. The results confirmed the view of an incomplete compensation and were used by the authors for a model of time-intensity trading (see also 6, 46, 68, 82).

The Effect of Masking-Level Difference (MLD)

In other approaches, the effect of MLD, usually defined as the improvement in the binaural masked threshold when the polarity of either the masker or the signal to one ear is reversed, was included. In an earlier experiment, Hafter & Carrier (80) had studied MLD for a tonal masker and a tonal signal of the same frequency and duration. Introduction of interaural time and interaural intensity differences of the signal suggested that the trading ratio depends upon experimental condition. Yost (276) observed that at high frequencies the interaural phase difference is no longer usable as a cue. Contrary to the homophasic condition, the Weber fraction decreases for the antiphasic condition for increasing values of the phase angle of addition (277). (For a discussion on possible artifacts in this type of experiment see 267.) Similar experiments, but with both the masker and the signal derived from the same 50-Hz band of noise, supported the view that the time and intensity cues do not cancel perfectly (105, 118, 119). McFadden, Russell & Pulliam (121) found that in binaural listening the masking pattern of an antiphasic 100-msec tone signal with a homophasic 4000-Hz continuous masker is characterized by two local minima at about ± 10 Hz from the masker. Further related experiments are found elsewhere (30, 122, 143, 195, 207; see for a survey 104).

In the more traditional MLD experiments, wide-band noise is used as a masker. MLD appears to be independent of signal duration and, probably due to physiological noise, is reduced at low sensation levels (204). At hearing threshold, the effect is very small (67). McFadden & Pulliam (120) observed that a lower level of a monaurally presented signal in a binaurally presented noise masker is sufficient for detection rather than for lateralization. Wilbanks (270) varied the interaural correlation of both his 135-Hz wide noise signal, centered at 250 Hz, and the masker, and noticed that with a correlated masker detection is about 14 dB better with an uncorrelated signal than with a correlated signal (see also 206). Robinson & Dolan (182) confirmed that for uncorrelated noise, MLD for tones decreases for increasing signal frequency. For correlated noise, the detection threshold of a 500-Hz tone in the antiphasic condition is lower for large than for small time intervals between the onsets of the noise and the signal (183; see also 9, 240). Townsend & Goldstein (239) investigated MLD at suprathreshold levels by means of loudness matching. It appeared that the antiphasic advantage is greatly reduced or absent for sensation levels above 20 dB. It is likely that loudness determines the frequency discrimination performance for binaural signals (65). Using complex sounds (natural and synthetic vowels) as signals, Mosko & House (131) confirmed that maximal MLD occurs when the components in the region of 250 to 500 Hz are interaurally out of phase. At low sensation levels, resolution of frequency and amplitude is better with antiphasic than with homophasic signals (96). (Further studies include 181, 222–224, 278.)

This large number of recent MLD studies illustrates how fashionable this topic is. Perhaps the most interesting finding is that MLD exists also in forward and backward masking (170, 199). This means that the detection of a low-frequency tone, separated from the masker by a short silent interval, improves if the phase is reversed at one ear. This may have important implications for models related to MLD, such as the lateralization model proposed by Hafter (79) and the correlation model proposed by Osman (141, 142).

Literature Cited

1. Abel, S. M. 1972. Duration discrimination of noise and tone bursts. *J. Acoust. Soc. Am.* 51:1219–23
2. Ibid. *Discrimination of temporal gaps.* 52:519–24
3. Ahumada, A. Jr., Lovell, J. 1971. Stimulus features in signal detection. *J. Acoust. Soc. Am.* 49:1751–56
4. Anderson, C. M. B., Whittle, L. S. 1971. Physiological noise and the missing 6 dB. *Acustica* 24:261–72
5. Babkoff, H., Sutton, S. 1971. Monaural temporal interactions. *J. Acoust. Soc. Am.* 50:459–65
6. Babkoff, H., Sutton, S., Barris, M. 1973. Binaural interaction of transients: interaural time and intensity asymmetry. *J. Acoust. Soc. Am.* 53:1028–36
7. Banks, M. S., Green, D. M. 1973. Localization of high- and low-frequency transients. *J. Acoust. Soc. Am.* 53:1432–33
8. Bauer, B. B., Torick, E. L., Allen, R. G. 1971. The measurement of loudness level. *J. Acoust. Soc. Am.* 50:405–14
9. Bell, D. W. 1972. Effect of fringe on masking-level difference when gating from uncorrelated to correlated noise. *J. Acoust. Soc. Am.* 52:525–29
10. Berliner, J. E., Durlach, N. I. 1973. Intensity perception. IV. Resolution in roving-level discrimination. *J. Acoust. Soc. Am.* 53:1270–87
11. Bertelson, P., Tisseyre, F. 1970. Perceiving the sequence of speech and nonspeech stimuli. *Quart. J. Exp. Psychol.* 22:653–62
12. Bilsen, F. A. 1973. On the influence of the number and phase of harmonics on the perceptibility of the pitch of complex signals. *Acustica* 28:60–65
13. Bilsen, F. A., Goldstein, J. L. 1974. Pitch of dichotically delayed noise and its possible spectral basis. *J. Acoust. Soc. Am.* 55:292–96
14. Bilsen, F. A., Raatgever, J. 1973. Spectral dominance in binaural lateralization. *Acustica* 28:131–32
15. Bilsen, F. A., Ritsma, R. J. 1969/70.

Repetition pitch and its implication for hearing theory. *Acustica* 22:63-73

16. Bilsen, F. A., Ritsma, R. J. 1970. Some parameters influencing the perceptibility of pitch. *J. Acoust. Soc. Am.* 47:469-75

17. Blauert, J. 1969/70. Sound localization in the median plane. *Acustica* 22: 205-13

18. Ibid 1970. Zur Trägheit des Richtungshörens bei Laufzeit- und Intensitätsstereophonie. 23:287-93

19. Blauert, J. 1971. Localization and the law of the first wavefront in the median plane. *J. Acoust. Soc. Am.* 50:466-70

20. Blauert, J. 1972. On the lag of lateralization caused by interaural time and intensity differences. *Audiology* 11:265-70

20a. Blauert, J. 1974. *Räumliches Hören.* Stuttgart: Hirzel Verlag. 256 pp.

21. Blauert, J., Laws, P. 1973. Verfahren zur orts- und klanggetreuen Simulation von Lautsprecherbeschallungen mit Hilfe von Kopfhörern. *Acustica* 29:273-77

22. Boone, M. M. 1973. Loudness measurements on pure tones and broad band impulsive sounds. *Acustica* 29:198-204

23. Braida, L. D., Durlach, N. I. 1972. Intensity perception. II. Resolution in one-interval paradigms. *J. Acoust. Soc. Am.* 51:483-502

24. Bray, D. A., Dirks, D. D., Morgan, D. E. 1973. Perstimulatory loudness adaptation. *J. Acoust. Soc. Am.* 53:1544-48

25. Brinkmann, K. 1973. Audiometer-Bezugsschwelle und Freifeld-Hörschwelle. *Acustica* 28:147-54

26. Burghardt, H. 1972. *Zusammenhang zwischen subjektiver und objektiver Dauer von Schallen.* PhD thesis. Technological Univ., München. 81 pp.

27. Burghardt, H. 1972/73. Einfaches Funktionsschema zur Beschreibung der subjektiven Dauer von Schallimpulsen und Schallpausen. *Kybernetik* 12:21-29

28. Burghardt, H. 1973. Die subjektive Dauer schmalbandiger Schalle bei verschiedenen Frequenzlagen. *Acustica* 28:278-84

29. Ibid. Ueber die subjektive Dauer von Schallimpulsen und Schallpausen, 284-90

29a. Buunen, T. J. F., Festen, J. M., Bilsen, F. A., van den Brink, G. 1974. Phase effects in a three-component signal. *J. Acoust. Soc. Am.* 55:297-303

30. Canahl, J. A. Jr. 1970. Binaural masking of a tone by a tone plus noise. *J. Acoust. Soc. Am.* 47:476-79

31. Ibid 1971. Two- versus four-tone masking at 1000 Hz. 50:471-74

32. Carter, N. L. 1972. Effects of rise time and repetition rate on the loudness of acoustic transients. *J. Sound. Vib.* 21:227-39

33. Carter, N. L., Dunlop, J. I. 1973. The effects of rise time and repetition rate on the thresholds for acoustic transients. *J. Sound Vib.* 30:359-66

34. Carvellas, T., Schneider, B. 1972. Direct estimation of multidimensional tonal dissimilarity. *J. Acoust. Soc. Am.* 51:1839-48

35. Chocholle, R. 1972. Effets de masque homolatéraux et contralatéraux, totaux et partiels, sur un son pur de deux autres sons purs placés de part et d'autre du premier. *Acustica* 27:267-77

36. Clack, T. D., Erdreich, J., Knighton, R. W. 1972. Aural harmonics: the monaural phase effects at 1500 Hz, 2000 Hz, and 2500 Hz observed in tone-on-tone masking when $f_1 = 1000$ Hz. *J. Acoust. Soc. Am.* 52:536-41

37. Crane, H. D. 1972. Mechanical impact and fatigue in relation to nonlinear combination tones in the cochlea. *J. Acoust. Soc. Am.* 51:508-14

38. Damaske, P. 1969/70. Richtungsabhängigkeit vom Spektrum und Korrelationsfunktionen der an den Ohren empfangenen Signale. *Acustica* 22: 191-204

39. Damaske, P. 1971. Head-related two-channel stereophony with loudspeaker reproduction. *J. Acoust. Soc. Am.* 50:1109-15

40. Damaske, P., Mellert, V. 1969/70. Ein Verfahren zur richtungstreuen Schallabbildung des oberen Halbraumes über zwei Lautsprecher. *Acustica* 22:153-62

41. Ibid 1971. Zur richtungstreuen stereo-

phonen Zweikanalübertragung. 24: 222-25
42. Davies, R. O., Greenhough, M., Williams, R. P. 1973. The pitch of pulse trains with random arrangements of two basic interpulse times. *Acustica* 29:93-100
43. de Barbenza, C. M., Bryan, M. E., McRobert, H., Tempest, W. 1970. Individual loudness susceptibility. *Sound* 4:75-79
44. de Boer, E. 1956. On the "residue" in hearing. PhD thesis. Univ. Amsterdam. 106 pp.
45. Dirks, D. D., Bower, D. 1970. Effect of forward and backward masking on speech intelligibility. *J. Acoust. Soc. Am.* 47:1003-8
46. Domnitz, R. 1973. The interaural time jnd as a simultaneous function of interaural time and interaural amplitude. *J. Acoust. Soc. Am.* 53:1549-52
47. Duifhuis, H. 1970. Audibility of high harmonics in a periodic pulse. *J. Acoust. Soc. Am.* 48:888-93
48. Ibid 1971. Audibility of high harmonics in a periodic pulse. II. Time effect. 49:1155-62
49. Duifhuis, H. 1972. *Perceptual analysis of sound.* PhD thesis. Technological Univ., Eindhoven. 178 pp.
50. Dunn, B. E. 1971. Effect of unilateral masking on the lateralization of binaural pulses. *J. Acoust. Soc. Am.* 50:483-89
51. Egan, J. P. 1971. Auditory masking and signal detection theory. *Audiology* 10:41-47
52. Elfner, L. F. 1971. Continuity in alternately sounded tonal signals in a free field. *J. Acoust. Soc. Am.* 49:447-49
53. Elfner, L. F., Bothe, G. G., Simrall, D. S. 1970. Monaural localization: effects of feedback, incentive, and interstimulus interval. *J. Aud. Res.* 10:11-16
54. Elliott, L. L. 1971. Backward and forward masking. *Audiology* 10:65-76
55. Erdreich, J., Clack, T. D. 1972. An algorithm for analysis of phase effects: application to monaural distortion product estimation. *J. Acoust. Soc. Am.* 52:1124-26
56. Erulkar, S. D. 1972. Comparative aspects of spatial localization of sound. *Physiol. Rev.* 52:237-360

57. Evans, D. H. 1971. An experimental determination of the growth of auditory sensation for time periods greater than 125 ms. *J. Aud. Res.* 11:374-84
58. Fastl, H. 1971. Ueber Tonhöhenempfindungen bei Rauschen. *Acustica* 25:350-54
59. Feth, L. L. 1972. Combinations of amplitude and frequency differences in auditory discrimination. *Acustica* 26: 67-77
60. Fidell, S. 1970. Sensory function in multimodal signal detection. *J. Acoust. Soc. Am.* 47:1009-15
61. Fourcin, A. J. 1970. Central pitch and auditory lateralization. See Ref. 162, 319-28
62. Fraser, W. D., Petty, J. W., Elliott, D. N. 1970. Adaptation: central or peripheral? *J. Acoust. Soc. Am.* 47: 1016-21
63. Galambos, R., Bauer, J., Picton, T., Squires, K., Squires, N. 1972. Loudness enhancement following contralateral stimulation. *J. Acoust. Soc. Am.* 52:1127-30
64. Gardner, M. B., Gardner, R. S. 1973. Problem of localization in the median plane: effect of pinnae cavity occlusion. *J. Acoust. Soc. Am.* 53:400-8
65. Gebhardt, C. J., Goldstein, D. P., Robertson, R. M. 1972. Frequency discrimination and the MLD. *J. Acoust. Soc. Am.* 51:1228-32
66. Gengel, R. W. 1972. Auditory temporal integration at relatively high masked-threshold levels. *J. Acoust. Soc. Am.* 51:1849-51
67. Gerber, S. E., Jaffe, P. G., Alford, B. L. 1971. Binaural threshold and interaural phase differences. *J. Aud. Res.* 11:65-68
68. Gilliom, J. D., Sorkin, R. D. 1972. Discrimination of interaural time and intensity. *J. Acoust. Soc. Am.* 52: 1635-44
69. Gjaevenes, K., Rimstad, E. R. 1972. The influence of rise time on loudness. *J. Acoust. Soc. Am.* 51:1233-39
70. Glave, R. D. 1973. *Untersuchungen zur Tonhöhenwahrnehmung stochastischer Schallsignale.* Hamburg: Helmut Buske Verlag. 240 pp.
71. Goldstein, J. L. 1973. An optimum processor theory for the central forma-

tion of the pitch of complex tones. *J. Acoust. Soc. Am.* 54:1496–1516

72. Green, D. M. 1971. Temporal auditory acuity. *Psychol. Rev.* 78:540–51

73. Green, D. M. 1973. Temporal acuity as a function of frequency. *J. Acoust. Soc. Am.* 54:373–79

74. Greenhough, M., Williams, R. P., Wright, S. J. 1973. Some experiments on the second effect of pitch shift in three-tone complexes. *J. Sound. Vib.* 26:277–82

75. Greenwood, D. D. 1971. Aural combination tones and auditory masking. *J. Acoust. Soc. Am.* 50:502–43

76. Ibid 1972. Masking by narrow bands of noise in proximity to more intense pure tones of higher frequency: application to measurement of combination band levels and some comparisons with masking by combination noise. 52:1137–43

77. Ibid. Masking by combination bands: estimation of the levels of the combination bands $(n + 1)f_l\text{-}nf_h$, 1144–54

78. Ibid. Combination bands of even order: masking effects and estimation of level of the difference bands $(f_h\text{-}f_l)$ and $2(f_h\text{-}f_l)$, 1155–67

79. Hafter, E. R. 1971. Quantitative evaluation of a lateralization model of masking-level differences. *J. Acoust. Soc. Am.* 50:1116–22

80. Hafter, E. R., Carrier, S. C. 1970. Masking-level differences obtained with a pulsed tonal masker. *J. Acoust. Soc. Am.* 47:1041–47

81. Ibid 1972. Binaural interaction in low-frequency stimuli: the inability to trade time and intensity completely. 51:1852–62

82. Hafter, E. R., Carrier, S. C., Stephan, F. K. 1973. Direct comparison of lateralization and the MLD for monaural signals and gated noise. *J. Acoust. Soc. Am.* 53:1553–59

83. Hall, J. L. 1972. Auditory distortion products $f_2\text{-}f_1$ and $2f_1\text{-}f_2$. *J. Acoust. Soc. Am.* 51:1863–71

84. Ibid. Monaural phase effect: cancellation and reinforcement of distortion products $f_2\text{-}f_1$ and $2f_1\text{-}f_2$, 1872–81

85. Hall, J. L., Lummis, R. C. 1973. Thresholds for click pairs masked by band-stop noise. *J. Acoust. Soc. Am.* 54:593–99

86. Hall, J. L., Schroeder, M. R. 1972. Monaural phase effects for two-tone signals. *J. Acoust. Soc. Am.* 51:1882–84

87. Harris, J. D. 1972. Audition. *Ann. Rev. Psychol.* 23:313–46

88. Harris, J. D. 1972. A florilegium of experiments on directional hearing. *Acta Otolaryngol. Suppl.* 298. 26 pp.

89. Harris, J. D., Myers, C. K. 1971. Tentative audiometric threshold-level standards from 8 through 18 kHz. *J. Acoust. Soc. Am.* 49:600–1

90. Harris, J. D., Sergeant, R. L. 1971. Monaural/binaural minimum audible angles for a moving sound source. *J. Speech Hear. Res.* 618–29

91. Harrison, J. M., Downey, P. 1970. Intensity changes at the ear as a function of the azimuth of a tone source: a comparative study. *J. Acoust. Soc. Am.* 47:1509–18

92. Hattler, K. W., Stokinger, T. E. 1972. Loudness balances employing signals with unequal duty cycles. *J. Acoust. Soc. Am.* 52:558–65

93. Helle, R. 1969/70. Amplitude und Phase des im Gehör gebildeten Differenztones dritter Ordnung. *Acustica* 22:74–87

94. Hellman, R. P. 1970. Effect of noise bandwidth on the loudness of a 1000-Hz tone. *J. Acoust. Soc. Am.* 48:500–4

95. Hellman, R. P. 1972. Asymmetry of masking between noise and tone. *Percept. Psychophys.* 11:241–46

96. Henning, G. B. 1973. Effect of interaural phase on frequency and amplitude discrimination. *J. Acoust. Soc. Am.* 54:1160–78

97. Houtgast, T. 1972. Psychophysical evidence for lateral inhibition in hearing. *J. Acoust. Soc. Am.* 51:1885–94

98. Houtgast, T. 1973. Psychophysical experiments on "tuning curves" and "two-tone inhibition." *Acustica* 29:168–79

99. Houtgast, T. 1974. *Lateral suppression in hearing.* PhD thesis. Free Univ., Amsterdam. 114 pp.

100. Houtgast, T. 1974. Lateral suppression and loudness reduction of a tone in noise. *Acustica* 30:214–21

101. Houtsma, A. J. M., Goldstein, J. L. 1972. The central origin of the pitch of

complex tones: evidence from musical interval recognition. *J. Acoust. Soc. Am.* 51:520-29

102. Howes, W. L. 1971. Loudness determined by power summation. *Acustica* 25:343-49

103. Irwin, R. J., Zwislocki, J. J. 1971. Loudness effects in pairs of tone bursts. *Percept. Psychophys.* 10:189-92

104. Jeffress, L. A. 1971. Detection and lateralization of binaural signals. *Audiology* 10:77-84

105. Jeffress, L. A., McFadden, D. 1971. Differences of interaural phase and level in detection and lateralization. *J. Acoust. Soc. Am.* 49:1169-79

106. Karlovich, R. S. et al 1971. Auditory threshold at 125 Hz as a function of signal duration and signal filtering. *J. Acoust. Soc. Am.* 49:1897-99

107. Kay, R. H., Matthews, D. R. 1972. On the existence in human auditory pathways of channels selectively tuned to the modulation present in frequency-modulated tones. *J. Physiol.* 225: 657-77

108. Keen, K. 1972. Preservation of constant loudness with interaural amplitude asymmetry. *J. Acoust. Soc. Am.* 52:1193-96

109. Kuhl, W., Plantz, R. 1972. Die Lokalisierung einer vorderen und einer hinteren Schallquelle bei frei beweglichem Kopf. *Acustica* 27:108-10

110. Laws, P. 1973. Entfernungshören und das Problem der Im-Kopf-Lokalisiertheit von Hörereignissen. *Acustica* 29:243-59

111. Leshowitz, B. 1971. Measurement of the two-click threshold. *J. Acoust. Soc. Am.* 49:462-66

112. Leshowitz, B., Cudahy, E. 1972. Masking with continuous and gated sinusoids. *J. Acoust. Soc. Am.* 51: 1921-29

113. Ibid 1973. Frequency discrimination in the presence of another tone. 54: 882-87

114. Leshowitz, B., Wightman, F. L. 1971. On-frequency masking with continuous sinusoids. *J. Acoust. Soc. Am.* 49:1180-90

115. Levelt, W. J. M., Riemersma, J. B., Bunt, A. A. 1972. Binaural additivity of loudness. *Brit. J. Math. Statist. Psychol.* 25:51-68

116. Luce, R. D., Green, D. M. 1972. A neural timing theory for response times and the psychophysics of intensity. *Psychol. Rev.* 79:14-57

117. Lummis, R. C., Guttman, N. 1972. Exploratory studies of Zwicker's "negative afterimage" in hearing. *J. Acoust. Soc. Am.* 51:1930-44

118. McFadden, D., Jeffress, L. A., Ermey, H. L. 1971. Differences of interaural phase and level in detection and lateralization: 250 Hz. *J. Acoust. Soc. Am.* 50:1484-93

119. McFadden, D., Jeffress, L. A., Lakey, J. R. 1972. Differences of interaural phase and level in detection and lateralization: 1000 and 2000 Hz. *J. Acoust. Soc. Am.* 52:1197-1206

120. McFadden, D., Pulliam, K. A. 1971. Lateralization and detection of noise-masked tones of different durations. *J. Acoust. Soc. Am.* 49:1191-94

121. McFadden, D., Russell, W. E., Pulliam, K. A. 1972. Monaural and binaural masking patterns for a low-frequency tone. *J. Acoust. Soc. Am.* 51:534-43

122. McFadden, D., Sharpley, A. D. 1972. Detectability of interaural time differences and interaural level differences as a function of signal duration. *J. Acoust. Soc. Am.* 52:574-76

123. Metters, P. J., Williams, R. P. 1973. Experiments on tonal residues of short duration. *J. Sound Vib.* 26:432-36

124. Molino, J. A. 1973. Pure-tone equal-loudness contours for standard tones of different frequencies. *Percept. Psychophys.* 14:1-4

125. Moore, B. C. J. 1972. Some experiments relating to the perception of pure tones: possible clinical applications. *Sound* 6:73-79

126. Moore, B. C. J. 1973. Frequency difference limens for short-duration tones. *J. Acoust. Soc. Am.* 54:610-19

127. Ibid. Frequency difference limens for narrow bands of noise, 888-96

128. Moore, B. C. J. 1973. Some experiments relating to the perception of complex tones. *Quart. J. Exp. Psychol.* 25:451-75

129. Moore, T. J., Welsh, J. R. Jr. 1970. Forward and backward enhancement of sensitivity in the auditory system. *J. Acoust. Soc. Am.* 47:534–39

130. Morgan, D. E., Dirks, D. D. 1973. Suprathreshold loudness adaptation. *J. Acoust. Soc. Am.* 53:1560–64

131. Mosko, J. D., House, A. S. 1971. Binaural unmasking of vocalic signals. *J. Acoust. Soc. Am.* 49:1203–12

132. Moulin, L. K. 1972. The effects of physiological noise on the auditory threshold. *J. Speech Hear. Res.* 15:837–44

133. Mulligan, B. E., Elrod, M. 1970. Monaural detection and filtering. *J. Acoust. Soc. Am.* 47:1548–56

134. Nábělek, I. V., Nábělek, A. K., Hirsh, I. J. 1970. Pitch of tone bursts of changing frequency. *J. Acoust. Soc. Am.* 48:536–53

135. Ibid 1973. Pitch of sound bursts with continuous and discontinuous change of frequency. 53:1305–12

136. Nielsen, D. W., Fraser, W. D., Elliott, D. N. 1970. Frequency discrimination in the adapted ear. *J. Acoust. Soc. Am.* 47:540–45

137. Nixon, J. C., Raiford, C. A., Schubert, E. D. 1970. Technique for investigating monaural phase effects. *J. Acoust. Soc. Am.* 48:554–56

138. Noffsinger, P. D., Olsen, W. O. 1970. Postexposure responsiveness in the auditory system. II. Sensitization and desensitization. *J. Acoust. Soc. Am.* 47:552–64

139. Noffsinger, P. D., Tillman, T. W. 1970. Postexposure responsiveness in the auditory system. I. Immediate sensitization. *J. Acoust. Soc. Am.* 47:546–51

140. Northern, J. L., Downs, M. P., Rudmose, W., Glorig, A., Fletcher, J. L. 1972. Recommended high-frequency audiometric threshold levels (8000–18000 Hz). *J. Acoust. Soc. Am.* 52:585–95

141. Osman, E. 1971. A correlation model of binaural masking level differences. *J. Acoust. Soc. Am.* 50:1494–1511

142. Ibid 1973. Correlation model of binaural detection: interaural amplitude ratio and phase variation for signal. 54:386–89

143. Pastore, R. E., Sorkin, R. D. 1972. Simultaneous two-channel signal detection. I. Simple binaural stimuli. *J. Acoust. Soc. Am.* 51:544–51

144. Patterson, J. H. 1971. Additivity of forward and backward masking as a function of signal frequency. *J. Acoust. Soc. Am.* 50:1123–25

145. Ibid. Masking of tones by transient signals having identical energy spectra, 1126–32

146. Patterson, J. H., Green, D. M. 1970. Discrimination of transient signals having identical energy spectra. *J. Acoust. Soc. Am.* 48:894–905

147. Patterson, J. H., Green, D. M. 1971. Masking of transient signals having identical energy spectra. *Audiology* 10:85–96

148. Patterson, R. D. 1973. The effects of relative phase and the number of components on residue pitch. *J. Acoust. Soc. Am.* 53:1564–72

149. Paulus, E., Zwicker, E. 1972. Programme zur automatischen Bestimmung der Lautheit aus Terzpegeln oder Frequenzgruppenpegeln. *Acustica* 27:253–66

150. Pedersen, C. B., Elberling, C. 1972. Temporal integration of acoustic energy in normal hearing persons. *Acta Otolaryngol.* 74:398–405

151. Penner, M. J., Robinson, C. E., Green, D. M. 1972. The critical masking interval. *J. Acoust. Soc. Am.* 52:1661–68

152. Penner, M. J., Viemeister, N. F. 1973. Intensity discrimination of clicks: the effects of click bandwidth and background noise. *J. Acoust. Soc. Am.* 54:1184–88

153. Perrott, D. R. 1970. A further note on "Limits for the detection of binaural beats." *J. Acoust. Soc. Am.* 47:663–64

154. Perrott, D. R. 1970. Signal and interaural level difference effects on binaural critical band. *J. Aud. Res.* 10:1–4

155. Perrott, D. R., Briggs, R., Perrott, S. 1970. Binaural fusion: its limits as defined by signal duration and signal onset. *J. Acoust. Soc. Am.* 47:565–68

156. Perrott, D. R., Williams, K. N. 1970. Effects of interaural frequency differences on the lateralization function. *J.*

Acoust. Soc. Am. 48:1022–23
157. Petty, J. W., Fraser, W. D., Elliott, D. N. 1970. Adaptation and loudness decrement: a reconsideration. *J. Acoust. Soc. Am.* 47:1074–82
158. Pfeiffer, R. R. 1970. A model for two-tone inhibition of single cochlear-nerve fibers. *J. Acoust. Soc. Am.* 48:1373–78
159. Plenge, G. 1972. Ueber das Problem der Im-Kopf-Lokalisation. *Acustica* 26:241–52
160. Plomp, R. 1964. The ear as a frequency analyzer. *J. Acoust. Soc. Am.* 36:1628–36
161. Ibid 1967. Pitch of complex tones. 41:1526–33
162. Plomp, R., Smoorenburg, G. F., Eds. 1970. *Frequency Analysis and Periodicity Detection in Hearing.* Leiden: Sijthoff. 482 pp.
163. Plomp, R., Steeneken, H. J. M. 1973. Place dependence of timbre in reverberant sound fields. *Acustica* 28:50–59
164. Plomp, R., Wagenaar, W. A., Mimpen, A. M. 1973. Musical interval recognition with simultaneous tones. *Acustica* 29:101–9
165. Pollack, I. 1971. Interaural correlation detection for auditory pulse trains. *J. Acoust. Soc. Am.* 49:1213–17
166. Ibid. Spectral basis of auditory "jitter" detection. 50:555–58
167. Ibid. Amplitude and time jitter thresholds for rectangular-wave trains, 1133–42
168. Ibid. Discrimination of the interval between two brief pulses, 1203–4
169. Pollack, I. 1973. Forward, backward and combined masking: implications for an auditory integration period. *Quart. J. Exp. Psychol.* 25:424–32
170. Punch, J., Carhart, R. 1973. Influence of interaural phase on forward masking. *J. Acoust. Soc. Am.* 54:897–904
171. Pynn, C. T., Braida, L. D., Durlach, N. I. 1972. Intensity perception. III. Resolution in small-range identification. *J. Acoust. Soc. Am.* 51:559–66
172. Raiford, C. A., Schubert, E. D. 1971. Recognition of phase changes in octave complexes. *J. Acoust. Soc. Am.* 50:559–67
173. Rainbolt, H., Small, A. M. 1972. Mach bands in auditory masking: an attempted replication. *J. Acoust. Soc. Am.* 51:567–74
174. Reed, C. M., Bilger, R. C. 1973. A comparative study of S/N_0 and E/N_0. *J. Acoust. Soc. Am.* 53:1039–44
175. Ritsma, R. J. 1962. Existence region of the tonal residue. I. *J. Acoust. Soc. Am.* 34:1224–29
176. Ibid 1967. Frequencies dominant in the perception of the pitch of complex sounds. 42:191–98
177. Ritsma, R. J., Bilsen, F. A. 1970. Spectral regions dominant in the perception of repetition pitch. *Acustica* 23:334–39
178. Ritsma, R. J., Engel, F. L. 1964. Pitch of frequency-modulated signals. *J. Acoust. Soc. Am.* 36:1637–44
179. Robinson, C. E., Pollack, I. 1971. Forward and backward masking: testing a discrete perceptual-moment hypothesis in audition. *J. Acoust. Soc. Am.* 50:1512–19
180. Ibid 1973. Interaction between forward and backward masking: a measure of the integrating period of the auditory system. 53:1313–16
181. Robinson, D. E. 1971. The effect of interaural signal-frequency disparity on signal detectability. *J. Acoust. Soc. Am.* 50:568–71
182. Robinson, D. E., Dolan, T. R. 1972. Effect of signal frequency on the MLD for uncorrelated noise. *J. Acoust. Soc. Am.* 51:1945–46
183. Robinson, D. E., Trahiotis, C. 1972. Effects of signal duration and masker duration on detectability under diotic and dichotic listening conditions. *Percept. Psychophys.* 12:333–34
184. Rochester, S. 1971. Detection and duration discrimination of noise increments. *J. Acoust. Soc. Am.* 49:1783–89
185. Rodenburg, M. 1972. *Sensitivity of the auditory system to differences in intensity.* PhD thesis. Medical Faculty, Rotterdam. 96 pp.
186. Ronken, D. A. 1970. Monaural detection of a phase difference between clicks. *J. Acoust. Soc. Am.* 47:1091–99
187. Ibid 1971. Some effects of bandwidth-duration constraints on frequency discrimination. 49:1232–42
188. Ibid 1972. Changes in frequency discrimination caused by leading and trailing tones. 51:1947–50
189. Ibid 1973. Masking produced by sinusoids of slowly changing frequency. 54:905–15

190. Rowley, R. R., Studebaker, G. A. 1971. Loudness-intensity relations under various levels of contralateral noise. *J. Acoust. Soc. Am.* 49:499–504

191. Schacknow, P. N., Raab, D. H. 1973. Intensity discrimination of tone bursts and the form of the Weber function. *Percept. Psychophys.* 14:449–50

192. Scharf, B. 1971. Fundamentals of auditory masking. *Audiology* 10:30–40

193. Scharf, B., Fishken, D. 1970. Binaural summation of loudness, reconsidered. *J. Exp. Psychol.* 86:374–79

194. Schneider, B., Wright, A. A., Edelheit, W., Hock, P., Humphrey, C. 1972. Equal loudness contours derived from sensory magnitude judgments. *J. Acoust. Soc. Am.* 51:1951–59

195. Schoeny, Z. G., Carhart, R. 1971. Effects of unilateral Ménière's disease on masking-level differences. *J. Acoust. Soc. Am.* 50:1143–50

196. Schouten, J. F., Ritsma, R. J., Cardozo, B. L. 1962. Pitch of the residue. *J. Acoust. Soc. Am.* 34:1418–24

197. Schulman, A. I. 1971. Detectability of the deletion of a tone from a tone-plus-noise background. *Percept. Psychophys.* 9:496–98

198. Slaymaker, F. H. 1970. Chords from tones having stretched partials. *J. Acoust. Soc. Am.* 47:1569–71

199. Small, A. M. et al 1972. MLDs in forward and backward masking. *J. Acoust. Soc. Am.* 51:1365–67

200. Smoorenburg, G. F. 1970. Pitch perception of two-frequency stimuli. *J. Acoust. Soc. Am.* 48:924–42

201. Ibid 1972. Audibility region of combination tones. 52:603–14

202. Ibid. Combination tones and their origin, 615–32

203. Soderquist, D. R. 1970. Frequency analysis and the critical band. *Psychon. Sci.* 21:117–19

204. Soderquist, D. R., Lindsey, J. W. 1970. Masking-level differences as a function of noise spectrum level, frequency, and signal duration. *J. Aud. Res.* 10:276–82

205. Soderquist, D. R., Lindsey, J. W. 1972. Physiological noise as a masker of low frequencies: the cardiac cycle. *J. Acoust. Soc. Am.* 1216–20

206. Sorkin, R. D., Pastore, R. E., Pohlmann, L. D. 1972. Simultaneous two-channel signal detection. II. Correlated and uncorrelated signals. *J. Acoust. Soc. Am.* 51:1960–65

207. Sorkin, R. D., Pohlmann, L. D., Gilliom, J. D. 1973. Simultaneous two-channel signal detection. III. 630- and 1400-Hz signals. *J. Acoust. Soc. Am.* 53:1045–50

208. Srinivasan, R. 1971. Auditory critical bandwidth for short-duration signals. *J. Acoust. Soc. Am.* 50:616–22

209. Steed, O. T., Martin, A. M. 1973. Studies on quiet threshold shift in the absence of noise. *J. Sound. Vib.* 26:353–60

210. Stephens, S. D. G. 1970. Studies on the uncomfortable loudness level. *Sound* 4:20–23

211. Stephens, S. D. G. 1973. Auditory temporal integration as a function of intensity. *J. Sound Vib.* 30:109–26

212. Stephens, S. D. G. 1973. Some experiments on the detection of short duration stimuli. *Brit. J. Audiol.* 7:81–94

213. Stephens, S. D. G., Anderson, C. M. B. 1971. Experimental studies on the uncomfortable loudness level. *J. Speech Hear. Res.* 14:262–70

214. Stevens, S. S. 1972. Perceived level of noise by Mark VII and decibels (E). *J. Acoust. Soc. Am.* 51:575–601

215. Stevens, S. S. 1972. 1971 Rayleigh gold medal address: calculating the perceived level of light and sound. *J. Sound Vib.* 23:297–306

216. Stokinger, T. E., Cooper, W. A. Jr., Lankford, J. E. 1970. Effect of interval durations on interaural loudness balancing. *J. Aud. Res.* 10:35–44

217. Stokinger, T. E., Cooper, W. A. Jr., Meissner, W. A. 1972. Influence of binaural interaction on the measurement of perstimulatory loudness adaptation. *J. Acoust. Soc. Am.* 51:602–7

218. Stokinger, T. E., Cooper, W. A. Jr., Meissner, W. A. 1972. Loudness tracking and the staircase method in measurement of adaptation. *Audiology* 11:161–68

219. Stokinger, T. E., Cooper, W. A. Jr., Meissner, W. A., Jones, K. O. 1972. Intensity, frequency, and duration effects in the measurement of monaural perstimulatory loudness adaptation. *J. Acoust. Soc. Am.* 51:608–16

220. Sundberg, J. E. F., Lindqvist, J. 1973.

Musical octaves and pitch. *J. Acoust. Soc. Am.* 54:922–29

221. Sutton, R. A., Williams, R. P. 1970. Residue pitches from two-tone complexes. *J. Sound Vib.* 13:195–99

222. Taylor, M. M., Clarke, D. P. J. 1971. Monaural detection with contralateral cue (MDCC). II. Interaural delay of cue and signal. *J. Acoust. Soc. Am.* 49:1243–53

223. Taylor, M. M., Clarke, D. P. J., Smith, S. M. 1971. Monaural detection with contralateral cue (MDCC). III. Sinusoidal signals at a constant performance level. *J. Acoust. Soc. Am.* 49:1795–1804

224. Taylor, M. M., Smith, S. M., Clarke, D. P. J. 1971. Monaural detection with contralateral cue (MDCC). IV. Psychometric functions with sinusoidal signals. *J. Acoust. Soc. Am.* 50:1151–61

225. Tempest, W., Bryan, M. E. 1971. The auditory threshold for short-duration pulses. *J. Acoust. Soc. Am.* 49:1901–2

226. Terhardt, E. 1969/70. Oktavspreizung und Tonhöhenverschiebung bei Sinustönen. *Acustica* 22:345–51

227. Terhardt, E. 1970. Frequency analysis and periodicity detection in the sensations of roughness and periodicity pitch. See. Ref. 162, 278–90

228. Terhardt, E. 1971. Die Tonhöhe harmonischer Klänge und das Oktavintervall. *Acustica* 24:126–36

229. Ibid 1972. Zur Tonhöhenwahrnehmung von Klängen. I. Psychoakustische Grundlagen. 26:173–86

230. Ibid. Zur Tonhöhenwahrnehmung von Klängen. II. Ein Funktionsschema, 187–99

231. Terhardt, E. 1974. Pitch, consonance, and harmony. *J. Acoust. Soc. Am.* 55:1061–69

232. Terhardt, E., Fastl, H. 1971. Zum Einfluss von Störtönen und Störgeräuschen auf die Tonhöhe von Sinustönen. *Acustica* 25:53–61

233. Thurlow, W. R. 1957. An auditory figure-ground effect. *Am. J. Psychol.* 70:653–54

234. Thurlow, W. R., Jack, Ch.E. 1973. Some determinants of localization-adaptation effects for successive auditory stimuli. *J. Acoust. Soc. Am.* 53:1573–77

235. Thurlow, W. R., Mergener, J. R. 1970. Effect of stimulus duration on localization of direction of noise stimuli. *J. Speech Hear. Res.* 13:826–38

236. Tobias, J. V., Ed. 1970. *Foundations of Modern Auditory Theory*, Vol. I. New York: Academic. 466 pp.

237. Tobias, J. V., Ed. 1972. *Foundations of Modern Auditory Theory*, Vol. II. New York: Academic. 508 pp.

238. Toole, F. E. 1970. In-head localization of acoustic images. *J. Acoust. Soc. Am.* 48:943–49

239. Townsend, T. H., Goldstein, D. P. 1972. Suprathreshold binaural unmasking. *J. Acoust. Soc. Am.* 51:621–24

240. Trahiotis, C., Dolan, T. R., Miller, T. H. 1972. Effect of "backward" masker fringe on the detectability of pulsed diotic and dichotic tonal signals. *Percept. Psychophys.* 12:335–38

241. Tsumura, T., Sone, T., Nimura, T. 1973. Auditory detection of frequency transition. *J. Acoust. Soc. Am.* 53:17–25

242. van den Brink, G. 1970. Two experiments on pitch perception: diplacusis of harmonic AM signals and pitch of inharmonic AM signals. *J. Acoust. Soc. Am.* 48:1355–65

243. Ventry, I. M., Woods, R. W., Rubin, M., Hill, W. 1971. Most comfortable loudness for pure tones, noise, and speech. *J. Acoust. Soc. Am.* 49:1805–13

244. Viemeister, N. F. 1972. Intensity discrimination of pulsed sinusoids: the effects of filtered noise. *J. Acoust. Soc. Am.* 51:1265–69

245. Vitz, P. C. 1972. Preference for tones as a function of frequency (hertz) and intensity (decibels). *Percept. Psychophys.* 11:84–88

246. von Békésy, G. 1963. Hearing theories and complex sounds. *J. Acoust. Soc. Am.* 35:588–601

247. Ibid 1972. The missing fundamental and periodicity detection in hearing. 51:631–37

248. von Bismarck, G. 1972. *Extraktion und Messung von Merkmalen der Klangfarbenwahrnehmung stationärer Schalle.* Communication of Sonderforschungsbereich 50 *Kybernetik.* München. 110 pp.

249. von Bismarck, G. 1974. Timbre of steady sounds: a factorial investigation of its verbal attributes. *Acustica* 30:146–59

250. Ibid. Sharpness as an attribute of the timbre of steady sounds, 159–72

251. Walliser, K. 1969. Zusammenhänge zwischen dem Schallreiz und der Periodentonhöhe. *Acustica* 21:319–29

252. Ibid. Zur Unterschiedsschwelle der Periodentonhöhe, 329–36

253. Walliser, K. 1969. Ueber ein Funktionsschema für die Bildung der Periodentonhöhe aus dem Schallreiz. *Kybernetik* 6:65–72

254. Ward, L. M. 1972. Category judgments of loudnesses in the absence of an experimenter-induced identification function: sequential effects and power-function fit. *J. Exp. Psychol.* 94:179–84

255. Ward, L. M. 1973. Repeated magnitude estimations with a variable standard: sequential effects and other properties. *Percept. Psychophys.* 13:193–200

256. Warren, R. M. 1970. Elimination of biases in loudness judgments for tones. *J. Acoust. Soc. Am.* 48:1397–1403

257. Warren, R. M. 1970. Perceptual restoration of missing speech sounds. *Science* 167:392–93

258. Warren, R. M. 1973. Anomalous loudness function for speech. *J. Acoust. Soc. Am.* 54:390–96

259. Warren, R. M., Obusek, C. J. 1971. Speech perception and phonemic restorations. *Percept. Psychophys.* 9:358–62

260. Warren, R. M., Obusek, C. J., Ackroff, J. M. 1972. Auditory induction: perceptual synthesis of absent sounds. *Science* 176:1149–51

261. Warren, R. M., Warren, R. P. 1970. Auditory illusions and confusions. *Sci. Am.* 223, No. 6:30–36

262. Watson, C. S., Franks, J. R., Hood, D. C. 1972. Detection of tones in the absence of external masking noise. I. Effects of signal intensity and signal frequency. *J. Acoust. Soc. Am.* 52:633–43

263. Weiler, E. M., Loeb, M., Alluisi, E. A. 1972. Auditory adaptation and its relationship to a model for loudness. *J. Acoust. Soc. Am.* 51:638–43

264. Wettschureck, R. G. 1973. Die absoluten Unterschiedsschwellen der Richtungswahrnehmung in der Medianebene beim natürlichen Hören, sowie beim Hören über ein Kunstkopf-Uebertragungssystem. *Acustica* 28:197–208

265. Wettschureck, R. G., Plenge, G., Lehringer, F. 1973. Entfernungswahrnehmung beim natürlichen Hören sowie bei kopfbezogener Stereofonie. *Acustica* 29:260–72

266. Whitfield, I. C. 1967. *The Auditory Pathway.* London: Arnold. 209 pp.

267. Wightman, F. L. 1971. Detection of binaural tones as a function of masker bandwidth. *J. Acoust. Soc. Am.* 50:623–36

268. Ibid 1973. Pitch and stimulus fine structure. 54:397–406

269. Ibid. The pattern-transformation model of pitch, 407–16

270. Wilbanks, W. A. 1971. Detection of a narrow-band noise as a function of the interaural correlation of both signal and masker. *J. Acoust. Soc. Am.* 49:1814–17

271. Wiley, T. L., Small, A. M. Jr., Lilly, D. J. 1973. Monaural loudness adaptation. *J. Acoust. Soc. Am.* 53:1051–55

272. Williams, K. N., Perrott, D. R. 1972. Temporal resolution of tonal pulses. *J. Acoust. Soc. Am.* 51:644–47

273. Wilson, J. P., Johnstone, J. R. 1973. Basilar membrane correlates of the combination tone $2f_1 - f_2$. *Nature* 241:206–7

274. Wilson, R. H., Carhart, R. 1971. Forward and backward masking: interactions and additivity. *J. Acoust. Soc. Am.* 49:1254–63

275. Woods, R. W., Ventry, I. M., Gatling, L. W. 1973. Effect of ascending and descending measurement methods on comfortable loudness levels for pure tones. *J. Acoust. Soc. Am.* 54:205–6

276. Yost, W. A. 1972. Tone-on-tone masking for three binaural listening conditions. *J. Acoust. Soc. Am.* 52:1234–37

277. Yost, W. A. 1972. Weber's fraction for the intensity of pure tones presented binaurally. *Percept. Psychophys.* 11:61–64

278. Yost, W. A., Penner, M. J., Feth, L. L.

232   PLOMP

1972. Signal detection as a function of contralateral sinusoid-to-noise ratio. *J. Acoust. Soc. Am.* 51:1966–70

279. Yost, W. A., Wightman, F. L., Green, D. M. 1971. Lateralization of filtered clicks. *J. Acoust. Soc. Am.* 50:1526–31

280. Young, I. M., Wenner, C., Kanofsky, P. 1970. Three factors affecting binaural loudness balance. *J. Aud. Res.* 10:251–56

281. Zwicker, E. 1969/70. Subjektive und objektive Dauer von Schallimpulsen und Schallpausen. *Acustica* 22:214–18

282. Zwicker, E., Fastl, H. 1972. Zur Abhängigkeit der Nachverdeckung von der Störimpulsdauer. *Acustica* 26:78–82

283. Zwicker, E., Fastl, H. 1972. On the de-velopment of the critical band. *J. Acoust. Soc. Am.* 52:699–702

284. Zwicker, E., Fastl, H. 1973. Cubic difference sounds measured by threshold- and compensation-method. *Acustica* 29:336–43

285. Zwicker, E., Schütte, H. 1973. On the time pattern of the threshold of tone impulses masked by narrow band noise. *Acustica* 29:343–47

286. Zwislocki, J. J. 1971. Central masking and neural activity in the cochlear nucleus. *Audiology* 10:48–59

287. Zwislocki, J. J. 1972. A theory of central auditory masking and its partial validation. *J. Acoust. Soc. Am.* 52:644–59

ELECTROPHYSIOLOGY AND BEHAVIOR[1]

Edward C. Beck[2]

Veterans Administration Hospital and University of Utah
Salt Lake City, Utah 84113

Space limitation in the *Annual Review of Psychology* prevents serious in-depth treatment of a topic to a degree that would satisfy the expert. Nor does it allow for background information so necessary for clear exposition for the student. The voluminous material that emerges during the several years between particular reviews can only be skimmed, thereby neglecting and possibly offending a number of deserving researchers. This is particularly true with the present review. It will attempt to cover studies using two widely accepted techniques, the Average Evoked Response and the Contingent Negative Variation that have provided volumes of research over the past decade. Neither of these has been systematically reviewed in the *Annual Review*. Research utilizing these techniques has literally metastasized to include practically every aspect of behavior, species ranging from rat to man, and clinical applications from dentistry to psychiatry. To review this vast area in the limited number of pages allotted is presumptuous. But this I do hoping that in broad outline most of the major areas can be covered, and this I do with an apology to many investigators and friends whose interesting work is deserving of more description and elaboration than space will permit.

The following general references (33, 72, 73, 104, 127, 201, 203, 218, 233, 265, 291, 292, 318) provide invaluable background. Four deserve special comment. Regan's (233), the most complete, covers all aspects of most techniques; Shagass'

---

[1] See NAPS document No. 02430 for 89 pages of supplementary material. Order from ASIS/NAPS c/o Microfiche Publications, 305 E. 46th Street, New York, NY 10017. Remit in advance for each NAPS accession number. Make checks payable to Microfiche Publications. Microfiche are $1.50, and photocopies are $13.85. Outside of U.S. or Canada, postage is $.50 for a fiche or $2.00 for a photocopy.

[2] Approved research projects 0864–01, 02 of the Veterans Administration, and supported in part by NIMH Research Grant 1 RO1 DA00388–01 and NICHD Contract PH-43–67–1451.

Special acknowledgment is given to Dr. L. W. Jarcho, Professor and Chairman, Department of Neurology, who gave unstintingly of his time with invaluable comment and review.

(265) is especially valuable to psychologists and psychiatrists; Perry & Childers' (218) covers the visual response; McCallum & Knott's (203) is based on reviews and papers at the 2nd International CNV Congress. All are scholarly and informative.

THE EVOKED RESPONSE (ER) AND THE CONTINGENT NEGATIVE VARIATION (CNV)

The growing popularity of evoked response research has been paralleled by technological advances in the development of small and inexpensive computers which enable investigators to sum and average evoked responses rapidly and efficiently. Also contributing has been the repeatedly reinforced expectation that the evoked response (ER) technique will be more useful in assessing brain function than the conventional EEG and other electrophysiological analyses. In contrast to the EEG, ERs are under stimulus control, thus providing additional information about the different sensory systems, functionally different pathways, and brain areas involved in the response. ERs lend themselves to more quantifiable analysis than does the EEG trace.

The computerized ER that emerges from the brain's background electrical turbulence is a complex pattern of as many as 15 identifiable wave components or reproducible patterns of polarity, amplitude, and duration that lasts for hundreds of milliseconds. Each component can be accurately measured in amplitude and latency. Characteristics of these electrical cerebral patterns indicate that they represent activity initiated by sense organs, cortical and subcortical brain areas, and anatomically and functionally different neuronal aggregates. These patterns may also indicate a relationship between the evoked neuronal activity and the subject's perception of the evoking stimulus and its significance to him at the time of perception. Finally, the ER faithfully reflects the nature of the evoking stimulus; responses to light, sound, and touch all differ, as do ERs to patterned and colored light, or auditory stimuli when they convey meaning.

The Contingent Negative Variation (CNV), a slow-rising, surface-negative brain potential usually depends upon the association or contingency of two successive stimuli. Conditions to produce the CNV are so similar to Pavlovian conditioning that the technique gained immediate and widespread acceptance by psychologists.

Reliability, Stability, Validity: Methods and Techniques: Statistical and Mathematical Analyses

Reliability and stability of ERs were early concerns of evoked response investigators as responses were reported to be affected by a variety of conditions. However, most studies indicated that the ER was reliable in the adult (71, 109, 182, 267). In some, mean product-moment correlations of 0.88 were obtained between visually evoked responses (VERs) separated by months (109). Recent studies have involved infants and children and report that reliability and stability increase with age (53, 119–121). Callaway & Halliday (53), recording from 120 children 6 to 15 years of age, reported that variability of the visual (VER) and auditory (AER) evoked response decreased with increasing age. Ellingston et al (120, 121), studying variability of the VER in the human infant and adult, found that the adult response was far more reliable than that of the infant. Despite the impressive correlations, a procedure often adopted is to include a reliability measure in each study itself.

Validity of the ER as representative of neural activity was a source of concern and argument. Are components of the ER of neural origin or are they the sum of artifacts, myogenic responses, extracerebral activity, or all of these? These possibilities were seriously investigated by Bickford and others (34–36, 104). Bickford's criticisms were worrisome. With enthusiastic admonishment he reported data showing that with different postures, such as a change in facial expression, frowning, raising the eyebrows, muscle tension, etc, new waves emerged, others changed, still others disappeared.

The only answer to Bickford's criticism was to show a relationship between the gross wave components of the ER recorded at scalp and those recorded at cortex. A number of experimenters succeeded in doing just that (44, 47, 75, 95, 96, 140, 159, 171, 177, 305). There was good concordance between the response recorded from scalp and that from dura, although the amplitudes of the scalp recordings were often smaller. Differences that did occur among the various studies could be accounted for by the methods used. For example, some studies (96, 140) analyzed only the first 125 msec of the response as contrasted to others (159) which described both "early" and "late" ER components separately. There remained the question of the differences in the wave form of the ER when electrodes were placed *over* and *under* the dura. Geisler & Gerstein (139) demonstrated that the major part of the diffusion or spreading of the potential distribution may actually be due to dura and cerebro-spinal fluid under the dura. Potentials recorded from dura and scalp tended to resemble each other more than those recorded subdurally.

Methods and techniques received systematic attention not only in papers but in a number of symposia and books. The NASA symposium (104) dealt specifically with these problems: methods involved in cross-modality comparison of ERs (Goff 144); methods in the CNV (Cohen 73); data analysis techniques in ER research (Donchin 100); and the topic of psychological variables in the ER research (Sutton 288). The nature of the evoking stimuli—visual, auditory, etc—was found to be critical to ER research and received systematic attention in a number of studies. Visual stimuli were reviewed and evaluated in detail by Perry & Childers (218, Chapter 2) and Regan (233, Chapters 2 and 5) and included studies in which color, pattern, frequency, intensity, steady state, binocular, and moving stimuli were utilized. Similarly treated were somatosensory stimuli by Shagass (265) and auditory by Davis (86, 87, 89, 90) and Rapin & Graziani (224, 225).

Statistical and mathematical analyses of bioelectrical data were the topic of a number of studies directed towards quantifying and comparing ERs (32, 53, 98–100, 123, 175, 233, 286, 287, 299, 308–310). The multidimensionality of the ER made it difficult to state with any certainty how two or more responses were different. They may have identical wave shapes but different amplitudes; some segments may differ while others are identical, or one or more components may differ. *Multivariate analysis* (98–100) circumvented these problems and provided a reliable technique for judging the significance of differences. Factor analysis of principal components of the ER (175) was found to provide a meaningful, quantitative description when the resulting factor components were rotated following a Varimax procedure (175). Promise for this technique was found in results from drug studies wherein ERs computed under different doses of the *same* drug were described by *similar* regression equations, while markedly different equations were needed to describe effects for different drugs.

Neurogenesis, the Underlying Neuroanatomy and Neurophysiology of the ER

A detailed knowledge of the intracranial sources and neural pathways that determine the wave form of the ER will provide a powerful technique for both researchers and diagnosticians. When such knowledge is definitive, the ER may be used to identify with reasonable certainty the areas of the brain most affected by psychological processes or by disease or injury. We may even know what systems or brain areas participate in certain mental processes. There have been a number of approaches to this problem.

One has been the individual neuron or single cell model wherein an explanation of the configuration of the ER was sought in the sum of time-locked neuronal activities of many cells. Advocates of this hypothesis, Creutzfeldt & others (80–84, 133), proposed that averaged single neuron activity was responsible for *all* the different components of the surface ER. From purely visual inspection of the intracellular frequency and the wave form of the surface ER there appeared to be support for this notion since the frequency of intracellular activity and gross surface waves were at least superficially similar. Also the frequencies of both changed in a similar manner during sleep and wakefulness (81, 83, 133). With careful scrutiny and examination of longer sections of the record, the relationships between intracellular activity and ER waves were found to be fleeting (124). As different laboratories have reported different relationships between unit firing and local surface slow wave activity (80, 81, 94, 124, 133), evidence is accumulating that there is really no fixed relation between unit firing frequency and local slow wave ER activity. The phenomenon may be an *ignis fatuus*.

Anatomical pathways have been another approach to tracing the source of components of the ER. A long-standing and convenient hypothesis regarding these sources was that the ER could be divided into two main temporal sequences known as the *primary* or early response and *postprimary* or late response. These were believed to represent two anatomically different systems. Identifying features of the earlier primary response were that conduction was via specific thalamo-cortical pathways to specific primary sensory areas of the cortex (38) and that it remained unchanged or in some cases enhanced under anesthesia and during sleep. The postprimary response, arriving 50–100 msec after the stimulus, was thought to result from neural volleys traveling through extralemniscal pathways and hence involves the reticular formation and unspecific thalamic nuclei in their conduction. The postprimary response was characterized as being polysensory in nature, widely and bilaterally distributed over the cortex, and markedly sensitive to changes in levels of consciousness, as with attention, anesthesia, and sleep. Because of these features the early response was regarded by many to be "sensory receiving" in function, as contrasted to the presumed function of "information processing" assigned to the late components.

While there remains general agreement about the neural systems and pathways that give rise to the early components, the source of the late response has been seriously challenged (142, 304, 307, 324). From careful isopotential mapping based on the notion that intracranial sources were reflected in scalp recording according to the principles of volume conduction, Vaughn (304) reported that *all* components of the human auditory evoked response, including the long latency vertex potentials, derived from a dipole source reversing polarity at the level of the Sylvian fissure. In a similar manner, the somatosensory evoked response was generated solely in the primary somatosensory projection area. This assertion, if taken at face value, was in conflict with long established beliefs concerning the localization and presumptive origin of the late or long latency components, particularly the vertex wave.

These findings were challenged by Kooi, Tipton & Marshall (183), who repeated isopotential mapping but did not use, as Vaughn did, a cephalic reference. They found no evidence of a polarity reversal. Others (221) have confirmed Kooi's observations. The existence of a deeply located dipole in the primary auditory cortex as the source of *all* components of ER is thus questionable. Others attempting to calculate the potential distribution on the scalp produced by hypothetical sources within the skull and to relate these to the neuroanatomy underlying the evoked response (144, 183, 185) have met with a number of problems. Some even express doubt that it is reasonable to regard the brain as an isotropic volume conductor (194, 209).

Other evidence against the "extralemniscal hypothesis" was more convincing. The suggestion that the late longer latency components of the ER derive from nonspecific impulses transmitted along extralemniscal bilaterally projecting reticular and thalamic pathways was refuted by a number of experiments (142, 184, 187, 284, 324). These studies involved patients with unilateral cerebral lesions which disrupted primary somatic pathways at or above the thalamic level. The "extralemniscal hypothesis" predicts that stimulation of the affected side of the body should produce ERs over the unaffected hemisphere. That is, the extralemniscal conduction would escape or bypass the point of injury or lesions. A startling result, however, was the bilateral loss of *all* evoked response components, including those over the unaffected hemisphere, with stimulation of the affected side of the body.

Despite these findings, data continue to accumulate which indicate that different components and different time segments of the ER change differentially. There must be two or more systems or neuroanatomical pathways that determine the wave form configuration of the evoked response to account for the repeatedly observed changes in ER components differentially determined by a number of conditions—physiological, psychological, pharmacological, and developmental. So, while we must abandon the notion that there is a *parallel* projecting nonspecific system, late components could reflect activity arising from this system but activated serially through corticifugal fibers deriving from the primary area or its immediate associational areas. Once activated in this manner through primary cortex, the nonspecific system could then project actively to the cortex in the diffuse manner observed. The evidence does not permit us to distinguish this possibility from others involving corticifugal and commissural conduction.

Sensory Receiving

ERs faithfully reflect the nature of the evoking stimulus. Not only do different sensory modalities evoke different responses, i.e. VERs, AERs, and SERs are uniquely different, but qualitative aspects of each stimulus may also be reflected in the wave form configuration of the ER. For instance, the VER changes differentially to patterned light, colored light, etc. ERs also change to "meaningful" stimuli. By an arbitrary separation ERs may be classified as those reflecting "qualitative" aspects of the stimulus, such as pattern or color, and those reflecting psychological state or "meaningfulness." This section reviews those studies in which ERs are thought to reflect characteristics or qualities of the stimulus. *Information processing* will review those studies that deal mainly with psychological variables.

VISUAL EVOKED RESPONSES   Possibly because it was the first to be described (71, 92), the VER has received more systematic attention than other ERs. Despite the variety of techniques, electrode placement, stimulating procedures, etc, there is a surprising agreement in the literature as to the wave form configuration of the VER. Schematic comparisons of mean VERs obtained from different laboratories appear in several reviews (33, 218, 265). Comparisons derive from investigators using a flash stimulus of brief duration and diffuse light (10, 63, 71, 110, 138, 182, 238, 259, 301, 302). In these studies from 6 to 9 peaks or components were described. Serious effort has been directed towards reliable identification of the peaks of the VER. In one study (153) wave form patterns evoked by 4 intensities of flash were studied in relation to intersubject variability. An algorithm was developed which identified, with 67–100 percent accuracy, instances when a single peak event occurred within the time range of each of 6 peak distributions, indicating that there are at least 6 reliable components.

Brightness, frequency and movement all affected the VER in unique ways. Latencies of VER components decreased with increased intensity. This held true for components peaking up to 500 or more msec after the stimulus (272, 294, 295, 306, 321). With increasing intensity the peak to trough amplitude of VER components increased but leveled off and even decreased when higher intensities were reached (8, 66, 93, 239, 294, 295, 303). A single moving spot of light elicited a VER (11–13) as did moving patterned stimuli (195). The amplitude of the VER elicited by movement was found to be a function of the change of the angular velocity of the stimulus. Steady-state VERs, visual responses elicited by sinusoidally modulated light (67–69, 208, 230, 232, 299, 300), contributed a new and promising dimension to ER research. The response to this form of stimulation was roughly sinusoidal, following faithfully the frequency of the undulating light within certain limits. Intensity, frequency, spectra, and other variables were investigated. Regan (233) provides a scholarly, in-depth review of these techniques.

This situation piqued the curiosity of some psychiatrists, notably Callaway (51), who found individual differences in the steady-state response. Subjects could be divided according to their response to sinusoidal photic stimulation. There were those who responded with augmented responses and those whose responses were reduced with sinusoidal stimuli.

Pattern and contour Spehlman (279) noted marked differences between VERs evoked by a uniform field and those by a patterned field. A positive wave peaking at 180–250 msec increased markedly in amplitude with patterned stimuli. It was noted that a critical factor appeared to be the density of contrast borders or the check-size of the pattern; the greater the contrast, the larger the response (118, 155–157, 319, 320). In addition to the enhancement of a late wave, it appeared that when VERs to a uniform stimulus field were compared with VERs to a highly contrasted patterned field, the polarity of a prominent positive wave at about 100 msec reversed, becoming negative without any apparent change in latency (155, 240). This polarity could be reversed merely by changing the retinal location of the patterned stimulus or by defocusing the pattern itself (155). Patterns with corners evoked larger VERs than striped patterns (194, 240). These studies have provided the basis for a possible method of refraction, particularly with children. Amplitude and configuration of VERs to patterned light will indicate when the image is in best focus.

Color and spectra Shipley, Jones & Fry (271–273) reported that the wave form of the ER to various spectra showed color-specific differences which persisted over a wide range of intensities. They not only equated the luminance of the different colored stimuli by heterochromatic flicker photometry, but varied intensities over a range of 5 log units. Clynes (66–70) extracted different color-specific components of the VER and reported that distinguishable ER wave forms were specific to different stimulus colors. When red, green, and blue stimuli were abruptly switched on, different wave forms were evoked. Subjects with normal color vision showed a gradual change in their VER wave form as the wave length was progressively changed from 680 nm (deep red) to 380 nm (far violet). Three distinct ERs could be recognized by purely visual inspection. Certain components were missing or distorted in color-blind subjects, depending on the type of the disorder. Other investigators have confirmed and extended these findings (9, 58, 64, 229, 231, 234, 241).

VERs to word stimuli have been studied by several investigators who could not unequivocally show that VERs to word stimuli could be distinguished from responses to nonword or nonsense syllable stimuli equated for brightness (29, 30, 48, 49, 174, 188). Although a difference was reported, Shelburne (270) had an alternate explanation. The difference that did occur was generally an increased positivity, maximal at latencies of 450 to 500 msec after the stimulus presentation. As the CNV usually terminates with a positive wave at about this time, it seemed possible to Shelburne that the CNV was involved in such experiments.

Species differences   The VERs of various species are unique. Rodents (rat, guinea pig, rabbit) all demonstrate markedly similar VERs, as do various strains of cats; VERs of primates, various monkeys and man, are strikingly similar (76–79, 141, 178, 236). Within a genus there may be notable differences (76, 77, 79) that may influence experimental interpretation, e.g. the VERs of albino and hooded rats are different. The VERs differ because the visual system of the albino rat is defective, as are those of other albino species (77). Differences between VERs in strains of rats probably account for the apparent conflict in a number of studies, as these animals are so extensively used in perceptual research (77).

Changes with maturation and aging   VERs change markedly during infancy (119–122, 125, 129, 167, 243, 244), throughout maturation and development (19, 22–24, 28, 112, 113, 115, 116), and during aging and senescence (257, 258, 265). As the ER may change twofold or more in amplitude at different age levels, the need for developmental normative data before clinical application is obvious. Apparently there are hereditary factors in the VER, as monozygotic twins demonstrate almost identical responses while dizygotic twins do not (108, 111, 186, 215, 326).

AUDITORY EVOKED RESPONSES (AERS)   The vicissitudes of the AER have been the most numerous of all the responses. Efforts to define the various components (86, 87, 89, 90, 146, 224, 225, 247) were frustrated because earlier components could be recorded from posterior neck muscles and were presumed to be myogenic, the result of reflex muscle contraction to sound. As this came to be generally accepted (33, 89, 90, 144), investigators directed their attention to later components, the most prominent of which were the N1 and P2 deflections with latencies of 95 to 105 and 170 to 200 msec, respectively (14–17, 86–90, 224, 225). Late components were studied in some detail with a view to applying the findings to audiology. It was reported that latency of these waves did not vary greatly with a change in intensity of the stimulus, nor were the latency and amplitude of these waves affected by changes in frequency between 300 and 4800 Hz. It was reported that the interval between stimuli must exceed 6 sec for recovery of maximal amplitude. Stimulating every second, as is often done, reduced the amplitude of the AER to one-quarter maximum (89, 90).

By reducing the intensity of the auditory stimulus and by averaging thousands of single responses, new insights into the components of the AER have emerged (165, 172, 221–223). We can now say with some certainty that *early* components of the AER, of which there are 6 in the first 8 msec of the response, probably represent activation of cochlear and auditory nuclei in the brain stem. The *middle latency* components, probably 5 in number, occurring between 8 and 50 msec, represent activation of both thalamus and auditory cortex, but can reflect concurrent scalp muscle reflexes. The *long latency* component, occurring after 50 msec and commonly known as P1-N1-P2-N2, represents widespread activiation of the frontal cortex and derives from a source other than that responsible for the earlier components.

The AER to speech stimuli   It has been proposed that there are specialized neuromechanisms required for the perception of speech and, as is well known, speech is lateralized to the left hemisphere in most people. Since patterned light evokes unique VERs, what are the effects of patterned sound, speech, on the AER? Three studies emerged recently, reporting that the AER to speech stimuli demonstrated hemispheric differences that other auditory stimuli did not (197, 210, 325). Space permits mention of only one strategy (325). Stop consonants, *Ba* and *Da*, equated for identical stimulus qualities, were used in two different tasks. In one instance the subject was to judge the *frequency* of the two stop consonants, that is, *Ba* or *Da* were delivered at two different pitches. In the other, *linguistic* content was the critical variable, i.e. the subject was to distinguish whether the stop consonant was *Ba* or *Da*. The two situations produced different AERs, but only linguistic content resulted in AER asymmetries with larger responses in the left hemisphere.

SOMATOSENSORY EVOKED RESPONSES (SERS)   The wave components and distribution of the SER over the scalp have been carefully studied by Goff, Shagass, and others (1, 5, 142–145, 265–268). On the basis of the scalp distribution of the SER and other factors, Goff's group has divided the components into a schema of 5 epochs. The earliest epoch contained wave components which were very small or absent on the side ipsilateral to stimulation. These consisted of *component 1*, a positive-negative-positive sequence with peaks at 16, 20 and 25 msec, respectively; *component 2*, a positive peak at about 30 msec; *component 3*, a positive peak at about 50 msec. The later *components, 4* and *5*, were bilaterally represented with component 4 comprising two peaks, a negative at 65 and a positive at 85 msec. Finally, component 5 comprised 2 peaks, a negative peak at 135 and a positive peak at about 200 msec.

When SERs of blind and sighted subjects were compared (128), the SERs of the blind had markedly shorter latencies. A late negative component arriving at about 150 msec in the normals' SERs arrived approximately 20 msec earlier in SERs of the blind subjects. Another interesting observation (253) was that a procedure related to acupuncture (electrical cutaneous stimulation) markedly attenuated SERs for as long as 20 min.

EVOKED RESPONSES TO OTHER STIMULI   Olfactory evoked responses have been recorded from the human (3, 129a, 278a) and quite extensively from the cat and rabbit (134). The olfactory ER was reexamined (278a) and stimulation of nasal trigeminal afferents found to be a principal source of the "olfactory" ER. Electrical stimulation of the tongue elicits a sensation of taste and also an ER (135). Vestibular ERs were reported (148).

CONTINGENT NEGATIVE VARIATION (CNV)   The slow negative shift of brain electrical potential that bridges the temporal gap between two stimuli, S_1 and S_2, when the first acts as a warning and the other as an imperative stimulus, has been termed the Contingent Negative Variation (CNV). Generally an alerting or warning signal precedes the delivery of an imperative signal to which the subject must make some kind of response. The interval between S_1 and S_2, usually 1 to 2 sec, is adequate for the full development of the slowly rising negative wave. In the decade since this phenomenon was first described and elaborated (205, 311–315), there has been an avalanche of studies, but still no consensus has emerged concerning the psychological concomitants of the CNV. Different viewpoints can be summarized in terms of four hypotheses or interpretations: *expectancy* (74, 312, 314); *motivation* (168, 228); *conation* (189, 190, 192, 198); and *attention* (161, 201, 292, 293).

A pitfall in analysis of the CNV is involuntary eye movements during the S_1–S_2 interval (164, 190, 285). Source and topographic distribution of the CNV was originally presumed to be in anterior regions of the frontal cortex, spreading posteriorly to precentral motor areas (313, 315). Järvilehto & Fruhstorfer (170), however, were able to differentiate three slow potentials (SPs) by manipulating the tasks of subjects. Borda (41) recorded from frontal and central cortical regions in the rhesus monkey and reported that SPs recorded from each of these areas occurred independently. Rebert (226) confirmed this finding and reported that frontal SPs were larger and more consistent than those found in the motor areas. Others (105, 245) studied the topographical distribution of the CNV in the monkey and reported a frontal-precentral or a postcentral slow potential depending upon the nature of the task.

Numerous studies suggest that the CNV is symmetrically distributed over the two hemispheres (189, 190, 196, 314). However, there have been claims for slightly larger SPs over the hemisphere contralateral to the hand used for a response (216), or over the dominant hemisphere in experimental designs involving numerical stimuli and arithmetic operations (50). McCallum & Cummings (202) investigated the effects of brain lesions on the CNV and reported convincing correspondence between asymmetry of the distribution of the CNV and the site of the lesion in those cases where the lesions were localized. With more diffuse lesions there was a generalized suppression of the CNV.

Skinner & Lindsley (276, 277) inserted cryogenic probes into midline anterior thalamus of experimental animals. During transient cryogenic blockade of this area, slow potentials were abolished; VERs and SERs were enhanced. Further evidence that the diffuse nonspecific thalamic system may play some role in the genesis of the CNV was provided by Hablitz (150), who demonstrated that CNV potentials were seen earlier from leads implanted in nonspecific thalamic nuclei than from those in cerebral cortex. This relationship, however, was not true in all situations.

Information Processing, Psychological Variables

In this area there were daring excursions not only into the brain but into the mind. Cerebral potentials recorded from gold electrodes implanted in the human brain were related to "real" and "imaginary" stimuli (317). Extrasensory cerebral potentials were reported to be passed from one identical twin to the other (107). Despite a number of excellent experiments, there was such a welter of techniques and subjective description that one had difficulty separating results from interpretation. Encountered was "information delivery," "read-out components," "bias level," "decision making," "expectancy waves," and 20 or more anthropocentric descriptions. One would not be greatly surprised to encounter a slow rising late wave of "brotherly love." Despite these difficulties, evidently this is where the action is for psychologists. Possibly we are moving, as some have claimed, towards a technique that will provide a "window to the mind."

ATTENTION, HABITUATION, SELECTIVE ATTENTION   A number of investigators have reported that attending, learning, and other mental processes may be reflected in the size and wave form of the cerebral evoked response. During inattention or during habituation the response has been reported to diminish, while during attention it has been observed to increase in size. For example, attenuation of the ER in the visual system to a repeated presentation of light (habituation) has been reported all along the visual pathways from the optic tract to the primary visual cortex, implying some inhibitory influence at all levels of that system. Similarly, attenuation of the auditory evoked response to a repeated click has been reported in the auditory pathways from the dorsal cochlear nucleus to the auditory cortex, and somatosensory ERs declined as a function of time in the medial lemniscus, the ventral posterolateral nucleus of the thalamus, and the somatosensory cortex (1, 39, 40, 62, 137, 160, 193, 206, 219, 296, 316). Likewise, with increased attention to an auditory stimulus, such as a conditioned response to a click, enhancement of the auditory response has been reported at dorsal cochlear nucleus, medial geniculate body, and auditory cortex. Increased attention to visual stimuli altered the form and amplitude of VERs recorded along the visual pathways including the lateral geniculate and the striate and parastriate cortices (27, 151, 158, 160, 169, 173, 220, 246, 249, 251, 260–63). ERs were also reported to be enhanced in human subjects when they were attending to a click (85, 149, 165, 166, 171a, 214a, 221, 222, 280, 323) or to a flash (27, 117, 137, 152, 156a). In the majority of these experiments the late components were most affected.

When two stimuli were presented simultaneously and subjects were asked to attend to one and ignore the other, the amplitude of the late components to the ignored stimulus was attenuated while the opposite effect was noted with the response to the attended stimulus (60, 61, 101, 152, 254, 255, 280). Näätänen (214) and Karlin (176) argued a noncognitive explanation for these results. It will be recalled that when changes occurred during attention these changes were confined mainly to the late components of the ER. It is well known that during periods of increased arousal these components change. As heightened states of arousal enhance components of the ER, Karlin and Näätänen pressed the point of view of a "prior-state hypothesis." That is, as stimuli in most of the studies were presented in a more or less orderly fashion, the subject had time to prepare for the critical stimulus, and thus enhancement was due to a level of increased arousal, not to selective attention, hence noncognitive. They also argued a "reactive change hypothesis," which meant that after the critical stimulus had occurred and the noncritical stimulus was presented the subject was in a relaxed state and hence there was attenuation of these components. These arguments were disturbing but valid. A flurry of disagreement found its way into the literature (102, 103, 212, 213) and was summarized by Regan (233) with a characteristically British comment: "This exchange of letters serves to confirm that any ambiguity or imprecision in defining the psychological terms used in evoked response research is a most potent source of misunderstanding and confusion." Even prior to the admonitions of Näätäten and Karlin, some experiments had been reported that met their objections (27, 117, 251).

Recently the effects of selective attention on both VERs and SERs have been investigated with conditions regarding transient changes in arousal level and peripheral orienting factors reduced to a minimum, with stimuli presented in a random and unpredictable sequence, and time epochs studied which could not be related to the effects of CNV. Harter & Salmon (156a) investigated the effects of selective attention on VERs. When the stimulus was attended, a reliable enhancement of a surface negative wave peaking at about 220 msec and a surface positive wave at about 315 msec occurred. Ford et al (132a) extended this approach to include both VERs and AERs. They reported that a negative component (arriving at about 200 msec in both systems) reflected selection between sensory modalities, while a later positive wave, peaking after 400 msec, indicated more complex intramodal discrimination. In what appeared to be a decisive experiment, Picton & Hillyard (223) investigated the effects of attention on the AER. With attention directed towards auditory stimuli to detect an occasional faint signal, there was a significant increase in the amplitude of two late waves: N1 occurring at 83 msec, and P2 occurring at 161 msec (mean time). A striking effect in these experiments was the appearance of a large "P3" component at about 450 msec in response to the detected signals. This was topographically distinct from the preceding components and could be recorded only in response to a detected stimulus or a detected omission of the stimulus in a regular train. From this it appeared that two systems are operating in selective attention, one indicated by the increased amplitude of the N1–P2 waves, the second reflected in the later more widespread P3 complex. The first may involve the selection of a particular input channel to be examined, while the second may indicate information processing. It should be noted that these last two studies (132a, 223) are in close agreement.

INFORMATION DELIVERY—STIMULUS UNCERTAINTY, THE P3 WAVE   Sutton, Braren, Tueting, and Zubin (289,290) were the first to describe the late positive component that was uniquely sensitive to what appeared to be the internal state of the subject. This was a slow (250–500 msec) positive wave similar to the vertex wave originally described by Davis (88). Sutton described the late positive wave as occurring around 300 msec and hence referred to it as P300, later to be called the P3 wave. The P3 wave appeared to be far less closely coupled to the evoking stimuli than any other wave. In fact, the absence of a stimulus could evoke the P3 wave, provided it was attributed to the "resolution of some uncertainty" (290,317). An exciting example of this was found in recordings made from intracerebral electrodes in five patients under treatment for chronic obsessional and anxiety disorders (317). Clear cerebral electrical potentials termed "omitted potentials" were observed when stimuli were expected but did not occur. These "omitted potentials" resembled those evoked when the real stimuli were presented.

The P3, occurring during a similar time epoch as the CNV, has been thought by some to be a manifestation of CNV activity. However, Donald & Goff (97) have demonstrated that these two phenomena, the P3 and the CNV, are dissociated.

Since the P3 has been found to be exquisitely sensitive to a variety of experimental maneuvers, it has excited considerable research and a variety of opinions. Defined operationally, an enhanced P3 may indicate: an occasional stimulus change (179, 222, 242, 278); a signal for a simple or choice reaction (106, 322); the detection of a threshold level auditory signal (166, 217, 281); a signal which confirms or refutes a prior guess (289, 290, 298); a signal to shift motor set (97); and finally a letter which completes a word (270). A number of formulations of the psychological processes that accompany the P3 have been offered. To this reviewer the most acceptable is that from the studies of Hillyard & Picton (165, 221, 222). The P3 wave is enhanced only when stimulus information is being actively processed and is uniquely associated with the occurrence of a signal and its correct detection.

PSYCHOLOGICAL VARIABLES AND THE CNV   The magnitude of the CNV was found to be dependent upon: qualities of the stimulus such as the intensity of S2, the imperative stimulus (166, 191, 228); uncertainty in the delivery of S2 (190, 312); distraction (205, 293); information contained in S2 (312, 313); duration of the S1–S2 interval as well as reaction time (162, 163, 199, 293); effort expended (41, 192, 227); response accuracy (162, 191, 198, 200); concentration and anxiety (180, 191, 198); sex differences (180); and finally psychopathology (42, 202, 204, 205). Results from nonhuman primates (41, 105, 150, 207, 226) generally support the conclusions drawn from some human studies (57, 170) that (a) the CNV is not a single process, and (b) that its nature and cerebral topography are dependent upon the state of the organism and the task imposed.

SLEEP, ANESTHESIA, HYPNOSIS, AND ALTERED CONSCIOUSNESS   VERs, AERs, and SERs have been investigated during various stages of sleep. They were found to change during sleep in man (45, 46, 138, 143, 182, 248) and in animals (2, 4, 6, 7), yielding responses that characterized the level of sleep. Late components of ERs were generally the waves most affected. Reviews of sleep research and sleep disorders by Broughton (45, 46) provide additional detail and pertinent background. The evolution of sleep received careful and systematic attention in symposia and papers (2, 6, 7), with reports indicating that "slow wave" and "para-doxical" sleep first developed phylogenetically with birds and mammals in paral-lel with the evolution of homeothermy, possibly as a mechanism to minimize energy expenditure. The effects of *anesthesia* on the VER were reviewed by Brazier (43), and effects of general anesthetics on VERs, AERs, and SERs in man and animal by Clark & Rosner (65).

Hypnosis, initially reported to have marked effects on the amplitude of the ER (69, 160), was found with larger groups of subjects to effect no reliable change other than increased stability (20, 25, 154). The ER appears to be a more accurate measure of *cerebral death* than the conventional EEG. In both man (297) and animals (21, 31) the ER was found to be more durable than the EEG during periods of serious cerebral embarassment and more predictive of the time of "brain death." This technique may prove valuable in determining cerebral death in the presence of ambiguous cerebral electrical activity, particularly with sus-pected death due to barbiturates and other depressants (21, 31, 297).

INTELLIGENCE AND MENTAL RETARDATION   Ertl and co-workers (18, 59a, 126a) reported reliable and significant relationships between latency of certain VER components and IQ test measures. The peak delays of components of subjects with high IQ arrived significantly earlier than did those of subjects with low IQ. The differences were large, often more than 100 msec (59). Reported Pearson *r* corre-lations were equally convincing (18), ranging from -.70 and -.80 for measured IQ and latency of some waves. While these data suggested that the ER was a prom-ising, reliable measure of "biological intelligence," there has been a general inability of others to replicate them (24, 55, 56, 114–116, 235, 259). Although Shucard & Horn (274, 275) correlated 16 ability tests, with measurable VER components, few significant correlations emerged, none beyond .25. In another approach (235) two groups of 20 children matched for age differed in mean group IQ by more than 50 points. VERs of the groups differed reliably in amplitude but not in latency. Amplitude of certain components and hemispheric asymmetry differentiated the groups, brighter children having larger overall responses and asymmetry characterized by larger responses in the right hemisphere. As higher IQ children were more alert than those of lower intelligence, this difference could be due to enhancement of late components because of increased level of attention. Engel & Fay (126) investigated the possible relationship of VERs derived in neonates with IQ measurement at ages 3 and 4 years. Studying 828 infants, they found some indication that the latency measurements of the neonatal VER pre-dicted certain *motor* development at 3 and 4 years, but there was no correlation between latency of VER and subsequent intellectual development. Schafer & Marcus (256) reported that when the stimuli evoking a response were *self-administered*, both AERs and VERs reduced in amplitude and later components arrived earlier. This effect, greater with AERs than VERs, was more marked with the brighter subjects. Scientists, technicians, and institutionalized retar-dates were compared.

Mental retardation has been an area of interest to ER researchers. Barnet and co-workers (14–17), noting the differences in normal and developmentally retarded newborns, reported that click evoked responses were significantly larger in infants with Down's syndrome than in matched normal infants. Others have studied VERs of older retarded children (37, 136, 237). Beyond longer latencies and missing components in the responses, the most striking difference was that reported by Bigum, Dustman & Beck (37). The SERs of mongoloid children not only differed from normals but were sufficiently unique to be recognized on relatively casual inspection. Somewhat like the disorder itself, characteristics of the response were strikingly similar among the Down's syndrome children.

EVOKED RESPONSES AND ANIMAL LEARNING; OTHER ELECTRICAL ACTIVITY AND BEHAVIOR   John (173) demonstrated "generalization" of ERs. Cats trained to one task utilizing a stimulus S_1, when learning another similar task to stimulus S_2, yielded ERs with periodicity and waves common to both S_1 and S_2.

While hippocampal theta activity has been previously associated with arousal, attention, and orienting behavior, lately remarkable correlations have been shown with the rate of theta rhythm and bursts of sniffing and associated vibrissal movement in the rat (147, 181). This implies that theta rhythm is associated with *movement* related to orienting, not orienting itself. Eye movement (250, 252), and other activity such as exploratory behavior, drinking, grooming, crouching, etc, also showed correlations with hippocampal frequencies (147, 181, 250, 252, 260–264). Schwartzbaum & co-workers (260–263) have related VER amplitude, behavioral reactivity, and hippocampal theta in the rat. The animals were confronted with two situations: in one the series of flashes signaled no contingency; and in the other the flashes indicated the delivery of food. In the first, wherein the animals became habituated, amplitude of VERs increased and hippocampal rhythms shifted to lower frequencies. In the food delivery situation VERs were reduced in amplitude and hippocampal activity increased in frequency. Other excellent animal studies utilizing the ER as an electrophysiological correlate to various behaviors were reported (151, 169, 178, 220, 242, 249). Among the studies cited (151, 178, 220) an interesting phenomenon was repeatedly observed. A large enduring rhythmical after-discharge of several waves was produced by iterative flashes, mainly when the animal was "relaxed." Fleming & co-workers (130–132) applied this reliably occurring phenomenon to the evaluation of drug effects on CNS activity, reporting that those drugs associated with physiological arousal, such as amphetamine, pilocarpine, and physostigmine, suppressed the after-discharge. When anticonvulsant drugs were evaluated, it was found that diphenylhydantoin (Dilantin) had little effect, while those such as trimethadione, generally used in the control of petit mal, greatly attenuated the after-discharge.

Brief mention should be made of two other electrical patterns, the *40 Hz* and the *12–14 Hz* rhythms, that lately have been related to behavior. Recording from cats implanted with cortical and subcortical electrodes, and analyzing the cerebral electrical activity by frequency analyses, Sheer (269) reported that after a criterion level of performance was achieved, there was a repeatedly marked increase in 40 Hz activity at the time the animals made a "relevant" response. This he interpreted to be an electrophysiological correlate of memory consolidation. While Mulholland (211) and others have demonstrated the ability of human subjects to modify the amount of alpha activity in their EEGs, Sterman & Friar (282) demonstrated a unique application of this technique, claiming a reduction in the incidence of seizures in an epileptic when the patient was trained to produce rhythmic activity over the sensory motor area. This application evolved from studies of a rhythm, 12–14 Hz, occurring over the sensory motor cortex of the cat, seen during voluntary suppression of movement (283). The cat could be "shaped" to produce such a rhythm. Furthermore, Sterman & co-workers have been fairly successful in tracing out the source of this rhythm which they believe to be generated by neurons within the ventral basal thalamus.

At the time this review was submitted, an International Symposium on Cerebral Evoked Potentials was in progress in Brussels. Volumes will be published on new findings of the more than 100 contributors. These will be edited by Professor John E. Desmedt and will cover new aspects of both ER and CNV research.

As may be seen, there has been an avalanche of research since Dawson (91) opened the door for such techniques. Clinicial and other applications are developing rapidly (26, 33, 52, 54, 202, 233, 265). A future reviewer of this area will no doubt be as impressed as this reviewer with the diversity and extent of the technique.

Literature Cited

1. Allison, T. 1962. Recovery functions of somatosensory evoked responses in man. *Electroencephalogr. Clin. Neurophysiol.* 14:331–43
2. Allison, T. 1972. Comparative and evolutionary aspects of sleep. In *The Sleeping Brain, Perspectives in the Brain Sciences,* ed. M. H. Chase, 1:1–57. UCLA Brain Inform. Serv.
3. Allison, T., Goff, W. R. 1967. Human cerebral evoked responses to odorous stimuli. *Electroencephalogr. Clin. Neurophysiol.* 23:558–60
4. Allison, T., Goff, W. R., Sterman, M. B. 1966. Cerebral somatosensory responses evoked during sleep in the cat. *Electroencephalogr. Clin. Neurophysiol.* 21:461–68
5. Allison, T., Goff, W. R., Williamson, P. D., VanGilder, J. C., Fisher, T. C. 1973. *On The Origin of Early Components of the Human Somatic Evoked Response.* Presented at 27th Ann. Meet. Am. Electroencephalogr. Soc. Boston
6. Allison, T., Van Twyver, H. 1970. The evolution of sleep. *Natural History* Vol. 79, No. 2
7. Allison, T., Van Twyver, H., Goff, W. R. 1972. Electrophysiological studies of the echidna, *Tachyglossus aculeatus.* I. Waking and sleep. *Arch. Ital. Biol.* 110:145–84
8. Armington, J. C. 1964. Adaptational changes in the human electroretinogram and occipital response. *Vision Res.* 4:179–92
9. Armington, J. C. 1966. Spectral sensitivity of simultaneous electroretinograms and occipital responses. *Vision Res.* Suppl. 1:225–33
10. Barlow, J. S. 1957. An electronic method for detecting evoked responses of the brain and for reproducing their average waveforms. *Electroencephalogr. Clin. Neurophysiol.* 9:340–43
11. Barlow, J. S. 1963. Some statistical characteristics of electrocortical activity in relation to visual-oculomotor tracking in man. *Bol. Inst. Estud. Med. Biol.* (Mex.) 21:497–518

12. Barlow, J. S. 1964. Evoked responses in relation to visual perception and oculomotor reaction times in man. *Ann. NY Acad. Sci.* 112:432–67

13. Barlow, J. S., Cigánek, L. 1969. Lambda responses in relation to visual evoked responses in man. *Electroencephalogr. Clin. Neurophysiol.* 26:183–92

14. Barnet, A. B. 1971. EEG and evoked response correlates of mental retardation. *Clin. Proc. Child. Hosp.* 27:250–60

15. Barnet, A. B., Goodwin, R. S. 1965. Averaged evoked electroencephalographic responses to clicks in the human newborn. *Electroencephalogr. Clin. Neurophysiol.* 18:441

16. Barnet, A. B., Lodge, A. 1967. Click evoked EEG responses in normal and developmentally retarded infants. *Nature* 214:252–55

17. Barnet, A. B., Ohlrich, E. S., Shanks, B. L. 1971. EEG evoked responses to repetitive auditory stimulation in normal and Down's syndrome infants. *Develop. Med. Child. Neurol.* 13:321–29

18. Barry, W. M., Ertl, J. P. 1965. Brain waves and human intelligence. In *Modern Educational Developments: Another Look*, ed. F. B. Davis. New York: Educ. Rec. Bur. 257 pp.

19. Beck, E. C. 1969. Interhemispheric differences in the amplitude of the evoked potential in children. *Soc. Neurosci. Progr. Abstr.* 1:85

20. Beck, E. C., Barolin, G. S. 1965. The effect of hypnotic suggestion on evoked potentials. *J. Nerv. Ment. Dis.* 140:154–61

21. Beck, E. C., Behrens, E. M., Dustman, R. E. 1973. The averaged visual evoked potential as a technique for assessing cerebral death. *Soc. Neurosci. Progr. Abstr.* 3:326

22. Beck, E. C., Dustman, R. E. 1972. Developmental electrophysiology of brain function in normal and abnormal children. In *Current Status of Physiological Psychology: Readings*, ed. D. Singh, C. Morgan, 362–69. Monterey, Calif.: Brooks/Cole. 398 pp.

23. Beck, E. C., Dustman, R. E. 1974. Developmental electrophysiology of brain function as reflected by changes in the evoked response. In *Neuropsychological Methods for the Assessment of Impaired Brain Function*, ed. J. W. Prescott. Washington, D.C.: GPO. In press

24. Beck, E. C., Dustman, R. E. 1974. Changes in the evoked response in maturation and aging in man and macaque. In *Behavior and Brain Electrical Activity*, ed. N. R. Burch. New York: Plenum. In press

25. Beck, E. C., Dustman, R. E., Beier, E. G. 1966. Hypnotic suggestions and visually evoked potentials. *Electroencephalogr. Clin. Neurophysiol.* 20:397–400

26. Beck, E. C., Dustman, R. E., Lewis, E. G. 1974. The use of the averaged evoked potential in the evaluation of central nervous system disorders. *Int. J. Neurol.* In press

27. Beck, E. C., Dustman, R. E., Sakai, M. 1969. Electrophysiological correlates of selective attention. See Ref. 127, 396–416

28. Beck, E. C., Dustman, R. E., Schenkenberg, T. 1974. Life span changes in the electrical activity of the human brain as reflected in the cerebral evoked response. In *Neurobiology and Aging*, ed. J. M. Ordy, K. R. Brizzee, P. Gerone. New York: Plenum. In press

29. Begleiter, H., Platz, A. 1969. Evoked potentials: Modifications by classical conditioning. *Science* 166:769–71

30. Begleiter, H., Platz, A. 1969. Cortical evoked potentials to semantic stimuli. *Psychophysiology* 6:91–100

31. Behrens, E. M., Beck, E. C., Dustman, R. E. 1973. *The Use of the Computer Averaged Visual Evoked Response as a Technique for Assessing Cerebral Death*. Presented at 81st Ann. Conv. APA Montreal, Canada

32. Bennett, J. R., MacDonald, J. S., Drance, S. M., Uenoyama, K. 1971. Some statistical properties of the visual evoked potential in man and their application as a criterion of normality. *IEEE Trans. Biomed. Eng.* 18:23–34

33. Bergamini, L., Bergamasco, B. 1967. *Cortical Evoked Potentials in Man*. Springfield, Ill.: Thomas. 116 pp.

34. Bickford, R. G. 1964. Properties of the

photomotor response system. *Electroencephalogr. Clin. Neurophysiol.* 17: 456

35. Ibid 1967. Effect of facial expression on the averaged evoked response to light in man. 23:78–79

36. Bickford, R. G., Jacobson, J. L., Cody, D. T. R. 1964. Nature of average evoked potentials to sound and other stimuli in man. *Ann NY Acad. Sci.* 112:204–23

37. Bigum, H. B., Dustman, R. E., Beck, E. C. 1970. Visual and somatosensory evoked responses from mongoloid and normal children. *Electroencephalogr. Clin. Neurophysiol.* 28:202–5

38. Bishop, G. H., Clare, M. H. 1953. Responses of cortex to direct electrical stimuli applied at different depths. *J. Neurophysiol.* 16:1–19

39. Bogacz, J., Vanzulli, A., García-Austt, E. 1962. Evoked responses in man. IV. Effects of habituation, distraction and conditioning upon auditory evoked responses. *Acta Neurol. Lat. Am.* 8: 244–52

40. Bogacz, J., Vanzulli, A., Handler, P., García-Austt, E. 1960. Evoked responses in man. II. Habituation of visual evoked response. *Acta Neurol. Lat. Am.* 6:353–62

41. Borda, R. P. 1970. The effect of altered drive states on the contingent negative variation (CNV) in rhesus monkey. *Electroencephalogr. Clin. Neurophysiol.* 29:173–80

42. Bostem, F., Rousseau, J. C., Degossely, M., Dongier, M. 1967. Psychopathological correlations of the non-specific portion of visual and auditory evoked potentials and the associated contingent negative variation. *Electroencephalogr. Clin. Neurophysiol.* 26:131–38

43. Brazier, M. A. B. 1970. Effect of anesthesia on visually evoked responses. *Int. Anesth. Clin.* 8:103–28

44. Broughton, R. J. 1967. *Somatosensory evoked potentials in man: Cortical and scalp recordings.* PhD thesis. McGill Univ. Montreal, Canada

45. Broughton, R. J. 1968. Sleep disorders: Disorders of arousal? *Science* 159: 1070–78

46. Broughton, R. J. 1971. Neurology and sleep research. *Can. Psychiat. Assoc. J.* 16:283–93

47. Broughton, R. J., Rasmussen, T., Branch, C. 1968. Cortex and scalp recorded somatosensory evoked potentials in man. *Electroencephalogr. Clin. Neurophysiol* 24:285

48. Buchsbaum, M., Fedio, P. 1969. Visual information and evoked responses from the left and right hemispheres. *Electroencephalogr. Clin. Neurophysiol.* 26:266–72

49. Buchsbaum, M., Fedio, P. 1970. Hemispheric differences in evoked potentials to verbal and nonverbal stimuli in the left and right visual fields. *Physiol. Behav.* 5:207–10

50. Butler, S. R., Glass, A. 1971. Interhemispheric asymmetry of contingent negative variation during numeric operations. *Electroencephalogr. Clin. Neurophysiol.* 30:366

51. Callaway, E. 1972. Pharmacology of evoked potentials in man. See Ref. 265, 74–76

52. Callaway, E. 1969. Diagnostic uses of the average evoked potentials. See Ref. 104, 299–317

53. Callaway, E., Halliday, R. A. 1973. Evoked potential variability: Effects of age, amplitude and methods of measurement. *Electroencephalogr. Clin. Neurophysiol.* 34:125–33

54. Callaway, E., Jones, R. T., Donchin, E. 1970. Auditory evoked potential variability in schizophrenia. *Electroencephalogr. Clin. Neurophysiol.* 29: 421–28

55. Callaway, E., Naylor, H., VanBeenan, S. 1973. Average evoked potential/Intelligence correlations: Long auditory AEP latencies with high IQ *Soc. Neurosci. Progr. Abstr.* 3:323

56. Callaway, E., Stone, G. C. 1969. Evoked response methods for the study of intelligence. *Agressologie* 10:1–5

57. Cant, B. R., Bickford, R. G. 1967. The effect of motivation on the contingent negative variation (CNV). *Electroencephalogr. Clin. Neurophysiol.* 23:594 (abstr.)

58. Cavonius, C. R. 1965. Evoked response of the human visual cortex: Spectral sensitivity. *Psychon. Sci.* 2:185–86

59. Celesia, G. G., Puletti, F. 1971. Auditory input to the human cortex during states of drowsiness and surgical anesthesia. *Electroencephalogr. Clin. Neurophysiol* 31:603–9

59a. Chalke, F. C. R., Ertl, J. 1965. Evoked potentials and intelligence. *Life Sci.* 4:1319–21

60. Chapman, R. M. 1965. Evoked responses to relevant and irrelevant visual stimuli while problem solving. *Proc. Am. Psychol. Assoc.,* 177–78

61. Chapman, R. M., Bragdon, H. R. 1964. Evoked responses to numerical visual stimuli while problem solving. *Nature* 203:1155–57

62. Chow, K. L., Randall, W., Morrell, F. 1966. Effect of brain lesions on conditioned cortical electropotentials. *Electroencephalogr. Clin. Neurophysiol.* 20: 357–69

63. Cigánek, L. 1961. The EEG response (evoked potential) to light stimulus in man. *Electroencephalogr. Clin. Neurophysiol.* 13:165–72

64. Cigánek, L., Ingvar, D. H. 1969. Colour specific features of visual cortical responses in man evoked by monochromatic flashes. *Acta Physiol. Scand.* 76:82–92

65. Clark, D. L., Rosner, B. S. 1973. Neurophysiologic effects of general anesthetics: 1. The electroencephalogram and sensory evoked responses in man. *Anesthesiology* 38:564–82

66. Clynes, M., Kohn, M. 1964. Specific responses of the brain to colour stimuli. *Proc. 17th Conf. Eng. Med. Biol.,* 32

67. Clynes, M., Kohn, M. 1967. Spatial visual evoked potentials as physiologic language elements for colour and field structure. See Ref. 72, 82–96

68. Clynes, M., Kohn, M., Gradijan, J. 1967. Computer recognition of the brain's visual perception through learning and brain's physiologic language. *IEEE Int. Conv. Rec.* 9:125–42

69. Clynes, M., Kohn, M., Lifshitz, K. 1964. Dynamics of spatial behavior of light evoked potentials, their modification under hypnosis, and on-line correlation in relation to rhythmic components. *Ann. NY Acad. Sci.* 112:468–508

70. Clynes, M., Kohn, M., Litchfield, D. 1965. Chromaticity waves of evoked human brain potentials in normal and colour-blind vision. *Fed. Proc.* 24:274

71. Cobb, W. A., Dawson, G. D. 1960. The latency and form in man of the occipital potential evoked by bright flashes. *J. Physiol.* 152:108–21

72. Cobb, W., Morocutti, C., Eds. 1967. *The Evoked Potentials. Electroencephalogr. Clin. Neurophysiol. Suppl. 26.* Amsterdam: Elsevier. 218 pp.

73. Cohen, J. 1969. Very slow brain potentials relating to expectancy: The CNV. See Ref. 104, 143–63

74. Cohen, J., Walter, W. G. 1966. The interaction in the brain to semantic stimuli. *Psychophysiology* 2:187–96

75. Cooper, R., Winter, A. L., Crow, H. J., Walter, W. G. 1965. Comparison of subcortical, cortical and scalp activity using chronically indwelling electrodes in man. *Electroencephalogr. Clin. Neurophysiol.* 18:217–28

76. Creel, D. J. 1971. Differences of ipsilateral and contralateral visually evoked responses in the cat: Strains compared. *J. Comp. Physiol. Psychol.* 77:161–65

77. Creel, D. J., Dustman, R. E., Beck, E. C. 1970. Differences in visually evoked responses in albino versus hooded rats. *Exp. Neurol.* 29:298–309

78. Ibid 1973. Visually evoked responses in the rat, guinea pig, cat, monkey and man. 40:351–66

79. Creel, D. J., Giolli, R. A. 1972. Retinogeniculate projections in guinea pigs: Albino and pigmented strains compared. *Exp. Neurol.* 36:411–25

80. Creutzfeldt, O. D., Fuster, J. M., Lux, H. D., Nacimiento, A. C. 1964. Experimenteller Nachweis von Beziehungen zwischen EEG-Wellen und Aktivitat corticaler Nervenzellen. *Naturwissenschaften* 51:166–67

81. Creutzfeldt, O. D., Jung, R. 1961. Neuronal discharge in the cat's motor cortex during sleep and arousal. In *The Nature of Sleep,* ed. G. E. W. Wolstenholme, M. O'Connor, 131–70. London: Churchill. 591 pp.

82. Creutzfeldt, O. D., Rosina, A., Ito, M., Probst, W. 1969. Visual evoked re-

sponse of single cells and of the EEG in primary visual area of the cat. *J. Neurophysiol.* 32:127–39

83. Creutzfeldt, O. D., Watanabe, S., Lux, H. D. 1966. Relations between EEG phenomena and potentials of single cortical cells. I. Evoked responses after thalamic and epicortical stimulation. *Electroencephalogr. Clin. Neurophysiol.* 20:1–18

84. Ibid. Relations between EEG phenomena and potentials of single cortical cells. II. Spontaneous and convulsoid activity, 19–37

85. Davis, H. 1964. Enhancement of evoked cortical potentials in humans related to a task requiring a decision. *Science* 145:182–83

86. Davis, H. 1965. The young deaf child: Identification and management. *Acta Otolaryngol.* 59:170–85

87. Davis, H. 1966. Validation of evoked-response audiometry (ERA) in deaf children. *Int. Audiol.* 5:77–81

88. Davis, H., Davis, P. A., Loomis, A. L., Harvey, N., Hobart, G. A. 1939. Electrical reactions of the brain to auditory stimulation during sleep. *J. Neurophysiol.* 2:500–14

89. Davis, H., Hirsch, S. K., Shelnutt, J., Bowers, C. 1967. Further validation of evoked response audiometry (ERA). *J. Speech Hear. Res.* 10:717–32

90. Davis, H., Mast, T., Yoshie, N., Zerlin, S. 1966. The slow response of the human cortex to auditory stimuli: Recovery process. *Electroencephalogr. Clin. Neurophysiol.* 21:105–13

91. Dawson, G. D. 1947. Cerebral responses to electrical stimulation of peripheral nerve in man. *J. Neurol. Neurosurg. Psychiat.* 10:134–40

92. Dawson, G. D. 1954. A multiple scalp electrode for plotting evoked potentials. *Electroencephalogr. Clin. Neurophysiol.* 6:153–54

93. Diamond, S. P. 1964. Input-output relations. *Ann. NY Acad. Sci.* 112:160–71

94. Dill, R. C., Vallecalle, E., Verzeano, M. 1968. Evoked potentials, neuronal activity and stimulus intensity in the visual system. *Physiol. Behav.* 3:797–801

95. Domino, E. F., Corssen, G. 1964.

Visually evoked response in man with and without induced muscle paralysis. *Ann. NY Acad. Sci.* 112:226–37

96. Domino, E. F., Matsuoka, S., Watty, J., Cooper, I. 1964. Simultaneous recording of scalp and epidural somatosensory-evoked responses in man. *Science* 145:1199–1200

97. Donald, M. W., Goff, W. R. 1971. Attention-related increases in cortical responsivity dissociated from the contingent negative variation. *Science* 172:1163–66

98. Donchin, E. 1966. A multivariate approach to the analysis of average evoked potentials. *IEEE Trans. Biomed. Eng.* 13:131–39

99. Donchin, E. 1969. Discriminant analysis in average evoked response studies: the study of single trial data. *Electroencephalogr. Clin. Neurophysiol.* 27:311–14

100. Donchin, E. 1969. Data analysis techniques in average evoked potential research. See Ref. 104, 199–236

101. Donchin, E., Cohen, L. 1967. Average evoked potentials and intramodality selective attention. *Electroencephalogr. Clin. Neurophysiol.* 22:537–46

102. Donchin, E., Cohen, L. 1969. Anticipation of relevant stimuli and evoked potentials: A reply to Näätänen. *Percept. Mot. Skills* 29:115–17

103. Ibid. Further reply to Näätänen, 270

104. Donchin, E., Lindsley, D. B. 1969. *Average Evoked Potentials: Methods, Results and Evaluations.* Washington, D. C.: NASA SP-191. 400 pp.

105. Donchin, E., Otto, D., Gerbrandt, L. K., Pribram, K. H. 1971. While a monkey waits: Electrocortical events recorded during the foreperiod of a reaction time study. *Electroencephalogr. Clin. Neurophysiol.* 31:115–27

106. Donchin, E., Smith, D. B. D. 1970. The contingent negative variation and the late positive wave of the average evoked potential. *Electroencephalogr. Clin. Neurophysiol.* 29:201–3

107. Duane, T. D., Behrendt, T. 1965. Extrasensory electroencephalic induction between identical twins. *Science* 150:367

108. Dumermuth, G. 1968. Variance spec-

tra of electroencephalograms in twins. In *Clinical Electroencephalography of Children*, ed. P. Kellaway, I. Petersen, 119–54. New York: Grune & Stratton, 332 pp.

109. Dustman, R. E., Beck, E. C. 1963. Long term stability of visually evoked potentials in man. *Science* 142:480–82

110. Dustman, R. E., Beck, E. C. 1965. Phase of alpha waves, reaction time and visually evoked potentials. *Electroencephalogr. Clin. Neurophysiol.* 18:433–40

111. Ibid. The visually evoked potential in twins. 19:570–75

112. Dustman, R. E., Beck, E. C. 1966. Visually evoked potentials: Amplitude changes with age. *Science* 151:1013–15

113. Dustman, R. E., Beck, E. C. 1968. The effects of maturation and aging on the wave form of visually evoked potentials. *Electroencephalogr. Clin. Neurophysiol.* 26:2–11

114. Ibid 1972. Relationship of intelligence to visually evoked responses. 33:254 (abstr.)

115. Dustman, R. E., Beck, E. C. 1974. The evoked response: Its use in evaluating brain function of children and young adults. In *Psychiatric and Psychological Problems of Childhood*, ed. D. V. Siva Sankar. Westbury, NY: P.J.D. Publ. In press

116. Dustman, R. E., Schenkenberg, T., Beck, E. C. 1974. The development of the evoked response as a diagnostic and evaluative procedure. In *Developmental Psychophysiology in Mental Retardation and Learning Disability*, ed. R. Karrer. Springfield, Ill.: Thomas. In press

117. Eason, R. G., Harter, M. R., White, C. T. 1969. Effects of attention and arousal on visually evoked cortical potentials and reaction time in man. *Physiol. Behav.* 4:283–89

118. Eason, R. G., White, C. T., Bartlett, N. 1970. Effects of checkerboard pattern stimulation on evoked cortical responses in relation to check size and visual field. *Psychon. Sci.* 21:113–15

119. Ellingson, R. J. 1970. Variability of visual evoked responses in the human newborn.*Electroencephalogr. Clin. Neu-*

rophysiol. 29:10–19

120. Ellingson, R. J., Danahy, T., Nelson, B., Lathrop, G. H. 1974. Variability of auditory evoked potentials in human newborns. *Electroencephalogr. Clin. Neurophysiol.* 36:155–62

121. Ellingson, R. J., Lathrop, G. H., Danahy, T., Nelson, B. 1973. Variability of visual evoked potentials in human infants and adults. *Electroencephalogr. Clin. Neurophysiol.* 34:113–24

122. Ellingson, R. J., Rose, G. H. 1970. Ontogenesis of the electroencephalogram. In *Developmental Neurobiology*, ed. W. A. Himwich, 441–74. Springfield, Ill.: Thomas. 770 pp.

123. Elmgren, J., Lowenbard, P. 1969. A factor analysis of the human EEG. *Psychol. Lab. Univ. Goteborg Rep.* No. *2*

124. Elul, R. 1968. Brain waves: Intracellular recording and statistical analysis help clarify their physiological significance. In *Data Acquisition and Processing in Biology and Medicine*, 5:93–115. Oxford, New York: Pergamon

125. Engel, R., Butler, B. V. 1963. Appraisal of conceptual age of newborn infants by EEG methods. *J. Pediat.* 63:386

126. Engel, R., Fay, W. 1972. Visual evoked responses at birth, verbal scores at three years and IQ at four years. *Develop. Med. Child Neurol.* 14:283–89

126a. Ertl, J., Schafer, E. W. P. 1969. Brain response correlates of psychometric intelligence. *Nature* 223:421–22

127. Evans, C. R., Mulholland, T. B., Eds. 1969. *Attention in Neurophysiology*. London: Butterworth. 447 pp.

128. Feinsod, M., Bach-y-Rita, P., Madey, J. M. J. 1973. Somatosensory evoked responses: Latency differences in blind and sighted persons. *Brain Res.* 60:219–23

129. Ferriss, G. S., Davis, G. D., Dorsen, M. McF., Hackett, E. R. 1967. Changes in latency and form of the photically induced average evoked response in human infants. *Electroencephalogr. Clin. Neurophysiol.* 22:305–12

129a. Finkenzeller, P. 1966. Gemittelte EEG–Potentiale bei olfactorischer Reizung. *Pflügers Arch.* 292:76–80

130. Fleming, D. E., Rhodes, L. E., Wilson, C. E., Shearer, D. E. 1972. Time-drug modulations of photically evoked after-discharge patterns. *Physiol. Behav.* 8:1045–49

131. Fleming, D. E., Rhodes, L. E., Wilson, C. E., Shearer, D. E. 1973. Differential effects of convulsive drugs on photically evoked after-discharge parameters. *Psychopharmacology* 29:77–84

132. Fleming, D. E., Shearer, D. E., Creel, D. J. 1974. Effect of pharmacologically induced arousal on the evoked potential in the unanesthetized rat. *Pharmacol. Biochem. Behav.* 2:187–92

132a. Ford, J. M., Roth, W. T., Dirk, S. J., Kopell, B. S. 1973. Evoked potential correlates of signal recognition between and within modalities. *Science* 181:465–66

133. Fox, S. S., O'Brien, J. H. 1965. Duplication of evoked potential wave-form by curve of probability of firing of a single cell. *Science* 147:888–90

134. Freeman, W. J. 1974. Topographic organization of primary olfactory nerve in cat and rabbit as shown by evoked potentials. *Electroencephalogr. Clin. Neurophysiol.* 36:33–45

135. Funakoshi, M., Kawamura, Y. 1971. Summated cerebral evoked responses to taste stimuli in man. *Electroencephalogr. Clin. Neurophysiol.* 30: 205–9

136. Galbraith, G. C., Gliddon, J. B., Busk, J. 1970. Visual evoked responses in mentally retarded and nonretarded subjects. *Am. J. Ment. Defic.* 75:341–48

137. García-Austt, E., Bogacz, J., Vanzulli, A. 1964. Effects of attention and inattention upon visual evoked response. *Electroencephalogr. Clin. Neurophysiol.* 17:136–43

138. Gastaut, H. et al 1963. A transcranial chronographic and topographic study of cerebral potentials evoked by photic stimulation in man. In *Brain Mechanisms*, ed. G. Moruzzi, A. Fessard, H. H. Jasper, 374–92. Amsterdam: Elsevier. 493 pp.

139. Geisler, C. D., Gerstein, G. L. 1961. The surface EEG in relation to its sources. *Electroencephalogr. Clin. Neurophysiol.* 13:927–34

140. Giblin, D. R. 1964. Somatosensory evoked potentials in healthy subjects and in patients with lesions of the nervous system. *Ann. NY Acad. Sci.* 112:93–142

141. Giolli, R. A., Guthrie, M. D. 1971. Organization of subcortical projections of visual areas I and II in the rabbit. An experimental degeneration study. *J. Comp. Neurol.* 142:351–76

142. Goff, W. R. 1969. Evoked potential correlates of perceptual organization in man. See Ref. 127, 169–93

143. Goff, W. R., Allison, T., Shapiro, A., Rosner, B. S. 1966. Cerebral somatosensory responses evoked during sleep in man. *Electroencephalogr. Clin. Neurophysiol* 21:1–9

144. Goff, W. R., Matsumiya, T., Allison, T., Goff, G. D. 1969. Cross-modality comparisons of averaged evoked potentials. See Ref. 104, 95–141

145. Goff, W. R., Rosner, B. S., Allison, T. 1962. Distribution of cerebral somatosensory evoked responses in normal man. *Electroencephalogr. Clin. Neurophysiol.* 14:697–713

146. Goldstein, R., Rodman, L. B. 1967. Early components of averaged evoked responses to rapidly repeated auditory stimuli. *J. Speech Hear. Res.* 10: 697–705

147. Gray, J. A. 1971. Medial septal lesions, hippocampal theta thythm and the control of vibrissal movement in the freely moving rat. *Electroencephalogr. Clin. Neurophysiol.* 30:189–97

148. Greiner, G. F., Collard, M., Conraux, C., Picart, P., Rohmer, F. 1967. Recherche de potentiels évoqués d'origine vestibulaire chez l'homme. *Acta Otolaryngol.* 63:320–29

149. Gross, M. M., Begleiter, H., Tobin, M., Kissin, B. 1965. Auditory evoked response comparison during counting clicks and reading. *Electroencephalogr. Clin. Neurophysiol.* 18:451–54

150. Hablitz, J. J. 1973. Operant conditioning and slow potential changes from monkey cortex. *Electroencephalogr. Clin. Neurophysiol.* 34:399–408

151. Hackett, J. T., Marczynski, T. J. 1971. Positive reinforcement and visual evoked potentials in cat. *Brain Res.* 26:57–70

152. Haider, M., Spong, P., Lindsley, D. B.

1964. Attention, vigilance, and cortical evoked potentials in humans. *Science* 145:180–82

153. Hall, R. A., Rappaport, M., Hopkins, H. K., Griffin, R. B. 1973. Peak identification in visual evoked potentials. *Psychophysiology* 10:52–60

154. Halliday, A. M., Mason, A. A. 1964. Cortical evoked potentials during hypnotic anaesthesia. *Electroencephalogr. Clin. Neurophysiol.* 16:312–14

155. Harter, M. R. 1968. Effects of contour sharpness and check size on visually evoked cortical potentials. *Vision Res.* 8:701–11

156. Harter, M. R., Salmon, L. E. 1971. Evoked cortical responses to patterned light flashes: Effects of ocular convergence and accomodation. *Electroencephalogr. Clin. Neurophysiol.* 30:527–33

156a. Harter, M. R., Salmon, L. E. 1972. Intra-modality selective attention and evoked cortical potentials to randomly presented patterns. *Electroencephalogr. Clin. Neurophysiol.* 32:605–13

157. Harter, M. R., White, C. T. 1969. Evoked cortical responses to checkerboard patterns: Effect of check-size as a function of visual acuity. *Electroencephalogr. Clin. Neurophysiol.* 28:48–54

158. Hearst, E., Beer, B., Sheatz, G. C., Galambos, R. 1960. Some electrophysiological correlates of conditioning in the monkey. *Electroencephalogr. Clin. Neurophysiol.* 12:137–52

159. Heath, R. G., Galbraith, G. C. 1966. Sensory evoked responses recorded simultaneously from human cortex and scalp. *Nature* 212:1535–37

160. Hernández-Péon, R. 1960. Neurophysiological correlates of habituation and other manifestations of plastic inhibitions. In *The Moscow Colloquium on Electroencephalography of Higher Nervous Activity*, ed. H. H. Jasper, G. D. Smirnov, 101–12. *Electroencephalogr. Clin. Neurophysiol. Suppl. 13.* Amsterdam: Elsevier. 420 pp.

161. Hillyard, S. A. 1969. The CNV and the vertex evoked potential during signal detection: A preliminary report. See Ref. 104, 349–53

162. Hillyard, S. A. 1969. Relationships between the contingent negative variation (CNV) and reaction time. *Physiol. Behav.* 4:351–58

163. Hillyard, S. A., Galambos, R. 1967. Effects of stimulus and response contingencies on a surface negative slow potential shift in man. *Electroencephalogr. Clin. Neurophysiol.* 22:297–304

164. Ibid 1970. Eye movement artifact in the CNV. 28:173–82

165. Hillyard, S. A., Hink, R. F., Schwent, V. L., Picton, T. W. 1973. Electrical signs of selective attention in the human brain. *Science* 182:177–80

166. Hillyard, S. A., Squires, K. C., Bauer, J. W., Lindsay, P. H. 1971. Evoked potential correlates of auditory signal detection. *Science* 72:1357–60

167. Hrbek, A., Mares, P. 1964. Cortical evoked responses to visual stimulation in full-term and premature newborns. *Electroencephalogr. Clin. Neurophysiol.* 16:575–81

168. Irwin, D. A., Knott, J. R., McAdam, D. W., Rebert, C. S. 1966. Motivational determinants of the "contingent negative variation." *Electroencephalogr. Clin. Neurophysiol.* 21:538–43

169. Jane, J. A., Smirnov, G. D., Jasper, H. H. 1962. Effects of distraction upon simultaneous auditory and visual evoked potentials. *Electroencephalogr. Clin. Neurophysiol.* 14:344–58

170. Järvilehto, T., Fruhstorfer, H. 1970. Differentiation between slow cortical potentials associated with motor and mental acts in man. *Exp. Brain Res.* 11:309–17

171. Jasper, J., Lende, R., Rasmussen, T. 1960. Evoked potentials from exposed somatosensory cortex in man. *J. Nerv. Ment. Dis.* 130:526–37

171a. Jenness, D. 1972. Auditory evoked response differentiation with discriminate learning in humans. *J. Comp. Physiol. Psychol.* 80:75–90

172. Jewett, D. L., Romano, M. N., Williston, J. S. 1970. Human auditory evoked potentials: Possible brain stem components detected on the scalp. *Science* 167:1517–18

173. John, E. R. 1972. Switchboard versus statistical theories of learning and memory. *Science* 177:850–64

174. John, E. R., Herrington, R. N., Sutton,

S. 1967. Effects of visual form on the evoked response. *Science* 155:1439–42

175. John, E. R., Walker, D., Cawood, M. R., Gehrmann, J. 1973. Factor analysis of evoked potentials. *Electroencephalogr. Clin. Neurophysiol.* 34:33–43

176. Karlin, L. 1970. Cognition, preparation, and sensory-evoked potentials. *Psychol. Bull.* 73:122–36

177. Kelly, D. L., Goldring, S., O'Leary, J. L. 1965. Averaged evoked somatosensory responses from exposed cortex of man. *Arch. Neurol.* 13:1–9

178. Kimura, D. 1962. Multiple response of visual cortex of the rat to photic stimulation. *Electroencephalogr. Clin. Neurophysiol.* 14:115–22

179. Klinke, R., Fruhstorfer, H., Finkenzeller, P. 1968. Evoked responses as a function of external stored information. *Electroencephalogr. Clin. Neurophysiol.* 25:119–22

180. Knott, J. R., Irwin, D. A. 1967. Anxiety, stress and the CNV. *Electroencephalogr. Clin. Neurophysiol.* 22:188

181. Komisaruk, B. R. 1970. Synchrony between limbic system theta activity and rhythmical behavior in rats. *J. Comp. Physiol. Psychol.* 70:482–92

182. Kooi, K. A., Bagchi, B. K. 1964. Visual evoked responses in man: Normative data. *Ann. NY Acad. Sci.* 112:254–69

183. Kooi, K. A., Tipton, A. C., Marshall, D. E. 1971. Polarities and field configurations of the vertex components of the human auditory evoked response: A reinterpretation. *Electroencephalogr. Clin. Neurophysiol.* 31:166–69

184. Larson, S. J., Sances, A., Christenson, P. C. 1966. Evoked somatosensory potentials in man. *Arch. Neurol.* 15:88–91

185. Lehmann, D., Kavanagh, R. N., Fender, D. H. 1969. Field studies of averaged visually evoked potentials in a patient with a split chiasm. *Electroencephalogr. Clin. Neurophysiol.* 26:193–99

186. Lewis, E. G., Dustman, R. E., Beck, E. C. 1972. Evoked response similarity in monozygotic, dizygotic and unrelated individuals: A · comparative study. *Electroencephalogr. Clin. Neurophysiol.* 32:309–16

187. Liberson, W. T. 1966. Study of evoked potentials in aphasics. *Am. J. Phys. Med.* 45:135–42

188. Lifshitz, K. 1966. The average evoked cortical response to complex visual stimuli. *Psychophysiology* 3:55–68

189. Low, M. D. 1969. Comment on Cohen's paper. See Ref. 104, 163–71

190. Low, M. D., Borda, R. P., Frost, J. D., Kellaway, P. 1966. Surface-negative, slow-potential shift associated with conditioning in man. *Neurology* 16:771–82

191. Low, M. D., Coats, A. C., Rettig, G. M., McSherry, J. W. 1967. Anxiety, attentiveness-alertness: A phenomenological study of the CNV. *Neuropsychologia* 5:379–84

192. Low, M. D., McSherry, J. W. 1968. Further observations of psychological factors involved in CNV genesis. *Electroencephalogr. Clin. Neurophysiol.* 25:203–7

193. Macadar, O., Ginés, A., Bove, I. C., García-Austt, E. 1963. Effect of habituation, interference and association of stimuli upon the visual evoked response in the rat. *Acta Neurol. Lat. Am.* 9:315–27

194. Mackay, D. M. 1969. Evoked brain potentials as indicators of sensory information processing. *Neurosci. Res. Progr. Abstr.* 7:3

195. Mackay, D. M., Rietveld, W. J. 1968. Electroencephalogram potentials evoked by accelerated visual motion. *Nature* 217:677–78

196. Marsh, G. R., Thompson, L. W. 1973. Effects of age on the contingent negative variation in a pitch discrimination task. *J. Gerontol.* 28:56–62

197. Matsumiya, Y., Tagliasco, V., Lombroso, C. T., Goodglass, H. 1972. Auditory evoked response: Meaningfulness of stimuli and interhemispheric asymmetry. *Science* 175:790–92

198. McAdam, D., Irwin, D. A., Rebert, C. S., Knott, J. R. 1966. Conative control of the contingent negative variation. *Electroencephalogr. Clin. Neurophysiol.* 21:195–95

199. McAdam, D., Knott, J. R., Rebert, C. S. 1969. Cortical slow potential changes in man related to interstimulus interval and to pre-trial prediction of

interstimulus interval. *Psychophysiology* 5:349-58

200. McAdam, D., Rubin, E. H. 1971. Readiness potential, vertex positive wave, contingency negative variation and accuracy of perception. *Electroencephalogr. Clin. Neurophysiol.* 30: 511-17

201. McCallum, W. C. 1969. The contingent negative variation as a cortical sign of attention in man. See Ref. 127, 40-63

202. McCallum, W. C., Cummings, B. 1973. The effects of brain lesions on the contingent negative variation in neurosurgical patients. *Electroencephalogr. Clin. Neurophysiol.* 35:449-56

203. McCallum, W. C., Knott, J. R., Eds. 1973. *Event Related Slow Potentials of the Brain: Their Relations to Behavior. Electroencephalogr. Clin. Neurophysiol. Suppl. 33.* Amsterdam: Elsevier. 390 pp.

204. McCallum, W. C. et al 1973. Event related slow potential changes in human brain stem. *Nature* (London) 242: 465-67

205. McCallum, W. C., Walter, W. G. 1968. The effects of attention and distraction on the contingent negative variation in normal and neurotic subjects. *Electroencephalogr. Clin. Neurophysiol.* 25: 319-29

206. McGowan-Sass, E. E. 1972. Habituation of somatosensory evoked potentials in the lemniscal system of the cat. *Electroencephalogr. Clin. Neurophysiol.* 32:373-81

207. McSherry, J. W. 1971. *Intracortical origin of the contingent negative variation in the rhesus monkey.* PhD thesis. Baylor Coll. Med., Houston

208. Milsum, J. H. 1969. The role of unidirectional rate sensitivity in biological control system stabilization. *Ann. NY Acad. Sci.* 156:731-39

209. Morrell, F., Morrell, L. 1965. Computer aided analysis of brain electrical activity. In *The Analysis of Central Nervous System and Cardiovascular Data Using Computer Methods,* ed. L. D. Proctor, W. R. Adey, 441-78. Washington, D. C.: NASA SP-72

210. Morrell, L. K., Salamy, J. G. 1971. Hemispheric asymmetry of electrocor-

tical responses to speech stimuli. *Science* 174:164-66

211. Mulholland, T. B. 1972. Occipital alpha revisited. *Psychol. Bull.* 78:176-82

212. Näätänen, R. 1969. Anticipation of relevant stimuli and evoked potentials: A comment on Donchin's and Cohen's 'Averaged Evoked Potentials and Intramodality Selective Attention'. *Percept. Mot. Skills* 28:639-46

213. Ibid. Anticipation of relevant stimuli and evoked potentials: A reply to Donchin and Cohen. 29:233-34

214. Näätänen, R. 1970. Evoked potential, EEG, and slow potential correlates of selective attention. *Acta Psychol.* 33: 178-92

214a. Öhman, A., Lader, M. 1972. Selective attention and "habituation" of the auditory averaged evoked response in humans. *Physiol. Behav.* 8:79-85

215. Osborne, R. T. 1970. Heritability estimates for the visual evoked response. *Life Sci.* 9:381-90

216. Otto, D. A., Leifer, L. J. 1973. The effect of modifying response and performance feedback parameters on the CNV in humans. See Ref. 203, 29-37

217. Paul, D., Sutton, S. 1972. Evoked potential correlates of response criterion in auditory signal detection. *Science* 177:362-64

218. Perry, N. W., Childers, D. G. 1969. *The Human Visual Evoked Response: Method and Theory.* Springfield, Ill.: Thomas. 187 pp.

219. Perry, N. W., Copenhaver, R. M. 1965. Differential cortical habituation with stimulation of central and peripheral retina. *Percept. Mot. Skills* 20:1209-13

220. Pickenhein, L., Klingberg, F. 1965. Behavioral and electrical changes during avoidance conditioning to light flashes in the rat. *Electroencephalogr. Clin. Neurophysiol.* 18:464-76

221. Picton, T. W., Hillyard, S. A. 1974. Human auditory evoked potentials. II. Effects of attention. *Electroencephalogr. Clin. Neurophysiol.* 36:191-200

222. Picton, T. W., Hillyard, S. A., Galambos, R., Schiff, M. 1971. Human auditory attention: A central or peripheral process? *Science* 173:351-53

223. Picton, T. W., Hillyard, S. A., Krausz,

H. I., Galambos, R. 1974. Human auditory evoked potentials. I: Evaluation of components. *Electroencephalogr. Clin. Neurophysiol.* 36(2):179–90

224. Rapin, I. 1964. Evoked responses to clicks in a group of children with communication disorders. *Ann. NY Acad. Sci.* 112:182–203

225. Rapin, I., Graziani, L. J. 1967. Auditory evoked responses in normal, brain damaged and deaf infants. *Neurology* 17:881–94

226. Rebert, C. S. 1972. Cortical and subcortical slow potentials in the monkey's brain during a preparatory interval. *Electroencephalogr. Clin. Neurophysiol.* 33:389–402

227. Rebert, C. S., Irwin, D. A. 1969. Slow potential changes in cat brain during classical appetitive and aversive conditioning of jaw movement. *Electroencephalogr. Clin. Neurophysiol.* 27: 152–61

228. Rebert, C. S., McAdam, D. W., Knott, J. R., Irwin, D. A. 1967. Slow potential change in human brain related to level of motivation. *J. Comp. Physiol. Psychol.* 63:20–23

229. Regan, D. 1966. An effect of stimulus colour on average steady-state potentials evoked in man. *Nature* 210: 1056–57

230. Regan, D. 1966. Some characteristics of average steady-state and transient responses evoked by modulated light. *Electroencephalogr. Clin. Neurophysiol.* 20:238–48

231. Regan, D. 1970. Evoked potential and psychophysical correlates of changes in stimulus colour and intensity. *Vision Res.* 10:163–78

232. Regan, D. 1972. Cortical evoked potentials. *Advan. Behav. Biol.* 5:177–92

233. Regan, D. 1972. *Evoked Potentials in Psychology, Sensory Physiology and Clinical Medicine.* London: Chapman & Hall. 328 pp.

234. Regan, D., Tyler, C. W. 1971. Wavelength-modulated light generator. *Vision Res.* 11:43–56

235. Rhodes, L. E., Dustman, R. E., Beck, E. C. 1969. The visual evoked response: A comparison of bright and dull children. *Electroencephalogr. Clin. Neurophysiol.* 27:364–72

236. Rhodes, L. E., Fleming, D. E. 1970. Sensory restriction in the albino rat: Photically evoked after-discharge correlates. *Electroencephalogr. Clin. Neurophysiol.* 29:488–95

237. Richlin, M., Weisinger, M., Weinstein, S., Giannini, M., Morganstern, M. 1971. Interhemispheric asymmetries of evoked cortical responses in retarded and normal children. *Cortex* 7:98–105

238. Rietveld, W. J. 1963. The occipitocortical response to light flashes in man. *Acta Physiol. Pharmacol. Neer.* 12: 373–407

239. Rietveld, W. J., Tordoir, W. E. M. 1965. The influence of flash intensity upon the visual evoked response in the human corex. *Acta Physiol. Pharmacol. Neer.* 13:160–70

240. Rietveld, W. J., Tordoir, W. E. M., Hagenouw, J. R., Lubbers, J. A., Spoor, T. A. C. 1967. Visual evoked responses to blank and to checkerboard patterned flashes. *Acta Physiol. Pharmacol. Neer.* 14:259–85

241. Riggs, L. A., Sternheim, C. E. 1969. Human retinal and occipital potentials evoked by changes of the wavelength of the stimulating light. *J. Opt. Soc. Am.* 59:635–40

242. Ritter, W., Vaughan, H. G., Costa, L. D. 1968. Orienting and habituation to auditory stimuli: A study of short term changes in average evoked responses. *Electroencephalogr. Clin. Neurophysiol.* 25:550–56

243. Rose, G. H., Lindsley, D. B. 1965. Visually evoked electrocortical responses in kittens: Development of specific and nonspecific systems. *Science* 148:1244–46

244. Rose, G. H., Lindsley, D. B. 1968. Development of visually evoked potentials in kittens: Specific and nonspecific responses. *J. Neurophysiol.* 31:607–23

245. Rosen, S. C., Stamm, J. S. 1969. Cortical steady potential shifts during delayed response performance by monkeys. *Electroencephalogr. Clin. Neurophysiol.* 27:684–85

246. Rothblat, L., Pribram, K. H. 1972. Selective attention: Input filter or response selection? An electrophysiological analysis. *Brain Res.* 39:427–36

247. Ruhm, H., Walker, E., Flanigin, H.

1967. Acoustically-evoked potentials in man: Mediation of early components. *Laryngoscope* 77:806–22

248. Saier, J., Régis, H., Mano, T., Gastaut, H. 1968. Potentiels évoqués visuels et somesthesiques pendant le sommeil de l'homme. *Brain Res.* 10:431–40

249. Saito, H., Yamamoto, M., Iwai, E., Nakahama, H. 1973. Behavioral and electrophysiological correlates during flash-frequency discrimination learning in monkeys. *Electroencephalogr. Clin. Neurophysiol.* 34:449–60

250. Sakai, K., Sano, K., Iwahara, S. 1973. Eye movements and the hippocampal theta activity in cats. *Electroencephalogr. Clin. Neurophysiol.* 34:547–49

251. Sakai, M., Dustman, R. E., Beck, E. C. 1968. Summed evoked responses from primary and associational cortices of cats at different levels of awareness. *Proc. Am. Psychol. Assoc.* 3:309–10

252. Sano, K., Iwahara, S., Senba, K., Sano, A., Yamazaki, S. 1973. Eye movements and hippocampal theta activity in rats. *Electroencephalogr. Clin. Neurophysiol.* 35:621–25

253. Satran, R., Goldstein, M. N. 1973. Pain perception: Modification of threshold of intolerance and cortical potentials by cutaneous stimulation. *Science* 180:1201–2

254. Satterfield, J. H. 1965. Evoked cortical response enhancement and attention in man. A study of responses to auditory and shock stimuli. *Electroencephalogr. Clin. Neurophysiol.* 19:470–75

255. Satterfield, J. H., Cheatum, D. 1964. Evoked cortical potential correlates of attention in human subjects. *Electroencephalogr. Clin. Neurophysiol.* 17:456

256. Schafer, E. W. P., Marcus, M. M. 1973. Self-stimulation alters human sensory brain responses. *Science* 181:175–77

257. Schenkenberg, T. 1970. *Visual, auditory, and somatosensory evoked responses of normal subjects from childhood to senescence.* PhD thesis. Univ. Utah, Salt Lake City. 247 pp.

258. Schenkenberg, T., Dustman, R. E. 1970. Visual, auditory and somatosensory evoked response changes related to age, hemisphere and sex. *Proc. Am.*

Psychol. Assoc. 183–84

259. Schwartz, M., Shagass, C. 1964. Recovery functions of human somatosensory and visual evoked potentials. *Ann. NY Acad. Sci.* 112:510–25

260. Schwartzbaum, J. S., DiLorenzo, P. M., Mello, W. F., Kreinick, C. J. 1972. Further evidence of dissociation between reactivity and visual evoked response following septal lesions in rats. *J. Comp. Physiol. Psychol.* 80:143–49

261. Schwartzbaum, J. S., Kreinick, C. J. 1973. Interrelationships of hippocampal electroencephalogram visually evoked response, and behavioral reactivity to photic stimuli in rats. *J. Comp. Physiol. Psychol.* 85(3):470–90

262. Schwartzbaum, J. S., Kreinick, C. J., Gustafson, J. W. 1971. Cortical evoked potentials and behavioral reactivity to photic stimuli in freely moving rats. *Brain Res.* 27(2):295–307

263. Schwartzbaum, J. S., Kreinick, C. J., Levine, M. S. 1972. Behavioral reactivity and visual evoked potentials to photic stimuli following septal lesions in rats. *J. Comp. Physiol. Psychol.* 80:123–42

264. Segal, M. 1973. Flow of conditioned responses in limbic telecephalic system of the rat. *J. Neurophysiol.* 36(5): 840–54

265. Shagass, C. 1972. *Evoked Brain Potentials in Psychiatry.* New York: Plenum. 274 pp.

266. Shagass, C. 1972. Electrophysiological studies of psychiatric problems. *Rev. Can. Biol.* 31:77–95

267. Shagass, C., Schwartz, M. 1964. Recovery functions of somatosensory peripheral nerve and cerebral evoked responses in man. *Electroencephalogr. Clin. Neurophysiol.* 17:126–35

268. Shagass, C., Schwartz, M. 1964. Evoked potential studies in psychiatric patients. *Ann. NY Acad. Sci.* 112: 526–42

269. Sheer, D. E. 1970. Electrophysiological correlates of memory consolidation. *In Molecular Mechanisms in Memory and Learning*, ed. G. Ungar, 177–211. New York: Plenum. 296 pp.

270. Shelburne, S. A. 1972. Visual evoked responses to word and nonsense sylla-

ble stimuli. *Electroencephalogr. Clin. Neurophysiol.* 32(1):17–25

271. Shipley, T., Jones, R. W., Fry, A. 1965. Evoked visual potentials and human colour vision. *Science* 150:1162–64

272. Shipley, T., Jones, R. W., Fry, A. 1966. Intensity and the evoked occipitogram in man. *Vision Res.* 6:657–67

273. Ibid 1968. Spectral analysis of the visually evoked occipitogram in man. 8:409–31

274. Shucard, D. W., Horn, J. L. 1972. Evoked cortical potentials and measurement of human abilities. *J. Comp. Physiol. Psychol.* 78:59–68

275. Shucard, D. W., Horn, J. L. 1973. Evoked potential amplitude change related to intelligence and arousal. *Psychophysiology* 10:445–52

276. Skinner, J. E. 1971. Abolition of a conditioned, surface-negative, cortical potential during cryogenic blockade of the nonspecific thalamo-cortical system. *Electroencephalogr. Clin. Neurophysiol* 31:197–209

277. Skinner, J. E., Lindsley, D. B. 1971. Enhancement of visual and auditory evoked potentials during blockade of the non-specific thalamo-cortical system. *Electroencephalogr. Clin. Neurophysiol.* 31:1–6

278. Smith, D. B., Donchin, E., Cohen, L., Starr, A. 1970. Auditory averaged evoked potentials in man during selective binaural listening. *Electroencephalogr. Clin. Neurophysiol.* 28:146–52

278a. Smith, D. B., Allison, T., Goff, W. R., Principato, J. J. 1971. Human odorant evoked response: Effects of trigeminal or olfactory deficit. *Electroencephalogr. Clin. Neurophysiol.* 30:313–17

279. Spehlman, R. 1965. The averaged electrical responses to diffuse and to patterned light in the human. *Electroencephalogr. Clin. Neurophysiol.* 19:560–69

280. Spong, P., Haider, M., Lindsley, D. B. 1965. Selective attentiveness and cortical evoked responses to visual and auditory stimuli. *Science* 148:395–97

281. Squires, K. C., Hillyard, S. A., Lindsay, P. H. 1973. Cortical potentials evoked by confirming and disconfirming feedback following an auditory discrimination. *Percept. Psychophys.* 13:25–31

282. Sterman, M. B., Friar, L. 1972. Suppression of seizures in an epileptic following sensorimotor EEG feedback graining. *Electroencephalogr. Clin. Neurophysiol.* 33:89–95

283. Sterman, M. B., Howe, R. C., MacDonald, L. R. 1970. Facilitation of spindleburst sleep by conditioning of electroencephalographic activity while awake. *Science* 167:1146–48

284. Stohr, P. E., Goldring, S. 1969. Origin of somatosensory evoked scalp responses in man. *J. Neurosurg.* 31:117–27

285. Straumanis, J. J., Shagass, C., Overton, D. A. 1969. Problems associated with application of the contingent negative variation to psychiatric research. *J. Nerv. Ment. Dis.* 148:170–79

286. Suter, C. 1969. *Computer Analysis of Evoked Potential Correlates of the Critical Band.* Tech. Rep. Computer Sci. Center, Univ. Maryland, 68–98

287. Suter, C. M. 1970. Principal component analysis of average evoked potentials. *Exp. Neurol.* 29(2):317–27

288. Sutton, S. 1969. The specification of psychological variables in an average evoked potential experiment. See Ref. 104, 237–97

289. Sutton, S., Braren, M., Zubin, J. 1965. Evoked potential correlates of stimulus uncertainty. *Science* 150:1177–88

290. Sutton, S., Tueting, P., Zubin, J. 1967. Information delivery and the sensory evoked potential. *Science* 155:1436–39

291. Tecce, J. J. 1970. Attention and evoked potentials in man. In *Attention—Contemporary Theory and Analysis*, ed. D. I. Mostofsky, 331–65. New York: Appleton. 433 pp.

292. Tecce, J. J. 1972. Contingent negative variation (CNV) and psychological process in man. *Psychol. Bull.* 77(2):73–108

293. Tecce, J. J., Scheff, N. M. 1969. Attention reduction and suppressed direct current potentials in the human brain. *Science* 164:331–33

294. Tepas, D. I., Armington, J. C. 1962. Evoked potentials in the human visual system. In *Biological Prototypes and Synthetic Systems*, 1:13–21. New York:

Plenum. 397 pp.

295. Tepas, D. I., Armington, J. C. 1962. Properties of evoked visual potentials. *Vision Res.* 2:449–61

296. Thompson, R. F., Spencer, W. A. 1966. Habituation: A model phenomenon for the study of neuronal substrates of behavior. *Psychol. Rev.* 73:16–43

297. Trojaborg, W., Jorgenson, E. O. 1973. Evoked cortical potentials in patients with "isoelectric" EEGs. *Electroencephalogr. Clin. Neurophysiol.* 35: 301–9

298. Tueting, P., Sutton, S., Zubin, J. 1970. Quantitative evoked potential correlates of the probability of events. *Psychophysiology* 7:385–94

299. van der Tweel, L. H., Spekreijse, H. 1969. Signal transport and rectification in the human evoked-response system. *Ann. NY Acad. Sci.* 156:678–95

300. van der Tweel, L. H., Verduyn, H. F. E. 1965. Human visual responses to sinusoidally modulated light. *Electroencephalogr. Clin. Neurophysiol.* 18: 587–98

301. van Hof, M. W. 1960. Open-eye and closed-eye occipitocortical response to photic stimulation of the retina. *Acta Physiol. Pharmacol. Neer.* 9:443–51

302. Ibid. The relation between the cortical responses to flash and to flicker in man, 210–24

303. Vaughan, H. G. 1966. The perceptual and physiologic significance of visual evoked responses recorded from the scalp in man. In *Clinical Electroretinography*, ed. H. M. Burian, J. H. Jacobson, 203–23. Oxford: Pergamon. 376 pp.

304. Vaughan, H. G. 1969. The relationship of brain activity to scalp recordings of event-related potentials. See Ref. 104, 45–94

305. Vaughan, H. G., Gross, C. G. 1969. Cortical responses to light in unanesthetized monkeys and their alteration by visual system lesions. *Exp. Brain Res.* 8:19–36

306. Vaughan, H. G., Hull, R. C. 1965. Functional relation between stimulus intensity and photically evoked cerebral responses in man. *Nature* 206: 720–22

307. Vaughan, H. G., Ritter, W. 1970. The sources of auditory-evoked responses recorded from the human scalp. *Electroencephalogr. Clin. Neurophysiol.* 28: 360–67

308. Walter, D. O. 1963. Spectral analysis for electroencephalograms: Mathematical determination of neurophysiological relationships from records of limited duration. *Exp. Neurol.* 8:155

309. Walter, D. O. 1971. Two approximations to the median evoked response. *Electroencephalogr. Clin. Neurophysiol.* 30:246–47

310. Walter, D. O., Brazier, M. A. B., Eds. 1969. Advances in EEG Analysis. *Electroencephalogr. Clin. Neurophysiol. Suppl. 27.* Amsterdam: Elsevier

311. Walter, W. G. 1964. The convergence and interaction of visual, auditory, and tactile responses in human nonspecific cortex. *Ann. NY Acad. Sci.* 112:320–61

312. Walter, W. G. 1965. Effects on anterior brain responses of an expected association between stimuli. *J. Psychosom. Res.* 9:45–49

313. Walter, W. G. 1967. Slow potential changes in the human brain associated with expectancy, decision and intention. See Ref. 72, 123–30

314. Walter, W. G., Cooper, R., Aldridge, V. J., McCallum, W. C., Winter, A. L. 1964. Contingent negative variation: an electric sign of sensorimotor association and expectancy. *Nature* 203: 380–84

315. Walter, W. G., Crow, H. J. 1964. Depth recording from the human brain. *Electroencephalogr. Clin. Neurophysiol.* 16:68–72

316. Webster, W. R., Dunlop, C. W., Simons, L. A., Aitkin, L. M. 1965. Auditory habituation: A test of a centrifugal and a peripheral theory. *Science* 148:654–56

317. Weinberg, H., Walter, W. G., Crow, H. J. 1970. Intracerebral events in humans related to real and imaginary stimuli. *Electroencephalogr. Clin. Neurophysiol.* 29:1–9

318. Whipple, H. E., Ed. 1964. *Sensory Evoked Response in Man. Ann. NY Acad. Sci.* 112. 546 pp.

319. White, C. T. 1969. Evoked cortical responses and patterned stimuli. *Am. Psychol.* 24:212–14

320. White, C. T., Eason, R. G. 1966. Evoked cortical potentials in relation to certain aspects of visual perception. *Psychol. Monogr.* 80:1–14

321. Wicke, J. D., Donchin, E., Lindsley, D. B. 1964. Visual evoked potentials as a function of flash luminance and duration. *Science* 146:83–85

322. Wilkinson, R. T., Morlock, H. C. 1967. Auditory evoked response and reaction time. *Electroencephalogr. Clin. Neurophysiol.* 23:50–56

323. Williams, H. L., Morlock, H. C., Morlock, J. V., Lubin, A. 1964. Auditory evoked responses and the EEG stages in sleep. *Ann. NY Acad. Sci.* 112:172–81

324. Williamson, P. D., Goff, W. R., Allison, T. 1970. Somatosensory evoked responses in patients with unilateral cerebral lesions. *Electroencephalogr. Clin. Neurophysiol.* 28:566–75

325. Wood, C. C., Goff, W. R., Day, R. S. 1971. Auditory evoked potentials during speech perception. *Science* 173:1248–51

326. Young, J. P. R., Lader, M. H., Fenton, G. W. 1972. A twin study of the genetic influences on the electroencephalogram. *J. Med. Genet.* 9:13–16

PERCEPTION

§234

Daniel J. Weintraub

Human Performance Center, Department of Psychology
University of Michigan, Ann Arbor, Michigan 48104

The field of perception reaches to the corners of the psychological landscape. Therefore, this review, which primarily covers the literature published during calendar years 1972 and 1973, is unapologetically idiosyncratic. The topic is visual perception. Color vision and perceptual development receive frequent treatment in *Annual Review* chapters, so these topics will be slighted. Sekuler's (172) admirable chapter in last year's *Annual Review of Psychology* covering "spatial vision" permits me to tread lightly across that ground.

I have surveyed the remaining terrain like a helicopter pilot. The simile is apt because helicoptering allows one to pull back in order to appreciate the panorama, hover low for closer observation, alight to reconnoiter, but it does not permit a microscopic examination of every square centimeter of soil. Any pilot is well acquainted with the territory near home base; he is more likely to know only landmarks farther out. The territory was found to be wide, varied, and interesting. However, I must report that there's a jungle down there, trails that lead nowhere overgrown with tangled roots, vegetation that is perpetually green but never flowers, and unfriendly tribes separated by nearly impenetrable forest. The tribes skirmish only occasionally because they seldom venture from their own clearings, which they stand ready to defend at a moment's notice.

Two large tribes will be described before the analogy is abandoned. There are neurophysiological theorists and psychological-process theorists (functionalists). The former deal in flesh and blood mechanisms (e.g. neural lateral interactions), the latter in descriptive labels for psychological functions (e.g. size comparator), the labels sometimes enclosed in rectangles and connected by lines to form a flow diagram, irreverently termed the "Boxology" by a charming Ms. who is a fellow tribesperson.

The tribes can be distinguished by language, habits, and lifestyle. A truly remarkable distinguishing feature discovered from this survey is the number and character of human subjects deemed appropriate for a psychophysical experiment. One tribe characteristically tests two or three subjects, and often only one. These few subjects are considered as representative, and it is common for multiple authors of a research report to have tested each other. The other tribe strives for large samples, tries to estimate population variability, and employs experimenters as subjects with great caution fearing experimenter and subject bias. Any investigator can be categorized as to tribe on the basis of a simple test. Compute the median number of human subjects used per experimental condition as determined from the investigator's published research. The criterion cut for deciding the theoretical orientation of any investigator lies near 5; functionalists lie above the cut.

Each group finds the language of the other not to its liking. A potentially more serious failing is that each tends to ignore the evidence developed by the other. Fortunately, both kinds of theorists and theories are thriving. Unfortunately, apartheid stands in the way of advancing the science of perception.

DRAWING INFERENCES FROM DATA

Brindley (25) proposed an hypothesis linking experience to its neural substrate ". . . namely that physically indistinguishable signals sent from the sense organs to the brain cause indistinguishable sensations" (p. 134). Brindley proposed that psychophysical procedures requiring judgments of indistinguishability are highly to be preferred. Data from matching and threshold determinations were labeled as Class A observations. Null-match methods do have high face validity for investigating neurophysiological hypotheses. Stimuli that are indistinguishable might be presumed to have identical neural concomitants [which is the converse of Brindley's statement, as Boynton & Onley (24) pointed out]. Indistinguishability must mean, however, indistinguishability in all respects. In colorimetry, for example, an observer's task is to produce a metameric (look alike) match. Indistinguishability demands further verification. The observer must be unable to detect any difference between the metamers when they are then presented to him in a two-alternative forced-choice experiment requiring a temporal or spatial discrimination. [Compare the above treatment of Class A observations with that of Cornsweet & Pinsker (33) and of Sekuler (172).]

Unfortunately, complete perceptual identity is impossible in the most interesting experiments because the stimuli are indelibly tagged by their contexts. In an experiment on simultaneous hue contrast, a stimulus in a chromatic (colored) surround might be matched by a stimulus in an achromatic (neutral) surround. After the match has been achieved the stimuli are nevertheless distinguishable by their respective surrounds. The line segments to be matched for length in the Müller-Lyer display are tagged by distinguishable arrowheads. Since stimuli are seldom context free, null matches, of necessity, are null with respect to selected attributes only. Observers are asked to disregard all other differences. These less than ideal matches are the best that can be done when it is context that makes objectively equal stimuli appear unequal. [Compare with the Class IV observations of Boynton & Onley (24).]

I propose that *all* null-match techniques be promoted to Class A status, reserving for Brindley's indistinguishability-in-all-respects criterion the title Class A' to designate their prime (i.e. high grade) quality. It requires no great leap to assume, when two stimuli look alike under conditions where their contexts differ, that at some level the neural activities corresponding to the stimuli are identical. The important point is that no matter what the conditions, conferring neural indistinguishability by virtue of perceptual indistinguishability is an inference. In principle, only Class A' null matches can be confirmed through forced-choice techniques. Even when there is no objective criterion of correct and incorrect choice, perceptual indistinguishability can be confirmed via forced-choice techniques.

Regardless of class, the convergence of various psychophysical techniques is important. If null-match data are comparable to those obtained by ratings or by magnitude estimates, then confidence increases concerning what is being measured. Suppose operations presumably assessing the same attribute disagree? Wagner & Boynton (207) compared several methods of heterochromatic photometry. They recommended that null matches for brightness (disregarding other color attributes, i.e. hue and saturation) be abandoned in favor of producing a minimally distinct border between contiguous color patches for a substantial number of very practical reasons. Nevertheless, such a recommendation clearly violates functionalist (and phenomenological) tenets. Brightness matching addresses the very fundamental meaning of the term *brightness*. If two stimuli meeting the criterion of a minimally distinct border do not appear equally bright, then the tractability or reliability of the measures would seem irrelevant.

Because they are so basic and simple, null-match techniques may lull the experimenter into believing that he has found the ultimate in psychophysical security. Not so. Always implied is the proviso that the effect has been measured *relative to the comparison stimulus*. On what basis can it be inferred that the comparison stimulus is perceived veridically? For example, do parallel lines attract? Quina & Pollack (163) required subjects to judge the distance between parallel lines by determining an equal distance between two dots. Relative to the dots, parallels are perceived as closer together. However, dots might repel one another, and parallels might also repel, but less strongly, as Weintraub & Tong (216) concluded on the basis of other converging evidence.

Another serious problem is that the comparison stimulus used to "measure" an experimental outcome is itself being influenced by the independent variable. Howard, Evans & McDonald (93) showed that in a figural-aftereffects paradigm the inducing figure affected the location of the comparison figure as well as the test figure. An annular surround with only slightly greater luminance than the center test disk causes a drastic reduction in the perceived brightness of the disk. Yet Guth (76) found little or no change in ΔIs superimposed on the disk when the surround luminance was varied. But given a base intensity (I), the just-noticeable-increase in intensity (ΔI) used as an index may covary with the independent variable. To quote Guth,

> These facts may be explained by the possibility that the inhibition that causes a reduction in the neural activity associated with the disk or image also causes a similar

reduction in the neural activity associated with the ΔI flash. If the inhibitory reductions occur over the range where $\Delta I/I$ is constant, and if they reduce neural activity from I and from ΔI by the same factor, then absolutely no change is to be expected in the ΔI required for threshold, even though the apparent brightness of the test field decreases markedly. . . . To the extent that our measuring instrument (the ΔI or threshold light) is affected by the same inhibition that we are trying to evaluate, our efforts may prove useless (76, p. 952).

ASPECTS OF THE WORLD AS PERCEIVED

Evidence is accumulating that psychological plane geometry corresponding to operations accomplished in the real world with compass and straightedge is complex indeed. Perceived rectilinearity among line and/or dot elements depends critically upon their orientation and also eye fixation relative to the elements being judged (39, 153, 162). Psychological parallelism is a function of the orientation of the pair of lines (27). Errors in the perceived size of angles depend upon the size of the angle, the orientation of the angle, and the technique used in assessing the errors (27, 91, 218). There is considerable agreement that obtuse angles are underestimated, but it is not so certain that acute angles are overestimated. Perkins (154) presented line drawings of rectangular solids and asked subjects to judge whether the drawings represented three-dimensional rectangular boxes. On the basis of projective geometry, half the set of drawings could have been projections of a rectangular solid, the rest could not. Subjects tended strongly to judge as rectangular boxes only the drawings that could have been rectangular boxes. Thus perceivers seemed to impose perpendicularity on their angles. The Perkins experiment would seem to be a very fruitful one to try cross-culturally in environments that are not so carpentered.

PATTERN   An excellent tempered review of infant form perception has been provided by Bond (20). The notion of figural goodness has received considerable experimental and theoretical support in recent years from Garner, whose new book (60) summarizes a large body of evidence concerning stimulus structure existing in various types of patterns, especially in dots selected from a matrix. [A paper by Bear (12) has a similar orientation.]

Rock (169), in his new book, argues that patterns encompass the notion of uprightness with respect to gravity. Familiar patterns possess assigned direction, e.g. the "top" of a form. Since gravity defines the orientation of a form for the perceiver, tilting the head has little effect on shape constancy, whereas tilting a relatively unfamiliar form will affect its phenomenal shape, even though the head is tilted to preserve retinal orientation. Wenderoth (14, 221) demonstrated the converse, that the axes of figures or intersecting lines used as contextual frames of reference influence judgments of apparent verticality (as in the rod-and-frame test).

Schuck (171), by means of a clever series of controls, studied the fragmenting of visual images as subjects fixate an HB stimulus. He found that continuous verbal reporting during a trial produced a significant bias to *report* meaningful fragments of the fixated stimulus when compared with other response methods. He was not able to support Hebb's hypothesis concerning the proponderance of meaningful fragments among those reappearing.

PATTERN ANOMALIES (ILLUSIONS)   The word *illusion*, conveying as it does the unfortunate connotations of magic and deception, should probably by exorcised from the vocabulary of perception. With the exception of the literature on pattern, very few perceptual anomalies are called illusions. Judged by the quantity of published material, pattern anomalies is one of the most popular topics in perceptual research and theory. An entire issue of the new journal *Perception* was devoted to anomalies, primarily pattern. The handbook of pattern anomalies has been written. It is well organized, comprehensive, up-to-date, and suprisingly undogmatic. To find out what theoretical viewpoints prevail and what data exist, go directly to Robinson's *The Psychology of Visual Illusion* (168)—before starting to experiment.

Cowan's (34) research on the twisted-cord effect, essentially a concentric set of lines that appear to be spiraling inward, represents a systematic attack on a relatively untouched problem.

The literature reveals that the field has passed beyond merely demonstrating that an effect exists. For the most part directionality (positive versus negative errors, assimilation versus contrast) is also settled; magnitudes have become important.

Poggendorff effect   A current research question that hinges upon the directionality and magnitude of errors is whether the Poggendorff display (parallel lines interrupting a transversal) produces a Poggendorff or anti-Poggendorff effect when only the portions of parallels forming an acute angle with the transversal are represented. A tally just for the period under review shows two papers claiming a small Poggendorff effect (Houck & Mefferd 94, Imai 95; both papers presenting a gold mine of additional parametric data as well), two claiming a small anti-Poggendorff effect (Krantz & Weintraub 105, Pressey & Sweeney 160), and one presenting mixed results depending upon psychophysical method among other things (Day 40). Granting other complicating variables like the particular acute angle employed, one wonders whether to disregard one or another result, or average the results and conclude that acute angles alone have little or no effect upon judgmental errors in the Poggendorff display. Fortunately, there is unanimous agreement that obtuse-angle-only displays yield a strong Poggendorff effect. But overestimation of acute angle bears on the admissibility of certain theories like the regression-to-right-angle tendency (Hotopf & Ollerearnshaw 91, 92). Regression to right angles could be given a functionalist or a neurophysiological interpretation. Perceivers tend, because of a carpentered environment, to interpret any angle as closer to a right angle than it actually is; or contour interactions cause the sides of acute angles to be represented neurally as diverging more than they ought.

Müller-Lyer effect   The Müller-Lyer arrowhead display remains popular as a testing ground for theories, which can be loosely categorized as either context or contour theories. Gregory (72-74) continues to defend his misapplied-constancy scaling theory. Context, in the form of perspective features in the display, automatically triggers a size-scaling response below the level of awareness. Georgeson & Blakemore (61) presented the display stereoscopically so that the arrowhead figure was perceived as flat or with fins tilted in depth either toward or away from the subject. Thus the implied depth could be reinforced or counteracted. The data did not support the theory; tilting the fins either forward or back reduced errors somewhat. Pressey's assimilation theory (159) postulates that the stimulus context determines the observer's attentive field. A more precise specification of the relationship between stimulus parameters and the size and location of the hypothetical attentive field would appear to be the direction in which theory refinement should proceed. Other interesting papers bearing on versions of context theory are Chiang (28), Coren & Girgus (32), Day (38), Fellows & Thorn (50), and Massaro (125). Smets & Haesen (182) suggest a clever demonstration and argue from it that the Müller-Lyer effect must be centrally caused. Place an identical vertical line in each field of a stereoscope so that they will fuse stereoscopically. Add inward-pointing arrowheads to the ends of one line and outward-pointing arrowheads to the ends of the other line. Fuse the two vertical lines stereoscopically. If the anomaly occurs peripherally, then the vertical lines will be perceived as unequal in length and the arrowheads will not join to form Xs. In fact, they do join to form Xs.

Pollack has proposed a theory based upon brightness contrast that explains the decline in the Müller-Lyer effect with age as a decline in sensitivity to contours. Pollack & Silvar (158) reported that subjects with more dense pigmentation of the fundus oculi of the eye produced smaller errors. Bayer & Pressey (11) could not replicate that finding in a within-race design. Ebert & Pollack (48, 49), in more recent work, have not demonstrated a consistent relationship between ocular pigmentation and error magnitude when variables such as stimulus duration are altered. The converse of Pollack's hypothesis can be argued on logical grounds, namely, that ocular pigmentation reduces stray light thereby sharpening retinal contrast and increasing judgmental errors. Weintraub, Tong & Smith (217) emphasized the role of differences in contour contrast. Increasing the contrast of arrowheads, while decreasing the contrast of the shaft, enhanced errors.

Ponzo effect   Misapplied-constancy scaling applies directly to a display that can be likened to viewing railroad tracks with segments of cross ties at different distances. Fisher (54) interpreted his results as supporting a contour-proximity theory. Fineman & Carlson (53) embedded the test lines in a texture gradient of dots à la Gibson; the effect did not differ from what was obtained with a textureless background—evidence against misapplied-constancy scaling. Leibowitz & Pick (109) compared Ugandan villagers with college students from America, Guam, and Uganda. The villagers showed no Ponzo effect under any circumstances, while the others produced increasing errors as depth cues were introduced into the stimulus display. A contour-interaction theory cannot explain why the Ponzo display was totally ineffective among villagers.

Theory Girgus & Coren (64) have been exploiting short-term error decrement as a theoretical tool. Through practice or mere inspection over a period of minutes many pattern anomalies show a decrease in error magnitude. These patterns, they assert, must have a judgmental (cognitive) component. Stadler (186) effectively criticizes Ganz's equating of figural aftereffects and simultaneous effects. Walker (208) has laid it on the line with an explicit contour-interaction model based upon spurious excitation in the vicinity of intersecting contours at the retinal level. The first return volley is on its way (MacLeod, Virsu & Carpenter 121). This theory was designed for intersecting-line displays like the Pogendorff. Assimilation theory (Pressey & Sweeney 161) and cognitive mistracking (Weintraub & Tong 216) also claim to explain the Poggendorff display.

What sorts of theory are tenable? My biases are that most pattern anomalies are multiply caused, and that all anomalies do not share the same set of factors. Can any theories be excluded? Judging by the amount of negative evidence, misapplied-constancy scaling should be playing only a minor role in most anomalies. Other types of context effects, perhaps acquired as the child interacts with his environment, may be involved, but I predict that for the pattern anomalies considered above (but not for all pattern anomalies), the sine qua non is some form of contour interaction, one probably very little affected by learning. The task is to determine the nature and locus (central? peripheral?) of the contour effect or effects. Perhaps one or more of the above theoretical formulations is close to the truth.

COLOR Blending phenomenal description and experimental observation is Beck's book on surface color (13). As an example of the flavor of the book, the following terms describe subjectively different aspects of the luminousness of light: brightness, lightness, perceived intensity of illumination, apparent luminance. Plastic soupspoons over the eyes provide cheap, convenient, and effective Ganzfeld conditions. Crovitz (35) studied binocular color rivalry by painting one soupspoon red and one green. Observers tended to see a field divided down the middle into two colors with the nasal part of each field being suppressed. Loomis (118) eliminated the photopigment-bleaching hypothesis for the Bidwell subjective-color phenomenon. A red interval sandwiched between a black and a white interval presented in a repeating sequence appears as a flickering blue-green hue. Loomis compared the afterimage of the Bidwell color with an adjacent afterimage formed by a reordering of the same three light intervals, which appeared red. He showed that the two afterimages were not identical (but instead were complementary to their respective perceived hues) even though the retinal bleaches were identical. Kitterle (103) found that simultaneous lightness contrast was a function of the orientation of the test bar, and argued that the contrast effect could not, therefore, take place at the retinal level.

Drawing on a huge resource of published data, Bornstein (21) has proposed a provocative physiologically based theory to explain cultural differences in color naming. The hypothesis states that, as a result of diet and/or environmental adaptation to the ultraviolet components of sunlight, vision can become short-wavelength insensitive. Thus blues and greens, colors in which short wavelengths predominate, would tend to be confused and, therefore, be lumped into the same verbal color category.

SIZE AND DISTANCE   An agreed-upon terminology is a must in order to avoid confusion. Four levels of discourse will be illustrated with size terms: the stimulus as it exists in the physical world, that is, the distal stimulus (e.g. *physical* size); unobservable variables relating to the world of experience (*perceived* size); response variables (*judged* size); and the proximal stimulus (*retinal* size), the physical representation of a particular cue at the retinal level. (In my opinion, retinal size, since it is not represented directly in experience, has no necessarily preferred status in any function relating perceived size to perceived distance.)

There are various means of judging size. A null-match experiment might involve an adjustable comparison stimulus at a fixed physical distance that is to be matched with other stimuli differing in physical size and physical distance. Extreme caution is necessary in inferring perceived size from various measures of judged size. Under what circumstances might a theorist decide that the setting of the comparison stimulus measures perceived size? Perhaps when the comparison stimulus is reasonably close to the observer, and all distance cues are available, then the argument could be made that the comparison stimulus, since it is perceived veridically in some sense, measures the perceived sizes of other stimuli.

Although there is good reason to believe that retinal size is not directly registered in experience, its physical equivalent, visual angle, would seem to have a perceptual equivalent. Under reduced cue conditions the perceptual equivalents of physical size, physical distance, and physical visual angle were shown by Foley (55) to characterize a perceptual space that could not be Euclidean. A stimulus observed in the periphery along a horizontal meridian must be moved closer to appear equal to the same stimulus judged foveally (Newsome 149). The outcome might be interpreted in terms of a change in perceived visual angle rather than the experimenter's interpretation of change in perceived size. Moon illusioners take note: If the distortion, which is large, also takes place along the vertical retinal meridian, then objects higher in the visual field will be perceived as smaller. [Incidentally, vestibular stimulation induced by acceleration in a parallel swing had no effect on a luminous-disk equivalent of the moon illusion, according to Van Eyl (202)].

Observer cues, convergence, accommodation, binocular disparity, and voluntary eye movements were investigated with respect to size and distance (56, 110, 151). In (110) accommodation was determined in unintrusive fashion by asking the subject to detect the motion of speckle in his visual field produced by a laser-scintillation technique. When an observer wears glasses that alter accommodation and convergence, Wallach and co-workers (212, 213) have discovered alterations in judged size, stereoscopic depth, and pointing with a previously unviewed arm, implying that changes in perceived distance were involved. It is easy to train observers to rotate their heads while viewing a stimulus monocularly in order to create motion parallax for themselves. Observers make very accurate judgments of depth after ten practice trials (Ferris 51). Johansson (96) also demonstrated the efficacy of voluntary head movements in judging depth.

Gogel (66, 69) has continued his systematic experimental and theoretical attack on size-distance problems; back-to-back papers (67, 68) summarize his position. Two tendencies are postulated. The specific-distance tendency says that an object will tend toward being perceived at a near distance (about 2 meters) from the observer as cues to physical distance degenerate. The equidistance tendency says that objects will tend toward being perceived at the same distance from the observer as cues to physical distance degenerate. Thus a perceived distance is associated with every object even under the most severe reduction conditions. Gogel proposes an hypothesis about perceptual interactions. The proximal cues for physical distance do not alone specify perceived distance (see the two tendencies described above). One can determine what Gogel calls a perceptual equation describing the interaction between perceived size and perceived distance. The equation is not truly a perceptual equation because nonperceptual proximal stimuli are also represented. A completely perceptual equation is a mathematical representation of perceptual space.

Over the years a comprehensive set of proximal cues has been assembled and a beginning made of specifying interactions among subsets. Needed badly are overlying principles that encompass many specific cues-to-percept relationships. Gogel's approach is to be commended. (I feel that his theoretical principles are aimed in the proper direction.)

Two interesting papers considered shape constancy for slanted plane stimuli Perkins (155) presented outline drawings of boxes, some of which could not be projections of rectangular boxes and asked subjects to state whether each box was rectangular. Even at a severe slant, subjects tended to respond to the outline, not in terms of its retinal projection but in terms of the outline on the card. Massaro (127) measured reaction times and errors in classifying a stimulus as circular or elliptical. Reaction times for correct judgments and percent errors increased with increasing slant.

Gibson (62) has re-elaborated his theoretical position; Gyr (78) marshalled cogent criticisms; Gibson responded (63). Parenthetically, texture may be overrated as a cue to depth (Newman 148).

The Pulfrich stereophenomenon (viewing pendular oscillation binocularly with a neutral-density filter over one eye leads to perceived orbital motion) continues to attract attention. Harker (80) has incorporated it into a testing procedure as one of the indicators of binocular vision with clinical use in mind. Levick, Cleland & Coombs (113) lay out the calculations to show that the expected orbit of pendular motion is a conic section, assuming the simple explanation of the phenomenon to be time lag between eyes for signals reaching the brain. New data are provided by Rogers & Antis (170).

And finally, a review by Miller (140) of cross-cultural research on the perception of pictorial materials, its perils and pitfalls, is highly recommended for those interested in supporting theories of depth perception with cross-cultural data.

CONTEXT

Regardless of whether one believes with Gibson that perceptual experience leads the perceiver toward veridicality, there is no question that a variety of stimulus factors interfere with the achievement of veridicality. When stimuli from a set are presented one at a time to be identified by observers—the method of single stimuli or absolute judgments—the data bear strong resemblances to the outcomes of paired-associate learning experiments. Much as in the learning experiment, subjects are first shown how to assign a number to each stimulus; the stimuli are then presented in a random order and the correct number is called for. The outcomes are influenced by many of the variables known to influence learning (see Siegel & Siegel 177). In a pitch-discrimination task clear sequential dependencies are revealed for trials on which the just-previous stimulus is repeated (Siegel 179, confirmed by Aiken, Abrams & Shennum 2). Lockhead (116), in his latest summary article, also documents memory effects as a function of sequential dependencies. The conclusion is that a large portion of the limitation on performance may be a memory limitation on remembering the assignment of responses to stimuli. The subject will tend to repeat his previous response on repetition trials with no feedback independently of whether he was previously correct or incorrect (179, but not confirmed by 2).

Another documented tendency is that an observer reveals a propensity to employ all the available response categories equally often. Steinberg & Sekuler (190) obtained confirming evidence using category judgments.

The range of stimuli being judged also strongly influences judgments. Parducci (152) developed a range-frequency model that is the prototype for the more recent formulations. Gravetter & Lockhead (70) presented a similar model, which, like Parducci's, is in the tradition of Thurstonian category scaling.

In contrast to the above approach to context, Helson's adaptation-level theory has tended to accept judgments as valid indicators of the perceived stimulus. Anchor stimuli do shift judgments [Ellis, with comparative judgments to avoid response bias (47); Steger, Wilkinson & Carter (189)]. The shift can be moderated by telling subjects after practice that they are excellent judgers and to keep up the good work (Levine 114). In principle, forced-choice techniques and Thurstonian scaling (and, therefore, signal-detection analysis) can eliminate or separate response bias (response-criterion effects) from perceiving (discriminability) (see McNicol & Pennington 134). I predict that the pioneering adaptation-level formulation will be absorbed by the approaches capable of treating the effects of context in more sophisticated ways. Incidentally, I am convinced that no possible appeal to response bias can explain away the differences in hue of Helson's original work on adaptation level in which nonselective stimuli (grays under normal illumination) can appear to have any of a wide range of hues—red through achromatic through green—as a function of reflectance relative to the adapting reflectance of long wavelength (red) light (Helson 86). What I am suggesting is that theories attempting to explain adaptation-level effects in terms of response bias must be specific about the kinds of stimuli to which the explanation applies. I believe that adaptation-level theory itself went awry when it became a general theory of context effects.

Context can be provided by knowledge of the characteristics of an object. Borresen (22) found that stimuli with characteristics that implied motion in a given direction (e.g. an automobile) led to a significant number of autokinetic movements in the proper direction. Biederman and co-workers (15) scrambled the context by sectioning a picture into blocks and rearranging them. Search time for an object was the dependent variable. Jonides & Gleitman (99) obtained reaction-time differences depending upon whether the subject was searching for an item in the same category or one in a different category from the rest of the items in the array. The symbol 0 is ambiguous until conceptually categorized by the subject as either a letter or digit. The symbol was processed during search as though it were a member of the set to which it was assigned conceptually.

The Stroop Color Word Test contains interference trials on which subjects are asked to name the hue of the ink in which each word is printed while ignoring the word, which spells an incongruent color name. Dyer (44) summarized and integrated the recent experimental literature. There is strong consensus that response competition is involved. If so, then the next step is to explain response competition. To response competition Dyer adds a second factor, a breakdown in selective attention, to be specific, an inability to focus on a color and at the same time gate the word itself. Dyer & Severance (45) have tested a technique useful in Stroop-like situations involving pairs of dimensions that cannot be combined spatially, or useful in studying the time course of the interference. The two dimensions can be presented sequentially. When a color patch is preceded by the flashing of a color name in black, a reliable Stroop effect is obtained, but it is smaller by about half. The following references were published during the time period covered by this review but not listed in Dyer's review (43, 58, 90, 115, 157, 173).

Not all word contexts are detrimental as in the Stroop test. A word-superiority effect was obtained by Reicher (165). A letter can be identified more easily when it is embedded in a word than when it is presented alone or in a sequence of unrelated letters. The finding is counterintuitive. How can an observer gain more information about each letter in a four-letter word than about a single letter in a one-letter array? The phenomenon has, therefore, attracted considerable attention. Bouma (23), in an investigation directed at the process of reading, found that recognition declines with distance from the fovea (less so toward the right). For a letter of a given eccentricity, i.e. distance from the fovea, recognition is better for that letter if the rest of the word lies closer to the fovea. Thus, for a letter to the right of fixation, if that letter begins a word, then it is recognized less well than if it remains in the same location and ends a word. The opposite is true to the left of fixation. A reasonable conclusion is that some type of lateral masking among adjacent stimuli acts more strongly in the direction of the fovea than against it. (Both words and nonwords were used as stimuli. Stimuli were presented for 100 milliseconds, and no mask was used.) The Taylor & Brown (194) U-shaped recognition function, found to the right of fixation with unlimited viewing, seems to be accounted for by Bouma's two factors. Compare the data of Monti (144) also. When Shaw & Weigel (175) replaced letters in a string with bars or blanks, recognition was facilitated. If a string of letters is fixated at its center, then the lateral masking of adjacent contours diminishes as one proceeds toward the initial and final letters of the string. However, this is more than counteracted by the general decline in recognition toward the periphery.

What is the effect of adding a mask? The ends of a string seem less affected by the mask. Is this because the ends are processed first and masking has its greatest impact on the remainder of the string? Henderson & Park (87), through the use of monetary payoffs favoring the middle, still found that a pattern mask most interferes with the middle of a string. Johnston & McClelland (98) reported that the word-superiority effect depended critically on the type of postexposure field. A pattern mask produces the effect; a plain white field as mask abolishes it.

What cognitive factors are involved? Mezrich (138) hypothesized that a single letter was processed as a spatial pattern rather than a verbal code presumed for words. Mezrich required subjects to vocalize each stimulus, letter or word, to make processing more similar. The result was a letter-superiority effect. Redundancy should be important in these types of situations and it is (see Colegate & Eriksen 30). On the question of controlling for redundancy the data of Thompson & Massaro (196) conflict with those of Smith & Haviland (183). In what is the latest word, but surely not the last word, Massaro (126) demonstrated that what he called lateral masking, but what may well be the laterality effects of pattern masking, is the culprit. Controlling both for redundancy and laterality effects reduced the word-superiority effect to near zero.

Repeatedly flashing the same visual stimulus improves its identification (Haber & Hershenson 79), but doubt has been cast upon Haber's hypothesis that repeated presentations improve the clarity of the perceived stimulus (89, 215). Doherty & Keeley (42) marshalled the past evidence against the hypothesis that clarity enhancement is the cause of the well-documented improvement in identifiability. They proposed instead that the evidence strongly favors the hypothesis that independent perceptual inputs are aggregated from each succeeding presentation of the stimulus.

The Rod-and-frame test (RFT) is a perceptual distortion of the perceived verticality of a luminous rod as the result of a tilted luminous square frame. The RFT is used as a tool in personality research. Since the phenomenon is not well understood, it is fortunate that psychophysical work is also proceeding. Increased exposure time increases RFT errors (84); the most obvious hypothesis is adaptation to a tilted visual field. Long (117) found that low illumination affected RFT scores, and series of trials in which the experimenter moved the rod as soon as the subject responded gave different data from a predetermined experimenter pace. Small (181) verbally reinforced subjects either toward or away from true verticality by saying "very good" at opportune times. The resulting perturbations in judgments remained on a follow-up test one month later. If short-term conditioning procedures have long-term consequences, then what is the usefulness of the RFT for predicting presumably stable personality structures (field dependence and independence)? Psychiatric inpatients often do not understand instructions for the RFT (Johnson, Neville & Beutler 97), which partly explained the extreme field dependence found consistently among their own inpatients in the past. Walker (211) found no significant correlation between field dependence measured visually and tactually. Instead of the square frame, an open grillwork was used, which the subject either looked through or reached through to determine verticality.

PERCEPTUAL MECHANISMS

Stimulating the visual sense requires not only sufficient electromagnetic energy in the proper wavelength range delivered to the retina but also a *temporal change* in stimulus energy. Temporal modulation must occur on the retina via eye movements or motion of the stimulus. Stabilized-image work has shown that not only homogeneous fields but also patterned fields fade and disappear perceptually in seconds. If stabilization is complete, then nothing reappears. Tulunay-Keesey (199) contributed additional key evidence. In brief, slow flicker is the main determiner of target visibility under stabilized-image conditions. Arend (5) has begun the important work of incorporating temporal energy change into a model of the visual system that must, of course, be responsive to the spatial distributions of energy signaling contour (and thus pattern), brightness, hue, etc.

FEATURE DETECTORS   Sekuler's (172) review emphasized feature detection; interest and research in the area has expanded rapidly, ranking with pattern anomalies (illusions) in appeal. Research centers around two basic adaptation procedures.

The simple aftereffect paradigm requires one adapting stimulus to which the observer attends for a specified time. Normally the observer scans the adapting stimulus to prevent the formation of a conventional afterimage. Stimulus dimensions most often investigated are type of pattern (usually either a line or a repeating pattern of parallel elements—square-wave or sinusoidal grating), orientation (i.e. tilt), motion, and adapting contrast. The test stimulus is modified in some way as a consequence of adaptation. Its detection threshold is increased, suprathreshold contrast is reduced, perceived tilt or frequency or velocity is changed. Blakemore and co-workers (18) have been exploiting a derived measure developed by Blakemore & Nachmias (19), specifying any threshold elevation, however it is produced, in terms of equivalent contrast, i.e. the contrast of a vertical adapting grating that produces the same amount of threshold elevation (on a vertical test grating). Movshon & Blakemore (145) showed, for example, that the change in orientation of an adapting grating that halves the equivalent contrast is reasonably constant regardless of spatial frequency. The untransformed outcome, the range of orientations adapted (i.e. how many degrees on either side of vertical were adapted by a vertical grating), is heavily dependent on the particular spatial adapting frequency employed. Sharpe & Tolhurst (174) used the equivalent-contrast transformation to evaluate effects of grating drift and flicker.

With respect to the specificity of neural units, there are those willing to argue on the basis of psychophysical data in favor of velocity-specific detectors (Tolhurst, Sharpe & Hart 198) and narrowly tuned spatial-frequency analyzers (Abadi & Kulikowski 1). Blakemore, Muncey & Ridley (18) discussed the possibility that spatial-frequency channels are relatively broad, but they inhibit each other (Tolhurst 197), thus sharpening the tuning of the system. "If this is the case, then aftereffects of adaptation may be due to prolonged inhibition rather than to over-excitation. . . . In that case, adaptation experiments (and those involving simultaneous masking) may be measuring the broad tuning properties of this inhibition, rather than the excitatory tuning characteristics themselves" (18, p. 1929).

Two important articles raise problems for the concept of spatial-frequency analyzers. Stecher, Sigel & Lange (188) worked with grating adaptation among frequencies so close as to be considered within the same spatial-frequency channel. As one example, a frequency of 8 cycles per degree was added to an adapting frequency of 13.3 cycles. The combination not only did not increase the adapting effect on a test grating of 13.3 cycles, it actually reduced it. That is, adding an adjacent spatial frequency weakened the potency of the adapting stimulus. Nachmias et al (147) presented a square-wave adapting stimulus, which has a Fourier spectrum of all the odd harmonics, and checked for a threshold increase in the vicinity of the third harmonic. Under temporal two-alternative forced-choice conditions, adaptation was not obtained. Partial success was achieved with the method of adjustment.

Ocular defects in the newborn lead to selective deprivation of certain line orientations. The most recent selective-deprivation work with kittens continues to support the view that permanent acuity deficits occur (146), and that anomalies are found at the cortical level (17, 156). In humans loss of acuity can be demonstrated for orientations affected by astigmatism, and the severity depends upon the degree of astigmatism (143). In conjunction with the reduced resolution as a function of astigmatism, Freeman & Thibos (57) noted a concomitant decrease in evoked potentials. Annis & Frost (3) claim that different visual environments provide different opportunities for observing obliques compared to horizontals and verticals, and these experiences are mirrored in visual-resolution tests using gratings in various orientations. In addition to visual acuity, it has been well established that targets presented either horizontally or vertically show a consistent, though often small, superiority in performance over oblique orientations for visual tasks like stimulus detection, tracking, and judgments of orientation (Appelle 4). Are all such meridional effects determined by early stimulation? Although gravitational cues appear to maintain orientation constancy (195), two studies (52, 142) showed that adaptation to gratings was dependent upon the retinal coordinates of the gratings. Vestibular input as a consequence of head tilt did not affect the adaptation process. Thus far, with counterevidence lacking, the message is unambiguous: Astigmatism and, by implication, any ocular defect that blurs or distorts the retinal image, seem to lead to permanent visual dysfunction.

The second basic type of experiment is the contingency-aftereffects paradigm pioneered by McCullough (131) and her students. Two values are chosen from each of two stimulus dimensions (e.g. hue, either orange or blue; bar grating oriented vertically or horizontally). Pairing one value from each dimension provides two adapting stimuli (orange verticals, blue horizontals), which are presented alternatingly. The test stimulus probes with one dimension to check whether the other is elicited. For the McCullough effect a black and white stimulus of horizontal and vertical bars produces complementary hues contingent upon bar orientation.

Useful variations have been developed. Lovegrove & Over (119) linked two dimensions in one adapting stimulus (hue and grating orientation) and obtained a greater tilt aftereffect when the test grating matched the adapting grating in hue. Virsu & Haapasalo (203) alternated square-wave gratings of different frequencies, each paired with a different hue, and after adaptation, presenting a hue caused an intermediate frequency to shift away from the spatial frequency paired with that hue.

Successful contingency pairings permit the inference of various types of higher-order neural cells. The following have been successfully paired: hue with curved lines (167), hue with rotation clockwise and counterclockwise (129), fine and coarse texture with rotation (209), hue with motion up or down (120), rotation with direction of gaze left or right (128). Hay & Goldsmith (83) linked head movements up or down with movements of a spot right or left. Woolsey & Newman (222) presented contrarotating disks on the same shaft. Each disk had transparent and dotted sectors, and subjects observed simultaneous contrarotation, one disk seen through the other. A rotation aftereffect was linked with each disk when rotation ceased (rotation had been paired with depth?). Stromeyer, Lange & Ganz (191) paired a different hue with each of two vertical gratings having identical frequency spectra but differing in phase angle between frequency components. Not all sinusoid sets were effective in producing a hue-contingent effect.

Over, Long & Lovegrove (150) could not generate a McCullough effect with contour to one eye and pattern to the other; Coltheart (31) obtained no interocular transfer. Therefore, hue and orientation may be linked somewhat peripherally. Mayhew (130) showed how to produce movement aftereffects contingent on size. The effect will not transfer to a black and white reversal of the adapting pattern; it is short-lived, one to two seconds, but can be re-elicited many times.

No doubt even more exotic contingencies are just around the corner. Is it logical to argue that every successful pairing demonstrates the existence of analyzers for each dimension?

Other methods of approaching feature detection are via afterimages (Atkinson 6, Wade 205), binocular rivalry (Wade 204), and even monocular rivalry (7, 26). For two papers addressed to feature detection from a more cognitive point of view see Weisstein, Montalvo & Ozog (219) and Harmon & Julesz (81).

The model of spatial-frequency analyzers transmitting information along separate pathways can be taken literally. The work of Maffei & Fiorentini (122), for example, recording the responses of single neurons at various levels of the visual system of the cat, would indicate that a visual system is capable of coding and transmitting information in that manner. However, when a higher-order cell is found that responds to a limited set of stimulus features or a narrow frequency band, does that measurable neural concomitant of retinal stimulation have anything to do with the process of perception? Uttal's (201) distinction between sign and code confronts the matter explicitly. A sign is a neural concomitant of stimulation that is lost at some more central level of the nervous system. A code, on the other hand, is a true conveyor of stimulus information; it must be both necessary and sufficient for producing a sensory experience.

The neurophysiological theories of the future will address themselves to higher-order functions like perceived depth, and ultimately to the constancies (size, distance, brightness, etc). The perception of depth from stereoscopic cues requires the existence of disparity detectors. Three papers presented psychological evidence buttressed by arguments favoring the existence of such detectors (141, 164, 166). With respect to the constancies, a variety of papers presented data that could not be accounted for by appealing to the retinal distance between contours. Instead, perceived distance including perceived separation in depth explained the outcomes, as though neural interaction were taking place at the level of distance constancy. Mershon (136) investigated whiteness contrast, Greene, Lawson & Godek (71) the Ponzo effect, and Attneave & Block (8) apparent motion. Blakemore, Garner & Sweet (16) found interocular transfer of grating-frequency adaptation, but did not find a size-constancy effect for gratings, i.e. when the test grating was the same as the adapting grating but at a different distance. Supporting, but perhaps rather speculative, neurophysiological evidence also exists (124, 185).

BACKWARD MASKING   Lefton (112) reported that in metacontrast the duration of the mask had little effect, as did mask width (compare with 100), and that maximum masking occurred when the mask was presented at the offset of the stimulus (compare with 75). Dember & Stefl (41) with various black-and-white sectored test stimuli obtained detection enhancement for the metacontrast paradigm compared to detection in the absence of the mask. Standing & Dodwell (187) flashed a subthreshold stimulus upon a steady background, and if the background terminated shortly after the offset of the subthreshold stimulus, then the flash became visible. Lefton (111) reviewed the field of metacontrast.

PRISMATIC ADAPTATION   Research on touch/vision coordination and rearrangement seems to be undergoing a period of consolidation. Nonfocal factors have been emphasized, and at present it is difficult to provide a synthesis or integration of the findings. With spaced practice under prismatic viewing conditions, considerable transfer of adaptation to the unexposed hand occurs, but not under massed practice (Taub & Goldberg 193, but compare with Cohen 29). The goggles holding the prisms are an important component of the stimulus context, and after adaptation, goggles alone contribute to the effects (Kravitz 106). The conditioned stimulus for adaptation effects need not be a relevant aspect of adaptation. A concomitant tone during adaptation also acquired the properties of a conditioned stimulus (107). In an important experiment, Welch (220) employed a pseudoprismatic situation in which the observer viewed the luminous finger of another person that was displaced as though the observer were viewing his own finger through prisms. Prismlike adaptation occurred even for informed observers who knew that the luminous adapting finger was not their own. Walker (210) demonstrated the natural visual capture that occurs with a size anomaly in the visual field. Cognitive factors are important (139, 200). Unnoticed head deviations systematically occur (108). Passive arm movements led to adaptation when the arm remained outstretched (Baily 9); passive adaptation depended on the use of a structured visual background (Melamed, Halay & Gildow 135). But perhaps we are too enraptured by visual capture (McDonnell & Duffett 132).

APPLICATIONS

A report on the value of the stereoscopic viewing of aerial photographs by Zeidner, Sadacca & Schwartz (224) is a neglected classic. Experienced photointerpreters, using aerial photographs obtained on actual missions, were asked to detect and identify objects of military significance. (No depth information is necessarily required for such a task.) Contrary to the prejudices of even today's image interpreters, there was no evidence favoring stereo over nonstereo procedures (which employed the same photographs with one of the stereo pair removed, and a plausible cover story concerning the absence of stereo) on the task. Some measures showed a slight superiority for nonstereo.

Facial recognition, in light of its importance in eyewitness testimony in court, is a worthy topic. Shepherd & Ellis (176) found that for a set of female faces memory was excellent for those considered as either beautiful or ugly, but not as good for the remainder. A cross-racial bias has been shown favoring remembering the faces of members of one's own race (123). However, a short-term training session of 100 trials on white subjects obliterated the bias. Galper (59) found the usual cross-racial bias except that white students enrolled in a Black studies course showed better recognition for black faces.

Reading is an activity with perceptual components. The danger for those in perception is to treat it as a purely perceptual phenomenon. A collection of papers on the relationship between speech and reading (101) contains excellent selections to titillate theorist and experimentalist. Frank Smith (184) has proposed an information-processing/psycholinguistic/cognitive (George Miller/Chomsky/Bruner) theory of reading, which is presented in sprightly and persuasive style in a little book called *Understanding Reading*. I have used the book as a text in an undergraduate perception course and find that a great deal of the modern data and theories of perception can be integrated into a topic that appeals to many students. Baron (10) published evidence that supports Smith's stance

quite nicely. Baron argued from his data that a reader does not need an intermediate phonemic code to read. The reader can instead proceed directly to meaning
from a visual analysis. Guthrie (77) used children with a reading disability to
investigate two classes of reading models. Two groups of normal children served as
control subjects, one matching the disabled children for age, and the other, much
younger, matching for level of reading ability.

METHODOLOGY

The word is out. Beware of response bias. Consider forced-choice procedures as a
substitute for the less tedious and more informative method of adjustment. There
is merit in testing crucial data using a forced-choice arrangement as a check [note
the Nachmias, Sansbury, Vassilev & Weber (147) study]. Even checking a few data
points with each method is valuable. One owes it to oneself as an informed
scientist to grasp the basics of signal-detection theory. Try McNicol's primer (133).
Swets (192) again argues convincingly about the value of the approach; response
bias cannot, in fact, be overlooked or disregarded; interpreting data in terms of an
operating characteristic has superior practical advantages. Simpson & Fitter (180)
discuss various indices of detection and give reasons for recommending a particular one, d_a, which is equal to $\sqrt{2}$ times the normal deviate of the area under the
ROC curve. Consider the advantages of staircase procedures in which the observer's response determines the stimulus sequencing, keeping the stimuli being
presented within the observer's uncertainty region. Simpler versions are an
efficient variant of the method of constant stimuli. If necessary, the procedure can
be used with small numbers of observations; statistical computations are easy. [A
brief discussion and examples of the procedure in action appeared in (214).] The
staircase method should be compared with Herrick's (88) random method of
limits, a constant-stimulus variant that I do not recommend. Without adaptations
the staircase approach will not guard against response bias. However, null-match
judgments that are not context free cannot be safeguarded anyway.

Wright (223) used signal detectability procedures to determine the wavelength
discrimination function of the pigeon. Compare signal detection with pigeons
(Wright) to the method of constant stimuli with humans (Siegel & Siegel 178);
both experiments probe wavelength discrimination. [Not everyone is enchanted
with signal detectability. See Ellis (46), Wagenaar (206), and Hébert (85).]

A model psychophysical experiment by Kelly & Savoie (102) compared the
method of adjustment with a modified staircase procedure. A forced-choice decision was required to choose which of the two temporal intervals the stimulus
appeared in. Stairstepping to the next level was contingent upon whether the
subject had chosen the incorrect interval. This paper and the Wright paper cited
above should be required reading for practicing psychophysicists. Incidentally, the
data obtained in detecting sinusoidal gratings by the forced-choice staircase
procedure differ very little in shape from the adjustment data. Overall sensitivity
was shown to be far better by the staircase method.

Another way to avoid certain types of response bias is to use an "involuntary" response. Metz & Balliet (137) assessed human scotopic luminosity functions by means of optokinetic nystagmus generated with moving stripes. Kleespies & Wiener (104) investigated subception with an initial eye-movement response (orienting reflex) not normally monitored consciously.

IN CONCLUSION

Two topics lying outside the traditional lines of perceptual research deserve mention because of uniqueness. Harris (82) plotted the log times against log distances of current world sports records in swimming, running, walking, speed skating, and horse racing. The data are strongly linear for each type of activity and slopes are nearly identical. Thus the data conform closely to Stevens' power law with an all-encompassing exponent of 1.1! Harris hazards a perceptual explanation. Hypotheses anyone?

Suppose that an intense flash of light forms a long-lasting afterimage of one's own hands being held in front of a grid of lines. Now, in total darkness, one hand is lowered "out of the picture" of the afterimage. Suppose instead that the afterimage of a corridor is produced, and then one physically walks down the corridor in the dark. Davies (36, 37) collected subjective reports. A black hole often appeared in the afterimage where the hand had been; the sensation of walking along the corridor, i.e. through one's own afterimage, was also reported.

For me, the phenomenological aspects are an appealing aspect of the study of perception. Given that a physical world exists, what is the nature of the phenomenal world? How did it get that way? What can be determined about the neural substrate without which there is no perception? Some pieces of the puzzle are amenable to scientific investigation. For the investigators involved, I propose the title, Experimental Phenomenologist. Much of the puzzle invades the domain of philosophy. An essay by Globus (65) argues that monist and dualist views are symmetric, and treats the symmetry in terms of Bohr's complementarity principle. Be advised that the arguments are presented clearly, the philosophical terminology is not overpowering, and the arguments are likely to appeal to the experimental phenomenologist.

Progress comes slowly. Impressive improvements in psychophysical techniques and apparatus technology can be discerned. Commendable work has been accomplished in defining issues and constructing theories that can account for highly selected subsets of experimental findings. Important conflicts in the data base of perception have yet to be resolved. We now have bigger and more sophisticated controversies, but how many issues have been laid to rest?

If I were to try to capture the essence of the area of perception in a word, then that word would be *ferment*. These are exciting times for perception. Nevertheless, the advantages that accrue to hindsight will be required to determine whether 1972 and 1973 were truly vintage years.

Literature Cited

1. Abadi, R. V., Kulikowski, J. J. 1973. Linear summation of spatial harmonics in human vision. *Vision Res.* 13: 1625–28
2. Aiken, E. G., Abrams, A. J., Shennum, W. A. 1973. Memory processes in the method of absolute judgment: a robust effect. *Percept. Mot. Skills* 36:338
3. Annis, R. C., Frost, B. 1973. Human visual ecology and orientation anisotropies in acuity. *Science* 181:729–31
4. Appelle, S. 1972. Perception and discrimination as a function of stimulus orientation: The "oblique effect" in man and animals. *Psychol. Bull.* 78: 266–78
5. Arend, L. E. Jr. 1973. Spatial differential and integral operations in human vision: Implications of stabilized retinal image fading. *Psychol. Rev.* 80: 374–95
6. Atkinson, J. 1973. Properties of human visual orientation detectors: new approach using patterned afterimages. *J. Exp. Psychol.* 98:55–63
7. Atkinson, J., Campbell, F. W., Fiorentini, A., Maffei, L. 1973. The dependence of monocular rivalry on spatial frequency. *Perception* 2:127–33
8. Attneave, F., Block, G. 1973. Apparent movement in tridimensional space. *Percept. Psychophys.* 13:301–7
9. Baily, J. S. 1972. Arm-body adaptation with passive arm movements. *Percept. Psychophys.* 12:39–44
10. Baron, J. 1973. Phonemic stage not necessary for reading. *Quart. J. Exp. Psychol.* 25:241–46
11. Bayer, C. A., Pressey, A. W. 1972. Geometric illusions as a function of pigmentation of the Fundus oculi and target size. *Psychon Sci.* 26:77–79
12. Bear, G. 1973. Figural goodness and the predictability of figural elements. *Percept. Psychophys.* 13:32–40
13. Beck, J. 1972. *Surface Color Perception.* Ithaca, NY: Cornell Univ. Press. 206 pp.
14. Beh, H. C., Wenderoth, P. M. 1972. The effect of variation of frame shape on the angular function of the rod-and-frame illusion. *Percept. Psychophys.* 11:35–37
15. Biederman, I., Glass, A. L., Stacy, E.

W. Jr. 1973. Searching for objects in real-world scenes. *J. Exp. Psychol.* 97:22–27
16. Blakemore, C., Garner, E. T., Sweet, J. A. 1972. The site of size constancy. *Perception* 1:111–19
17. Blakemore, C., Mitchell, D. E. 1973. Environmental modification of the visual cortex and the neural basis of learning and memory. *Nature* 241: 467–68
18. Blakemore, C., Muncey, J. P. J., Ridley, R. M. 1973. Stimulus specificity in the human visual system. *Vision Res.* 13:1915–31
19. Blakemore, C., Nachmias, J. 1971. The orientation specificity of two visual aftereffects. *J. Physiol.* 213:157–74
20. Bond, E. K. 1972. Perception of form by the human infant. *Psychol. Bull.* 77:225–46
21. Bornstein, M. H. 1973. Color vision and color naming: A psychophysiological hypothesis of cultural difference. *Psychol. Bull.* 80:257–85
22. Borresen, C. R. 1973. Autokinetic movement as a function of the implied movement of target shape. *J. Exp. Psychol.* 97:89–92
23. Bouma, H. 1973. Visual interference in the parafoveal recognition of initial and final letters of words. *Vision Res.* 13:767–82
24. Boynton, R. M., Onley, J. W. 1962. A critique of the special status assigned by Brindley to "psychophysical linking hypotheses" of "Class A." *Vision Res.* 2:383–90
25. Brindley, G. S. 1970. *Physiology of the Retina and Visual Pathway.* Baltimore: Williams & Wilkins. 315 pp. 2nd ed.
26. Campbell, F. W., Gilinsky, A. S., Howell, E. R., Riggs, L. A., Atkinson, J. 1973. The dependence of monocular rivalry on orientation. *Perception* 2: 123–25
27. Carpenter, R. H. S., Blakemore, C. 1973. Interactions between orientations in human vision. *Exp. Brain Res.* 18:287–303
28. Chiang, C. 1973. A theory of the Müller-Lyer illusion. *Vision Res.* 13: 347–53
29. Cohen, M. M. 1973. Visual feedback,

distribution of practice, and intermanual transfer of prism aftereffects. *Percept. Mot. Skills* 37:599–609

30. Colegate, R. L., Eriksen, C. W. 1972. Form of redundancy as a determinant of tachistoscopic word recognition. *Percept. Psychophys.* 12:477–81

31. Coltheart, M. 1973. Colour-specificity and monocularity in the visual cortex. *Vision Res.* 13:2595–98

32. Coren, S., Girgus, J. S. 1972. Differentiation and decrement in the Müller-Lyer illusion. *Percept. Psychophys.* 12:466–70

33. Cornsweet, T. N., Pinsker, H. M. 1965. Luminance discrimination of brief flashes under various conditions of adaptation. *J. Physiol.* 176:294–310

34. Cowan, T. M. 1973. Some variation(s) of the twisted cord illusion and their analyses. *Percept. Psychophys.* 14:553–64

35. Crovitz, H. F. 1972. Transient binasal hemianopia in a pair of plastic soupspoons. *Psychon. Sci.* 28:234

36. Davies, P. 1973. Effects of movements upon the appearance and duration of a prolonged visual afterimage: 1. Changes arising from the movement of a portion of the body incorporated in the afterimage scene. *Perception* 2:147–53

37. Ibid. Effects of movements upon the appearance and duration of a prolonged visual afterimage: 2. Changes arising from movement of the observer in relation to the previously afterimaged scene. 155–60

38. Day, R. H. 1972. Visual spatial illusions: a general explanation. *Science* 175:1335–40

39. Day, R. H. 1973. The oblique line illusion: the Poggendorff effect without parallels. *Quart. J. Exp. Psychol.* 25:535–41

40. Day, R. H. 1973. The Poggendorff illusion with obtuse and acute angles. *Percept. Psychophys.* 14:590–96

41. Dember, W. N., Stefl, M. 1972. Backward enhancement? *Science* 175:93–95

42. Doherty, M. E., Keeley, S. M. 1972. On the identification of repeatedly presented, brief visual stimuli. *Psychol. Bull.* 78:142–54

43. Dyer, F. N. 1973. Same and different judgments for word-color pairs with "irrelevant" words or colors: evidence for word-code comparisons. *J. Exp. Psychol.* 98:102–8

44. Dyer, F. N. 1973. The Stroop phenomenon and its use in the study of perceptual, cognitive, and response processes. *Mem. & Cogn.* 1:106–20

45. Dyer, F. N., Severance, L. J. 1973. Stroop interference with successive presentations of separate incongruent words and colors. *J. Exp. Psychol.* 98:438–39

46. Ellis, H. D. 1972. Adaptation-level theory and context effects on sensory judgments: Perception or response? *Perception* 1:101–9

47. Ibid. Two empirical tests of informal predictions from Helson's adaptation-level theory, 331–39

48. Ebert, P. C., Pollack, R. H. 1972. Magnitude of the Müller-Lyer illusion as a function of hue, saturation, and fundus pigmentation. *Psychon. Sci.* 26:225–26

49. Ibid. Magnitude of the Müller-Lyer illusion as a function of lightness contrast, viewing time, and fundus pigmentation, 347–48

50. Fellows, B., Thorn, D. 1973. A test of Piaget's explanation of the Müller-Lyer illusion. *Brit. J. Psychol.* 64:83–90

51. Ferris, S. H. 1972. Motion parallax and absolute distance. *J. Exp. Psychol.* 95:258–63

52. Findlay, J. M., Parker, D. M. 1972. An investigation of visual orientation constancy using orientation-specific properties of acuity and adaptation. *Perception* 1:305–13

53. Fineman, M.B., Carlson, J. 1973. A comparison of the Ponzo illusion with a textural analogue. *Percept. Psychophys.* 14:31–33

54. Fisher, G. H. 1973. Towards a new explanation for the geometrical illusions: II. Apparent depth or contour proximity? *Brit. J. Psychol.* 64:607–21

55. Foley, J. M. 1972. The size-distance relation and intrinsic geometry of visual space: implications for processing. *Vision Res.* 12:323–32

56. Foley, J. M., Richards, W. 1972. Effects of voluntary eye movement and convergence on the binocular appreciation of depth. *Percept. Psychophys.* 11:423–27

57. Freeman, R. D., Thibos, L. N. 1973. Electrophysiological evidence that abnormal early visual experience can modify the human brain. *Science* 180:876–78

58. Friedman, H., Derks, P. L. 1973. Simultaneous motor and verbal processing of visual information in a modified Stroop test. *Percept. Psychophys.* 13:113–15

59. Galper, R. E. 1973. "Functional race membership" and recognition of faces. *Percept. Mot. Skills* 37:455–62

60. Garner, W. R. 1974. *The Processing of Information and Structure.* Potomac, Md: Erlbaum. 203 pp.

61. Georgeson, M. A., Blakemore, C. 1973. Apparent depth and the Müller-Lyer illusion. *Perception* 2:225–34

62. Gibson, J. J. 1972. A theory of direct visual perception. In the *Psychology of Knowing*, ed. J. R. Royce, W. W. Rozeboom, 215–27. New York: Gordon & Breach. 496 pp.

63. Gibson, J. J. 1973. Direct visual perception: A reply to Gyr. *Psychol. Bull.* 79:396–97

64. Girgus, J. S., Coren, S. 1973. Peripheral and central components in the formation of visual illusions. *Am. J. Optom.* 50:533–40

65. Globus, G. G. 1973. Unexpected symmetries in the world knot. *Science* 180:1129–36

66. Gogel, W. C. 1972. Depth adjacency and cue effectiveness. *J. Exp. Psychol.* 92:176–81

67. Gogel, W. C. 1973. The organization of perceived space. I. Perceptual interactions. *Psychol. Forsch.* 36:195–221

68. Ibid. The organization of perceived space. II. Consequences of perceptual interactions, 223–47

69. Gogel, W. C., Sturn, R. D. 1972. A test of the relational hypothesis of perceived size. *Am. J. Psychol.* 85:201–16

70. Gravetter, F., Lockhead, G. R. 1973. Criterial range as a frame of reference for stimulus judgment. *Psychol. Rev.* 80:203–16

71. Greene, R. T., Lawson, R. B., Godek, C. L. 1972. The Ponzo illusion in stereoscopic space. *J. Exp. Psychol.* 95:358–64

72. Gregory, R. L. 1972. Comments on L. E. Krueger's "disconfirming evidence" of R. L. Gregory's theory of illusions. *Psychol. Rev.* 79:540–41

73. Gregory, R. L. 1973. A discussion of G. H. Fisher's "towards a new explanation for the geometrical illusions: apparent depth or contour proximity?" and the inappropriate constancy-scaling theory. *Brit. J. Psychol.* 64:623–26

74 Gregory, R. L. 1973. Reply to Massaro. *Psychol. Rev.* 80:304

75. Growney, R., Weisstein, N. 1972. Spatial characteristics of metacontrast. *J. Opt. Soc. Am.* 62:690–96

76. Guth, S. L. 1973. On neural inhibition, contrast effects and visual sensitivity. *Vision Res.* 13:937–57

77. Guthrie, J. T. 1973. Models of reading and reading disability. *J. Educ. Psychol.* 65:9–18

78. Gyr, J. W. 1972. Is a theory of direct visual perception adequate? *Psychol. Bull.* 77:246–61

79. Haber, R. N., Hershenson, M. 1965. Effects of repeated brief exposures on the growth of a percept. *J. Exp. Psychol.* 69:40–46

80. Harker, G. S. 1973. Assessment of binocular vision utilizing the Pulfrich and Venetian blind effects. *Am. J. Optom.* 50:435–45

81. Harmon, L. D., Julesz, B. 1973. Masking in visual recognition: Effects of two-dimensional filtered noise. *Science* 180:1194–96

82. Harris, A. H. 1972. Time-distance records and the power function. *Percept. Psychophys.* 12:289–90

83. Hay, J. C., Goldsmith, W. M. 1973. Space-time adaptation of visual position constancy. *J. Exp. Psychol.* 99:1–9

84. Hayes, R. W., Venables, P. H. 1972. An exposure time effect in the Witkin rod-and-frame test. *Psychon. Sci.* 28:243–44

85. Hébert, J. A. 1973. Adaption-level and theory of signal detection: An examination and integration of two judgment models for voluntary stimulus generalization. *Acta Psychol.* 37:15–29

86. Helson, H. 1938. Fundamental problems in color vision: I. The principle governing changes in hue, saturation, and lightness of non-selective samples

in chromatic illumination. *J. Exp. Psychol.* 23:439–76

87. Henderson, L., Park, N. 1973. Are the ends of tachistoscopic arrays processed first? *Can. J. Psychol.* 27:178–83

88. Herrick, R. M. 1973. Psychophysical methodology: VI. Random method of limits. *Percept. Psychophys.* 13:548–54

89. Herzog, T. R. 1973. The repetition effect: A further test of the clarity-enhancement explanation. *Can. J. Psychol.* 27:450–55

90. Hock, H., Petrasek, J. 1973. Verbal interference with perceptual classification: The effect of semantic structure. *Percept. Psychophys.* 13:116–20

91. Hotopf, W. H. N., Ollerearnshaw, C. 1972. The regression to right angles tendency and the Poggendorff illusion. I. *Brit. J. Psychol.* 63:359–67

92. Ibid. The regression to right angles tendency and the Poggendorff illusion. II, 369–79

93. Howard, R. B., Evans, G. W., McDonald, J. K. 1973. Induction-, test-, and comparison-figure interactions under illusion and figural aftereffect conditions. *Percept. Psychophys.* 14:249–54

94. Houck, R. L., Mefferd, R. B. Jr. 1973. The Poggendorff illusion: a neurologically based hypothesis. *Am. J. Psychol.* 86:283–309

95. Imai, S. 1973. Experiments on Poggendorff illusion. *J. Soc. Sci. & Humanities* (JIMBUN GAKUHO), Tokyo Metrop. Univ. 90:1–39

96. Johansson, G. 1973. Monocular movement parallax and near-space perception.*Perception* 2:135–46

97. Johnson, D. T., Neville, C. W. Jr., Beutler, L. E. 1972. Differences between rod-and-frame test distributions of psychiatric inpatients and college students: A partial resolution. *Psychon. Sci.* 28:77–78

98. Johnston, J. C., McClelland, J. L. 1973. Visual factors in word perception. *Percept. Psychophys.* 14:365–70

99. Jonides, J., Gleitman, H. 1972. A conceptual category effect in visual search: O as letter or as digit. *Percept. Psychophys.* 12:457–60

100. Kao, K. C., Dember, W. N. 1973. Effects of size of ring on backward masking of a disk by a ring. *Bull. Psychon. Soc.* 2:15–17

101. Kavanagh, J. F., Mattingly, I. G., Eds. 1972. *Language by Ear and by Eye: The Relationship between Speech and Reading.* Cambridge, Mass.: MIT Press. 398 pp.

102. Kelly, D. H., Savoie, R. E. 1973. A study of sine-wave contrast sensitivity by two psychophysical methods. *Percept. Psychophys.* 14:313–18

103. Kitterle, F. L. 1973. The possible locus of lightness contrast. *Percept. Psychophys.* 14:585–89

104. Kleespies, P., Wiener, M. 1972. The "orienting reflex" as an input indicator in "subliminal" perception. *Percept. Mot. Skills* 35:103–10

105. Krantz, D. H., Weintraub, D. J. 1973. Factors affecting perceived orientation of the Poggendorff transversal. *Percept. Psychophys.* 14:511–17

106. Kravitz, J. H. 1972. Conditioned adaptation to prismatic displacement. *Percept. Psychophys.* 11:38–42

107. Kravitz, J. H., Yaffe, F. 1972. Conditioned adaptation to prismatic displacement with a tone as the conditional stimulus. *Percept. Psychophys.* 12:305–8

108. Lackner, J. R. 1973. The role of posture in adaptation to visual rearrangement. *Neuropsychologia* 11:33–44

109. Leibowitz, H. W., Pick, H. L. Jr. 1972. Cross-cultural and educational aspects of the Ponzo perspective illusion. *Percept. Psychophys.* 12:430–32

110. Leibowitz, H. W., Shiina, K., Hennessy. R. T. 1972. Oculomotor adjustments and size constancy. *Percept. Psychophys.* 12:497–500

111. Lefton, L. A. 1973. Metacontrast: A review. *Percept. Psychophys.* Suppl. 13 (No. 18):161–71

112. Lefton, L. A. 1973. Spatial factors in metacontrast. *Percept. Psychophys.* 14: 497–500

113. Levick, W. R., Cleland, B. G., Coombs, J. S. 1972. On the apparent orbit of the Pulfrich pendulum. *Vision Res.* 12: 1381–88

114. Levine, S. 1972. The effect of the induction of involvement on psychophysical judgments. *Percept. Psychophys.* 11:49–55

115. Liu, A. 1973. Decrease in Stroop effect by reducing semantic interference. *Percept. Mot. Skills* 37:263–65

116. Lockhead, G. R. 1973. Choosing a response. In *Attention and Performance IV*, ed. S. Kornblum, 289–301. New York: Academic. 771 pp.

117. Long, G. M. 1973. The Rod-and-frame test: further comments on methodology. *Percept. Mot. Skills* 36:624–26

118. Loomis, J. M. 1972. The photopigment bleaching hypothesis of complementary after-images: a psychophysical test. *Vision Res.* 12:1587–94

119. Lovegrove, W. J., Over, R. 1973. Colour selectivity in orientation masking and aftereffect. *Vision Res.* 13:895–902

120. Lovegrove, W. J., Over, R., Broerse, J. 1972. Color selectivity in motion after-effect. *Nature* 238:334–35

121. MacLeod, D. I. A., Virsu, V., Carpenter. R. H. S. 1974. On mathematical illusions. *Percept. Psychophys.* In press

122. Maffei, L., Fiorentini, A. 1973. The visual cortex as a spatial frequency analyser. *Vision Res.* 13:1255–67

123. Malpass, R. S., Lavigueur, H., Weldon, D. E. 1973. Verbal and visual training in face recognition. *Percept. Psychophys.* 14:285–92

124. Marg, E., Adams, J. E. 1970. Evidence for a neurological zoom system in vision from angular changes in some receptive fields of single neurons with changes in fixation distance in the human visual cortex. *Experientia* 26: 270–71

125. Massaro, D. W. 1973. Constancy scaling revisited. *Psychol. Rev.* 80:303

126. Massaro, D. W. 1973. Perception of letters, words, and nonwords. *J. Exp. Psychol.* 100:349–53

127. Massaro, D. W. 1973. The perception of rotated shapes: A process analysis of shape constancy. *Percept. Psychophys.* 13:413–22

128. Mayhew, J. E. W. 1973. After-effects of movement contingent on direction of gaze. *Vision Res.* 13:877–80

129. Mayhew, J. E. W. 1973. Luminance thresholds for motion contingent on color. *Perception* 2:41–51

130. Mayhew, J. E. W. 1973. Movement aftereffects contingent on size: Evidence for movement detectors sensitive to direction of contrast. *Vision Res.* 13:1789–95

131. McCullough, C. 1965. Color adaptation of edge-detectors in the human visual system. *Science* 149:1115–16

132. McDonnell, P. M., Duffett, J. 1972. Vision and touch : a reconsideration of conflict between the two senses. *Can. J. Psychol.* 26:171–80

133. McNicol, D. 1972. *A Primer of Signal Detection Theory.* London: Allen & Unwin. 242 pp.

134. McNicol, D., Pennington, C. W. 1973. Sensory and decision processes in anchor effects and aftereffects. *J. Exp. Psychol.* 100:232–38

135. Melamed, L. E., Halay, M., Gildow, J. W. 1973. Effect of external target presence on visual adaptation with active and passive movement. *J. Exp. Psychol.* 98:125–30

136. Mershon, D. H. 1972. Relative contributions of depth and directional adjacency to simultaneous whiteness contrast. *Vision Res.* 12:969–79

137. Metz, J. W., Balliet, R. F. 1973. Visual threshold: human scotopic luminosity functions determined with optokinetic nystagmus. *Vision Res.* 13:1001–4

138. Mezrich, J. 1973. The word superiority effect in brief visual displays: Elimination by vocalization. *Percept. Psychophys.* 13:45–48

139. Miller, E. A. 1972. Interaction of vision and touch in conflict and nonconflict form perception tasks. *J. Exp. Psychol.* 96:114–23

140. Miller, R. J. 1973. Cross-cultural research in the perception of pictorial materials. *Psychol. Bull.* 80:135–50

141. Mitchell, D. E., Baker, A. G. 1973. Stereoscopic aftereffects: evidence for disparity-specific neurones in the human visual system. *Vision Res.* 13: 2273–88

142. Mitchell, D. E., Blakemore, C. 1972. The site of orientational constancy. *Perception* 1:315–20

143. Mitchell, D. E., Freeman, R. D., Millodot, M., Haegerstrom, G. 1973. Meridional amblyopia: evidence for modification of the human visual system by early visual experience. *Vision Res.* 13:535–58

144. Monti, P. M. 1973. Lateral masking of end elements by inner elements in tachistoscopic pattern perception. *Percept. Mot. Skills* 36:777–78

145. Movshon, J. A., Blakemore, C. 1973. Orientation specificity and spatial selectivity in human vision. *Perception* 2:53–60

146. Muir, D. W., Mitchell, D. E. 1973. Visual resolution and experience: acuity deficits in cats following early selective visual deprivation. *Science* 180:420–22

147. Nachmias, J., Sansbury, R., Vassilev, A., Weber, A. 1973. Adaptation to square-wave gratings: In search of the elusive third harmonic. *Vision Res.* 13:1335–42

148. Newman, C. V. 1972. Familiar and relative size cues and surface texture as determinants of relative distance judgments. *J. Exp. Psychol.* 96:37–42

149. Newsome, L. R. 1972. Visual angle and apparent size of objects in peripheral vision. *Percept. Psychophys.* 12:300–4

150. Over, R., Long, N., Lovegrove, W. 1973. Absence of binocular interaction between spatial and color attributes of visual stimuli. *Percept. Psychophys.* 13:534–40

151. Oyama, T., Iwawaki, S. 1972. Role of convergence and binocular disparity in size constancy. *Psychol. Forsch.* 35:117–30

152. Parducci, A. 1965. Category judgment: A range-frequency model. *Psychol. Rev.* 72:407–18

153. Parlee, M. B. 1972. Differences in apparent straightness of dot and line stimuli. *Vision Res.* 12:735–42

154. Perkins, D. N. 1972. Visual discrimination between rectangular and nonrectangular parallelopipeds. *Percept. Psychophys.* 12:396–400

155. Ibid. 1973. Compensating for distortion in viewing pictures obliquely. 14:13–18

156. Pettigrew, J. D., Freeman, R. D. 1973. Visual experience without lines: Effect on developing cortical neurons. *Science* 181:599–602

157. Pick, A. D., Pick, H. L. Jr., Hales, J. J. 1972. Selective attention to words and colors. *Psychon. Sci.* 29:85–87

158. Pollack, R. H., Silvar, S. D. 1967. Magnitude of the Müller-Lyer illusion in children as a function of pigmentation of the Fundus oculi. *Psychon. Sci.* 8:83–84

159. Pressey, A. W. 1972. The assimilation theory of geometric illusions: An additional postulate. *Percept. Psychophys.* 11:28–30

160. Pressey, A. W., Sweeney, O. 1972. Acute angles and the Poggendorff illusion. *Quart. J. Exp. Psychol.* 24:169–174

161. Pressey, A. W., Sweeney, O. 1972. Some puzzling results on the Poggendorff illusion. *Percept. Psychophys.* 12:433–37

162. Prytulak, L. S. 1973. Interaction of fixation point and stimulus orientation on the appearance of rectilinearity. *Percept. Psychophys.* 14:493–96

163. Quina, K., Pollack, R. H. 1973. Attraction of parallels as a function of intercontour distance. *Percept. Mot. Skills* 36:934

164. Regan, D., Beverley, K. I. 1973. Disparity detectors in human depth perception: Evidence for directional selectivity. *Science* 181:877–79

165. Reicher, G. M. 1969. Perceptual recognition as a function of meaningfulness of stimulus material. *J. Exp. Psychol.* 81:275–80

166. Richards, W. 1972. Response functions for sine- and square-wave modulations of disparity. *J. Opt. Soc. Am.* 62:907–11

167. Riggs, L. A. 1973. Curvature as a feature of pattern vision. *Science* 181:1070–72

168. Robinson, J. O. 1972. *The Psychology of Visual Illusion.* London: Hutchinson. 288 pp.

169. Rock, I. 1973. *Orientation and Form.* New York: Academic. 165 pp.

170. Rogers, B. J., Anstis, S. M. 1972. Intensity versus adaptation and the Pulfrich stereophenomenon. *Vision Res.* 12:909–28

171. Schuck, J. R. 1973. Factors affecting reports of fragmenting visual images. *Percept. Psychophys.* 13:382–90

172. Sekuler, R. 1974. Spatial vision. *Ann. Rev. Psychol.* 25:195–232

173. Seymour, P. H. K. 1973. Stroop interference in naming and verifying spatial locations. *Percept. Psychophys.* 14:95–100

174. Sharpe, C. R., Tolhurst, D. J. 1973. The effects of temporal modulation on the orientation channels of the human

visual system. *Perception* 2:23–29
175. Shaw, P., Weigel, G. A. 1973. Effects of bars and blanks on recognition of words and nonwords embedded in a row of letters. *Percept. Psychophys.* 14:117–24
176. Shepherd, J. W., Ellis, H. D. 1973. The effect of attractiveness on recognition memory for faces. *Am. J. Psychol.* 86:627–33
177. Siegel, J. A., Siegel, W. 1972. Absolute judgment and paired-associate learning : Kissing cousins or identical twins? *Psychol Rev.* 79:300–16
178. Siegel, M. H., Siegel, A. B. 1972. Hue discrimination as a function of stimulus luminance. *Percept. Psychophys.* 12:295–99
179. Siegel, W. 1972. Memory effects in the method of absolute judgment. *J. Exp. Psychol.* 94:121–31
180. Simpson, A. J., Fitter, M. J. 1973. What is the best index of detectability? *Psychol. Bull.* 80:481–88
181. Small, M. M. 1973. Modification of performance on the Rod-and-frame test. *Percept. Mot. Skills* 36:715–20
182. Smets, G., Haesen, W. 1973. Confirmation of central explanations of the Müller-Lyer illusion. *Percept. Mot. Skills* 37:305–6
183. Smith, E. E., Haviland, S. E. 1972. Why words are perceived more accurately than nonwords: Inference versus unitization. *J. Exp. Psychol.* 92:59–64
184. Smith, F. 1971. *Understanding Reading.* New York: Holt, Rinehart & Winston. 239 pp.
185. Spinelli, D. N. 1970. Recognition of visual patterns. In *Perception and its Disorders*, ed. D.A. Hamburg, K.H. Pribram, A. J. Stunkard, 139–49. Baltimore: Williams & Wilkins. 405 pp.
186. Stadler, M. 1972. Figural aftereffects as optical illusions? *Am. J. Psychol.* 85: 351–75
187. Standing, L. G., Dodwell, P. C. 1972. Retroactive contour enhancement: A new visual storage effect. *Quart. J. Exp. Psychol.* 24:21–29
188. Stecher, S., Sigel, C., Lange, R. V. 1973. Composite adaptation and spatial frequency interactions. *Vision Res.* 13:2527–31
189. Steger, J. A., Wilkinson, J., Carter, R.

1973. Test of integration theory and adaptation level theory in anchored judgments. *Percept. Mot. Skills* 36: 271–74
190. Steinberg, W., Sekuler, R. 1973. Changes in visual spatial organization: Response frequency equalization versus adaptation level. *J. Exp. Psychol.* 98:246–51
191. Stromeyer, C. F. III, Lange, A. F., Ganz, L. 1973. Spatial frequency phase effects in human vision. *Vision Res.* 13:2345–60
192. Swets, J. A. 1973. The relative operating characteristic in psychology. *Science* 181:990–1000
193. Taub, E., Goldberg, I. A. 1973. Prism adaptation: Control of intermanual transfer by distribution of practice. *Science* 180:755–57
194. Taylor, S. G., Brown, D. R. 1972. Lateral visual masking: Supraretinal effects when viewing linear arrays with unlimited viewing time. *Percept. Psychophys.* 12:97–99
195. Templeton, W. B. 1973. The role of gravitational cues in the judgment of visual orientation. *Percept. Psychophys.* 14:451–57
196. Thompson, M. C., Massaro, D. W. 1973. Visual information and redundancy in reading. *J. Exp. Psychol.* 98:49–54
197. Tolhurst, D. J. 1972. Adaptation to square-wave gratings: inhibition between spatial frequency channels in the human visual system. *J. Physiol. London.* 226:231–49
198. Tolhurst, D. J., Sharpe, C. R., Hart, G. 1973. The analysis of the drift rate of moving sinusoidal gratings. *Vision Res.* 13:2545–55
199. Tulunay-Keesey, U. 1973. Stabilized target visibility as a function of contrast and flicker frequency. *Vision Res.* 13:1367–73
200. Uhlarik, J. J. 1973. Role of cognitive factors on adaptation to prismatic displacement. *J. Exp. Psychol.* 98:223–32
201. Uttal, W. R. 1973. *The Psychobiology of Sensory Coding.* New York: Harper & Row. 679 pp.
202. Van Eyl, F. P. 1972. Induced vestibular stimulation and the moon illusion. *J. Exp. Psychol.* 94:326–28

203. Virsu, V., Haapasalo, S. 1973. Relationships between channels for colour and spatial frequency in human vision. *Perception* 2:31–40
204. Wade, N. J. 1973. Binocular rivalry and binocular fusion of afterimages. *Vision Res.* 13:999–1000
205. Wade, N. J. 1973. Orientation and spatial frequency effects on linear afterimages. *Percept. Psychophys.* 13: 446–50
206. Wagenaar, W. A. 1973. The effect of fluctuations of response criterion and sensitivity in a signal detection experiment. *Psychol. Forsch.* 36:27–37
207. Wagner. G., Boynton, R. M. 1972. Comparison of four methods of heterochromatic photometry. *J. Opt. Soc. Am.* 62:1508–15
208. Walker, E. H. 1973. A mathematical theory of optical illusions and figural aftereffects. *Percept. Psychophys.* 13:467–86
209. Walker, J. T. 1972. A texture-contingent visual motion aftereffect. *Psychon. Sci.* 28:333–35
210. Walker, J. T. 1972. Natural visual capture in bilateral length comparisons. *Percept. Psychophys.* 11:247–51
211. Walker, J. T. 1972. Tactual field dependence. *Psychon. Sci.* 26:311–13
212. Wallach, H., Frey, K. J. 1972. Adaptation in distance perception based on oculomotor cues. *Percept. Psychophys.* 11:77–83
213. Wallach, H., Frey, K. J., Bode, K. A. 1972. The nature of adaptation in distance perception based on oculomotor cues. *Percept. Psychophys.* 11:110–16
214. Weintraub, D. J., Herzog, T. R. 1973. The kinesthetic aftereffect: ritual versus requisites. *Am. J. Psychol.* 86: 407–23
215. Weintraub, D. J., McNulty, J. A. 1973. Clarity versus identifiability of repeatedly flashed patterns. *J. Exp. Psychol.* 99:293–305
216. Weintraub, D. J., Tong, L. 1974. Assessing Poggendorff effects via collinearity, perpendicularity, parallelism, and Oppel (distance) experiments. *Percept. Psychophys.* 16:213–31
217. Weintraub, D. J., Tong, L., Smith, A. J. 1973. Müller-Lyer versus size/reflectance-contrast illusion: Is the age-related decrement caused by a declining sensitivity to brightness contours? *Develop. Psychol.* 8:6–15
218. Weintraub, D. J., Virsu, V. 1972. Estimating the vertex of converging lines: Angle misperception? *Percept. Psychophys.* 11:277–83
219. Weisstein, N., Montalvo, F., Ozog, G. 1972. Differential adaptation to gratings blocked by cubes and gratings blocked by hexagons: A test of the neural symbolic activity hypothesis. *Psychon. Sci.* 27:89–92
220. Welch, R. B. 1972. The effect of experienced limb identity upon adaptation to simulated displacement of the visual field. *Percept. Psychophys.* 12:453–56
221. Wenderoth, P. M. 1973. The effects of tilted outline frames and intersecting line patterns on judgment of vertical. *Percept. Psychophys.* 14:242–48
222. Woolsey, J. A., Newman, C. V. 1973. Motion aftereffects following inspection of contrarotating stimuli. *Vision Res.* 13:2587–89
223. Wright, A. A. 1972. Psychometric and psychophysical hue discrimination functions for the pigeon. *Vision Res.* 12:1447–64
224. Zeidner, J., Sadacca, R., Schwartz, A. I. 1961. *Human factors studies in image interpretation: The value of stereoscopic viewing.* Human Factors Res. Branch Tech. Res. Note 114. 37 pp.

VERBAL LEARNING AND MEMORY

Leo Postman[1]

Institute of Human Learning, University of California
Berkeley, California 94720

HISTORICAL TRENDS

The last review of memory and verbal learning by Tulving & Madigan (180) painted a deeply pessimistic picture of the theoretical and experimental progress during the nearly 100 years of the post-Ebbinghaus era. As these critics saw it, tireless investigators compiled endless measurements of performance in laboratory tasks which bear little or no relation to the complexities and subtleties of human memory. For the most part, the experiments demonstrated and quantified what Aristotle expounded in the remote days of antiquity—that memory is likely to reflect the contiguity and similarity of past events. While that proposition may have some empirical validity, it offers no purchase on the dynamics of remembering. Yet the students of learning and memory were excruciatingly slow to break out of the constraints imposed by the pretheoretical schema of mechanical chaining of mental representations. A discouraging manifestation of the futility of it all was the fact that laboratory procedures, such as serial and paired-associate learning, which obviously can be no more than a means to an end, became an object of experimental and theoretical analysis, i.e. an end by themselves. Thus it came about that in the middle of the twentieth century, man still thought "about his own memory processes in terms readily translatable into ancient Greek" (180, p. 437). It is only fair to add that the picture painted by Tulving and Madigan was not one of unrelieved gloom. They saw many promising leads as attention shifted away from the traditional problems of association to questions about the processing, storage, and retrieval of the multiplex information to which man is exposed both inside and outside the laboratory.

This chapter is being written about 5 years after the last review, but the lines of historical development appear quite different to the present writer, and not only

[1] The preparation of this report was facilitated by grant MH 12006 from the National Institute of Mental Health.

because of the advances and changes in the field that have occurred during the intervening period. Perhaps the first point that is worth making is that the antiquity of concepts is not a measure of their triviality in psychology any more than it is in mathematics. Contiguity and similarity have, in fact, turned out to be fundamental determinants of remembering. We know a great deal now, but not nearly enough, about their mode of operation. Those who have made a determined effort to break out of the traditional mold have nevertheless been constrained to treat contiguity and similarity as fundamental variables, for example in the formulation of the principles of grouping in perception and memory, originally proposed by the Gestaltists and now newly demonstrated by proponents of organization theory (20). It is essentially by virtue of contiguity and similarity that higher-order units in memory are assumed to be formed, although one may now prefer to describe the consequences as seriation (103) and subjective organization. The examples could be multiplied to show that there is an abundance of old wine in new bottles on the shelves of those who are deeply disappointed in the plodding accomplishments of the past.

It is not the age and the tradition-encrusted aura of the concepts and variables that matter, but the use to which they are put. Consider, for example, frequency, which is no less hoary a principle than contiguity and similarity in the history of thought about memory. One of the most promising and productive approaches to the problem of recognition today is built on the elegantly simple assumption that the discrimination between old and new events is based on the attribute of frequency (186). Let us also note that the most recent, and probably most sophisticated and comprehensive, model of human information processing and memory is described by its authors as a neo-Aristotelian theory of association (3). This is a model which is written in the language of computers; thus the voice of Aristotle is heard again in this electronic age.

One cannot judge the fruits of past labors just by the advances that have been made in theory. It is necessary to consider the cumulative growth in empirical knowlege as well. Tulving and Madigan tell us that of the many hundreds of papers they examined they were able to classify less than 10 percent as "worthwhile." These were papers that clarified existing problems, "opening up new areas of investigation, and providing titillating glimpses into the unknown" (180, p. 442). As for the rest of the publications, they were consigned to the categories of "utterly inconsequential" or "run-of-the-mill." We must concede without demurrer that the literature on verbal learning and memory contains more than its share of hack products reporting trivial parametric manipulations and unnecessary variations on old and tired themes. It is (perhaps deceptively) easy to do routine studies of verbal learning, and many are done because the variables are there to be manipulated. There would probably be fair agreement on what is "utterly inconsequential."

It is the evaluation of the "run-of-the-mill" work that is open to debate. There have been few, if any, truly crucial experiments on memory which signaled a theoretical breakthrough. Unfortunately, unexpected and counterintuitive results more often than not ultimately are found to be artifacts or interpretable in terms of already known principles. The theoretical blast of Rock's thesis of one-trial learning (148) ended on a whimper amidst confusion about uncontrollable variables and uncertainties of measurement (147). A recent cause in point is the phenomenon of negative part-to-whole transfer (175), which we discuss below. In the current state of the psychology of verbal learning and memory, theoretical advances are most likely to occur through the integration of stable and repeatable experimental results and the resolution of apparent inconsistencies among observed empirical phenomena. The "run-of-the-mill" studies are useful in contributing stable facts and in alerting us to the lack of order in empirical relationships. Thus the products may be valuable, even though the context of discovery may now be judged by some to have been routine or pedestrian.

A few examples will help to show how new and challenging theoretical issues are anchored to (and perhaps in some cases arise out of) both the orderliness and the disorderliness of run-of-the-mill facts. One of the central issues in current discussions of the nature of memory is the validity of the distinction between a short-term and a long-term store. The resolution of this question has hinged in large measure on the reexamination of the effects of such old and familiar variables as serial position, presentation rate, and the similarity between the memory task and the activities filling the retention interval (e.g. 54, 87). Theorists knew what the expected effects in conventional rote-learning situations were; by showing that these relations failed to materialize in certain tests of short-term retention, they were trying to make a case for a separate and different memory system.

Consider next the conditions and characteristics of encoding which today occupy the center of the theoretical stage—encoding variability (106, 115), encoding persistence (61), and encoding specificity (182), dimensions of encoding or depth of processing (36), and so forth. In each case the arguments pro and con take their point of departure from phenomena of old standing; new experimental arrangements are devised to permit these classes of phenomena to exhibit the operation of the postulated intervening mechanisms. Investigations of the effects of spacing on recall and reexaminations of the conventional paradigms of paired-associate transfer have been the primary testing grounds of the principles of encoding variability and persistence. Contextual stimuli at input and output have been manipulated to demonstrate encoding specificity, and the time-honored question of differences between recall and recognition has emerged as a critical dependent variable in the evaluation of this hypothesis. Those concerned with levels and varieties of processing have brought us back to an examination of the consequences of sheer repetition and the variations in incidental memory attendant upon the performance of different orienting tasks. We will comment on these theoretical developments later. For the present, these examples are intended to serve as a reminder of the symbiotic relationship between patient fact-finders and innovative theorists. What kinds of evidence are "worthwhile" and "run-of-the-mill" changes continuously, and there is a high risk in applying these categorical judgments prematurely.

The degree to which one sees the field of verbal learning and memory as static or changing depends on his temporal perspective. In a broad sweep over the "period from approximately 350 B.C. to 1969 A.D." (180, p. 437), Tulving and Madigan saw painfully little change. When one focuses on the brief span of the last two decades or so, recent changes in concepts, theories, and methods appear drastic and loom large. During these years, the methodological constraints of behaviorism and the frugal tenets of functionalism were eagerly set aside by many influential investigators. Concepts that had lain dormant because they had appeared to lack complete scientific respectability made a spectacular comeback—organization, imagery, attention, consciousness, to name just a few. The language of the computer replaced the vocabulary of habit theory and conditioning: the basic sequence of events in learning and remembering is described in terms of coding, processing, storage, and retrieval. Model building became a major preoccupation. The number of models—boxes joined by intricate arrangements of arrows and loops, flow diagrams, computer programs, systems of equations, and multifarious combinations thereof—proliferated at a remarkable rate. Today the ratio of models to experiments is quite high, although happily still less than unity. As part of the modelers' armamentarium, the proverbial homunculus has gained a measure of implicit tolerance, sometimes in the guise of an executive routine, selecting codes, deciding on processing strategies, and searching through the recesses of the memory store(s). None of these pretheoretical and theoretical orientations is intrinsically good or bad. There is no question but that investigations formulated within an information-processing framework have yielded important facts about learning and memory. The critical issue which has to be faced is whether the multiplicity and complexity of hypothetical mechanisms are outdistancing the observable facts at a rate that is cause for alarm. This question is the underlying theme of the selective review of the recent literature that follows.

One more point about the current intellectual climate may be in order. Against the background of the functionalist tradition, the developments which we have described had the earmarks of a theoretical and methodological revolution. Now it is a commonplace observation that revolutionaries tend to turn conservative once they seize the reins of government. It is to be feared that intellectual revolutionaries are no exception. There are worrisome signs that a new orthodoxy and a normative nominalism may be in the making. Consider, for example, the following remarkable statement which appeared in the discussion section of a paper in which the authors argued for an interpretation of incidental learning in terms of type of processing as opposed to differential responding to the stimulus items:

> Of course, we do not understand processes better than responses nor do we argue that processes are more objective or more scientific. Indeed, we probably know as little about processes as we do about hypothetical responses. We do argue, however, that the notion of processes involved in a task offers more adequate, productive, and interesting experimental ideas than the relatively constricted (and equally hypothetical) notion of responses (77, p. 479).

Surely the name that one attaches to an hypothetical event should not matter in and of itself when the nature of the event is only vaguely understood. We must guard against the obvious fallacy that a change to a preferred language entails, or even holds out the promise of, better understanding.

THE SHORT AND HAPPY REIGN OF
DUAL-PROCESS THEORY

Few theoretical ideas have influenced our field of research as profoundly as the formulation of the multiple-store conception of memory. While there have been various versions differing in detail (cf. 130), the modal scheme encompasses three stages: a sensory register, a short-term store and a long-term store (e.g. 4). Since our concern here is with verbal learning and memory, we will not consider the sensory component any further but will address ourselves only to the dichotomy between a short-term store (STS) and a long-term store (LTS). The question to be examined is how tenable this distinction appears to be in the light of the most recent experimental evidence.

Before the present status of the theory is appraised, it is well to remind ourselves of the type of evidence that motivated and sustained the formulation of a dual-store hypothesis. The finding that massive forgetting of a subspan amount of material can occur in a matter of seconds, as in the Brown-Peterson paradigm, was undoubtedly influential but would not have been sufficient in itself. There is nothing in the fact that forgetting is much more rapid under some experimental arrangements than others which compels the inference of qualitatively distinct processes. The conviction that there are separate stores was founded on indications that short-term and long-term traces had different properties, and that the establishment of the latter was dependent on the survival of the former. As is well known, the major lines of evidence which have been invoked to support a functional dichotomy of memory processes include (a) the specificity of memory deficits in brain-damaged patients; (b) apparent differences in encoding related to the length of the interval between input and retention test; (c) the effects of presentation modality on performance; and (d) the interaction of the serial position at input with a variety of experimental manipulations, with recall of the terminal items presumably reflecting output from STS and that of early and middle items from LTS.

While models vary with respect to the characteristics assigned to the two stores, there is substantial agreement on the major functional differences between the hypothesized long-term and short-term systems. A useful composite summary of these differences was recently presented by Craik & Lockhart (36): STS is a system of limited capacity in which information is maintained by continued attention and rehearsal. The format of the information is predominantly phonemic, probably also visual, and "possibly semantic." The trace is of short duration (up to 30 sec) and loss from the store occurs through displacement or "possibly decay." Retrieval is likely to be automatic or dependent on temporal and phonemic cues. Information that has been maintained by rehearsal in STS is transferred to LTS; a common assumption is that the probability of transfer is a direct function of the duration of an item's stay in STS (4, 54, 131). Once information has entered LTS, which has no determinate limits, it is maintained by repetition or organization. The format of the information is largely semantic but includes some visual and auditory representations as well. The long-term trace is of indefinite duration. Successful retrieval depends on the availability of appropriate cues and may be the outcome of a search process. Forgetting occurs when the stored information becomes inaccessible because of the loss of retrieval cues or discriminability is degraded through interference.

The title of the present section was chosen to reflect an emerging consensus that this compact and well articulated schema is rapidly losing both face validity and empirical support. The change in the climate of opinion is made all the more impressive by the fact that some of the most vigorous and persuasive criticisms have been advanced by investigators who in the past have contributed substantially to the supporting evidence (121, 167, 201). In discussing the experimental evidence, we will refer to the salient features of the two hypothetical stores listed by Craik & Lockhart (36). Since there have been several comprehensive reviews of the literature during the last few years, we will cite just a few of the many relevant recent studies.

Coding in STS

Note that Craik and Lockhart described the format of information in STS as "phonemic, probably visual, possibly semantic." This guarded and tentative description appropriately reflects the increasing weight of the evidence against the proposition that the coding of material in STS is necessarily or exclusively acoustic. The origin of this somewhat counter-intuitive hypothesis can be traced in the first instance to the identification of STS as a holding mechanism in which information is maintained through rehearsal. In order to be rehearsed, visual input has to be recoded into an auditory form (173).

It is less clear why it was further assumed by at least some theorists (6, 7, 90, 125) that semantic coding does not occur in STS but only in LTS. Such an assumption may have reflected in part a search for characteristics which would differentiate sharply between the two systems. It can also be seen as related once more to the rehearsal function of STS. Semantic processing of the items reduces the amount of time and effort that can be devoted to maintenance rehearsal. Atkinson & Shiffrin (4) pointed out explicitly that a trade-off might occur in STS between maintenance rehearsal on the one hand and elaborations and transformations of the input on the other. They suggested that the extent to which such a division of effort did in fact occur in any given situation was under the control of the learner.

Other exponents of dual-process theory, notably Glanzer (54), put the mnemonic organization of the material squarely in STS. The probability that a mnemonic relation can be established and used is seen by Glanzer as dependent on how closely the relevant items follow each other, i.e. how likely they are to be together in STS. Norman & Rumelhart (131) suggest that the primary distinction between long-term and short-term memory lies in the degree of permanence with which contextual information is attached to stored representations. "When information is retrieved, all that matters is the number of attributes that are still retained: no distinction is made between short- and long-term storage" (p. 29). In retrospect, one cannot help but wonder why the proposition that semantic encoding does *not* occur in STS attained the prominence that it did. Support for this particular hypothesis has surfaced only occasionally (e.g. 90, 98). Nevertheless, a significant proportion of the papers on short-term memory during the last few years was directed to the disproof of the hypothesis. There appears to be a functional autonomy of hypotheses as well as of methods (180).

It is necessary then to distinguish between two quite separate questions subsumed under the hypothesis that coding in STS is primarily phonemic. First, can information entering in a nonverbal format be maintained only if it is recoded phonemically? Second, can information be coded semantically in STS and what are the conditions determining whether it is or not? The evidence most commonly cited for phonemic recording of visual inputs is (*a*) the impairment in the recall of visually presented letters as the acoustic similarity of the letters is increased, and (*b*) the correspondence between the pattern of errors in recall to the confusions that occur in tests of auditory perception of the letters (30). It is doubtful that any general conclusions about the coding limitations of STS should have been drawn from such results. The only valid inference is that phonemic coding does occur in STS, not that it is the exclusive form of coding (cf 62). Visual coding could have occurred without being reflected in confusion errors, perhaps because the visual and phonemic traces decay at different rates (201). In any event, it has now become apparent that the mechanisms underlying phonemic confusion errors are more complex than had been originally supposed and that there is no simple and direct line of argument from the occurrence of such errors to fixed coding characteristics of STS.

Two important recent studies bearing on this question should be mentioned here. Peterson & Johnson (138) returned to the question raised earlier (66, 123) of the relationship between articulation and acoustic confusion effects in immediate recall. To minimize articulation, subjects were required to count aloud during the visual presentation of letter strings. The input sequences were of either low or high acoustic confusability. Control subjects remained silent during the presentation of the strings. The usual inverse relation between acoustic similarity and recall was found in the silent condition, but this effect was entirely eliminated when counting was required. In a second experiment, the effects of silence and counting were compared under conditions of auditory presentation. As in the previous situation, performance was substantially reduced by counting but the acoustic similarity effect was now present under both conditions. The conclusion was that both acoustic and articulatory cues can function in short-term retention. "The subject will use what is convenient" (p. 350). That is, he adds articulatory cues when presentation is visual and utilizes acoustic ones when presentation is auditory.

In the experiments of Estes (47, 48), the dependence of phonemic encoding on vocalization is clearly demonstrated. As expected, confusions among acoustically similar letters presented visually rose to a sharp peak and then declined as a function of retention interval when vocalization was permitted at input. However, when vocalization was prevented by the concurrent performance of a verbal task (categorizing the individual letters according to their position in the alphabet) or by reduced exposure duration, the probability of confusion errors was no greater for acoustically similar than dissimilar letters (at chance). Furthermore, there was evidence for phonemic encoding when vocalization was suppressed during input but a brief pause for rehearsal was introduced within less than 2 sec after the visual display. It appears, therefore, that nonauditory representations of the letters remain available for rehearsal for a second or more even though other visual characters have been displayed in the same location. Estes concludes that the phonemic encoding of visually presented items is not effected by a central recoding process; rather it is based on an auditory-articulatory input which occurs in parallel with or subsequent to the visual presentation. It is important to note that in both the studies we have summarized retention is well above chance even when vocalization is prevented and the use of acoustic cues is minimized. It is true that vocalization enhances item availability, but some of the information is maintained without vocalization, although it remains to be determined how.

The question of how the trace of the visual input is maintained for a delayed phonemic readout is of considerable theoretical importance. As Estes points out, it would not be reasonable to explain this finding in terms of the maintenance of visual features in a short-term visual memory system. Under the fast rate of presentation used, the image of a given letter would have been overwritten during the period of delay by subsequent items displayed in the same location. Existing models obviously do not provide an exhaustive account of the ways in which information can be maintained for purposes of further processing immediately after input. The idea that an auditory-verbal-linguistic format is essential for sustained short-term storage has more generally been called into serious question by the results of a series of recent studies comparing retention for visual and auditory inputs.

In the experiments by Kroll, Parkinson, and their associates (91, 93, 94, 135, 136, 159) the subjects are engaged in shadowing aurally presented letters while trying to remember a single "memory letter" that is presented either visually or aurally. The rationale of this manipulation is that the amount of interference produced by the interpolated shadowing task should be equivalent if the visual display were recoded into an auditory format. The results consistently fail to confirm this prediction. Immediate retention of the auditory and visual letter is equivalent or may favor the former; however, after a shadowing interval of the order of 10–20 sec, retention of the visual memory letter is superior. Phonemic similarity between the target letter and the interpolated shadowing material reduces recall when the presentation is aural but not when it is visual. This finding reinforces the conclusion that the visual input is not recoded into an auditory format in this situation. Furthermore, immediate and delayed serial position curves are similar in the recall of visually presented stimuli, showing both primacy and recency effects. With auditory presentation, only a primacy effect is typically obtained after a delay.

It is interesting to note that superiority of visually presented trigrams was recently observed in the standard Brown-Peterson paradigm, with backward counting as the distractor activity (160). This result is reasonable when the similarity (with respect to the modality engaged) between the original and the interpolated task is considered. The apparent persistence of visual information over the short term, although not to a greater extent than of auditory inputs, has been demonstrated under other experimental arrangements as well (e.g. 96). Taken together, these studies make it clear that coding in an acoustic format is not mandatory for short-term retention, even though that format may be dominant in many situations. It would be unfortunate if recognition of this state of affairs led to a subdivision of the storage compartment into autonomous auditory and visual boxes. Some investigators are tempted to speculate along these lines. A more reasonable conclusion would seem to be that if one has to think in terms of a short-term store, one should conceive of it in functional rather than structural terms (138).

A brief general comment on modality differences may be interjected here. Except in special situations like those used by Kroll et al, performance is typically better after auditory than visual presentation. The difference is usually confined to the terminal items in a list (e.g. 32, 101, 122, 197). When visual and auditory presentations are mixed within a list, recall tends to be organized by modality (122, 129). The effects are impressive, but it remains rather unclear what they imply. A variety of explanations have been suggested (cf 121, 197). One hypothesis which has received considerable attention is that the input to STS may be augmented from a precategorical acoustic store (39, 120). However, such an interpretation appears to be untenable since decay from this store is too rapid to encompass the time span over which the modality differences have been shown to extend (121). To postulate separate visual and auditory prelinguistic stores which differ in capacity (122) is essentially to restate the explanatory problem in structural terms.

Recent experiments have shown that the advantage of auditory over visual presentation is independent of word length in both free and serial recall (197, 198). Since the unit of information in the precategorical store must be taken to be less than a word, the results indicate that the modality effect probably reflects a postcategorical stage of processing. Watkins (197) suggests that recency and modality effects, which are both independent of word length, are determined by the same process in primary memory, but the exact nature of this process remains to be specified. In any event, as Murdock (121) points out, the modality effect presents a problem for dual-store theories which assume that items pass from STS to LTS since the superiority of the auditory mode is usually limited to the recency portion of the serial position curve.

We turn now to evidence bearing on the question of whether or not semantic encoding occurs in STS. As already noted, the hypothesis that it does not was rather implausible to begin with, nor has it been entertained in a serious way by many dual-store theorists. It is sufficient, therefore, to cite the recent careful experiments by Shulman (166, 168) which leave little doubt that the semantic characteristics of words can significantly influence performance in a short-term memory situation. Shulman used a probe recognition procedure in which the subject was required to judge whether a test item was identical to one of the words in a 10-word list, a synonym of one of the words, or a homonym. The subject did not know in advance which type of probe would occur and thus was presumably forced to encode the items semantically as well as phonemically. The functions relating correct recognition to serial position were closely similar in shape and in each case showed a pronounced recency effect. While the level of recognition for synonyms was high, it fell below that for homonyms. The implications of such a difference are equivocal, however, since the degree of semantic similarity cannot necessarily be assumed to be as great as that of phonemic similarity. In a subsidiary experiment Shulman found that subjects' ability to recognize synonymity is less than perfect even when memory is not involved. It may be noted in passing that comparing the effects of two types of similarity is always extremely risky, precisely because of the difficulty of equating the degree of relationship along the different dimensions.

Shulman's results show that semantic encoding in a short-term memory situation can be highly effective when the task demands it. The author proposes a principle of time-dependent encoding: it takes longer to process an item semantically than to process it phonemically. Hence subjects may confine themselves to the latter dimension when that is sufficient to meet the experimental requirements. This interpretation receives some support from the fact that recognition of synonyms improves as rate of presentation decreases, whereas that of identical and homonymous targets does not. There remained the unlikely possibility that words are always stored phonemically but are recoded into a semantic form when synonym recognition is required. This hypothesis was tested in an ingenious experiment by Raser (144) and not unexpectedly found wanting. Hopefully, the question of whether words can be encoded semantically in short-term memory situations is now settled. The idea that people would mouth the sounds of words for several seconds at a stretch without knowing what they were saying was always a bit unsettling.

Rehearsal and Transfer to LTS

The typical flow chart of a dual-process model shows some, but not all, of the information that has entered STS as being transferred to LTS. Exactly how this transfer might occur is usually not specified. We see an arrow pointing from one box to another, but few if any theorists would have wanted us to take the box schema literally, perhaps signifying that excitation flows from a short-term to a long-term location. In any event, it seemed reasonable to suppose that the probability of transfer was related directly to the length of an item's stay in STS. While an item remains in STS, it can be maintained through rehearsal, the corresponding LTS trace is built up, and there is time for useful coding operations and other storage processes to be accomplished (4, 54). Apparent strong support for this conception was obtained in experiments on free recall when the frequency with which individual items were rehearsed during study trials was correlated with the probability of their being reproduced on a subsequent test of retention (154, 156, 157). This correlation was very high (thus accounting for the effects of primacy), with the notable exception of the last few positions in the list. For the terminal portion, the frequency of rehearsals was very low but the probability of recall was high, particularly in the last position. The last few items may be retrievable from STS, and to that extent the probability of recall should be independent of the number of rehearsals. That is, an item is available and accessible if it is still in STS, regardless of how often it has been rehearsed. The earlier items, however, must be retrieved from LTS; hence the probability of their recall is determined by the amount of information in LTS, which in turn is a function of the number of rehearsals.

This line of reasoning was further strengthened by the demonstration of a negative recency effect in delayed free recall (33, 35). When subjects learn a series of lists, each presented for a single study trial, a pronounced recency effect is obtained on the immediate test of recall for each individual list. However, when recall of all the lists is requested at the end of the session, the items that had occupied the terminal positions in the successive lists are remembered least well. It had, of course, been known that the recency effect in single-trial free recall is eliminated by a few seconds of interpolated activity (54); the additional finding now was that in final free recall for a series of lists retention for the terminal items fell below that for the middle ones (hence the phrase, negative recency). The negative recency effect has considerable generality: it has been found with serial as well as free recall (27), with probe recall of paired associates (102, 110), and holds both for items that were recalled on the immediate test and those that were not (although initial recall raises the level of final retention). It has been observed for recognition as well (35, 41), although not invariably so (27). The obvious explanation within the framework of a two-store model is that terminal items, while highly accessible from STS on an immediate test, are inadequately registered in LTS, in fact more inadequately than any other items, and hence cannot be retrieved from LTS on the final test.

So far so good. Unfortunately, subsequent work has shown that in spite of its face validity the dual-process interpretation of the negative recency effect was apparently wrong, at least insofar as inadequate registration in LTS was attributed to shortness of stay in STS and lack of opportunity for rehearsal. Several related experiments have now converged on the conclusion that long-term retention is not determined by either the sheer amount of rehearsal or the duration of an item's stay in STS. Rather what is critical is the type of rehearsal or processing that takes place during the input period. Rehearsal that serves only to maintain the immediate availability of an item, such as simple repetition, does little if anything to enhance subsequent recall. Active processing of the item—elaboration, transformation, recoding, and so on—does enhance subsequent recall. For purposes of further discussion we will adopt the terminology used in a recent article and distinguish between maintenance rehearsal on the one hand and constructive rehearsal on the other (213). Some of the major findings which appear to lend support to this distinction will be summarized briefly:

1. When a distractor task is performed after the presentation of each of a series of lists, recall of the terminal items is depressed as compared to conditions in which intervals of either silent or overt rehearsal periods are interpolated. However, on the final test of recall for all lists, retention of these items is highest under the distractor treatment. Similar results are obtained with lists of subspan length (78, 79). The proposed interpretation is that in anticipation of the rehearsal-preventing activity the critical items are processed more thoroughly, i.e. rehearsal

becomes more constructive. Since no differences are found on a final test of recognition, the generation of effective retrieval cues is implicated. An examination of the results suggests that such an interpretation should be made with considerable caution. While the differences in final performance are significant, they are by no means of impressive proportions. The subjects' ability to improve their efficiency of processing must have been rather limited. Perhaps more important, with reference to immediate recall, a comparison is effectively made between the final retention of lists varying in length. For various reasons, losses may be greater for a relatively long than short list. Such pedestrian variables have a way of intruding themselves and should not be overlooked.

2. Craik & Watkins (37) undertook to manipulate directly the length of STS storage and the amount of overt rehearsal for items to be recalled subsequently, presumably from LTS. Neither storage time nor the number of overt rehearsals was directly related to long-term recall. One of their experiments bears directly on the interpretation of the negative recency effect. Subjects were induced to rehearse aloud the terminal items in successive lists as often as the initial ones. If the poor delayed recall of terminal items is due to a lack of rehearsal, the retention deficit should be eliminated under these conditions. It was not. It appears that the additional rehearsal was not constructive enough. One is left with the question, however, of whether massed rehearsals of terminal items should be expected to be as effective as the typically distributed rehearsals (156) of the initial items.

3. In the context of a study of directed forgetting, Woodward, Bjork & Jongeward (213) investigated the relation between amount of rehearsal and subsequent retention. For present purposes, the critical manipulation was that the cue to remember or forget was presented for individual words after varying periods of delay. The subjects had to hold each word in memory until the cue appeared. The length of the rehearsal period had no effect on the initial recall of the to-be-remembered items nor on the final recall of either the to-be-remembered or the to-be-forgotten items [similar results had been reported previously (43, 212)]. There was, however, a strong relationship between rehearsal time and final recognition for both classes of items. The basic conclusion is again that there was no constructive rehearsal of the type required for recall. However, rote maintenance rehearsal apparently will strengthen an item's representation sufficiently to improve long-term recognition. What is not known is how much of each of the delay periods was actually spent in rehearsal. If the range in the number of rehearsals was limited, there might have been sufficient variation to affect recognition but not recall.

4. To round out the picture, it should be mentioned that a lack of relation between rehearsal frequency and end-of-session recall has also been found in the traditional Brown-Peterson situation (117). The retention intervals were either filled with the usual backward-counting task or left free for rehearsal. On the tests for individual trigrams the experimental manipulation produced the expected differences—there was heavy forgetting under the distractor condition and nearly perfect recall over all retention intervals when rehearsal was allowed. However, the final recall scores were virtually identical. According to the authors, unre-

stricted rehearsal served to maintain the items in STS but not to encode them in LTS. Unfortunately, it is difficult to draw any conclusions from these results since the probability of final recall was only .10. A list of 25 CCCs of low association value is just extremely difficult to recall. The problem of low sensitivity produced by floor effects arises, to varying degrees, in the assessment of most of the final recall scores that have been considered in this section.

We have discussed these studies in some detail not only because of their critical importance for dual-process theory but also because they call into serious question a widely held and rarely questioned assumption that there is a direct relation between retention and amount of rehearsal or study time. The proposition that rehearsal activities can vary in effectiveness should cause little surprise. What is rather startling is the flat assertion that sheer repetition or "maintenance rehearsal" has only momentary effects and fails to influence recall even a few minutes later. Not long ago, Cooper & Pantle (31) came to a very different conclusion on the basis of their review of the evidence concerning the total-time hypothesis: "When task requirements do not exceed simple rehearsal . . . a fixed amount of time is necessary to learn a fixed amount of material" (p. 232). The apparent conflict with the total-time principle has been noted by others (37). That principle has, of course, limited validity, but there certainly have been no indications of a zero correlation between study time and performance. One might try to reconcile the divergent conclusions by claiming that rehearsal was adequately constructive whenever a positive relation to study time was found. Possibly so, but there is also the finding that sheer "mindless" repetition—pronouncing items aloud over and over—has very substantial effects on the level of incidental learning (113, 114). Performance of orienting tasks which are alleged to involve no "semantic processing" does result in respectable amounts of incidental learning, even though not as much as observed under conditions believed to induce such processing (77).

For the time being, it will be prudent to view the proposed dichotomy between maintenance rehearsal and constructive rehearsal with great caution. Dichotomies have a way of becoming points on a continuum. Null effects such as those observed in the last three studies described above do not provide a firm basis for broad generalizations, especially when there are reasonable questions about the degree of control over the variables and the sensitivity of the measures of retention. It may be that a classification of rehearsal activities with respect to degree of "constructiveness" will prove very useful, but if that is to happen, one has to be mindful of the danger of circular reasoning in the use of vague and unspecified qualitative distinctions. The experiment by Jacoby & Bartz (79) showing the beneficial effect of an interpolated distractor activity on subsequent recall is a case in point. The inference that subjects anticipating an interfering task can proceed at a moment's notice to generate more effective retrieval cues (whatever these may be) is entirely ad hoc. There is nothing in the experimental manipulations related to retrieval cues; to argue that the quality or usefulness of the cues was improved does no more than to restate the apparent effect of the independent variable. We return below to the difficulties that arise in attempts to establish taxonomies of processing.

The Limited Capacity of STS and Short-Term Forgetting

Short-term forgetting is closely linked to the limited capacity of STS in dual-process theories. As Atkinson & Shiffrin (4) see it, information decays from the store unless it is maintained by rehearsal. But the number of units that can be so maintained is strictly limited. Each new item entered into the rehearsal buffer displaces one already there. One can of course postulate displacement as the basic mechanism of loss and discount decay (200). Within this general framework two major uncertainties concern the capacity of the store and the relative importance of decay and displacement.

As Craik & Lockhart (36) point out, the concept of limited capacity has ambiguous connotations since it is often unclear whether the limitation is meant to apply to the number of units that can be stored or the rate at which successive units can be processed. They suggest that existing numerical estimates bear more on storage than processing limitations. In any event, the available estimates vary with the definition of functional units and the method of measurement (often deviating drastically from the magic number seven plus or minus two). The interpretative difficulties that beset the assessment of STS storage capacity may be illustrated with reference to the work of Glanzer and his associates (summarized in 54). The point of departure in this series of studies is the assumption that the serial position curve in free recall reflects the output from two different stores: for all positions except the terminal ones retrieval is primarily or entirely from LTS; terminal items may be retrieved from either LTS or STS but on an immediate test of recall may be expected to come primarily from the latter. This basic assumption is taken to be validated by the interaction of task and presentation variables with the serial position of the items at input. Factors such as rate of presentation, list length, word frequency, and interitem associative relations have systematic effects on recall at all but the terminal serial positions.

The raw interactions obviously do not imply anything about output from separate stores. Given the purely descriptive phenomenon of a recency peak, nothing more may be involved than a ceiling effect. Some estimate of the amount of information retrieved from each of the stores is needed to interpret the interactions. To accomplish this objective, Glanzer, like numerous other investigators, has applied a formula devised by Waugh & Norman (200). The asymptote of the serial position curve or the level of recall after a delay furnishes a measure of LTS. The output of STS is then calculated by means of a subtraction procedure. The worrisome feature of this approach is that the logic of measurement comes close to being circular. The existence of two separate stores is assumed, not independently demonstrated, and the choice of measures of LTS essentially begs the question or at the very least makes an arbitrary assumption about the sources of output at different positions or after different retention intervals. Solving a single equation with two unknowns is necessarily a bootstrap operation, and measures flowing from such a solution have to be viewed with considerable reservations.

These difficulties should be borne in mind when we consider Glanzer's major conclusions regarding the capacity of STS, which hinge critically on the validity of the subtraction measures. He found the capacity of the store limited to "about three items." Such a low estimate was bound to strain credulity, if for no other reason than because "it is incompatible with what we know about understanding grammatical utterances" (121, p. 91). Recently Glanzer & Razel (56) attempted to meet this criticism by showing that the capacity limitations (which they revised downward from about three to two) apply to units that may vary in length rather than to fixed elements such as phonemes, morphemes, or words. They found that the estimated number of units in STS remained constant at about two, regardless of whether the units were monosyllabic words, disyllabic words, compound words, cliché sentences, or unfamiliar sentences. It should be understood that the near invariance in the number of units represents the derived estimates, specifically the sums of the estimates for the last six serial positions. The actual data often show substantial differences in the level of recall except for the ubiquitous recency peak. The authors' conclusion is that the number of units held in STS is essentially fixed but that the size and complexity of the units can vary freely and may be as long as a complete sentence. Thus, the limited-capacity store can function effectively in linguistic processing.

The argument is not convincing. The phenomenon of chunking is hardly new. The recency peak is also here to stay, but whether it largely reflects the output of a distinct and separate system is something to be proved rather than postulated. What is most troublesome is the reconstruction of the fine grain of the memory system by means of a formula of highly dubious validity. The Waugh-Norman equation does yield numbers that are systematically related to the changing probabilities of recall as a function of serial position. It seems overly sanguine to reify these numbers into "real" units in a hypothetical store. One might well be pulled up short in pursuing this tack when he finds that this formula yields zero, and even negative, estimates of STS output for individual subjects. However that may be, this exercise still leaves unaltered the astounding claim that during the acquisition of a list of unrelated words the STS can hold only two such units.

Is the apparent evanescence of the contents of STS attributable to decay, displacement, or both? This once highly controversial question has not been debated much of late, undoubtedly because of the apparent difficulty of arriving at an experimental decision between the alternatives. Recently an ingenious new procedure developed by Reitman (145) has served to reopen the question. The innovation was to fill the interval between item presentation and test with an exacting tone detection task that would preclude verbal interference and at the same time minimize if not eliminate rehearsal. Thus one might come reasonably close to assessing the effects of the sheer passage of time on short-term retention. There was no forgetting over a 15-sec period under this arrangement. Similar results were obtained by Shiffrin (165) in an extension of Reitman's experiment. The implication that a strictly nonverbal distractor task does not result in the loss of verbal items from STS has not unexpectedly been called into question. The objection was raised that Reitman's signal-detection task was not sufficiently demanding to prevent some recycling of the material held in memory. With a tone-shadowing task considered to be more demanding, progressive declines in retention were observed; furthermore, interpolated pursuit-rotor activity led to a reduction of the terminal peak in free recall (199). The investigators concluded that two different factors may contribute to the loss of items from STS: (*a*) a diversion of attention from the to-be-remembered items which may be effected by nonverbal distractors, and (*b*) the similarity between the items in store and the interpolated materials which produces difficulty in retrieval. Thus the standoff between decay (either in its pristine sense or in the guise of diversion of attention) and interference will have to continue for a while longer.

In general, there has been little systematic progress in the exploration of the mechanisms responsible for forgetting from STS (whatever its capacity). Glanzer has remained a staunch defender of an essentially pure displacement principle. In his free-recall experiments, the similarity between interpolated and list items appears to have no effect (55). To draw a strong conclusion that the similarity between the target items and the interpolated activity is irrelevant obviously flies in the face of a great deal of evidence (which need not be enumerated here) that both phonemic and semantic similarity significantly influence the amount of retroactive interference in short-term memory situations. Glanzer (54) suggests that such results may reflect effects on LTS rather than STS. The same argument has been made about proactive interference in short-term memory, with the aid of the Waugh-Norman subtraction formula (34). Whether one accepts this argument depends to a considerable extent on his faith in the precision of the measurement of STS by subtraction formulas.

As in the work on long-term retention of lists, the understanding of the conditions and mechanisms of proactive inhibition (PI) in short-term memory appears to be decreasing rather than increasing. Earlier there was good reason to believe that such principles as unlearning and spontaneous recovery were directly applicable to the explanation of proactive losses in short-term memory, and the Brown-Peterson situation in particular (86). It has now been shown that there may be little or no unlearning of successive items under the very conditions that lead to a progressive buildup of PI. The most direct demonstration of this fact comes from a study by Dillon (44), whose subjects were required to recall their previous responses at various stages of a critical trial (either before the presentation of the new item or at one of several points during the retention interval). There was no evidence for either unlearning or spontaneous recovery. Absence of unlearning can also be inferred from the substantial proactive facilitation that is found when items are repeated after a lag of several trials (26). Repetition enhances recall more than does release from PI effected by a shift in taxonomic category (63).

The effectiveness of competition at recall as a determinant of short-term PI has also been questioned. One line of evidence is that recall does not increase when the subject has the preceding items before him at the time of test (25, 44). This fact does not, however, constitute as strong an argument against competition as might appear at first blush. The actual presence of the prior items may enhance their competitive potential. The situation is reminiscent of the negative effects of list cues in free recall (155). However, these results do raise questions about the importance of the role played by failures of item differentiation. If not unlearning and competition, then what? There are several other possibilities. One recurrent suggestion is retrieval failure. For example, in experiments on release from PI, the effectiveness of item-specific retrieval cues may decline as members of the same class follow each other; when there is a shift in class, the power of the most recent retrieval cue is restored. Gardiner, Craik & Birtwistle (52) have presented evidence that appears to favor this interpretation. When the shift is from one subset to another within a broad category, release from PI occurs only when the name of the new subset is presented either at input or at the time of recall. Retrieval difficulties are implicated because of the effectiveness of a subset cue that is first introduced in the test phase.

It is not clear to what extent such findings can be generalized to situations in which successive items do not belong to a circumscribed category. There is not enough evidence to attribute the buildup of PI for all types of materials to the progressive weakening of retrieval cues. The explanation would soon falter or become ad hoc. When successive items do not fall into normative groupings, we usually do not know what the retrieval cues might be, or whether it is even useful to think in terms of changes in the effectiveness of such cues. The possible role of retrieval cues in the buildup of, and release from, PI must also be examined in the light of several demonstrations that tests of recognition show changes in performance over trials quite similar to those observed with recall (25, 59, 60, 64, 139). If one assumes that retrieval does not play a critical part in recognition, then the implication is that PI reflects deficiencies of storage or perhaps forgetting during storage in the sense of Posner's (141) "acid bath" hypothesis. If the proposition that recognition is relatively retrieval-free is rejected (181), the inference obviously does not follow.

The available recognition data have failed to yield conclusive information about the role of item differentiation in PI. Previous items have been found to be more powerful distractors than new ones in some cases (60, 64) but not in others (59, 139). The total picture remains blurred. A search for a single locus or single mechanism of proaction is not likely to prove any more successful for short-term retention than it has in research on long-term retention of lists. Analyses in terms of conventional principles of interference have begun to yield diminishing returns. Among alternative hypotheses the possibility mentioned by Dillon (44) that PI may reflect the progressive degradation of the quality of learning deserves especial attention. The same possibility has been brought to the fore in studies of PI in the long-term retention of paired-associate lists. The principles of PI may in the end turn out to be the same in short-term and long-term retention but are likely to include mechanisms not now encompassed by theories of interference.

The Moral of the Story of Dual-Process Theory

The moral one may well draw from the history of dual-process theory is that there are important risks in the rush to modeling which has of late been so characteristic of the field of memory. What happened in retrospect is that certain observed phenomena of memory, e.g. the forgetting of a single trigram in a matter of seconds, looked strikingly different from those typically recorded under conventional experimental arrangements. The difference in appearances was so great that there was a strong disposition to look for other evidence implying the operation of qualitatively different processes in spite of the obvious objections to postulating discontinuities of function.[2] The computer-oriented nomenclature of information processing was there, waiting to be used, and the processes were soon translated into structures. Protestations to the contrary notwithstanding, the structures became reified. Counting the exact number of units or slots in STS signifies nothing less.

Now a structural model with bins connected by arrows is potentially as useful as any other theoretical framework, i.e. it should be judged by its heuristic value. Fair enough. In practice, however, structural models appear to entail risks that are endemic to them: premature precision, internal fission, and proliferation. Once an STS was proposed, its capacity, the characteristics of the units held in it and displaced from it, and its temporal parameters had to be specified. As we have suggested, the measurement procedures have tended to be circular and to involve arbitrary assumptions. Once the estimates are made, however, the validity of the formulas is rarely questioned, and the numbers are taken literally; that is premature precision. As for internal fission, it occurs predictably when new or unexpected findings have to be accommodated. It is easy enough to add another box and pair of arrows, for example an intermediate-term as well as short-term and long-term memory, or to subdivide the store into compartments for different modalities. The data promoting internal fission are often important, but patching up a flow chart does not really aid in understanding and explaining them. Finally, there is proliferation. Diagrams representing the successive stages of information processing are easy to construct, and there are no apparent rules delimiting the kinds of structures that one can incorporate into them. So the number of general models inevitably grows apace, to say nothing of specialized models for such processes as recall and recognition. For a sampling see pages 21, 118, 205, 241, 347, 377, and 382 in *Models of Human Memory* (130). There would be more if some of the models had not been described verbally. Variety may be the spice of life and heterodoxy an essential condition of scientific progress, but modeling license does contribute to theoretical chaos. The time may have come to unsheath Occam's razor once more: Models should not be multiplied beyond necessity.

If this picture is somewhat overdrawn, it was done deliberately to call attention to the dangers of the theoretical particularism which has been rife in the study of learning and memory. We have traced the source of this trend to the formulation of two-store models. The retreat from such models began as their assumptions were subjected to increasingly searching scrutiny. The implications of these developments are well worth pondering.

[2] We have not considered the results obtained with brain-damaged patients which continue to be cited as evidence for dual-process theory (201). The existing data do not impress us as unequivocal; more important, extrapolations from pathological deficits to the structure of normal memory are of uncertain validity. We must also note a temptation to reverse the argument and to identify STS and LTS on the basis of comparisons between normal subjects and patients (8, p. 181).

LEVELS OF PROCESSING AND DIMENSIONS OF ENCODING

Levels of Processing

In what promises to be a very influential paper, Craik & Lockhart (36) suggested that the broad range of phenomena which had motivated the postulation of multiple stores can be conceptualized more adequately in terms of levels of processing. The guiding assumption is that the presentation of any stimulus initiates a series or hierarchy of processing stages which can be graded along a continuum of depth. Sensory analysis and semantic-cognitive elaboration define the end points of this continuum. Subsequent retention is a function of depth. "Thus, memory, too, is viewed as a continuum from the transient products of sensory analyses to the highly durable products of semantic-associative operations" (p. 676). Regardless of depth, information can be maintained in memory by being recirculated at a currently activated level of processing. Recirculating means keeping the items, as analyzed up to a given point, in consciousness and is essentially synonymous with the maintenance rehearsal of dual-process theory. The recycling operation is designated as Type I processing and defines primary memory. By contrast, Type II processing occurs when the analysis proceeds to a new and deeper level. At any one level, Type I processing will not improve retention beyond that characteristic of that level, only Type II processing will. The depth to which analysis proceeds and the amount of material that can be encompassed are constrained by the limited capacity of a central processor which can be deployed flexibly "to one of several levels in one of several encoding dimensions" (p. 679). The limited-capacity processor expends its energy economically and initiates maintenance rehearsal at a relatively shallow level, e.g. the acoustic-articulatory one, when that is sufficient to satisfy the task demands. The length of the sequences that can be maintained depends on their compatibility with existing cognitive structures: the greater the consistency, the more readily the components can be grouped or chunked for purposes of processing.

One apparent advantage of this approach is that observed differences between short-term and long-term memory can be referred to the flexible mode of operation of the information-processing system. There are no longer any fixed expectations about either the number or the characteristics of units that should be retained under the experimental arrangements used to define short-term and long-term memory. However, the way in which the flexible central processor is believed to advance to successively deeper levels of analysis, and the conditions which are assumed to be conducive to maintenance rehearsal, are fully consistent with the functional differences previously attributed to STS and LTS. Findings which have created fundamental difficulties for dual-process interpretations, such as the lack of correlation between the sheer amount of rehearsal and subsequent retention, can be readily referred to the failure of stimulus analysis to have reached a sufficient level of depth. And the critical serial position effects in immediate and delayed recall can be handled easily by assuming that depth of encoding varies with the position of an item in the list.

Craik and Lockhart view their approach not as a full-fledged theory (for example, problems of retrieval are omitted from consideration at this point) but rather as a conceptual framework for research on memory. It should be considered in this spirit. The analysis is timely and significant to the extent that it makes a convincing case for an interpretation of the apparent differences between short-term and long-term memory without recourse to a structural two-store model. The argument makes it clear that the existing facts do not compel us to accept as axiomatic a dichotomy of nonsensory memories with structural properties. It is less clear, however, that the fundamental issue of continuity versus discontinuity of memory functions has been resolved satisfactorily. Does the discontinuity not surface once more in the guise of stages of processing? The levels of processing evolve in stages, but the authors assure us that they envisage these levels as a continuum of analysis. But if there is a true continuum, then the identification of separate stages is either impossible or arbitrary. When we see the scheme applied to specific phenomena, we come away with the impression that the successive levels follow each other in a stop-and-go fashion. Recycling can be initiated at any of the postsensory stages. Thus there are in effect qualitative discontinuities in memory; for example what is retained may be primarily acoustic rather than semantic information. The final level that will be reflected in retention is not, however, correlated in a one-to-one fashion with processing time; the authors recognize that analysis does not necessarily proceed in an orderly sequence from superficial to deep. Why then insist on time-dependent stages? The basic conclusion that emerges from the analysis is that information can be processed in many different ways, and what is remembered depends on the kind of processing that has occurred. That sounds like a truism, but it was probably an important truism to restate at this point. The arrangement of levels of encoding in temporal lockstep appears to be a continuing concession to the claim that there are systematic changes in mode of encoding as one moves from short-term to long-term memory. Yet, given the ambiguous implications of confusion errors, there is no hard evidence for this claim. It has yet to be shown that under normal circumstances an individual hearing a word will process and recycle only the sound without knowing what the word means. What we are questioning here is not the assumption that processing takes time, and that the more diversified the processing the more time is required; it is rather the more or less orderly progression from surface to depth that is at issue.

The normative concept of depth is likely to prove troublesome. It is taken for granted that the semantic-associative elaborations represent the deeper levels of analysis. That assumption has face validity when one thinks of associative or free recall. But there are situations in which the processing of other features, particularly of frequency and contextual information, becomes critical. Much of the current work on recognition points to this conclusion. Must the definition of depth then change with task requirements? Is "optimal processing" different from processing to maximal depth? It should also not be taken as self-evident that trace strength and durability increase directly with depth of analysis. It is true that there is some evidence that acoustic features are forgotten more rapidly than semantic ones (e.g. 5, 24), but the differences are not very large and it is not clear whether they are a function of trace strength or variations in interpolated interference. It had once seemed intuitively obvious that there is an inverse relation between meaningfulness and rate of forgetting, but this expectation has not been borne out empirically.

If a conceptualization in terms of levels of processing is to provide a productive framework for research on memory, we must ask how likely it is to generate experimentally testable hypotheses. The very flexibility which is attributed to the processing system carries with it the danger of circularity. The specific danger is that one would be tempted to infer what the level of processing was from the results of retention tests. But such evidence is obviously post hoc. What is needed is to bring the level of encoding under experimental control and to observe the effects on retention. Craik and Lockhart point out that the incidental learning paradigm permits one to do just that. The experimenter can determine how the subject processes the material by his choice of orienting task. They cite numerous studies which show that amount of incidental memory is directly related to the depth of processing required by the orienting task. This line of evidence bears closer scrutiny.

TYPE OF PROCESSING AND INCIDENTAL MEMORY   In an extensive series of experiments, Jenkins and his associates (75–77, 82, 178, 196) have marshalled evidence for the proposition that, regardless of instructions to learn, the amount of retention is determined by whether or not the subject engages in semantic processing. Other investigators have likewise concluded that incidental memory is a function of the degree of semantic processing involved in the orienting task (45, 80, 118). For purposes of examining some of the interpretative problems that remain to be resolved, we confine ourselves to a consideration of the studies of Jenkins' group. In these experiments, the typical pattern of results is that incidental subjects performing a semantic task recall as much as those who perform the same task and also expect to be tested for recall; furthermore, there is no difference between these two groups and a control group that is simply instructed to learn the words and does not perform an orienting task. When the orienting task is nonsemantic, retention is considerably lower, and equally so for subjects who do, and subjects who do not, expect to be tested for recall. The conclusion is that the only critical determinant of recall is the type of processing, and this holds true regardless of the difficulty of the orienting task.

This conclusion is very strong, but there are some rather troublesome features of both the experimental manipulations and the results which call for caution. The first concerns the a priori differentiation between semantic and nonsemantic tasks. The semantic task used most often was rating the stimulus words as to their pleasantness or unpleasantness; in other cases the frequency of usage of the words was rated, or a word that could be appropriately paired with the target item was generated. A variety of nonsemantic orienting tasks was devised to induce the subject to "treat the word as an object without considering its semantic characteristics (or meaning)" (82, p. 92). The activities falling under this heading included checking for the presence of certain letters in the words, estimating the number of letters, and producing rhymes. Also included in this category were syntactic tasks, e.g. determining the part of speech and deciding whether a given word did or did not fit into a particular sentence frame. How valid is the classification of the tasks? Few would be disposed to deny that checking for the presence of certain letters need not involve processing the meaning of a word, but credulity is strained when the same assertion is made about identification of parts of speech and judgments of the appropriateness of a word for a sentence frame. On the other hand, why is judging the frequency of a word a deeply semantic activity? One does not have to think very much about the meaning of a word to decide whether or not it is a familiar "object." The point of these carping comments is that "semantic processing" is a concept lacking in precision and invoked on the strength of the investigator's intuition which may not be shared by others. The same applies to the delimitation of situations in which such processing presumably does not occur.

In any event, there is every reason to worry about the implications of the results because the experimental manipulations work, as it were, too well. Specifically, there are two warning signs. First, subjects forewarned about the test of retention do no better than purely incidental learners, even when the orienting tasks are nonsemantic. That is an unusual result which is at variance with most of the available evidence (112). Surely the instructed subjects should have engaged in at least a modicum of semantic processing. Second, the subject's ability to grasp and store the semantic characteristics of a word is apparently so great that it is not affected by normal limitations on processing capacity. That is implied by the finding that retention is not significantly lowered when the subject must perform a nonsemantic as well as a semantic task. (Actually, the difference is always in the expected direction and in some cases sizeable.)

The results may not be nearly as decisive as the investigators supposed. A question that invites careful examination is whether there are systematic differences between the supposedly semantic and nonsemantic tasks. One potentially important difference is that the semantic tasks call for subjective ratings which cannot be either right or wrong. Most of the nonsemantic tasks, on the other hand, require the subject to make a response the correctness of which can be evaluated objectively. The subjects can monitor their own performance and are likely to do so. To put it somewhat differently, the nonsemantic tasks involve a determinate amount of information reduction whereas the semantic ones do not. Now it is known that in short-term memory situations retention declines in an orderly fashion as the amount of information to be reduced by performance of the interpolated task increases (141). The assertion that it is the degree of semantic processing which constitutes the only, or the critical, difference between the two classes of orienting tasks remains, therefore, to be validated. If the processing demands of the orienting task are sufficiently great, the absence of differences between instructed and uninstructed subjects would become understandable. As for the failure of concurrent tasks to reduce the effectiveness of semantic processing, reconciliation with other evidence that leads to the opposite conclusion is clearly needed. Quite recently, Mandler & Worden (104) presented evidence which they interpreted as demonstrating that the performance of a subsidiary task does significantly impair subsequent recall and recognition. (It is interesting to note that these authors classified the identification of words as nouns or verbs as a semantic processing task!) The actual data obtained by Jenkins and his associates also bear careful reexamination. In one relevant study, six out of six comparisons showed higher recall when a semantic task was performed by itself rather than in conjunction with a nonsemantic task (196, experiments I and III). More evidence will be needed before it becomes reasonable to conclude that semantic activity is immune to the constraints of limited processing capacity.

The Multiple Dimensions of Word Encoding

Few students of memory today would be willing to assert in the manner of Gertrude Stein that a word is a word is a word. On the contrary, they are becoming increasingly impressed with the multitude of features and attributes which the learner can perceive and encode when a word is presented to him. What remains uncertain is which and how many of such characteristics are processed and encoded on the occasion of a brief presentation during a learning experiment. As we have seen, Craik and Lockhart would have us think in terms of a sequence of successive encoding steps, with the sequence subject to termination at any convenient stage. A very different picture is painted by Wickens (202) on the basis of his programmatic series of experiments in which release from PI was effected by shifts in item characteristics along many diverse dimensions. He concludes that in the "split second" while a word is processed by an individual "it is granted a locus on many . . . dimensions or aspects—encoded, in short, in a multiplicity of ways" (202, p. 12). These dimensions are both semantic and nonsemantic, and Wickens views their activation as essentially simultaneous and automatic. As the test of release from PI continues to be applied, the number of encoding dimensions that appear to be activated during the presentation of a word keeps growing. Some recent additions include sense impressions (205), syntactic features (65), language of presentation to bilingual subjects (58), and phonological features (29). There are also some puzzles such as the asymmetry of modality shifts which is observed under some conditions but not others (71–73, 92).

The conclusion that all the dimensions for which release from PI has been observed are simultaneously encoded during the presentation of a word can be questioned. As Underwood (187) has pointed out, there are potentially serious objections to such an inference. First, it is doubtful that all the attributes that have been investigated are independent. However, even if some of them are tied together, an impressively large number of independently encoded characteristics would be likely to remain. A more basic question is raised by Underwood's suggestion that the experimental arrangements of the release experiment carry an instruction to the subject to encode successive items along a particular dimension. That is, the critical dimension is primed; for example, treating the items as members of a specific taxonomic class becomes more and more likely as one instance after another is presented. To the extent that priming occurs, the number of attributes that are encoded automatically and simultaneously may be greatly overestimated. One cannot, therefore, add together all the features that have been shown to be effective in separate release experiments and thus reconstruct the total ensemble of encodings that are activated simultaneously. It is altogether reasonable to suppose that more than one feature of a word is registered, and there is some evidence that the release effect is greater when there is a shift with respect to two characteristics rather than one (203). What the limits of multiple encoding might be under normal circumstances remains uncertain.

Encoding of Phonological Attributes

The role of phonological attributes in the acquisition of lists of words has begun to receive systematic attention only fairly recently. There may have been a disposition to take it for granted that such attributes are of little significance in long-term memory, in accordance with the assumption of two-store theories. There is now abundant evidence that such an assumption would have been incorrect. Perhaps the best documentation is contained in a programmatic series of studies by Nelson and his associates (summarized in 126) in which the ordinal position effects of letter duplication were carefully examined. The essential finding is that the magnitude of such effects is greatest in the initial, second greatest in the terminal, and least in the medial, positions of stimulus words. The direction of the effects depends on task requirements. In paired-associate learning, where stimulus discrimination is essential, difficulty of acquisition conforms to this pattern. On the other hand, when recall is free, the ranking of conditions is reversed; the same is true when the position of elements shared by stimulus and response terms is manipulated in paired-associate learning. Nelson suggests that words are processed as phonological sequences, essentially like miniature serial lists. The ease with which access is gained to this code varies with the serial position of the elements, with the initial position dominant. Response recall is facilitated by the presence of overlapping features, whereas the associative stage of learning is delayed. An interesting recent finding is that the typical ordinal position effect is present during the acquisition of pairs of concrete as well as abstract words, even when the former are learned under instruction to generate interacting images (127). The implication is that the imaginal attributes and phonological features are processed independently. There is little doubt that phonological similarity can play an important role even when familiar words are used as the learning materials. Evidence obtained in studies of transfer (97, 204) and false recognition (e.g. 38, 128, 158) fully supports this conclusion.

Are Words Stored When Sentences Are Encoded?

We have been discussing the encoding of individual words in the context of list learning. This may be the appropriate place to mention the hypothesis, which has gained some popularity, that when individuals are exposed to interrelated sentences, they may not encode and store individual strings of words at all but rather "wholistic semantic ideas" that represent the total propositional content of the sentences. This hypothesis was advanced by Bransford & Franks (23, 49). The individual sentences presented to their subjects contained from one to three atomic propositions which were drawn from a complex integrated statement that comprised four such components. On a subsequent test of recognition the confidence with which the subjects recognized a sentence was a direct function of the number of atomic propositions contained in it. As long as a test sentence was consistent with the total integrated idea, it did not make any difference whether that particular sentence had actually been presented or not. Thus the full four-proposition sentence received the highest confidence ratings even when it had not been presented. Test sentences which were inconsistent with the total idea were readily rejected. This pattern of results was taken to imply that unified semantic representations reflecting the total complex ideas were stored in memory; recognition then depends on the propositional overlap between the stored representation and the test sentence. Subsequent work has served to cast doubt on the conclusion, at least in its strong form. The strength of the relation between recognition and the number of component propositions in a test sentence was shown to depend on instructions. This relation is attenuated when the recognition decision is based on identity of meaning rather than on the actual prior occurrence of a test sentence (84). Subjects are able to recognize component propositions to which they have been exposed, even though they may be uncertain whether they heard them alone or in conjunction with other components. Furthermore, as Anderson & Bower (3, pp. 347 ff.) have demonstrated, the difficulty of discriminating between old and new sentences is predictable on the basis of the overlap in amount of contextual information attached to target and distractor sentences. The discrimination between old and new sentences is improved when a forced-choice recognition procedure is used. Finally, when simpler elements (letters and numbers) are used in a formal arrangement corresponding to that used in the semantic studies, it is found that subjects can abstract the rules but also retain specific items (146). It is clearly premature to conclude that specific verbal information is not stored when general linguistic ideas are abstracted from the input.

THE VARIABILITY AND SPECIFICITY OF ENCODING

We have used the concept of encoding freely without stopping to define it. That is characteristic of much contemporary writing on learning and memory. References to encoding are ubiquitous because it is taken as axiomatic that verbal inputs are somehow selectively processed or transformed before they are stored in memory. For purposes of the discussion that follows it is useful to examine the various connotations of encoding explicitly. A valuable classification of the types of encoding that are assumed to occur has been provided by Bower (21): (a) selection—a component is selected out of a complex pattern; (b) rewriting—an input is translated into another format, e.g. a sequence of visual symbols is transformed into a verbal description; (c) componential description—a nominal item such as a word is registered as a list or complex of attributes or features; (d) elaboration—additions are made to the nominal input in order to transform it and render it more memorable, e.g. natural language mediators (142).

The basic question of interest to the investigator of memory is how these different kinds of encodings influence acquisition and retention. Demonstrations that some type of encoding, such as the use of natural language mediators, is useful under some circumstances (119) does not carry us very far theoretically. (The evidence in support of this widely made claim is not very impressive.) The theoretical implications assume more fundamental importance when relationships between systematic characteristics of encoding and subsequent retrieval and recognition are considered. Two such characteristics are the variability and the specificity of encoding.

Encoding Variability

The principle of encoding variability was developed by Martin (106, 108) in the context of associative learning and applied by him principally to the analysis of problems of transfer and interference. The essential argument is that the encoding of a nominal stimulus (A) has some probability of varying from one occasion to the next. Since associations (A-B) are formed to stimuli-as-encoded, variability retards acquisition. As the encodings stabilize, so does acquisition performance. Encoding variability becomes a positive factor when a new response must be attached to an old stimulus (A-D). The guiding assumption here is that two different responses cannot be attached to the same stimulus-as-encoded. A failure to change encodings results in negative transfer and unlearning. When both B and D must be recalled, success in retrieval will depend on the probabilities of sampling the encodings specific to each response.

The idea of encoding variability has also been applied in a quite different way, namely in contrasting the effects on the probability of recall of multiple as compared with single encodings of an item (115). Stated in its simplest terms, the proposition is that multiple encodings entail multiple retrieval cues which can provide access to the to-be-remembered item at the time of recall. Hence there should be a direct relation between the number of different encodings and the probability of recall of an item. One way in which encoding variability may be induced is by presenting an item at different times or in varied contexts. Thus this argument has become of major interest in the many current investigations of the differences between massed and spaced repetitions. particularly in free recall.

THE SPACING EFFECT IN FREE RECALL   It has been shown many times, and no longer needs to be referenced, that recall is higher when repetitions are spaced rather than massed. Furthermore, it has been found in some, but not all, studies that the beneficial effects of spacing increase as a function of the lag between successive repetitions. (Some of the possible reasons for the discrepant findings regarding the effects of lag are discussed in 115.) Several explanations of the spacing effect have been proposed (cf 17), but, as measured by the sheer number of studies, the encoding variability hypothesis appears to have engaged the interest of the majority of investigators.

The explanation of the superiority of distributed practice (DP) over massed practice (MP) in free recall took its point of departure from the assumption that the formation of subjective units facilitates retrieval. Given this assumption, the hypothesis was formulated by Melton (115, p. 605) as follows:

The prediction of the beneficial effects of DP, and the gradation of this beneficial effect as a function of lag, is obtained by assuming, first, that the coding of a word in two different subjective units (or in a larger subjective unit) increases the cues or the access routes to its retrieval, and second, that as the lag between two or more occurrences of a word increases, the word contexts in which it occurs become less and less correlated (more independent) and the total number of different cues to its retrieval increases.

Note that the basic assumption that is made here questions the generality of another principle that underlies much of the analysis of organizational processes in free recall, namely, that successful retrieval depends on the development of consistent, rather than variable, higher-order units. What little evidence there is indicates that the incorporation of an item into more than one grouping during successive presentations does not in fact aid free recall and indeed may impair it (22, 211). However, the situation may be different under conditions of spaced presentation during a single study trial.

The encoding-variability interpretation of the MP-DP effect has two related testable implications: (a) the lag effect should be eliminated if variability can be induced in the encoding of all items regardless of spacing of repetitions; (b) the effect should likewise be eliminated if variable encoding of repeated items is minimized. An early experiment by Madigan (100) was based on this logic. To control encoding, each item was accompanied by a cue during presentation. When an item was repeated, the cue either remained the same or was changed. In the former case, the encodings of all repeated items should have remained constant, in the latter case they should have varied. Unfortunately, a lag effect was observed in free recall under both treatments. It should be noted, however, that the conditions of encoding were manipulated by means of item-specific cues, whereas Melton's original formulation had emphasized the influence of the verbal context created by preceding items. The majority of subsequent studies have been based on the same rationale as Madigan's investigation. Cued as well as uncued recall has been used, but for present purposes we need be concerned only with the latter since results obtained with cued recall do not bear directly on the proposed explanation of the MP-DP differences in free recall.

Numerous investigators have taken advantage of the existence of homographs to control encoding, manipulating the contexts in which the homographs were repeated (sentences or preceding items) so as to induce either the same or a different interpretation of these ambiguous words. The results are so inconsistent as to be utterly perplexing, and there would be little point in a detailed review. Suffice it to say that there is support for a variety of incompatible conclusions: (a) controlled encoding neither influences the level of recall nor does it attenuate the lag effect (83); (b) controlled encoding does produce substantial differences in recall and does attenuate the lag effect (53); (c) there is a lag effect when encoding is forced to remain the same, but not when it is caused to vary (111). This pattern has also been observed on a test of recognition (208). So much for homographs.

In other studies, nonhomographs were used and the sentence context varied, bringing to light additional problems; for example, differential encoding is said to eliminate the lag effect only when the subject's rehearsal pattern is strictly controlled (40). With other materials, the effectiveness of a second encoding has been described as being contingent on the forgetting of the first (183), but so far we have not been able to figure out how the subject ends up having the benefit of two retrieval routes under such circumstances.

Another approach to the explanation of the MP-DP effect promises to yield more palpable results. The effect might not reflect an advantage of DP but rather a deficit under MP (185). Perhaps the subject spends less time processing a repeated item under massed than under distributed conditions. Direct confirmation of this hypothesis was obtained when subjects were allowed to pace themselves during the presentation of a long list containing both massed and distributed repetitions (164). However, internal analyses showed that the differences in recall could not be attributed entirely to the variations in exposure time. Some of the difference that remains unaccounted for may reflect differential rehearsal after the second repetition. The opportunity for rehearsals between presentations is directly related to lag; furthermore, the number of rehearsals after the second presentation has been shown to increase as a function of lag (154). Such bread-and-butter types of explanations may yet carry us well forward in understanding the MP-DP effect.

Before we conclude this section on encoding variability, we return briefly to the evidence obtained in studies of transfer. The results and conclusions are not appreciably more clear-cut than with reference to the MP-DP effect. The idea that transfer should be profoundly influenced by the degree to which there are changes in the encodings of nominal stimuli is eminently reasonable. In particular, negative transfer under paradigms such as A-B, A-D and A-B, A-Br should be capable of being reduced or eliminated if the common A term is appropriately recoded during the acquisition of the second task. Yet substantial interference under these conditions is the rule. One reason for this state of affairs seems to be that subjects are not disposed to recode stimuli but rather prefer to retain their old encodings. When compound stimuli with distinctive components are used, a shift in functional cue sometimes occurs under conditions of negative transfer (116) but often it does not (57, 161). The evidence is mixed as to whether a shift is necessarily beneficial (140, 206). Subjects may be conservative because in the long run they do better, or at least as well, working through associative interference with a familiar cue than trying to develop an entirely new encoding. The discouraging results obtained with compound stimuli, where the possibilities of recoding are obvious, do not tell us much about what happens when the nominal stimuli are integrated units such as words. Here there is little or no hard evidence for spontaneous recoding in the transfer phase. If recoding occurs but is apt to be so subtle as to escape detection by available methods (107), the matter has to be held in abeyance for the time being.

Is encoding variability a basic phenomenon of learning and memory? No one knows for certain. The alleged phenomenon is a highly subjective one, and the evidence has, to say the least, been elusive. Yet we expect no diminution in the number of ingenious and complex experiments designed to capture the elusive variability on the wing. A future reviewer might well say, "They sought it with thimbles, they sought it with care; they pursued it with forks and hope . . ."

Encoding Specificity

We introduce this section with a well-known quotation from an article by Thomson & Tulving: "No cue, however strongly associated with the TBR [to-be-remembered] item or otherwise related to it, can be effective unless the TBR item is specifically encoded with respect to that cue at the time of storage" (177, p. 255). Before we consider the evidence bearing on this hypothesis, it is important to make clear under what conditions an item would be considered to have been specifically encoded with respect to a particular cue. This is not to be taken to mean that the learner habitually stores a potential retrieval cue with each item, internally generating paired associates, as it were. The assertion is rather that a retrieval cue will be effective only when the stored information includes the relation between the target word and the cue. Thus *chair* will be an effective retrieval cue for *table* only if the information about the table-chair relationship has been stored at the time of input (182, p. 359). This information will not necessarily be part of the trace of *table* because retrieval is from the episodic rather than the semantic store (179). The table-chair relationship is a permanent part of semantic memory but may not be part of the trace in the episodic system laid down by a particular presentation of *table*.

The principle of encoding specificity, formulated within the framework of the distinction between semantic and episodic memory, is put squarely in opposition to the "generation-recognition models." According to the latter, a retrieval cue initiates the search for, or generation of, potential responses. A response that is recognized, on the basis of contextual or occurrence information, is then given overtly. This position has been espoused by Bahrick (9–11), who found that the effectiveness of a retrieval cue first introduced at the time of recall could be expressed as the joint probability of successful generation and correct recognition of the target item. Thus recall is conceptualized as a two-stage process, involving both retrieval and recognition (2, 88). Tulving & Thomson (182) question two basic assumptions of the two-stage position: (*a*) that words have "transsituational identity," i.e. unique representations in memory; and (*b*) that the presentation of a word results in immediate access to its location in memory. Neither of these assumptions is acceptable if the encoding of words is context-specific and storage is in an episodic system.

There are three important experiments by Tulving and Thomson which, singly and in combination, have been interpreted as supporting the principle of encoding specificity. These studies are well known and widely cited, and a brief recapitulation of the major findings should be sufficient here. 1. When TBR items are presented in the context of weakly associated cues, recall cued by these weak cues is considerably higher than uncued recall. By contrast, recall cued by strong normative associates is no better than uncued recall (177). 2. On tests of recognition, either additions to or subtractions from the context present at the time of recognition impair performance. Context here refers to the presence of associates of the target item (181). 3. Items recalled in a context different from that at input frequently fail to be recognized. Words are again presented in the presence of weak cues. Many of the target items are reproduced when subjects subsequently generate free associates to strong normative cues, but in a high proportion of the cases the target items fail to be recognized as members of the input list. In this situation cued recall is higher than recognition (182).

The theoretical issues raised by these results are fundamental indeed. It should not be surprising that they can be seen as open to different interpretations. In considering the ineffectiveness of strong cues after input in the presence of weak ones, we have to ask whether learning a pairwise contingency—in the presence of A respond with B—ipso facto entails the encoding of B with respect to A, in the sense that the semantic features of the target item (B) become assimilated to those of the cue (A). Suppose that does not happen to any significant extent. A strong normative associate (C) presented at the time of test may not facilitate, or may indeed hinder, recall simply by virtue of the fact that it is a new cue. It is known that failure to recognize a stimulus may lead to failure of recall. Furthermore, to the extent that the subject makes use of backward associations (B-A) to check on the correctness of potential responses (cf 209), the presence of the new cue may lead him to the erroneous rejection of target items. There is an obvious parallel here to the A-B, C-B paradigm of transfer where associative interference is observed with responses of high meaningfulness.

Similar questions arise with respect to the finding that many target items are not recognized when they are generated by the subjects under free-association instructions. Again there is a new cue, namely, the stimulus used to elicit the free associates. Thus erroneous rejection of target items becomes likely, for the reasons already mentioned. A complicating factor is that each target item had to be picked out from among four or six free associates given to the same test stimulus. The semantic similarity between generated targets and generated distractors was, therefore, probably quite high and the recognition task correspondingly difficult. Under these circumstances, one would expect subjects to adopt a stringent criterion in making their recognition decisions. There is no conclusive evidence on this point, but it is to be noted that in the study of Tulving and Thomson the raw hit rate was more than doubled when a forced-choice test of recognition was used. The implications of this study are sufficiently important to warrant a detailed consideration of all the factors that might be responsible for the reversal of the usual relation between recognition and recall. Whatever the outcome of further analyses may be, the fact that such a reversal can occur under some circumstances is of considerable theoretical interest.

The major interpretative problem stems from the operations used to effect changes in encoding between presentation and test. The thrust of the theoretical argument is that the encoding of the target item per se is profoundly influenced by the cognitive environment in which it appears. In the studies under discussion, the weak cues accompanying the target items at input constitute the cognitive environment. However, the experimental operations are essentially those of paired-associate learning and, especially after a series of set-inducing lists, emphasize pairwise contingencies. To the extent that encoding specificity lies in the information about these contingencies, the broad theoretical implications of the results would be changed.

We turn now to the effects of contextual changes on recognition. The original findings have been confirmed and extended by Thomson (176). Although there are exceptions, either the addition or the deletion of context reduces recognition performance. The presence or absence of a second item is viewed as constituting a cognitive environment which has a critical influence on the encoding of the target item. Would it be equally reasonable to say that the mode of presentation of an item—whether it appeared alone or in juxtaposition with another word—is one of the attributes of the input event that is stored? It is known that subjects remember other "extraneous" features of input events reasonably well, such as serial position and modality of presentation. When a recognition decision is difficult, the subject may rely on whatever information remains available about the physical conditions of the original presentation. There is some apparent support for this interpretation in Thomson's data: he found that the inclusion of both single items and pairs in the input list was a necessary condition of the impairment of recognition by addition of context. The same was not true for the deletion of context, but the interpretation of the latter results is complicated by the use of strongly associated pairs.

The demonstration of context effects is taken as evidence for the operation of retrieval processes in recognition. Recognition depends on access to the stored representation of the item as originally encoded. If at the time of test the encoding of the target differs substantially from that during input, the probability of access is correspondingly reduced. Thus retrieval would be involved since the "location" of the target item in memory must be found. The thrust of this argument is that words, qua strings of letters or sound sequences, do not occupy a fixed "location" in memory. (It is not clear whether this position has actually been advocated in an unqualified form by any two-stage theorist.) The effectiveness of contextual manipulations does not, however, seem to imply anything very definite about the immediacy or automaticity of access to stored representations of target items. If the encodings during input and at the time of test are sufficiently similar, no retrieval search may be necessary and access may be both immediate and automatic. In the everyday world one often experiences a sudden shock of recognition without previously engaging in retrieval operations.

There have been several demonstrations that the recognition of homographs depends on the relation between the semantic contexts in which such polysemous words are presented during input and at the time of test. Changes in context designed to induce different interpretations of the homograph impair recognition (99, 105). After seeing "strawberry jam" in the input list it is harder to recognize "jam" when confronted with "traffic jam" on the test rather than with the repetition of "strawberry jam" or "raspberry jam." The only surprising finding is that the effect of such manipulations is sometimes quite small, clearly implicating a context-free component of recognition learning (42). It has also been shown, perhaps not unexpectedly, that homographs studied as isolated words are more likely to be recognized when embedded in test sentences suggesting a common, rather than an uncommon, interpretation of the word (207). The implication of all these results is, of course, that homographs are encoded in a specific semantic sense. When "strawberry jam" is presented, the episodic trace contains information related to fruit preserves but not to traffic congestion. The problem would not arise were it not for the peculiar economy of English spelling. There should not have been any doubt that semantic as well as orthographic and phonemic information is stored when a word is presented. In contrast to what is true of other words, there is no relation between alternative meanings of homographs. Thus this case is too atypical to permit any broad generalizations about the role of retrieval in recognition.

IMAGERY

No discussion of coding processes would be complete without a section on the role of imagery in learning and retention. Regrettably, we find little to report about broad new developments. The empirical evidence for the effectiveness of imaginal encoding was reviewed thoroughly in Paivio's book (133). Since the appearance of the book, there has been a large number of new experiments demonstrating positive effects of rated imagery value and imagery instructions on performance in a great variety of tasks, ranging from the Brown-Peterson short-term memory situation to recall of meaningful sentences. There would be no point in enumerating them. Concreteness is better than abstractness and pictures are better than words. If one wants one good new reference for documenting these assertions, he can use the series of experiments reported by Paivio & Csapo (134). If anyone doubts that pictures are easy to remember, he should read a recent paper by Standing, entitled Learning 10,000 Pictures (174). This author concludes that the capacity of recognition memory for pictures has for all practical purposes no limits. It is also possible to report that, contrary to popular misconceptions, bizarre images and pictures are no better as memory aids than common ones (28, 124, 210).

Imagery value is found to have substantial effects in situations where one does not have very good reasons for expecting it. Verbal discrimination is a case in point. The effect has been repeatedly demonstrated, and an effort has been made to show that imagery exerts its influence independently of situational frequency (151-153). It remains uncertain what the source of the imagery effect is. One possibility is that correct alternatives receive more implicit rehearsals when they have high rather than low imagery value. Attempt to establish a direct relation between imagery value and subjective frequency in the context of verbal-discrimination studies led to inconclusive results (195).

While empirical demonstrations of the apparent power of imaginal encodings continue, theoretical analyses of the underlying processes are inching forward slowly at best. Paivio still favors a dual-encoding interpretation, but evidence for it remains circumstantial (e.g. 134). Begg (15, 16) has been arguing that imaginal encoding favors unitization and thus results in a reduction of memory load. For example, concreteness of the component items favors the recall of phrases; moreover, the pairs are recalled in an all-or-none manner. Little attention is paid in such discussion to the problem of decoding.

Increasing doubts are being expressed about the use of the concept of image as an explanatory construct. A thoughtful critique may be found in a recent article by Pylyshyn, who asks the question of "what the mind's eye tells the mind's brain"

(143). He argues that subjective experiences such as images may not play an essential causal role at all in psychological processes. "Cognition may be 'mediated' by something quite different from either pictures or words, different in fact from anything that can be observed from either within or without" (p. 4). Some abstract underlying representation must be postulated since one can move easily back and forth between pictures and words. In a similar vein, Anderson & Bower (3) reject the "mental-picture metaphor" and argue for conceptualizing what is stored in propositional terms. Imagery is seen as helpful because it favors the encoding of propositions that are effective for storage. What is clearly needed in this area of research is a sustained fresh look at the complex problems of conceptualization that arise in the interpretation of imagery effects. What is *not* needed is a continuing flow of demonstrations that performance is correlated with imagery value, and that instructions to use interacting images enhance recall. Since such investigations will undoubtedly continue to be carried out at a rapid rate, it is to be hoped at least that greater attention will be paid to potential confounding variables such as the correlation between lexical complexity and abstractness (89). Galbraith & Underwood (51) reported recently that abstract words are perceived as having higher frequency and as occurring in a greater variety of contexts than concrete ones. It is far too early to take it for granted that the only important difference between concrete and abstract words is the ease of imaginal encoding.

ORGANIZATION

The ultimate sign of the success of a theoretical idea is that it comes to be taken for granted as part of the current body of knowledge in a discipline. This is what has happened to the concept of organization in recall, although some investigators still seem to find it useful to document it anew. There is no longer a sharp confrontation between the organizational and associationistic points of view. Transition experiments have shown that the operations defining the development of organization and the establishment of associations shade into each other. Thus there are predictable transfer effects from free-recall to paired-associate learning which imply that the existence of higher-order units can significantly influence the development of associative relations between the members of such units (12, 13, 81, 150). It has been shown that a program based on an associative model can simulate output organization with some success (1).

There is still a great deal of exploration of the conditions conducive to the development of higher-order units and consistency of output order. The analysis is becoming increasingly fine-grained. Data keep coming in on the effectiveness of different kinds and numbers of categories (e.g. 14, 95) and the exact spacing of category instances within a list (19). The ways in which interresponse times reflect organization (85, 137) and the mechanisms of output interference in the recall of categorized lists (172) are being investigated. Studies such as these add useful information, but we do not discuss them in detail, and omit many others, because they do not seem to call for drastic changes in extant theoretical formulations. However, there have been some interesting theoretical developments in this area as well. We will consider two problem areas in which significant changes in the interpretation of organizational processes have recently emerged. These concern the mechanism of part-to-whole and whole-to-part transfer in free recall and the issue of independent vs dependent item storage.

The original demonstrations of negative part-to-whole and whole-to-part transfer were of considerable importance, not so much because the results were counterintuitive but because they gave support to a strong prediction derived from organization theory. The persistence of inappropriate higher-order units was shown to retard learning in the teeth of the advantage accruing from prior famil- iarization with the TBR items. It could also be inferred that for each list, short or long, there was an optimal organization that maximized speed of learning. Among the later findings serving to cast doubt on the organizational interpretation were the following: (*a*) informing the subject about the relation between the successive lists eliminated the apparent negative transfer effects (132); (*b*) there was positive rather than negative transfer when subjects were led to adopt a lenient criterion for responding (171); and (*c*) typical part-whole effects were obtained when successive lists were in fact identical (162). These results implicated difficulties of list dis- crimination rather than the carryover of inappropriate higher-order units as the source of negative transfer. That negative transfer occurs at the level of "list tagging" now appears to have been firmly established by Sternberg & Bower (175), who measured list identification as well as recall during the transfer phase. They show that their analysis can account satisfactorily for most of the existing transfer results.

A chronic thorn in the side of organization theorists has been Slamecka's (169) finding that cuing subjects with words from within the list failed to enhance free recall. This finding led him to the conclusion that organization is not a character- istic of trace storage. Recall becomes organized only by virtue of the adoption of a retrieval plan based on the subject's perception of the list. This argument was pressed home when Slamecka (170) found that in the recall of categorized lists cuing by specific instances from within the list served to increase access to cate- gories but not the recall of items within a category. Thus multiple cues were no more effective than single ones. The conclusion was that there is no growth of associative linkages among individual items within higher-order units. Subse- quent work served to make the theoretical issue even more acute: a negative relation was demonstrated between the number of instances presented as cues and the probability of recall of the remaining items (149, 155). As a consequence, a drastically revised picture of the retrieval process in the recall of organized lists is now being proposed. The essence of the argument is that the effective associations are not among the individual items but rather between the items and a retrieval cue (155) or control element (109, 149). The higher-order unit is seen as being organized hierarchically. Access to individual items is not horizontal but rather through the control element. Cuing by individual instances has a negative effect because the strength of the association of the presented items to the control element is increased by virtue of their presentation, and the accessibility of other items is correspondingly reduced. It is too early to evaluate the promise of this new theoretical formulation which does indeed represent a radical departure from established principles and is counter-intuitive in denying the operation of inter-item associations in recall. An early question to consider is how applicable this interpretative schema is to the recall of noncategorized lists. There is an obvious risk that principles derived from results obtained with categorized lists may prove to have limited generality.

ATTRIBUTES OF MEMORY

One of the most important new developments in our field is the steady growth of interest in the multiplicity of attributes that constitute the memory of an event. We remember not only what occurred, but also when, where, how frequently, and so on. This conception of memory was set forth in a seminal paper by Underwood (184), which also introduced the distinction between two major classes of attributes—those serving a discriminative function on the one hand and those instrumental in retrieval on the other. Research on attributes has been directed toward two general objectives: (*a*) to explore the range of attributes that are remembered and thereby to gain some understanding of the characteristics of the memory trace; (*b*) to determine by experimental analysis the function of specific attributes in the processes of remembering. We will illustrate these two approaches with the aid of some representative studies.

Repetition and the Representation of Events in Memory

How is the repeated experience of the same nominal event recorded in memory? The historical answer was, of course, that the trace of that event was strengthened. The results obtained in a programmatic series of studies by Hintzman and his associates on memory for attributes has provided decisive evidence against this conception. Some of the basic findings are these : (*a*) Subjects can judge with some accuracy not only the frequency with which items have been repeated within a list but also whether the repetitions were massed or spaced (67). (*b*) When a word is presented twice within a list, subjects retain information about the serial positions in which the repetitions occurred; moreover, the judgments of the two serial positions are essentially independent (68). (*c*) When repetitions of a word are distributed over two lists, the subjects retain information about the separate frequencies of occurrence in each of the target lists, although there is also some effect of overall frequency (68). (*d*) The identification of the list membership of an item is mediated by both frequency and recency information (70). Results such as these show clearly that information about the time of occurrence and the spacing of repeated events is retained in memory; information about spacing may be derived from implicit judgments of recency (69). It is apparent that these discriminations could not be based on the changes in strength of a single trace which is incremented by each repetition; the facts are more consistent with a multiple-trace hypothesis which holds that repeated occurrences of an event produce multiple representations in memory that preserve information about the temporal order of repetitions (cf 74).

Frequency Discrimination and Recognition

In a programmatic series of investigations, Underwood and his associates have accumulated an impressive body of data in support of the hypothesis that frequency discrimination is a basic mechanism of recognition. Information is stored about both the background frequency and the situational frequency of events. The former represents the record of long-term cumulative experience and the latter the number of occurrences in a specific context such as an experimental situation. (One may note a parallel here to the distinction between semantic and episodic memory.) In experiments on recognition, the discrimination between situational frequencies of 0 (distractors) and 1 (targets) is sufficient for a correct decision. The fact that accurate relative judgments of situational frequency can be made even when distractors have higher background frequencies than targets argues directly against trace strength as the basis of the discrimination and in favor of viewing frequency as a distinctive attribute of memory. Perhaps the most direct demonstration of the dependence of recognition on frequency discrimination is the close correspondence between frequency judgments and recognition decisions following a given verbal input (188). Absolute and relative frequency judgments are highly correlated and both predict the accuracy of recognition (194).

A number of interesting predictions have been derived from frequency theory and confirmed experimentally. One of these concerns the development of systematic changes in performance in the course of a recognition test. When the same distractor is used repeatedly with different targets, recognition accuracy declines progressively because the distractors gain situational frequency; correspondingly, performance improves when the same target is presented repeatedly, each time with a different distractor (191). While these results provided impressive support for the theory, they also made it clear that attributes other than frequency can serve to mediate recognition: performance failed to decline to a chance level when the situational frequency of the distractors exceeded that of the targets. Other factors, such as the semantic characteristics of individual words (cf 189), undoubtedly influence recognition decisions. However, it is also a fact that the learner is remarkably sensitive to variations in situational frequency. For example, the frequency that accrues to the syllables of input words is reflected in the error probabilities when the syllables are subsequently combined into new words on the recognition test (193). But there are also important limitations on the individual's ability to store and utilize information about the situational frequency of specific items. Thus the presence of conceptually related items in a list leads to the overestimation of the frequencies of individual words, probably because the subject is unable to differentiate between presented frequencies and those produced by displaced rehearsals (163).

The frequency theory of verbal discrimination learning continues to receive impressive empirical support. Study after study shows that performance in a verbal discrimination task reflects directly the relative frequencies that accrue, through either overt or covert processing, to the correct and incorrect alternatives. Other factors undoubtedly play a part; as in the case of recognition, performance often fails to deteriorate as severely as it should when discrimination on the basis of frequency can be assumed to be difficult or impossible (e.g. 192). What these other factors might be remains uncertain. The hypothesis that associations incidentally formed between the members of pairs play a significant causal role in verbal discrimination learning (50) can now be ruled out on the basis of a number of critical tests (214).

Perhaps the most urgent problem facing frequency theory is to account for the loss of frequency information over time. The losses are extensive, but how do they come about? A promising hypothesis was that there is a progressive assimilation of situational frequency to background frequency, but this interpretation has received only partial empirical support. Retroactive and proactive inhibition occur, but the observed functional relations do not always conform to the predictions of frequency theory (190, 194). If these difficulties can be resolved, we may gain a new purchase not only on the forgetting of frequency information but also on the conditions determining the loss over time of other attributes of memory.

SOME IMPORTANT OMISSIONS FROM THIS REVIEW

This review does not contain a section on interference theory and forgetting. Interference theory today is in a state of ferment if not disarray. There have been powerful challenges to traditional formulations (61, 107), and responses to these challenges, but the critical experiments that will permit a decision between the contending theories remain to be performed. There is no lack of new data on retroaction and proaction, but so far they have failed to resolve the basic theoretical issues. The literature is both voluminous and technical. Since it has been reviewed elsewhere, it seemed reasonable to omit it from this review. We have also not discussed the recent work on intentional or directed forgetting. Excellent summaries of this literature are available (18, 46). While there are specific experimental operations that define directed forgetting, it appears to us that the concept is an essentially hybrid one. The results of the experiments have given us valuable information about the effects of selective rehearsal, the functional grouping of items in memory, and the consequences of selective memory search. But they tell us little about forgetting in the basic sense—why information that has been acquired and used is subsequently lost. Many other important topics have not been mentioned lest one's limited-capacity processor be strained unduly.

Literature Cited

1. Anderson, J. R. 1972. FRAN: A simulation model of free recall. *The Psychology of Learning and Motivation*, ed. G. H. Bower, 5:315–78. New York: Academic
2. Anderson, J. R., Bower, G. H. 1972. Recognition and retrieval processes in free recall. *Psychol. Rev.* 79:97–123
3. Anderson, J. R., Bower, G. H. 1973.

Human Associative Memory. Washington: Winston
4. Atkinson, R. C., Shiffrin, R. M. 1968. Human memory: A proposed system and its control processes. *The Psychology of Learning and Motivation*, ed. K. W. Spence, J. T. Spence, 2:89–195. New York: Academic
5. Bach, M. J., Underwood, B. J. 1970.

Developmental changes in memory attributes. *J. Educ. Psychol.* 61:292–96

6. Baddeley, A. D. 1966. Short-term memory for word sequences as a function of acoustic, semantic and formal similarity. *Quart. J. Exp. Psychol.* 18: 362–68

7. Baddeley, A. D., Levy, B. A. 1971. Semantic coding and short-term memory. *J. Exp. Psychol.* 89:132–36

8. Baddeley, A. D., Warrington, E. K. 1970. Amnesia and the distinction between long- and short-term memory. *J. Verb. Learn. Verb. Behav.* 9:176–89

9. Bahrick, H. P. 1969. Measurement of memory by prompted recall. *J. Exp. Psychol.* 79:213–19

10. Bahrick, H. P. 1970. Two-phase model for prompted recall. *Psychol. Rev.* 77:215–22

11. Bahrick, H. P. 1971. Accessibility and availability of retrieval cues in the retention of a categorized list. *J. Exp. Psychol.* 89:117–25

12. Barton, A. K. 1973. An empirical analysis of free-recall to paired-associate transfer. *J. Exp. Psychol.* 97: 79–88

13. Barton, A. K., Young, R. K. 1972. Transfer from free-recall to paired-associate learning. *J. Exp. Psychol.* 95:240–41

14. Basden, D. R., Higgins, J. 1972. Memory and organization: Category recall and retrieval capacity. *J. Verb. Learn. Verb. Behav.* 11:157–63

15. Begg, I. 1972. Recall of meaningful phrases. *J. Verb. Learn. Verb. Behav.* 11:431–39

16. Begg, I. 1973. Imagery and integration in the recall of words. *Can. J. Psychol.* 27:159–67

17. Bjork, R. A. 1970. Repetition and rehearsal mechanisms in models for short-term memory. See Ref. 130, 307–30

18. Bjork, R. A. 1972. Theoretical implications of directed forgetting. *Coding Processes in Human Memory*, ed. A. W. Melton, E. Martin, 217–35. Washington: Winston

19. Borges, M. A., Mandler, G. 1972. Effect of within-category spacing on free recall. *J. Exp. Psychol.* 92:207–14

20. Bower, G. H. 1972. A selective review of organizational factors in memory. *Organization of Memory*, ed. E. Tulving, W. Donaldson, 93–137. New York: Academic

21. Bower, G. H. 1972. Stimulus-sampling theory of encoding variability. See Ref. 18, 85–123

22. Bower, G. H., Lesgold, A. M., Tieman, D. 1969. Grouping operations in free recall. *J. Verb. Learn. Verb. Behav.* 8:481–93

23. Bransford, J. D., Franks, J. J. 1971. The abstraction of linguistic ideas. *Cogn. Psychol.* 2:331–50

24. Bregman, A. S. 1968. Forgetting curves with semantic, phonetic, graphic, and contiguity cues. *J. Exp. Psychol.* 78: 539–46

25. Carey, S. T. 1973. Delayed recognition testing, incidental learning, and proactive-inhibition release. *J. Exp. Psychol.* 100:361–67

26. Cermak, L. S., Sampson, J. B. 1972. Decay of acoustic proactive facilitation. *J. Exp. Psychol.* 96:237–38

27. Cohen, R. L. 1970. Recency effects in long-term recall and recognition. *J. Verb. Learn. Verb. Behav.* 9:672–78

28. Collyer, S. C., Jonides, J., Bevan, W. 1972. Images as memory aids: Is bizarreness helpful? *Am. J. Psychol.* 85:31–38

29. Coltheart, M., Geffen, G. 1970. Grammar and memory. I. Phonological similarity and proactive interference. *Cogn. Psychol.* 1:215–24

30. Conrad, R., Hull, A. 1964. Information, acoustic confusion and memory span. *Brit. J. Psychol.* 55:429–32

31. Cooper, E. H., Pantle, A. J. 1967. The total-time hypothesis in verbal learning. *Psychol. Bull.* 68:221–34

32. Craik, F. I. M. 1969. Modality effects in short-term storage. *J. Verb. Learn. Verb. Behav.* 8:658–64

33. Ibid 1970. The fate of primary memory items in free recall. 9:143–48

34. Craik, F. I. M., Birtwistle, J. 1971. Proactive inhibition in free recall. *J. Exp. Psychol.* 91:120–23

35. Craik, F. I. M., Gardiner, J. M., Watkins, M. J. 1970. Further evidence for a negative recency effect in free recall. *J.*

Verb. Learn. Verb. Behav. 9:554–60
36. Craik, F. I. M., Lockhart, R. S. 1972. Levels of processing: A framework for memory research. *J. Verb. Learn. Verb. Behav.* 11:671–84
37. Craik, F. I. M., Watkins, M. J. 1973. The role of rehearsal in short-term memory. *J. Verb. Learn. Verb. Behav.* 12:599–607
38. Cramer, P., Eagle, M. 1972. Relationship between conditions of CrS presentation and the category of false recognition errors. *J. Exp. Psychol.* 94:1–5
39. Crowder, R. G., Morton, J. 1969. Precategorical acoustic storage (PAS). *Percept. Psychophys.* 5:365–73
40. D'Agostino, P. R., DeRemer, P. 1973. Repetition effects as a function of rehearsal and encoding variability. *J. Verb. Learn. Verb. Behav.* 12:108–13
41. Darley, C. F., Murdock, B. B. Jr. 1971. Effects of prior free recall testing on final recall and recognition. *J. Exp. Psychol.* 91:66–73
42. Davis, J. C., Lockhart, R. S., Thomson, D. M. 1972. Repetition and context effects in recognition memory. *J. Exp. Psychol.* 92:96–102
43. Davis, J. C., Okada, R. 1971. Recognition and recall of positively forgotten items. *J. Exp. Psychol.* 89:181–86
44. Dillon, R. F. 1973. Locus of proactive interference effects in short-term memory. *J. Exp. Psychol.* 99:75–81
45. Elias, C. S., Perfetti, C. A. 1973. Encoding task and recognition memory: The importance of semantic encoding. *J. Exp. Psychol.* 99:151–56
46. Epstein, W. 1972. Mechanisms of directed forgetting. *The Psychology of Learning and Motivation*, ed. G. H. Bower, 6:147–191. New York: Academic
47. Estes, W. K. 1972. An associative basis for coding and organization in memory. See Ref. 18, 161–90
48. Estes, W. K. 1973. Phonemic coding and rehearsal in short-term memory for letter strings. *J. Verb. Learn. Verb. Behav.* 12:360–72
49. Franks, J. J., Bransford, J. D. 1972. The acquisition of abstract ideas. *J. Verb. Learn. Verb. Behav.* 11:311–15
50. Fulkerson, F. E., Kausler, D. H. 1969.

Effects of intrapair and interpair bidirectional associates on verbal-discrimination learning. *J. Verb. Learn. Verb. Behav.* 8:307–10
51. Galbraith, R. C., Underwood, B. J. 1973. Perceived frequency of concrete and abstract words. *Mem. & Cogn.* 1:56–60
52. Gardiner, J. M., Craik, F. I. M., Birtwistle, J. 1972. Retrieval cues and release from proactive inhibition. *J. Verb. Learn. Verb. Behav.* 11:778–83
53. Gartman, L. M., Johnson, N. F. 1972. Massed versus distributed repetition of homographs: A test of the differential-encoding hypothesis. *J. Verb. Learn. Verb. Behav.* 11:801–8
54. Glanzer, M. 1972. Storage mechanisms in recall. See Ref. 1, 5:129–93
55. Glanzer, M., Koppenaal, L., Nelson, R. 1972. Effects of relations between words on short-term storage and long-term storage. *J. Verb. Learn. Verb. Behav.* 11:403–16
56. Glanzer, M., Razel, M. 1974. The size of the unit in short-term storage. *J. Verb. Learn. Verb. Behav.* 13:114–31
57. Goggin, J., Martin, E. 1970. Forced stimulus encoding and retroactive interference. *J. Exp. Psychol.* 84:131–36
58. Goggin, J., Wickens, D. D. 1971. Proactive interference and language change in short-term memory. *J. Verb. Learn. Verb. Behav.* 10:453–58
59. Gorfein, D. S., Jacobson, D. E. 1972. Proactive effects in short-term recognition memory. *J. Exp. Psychol.* 95:211–14
60. Ibid 1973. Memory search in a Brown-Peterson short-term memory paradigm. 99:82–87
61. Greeno, J. G., James, C. T., DaPolito, F. J. 1971. A cognitive interpretation of negative transfer and forgetting of paired associates. *J. Verb. Learn. Verb. Behav.* 10:331–45
62. Gruneberg, M. M., Sykes, R. N. 1971. 'Coding' in studies of acoustic and semantic interference and confusion. *Am. J. Psychol.* 84:473–76
63. Hasher, L., Goggin, J., Riley, D. A. 1973. Learning and interference effects in short-term memory. *J. Exp. Psychol.* 101:1–9

64. Hawkins, H. L., Pardo, V. J., Cox, R. D. 1972. Proactive interference in short-term recognition: Trace interaction or competition? *J. Exp. Psychol.* 92:43–48

65. Heisey, J. A., Duncan, C. P. 1971. Syntactical encoding in short-term memory. *J. Verb. Learn. Verb. Behav.* 10:95–100

66. Hintzman, D. L. 1967. Articulatory coding in short-term memory. *J. Verb. Learn. Verb. Behav.* 6:312–16

67. Hintzman, D. L., Block, R. A. 1970. Memory judgments and the effects of spacing. *J. Verb. Learn. Verb. Behav.* 9:561–66

68. Hintzman, D. L., Block, R. A. 1971. Repetition and memory: Evidence for a multiple-trace hypothesis. *J. Exp. Psychol.* 88:297–306

69. Ibid 1973. Memory for the spacing of repetitions. 99:70–74

70. Hintzman, D. L., Waters, R. M. 1970. Recency and frequency as factors in list discrimination. *J. Verb. Learn. Verb. Behav.* 9:218–21

71. Hopkins, R. H., Edwards, R. E., Cook, C. L. 1973. Presentation modality, distractor modality, and proactive interference in short-term memory. *J. Exp. Psychol.* 98:362–67

72. Hopkins, R. H., Edwards, R. E., Gavelek, J. R. 1971. Presentation modality as an encoding variable in short-term memory. *J. Exp. Psychol.* 90:319–25

73. Hopkins, R. H., Edwards, R. E., Tamayo, F. M. V., Holman, M. A., Cook, C. L. 1973. Presentation modality and proactive interference in short-term retention using a mixed-modality distractor task. *Mem. & Cogn.* 1:439–42

74. Howell, W. C. 1973. Representation of frequency in memory. *Psychol. Bull.* 80:44–53

75. Hyde, T. S. 1973. Differential effects of effort and type of orienting task on recall and organization of highly associated words. *J. Exp. Psychol.* 97:111–13

76. Hyde, T. S., Jenkins, J. J. 1969. Differential effects of incidental tasks on the organization of recall of a list of highly associated words. *J. Exp. Psychol.* 82:472–81

77. Hyde, T. S., Jenkins, J. J. 1973. Recall for words as a function of semantic, graphic, and syntactic orienting tasks. *J. Verb. Learn. Verb. Behav.* 12:471–80

78. Jacoby, L. L. 1973. Encoding processes, rehearsal, and recall requirements. *J. Verb. Learn. Verb. Behav.* 12:302–10

79. Jacoby, L. L., Bartz, W. H. 1972. Rehearsal and transfer to LTM. *J. Verb. Learn. Verb. Behav.* 11:561–65

80. Jacoby, L. L., Goolkasian, P. 1973. Semantic versus acoustic coding: Retention and conditions of organization. *J. Verb. Learn. Verb. Behav.* 12:324–33

81. Johnson, M. K. 1972. Organizational units in free recall as a source of transfer. *J. Exp. Psychol.* 94:300–7

82. Johnston, C. D., Jenkins, J. J. 1971. Two more incidental tasks that differentially affect associative clustering in recall. *J. Exp. Psychol.* 89:92–95

83. Johnston, W. A., Coots, J. H., Flickinger, R. G. 1972. Controlled semantic encoding and the effect of repetition lag on free recall. *J. Verb. Learn. Verb. Behav.* 11:784–88

84. Katz, S. 1973. Role of instructions in abstraction of linguistic ideas. *J. Exp. Psychol.* 98:79–84

85. Kellas, G., Ashcraft, M. H., Johnson, N. S., Needham, S. 1973. Temporal aspects of storage and retrieval in free recall of categorized lists. *J. Verb. Learn. Verb. Behav.* 12:499–511

86. Keppel, G., Underwood, B. J. 1962. Proactive inhibition in short-term retention of single items. *J. Verb. Learn. Verb. Behav.* 1:153–61

87. Kintsch, W. 1970. *Learning, Memory, and Conceptual Processes.* New York: Wiley

88. Kintsch, W. 1970. Models for free recall and recognition. See Ref. 130, 331–73

89. Kintsch, W. 1972. Abstract nouns: Imagery versus lexical complexity. *J. Verb. Learn. Verb. Behav.* 11:59–65

90. Kintsch, W., Buschke, H. 1969. Homophones and synonyms in short-term memory. *J. Exp. Psychol.* 80:403–7

91. Kroll, N. E. A. 1972. Short-term memory and the nature of interference from concurrent shadowing. *Quart. J. Exp. Psychol.* 24:414–19

92. Kroll, N. E. A., Bee, J., Gurski, G. 1973. Release of proactive interference as a result of changing presentation modality. *J. Exp. Psychol.* 98:131-37
93. Kroll, N. E. A., Kellicutt, M. H. 1972. Short-term recall as a function of covert rehearsal and of intervening task. *J. Verb. Learn. Verb. Behav.* 11:196-204
94. Kroll, N. E. A., Parks, T., Parkinson, S. R., Bieber, S. L., Johnson, A. L. 1970. Short-term memory while shadowing: Recall of visually and of aurally presented letters. *J. Exp. Psychol.* 85:220-24
95. Lauer, P. A., Battig, W. F. 1972. Free recall of taxonomically and alphabetically organized word lists as a function of storage and retrieval cues. *J. Verb. Learn. Verb. Behav.* 11:333-42
96. Laughery, K. R., Welte, J. W., Spector, A. 1973. Acoustic and visual coding in primary and secondary memory. *J. Exp. Psychol.* 99:323-29
97. Laurence, M. W. 1970. Role of homophones in transfer learning. *J. Exp. Psychol.* 86:1-7
98. Levy, B. A., Murdock, B. B. Jr. 1968. The effect of delayed auditory feedback and intralist similarity in short-term memory. *J. Verb. Learn. Verb. Behav.* 7:887-94
99. Light, L. L., Carter-Sobell, L. 1970. Effects of changed semantic context on recognition memory. *J. Verb. Learn. Verb. Behav.* 9:1-11
100. Madigan, S. A. 1969. Intraserial repetition and coding processes in free recall. *J. Verb. Learn. Verb. Behav.* 8:828-35
101. Madigan, S. A. 1971. Modality and recall order interactions in short-term memory for serial order. *J. Exp. Psychol.* 87:294-96
102. Madigan, S. A., McCabe, L. 1971. Perfect recall and total forgetting: A problem for models of short-term memory. *J. Verb. Learn. Verb. Behav.* 10:101-6
103. Mandler, G., Dean, P. J. 1969. Seriation: Development of serial order in free recall. *J. Exp. Psychol.* 81:207-15
104. Mandler, G., Worden, P. E. 1973. Semantic processing without permanent storage. *J. Exp. Psychol.* 100:277-83
105. Marcel, A. J., Steel, R. G. 1973. Semantic cueing in recognition and recall. *Quart. J. Exp. Psychol.* 25:368-77
106. Martin, E. 1968. Stimulus meaningfulness and paired-associate transfer: An encoding variability hypothesis. *Psychol. Rev.* 75:421-41
107. Ibid 1971. Verbal learning theory and independent retrieval phenomena. 78:314-32
108. Martin, E. 1972. Stimulus encoding in learning and transfer. See Ref. 18, 59-84
109. Mathews, R. C., Tulving, E. 1973. Effects of three types of repetition on cued and noncued recall of words. *J. Verb. Learn. Verb. Behav.* 12:707-21
110. McCabe, L., Madigan, S. 1971. Negative effects of recency in recall and recognition. *J. Verb. Learn. Verb. Behav.* 10:307-10
111. McCormack, P. D., Carboni, N. L. 1973. Lag invariance with forced encodings in free recall. *Can. J. Psychol.* 27:144-51
112. McLaughlin, B. 1965. "Intentional" and "incidental" learning in human subjects: The role of instructions to learn and motivation. *Psychol. Bull.* 63:359-76
113. Mechanic, A. 1964. The responses involved in the rote learning of verbal materials. *J. Verb. Learn. Verb. Behav.* 3:30-36
114. Mechanic, A., Mechanic, J. D. 1967. Response activities and the mechanism of selectivity in incidental learning. *J. Verb. Learn. Verb. Behav.* 6:389-97
115. Melton, A. W. 1970. The situation with respect to the spacing of repetitions and memory. *J. Verb. Learn. Verb. Behav.* 9:596-606
116. Merryman, C. T., Merryman, S. S. 1971. Stimulus encoding in the A-B', AX-B and the A-B'r, AX-B paradigms. *J. Verb. Learn. Verb. Behav.* 10:681-85
117. Meunier, G. F., Ritz, D., Meunier, J. A. 1972. Rehearsal of individual items in short-term memory. *J. Exp. Psychol.* 95:465-67
118. Mondani, M. S., Pellegrino, J. W., Battig, W. F. 1973. Free and cued recall as a function of different levels of word processing. *J. Exp. Psychol.* 101:324-29

119. Montague, W. E. 1972. Elaborative strategies in verbal learning and memory. See Ref. 46, 6:225–302

120. Morton, J. 1970. A functional model for memory. See Ref. 130, 203–54

121. Murdock, B. B. Jr. 1972. Short-term memory. See Ref. 1, 5:67–127

122. Murdock, B. B. Jr., Walker, K. D. 1969. Modality effects in free recall. *J. Verb. Learn. Verb. Behav.* 8:665–76

123. Murray, D. J. 1968. Articulation and acoustic confusability in short-term memory. *J. Exp. Psychol.* 78:679–84

124. Nappe, G. W., Wollen, K. A. 1973. Effects of instructions to form common and bizarre mental images on retention. *J. Exp. Psychol.* 100:6–8

125. Neisser, U. 1966. *Cognitive Psychology.* New York: Appleton

126. Nelson, D. L. 1972. Words as sets of features: The role of phonological attributes. *Topics in Learning and Performance*, ed. R. F. Thompson, J. F. Voss, 215–39. New York: Academic

127. Nelson, D. L., Brooks, D. H. 1973. Independence of phonetic and imaginal features. *J. Exp. Psychol.* 97:1–7

128. Nelson, D. L., Davis, M. J. 1972. Transfer and false recognitions based on phonetic identities of words. *J. Exp. Psychol.* 92:347–53

129. Nilsson, L. 1973. Organization by modality in short-term memory. *J. Exp. Psychol.* 100:246–53

130. Norman, D. A., Ed. 1970. *Models of Human Memory.* New York: Academic

131. Norman, D. A., Rumelhart, D. E. 1970. A system for perception and memory. See Ref. 130, 19–64

132. Novinski, L. S. 1972. A reexamination of the part/whole effect in free recall. *J. Verb. Learn. Verb. Behav.* 11:228–33

133. Paivio, A. 1971. *Imagery and verbal processes.* New York: Holt

134. Paivio, A., Csapo, K. 1973. Picture superiority in free recall: Imagery or dual coding? *Cogn. Psychol.* 5:176–206

135. Parkinson, S. R. 1972. Short-term memory while shadowing: Multiple-item recall of visually and of aurally presented letters. *J. Exp. Psychol.* 92:256–65

136. Parkinson, S. R., Parks, T. E., Kroll, N. E. A. 1971. Visual and auditory short-term memory: Effects of phonemically similar auditory shadow material during the retention interval. *J. Exp. Psychol.* 87:274–80

137. Patterson, K. E., Meltzer, R. H., Mandler, G. 1971. Inter-response times in categorized free recall. *J. Verb. Learn. Verb. Behav.* 10:417–26

138. Peterson, L. R., Johnson, S. T. 1971. Some effects of minimizing articulation on short-term retention. *J. Verb. Learn. Verb. Behav.* 10:346–54

139. Petrusic, W. M., Dillon, R. F. 1972. Proactive interference in short-term recognition and recall memory. *J. Exp. Psychol.* 95:412–18

140. Polzella, D. J., Martin, E. 1973. Stimulus encoding in A-B, A-D transfer. *Am. J. Psychol.* 86:589–600

141. Posner, M. I., Konick, A. F. 1966. On the role of interference in short-term retention. *J. Exp. Psychol.* 72:221–31

142. Prytulak, L. S. 1971. Natural language mediation. *Cogn. Psychol.* 2:1–56

143. Pylyshyn, Z. W. 1973. What the mind's eye tells the mind's brain: A critique of mental imagery. *Psychol. Bull.* 80:1–24

144. Raser, G. A. 1972. Recoding of semantic and acoustic information in short-term memory. *J. Verb. Learn. Verb. Behav.* 11:692–97

145. Reitman, J. S. 1971. Mechanisms of forgetting in short-term memory. *Cogn. Psychol.* 2:185–95

146. Reitman, J. S., Bower, G. H. 1973. Storage and later recognition of exemplars of concepts. *Cogn. Psychol.* 4:194–206

147. Restle, F. 1965. Significance of all-or-none learning. *Psychol. Bull.* 64:313–25

148. Rock, I. 1957. The role of repetition in associative learning. *Am. J. Psychol.* 70:186–93

149. Roediger, H. L. III. 1973. Inhibition in recall from cueing with recall targets. *J. Verb. Learn. Verb. Behav.* 12:644–57

150. Rogers, J. L., Battig, W. F. 1972. Effect of amount of prior free recall learning on paired-associate transfer. *J. Exp. Psychol.* 92:373–77

151. Rowe, E. J. 1972. Imagery and fre-

quency processes in verbal discrimination learning. *J. Exp. Psychol.* 95:140-46

152. Rowe, E. J., Paivio, A. 1971. Word frequency and imagery effects in verbal discrimination learning. *J. Exp. Psychol.* 88:319-26

153. Ibid 1972. Effects of noun imagery, pronunciation, method of presentation, and intrapair order of items in verbal discrimination. 93:427-29

154. Rundus, D. 1971. Analysis of rehearsal processes in free recall. *J. Exp. Psychol.* 89:63-77

155. Rundus, D. 1973. Negative effects of using list items as recall cues. *J. Verb. Learn. Verb. Behav.* 12:43-50

156. Rundus, D., Atkinson, R. C. 1970. Rehearsal processes in free recall: A procedure for direct observation. *J. Verb. Learn. Verb. Behav.* 9:99-105

157. Rundus, D., Loftus, G. R., Atkinson, R. C. 1970. Immediate free recall and three-week delayed recognition. *J. Verb. Learn. Verb. Behav.* 9:684-88

158. Runquist, W. N., Blackmore, M. 1973. Phonemic storage of concrete and abstract words with auditory presentation. *Can. J. Psychol.* 27:456-63

159. Salzberg, P. M., Parks, T. E., Kroll, N. E. A., Parkinson, S. R. 1971. Retroactive effects of phonemic similarity on short-term recall of visual and auditory stimuli. *J. Exp. Psychol.* 91:43-46

160. Scarborough, D. L. 1972. Stimulus modality effects on forgetting in short-term memory. *J. Exp. Psychol.* 95:285-89

161. Schneider, N. G., Houston, J. P. 1968. Stimulus selection and retroactive inhibition. *J. Exp. Psychol.* 77:166-67

162. Schwartz, R. M., Humphreys, M. S. 1973. List differentiation in part/whole free recall. *Am. J. Psychol.* 86:79-88

163. Shaughnessy, J. J., Underwood, B. J. 1973. The retention of frequency information for categorized lists. *J. Verb. Learn. Verb. Behav.* 12:99-107

164. Shaughnessy,, J. J., Zimmerman, J., Underwood, B. J. 1972. Further evidence on the MP-DP effect in free-recall learning. *J. Verb. Learn. Verb. Behav.* 11:1-12

165. Shiffrin, R. M. 1973. Information persistence in short-term memory. *J. Exp. Psychol.* 100:39-49

166. Shulman, H. G. 1970. Encoding and retention of semantic and phonemic information in short-term memory. *J. Verb. Learn. Verb. Behav.* 9:499-508

167. Shulman, H. G. 1971. Similarity effects in short-term memory. *Psychol. Bull.* 75:399-415

168. Shulman, H. G. 1972. Semantic confusion errors in short-term memory. *J. Verb. Learn. Verb. Behav.* 11:221-27

169. Slamecka, N. J. 1968. An examination of trace storage in free recall. *J. Exp. Psychol.* 76:504-13

170. Slamecka, N. J. 1972. The question of associative growth in the learning of categorized material. *J. Verb. Learn. Verb. Behav.* 11:324-32

171. Slamecka, N. J., Moore, T., Carey, S. 1972. Part-to-whole transfer and its relation to organization theory. *J. Verb. Learn. Verb. Behav.* 11:73-82

172. Smith, A. D. 1973. Input order and output interference in organized recall. *J. Exp. Psychol.* 100:147-50

173. Sperling, G. 1967. Successive approximations to a model of short-term memory. *Acta Psychol.* 27:285-92

174. Standing, L. 1973. Learning 10,000 pictures. *Quart. J. Exp. Psychol.* 25:207-22

175. Sternberg, R. J., Bower, G. H. 1974. Transfer in part-whole and whole-part free recall: A comparative evaluation of theories. *J. Verb. Learn. Verb. Behav.* 13:1-26

176. Thomson, D. M. 1972. Context effects in recognition memory. *J. Verb. Learn. Verb. Behav.* 11:497-511

177. Thomson, D. M., Tulving, E. 1970. Associative encoding and retrieval: weak and strong cues. *J. Exp. Psychol.* 86:255-62

178. Till, R. E., Jenkins, J. J. 1973. The effects of cued orienting tasks on the free recall of words. *J. Verb. Learn. Verb. Behav.* 12:489-98

179. Tulving, E. 1972. Episodic and semantic memory. *Organization of Memory*, ed. E. Tulving, W. Donaldson, 381-403. New York: Academic

180. Tulving, E., Madigan, S. A. 1970. Memory and verbal learning. *Ann.*

Rev. Psychol. 21:437–84
181. Tulving, E., Thomson, D. M. 1971. Retrieval processes in recognition memory: Effects of associative context. *J. Exp. Psychol.* 87:116–24
182. Tulving, E., Thomson, D. M. 1973. Encoding specificity and retrieval processes in episodic memory. *Psychol. Rev.* 80:352–73
183. Tzeng, O. J. L. 1973. Stimulus meaningfulness, encoding variability, and the spacing effect. *J. Exp. Psychol.* 99:162–66
184. Underwood, B. J. 1969. Attributes of memory. *Psychol. Rev.* 76:559–73
185. Underwood, B. J. 1970. A breakdown of the total-time law in free recall learning. *J. Verb. Learn. Verb. Behav.* 9:573–80
186. Underwood, B. J. Recognition memory. 1971. *Essays in Neobehaviorism*, ed. H. H. Kendler, J. T. Spence, 313–35. New York: Appleton
187. Underwood, B. J. 1972. Are we overloading memory? See Ref. 18, 1–23
188. Underwood, B. J. 1972. Word recognition memory and frequency information. *J. Exp. Psychol.* 94:276–83
189. Underwood, B. J., Freund, J. S. 1970. Relative frequency judgments and verbal discrimination learning. *J. Exp. Psychol.* 83:279–85
190. Ibid 1970. Retention of a verbal discrimination. 84:1–14
191. Underwood, B. J., Freund, J. S. 1970. Testing effects in the recognition of words. *J. Verb. Learn. Verb. Behav.* 9:117–25
192. Underwood, B. J., Shaughnessy, J. J., Zimmerman, J. 1972. List length and method of presentation in verbal discrimination learning with further evidence on retroaction. *J. Exp. Psychol.* 93:181–87
193. Underwood, B. J., Zimmerman, J. 1973. The syllable as a source of error in multisyllable word recognition. *J. Verb. Learn. Verb. Behav.* 12:701–6
194. Underwood, B. J., Zimmerman, J., Freund, J. S. 1971. Retention of frequency information with observations on recognition and recall. *J. Exp. Psychol.* 87:149–62
195. Wallace, W. P., Murphy, M. D., Sawyer, T. J. 1973. Imagery and frequency in verbal discrimination learning. *J. Exp. Psychol.* 101:201–19
196. Walsh, D. A., Jenkins, J. J. 1973. Effects of orienting tasks on free recall in incidental learning: "Difficulty," "effort," and "process" explanations. *J. Verb. Learn. Verb. Behav.* 12:481–88
197. Watkins, M. J. 1972. Locus of the modality effect in free recall. *J. Verb. Learn. Verb. Behav.* 11:644–48
198. Watkins, M. J., Watkins, O. C. 1973. The postcategorical status of the modality effect in serial recall. *J. Exp. Psychol.* 99:226–30
199. Watkins, M. J., Watkins, O. C., Craik, F. I. M., Mazuryk, G. 1973. Effect of nonverbal distraction on short-term storage. *J. Exp. Psychol.*, 101:296–300
200. Waugh, N. C., Norman, D. A. 1965. Primary memory. *Psychol. Rev.* 72:89–104
201. Wickelgren, W. A. 1973. The long and the short of memory. *Psychol. Bull.* 80:425–38
202. Wickens, D. D. 1970. Encoding categories of words: An empirical approach to meaning. *Psychol. Rev.* 77:1–15
203. Wickens, D. D. 1972. Characteristics of word encoding. See Ref. 18, 191–215
204. Wickens, D. D., Ory, N. E., Graf, S. A. 1970. Encoding by taxonomic and acoustic categories in long-term memory. *J. Exp. Psychol.* 84:462–69
205. Wickens, D. D., Reutener, D. B., Eggemeier, F. T. 1972. Sense impression as an encoding dimension of words. *J. Exp. Psychol.* 96:301–6
206. Williams, R. F., Underwood, B. J. 1970. Encoding variability: tests of the Martin hypothesis. *J. Exp. Psychol.* 86:317–24
207. Winograd, E., Conn, C. P. 1971. Evidence from recognition memory for specific encoding of unmodified homographs. *J. Verb. Learn. Verb. Behav.* 10:702–6
208. Winograd, E., Raines, S. R. 1972. Semantic and temporal variation in recognition memory. *J. Verb. Learn. Verb. Behav.* 11:114–19
209. Wolford, G. 1971. Function of distinct associations for paired-associate performance. *Psychol. Rev.* 78:303–13
210. Wollen, K. A., Weber, A., Lowry, D. H. 1972. Bizarreness versus interaction

of mental images as determinants of learning. *Cogn. Psychol.* 3:518–23

211. Wood, G. 1972. Organizational processes and free recall. See Ref. 20, 49–91

212. Woodward, A. E. Jr., Bjork, R. A. 1971. Forgetting and remembering in free recall: intentional and unintentional. *J. Exp. Psychol.* 89:109–16

213. Woodward, A. E. Jr., Bjork, R. A., Jongeward, R. H. Jr. 1973. Recall and recognition as a function of primary rehearsal. *J. Verb. Learn. Verb. Behav.* 12:608–17

214. Zimmerman, J., Shaughnessy, J. J., Underwood, B. J. 1972. The role of associations in verbal-discrimination learning. *Am. J. Psychol.* 85:499–518

COUNSELING AND STUDENT DEVELOPMENT

236

John M. Whiteley,[1] *Mary Quinn Burkhart,*[2]
Michele Harway-Herman,[3] *and Rita M. Whiteley*[4]
University of California, Irvine, California 92664

The scope and volume of the literature on both counseling and student development has increased dramatically over the past several years. The literature on both subjects has diverged to the point where we have recommended to the editorial board of the *Annual Review of Psychology* that the topics be separated in future issues. We have chosen to separate them in our presentation.

It should be underscored that the limitations of space and the intent of the editor's charge to us was "to present a broad view of the progress, direction, and purpose of current research. . ." in the context of a "selective—not comprehensive—review of the literature, and a critical analysis of the present state of the subject assigned."

Our initial draft was twice the length of our allotted pages. At that we did not feel that we had done the subjects justice. It must be recognized that it is possible, and indeed it has been done, to write books on much less subject matter than is covered here.

THE COUNSELING LITERATURE

This has been an extraordinary period in the development of the counseling literature. The initial research forays, particularly in client-centered and behavioral counseling in the 1950s and 1960s, have resulted in the development of a range of valid and reliable research instruments which have made possible much productive basic research.

On a number of topics it has been necessary to cite findings from literature prior to 1971, because they are necessary to understanding the growth of our knowledge,

[1] Associate Professor of Social Ecology and Dean of Students.
[2] Assistant Dean of Students, Career Planning and Placement.
[3] Director of Women's Programs and Assistant Dean of Students.
[4] Counseling Psychologist, Counseling Service.

337

particularly as they relate to the problems of replication, therapist-offered conditions such as empathy, the use of confrontation to promote client self-exploration, counselor selection, criterion of outcome issues, and the role of self-disclosure for both counselor and client in effecting change as a result of the counseling process.

We have tried to strike a balance between alerting readers to important areas of inquiry by citing significant research results, and directing attention to methodological issues which can assist future researchers in further improving the power of our counseling research tools. Lastly, we have attempted to identify certain areas which merit intensive research activity in the immediate future.

Empathy and Other Therapist-Offered Conditions

Meltzoff & Kornreich (105) critiqued the research done prior to 1970 on empathy and other, what they termed, "therapist-offered conditions." Their concerns provide a useful baseline for analysis of the studies since then. A first concern is the limitation inherent in studying therapist-offered conditions, as that topic fails to consider the interaction between counselor and client, and any relevant client-offered conditions.

A second concern identified by Meltzoff & Kornreich (105) is that in most process studies the various facilitative variables are: "... related only to the patient's self-exploration. The implicit, and sometimes explicit, argument is that the facilitative conditions lead to self-exploration, which in turn leads to favorable outcome. Both hypotheses remain to be firmly established" (p. 402). There are, of course, major differences of opinion about whether the hypotheses remain to be established. Patterson (117), Carkhuff (30), Carkhuff & Berenson (38), Truax & Carkhuff (135) and Truax & Mitchell (137) offer considerable evidence in support of the relationship between what Meltzoff & Kornreich (105) label therapist-offered conditions and client change.

A third concern of Meltzoff & Kornreich (105) is that it would be a mistake "to freeze therapeutic research in process into the current versions of these facilitative conditions when the results are ambiguous and much remains to be explored" (p. 402). This concern appeared to be based on indications from research that self-exploration may not be the only vehicle to change, or may not lead to change, that the therapeutic conditions may be accounted for by one major variable, or that some simpler, specifiable therapist behaviors may underlie these conditions.

With the concerns of Meltzoff & Kornreich (105) as a preamble, the literature on empathy from 1970 through March 1974 is not likely to produce converts to the idea that the basic research problems have been solved.

Heck & Davis (68), using a counseling analogue format, investigated the nature of the interaction between counselor and client as it contributes to the differential level at which empathy is offered. As such, it is research that directly investigates the first problem area identified by Meltzoff & Kornreich (105)—namely, the interaction between counselor and client as that interaction affects the behavior of the counselor.

In this study, Heck & Davis (68) were interested in whether certain counselor-client characteristics interact and produce an effect upon the counselor's level of expressed empathy. They report that the level at which empathy is expressed is affected by differences in clients. Another finding of the study bears reporting; namely, evidence supporting the contention "derived from conceptual system theory that counselors who differ in conceptual level have different base levels of empathy" (p. 103). This may indicate one source of the differences between people in their capacity to offer an empathic response. Further research ought to be undertaken to explore the implications of this and its potential utility as a selection device for counselor training.

Gurman's (66) study of the therapeutic conditions of empathy, warmth, and genuineness within each session by an individual therapist clearly demonstrates the increasing sophistication of the current investigations in the area of therapist-offered conditions.

This is an important area of inquiry since implicit in prior research models (Wogan 147) has been the assumption that these helping variables were a constant for a therapist at some fixed level of facilitativeness. Rogers et al (123, p. 11), for example, had taken the position that the helping variables reflected "underlying attitudes" or "basic feelings."

A series of earlier investigators (Kiesler, Mathieu & Klein 92; Moos & MacIntosh 109; Vesprani 139) starting with Truax (133) began to question the stability of these therapist variables. Wogan (147) further questioned the reliability of the usual measure of empathy, noting that "since most research uses single measures of empathy, taken at one point in time, there are questions of the reliability of empathy itself " (p. 112).

The purpose of Gurman's (66) study was to assess the "consistency of therapeutic functioning within and across sessions with repeated measures of facilitativeness within the same therapist-patient dyads" (p. 16). Gurman employed "systematically selected therapists in a multiple, single case format," utilizing a research approach presented by Bergin & Strupp (20), Chassan (40), and Davidson & Costello (49). Therapist functioning was rated on the Bergin & Solomon (19) revision of the Truax Accurate Empathy Scale and on the Truax scales of Nonpossessive Warmth and Genuineness (Truax & Carkhuff 135).

Two significant findings resulted from this study. First, both high- and low-functioning therapists vary in their functioning, both within and across sessions. Second, therapeutic conditions tend to reach peak levels within sessions in the mid-late and late segments of the therapy hour.

This study directly challenges the usual methodology in studies of therapeutic facilitativeness with respect to sampling of therapist functioning for rating purposes. It gives added impetus to Kiesler's (90) point that determination of which segments to sample ought to be based on the theory from which the therapist is rating. Further, the Mintz & Luborsky (106) finding that ratings based on brief segments could not be considered as accurate approximations to session-based judgments deserves even more careful attention from researchers in light of this finding.

A final issue raised by Gurman (66) is the question of whether all therapist responses are of equal importance in therapy. Truax & Carkhuff (135) had earlier questioned whether or not peak levels of functioning might not be more predictive of outcome than overall level. Gurman asserts quite persuasively that this area represents an important one for future inquiry.

Grief & Hogan (65) presented a paper on the theory and measurement of empathy from quite a different perspective than the client-centered tradition. Their work begins by indicating that empathy refers to "a sensitivity to the needs and values of others," and identifies it as a "major element in role-theoretical accounts of interpersonal behavior." The role-theoretical literature was noted by the authors to include such references as Cottrell (45), Goffman (61), Kelly (89), McDougall (102), Mead (103), and Sarbin & Allen (125).

The work of Grief & Hogan (65), based on a scale derived from the California Personality Inventory and the Minnesota Multiphasic Personality Inventory, adds a potentially different definition to the term of empathy in the literature. This brings to mind the research questioning the meaning of accurate empathy ratings (Chinsky & Rappaport 43; Kiesler, Mathieu & Klein 92).

A second thread of literature introduced by Grief & Hogan focused on the relationship of the concept of empathy to understanding moral development and moral conduct. Cited here are such references as Baier (10), Hogan (76), and Wright (149). What is particularly interesting about this set of literature citations is that there exists an entirely different set of researchers (Mosher & Sprinthall 111) independently drawing upon the relationship of empathy to moral development. Mosher & Sprinthall (111) were teaching counseling empathy skills to high school students in order to promote moral development as defined by Kohlberg (94–97).

Both Grief & Hogan (65) and Mosher & Sprinthall (111) appear to the writers of this review article to be investigating one of the frontier areas in counseling research. The fact that they began publishing about the same time from such different schools of thought and methodology reflects both the nature of interdisciplinary scientific inquiry and the fact that the counseling literature is suffering from an information retrieval problem of the first magnitude, particularly in the area of the applicability of work from other disciplines.

Self-Disclosure

The passage of time has allowed systematic investigation to broaden our knowledge in important ways. Our increased understanding of self-disclosure is a case in point. Jourard's (82) and Mowrer's (112) initial work, further developed by Carkhuff & Berenson (38), Truax & Carkhuff (135), Brahan (25), Strong & Schmidt (132), Schmidt & Strong (128), Strong & Dixon (131), has laid the groundwork for detailed research to the point that Murphy & Strong (113) were able to demonstrate the influence of self-disclosure in helping another person feel warmth, friendliness, and being understood, and the significance of the timing of a self-disclosure. Giannandrea & Murphy (60), in an extension of the Murphy & Strong (113) work, investigated the relationship between frequency of similarity self-disclosure and return for a second interveiw. A curvilinear relationship was found in which more students return for a second interview after receiving a moderate number of disclosures than after receiving few or many disclosures.

Heilbrun (75) investigated the relationship between difficulty in self-disclosure to early termination in therapy. This research brings together several different threads of investigation, including role expectancy theory (69–74) and the self-disclosure of Jourard (82). The hypothesis that females who terminate prematurely from therapy are those who have greater difficulty engaging in self-disclosure, especially with males, was tested. He found the opposite to be the case. Probable terminators were higher self-disclosers than probable continuers. All females, however, disclosed more to females than to males. The use of role-expectancy theory was helpful in his interpretation of the results, particularly in suggesting implications for further research.

Weigel et al (143) reported that therapist self-disclosure may lead to client opinions of unprofessional conduct or questions about the therapist's mental health. While a therapist may be better liked by group members if he is self-disclosing, Weigel & Warnath (144) found the therapist may be judged as less healthy mentally. In a related study, Truax, Carkhuff & Kodman (136) found that deviation from a "professional role" through self-revelation may lead to being viewed as less helpful.

The notion of what is expected therapist conduct is, of course, central. It is beyond the scope of this paper to review the many differing conceptions. Suffice it to say that the few previous studies (Culbert 47, Bolman 23, Kangas 86) which have investigated the effects of therapist self-disclosure do not provide any definitive conclusions.

Dies (51) continued this line of inquiry by getting clients from ten different therapy groups to evaluate their leaders on the Group Therapist Orientation Scale (50), which assesses opinions about the appropriateness of therapist self-disclosure. Clients were also asked to evaluate their therapists on a set of 20 bipolar adjectives designed to obtain information on therapist likability, perceived levels of helpfulness, and emotional stability. The results of this study found that self-disclosing therapists were judged by their clients as more friendly, disclosing, trusting, intimate, helpful, and facilitating (Factor 1), yet also as being less relaxed, strong, stable, and sensitive (Factor 2). A related finding was that the longer a client was in therapy, the more favorable were his attitudes likely to be toward therapist self-disclosure.

May & Thompson (100), in a study related to the Dies (51) work, investigated further the relationship between therapist self-disclosure, mental health, and helpfulness as perceived by group members. Another part of this work was whether the group member's opinion of therapist self-disclosure and mental health was related to the member's own self-disclosure level and mental health. Significant positive correlations were found among the three therapist dimensions of self-disclosure, helpfulness, and mental health. No significant differences were found in the ratings of group leaders by those group members ranked highest and those ranked lowest on the member variables of self-disclosure and mental health. May & Thompson provide a thoughtful discussion of possible reasons why the findings from their study are at variance with those of Weigel et al (143). Since Dies (51) appeared in the same journal issue as did May & Thompson (100), neither was able to discuss the other's results. There is much yet to clarify in this area of inquiry. Further research is essential.

Confrontation and Self-Exploration

The work on confrontation is another example of progressive, systematic research which has advanced our knowledge of key counseling concepts. Berenson and co-workers (16, 17), in their investigations of characteristics of high and low facilitators, found that high facilitators more frequently used confrontation. Anderson (2) found that within the first therapy hour client self-exploration was influenced by confrontation in a differential manner depending on whether the counselor was a high or a low facilitator. Confrontation was related to increased client self-exploration when accompanied by high levels of the facilitative conditions. Under low levels of facilitative conditions, confrontation was not followed by increased self-exploration. In further research, Anderson (3) used an analysis of variance design to compare the effect of therapist level, client level, confrontation type, and whether it was the first or fourth interview. She found three significant results: (a) confrontations were followed by increased client self-exploration to a significantly greater degree from high-functioning therapists than from low-functioning therapists; (b) the fourth interview as compared to the first produced greater variability in client depth of self-exploration; (c) greater variability in type of confrontation was found in high-functioning therapists.

Mitchell & Namanek (108) undertook a replication of the Anderson (2) study as well as a considerable extension of confrontation research. They investigated the effects of therapist confrontation on subsequent client and therapist behavior within the first therapy interview. Importantly, Anderson's (2) findings were not replicated. No mention was made of the related Anderson (3) study.

Confrontation was found by Mitchell & Namanek (108) to have had little overall impact on client self-exploration within the first session of therapy. A number of intriguing avenues for further research were outlined, including the study of the effects of confrontation over the entire course of psychotherapy.

Kaul, Kaul & Bednar (87) investigated the response styles of eight counselors, all functioning at or above minimally facilitative levels of therapeutic core conditions. These counselors were classified as confrontative or speculative in order to study the effects of response style upon client self-exploration. Estimates were made by the counselors, the clients, and by trained raters of client depth of self-exploration.[5] In summarizing the previous literature,[5] Kaul, Kaul & Bednar (87) noted that an implication from previous studies is that counselor confrontation leads to increased self-exploration by clients, "at least when the counselor is judged to be performing at minimally facilitative levels of therapeutic core con-

---

[5] A problem in the Kaul, Kaul & Bednar literature review is that the Mitchell & Namanek paper (108) had not appeared at the time they submitted their review. Mitchell & Namanek (108) importantly failed to replicate Anderson (2), a fact Kaul, Kaul & Bednar could not have known. They also failed to review Berenson, Mitchell & Laney (16), and Mitchell & Berenson (107).

ditions" (p. 132). Such an implication they believe to be tenuous, since "the technique of confrontation has been confounded with therapeutic levels." Another research problem they note is that the consequences of confrontations have been assessed immediately following the technique, and that no compelling evidence exists to support the belief that "the consequences of confrontations will manifest themselves immediately."

Results of the research by Kaul, Kaul & Bednar (87) were as follows: 1. Confrontative counselors perceived greater self-exploration in their clients than did speculative counselors, but clients perceived greater self-exploration than did counselors or judges. 2. Clients of confrontative and speculative counselors did not differ in their perceptions of their self-exploration. 3. Importantly, trained raters did not differ in their perceptions of self-exploration between clients of confrontative or speculative counselors.

There certainly was not support for the general hypothesis that counselor confrontation leads to client self-exploration. Because of certain methodological differences, the authors caution that their results "cannot be interpreted as completely contradictory to the results of earlier studies." They do note that the fact trained raters did not differ in their assessment of self-exploration "across confrontive and speculative response styles contradicts Anderson's (2, 3) data" (87, p. 135).

The explanation offered by Kaul, Kaul & Bednar (87) is that:

> ... both groups of counselors were functioning at high levels of facilitative conditions and both were actively engaged in productive, therapeutic activities. The implication is that client self-exploration is more a function of the counselor's overall effectiveness than of the specific modality through which it may be expressed (p. 135).

The authors note that investigating the above line of reasoning represents a potentially fruitful area for further research.

The studies on confrontation cited above, taken together, are important in that they indicate the extraordinary complexity of research on counseling variables, the difficulty inherent in the isolation of the effect of a single therapist-offered condition imbedded in overall therapist behavior, the necessity of careful replication, the appraising of all the relevant literature, and the benefits in increased understanding which accrue from systematic investigation over a period of time. While confrontation as a counselor skill may have promise, its effects on clients over the course of counseling have barely begun to be studied.

Training in Basic Human Helping Skills

The last decade, and particularly the period of time covered by this review, has marked a major advance in the methodology of training counselors. Adopting very specific, observable skills as the basis, a number of innovators have developed training packages which are now receiving research scrutiny. A partial listing of these training innovators would include, along with their associates, Carkhuff (30, 32–36), Kagan (83–85), Hosford (80), Ivey (81), Gazda (59), Danish & Hauer (48), and Brammer (26). It is beyond the scope of this review to undertake a systematic evaluation of these various approaches to teaching human helping skills. The relative newness has precluded the development of an empirical assessment of their comparative effectiveness, though there has been considerable research done within each system. Given the importance to society of developing potent methods for teaching human helping skills which will benefit both counselors in training and members of the general public who wish to be paraprofessionals, this area must be assigned priority for investigation in the immediate future.

Several research studies which have investigated elements of training deserve mention. Fry (58) found that pairing helping skills training with desensitization improves post-training ratings of the trainee's helping function.

Butler & Hansen (28) investigated two important questions in training: whether persons rated prior to training as being low or moderate in level of facilitation experience differential effects from counselor training, and whether the post-training level of each group persists over time. The authors found that levels of facilitation can be increased for both groups, and that these levels are maintained over a 4-week post-training period. The results suggested that moderately functioning persons benefited more from training, though this finding was not definitive.

Saltmarsh (124) and Birk (22) both presented approaches for assisting counselors in developing empathy skills. Saltmarsh's approach was to utilize programmed instruction consisting of printed materials and tape-directed interaction focusing on each of the five identified components which he assumed to be supportive of empathy. The evidence for the validity of the components was not presented. He did find significant differences between the experimental group which had his training program and a control group which had discussions about "relationship dynamics" on the Kagan et al (85) Michigan State Affective Sensitivity Scale, which is a valid and reliable instrument for measuring affective sensitivity. A weakness in this particular study which the author noted was that the experimental group focused intensely on empathy while the control group did not. The specific defects of this study are correctable in future research. The idea of using alternate approaches such as programmed instruction to teaching empathy is worthy of further study.

Birk (22) investigated the effects of a didactic and an experiential counseling supervision method in developing empathy. In addition, she found that supervisee preference for a particular supervision had no effect. With respect to which type of supervision was most effective in developing empathy, her findings supported the didactic over the experiential, as did Payne & Gralinski's (119).

Selection of Counselors and the Criterion Problem

Counselor selection studies constitute a research area where little progress has been made, in contrast with developments in training research. A central issue has been the definitions of effectiveness and ineffectiveness employed in labeling subject groups and their relation to an outcome criterion for client behavior. In reviewing developments in thinking and research regarding the criterion problem, it was considered useful to draw on psychotherapy as well as counseling literature to provide a complete examination of the issues.

In the last 7 years, three reviews of the literature on counselor selection—Patterson (116), Allen & Whiteley (1) and Whiteley (146)—have agreed specifically on two criticisms of predictive studies: the inadequate definition of the criterion, and the lack of a theoretical rationale for selection of variables. The two are obviously interrelated.

Allen & Whiteley's (1) analysis of the difficulties in yielding predictive validities in the studies they reviewed is that researchers proceeded in the assumption that since personality differences exist between "good" and "bad" counselors, all one had to do is "administer the standard personality tests and tabulate the differences" (p. 7). They further observed that no existing test of personality can carry the measurement and conceptualization of the whole personality, and that it is unlikely that any "specifiable aggregates of individual personality traits" will be found to discriminate between effective and ineffective counselors. Clearly, the direction of theory is required.

The relevance to counselor behavior of personality measurements developed for assessment of psychopathology in patient populations must also be seriously questioned. The use of these and other standardized measurements in counselor selection research "implicitly makes," as Meltzoff & Kornreich note in their 1970 review, "their authors usurp the place of the researcher as the creator of hypotheses for his experiment" (105, p. 310). The record of research in this area indicates a willingness on the part of many investigators to relinquish this function, in the absence of viable theoretical models, perhaps in the hope of discovering by coincidence the "right fish" with which to begin to stock one's own pond.

The quest for a theoretical formulation takes us back to the criterion problem. Whiteley (146) has argued that "By assessing what the counselor does (his actual behavior), criteria of competence can be developed.... by attempting first to specify the counselor behaviors which are associated with client change, it becomes possible to relate these behaviors to higher-order personality factors within a systematic rationale" (pp. 175-76). In summary, before any progress can be made in a theoretical formulation of the personality dimensions related to effectiveness in counseling, more rigorous consideration must be given to the definition of the criterion—effectiveness—and that definition must be in terms of specifiable counseling behaviors which are clearly and predictably associated with client change.

THE CRITERION PROBLEM—PSYCHOTHERAPY: EFFECTIVE OR INEFFECTIVE?   The publication in 1952 of the first of a series of papers by Hans Eysenck, questioning the efficacy of traditional psychotherapy, brought forth a flurry of research activity to demonstrate the effects of psychotherapy and a refocus and reevaluation of the investigative models employed in studying the process and outcome of therapy.

Eysenck's (53) challenge spearheaded the impact of behavioral science on the theory and practice of psychotherapy, particularly on the criteria for specifying outcome and measures of change. At the same time there was a marked increase in preference for behavioral models of therapy and their more operationally specifiable treatment and outcome variables. While some were turning to learning theory for techniques demonstrably potent in changing behavior, many others renewed their efforts to validate the more traditional forms of psychotherapy.

Eysenck's critique continues to be the subject of debate regarding assessment of outcome, and every review of the literature in this area begins with his survey, although Bergin (18), in a refreshing departure, remarks, ". . . even though some people like myself are still writing about it, I, at least, know that I am writing history, not news" (p. 218).

Bergin (18), in his review of Eysenck's work and the ensuing 20 years of controversy and productivity it provoked, concludes that the bases for the issues raised by Eysenck have quietly dissipated and that there *is* evidence of significant change in clients receiving the more traditional forms of psychotherapy.

In a review of 48 recent studies of outcome, Bergin (18) demonstrated a slight positive relationship between more rigorous design and more positive outcome. Bergin examined these studies for, among other things, thoroughness and adequacy of design. He considers his evidence conclusive enough to "dispel the notion that experimental rigor washes out significance of results in tests of therapy effectiveness" (p. 238).

Meltzoff (104) and Meltzoff & Kornreich (105), in their thorough reviews of the research literature, assert definitively that the evidence for the effectiveness of psychotherapy is in. Among the 101 studies they examined, 56 percent (57 studies) were considered "sufficiently adequate in design and execution for valid conclusions to be drawn." Of these, 84 percent (48 studies) yielded positive outcomes of psychotherapy.

Meltzoff & Kornreich (105) attribute the differences between the conclusions arrived at in their review and earlier ones (Eysenck 53–55, Truax & Carkhuff 135) to the greater scope and comprehensiveness of the literature they reviewed, as well as to the use of stringent criteria for assessing the adequacy of design of studies reviewed. They selected material sufficiently inclusive in scope to investigate adequately the issues central to the question of effectiveness (which it can be argued had never been done prior to these reviews and Bergin's which followed shortly after). By assigning differential values to the evidence in terms of design adequacy, they were able to conclude, in agreement with Bergin, that "the better the quality of research, the more positive the results obtained" (105, p. 177).

While the studies reviewed by Bergin (18), Meltzoff & Kornreich (105), and Kellner (88) represent significant improvement in design and in the specificity of the criterion, the criterion itself remains a problem in interpretation. The use of subjective ratings by therapists or patients as criterion measures has declined considerably. Meltzoff & Kornreich (105) found only 6 to 7 percent of all studies, regardless of adequacy of design, were using these kinds of ratings. Rather, observed behavior, personality inventories, and rated behavior were more utilized, often in combination, and were particularly prevalent in studies which the authors rated as adequate in design.

However, these less subjective criteria are still sources of difficulty in interpretation due to the differences among various theoretical systems in assumptions about what constitutes change and the valence of its direction. More importantly, these kinds of outcome criteria have not been more efficacious than the more subjective ones in the task of identifying the therapist behaviors relevant to them. Kiesler (91), in his analysis of what he has labeled the "uniformity myth," i.e. the "quest for the *one system* of therapist behavior that would produce constructive personality change for patients" argues that "our psychotherapy research designs can no longer incorporate these uniformity myths" (p. 40).

The uniformity assumption is that clients on the one hand and therapists on the other represent "uniform, homogenous groups, more alike than different," and that outcome represents "a uniform and homogenous patient-change dimension . . . that would reflect for *any patient* the effects of psychotherapy" (p. 40).

Increasingly the argument is being made for specific rather than global criteria for client change in outcome studies. Individually specified criteria for constructive personality change would take into account the fact that what represents improvement for one client in a particular direction on a particular variable may not represent improvement for another. Bergin (18) raises an interesting question on this point by asking whether a reevaluation of past outcome research would show that "meager results of many studies may have resulted from misapplications of the same criteria to different patients" (p. 259).

Clearly, the central issues in outcome research have moved beyond the effective-ineffective debate, and the assumption of a unitary process applied to a unitary problem has been firmly dispatched. Such a conceptualization lacks the potency and relevance to generate further progress in counseling and psychotherapy research. Bergin & Strupp's (21) position is indicative of the direction outcome research must now take: "We feel the problem of psychotherapy research in its more general terms should be reformulated as a standard scientific question: What specific therapeutic interventions produce specific changes in specific patients under specific conditions?" (p. 8).

Certainly another long-standing difficulty in outcome research has been the tendency to utilize counselors and therapists who are in training rather than experienced, professionally qualified persons. It is unlikely that any other profession would attempt to examine the nature of its skills and the effects of its treatments by studying minimally or inadequately trained members. Bergin's review (18) offers some evidence that "outcomes differ significantly as a function of experience level" (p. 237). He reports that "53 percent of the studies involving experienced therapists (20 of 38) yielded positive results, while 18 percent (2 of 11) by inexperienced therapists were positive" (p. 237).

Bergin's data and the lack of logic behind this practice should be enough to dissuade researchers tempted by the all-too-available student-therapist population. A further argument against this practice can be found in the evidence for change in therapists' attitudes and self-reported change in technique between internship and attainment of several years' experience.

THE RELATIONSHIP AS AN INTERMEDIATE OUTCOME   The quest to determine what behaviors of the therapist are associated with positive outcome has led some researchers to look for commonalities among therapists of different schools and training backgrounds. The assumption is that one can abstract the essence of the therapeutic process from a discovery of the commonalities. These efforts are predicated upon a unitary view of psychotherapy in contrast to the multidimensional position taken by Bergin & Strupp (21) and Kiesler (91).

Diversity of opinion among therapeutic systems is greatly in evidence in the theoretical literature in (a) the wide variety of conceptualizations utilized to explain a client's behavior; (b) the difference in time period of the client's life which is regarded important for therapeutic focus; (c) the nature of the therapeutic interventions; (d) the implicit and explicit tasks required of the client by the therapist; and (e) the forms of verbal interactions in the therapeutic process. The one area of agreement does appear to be in the centrality of the interpersonal relationship between the therapist and the client, particularly in the more traditional psychotherapy literature. Bordin (24) affirms this in his observation: "Virtually all efforts to theorize about psychotherapy are intended to describe and explain what attributes of the interactions between the therapist and the patient will account for whatever behavior change results" (p. 235).

The work of Truax & Carkhuff (135) and their associates, who represent their efforts as having identified "certain prepotent therapist variables that cut across most theoretical models of therapy," and which they offer as constituting the basic conditions of a therapeutic relationship, is the most extensively developed and rigorously research-supported endeavor arising from the experiential, client-centered, relationship-oriented (as opposed to technique-oriented) school of therapy which traces its theoretical paternity to Carl Rogers (120–122).

The definition and delineation of these therapist conditions and their relation to outcome have been presented and summarized in a number of articles and books, the most comprehensive being those by Carkhuff and his associates (31, 37, 38, 135, 137). Recent research in this area has been reviewed elsewhere in this chapter.

Process research from a variety of areas of study have demonstrated the effects of therapist and relationship variables on client behavior. Bandura, Lipsher & Miller (12) found that therapist avoidance responses to client expressions of hostility inhibited further expressions of hostility or caused clients to change the object of hostility. Goldstein, Heller & Sechrest (62) demonstrated a relationship between the degree of facilitative conditions present in the therapy relationship and the degree of interpersonal attraction between therapist and client. Goldstein & Simonson (63) found interpersonal attraction to be significantly related to the type of client behavior engaged in during the interview, i.e. during a condition of positive attraction the client "(1) was less covertly resistive, (2) talks more, (3) is self-descriptively sicker, and (4) has more favorable prognostic expectancies for himself." Correspondingly, the more attracted the therapist is to the client, "(1) the more the client talks, (2) the more open he is in the content of his communications, and (3) the less overtly and covertly resistive he is" (p. 164).

Kratochvil et al (98) presented evidence that changes in the direction of counselor functioning had more effect on client functioning than did the counselor's absolute level; i.e. low-functioning (on the "core conditions") counselors changing in a positive direction had more positive effect on client's functioning than did higher-functioning counselors who were deteriorating in functioning over a period of time. Carkhuff (31, 39) reported similar effects of counselor trainers on trainees. In interaction with a low-functioning trainer, the higher the trainee's initial level of functioning, the greater the probability that he will deteriorate in functioning or terminate training.

Vitalo (140) found that high-functioning (in terms of the "core conditions") experimenters in a conditioning study were significantly more successful in producing high acquisition rates in subjects than were low-functioning experimenters. Truax (134) presented evidence that the therapist's differential interpersonal reinforcement of client self-exploration led to an increase of self-exploration and greater therapeutic improvement in outcome measures.

At the same time that the body of opinion among research leaders is moving toward a multidimensional model for outcome in which specific gains representing the goals of the particular therapy and client sample are hypothesized and tested, there appear to be seeds of a consensual view of the therapeutic relationship as a criterion in the literature. Even the technique-oriented therapies are now according the relationship some significance, as evidenced in this statement by Goldstein & Wolpe (64): "In the case of interpersonal anxiety, behavior therapists might be giving instruction in assertive training, employing systematic desensitization, advising, giving 'homework,' correcting misconceptions, all in the context of a warm and accepting atmosphere" (p. 222).

Patterson (116, 118) has posited the relationship as an "intermediate criterion" in that it is the medium or vehicle through which change is mediated. There appears to be support for Patterson's view in the conclusions of the more recent major reviews of the literature. Bergin & Strupp (21) list the psychological mechanisms in most prominent use in the major systems of psychotherapy and note that "a crucial requisite for determining the extent to which the foregoing mechanisms can become operative is the patient's *amenability* or *receptivity* to the therapist's influence" (p. 13).

Truax & Mitchell (137), reviewing the work of Truax, Carkhuff, and their associates, conceptualize the therapeutic effects of the core conditions drawing from a learning theory model. Their hypotheses support Patterson's position and represent further convergence of conceptualization of the therapeutic process among theoretical systems.

Bergin & Strupp (21), in their summary, appear to be arguing explicitly for the relationship as an intermediate criterion for outcome:

Our critical look at the field suggests . . . that regardless of the therapeutic objectives and the technical procedures, the therapist must succeed in the following: 1. He must create conditions which make the patient amenable to his influence. Usually this is spoken of in terms of a therapeutic relationship in which the patient experiences respect, trust, and acceptance, which render him receptive to the therapist's suggestions, interpretations, and the like. 2. While these conditions are being created, the therapist employs a variety of technical procedures (desensitization, interpretations, etc.) to influence the patient in directions considered therapeutically desirable and ultimately intended to increase the patient's independence, self-direction, and autonomy (p. 17).

Goldstein & Simonson (63) conceptualized the relationship as an intermediate criterion in their investigation of interpersonal attraction in psychotherapy. They describe their efforts as

... developing techniques for "hooking" the patients, that is, for maximizing the favorableness of the initial relationship so that the patient, at a minimum, returns for further sessions and, more maximally, is open to the therapist's influence attempts. We propose no *direct* relationship between *initial* patient attraction to his therapist and the subsequent therapy outcome. Instead, we view the initial relationship as a possible potentiator or catalyst whose consequents can lead to a more favorable outcome (pp. 161–62).

The relationship as an intermediate outcome criterion is a promising source for identifying the counselor behaviors related to effectiveness in that it allows us to look for a set of behaviors that are basic to influencing another person, irrespective of ultimate therapeutic goal. The selection task then becomes that of ascertaining whether there are individual differences in capacity to engage in the kinds of behaviors which are basic to the establishment of a therapeutic relationship.

Previous studies which utilize either the relationship itself as an intermediate criterion (Goldstein & Simonson 63) or the relationship behaviors which themselves are regarded as therapeutic (which would include most of the studies employing the Truax scales or Carkhuff's revision) have in common a criterion of effectiveness that reflects a response style of the counselor toward the client's expressions of feelings. This response style is basically one of receptivity or approach of the client's affective behavior.

The assumptions concerning the process of effectiveness differ. For some researchers the approach response style serves variously in different stages of therapy as a positive reinforcer (Bandura et al 12) and desensitizer (Truax & Mitchell 137). For others, implicitly therapeutic interpersonal nurturance is the effect of approach behaviors constituting the criterion (empathy, self-disclosure, confrontation) (Carkhuff 30). What is central, however, is the use of a criterion reflecting an approach response to client's verbalizations of feelings.

THE STUDENT DEVELOPMENT LITERATURE

Preparing a synopsis of the literature on student development presents many problems due to the tremendous variety of studies on this topic. Not only are there vast numbers of individual studies, but these studies themselves differ in philosophical approach, methodology and content.

Methodological Issues

COMMON DESIGNS   Student development research is not developmental research in general. Wohlwill (148) has listed the tasks of developmental psychology as: (*a*) determining the structural relationships and temporal patternings of change among sets of variables, and (*b*) specifying functional relationships between particular, situational, experiential, or organismic variables and selected parameters of change. The task of student development research is to study the relationship between situational and experiential variables and change in behavior, attitudes, and values during the college years while ignoring the change caused by organismic variables.

THE LONGITUDINAL DESIGN   Just as in developmental psychology, methodological problems beset researchers who study changes in students over time. Astin (5) criticizes much of the research conducted in this area and proposes multidimensional and longitudinal approaches. A longitudinal (or time series) design requires several measurements of student attitudes, usually over a period of several years. The process can be repeated as many times and for as long a period as is necessary. The advantage of this design is that subjects are members of the same cohort; that is, that they are all freshmen or sophomores at the same time, and accordingly have been exposed to similar experiences (e.g. the philosophy of the college was the same for all). In addition, a baseline for early behavior of the subject is established and can be subtracted from later measurements.

However, there are disadvantages to employing this design. It is time-consuming, and it does not control for the effect of history (Campbell & Stanley 29). History, or the effect of events extraneous to the college experience, may account for differences between the first and second measures. For example, the gasoline crisis of winter 1974 may result in great changes in the behavior of last year's freshmen, although such changes would be unrelated to these students' college experience. There are also sampling problems inherent in the longitudinal design, since those who leave college are usually eliminated from the sample. This in turn limits the generalizability and interpretation of the results.

THE CROSS-SECTIONAL DESIGN   If freshmen and sophomores were both subjects at the same time and compared on some variable, results would be very different. This cross-sectional type of design confounds a number of variables, such as the year of the subject and the cohort. In terms of the college population it is also subject to sampling problems: the upperclassmen are not usually comparable to the freshmen samples because the designs do not take into account dropouts, transfers, and other shifts in the college population. This occurrence, called experimental mortality (Campbell & Stanley 29) could produce effects which are confounded with the effect of the college experience. Unfortunately, this is a common design in student development research.

MORE SOPHISTICATED ALTERNATIVES   A noted developmental researcher, Schaie (127), suggests several alternatives to the longitudinal and cross-sectional designs which might be more effective in student development research. According to Schaie, responses are a function of the subject's age (or year in school, in this case), the time the measurement is taken, and the cohort of the subject. The designs described earlier usually only take into account one of these variables at a time. The designs Schaie suggests, while not considering all three variables, are an improvement in that two variables are considered simultaneously.

THE TIME-SEQUENTIAL DESIGN   The first design, the time-sequential, considers both the year of the subject and time of measurement. In a time-sequential design, for example, four groups of subjects might be used: (a) a group of subjects who were freshmen in 1974 and measured in 1976 when they were juniors; (b) a group of subjects who were freshmen in 1975 and measured in 1976 when they were sophomores; (c) a group of subjects who were freshmen in 1975 and measured in 1977 when they were juniors; and (d) a group who were freshmen in 1976 and measured in 1977 when they were sophomores. Year is taken into account, since there are two groups of each year, as is time of measurement, since some of the subjects are measured at the same time as the others, but at a different time than the other half of the sample. Cohort is not considered in this design.

THE COHORT-SEQUENTIAL DESIGN   Another new design is called the cohort-sequential. This design takes into account cohort and year but not time of measurement. Here again two groups from different years would be recorded as subjects. These would be (a) one group of subjects who were freshmen in 1974 and measured in 1976 when they were juniors; (b) one group of subjects who were freshmen in 1974 and measured in 1977 when they were seniors; (c) one group who were freshmen in 1975 and measured in 1977 when they were juniors; and (d) a group of freshmen in 1975 measured in 1978 when they were seniors.

THE CROSS-SEQUENTIAL DESIGN   The final design of this type is called a cross-sequential design. It takes into account the time of measurement and the cohort but not the year of the subject. For example, sophomores and juniors would be measured in 1977 (having entered in 1976 and 1975 respectively). Juniors and seniors would be measured in 1978 (having entered in 1976 and 1975 also). The subjects would not be of comparable years.

So, although these designs are an improvement over the simple longitudinal design, they fail to consider one variable. Selection of a particular design depends on which of the three variables (time of measurement, year, and cohort) the researcher wishes to be confounded.

ADDITIONAL VARIABLES   Two additional variables which are not applicable to developmental research in general but are most important to student development research are intercollege comparisons and comparisons of students and non-students. The first variable suggests that by comparing the effect of various colleges on students it is possible to learn about the college experience. The second is predicated on comparing the effects of college attendance to nonattendance. Unfortunately, most of the research in this area examines only college students and completely ignores those young adults who have not gone on to college. When these variables are considered, however, researchers should be careful that those variables mentioned earlier are also taken into account.

Statistical Issues

Aside from these methodological techniques for improving student developmental studies, there have been numerous statistical techniques suggested by researchers in the field. Astin (4) suggests a three-step model examining students at different universities. This model considers the contributions of three types of variables: (*a*) input—those "talents, skills, aspirations, and other potentials for growth and learning that the student brings with him"; (*b*) the college environment—"those aspects of the higher educational institution that are capable of effecting the development of the student"; and (*c*) output—"those skills, attitudes, and behaviors of students the higher educational institution either does influence or attempts to influence." The advantages of this model, according to Astin, are several. In the typical study, an instrument is given to students over a period of time (longitudinal study). The difference between various administrations of the instrument is said to reflect the changes caused by the college experience. The problem with this assumption, as mentioned earlier and noted by Astin (8), is that ". . . any obtained relationship between educational practice and student output is necessarily ambiguous so long as no control is exercised over differential student input" (p. 301). His design eliminates the problem by taking into account student input. With his three-step model, Astin partials the effect of the input out of the output and also out of the college environment.

Astin's research model represents an improvement over many used in past studies in that it incorporates (*a*) students from a representative sample of colleges and universities instead of biased samples; (*b*) uniform measurement instruments, sampling techniques, and methods of subject identification to make data from different investigations interchangeable; and (*c*) both longitudinal and cross-sectional measurements of subjects to result in an approximation of the time-sequential design described earlier. Astin's research utilizing this model was initiated in 1965 with a collection of student input information. The second stage of his model consisted of follow-up criterion data and data about environmental variables. This project has been ongoing ever since and has provided an enormous amount of information about college students.

Astin (4) criticizes suggested statistical alternatives to his techniques. Matching students at different colleges is undesirable because the subsamples thus attained are unrepresentative of their institutions. There are also statistical problems inherent in using actuarial tables to control differential input.

Astin (4), aware of the shortcomings of his own design, concludes that no matter how good the design is, the investigator can be certain that he has isolated the true college impact only in those fortuitous situations where environmental variables are uncorrelated with the input variables in his multiple regression process or where the correlation between the environmental variables and the output variables is much higher than that between environmental variables and the input variables.

Feldman (57) suggests several alternatives to the Astin model. These include: path analysis (Feldman 57); Werts' (145) method in which he partitions the explained variance in the outcome variable into components in order to examine both the independent effects of the predicted variables and the joint effects; and Creager's (46) method of partitioning variance of the output variables into the unique contribution of subsets of variables and the commonality of all subsets. Which method is to be used, Feldman concludes, depends largely on the focus of the research—whether it is correlational prediction or causal analysis.

Philosophical Issues

Moving out of the methodological and statistical arena, research in the area of student development also varies in terms of philosophical and theoretical stance. Most often studies seem to lack systematic theoretical development. Investigators appear to be more concerned with a particular subgrouping of the university population and how it reacts to a particular program at a particular university, than in advancing the body of knowledge of student development research on the impact of the college experience on the student.

Some studies do consider the issue of impact, but few of those investigations are founded in theory. A limited number of studies do construct a theoretical framework on which to view student development research. This framework usually takes one of four major approaches: (a) the goals of higher education; (b) personality development of the student; (c) preparing students to occupy certain occupational and social roles; and (d) variation among colleges (Feldman 56).

GOALS OF HIGHER EDUCATION   Studies of the first type usually center around the academic achievement of students. These include Astin's (8) study of the impact of dormitory living on students. Although this particular study goes beyond simply looking at the educational progress of the students into an examination of attitudinal and personality variables, it does provide a useful model. Results of the study indicate that at a four-year college, living away from home has positive effects on the student's educational development. Students who live away from home are likely to be more successful than students who live with their parents on a number of dimensions: (a) they are less likely to drop out; (b) they are more likely to receive a high grade point average; (c) they are more likely to complete a baccalaureate in 4 years; and (d) they are more likely to apply to graduate school than are students who live at home. Dormitory living has somewhat of an advantage over living in a private room. This study attempts to look at the impact of college residential patterns on educational attainment. In another study, Hall (67) compares the academic performance of community college students with that of 4 year colleges students and finds that the community college students fare better. After 4 years, however, the students who transferred to 4 year colleges do no better than do 4 year students. Unfortunately, to conclude that community colleges have a superior program to 4-year colleges would be erroneous because of methodological inadequacies of Hall's design.

Teaching techniques are often investigated under this format. Leatherwood (99) investigated the effects of different teaching procedures on junior college students. Students found the lecture method to be the least effective when compared with leaderless discussion and role playing. Van Dyne (138) investigated the impact of experimental college on the students. He found that most learning in this situation takes place in small seminars, independent study, and off-campus field study. For some students the freedom was hard to handle, and for others this type of education resulted in greater self-discipline and better awareness of goals, limitations, and strengths. The investigator points to difficulties inherent in evaluating student growth in these programs.

PERSONALITY DEVELOPMENT   A second approach to student development research based upon a theoretical framework is to conduct studies on the personality development of students (Chickering 41). Chickering identified seven significant areas of development, showed the progression of development in these areas using students' evaluation of themselves, and proceeded to discuss the types of programs which would foster change in these areas. Underlying Chickering's research is the Piagetian concept that development occurs through a sequence of differentiation and integration. From this theoretical base, Chickering has then suggested ways of setting up college programs to foster development. More importantly, Chickering has isolated variables of student development: competence, management of emotion, autonomy, identity development, interpersonal development, integrity development, and goal development.

One recently completed study (Barton, Cattell & Vaughan 13) does come closer than most to pinpointing change due to the college experience. It is also one of the rare studies which compares college students to those that do not attend college. Barton et al were particularly interested in specifying changes in personality which occur as a function of college attendance.

Subjects in this study completed Cattell's 16 personality factor questionnaire in 1965 and in 1970 filled out another questionnaire designed to assess the major environmental events which occurred in each subject's life between 1965 and 1970. On the basis of the second questionnaire, subjects were divided into a college group and a work group.

Results indicate that college students score higher on the Cattell questionnaire both before and after college. For both groups, intelligence and radicalism factors increased and suspicion decreased. The authors conclude that these changes indicate age trends (naturally occurring development).

For the factors of tendermindedness and imagination, the college group increased at a higher rate than did the work group, while the work group showed a significantly higher increase in self-sentiment than did the college group. The work group also showed a significant decrease in independence.

King (93) was project director for an important study in the field of college student developmental research. Known as the Harvard Student Study, this was a longitudinal study of personality development during late adolescence and early adulthood. There were four objectives: 1. investigation of the process of personality change and stability as this was related to personality structure and interaction with the college; 2. study of the socializing and allocating functions of the college as an organization in society; 3. development of research methods and general research strategies; 4. development of theory. This latter point is particularly important. The study was unable to proceed on the basis of hypothesis testing based on well-established theory, according to King, because such theory did not exist.

The complexity of this interdisciplinary research (the research team consisted of representatives from sociology, statistics, clinical psychology, psychiatry, and psychoanalysis) is reflected in the translation of general aims into an operational framework consisting of six major variables. Independent variables were the organizational characteristics of Harvard College and the social, cultural, and personality characteristics of the staff and students. Role theory was utilized as a mediating mechanism between the student's personality and the college environment. Finally, criterion variables were patterns of student personality change and stability, stabilization and adaptation, and postcollege roles. A panel design was utilized to ascertain personality changes over time, including both survey and intensive case study approaches. An organizational analysis was undertaken which assessed the structures and functions of the college, with particular emphasis on the academic departments, residential units, and extracurricular organizations. It is well beyond the scope of this review to consider all of the contributions to basic student developmental theory which will be generated by this seminal work.

King (93) published the first in a series of book reports on this project. The "continuity model" of evolutionary personality change which he postulated should provide a basis for hypothesis testing from established theory for subsequent researchers.

Research in other college environments which will generalize beyond the confines of the predominantly eastern selective college subculture should be a first task in future research.

OCCUPATIONAL DEVELOPMENT   The third area, the employment area, includes McCrea's (101) study of the occupational outlook of students. Basically a survey of student expectations of educational and occupational attainment, this type of study provides little information about the impact of college.

VARIATIONS AMONG COLLEGES   Finally, studies of the college environment are more logically related to a conceptual framework. It is not always possible to interpret the correlations between variations in demographic features of a college and variations in student change. What is important is studying how the demographic characteristics create conditions which in turn have an impact on the college student. For this reason, environments are studied. Baird (11) distinguishes eight different functions of college environmental measures which are related to three philosophies of measurement: (a) general research versus applied; (b) inter-versus intra-university; and (c) institution versus individual. Some of the common types include general intrauniversity studies of institution such as the College and University Environment Scale (CUES) by Page (114), and the College Characteristics Index (CCI) by Stern (130), indicating features and characteristics of college environments, and the general interuniversity studies of individuals (ACE type) of Astin et al (8), in which norms of freshmen student characteristics across colleges are developed. Baird cautions that no research can possibly serve all eight functions.

Because students' responses to these standard college environment measures are in part determined by their own demographic characteristics (sex, year in school, major field, residence), some researchers have found it more expedient to partition the total population into several subsamples which can be compared, or to study one subsample of the university population and the impact the educational process has had on that group. As long as no attempt is made to generalize to a larger college population, some useful information can be gathered from these data.

Breakdown of the Student Population

DROPOUTS   As was mentioned earlier, most research in student development looks only at students in college without comparing the data to those gathered from students who have never attended college. There has been great interest, however, in studying students who were once in college but who no longer are at the time of measurement. Studies of dropouts are done, not in order to partition out college impact from general development, but to find out where colleges have failed. Cope & Hewitt (44) studied 1131 students who dropped out within 2 years of college enrollment. Since these investigators were primarily interested in students who chose to drop out, those leaving for involuntary reasons (e.g. illness) were excluded from the analysis. Their results indicate that the most frequent reasons given for leaving college were social, followed by academic, family, religious, financial, fraternity and sorority, and discipline. Morrisey (110) studied dropouts but only among freshmen. With this group, scholastic reasons were most often responsible for the attrition. Persisters were compared to dropouts and it was found that persistence was positively related only to high school rank and fall grade-point average in college. Zaccaria & Creaser (150), who compared graduates, achieving withdrawals, nonachieving withdrawals, and failures, found differences on high school rank and ACT between the former two as compared to the latter two. However, the Edwards Personal Preference Schedule shows that persisting students have somewhat different personal needs than those of students who withdraw. Taken together, these results suggest that, after an initial period of adjustment to the academic rigors of college, social pressures become more important in decisions of whether to stay in school or leave. Astin's (6) national profile of dropouts seems to contradict this finding. His data indicate that the principal predictors of persistence were high school grades and tests of academic ability. However, his definition of persistence is more conservative than that of most other researchers—persisters are those who complete a BA in 4 years. The criterion therefore excludes all students who take reduced course loads, who "stop out", or who need additional time to make up academic failures. It is not surprising therefore to find that academic data provide the best predictors of those students who are indeed the top students.

Residents versus Commuters

Comparing on-campus residents with nonresidents is another way in which student development researchers have partitioned the overall student population. Sauber (126) investigated the effect of place of residence on college adjustment at Florida State University. Place of residence did not affect the frequency and severity of problems studied. Those living at home or in university residence halls had slightly fewer problems with sociopsychological and personal psychological relations. Paolone (115) investigated the relationship between place of residence and maturity and found little relationship. He did find that those students living off campus were less dogmatic and authoritarian than those living on campus. Chickering & Kuper (42) compared educational outcomes for commuter and resident students. Results indicated that commuters and residents have similar academic experiences but that there are large differences between the two groups in terms of extracurricular activities and relationships with peers and parents. Commuters participate less in extracurricular activities and hold fewer leadership positions. They also have closer ties with their parents and fewer campus friends and fewer dating relationships. Over a 4 year period, commuters changed more often than residents in the direction of increasing their intellectual interests while residents changed more in nonintellectual measures such as complexity and autonomy. Finally, Astin's (7) study, mentioned earlier, found that living away from home has positive benefits on the student's education: these students were less likely to drop out and were more likely to apply to graduate school and receive high grade point averages. Living away from home also had consistently positive effects on students' perceptions of their own interpersonal competency. Living away from home increased the probability that students would be satisfied with the overall undergraduate experience. Astin concludes that institutions considering abandoning dormatories may want to take a second look.

It is difficult to draw conclusions about the impact that place of residence has on student development in view of these contradictory findings. Since, as discussed earlier, most of the methodologies employed by the above investigators are imperfect, perhaps unequivocal results might yet be found.

THE DISADVANTAGED STUDENT   Aside from partitioning the student population in informative ways, student development researchers have also chosen frequently to concentrate on a particular subgroup of the total population.

In the last few years, the disadvantaged student has received close scrutiny. A comprehensive study done by Astin et al (9) assesses the effectiveness of special programs designed to serve high risk students. The investigators were particularly interested in isolating those program components which promised to be of greatest benefit in educating the disadvantaged student. Although the study suffers the common drawback of not distinguishing between naturally occurring development and that development which is specifically related to college experience, it does isolate certain environmental variables which influence developmental outcome. Using the three-step model of student input characteristic, environmental characteristic, and student output, the study determined: 1. Disadvantaged students are more likely to persist in a larger, more selective university than at a less selective institution. They are also more likely to stay at a 2-year college, but the important factors appear to be structure, faculty and curricula. 2. Black students and students of low socioeconomic background receive lower grades in college than those predicted on the basis of high school grades; however, if those same students went to selective colleges they would have received better grades than predicted. 3. Predominantly Black colleges had the effect of strengthening student interest in becoming an authority in a special field or a community leader. 4. The source of financial support is an important factor as to college satisfaction and persistence; scholarships are particularly effective in this regard, while loans had no effect.

Some of the studies in this area focus on particular types of special programs, such as the Open Admission Program at the City University of New York, through which all New York City high school graduates are promised admission to one of the city's 2-year or 4-year colleges. The program was under attack from many quarters following its inception, with the accusations being that it would lower the standards of the colleges and that Open Admission students were failing in larger numbers than regular admission students. Benjamin & Powell (15) counter these charges with data indicating that at least at one college the program was not having the expected deleterious results. While students admitted under the Open Admission Program earned fewer credits during their first semester, 35% successfully completed the semester. The results are viewed as positive by the authors of the study.

Other studies on disadvantaged students include Sedlacek & Brooks' (129) attempt to predict academic success of students in special programs. Because of their largely Black sample, results are mostly applicable to Blacks. They found that SAT scores and high school grades did not correlate with college grades, and that better predictors were the number of credit hours attempted and a positive reaction to external control. They conclude that there are differences in the variables relating to Black student success and that these should be considered in the admission process.

MINORITY STUDENTS   The impact of a college experience on minority students as a subgroup of the total student population has also been examined by several researchers. Bayer (14) reports on trend characteristics of Black freshmen as compared to non-Blacks. His results indicate few changes in trends among Black college freshmen since 1968 and a remarkable similarity between Black and non-Black students in predominantly White universities. Watley (142) investigated the effects of marriage on college attendance among both Black and non-Black students. In general, married students are less likely to complete their freshman year than are nonmarried students. They are also likely to get poorer grades than their single peers. His findings also indicate that a greater portion of Black men are married than non-Black men. Watley (141) also looked at the effect of finances on college attendance among Black and non-Black students who had taken the

National Merit Scholarship Qualifying Test. Blacks had more scholarships, government aid, and college loans, while non-Blacks received more parental aid, summer jobs, and savings. Students who did not attend college indicated that they needed money for at least one half of their college expenses.

These studies delineate characteristics of students in this subgroup, but give us very little information about the impact college has had on this subgroup. Some research suggests ways in which the university may have some impact on the lives of its students. Burback & Thompson (27) studied alienation among Puerto Rican, Black, and White college students. They found that Blacks scored higher than the other subgroups on total alienation, higher than Whites on powerlessness and normlessness, and higher than Puerto Ricans on social isolation. The authors conclude that Black students face more contradictory norm patterns and feel less in control of their own lives than do other students. They also suggest that the university must work to reduce their negative feelings and change their attitude in order to help them adjust to the college environment.

OTHER SUBGROUPS   Other subgroups that have been studied by student development researchers include low-income students, "older" freshman, "low achievers," and veterans. Holmstrom (77) looks at low-income students as compared to the other undergraduates. Using the Astin technique, she found that they are more likely to be found in public institutions, that they are more often Black and older, that their high school grades were generally higher than those of other students, but that in college they have slightly lower grade-point averages and fewer of them receive baccalaureates. Among low-income students, the sex of the student appears to be an important variable, in that more women in this category are likely to receive their degrees than are men. As in earlier findings, those low-income students at highly selective institutions are more likely to obtain the BA in 4 years than are those in less selective schools. For both low-income students and others, financial support is an important factor for academic success, but the low-income student is particularly dependent on support if he is to make satisfactory progress.

Holmstrom (78) also studied "older" freshmen. She found that most of these students tended to enroll in public institutions in the liberal arts fields rather than technical fields. Usually they enrolled in small, less selective schools. Most were men and economically disadvantaged. Their high school grades were lower than those of the "typical" student, as were their college grades. In a third study completed by Holmstrom (79), low achievers were compared to "other" undergraduates. Low achievers were mostly men and tended to be older. In general, low achievers differed from other students in college experience, plans, achievements, and attitudes.

Drew & Creager (52) studied the veterans who returned to college. Results indicate that veterans are older than the average freshman and from a lower socioeconomic status. More veterans were Black than White, most had poor high school academic records, and had lower educational aspirations than the average freshman.

Most of these studies are in the category of descriptive studies. The different variables that are studied are unrelated and thus lack meaning. Again, the impact of college is not directly the focus of the study, nor is it useful to speculate regarding the impact from the data presented.

Student Development Research: Where It Stands

While the general state of the literature is less than satisfactory, there are several positive aspects of student development research that need to be emphasized. Astin and his colleagues deserve credit for generating a great wealth of information on the college student. Their three-step model has been the basis for many of the studies completed in the last few years. Within this review, several studies employ this research model (5, 7-9, 14, 52, 77-79). Certainly the heuristic value of his model is great.

The continued attempt by others in the field to modify the research methodology is encouraging. It is also encouraging that researchers such as King (93) are seeing the importance of studies of student development in a theoretical framework. This approach will hopefully lead to an elimination of the piecemeal approach that has occurred in the past.

Literature Cited

1. Allen, T. W., Whiteley, J. M. 1968. *Dimensions of Effective Counseling.* Columbus, Ohio: Merrill
2. Anderson, S. C. 1968. Effects of confrontation by high- and low-functioning therapists. *J. Couns. Psychol.* 15:411–16
3. Ibid 1969. Effects of confrontation by high- and low-functioning therapists on high- and low-functioning clients. 16:299–302
4. Astin, A. W. 1970. The methodology of research on college impact, parts one and two. *Sociol. Educ.* 43:223–54, 437–50
5. Astin, A. W. 1972. The measured effects of higher education. *Ann. Am. Acad. Polit. Soc. Sci.* 404:1–20
6. Astin, A. W. 1972. *College Dropouts—A National Profile.* Washington D.C.: Am. Counc. Educ. 71 pp.
7. Astin, A. W. 1973. The impact of dormitory living on students. *Educ. Rec.* 54:204–10
8. Astin, A. W., King, M. R., Light, J. M., Richardson, G. T. 1973. *The American Freshman: National Norms for Fall 1973.* Los Angeles: Coop. Inst. Res. Program
9. Astin, H. S., Astin, A. W., Bisconti, A.

S., Frankel, H. H. 1972. *Higher Education and the Disadvantaged Student.* Washington D.C.: Hum. Serv. Press. 359 pp.
10. Baier, K. 1965. *The Moral Point of View.* New York: Random House
11. Baird, L. L. 1971. The functions of college environmental measures. *J. Educ. Meas.* 8:83–86
12. Bandura, A., Lipsher, D., Miller, P. E. 1960. Psychotherapists' approach-avoidance reactions to patients' expressions of hostility. *J. Consult. Psychol.* 24:1–8
13. Barton, K., Cattell, R. B., Vaughan, G. M. 1973. Changes in personality as a function of college attendance on work experience. *J. Couns. Psychol.* 20:162–65
14. Bayer, A. E. 1972. *The Black College Freshman: Characteristics and Recent Trends.* Washington: Am. Counc. Educ. 98 pp.
15. Benjamin, J. A., Powell, P. E. 1971. Open admissions: Expanding educational opportunity. *J. Nat. Assoc. Women Deans Couns.* 34:146–48
16. Berenson, B. G., Mitchell, K. M., Laney, R. C. 1968. Level of therapist functioning, types of confrontation and

type of patient. *J. Clin. Psychol.* 24:111–13

17. Berenson, B. G., Mitchell, K. M., Moravec, J. A. 1968. Level of therapist functioning, patient depth of self-exploration and type of confrontation. *J. Couns. Psychol.* 15:136–39

18. Bergin, A. E. 1971. The evaluation of therapeutic outcomes. In *Handbook of Psychotherapy and Behavior Change: An Empirical Analysis*, ed. A. E. Bergin, S. Garfield. New York: Wiley

19. Bergin, A. E., Solomon, B. 1970. Personality and performance correlates of empathic understanding in psychotherapy. In *New Directions in Client-Centered Therapy*, ed. T. Tomlinson, J. Hart. Boston: Houghton-Mifflin

20. Bergin, A. E., Strupp, H. H. 1970. New directions in psychotherapy research. *J. Abnorm. Psychol.* 76:13–26

21. Bergin, A. E., Strupp, H. H. 1972. *Changing Frontiers in the Science of Psychotherapy*. Chicago: Aldine-Atherton

22. Birk, J. M. 1972. Effects of counseling supervision method and preference on empathic understanding. *J. Couns. Psychol.* 19:542–46

23. Bolman, L. 1971. Some effects of trainers on their T groups. *J. Appl. Behav. Sci.* 7:309–26

24. Bordin, E. S. 1959. Inside the therapeutic hour. In *Research in Psychotherapy*, ed. E. A. Rubenstein, M. B. Parloff, 235–46. Washington D.C.: Am. Psychol. Assoc.

25. Brahan, J. M. Client reaction to counselor's use of self-experience. *Personnel Guid. J.* 45:568–72

26. Brammer, L. M. 1973. *The Helping Relationship: Process and Skills*. Englewood Cliffs: Prentice-Hall

27. Burbach, H. J., Thompson, M. A. 1971. Alienation among college freshmen: a comparison of Puerto Rican, Black and white students. *J. Coll. Stud. Personnel* 12:248–52

28. Butler, E. R., Hansen, J. C. 1973. Facilitative training: acquisition, retention, and modes of assessment. *J. Couns. Psychol.* 20:60–65

29. Campbell, D. T., Stanley, J. C. 1963. *Experimental and Quasi-Experimental Designs for Research*. Chicago: Rand McNally

30. Carkhuff, R. R. 1969. *Helping and Human Relations: A Primer for Lay and Professional Helpers. Vol. 1 Selection and Training*. New York: Holt, Rinehart & Winston

31. Carkhuff, R. R. 1969. The prediction of the effects of teacher-counselor education: the development of communication and discrimination selection indexes. *Couns. Educ. Superv.* 8:265–72

32. Carkhuff, R. R. 1971. *The Development of Human Resources*. New York: Holt, Rinehart & Winston

33. Carkhuff, R. R. 1972. *The Art of Helping*. Amherst: Hum. Resource Develop. Press

34. Carkhuff, R. R. 1972. *The Art of Problem-Solving*. Amherst: Hum. Resource Develop. Press

35. Carkhuff, R. R. 1972. *The Art of Training*. Amherst: Hum. Resource Develop. Press

36. Carkhuff, R. R. 1972. The development of systematic human resource development models. *Couns. Psychol.* 3:4–11

37. Ibid. New directions in training for the helping professions: toward a technology for human and community resource development, 12–30

38. Carkhuff, R. R., Berenson, B. G. 1967. *Beyond Counseling and Psychotherapy*. New York: Holt, Rinehart & Winston

39. Carkhuff, R. R., Kratochvil, D., Friel, T. 1968. Effects of professional training: Communication and discrimination of facilitative conditions. *J. Couns. Psychol.* 15:68–74

40. Chassan, J. B. 1967. *Research Design in Clinical Psychology and Psychiatry*. New York: Appleton-Century-Crofts

41. Chickering, A. W. 1969. *Education and Identity*. San Francisco: Jossey-Bass

42. Chickering, A. W., Kuper, E. 1971. Educational outcomes for commuters and residents. *Educ. Rec.* 52:255–61

43. Chinsky, J. M., Rappaport, J. 1970. Brief critique of the meaning and reliability of "accurate empathy" ratings. *Psychol. Bull.* 73:379–82

44. Cope, R. G., Hewitt, R. G. 1971. Types of college dropouts: an environmental press approach. *Coll. Stud. J.* 5:46–51

45. Cottrell, L. S. Jr. 1971. Covert behavior in interpersonal interaction. *Proc. Am. Phil. Soc.* 115:462–69

46. Creager, J. A. 1969. *On Methods for Analysis and Interpretation of Input and Treatment Effects on Education Outcomes.* Washington D.C.: Am. Counc. Educ.

47. Culbert, S. A. 1968. Trainer self-disclosure and member growth in two T groups. *J. Appl. Behav. Sci.* 4:47–73

48. Danish, S., Hauer, A. 1973. *Helping Skills: A Basic Training Program.* New York: Behavioral Publ.

49. Davidson, P. O., Costello, C. G. 1969. *N = 1: Experimental Studies of Single Cases.* New York: Van Nostrand Reinhold

50. Dies, R. R. 1972. Group therapist self-disclosure: Development and validation of a scale. *Proc. 80th Ann. Conv. APA* 7:369–70 (Summary)

51. Dies, R. R. 1973. Group therapist self-disclosure: an evaluation by clients. *J. Couns. Psychol.* 20:344–48

52. Drew, D. E., Creager, J. A. 1972. *The Vietnam era: veterans enter college.* Washington D.C.: Am. Counc. Educ. Res. Rep.

53. Eysenck, H. J. 1952. The effects of psychotherapy: an evaluation. *J. Couns. Psychol.* 16:319–24

54. Eysenck, H. J. 1960. *Handbook of Abnormal Psychology.* London: Pitman

55. Eysenck, H. J. 1965. The effects of psychotherapy. *Int. J. Psychiat.* 1:97–178

56. Feldman, K. A. 1969. Studying the impact of college on students. *Sociol. Educ.* 42:207–37

57. Ibid 1970. Some methods for assessing college impacts. 44:133–50

58. Fry, P. S. 1973. Effects of desensitization treatment on core-condition training. *J. Couns. Psychol.* 20:214–19

59. Gazda, G. M. 1973. *Human Relations Development: A Manual for Educators.* Boston: Allyn & Bacon

60. Giannandrea, V., Murphy, K. C. 1973. Similarity self-disclosure and return for a second interview. *J. Couns. Psychol.* 20:545–58

61. Goffman, E. 1959. *The Presentation of Self in Everyday Life.* New York: Doubleday Anchor

62. Goldstein, A. P., Heller, K., Sechrest, L. B. 1966. *Psychotherapy and the Psychology of Behavior Change.* New York: Wiley

63. Goldstein, A. P., Simonson, N. R. 1971. Sociological approaches to psychotherapy research. See Ref. 18, 154–95

64. Goldstein, A., Wolpe, J. 1971. A critique by Alan Goldstein and Joseph Wolpe. *Comparative Psychotherapy,* ed. A. O. DiLoreto, 222–32. Chicago: Aldine-Atherton

65. Grief, E. B., Hogan, R. 1973. The theory and measurement of empathy. *J. Couns. Psychol.* 20:280–84

66. Gurman, A. S. 1973. Instability of therapeutic conditions in psychotherapy. *J. Couns. Psychol.* 20:16–24

67. Hall, L. H. 1971. Academic performances of matched groups of community college and 4-year college students. *J. Educ. Res.* 64:475–77

68. Heck, E. J., Davis, C. S. 1973. Differential expression of empathy in a counseling analogue. *J. Couns. Psychol.* 20:101–4

69. Heilbrun, A. B. 1961. Client personality patterns, counselor dominance, and duration of counseling. *Psychol. Rep.* 9:15–25

70. Heilbrun, A. B. 1961. Male and female personality correlates of early termination in counseling. *J. Couns. Psychol.* 8:31–36

71. Heilbrun, A. B. 1968. Counseling readiness and the problem-solving behavior of clients. *J. Consult. Clin. Psychol.* 32:396–99

72. Ibid 1970. Toward resolution of the dependency-premature termination paradox for females in psychotherapy. 34:382–86

73. Heilbrun, A. B. 1971. Female preference for therapist initial interview style as a function of "client" and therapist social role variables. *J. Couns. Psychol.* 18:285–91

74. Heilbrun, A. B. 1972. Effects of briefing upon client satisfaction with the initial counseling contact. *J. Consult. Clin. Psychol.* 38:30–56

75. Heilbrun, A. B. 1973. History of self-disclosure in females and early defection from psychotherapy. *J. Couns. Psychol.* 20:250–57

76. Hogan, R. 1973. Moral conduct and moral character: A psychological perspective. *Psychol. Bull.* 79:217–32

77. Holmstrom, E. I. 1973. Low income students: Do they differ from "typical"

undergraduates. *ACE Res. Rep.* 8:46

78. Ibid. "Older" freshmen: Do they differ from "typical" undergraduates?, 46

79. Ibid. Low Achievers: Do they differ from "typical" undergraduates?, 44

80. Hosford, R. E. 1974. A behavioral counseling training curriculum—8 part film series and book. Washington, D.C.: Am. Personnel Guid. Assoc.

81. Ivey, A. 1971. *Microcounseling.* Springfield: Thomas

82. Jourard, S. M. 1964. *The Transparent Self.* Princeton: Van Nostrand

83. Kagan, N. 1971. *Influencing Human Interaction* (a filmed six-hour mental health training series and accompanying 186-page instructor's manual). Instructional Media Center, Michigan State Univ., East Lansing

84. Kagan, N. 1974. Influencing human interaction in schools. *Unit I Elements of Facilitating Communication.* Washington, D.C.: Am. Personnel Guid. Assoc.

85. Kagan, N. et al 1967. *Studies in Human Interaction.* East Lansing, Mich.: Educ. Publ. Serv.

86. Kangas, J. A. 1971. Group members' self-disclosure: A function of preceding self-disclosure by leader or other group member. *Comp. Group Stud.* 2:65–70

87. Kaul, T. J., Kaul, M. A., Bednar, R. L. 1973. Counselor confrontation and client depth of self-exploration. *J. Couns. Psychol.* 20:132–36

88. Kellner, R. 1967. The evidence in favor of psychotherapy. *Brit. J. Med. Psychol.* 40:341–58

89. Kelly, G. A. 1955. *The Psychology of Personal Constructs.* Vol. 1. *A Theory of Personal Constructs.* New York: Norton

90. Kiesler, D. J. 1966. Basic methodological issues implicit in psychotherapy process research. *Am. J. Psychother.* 20:135–55

91. Kiesler, D. J. 1971. Experimental designs in psychotherapy research. See Ref. 18, 36–74

92. Kiesler, D. J., Mathieu, P. L., Klein, M. H. 1967. A summary of the issues and conclusions. See Ref. 123, 295–311

93. King, S. H. 1973. *Five Lives at Harvard: Personality Change During College.* Cambridge, Mass.: Harvard Univ. Press

94. Kohlberg, L. 1964. Development of moral character and moral ideology. In *Review of Child Development Research,* ed. M. Hoffman, L. Hoffman, 383–431. New York: Russell Sage Found.

95. Kohlberg, L. 1968. Moral development. *International Encyclopedia of Social Science,* 489–94. New York: Crowell, Collier & MacMillan

96. Kohlberg, L. 1972. A cognitive-developmental approach to moral education. *Humanist* 6:13–16

97. Kohlberg, L., Turiel, E. 1971. Moral development and moral education. In *Psychology and Educational Practice,* ed. G. Lesser, 410–64. Glenview, Ill.: Scott Foresman

98. Kratochvil, D., Aspy, D., Carkhuff, R. 1967. The differential effects of absolute level and direction of growth in counselor functioning upon client level of functioning. *J. Clin. Psychol.* 23:216–17

99. Leatherwood, H. W. 1972. The effectiveness of small-group procedures in the classroom as aids in movement toward self-actualization in junior college students. *Diss. Abstr. Int.* 32:4988

100. May, O. P., Thompson, C. L. 1973. Perceived levels of self-disclosure, mental health, and helpfulness of group leaders. *J. Couns. Psychol.* 20:349–52

101. McCrea, J. M. 1971. *The College Student's Occupational Outlook.* Presented at West. Econ. Assoc., Vancouver, B.C.

102. McDougall, W. 1908. *An Introduction to Social Psychology.* London: Methuen

103. Mead, G. H. 1934. *Mind, Self, and Society.* Univ. Chicago Press

104. Meltzoff, J. 1969. Effectiveness of psychotherapy is amply demonstrated. *Int. J. Psychiat.* 7:149–52

105. Meltzoff, J., Kornreich, M. 1970. *Research in Psychotherapy.* New York: Atherton

106. Mintz, J., Luborsky, L. 1971. Segments versus whole sesssions: Which is the better unit for psychotherapy process research? *J. Abnorm. Psychol.* 78:180–91

107. Mitchell, K. M., Berenson, B. G. 1970. Differential use of confrontation by high and low facilitative therapists. *J. Nerv. Ment. Dis.* 151:303–9

108. Mitchell, K. M., Namanek, T. M. 1972. Effects of therapist confrontation on subsequent client and therapist behavior during the first therapy interview. *J. Couns. Psychol.* 19:196–201

109. Moos, R. H., MacIntosh, S. 1970. Multivariate study of the patient-therapist system: A replication and extension. *J. Consult. Clin. Psychol.* 35:298–307

110. Morrisey, R. J. 1971. Attrition in probationery freshmen. *J. Coll. Stud. Personnel* 12:279–85

111. Mosher, R. L., Sprinthall, N. A. 1971. Psychological education: A means to promote personal development during adolescence. *Couns. Psychol.* 2:3–82

112. Mowrer, O. H. 1964. *The New Group Therapy*. Princeton: Van Nostrand

113. Murphy, K. C., Strong, S. R. 1972. Some effects of similarity self-disclosure. *J. Couns. Psychol.* 19:121–24

114. Pace, C. R. 1963. *Preliminary Technical Manual: College and University Environmental Scales*. Princeton, N. J.: Educ. Test. Serv.

115. Paolone, F. J. 1972. *Collegiate residence and student background: an exploration study into their relationship to student maturity*. PhD thesis. Pennsylvania State Univ. 176 pp.

116. Patterson, C. H. 1967. Research on the selection of counselors. In *Research in Counseling: Evaluation and Refocus*, ed. J. M. Whiteley, 69–101. Columbus, Ohio: Merrill

117. Patterson, C. H. 1969. A current view of client-centered or relationship therapy. *Couns. Psychol.* 1:2–25

118. Patterson, C. H. 1971. *An Introduction to Counseling in the School*. New York: Harper & Row

119. Payne, P., Gralinski, D. M. 1968. Effects of supervisor style and empathy upon counselor learning. *J. Couns. Psychol.* 15:517–21

120. Rogers, C. R. 1951. *Client-Centered Therapy*. Boston: Houghton-Mifflin

121. Rogers, C. R. 1957. Necessary and sufficient conditions of therapeutic personality change. *J. Consult. Psychol.* 21:95–103

122. Rogers, C. R. 1962. The interpersonal relationship: the core of guidance. *Harvard Educ. Rev.* 32:416–29

123. Rogers, C. R., Gendlin, E. T., Kiesler, D. J., Truax, C. B., Eds. 1967. *The Therapeutic Relationship and Its Impact: A Study of Psychotherapy with Schizophrenics*. Madison: Univ. Wisconsin Press

124. Saltmarsh, R. E. 1973. Development of empathic interview skills through programmed instruction. *J. Couns. Psychol.* 20:375–77

125. Sarbin, T. R., Allen, V. L. 1968. Role theory. In *Handbook of Social Psychology*, ed. G. Lindzey, E. Aronson. Reading, Mass.: Addison-Wesley

126. Sauber, S. R. 1972. College adjustment and place of residence. *J. Coll. Stud. Personnel* 13:205–8

127. Schaie, K. W. 1965. A general model for the study of developmental problems. *Psychol. Bull.* 64:92–107

128. Schmidt, L. D., Strong, S. R. 1971. Attractiveness and influence in counseling. *J. Couns. Psychol.* 18:348–51

129. Sedlacek, W. E., Brooks, G. C. 1972. Predictors of academic success for university students in special programs. *Cult. Study Center Res. Rep.*, Univ. Maryland 4:1–13

130. Stern, R. 1966. *Studies of College Environments*. U.S. Dep. HEW Coop. Res. Project #378. Syracuse Univ.

131. Strong, S. R., Dixon, D. N. 1971. Expertness, attractiveness, and influence in counseling. *J. Couns. Psychol.* 18:562–70

132. Strong, S. R., Schmidt, L. D. 1970. Trustworthiness and influence in counseling. *J. Couns. Psychol.* 17:197–204

133. Truax, C. B. 1966. Reinforcement and nonreinforcement in Rogerian psychotherapy. *J. Abnorm. Psychol.* 71:1–9

134. Truax, C. B. 1968. Therapist interpersonal reinforcement of client self-exploration and therapeutic outcome in group psychotherapy. *J. Couns. Psychol.* 15:225–31

135. Truax, C. B., Carkhuff, R. R. 1967. *Toward Effective Counseling and Psychotherapy*. Chicago: Aldine

366 WHITELEY, BURKHART, HARWAY-HERMAN & WHITELEY

136. Truax, C. B., Carkhuff, R. R., Kodman, F. 1965. Relationships between therapist-offered conditions and patient change in group psychotherapy. *J. Clin. Psychol.* 21:327–29
137. Truax, C. B., Mitchell, K. M. 1971. Research on certain therapist interpersonal skills in relation to process and outcome. See Ref. 18, 299–344
138. Van Dyne, L. A. 1972. Experimental colleges: Uneasy freedom, mind-bending strains—and hope. *Chron. Higher Educ.* 6:1
139. Vesprani, G. J. 1969. Personality correlates of accurate empathy in a college companion program. *J. Consult. Clin. Psychol.* 33:722–27
140. Vitalo, R. L. 1970. Effects of facilitative interpersonal functioning in a conditioning paradigm. *J. Couns. Psychol.* 17:141–44
141. Watley, D. J. 1971. Black and non-Black youth: finances and college attendance. *NMSC Res. Rep.* 7:17
142. Ibid. Black and non-Black youth: does marriage hinder college attendance?, 28
143. Weigel, R. G., Dinges, N., Dyer, R.,

Straumfjord, A. A. 1972. Perceived self-disclosure, mental health, and who is liked in group treatment. *J. Couns. Psychol.* 19:47–52
144. Weigel, R. G., Warnath, C. F. 1968. The effects of group therapy on reported self-disclosure. *Int. J. Group Psychother.* 18:31–41
145. Werts, C. E. 1968. Path analysis: testimonial of a proselyte. *Am. J. Sociol.* 73:509–12
146. Whiteley, J. M. 1969. Counselor education. *Rev. Educ. Res.* 30:173–87
147. Wogan, M. 1969. Investigation of a measure of empathic ability. *Psychother. Theory, Res. Pract.* 6:109–12
148. Wohlwill, J. 1970. Methodology and research in developmental change. In *Life Span Developmental Psychology*, ed. L. R. Goulet, P. B. Balks, 150–91. New York: Academic
149. Wright, D. 1971. *The Psychology of Moral Behavior.* Baltimore: Penguin
150. Zaccaria, L., Creaser, J. 1971. Factors related to persistence in an urban commuter university. *J. Coll. Stud. Personnel* 12:286–91

NEUROPHYSIOLOGY OF LEARNING

237

Irving Kupfermann
New York State Psychiatric Institute and
Department of Psychiatry, Columbia University
College of Physicians and Surgeons, New York, NY 10016

A typical learning task involves a motivated organism that perceives a stimulus, reacts to it, and subsequently modifies its behavior. A complete analysis of the neurophysiology of learning thus involves aspects of sensory function and control of movement as well as aspects of motivation and drive. Indeed, the analysis of learning encompasses almost all areas of interest to psychologists, and the broad scope of the problem is reflected in the bewildering number of approaches and techniques that have been applied to its study. In the present review, only a very limited selection of the total literature will be considered. An important basis for selection has been the degree to which it is possible from the research to draw conclusions regarding cellular *mechanisms* of neuronal plasticity. The review is divided into two main parts. The first part deals with research that attempts to study the cellular mechanisms of actual examples of behavioral modifications, either habituation or associative forms of learning. The second part deals with model studies of neuronal plasticity, in which the behavioral relevance of the plasticity has not yet been directly ascertained.

As a result of the emphasis on plastic mechanisms, the review primarily covers electrophysiological studies on invertebrates or simplified vertebrate preparations. By and large, with present day techniques, it is only in such preparations that it is possible to do the types of experiments that *definitively* establish mechanisms. Largely excluded from the present review are studies utilizing such techniques as spreading depression, inhibition of protein synthesis, and lesions. With few exceptions, the interpretation of results of experiments utilizing these techniques depends upon a number of assumptions whose validity cannot be determined. Because of space limitations, the present review also excludes the numerous biochemical studies of learning that have appeared in the past few years.

This review will emphasize the most recent findings, but in order to maintain some degree of historical perspective, studies within the past 5 years will also be considered. For this reason, the review will slighly overlap the previous chapter in the *Annual Review of Psychology* on the neurophysiology of learning (119).

367

As far back as the turn of the century, there was speculation that learning involves alterations of synaptic interactions between neurons. This hypothesis has been supported by numerous experiments demonstrating that synapses have a great capacity for plasticity, but only in the last 5 years has there been convincing evidence that synaptic plasticity mediates alterations of actual behavior. Not surprisingly, the first demonstrations of the behavioral relevance of synaptic plasticity involved studies of habituation, one of the simplest forms of behavioral modification.

HABITUATION

It is gratifying to see that there has been relatively little debate about whether or not habituation qualifies as "true" learning. There seems to be general agreement that habituation is an important class of behavior modification in the life of all organisms, and that habituation has many of the features of more complex forms of learning (e.g. 69, 98, 99).

Vertebrate Studies

The studies of Spencer, Thompson & Neilson (115, 115a) on decrement of the flexion reflex in spinal cats were the first to provide convincing data on the possible mechanisms of habituation. The flexion reflex has also been used to show that dishabituation is a superimposed facilitatory process not directly linked to habituation (115, 118). On the basis of studies of habituation and dishabituation, it has been postulated that every stimulus simultaneously evokes two independent processes—one leading to decrement, the other to increment of responsiveness (118). This simple idea provides a powerful explanatory principle for a great number of experimental observations.

On the basis of the research of habituation of the flexion reflex, several possible mechanisms have been excluded. For example, habituation of the flexion reflex is not due to plastic changes affecting the excitability of the motor neurons (115a, 127). It is also unlikely that habituation is due to a type of presynaptic inhibition at the sensory fiber terminal (49, 127) and, in fact, indirect data suggest that it is unlikely that any type of active inhibitory process underlies habituation of the flexion reflex. One report (128), however, claims to have obtained evidence that on theoretical grounds suggests the operation of an active inhibitory process. These findings, however, could not be replicated in a later study by another laboratory (45), and the theoretical grounds for the argument have been questioned (55). The bulk of evidence suggests that habituation of the flexion withdrawal reflex in spinal cats is due to decrement of excitatory synaptic potentials at the level of the interneurons in the circuit (115a, 128). Some indirect data argue against the possibility that significant decrement occurs at the first synapse (between sensory afferents and interneurons) in the flexion reflex of the cat. For example, decrement at the primary afferents would result in there being little or no generalization between receptive fields, and yet there is virtually complete generalization of habituation from one receptive field to another (45, 115). Furthermore, those interneurons that appear to receive monosynaptic connections from cutaneous afferents do not show a decrease of evoked spike activity when repeatedly activated (115a, 128). It should be noted, however, that in a study of generalization of habituation of the flexion reflex in humans with spinal transection, when a single test stimulus presentation was used to assess generalization, there was virtually no generalization, even when the test point on the skin was as close as 4 cm away from the point that was originally habituated (35). On the other hand, when generalization was assessed by means of repeated stimuli presented at one point following habituation at a nearby point, there was evidence of some generalization, since there was an apparent savings in the rate of habituation. Because of methodological differences, it is difficult to compare various studies of generalization, but further studies of this phenomenon would be valuable and could provide insights into the mechanism of habituation.

Consistent with the hypothesis that the plastic changes underlying habituation and sensitization of the flexion reflex are located at the level of the interneurons is the observation that the responsiveness of interneurons is parallel to the behavioral responses. Two classes of interneurons have been described (48). One class shows a purely decremental response with repeated stimulation, while a second class initially increases in responsiveness but eventually decreases. Behaviorally, with repeated stimulation the flexion reflex can initially show incrementing responses (sensitization) before showing decrement (habituation) (118). Similar classes of neurons found in the spinal cord are also found in the reticular formation (50), and it is likely that mechanisms of tactile habituation present in the spinal cord are also present in the brain. It seems likely that the mechanisms operating in lower animals also operate in humans, since on the behavioral level habituation and dishabituation of the flexion reflex in humans with spinal transection (35, 42, 43) is very similar to that of spinal cats.

Invertebrate Studies

In order to study synaptic mechanisms most effectively, it is necessary to work with a monosynaptic pathway in which it is possible to stimulate the presynaptic unit and record from the postsynaptic unit without the mediation of polysynaptic pathways. In other words, it is necessary to locate both the presynaptic and postsynaptic unit at which the critical change mediating the behavioral plasticity is located. This has not yet been possible in the spinal cord, but it has been possible in several different invertebrates, including the crayfish, the sea hare *Aplysia*, and the cockroach. Habituation of the gill-withdrawal reflex in the marine mollusk *Aplysia* has been extensively studied by Kandel in collaboration with Carew, Castelluci, Kupfermann, and Pinsker (19–22, 78, 99, 100). Habituation in the crayfish has been studied by several investigators including Krasne in collaboration with Bryan, Roberts, Wine, and Woodsmall (72–74b, 131) and by Zucker, Kennedy, and Selverston (139, 141). Studies of habituation in the cockroach are not as complete as in *Aplysia* and the crayfish, but several investigators have recently made important contributions, including Callec, Guillet, Pichon & Boistel (18) and Zilber-Gachelin & Chartier (137, 138). The picture that has so far emerged is surprisingly consistent, indicating that in all cases habituation is due, at least in part, to a decrease of excitatory synaptic efficacy at the central synapses of the sensory units in the reflex pathways.

BEHAVIORAL STUDIES   Habituation of escape responses to tactile stimuli have proved to be the most easily analyzed. These responses typically habituate rapidly. Like higher forms of learning, habituation can be retained for days and even weeks. In a very thorough and well-controlled study of habituation of siphon and gill withdrawal in *Aplysia*, Carew, Pinsker & Kandel (21) showed that habituation in this animal has several parametric features characteristic of higher forms of learning. First, they demonstrated that habituation in *Aplysia* can be retained for a very long period of time. At least 3 weeks after initial habituation experience, acquisition of habituation was more rapid than in control animals. Long-term habituation was produced by training animals daily with 10 trials a day for 5 days. It was also shown that, as is characteristic of higher forms of learning, retention of habituation was better following spaced training (10 trials/day for 4 days) than after massed training (40 trials in one day). A long-term effect was also seen when the spacing between groups of 10 trials was as little as 1½ hours, thus permitting long-term habituation to be readily studied in an acute preparation. Wine and Krasne (73, 131) have found that the escape response in crayfish also shows long-term retention, and full recovery did not occur 24 hours after just 10 trials of previous habituation.

Parallel to the vertebrate flexion reflex, a strong stimulus can produce increased responsiveness of either a habituated response (dishabituation) or a nonhabituated withdrawal response in *Aplysia*. Similar to habituation, sensitization of the withdrawal reflex of *Aplysia* can be retained for several weeks (100). Dishabituation also occurs in the cockroach (138), but probably does not occur in the escape response of crayfish (73).

PERIPHERAL MECHANISMS   Habituation of tail-flip escape responses in the crayfish (73, 141) and of the gill-withdrawal reflex in *Aplysia* (22, 78) does not ordinarily involve peripheral changes either of the sensory end organs or of the muscle and neuromuscular synapse. A source of confusion in the literature on habituation is the fact that under certain specialized conditions, peripheral changes may contribute to response modifications in invertebrates. Thus, for example, in *Aplysia* if tactile stimuli are repeatedly applied directly to a pinnule of the gill instead of to the skin surrounding the gill, the withdrawal response of the pinnule habituates even if the central nervous system is removed (81a, 96). Under some circumstances these peripheral mechanisms may interact with central factors (86). The nature of the peripheral factors is not known, and it is not even clear whether or not the peripheral mechanisms involve peripherally located neurons or are mediated by direct excitation of muscle. The central mechanisms have proven more amenable to cellular analysis, and fortunately peripheral mechanisms can be bypassed by utilizing a weak or moderate stimulus applied to the receptive surface surrounding the gill (81a) instead of directly to the gill itself. Thus the gill can be involved in two distinct reflexes: a gill-withdrawal reflex that habituates via central mechanisms, and a pinnule response that habituates via a peripheral mechanism.

As in *Aplysia*, peripheral mechanisms may, in principle, contribute to reflex habituation in the crayfish, but they probably do not substantially contribute to normal habituation of the lateral giant escape reflex. Thus, for example, the neuromuscular synapse for one of the motor neurons of the escape response shows depression when stimulated at rates of one per minute or less (15). However, the decrement that may occur at this synapse appears to be offset by the facilitation that occurs at the neuromuscular synapses of other motor neurons involved in the escape response (139).

Habituation of the withdrawal response to light in *Pleurobranchaea* appears to invole sensory adaptation, but central mechanisms are probably also involved (33). Finally, there are some data suggesting that a certain degree of sensory adaptation of some types of tactile receptors may accompany repeated tactile stimulation of cockroaches (137). This sensory adaptation is not sufficient to fully explain the response decrement observed in neurons in the central nervous system (137, 138), but it presumably does contribute somewhat.

NEURAL CIRCUITS MEDIATING ESCAPE RESPONSES   In order to study the mechanisms of habituation, it was first necessary to study the neural circuitry controlling the reflexes that habituate. In *Aplysia* the motor neurons that innervate the organs involved in the defensive withdrawal reflex have been identified (79, 95). A possible complication in the neural analysis of molluscan behavior is that molluscan "motor neurons" may not connect directly to muscle. It has recently been shown, however, that gill motor neurons in *Aplysia* produce discrete junction potentials in gill muscle (21a, 81a). It thus appears very likely that despite the presumed existence of an extensive peripheral "nerve net" in the muscles of *Aplysia*, the gill motor neurons make direct connections to muscle. In *Tritonia*, on the other hand, the motor neurons mediating the swimming escape response may not make direct connections to muscle (59).

Gill motor neurons in *Aplysia* receive both a monosynaptic and polysynaptic excitatory synaptic input from the mechanoreceptors that mediate the reflex (17, 22). The cell bodies of the mechanoreceptors are located within the ganglion containing the motor neurons, permitting simultaneous recording and stimulation of the sensory neurons and their follower cells—either motor neurons or interneurons that in turn excite motor neurons.

In the crayfish, the motor neurons mediating the tactile escape reflex may receive direct connections from tactile sensory units (73, 139), but their main input comes from the lateral giant fibers, which are a series of electrically connected neurons that function as a single fiber (141). The lateral giant fibers receive input either directly from sensory units via electrical synapses or indirectly from a small number of interneurons that produce excitatory synaptic potentials in the giant fibers. These interneurons, in turn, very likely receive a direct (monosynaptic) chemical excitatory input from mechanoreceptor units.

In the cockroach, the neural circuit of the escape reflex has not yet been worked out in detail. For many years it was felt that the escape reflex in cockroaches is mediated by the giant fibers of the ventral nerve cord, but recently it was shown that direct stimulation of the largest giant fibers does not result in an escape response (32).

LOCUS OF PLASTIC CHANGES UNDERLYING HABITUATION AND DISHABITUATION   In order to study the central neuronal changes mediating habituation, it was necessary to develop semi-intact preparations in which it is possible to simultaneously record behavior and intracellular neural activity. Such semi-intact preparations were developed independently for the study of gill withdrawal in *Aplysia* (79) and for the swimming response in *Tritonia* (129). In the semi-intact preparation in *Aplysia*, it was shown that the short-term decrease of reflex responsiveness of the gill was due to progressively fewer spikes elicited in gill motor neurons by repeated tactile stimulation. The identified gill motor neuron L7 was studied in detail since its action could be shown to account quantitatively for a substantial (30–40%) proportion of the total gill contraction elicited by a tactile stimulus (81a). In some *Aplysia* neurons *not* related to the gill, repeated direct firing by means of depolarizing pulses leads to progressively fewer spikes (80, 116a), but this is not the case for gill motor neurons (21a). Thus the decreased firing of L7 during habituation is not. due to decreased excitability of the neuron. Instead, decreased firing was shown to be due to a progressive decrease in the size of the complex excitatory synaptic potential that is evoked in L7 by tactile stimuli applied to the skin of the animal. In order to study the mechanism of the decreased synaptic input, a simplified preparation was used in which it was possible to record the monosynaptic potentials that mechanoreceptor neurons produce on interneurons and motor neurons (22). These monosynaptic potentials progressively diminish in size when repeatedly elicited at low rates (22), indicating that at least part and perhaps all of the reflex decrement is due to a change occurring at the primary afferent synapse. When another afferent pathway was stimulated strongly, the same synapse that showed decrement showed facilitation. Thus neural changes mediating both habituation and dishabituation in *Aplysia* were shown to have the same locus in the nervous system. In addition, changes at that locus also contribute to the phenomenon of sensitization, since dishabituation in *Aplysia* is a special case of sensitization (19).

In crayfish, behavioral decrement was shown to be associated with a decrement of the later component of a two-component excitatory synaptic potential at the lateral giant fiber (72). The later synaptic component is a complex synaptic potential composed of individual potentials produced by several interneurons that are excited by tactile afferents (141). Further analysis showed that during habituation there was a decrease in the number of these interneurons fired by the afferent input (72, 139). The decreased firing of the interneurons in turn was due to a decrease of the monosynaptic excitatory synaptic input from mechanoreceptor afferents (140). Thus, both in crayfish and *Aplysia* decrement occurs at the first central synapses of the primary receptors.

In the cockroach, the behavioral significance of neurophysiological studies is less certain than in the crayfish or *Aplysia*, but there is evidence that habituation of the escape response is due to decrement of excitatory synaptic potentials at the central synapses of the primary afferent fibers (18, 137), as well as higher order synapses (138). Unlike *Aplysia*, dishabituation in the cockroach may not involve the primary afferent synapse, but may operate only at higher levels (138).

MECHANISM OF SYNAPTIC CHANGE DURING HABITUATION   Since in the examples discussed, synaptic decrement occurs in a monosynaptic pathway in which only a single presynaptic element is stimulated, it is virtually certain that the decrement represents a depression of excitatory snynaptic transmission rather than active inhibition. Although presynaptic inhibition can occur at the central terminals of the mechanoreceptor neurons in the crayfish (74), such presynaptic inhibition does not mediate synaptic decrement during behavioral habituation. Instead, presynaptic inhibition appears to be active only during tail flips, and thereby prevents excessive decrement of the central mechanoreceptor synapses.

Since habituation in invertebrates is not due to an active inhibitory process, it is unlikely that dishabituation is due to the blocking of inhibition. As was suggested in vertebrates (115a), dishabituation appears to be an independent facilitatory process (19, 22). The most parsimonious explanation of dishabituation in *Aplysia* is that it results from a type of presynaptic facilitation (67), although direct data are lacking.

A major question concerning the mechanism of the decrement of excitatory synaptic potentials during habituation is whether the decrement is due to presynaptic or postsynaptic factors. A presynaptic cause of decrement implies that synaptic decrement is due to progressively less transmitter substance being released for each presynaptic spike. Postsynaptic causes of synaptic decrement imply that there is a constant amount of transmitter release with repeated presynaptic spikes, but that the transmitter becomes progressively less effective in depolarizing the postsynaptic cell. Postsynaptic factors could include such things as changes in the resistance of the postsynaptic cell or desensitization of the postsynaptic receptors that react with the transmitter substance. Evidence from neuromuscular junctions and other model synaptic systems exhibiting synaptic decrement indicates that decrement usually results from a presynaptic process that operates to reduce transmitter output with repeated release (see p. 379). At certain synapses, synaptic decrement (of unknown behavioral significance) may also be due to a postsynaptic process involving receptor desensitization (31, 122). In both the crayfish (140) and *Aplysia* (21b), however, the available data indicate that behaviorally relevant decrement is due to decreased transmitter release rather than receptor desensitization. This conclusion was made on the basis of a quantal analysis of the decremented and nondecremented excitatory synaptic potential (see p. 378 et seq on model studies for a discussion of quantal analysis). Because of technical difficulties in the crayfish (140), it was not possible to apply the most direct and powerful methods of quantal analysis. The method that was used (variance method) is based upon an analysis of fluctuations of the size of the synaptic potential, and this method is valid only if a number of underlying assumptions are applicable. Unfortunately, it was not possible to directly assess whether these assumptions were indeed applicable. Nevertheless, the data obtained were consistent with the interpretation that the decrement was due to the release of less transmitter per presynaptic spike, i.e. there was a decrease of quantal content.

A similar conclusion was reached in preliminary studies of the sensory-to-motor-neuron synapse that mediates habituation of the gill-withdrawal reflex in *Aplysia* (21b). At this synapse it was possible to apply more direct techniques for assessment of quantal content, and it could be shown that repeated presynaptic spikes released progressively less quantal units (m) of transmitter. In some experiments the magnesium ion concentration in the bathing solution was raised in order to decrease the release per presynaptic spike to an average of only one or a few quanta. Under these conditions, during successive presynaptic spikes, there was no change of the size of the voltage change produced by individual quanta (q), but there was an increase in the number of failures (lack of any release). An increase of failures argues very strongly against a postsynaptic mechanism of depression, such as receptor desensitization.

The analysis of the synaptic mechanisms underlying habituation thus far have been limited to short-term habituation. For reasons that are not understood, habituation obtained in acute crayfish preparations exhibits only very brief retention, even though habituation of the same response in intact crayfish exhibits long-term retention of greater than 24 hours (73). On the other hand, electrophysiological evidence from the isolated abdominal ganglion of *Aplysia* indicates that this preparation can exhibit retention of synaptic decrement at gill motor neurons for a period of at least 24 hours (20). It should therefore prove possible to analyze the mechanism of long-term habituation of withdrawal reflexes in *Aplysia* and to gain important insights into the relationship of short-term to long-term storage processes.

ASSOCIATIVE LEARNING

Vertebrate Studies

Research on the mechanisms of associative learning has been done primarily on vertebrate preparations. In many invertebrates it has not been possible to demonstrate associative learning, and those invertebrates that exhibit the clearest examples of associative learning by and large do not have the most favorable nervous systems for study.

The great majority of studies of vertebrate associative learning have not been concerned with cellular mechanisms of learning and consequently will not be reviewed in detail. These studies try to trace the flow of information from one neural structure to another during the course of acquisition, retention, and extinction. In an attempt to separate secondary changes of neuronal activity from primary changes, a number of studies from the laboratory of Olds (e.g. 70, 109) have looked at those changes of single unit activity that occur with the shortest latency following the presentation of a conditioned stimulus. The interpretation of findings utilizing this method is highly dependent upon detailed anatomical knowledge, not only of what is connected to what, but also of the conduction velocity of the interconnecting pathways. At present such anatomical knowledge is not sufficient to provide unambiguous interpretation of experiments that utilize latency information to discriminate primary from secondary neural changes.

An important series of recent studies by Woody and his collaborators (134, 135) have attempted to analyze the cellular mechanisms of classical conditioning in the cat. Although these studies constitute one of the most promising approaches toward identifying the nature of the plastic changes underlying associative learning in vertebrates, because of statistical and methodological problems it is imperative that these studies be independently confirmed.

A key element in the studies of Woody and collaborators is the physiological identification of the single units that are studied. By means of microstimulation through a microelectrode, cells (or small populations of cells) were classified as belonging to different motor systems. Confirming previous findings by others, closely spaced neurons within a single cortical electrode tract were found to project (polysynaptically) to distinctly different motor fields. In groups of cats classically conditioned with one or another response as the unconditioned response, there was a corresponding shift in the prevalence and in the threshold for activation of the type of cell whose motor projection corresponded to the conditioned response. Thus, for example, in cats trained to eyeblink (unconditioned stimulus, glabella tap) in response to a click (conditioned stimulus), a click stimulus activated more cells that projected to eyeblink muscles than to nose muscles, and vice versa for cats trained to exhibit a nose twitch to a conditioned stimulus. Thus, after conditioning, within a population of intermingled cells the conditioned stimulus tended to excite a specific subpopulation of cells more than other subpopulations. A significant finding from these studies was the observation that although with conditioning there was an increase in the *number* of motor-specific cells that responded to the conditioned stimulus, there was no consistent increase in the average number of spikes elicited per unit. Thus it was concluded that a response occurs when the total number of units activated by a stimulus exceeds a certain value (135).

In addition to an increase in the number of responsive motor-specific cells in conditioned cats, Woody & Engel (135) found that there was a decrease in the electrical threshold for activation of cells projecting to the motor field of the conditioned response. Since electrical stimulation of the brain can excite cells either directly or synaptically by exciting presynaptic fibers, these experiments cannot determine whether the threshold change is due to presynaptic or postsynaptic changes at the neuron.

In order to explore the nature of threshold changes during learning, Woody & Black-Cleworth (134) utilized intracellular recording techniques in an attempt to directly measure the threshold and input resistance of cells projecting to the motor field of the conditioned response. They found that in cats trained to eyeblink, eye projection motor cells had significantly lower threshold for firing than did nose projection cells. Since in this case the electrode was intracellular, the threshold was measured by current limited to the stimulated cells, and it is therefore very likely that the threshold change represents a change in the neuron itself rather than a change in its presynaptic input. This represents the first systematic study which claims to have demonstrated a postsynaptic locus for a plastic change associated with learning, and as such deserves very careful scrutiny. Unfortunately, this study did not include either a nonconditioned control group or a group conditioned to make a different conditioned response. Consequently, it is impossible to unequivocally eliminate the possibility that neurons that project to eye muscles are different from other cells, independent of whether the cat is conditioned or not.

Invertebrate Studies

INSECTS   In 1962, Horridge reported that it was possible to train headless cockroaches to position a leg so as to minimize an electric shock that was given whenever the leg dropped below some preset level. This type of learning appeared to be highly promising for neural analysis. The learning could occur even when all of the central nervous system was removed except for a single ganglion in the ventral nerve cord. Following the initial reports of learning of leg position in insects, there were a number of behavioral and physiological studies of this phenomenon (reviewed by Eisenstein 37), but progress in understanding the neural mechanisms at a cellular level has been disappointing. Hoyle & Burrows (58), however, have recently reported a very promising development. They have identified the locust motor neuron that was previously shown to undergo modification of tonic firing rate contingent upon an operant conditioning regimen (57). This neuron, the tonic motor neuron of the anterior aductor of the coxa (AAdC), could be impaled by intracellular electrodes for morphological and electrophysiological studies. By means of dye injection techniques, they studied the morphology of the AAdC (16). Unlike the other motor neurons studied in the metathoracic ganglion, this cell was devoid of branches on a particular segment of its axonal process in the neuropile. Intracellular recordings from the AAdC suggested that the spike activity of this cell is not driven one-for-one by an underlying excitatory synaptic potential. Rather, the cell shows tonic activity that appears to be modulated by a background level of synaptic activity. These data indicate that modification of the firing frequency of this cell could be due to either a change in its tonic level of excitatory or inhibitory synaptic input, or to a change in the firing threshold of the cell. Tosney & Hoyle (120) have reported a new automated operant training technique for producing alterations in the firing rate of the AAdC.

GASTROPOD MOLLUSKS   The gastropod mollusks are ideal for cellular neurophysiological study, but up until very recently there was no convincing evidence that they are capable of associative learning. Widely quoted studies of maze learning or classical conditioning in snails (see Willows 130 for review) on close examination reveal a total lack of appropriate controls for nonassociative forms of learning. Far better controlled than these early reports are recent studies of conditioning of feeding responses in the marine mollusk *Pleurobranchaea* (33) or the pulmonate slug *Limax* (Gelperin, submitted for publication). It is nevertheless still premature to conclude that associative conditioning has been unequivocally demonstrated. These recent studies have not yet received independent replication, and additional controls would be desirable. In at least one instance, an attempt to replicate (77) a study of conditioning of feeding in *Aplysia* (63) was unsuccessful. In addition, some of the parametric features of conditioning in gastropod mollusks are very different from what is generally considered to be characteristic of conditioning in vertebrates. For example, conditioning in *Pleurobranchaea* (33) occurs even when there is zero time interval between the conditioned stimulus (tactile stimulation with a glass rod) and the unconditioned stimulus (extract of squid juice). The glass rod was dipped in the squid extract and then rubbed on the oral veil of the animal. Unfortunately, this technique of simultaneous presentation of the conditioned and unconditioned stimulus makes it impossible to do a control experiment in which an identical unconditioned stimulus can be presented unpaired with the conditioned stimulus.

There is a preliminary report of neural correlates associated with conditioning of feeding responses in *Pleurobranchaea* (33). Although promising, these studies are not yet complete enough to permit any conclusions.

PRELUDES TO ASSOCIATIVE CONDITIONING   Several different features of nonassociative behavioral modification in gastropod mollusks could provide an insight into associative forms of learning. Sensitization can be demonstrated readily in mollusks, and it has been argued that sensitization may be an evolutionary precursor of associative conditioning (124).

Two features of habituation in *Aplysia* that may be relevant to associative learning are greater retention with spaced compared to massed training (21), and less rapid habituation with strong compared to weak stimuli (99). These features may represent primordial elements of associative conditioning. It may well be that detailed understanding of the temporal and spatial features of nonassociative forms of learning will provide important clues to the mechanism of associative learning.

MODEL STUDIES OF NEURONAL PLASTICITY

Alterations in behavior presumably involve neuronal plasticity, or the property of neurons to undergo functional alterations. Until recently all of our knowledge of neuronal plasticity came from studies of "model" systems that were not involved in actual behavioral changes, or whose behavioral relevance was unknown. Although it is now possible in a few instances to analyze the mechanisms of neuronal plasticity known to mediate actual changes of behavior, model studies of plasticity still constitute an important source of data relevant to the neurophysiology of learning. Model studies help define the biologically meaningful boundaries for theoretical treatments of the neurophysiology of learning. In addition, studies of experimentally favorable model systems, such as neuromuscular junctions, can provide the basic concepts and techniques for the study of less experimentally favorable systems that are behaviorally relevant. There is an unfortunate tendency for some authors to utilize behavioral terms such as habituation to describe neurophysiological processes such as synaptic depression (e.g. 15, 137), thereby blurring the distinction between studies of established behavioral significance with model studies that have only theoretical significance.

Protozoa

Because of the great differences of the behavioral integrative systems between protozoans and metazoans, it can be questioned whether behavioral modification in protozoans should be termed learning. Protozoans, however, exhibit response decrement (5, 93, 133) similar to metazoan habituation, and they may prove useful as model systems for what may occur at vertebrate synapses during habituation.

There is good evidence that response decrement in protozoa is not due to fatigue of the motor apparatus (5, 133). Decrement may be due to the waning of some process associated with sensory transduction. By means of intracellular recording from *Stentor*, Wood (132) found that repeated mechanical stimulation evokes a progressively smaller prepotential. The prepotential ordinarily appears to trigger an action potential and associated movement. As the prepotential becomes smaller, it appears to no longer trigger an action potential and contraction fails to occur.

Studies on the biophysical or biochemical basis of response decrement in protozoa have largely yielded negative results. For example, there was no detectable increase or decrease of the total quantity of inorganic ions in unstimulated or stimulated protozoa (3). Similarly, alteration of protein synthesis does not appear to be associated with response decrement (2) and, in fact, decrement still occurs in cell ghosts of animals that have had their macronuclei removed (6). Applewhite & Gardner (3) have postulated that response decrement in protozoa is not due to an energy-consuming process, since the rate of decrement is constant over a wide temperature range. They suggest that alterations of the distribution of magnesium or calcium stores within the organism may underlie response decrement.

Despite continued attempts to demonstrate associative behavioral modifications in protozoa, there are still no convincing examples that have been generally accepted (see e.g. 4, 51).

Synaptic Plasticity

QUANTAL ANALYSIS   At one time, studies of synaptic plasticity were largely of academic interest to psychologists interested in mechanisms of learning. The demonstration that synaptic plasticity can indeed mediate behavioral modifications gives renewed significance to model studies of synaptic function, and it is becoming increasingly clear that psychologists interested in mechanisms of learning must understand synaptic physiology. An excellent elementary treatment of synaptic function is provided by Katz (67a), and several more technical reviews are also available (e.g. 60, 61, 76, 88a). To a psychologist, the literature on synaptic plasticity may appear highly complex and technical, but much of this literature can be understood on the basis of a few elementary concepts regarding the "quantal theory" of Del Castillo & Katz (34). Quantal theory provides the basic concepts and theoretical tools for the physiological analysis of synaptic function and modification of synaptic function. The basic postulate of quantal theory is that the transmitter substance at the presynaptic terminal of a synapse is released in discrete packets. A synaptic potential of size $\bar{V}$ millivolts is composed of m number of quantal units each of which contributes q millivolts, that is, $\bar{V} = mq$. The release of each quantal unit is a statistical process. In the resting state the probability of release (p) is very small, but invasion of the terminal by an action potential very briefly results in a large increase of p.

Empirically it has been found that at many synapses, for relatively low levels of release the statistical properties of transmitter release follows a Poisson or close to Poisson distribution. The discovery that the synapse contains morphologically discrete synaptic vesicles led to a hypothetical identification of the constants of the Poisson equation with real entities. One notion is that if there is a population of n vesicles that can be readily released, and each vesicle has a probability p of being released during an action potential, then m (the number of quanta released per action potential) $= pn$. The value of m will vary from spike to spike since it is determined by a probabilistic constant p. The frequency distribution of repeated values of m will be Poisson if p is not too large, n is very large and the release of quanta are independent events. A variety of methods exist for estimating the values of q, m, n, and p at synaptic terminals, and an important thrust in the analysis of synaptic plasticity has been an attempt to characterize altered synaptic potentials in terms of alterations of these parameters.

With rare exceptions, during the decade following the first description of the quantal hypothesis, it was found that both increases as well as decreases of synaptic efficacy were due to a presynaptic factor, i.e. a change in m, reflected in a change in the amount of transmitter released (61). As described earlier, quantal analysis has been used to help establish that habituation in crayfish and *Aplysia* is due to a decrease of quantal content (m) at the synapses of primary afferent fibers. During the past 5 years, in model studies of synaptic plasticity, there have been many attempts to relate changes in m to a change of either the probability of release (p) or the number of releasable quanta (n). A number of investigators have concluded that both increases and decreases of successively evoked synaptic potentials can be due to changes of either p or n or both (9, 25, 125).

Complicating the analysis of synaptic plasticity in terms of changes in p and n is the suggestion that p and n may not be so readily translated into simple representations of a quantity of synaptic vesicles and the probability of release. For example, p may represent the combined probability of a vesicle moving into a release site and the probability of release from that site (140).

CALCIUM AND INCREASED TRANSMITTER RELEASE   Of the numerous hypotheses put forth to explain the mechanism of alterations of transmitter release that occurs following preceding release, the most viable has been the suggestion of Katz & Miledi (68) to explain facilitation or increased transmitter release for a period up to approximately 250 msec following a single presynaptic spike. They suggested that facilitation is the result of residual calcium that remains in the presynaptic terminal following the initial inflow of calcium during the first presynaptic spike. This hypothesis is based in part on the finding that at the vertebrate neuromuscular junction the amount of transmitter release per presynaptic impulse is related to the fourth power of the external (and presumably internal) calcium concentration (36, but see also 29, 92). An exponential relationship between internal calcium concentration and transmitter release would mean that small changes of the concentration of calcium in the presynaptic terminal would produce large changes in transmitter release.

The basic observation in support of the residual calcium hypothesis is that the amount of calcium present at the terminal during the first presynaptic spike determines the degree of increase of the amount of transmitter released by the second presynaptic spike. Both an early (68) as well as later stage of facilitation (136) can be acounted for by the residual calcium hypothesis. It has been speculated that because of the great affinity of mitochondria for calcium, mitochondria may regulate neuronal levels of calcium (83) and may thereby help terminate transmitter release following the inrush of calcium at the presynaptic terminal (103).

A role for calcium in mediating the relatively long lasting potentiation following a train of presynaptic spikes (post-tetanic potentiation) has been suggested on the basis of experiments similar to those studying facilitation. Increasing the external calcium ion concentration present during tetanic stimuli increases the *duration* of the following post-tetanic potentiation (105, 123). The maximum *degree* of potentiation, however, is not much affected, and there does not appear to be a good quantitative fit between observed potentiation and potentiation to be expected on the basis of the calcium ion concentration present during the tetanic stimulation.

It has been claimed recently that synapses in the hippocampus can show very prolonged potentiation following stimulation of the perforant pathway (11, 12). Prolonged potentiation, in the range of hours, has also been reported at certain neuromuscular synapses in crustaceans (111) and at the synapse between the lateral column fibers and motor neurons in the frog (38). The role of calcium in very prolonged post-tetanic potentiation has not been studied.

As well as calcium directly regulating the amount of transmitter release, there is evidence that calcium may regulate the rate of synthesis of transmitter agents. Banks, Magor & Mraz (8) have found that reducing the calcium ion concentration leads to a decreased rate of synthesis of noradrenalin.

SYNAPTIC DECREMENT AND TRANSMITTER DEPLETION   Until recently, most experimental evidence suggested that synaptic decrement was related to a depletion of n or the readily available store of transmitter quanta. For example, as would be predicted by the depletion hypothesis, at the vertebrate neuromuscular junction the degree of depression is directly related to the amount of transmitter released per presynaptic spike (117).

The first evidence suggesting that simple depletion of transmitter stores cannot explain synaptic decrement came from a study of Kuno (75) on the monosynaptic excitatory connection between muscle afferents and motor neurons in the spinal cord. Previous studies indicated that this synapse shows decrement at rates of stimulation as low as one every 10 seconds (84). If activity of the synapse led to transmitter depletion, it might be expected that the quantal content of each afferent terminal would be relatively large or n would be small. A quantal analysis of this synapse revealed that the actual quantal content per afferent terminal is very low, each fiber releasing an average of only a single quantum per spike (75). Furthermore, the size of the second of a pair of evoked synaptic potentials was not related to the size of the previous potential. An inverse relationship would be expected if n was small and the transmitter store was easily depleted. It would be of interest to see whether the dorsal column synapse onto motor neurons also has properties similar to the muscle afferent synapse. The dorsal column synapse recently has been found to show decremental responses at low rates of stimulation and, similar to the muscle afferent synapse, the decrement cannot be explained by an active inhibitory process (38).

Recent data on two other rapidly decrementing synapses also suggest that a simple decrease of n cannot explain synaptic decrement. Bruner & Kennedy (15) have found that the depression of synaptic efficacy at the giant-to-motor synapse in crayfish is unaltered (as a percent of initial value) even when transmitter release per presynaptic spike is greatly reduced by raising the magnesium ion concentration in the bathing solution. Similar results have been obtained in preliminary studies of the behaviorally relevant decrementing synapse in *Aplysia* (21b).

Despite the recent data, the actual mechanism of transmitter release is not well enough understood to completely rule out the possibility that synaptic decrement is due to a decrease of the amount of available transmitter, but it is becoming increasingly attractive to consider that decrement, especially at rapidly decrementing synapses, is due to a decrease of the probability of release of a constant store of transmitter. An attractive feature of this hypothesis is that both synaptic increment and synaptic decrement could be explained by a similar mechanism involving alteration of presynaptic calcium levels. Just as increased presynaptic levels of calcium ions could, in principle, explain increased transmitter release, a decrease of presynaptic calcium levels could explain synaptic depression.

CYCLIC ADENOSINE MONOPHOSPHATE   Cyclic adenosine monophosphate (cAMP) has been identified as a substance that mediates many different cellular events triggered by external stimuli (46), and as such it is natural that it should figure in speculation regarding mechanisms of learning. In one symposium concerned with the role of cAMP in the nervous system, no less than four papers concluded by speculating that cAMP may be involved in both short-term and long-term memory (13, 47, 54, 82). Several different transmitters have been shown to stimulate neuronal production of cAMP (46), and there is reason to believe that cAMP could have effects on the genetic readout of the cell (82), as well as on membrane properties (104). Particularly intriguing are the data suggesting that epinephrine may increase the release of acetylcholine at the neuromuscular junction by stimulating increased presynaptic levels of cAMP (112). On the basis of analogy to other systems, it has been suggested that cAMP may affect neuronal function by altering membrane permeability or binding to calcium (104). cAMP could affect movement of calcium into organelles within the terminal such as microsomal vesicles (14, 112) or mitochondria. Alternatively, it might regulate movement of calcium across the membrane, out of presynaptic terminals into the intracellular space.

THEORETICAL MODELS   The basic features of classical or operant conditioning can be realized by means of elementary neuronal plastic properties combined with very simple connectivity patterns of the constituent neurons (e.g. 44, 81). Several authors have pointed out that by means of appropriate circuitry, conditioning can result from a *decrease* as well as *increase* of synaptic effectiveness (44, 56, 81, 107). Speculation regarding the role of decreased synaptic effectiveness in learning is of added interest given the fact that at present the only documented neuronal mechanism of a behavioral change is a decrease of synaptic efficacy (see pp. 373–74). Further, many of the trophic interactions between neurons, as discussed below, involve decreases of synaptic effectiveness or connectivity.

TROPHIC INTERACTIONS AND CONTINGENT ALTERATIONS OF SYNAPTIC INTER-ACTION   Since associative learning involves alteration of behavior as a function of some contingent relationship between stimuli or responses, researchers have been interested in whether or not long-term changes of synaptic effectiveness of a presynaptic element can be contingent upon the activity either of the postsynaptic unit or of other presynaptic terminals on the same postsynaptic element. A number of experiments suggest that contingent modifications of synaptic function is possible, but in no case have such modifications been causally related to learning.

One intriguing possibility of an interaction between presynaptic and postsynaptic activity arises from the observations of Lømo & Rosenthal (85) and Cohen & Fischbach (27). These workers have found that lack of activity of muscle leads to a spread of acetylcholine sensitivity over the whole muscle membrane, and that conversely, activity of the muscle results in shrinkage of active receptor areas to the region of the end plate. Thus the spread of receptor sensitivity following denervation of muscle or neurons (supersensitivity) may not be due to the removal of a trophic substance contained in the nerve, but rather may be due to lack of activity of the postsynaptic element. Stent (116) has speculated that reversal of the sign of the membrane potential during the action potential of a neuron (or muscle) "destroys" receptors on the surface, but that the postsynaptic receptors immediately under the region of terminals that have been active are spared because this region is not as severely depolarized by the postsynaptic action potential. This mechanism could provide the physical basis of the Hebb hypothesis of associative learning. Only those synapses that have participated in firing the postsynaptic cell would remain effective, whereas synapses not involved in firing the neuron would become ineffective due to the disappearance of active receptors.

Although there are data that suggest that the spread of receptor sensitivity following denervation is not due to the removal of a trophic substance (as was previously believed), some experiments suggest that under certain conditions lack of a trophic substance in nerve may also result in spread of active receptors (64). Harris has recently reviewed the trophic functions of nerve cells (52).

Several experiments suggest that a trophic substance in one nerve terminal may affect the spatial distribution of other terminals. Aguilar et al (1), for example, have found evidence consistent with the hypothesis that axoplasmic flow within a neuron continually provides the terminal with a substance that diffuses out and functions to prevent the invasion of nearby terminals. When axoplasmic flow of a nerve was blocked, the sensory field of the nerve appeared to be "invaded" by the terminals of nearby nerves. Marotte & Mark (88) have reported evidence (carefully confirming older findings) that one synaptic terminal on a muscle fiber can cause other terminals on the same muscle fiber to become nonfunctional. Nerves innervating eye muscles of fish were sectioned and then permitted to regenerate. When a nerve not normally innervating a muscle made synaptic contact, the muscle showed reflex activity appropriate for that nerve but inappropriate for its normal function. Shortly after the muscle became innervated by its normal nerve, the abnormal reflex disappeared and was replaced by normal reflex activity. A reasonable interpretation of this result is that inappropriate synapses can function, but are made nonfunctional by more appropriate synaptic connections.

There is increasing evidence that in the central nervous system the existence of one set of synaptic terminals on a neuron prevents the invasion of other terminals, and that if the normal input to a neuron is removed or prevented from forming, terminals from other systems will fill in the area devoid of its normal synaptic terminals (e.g. 87, 91, 103a, 108). On the basis of electrophysiological (87) and behavioral evidence (108), it appears that such abnormal connections are functional.

MORPHOLOGICAL CHANGES   Up until approximately 5 years ago, there were very few reports of synaptic morphological changes due to experience or synaptic use. Recently a large number of studies have appeared reporting various types of morphological changes. One group of studies has examined short-term changes (lasting on the order of minutes) as a consequence of relatively brief periods of synaptic activity. Another group of studies, usually done with young animals whose nervous system is in the process of development, has examined long-term changes (lasting days or weeks) in response to injury or long-term exposure to environmental stimuli.

Short-term changes   The most dramatic short-term morphological changes in synaptic terminals are the result of very high levels of stimulation (23, 41, 65, 71, 89, 97) or conditions in which the metabolic activity of the presynaptic terminal is impaired (7, 65, 94). But changes have also been reported under more physiological conditions (101, 102). Alterations reported include increases or decreases of the number of synaptic vesicles and their volume (65, 71, 89, 97, 102), alterations of the morphology and position of nerve-terminal mitochondria (65), increases of the amount of external membrane at the terminal (53, 101), and increases of the size of synaptic boutons (62). The data on ultrastructural changes at synapses following use provide added support for the notion that transmitter release consists of a process in which synaptic vesicles fuse with the presynaptic terminal and release their contents into the synaptic cleft. Although there can be morphological changes at synapses following use, it is by no means established that any alterations of *normal* synaptic function is related to such morphological changes. In fact, there are already data that suggest that short-term synaptic decrement need *not* necessarily correlate with presynaptic morphological changes (66).

Long-term changes   Sotelo & Palay have reported ultrastructural evidence of terminal degeneration in normal brains, and they suggest that constant death and regrowth of terminals may be a normal state of affairs (114, see also 26). Furthermore, they have seen ultrastructural evidence indicating active growth of dendrites, and have hypothesized that the postsynaptic as well as presynaptic elements may be involved in a constant renewal process (113). Although there are no direct physiological data demonstrating support of this hypothesis, several morphological studies have found long-term changes of both presynaptic and postsynaptic structures. Early studies on the visual system reported alterations of the size and number of synapses or of the branching patterns of dendrites following damage to afferent fiber systems or following long periods of sustained exposure to abnormally low levels of afferent input (28, 30, 121). Fifková (39, 40) reported morphological changes of synapses in the visual cortex of rats raised with one eye sutured closed. Since diffuse light can still penetrate through the sutured eyelid, the morphological changes may be due to a lack of pattern vision rather than lack of light stimulation per se. These results, as well as others (30), indicate that the nature of morphological changes induced by environmental conditions cannot be expressed by simple generalizations. For example, axodendritic synapses in the cortex receiving the projection from the sutured eye were decreased in number but increased in size. By contrast, axosomatic synapses decreased in size, particularly those synapses containing round as opposed to oval vesicles (39, 40).

The visual system of the cat appears to be particularly sensitive to environmental contingencies up until about 4 months of age. The morphological, physiological, and behavioral effects of unilateral lid closure in cats are most readily produced in cats no older than 4 months, and during this same period, substantial reversal of the effects of unilateral closure can be produced by reversing the eye that is sutured closed (10). However, there is evidence that under appropriate conditions at least some degree of recovery of visual function can be produced in cats that have had unilateral lid closure from birth up to a year (24).

Recently changes of synaptic morphology (39, 90, 126) or dendritic branching (47a, 110) have been correleated with more normal variations of environmental stimulation. One line of research has demonstrated morphological correlates related to relatively mild variations in the degree of environmental complexity in which young animals are raised. Alterations of both synaptic (90, 126) and dendritic (47a) structures have been reported. On the whole, these changes closely parallel the earlier as well as more recently reported changes of gross cortical morphology or biochemical characteristics related to environmental complexity (106). Some of the cerebral effects of environmental complexity have been found in adult animals (104a), strengthening the possibility of relating these effects to learning rather than to development.

CONCLUSION

During the past 5 years there has been a great acceleration of cellular studies of mechanisms of learning and behavioral plasticity. As is usually the case in science, few recent studies have revealed dramatically new principles, but older isolated observations or hypotheses have received substantial confirmation or rebuttal. Particularly significant has been the movement toward relating model studies of short-term synaptic plasticity to short-term alterations of behavior.

Alterations of synaptic efficacy have been definitively related to short-term alterations of behavior in invertebrates. The available data indicate that similar alterations underlie short-term behavioral changes in vertebrates. An important advance in the analysis of the neural mechanisms of learning will be to determine if the existing model systems of long-term neural plasticity are relevant to long-term behavioral modification. Most model studies of long-term neural plasticity have been done in developing nervous systems or in neural systems recovering from damage. It will be a challange to demonstrate whether or not the existing examples of the capacity of the nervous system to undergo long-term plastic changes have relevance to behavioral modifications, or whether such changes represent unique adaptations of growth or response to injury. An additional challenge for future research will be to determine to what degree the neural mechanisms of nonassociative learning such as habituation apply to associative forms of learning.

ACKNOWLEDGMENTS

I thank Drs. T. Carew, V. Castellucci, E. Kandel, and K. Weiss for their constructive criticism of the manuscript. Preparation supported in part by NIH Grant NS 10757.

Literature Cited

1. Aguilar, C. E., Bisby, M. A., Cooper, E., Diamond, J. 1973. Evidence that axoplasmic transport of trophic factors is involved in the regulation of peripheral nerve fields in salamanders. *J. Physiol.* 234:449–64
2. Applewhite, P. B., Gardner, F. T. 1970. Protein and RNA synthesis during protozoan habituation after loss of macronuclei and cytoplasm. *Physiol. Behav.* 5:377–78
3. Applewhite, P. B., Gardner, F. T. 1971.

Theory of protozoan habituation. *Nature, New Biol.* 230:285–87
4. Applewhite, P. B., Gardner, F. T. 1973. Tube-escape behavior of *Paramecia*. *Behav. Biol.* 9:245–50
5. Applewhite, P. B., Gardner, F. T., Lapan, E. 1969. Physiology of habituation learning in a protozoan. *Trans. NY Acad. Sci.* 31:842–49
6. Applewhite, P. B., Lapan, E. A., Gardner, F. T. 1969. Protozoan habituation learning after loss of macro-

nuclei and cytoplasm. *Nature* 222: 491–92

7. Atwood, H. L., Lang, F., Morin, W. A. 1972. Synaptic vesicles: selective depletion in crayfish excitatory and inhibitory axons. *Science* 176:1353–55

8. Banks, P., Magor, D., Mraz, P. 1973. Metabolic aspects of the synthesis and intra-axonal transport of noradrenaline storage vesicles. *J. Physiol.* 229:383–94

9. Betz, W. J. 1970. Depression of transmitter release at the neuromuscular junction of the frog. *J. Physiol.* 206:629–44

10. Blakemore, C., Van Sluyters, R. C. 1974. Reversal of the physiological effects of monocular deprivation in kittens: Further evidence for a sensitive period. *J. Physiol.* 237:195–216

11. Bliss, T. V. P., Gardner-Medwin, A. R. 1973. Long-lasting potentiation of synaptic transmission in the dentate area of the unanesthetized rabbit following stimulation of the perforant path. *J. Physiol.* 232:357–74

12. Bliss, T. V. P., Lϕmo, T. 1973. Long-lasting potentiation of synaptic transmission in the dentate area of the anesthetized rabbit following stimulation of the perforant path. *J. Physiol.* 232:331–56

13. Breckenridge, B. M., Bray, J. J. 1970. Cyclic AMP in nerve. See Ref. 46, 325–33

14. Brooker, G. 1973. Oscillation of cyclic adenosine monophosphate concentration during the myocardial contraction cycle. *Science* 182:933–34

15. Bruner, J., Kennedy, D. 1970. Habituation: Occurrence at a neuromuscular junction. *Science* 169:92–94

16. Burrows, M., Hoyle, G. 1973. Neural mechanisms underlying behavior in the locust *Schistocerca gregaria*. III. Topography of limb motorneurons in the metathoracic ganglion. *J. Neurobiol.* 4:167–86

17. Byrne, J. 1973. *Receptive fields and response properties of Aplysia mechanoreceptor neurons.* PhD thesis. Polytechnic Inst., Brooklyn, NY

18. Callec, J. J., Guillet, J. C., Pichon, Y., Boistel, J. 1971. Further studies on synaptic transmission in insects. II. Relations between sensory information

and its synaptic integration at the level of a single giant axon in the cockroach. *J. Exp. Biol.* 55:123–49

19. Carew, T. J., Castellucci, V. F., Kandel, E. R. 1971. An analysis of dishabituation and sensitization of the gill-withdrawal reflex in *Aplysia. Int. J. Neurosci.* 2:79–98

20. Carew, T. J., Kandel, E. R. 1973. Acquisition and retention of long-term habituation in *Aplysia*: Correlation of behavioral and cellular processes. *Science* 182:1158–60

21. Carew, T. J., Pinsker, H. M., Kandel, E. R. 1972. Long-term habituation of a defensive withdrawal reflex in *Aplysia. Science* 175:451–54

21a. Carew, T. J., Pinsker, H., Rubinson, K., Kandel, E. R. 1974. Physiological and biochemical properties of neuromuscular transmission between identified motoneurons and gill muscle in *Aplysia. J. Neurophysiol.* 37(5). In press

21b. Castellucci, V., Kandel, E. R. 1974. *Further analysis of the synaptic decrement underlying habituation of the gill-withdrawal reflex in Aplysia.* Presented at 4th Ann. Meet. Soc. Neurosci. Abstr.

22. Castellucci, V., Pinsker, H., Kupfermann, I., Kandel, E. R. 1970. Neuronal mechanisms of habituation and dishabituation of the gill-withdrawal reflex in *Aplysia. Science* 167:1745–48

23. Ceccarelli, B., Hurlburt, W. P., Mauro, A. 1973. Turnover of transmitter and synaptic vesicles at the frog neuromuscular junction. *J. Cell Biol.* 57:499–524

24. Chow, K. L., Stewart, D. L. 1972. Reversal of structural and functional effects of long-term visual deprivation in cats. *Exp. Neurol.* 34:409–33

25. Christensen, B. N., Martin, A. R. 1970. Estimates of probability of transmitter release at the mammalian neuromuscular junction. *J. Physiol.* 210:933–45

26. Cohen, E. B., Pappas, G. D. 1969. Dark profiles in the apparently normal nervous system. A problem in the electron microscopic identification of early anterograde degeneration. *J. Comp. Neurol.* 136:375–96

27. Cohen, S. A., Fischbach, G. D. 1973. Regulation of muscle acetylcholine sensitivity by muscle activity in cell

culture. *Science* 181:76–78

28. Coleman, P. D., Riesen, A. H. 1968. Environmental effects on cortical dendritic fields. I. Rearing in the dark. *J. Anat.* 102:363–74

29. Cooke, J. D., Okamoto, K., Quastel, D. M. J. 1973. The role of calcium in depolarization-secretion coupling at the motor nerve terminal. *J. Physiol.* 228:459–97

30. Cragg, B. G. 1969. The effects of vision and dark-rearing on the size and density of synapses in the lateral geniculate nucleus measured by electron microscopy. *Brain Res.* 13:53–67

31. Curtis, D. R., Ryall, R. W. 1966. The synaptic excitation of Renshaw cells. *Exp. Brain Res.* 2:81–96

32. Dagan, D., Parnas, I. 1970. Giant fibre pathways involved in evasive response of the cockroach, *Periplaneta americana. J. Exp. Biol.* 52:313–24

33. Davis, W. J., Mpitsos, G. J. 1971. Behavioral choice and habituation in the marine mollusk *Pleurobranchaea californica* MacFarland (Gastropoda, Opisthobranchia). *Z. Vergl. Physiol.* 75:207–32

34. Del Castillo, J., Katz, B. 1954. Quantal components of the end-plate potential. *J. Physiol.* 124:560–73

35. Dimitrijević, M. R., Nathan, P. W. 1970. Studies of spasticity in man. 4. Changes in flexion reflex with repetitive cutaneous stimulation in spinal man. *Brain* 93:743–68

36. Dodge, F. A., Rahamimoff, R. 1967. Co-operative action of calcium ions in transmitter release at the neuromuscular junction. *J. Physiol.* 193:419–32

37. Eisenstein, E. M. 1972. Learning and memory in isolated insect ganglia. *Advan. Insect Physiol.* 9:111–81

38. Farel, P. B., Glanzman, D. L., Thompson, R. F. 1973. Habituation of a monosynaptic response in the vertebrate central nervous system: Lateral column-motoneuron pathway in isolated frog spinal cord. *J. Neurophysiol.* 36:1117–30

39. Fifková, E. 1970. The effect of monocular deprivation on the synaptic contacts of the visual cortex. *J. Neurobiol.* 1:285–94

40. Ibid 1970. Changes of axosomatic synapses in the visual cortex of monocularly deprived rats. 2:61–71

41. Friesen, A. J. D., Khatter, J. C. 1971. Effect of stimulation on synaptic vesicles in the superior cervical ganglion of the cat. *Experientia* 27:285–87

42. Fuhrer, M. J. 1972. Habituation of skin conductance responses and flexor withdrawal activity mediated by the functionally transected human spinal cord. *Brain Res.* 42:353–66

43. Ibid 1973. Dishabituation of flexor withdrawal activity mediated by the functionally transected human spinal cord. 63:93–102

44. Gardner-Medwin, A. R. 1969. Modifiable synapses necessary for learning. *Nature* 223:916–19

45. Glanzman, D. L., Groves, P. M., Thompson, R. F. 1972. Stimulus generalization of habituation in spinal interneurons. *Physiol. Behav.* 8:155–58

46. Greengard, P., Costa, E., Eds. 1970. *Role of Cyclic AMP in Cell Function. Advances in Biochemical Psychopharmacology.* New York: Raven. 386 pp.

47. Greengard, P., Kuo, J. F. 1970. On the mechanism of action of cyclic AMP. See Ref. 46, 287–306

47a. Greenough, W. T., Volkmar, F. R. 1973. Pattern of dendritic branching in occipital cortex of rats reared in complex environments. *Exp. Neurol.* 40:491–504

48. Groves, P. M., De Marco, R., Thompson, R. F. 1969. Habituation and sensitization of spinal interneuron activity in acute spinal cats. *Brain Res.* 14:521–25

49. Groves, P. M., Glanzman, D. L., Patterson, M. M., Thompson, R. F. 1970. Excitability of cutaneous afferent terminals during habituation and sensitization in acute spinal cat. *Brain Res.* 18:388–92

50. Groves, P. M., Miller, S. W., Parker, M. V. 1972. Habituation and sensitization of neuronal activity in the reticular formation of the rat. *Physiol. Behav.* 8:589–93

51. Hanzel, T. E., Rucker, W. B. 1972. Trial and error learning in paramecium: A replication. *Behav. Biol.* 7:873–80

52. Harris, A. J. 1974. Inductive functions

of the nervous system. *Ann. Rev. Physiol.* 36:251–305

53. Heuser, J. E., Reese, T. W. 1973. Evidence for recycling of synaptic vesicle membrane during transmitter release at the frog neuromuscular junction. *J. Cell Biol.* 57:315–44

54. Hoffer, B. J., Siggins, G. R., Bloom, F. E. 1970. Possible cyclic AMP-mediated adrenergic synapses to rat cerebellar purkinje cells: combined structural, physiological and pharmacological analyses. See Ref. 46, 349–70

55. Horn, G. 1970. Changes in neuronal activity and their relationship to behaviour. In *Short-term Changes in Neural Activity and Behaviour*, ed. G. Horn, R. A. Hinde, 567–606.

56. Horn, G. 1971. Habituation and memory. In *Biology of Memory*, ed. G. Adam, 267–86. Budapest: Press of Hungarian Acad. Sci.

57. Hoyle, G. 1965. Neurophysiological studies on "learning" in headless insects. In *The Physiology of the Insect Central Nervous System*, ed. J. E. Treherne, J. W. L. Beament, 203–32. London-New York: Academic

58. Hoyle, G., Burrows, M. 1973. Neural mechanisms underlying behavior in the locust *Schistocerca gregaria*. I. Physiology of identified motorneurons in the metathoracic ganglion. *J. Neurobiol.* 4:3–41

59. Hoyle, G., Willows, A. O. D. 1973. Neuronal basis of behavior in *Tritonia*. II. Relationship of muscular contraction to nerve impulse pattern. *J. Neurobiol.* 4:239–54

60. Hubbard, J. I. 1970. Mechanisms of transmitter release. In *Progress in Biophysics and Molecular Biology*, ed. J. A. V. Butler, D. Noble, 33–124. Oxford-New York: Pergamon

61. Hubbard, J. I., Llinas, R., Quastel, D. M. J. 1969. *Electrophysiological Analysis of Synaptic Transmission*. Baltimore: Williams & Wilkins

62. Illis, L. S. 1969. Enlargement of spinal cord synapses after repetitive stimulation of a single posterior root. *Nature* 223:76–77

63. Jahan-Parwar, B. 1970. Conditioned response in *Aplysia californica*. *Am. Zool.* 10:287 (Abstr.)

64. Jones, R., Vrbová, G. 1974. Two factors responsible for the development of denervation hypersensitivity. *J. Physiol.* 236:517–38

65. Jones, S. F., Kwanbunbumpen, S. 1970. The effects of nerve stimulation and hemicholinium on synaptic vesicles at the mammalian neuromuscular junction. *J. Physiol.* 207:31–50

66. Ibid. Some effects of nerve stimulation and hemicholinium on quantal transmitter release at the mammalian neuromuscular junction, 51–61

67. Kandel, E. R., Tauc, L. 1965. Mechanism of heterosynaptic facilitation in the giant cell of the abdominal ganglion of *Aplysia depilans*. *J. Physiol.* 181:28–47

67a. Katz, B. 1966. *Nerve, Muscle and Synapse*. New York: McGraw-Hill

68. Katz, B., Miledi, R. 1968. The role of calcium in neuromuscular facilitation. *J. Physiol.* 195:481–92

69. Kimmel, H. D. 1973. Habituation, habituability and conditioning. In *Habituation. Behavioral Studies*, ed. H. V. S. Peeke, M. J. Herz, 219–38. New York-London: Academic

70. Kornblith, C., Olds, J. 1973. Unit activity in brain stem reticular formation of the rat during learning. *J. Neurophysiol.* 36:489–501

71. Korneliussen, H. 1972. Ultrastructure of normal and stimulated motor end plates. *Z. Zellforsch. Mikrosk. Anat.* 130:28–57

72. Krasne, F. B. 1969. Excitation and habituation of the crayfish escape reflex: The depolarizing response in lateral giant fibers of the isolated abdomen. *J. Exp. Biol.* 50:29–46

73. Krasne, F. B. 1973. Learning in crustacea. In *Invertebrate Learning. Arthropods and Gastropod Mollusks*, ed. W. C. Corning, J. A. Dyal, A. O. D. Willows, 49–130. New York-London: Plenum

74. Krasne, F. B., Bryan, J. S. 1973. Habituation: Regulation through presynaptic inhibition. *Science* 182:590–92

74a. Krasne, F. B., Roberts, A. M. 1967. Habituation of the crayfish escape response during release from inhibition induced by picrotoxin. *Nature* 215:769–70

74b. Krasne, F. B., Woodsmall, K. S. 1969.

Waning of the crayfish escape response as a result of repeated stimulation. *Anim. Behav.* 17:416–24

75. Kuno, M. 1964. Mechanism of facilitation and depression of the excitatory synaptic potential in spinal motoneurones. *J. Physiol.* 175:100–12

76. Kuno, M. 1971. Quantum aspects of central and ganglionic synaptic transmission in vertebrates. *Physiol. Rev.* 51:647–78

77. Kupfermann, I. 1974. Feeding behavior in *Aplysia*: A simple system for the study of motivation. *Behav. Biol.* 10:1–26

78. Kupfermann, I., Castellucci, V., Pinsker, H., Kandel, E. R. 1970. Neuronal correlates of habituation and dishabituation of the gill-withdrawal reflex in *Aplysia. Science* 167:1743–45

79. Kupfermann, I., Kandel, E. R. 1969. Neuronal controls of a behavioral response mediated by the abdominal ganglion of *Aplysia. Science* 164:847–50

80. Kupfermann, I., Kandel, E. R. 1970. Electrophysiological properties and functional interconnections of two symmetrical neurosecretory clusters (bag cells) in abdominal ganglion of *Aplysia. J. Neurophysiol.* 33:865–76

81. Kupfermann, I., Pinsker, H. 1969. Plasticity in *Aplysia* neurons and some simple neuronal models of learning. In *Reinforcement and Behavior*, ed. J. Tapp, 356–86. New York: Academic

81a. Kupfermann, I., Pinsker, H., Castellucci, V., Kandel, E. R. 1971. Central and peripheral control of gill movements in *Aplysia. Science* 174:1252–56

82. Langan, T. A. 1970. Phosphorylation of histones *in vivo* under the control of cyclic AMP and hormones. See Ref. 46, 307–23

83. Lehninger, A. L. 1967. Cell organelles: The mitochondrion. In *The Neurosciences*, ed. G. C. Quarton, T. Melnechuck, F. O. Schmitt, 91–100. New York: Rockefeller Univ. Press

84. Lloyd, D. P., Wilson, V. J. 1957. Reflex depression in rhythmically active monosynaptic reflex pathways. *J. Gen. Physiol.* 4:409–26

85. Lφmo, T., Rosenthal, J. 1972. Control of ACh sensitivity by muscle activity in the rat. *J. Physiol.* 221:493–513

86. Lukowiak, K., Jacklet, J. W. 1972. Habituation and dishabituation: Interactions between peripheral and central nervous systems in *Aplysia. Science* 178:1306–8

87. Lynch, G., Deadwyler, S., Cotman, C. 1973. Postlesion axonal growth produces permanent functional connections. *Science* 180:1364–66

88. Marotte, L. R., Mark, R. F. 1970. The mechanism of selective reinnervation of fish eye muscle. I. Evidence from muscle function during recovery. *Brain Res.* 19:41–51

88a. Martin, A. R. 1966. Quantal nature of synaptic transmission. *Physiol. Rev.* 46:51–66

89. Model, P. G., Highstein, S. M., Bennett, M. V. L. 1973. *Depletion of vesicles and fatigue of transmission at a vertebrate central synapse. Expanded Abstracts 27.* Presented at 3rd Ann. Meet. Soc. Neurosci.

90. Mφllgaard, K., Diamond, M. C., Bennett, E. L., Rosenzweig, M. R., Lindner, B. 1971. Quantitative synaptic changes with differential experience in rat brain. *Int. J. Neurosci.* 2:113–28

91. Moore, R. Y., Björklund, A., Stenevi, U. 1971. Plastic changes in the adrenergic innervation of the rat septal area in response to denervation. *Brain Res.* 33:13–35

92. Ortiz, C. L., Bracho, H. 1972. Effect of reduced calcium on excitatory transmitter release at the crayfish neuromuscular junction. *Comp. Biochem. Physiol.* 41A:805–12

93. Osborn, D., Blair, H. J., Thomas, J., Eisenstein, E. M. 1973. The effects of vibratory and electrical stimulation on habituation in the ciliated protozoan, *Spirostomum ambiguum. Behav. Biol.* 8:655–64

94. Páraducz, Á., Fehér, O., Joó, F. 1971. Effects of stimulation and of hemicholinium (HC-3) on the fine structure of nerve endings in the superior cervical ganglion of the cat. *Brain Res.* 34:61–72

95. Peretz, B. 1969. Central neuron initiation of periodic gill movements. *Science* 166:1167–72

96. Ibid 1970. Habituation and dishabit-

uation in the absence of a central nervous system. 169:379–81

97. Perri, V., Sacchi, O., Raviola, E., Raviola, G. 1972. Evaluation of the number and distribution of synaptic vesicles at cholinergic nerve endings after sustained stimulation. *Brain Res.* 39:526–29

98. Petrinovich, L. 1973. A species-meaningful analysis of habituation. See Ref. 69, 141–62

99. Pinsker, H., Castellucci, V., Kupfermann, I., Kandel, E. R. 1970. Habituation and dishabituation of the gill-withdrawal reflex in *Aplysia. Science* 167:1740–42

100. Pinsker, H. M., Hening, W. A., Carew, T. J., Kandel, E. R. 1973. Long-term sensitization of a defensive withdrawal reflex in *Aplysia. Science* 182:1039–42

101. Pysh, J. J., Wiley, R. G. 1974. Synaptic vesicle depletion and recovery in cat sympathetic ganglia electrically stimulated *in vivo. J. Cell Biol.* 60:365–74

102. Quilliam, J. P., Tamarind, D. L. 1973. Some effects of preganglionic nerve stimulation on synaptic vesicle populations in the rat superior cervical ganglion. *J. Physiol.* 235:317–31

103. Rahamimoff, R., Alnaes, E. 1973. Inhibitory action of ruthenium red on neuromuscular transmission. *Proc. Nat. Acad. Sci.* 70:3613–16

103a. Raisman, G., Field, P. M. 1973. A quantitative investigation of the development of collateral reinnervation after partial deafferentation of the septal nuclei. *Brain Res.* 50:241–64

104. Rasmussen, H., Tenenhouse, A. 1968. Cyclic adenosine monophosphate, Ca^{++}, and membranes. *Proc. Nat. Acad. Sci.* 59:1364–70

104a. Riege, W. H. 1971. Environmental influences on brain and behavior of year-old rats. *Develop. Psychobiol.* 4:157–67

105. Rosenthal, J. 1969. Post-tetanic potentiation at the neuromuscular junction of the frog. *J. Physiol.* 203:121–33

106. Rosenzweig, M. R., Bennett, E. L. 1972. Cerebral changes in rats exposed individually to an enriched environment. *J. Comp. Physiol. Psychol.* 80:304–13

107. Rosenzweig, M. R., Møllgaard, K., Diamond, M. C., Bennett, E. L. 1972.

Negative as well as positive synaptic changes may store memory. *Psychol. Rev.* 79:93–96

108. Schneider, G. E. 1973. Early lesions of superior colliculus: Factors affecting the formation of abnormal retinal projections. *Brain, Behav. Evol.* 8:73–109

109. Segal, M. 1973. Flow of conditioned responses in limbic telencephalic system of the rat. *J. Neurophysiol.* 36:840–54

110. Shapiro, S., Vukovich, K. R. 1970. Early experience effects upon cortical dendrites: A proposed model. *Science* 167:292–94

111. Sherman, R. G., Atwood, H. L. 1971. Synaptic facilitation: Long-term neuromuscular facilitation in crustaceans. *Science* 171:1248–50

112. Singer, J. J., Goldberg, A. L. 1970. Cyclic AMP and transmission at the neuromuscular junction. See Ref. 46, 335–48

113. Sotelo, C., Palay, S. L. 1968. The fine structure of the lateral vestibular nucleus in the rat. *J. Cell Biol.* 36:151–79

114. Sotelo, C., Palay, S. L. 1971. Altered axons and axon terminals in the lateral vestibular nucleus of the rat. Possible example of axonal remodeling. *Lab. Invest.* 25:653–71

115. Spencer, W. A., Thompson, R. F., Neilson, D. R. Jr. 1966. Response decrement of the flexion reflex in the acute spinal cat and transient restoration by strong stimuli. *J. Neurophysiol.* 29:221–39

115a. Ibid. Alterations in responsiveness of ascending and reflex pathways activated by iterated cutaneous afferent volleys, 240–52

116. Stent, G. 1973. A physiological mechanism for Hebb's postulate of learning. *Proc. Nat. Acad. Sci.* 70:997–1001

116a. Stephens, C. L. 1973. Relative contribution of synaptic and non-synaptic influences to response decrements in a post-synaptic neurone. *J. Exp. Biol.* 59:315–21

117. Thies, R. E. 1965. Neuromuscular depression and the apparent depletion of transmitter in mammalian muscle. *J. Neurophysiol.* 28:427–42

118. Thompson, R. F., Groves, P. M., Teyler, T. J., Roemer, R. A. 1973. A dual-process theory of habituation:

Theory and behavior. See Ref. 69, 239–71

119. Thompson, R. F., Patterson, M. M., Teyler, T. J. 1972. The neurophysiology of learning. *Ann. Rev. Psychol.* 23:73–104

120. Tosney, T., Hoyle, G. 1973. *Automatic entrainment for a cellular learning study.* Presented at 3rd Ann. Meet. Soc. Neurosci. 238 Abstr.

121. Valverde, F. 1971. Rate and extent of recovery from dark rearing in the visual cortex of the mouse. *Brain Res.* 33:1–11

122. Wachtel, H., Kandel, E. R. 1971. Conversion of synaptic excitation to inhibition at a dual chemical synapse. *J. Neurophysiol.* 34:56–68

123. Weinreich, D. 1971. Ionic mechanisms of post-tetanic potentiation at the neuromuscular junction of the frog. *J. Physiol.* 212:431–46

124. Wells, M. J. 1971. Conditioning and sensitization in snails. *Anim. Behav.* 19:305–12

125. Wernig, A. 1972. Changes in statistical parameters during facilitation at the crayfish neuromuscular junction. *J. Physiol.* 226:751–59

126. West, R. W., Greenough, W. T. 1972. Effect of environmental complexity on cortical synapses of rats: Preliminary results. *Behav. Biol.* 7:279–84

127. Wickelgren, B. G. 1967. Habituation of spinal motoneurons. *J. Neurophysiol.* 30:1404–23

128. Ibid. Habituation of spinal interneurons, 1424–38

129. Willows, A. O. D. 1968. Behavioral acts elicited by stimulation of single identifiable nerve cells. In *Physiological and Biochemical Aspects of Nervous Integration*, ed. F. D. Carlson, 217–43. Englewood Cliffs, NJ: Prentice-Hall

130. Willows, A. O. D. 1973. Learning in gastropod mollusks. See Ref. 73, 187–273

131. Wine, J. J., Krasne, F. B. 1969. Independence of inhibition and habituation in the crayfish lateral giant fiber

escape reflex. *Proc. 77th Ann. Conv. APA* 237–38

132. Wood, D. C. 1970. Electrophysiological correlates of the response decrement produced by mechanical stimuli in the protozoan *Stentor coeruleus. J. Neurobiol.* 2:1–11

133. Wood, D. C. 1973. Stimulus specific habituation in a protozoan. *Physiol. Behav.* 11:349–54

134. Woody, C. D., Black-Cleworth, P. 1973. Differences in excitability of cortical neurons as a function of motor projection in conditioned cats. *J. Neurophysiol.* 36:1104–16

135. Woody, C. D., Engel, J. Jr. 1972. Changes in unit activity and thresholds to electrical microstimulation at coronal-pericruciate cortex of cat with classical conditioning of different facial movements. *J. Neurophysiol.* 35:230–41

136. Younkin, S. G. 1974. An analysis of the role of calcium in facilitation at the frog neuromuscular junction. *J. Physiol.* 237:1–14

137. Zilber-Gachelin, N. F., Chartier, M. P. 1973. Modification of the motor reflex responses due to repetition of the peripheral stimulus in the cockroach. I. Habituation at the level of an isolated abdominal gnaglion. *J. Exp. Biol.* 59:359–81

138. Ibid. Modification of the motor reflex responses due to repetition of the peripheral stimulus in the cockroach. II. Conditions of activation of the motoneurones, 383–403

139. Zucker, R. S. 1972. Crayfish escape behavior and central synapses. II. Physiological mechanisms underlying behavioral habituation. *J. Neurophysiol.* 35:621–37

140. Zucker, R. S. 1973. Changes in the statistics of transmitter release during facilitation. *J. Physiol.* 229:787–810

141. Zucker, R. S., Kennedy, D., Selverston, A. I. 1971. Neuronal circuit mediating escape responses in crayfish. *Science* 173:645–50

PERSONALITY

238

Rae Carlson [1]

Department of Psychology, Livingston College, Rutgers University
New Brunswick, New Jersey 08903

This year may mark the beginning of the major turnaround in personality study we have long awaited. Not that "progress" is compellingly visible; flaws noted by previous reviewers continue: "sprawl and diversity" abide, as does that chilling absence of larger theoretical aims and synthesizing concerns which Adelson (1) deplored so eloquently. Yet there are grounds for predicting the rebirth of a solid personology, and the reviewer's task must now be that of nurturing the promising new life. Six years ago Adelson construed the task as largely reportorial, and regretfully focused on mainstream research at the expense of studies that were "off beat or ahead of their time." Here I have chosen the opposite approach; working within drastically reduced page limitations, I have neglected a good deal of competent mainstream research to focus upon developments which seem most promising for the future. This selectivity surely betrays my own bias; but the *use* of personal intellectual convictions is in itself one of the promising trends to be reported.

Most observers would agree that personology, in any nontrivial sense, virtually disappeared during the 1960s. To be sure, a number of investigators managed to maintain a steady concern with "real" personology, the elaboration of comparative theories of personality flourished, and the proliferation of psychometric approaches continued unabated. However, as an area of inquiry, the field was largely swamped by the vigorous development of experimental social psychology, conquests in cognitive-developmental work, the burgeoning technology of behavior modification, and the celebrations of humanistic ideology. That we now confront a period in which personology seems likely to be rediscovered—when, if it did not exist, it would have to be invented—is owed more to successes in some related fields, and to failures in others, than to the coherent development of personology itself. Within general psychology, the ascendance of biological-evolutionary and cognitive approaches have been liberating forces, along with the collapse of the laboratory-experimental method as the major source of knowledge in social and

---

[1] I am grateful to colleagues at New York State University College at Brockport, where this review was prepared.

developmental psychology. Beyond psychology, the pace of social change—especially the impact of Black consciousness, women's liberation, and the counterculture—has produced searching reexaminations of our traditional assumptions.

Personality research is difficult to organize, even in the most tranquil times. One must deal with structural, dynamic, and developmental questions—and from the perspectives of general, differential, and individual psychology. The task is compounded during periods of major paradigm-shifts, since any contribution may simultaneously speak to quite different substantive, conceptual, and methodological issues. Here the presentation is organized on the basis of my intuitive judgment of "importance." Conceptual and methodological issues now lie at the forefront of personology; if there is disappointingly little to report by way of "advances" in substantive research, the empirical literature may serve to mark problems of importance and possible ways of redirecting inquiry.

REORIENTATIONS IN THEORY AND METHOD

Far more significant than any specific advances during the past year is the distinct change in the climate of psychological research. Widespread dissatisfaction with dominant modes of inquiry—the reliance upon simple, linear, quantitative, causal models for prediction of overt behaviors—has ushered in a period in which a serious personology may flourish. The year has seen several proposals for fundamental reorientations in conceptualization and inquiry. Spence (89) offered a provocative contrast between digital and analog descriptions of behavior, noting the sensitivity and flexibility of analog systems, and their particular relevance for fields of inquiry where the molar phenomena are more important than their molecular ingredients.

Urging the need for a thorough conceptual exploration of personality description, Alston (3, 4) contributed an extremely useful analysis of the distinction between T-concepts (essentially "trait" notions, defined by frequency of responses over a range of situations) and D-concepts ("desires" and other "deeper-lying" dispositions). T's and D's are shown to have opposite strengths and weaknesses in nomological relations to behavior; an analogy is the contrast between a language (D's) and a signaling system that lacks a grammar (T's). Importantly, Alston observed that: ". . . T's and D's do not fit together into a single coherent scheme. Hence in developing a model for personality description we must choose between them, and as far as a theory of basic underlying structure is concerned, the preference must be for D's." This welcome gift from a philosopher is worth the serious attention of personologists.

Two papers by Olweus (71, 72) advance similar conceptual distinctions in reporting a program of research on aggression. Olweus argued (and demonstrated empirically) that it is necessary to distinguish between theoretical and observable variables, between action and inhibitory tendencies, between situational and habitual components of behavior. Noting that a simple, linear model proves inadequate, he warned that such powerful linear techniques as multiple regression and factor analysis may be of little value when not guided by theoretical considerations. In a series of studies of aggression in boys, markedly different relationships were obtained between projective and overt aggressive responses for boys with different levels of inhibition, but both projective and inventory approaches could predict aggression with considerable accuracy. There may exist a good deal of consistency on a genotypic level, despite absence of phenotypic consistency. Olweus's findings strongly support his contention that "prediction is not enough, and cannot substitute for understanding and explanation" (71, p. 315).

Still another voice urging a compatible message is Livson's (63) discussion of developmental dimensions of personality. The life-span developmental perspective, he suggests, offers a necessary corrective to approaches which have confused substantive and methodological issues. Such an approach is necessarily concerned with continuities, seeks to identify genotypes which have eluded investigators preoccupied with phenotypic data, must necessarily establish typologies, rely upon life-record data (observations and interviews), and readmit clinical judgments and rating methods as indispensable tools of inquiry.

While the message of current contributors strongly challenges the value of familiar trait conceptions and quantitative, linear measurement approaches, the issues are by no means resolved. Cattell (16) offered a comprehensive treatment of personality and mood as assessed with questionnaires. Although much of this volume is directed toward technical issues and internal conflicts among workers in the psychometric tradition, Cattell, as usual, has organized an extremely broad domain, providing a conceptual structure which includes the hierarchical organization of dispositions, their course through the life history, manifestations in pathology, and much more. The volume deserves to have considerable impact beyond the immediate circle of questionnaire afficionados.

Person, Situation, Interaction

Pseudo-issues manage to consume as much time and effort as real ones, and few controversies have seemed so noisy in recent years as the situationists' attack on the legitimacy of "personality" variables in psychological science. The controversy seems to have dissipated during the period of this review, and the "disposition vs situation" issue resolved in mutual agreement that "interactional" frameworks are required. A good deal of rather naive and redundant argument has been put into perspective by Bowers' (11) timely and useful analysis. Examining the metaphysical, psychological, and methodological biases of situationism, he noted the consequences of the misidentification of an S-R viewpoint with the experimental method, and of the nearly exclusive reliance upon laboratory experimentation as a mode of inquiry. His perceptive analysis of the recent literature should be useful to many workers.

Reviewing the entire "disposition vs situation" controversy it seems astonishing that so much effort and intelligence has been expended in attacking or defending a narrow "trait" conception of personality. Serious personologists have never construed behavioral consistencies as defining personality. Situationists, holding a somewhat different scientific ideology, have tended to misconstrue belief in personality dispositions as somehow equivalent to "person blame." Hopefully, we have passed through an awkward age, and are now belatedly prepared to search earnestly for keys to understanding individuality.

While the triumph of a Lewinian "interactionist" view comes as a welcome relief, it is not entirely clear how such a research program is to be theoretically guided. Neither of the two most vigorous research traditions with serious claims in this area—those identified with attribution theory or with locus of control—appears to hold great promise. Attribution theory, ably represented by Jones et al (51), among many others, tends to focus rather narrowly upon cognitive processes under situational constraints. The disregard of preexisting subject variables, and of more complex cognitive-affective processes, seems to limit what current attribution theory research may contribute to personology. Locus of control literature, although conceptually dealing with an important personality variable, has been so instrument-bound as to offer little theoretical clarity. Undoubtedly, this is the single most popular topic in current personality research, so one hesitates to offer a cavalier and perhaps premature dismissal of this work. At this point, the internal-external control variable appears to be one of the fads which periodically captures the field. Collins and his associates (22, 23), placing the internal-external metaphor in a broader context, explored empirically alternative explanations of the I-E work. They concluded that at least four separate dimensions of individual difference are involved, and that the metaphor can be (and should be) decomposed. Recent work with multidimensional assessment of I-E appears to generate firmer relationships with outside criteria. However, refinement of I-E assessment methods would not seem to transcend basic limitations. Until fundamental issues are addressed with greater theoretical depth and methodological breadth, current locus of control research seems unlikely to clarify critical questions about person-situation relationships.

In Search of Personality Theory

A most serious problem remains the absence of any widely shared, comprehensive, and dynamic theoretical framework capable of posing significant, researchable questions or tying together research findings. The resulting fragmentation in the field, with its unsatisfying array of researches guided by "middle-range theories," scientific ideologies, or simply the availability of popular ideas and instruments, is troublesome enough; a further problem is our doubtful capacity to assimilate advances in neighboring fields which pose exciting challenges to the personologist. Implications of work in biology and ethology (e.g. right-left brain functions, evolutionary adaptedness of dreaming, of facial expression, and so on), in anthropology, psycholinguistics, and cognitive-developmental psychology have posed an implicit agenda for personology. Our most urgent task may well be that of the difficult, systematic, theoretical stock-taking we have avoided in recent years.

Psychoanalytic theory, which served this guiding, integrating function through many years of personological inquiry, was just such a comprehensive and dynamic formulation. To an unacknowledged degree, psychoanalytic theory still guides research—if in an implicit, diffuse fashion—in the choice of problems (e.g. ego development) or research variables (e.g. defenses). Despite considerable disillusionment with aspects of Freudian theory (for example, the energy model and the treatment of sex differences, which stands among its more dramatic "failures"), the sheer scope and depth of the theory—and its viability in contemporary ego psychology—remain invaluable to personologists. Jahoda's (49) thoughtful analysis of the mutual challenges of social psychology and psychoanalysis concluded that the controversial position of psychoanalysis must be kept alive. Stoller (90) recently reviewed Freudian formulations of psychosexuality in the light of recent biological inquiry, noting both the revisions required and the stability of the basic structure. Kline's (53) assessment of the status of psychoanalytic propositions yielded a rather positive verdict. This work, which stands as an updating of Sears' assessment 30 years ago, will be a useful resource for many workers. More recently, LeVine (59) explicitly invoked psychoanalytic theory and method in his reformulation of the culture-and-personality field. He offered an exceedingly useful review of the earlier culture and personality work, a critique of personality assessment methods, along with a proposal for a "population psychology" in which the method of clinical psychoanalysis could be translated into a program for cross-cultural work. While this last feature may raise doubts among many personologists, LeVine's analysis of contemporary personality research is perceptive, and his ideas worth serious attention.

The promise of a "new" theoretical framework of complexity and power may be found in the accelerated rediscovery of Jungian thought. The past year has seen the publication of the first volume of Jung's letters (2), the Freud-Jung correspondence (66), and the appearance of several new books presenting Jung's theory to various audiences (38, 78, 86, 91). The very bases for psychologists' earlier neglect of Jung's work now seem to commend it to our attention: the emphases upon nativism, symbolism, the intrinsic duality in human nature, and upon the proactive quality of inner experience are obviously compatible with the emerging *Zeitgeist*. Doubtless our students—and the ubiquitous "intelligent layman"—are mainly responsible for the Jungian revival. Jung's own writings, like those of his current interpreters, tend more toward metapsychological and therapeutic issues than toward providing an explicit framework for empirical inquiry. Thus considerable effort may be required in aligning Jungian theoretical insights with appropriate research procedures. However, this task seems both feasible and worthwhile, as several recent contributions demonstrate.

For a number of years, Helson's researches into creative styles have invoked Jungian thought in delineating the personal qualities and imaginative processes involved in creative work. Two new papers (39, 40) provide excellent examples of the use of Jung's theoretical ideas in organizing psychometric data to capture the subtle relationships between dimensions of literary fantasy and the personality and work style of the author. Among several provocative implications of Helson's work are the possibilities of integrating Rankian and Jungian concepts, and the use of Jung's typology—and concepts of "anima" and "animus"—in accounting for masculine and feminine styles of creative work.

Jung's theory of psychological types, while representing only a part of the entire theoretical apparatus, may prove to be the aspect of Jungian thought most accessible to (and testable by) academic psychologists. For the mainstream psychologist, Jung's type theory plays a role comparable to that of Freudian "defense mechanisms" for earlier generations: the constructs offer a coherent descriptive system which accords well with (and helps to organize) the individual differences one encounters in real life, and may be adopted somewhat independently of a commitment to the entire theory. Unfortunately, the type theory seems to be widely misunderstood as mostly involving "introversion vs extraversion," so that the dynamic complexity of the typology has been little explored. Carlson & Levy (14) proposed the type theory as a framework for studying person-situation interactions, and reported a series of empirical studies directed toward its construct validation. Using rather conventional research methods to test derivations from Jungian theory, they found that introverted-thinking and extraverted-feeling types (assessed via the Myers-Briggs Type Indicator) differed in performance on two types of short-term memory tasks; intuitive-perceptive types were more accurate than sensing-judging types in interpreting facial expressions of emotion; and extraverted-intuitives were overrepresented among social service volunteers.

Research on Jungian typology may be greatly facilitated by the availability of a standardized instrument—the Myers-Briggs Type Indicator (69)—which combines intuitive appeal to subjects with psychometric stability (60) and an increasingly firm record for construct validity. Hopefully, publications from an ongoing program of typological research at the University of Florida (M. McCaulley, personal communication, December 1973) and from intensive work by the test developer (I. Myers, personal communication, December 1973) may be available to future reviewers for the *Annual Review of Psychology*.

What of other theories of personality traditionally discussed in our textbooks? Adler's influence was noted in a new commemorative volume (68) and in the development of a measure of the social-interest variable (36). McDougall's seminal ideas are presented in Boden's (10) scholarly discussion of purposive explanation in psychology. Humanistic and social learning viewpoints motivated several papers reviewed in later sections. However, one discovers that there are rather few formulations of sufficient breadth, depth, and complexity to qualify as "theories of personality." Alternative viewpoints seem to represent different emphases, or to be largely identified with particular variables, particular methods. The complementary, rather than competing, nature of alternative formulations is a core notion in Cartwright's (15) new textbook which develops "realistic eclecticism" as a framework for teaching the basic personality course.

Meanwhile, exploration of metatheoretical issues promises to enliven the literature and should ultimately contribute to conceptual clarity and methodological advance. Prominent are recent discussions of dialectic (81), positivist vs organicist (75), and relational (64) models, along with such unpublished work as Tomkins' (S. S. Tomkins, personal communication, April 1974) formulation of "power vs purity" in models of inquiry.

A SELECTIVE REVIEW OF PERSONALITY RESEARCH

Ideally, it should be possible to organize a year's output of personality research in terms of a coherent conceptual framework. This has not been possible, and the research literature is here grouped under somewhat arbitrary and overlapping thematic labels. Regrettably, several important topics are entirely neglected and others treated incompletely—largely from space limitations which required the exercise of the reviewer's (clearly fallible) judgment as to the "promise" of current work.

Ego Development, Moral Development

Personologists' concern with truly molar levels of analysis is reflected in continuing work on ego development and moral development. Haan et al (37) attempted to assess the interrelationships among three formulations of development and process—Loevinger's model of ego development, Kohlberg's moral development sequence, and Haan's model of ego functions—in a study of hippies. While the sample was too small and too special to permit a thorough exploration of theoretical issues, there emerged a useful picture of the dynamics of hippie youth Coping ego functions were related to level of moral development, but not to ego development; if anything, ego development appeared to be related to increasingly "successful" defense. Hippie youth appeared to be in a transitional stage beyond convention, but not yet principled in moral reasoning or conscientious in ego development. The investigators offered new ideas about the "fit" of normative theories to persons who have chosen a socially dissident, morally uncertain, and personally hazardous life style.

Erikson's formulation of psychosocial crises was explored in a study (73) which described a new ego identity status—"alienated achievement"—and modes of coping with the intimacy vs isolation crisis among college men. One in "alienated achievement" status seems to equal the identity-achievement person in ego strength and degree of identity resolution, but bases his identity more on interpersonal relationships than on matters of occupational or ideological choice. Three major "intimacy" statuses were identified and related to identity statuses. Tentative support emerged for the basic premise that genuine intimacy occurs only after a reasonable sense of identity has been established. In another study (93), college women of different ego identity statuses were presented the Asch conformity task. Those in "stable" identity statuses (achievement and foreclosure) conformed less than those in "unstable" statuses (moratorium and diffusion). Erikson's conception of basic trust as the outcome of successful resolution of the earliest psychosocial crisis motivated a study of trust and academic achievement (47). Girls were generally more trusting; the child's trust of the teacher and the teacher's ratings of trust were independent of intelligence and significantly related to academic performance of school children.

A rapprochement with Erikson's theory appears in Kohlberg's (55) recent essay on moral development. Kohlberg has dramatically shifted from his earlier contention that moral development ended with adolescence; stages of principled moral reasoning are now seen as appearing first in early adulthood. Further, there is sketched a hypothetical seventh stage of moral development corresponding to the basically religious Eriksonian stage whose outcomes are a sense of integrity vs a sense of despair. Kohlberg's discussion of theoretical issues involved in integrating structural stages and ego development stages poses many stimulating ideas. In the structural model, stages are different structures for a single function (e.g. moral development, logical reasoning); in Eriksonian theory, stages represent choices or uses of new functions by an ego. In structural theory, developmental change is primarily a changed perception; later stages are more cognitively adequate and more universally applicable. In contrast, Erikson's theory involves developmental change as a self-chosen identification with goals, resulting in relatively permanent choices or commitments; later stages are more adequate, not in cognitive inclusiveness, but in their ability to order personal experience in more stable, positive, and purposive form. The basic differences are those of logical vs psychological formulations; as Kohlberg notes, an integrated theory of social and moral stages would attempt to combine the two perspectives.

An alternative model of moral conduct and moral character has been introduced by Hogan (42), who assumes that moral conduct is fundamentally "irrational" and that differences in even such clearly cognitive phenomena as moral judgments derive from more basic personological structures. Five dimensions are proposed: moral knowledge, socialization, empathy, autonomy, and a dimension of moral judgment (ethics of conscience vs ethics of responsibility). He offers conceptual and empirical definitions, developmental antecedents, and empirical findings supporting each of the five dimensions. Elsewhere (41, 43) Hogan has placed the problem of moral development in a dialectical framework and outlined a role-theoretical perspective to the problem of compliance.

Fishkin et al (33) examined the relationships between moral reasoning and political ideology in an attempt to replicate and extend findings from earlier Berkeley studies of student activists. College students on eight campuses, studied during the Cambodia-Kent State crisis, responded to the Kohlberg moral dilemmas and rated political slogans. "Law-and-order" moral reasoning was strongly related to conservative ideology; preconventional subjects favored violent radicalism, while postconventionalists rejected conservative views but did not accept radical ideology.

Moral development inevitably involves consideration of altruism and prosocial behavior—a topic which continues to command much research interest. The past year produced a "great" study which restores one's faith in the experimental method by the competence and care with which basic issues were considered in the conduct of research and interpretation of findings. This is a study by Yarrow and her associates (102) of preschool children's "learning concern for others." Experimental treatments were based on analyses of natural socialization experiences in which parents may simply teach principles or may also exemplify them in practice, and where either procedure may vary in the warmth and nurturance of relationships. In constructing four experimental environments, several weeks were taken to establish the experimenters as meaningful adults in the children's natural (nursery school) settings. Various modes of presenting distress situations were developed; baseline tests of helping behavior preceded exposure to experimental histories of high or low nurturance; and were followed by posthistory evaluation before introduction of training conditions; both immediate and long-range tests for retention of experimental influences were made; and basic findings were replicated in a second experiment with children from a different socioeconomic background. (Surprisingly, one flaw in this otherwise exemplary study was the failure to report sex-composition of the sample or analyses for sex differences.) Findings were complex, but unequivocal: symbolic altruism increased in all experimental groups, but was unaffected by adults' nurturance; nurturance increased altruism in nonpressured, realistic encounters with distress, and children with nurturant caretakers who had modeled helping in both symbolic and live distress gave more help, verbalized more sympathy, and were more consistent in their altruism.

The elegance and clarity of Yarrow's design and results are matched by the rich and insightful discussion of theoretical and methodological issues in altruism research, and useful extrapolations to "real life" settings. This is a landmark study which sets standards for future work in the area.

Masculine, Feminine

Nowhere is the impact of social change more striking than in psychologists' increased concern with sex differences in personality. Psychosexuality, although a central construct in personology, has been ignored in much research, or treated simply in terms of normative conceptions of "sex roles." The consciousness-raising among psychologists induced by Women's Liberation has produced a torrent of critical, substantive, and sometimes polemical work. The year's harvest may be captured under two rubrics: the "psychology of women" (treated in a separate chapter of this volume), and conceptual and methodological issues in personality research arising in the study of psychosexuality.

Implicit "masculine bias" in the structure of psychological inquiry has been noted with increasing frequency over the past few years. Carlson (13) addressed the impoverished conceptions of personality reflected in recent empirical work, and suggested that dominant modes of inquiry are "agentic" (masculine) in Bakan's (5) sense; the complementary development of "communal" (feminine) styles of research are required for investigation of important problems. Among deficiencies noted in current work, three interlocking issues were proposed for future personality research: duality in human nature (the coexistence of "opposite" tendencies within the individual), typology (attention to qualitative constructs as a corrective to dimensional thinking), and biological bases of individuality.

The significance of a dualistic approach to masculinity-femininity was underscored by Constantinople's (24) review of M-F assessment literature. Her close scrutiny of major tests of M-F sharply questioned three basic untested assumptions: (a) that M-F is best defined in terms of sex differences in item responses; (b) that it is a single bipolar dimension ranging from extreme masculinity to extreme femininity; and (c) that it is unidimensional in nature and can be adequately measured by a single score. Some recognition of the "bisexuality" assumed in psychodynamic theories (e.g. Freud, Jung) now seems equally demanded by psychometric and theoretical imperatives.

The power of a theoretical framework, when wedded to a broad-gauged methodology, is nicely illustrated by Jeanne Block's (8) elegant summary of longitudinal and cross-national studies of sex-role socialization. Invoking Bakan's conceptions of agency and communion and Loevinger's formulation of ego development, Block succeeded in charting the course of development under varying personal, family, and societal conditions. Among other important findings, her work reveals: striking cross-national consistency in demands for agentic qualities in boys and communal qualities in girls (but with predictable overemphasis on "agency" in both sexes in the more capitalistic American society); a corrective emphasis upon the father's role in psychosexual development for both sexes; and a clear tendency for more mature levels of ego development to involve the integration of agentic and communal qualities.

This line of inquiry was extended in another study (9) exploring data from the California longitudinal studies. Using Socialization and Femininity scores from the California Personality Inventory as the basis of a fourfold typology (high-low socialization, appropriate-inappropriate sex typing), Block et al examined personality data from adult years and earlier family and childhood data in discovering rather different "recipes" for sex-role socialization. A differentiated conception of identification emerged, along with convincing evidence that traditional sex-role typing for men appears to extend the personal options available, while for women this has tended to restrict alternatives of action and expression. Among the emergent patterns, that of an "androgynous" identification—in which neither parent presented a stereotypic sex-role model, but both provided models of competence, tolerance, and shared responsibilities—appears to define a developmental course both salutory in its consequences and in tune with current social trends.

Psychological formulations of sex-role socialization (as of most important issues) may inevitably carry normative implications. If "appropriate" masculine or feminine sex-typing was the message urged in recent decades, it is rapidly being replaced by an "androgynous" norm which asserts that *both* masculine and feminine modes of experience and action are involved in optimal development. Bem (6, 7) has developed an adjective checklist distinguishing masculine, feminine, and androgynous sex typing, and has offered early evidence on its construct validity. Her work with collegiate samples indicates that these options can be assessed reliably, and that (with a few wrinkles) androgynous subjects of both sexes are more competent in performing experimental tasks associated with both stereotypic masculine and feminine roles. The notion of psychological androgyny has become increasingly influential since Rossi's (80) early paper; thus it deserves a more searching conceptual analysis than the current literature affords. To what extent are androgynous subjects more task-oriented than ego-oriented in a Lewinian sense? Is psychological androgyny more usefully construed as a "unisex" escape from normative constraints, or as the development of (bisexual) potentialities within a secure gender identity? Are there risks that an androgynous norm may prove as constrictive as earlier norms of "appropriate" sex typing (e.g. Bem's characterization of feminine women who "flunked" experimental tasks as showing "behavioral deficits")? Might more complex dualistic formulations (e.g. Bakan's constructs of agency and communion, Jung's conceptions of anima and animus) enrich inquiry on psychological androgyny? Such questions, of course, must be answered by future research.

Socialization is but part of the pattern of psychosexuality; there remains the task of integrating new biological knowledge with current psychological formulations. An important work by Money & Ehrhardt (67), which lives up to its subtitle, Differentiation and Dimorphism of Gender Identity from Conception to Maturity, provides an extremely useful integration of concepts and data from genetics, embryology, endocrinology, neurosurgery, social anthropology, and psychology. The publication of the American Psychopathological Association symposium on contemporary sexual behavior (105) offers several valuable formulations of biological aspects of sexuality and their implications for psychological inquiry and therapeutic work.

The Biology of Personality

In an era when the biological-evolutionary viewpoint amounts to a "revolution" (27) in general psychology, we may expect that personologists will increasingly attend to psychobiological work for the enrichment and extension of our inquiry. Within the past year, the most prominent lines of influence involve the assimilation or accomodation of work in genetics, psychophysiology, and morphology; on the personality side, these deal with aggression, temperament, extroversion, and obesity.

Jarvik et al (50) reviewed the evidence bearing upon the rare but theoretically important XYY genotype as a key to understanding human aggression. While many unresolved issues were noted, the authors suggested that the XYY genotype may be seen as highlighting the association between maleness and violence, and that the power of this approach to aggression lies in its basis in an inherent predisposition, along with the search for a solution in an understanding of environmental variables. Inheritance of temperaments was examined in a study (12) of 127 pairs of monozygotic and dizygotic twins (aged 4 months to 16 years), with questionnaire assessments of emotionality, activity, sociability, and impulsivity provided by members of the Mothers of Twins Clubs in eight states. The findings argued strongly for a genetic component in the four temperaments, with a single exception (impulsivity in girls); heritabilities were generally higher for boys than for girls, and the impact of the environment was also strongly suggested by the patterning and age trends in the correlations.

A Pavlovian view of "nervous typology" appears in both British and American work. Claridge and his associates (17) reported an ambitious twin study aimed at examining both psychophysiological and genetic bases of individual differences, and testing a theoretical model developed originally with psychiatric patients.

Personality questionnaires, cognitive tasks, and physiological measures were administered to a group of 95 pairs of normal adult twins; correlational and factor analytic methods examined issues dictated by the underlying theory. While the findings were too complex for summary here, several implications of the results may be noted. "Tonic arousal" and "arousal modulation" were identified as components of psychophysiological patterns which could be used as a basis for nervous typological classification and meaningfully related to dimensions of neuroticism and psychoticism. Arousal modulation appeared to be strongly influenced by heredity, and tonic arousal apparently subject to considerable environmental variation. With respect to more familiar personality variables, the findings were complex and perhaps disappointing to the investigators: genetic bases of extraversion appear mainly via the "sociability" component, and there was no evidence for any marked genetic contribution to anxiety/neuroticism; genetic contributions to cognitive variables appeared mainly via general intelligence. The thrust of the work, however, supported the underlying conceptual approach: that differences in the interaction between the same set of nervous typological processes are crucial, and that the problem is one of discovering the varieties of nervous typological organization rather than of specifying the particular causal process which is separately responsible for each personality dimension.

"Strength of nervous system" in Pavlov's sense was linked to "need for stimulation" in two studies by Sales et al (84). Strong subjects ("reducers") presumably need higher levels of stimulation, while weak subjects ("augmenters") perform better at lower levels of stimulus input. Substituting a measure of auditory threshold for the usual kinesthetic aftereffects task, the investigators confirmed predictions over a wide range of dependent variables. Strong (high threshold) subjects were more likely to prefer complex stimuli, become bored with simple tasks, drink coffee, have been raised in urban environments, and group social stimulus figures more densely, as compared with weak subjects. Somewhat compatible findings come from another study (52) relating personality variables to tolerance to an irritant compound.

While in no sense biologically based, Coan's (18) thorough exploration of personality factors in smoking is of some relevance here. He noted that smokers ". . . tended to show more tolerance, if not actual hunger, for varied ideas, emotional and perceptual effects, complexity, and perhaps even confusion"; smokers tended to be more extraverted than nonsmokers, although this rule applied more markedly to women, and the links between smoking and extraversion seem to require more thorough analysis of the nature of extraversion.

The possibilities, as well as the problems, in psychophysiological approaches to personality are set forth in Gale's (34) review of the extraversion-and-EEG literature. Psychophysiology (which he sharply distinguishes from physiological psychology) considers simultaneously behavior, subjective experience, and physiological state, and thus examines the "whole man." Nearly four decades of research on extraversion-EEG relationships, however, have yielded contradictory findings, largely through failures to consider the conceptual and practical demands of the three component fields. Gale outlined necessary precautions to be taken in future work, along with some alternative paradigms (those associated with vigilance, social interaction, stimulus complexity, and imagery) which may be developed to yield useful data. Particularly important—as is clear in his analysis of existing work—will be greater concern with conceptual clarity and attention to subjects' phenomenology.

Clearly, there are potentially important relationships between much of the biologically oriented work on "temperament" and the cognitively oriented work on "style." As yet these relationships cannot be described with much assurance, but it seems safe to predict lively attention to this problem area in the near future.

From social and phenomenological standpoints, few personality data are more "biological" than body build. Morphology appears in the current literature mainly through the continuing interest in obesity. Here current concerns are with explaining behavioral differences between obese and normal persons in terms of responsiveness to external cues (76, 77) or in terms of deficit in response inhibition (88).

Evolutionary and ethological approaches continue to gain influence in psychologists' thinking. The impact may be clearest in the growth of work on nonverbal communication—an area nicely presented in a new anthology by Weitz (97)—and more specifically in studies of eye contact and of emotional expression. For example, Ellsworth & Carlsmith (32) specifically drew upon work in ethology in formulating the role of gaze aversion in aggressive encounters. (Their very complex findings from a complex research design are inevitably more provocative than definitive. The basic finding that human subjects try to eliminate or avoid aversive eye contact of a victim reflects both ethological and social psychological interpretation.)

The centennial anniversary of Darwin's basic work on emotional expression prompted an important volume (30) tracing the history of this field and presenting conceptual and methodological issues from several perspectives. Ekman's introductory chapter offers a useful case study of the bases for the rejection and later rediscovery of Darwin's work; other chapters present the evolution of facial musculature and its role in emotional expression, an account of recent primate work, the history and unfinished business of developmental inquiry on emotional expression, an analysis of cultural universals and cultural constraints, and a discussion of theoretical and methodological issues in Darwin's work.

Implications of the biological perspective for personology go far beyond the brief summary possible here. If the importances of biological thinking is not as yet matched by clear indications of *how* we may best exploit advances in these neighboring areas, this may prove to be a blessing in at least two ways: toward the enrichment of personology and its contribution to other fields. Personologists have every reason to welcome and to understand the "biological revolution"—which, after all, affirms the importance of organismic variables—and to formulate seriously and critically our own biological assumptions. At this point, well-formulated ideas and disciplined speculation may be more important than data or tight designs. (For example, might not the "opponent process" model of neural organization (45) suggest an approach to the study of duality in human nature?) Further, several areas of psychobiology appear to welcome clearer definition of psychological variables which could better focus their inquiry. [For example, what might personologists contribute toward identifying those genotypes useful in shifting quantitative genetics toward a true behavior genetics (96)?] While it is far easier to pose questions than to suggest answers, the biological field will clearly command—and deserve—sharply increased attention.

Personality Style

"Style" offers a potential key for capturing individuality in a dynamic and truly personal way, as Allport long held. Yet it is difficult to arrive at a conceptualization which clearly differentiates stylistic variables from abilities, defenses, temperament, and a good many other constructs; viewed at close range, these constructs interact and interpenetrate in disconcerting ways. Indeed, perhaps style *is* that interaction. The notion of style as "how" one acts, thinks, feels—as contrasted with "what" one does, thinks, or feels—must serve. Several studies included in this section, however, might equally claim attention elsewhere.

One of the most promising efforts to capture personal style comes from Rice's (79) continuing study of voice qualities. Vocal style has intuitive appeal as a potentially important variable: it is a directly behavioral and "unobtrusive" measure, elicited in natural settings, and one which has been reliably assessed and related to therapeutic outcomes. In contrast to recent concerns with microscopic linguistic analysis of nonverbal communication, Rice classified a limited number of vocal styles on the basis of a "melodic line"—pitch range, tempo, emphasis patterns, as well as (reliably assessed) judgments of inwardness, instrumental quality, involvement, and the like. Three such vocal styles, previously identified in a study of clients in Rogerian therapy, were related to pretherapy Rorschach and MMPI data. A "focused" style (high energy, narrow pitch fluctuation, irregularities of tempo, a quality of inward-turning), an "externalizing" style (high energy, wide pitch range, regular stress patterns, a "talking-at" quality), and a "limited" style (low energy, narrow pitch range, even tempo, weak stress patterns, and a fragile, distancing quality) were related in predicted ways to Rorschach scores associated with creative functioning; as predicted, they were unrelated to Rorschach scores reflecting normative-adjustment criteria or to MMPI scores.

This line of inquiry was extended in Wexler's (99) study relating voice quality to cognitive processes (differentiation and integration; vividness and variety) assumed to reflect ongoing processes of self-actualization, as well as to a more conventional measure (the Personal Orientation Inventory) of self-actualization. Subjects were undergraduates describing feelings when experiencing various emotions. Again, a "focused" vocal style was strongly associated with both the meaning-structure and questionnaire measures of self-actualization; "externalizing" vocal style was negatively related to both types of measures, and a "limited" style showed weak negative relationships to both. This approach to assessment of vocal style seems promising for other research contexts, as well.

Expressive movement remains a classic but surprisingly undeveloped field for studying personal style. A series of neat little studies by Zweigenhaft & Marlowe (104) clearly established links between signature size and various indices of status and self-esteem. Taken together with Zweigenhaft's (103) earlier findings, these studies point to the promise of work on graphic expression, and invite more searching looks at theoretical implications.

The explosion of work on nonverbal communication gives new impetus to the study of expressive styles—particularly work on eye contact and emotional expressiveness. While most of the current interest in eye contact is concerned with communication processes, the eyes also provide cues to deeper, more permanent aspects of personality. Libby & Yaklevich (61) studied the effects of three personality needs on maintenance of eye contact and gaze aversion during structured interviews. As predicted, nurturant subjects returned the interviewer's gaze; subjects high in abasement looked leftward (not downward) when shame and humiliation were invoked; intraception was unrelated to ocular responses; and women maintained eye contact more often than men. The complex findings, discussed in terms of theories of Ekman and Tomkins as well as findings from ethological and right-left hemisphere research, offer provocative leads for further inquiry. Conscious attempts at duplicating emotional expressions, however, are not strictly "expressive" and involve other considerations, as Draughan's (29) study reveals. Most subjects improved when a mirror was used; however, anxious people were inhibited by the use of a mirror, and nonanxious people were not.

Interest in personality style remains centered in cognitive styles—and the analytic vs global style (field dependence-independence) remains the hardiest of our stylistic variables. Yet serious questions are raised: about the implicitly evaluative nature of the construct (with field independence defining the "desirable" style in most studies), about implicit sex bias (with males typically more field-independent), and about the generality of field dependence-independence (since the defining tasks involve spatial abilities). Several contributions this year have addressed these questions. DeFazio (28) examined the analytic-global style in a linguistic context and found that field independents performed better on the Cloze Test and speech-shadowing tasks. Thus the analytic style seems to represent more than spatial ability. Within his carefully drawn (and thus somewhat special) sample, field-independence was associated with language competence, but sex was not. Other studies found field independence related to empathy (65) and enhanced by children's practice in meditation (62). Nevill (70) studied the effects of dependency arousal upon both eye contact and field dependence-independence. Among her findings were the following: dependency arousal increased duration (but not frequency) of eye contact, as well as field-dependent responding; field dependence was consistently related to duration of eye contact; women were more often field dependent, and tended to maintain eye contact.

Sex differences in two cognitive-perceptual styles—differentiation and stimulus intensity control—were studied by Silverman et al (85). This work introduced several new features: assessment of other dispositional variables, the use of an EEG measure of perceptual differentiation, and replication with a clinical sample. The results point to significant sex differences and pose new questions. For example, among males high anxiety and neuroticism were associated with undifferentiated perceptual responsiveness and with stimulus intensity augmentation; among females, these were associated with differentiation and with stimulus intensity reduction. Sex-typed results with "normal" samples were reversed with clinical subjects (mainly acting-out adolescents). Further, EEG-evoked-response measures of perceptual differentiation (offered as a promising way of studying basic phenomena among infants, psychotics, subjects in drugged states) point to the role of neurophysiological functioning in perceptual style which demands further inquiry.

An information-processing approach to cognitive differences between repressors and sensitizers is well illustrated by Pagano's (74) use of the Sternberg choice reaction-time memory-search task. Taken as a whole, his findings imply that cognitive style differences between repressors and sensitizers are not to be found at the level of "taking in" external stimuli; rather, events occurring at the level of memory organization and internal coding of experience are implicated. Other links between new work in cognition and personologists' concern with personal style seem clearly worth developing.

Emotions and Personality

Emotions hold a secure and central place in any account of personality—yet it remains difficult to define that place. With the growing discontent that psychology has become "too cognitive," neglecting the affective side of experience and behavior, considerable recent work has sought to look more closely at cognitive-affective dynamics. Efforts are still handicapped by the lack of any widely shared theory or well defined concepts of emotion. Most personality theories, as Izard (48) noted, have tended to ignore the problem of delineating the separate emotions and their effects on cognitive and motor processes. Even general concepts of emotion are discussed in confusing or contradictory terms; thus, for example, "feeling" means quite different things to Rogers and to Jung. A sampling of this year's contributions reveals the scattered quality of the growing body of work on emotions, and invites further efforts at clarification and integration.

Strongman (92) offered a broad survey of approaches to the psychology of emotion, drawing together, comparing, and evaluating representative views. While this is a useful volume, it does not fully address personologists' concerns, and in its stress upon methodological and behavioral criteria it seems unlikely to replace Izard's (48) recent survey. Ekman's (31) contribution to the Darwin centennial volume closely examined the "culture-specific" vs "universal" views of emotional expression, noted the problems in conducting cross-cultural inquiry, and weighed the evidence on both sides of the controversy. This extensive, in-depth review (which includes a valuable summary of work by the Ekman and Izard research groups) substantiates a clear conclusion: there *are* universal facial expressions of emotion. In attempting to explain the basis for the demonstrated pan-cultural facial expressions of emotion, Ekman (following Tomkins) offers a neurocultural theory postulating innate facial affect programs along with socially learned and culturally variable elicitors of the affect programs.

While the intricacies of emotion theories are beyond the scope of this review, it appears that neo-Jamesian theories are now in ascendance; among these, Schachter's arousal-plus-cognition formulation seems the most influential. In this context, recent work on facial expressions suggests the need to give greater recognition to discrete emotions and to the role of feedback from facial and postural (rather than merely visceral) responses in accounting for the experience of emotion.

Laird (58) found that subjects led to "frown" or to "smile" without awareness of the nature of their expressions reported feelings of anger and happiness, respectively, and found cartoons funnier when smiling. This demonstration that facial expressions can induce appropriate emotional expressions bears upon theoretical questions. While the study is presented in terms of self-attribution theory, Laird noted that the results are equally compatible with any of the neo-Jamesian formulations; the preference for an attribution model rests mainly on the salience of cognitive variables in Schachter's studies, and on continuity with attributional processes in social psychology (as contrasted with the "sensory" emphasis seen in alternative models). However, several features of the study (including the primary concern with facial expressions) suggest that its contribution might more readily be assimilated to the Tomkins-Izard formulations.

Openness and depth in the experiencing of feelings are central in several versions of humanistic psychology. Wexler (98) addressed this issue, proposing that "depth of experiencing" reflects the amount of cognitive activity expended in elaborating and synthesizing facets of meaning with respect to the emotional state. Students described their feelings while experiencing three different emotions and subsequently rated their "involvement" in each; independent judges reliably rated depth of experiencing, and the tape-recorded narratives were content-analyzed for differentiation and integration of meaning. As predicted, self-report and external judgments of "depth" were related to the cognitive measures; further, positive affects were both more involving to the subjects and produced more differentiated and integrated meanings. The findings seem to go beyond the theoretical frameworks invoked (humanistic psychology, Schachter's theory of emotions) to require a more complete account of the processes involved. Again, Tomkins' theory would seem more apposite in its account of the recruitment of thought and imagery in the notion of "ideo-affective density."

For the personologist, the area of cognitive-affective dynamics poses some of the most exciting and formidable challenges to be found in contemporary psychology. This is an extremely broad domain, incompletely mapped by several tenuous, complex, and perhaps contradictory formulations. Only a few new explorations can be noted here.

Radical reformulations of traditional approaches to learning and concept formation are implicit in work on affects. Unpublished work by Levy (N. Levy, personal communication, March 1974) points out that most analyses of emotion have failed to note that emotions are ideas, and thus can be studied as concepts. A compatible formulation has been advanced in Rychlak's (82) program of research on "reinforcement value" in learning. He observed:

The term 'conceptual' is used widely in psychological theory, usually in inappropriate fashion. To conceptualize is to actively *create* ideas ... The essential nature of affect (feelings, emotions, and so forth) is that it all comes down to judgments ... the student of affective factors wishes to raise his dimension to the status of a basic dimension in human learning. The conceptual and nonmotivational side to affective influences on learning is that they are ... acts of evaluation ... This evaluative capacity is far more central to human learning than laboratory-centered theories of learning using lower animals and IBM machines as analogues have made it appear (82, pp. 253–54).

This basic conceptualization has been developed in a series of researches on learning styles which have major implications for the assessment of ability, racial differences in intellectual styles, and more fundamentally, for understanding personological bases of learning. Importantly, Rychlak also seems to provide an independent formulation of the "feeling function" of Jungian theory, and thus offers another potential bridge between disparate lines of inquiry.

The extremely rich formulation of cognitive-affective dynamics available in Tomkins' (94, 95) theory has not as yet been sufficiently exploited in empirical work. Within the year, Singer's (87) program of research on play and imagination invoked the theory as a conceptual framework, and a series of studies of an affect-based typology of smoking (46) added to its construct validity. However, more central aspects of the theory deserve translation into testable formulations and increased attention in other research contexts.

Neglected Themes: An Apology

With dismay I recognize how much has been left out of this chapter, and offer a deep apology to readers whose major research interests have been totally ignored. One might properly expect to find discussion of new work on dreams (20, 21, 26, 100), fantasy and imagination (87), on ego strength and ego defense (35), on anxiety and aggression, the formulation and functioning of the self-concept, on creativity, and much more. Neglected, too, are examples of methodological alternatives available to personologists (19, 25, 83) and critical discussions of more familiar methods (54, 101). Since "personality" includes the whole human being —and thus most of what psychologists study—one must be severely selective. Selection based upon the ripeness of problem areas for contributing to theoretical development of the field carries the enormous price of neglecting many valuable contributions.

SOME FINAL WORDS

The optimism of the opening sentence may seem more a wish than a prediction; a review of the field shows more possibilities than performance. But the message is still optimistic. Psychology seems to have entered a liberal and humane intellectual climate, appreciating the complexity of the human being, and prepared to reclaim a neglected heritage of ideas. We have "caught up" with James, Jung, and McDougall and can begin to build upon their ideas. Personologists have an important task: to capture the organization of psychological processes within persons-in-societies. This surely requires a return to theory—but not in the sense of "comparing theories" as objects of study. Our efforts are better directed toward the conceptual clarification and integration that will enable us to pull together a vast empirical literature and better read its meaning.

Personologists have always realized that we must look in two directions—toward biology and toward culture—and attempt some synthesis. Perhaps we might also look inward, remembering that the enduring theories were written out of the experience of Freud, Jung, James, and others. On a more modest level, ideas can be tested against our own experience—as can our choices of problems and methods. Here Hudson's (44) autobiographical critique of psychology and Krawiec's (56, 57) collection of psychologists' autobiographies offer delightful and abundant evidence that "personality" is alive, well, and functioning.

Literature Cited

1. Adelson, J. 1969. Personality. *Ann. Rev. Psychol.* 20:217-52
2. Adler, G., Ed. 1973. *C. G. Jung: Letters, Volume 1, 1906-1950.* Princeton, NJ: Princeton Univ Press. 596 pp.
3. Alston, W. P. 1973. *A conceptual divide in personality description.* Presented at 81st Ann. Meet. Am. Psychol. Assoc. Montreal
4. Alston, W. P. 1970. Toward a logical geography of personality. In *Mind, Science and History*, ed. H. E. Kiefer, M. K. Munitz, 59-92. Albany: State Univ. New York Press. 321 pp.
5. Bakan, D. 1966. *The Duality of Human Existence.* Chicago: Rand McNally
6. Bem, S. 1975. Sex role adaptability: One consequence of psychological androgyny. *J. Pers. Soc. Psychol.* In press
7. Bem, S. 1974. The measurement of psychological androgyny. *J. Consult. Clin. Psychol.* 42:155-62
8. Block, J. H. 1973. Conceptions of sex-role: Some cross-cultural and longitudinal perspectives. *Am. Psychol.* 28:512-26
9. Block, J., Von der Lippe, A., Block, J. H. 1973. Sex-role and socialization patterns: Some personality concomitants and environmental antecedents. *J. Consult. Clin. Psychol.* 41:321-41
10. Boden, M. A. 1972. *Purposive Explanation in Psychology.* Cambridge: Harvard Univ. Press
11. Bowers, K. S. 1973. Situationism in psychology: An analysis and a critique. *Psychol. Rev.* 80:307-36

12. Buss, A. H., Plomin, R., Willerman, L. 1973. The inheritance of temperaments. *J. Pers.* 41:513-24
13. Carlson, R. 1972. Understanding women: Implications for personality theory and research. *J. Soc. Issues* 28:17-32
14. Carlson, R., Levy, N. 1973. Studies of Jungian typology: I. Memory, social perception, and social action. *J. Pers.* 41:559-76
15. Cartwright, D. S. 1974. *Introduction to Personality.* Chicago: Rand McNally. 559 pp.
16. Cattell, R. B. 1973. *Personality and Mood by Questionnaire.* San Francisco: Jossey-Bass
17. Claridge, G., Canter, S., Hume, W. L. 1973. *Personality Differences and Biological Variations: A Study of Twins.* Oxford: Pergamon. 175 pp.
18. Coan, R. W. 1973. Personality variables associated with cigarette smoking. *J. Pers. Soc. Psychol.* 26:105-9
19. Cody, J. 1971. *After Great Pain: The Inner Life of Emily Dickinson.* Cambridge, Mass: Harvard Univ. Press
20. Cohen, D. B. 1973. Sex role orientation and dream recall. *J. Abnorm. Psychol.* 82:246-52
21. Cohen, D. B. 1974. Toward a theory of dream recall. *Psychol. Bull.* 81:135-55
22. Collins, B. E. 1974. Four components of the Rotter Internal-External scale. *J. Pers. Soc. Psychol.* 29:381-91
23. Collins, B. E., Martin, J. C., Ashmore, R. D., Ross, L. 1973. Some dimensions

of the internal-external control metaphor in theories of personality. *J. Pers.* 41:471–92

24. Constantinople, A. 1973. Masculinity-femininity: An exception to a famous dictum? *Psychol. Bull* 80:389–407

25. Dailey, C. A. 1971. *Assessment of Lives.* San Francisco: Jossey-Bass. 243 pp.

26. Dallett, J. 1973. Theories of dream function. *Psychol. Bull.* 79:408–16

27. D'Amato, M. R. 1974. Derived motives. *Ann. Rev. Psychol.* 25:83–106

28. DeFazio, V. J. 1973. Field articulation differences in language abilities. *J. Pers. Soc. Psychol.* 25:351–56

29. Draughan, M. 1973. Duplication of facial expressions: conditions affecting task and possible clinical usefulness. *J. Pers.* 41:140–49

30. Ekman, P., Ed. 1973. *Darwin and Facial Expression.* New York: Academic. 288 pp.

31. Ekman, P. 1973. Darwin and cross-cultural studies of facial expression. See Ref. 30

32. Ellsworth, P., Carlsmith, J. M. 1973. Eye contact and gaze aversion in an aggressive encounter. *J. Pers. Soc. Psychol.* 28:280–92

33. Fishkin, J., Keniston, K., MacKinnon, C. 1973. Moral reasoning and political ideology. *J. Pers. Soc. Psychol.* 27: 109–19

34. Gale, A. 1974. The psychophysiology of individual differences: Studies of extraversion and the EEG. See Ref. 54, 211–56

35. Gleser, G. C., Sacks, M. 1973. Ego defenses and reaction to stress: A validation study of the defense mechanisms inventory. *J. Consult. Clin. Psychol.* 40:181–87

36. Greever, K. B., Tseng, M. S., Friedland, B. U. 1973. Development of the social interest index. *J. Consult. Clin. Psychol.* 41:454–58

37. Haan, N., Stroud, J., Holstein, C. 1973. Moral and ego stages in relationship to ego processes: A study of "hippies." *J. Pers.* 41:598–612

38. Hall, C. S., Nordby, V. J. 1973. *A Primer of Jungian Psychology.* New York: Toplinger. 136 pp.

39. Helson, R. 1973. Heroic and tender

modes in women authors of fantasy. *J. Pers.* 41:493–512

40. Helson, R. 1973. The heroic, the comic, and the tender: Patterns of literary fantasy and their authors. *J. Pers.* 41:163–84

41. Hogan, R. 1972. *Dialectical aspects of moral development.* Presented at 80th Ann. Meet. Am. Psychol. Assoc. Honolulu

42. Hogan, R. 1973. Moral conduct and moral character: A psychological perspective. *Psychol. Bull.* 79:217–32

43. Hogan, R. 1973. *On theoretical egocentrism and the problem of compliance.* Presented at 81st Ann. Meet. Am. Psychol. Assoc. Montreal

44. Hudson, L. 1973. *The Cult of the Fact.* New York: Harper & Row. 188 pp.

45. Hurvich, L. M., Jameson, D. 1974. Opponent processes as a model of neural organization. *Am. Psychol.* 29: 88–102

46. Ikard, F. F., Tomkins, S. 1973. The experience of affect as a determinant of smoking behavior. *J. Abnorm. Psychol.* 81:172–81

47. Imber, S. 1973. Relationship of trust to academic performance. *J. Pers. Soc. Psychol.* 28:145–50

48. Izard, C. E. 1971. *The Face of Emotion.* New York: Appleton-Century-Crofts. 468 pp.

49. Jahoda, M. 1974. Social psychology and psycho-analysis: A mutual challenge. *Brit. J. Soc. Psychol.* In press

50. Jarvik, L. F., Klodin, V., Matsuyama, S. S. 1973. Human aggression and the extra Y chronosome: Fact or fantasy? *Am. Psychol.* 28:674–82

51. Jones, E. E. et al 1972. *Attribution: Perceiving the Causes of Behavior.* Morristown, NJ: General Learning Press. 186 pp.

52. Klapper, J. A., McColloch, M. A., Merkey, R. P. 1973. The relationship of personality to tolerance of an irritant compound. *J. Pers. Soc. Psychol.* 26: 110–12

53. Kline, P. 1972. *Fact and Fantasy in Freudian Theory.* London: Methuen

54. Kline, P., Ed. 1974. *New Approaches in Psychological Measurement.* New York: Wiley. 269 pp.

55. Kohlberg, L. 1973. Continuities in childhood and adult moral development revisited. In *Life-Span Developmental Psychology: Personality and Socialization*, ed. P. B. Baltes, K. W. Schaie, 179–204. New York: Academic. 452 pp.

56. Krawiec, T. S. 1972. *The Psychologists*, Vol 1. New York: Oxford. 376 pp.

57. Krawiec, T. S. 1974. *The Psychologists*. Vol 2. New York: Oxford. 400 pp.

58. Laird, J. D. 1974. Self-attribution of emotion: The effects of expressive behavior on the quality of emotional experience. *J. Pers. Soc. Psychol.* 29:475–86

59. LeVine, R. A. 1973. *Culture, Behavior, and Personality*. Chicago: Aldine. 319 pp.

60. Levy, N., Murphy, C., Carlson, R. 1972. Personality types among Negro college students. *Educ. Psychol. Meas.* 32:641–53

61. Libby, W. L., Yaklevich, D. 1973. Personality determinants of eye contact and direction of gaze aversion. *J. Pers. Soc. Psychol.* 27:197–206

62. Linden, W. 1973. Practicing of meditation by school children and their levels of field dependence-independence, test anxiety, and reading achievement. *J. Consult. Clin. Psychol.* 41:139–43

63. Livson, N. 1973. Developmental dimensions of personality: A life-span formulation. See Ref. 55, 98–123

64. Looft, W. R. 1973. Socialization and personality throughout the life span: An examination of contemporary psychological approaches. See Ref. 55, 26–52

65. Martin, P. L., Toomey, T. C. 1973. Perceptual orientation and empathy. *J. Consult. Clin. Psychol.* 41:313

66. McGuire, W., Ed. 1974. *The Freud/-Jung Letters*. Princeton, NJ: Princeton Univ. Press

67. Money, J., Ehrhardt, A. A. 1972. *Man & Woman, Boy & Girl*. Baltimore: Johns Hopkins. 311 pp.

68. Mosak, H., Ed. 1973. *Alfred Adler, His Influence on Psychology Today*. Park Ridge, N.H.: Noyes

69. Myers, I. B. 1962. *Myers-Briggs Type Indicator Manual*. Princeton, NJ: Educ. Test. Serv.

70. Nevill, D. 1974. Experimental manipulation of dependency motivation and its effects on eye contact and measures of field dependency. *J. Pers. Soc. Psychol.* 29:72–79

71. Olweus, D. 1973. Personality and aggression. In *Nebraska Symposium on Motivation 1972*, ed. J. K. Cole, D. D. Jensen, 261–321. Lincoln: Univ. Nebraska Press

72. Olweus, D. 1973. Personality factors and aggression. *Rep. Inst. Psychol. Univ. Bergen.* 36 pp.

73. Orlofsky, J. L., Marcia, J. E., Lesser, I. M. 1973. Ego identity status and the intimacy versus isolation crisis of young adulthood. *J. Pers. Soc. Psychol.* 27:211–19

74. Pagano, D. F. 1973. Information-processing differences in repressors and sensitizers. *J. Pers. Soc. Psychol.* 26:105–9

75. Pepper, S. C. 1942. *World Hypotheses*. Berkeley: Univ. California Press

76. Pliner, P. L. 1973. Effects of cue salience on the behavior of obese and normal subjects. *J. Abnorm. Psychol.* 82:226–32

77. Ibid. Effect of external cues on the thinking behavior of obese and normal subjects, 233–38

78. Progoff, I. 1973. *Jung's Psychology and its Social Meaning*. Garden City, NY: Anchor. 290 pp.

79. Rice, L. N., Gaylin, N. L. 1973. Personality processes reflected in client vocal style and Rorschach performance. *J. Consult. Clin. Psychol.* 40:133–38

80. Rossi, A. S. 1964. Equality between the sexes: An immodest proposal. *Daedalus* 93:607–52

81. Rychlak, J. F. 1968. *A Philosophy of Science for Personality Theory*. Boston: Houghton Mifflin

82. Rychlak, J. F., Hewitt, C. W., Hewitt, J. 1973. Affective evaluation, word quality, and the verbal learning styles of black versus white junior college females. *J. Pers. Soc. Psychol.* 27:248–55

83. Sales, S. M. 1973. Threat as a factor in authoritarianism: An analysis of ar-

chival data. *J. Pers. Soc. Psychol.* 28:44–57

84. Sales, S. M., Guydosh, R. M., Iacono, W. 1974. Relationship between "strength of the nervous system" and the need for stimulation. *J. Pers. Soc. Psychol.* 29:16–22

85. Silverman, J., Buchsbaum, M., Stierlin, H. 1973. Sex differences in perceptual differentiation and stimulus intensity control. *J. Pers. Soc. Psychol.* 25: 309–18

86. Singer, J. 1972. *Boundaries of the Soul: The Practice of Jung's Psychology.* Garden City, NY: Doubleday. 420 pp.

87. Singer, J. L. 1973. *The Child's World of Make-Believe.* New York: Academic. 294 pp.

88. Singh, D. 1973. Role of response habits and cognitive factors in determination of behavior of obese humans. *J. Pers. Soc. Psychol.* 27:220–38

89. Spence, D. P. 1973. Analog and digital descriptions of behavior. *Am. Psychol.* 28:479–88

90. Stoller, R. J. 1973. Overview: the impact of new advances in sex research on psychoanalytic theory. *Am. J. Psychiat.* 130:241–51

91. Storr, A. 1973. *C. G. Jung.* New York: Viking, 116 pp.

92. Strongman, K. T. 1973. *The Psychology of Emotion.* London: Wylie. 235 pp.

93. Toder, N. L., Marcia, J. E. 1973. Ego identity status and response to conformity pressure in college women. *J. Pers. Soc. Psychol.* 26:287–94

94. Tomkins, S. S. 1962. *Affect, Imagery, Consciousness,* Vol. 1. New York: Springer. 522 pp.

95. Tomkins, S. S. 1963. *Affect, Imagery, Consciousness,* Vol. 2. New York: Springer

96. Vale, J. R. 1973. Role of behavior genetics in psychology. *Am. Psychol.* 28: 871–82

97. Weitz, S. 1974. *Nonverbal Communication.* New York: Oxford. 368 pp.

98. Wexler, D. A. 1974. *Depth of experiencing of emotion and the elaboration of meaning.* Presented at West. Psychol. Assoc. San Francisco

99. Wexler, D. A. 1974. Self-actualization and cognitive processes. *J. Consult. Clin. Psychol.* 42:47–53

100. Wiseman, R. J., Reyher, J. 1973. Hypnotically induced dreams using the Rorschach inkblots as stimuli: A test of Freud's theory of dreams. *J. Pers. Soc. Psychol.* 27:36

101. Wylie, R. C. 1974. *The Self-Concept,* Vol 1. Lincoln: Univ. Nebraska Press. 433 pp. Rev. ed.

102. Yarrow, M. R., Scott, P. M., Waxler, C. Z. 1973. Learning concern for others. *Develop. Psychol.* 8:240–60

103. Zweigenhaft, R. L. 1970. Signature size: A key to status awareness. *J. Soc. Psychol.* 81:49–54

104. Zweigenhaft, R. L., Marlowe, D. 1973. Signature size: Studies in expressive movement. *J. Consult. Clin. Psychol.* 40:469–73

105. Zubin, J., Money, J., Eds. 1973. *Contemporary Sexual Behavior: Critical Issues in the 1970s.* Baltimore: Johns Hopkins. 468 pp.

ATTITUDES AND OPINIONS[1]

239

Charles A. Kiesler[2] and Paul A. Munson

Department of Psychology, University of Kansas
Lawrence, Kansas 66045

Our original review uncovered over 1500 articles and books related in some way to the study of attitudes and opinions. Of course, a much more modest number actually has been included in this review. The study of attitudes and opinions, broadly defined, has historically occupied much of the attention of social psychology and underlies a good deal of research in other areas as well. To cut the field to a more manageable size, we have attended quite closely to the structure of the previous four chapters by Fishbein & Ajzen (92), Sears & Abeles (278), McGuire (206), and Moscovici (226).

SURVEYS OF THE ATTITUDE AREA

MONOGRAPHS   One of the most discussed monographs published during the period of review was *Attribution: Perceiving the causes of behavior*, by Jones et al (151), which includes a number of provocative chapters. This important work is examined at several points later and need not be detailed here. Triandis (311) also has published an excellent brief review of the literature on attitude and attitude change, although there are others at a lower level (9, 106). Kiesler (171) and Duval & Wicklund (77) published research monographs on, respectively, commitment and objective self-awareness, each with rather extensive theoretical discussion. Rokeach (257) has published another volume in his continuing study of human values. Dawes' (67) thorough introduction to attitude measurement should prove useful in a variety of educational settings. At a substantially higher level is the monograph on multidimensional scaling, edited by Shepard, Romney & Nerlove (282).

---

[1] This review covers the period from January 1, 1971, to December 31, 1973, although we tried to include especially important articles published in the first quarter of 1974. For the most part we have not included preprints or unpublished work, and certainly made no systematic attempt to gather such material. Our debt to McGuire and Sears & Abeles for previous *Annual Review* chapters will be obvious to the reader.

[2] Preparation of this chapter was facilitated by a grant to the senior author from the National Science Foundation GS-29722X2.

SOCIAL PSYCHOLOGY TEXTS   Seven good new texts on social psychology appeared during our review. We are overcome by a plethora of riches. For slightly different reasons, we like best the works of Aronson (15) and Wrightsman (337, 338), although it is surely a matter of taste, since the others are very good by any standards. McClintock (204) and Insko & Schopler (138) take a more experimental approach, while Elms (84) and Sampson (271) emphasize issues of social relevance. McLaughlin (209) stresses learning and social behavior. The level at which these books are written varies substantially. Insko & Schopler's (138) book, because of their inclusion of a number of reprinted articles interspersed with text, could be used for a more advanced course too. We note also solid books by Crano & Brewer (63) and Hendrick & Jones (126) on research methods in social psychology that are suitable for undergraduates.

NEW JOURNALS   Three new journals appeared on the scene: *The Journal of Applied Social Psychology* (a new JASP!), edited by Siegfried Streufert, Howard Fromkin, and Joan Suppes; *The European Journal of Social Psychology*, edited by Mauk Mulder, Gustaf Jahoda, Serge Moscovici, and Peter Schönbach; and the *Journal for the Theory of Social Behavior*, edited by Paul Secord and Rom Harré.
    EJSP publishes especially good work, in our judgment, and is indicative of the progress of social psychology in Europe in recent years. The other two journals are competitive and illustrate the burgeoning nature of social psychology.

COLLECTIONS OF READINGS   Ordinarily collections of readings have not been mentioned in this series of reviews. However, since they may prove useful to the reader, we will list a few. Probably most central to the study of attitude and opinion change are the readers edited by Himmelfarb & Eagly (130), Malec (196), Suedfeld (302), Thomas (307), Freedman, Carlsmith & Sears (94), King & McGinnies (180), and McGinnies & Ferster (205). Several other edited works are concerned with various social issues (43, 115, 134, 249). A book edited by Rappaport & Summers (253) contains a number of original and thoughtful articles on human judgment and social interaction.

RELATED WORK   Triandis' (312) book on subjective culture and the work of Glass & Singer (101) on urban stress should be of special interest to our readers. Thoughtful work on prejudice was published by Campbell (49), LeVine & Campbell (191), Coleman (55), and Jones (156). The last is a stimulating paperback designed for use in an introductory course in social psychology.
    Experimental social psychologists are becoming much more interested in problems of program evaluation, a field logically intertwined with the study of attitude change. The interested reader is commended to the recent books by Caro (50), Rossi & Williams (266), Williams (331), Zaltman (342), and Zurcher & Bonjean (350), all of which are substantial additions to the field.
    Our readers might also be interested in books on interpersonal attraction (47, 229); personality (222, 330); the social psychology of groups (17, 197, 343); the self (348); motivation and emotion (32, 54, 83, 321); and several books critical of theory and method in social psychology (70, 116, 141, 161, 286).

METHODOLOGICAL ISSUES

MEASUREMENT AND SCALE CONSTRUCTION   Phifer (252) has shown that in the own-categories procedure an individual may select a disproportionate number of acceptable statements as a result of greater ability to discriminate among items that fall within the latitude of acceptance. Ostrom (241) has proposed a technique to increase the range of items sampled from the "universe of content," but the procedure appears to rest heavily on obtaining a representative sample of subjects to generate items.

The problem of interpretation and assessment of neutral attitudes has also received some attention. Edwards & Ostrom (81) have investigated the influence of underlying cognitive structure, based on the premise that the certainty with which neutral attitudes are held is a function of the homogeneity of information regarding the object. Kaplan (162a) has approached the ambivalence-indifference issue with a modification of the semantic differential measurement technique, where the problem is most apparent in the double labeling of the neutral midpoint of the scale.

A new problem may exist for scales using bipolar adjectives. Reich (254) has found that the subjectivity of the judgment scale interacts with the subject's involvement with the issue. Subjects low on involvement tended to show greater uncertainty when a subjective dimension was employed in a modified Thurstone categorization task.

The most innovative recent approach to attitude measurement is the bogus pipeline paradigm presented by Jones & Sigall (153). For those unfamiliar with this *ignis minimus*, the procedure is one in which a subject is led to believe that a physiological index of his true attitude response tendency is obtained by a piece of sophisticated electronic equipment. The paradigm possesses the advantages of increased sensitivity of measurement (58) and the inhibition of the influence of social desirability (285). Although the extent to which the technique can be generally employed may be limited (240), its potential pitfalls appear to lie more with the user than with the procedure itself (154).

Miron (221) has questioned the wide application of the semantic differential scale (and underlying factors) to specific semantic domains substantially removed from the original derivation. For an interesting discussion of semantic mediation, see Miron (220) and Osgood (239).

ATTITUDE-BEHAVIOR RELATIONSHIP   The historic problem of the "failure" of attitudes to predict behavior continues to receive considerable attention. The most common tack to increase the predictability of behavior from attitude has been the "other variables" approach. In addition to the central attitude, measures are also obtained of related and possibly conflicting attitudes and of the individual's perception of situational constraints which are thought to mediate or influence the attitude-behavior relationship. Wicker (325) found that the best predictor of behavior was the person's estimate of his response given the occurrence of unplanned extraneous events. Weinstein (322) assessed attitudes toward the issue, toward potential action, and toward the combined referent and action stimuli, with the latter measure yielding the highest correlation with behavior. In a refinement of this approach, Rosen & Komorita (259) used perceived effectiveness of actions (to result in change) as weights for a series of actions which differed in level of behavioral commitment, and assessed subjects' willingness to engage in behavior. By summing over the weighted behavior, an Action Potential Index was derived which correlated .59 with the behavioral criterion. Factors which have been included in the other variables approach to the attitude-behavior relationship are potential consequences of behavior (96), perception of social norms and reference group expectancies (2, 7), and personal norms (277).

The solution of the attitude-behavior problem by the "other variables" approach may not be as straightforward as it appears. Sample & Warland (270) have found that the certainty with which the central attitude is held moderates the increase in predictability contributed by measuring other variables. Problems may also exist in deciding when a variable is an "other" variable. Rokeach & Kliejunas (258) found that attitude toward the situation, cutting class, was a better predictor of behavior than attitude toward the object, the specific instructor. In this case, the attitude toward the situation could be considered the more basic construct, and illustrates the somewhat artificial distinctions among attitude, behavior, and related variables (173).

BEHAVIORAL INTENTION   The term behavioral intention is not defined consistently in the literature. It has been used both as a predictor of behavior (in the sense of being a measure sensitive to other variables that may influence behavior) and as a dependent measure of behavior. Perhaps the most comprehensive assessment of the role of behavioral intention in predicting behavior has been conducted by Kothandapani (181), employing the issue of attitude toward birth control. Four verbal measures (Thurstone, Likert, Guttman, and Gilford) were independently constructed for each of three components of attitude—feeling, belief, and intention to act. The twelve scales were administered to 50 users and nonusers and yielded a 12×12 multitrait-multimethod correlational matrix. The three components of feeling, belief, and intention to act were confirmed by two factor-analytic techniques. Regardless of method of measurement, intention to act served as the best predictor of behavior.

Much of the work regarding behavioral intention has been done by Fishbein and his associates (e.g. 5) and has been summarized by Ajzen & Fishbein (6). According to Fishbein's model, an individual's attitude toward the act (Aact) and motivation to comply with normative expectancies of others [NB(Mc)] are the predictors of behavioral intention (BI). Behavioral intentions are presumed to correlate highly with behavior as denoted in the symbolic representation of the model (B ∼ BI). Ajzen & Fishbein state that "the more abstract or generalized the measure of intention the lower will be its correlation with a specific behavior." Consistent with this statement, the studies which they review show correlations of BI with B to range from .21 to .97. The model as it now stands has received criticism from Schwartz (277) for its exclusion of personal normative beliefs as a predictor of BI. At a more fundamental level, Smith & Clark (289) take issue with the formulation of attitude as a function of attributed characteristics and belief strength ($A_o = \Sigma B_i a_i$), finding that an individual component (a) predicted A_o better than $\Sigma B_i a_i$. They conclude that the approach precludes the possibility of rigorously sorting out traits associated with the attitude object from those that are subsequently inferred and attributed to the object.

As a final note on the attitude-behavior relationship, we find ourselves in agreement with Dillehay (72) "on the irrelevance of the classical negative evidence concerning the effect of attitudes on behavior." Yet it is somewhat disconcerting that Bickman (34) reports interviewing over 500 individuals regarding personal responsibility to pick up litter when they see it and receiving affirmative responses for 94% of his sample, only to have less than 2% of the respondents pick up a piece of planted litter as they departed from the interview.

SOCIAL PSYCHOLOGY OF THE EXPERIMENT   Frequent references to methodological safeguards and the sometimes cautious interpretation of results reflect the general awareness and concern with the influence of subjects' role, demand characteristics, and experimenter bias on the internal and external validity of experimental results. These variables are worthy of study in their own right, and the research on them probably helps us to become better experimental social psychologists. However, the data accrued under the rubric of the social psychology of the experiment do not offer a convincing explanation of other research. Of course, if one is predicting only main effects in an experiment, then alternative explanations are easy to come by, including the ones to be discussed in this section.

Although it is not the most important methodological issue, interest in the nature of subjects' role behavior in the experimental setting has instigated the most research. An excellent review by Weber & Cook (318) looks at the evidence for the most frequently hypothesized forms of such roles (the good subject, faithful subject, negative subject, and apprehensive subject) in a number of research paradigms and provides some resolution of the overall picture. Adair & Schachter (3) reexamined the conclusion of Sigall et al (284a) that subjects were motivated by evaluation apprehension to "look good" rather than to cooperate. When the experimenter's expectation was not explicit, subjects showed an increase in performance, replicating the finding of Sigall et al. However, when the experimenter's expectation was made explicit, subjects decreased performance. Adair & Schachter conclude that subjects tended to confirm the hypothesis they perceived as correct (although perception of correctness was assessed after behavior). However, the design of the study does not allow discrimination between interpretations based on good subject or apprehensive subject behavior. Rosnow et al (262) employed an attitude change paradigm in which subjects were made aware of the demand to change by pretest cueing and found that when subjects believed yielding reflected negatively on their self image (indicated by a low IQ), there was less change than when the implication for self image was positive. The findings of this study are consistent with the conclusion of Weber & Cook that when the good subject and apprehensive subject roles are pitted against each other, the subject's responses are consistent with those expected for evaluation apprehension. Rosnow

& Aiken (261) have taken a different tack in approaching the investigation of bias in the psychological experiment. According to their formulation the manner in which a subject reacts to demand characteristics depends upon three mediating variables: (*a*) subject receptivity to demand; (*b*) motivation to comply in a positive, negative, or neutral manner; and (*c*) ability to comply.

VOLUNTEERING   In the Rosnow (262) study the subject samples included both volunteers and nonvolunteers, but source of subject was not related to attitude change behavior. Hood & Back (133) have stated that subjects volunteer because of a cathartic need for self-disclosure. However, their data show the effect occurred only for males. Further, their data revealed the somewhat inconsistent finding that among volunteers there was a preference for a study involving competition rather than alternatives allowing more self-disclosure. Kruglanski (183) has proposed that the continued investment of resources in research investigating volunteer artifacts is unwarranted. He concludes that although volunteer artifacts may always be a potential source of bias, it has not been demonstrated that they act as a "unitary psychological variable" or as a pervasive source of bias. Kruglanski's conclusion regarding the consistency and pervasiveness of the volunteer artifact has not gone undisputed (263).

DECEPTION AND SUSPICION   Rubin & Moore (267) have found that subjects in a social influence study showed a tendency to resist influence with increasing levels of suspicion. They also tested the effectiveness of an open-ended questionnaire for detecting suspicion against a criterion of an extended debriefing interview. The questionnaire was effective in discriminating three levels of suspicion, and a form using an impression set was somewhat more effective than one using a simple recall approach.

The effects of a subject's awareness of deception on experimental behavior has received further attention from Cook & Perrin (57). Whereas subjects who had previously experienced deception tended to respond in a biased manner, those who had learned about deception in the abstract did not. When subjects were cued that the study might involve deception, the difference in performance between those who had experienced deception and those who had knowledge of deception was eliminated. An additional finding of interest was that suspiciousness and reported legitimacy of deception were positively related. In one of a series of studies investigating the role of deception in psychological research, Holmes & Bennett (132) found that awareness of possible deception did not influence subjects' physiological or self-report responses to threat of shock.

According to Newberry (230), a questionnaire was more effective than direct questioning in inducing subjects to admit to having foreknowledge on a problem solving task regardless of whether the approach was characterized by positive or negative demand. Those subjects who had received information about the task, including those who would admit it, used it to improve their performance although perhaps not intentionally.

Judging from the distribution of research in this area, it is the subject who is perceived to be the source of bias in psychological research. Research directed at elucidating the variables that contribute to experimenter bias has received little recent attention. A notable exception is a study by Jones & Cooper (158), which showed experimenter-subject eye contact to be associated with subject affect which influenced responding on a person perception task.

SUBJECTS' PERCEPTIONS AND EXPECTATIONS OF THE EXPERIMENTAL SETTING   From research in this area it appears that subjects do not find the use of deception and encountering certain noxious events (such as being shocked or asked personal questions) to be inappropriate (86, 300). However, this may not be the case if from the subject's point of view the behavior in question is not justified or the research does not contribute to science. Sullivan & Deiker (303) have also found that a sample of psychologists responded more conservatively to questions of experimental ethics than did students. Those who read the report of the APA Ethics Committee (8) were already aware of psychologists' conservatism in this area.

One of the approaches used to obtain information of subjects' reactions to experimental settings is the simulated experiment. This method has also been presented as a device to circumvent the restrictions imposed by requirements for informed consent, by obtaining a subject's consent on the basis of his reaction to a description of a similar study (33). However, today's experimental simulation is yesterday's role playing with a little less action, and some caution should be exercised in generalizing from the armchair speculations of college sophomores. For a review of role playing, see Miller (214).

DISSONANCE

FORCED COMPLIANCE   Previous reviews have noted the controversy over the effects predicted by dissonance theory in the forced compliance paradigm (92, 206, 278). Recent research has concentrated on investigation of the conditions under which the dissonance effect occurs in the forced compliance paradigm. Several studies seem worth noting in detail. All focus on the phenomenological aspects of the behavior. That is, assume a person has acted (or been induced to act) inconsistently with his beliefs. The dissonance model predicts that the person will change this attitude to fit with his behavior to the extent that he freely chose to act, or was financially unrewarded for it, or perceived the behavior to be relatively unjustified on other grounds. Almost no investigator disagrees that such an effect occurs, but almost everyone agrees that the effect is substantially more limited than originally supposed. Recent research has focused on the dissonant behavior itself: whether it has negative consequences for self or others; whether the consequences were foreseeable or expected; whether the person felt responsible for the consequences or otherwise intended them to occur.

Cooper (58) has suggested that dissonance occurs only when one feels personally responsible for his behavior. In his study, subjects chose (or were forced) to work with a partner with a negative personal characteristic which ultimately led to their joint failure on a task. All partners possessed a negative characteristic; but the degree of negativity was systematically varied, as well as whether the subject expected the partner to have that particular negative characteristic or a different one. The dependent variable was liking for the partner. Cooper found, as expected, that the subject increased the perceived attractiveness of the partner only under high choice *and* when the negative trait had been expected or foreseeable, but especially when the trait was very negative. Cooper concludes that only when the subject could foresee, and therefore presumably feel personally responsible for, the negative implications of his choice did he experience dissonance. In a sequel to Cooper's study, Worchel & Brand (334) varied the source of the subject's expectation regarding the partner. They found the dissonance effect to occur only when the subject was responsible for his expectation (as opposed to the expectation being based on a test score).

Goethals & Cooper (102) varied choice and consequences of one's behavior independently of one's intention to produce those consequences. They found that if the subject chose to make a counterattitudinal speech, and if the listener were convinced by the speech, then the subject changed his own attitude to fit more closely with his behavior, regardless of whether he intended to convince the other or not. A second experiment, clarifying the manipulation of intention, replicated the basic results. Thus when subjects freely chose to engage in counterattitudinal behavior, they changed their attitudes only when the behavior had aversive consequences and regardless of whether the actor intended to effect those consequences. Cooper (58) and Worchel & Brand (334) emphasize that the perceived responsibility for one's behavior is critical in producing dissonance, while Goethals & Cooper (102) stress the consequences of one's behavior. The two lines of thought do not conflict, if one assumes that although the subjects of Goethals & Cooper unintentionally convinced the listener, they still might feel personally responsible for the effect. Indeed, Pallak, Sogin & Van Zante (246) found that negative consequences increased task evaluation only under high choice and when subjects made an internal attribution of causality for the consequences of the choice.

Collins & Hoyt (56) had subjects write a counterattitudinal essay, and independently varied financial inducement, consequences, and self-responsibility for the effects. Significant attitude change occurred only under low financial inducement and when the subject perceived that not only did his dissonant behavior have serious possible consequences, but that he would be personally responsible for them. This same basic result was also found after 14 days in a delayed posttest. In a separate study, Hoyt, Henley & Collins (136) found a similar interaction between choice and consequences. Collins & Hoyt had further predicted that without consequences or responsibility, incentive would have a positive relationship to attitude change, but this prediction was not borne out (indeed, the data were in the opposite direction). Nonetheless, Collins & Hoyt are to be commended for the inclusion of a delayed posttest as well as their unique attempt to manipulate independently both the consequences of subjects' behavior and their perceived responsibility for those consequences. The reader may also be interested in the Collins & Hoyt article for its extensive review of the literature on the forced compliance paradigm [also see Tate (304) for an annotated bibliography of the literature on counterattitudinal advocacy].

Calder, Ross & Insko (48) varied choice, incentive, and consequences (as well as also having subject-observers in each variation). Their results are complicated. With serious consequences, there was an interaction of choice and incentive: high choice/low incentive subjects changed more, as expected, than high choice/high incentive subjects. The effect was reversed under low choice. There was also an interaction of choice and incentive with more trivial consequences, and the two contributing comparisons were opposite those found with serious consequences. In other words, high choice, low incentive and serious consequences were necessary to produce the dissonance effect, a finding that fits with other results. The implications are less clear regarding a positive relationship between incentive and change with combinational conditions of both high consequence/low choice and low consequence/high choice.

The results from the subjects-observers of Calder, Ross & Insko (48) are interesting, although their theoretical meaning is unclear. In general, observers' guesses were more depressed than subjects' responses (a main effect), although the general array of means was more or less the same. However, an inference of change is less clear in the case of observers. For example, consider their high choice/serious consequences conditions. For involved subjects the control mean was 13.20, the high incentive mean was 14.80, and the low incentive mean was 21.33. The inference that low incentive subjects changed their attitude is quite straightforward. However, for observers, the three means are 11.00, 5.80, and 11.70. Even though the difference between incentive conditions is in the same direction (low greater than high) it is not at all clear that observers were engaging in the same process that involved subjects did. It seems instead that observers see the change occurring in the high incentive cell rather than the low incentive cell. It is commendable that Calder et al included observers in their design, but further work needs to be done before the meaning of this comparison becomes clear.

Frey & Irle (95) varied choice, incentive, and whether the subject's counterattitudinal essay would be anonymous or made public. In the public variation, the essays would be published with the subject's name and would be used in classroom discussions in which the subject would be asked to defend himself. The public variation bears some resemblance to the manipulation of aversive consequences used by others. Consistent with other studies, Frey & Irle found dissonance effects only under conditions of publicity, high choice, and low incentive. Unlike some other studies, they also found increased attitude change when the essay was to be made public (aversive consequences) and the subject had no choice but received a high incentive.

Typically in forced compliance studies the subject is induced to perform an act inconsistent with his beliefs. Darley & Cooper (66) conducted an experiment in which the subject was induced to refuse to act inconsistently [see Kiesler (171) for a description of a very similar study]. They reasoned that if the subject refused to comply, then the greater the money offered (and refused) the greater the dissonance. Having rejected the money, subjects should justify their behavior by developing an even more extreme attitude, thereby producing greater discrepancy between attitude and requested behavior. By altering the demands of the setting somewhat, Darley & Cooper were able to induce every subject to refuse to write a counterattitudinal essay. Subjects who refused $1.50 to comply became more extreme in their beliefs, and more so than controls or subjects who only refused 50¢. As Darley & Cooper (and Kiesler) point out, there is some danger in extrapolating forced compliance results simplistically to applied settings. If applied social scientists attempt to change attitudes through the forced compliance technique, they should be careful. If subjects refuse to comply, they may well develop more extreme attitudes than they previously held.

These experiments on the forced compliance paradigm suggest that the most reasonable current statement of both the definition of dissonance and the conditions under which the dissonance effect will occur is the following. The person will experience and reduce dissonance if he performs an act inconsistent with his beliefs and if the act has aversive consequences for the person or others, and if the person perceives that he bears some personal responsibility for the act. The exact meaning of personal responsibility is unclear; the various experiments indicate that it cannot be simply equated with intentionality, choice, justification of financial inducement, or expectation. For example, Calder, Ross & Insko (48) found dissonance effects only under low incentive and high choice. Neither variable alone produced the effect. If we presume that responsibility for one's behavior is the mediating variable for dissonance-like effects, then neither choice nor incentive could be equated with responsibility. Future research will undoubtedly delve more deeply into this interesting question.

Cooper & Duncan (60) worked on a different aspect of the definition of dissonance. They tried to test Aronson's (13) idea that dissonance results from a violation of one's self-image (e.g. lying to others produces dissonance because one is not the sort of person who lies to others). Cooper gave positive, negative, or neutral personal feedback to subjects about self. Subjects then wrote a counterattitudinal essay for either 50¢ or $2.50. Contrary to expectations based on the Aronson notion, manipulated self-esteem did not interact with incentive (although, of course, subjects receiving the smaller incentive showed greater attitude change). Subjects were further divided on self-reported self-esteem; again self-esteem did not significantly relate to attitude change. Indeed, contrary to expectation, there was a nonsignificant tendency for low self-esteem subjects to change more than those reporting high self-esteem. Aronson's idea, that one's concept of self supplies the cognitive implication ("I am not the sort of person who ...") that is violated by dissonant behavior, is intuitively appealing and certainly relates to the concept of self-responsibility for one's behavior mentioned previously. However, the study of Cooper & Duncan suggests that this theoretical cloak is ill-fitting.

ALTERNATIVE MODES OF DISSONANCE REDUCTION   Götz-Marchand (108) has completed three intriguing experiments which show that how one reduces dissonance depends upon the alternative ways offered and when. For example, in one study, subjects were led to believe that their IQ score was considerably below their expectations. Subjects were given a questionnaire of five items on separate pages relating to five different ways of resolving the dissonant input. Conformity (of IQ estimate) and test derrogation were presented either first or last (the rest of the sequence was constant). Subjects either completed the five items in order or looked at all five before beginning. Götz-Marchand found the dissonance reduction alternative emphasized depended heavily upon both order and knowledge of the sequence. When the conformity item was first in the sequence and subjects were unaware of the content of subsequent items, they changed their estimates of self-intelligence 10.1 units; when they knew the subsequent items they changed 4.7 units ($p < .01$). The results for the test derrogation item show a similar interaction pattern ($p < .01$). How subjects reduced dissonance in this study depended greatly on which alternative methods seemed readily available. When they were not aware of subsequent items, they emphasized the first one presented to them. In other studies, similar effects occurred when the subject was allowed to change his answers or when one item was arbitrarily deleted from the list. This dissertation illustrates how cognitively flexible people are in resolving dissonant situations and how little we know about such processes. At minimum, these results suggest future studies should use much more sophisticated research designs.

DISSONANCE AND OTHER VARIABLES   In the period covered by this review, most of the empirical work in dissonance has focused on either the forced compliance paradigm described earlier or on comparisons with attribution theory, yet to be described. Less concentrated, but noteworthy, effort has gone into the study of: temptation (187, 347a); decision-making (22, 128, 193, 198); the consistency of dissonance effects across experiments (310) and other long-term effects (314); *fait accompli* (59) and other postdecisional inputs (127, 144, 339); behavioral success in conditioning others (52); the commitment or reaction of the audience (36, 112, 287, 328); the effect of skill in role playing (201, 317); the relationship of dissonance to social judgment theory and involvement (28, 30, 37); personality variables (29, 46, 284, 329); effort (140, 251, 279); disconfirmed expectancies (41); inequity theory (225, 316); and declining to perform alternative behaviors (121, 216, 218, 309).

SUMMARY   Dissonance research has concentrated on discovering the critical variables underlying the forced compliance effect. Other research yet to be described has been concerned with comparing dissonance and attribution predictions. The sheer amount of research on dissonance theory has decreased quite dramatically over that contained in previous reviews, and the excitement generated by dissonance theory in social psychology has obviously been dampened. The hope of a previous review that, " . . . the spectacular though currently unrealized promise of dissonance theory does not go the way of the brontosaurus" (278) has not been completely violated, but the theory might be put on the endangered species list.

ATTRIBUTION THEORY

Attribution theory (25, 124, 149, 164, 165) appears to have replaced dissonance theory as the most popular theoretical model in social psychology. Further, the Dissertation Prize offered by the Society of Experimental Social Psychology was won in 1972 and 1973 for work generally related to attribution theory. Newtson (232) studied the implications for the attribution process of variations in the units of perception. Snyder (292) developed a scale to measure the degree to which individuals monitor and change their own behavior as a function of situational variations. Attribution theory is making its contributions to experimental work in attitude change in both quantity and quality.

The sheer frequency of appearance of attributional analyses in the literature serves to document literally the heuristic value of the approach. Attribution theory has indeed served to stimulate investigation, and represents a goodly portion of the empirical excitement in social psychology today. Overall, however, the comments of the last reviewers still appear to hold: " . . . few of the recently published studies seem to be direct extensions or tests of the underlying theory. Instead, most of these studies seem to be based on intuitive hypotheses, and their relationships to a systematic theory of attribution are usually left unstated, although there are some notable exceptions" (92, p. 502).

Aside from direct tests of attribution theory, its status qua theory is still questionable. Phenomenological analysis and the empirical study of attributional contingencies are legitimate approaches and of interest in their own right. On the other hand, to focus exclusively on experience and observation is to ignore both science and theory. In the present review we emphasize those studies which explicitly or implicitly help to illuminate the theoretical underpinnings of attributional psychology. In the history of psychology, confrontation among theories has produced significant advances in knowledge and should be a sign of scientifically healthy and exciting times. Consequently, direct attempts to test attribution theory and other theories are especially important. "Other theories" thus far have consisted mainly of dissonance theory, but there is no reason why theoretical confrontations should be so limited in the future. We also emphasize studies which reflect upon variables or issues unique to attribution theory and thereby help to clarify or explicate the theory, such as observer/actor differences. Lastly, we note that this is a review of attitude change, theoretically an attribution or inference about self. We therefore do not attempt to review thoroughly the multitude of studies in which attributions to others are the primary or sole dependent measure.

Theoretical Issues

PRETEST SALIENCE   For reasons that are not clear to us, several investigators have seized upon the salience of one's pretest attitude as a variable for which theoretical distinctions can be made between dissonance and attribution theory. Bem & McConnell (27) found that in a forced compliance experiment, subjects' recall of their pretest attitude was very similar to that shown on a posttest. Bem & McConnell concluded that their subjects did not experience dissonance between pretest attitude and counterattitudinal behavior, but rather simply inferred what their attitude must be on the basis of their behavior and its contingencies. An obvious alternative explanation of their results is that subjects did not want to admit to others, and possibly to self, that they had changed their attitudes. Subjects might not necessarily even be aware that they had changed; Goethals & Nelson (103) found, in a different setting, that subjects' perceived change and actual change did not correspond.

Several investigators (265, 293, 333) have posited that salience of pretest attitude is a variable about which dissonance theory and attribution theory make different predictions. A more salient pretest attitude, these investigators argue, should increase (dissonance and hence) attitude change from the point of view of dissonance theory, but decrease attitude change from the point of view of attribution theory. We do not completely agree with the theoretical prediction. To be sure, if one increases the salience of a pretest attitude, then one ordinarily increases the dissonance between that attitude and subsequent counterattitudinal behavior. However, this does not mean theoretically that more dissonance should be reduced, since increasing the salience of the pretest attitude should also increase its resistance to change. The confound between two variables theoretically leading to opposite predictions means that the prediction from dissonance theory is problematical at best.

The results still may have empirical utility. Snyder & Ebbesen (293) found that increasing the salience of the pretest attitude led to decreased change in the high dissonance condition, but also increased change in the low dissonance condition. They conclude against dissonance, but acknowledge that their results do not really fit with attribution theory either. They offer as explanation a variation of attribution theory in which volition affects the perception of one's behavior. Ross & Shulman (265) found that reinstatement of initial attitude did not decrease attitude change in a forced compliance experiment. Indeed the difference between their high and low choice conditions increased slightly when the initial attitude was made more salient. They conclude in favor of dissonance theory. Harris & Tamler (118) found a similar result. These studies are of empirical interest since they provide clues about the process of change in the forced compliance paradigm. However, since the dissonance prediction is ambiguous, the setting does not provide the necessary conditions for a clear test between the two theories.

THE ILLUSION OF UNIQUENESS   Kelley (164) has suggested that subjects in high dissonance conditions perceive themselves to be uniquely agreeing to act contrary to their beliefs. In Kelley's view the subject who complies under low incentive assumes (incorrectly) that he is unique in complying and infers therefore that the compliant behavior is actually consonant with true attitude. Cooper, Jones & Tuller (61) tested this proposition by telling some subjects that 90% of subjects had complied with the request to write a counterattitudinal essay and telling others that only 15–20% had complied. They found this manipulation of "uniqueness" to affect perceived concensus but it did not affect attitude change. Subjects receiving a small incentive for writing the essay changed their attitude more than subjects receiving a larger incentive, regardless of perceived uniqueness. Further, in control conditions in which uniqueness was not mentioned, perceived uniqueness did not vary as a function of incentive.

Motivational Issues

The areas of arousal and motivation seem to offer potential for differentiating between attribution theory and dissonance: attribution being a more dispassionate inferential process, while dissonance is a theoretical state of arousal which the individual presumably experiences as a negative state.

Zanna & Cooper (346) gave placebos to subjects in a forced compliance experiment. Some subjects were told that the pills would make them feel tense; others were told it would relax them; control subjects were told the pills would have no side effects. Zanna & Cooper based their theoretical derivation on two assumptions: (*a*) dissonance is a state of arousal; and (*b*) subjects can be led to misattribute states of arousal. If both assumptions are valid, Zanna & Cooper reasoned, then subjects could be misled into attributing the source of arousal to the pill rather than their own counterattitudinal behavior, and therefore not change their attitudes to reduce dissonance. Their data followed their theoretical predictions. Control subjects, who expected no side effects from the pill, showed a dissonance effect with high-choice subjects changing their attitudes to correspond with their behavior. When subjects could attribute their arousal to the pill, the dissonance effect was virtually eliminated. When subjects were told the pill would be relaxing, the high-choice subjects changed their attitudes significantly more than in the control condition. Zanna & Cooper conclude that such an array of data could not have occurred unless dissonance produced a state of arousal recognizable to subjects (otherwise subjects would not attribute the source of arousal to the pill). They say, "While Bem's and Kelley's model may be considered as useful heuristic devices, and while they may accurately reflect the process employed by observer-subjects, the present results suggest that involved subjects do indeed perceive themselves to be aroused when participating in a counterattitudinal role-playing situation" (346, p. 708). It should be noted that Zanna & Cooper do not directly test the hypothesis that dissonance is arousing, but rather test the implications of assuming that it is arousing. An indirect test, but a provocative result.

Pallak (242, 245) has tested the dissonance-as-arousal hypothesis several times. In one study (245) he varied both shock and dissonance (separately but not orthogonally) and found dissonance and anxiety arousal (when subjects expected to be shocked in the future) to have very similar effects on incidental verbal learning, suggesting a parallel between anxiety and dissonance as drive states. Pallak & Pittman (245) found a significant interaction between level of dissonance and degree of response competition in two separate experiments. High dissonance subjects learned more than low dissonance subjects when response competition was low and learned less when response competition was high. This interaction with response competition has been repeatedly found with other drive states and supports the hypothesis that dissonance is arousing.

The work of Zanna & Cooper and Pallak and his colleagues is sufficiently compelling that one must explain it in some way if one wishes to maintain a theoretical position of attribution as relatively "cool." The more general issue is motivation. If one does attribute the cause of his behavior to self, why? If the person theoretically asks himself "Why did I do that?", then what makes him ask the question? The research described above deals with the issue of the activity or arousal level of the person, addressing itself to one of the two classical issues on motivation, that of instigation to action. The other traditional issue of motivation, that of direction of behavior, has yet to be raised. One suspects that motivational issues, never a popular topic in social psychology in the past, may yet become a major concern in the future (172).

Actor/Observer Differences

In an important article, Jones & Nisbett (152) discuss the differing perceptions of actors and observers of behavior. "Actors," they say, "tend to attribute the causes of their behavior to stimuli inherent in the situation, while observers tend to attribute behavior to stable dispositions of the actor." This bias presumably is partly due to the actor's greater knowledge of his own history, motives, and desires. However, there is also a directional bias in perceptual orientation, such that for the actor the situation is preeminent, whereas the observer focuses his attention on the actor. This statement has produced much discussion (see also 151, 155, 203).

Nisbett et al (234) conducted three different demonstrational studies which illustrate the different perspectives of actors and observers. In each case, actors were more inclined to attribute the cause of their own behavior to some aspect of the situation. Observers were more likely to see the cause as due to some predisposition of the actor.

The issue of the differing perspectives of actors and observers was directly attacked by Storms (299). Storms reasoned that if attributions are literally influenced by one's focus of attention, then it should be possible to change the way actors and observers interpret a behavior by changing their visual orientation. In this study, two strangers (actors) participated in a brief conversation while two observers watched. Each of the observers was visually oriented toward one of the actors. Through ingenious use of videotape, Storms subsequently was able to show the interaction again to actors and observers, either from the same visual perspective as before (i.e. actor sees other actor on tape and observer sees the same actor he previously was watching) or a different perspective (i.e. subject sees self on tape; observer sees the actor not previously the focus of his attention). In both the control (no-tape) condition and the same-orientation conditions, subjects attributed the causes of their own conversational behavior to situational influences more than did their observers, as expected. However, when their visual orientation was changed through the subsequent use of videotape, both subjects' and observers' causal attributions of behavior were changed also. When subjects saw their own behavior on videotape, they became much more dispositional when explaining their own behavior. When videotape allowed observers the visual perspective of involved actors, they became much more situational in attributing cause to actors' behavior. In short, Storms found that under ordinary circumstances, actors tended to see their own behavior as situationally determined and observers see the same behavior as dispositionally determined. However, when Storms subsequently changed their visual perspective, he found the attributions for behavior to change also.

Bem (25) originally proposed that observers and actors are "isomorphic," that the inferential processes they use and the conclusions they arrive at are identical [although he no longer endorses this view in its extreme form (26)]. Jones et al (159) objected to both proposals regarding process and conclusion. Jones & Nisbett now propose quite convincingly that observers and actors have different perceptual sets and hence infer different attributional causes. Storms has shown that the attribution by observers and actors can be quite similar if the perceptual sets are equated. Zanna & Cooper, among others, still maintain that the process, at least in dissonant situations, is quite different. The exact process of inference and the content of inference remain interesting empirical and theoretical issues.

Attitudinal Attributions to Self

In this section, we review the several studies in which the primary dependent measure is an attitudinal attribution to self. Since attitude change is the specific concern of this review, we take the point of view that studies involving attributions to self are more germane to the issue than those studies of attribution to others (although the latter are still of interest regarding theoretical issues). We note that the number of studies mentioned here does not necessarily circumscribe the interest in this topic, since a number of experiments previously described under the rubric of dissonance theory could as easily be explained by attribution theory.

There are few attributional studies within the traditional attitude change paradigms (182, 344, 345, 347). Some work has been done on attributions regarding influencing others and being influenced by them (75, 103). Munson & Kiesler (228) also studied the role of attributions by others in the acceptance of persuasive communications. Other studies concern effects of real (219) or false physiological feedback (19, 100, 117, 260, 313, 332), and the perception of personal causation (18, 185, 190, 202, 264, 276, 336) particularly with reference to the interpretation of incentives and rewards (69, 184, 188, 235).

Nisbett & Valins (235) present an interesting discussion of rewards and incentives. They propose an "overjustification" hypothesis, viz. that large incentives for consonant behavior can undermine one's attitudes related to the behavior. "Just as the information-processing view maintains that subjects in the insufficient justification conditions of dissonance experiments *discover* stimulus causes for their behavior, it can predict that subjects in 'overly sufficient' conditions of 'consonance' experiments will *ignore* the stimulus causes for their behavior" (235, p. 68;

quotes and italics in original).[3] Lepper, Greene & Nisbett (188) tested this notion by having children draw pictures for which they received no reward, an expected reward, or an unexpected reward. Several days later the children were observed using the materials in a free-play situation. The percentage of time the subjects played with the target activity was taken as a measure of intrinsic motivation. Children who had previously received an expected reward spent less time in the target activity than either those in the control or unexpected reward conditions. Surprisingly, from the point of view of the reviewers, the unexpected reward did not affect time spent in the target activity.

The overjustification hypothesis has interesting possibilities in the application of attribution theory to the study of incentives and rewards (38). Some existing data clearly are not in line with the hypothesis [(236); see also (238) for a review of token reinforcement programs in the classroom], which suggests a good deal of experimental work yet to be done. Reiss & Sushinsky (255a) find, for example, that the data of Lepper et al do not replicate if one uses a multiple trial, operant procedure.

One of the most intriguing and theoretically unique findings of attribution research has been Bem's (23, 24) research on truth and lie lights. Bem originally found that if a person sees himself making statements under circumstances previously associated with telling the truth, he will come to believe that the statements represent fact. In our laboratory, we have failed three times to replicate this finding. A replication by Maslach (200) also does not support the original finding. Maslach discusses an alternative explanation, based upon decreased vigilance induced by the truth stimulus (also see 172). She found that the lie stimulus promoted more cautious responding as evidenced by such vigilance indices as better recall, greater confidence, slower reaction time, and a different pattern of

---

[3] We find the hypothesis intriguing, but quibble with its roots in our own work. Kiesler & Sakumura (178; see 171 for related work) found that when subjects were induced to tape-record a speech consistent with their attitudes, incentives for doing so did not affect their attitude, but (as predicted) subjects receiving low incentives were more resistant to attack later. Nisbett & Valins describe an unpublished study by Carlsmith & Lepper, who report that subjects who received a small incentive for writing a consonant essay changed their attitude less in response to a counter-communication (than those receiving a larger incentive) regardless of whether the counter-communication came before or after writing the essay. This result fits neatly with Nisbett & Valin's hypothesis, but we have not been able to replicate it in our laboratory. We find the resistance effect for low incentive to occur only when the counter-communication comes after the essay. We feel that our finding, although obviously related to the interpretations of our work on commitment, does not necessarily undermine the overjustification hypothesis in other settings or when the overjustification is more extreme. Our manipulations have been rather innocuous by design. One suspects that an overjustification would have to be much more extreme or obvious before the Nisbett-Valins effect would occur. Further, there is a substantial amount of evidence (114, 171, 177, 269) that these commitment manipulations cue off an active process in the low-justification conditions (as opposed to an undermining of attitude in the high-justification conditions).

physiological activity. The original conclusion is suspect at best. Maslach says, "Further experiments on false confessions should use different paradigms which build in a greater degree of mundane realism, and in which the act of confession has greater consequences for the subject" (p. 146).

Attributions to Others

Research abounds in this area, but much of it is beyond a review of attitude and opinion change. In particular, the work on perceived ability of self and others continues to be a focus of experimental attention (e.g. 88–90, 97, 146, 168, 306, 308, 319, 320). Weiner's (321) book on motivation deserves special mention for its description of this work.

CHOICE AND CORRESPONDENT INFERENCES   An earlier study by Jones & Harris (150) found that subjects attributed an attitude to another consistent with his behavior even, although less so, when it was performed under low choice. Jones et al (155) found the attribution to low-choice others to depend upon the attitudinal explicitness of the behavior (essay strength in their experiment) and the prior attributions of the observer. When an actor wrote a weak essay under low choice, observers attributed an attitude to him opposite to his behavior. Lopes (195) shows how these data could be interpreted within the context of Anderson's integration model (10, 129). Jellison & Davis (145) found that the extremity of another's behavior also affects our perception of his competence, ability, and sincerity (also see 51, 166 and 210). Ajzen (4) found perceived probability of some behavior to depend upon both perceived choice and the utility of the behavior. Reisman & Schopler (255) point out that one could conceive of the person and his disposition to act as having a unit relationship and that the attributed responsibility for an act should vary as a function of the strength of the unit relationship.

Victims and Responsibility

Stokols & Schopler (298) found the evaluation of a victim to vary inversely with the severity of the victim's misfortune and directly with expectations of future interaction. The victim's responsibility for the outcome did not affect evaluations of her. Phares & Wilson (251a) found attributed responsibility to be a function not only of the severity of outcome but the ambiguity of the situation and the perceiver's internal control (measured by I-E scale). Jones & Aronson (148) found no differences in fault attributed to rape and attempted rape victims, but divorced women were seen as more responsible for the act than either virgins or married women, and their subjects recommended shorter imprisonment for the victimizers of divorced women (which may say something about the liberation of Texas undergraduates). Shaw & Skolnick (281) found support for a refinement of both Lerner (189) and Walster (315) such that they predicted "victims" should not be seen as responsible for very positive outcomes since the "insular function" of attributed responsibility would be less. Fishbein & Ajzen (93) emphasize "contextual levels" in their discussion of this study. In a developmental study Rule &

Duker (268) found severity of outcome to be less attributionally important for older boys than younger ones (12 vs 7; also see 248).

Interpersonal Simulations

To the relief of us all, there are not many of these and, as might be expected, results are not consistent (76, 119, 162, 163).

Related Work on Balance Theory

In a series of three excellent studies, Crano & Cooper (64) tested Newcomb's (231) distinction among positively balanced, positively imbalanced, and nonbalanced situations. Using all possible pairs of situations subjects were asked to judge which situation of the pair was more stable and which more pleasant, thereby using each stimulus situation as a comparison point for every other stimulus situation. Although overall judgments were comparable to previous work, in no case was rated pleasantness of the triadic situation scalable, and pleasantness was concluded not to be unidimensional. Newcomb's (231) extension of Heider's (123) model regarding nonbalanced triads was supported, particularly regarding perceived stability of the triad. In the third study, subjects rated the comprehensibility and involvingness of the triads. Situations having a positive P/O bond were rated as more involving (comprehensibility was not scalable), supporting Newcomb's notion that a negative P/O bond motivates P to disengage from the situation directly with a resulting ambivalence toward the situation rather than neutrality. We note that Wellens & Thistlethwaite (323) did not find support for Newcomb's model when subjects were asked to estimate the value of missing relationships in a P-O-X triad.

Other work dealt with distinguishing among perceived pleasantness, tension, and consistency, as dependent measures (113); the recall of balanced and unbalanced structures (62, 137); similarity between perceiver and actor (105); cross-cultural investigations of balance (324); the salience of or preference for inconsistency (125, 280); and further work on the role of ambivalent and neutral relationships in dyadic structures (215). Although beyond the scope of this review, we note also the detailed work by Anderson and his colleagues, criticizing balance theory for the simplicity of its predictions regarding interpersonal perception. A number of interesting tests of Anderson's integration theory have appeared (10–12, 129, 272).

Summary

Attribution theory has blossomed as a frame of reference for a wide variety of research enterprises. However, the theoretical details of this approach are still not well articulated, and to the extent that its proponents maintain their inductive bias, they may never be. Inductively oriented theorists have never been known for challenging or testing their own assumptions. Partly as a result, there seems to be really several theories of attribution. To sharpen our understanding of the attribution process, it would be helpful to bring the approach into more frequent experimental confrontation with other theories. We do not take the position that theory A is right and theory B wrong. Surely both have a germ of truth that resonates to all of us, but only through a process of theoretical confrontation can we separate the wheat from the chaff and discover the touch of reality that each represents. Some claim there is no such thing as a critical test of a theory and they are probably right, but we certainly progress more quickly when we try to confront theories with their own ambiguities. As yet, research on attribution to self is in the infant stage, and the theory has been used more often to explain other data than to generate interesting predictions on its own. However, the recent monograph by Jones et al (151) is promising in that regard.

The work on attributions to self is especially important theoretically from several perspectives, even though some of this research is only beginning. For example, Weiner (321) discusses how our causal attribution for our own performance affects out subsequent behavior. The idea that causal attributions for previous behavior affect the relationship between attitude and behavior deserves serious consideration and should be tied to previous work on the attitude/behavior problem. Valins & Nisbett (313) discuss how reattribution therapy can be effective in inducing substantial change in patients' behavior. Research on attitude change has always been weakest in its implications for gross behavioral change, and the thoughtful work of Valins & Nisbett is a step in the right direction.

Attribution theory has not yet been tied closely to previous work in attitude change. Part of the problem is that the question of change itself is ambiguous within the theory. One who espouses an extremist attributional position would maintain that we don't change our attitudes but rather simply discover what they are. This implicit denial of change not only runs counter to a substantial body of work on assessment of attitudes (and motives), but more importantly leaves the theorist free to ignore any data that are even remotely challenging. This isolationist position may please those studying for their preliminary examination, but disappoint those who enjoy the excitement of a theoretical or empirical confrontation.

LEARNING AND CONDITIONING OF ATTITUDES

The conditioning of attitudes continues to be a popular research topic (85, 295). O'Donnell & Brown (237) found conditioning effects of both positive and negative attitudes to increase with age (grades 3–12), although a part correlation suggested the effect was due to increased awareness of the contingencies. With awareness constant, the part correlation between conditioning and age was −.11. Brown & Hill (44) suggest that task complexity mediates the relationship between awareness and conditioning. Kerpelman & Himmelfarb (169) applied the learning theory principles of acquisition, partial reinforcement, and counter-conditioning to the learning of attitudes in a concept-formation paradigm. Partially rewarded subjects were slower to learn the attitude, but more resistant to counter-conditioning, as predicted. Nisan (233) found that delayed rewards were perceived as more valuable than more immediately expected ones, although the relationship of this finding to Mischel's (222) work on delay of gratification needs to be explored. Lohr & Staats (194) demonstrated the generality of their language conditioning paradigm by successfully demonstrating conditioning in three Sino-Tibetan languages.

Several interesting studies are less tightly tied to the learning/conditioning paradigm. Baron, Bass & Vietze (20) carried out a field study with lower class black youth and found, as predicted, that lower levels of praise from a white experimenter were more effective in changing subject's self-image than were higher levels. They explain their effect in terms of subjects' normative expectations of reward and the experimenter's lessened credibility when he deviated from expected reward levels. This idea of deviation from expected interaction rates could be applied also to other work. For example, Stang (296) found that interaction rate had a positive relationship to leadership ratings, but a curvilinear relationship to interpersonal attraction. Zillman (349) found the use of rhetorical questions (presumably producing agreeing responses) to be more effective in persuasion than the more typical declarative statements (also see 273).

ATTITUDINAL EFFECTS OF "MERE" EXPOSURE   Zajonc's (340, 341) finding that the repeated exposure of a stimulus enhances its attractiveness continues to provoke discussion. Burgess & Sales (45) explain the effect in terms of classical conditioning and suggest that contextual factors (e.g. attitude toward the experimenter or the laboratory) act as higher-order unconditioned stimuli. In two studies they found exposure contexts and frequencies to interact. Stimuli presented in positive contexts become more positive with increasing exposure, while stimuli in negative contexts became more negative with increasing frequency of exposure. A similar finding was also obtained by Perlman & Oskamp (250) and Brickman et al (42).

SOCIAL JUDGMENT THEORY

The most important paper in this area reported a series of five studies by Sherif et al (283) on involvement. In Study I, they found highly involved subjects to use fewer freely chosen categories to describe their attitudes, rejected more beliefs, and were noncommittal toward fewer statements (than were less involved subjects in each case). In Study II, a field study, involved subjects used fewer categories to describe their attitudes towards objects higher in the priorities of their reference group. In Study III, subjects judged fewer communicators as credible regarding involving issues than uninvolving issues. Sherif et al conclude that the greater the involvement the more selective a person becomes in judging a communicator as credible and the more likely the subject will contrast a position discrepant from his own on that issue, thereby widening the gap between the communication and his own position. The results of Study IV indicated less attitude change in response to a communication on an involving topic than to a communication on a less involving topic. In Study V, it was found that degree of involvement, but not attitude, predicted response to a request for acting on one's attitude. For example, 63% of subjects attended a meeting on a highly involving topic (defined by own-categories procedures), 48% on a somewhat less involving issue, and 38% on a moderately involving issue. Taken together these studies represent a substantial advance in our knowledge of the relationship of attitude to ego-involvement (also see 82, 275, 301).

Rhine & Polowniak (256) report finding an increase in degree of involvement following attitude change and note the relationship of involvement to the study of commitment. Halverson & Pallak (114) investigated the relationship of commitment and involvement directly by measuring the latitudes of acceptance, noncommitment, and rejection of subjects who had recorded a speech consistent with their opinion under conditions of public identification or anonymity. Committed (public identification) subjects decreased their latitude of noncommitment and increased both the latitudes of acceptance and rejection. Halverson & Pallak conclude that the effects of commitment on resistance to attack and susceptibility to extreme appeals (171) may be mediated by a process of cognitive restructuring.

REACTANCE

Brehm (39) hypothesized that when a person's perceived freedom is threatened, he feels reactance, and acts in a manner to restore his perceived freedom. The basic reactance effect was replicated several times during the period of this review and seems very reliable (40, 71, 110, 124, 243, 335), although one failure to replicate was noted (74). Several investigators demonstrated conditions under which the resistance effect may be attenuated, such as: when the restriction in freedom is implemented by a social norm (110); when the subject is committed to future interaction with the person restricting his freedom (243); and when the person is prevented from inferring that the other intended to restrict his freedom (124).

Various interesting extensions of the model were tested. Berkowitz (31) interprets people's unwillingness to respond to requests for help as being due to reactance and relates the reactance model to a wide variety of studies on helping behavior. Linder, Wortman & Brehm (193) found that the attractiveness of decision alternatives converges as the decision point approaches in time. This convergence should decrease reactance since apparently perceived choice increases when the difference in attractiveness between alternatives lessens (80, 120). Worchel & Brehm (335) found that reactance can be reduced almost vicariously. When another person under the same threat to freedom was observed to act so as to restore his freedom, the subject apparently felt little need to reduce his own reactance. Also, Brehm & Rozen (40) found that when an attractive new choice alternative was introduced to the subject, the attractiveness of old ones increased. Presumably, the subject felt his freedom to choose one of the old alternatives was threatened.

SELF-AWARENESS

Duval, Wicklund, and associates (77, 78, 192, 326, 327) present a very promising new theory of objective self-awareness. They treat the objects of conscious attention as a dichotomy and suggest that at any given point in time either self or external events are the major focus of attention. In subjective self-awareness the person's focus of attention is outward and evaluation of other people or objects takes place. In objective self-awareness (i.e. self as object) the person sees himself as a distinct event in the world, and is very sensitive to any incorrectness or inconsistency among his beliefs or behavior. Duval & Wicklund apply this notion rather broadly to such issues as conformity, dissonance, attribution theory, and social facilitation.

Wicklund & Duval (326) found that subjects completing an attitude scale while listening to a tape of their own voice presented their opinions as more like their peers' than did subjects listening to someone else's voice. In the same paper, a study is reported in which subjects copying counterattitudinal material while confronting a television camera changed their opinion to reduce the attitude/behavior discrepancy more than did subjects for whom the camera was turned away. Wicklund & Duval indicate that objective self-awareness can be seen as one mediator of dissonance reduction. In a third study, objective self-awareness is seen as mediating social facilitation. Subjects copying letters in front of a mirror copied more than subjects not facing a mirror. Duval & Wicklund (78) found the attribution of causality to self was increased when attention was focused on self, independently of whether the causal consequences were good or bad. Wicklund & Ickes (327) found that subjects making a decision while listening to a tape of their own voice requested more predecisional information and indicated they would be more certain of choice than did subjects hearing a recording of another's voice. These studies of objective self-awareness are original and stimulating, and the reader is referred to the book by Duval & Wicklund for further discussion and detail.

COMMITMENT

Kiesler (171) has continued his work in the field of commitment to consonant behavior. His monograph summarizes the work to that date, describes six new experiments, and outlines the relationship of commitment to attribution notions and the writing of Kurt Lewin. As mentioned previously, the process of commitment is not easily seen as a simple one of attribution to self. Several experiments are related to this issue. Halverson & Pallak (114) found publicly committed subjects to decrease their latitude of noncommitment in the absence of other manipulations. Hoyt & Centers (135) found that if subjects were allowed to write any essay they wished, publicly committed subjects chose to espouse a more moderate position than did subjects writing anonymously. Pallak et al (244) found increasing commitment led one to be more responsive to an extreme but consonant communication. Kiesler, Pallak & Archer (176) found this effect to be limited to legitimate communicators. When faced with an illegitimate communicator, committed subjects responded negatively and increased the distance between own attitude and that of the speaker, compared to less committed subjects, regardless of the position advocated by the communicator. Salancik & Kiesler (269), in a study of commitment and the learning and retention of attitudinally related word-pairs, found committed subjects to recall a significantly greater number of consistent word-pairs and significantly fewer inconsistent and irrelevant word-pairs than did less committed subjects (also see 291). They suggest that commitment can affect both the salience of certain cognitions and their relatedness. Kiesler, Roth & Pallak (177) found committed subjects to actively avoid thinking about the attitudinal implications of their behavior, a process that belies a simple inference following behavior. In two other studies (174, 175) committed subjects were more likely to act on their beliefs, but only if attacked. Jones & Kiesler (157) found in three studies that committed subjects responded negatively (boomerang effect) to forewarning of attack, while uncommitted subjects showed anticipatory attitude change in the direction of the expected attack.

STIMULUS INCONGRUITY THEORY

Kiesler (172) has proposed a motivational theory of stimulus incongruity to account for data on dissonance, attribution, reactance, commitment, and self-awareness. His model is based on previous work in perception, attention and vigilance, information processing, and ecological psychology. Others have shown that organisms become aroused when faced with incongruous stimuli (those which are novel, distinctive, or unusual). Kiesler hypothesizes that people become aroused when faced with such incongruous stimuli, whether the stimulus is physicalistic, their own behavior, or someone else's behavior. The aroused organism is presumed to reduce the incongruity by identifying or "explaining" the incongruous behavior. Thus the instigation to act and the direction of the action are central components of the theory. One's own behavior could appear less incongruous to self through such means as attitude change, distortion of volitional contingencies, distraction, or misattribution of the arousal state.

PERSONALITY VARIABLES

SELF-ESTEEM   Dinner, Lewkowicz & Cooper (73) followed up on the previous work by McGuire & Millman (208) on anticipatory attitude change. Dinner et al found high-esteem subjects to show more anticipatory attitude change when forewarned of a communication on a familiar issue, while low self-esteem subjects changed more when expecting a communication on an unfamiliar issue. Dinner et al point to the unclarity in McGuire & Millman's original distinction between emotional and technical issues (see also 68, 157) and suggest their concept of familiarity with the issue is easier to work with.

In a more traditional line of research, Skolnick & Heslin (288) argue that the relationship between self-esteem and persuasibility should depend on the quality of the arguments in a communication. Using arguments contained in communications in other studies, they were able to show that arguments producing an inverted-U or positive relationship between self-esteem and persuasibility in other research were rated as more persuasible, valid, and logical than were arguments from studies in which a negative relationship was found. They found no differences in rated difficulty or complexity of the arguments, leading them to conclude that quality of the persuasive communication is a more potent predictor of the relationship between self-esteem and opinion change than is difficulty or complexity of the communication.

Eagly & Acksen (79) were concerned with the bases for change in self-esteem. They found that ordinarily favorable information about self was accepted more readily than unfavorable information, but that this effect was reversed when the subject expected further evaluations in the future (also see 223). Presumably the potential consequences of changing beliefs about self determined one's receptivity to evaluative information about self. For a review of the literature on our evaluations of others as a function of own self-esteem, see Jones (160).

DOGMATISM   Hodges & Byrne (131) suggest that one reason we respond so negatively to dissimilar attitudes is that they challenge our competence. They hypothesized that simply changing the wording of an attitude statement to be phrased more dogmatically should increase the threatening nature of disagreeing attitudes. In two different studies, strangers either agreed or disagreed with the subject, and phrased their beliefs either as dogmatic or openminded. In both experiments the phrasing had little effect on perceived attractiveness of attitudinally similar strangers, but strangers with different attitudes were rejected more when their attitudes were dogmatically phrased.

In a study which lasted over a 10-week interaction period, Jacoby (143) found that people low in dogmatism were significantly more accurate in perceiving co-workers' dogmatism score than were those high in dogmatism. Apparently, dogmatic people are unable to improve their accuracy of perceiving others over time. (For other studies related to dogmatism, see 65, 87, 142, 224, 290.)

In a study of values (Rokeach Value Survey), Starck (297) found that one's preferences for information sources varied as a function of specific values. Although the majority of respondents preferred interpersonal sources of information (family, friends), those valuing "inner harmony" preferred printed sources of information (over electronic sources and public events), while those valuing a "comfortable life" preferred electronic sources. Either this says something about middle-class America, or else it is the final word on the real decibel level of TV commericals.

SOURCE OR COMMUNICATOR EFFECTS

Mills & Harvey (217) tested Kelman's (167) conceptualization of the processes of identification and internalization. In identification, one theoretically accepts an influence attempt because one likes the communicator and wants to be like him. In internalization, one accepts the influence attempt because the change is congruent with belief and is itself rewarding. The former, Mills & Harvey say, implies an attractive communicator, and the latter implies a credible communicator. They suggest the timing of information about the communicator would be critical in acceptance of his message. As predicted, it made little difference whether information regarding the attractiveness of the communicator came before or after the message. However, an expert communicator was effective only if his expertise was known prior to receipt of his message. The data are interpreted as support for Kelman's distinction between the processes of internalization and identification.

Ference (91) set up an experimental situation in which the subjects received information from two different sources on each of several trials. He varied both the conflict between the sources and their relative accuracy (ability). Subjects' acceptance of information (attitude change) from the sources varied as a joint function of both source conflict and accuracy. Ference's paradigm is a neat one for studying source effects. Subjects were asked to make judgments regarding admissions of new students to the university. Actual cases were used, with all applicants being accepted but some failing to graduate. Subject's task was to determine who had failed. Letters of evaluation were included from two different sources who had interviewed each applicant. The dependent measure was the extent to which subject's response approximated each source. It is a plausible paradigm for manipulating both source and message variables.

Landy (186) varied the attractiveness of an audience and its reaction to a speaker. Subjects were more influenced by a speaker when they felt an attractive audience had listened to him, regardless of the reaction of the audience. Attitude change was greatest when an attractive audience applauded the speaker and (surprisingly) least when an unattractive audience jeered the speaker. The speaker was perceived more positively when listened to by an attractive audience. Landy speculates that one evaluates a persuasive communicator by knowing who else is paying attention to what is said. [See also (247) regarding the effect of immediacy of the interaction between speaker and relevant others.] Snyder & Rothbart (294) found the increased impact of an attractive communicator to be due more to subject's liking for him than to his perceived credibility. Cialdini et al (53) found that when a person expects to interact with another on an issue, he will moderate his position prior to the interaction, although the effect was apparently only a strategic response and did not persist over time.

This seems as good a context as any to mention the provocative chapter by Moscovici & Faucheux (227) on minority influence in the Berkowitz series. They criticize the experimental paradigm in which the group is seen as the active influencing agent and in which the individual or minority must conform to or deviate from the group's prescriptions. They argue convincingly for research studying how and when minorities (or individuals) can influence majorities (or other groups), leading to a better understanding of innovation.

FOREWARNING

As mentioned, Dinner et al (73) found high self-esteem subjects to show more anticipatory attitude change when forewarned of a communication on a familiar topic, while low self-esteem subjects changed more when expecting a communication on an unfamiliar topic. Deaux (68) suggests that anticipatory change is not related to either high or low self-esteem (manipulated or measured), but rather occurs when one is uncertain of his self-esteem. Jones & Kiesler (157) found when subjects were uncommitted on an issue, forewarning of an attack led them to abandon their belief. Committed subjects, on the other hand, intensified their beliefs when forewarned of attack. Jones & Kiesler found their interaction to hold in three different experiments and three different variations in commitment ranging from issues to direct manipulations of commitment.

Hass & Linder (122) studied the interaction of forewarning and the order of arguments in one- and two-sided messages. Somewhat surprisingly, forewarned subjects responded negatively to the placement of implicit refutational arguments (versus pro-arguments) first in a countercommunication. Subjects who were not forewarned attended less to the sequence of the arguments. This result persisted over three studies. Perhaps the refutational arguments amounted to an inadequate attack which only aroused subjects' defenses.

INTERPERSONAL ATTRACTION

Space limitations and personal inclinations preclude a thorough review of research on interpersonal attraction. We will only touch lightly on some issues that have interested readers of this series of reviews in the past.

SIMILARITY AND ATTRACTION   Byrne's attraction/reinforcement paradigm has continued to receive empirical attention, and his monograph (47) systematically outlines the voluminous research in this area. Other workers have extended and modified the basic finding.

Mitchell & Byrne (224) applied the attraction paradigm to the study of jury decisions. In a mock hearing, similarity of attitudes of juror and defendent directly affected the perceived attractiveness of the defendent. For both authoritarians and egalitarians, jurors' attitude similarity increased the attractiveness of the defendent. Interestingly, attitude similarity interacted with juror's authoritarianism in affecting recommended punishment. Authoritarians recommended significantly more severe punishment for a dissimilar other, while egalitarians showed no bias in recommended punishment. Within this restricted situation, attitudes toward the other and behavior toward him did not fit together neatly, at least for egalitarians.

Mascaro & Graves (199) applied adaptation-level theory to the attraction paradigm. Their subjects evaluated two stimulus people. Perceived similarity and attraction to the second stimulus person (50% attitude agreement) varied as a function of the attitudinal similarity of the first person (90%, 50% or 10% agreement). When the first person had been very similar to the subject, the second was perceived negatively in contrast in both perceived similarity and attraction. When the first stimulus person was very dissimilar, the second was perceived more positively.

Other work found the basic similarity/attraction effect to depend at least somewhat on: self's affective state (109), the basis of the attitude (21, 104, 170,

305); the basis of future interaction with the other (147); how explicitly the potential evaluation of the other is suggested (139); the relevance of the situation for the subject (111, 213); and the salience of the attitudinal disagreements (107). As one last titilating note, Bleda (35) found that attitude similarity directly affected female subjects' perceptions of the height of the other; the greater the attitude similarity, the taller the other was perceived, regardless of the height of the subject.

ORDER EFFECTS   Mettee (211, 212) carried out two studies to extend and refine the well-known gain-loss model of attraction proposed by Aronson & Linder (14, 16; also see 154a). His findings indicate the effect depends upon both the degree of affect communicated in the separate parts of the sequence and the inferred discernment of the other. Discernment is suggested to involve two potentially independent factors, credibility and discrimination of the other. Mettee showed that when self is evaluated in a negative/positive sequence on two separate tasks, attraction to the evaluator is greater than in a positive/positive sequence (much as Aronson & Linder had found originally). However, the opposite effect occurs if the sequence of evaluations occurs within the same task. In the latter case, the other is presumably seen as a less credible source of information.

PREDICTABILITY OF OTHERS   S. Kiesler (179) proposes that generally we dislike unpredictable others. In two experiments, she demonstrated that (a) situational constraints can influence individual preferences for predictability or unpredictability in others; (b) one who acts inappropriately is perceived as relatively unpredictable; and (c) whether one dislikes the inappropriate, unpredictable other depends on specifiable situational variations.

OTHER WORK   We cannot leave this topic without commending to the reader the excellent little book on theories of attraction and love edited by Murstein (229) and containing excellent articles by Walster, Newcomb, and others, as well as a provocative critique by Murstein of research in the attraction paradigm.

CONCLUSION

We have continued a tradition of avoiding the definition of attitude and attitude change by simply reviewing that body of research that self-defined attitude researchers have carried out in the last 3 years. We were surprised, however, after a systematic review, to learn how little research had been done on a variety of issues that have received heavy attention in the past. To wit, astonishingly little research has been done recently on the classic breakdown of the persuasion setting: variables relating to the communicator, the communication, and the recipient of the communication. There has been little investigation of fear appeals, order effects, the dissonance-discrepancy controversy, immunization, selective exposure, or attitude change in natural settings.

Why? Part of the problem may be the decline of popularity of dissonance theory, partly due to attacks on the attitude concept itself (1), and partly due to dissatisfaction expressed by respected colleagues with deductive theory (98, 99) and laboratory experiments (207).

McGuire (207) has recently criticized both theory-derived hypotheses and current research in the field. He argues for systems theory and multivariate correlational designs, and emphasizes hypothesis generation rather than hypothesis testing. Gergen (98, 99) suggests theories are primarily a reflection of contemporary history; that science and society form a feedback loop, such that science affects society and is thereby itself changed. Both have a point, of course. However, we disagree on several grounds. Schlenker (274) has pointed out the difference between empirical generalizations, so tied to our own culture, and abstract universal propositions which underlie scientific theorizing. While we accept McGuire's criticism of social psychological thinking as being distressingly univariate in tone, he has failed to consider that the multivariate systems approach to social problems is especially susceptible to influence or domination by cultural variables (and random error) which change over time.

Systems theory, computer simulations, and inductive theorizing, while to be encouraged on other grounds, have a common fault: they don't lead very easily to empirical tests of one's thinking. One is reminded of the ancient enthusiasm about factor-analysis as a technique to handle one's longing for the "big picture." It is a useful technique with proven caution associated with conclusions. However, factor-analysis, like systems theory, often capitalizes on the error variance associated with a testing of a single instance. Like a computer simulation, it is limited by the sampling bias in the data thrown in the hopper. Like inductive theorizing. it seldom leads to informative tests of one's underlying assumptions. Space limits a more detailed consideration of these complicated and important issues here, but we expect these issues to be hotly contested in the near future.

We, of course, are much more committed to the experimental method than McGuire (207) currently claims to be, and more appreciative of deductive theory and the mathematical logic that underlies it than Gergen (98, 99) admits to. However, we are sympathetic to the feelings behind their words—that as a field we have become too rigidly deductive and too totally laboratory oriented. Social psychology must surely swing back to a better balance between theory and observation, between laboratory and social problems. *Yin* and *Yang* should be in balance, not in alternate cycles. Social psychology and the study of attitude change is in the middle of that swing now, we think. However, a method/topic shift demands new theory and new approaches, and we are only now pausing to ponder these issues. As a result, attitude change is not the thriving field it once was and will be again.

Literature Cited

1. Abelson, R. P. 1972. Are attitudes necessary? See Ref. 180, 19–32
2. Acock, A. C., Defleur, M. L. 1972. A configurational approach to contingent consistency in the attitude-behavior relationship. *Am. Sociol. Rev.* 37:714–26
3. Adair, J. G., Schachter, B. S. 1972. To cooperate or to look good?: The subjects' and experimenters' perceptions of each others' intentions. *J. Exp. Soc. Psychol.* 8:74–85
4. Ajzen, I. 1971. Attribution of dispositions to an actor: Effects of perceived decision freedom and behavioral utilities. *J. Pers. Soc. Psychol.* 18:144–56
5. Ajzen, I., Fishbein, M. 1972. Attitudes and normative beliefs as factors influencing behavioral intentions. *J. Pers. Soc. Psychol.* 21:1–9
6. Ajzen, I., Fishbein, M. 1973. Attitudinal and normative variables as predictors of specific behaviors. *J. Pers. Soc. Psychol.* 27:41–57
7. Albrecht, S. L., Defleur, M. L., Warner, L. G. 1972. Attitude-behavior relationships: A reexamination of the postulate of contingent consistency. *Pac. Sociol. Rev.* 15:149–68
8. American Psychological Association, ad hoc Committee on Ethical Standards in Psychological Research 1971. Ethical standards for psychological research. *APA Monitor* 2:9–28
9. Andersen, K. E. 1971. *Persuasion: Theory and Practice.* Boston: Allyn & Bacon
10. Anderson, N. H. 1971. Integration theory and attitude change. *Psychol. Rev.* 78:171–206
11. Anderson, N. H., Farkas, A. J. 1973. New light on order effects in attitude change. *J. Pers. Soc. Psychol.* 28:88–93
12. Anderson, N. H., Lindner, R., Lopes, L. L. 1973. Integration theory applied to judgments of group attractiveness. *J. Pers. Soc. Psychol.* 26:400–8
13. Aronson, E. 1969. The theory of cognitive dissonance: A current perspective. In *Advances in Experimental Social Psychology*, ed. L. Berkowitz, 4:1–34. New York: Academic
14. Aronson, E. 1969. Some antecedents of interpersonal attraction. In *Nebraska Symposium on Motivation*, ed. W. J. Arnold, D. Levine, 17:143–77. Lincoln: Univ. Nebraska Press
15. Aronson, E. 1972. *The Social Animal.* San Francisco: Freeman
16. Aronson, E., Linder, D. 1965. Gain and loss of esteem as determinants of interpersonal attractiveness. *J. Exp. Soc. Psychol.* 1:156–71
17. Back, K. W. 1972. *Beyond Words: The Story of Sensitivity Training and the Encounter Movement.* New York: Russell Sage
18. Barefoot, J. C., Girodo, M. 1972. The misattribution of smoking cessation symptoms. *Can. J. Behav. Sci.* 4:358–63
19. Barefoot, J. C., Straub, R. B. 1971. Opportunity for information search and the effects of false heart-rate feedback. *J. Pers. Soc. Psychol.* 17:154–57
20. Baron, R. M., Bass, A. R., Vietze, P. M. 1971. Type and frequency of praise as determinants of favorability of self-image: An experiment in a field setting. *J. Pers.* 39:493–511
21. Batchelor, T. R., Tesser, A. 1971. Attitude base as a moderator of the attitude similarity-attraction relationship. *J. Pers. Soc. Psychol.* 19:229–36
22. Behling, C. F. 1971. Effects of commitment and certainty upon exposure to supportive and nonsupportive information. *J. Pers. Soc. Psychol.* 19:152–59
23. Bem. D. J. 1965. An experimental analysis of self-persuasion. *J. Exp. Soc. Psychol.* 1:199–218
24. Bem, D. J. 1966. Inducing belief in false confessions. *J. Pers. Soc. Psychol.* 3:707–10
25. Bem, D. J. 1967. Self-perception: An alternative interpretation of cognitive dissonance phenomena. *Psychol. Rev.* 74:183–200
26. Bem, D. J. 1972. Self-perception theory. In *Advances in Experimental Social Psychology*, ed. L. Berkowitz, 6:1–62. New York: Academic
27. Bem, D. J., McConnell, H. K. 1970. Testing the self-perception explanation

of dissonance phenomena: On the salience of premanipulation attitudes. *J. Pers. Soc. Psychol.* 14:23–31

28. Bergamin, J. D. B. 1971. Value-bonded attitudes: Changes in involvement as a function of discrepant behavior. *J. Soc. Psychol.* 85:219–24

29. Berger, C. R. 1972. Influence motivation and feedback regarding influence outcomes as determinants of self-persuasion magnitude. *J. Pers.* 40:62–74

30. Berger, C. R. 1972. Toward a role enactment theory of persuasion. *Speech Monogr.* 39:260–76

31. Berkowitz, L. 1973. Reactance and the unwillingness to help others. *Psychol. Bull.* 79:310–17

32. Berlyne, D. E., Madsen, K. B., Eds. 1973. *Pleasure, Reward, Preference.* New York: Academic

33. Berscheid, E., Baron, R. S., Dermer, M., Libman, M. 1973. Anticipating informed consent: An empirical approach. *Am. Psychol.* 28:913–25

34. Bickman, L. 1972. Environmental attitudes and actions. *J. Soc. Psychol.* 87:323–24

35. Bleda, P. R. 1972. Perception of height as a linear function of attitude similarity. *Psychon. Sci.* 27:197–98

36. Bodaken, E. M., Miller, G. R. 1971. Choice and prior audience attitude as determinants of attitude change following counterattitudinal advocacy. *Speech Monogr.* 38:109–12

37. Bodaken, E. M., Sereno, K. K. 1971. *Attitude change following counterattitudinal advocacy: An attempt to resolve inconsistencies.* Presented at Speech Commun. Assoc., San Francisco

38. Bowers, K. S. 1974. The psychology of subtle control: An attributional analysis of behavioral persistance. *J. Pers. Soc. Psychol.* In press

39. Brehm, J. W. 1966. *A Theory of Psychological Reactance.* New York: Academic

40. Brehm, J. W., Rozen, E. 1971. Attractiveness of old alternatives when a new, attractive alternative is introduced. *J. Pers. Soc. Psychol.* 20:261–66

41. Brickman, P. 1972. Rational and nonrational elements in reactions to disconfirmation of performance expectancies. *J. Exp. Soc. Psychol.* 8:112–23

42. Brickman, P., Redfield, J., Harrison, A. A., Crandall, R. 1972. Drive and predisposition as factors in the attitudinal effects of mere exposure. *J. Exp. Soc. Psychol.* 8:31–44

43. Brigham, J. C., Weissbach, T. A., Eds. 1972. *Racial Attitudes in America: Analyses and Findings of Social Psychology.* New York: Harper & Row

44. Brown, J. L., Hill, F. A. 1973. The effect of task complexity and attitude conditioning. *J. Soc. Psychol.* 90:53–58

45. Burgess, T. D., Sales, S. M. 1971. Attitudinal effects of "mere exposure": A reevaluation. *J. Exp. Soc. Psychol.* 7:461–72

46. Burgoon, M., Miller, G. R., Tubbs, S. L. 1972. Machiavellianism, justification, and attitude change following counterattitudinal advocacy. *J. Pers. Soc. Psychol.* 22:366–71

47. Byrne, D. 1971. *The Attraction Paradigm.* New York: Academic

48. Calder, B. J., Ross, M., Insko, C. A. 1973. Attitude change and attitude attribution: Effects of incentive, choice, and consequences. *J. Pers. Soc. Psychol.* 25:84–99

49. Campbell, A. 1971. *White Attitudes Toward Black People.* Ann Arbor: Inst. Soc. Res., Univ. Michigan

50. Caro, F. G., Ed. 1971. *Readings in Evaluation Research.* New York: Russell Sage

51. Chaikin, A. L., Cooper, J. 1973. Evaluation as a function of correspondence and hedonic relevance. *J. Exp. Soc. Psychol.* 9:257–64

52. Cialdini, R. B. 1971. Attitudinal advocacy in the verbal conditioner. *J. Pers. Soc. Psychol.* 17:350–58

53. Cialdini, R. B., Levy, A., Herman, P. C., Evenbreck, S. 1973. Attitudinal politics: The strategy of moderation. *J. Pers. Soc. Psychol.* 25:100–8

54. Cofer, C. N. 1972. Motivation and Emotion. Glenview, Ill.: Scott, Foresman

55. Coleman, J. S. 1971. *Resources for Social Change: Race in the United States.* New York: Wiley

56. Collins, B. E., Hoyt, M. F. 1972. Personal responsibility-for-consequences: An integration and extension of the forced compliance literature. *J. Exp.*

Soc. Psychol. 8:558-93

57. Cook, T. D., Perrin, B. F. 1971. The effects of suspiciousness of deception and the perceived legitimacy of deception on task performance in an attitude change experiment. *J. Pers.* 39:204-24

58. Cooper, J. 1971. Personal responsibility and dissonance: The role of foreseen consequences. *J. Pers. Soc. Psychol.* 18:354-63

59. Cooper, J., Brehm, J. W. 1971. Prechoice awareness of relative deprivation as a determinant of cognitive dissonance. *J. Exp. Soc. Psychol.* 7:571-81

60. Cooper, J., Duncan, B. L. 1971. Cognitive dissonance as a function of self-esteem and logical inconsistency. *J. Pers.* 39:289-302

61. Cooper, J., Jones, E. E., Tuller, S. M. 1972. Attribution, dissonance, and the illusion of uniqueness. *J. Exp. Soc. Psychol.* 8:45-57

62. Cottrell, N. B., Ingraham, C. H., Franklin, W. 1971. The retention of balanced and unbalanced cognitive structures. *J. Pers.* 39:112-31

63. Crano, W. D., Brewer, M. B. 1973. *Principles of Research in Social Psychology.* New York: McGraw-Hill

64. Crano, W. D., Cooper, R. E. 1973. Examination of Newcomb's extension of structural balance theory. *J. Pers. Soc. Psychol.* 27:344-53

65. Cronkhite, G., Goetz, E. 1971. Dogmatism, persuasibility and attitude instability. *J. Commun.* 21:342-52

66. Darley, S. A., Cooper, J. 1972. Cognitive consequences of forced noncompliance. *J. Pers. Soc. Psychol.* 24:321-26

67. Dawes, R. M. 1971. *Fundamentals of Attitude Measurement.* New York: Wiley

68. Deaux, K. 1972. Anticipatory attitude change: A direct test of the self-esteem hypothesis. *J. Exp. Soc. Psychol.* 8:143-55

69. Deci, E. L. 1971. Effects of externally mediated rewards on intrinsic motivation. *J. Pers. Soc. Psychol.* 18:105-15

70. Deese, J. 1972. *Psychology as Science and Art.* New York: Harcourt Brace Jovanovich

71. Dickenberger, D., Grabitz-Gniech, G. 1972. Restrictive conditions for the occurrence of psychological reactance: Interpersonal attraction, need for social approval, and a delay factor. *Eur. J. Soc. Psychol.* 2:177-98

72. Dillehay, R. C. 1973. On the irrelevance of the classical negative evidence concerning the effect of attitudes on behavior. *Am. Psychol.* 28:887-91

73. Dinner, S. H., Lewkowicz, B. E., Cooper, J. 1972. Anticipatory attitude change as a function of self-esteem and issue familiarity. *J. Pers. Soc. Psychol.* 24:407-12

74. Doob, A. N., Zabrack, M. 1971. The effect of freedom-threatening instructions and monetary inducement on compliance. *Can. J. Behav. Sci.* 3:408-12

75. Dutton, D. G. 1973. Attribution of cause for opinion change and liking for audience members. *J. Pers. Soc. Psychol.* 26:208-16

76. Dutton, D. G., Douglas, R. L. 1972. *Cognitive* cognitive dissonance revisited: A further look at the dissonance-self perception controversy. *Can. J. Behav. Sci.* 4:64-74

77. Duval, S., Wicklund, R. A. 1972. *A Theory of Objective Self-Awareness.* New York: Academic

78. Duval, S., Wicklund, R. A. 1973. Effects of objective self-awareness on attribution of causality. *J. Exp. Soc. Psychol.* 9:17-31

79. Eagly, A. H., Acksen, B. A. 1971. The effect of expecting to be evaluated on change toward favorable and unfavorable information about oneself. *Sociometry* 34:411-22

80. East, R. 1973. The durations of attention to alternatives and reevaluation in choices with two and three alternatives. *Eur. J. Soc. Psychol.* 3:125-44

81. Edwards, J. D., Ostrom, T. M. 1971. Cognitive structure of neutral attitudes. *J. Exp. Soc. Psychol.* 7:36-47

82. Eiser, R. J. 1973. Judgment of attitude statements as a function of judge's attitudes and the judgmental dimension. *Brit. J. Soc. Clin. Psychol.* 12:231-40

83. Ekman, P., Friesen, W. V., Ellsworth, P. 1972. *Emotion in the Human Face:*

Guidelines for Research and an Integration of Findings. New York: Pergamon

84. Elms, A. C. 1972. Social Psychology and Social Relevance. Boston: Little, Brown

85. Endler, N. S., Minden, H. A., North, C. 1973. The effects of reinforcement and social approval on conforming behaviour. Eur. J. Soc. Psychol. 3:297-310

86. Epstein, Y. M., Suedfeld, P., Silverstein, S. J. 1973. The experimental contract: Subjects' expectations of and reactions to some behaviors of experimenters. Am. Psychol. 28:212-21

87. Farina, A., Chapnick, B., Chapnick, J., Misiti, R. 1972. Political views and interpersonal behavior. J. Pers. Soc. Psychol. 22:273-78

88. Feather, N. T. 1971. Organization and discrepancy in cognitive structures. Psychol. Rev. 28:355-79

89. Feather, N. T., Simon, J. G. 1971. Attribution of responsibility and valence of outcome in relation to initial confidence and success and failure of self and other. J. Pers. Soc. Psychol. 18:173-88

90. Feather, N. T., Simon, J. G. 1973. Fear of success and causal attribution for outcome. J. Pers. 41:525-42

91. Ference, T. P. 1971. Feedback and conflict as determinants of influence. J. Exp. Soc. Psychol. 7:1-16

92. Fishbein, M., Ajzen, I. 1972. Attitudes and opinions. Ann. Rev. Psychol. 23:487-544

93. Fishbein, M., Ajzen, I. 1973. Attribution of responsibility: A theoretical note. J. Exp. Soc. Psychol. 9:148-53

94. Freedman, J. L., Carlsmith, J. M., Sears, D. O. 1971. Readings in Social Psychology. Englewood Cliffs, N.J.: Prentice-Hall

95. Frey, D., Irle, M. 1972. Some conditions to produce a dissonance and an incentive effect in a 'forced compliance' situation. Eur. J. Soc. Psychol. 2:45-54

96. Frideres, J. S., Warner, L. G., Albrecht, S. L. 1971. The impact of social constraints on the relationship between attitudes and behavior. Soc. Forces 50:102-12

97. Frieze, I., Weiner, B. 1971. Cue utilization and attributional judgments for success and failure. J. Pers. 39:591-606

98. Gergen, K. J. 1971. Social psychology as history. J. Pers. Soc. Psychol. 26:309-20

99. Gergen, K. J. 1974. Social psychology, science, and history: A rejoinder. Unpublished paper, Swarthmore College

100. Girodo, M. 1973. Film-induced arousal, information search, and the attribution process. J. Pers. Soc. Psychol. 25:357-60

101. Glass, D. C., Singer, J. E. 1972. Urban Stress: Experiments on Noise and Social Stressors. New York: Academic

102. Goethals, G. R., Cooper, J. 1972. Role of intention and post-behavioral consequence in the arousal of cognitive dissonance. J. Pers. Soc. Psychol. 23:298-301

103. Goethals, G. R., Nelson, R. E. 1973. Similarity in the influence process: The belief-value distinction. J. Pers. Soc. Psychol. 25:117-22

104. Goldstein, M., Davis, E. E. 1972. Race and belief: A further analysis of the social determinants of behavioral intentions. J. Pers. Soc. Psychol. 22:346-55

105. Gollob, H. F., Fischer, G. W. 1973. Some relationships between social inference, cognitive balance, and change in impression. J. Pers. Soc. Psychol. 26:16-22

106. Gorden, G. N. 1971. The Theory and Practice of Manipulative Communication. New York: Hastings House

107. Gormly, J., Gormly, A., Johnson, C. 1971. Interpersonal attraction: Competence motivation and reinforcement theory. J. Pers. Soc. Psychol. 19:375-80

108. Götz-Marchand, B. 1973. Praferenz von Dissonanzreduktionalternativen in Abhangigkeit von Ihrer Stellung, Bekanntheit, Revidierbarkeit und Verfugbarkeit. PhD thesis. Univ. Mannheim, West Germany

109. Gouax, C. 1971. Induced affective states and interpersonal attraction. J. Pers. Soc. Psychol. 20:37-43

110. Grabitz-Gniech, G. 1971. Some restrictive conditions for the occurrence of psychological reactance. J. Pers. Soc.

Psychol. 19:188–96

111. Griffitt, W., Byrne, D., Bond, M. H. 1971. Proportion of positive adjectives and personal relevance of adjective descriptions as determinants of attraction. *J. Exp. Soc. Psychol.* 7:111–21

112. Gross, A. E., Riemer, B. S., Collins, B. E. 1973. Audience reaction as a determinant of the speaker's self-persuasion. *J. Exp. Soc. Psychol.* 9:246–56

113. Gutman, G. M., Knox, R. E. 1972. Balance, agreement, and attraction in pleasantness, tension, and consistency ratings of hypothetical social situations. *J. Pers. Soc. Psychol.* 24:351–57

114. Halverson, R. R., Pallak, M. S. 1974. The effect of commitment and attitude extremity on cognitive structure and resistance to attack. Unpublished ms. Univ. Iowa

115. Hamsher, J. H., Sigall, H., Eds. 1973. *Psychology and Social Issues.* New York: Macmillan

116. Harré, R., Secord, P. F. 1972. *The Explanation of Social Behavior.* Totowa, N.J.: Rowman & Littlefield

117. Harris, V. A., Jellison, J. M. 1971. Fear arousing communications, false psychological feedback, and acceptance of recommendations. *J. Exp. Soc. Psychol.* 7:269–79

118. Harris, V. A., Tamler, H. 1971. Reinstatement of initial attitude and forced-compliance attitude change. *J. Soc. Psychol.* 84:127–34

119. Harris, V. A., Tamler, H. 1973. Awareness of initial attitude and prediction of final attitude: A bystander replication. *J. Soc. Psychol.* 91:251–62

120. Harvey, J. A., Johnston, A. 1973. Determinants of the perception of choice. *J. Exp. Soc. Psychol.* 9:164–79

121. Harvey, J., Mills, J. 1971. Effect of a difficult opportunity to revoke a counterattitudinal act upon attitude change. *J. Pers. Soc. Psychol.* 18:201–9

122. Hass, R. G., Linder, D. E. 1972. Counterargument availability and the effects of message structure on persuasion. *J. Pers. Soc. Psychol.* 23:219–33

123. Heider, F. 1958. *The Psychology of Interpersonal Relations.* New York: Wiley

124. Heller, J. F., Pallak, M. S., Picek, J. M. 1973. The interactive effects of intent and threat on boomerang attitude change. *J. Pers. Soc. Psychol.* 26:273–79

125. Hendrick, C. 1972. Effects of salience of stimulus inconsistency on impression formation. *J. Pers. Soc. Psychol.* 22:219–22

126. Hendrick, C., Jones, R. A. 1972. *The Nature of Theory and Research in Social Psychology.* New York: Academic

127. Heslin, R., Amo, M. F. 1972. Detailed test of the reinforcement-dissonance controversy in the counterattitudinal advocacy situation. *J. Pers. Soc. Psychol.* 23:234–42

128. Heslin, R., Blake, B., Rotton, J. 1972. Information search as a function of stimulus uncertainty and the importance of the response. *J. Pers. Soc. Psychol.* 23:333–39

129. Himmelfarb, S. 1972. Integration and attribution theories in personality impression formation. *J. Pers. Soc. Psychol.* 23:309–13

130. Himmelfarb, S., Eagly, A. H., Eds. 1974. *Readings in Attitude Change.* New York: Wiley

131. Hodges, L. A., Byrne, D. 1972. Verbal dogmatism as a potentiator of intolerance. *J. Pers. Soc. Psychol.* 21:312–17

132. Holmes, D. S., Bennett, D. H. 1974. Experiments to answer questions raised by the use of deception in psychological research: I. Role playing as an alternative to deception; II. Effectiveness of debriefing after a deception; III. Effect of informed consent on deception. *J. Pers. Soc. Psychol.* 29:358–67

133. Hood, T. C., Back, K. W. 1971. Self-disclosure and the volunteer: A source of bias in laboratory experiments. *J. Pers. Soc. Psychol.* 17:130–36

134. Hornstein, H. A., Bunker, B. B., Burke, W. W., Gindes, M., Lewicki, R. J., Eds. 1971. *Social Intervention: A Behavioral Science Approach.* New York: Free Press

135. Hoyt, M. F., Centers, R. 1972. Temporal situs of the effects of anticipated publicity upon commitment and resistance to counter-communication. *J. Pers. Soc. Psychol.* 22:1–7

136. Hoyt, M. F., Henley, M. D., Collins, B. E. 1972. Studies in forced compliance:

Confluence of choice and consequence on attitude change. *J. Pers. Soc. Psychol.* 23:204-10

137. Innes, J. M. 1973. The influence of attitude on the learning of balanced and unbalanced social structures. *Eur. J. Soc. Psychol.* 3:91-94

138. Insko, C. A., Schopler, J. 1972. *Experimental Social Psychology.* New York: Academic

139. Insko, C. A. et al 1973. Implied evaluation and the similarity-attraction effect. *J. Pers. Soc. Psychol.* 25:297-308

140. Insko, C. A., Worchel, S., Songer, E., Arnold, S. E. 1973. Effort, objective self-awareness, choice, and dissonance. *J. Pers. Soc. Psychol.* 28:262-69

141. Israel, J., Tajfel, H. 1972. *The Context of Social Psychology: A Critical Assessment.* New York: Academic

142. Izzett, R. R. 1971. Authoritarianism and attitudes toward the Vietnam war as reflected in behavioral and self-report measures. *J. Pers. Soc. Psychol.* 17:145-48

143. Jacoby, J. 1971. Interpersonal perceptual accuracy as a function of dogmatism. *J. Exp. Soc. Psychol.* 7:221-36

144. Jastrebske, E. M. 1970. *Dissonance or social consequences.* PhD thesis. Univ. Alberta, Canada

145. Jellison, J. M., Davis, D. 1973. Relationships between perceived ability and attitude extremity. *J. Pers. Soc. Psychol.* 27:430-36

146. Jellison, J. M., Riskind, J., Broll, L. 1972. Attribution of ability to others on skill and chance tasks as a function of level of risk. *J. Pers. Soc. Psychol.* 22:135-38

147. Johnson, D. W., Johnson, S. 1972. The effects of attitude similarity, expectancy of goal facilitation, and the actual goal facilitation on interpersonal attraction. *J. Exp. Soc. Psychol.* 8:197-207

148. Jones, C., Aronson, E. 1973. Attribution of fault to a rape victim as a function of respectability of the victim. *J. Pers. Soc. Psychol.* 26:415-19

149. Jones, E. E., Davis, K. E. 1965. From acts to dispositions: The attribution process in person perception. In *Advances in Experimental Social Psychology*, ed. L. Berkowitz, 2:219-66. New York: Academic

150. Jones, E. E., Harris, V. A. 1967. The attribution of attitudes. *J. Exp. Soc. Psychol.* 3:1-24

151. Jones, E. E. et al 1971. *Attribution: Perceiving the Causes of Behavior.* Morristown, N.J.: General Learning Press

152. Jones, E. E., Nisbett, R. E. 1971. *The Actor and the Observer: Divergent Perceptions of the Causes of Behavior.* Morristown, N.J.: General Learning Press

153. Jones, E. E., Sigall, H. 1971. The bogus pipeline: A new paradigm for measuring affect and attitude. *Psychol. Bull.* 76:349-64

154. Ibid 1973. Where there is *ignis*, there may be fire. 79:260-62

154a. Jones, E. E., Wein, G. A. 1972. Attitude similarity, expectancy violation, and attraction. *J. Exp. Soc. Psychol.* 8:222-35

155. Jones, E. E., Worchel, S., Goethals, G. R., Grumet, J. F. 1971. Prior expectancy and behavioral extremity as determinants of attitude attribution. *J. Exp. Soc. Psychol.* 7:59-80

156. Jones, J. M. 1972. *Prejudice and Racism.* Reading, Mass.: Addison-Wesley

157. Jones, J. M., Kiesler, C. A. 1971. The interactive effects of commitment and forewarning: Three experiments. See Ref. 171, 94-108

158. Jones, R. A., Cooper, J. 1971. Mediation of experimenter effects. *J. Pers. Soc. Psychol.* 20:70-74

159. Jones, R. A., Linder, D. E., Kiesler, C. A., Zanna, M. P., Brehm, J. W. 1968. Internal states or external stimuli: Observers' attitude judgments and the dissonance-theory/self-persuasion controversy. *J. Exp. Soc. Psychol.* 4:247-69

160. Jones, S. C. 1973. Self and interpersonal evaluations: Esteem theories versus consistency theories. *Psychol. Bull.* 79:185-99

161. Jung, J. 1971. *The Experimenter's Dilemma.* New York: Harper & Row

162. Kahan, J. P., Pichevin, M. F. 1971. Free choice dissonance: An interpersonal simulation. *Rep. Res. Soc. Psychol.* 2:11-20

162a. Kaplan, K. J. 1972. On the ambivalence-indifference problem in attitude theory and measurement: A suggested modification of the semantic differential technique. *Psychol. Bull.* 77:361-72

163. Kauffman, D. R. 1971. Incentive to perform counterattitudinal acts: Bribe or gold star? *J. Pers. Soc. Psychol.* 19:82-91

164. Kelley, H. H. 1967. Attribution theory in social psychology. In *Nebraska Symposium on Motivation*, ed. D. Levine, 15:192-238. Lincoln: Univ. Nebraska Press

165. Kelley, H. H. 1971. *Attribution in Social Interaction.* Morristown, N.J.: General Learning Press

166. Kelley, H. H. 1971. Moral evaluation. *Am. Psychol.* 26:293-300

167. Kelman, H. 1961. Processes of opinion change. *Public Opin. Quart.* 25:57-78

168. Kepka, E. J., Brickman, P. 1971. Consistency versus discrepancy as clues in the attribution of intelligence and motivation. *J. Pers. Soc. Psychol.* 20:223-29

169. Kerpelman, J. P., Himmelfarb, S. 1971. Partial reinforcement effects in attitude acquisition and counterconditioning. *J. Pers. Soc. Psychol.* 19:301-5

170. Kian, M., Rosen, S., Tesser, A. 1973. Reinforcement effects of attitude similarity and source evaluation on discrimination learning. *J. Pers. Soc. Psychol.* 27:366-71

171. Kiesler, C. A. 1971. *The Psychology of Commitment: Experiments Linking Behavior to Belief.* New York: Academic

172. Kiesler, C. A. 1974. *A motivational theory of stimulus incongruity, with applications for such phenomena as dissonance and self-attribution.* Presented at Midwest. Psychol. Assoc. Chicago

173. Kiesler, C. A., Collins, B. E., Miller, N. 1969. *Attitude Change: A Critical Analysis of Theoretical Approaches.* New York: Wiley

174. Kiesler, C. A., Mathog, R. 1971. Resistance to influence as a function of number of prior consonant acts. See Ref. 171, 66-74

175. Kiesler, C. A., Mathog, R., Pool, P., Howenstine, R. 1971. Commitment and the boomerang effect: A field

study. See Ref. 171, 74-85

176. Kiesler, C. A., Pallak, M. S., Archer, R. 1974. The woodwork hypothesis: The interactive effects of self-commitment with the legitimacy and attitudinal stance of the communicator. *Psychol. Rep.* In press

177. Kiesler, C. A., Roth, T., Pallak, M. S. 1974. The avoidance and reinterpretation of commitment and its implications. *J. Pers. Soc. Psychol.* 30:705-15

178. Kiesler, C. A., Sakumura, J. 1966. A test of a model for commitment. *J. Pers. Soc. Psychol.* 3:349-53

179. Kiesler, S. B. 1973. Preference for predictability or unpredictability as a mediator of reactions to norm violations. *J. Pers. Soc. Psychol.* 27:354-59

180. King, B. T., McGinnies, E., Eds. 1972. *Attitudes, Conflict, and Social Change.* New York: Academic

181. Kothandapani, V. 1971. Validation of feeling, belief, and intention to act as three components of attitude and their contribution to prediction of contraceptive behavior. *J. Pers. Soc. Psychol.* 19:321-33

182. Krisher, H. P. III, Darley, S., Darley, J. M. 1973. Fear-provoking recommendations, intentions to take preventive actions, and actual preventive actions. *J. Pers. Soc. Psychol.* 26:301-8

183. Kruglanski, A. W. 1973. Much ado about the 'volunteer artifacts.' *J. Pers. Soc. Psychol.* 28:348-54

184. Kruglanski, A. W., Alon, S., Lewis, T. 1972. Retrospective misattribution and task enjoyment. *J. Exp. Soc. Psychol.* 8:493-501

185. Kruglanski, A. W., Cohen, M. 1973. Attributed freedom and personal causation. *J. Pers. Soc. Psychol.* 26:245-50

186. Landy, D. 1972. The effects of an overheard audience's reaction and attractiveness on opinion change. *J. Exp. Soc. Psychol.* 8:276-88

187. Lepper, M. R. 1973. Dissonance, self-perception, and honesty in children. *J. Pers. Soc. Psychol.* 25:65-74

188. Lepper, M. R., Greene, D., Nisbett, R. E. 1973. Undermining children's intrinsic interest with extrinsic reward: A test of the "over-justification" hypotheses. *J. Pers. Soc. Psychol.* 28:129-37

189. Lerner, M. J. 1965. Evaluation of per-

formance as a function of performer's reward and attractiveness. *J. Pers. Soc. Psychol.* 1:355–60

190. Leventhal, G. S., Weiss, T., Buttrick, R. 1973. Attribution of value, equity, and the prevention of waste in reward allocation. *J. Pers. Soc. Psychol.* 27:276–86

191. LeVine, R. A., Campbell, D. T. 1972. *Ethnocentrism: Theories of Conflict, Ethnic Attitudes, and Group Behavior.* New York: Wiley

192. Liebling, B. A., Shaver, P. 1973. Evaluation, self-awareness, and task performance. *J. Exp. Soc. Psychol.* 9:297–306

193. Linder, D. E., Wortman, C. B., Brehm, J. W. 1971. Temporal changes in predecision preferences among choice alternatives. *J. Pers. Soc. Psychol.* 19:282–84

194. Lohr, J. M., Staats, A. W. 1973. Attitude conditioning in Sino-tibetan languages. *J. Pers. Soc. Psychol.* 26:196–200

195. Lopes, L. L. 1972. A unified integration model for prior expectancy and behavioral extremity as determinants of attitude attribution. *J. Exp. Soc. Psychol.* 8:156–60

196. Malec, M. A., Ed. 1971. *Attitude Change.* Chicago: Markham

197. Maliver, B. L. 1973. *The Encounter Game.* New York: Stein & Day

198. Mann, L. 1971. Effects of a commitment warning on children's decision behavior. *J. Pers. Soc. Psychol.* 17:74–80

199. Mascaro, G. F., Graves, W. 1973. Contrast effects of background factors on the similarity-attraction relationship. *J. Pers. Soc. Psychol.* 25:346–50

200. Maslach, C. 1971. The 'truth' about false confessions. *J. Pers. Soc. Psychol.* 20:141–46

201. Matefy, R. E. 1972. Attitude change induced by role playing as a function of improvisation and role-taking skill. *J. Pers. Soc. Psychol.* 25:343–50

202. McArthur, L. A. 1973. Perceiving the cause of one's own behavior: An unexpected reversal of attribution theory. *Psychol. Rep.* 32:983–88

203. McArthur, L. A. 1972. The how and what of why: Some determinants and consequences of causal attribution. *J. Pers. Soc. Psychol.* 22:171–93

204. McClintock, C., Ed. *Experimental Social Psychology.* New York: Holt

205. McGinnies, E., Ferster, C. B., Eds. 1971. *The Reinforcement of Social Behavior.* Boston: Houghton-Mifflin

206. McGuire, W. J. 1966. Attitudes and opinions. *Ann. Rev. Psychol.* 17:475–514

207. McGuire, W. J. 1973. The yin and yang of progress in social psychology: Seven koan. *J. Pers. Soc. Psychol.* 26:446–56

208. McGuire, W. J., Millman, S. 1965. Anticipatory belief lowering following forewarning of a persuasive attack. *J. Pers. Soc. Psychol.* 2:471–79

209. McLaughlin, B. 1971. *Learning and Social Behavior.* New York: Free Press

210. Messick, D. M., Reeder, G. 1972. Perceived motivation, role variations, and the attribution of personal characteristics. *J. Exp. Soc. Psychol.* 8:482–91

211. Mettee, D. R. 1971. Changes in liking as a function of the magnitude and affect of sequential evaluations. *J. Exp. Soc. Psychol.* 7:157–72

212. Ibid. The true discerner as a potent source of positive affect, 292–303

213. Mettee, D. R., Wilkins, P. C. 1972. When similarity "hurts": Effects of perceived ability and a humorous blunder on interpersonal attractiveness. *J. Pers. Soc. Psychol.* 22:246–58

214. Miller, A. G. 1972. Role playing: An alternative to deception? A review of the evidence. *Am. Psychol.* 27:623–36

215. Miller, H., Geller, D. 1972. Structural balance in dyads. *J. Pers. Soc. Psychol.* 21:135–38

216. Mills, J., Egger, R. 1972. Effect on derogation of a victim of choosing to reduce his distress. *J. Pers. Soc. Psychol.* 23:405–08

217. Mills, J., Harvey, J. 1972. Opinion change as a function of when information about the communicator is received and whether he is attractive or expert. *J. Pers. Soc. Psychol.* 21:52–55

218. Ibid. Can self-perception theory explain the findings of Harvey and Mills (1971)? 22:271–72

219. Mintz, P. M., Mills, J. 1971. Effects of arousal and information about its source upon attitude change. *J. Exp.*

Soc. Psychol. 7:561–70

220. Miron, M. S. 1971. The semantic differential and mediation theory. *Linguistics* 66:74–87

221. Miron, M. S. 1972. Universal semantic differential shell game. *J. Pers. Soc. Psychol.* 24:313–20

222. Mischel, W. 1971. *Introduction to Personality.* New York: Holt, Rinehart & Winston

223. Mischel, W., Ebbesen, E. B., Zeiss, A. R. 1973. Selective attention to the self: Situational and dispositional determinants. *J. Pers. Soc. Psychol.* 27:129–42

224. Mitchell, H. E., Byrne, D. 1973. The defendant's dilemma: Effects of juror's attitudes and authoritarianism on judicial decisions. *J. Pers. Soc. Psychol.* 25:123–29

225. Moore, L. M., Baron, R. M. 1973. Effects of wage inequities on work attitudes and performance. *J. Exp. Soc. Psychol.* 9:1–16

226. Moscovici, S. 1963. Attitudes and opinions. *Ann. Rev. Psychol.* 14:231–60

227. Moscovici, S., Faucheux, C. 1972. Social influence, conformity bias, and the study of active minorities. In *Advances in Experimental Social Psychology,* ed. L. Berkowitz, 6:150–202. New York: Academic

228. Munson, P. A., Kiesler, C. A. 1974. The role of attributions by others in the acceptance of persuasive communications. *J. Pers.* 42:453–66

229. Murstein, B. I., Ed. 1971. *Theories of Attraction and Love.* New York: Springer

230. Newberry, B. H. 1973. Truth telling in subjects with informations about experiments: Who is being deceived? *J. Pers. Soc. Psychol.* 25:369–74

231. Newcomb, T. M. 1968. Interpersonal balance. In *Theories of Cognitive Consistency: A Sourcebook,* ed. R. Abelson et al, 28–51. Chicago: Rand-McNally

232. Newtson, D. 1973. Attribution and the unit of perception of ongoing behavior. *J. Pers. Soc. Psychol.* 28:28–38

233. Nisan, M. 1973. Evaluation of temporally distant reinforcements. *J. Pers. Soc. Psychol.* 26:295–300

234. Nisbett, R. E., Caputo, C., Legant, P., Marecek, J. 1973. Behavior as seen by the actor and as seen by the observer. *J. Pers. Soc. Psychol.* 27:154–64

235. Nisbett, R. E., Valins, S. 1971. *Perceiving the Causes of One's Own Behavior.* Morristown, N.J.: General Learning Press

236. Nuttin, J. M. Jr. 1966. Attitude change after rewarded dissonant and consonant 'forced compliance'. *Int. J. Psychol.* 1:39–57

237. O'Donnell, J. M., Brown, M. J. K. 1973. The classical conditioning of attitudes: A comparative study of ages 8 to 18. *J. Pers. Soc. Psychol.* 26:379–85

238. O'Leary, K. D., Drabman, R. 1971. Token reinforcement programs in the classroom: A review. *Psychol. Bull.* 75:379–98

239. Osgood, C. E. 1971. Commentary on Miron's The Semantic Differential and Mediation Theory. *Linguistics* 66:88–96

240. Ostrom, T. M. 1973. The bogus pipeline: A new *ignis fatuus?* *Psychol. Bull.* 79:252–59

241. Ostrom, T. M. 1971–1972. Item construction in attitude measurement. *Public Opin. Quart.* 35:593–600

242. Pallak, M. S. 1970. The effect of expected choice and relevant or irrelevant dissonance on incidental retention. *J. Pers. Soc. Psychol.* 14:271–80

243. Pallak, M. S., Heller, J. F. 1971. Interactive effects of commitment to future interaction and threat to attitudinal freedom. *J. Pers. Soc. Psychol.* 17:325–31

244. Pallak, M. S., Mueller, M., Dollar, K., Pallak, J. 1972. Effect of commitment on responses to an extreme consonant communication. *J. Pers. Soc. Psychol.* 23:429–36

245. Pallak, M. S., Pittman, T. S. 1972. General motivational effects of dissonance arousal. *J. Pers. Soc. Psychol.* 21:349–50

246. Pallak, M. S., Sogin, S. R., Van Zante, A. 1974. Bad decisions: The effect of volunteering, locus of causality, and negative consequences on attitude change. *J. Pers. Soc. Psychol.* 30:217–27

247. Pease, K. 1972. Attitudes in linguistic communication: A further study of immediacy. *J. Pers.* 40:298–307

248. Peevers, B. H., Secord, P. F. 1973. Developmental changes in attributions of descriptive concepts to persons. *J. Pers. Soc. Psychol.* 27:120–28

249. Penner, L. A., Dertke, M. C., Eds. 1972. *Social Psychology: The Students' Reader.* Reading, Mass.: Addison-Wesley

250. Perlman, D., Oskamp, S. 1972. The effects of picture content and exposure frequency on evaluations of Negroes and Whites. *J. Exp. Soc. Psychol.* 7:503–14

251. Perry, B. L. 1971. *Differential effort in counterattitudinal advocacy: Effects on attitude change and extinction.* PhD thesis. Michigan State Univ., East Lansing

251a. Phares, E. J., Wilson, K. G. 1972. Responsibility attribution: Role of outcome severity, situational ambiguity, and internal-external control. *J. Pers.* 40:392–406

252. Phifer, M. K. 1971–1972. Influence of the process of discrimination on the selection of statements for an attitude scale. *Public Opin. Quart.* 35:601–5

253. Rappaport, L., Summers, D. A., Eds. 1973. *Human Judgment and Social Interaction.* New York: Holt, Rinehart & Winston

254. Reich, J. W., Farr, S. P. 1973. Dimensional responding and affective involvement effects on categorization complexity. *J. Pers. Soc. Psychol.* 26:48–53

255. Reisman, S. R., Schopler, J. 1973. An analysis of the attribution process and an application to determinants of responsibility. *J. Pers. Soc. Psychol.* 25:361–68

255a. Reiss, S., Sushinsky, L. W. 1974. *Overjustification, competing responses, and acquisition of intrinsic interest.* Unpublished ms. Univ. Illinois Chicago Circle

256. Rhine, R. J., Polowniak, W. A. 1971. Attitude change, commitment and ego involvement. *J. Pers. Soc. Psychol.* 19:246–50

257. Rokeach, M. 1973. *The Nature of Human Values.* New York: Free Press

258. Rokeach, M., Kliejunas, P. 1972. Behavior as a function of attitude-toward-object and attitude-toward-sit-uation. *J. Pers. Soc. Psychol.* 22:194–201

259. Rosen, B., Komorita, S. S. 1971. Attitudes and action: The effects of behavioral intent and perceived effectiveness of acts. *J. Pers.* 39:189–203

260. Rosen, G. M., Rosen, E., Reid, J. B. 1972. Cognitive desensitization and avoidance behavior: A reevaluation. *J. Abnorm. Psychol.* 80:176–82

261. Rosnow, R. L., Aiken, L. S. 1973. Mediation of artifacts in behavioral research. *J. Exp. Soc. Psychol.* 9:181–201

262. Rosnow, R. L., Goodstadt, B. E., Suls, J. M., Gitter, G. A. 1973. More on the social psychology of the experiment: When compliance turns to self-defense. *J. Pers. Soc. Psychol.* 3:337–43

263. Rosnow, R. L., Rosenthal, R. 1974. The taming of the volunteer problem: On coping with artifacts by benign neglect. *J. Pers. Soc. Psychol.* 30:188–90

264. Ross, M., Insko, C. A., Ross, H. S. 1971. Self-attribution of attitude. *J. Pers. Soc. Psychol.* 17:292–97

265. Ross, M., Shulman, R. E. 1973. Increasing the salience of initial attitudes: Dissonance versus self-perception theory. *J. Pers. Soc. Psychol.* 28:138–44

266. Rossi, P. H., Williams, W., Eds. 1972. *Evaluating Social Programs.* New York: Seminar Press

267. Rubin, Z., Moore, J. C. Jr. 1971. Assessment of subjects' suspicions. *J. Pers. Soc. Psychol.* 17:163–70

268. Rule, B. G., Duker, P. 1973. Effects of intentions and consequences on children's evaluations of aggressors. *J. Pers. Soc. Psychol.* 27:184–89

269. Salancik, J. R., Kiesler, C. A. 1971. Behavioral commitment and retention of consistent and inconsistent attitude word-pairs. See Ref. 171, 109–21

270. Sample, J., Warland, R. 1973. Attitude and the prediction of behavior. *Soc. Forces* 51:292–304

271. Sampson, E. E. 1971. *Social Psychology and Contemporary Society.* New York: Wiley

272. Sawyers, B. K., Anderson, N. H. 1971. Test of integration theory in attitude change. *J. Pers. Soc. Psychol.* 18:230–33

273. Scherer, K. R., Rosenthal, R., Koivu-maki, J. 1972. Mediating interpersonal expectancies via vocal cues: Differential speech intensity as a means of social influence. *Eur. J. Soc. Psychol.* 2:163–76

274. Schlenker, B. R. 1974. Social psychology and science. *J. Pers. Soc. Psychol.* 29:1–15

275. Schönpflug, U., Schönpflug, W. 1972. Scaling of attitude items under stress: Response shift or change of personal reference scale. *Eur. J. Soc. Psychol.* 2:145–62

276. Schopler, J., Layton, B. 1972. Determinants of the self-attribution of having influenced another person. *J. Pers. Soc. Psychol.* 22:326–32

277. Schwartz, S. H., Tessler, R. C. 1972. A test of a model for reducing measured attitude-behavior discrepancies. *J. Pers. Soc. Psychol.* 24:225–36

278. Sears, D. O., Abeles, R. P. 1969. Attitudes and opinions. *Ann. Rev. Psychol.* 20:253–88

279. Shaffer, D. R., Hendrick, C. 1971. Effects of actual effort and anticipated effort on task enhancement. *J. Exp. Soc. Psychol.* 7:435–47

280. Shaw, J. I., Skolnick, P. 1973. An investigation of relative preference for consistency motivation. *Eur. J. Soc. Psychol.* 3:271–80

281. Shaw, J. I., Skolnick, P. 1971. Attribution of responsibility for a happy accident. *J. Pers. Soc. Psychol.* 18:380–83

282. Shepard, R. N., Romney, A. K., Nerlove, S. B., Eds. 1972. *Multidimensional Scaling: Theory and Applications in the Behavioral Sciences: 1. Theory.* New York: Seminar Press

283. Sherif, C. W., Kelly, M., Rodgers, H. L., Sarup, G., Tittler, B. I. 1973. Personal involvement, social judgment, and action. *J. Pers. Soc. Psychol.* 27:311–27

284. Sherman, S. J. 1973. Internal-external control and its relationship to attitude change under different social influence techniques. *J. Pers. Soc. Psychol.* 26:23–29

284a. Sigall, H., Aronson, E., Van Hoose, T. 1970. The cooperative subject: Myth or reality. *J. Exp. Soc. Psychol.* 6:1–10

285. Sigall, H., Page, R. 1971. Current stereotypes: A little fading, a little faking. *J. Pers. Soc. Psychol.* 18:247–55

286. Skinner, B. F. 1971. *Beyond Freedom and Dignity.* New York: Knopf

287. Skolnick, P. 1971. Reactions to personal evaluations: A failure to replicate. *J. Pers. Soc. Psychol.* 18:62–67

288. Skolnick, P., Heslin, R. 1971. Quality versus difficulty: Alternative interpretations of the relationship between self-esteem and persuasibility. *J. Pers.* 39:242–51

289. Smith, A. J., Clark, R. D. III. 1973. The relationship between attitudes and beliefs. *J. Pers. Soc. Psychol.* 26:321–26

290. Smith, P. W., Brigham, J. C. 1971. The functional approach to attitude change: An attempt at operationalism. *Rep. Res. Soc. Psychol.* 3:73–80

291. Smith, S. S., Jamieson, B. D. 1972. Effects of attitude and ego involvement on the learning and retention of controversial material. *J. Pers. Soc. Psychol.* 22:303–10

292. Snyder, M. 1974. The self-monitoring of expressive behavior. *J. Pers. Soc. Psychol.* 30:526–37

293. Snyder, M., Ebbesen, E. B. 1972. Dissonance awareness: A test of dissonance theory versus self-perception theory. *J. Exp. Soc. Psychol.* 8:502–17

294. Snyder, M., Rothbart, M. 1971. Communicator attractiveness and opinion change. *Can. J. Behav. Sci.* 3:377–87

295. Staats, A. W., Gross, M. C., Guay, P. F., Carlson, C. C. 1973. Personality and social systems and attitude-reinforcer-discriminative theory: Interest (attitude) formation function, and measurement. *J. Pers. Soc. Psychol.* 26:251–61

296. Stang, D. J. 1973. Effect of interaction rate on ratings of leadership and liking. *J. Pers. Soc. Psychol.* 27:405–8

297. Starck, K. 1973. Values and information source preferences. *J. Commun.* 23:74–85

298. Stokols, D., Schopler, J. 1973. Reactions to victims under conditions of situational detachment: The effects of responsibility, severity, and expected future interaction. *J. Pers. Soc.*

Psychol. 25:199–209
299. Storms, M. D. 1973. Videotape and the attribution process: reversing actor's and observer's points of view. *J. Pers. Soc. Psychol.* 27:165–75
300. Straits, B. C., Wuebben, P. L., Majka, T. J. 1972. Influences on subjects' perceptions of experimental research situations. *Sociometry* 35:499–518
301. Stroebe, W. 1971. The effect of judges' attitudes on ratings of attitude statements: A theoretical analysis. *Eur. J. Soc. Psychol.* 1:419–34
302. Suedfeld, P., Ed. 1971. *Attitude Change: The Competing Views.* Chicago: Aldine-Atherton
303. Sullivan, D. S., Deiker, T. E. 1973. Subject-experimenter perceptions of ethical issues in human research. *Am. Psychol.* 28:587–91
304. Tate, E. 1973. *An annotated bibliography of studies on counter-attitudinal advocacy.* Unpublished ms., Univ. Saskatchewan, Canada
305. Tesser, A. 1971. Evaluative and structural similarity of attitudes as determinants of interpersonal attraction. *J. Pers. Soc. Psychol.* 18:92–96
306. Tessler, R. C., Schwartz, S. H. 1972. Help seeking, self-esteem, and achievement motivation: An attributional analysis. *J. Pers. Soc. Psychol.* 21:318–26
307. Thomas, K., Ed. 1971. *Attitudes and Behavior.* Middlesex, England: Penguin
308. Thompson, D. D. 1972. Attributions of ability from patterns of performance under competitive and cooperative conditions. *J. Pers. Soc. Psychol.* 23:302–8
309. Touhey, J. C. 1972. Comment on Harvey & Mills' Effect of a Difficult Opportunity To Revoke a Counterattitudinal Act. *J. Pers. Soc. Psychol.* 22:269–70
310. Ibid 1973. Individual differences in attitude change following two acts of forced compliance. 27:96–99
311. Triandis, H. C. 1971. *Attitude and Attitude Change.* New York: Wiley
312. Triandis, H. C. 1972. *The Analysis of Subjective Culture.* New York: Wiley
313. Valins, S., Nisbett, R. E. 1971. *Attribu-*

tion Processes in the Development and Treatment of Emotional Disorders. Morristown, N.J.: General Learning Press
314. Vroom, V. H., Deci, E. L. 1971. The stability of post-decision dissonance: A follow-up study of the job attitudes of business school graduates. *Organ. Behav. Hum. Perform.* 6:36–49
315. Walster, E. 1967. "Second-guessing" important events. *Hum. Relat.* 20:239–50
316. Walster, E., Berscheid, E., Walster, G. W. 1973. New directions in equity research. *J. Pers. Soc. Psychol.* 25:151–76
317. Watts, W. A. 1973. Intelligence and susceptibility to persuasion under conditions of active and passive participation. *J. Exp. Soc. Psychol.* 9:110–22
318. Weber, S. J., Cook, T. D. 1972. Subject effects in laboratory research: An examination of subject roles, demand characteristics, and valid inference. *Psychol. Bull.* 77:273–95
319. Weiner, B. et al 1971. *Perceiving the Causes of Success and Failure.* Morristown, N.J.: General Learning Press
320. Weiner, B., Heckhausen, H., Meyer, W. U., Cook, R. E. 1972. Causal ascription and achievement motivation: A conceptual analysis of effort and reanalysis of locus of control. *J. Pers. Soc. Psychol.* 21:234–48
321. Weiner, B. 1972. *Theories of Motivation: From Mechanism to Cognition.* Chicago: Markham
322. Weinstein, A. G. 1972. Predicting behavior from attitudes. *Public Opin. Quart.* 36:355–60
323. Wellens, A. R., Thistlethwaite, D. L. 1971. Comparison of three theories of cognitive balance. *J. Pers. Soc. Psychol.* 20:82–92
324. Whitney, R. E. 1971. Agreement and positivity in pleasantness ratings of balanced and unbalanced social situations. *J. Pers. Soc. Psychol.* 17:11–14
325. Wicker, A. W. 1971. An examination of the "other variables" explanation of attitude-behavior inconsistency. *J. Pers. Soc. Psychol.* 19:18–30
326. Wicklund, R. A., Duval, S. 1971. Opinion change and performance facilitation as a result of objective self-

awareness. *J. Exp. Soc. Psychol.*
7:319-42
327. Wicklund, R. A., Ickes, W. J. 1972. The
effect of objective self-awareness on
predecisional exposure to information.
J. Exp. Soc. Psychol. 8:378-87
328. Widgery, R. N., Miller, G. R. 1972.
Audience commitment and source
knowledge of audience as determinants of attitude change following
counterattitudinal advocacy. *Speech
Monogr.* 39:213-15
329. Widgery, R. N., Tubbs, S. L. 1972.
*Machiavellianism and religiosity as de-
terminants of cognitive dissonance in a
counterattitudinal situation.* Presented
at Int. Commun. Assoc. Atlanta
330. Wiggins, J. S., Renner, K. E., Clore, G.
L., Rose, R. J. 1971. *The Psychology of
Personality.* Reading, Mass: Addison-
Wesley
331. Williams, W. 1971. *Social Policy Research and Analyses.* New York: Elsevier
332. Wilson, T. G. 1973. Effects of false
feedback on avoidance behavior:
"Cognitive" desensitization revisited.
J. Pers. Soc. Psychol. 28:115-22
333. Woodyard, H. D. 1972. Self-perception, dissonance, and premanipulation
attitudes. *Psychon. Sci.* 29:193-96
334. Worchel, S., Brand, J. 1972. Role of
responsibility and violated expectancy
in the arousal of dissonance. *J. Pers.
Soc. Psychol.* 22:87-97
335. Worchel, S., Brehm, J. W. 1971. Direct
and implied social restoration of freedom. *J. Pers. Soc. Psychol.* 18:294-304
336. Wortman, C. B., Costanzo, P. R., Witt,
T. R. 1973. Effect of anticipated performance on the attribution of causality to self and others. *J. Pers. Soc. Psychol.* 27:372-81
337. Wrightsman, L. S. 1972. *Social Psychology in the Seventies.* Monterey,
Calif.: Brooks/Cole
338. Wrightsman, L. S., Brigham, J. C.,
Eds. 1973. *Contemporary Issues in*

Social Psychology. Monterey, Calif.:
Brooks/Cole
339. Yelen, D. R. 1970. The effects of dissonance and reward on perceptual distortion. *Psychon. Sci.* 20:319-21
340. Zajonc, R. B. 1968. Attitudinal effects
of mere exposure. *J. Pers. Soc. Psychol.*
9:1-27
341. Zajonc, R. B., Swap, W. C., Harrison,
A. A., Roberts, P. 1971. Limiting conditions of the exposure effect: Satiation
and relativity. *J. Pers. Soc. Psychol.*
18:384-91
342. Zaltman, G., Ed. 1973. *Process and
Phenomena of Social Change.* New
York: Wiley
343. Zander, A. 1971. *Motives and Goals in
Groups.* New York: Academic
344. Zanna, M. P. 1972. Inference of belief
from rejection of an alternative action.
Rep. Res. Soc. Psychol. 3:85-96
345. Zanna, M. P. 1973. On inferring one's
beliefs from one's behavior in a low-
choice setting. *J. Pers. Soc. Psychol.*
26:386-94
346. Zanna, M. P., Cooper, J. 1974. Dissonance and the pill: An attribution approach to studying the arousal
properties of dissonance. *J. Pers. Soc.
Psychol.* 29:703-9
347. Zanna, M. P., Kiesler, C. A. 1971. Inferring one's belief from one's behavior
as a function of belief relevance and
consistency of behavior. *Psychon. Sci.*
24:283-85
347a. Zanna, M. P., Lepper, M. R., Abelson,
R. P. 1973. Attentional mechanisms in
children's devaluation of a forbidden
activity in a forced-compliance situation. *J. Pers. Soc. Psychol.* 28:355-59
348. Ziller, R. C. 1973. *The Social Self.*
Elmsford, N.Y.: Pergamon
349. Zillman, D. 1972. Rhetorical elicitation
of agreement in persuasion. *J. Pers.
Soc. Psychol.* 21:159-65
350. Zurcher, L. A., Bonjean, C. M., Eds.
1970. *Planned Social Intervention.*
Scranton, Pa.: Chandler

PERSONNEL ATTITUDES AND MOTIVATION

§ 240

Edwin A. Locke[1]

College of Business and Management and
Department of Psychology, University of Maryland
College Park, Maryland 20742

The literature published since the previous review of this topic by Miner & Dachler (65) shows several trends. There has been a dramatic decrease in the popularity of equity theory, especially with respect to explaining job and task performance. Since the Pritchard et al monograph (76), the few studies concerned with equity have stressed its role in influencing pay satisfaction. Competent criticisms of equity theory's vagueness (106) and limited applicability may have contributed to its current lack of popularity. Need for achievement is also encountering increasing criticism (25), and the validity of Herzberg's theory remains in doubt (56).

In the applied realm, job enrichment and Management by Objectives continue to attract the attention of practitioners. But participatory management is the most frequently recommended panacea for problems pertaining to employee motivation (61) despite equivocal evidence (18).

In the theoretical realm, expectancy or V-I-E (valence-instrumentality-expectancy) theory has clearly become the most popular approach to motivation among industrial researchers (e.g. 48). However, there are still those who consider factor analysis and/or huge correlation matrices involving measurements of dozens of variables to be the key to unlocking the secrets of motivational psychology. (For this writer's comments on the latter approach, see 52, 54, 56). Organizational climate has also become popular, but the problem lies in determining just what the concept means (36). Space limitations prevent further discussion of this concept here, but for a thorough review of the topic see (37a).

Two other areas which continue to attract the attention of researchers are pay (97) and the relationship between job attitudes and behavior (73).

This article will be a selective review and critique of major theoretical approaches and major research areas relevant to employee attitudes and motivation.

---

[1] The author would like to thank Dr. Harry Binswanger for his helpful suggestions and ideas regarding some of the issues involved in the theory of psychological hedonism.

EXPECTANCY (V-I-E) THEORY

Previous reviews of and commentaries on expectancy theory have identified many of the practical problems involved in testing the basic V-I-E model, e.g. the problem of how to measure the various components or which components to measure; the need to include measures of role perceptions; the need to specify both intrinsic and extrinsic outcomes; the need for relevant measures of performance; and the problem of causality when interpreting the results of concurrent studies, etc (20, 38, 65).

One could add to this the need to control extraneous variables carefully when testing the explanatory power of expectancy theory. For example, correlations between expectancy and performance are typically computed without controlling for past performance level or for ability. Since self-perceptions of ability (which are presumably based on past performance and on actual ability) are correlated with performance (72), such controls are crucial if spurious expectancy-performance correlations are to be avoided. Only a few studies have shown evidence for expectancy effects with ability controlled (3, 70). Goal level is another variable that has not been adequately controlled in most V-I-E studies (19).

An examination of the research reported since Miner & Dachler's review reveals that many of these problems are still prevalent. Thus the conclusions to be drawn from it are necessarily equivocal.

For example, there are no consistent findings regarding which components are the best predictors of performance. Sometimes V works best (77). Sometimes I works best (67). More often E works best (3, 29, 85). The total V-I-E formula may predict performance better than any component by itself, or it may not. An additive model may work better than a multiplicative one (85), or there may be no difference (68). There have been no convincing explanations offered as to why whatever does work works, or why whatever does not work does not.

The expectancy model usually predicts self-ratings of effort, attitudes, and/or performance more successfully than it predicts supervisor's performance ratings or objectively measured performance (4, 49, 66, 68, 77, 98). This immediately makes the former results suspect, since response bias could account for them.

Generally the correlations between V-I-E constructs and objective performance (or supervisory ratings) in real-life settings are low (4–6, 20, 35, 66, 68, 77, 85, 86). The results using longitudinal designs in order to rule out the possibility of spurious concurrent correlations [e.g. individuals attempting to account logically for their own behavior after-the-fact (11)] are no better (49, 87).

Dachler & Mobley have pointed out some limitations of expectancy theory by showing that its ability to predict actual performance may be restricted to situations in which the contingencies between performance and work outcomes are clearly established and are clearly perceived by the employees (20, 21). Consistent with this hypothesis is the finding that expectancy theory tends to work best in situations where rewards are objectively geared to effort and performance, e.g. piece rate incentive systems (20, 44). In such situations performance-reward instrumentalities tend to be highest (16, 20, 75, 84). Even under these ideal conditions, however, there are puzzling failures of the theory, such as low valence subjects outperforming high valence subjects, despite instrumentality and ability being controlled (75).

An increasingly popular area of research related to expectancy theory has been labeled "attribution theory," and entails the study of the factors to which individuals attribute their successes and failures (107). Most such studies have focused on the determinants or effects of attributing success or failure on a task to: effort, luck, ability, and/or task difficulty. There have been attempts to integrate attribution research with Rotter's concept of Internal vs External (I-E) locus of control (62, 107). However, the precise meaning of the I-E scale is equivocal (107), though some studies have found that individuals high on I persist longer after failure than those high on E (109). The types of causal attributions an individual makes after success and failure are relevant to expectancy theory, since such attributions can influence the degree of affect experienced (and therefore valence) as well as subsequent expectancies.

As noted earlier, most previous discussions of expectancy theory research have focused on design flaws in tests of the theory. While such methodological problems have received ample attention, problems with expectancy theory itself have gone largely unnoticed or unmentioned until recently.

This writer believes that a thorough critique of the basic assumptions of expectancy theory is not only appropriate but long overdue. Thus the remainder of this section will be devoted to it. It is hoped that this critique will stimulate thinking and discussion of the issues involved and will lead, at the very least, to a less naive approach to the study of human motivation in general and to the study of work motivation in particular.

Critique of Expectancy Theory

HEDONISM   As formulated by industrial psychologists (111), expectancy theory is a form of calculative, psychological *hedonism* in which the ultimate motive of every human act is asserted to be the maximization of pleasure and/or the minimization of pain. The individual always chooses that course of action which he expects will lead to the greatest degree of pleasure or which will produce the smallest degree of pain. In Vroom's model, which is the prototype of all expectancy theories in industrial psychology, the individual acts to maximize his "valences," which Vroom defines as "expected satisfactions" (111, p. 15). On this issue it is worth pointing out that the theories of motivation from which V-I-E theory was derived (e.g. Lewin, etc) did *not* make any explicit hedonistic assumptions (8).

There is a very crude sense in which it is true that individuals are motivated to attain pleasure and to avoid pain. All individuals (in fact, all animals) are born with an automatic sensory-level pleasure-pain mechanism. This mechanism operates to inform the organism that certain actions are compatible with its survival and well-being or contrary to its welfare. This built-in mechanisms is the basis for the development of values and emotions which the individual subsequently acquires through learning.

While the body's pleasure-pain mechanism provides the biological basis for the experience of valuing, it does not follow that individuals will necessarily choose objects or actions solely on the basis of the degree of pleasure they expect their choices to bring. If this were true, we would expect that virtually everyone except the very poorest "calculators" would be happy. If a person failed to maximize his pleasure by taking one course of action, he would automatically switch to another until happiness was attained. The existence of neurosis, drug and alcohol addiction, suicides, and large numbers of chronically unhappy people would seem to belie this implication.

Even more embarrassing for the theory of hedonism is the existence of individuals who deliberately renounce their own pleasure, e.g. because they believe pleasure to be evil, as with St. Francis of Assisi; or because they believe it is their duty to take actions which they dislike, as with some men who give up their chosen careers in order to enter the family business; or because they believe self-sacrifice to be virtuous, as with any practicing altruist.

The hedonist usually attempts to answer such criticisms by arguing that these individuals must have decided that they would get more pleasure or less pain from the actions they chose to perform than they would have attained from more obviously self-serving activities. But here the hedonist becomes equivocal. He assumes that simply because a person was *motivated* to act in a certain way, i.e. that because he *wanted* to do one thing rather than another, that this fact alone proves he was motivated by *pleasure*. Vroom himself uses the term "preference" as a synonym for "anticipated satisfaction" (111, p. 15) on the implicit premise that only (anticipated) pleasure can be a basis for preference.

If the hedonist were to argue that the existence of preferences as such was proof of the validity of the theory of hedonism, he would be, in effect, assuming in advance the validity of the theory which he was attempting to prove, i.e. the doctrine that choices are regulated by anticipated pleasure. In logic, this is known as the fallacy of question-begging.

To avoid the accusation of circularity, the hedonist must prove, not that all behavior is motivated or that people have preferences, but that expected pleasure is the sole *basis* for all preferences.

If he wished to assert instead that hedonism is not an hypothesis about motivation but an axiom (a fundamental assumption that forms the base of motivational psychology and which cannot be opposed without self-contradiction), then it would be incumbent upon him to show *why* (or that) it was axiomatic.

It should be added that if pleasure were defined so widely as to be taken as synonymous with the term "motivation" or "preference," the theory would not be very useful in explaining individual differences in choices and actions. For example, even though both sexual activity and sexual abstinence are motivated (i.e. caused), there is a radical difference in the motivational basis of these differing actions, e.g. in the view each practitioner has of himself, of his own body, in the nature of his self-esteem, in his view of pleasure, etc. Even if one were to argue that an ascetic gets pleasure by abstaining from pleasure, it would have to be acknowledged that what the ascetic means by pleasure is radically different from what the nonascetic means by it.

There is a related problem with the doctrine of hedonism which pertains to the relationship between pleasure and pain. Calculations of expected pleasure under expectancy theory are made on the implicit premise that "units" of pleasure and pain are interchangeable, e.g. that eliminating 10 units of pain is equivalent to adding 10 units of pleasure. In short, it assumes that pleasure and pain differ only quantitatively, not qualitatively.

This premise is difficult to reconcile with clinical and experimental observations to the effect that there is a fundamental difference *in kind* between motivation by positives and motivation by negatives. There are enormous qualitative differences between individuals who seek to attain values and those who seek to avoid losing them. Motivation by desire is not the same as motivation by fear (9). For example, a student who sets his grade aspirations at a very low level so that he will not be disappointed if he does poorly is guided by very different principles of choice than one who is motivated to attain the best grades that he can. And the experiences in the two cases are not the same. Relief is not the same as pleasure. The "pleasure" of drinking oneself into an alcoholic stupor in order to avoid thinking about one's problems is not equivalent to the pleasure of working hard to succeed on a job that one loves.

Thus, even if one were to grant the basic premise of hedonism, there would have to be at least two separate versions of it, one focused on attaining pleasure and the other on avoiding pain. Since, however, people can focus on both of these goals in varying degrees, (and in varying degrees at different times), this would make for several additional versions, each with its own guiding principles.

Unfortunately, even the above modification would not suffice. It has been pointed out that individuals often act to "satisfice," i.e. to attain some minimum level of satisfaction, rather than to maximize pleasure (11–13). Since presumably one can also "negafice" (avoid some maximum degree of dissatisfaction), these principles, combined with those above, would produce an enormous number of motivating principles (e.g. pleasure satisficers, pain minimizers, pleasure maximizers, pain negaficers, combination pleasure satisficers and pain minimizers, etc). Such elaborations would lead to the virtual collapse of hedonism as a fundamental motivational principle.

But we are not through with the problems of hedonism yet. Since any adequate theory of motivation has to explain thoughts as well as overt actions (since thoughts are a type of action and therefore must be caused, i.e. motivated), hedonism would lead to the prediction that people should do everything in their power to avoid unpleasant thoughts, i.e. thoughts which cause them anxiety, dissatisfaction, self-doubt, guilt, depression, etc.

A policy of consistently avoiding unpleasant thoughts through extensive use of defense mechanisms and the like would lead to mental illness, however. One requirement of psychological health is a policy of *not* resorting to defensive mechanisms in order to avoid disturbing thoughts (and, as a corollary, not letting pleasurable thoughts, e.g. wishes, substitute for one's rational judgment.)

A final critique of hedonism is that the doctrine is by its nature deterministic, i.e. it is a form of *psychological determinism*. Hedonism, in arguing that men *inevitably*, by their nature, base their choices and actions on calculations of expected pleasure and pain, implies that they *cannot* act otherwise. The doctrine in effect asserts that men are powerless to resist the urges of their feelings and emotions. They are assumed to be helplessly pushed and pulled by their desires and fears, their ultimate choices in a given situation being the resultant of the total forces (i.e. feelings) acting on them at the time. To the degree that rational thought is employed, it is only the the service of one's feelings.

The assumption of determinism wipes out the possibility of ethics (the science that identifies the principles that *should* guide men's actions), since ethics presupposes choice (78). This doctrine also wipes out the possibility of knowledge, since it implies that men can only believe what they were forced to believe by forces beyond their control. According to the theory of determinism, for example, the only reason people advocate the doctrine of hedonism is that they feel good when they think about it and cannot, therefore, resist endorsing it (50)!

Determinism ignores the fact that man has a conceptual form of cognition which allows him to identify his feelings and the values which give rise to them, and to decide whether or not to act on them (14). Man's rational faculty enables him to *choose* the standards which he will use to guide his choices and actions (78).

A final note with respect to the assumption of hedonism: it is interesting to observe that virtually none of the empirical studies designed to test expectancy theory have used measures of expected pleasure or expected satisfaction as their index of valence. Usually individual subjects or employees are asked to indicate their relative preferences for or the relative desirability or importance of various outcomes or actions. Such procedures, of course, avoid the assumption that an individual's choices are based on the relative degree of pleasure they will bring or the pain they will avoid. The consistency with which directly hedonistic measurements are avoided in these studies suggests the possibility that advocates of expectancy theory do not themselves fully accept its hedonistic assumptions.

One recent study used a measure of past pleasure experienced when carrying out various job activities *in addition* to the usual valence measures (stressing desirability) and found that the former correlated with actual performance better than the combined V-I-E measures (98). However, this study did not test the possibility that such past pleasure was the result of past effective performance (and associated rewards), in which case the correlation would be a spurious result of past performance correlating with present performance.

If individuals cannot properly be described as pursuing pleasure, then what does guide their actions? With respect to motivation, it would be more accurate to say that individuals strive to attain goals, values, or purposes than to say that they strive for pleasure. Even when pleasure is a causal factor in choice, an individual's focus in acting is typically on the object of the action (the goal) rather than on pleasure (2). If an individual's primary focus were on pleasure, he would probably not attain it, since it cannot be attained directly, only indirectly, i.e. by attaining goals and objects (2).

Describing human behavior (qua human) as goal-directed or purposive does not make the a priori assumption that pleasure and pain are the sole and necessary determinants of action.

TIME SPAN   A capacity which distinguishes man from the lower animals, and one which stems from his ability to conceptualize, is the capacity to project the long range consequences of his actions. However, since the use of one's conceptual faculty is volitional (since it is exercised by choice), men differ enormously in the consistency and persistence with which they project the future. In addition, men differ in the ability and accuracy with which they make such projections (depending upon their experience, knowledge, intelligence, and methods of thinking). Since the possible time span across which men may project their actions and their consequences ranges from zero to the range of a lifetime, one can know nothing about how a man will act without knowing what time span the individual is considering when making his choices.

Despite observable differences among individuals in the above characteristic, expectancy theory has nothing whatever to say about the subject. Evidently there is an implicit premise to the effect that all individuals are alike in this respect.

THE SEARCH-LOAD PROBLEM   Just as individuals differ widely in the time span across which they project their actions, they differ widely in the number and types of actions and consequences which they consider when making their decisions (11, 12). This is partly an issue of necessity, partly one of style, and partly one of motivation. The necessity pertains to differences in mental capacity (cognitive load capacity) and differences in knowledge (of the various possible alternatives and action outcomes). The style issue pertains to differences in methods of thinking (defense mechanisms; use of reason vs emotion; use of one's own judgment vs conformity to others, etc). The motivation issue involves differences in persistence, self-confidence, and what the individual considers important.

Without knowing what a man will consider when forecasting his actions (e.g. how he will go about searching for consequences; when he will stop searching; how he will integrate the information obtained), one can predict little or nothing about what actions he will take. Again, however, expectancy theory has nothing to say about this issue, the implication being that people are basically the same with respect to search habits and load capacity.

This assumption is exemplified in the typical research study in which the experimenter defines for the individual the precise outcomes and behaviors he is to consider when forecasting his actions, and even makes the subsequent mathematical V-I-E calculations for the subject—calculations which he could not make consciously [and may not actually make at all; see (11)].

SUBCONSCIOUS MOTIVATION   The previous point brings up an additional problem with expectancy theory, namely, the implicit assumption that all motivation is conscious. Expectancy theory assumes that the individual consciously calculates the expected pleasure and/or pain to be gained or avoided through various actions and makes his choice(s) accordingly.

One does not have to be a confirmed advocate of Freudian psychoanalysis to recognize that individuals are not always conscious of their motives, premises, values, expectancies, and the like. If an individual is not conscious of all his values and premises, he cannot, of course, make conscious calculations regarding how to maximize his pleasure and minimize his pain (even granting that these are his ultimate goals).

Just as individuals differ in the time span across which they project their actions and the number and type of alternatives they consider before acting, they differ in the degree to which they are aware of the contents and processes of their own mind. Like being aware of the external world, being aware of one's own psychology depends on the desire and the ability to use one's conceptual faculty (14).

Again, expectancy theory has nothing to say about subconscious motivation; thus it must assume implicitly that subconscious motivation either does not exist or is not important.

IMPULSIVE, EXPRESSIVE, NEUROTIC, AND HABITUAL BEHAVIOR   There are certain categories of action which even the most confirmed V-I-E advocate could not claim were taken calculatively. The main feature of impulsive behavior, for example, is that it is done *without calculation* (hedonistic or otherwise). For example, a worker gets angry at his foreman and suddenly, during an argument, punches him in the nose. Afterwards he may be very sorry, especially if he is fired and subjected to a lawsuit. His explanation will usually be: "I just hit him. I didn't think about what I was doing." Such action is impulsive rather than instrumental. The time span considered in projecting the consequences of such actions is zero. The individual is not consciously aiming at a goal, but simply expressing a feeling. The same can occur with positive emotions, e.g. running and jumping with joy over some happy event.

There are also actions which the individual recognizes as harmful to his own interests, but which he takes anyway because he cannot resist the impulse, as in the case of genuine compulsive behavior.

Neurotically rigid behavior is another example of behavior which does not respond consistently or predictably to environmental circumstances (11).

Habitual behavior is also done without extensive advance calculation, although such calculations may have occurred when the habit was first acquired.

Since the types of behavior described above are not at all uncommon, the failure to account for them constitutes another limitation of expectancy theory.

THE RATIO SCALE PROBLEM   It has been pointed out that the formulas involved in the basic expectancy theory postulates assume the existence of ratio scales, since multiplication of valences, expectancies, and instrumentalities are involved. However, there is as yet no known method of measuring values or valences on a ratio scale (or even a true interval scale). Thus the form of the theory assumes the existence of measurements which do not exist (83). If such measurements do not exist, it is difficult to see how individuals, in choosing among action and outcome alternatives, could act as if they do. Whatever individuals use to make their calculations, it cannot be a ratio scale for valences.

THE INFINITE REGRESS PROBLEM   Expectancy theorists argue that the valence of an outcome is the product of the valences of all other outcomes to which this outcome leads and the instrumentality for that outcome in producing these other outcomes. Thus (theoretically) each particular valence is explained on the basis of other valences. Taken literally, this leads to an infinite regress, since each valence would have to be calculated by associating it with other valences and so on ad infinitum. In practice, individuals could not possibly make such calculations when deciding upon a course of action. The cognitive load would be overwhelming.

This problem could be resolved by recognizing that valences (i.e. feelings) are not psychological primaries. Feelings (and expected feelings) are the consequences of (subconscious) value judgments (52, 56). The sum of one's value judgments toward an object or outcome are automatically integrated by the subconscious and are reflected in one's emotional reactions to that object or outcome. To experience an emotion, the individual does not have to consciously focus on everything that is associated with a given object or outcome. His subconscious will make these associations for him.[2] However, it does not follow that by knowing an individual's (automatic) emotional reaction to an object one can predict his actions toward it—since this assumes the validity of the doctrine of hedonism, which has been previously questioned.

Some of the above criticisms of expectancy theory point to errors of omission in the theory (e.g. time span, cognitive load). That is, they are issues about which the theory says nothing explicitly but about which something could be said, e.g. by expanding the theory.

Other criticisms, however, entail errors of commission, i.e. problems regarding the validity of what was actually said. Some of these, such as hedonism, are fundamental to the entire approach of the theory (if not to the practice of researchers). Others, such as the impulsive behavior problem point to broad areas where the theory simply does not apply. Others might be resolved by making substantial revisions in the theory, e.g. the subconscious motivation problem, the ratio scale problem, the infinite regress problem.

If the foregoing critiques are accepted and used as a basis for revising the theory, however, it is questionable how closely the revised version will resemble the theory in its present form.

An alternative to the hypothetico-deductive approach to motivation of expectancy theorists would be a more inductive approach designed to discover how employees *actually* make choices among action alternatives. A theory of employee motivation could eventually be constructed on the basis of these findings. Such a theory, of course, would be highly complex and would require decades to develop.

GOAL-SETTING AND MANAGEMENT BY OBJECTIVES

Goal-setting is more appropriately viewed as a motivational technique rather than as a formal theory of motivation, despite previous suggestions to the contrary (51). Historically, the study of goal-setting stems from two sources: one industrial and

[2] It must be stressed that to experience an emotion is not necessarily to be aware that one is experiencing it. To know that one is experiencing an emotion, and more importantly to know what emotion one is experiencing, requires an act of conceptual identification.

one academic. Taylor used assigned goals or "tasks" as one of the key techniques of his system of Scientific Management (96). Each workman was given a challenging but reachable work goal each day based on the results of time (and motion) study. The methods by which he was to reach the goal (e.g. tools to be used, work techniques, distribution of rest pauses, etc) were spelled out in detail.

A modern version of the task idea can be found in the system called Management by Objectives (MBO). MBO is basically a method of developing a hierarchically integrated network of goals throughout all managerial levels of an organization (18).

In the academic realm, concepts like "task," "set," and "intention" were used by psychologists in the Wurzburg school to explain the results of their laboratory experiments. During the 1930s American psychologists in this tradition performed extensive studies of "level of aspiration" (quantitative goal setting), but they were more interested in the causes of aspiration level than in its effects.

Recent studies of goal-setting and its effects have been summarized by Locke (51) and Ryan (82). Pritchard & Curtis (74) conducted one of the few laboratory studies of goal-setting since Miner & Dachler's review 2 years ago. They replicated Locke's finding that moderately hard goals lead to higher performance levels than no (i.e. low) goals. However, they did not support his finding that monetary incentives affect performance only through their effects on goal level or goal commitment. Subjects offered a high (piece-rate) incentive for performance showed higher output than subjects given no piece rate incentive or lower incentives, even though the goal levels of the various groups were apparently equivalent. Nor were differences found in the degree of conscious goal commitment expressed by subjects in the various incentive conditions. Possibly subconscious commitment differences could account for the results. On the other hand, difference scores rather than residual gain scores were used as the measure of output, which could have confounded the results.

Laboratory research on goal-setting has been criticized on the grounds that its findings have not been replicated in real-life settings. However, four recent studies by Latham and his colleagues indicate that these laboratory findings can be successfully replicated in and applied to actual industrial situations. Ronan, Latham & Kinne (80) found in two studies that high productivity among independent pulpwood producers was correlated with the presence of a supervisor who stays on the job with his men and who sets production goals for them.

In an experimental study, Latham & Kinne (47) found that overall crew output per man was higher over a 12 week period in crews where a specific, moderately difficult goal was assigned to the sawyers in each crew than in control crews in which the sawyers were assigned no such goals.

The fourth study (46a) was also experimental but used a time series design. (A control group, unfortunately, was not available). Logging operators were assigned the goal of loading their trucks to 94% of maximum legal net weight; the previous average attained had been close to 60% of net weight. Latham found that performance improved immediately upon the introduction of the goals and remained at a high level throughout the following 9 months of the study. For the final 6 months, the percent of maximum load attained averaged over 90%. The net savings to the company of this increase in performance, as compared with what it would have cost to attain it through the purchase of additional trucks, was a quarter of a million dollars!

One surprising fact about the above studies was that goal assignments were made and performance increases obtained without the offering of any extrinsic reward for goal acceptance or goal attainment, and without any overt punishments being threatened for nonattainment. Obviously such dramatic results could not be expected in all organizations.

In another industrial study, Dachler & Mobley (20) found significant correlations between employee's self-chosen production goals and subsequent performance in two different plants, although the correlations were not large.

A number of recent studies of MBO have been summarized and integrated by Carroll & Tosi (18). These studies emphasize "soft" criteria, i.e. attitudes towards MBO and ratings of performance by superiors, rather than "hard" measures of actual organizational or individual effectiveness.

A number of interesting correlational findings emerged from these studies. For example, high goal clarity was consistently related to high satisfaction and high rated performance. High goal difficulty was associated with high performance only when the subordinates were mature and self-assured. Otherwise, hard goals tended to produce lowered performance. Presumably the hard goals demoralized and/or were rejected by employees with low self-confidence. Providing frequent feedback or performance reviews was virtually always associated with positive changes in attitudes and performance.

Degree of participation in goal-setting had no consistent relation to subsequent performance. Generally employees performed better with participation if they were used to it, but not otherwise. Superiors were usually most willing to allow participation by those subordinates whom they considered to be most competent.

Carroll & Tosi emphasize repeatedly that upper management commitment to MBO is crucial to its success, as is the integration of the MBO process with other organizational systems (e.g. the reward structure, budgeting, appraisal, etc).

One element of MBO that has not received sufficient emphasis in the research literature is the development of action plans, i.e. identifying the means by which the goal(s) will be achieved. Nor has this element received much attention in laboratory studies of goal-setting because their main emphasis has been on directly inciting the individual to greater effort rather than on developing strategies for goal attainment. However, in real life settings, increased effort is not always the most efficient method (or even a possible method) of attaining a new or harder goal. The most successful goal achiever is often the individual who devises the most effective or creative tactics and strategies for goal attainment or who most thoroughly develops the prerequisite skills in himself or his subordinates. More studies of individual differences in strategies or methods of arriving at or choosing strategies and of their relative effectiveness would be welcome.

One final issue concerns the relationship between "goal theory" and expectancy theory. Expectancy theory, as originally developed (111), never incorporated an explicit goal-setting stage, although some writers have suggested that one be added to the model (17, 20). One interesting difference in research findings between the two approaches is that expectancy theorists typically find a positive correlation between expectancy and performance, while goal-setting studies find that harder goals (with lower expectancies) lead to higher performance than easier goals [with higher expectancies (51)].

A recent study by Cartledge (19) attempted to reconcile some of the seemingly contradictory findings by positing that expectancy theory (i.e. the V, I, and E components) should be used to predict goal choice rather than to predict performance directly. In an experimental laboratory study Cartledge found a positive association between both E and V and the acceptance of an assigned goal. [Dachler & Mobley (20) also found that V-I-E theory predicted goal choice.] However, when all other factors were controlled, there was no significant relation between these factors and a measure of task effort (performance quantity, with ability partialed out). The best predictor of effort was the individual's *intended work rate*; the next best was the individual's *perceived goal difficulty* (measured by having the individual indicate how fast he would have to work to achieve his assigned goal *if* he tried for it). Both relationships held up when expectancy of success was partialled out.

A positive association was found between expectancy of success and effort in one subgroup, however. This subgroup was composed of individuals whose subjective expectancies and "objective" probabilities of success (based on the difficulty of their assigned goal) were widely discrepant. Those whose expectancy estimates were "too high" had significantly more ability on the task than those whose estimates were "too low." This indicates that the positive expectancy-performance correlations obtained in some previous studies might have been an artifact of differences in ability, since expectancy is presumably correlated with ability (72).

Cartledge's results indicate that in cases where the individual makes a definite commitment to a specific goal, performance (as measured by effort) is proportional to the demands of the task rather than to expectancy.

In settings where the individual is not required to commit himself to a specific goal, one might expect somewhat different results, depending upon the goal level originally chosen and the changes in goal level that occur as a result of experience with the task.

THE HERZBERG THEORY AND JOB ENRICHMENT

The Herzberg theory (39) continues to draw the attention of researchers, and the results continue to throw doubt upon key aspects of the theory, e.g. the view that "Motivators" cause job satisfaction but not dissatisfaction, while "Hygienes" cause job dissatisfaction but not satisfaction (32, 37, 55–57, 94, 99, 104, 105). Only when Herzberg's basic methodology, including his classification scheme, is used is the theory consistently supported (56, 59).

Waters and his colleagues (104, 105) find that attitudes toward Motivators are more highly correlated with both job satisfaction and job dissatisfaction than are attitudes toward Hygienes. This finding replicates the results of several earlier studies using similar correlational methods, as well as those of studies using more direct rating methods (94).

The results using an "intensity" approach to determine the potency of Motivators and Hygienes in causing satisfaction and dissatisfaction, however, do not support the results using a frequency approach. Generally the former method finds that both Motivators and Hygienes are reported to cause more satisfaction than dissatisfaction (32, 56).

This writer has pointed out (56) that the Herzberg incident classification system confuses two levels of analysis, viz events (what event or condition occurred or was present) and agents (who or what caused the event to occur or brought about the condition). When employees are asked to describe satisfying and dissatisfying occasions, and the incidents are coded separately by event and agent, the Herzberg two-factor theory is not replicated. The consistent finding with respect to events is that Motivator events are more likely to produce both satisfaction and dissatisfaction than are Hygiene events (37, 55–57). In this respect the results agree with the typical result of the correlational studies mentioned above.

With respect to agents, the results are more complex. There is a tendency, possibly defensive, for the self to be given credit for satisfying events and for others (supervisors, co-workers, the organization, etc) to be blamed for dissatisfying events (57). Overall, however, the supervisor and the organization are seen as by far the most important causal agents for *both* satisfying and dissatisfying events (57).

On the issue of defensiveness, Wall (99) found that the tendency to list Hygienes as sources of dissatisfaction was significantly correlated with a measure of ego-defensiveness. Since many of Herzberg's Hygienes are agents (e.g. supervisor, organizational policies, co-workers), this supports the notion that his original results are at least partly an artifact of defensive tendencies within individuals.

Wall's findings also point up another aspect of the Herzberg controversy, that of individual differences. A number of researchers have observed that, at least with respect to verbal reports of job attitudes, all individuals do not react equally favorably to Motivators, e.g. to opportunities for growth, autonomy, job enrichment, etc (41).

The evidence suggests that there is a tendency for blue collar workers, especially those with urban, industrial backgrounds and those who choose to work in large firms to be more likely to report Hygienes and less likely to report Motivators as sources of satisfaction (37, 41, 42, 55, 57). Other studies, however, have questioned the validity of some of these conclusions (95). At root, of course, such differences must be an individual matter rather than a matter of demographics or occupational level, since there are substantial individual differences among employees within all of the above groups. One individual trait claimed to be causally related to satisfaction with enriched jobs is cognitive complexity (93). Another is "higher order need strength" (48, 102).

It should be noted, however, that what people say they get pleasure from on their jobs is partly a function of the type of experiences they have had; therefore individual differences in such descriptions are not necessarily evidence for basic underlying value differences among employees (57). The fact that people do not claim to gain satisfaction from Motivators does not mean that they will not respond to them when they are provided. Some people do not have enough experience to predict accurately how they will respond to an entirely new job situation. Furthermore, the degree of satisfaction they experience with a given condition may have no relation to its effect on their job performance, since the two are not necessarily related (56).

What would be interesting in this regard is an experimental study of the "hard" (performance) and "soft" (attitudinal) reactions of different types of employees (e.g. those who claim to value and those who claim not to value jobs with opportunities for cognitive growth) to job enrichment.

The idea of job enrichment, though not originally developed by Herzberg, was popularized by him and has stimulated a great deal of applied research. Even though Herzberg's theory appears mistaken, mainly with reference to the role of Motivators as dissatisfiers and the role of Hygienes as satisfiers, this has not led to severe problems in application, for the main thrust of job enrichment is to provide more Motivators as a means of increasing morale and motivation.

The evidence from field studies is generally quite favorable to job enrichment with respect to improvements in both motivation and morale (27, 60, 89). Ford observed that about 85% of employees respond favorably to enrichment at AT & T (27). Practitioners report that it is very difficult to predict who will respond most favorably in advance. The most troublesome employees sometimes respond quite favorably, suggesting that this troublesomeness was an expression of frustration due to unused mental capacity (60).

Experienced consultants in the job enrichment area warn against the danger of job enrichment becoming a fad rather than one solution to one type of problem, i.e. underutilization of employees' skills and capacities, especially mental capacities (89, 92). Sirota & Wolfson have made a useful contribution to the field of pointing out the various obstacles to job enrichment which can be encountered in the course of implementation (e.g. wrong preconceptions of managers, poor diagnosis, technological constraints, etc) as well as advice on how to overcome these obstacles (90, 91).

At the theoretical level, there is a need to begin identifying the particular elements of job enrichment and to identify their relative degree of effectiveness in producing higher morale and productivity. For example, the following types of changes have been made by practitioners under the guise of "job enrichment" (e.g. see 27, 31, 60, 89):

— increased responsibility (taken from supervisor);
— increased autonomy (elimination of rules which limit discretion);
— increased recognition for job accomplishment;
— development of work modules or "wholes";

— provision of objective performance feedback regarding quality and/or quantity;

— job rotation (greater variety of tasks at the same level);

— upgrading of employee skills through training;

— goal-setting;

— use of new tools, procedures, and equipment;

— development of cohesive work teams;

— increased participation in decision-making;

— pay raises;

— reorganization of the work task to improve "physical" efficiency (from a time-study viewpoint).

It is clear from the above that a great many things are done under the rubric of job enrichment; yet the relationship of many of these changes to the actual theory of enrichment (e.g. Herzberg's theory) is far from clear. It was mentioned above that job enrichment allegedly involves the provision of Motivators in order to increase satisfaction and performance. However, pay raises, participation, and the development of work teams are Hygiene factors not Motivator factors. Goal-setting, according to Ford, is not the way to enrich jobs (27, p. 28), even though considerable research indicates that goal achievement is a major source of job satisfaction. Finally, feedback and improvements in tools, equipment, and in general physical efficiency stem more from the theory of scientific management (96) than from job enrichment theory.

The fact that what people do under the guise of job enrichment usually seems to "work" is encouraging from an applied standpoint; but from a theoretical viewpoint (and from a long-range applied viewpoint) it would be useful to know *why* these changes work. Studying job enrichment in terms of its various elements is extremely difficult, especially in field settings, but studies of this type might prove very fruitful in explaining the results of job enrichment studies and in providing a basis for more complete theories of employee motivation. Such theories, of course, would subsequently aid practitioners.

Large scale experimental studies are not the only method by which this could be accomplished. Intensive studies of one or two groups, changing various work attributes in sequence, might provide useful information despite the drawbacks of such time series designs.

PAY AND MONETARY INCENTIVES

Despite decades of ritualistic attacks on the concept of "economic man," and despite Taylor's somewhat oversimplified assumptions about worker motivation (96), employees continue to want compensation in return for their work and researchers continue to find it a stimulating research area (97). No single theoretical viewpoint dominates thinking on this subject. Rather one could say that thinking about pay permeates all theoretical approaches to employee motivation.

For example, Herzberg's theory stresses its role as a Hygiene factor (39), although research indicates that it can serve both as a motivator of job performance (48) and as a source of job satisfaction (37, 57). Beer & Gery (10) argue that this depends on the type of pay system. Merit systems may be perceived as instrumental in satisfying "higher order needs," while security-type payment systems are seen as satisfying "lower order needs."

Job enrichment specialists argue that enrichment must be accompanied by pay raises to avoid feelings of inequity (88). There is ample evidence for the view that perceived equity is an important determinant of pay satisfaction (26, 46, 76), even though there is as yet no adequate theory which would account for the different ways in which equity is conceived by different employees (106).

Expectancy theorists have focused on the relationship between performance and the degree to which high output is seen as instrumental in leading to higher pay (20, 44, 84, 87). Other conditions facilitating the effectiveness of a pay incentive plan include: the absence of group norms opposing high production; high valuation of pay by the employees; ability of the employees to understand the incentive plan; and a feeling on the part of the employees of support by and trust of upper management (16).

Another recent study supporting the expectancy theory viewpoint found that productivity was higher when it was based on individual as well as group output than when it was based on group output alone (108).

On the opposite side of the coin, there is some evidence (from laboratory studies) that when money is made contingent upon performance, it reduces the individual's intrinsic motivation, whereas if money is noncontingent, it does not reduce intrinsic motivation (23). This would lead one to predict that employees under merit systems would be less intrinsically motivated than those employed under a civil service or seniority system, a prediction which does not accord well with the common-sense view of nonmerit systems as promoting inefficiency. Actually, the above studies only compared piece rate vs noncontingent hourly pay. There was no intermediate condition in which there was hourly pay, but where promotion and retention depended upon performance.

Advocates of the "human relations" school of employee motivation favor group incentive plans like the Scanlon plan in order to encourage teamwork and prevent inter- and/or intragroup competition. Research on the Scanlon plan indicates that management attitudes toward employees and management's degree of commitment to a participative style of management are among the most important elements contributing to its success or failure in a given organization (81, 110). Expectancy theorists would question the degree to which a company-wide incentive would aid performance because of the limited degree to which any single individual's effort could affect company performance (108). However, it has not been proven that the incentive aspect of the plan is responsible for its success. A key element of the Scanlon plan is the development of better communication between management and labor through group meetings combined with a suggestion plan. Possibly the latter elements of the Scanlon plan are actually responsible for its success in those organizations where it has worked.

Advocates of Management by Objectives also stress the importance of pay in facilitating the success of this approach. It is asserted that MBO must be integrated with the organization's appraisal and reward systems in order for the managerial personnel to be committed to the goal-setting approach and to attaining the goals which they set (18). Dearden (22) has pointed out the complexities and pitfalls involved in the installation of any type of incentive plan.

JOB SATISFACTION AND JOB PERFORMANCE

Recent studies have further confirmed a host of earlier studies (56) to the effect that job satisfaction exerts little or no causal influence on productivity. When the two are related at all, the evidence favors an interpretation in favor of productivity as a cause of satisfaction (34, 101) rather than vice versa. It has been argued that productivity and satisfaction will be related in this fashion to the extent that there is a relationship between productivity and the attainment of the individual's important work values and goals (53). Nathanson & Becker (69) found some support for this proposition in a study of physicians. In circumstances where it could be assumed that physicians derived intrinsic satisfaction from outpatient care activities, or that they received recognition for such activities, or that outpatient care was an end in itself rather than a means to an end, satisfaction and productivity were significantly correlated. When these circumstances did not hold, the two variables were unrelated.

Recent findings concerning the effect of job satisfaction on withdrawal from the job also confirmed earlier results. Porter & Steers (73) carefully reviewed over 60 studies from the last 15 years and found substantial support for a relation between satisfaction and both turnover and absenteeism. A number of longitudinal and field-experimental studies supported the results obtained with the more common concurrent or retrospective studies.

Studies published since Porter & Steers' review further support their results, regardless of whether job attraction is measured with the Cornell JDI (103), expectancy theory measures combining the V-I-E components (24), or Motivator-Hygiene deprivation (7, 45). However, Porter & Steers note that the *best* individual predictor of termination may be the individual's intention to terminate. [Others have found frequency of "thoughts about quitting" to work well (7).] Presumably the intent to leave takes account of the individual's attitude toward his job in addition to other factors which could affect his decision, e.g. economic need, availability of other jobs, family considerations, attractiveness of fringe benefits on present job, etc.

The specific variables which Porter & Steers found to be associated with a low degree of withdrawal included: pay equity; opportunities for promotion; considerate supervisory style; small group size; characteristics of the work itself such as responsibility, autonomy, variety, and low stress; age; long previous tenure; and interests compatible with present work requirements. Porter & Steers hypothesized that the highest probabilities of withdrawal are shown by two types of employees: those who are anxious and emotionally unstable; and those who are highly ambitious, self-confident, independent, and aggressive. Presumably the first type is easily threatened and impulsive about acting on his negative feelings, while the second type is easily frustrated if deprived of opportunities commensurate with his aspirations (e.g. see 39a).

Another interesting finding in the recent literature is that there is often a continuum of withdrawal from absenteeism to turnover with high (or increased) absenteeism preceding a final decision to terminate (15, 58).

Since it is well accepted that satisfaction is a function in some way of the fit between individual values and job conditions, this suggests that there are two possible ways of increasing satisfaction: changing the person and changing the job. There is some evidence that giving the individual a realistic job preview can reduce disappointment and increase attraction (100). While such previews have been credited with helping the individual develop more realistic job expectations, this writer has argued elsewhere that expectations as such (divorced from aspirations, i.e. what the individual wants or values) will not have a major effect on attitudes (56). It was hypothesized that changing expectations would affect attitudes through their effect on the individual's job aspirations (or more probably, his view of what he would consider to be minimally acceptable on a job).

An organization need not change an individual's values in order to insure that he will fit into the organization, however. It can cash in on existing differences between individuals by selecting those who have values and aspirations compatible with the organizational structure. To a considerable extent, of course, individuals select themselves into (and out of) organizations in this manner (30, 42). In addition, some value adaptation occurs as a result of experience in the organization (40).

It is easier, of course, for an organization to modify conditions than to modify individual values. The potential of the former approach (e.g. job enrichment, supervisory training, OD, incentives) is well known and needs no further discussion here (e.g. see 28).

It has been argued elsewhere that the relationship between attitudes and withdrawal is now well enough established that more studies of this type will not add to our understanding of employee motivation and behavior (56). What is needed are studies involving: explanations for off-quadrant cases, i.e. those who are satisfied and withdraw, and those who are dissatisfied and do not withdraw; the cognitive processes leading to the decision to withdraw; and the study of qualitative as well as quantitative attitudinal factors as they relate to withdrawal (e.g. see 42). Porter & Steers (73) recommend additional types of studies.

A recently studied variable which has been found to relate to withdrawal, satisfaction, and job performance is that of "role orientation," defined by Graen, et al as "the perceived relevance of the job for the [employee's] work career" (33, p. 401). New nonacademic employees of a large university who saw their job as being related to work they planned to perform in the future (presumably as part of their career plans) were more satisfied, were rated as better performers by their supervisors, and were less likely to terminate than those who saw their jobs as unrelated to their career plans. An explanation for this finding remains to be found, but presumably it entails the individual's willingness or desire to fully accept and to become involved in his work role. Further studies of role orientation seem warranted.

MISCELLANEOUS

Several interesting studies did not fall into any of the above categories. One was a longitudinal study of worker adjustment to the 4-day work week (71), apparently the only such study on this subject published to date. The effects of the change were generally favorable with respect to both job attitudes and reduced absenteeism. However, employees reported fewer favorable effects on home life after one year than after 6 or 13 weeks on the 4-day week.

Another interesting study examined, through extensive interviews, the reactions of key managers from 90 small business firms to the flood damage wrought by hurricane Agnes in June 1972 (1). Degree of perceived threat was most highly (and negatively) related to high I scores on Rotter's I-E scale. High I scores were also highly related to the number of task-oriented coping mechanisms used (e.g. trying to obtain loans). Those with high E scores, on the other hand, were more likely to employ coping mechanisms designed to reduce, control, or express dysfunctional emotions such as anxiety (e.g. withdrawal, aggression). While the number of *different types* of task-oriented or emotion-oriented coping mechanisms used were unrelated to coping effectiveness as rated by the interviewers, the *total frequency* with which task-relevant coping methods were employed was highly and positively related to coping effectiveness.

In this writer's opinion, one of the most important books to be published in psychology in some time is Irving Janis' *Victims of Groupthink* (43). Janis views groupthink as a product of pressures for conformity which arise within cohesive groups. He defines it as: "a mode of thinking that people engage in when they are deeply involved in a cohesive in-group, when the members' strivings for unanimity override their motivation to realistically appraise alternative courses of action ... Groupthink refers to a deterioration of mental efficiency, reality testing, and moral judgment that results from in-group pressures" (43, p. 9) Although the focus of Janis' book is on the effects of groupthink on the quality of selected American foreign policy decisions, the implications of his ideas for organization management are obvious. Especially interesting are Janis' suggestions for preventing groupthink. Advocates of the "human relations" approach to employee morale and motivation may find this book particularly enlightening.

Finally, recent studies by Miner lead him to forecast an alarming shortage of managerial manpower in the years ahead (63, 64). The reason for this, according to Miner, is a precipitous drop in the number of students with values compatible with the values required for managerial success. This will lead, argues Miner, to recruiting difficulties and/or to poor performance among those who are hired but who lack the requisite motivational structure. Miner proposes increased use of "role-motivation" training as the best solution to this problem (63), although it remains to be seen whether this will work in view of the wider cultural context in which these value changes are occurring, i.e. the philosophical assault on business and capitalism that is occurring in our colleges and universities (79).

1. Anderson, C. R., Hellriegel, D., Slocum, J. W. Jr. 1974. *Managerial Response to Environmental Hazard.* Presented at Nat. Acad. Manage., Seattle
2. Arnold, M. B. 1960. *Emotion and Personality, Volume I: Psychological Aspects.* New York: Columbia Univ. 296 pp.
3. Arvey, R. D. 1972. Task performance as a function of perceived effort-performance and performance-reward contingencies. *Organ. Behav. Hum. Perform.* 8:423–33
4. Arvey, R. D., Mussio, S. J. 1973. A test of expectancy theory in a field setting using female clerical employees. *J. Vocat. Behav.* 3:421–32
5. Arvey, R. D., Neel, C. W. 1974. Moderating effects of employee expectancies on the relationship between leadership consideration and job performance of engineers. *J. Vocat. Behav.* 4:213–22
6. Ibid. Testing expectancy theory predictions using behaviorally based measures of motivational effort for engineers. 4:299–310
7. Atchison, T. J., Lefferts, E. A. 1972. The prediction of turnover using Herzberg's job satisfaction technique. *Personnel Psychol.* 25:53–64
8. Atkinson, J. W. 1964. *An Introduction to Motivation.* Princeton: Van Nostrand. 335 pp.
9. Atkinson, J. W., Feather, N. T., Eds. 1966. *A Theory of Achievement Motivation.* New York: Wiley. 392 pp.
10. Beer, M., Gery, G. J. 1972. Individual and organizational correlates of pay system preferences. See Ref. 97, 325–49
11. Behling, O., Starke, F. A. 1973. *Some Limits on Expectancy Theories of Work Effort.* Presented at Midwest. Meet. Am. Inst. Decis. Sci., East Lansing, Mich.

12. Behling, O., Starke, F. A. 1973. The postulates of expectancy theory. *Acad. Manage. J.* 16:373–88
13. Behling, O., Schriesheim, C., Tolliver, J. 1973. *Alternative Cognitive Formulations of the Work-Effort Decision.* Presented at Midwest. Acad. Manage., Chicago
14. Blumenthal, A. 1969. The base of Objectivist psychotherapy. *The Objectivist* 8:(6)6–10; (7)4–9
15. Burke, R. J., Wilcox, D. S. 1972. Absenteeism and turnover among female telephone operators. *Personnel Psychol.* 25:639–48
16. Cammann, C., Lawler, E. E. III 1973. Employee reactions to a pay incentive plan. *J. Appl. Psychol.* 58:163–72
17. Campbell, J. P., Dunnette, M. D., Lawler, E. E. III, Weick, K. E. Jr. 1970. *Managerial Behavior, Performance, and Effectiveness.* New York: McGraw-Hill, 546 pp.
18. Carroll, S. J. Jr., Tosi, H. L. Jr. 1973. *Management by Objectives.* New York: Macmillan. 216 pp.
19. Cartledge, N. D. 1973. *An experimental study of the relationship between expectancies, goal utility, goals and task performance.* PhD thesis. Univ. Maryland, College Park. 173 pp.
20. Dachler, H. P., Mobley, W. H. 1973. Construct validation of an instrumentality-expectancy-task-goal model of work motivation: some theoretical boundary conditions. *J. Appl. Psychol.* 58:397–418
21. Dansereau, F. Jr., Cashman, J., Graen, G. 1973. Instrumentality theory and equity theory as complimentary approaches in predicting the relationship of leadership and turnover among managers. *Organ. Behav. and Hum. Perform.* 10:184–200
22. Dearden, J. 1972. How to make incentive plans work. *Harvard Bus. Rev.* 50(4):117–24

23. Deci, E. L. 1972. The effects of contingent and noncontingent rewards and controls on intrinsic motivation. *Organ. Behav. Hum. Perform.* 8:217–29
24. Dunnette, M. D., Arvey, R. D., Banas, P. A. 1973. Why do they leave? *Personnel* May/June: 25–38
25. Entwisle, D. R. 1972. To dispel fantasies about fantasy-based measures of achievement motivation. *Psychol. Bull.* 77:377–91
26. Finn, R. H., Lee, S. M. 1972. Salary equity: its determination, analysis and correlates. *J. Appl. Psychol.* 56:283–92
27. Ford, R. N. 1969. *Motivation Through the Work Itself.* New York: Am. Manage. Assoc. 267 pp.
28. Friedlander, F., Brown, L. D. 1974. Organization development. *Ann. Rev. Psychol.* 25:313–41
29. Gavin, J. F. 1973. Self-esteem as a moderator of the relationship between expectancies and job performance. *J. Appl. Psychol.* 58:83–88
30. Goldthorpe, J. H., Lockwood, D., Bechhofer, F., Platt, J. 1970. *The Affluent Worker: Industrial Attitudes and Behaviour.* Cambridge, England: Cambridge Univ. 206 pp.
31. Gooding, J. 1972. Imaginative new ways to create satisfying jobs. See Ref. 61, 20–29
32. Gordon, M. E., Pryor, N. M., Harris, B. V. 1974. An examination of scaling bias in Herzberg's theory of job satisfaction. *Organ. Behav. Hum. Perform.* 11:106–21
33. Graen, G. B., Orris, J. B., Johnson, T. W. 1973. Role assimilation processes in a complex organization. *J. Vocat. Behav.* 3:395–420
34. Greene, C. N. 1973. Causal connections among managers' merit pay, job satisfaction, and performance. *J. Appl. Psychol.* 58:95–100
35. Greenhaus, J. H., Gavin, J. F. 1972. The relationship between expectancies and job behavior for white and black employees. *Personnel Psychol.* 25:449–55
36. Guion, R. M. 1973. A note on organizational climate. *Organ. Behav. Hum. Perform.* 9:120–25
37. Harris, T. C., Locke, E. A. 1974. Replication of white collar-blue collar differences in sources of satisfaction and dissatisfaction. *J. Appl. Psychol.* 59:369–70
37a. Hellriegel, D., Slocum, J. W. Jr. 1974. Organizational climate: measures, research, and contingencies. *Acad. Manage. J.* 17:255–80
38. Heneman, H. G. III, Schwab, D. P. 1972. Evaluation of research on expectancy theory predictions of employee performance. *Psychol. Bull.* 78:1–9
39. Herzberg, F., Mausner, B., Snyderman, B. B. 1959. *The Motivation to Work.* New York: Wiley. 157 pp.
39a. Hines, G. H. 1973. Achievement motivation, occupations, and labor turnover in New Zealand. *J. Appl. Psychol.* 58:313–17
40. Hinrichs, J. R. 1972. Value adaptation of new PhDs to academic and industrial environments—a comparative longitudinal study. *Personnel Psychol.* 25:545–65
41. Hulin, C. L. 1971. Individual differences in job enrichment—the case against general treatments. See Ref. 60, 159–91
42. Ingham, G. 1970. *Size of Industrial Organization and Worker Behaviour.* Cambridge, England: Cambridge Univ. 170 pp.
43. Janis, I. L. 1972. *Victims of Groupthink.* Boston: Houghton Mifflin. 276 pp.
44. Jorgenson, D. O., Dunnette, M. D., Pritchard, R. D. 1973. Effects of the manipulation of a performance-reward contingency on behavior in a simulated work setting. *J. Appl. Psychol.* 57:271–80
45. Karp, H. B., Nickson, J. W. Jr. 1973. Motivator-hygiene deprivation as a predictor of job turnover. *Personnel Psychol.* 26:377–84
46. Klein, S. M. 1973. Pay factors as predictors to satisfaction: a comparison of reinforcement, equity and expectancy. *Acad. Manage. J.* 16:598–610
46a. Latham, G. P., Baldes, J. 1974. The "practical significance" of Locke's theory of goal setting. *J. Appl. Psychol.* In press
47. Latham, G. P., Kinne, S. B. III 1974. Improving job performance through training in goal setting. *J. Appl. Psychol.* 59:187–91

48. Lawler, E. E. III 1973. *Motivation in Work Organizations.* Monterey, Calif.: Brooks/Cole. 224 pp.

49. Lawler, E. E. III, Suttle, J. L. 1973. Expectancy theory and job behavior. *Organ. Behav. Hum. Perform.* 9:482–503

50. Locke, E. A. 1966. The contradiction of epiphenomenalism. *Brit. J. Psychol.* 57:203–4

51. Locke, E. A. 1968. Toward a theory of task motivation and incentives. *Organ. Behav. Hum. Perform.* 3:157–89

52. Ibid 1969. What is job satisfaction? 4:309–36

53. Ibid 1970. Job satisfaction and job performance: a theoretical analysis. 5:484–500

54. Locke, E. A. 1972. Critical analysis of the concept of causality in behavioristic psychology. *Psychol. Rep.* 31:175–97

55. Locke, E. A. 1973. Satisfiers and dissatisfiers among white-collar and blue-collar employees. *J. Appl. Psychol.* 58:67–76

56. Locke, E. A. 1974. The nature and consequences of job satisfaction. In *Handbook of Industrial and Organizational Psychology,* ed. M. D. Dunnette. Chicago, Rand-McNally. In press

57. Locke, E. A., Whiting, R. J. 1974. Sources of satisfaction and dissatisfaction among solid waste management employees. *J. Appl. Psychol.* 59:145–56

58. Lyons, T. F. 1972. Turnover and absenteeism: a review of relationships and shared correlates. *Personnel Psychol.* 25:271–81

59. Macarov, D. 1972. Work patterns and satisfactions in an Israeli Kibbutz: a test of the Herzberg hypothesis. *Personnel Psychol.* 25:483–93

60. Maher, J. R., Ed. 1971. *New Perspectives in Job Enrichment.* New York: Van Nostrand Reinhold. 226 pp.

61. Marrow, A. J. 1972. *The Failure of Success.* New York: Amacom. 339 pp.

62. McMahan, I. D. 1973. Some determinants of expectancy of success. *Trans. NY Acad. Sci.* 35:661–71

63. Miner, J. B. 1973. The real crunch in managerial manpower. *Harvard Bus. Rev.* 51(6):146–58

64. Miner, J. B. 1974. Student attitudes toward bureaucratic role prescriptions

and the prospects for managerial talent shortages. *Personnel Psychol.* In press

65. Miner, J. B., Dachler, H. P. 1973. Personnel attitudes and motivation. *Ann. Rev. Psychol.* 24:379–402

66. Mitchell, T. R., Albright, D. W. 1972. Expectancy theory predictions of the satisfaction, effort, performance, and retention of Naval aviation officers. *Organ. Behav. Hum. Perform.* 8:1–20

67. Mitchell, T. R., Knudsen, B. W. 1973. Instrumentality theory predictions of students' attitudes towards business and their choice of business as an occupation. *Acad. Manage. J.* 16:41–52

68. Mitchell, T. R., Nebeker, D. M. 1973. Expectancy theory predictions of academic effort and performance. *J. Appl. Psychol.* 57:61–67

69. Nathanson, C. A., Becker, M. H. 1973. Job satisfaction and job performance: an empirical test of some theoretical propositions. *Organ. Behav. Hum. Perform.* 9:267–79

70. Nelson, L .R., Furst, M. L. 1972. An objective study of the effects of expectation on competitive performance. *J. Psychol.* 81:69–72

71. Nord, W. R., Costigan, R. 1973. Worker adjustment to the four-day week: a longitudinal study. *J. Appl. Psychol.* 58:60–66

72. O'Reilly, A. P. 1973. Perception of abilities as a determinant of performance. *J. Appl. Psychol.* 58:281–82

73. Porter, L. W., Steers, R. M. 1973. Organizational work and personal factors in employee turnover and absenteeism. *Psychol. Bull.* 80:151–76

74. Pritchard, R. D., Curtis, M. I. 1973. The influence of goal setting and financial incentives on task performance. *Organ. Behav. Hum. Perform.* 10:175–83

75. Pritchard, R. D., DeLeo, P. J. 1973. Experimental test of the valence-instrumentality relationship in job performance. *J. Appl. Psychol.* 57:264–70

76. Pritchard, R. D., Dunnette, M. D., Jorgenson, D. O. 1972. Effects of perceptions of equity and inequity on worker performance and satisfaction. *J. Appl. Psychol.* 56:75–94

77. Pritchard, R. D., Sanders, M. S. 1973. The influence of valence, instrumen-

tality, and expectancy on effort and performance. *J. Appl. Psychol.* 57: 55–60

78. Rand, A. 1964. *The Virtue of Selfishness.* New York: New American Library. 151 pp.

79. Rand, A. 1971. *The New Left: The Anti-Industrial Revolution.* New York: New American Library. 204 pp.

80. Ronan, W. W., Latham, G. P., Kinne, S. B. III 1973. Effects of goal setting and supervision on worker behavior in an industrial situation. *J. Appl. Psychol.* 58:302–7

81. Ruh, R. A., Wallace, R. L., Frost, C. F. 1973. Management attitudes and the Scanlon plan. *Ind. Relat.* 12:282–88

82. Ryan, T. A. 1970. *Intentional Behavior: An Approach to Human Motivation.* New York: Ronald. 590 pp.

83. Schmidt, F. L. 1973. Implications of a measurement problem for expectancy theory research. *Organ. Behav. Hum. Perform.* 10:243–51

84. Schwab, D. P. 1973. Impact of alternative compensation systems on pay valence and instrumentality perceptions. *J. Appl. Psychol.* 58:308–12

85. Schwab, D. P., Dyer, L. D. 1973. The motivational impact of a compensation system on employee performance. *Organ. Behav. Hum. Perform.* 9:215–25

86. Sheridan, J. E., Slocum, J. W. Jr., Min, B. K. 1974. *Motivational Determinants of Job Performance.* Presented at East. Acad. Manage., College Park, Md.

87. Sheridan, J. E., Slocum, J. W. Jr., Richards, M. D. 1974. Expectancy theory as a lead indicator of job behavior. *Decis. Sci.* In press

88. Sirota, D. 1972. Employee motivation. *Perspect. Def. Manage.* Autumn:1–9

89. Sirota, D. 1973. Job enrichment— another management fad? *Conf. Board Rec.* 10(4):40–45

90. Sirota, D., Wolfson, A. D. 1972. Job enrichment: what are the obstacles? *Personnel* May/June: 8–17

91. Ibid 1972. Job enrichment: surmounting the obstacles. July/August: 8–19

92. Sirota, D., Wolfson, A. D. 1973. Pragmatic approach to people problems. *Harvard Bus. Rev.* 51(1):120–28

93. Standing, T. E. 1973. *Satisfaction with the Work Itself as a Function of Cognitive Complexity.* Presented at Am. Psychol. Assoc., Montreal

94. Starcevich, M. M. 1973. The relationship between the "central life interests" of first-line managers, middle managers, and professional employees and job characteristics as satisfiers and dissatisfiers. *Personnel Psychol.* 27:107–15

95. Susman, G. I. 1973. Job enlargement: effects of culture on worker responses. *Ind. Relat.* 12(1):1–15

96. Taylor, F. W. 1947. *The Principles of Scientific Management.* New York: Norton. 144 pp.

97. Tosi, H. L. Jr., House, R. J., Dunnette, M. D., Eds. 1972. *Managerial Motivation and Compensation.* East Lansing: Michigan State Univ. 539 pp.

98. Turney, J. R. 1974. Activity outcome expectancies and intrinsic activity values as predictors of several motivation indexes for technical-professionals. *Organ. Behav. Hum. Perform.* 11:65–82

99. Wall, T. D. 1973. Ego-defensiveness as a determinant of reported differences in sources of job satisfaction and job dissatisfaction. *J. Appl. Psychol.* 58: 125–28

100. Wanous, J. P. 1973. Effects of a realistic job preview on job acceptance, job attitudes, and job survival. *J. Appl. Psychol.* 58:327–32

101. Ibid 1974. A causal-correlational analysis of the job satisfaction and performance relationship. 59:139–44

102. Ibid. The role of individual differences in human reactions to job characteristics. In press

103. Waters, L. K., Roach, D. 1973. Job attitudes as predictors of termination and absenteeism: consistency over time and across organizational units. *J. Appl. Psychol.* 57:341–42

104. Waters, L. K., Roach, D., Batlis, N. 1973. Further correlational analyses of five versions of two-factor theory of job satisfaction. *Psychol. Rep.* 32:1127–30

105. Waters, L. K., Waters, C. W. 1972. An empirical test of five versions of the two-factor theory of job satisfaction. *Organ. Behav. Hum. Perform.* 7:18–24

106. Weick, K. E. Jr. 1972. The concept of equity in the perception of pay. See Ref. 97, 268–90

107. Weiner, B. 1972. *Theories of Motivation: From Mechanism to Cognition.* Chicago: Markham. 474 pp.
108. Weinstein, A. G., Holzbach, R. L. Jr. 1973. Impact of individual differences, reward distribution, and task structure on productivity in a simulated work environment. *J. Appl. Psychol.* 58: 296–301
109. Weiss, H., Sherman, J. 1973. Internal-external control as a predictor of task effort and satisfaction subsequent to failure. *J. Appl. Psychol.* 57:132–136
110. White, J. K. 1973. *Recent Research on the Scanlon Plan.* Presented at Am. Psychol. Assoc., Montreal
111. Vroom, V. H. 1964. *Work and Motivation.* New York: Wiley. 331 pp.

PERSONNEL SELECTION, CLASSIFICATION, AND PLACEMENT

§241

Philip Ash and Leonard P. Kroeker
Department of Psychology, University of Illinois at Chicago Circle
Chicago, Illinois 60680

The 1972 review of personnel selection by Bray & Moses (31) focused upon the unfair test controversy generated by the consequences of the Tower Amendment to Title VII (Employment) of the Civil Rights Act of 1964 (48). In the 3-year period covered by the present review, 1971 through 1973, the extent of involvement of legal process in selection procedures and policies has broadened enormously.

Despite the pressure, concern, interest, and effort invested, however, progress in both theory and practice in the development of selection procedures to meet these legal and the related technical challenges has been disappointingly limited.

The three most notable developments in the triennium include: (*a*) the concurrent publication of four major summaries of testing, each from a different frame of reference, and all contributing to a new, integrated view of the field [Buros' (35) *Seventh Mental Measurements Yearbook*, DuBois' (67) *History of Psychological Testing*, Byham & Spitzer's (37) study of *The Law and Personnel Testing*, and Holmen & Docter's (96) report on *Educational and Psychological Testing*]; (*b*) a review, consolidation, and revision of the professional standards for testing (5, 6), and at the federal government level a proposed set of *Uniform Guidelines on Employee Selection Procedures* (165) which will supercede the EEOC Guidelines (92) and the OFCC Order on Testing (124); and (*c*) a broadening critique of the notion of differential validity and the "moderator variable" approach to the establishment of differential validity.

Several minor developments are also worthy of note: alternatives to the objective-type multiple-choice test such as job element examining, man-job matching, and similar techniques; an expanded interest in job analysis; and the beginnings of systematic inquiry into the procedures and problems of content validity.

Assessment center technology, interviewing, and other "classical" techniques

481

and topics continued to receive attention over the review period but without any notable developments. We do not seem to do better in 1973 than our ancestors did in 1917.

This review is organized around five topics:

1. THE STATE OF THE ART
2. TESTING AND THE LAW
3. METHODOLOGICAL PROBLEMS
4. SPECIFIC SELECTION TECHNIQUES AND AREAS
5. CONCLUSIONS

THE STATE OF THE ART

DuBois (67) traces the history of testing from its genesis in China *circa* 2200 B.C. as a method to select government officials, to its adoption four millenia later by the French in 1796, the English in 1833, and the United States in 1883. Over these millenia, tests were anchored in job content. Two inventions, however, established the pattern most characteristic of testing today: Binet's use of a sample of generic human tasks to measure "intelligence," and then the reduction of such items to the objective-type multiple-choice paper-and-pencil format. A simplistic view of the generic abilities required to perform successfully in any employment was married to an economical (cheap) methodology; job content was largely deleted from selection procedures and survived, if at all, on the criterion side of what emerged as the predictor-criterion relationship. It is at least arguable that in the more than half a century of experience with objective-type multiple-choice testing, little improvement has been achieved in this prediction, even in the face of ever more complicated statistical methodology. Ghiselli (83), summarizing all available studies from 1920 through 1966, noted an average validity of .19 for proficiency criteria and .29 for training criteria. Updating the study to 1973 (85), the averages increased to .22 and .39 respectively. In the latter report, Ghiselli calls our attention to "maximal validity coefficients" (.35 for proficiency criteria and .45 for training criteria)—the average of the "highest average validity coefficient" for each job. The report, however, does not indicate the number of studies involved nor the distribution of *studies* by validity attained. Nor can it take into account the unreported studies, although negative results are more likely to go unreported than positive results. The current critique of personnel testing is based not only on the proposition that tests may discriminate on a racial or ethnic basis; the majority of studies reported show that they do not predict job performance for *any* group (29, 109, 124, 155).

General Treatments

New, comprehensive contributions to the literature were limited: a text by Tyler (162); a newly edited set of readings partly devoted to personnel selection by Fleishman & Bass (77); a short but thoughtful summary by Bass (24); a variety of semitechnical "how-to-do-it" publications such as those of Ash (13) and Taylor (158); and a useful classified bibliography by Tenopyr (159), supplemented by a spate of articles in the personnel journals (e.g. 157). Boyd & Shimberg (30) produced a helpful handbook on performance testing; Campion (42) describes the use of work sampling for personnel selection. Performance testing has been largely neglected in favor of the attractive economy of group-administered objective-type paper-and-pencil tests. The emphasis on "job-relatedness" in court decisions and federal test regulations, however, is likely to result in increased interest in the performance or work sample. Thomas (160), argues, however, that while the work-sample technique may have higher construct validity than paper-and-pencil psychological tests for manually oriented occupations, it has much less validity for those occupations requiring abstract reasoning.

Testing in the Seventies

Testing is a massive enterprise and a big business. Buros' (35) *Seventh Yearbook* attests to the first: two volumes listing 1157 tests and a variety of indexes based thereon. Holmen & Docter (96) adumbrate the second—six giants in the field collectively account for approximately three-quarters of the total U.S. test sales. It is not surprising to learn that the practices of test publishers fall somewhat short of professional standards.

The question of whether or not tests invade privacy continues to be of interest. In regard to personnel selection, Rosenbaum (145) found, however, that the perception of the invasion tends to be idiosyncratic, a function of personal characteristics. What is private to you is not necessarily private to me, and vice versa.

APA Standards

The 1966 *Standards* (5) were directed primarily toward test publishers; the emphasis was on the content of the test manual. The 1974 revision (6), a collaborative effort of the APA, the American Educational Research Association, and the National Council on Measurement in Education, addresses itself also to the qualifications of the test user and to the "equal employment opportunity" issues that have emerged in regard to testing since 1966.

Job Analysis

One effect of the U.S. Supreme Court decision in Griggs vs Duke Power (63) was to reaffirm legally both doctrine and received tradition in personnel selection: selection predictors should be job related. To attain that result, job analysis is an essential step [writ large in the proposed new federal guidelines (165)]. Brute force empiricism—a battery of tests selected willy-nilly and tried out against any available criteria—will probably not satisfy the "job relatedness" requirement unless a showing can be made of *both* satisfactory validity coefficients and a logical or rational relationship between test content and job tasks.

Job analysis methodology has become a major area for exploration and theorizing. Prien & Ronan (131) provide an extensive review of findings on methods of conducting job analysis and utilization of job analysis results. They identify six "basic considerations" for which further research is needed: the reliability and validity of responses obtained from informants; the relations between job function components and person characteristics; the relations between job functions and performance style; the relations between function characteristics (e.g. time requirements, level of difficulty) and person characteristics; the construct validation of job functions and function composites; and the appropriate experimental designs and statistical paradigms for analysis of job data.

With respect to specific developed approaches, Fine & Wiley (76) published an introduction to Fine's functional job analysis, Fleishman & Stephenson (78) reviewed progress on his motor-skilled-oriented taxonomy of human performance, and McCormick and his associates described applications of the Position Analysis Questionnaire to the study of jobs (114, 115) and to "indirect" validity (i.e. a version of synthetic validity) (113).

Public jurisdictions, because of the exigencies of merit system examining, are more likely than private employers to emphasize job relatedness in tests, and to attempt to justify them on the basis of content validity rather than criterion-related validity. Reflecting this need, several government agencies, state and federal, have published manuals on job analysis specifically designed for personnel selection (139, 164, 175).

Content Validity

Although content validity has been one of the three main approaches to test validation included in the APA *Standards*, and has been set forth as a permissible approach to validation in both OFCC and EEOC regulations, literature on a relevant methodology for demonstrating its existence is practically nonexistent. Lennon (108) explored in 1956 some of the assumptions underlying the technique, but left procedures to others. The 1972 amendments to CRA 64, however, bringing merit systems under EEOC scrutiny, have generated new interest in this approach to validation, especially since a significant fraction of Civil Service tests are designed to measure subject-matter knowledge. Mussio & Smith (121) put together what is probably the first procedural manual on how to conduct and document a content validity study.

Synthetic Validity

Developed to provide estimates of test validity in the absence of data on an adequate sample of examinees for whom both test scores and criterion scores are available, the various approaches to synthetic validity involve matching a test-element profile with a job-element profile. Gordon (89) presents a rousing challenge to the more usual criterion validity approach, and opts for synthetic validity analysis as preferable. Primoff has made the most significant contribution to the technique in his development of the J-coefficient (132, 133). A recent manual (136) outlines step-by-step application of the technique. One important limitation must be recognized: a J-coefficient analysis provides no data on possible differential validity on a racial or ethnic basis, since person-data are not involved. Cleff's (50) man-job matching technique is an interesting alternative to test-based synthetic validity approaches. Instead of correlating job attribute profiles with test attribute profiles, the Cleff technique directly correlates job-task profiles with self-rating task profiles obtained from applicants, and dispenses with tests altogether.

Job Element Examining

The typical objective-type multiple-choice test places a premium on reading skills and also in blue-collar jobs frequently screens out minority group applicants. The job element examination procedure developed by Primoff at the U.S. Civil Service Commission is one of the most creative innovations in selection technology to emerge in the past decade, but its spread has been limited due to the almost total absence of publication in professional journals. Materials are available, however, from the U.S. Civil Service Commission (134, 135, 137).

The three basic ideas behind the job element method are: 1. Work for a position may be described by a small set of rather broad job elements such as "ability to inspect," "ability to lead or supervise," "reliability and dependability," etc. 2. It is possible to discover systematically the level of ability attained or potential of each applicant by drawing upon several sources of information: (a) the application form; (b) a supplementary information questionnaire; (c) reference inquiry replies; (d) scores on aptitude, ability, and other kinds of tests. 3. Information about each applicant can be evaluated (rated) against "benchmark" behaviors for a position and classified at one of five levels of adequacy for each element: 4–demonstrated superior ability; 3–demonstrated satisfactory ability; 2–barely acceptable or potential ability; 1– ability of some value, but less than barely acceptable; 0– training, experience, or test performance of no value.

Ash et al (16) describe an application to a state civil service system. The technique has also been introduced into selection procedures in industry, for mechanics, servicemen, and a variety of laborer occupations.

Criteria

Test validation, in the usual case, is based upon criterion validity. The criterion remains the weak link in the chain. Smith et al (155) have produced a good journeyman analysis of the characteristics of criteria to be attended to and a detailed rundown of almost all types of criteria used to evaluate job performance. An appendix summarizes an analysis of 118 validation studies conducted in 37 governmental agencies showing that most current practice is far below the potential, however; in 85 studies only judgmental criteria, i.e. supervisory ratings, were used. In almost two-thirds of these studies the test-criterion correlations were not statistically significant. Cravens & Woodruff (59) present an interesting methodology for developing criteria of salesman performance based upon a model of sales territory performance.

In a study somewhat reminiscent of Ghiselli's (83, 86), Lent et al (109) computed Significance Batting Averages (SBAs) for various combinations of predictor and criterion categories for a sample of 406 studies that yielded a total of 1506 joint predictor-criterion uses. Combining all studies, the overall SBA was .43: 43 per-

cent of the reported relationships were significant. Maximum Performance predictors (e.g. aptitude tests) were more likely to yield significant results than Typical
Performance predictors (e.g. personality or interest tests) (55 percent to 21 percent). Predictive validity studies yielded more frequent significant results than
concurrent designs. The analysis has interesting possibilities for picking predictor-criterion categories most likely to yield significant validity results, and possibly
for identifying moderator variables for pairings where correlation results are
usually not significant.

As the foregoing "state of the art" summary is intended to suggest, the art has
largely remained *status quo ante*.

TESTING AND CIVIL RIGHTS

Of the approximately 70,000 complaints filed annually with the Equal Employment Opportunity Commission, 15 to 20 percent involve alleged discrimination by
unfair testing (72). The spate of court cases involving "expert" psychological
testimony has led to the witticism that Title VII of CRA 1964 is "the psychologists'
social security act." The overriding issue is the extent to which psychological tests
and other selection criteria which have documentable adverse impact against
minority group applicants, particularly Blacks and Spanish-surname individuals,
discriminate against them unfairly—i.e. underpredict their performance on the job
or simply fail to provide a useful prediction of job performance. Significant
differences of opinion have emerged with respect to two subsidiary issues: first,
what are the criteria by which the existence of discrimination may be said to exist
(the consensus is that the fact of adverse impact itself and the finding of significant
differences in mean predictor scores are not sufficient evidence of discriminatory
impact), and second, do the data in fact support as a general proposition the
existence of differential validity?

While industrial psychologists have largely rejected the point of view that the
inferior performance of Blacks, particularly on cognitive tests, is to be expected
because of hereditary racial differences, they seem equally unwilling to embrace
the notion, advanced by Richardson & Spears (141), that the whole fault lies with
the "psychometric approach"—that Blacks are different, not deficient, that psy-
chometrics has failed to take account of cognitive style, of the social context of
testing, of the diversity of human abilities, of the importance of nutrition, of the
differences of score distributions and trait distributions. Rather, admitting that
tests and other selection criteria measure the results of deprivation and discrimination, the emphasis is placed upon the prediction of job performance. This is
the principal thrust of federal and state regulation in the area of testing: if a
plaintiff, on whom the initial burden rests, can demonstrate adverse impact, the
burden shifts to the respondent to demonstrate that the selection procedure involved is a valid predictor of job performance, and that an alternative procedure
entailing less adverse impact is not available.

Byham & Spitzer (36, 37) bring together some of the literature from *Myart vs*

Motorola to *Douglas vs Hampton* in a volume that attempts to spell out the implications for personnel management of the EEOC Guidelines on Employment Selection Procedures and the Office of Federal Contract Compliances' Order on Testing, although little reference is made to the litigation on tests in federal or state courts. Their main focus is selection practices and procedures as they relate to equal employment opportunity. The discussions of job-relatedness (validity) and of differential validity should be helpful to personnel managers whose knowledge of the technical aspects of testing is limited.

In a follow-up of an earlier analysis by Cooper & Sobol (56), the *Harvard Law Review* summarized the implications of Title VII of CRA 1964 with an analysis of more recent cases (72). Peskin (128) offers guidelines for the development of a viable equal employment opportunity program. Both law and regulation on the one hand, and social and economic pressure on the other, increasingly have been shaping personnel selection practices in advance of, and sometimes in spite of, the specific results of psychometric research on test technology. Even if it could be unequivocally demonstrated that adverse impact was the necessary result of tests of high validity and accurate prediction of job performance—such a demonstration does not yet seem to be within reach of the psychometric art—the imperatives of redress for the past and "affirmative action" in the present leave us with a sterile finding only minimally applicable to the circumstances of employment today.

Testing Guidelines

The 1966 EEOC Guidelines on Testing (92), calling for validation in the face of adverse impact and strongly endorsed by the U.S. Supreme Court in *Griggs vs Duke Power* (63), was followed in 1968 by the Office of Federal Contract Compliance with an order (124) spelling out in greater detail the requirements for test validation and incorporating the standards of test validation incorporated in the APA *Standards* (5). EEOC amplified its Guidelines in 1970 (92) to make them essentially similar to the OFCC Order. Although OFCC could cancel government contracts for noncompliance, under the original law EEOC had only limited power to intervene and practically none to initiate cases or impose sanctions. The 1972 amendments to CRA 1964 (48), however, have given EEOC substantially greater authority: to initiate cases and sue in its own behalf with its own corps of attorneys, and to extend its regulations to the public sector, with the exception only of the federal government itself. The 1972 amendments also established an Equal Employment Opportunity Coordinating Council representing the five federal agencies involved (EEOC, OFCC, U.S. Civil Service Commission, Civil Rights Division of the Department of Justice, U.S. Commission on Human Rights). Among other duties, the council was charged with developing *Uniform Guidelines on Employee Selection Procedures* to be applicable to the federal agencies involved in test litigation. The new *Guidelines* (165) probably will be issued in final form in 1974.

In addition to EEOC and OFCC, other state and federal agencies have issued regulations governing selection procedures. Probably the most extensive effort at the state level has been that of the Technical Advisory Committee on Testing in California (38). The United States Civil Service Commission (163) has published standards for governmental jurisdictions.

The history of these guidelines is a good example of the disparity between theory and application. The APA *Standards* (5, 6) set forth a professional consensus with respect to how tests should be developed and applied, but their translation into requirements in the draft of *Uniform Guidelines* has evoked widespread response and extensive debate both within and outside the profession (e.g. 118) as to whether the regulations are realistic in content and achievable in practice. OFCC, however, has published an amendment to its order incorporating that section of the *Uniform Guidelines* which deals in very specific detail with requirements for the presentation of evidence of test validity (125).

Biddle (26) provides a summary of the laws involved, the type of job, the validity evidence offered, and the awards in 50 leading public and private sector cases brought under various laws against discrimination, and the National Employment Law Project has published (64) a similar summary of 28 cases involving discrimination in the public sector. As regulations proliferate and become more specific, the only sure prediction to be made is that litigation over selection procedures will increase.

Differential Validity or Ethnic Differences in the Prediction of Job Performance

The statistical questions centering on ethnic group membership as a moderator variable in the prediction of job performance from test results is treated in a subsequent section of this review. Here we examine the evidence for or against differential validity.

The first problem involves an analysis of the criteria under which it may be said that differential validity exists at all. Boehm (29) identifies differential validity as the case in which there is a significant difference between the validity coefficients of the two ethnic groups compared and one or both coefficients are significantly different from zero, and excludes single-group validity where the obtained correlations are not significantly different. Schmidt et al (148), reanalyzing the Boehm hypothesis, conclude that single-group validity is ". . . probably illusory in nature", a function of small sample size and other characteristics of the data for the minority group. Schmidt & Hunter (150) reexamine the Cleary (49) and Thorndike (161) definitions of test bias—a test is biased if criterion prediction scores are too low, or if the test fails to select the same proportion of minority applicants that would be selected on the criterion itself or on a perfectly valid test—and conclude that the former definition is the more defensible. Humphreys (99), using a different rationale, recommends a direct comparison of correlations in the minority and majority group samples, and that "only in the event that the minority correlation is significantly lower and the confidence limits around that correlation include no useful levels of the relationship should the correlation be considered essentially zero." Cole (52) presents a model of equal opportunity for potentially successful applicants. Einhorn & Bass (69) review the general methodological considerations involved.

The data on differential validity, however, fit uncomfortably with all of the theories.

Significant differences in validity correlations are found; single validity vs zero validity coefficients are found; and perhaps most frequently (126), zero validity for both groups is found. Bass & Turner (25) report ethnic group differences in relationships among criteria of job performance, suggesting that lower predictor scores for minority groups reflected accurate performance predictions. Campbell (40) and Crooks (60), on the basis of an elaborate study of three jobs in the federal service, conclude that differential validity is an artifact of poor criterion design. Einhorn & Bass (69) address their attention to methodological considerations. Gael & Grant (82) and Grant & Bray (90) report that for telephone company jobs, although mean predictor and criterion scores differed, the regression slopes were similar, indicating that minority group examinees fared less well on *both* predictors and criteria.

The ETS study (60) is probably the most elaborate of any to date, but the use of job knowledge tests as criteria probably inflated test-criterion relationships by way of commonality of such factors as reading facility, and the authors' extrapolation to test selection in general is extremely optimistic. Federal guidelines call for separate validation for each ethnic group where feasible (e.g. enough cases are available). In the present state of the art, given the limited amount of consistent hard data available, that would seem to be the most prudent course. Even if it may be generally true that differential validity or even single-group validity is the exception rather than the rule, neither currently observed test validities nor ethnic-comparison studies provide much assurance that, in particular situations, something *like* differential validity does not exist.

Merit Systems

When vacancies in a specific job occur in the typical state, municipal, county, or other governmental unit merit system, an "examination announcement" is issued, candidates are screened for admission to examination on the basis of credentials (such as completion of high school), assembled and tested, and the names of those who "pass" are entered on a register. To fill a particular opening, the top three, top five, or some larger group defined by a referral rule, are referred to the cognizant supervisor, who chooses from among the referees.

This procedure has tended to thwart the entry of minority group members into civil service employment at two points. First, much more frequently than non-minority group members, they fail to meet the entry qualifications requirements, particularly the high school graduation requirement. Second, they fail the written tests at a much higher rate.

The most extensive challenge to these results has been mounted against police selection procedures (4, 32, 45, 46, 64, 71). Sometimes independently, sometimes jointly, selection of firemen has also been challenged (45, 51, 81).

As in the Griggs case, where the high school education requirement is imposed, no evidence is adduced as to its validity. The tests used for police selection range from homemade lists of questions to such old warhorses as Army Alpha, the WWII Army General Classification Test, the Wonderlic, and a series of tests published by the International Personnel Management Association (formerly the Public Personnel Association). Evidence of test validity has been almost universally absent in these cases, and in most of them the courts have struck down both the tests and the education requirement. Under the 1972 amendments to CRA 64, merit systems must abide by the guidelines set forth in the Griggs case. The implementation of this requirement, given the differences in ground rules as between merit system hiring and private industry hiring, constitutes a major challenge to test methodology.

Among all the cases challenging merit system selection procedures, probably the most interesting and far-reaching is Douglas vs Hampton (66), which involves a classical application of the generic intellectual aptitude concept to selection for employment. From the early 1930s until 1955, the U.S. Civil Service Commission administered a series of content-oriented tests, collectively known as the Junior Professional Assistant examinations, to qualify college graduates for entrance into specialized technical and professional positions. In 1955, the Commission introduced the Federal Service Entrance Examination, a high-level two-part test of verbal facility and numerical reasoning, as a generic measure for entry into more than 200 widely varying professional, managerial, and technical positions in federal agencies. Its generic character was also attested to by the fact that college students who took the Graduate Record Examination could offer their scores on that exam for the FSEE, until the Educational Testing Service refused to release the GRE scores on the basis that GRE was not designed or validated for occupational selection and placement. The plaintiffs in Douglas vs Hampton (66), in a class-action suit, made a plausible case of adverse impact against Blacks, and the defending U.S. Civil Service Commission has thus far largely based its case upon a technique it describes as "job analytic" validity, involving a showing that the measured verbal facility and numerical facility are required in jobs as diverse as park ranger at Yellowstone Park, baggage and customs examiner at O'Hare Airport, and human relations counselor in a big city. As this review goes to press, the U.S. Civil Service Commission (163a) has announced that it will replace the FSEE in the Fall of 1974 with a new Professional and Administrative Career Examination (PACE). The replacement exam ". . . is expected to measure more accurately an applicant's ability to perform in a given job, which in turn will result in better placement.

"All candidates will compete in a new written test which measures five abilities needed for successful performance. Each of the five parts will be weighted in relationship to the work to be done." The use by merit systems of unvalidated tests of general intellectual ability may well be drawing to an end.

The Private Sector

While particular attention has been drawn to litigation involving tests and selection procedures in the public sector, the majority of cases over the past 3 years have been in the private sector. Since the Griggs case, few respondent companies have attempted to justify the use of tests without evidence of validity. Involving a set of facts almost identical to those in Griggs, the West Georgia Power Company defended its use of tests on the basis of statistical techniques that were challenged as improper (166). The District Court decision in favor of the company was so confusing, however, that fearing the setting of unrealistic precedents, the Division of Industrial and Organizational Psychology of the American Psychological Association filed an *amicus* brief on the subject of test validation (33).

Another landmark case, notable because of the out-of-court large back-pay relief extended to the classes of individuals allegedly discriminated against, was the proceeding before the Federal Communications Commission by the EEOC against the American Telephone and Telegraph Company (153). The suit alleged both discrimination on race and on sex: that women were segregated largely into low-level telephone operator occupations, and that Blacks were excluded from higher-level maintenance jobs. At issue in the latter situation was a test battery which allegedly screened out a higher proportion of Blacks than of Whites. While the hearing delved in detail into the validity of the test battery, the settlement addressed itself to the matter of retributive pay and a revision of employment practices and goals to increase the opportunities of females and minority groups in the company, without respect to testing.

A third important case, Arrington vs Massachusetts Bay Transit Authority (9), attacked the validity of the U.S.E.S. General Aptitude Test Battery for the selection of toll collectors and bus drivers. It led to a major national research program funded by the Urban Mass Transportation Administration to develop a nondiscriminatory bus driver selection battery (20).

In these and many other cases, psychologists played adversary roles as expert witnesses, undoubtedly leaving overall the impression that the validation of selection procedures is an art with respect to which no strong professional consensus yet exists.

Females

The inclusion of sex among the categories on the basis of which discrimination was to be prohibited was introduced into CRA 64 by senators who believed that it reduced the bill to an absurdity and would lead to its defeat. History has recorded otherwise: the Senate early and women later took it seriously. Title VII has provided a major avenue of redress for alleged sex discrimination. Although enforcement efforts have been less than vigorous (130), fully one-third of the cases filed before EEOC alleging discrimination have been brought on the basis of the sex provision (146), and of 500 EEOC bias complaints active in 1973 involving institutions of higher education, 45 percent involved discrimination on the basis of sex. Astin et al (19) document *in extenso* discrimination against women in almost all aspects of American society, including employment selection and promotion. Fidell (75), in a survey inviting psychology department chairmen to evaluate potential candidates for faculty appointment, demonstrated that male and female applicants with identical credentials, offering vitas differing only in the sex-linked name of the applicant (e.g. Jeanne Smith–John Smith) would be treated differently: on the average, women were less likely to be considered for employment, and if considered would be offered lower-status positions at lower salaries than men with the same credentials. Rosen & Jerdee (144), in a study of similar design, arrived at the same findings with respect to entry management positions in industry, although to the extent to which the studies are comparable, the male-female differences in industry seemed to be smaller than those in academia.

Discrimination against women has been based primarily upon sex stereotypes, not imputed ability or test performance differences, but Arvey & Mussio (10) did find that Civil Service tests showed unfair discrimination against culturally disadvantaged females. Probably the most significant sex-discrimination case reaching settlement was the one involving AT&T (153), described above.

Professionals

Access to practice in professional occupations is a two-step process, involving the successful completion of a specified course of study in an institution of higher education leading to an appropriate professional degree, and successful passage of an examination by a state certifying agency. In the major professions—medicine, law, teaching, dentistry, pharmacy, etc—no significant challenge has yet been mounted against the educational requirement. The state-administered entry examinations, however, are increasingly becoming subject to challenge under Title VII and related laws.

The Bar

In respect to admission to the bar, challenges are now being mounted in about 19 states. Typical proceedings are those in Alabama (3), California (73), Virginia (106), and Georgia (127). With minor variations, these cases all raise three or four test selection issues: (*a*) the tests result in adverse impact—typically, 80–90 percent of white examinees pass as against 10–60 percent of Black or Spanish-surname examinees; (*b*) the system suffers from procedural discrimination—the examiner knows the race of the examinee and grades accordingly (this issue is raised in some cases only); (*c*) the tests are unreliable—typically, each question on the exam is written by one examiner who then grades all responses to that question; (*d*) the tests have no demonstrated validity against criteria of actual law practice.

In relation to the criterion problem, it is alleged that the practice of Black attorneys, centered upon disadvantaged clients, is different from that of White attorneys. The examinations, it is alleged, reflect the kind of practice (corporate law, civil suits) more typical of white attorney practice.

To date the courts of original jurisdiction have all turned back challenges to the state bar examination, but appeals courts have yet to be heard from. Psychologists have served as expert witnesses on both sides in some of these cases, and the record includes psychological analysis of the reliability and validity issues.

The Education Profession

Admission to the teaching profession is, like admission to the practice of law, conditioned upon completion of a prescribed course of education and a subsequent certification by a state agency. Particularly in states in which a dual white-black system formerly existed, a second requirement has been added typically by the state certification agency, such as (*a*) a master's degree, (*b*) a specified number of graduate credit hours, or (*c*) special examinations.

The special examinations route, however, has led to additional challenges on the basis that the examinations themselves are discriminatory on race and not job related (8, 21, 47). In *Armstead vs Starkville Municipal Separate School District* (8) the test at issue was the Graduate Record Examination. Representatives of the publisher, among others, testified that it was not designed or appropriate for teacher certification. In *Baker vs Columbus Municipal Separate School District* (21), in the process of converting from a dual segregated system to a unitary system, the district adopted a cutoff score of 1000 on the National Teachers Examination as a condition of hire or rehire. All the teachers denied reemployment on the basis of failing the test had been recommended for rehire by their supervisors on the basis of performance. Adverse impact was evident: 90 percent of white examinees passed as against only 11 percent of black examinees. Expert witnesses for both sides testified that the validity of the test as a predictor of effective teaching was unknown. The court struck down use of the test.

Little attention has yet been paid to the question of the validity of professional certification exams. As in the bar cases, it is frequently argued that the criteria of successful professional practice are so diverse and elusive as to defy practical measurement; the entrance examinations must be accepted on the basis of the expertise of the peer professionals who devise them. In the face of adverse impact against protected minority groups, however, it is clear that challenges to professional entrance and certifying examinations will increase.

Reading Ease

Reading difficulty level is an often-neglected dimension of test construction, but it may be very important in determining an individual's ability to perform on an examination. In a little-noticed paper, Campbell (39) demonstrated that reducing the reading level difficulty of tests for police increased test-performance criterion correlations. The issue of test fairness has renewed interest in the problem, particularly in merit system jurisdictions where a stipulated level of educational attainment—from none to high school graduation—is imposed to qualify for entrance to an examination. If the exam requires a level of reading comprehension substantially higher than the job specification calls for, the possibility of unfair discrimination exists. Ash (15), using the SMOG index of readability (117) found that 36 of 76 examinations for positions with specified minimum educational requirements had reading level grades significantly higher than the educational requirement, and that of 58 tests for positions (frequently labor) with no minimum educational level requirement, 25 required a comprehension level beyond high school graduation. Ash suggests that the disparity between reading difficulty of the examinations and minimum educational qualifications for the job tends to make such tests racially discriminatory, given the disparity in average educational attainment between Blacks and other minority group members on the one hand and nonminority group members on the other. Hoffman (93) compared the Flesch, Forbes-Cottle (79), and Dale-Chall methods of estimating the reading grade level of tests for tests used in the Pennsylvania State Civil Service, and concluded that the Flesch formula gave more consistent results. Of 22 tests subjected to reading ease analysis, six had reading grade levels slightly higher or higher than the job's entrance qualification.

METHODOLOGICAL DEVELOPMENTS

Topics involving methodological considerations are prominent in the literature, including moderator variable research, sequential testing in decision making, and systems approaches to personnel selection. Considerable interest has also been displayed in the application of multivariate statistical technology to problems involving selection methodology.

Multivariate Statistical Techniques

Zedeck (176) has proposed the use of a multivariate discriminant analysis procedure to identify moderator variables and has compared the results derived from this procedure with the results obtained by the use of both the univariate simple algebraic and absolute difference techniques. The discriminant function has also been employed by Lissitz & Henschke-Mason (111) in an attempt to improve the hit rate of a multiple discriminant classification procedure.

Other multivariate research has been directed toward the solution of methodological problems involving linear composite scores utilized in selection and classification. Conger & Lipshitz (55) have developed a general index of reliability, called canonical reliability, for use with profiles. In the event that empirical weights are desired and factor analysis is required, the problem of determining what components of the model are invariant across a set of populations must be faced. Bloxom (27) deals with the invariance problem by developing special cases of the factor analysis model for four selection situations.

The question of reliability has also been addressed in other forums. Most questionnaires and surveys yield data with weak scale properties and much measurement error. Gleason & Staelin (87) have derived a procedure whereby questionnaire data may be transformed to reduce the error variance and to improve the metric properties of the individual variables. Cureton et al (61) reexamine test length in relation to the standard error of measurement.

A degree of methodological cross-pollination characterizes many emerging disciplines, and selection is no exception. Of particular interest in this regard is O'Connor's (123) application of biostatistical methodology to personnel classification and turnover.

The potential advantages of a sequential testing procedure for multidimensional dichotomous classifications have been investigated by Linn, Rock & Cleary (110). When comparing sequential testing strategies with conventional procedures with respect to efficiency in making dichotomous decisions, it was found that the latter require approximately twice as many items to achieve the level of accuracy obtainable by sequential tests. Rock, Barone & Boldt (143) have developed a mathematical solution to the two-stage selection problem which requires only predictor criterion intercorrelations and selection ratio information. Theoretical solutions suggest that a considerable amount of testing time may be saved with little or no decrease in the validity of the selection procedure for various values of the selection ratios.

Mathematical Modeling

There has been only slight activity in the general area of the mathematical modeling of decision strategies in personnel selection. To facilitate the development of a computer decision simulation model, Smith (156) has analyzed and programmed thought processes used by a psychologist dealing with personnel selection and placement problems. He discusses several implications concerning test validation and general decision making. Holdsworth (94) discusses the problem of failing to meet the underlying assumptions when modeling personnel selection decisions.

Moderator Variables

Several issues in moderator variable research provided the focus for a lively and informative exchange of views. Abrahams & Alf (1) describe several methodological difficulties encountered by investigators seeking to improve prediction by identifying and using moderator variables. The types of problems described include misuse of regression equations, residual scores, and validity coefficients, as well as failure to perform a complete evaluation of the moderator's actual contribution to prediction. Dunnette (68) criticized the arguments advanced by Abrahams & Alf against both quadrant analysis and Ghiselli's 'd' technique. In addition, Dunnette suggested several modifications of moderator search techniques. Abrahams & Alf's (2) reply involved a discussion of the limitations of the quadrant analysis modification and an evaluation of Dunnette's proposed two-stage strategy for combining Ghiselli's 'd' technique with a directional strategy.

Ghiselli's (84) moderator system for two predictors has also been criticized by Velicer (168) on the grounds of general inapplicability in practical prediction situations. Conger (53) concluded that the correlations between difference scores should be near zero for successful application of Ghiselli's system. Velicer (168) has provided theoretical results as well as a practical example indicating that this correlation coefficient is usually much closer to unity. In view of this, the applied researcher is advised to examine alternative models for moderated regression.

Zedeck (177) defines several alternative concepts of moderator variables in terms of whether they lead to differential validity or lead to differential predictability, or involve moderated regression techniques. He discusses the dissimilarity of results yielded by the three approaches in terms of the types of variable employed as a moderator and in terms of certain methodological problems. He concludes that the utility of moderator variable research is limited by statistical problems, by the limited understanding of the statistical operation of moderators, and by lack of a rapid systematic approach to the identification of moderators.

The position taken by Velicer (169) with respect to the conceptualization of moderator variables differs from that taken by Zedeck in that the former conceives the moderator variable as a case of heterogeneous regression. The heterogeneous model yields several useful statistical tests of significance as well as some indications concerning the type of variables likely to be good moderators.

Bartlett & O'Leary (22) illustrate the use of a differential prediction model to moderate the effects of heterogeneous groups. In fact, they present 11 different models utilizing the interactive effect between racial groups and validity. It is not surprising that improvement of predictor utility results from separate validation on all possible groups as opposed to validation on one large heterogeneous group. Lefkowitz (107) reports on the empirical use of ethnic group as a moderator in predicting tenure.

In an attempt to stimulate thought in previously unexplored directions, Ghiselli (86) has suggested that the most important contributions of the findings with respect to the existence of the moderator effect may lie in the implications for measurement theory. Moderator research indicates that the measurable properties of human beings are interrelated in a dynamic fashion, requiring new dynamic conceptualizations about the qualitative description of human beings as distinguished from the static concepts inherent in classical measurement theory. In addition, Ghiselli (86) contends that industrial psychologists may do well to focus their attention on the uniqueness of individuals as opposed to placing an emphasis on the uniqueness of categories of individuals.

Utility of Selection Devices

The evaluation of benefit obtained from selection devices is a problem of considerable interest. Schmidt & Hoffman (149) empirically compared three methods of assessing the utility of a selection device. In an earlier study, McCornack (116) compared three predictor selection techniques in an attempt to determine an optimal technique for use in cross-validation. Gross (91) attacked the problem analytically in terms of the gain from selection, which is defined as the standardized average performance of a group of subjects selected in a future sample using a regression equation derived on an earlier sample. He derived expressions for the density function and the expected value of the gain from selection statistic and has studied them in terms of sample size, number of predictors, and the prior distribution of the multiple correlation.

In an applied study, Inskeep (100) used relatively simple statistical techniques based on existing employee records in order to identify changes in the selection process leading to a reduction in labor turnover.

Systems Approaches to Selection

Systems approaches to selection and manpower problems received a greater share of attention than in the past. Sands (147) developed the CAPER model, which provides the personnel manager with the information necessary to minimize the estimated total cost of recruiting, selecting, inducting, and training a sufficient number of persons to meet a specified quota of satisfactory personnel. Systems of employee selection have been discussed in terms of the relationship between job requirements and employee objectives by both Sledr (154) and Winicky (174).

Fleishman & Stephenson (78) developed a taxonomy to evaluate systems for describing and classifying tasks than can improve generalization of research results about human performance.

Astin (18), in discussing a manpower placement system for APA, speculates on the nature of the system's basic features. Love (112) examines the problem from the individual's perspective and suggests plans for updating current job-marketing procedures via a computerized job placement system.

Miscellaneous Statistical Issues

A number of studies related to traditional validation problems have appeared. Articles by Fossum (80) and Bryson (34) are representative of attempts to shorten tests and increase validity. Elshout & Roe (70) considered the general problem of generalizing correlational results from a sample, known to be drawn from a population whose range is restricted, to an unrestricted population. An interesting paper on the application of Jöreskog's congeneric test model to the correction for attenuation problem is provided by Werts & Linn (172).

The elusive suppressor variable also received a measure of attention. Conger & Jackson (54) note that some of the confusion surrounding it is due to the investigator's failure to distinguish between its use in the prediction of a criterion, in the measurement of a construct, and in the delineation of relationships between constructs. They also explicate, definitionally and mathematically, the nature of the suppressor variable, and show the conditions under which there are formal identities between results based upon analyses using a suppressor variable and results based upon approaches involving multiple, part, and partial correlational procedures.

The development of a selection validation model incorporating both ipsative and normative approaches has been proposed by Howell (97). The model assumes that individuals are unique, and that despite this they can be grouped into typologies, where a type has meaning only to the extent that it is useful for measurement purposes.

Studies involving the use of convergent-discriminant validation techniques were somewhat under-represented in the articles surveyed. The multitrait multimethod approach was used effectively by Campbell et al (41) in a study designed to develop and evaluate behaviorally based rating scales. An interesting finding of the study is that a modified scaled expectations procedure, which is a performance rather than an effectiveness measure, yields less method variance, less halo error, and less leniency error than a summated ratings technique which is not behaviorally anchored.

SPECIFIC SELECTION TECHNIQUES AND AREAS

This section deals primarily with four areas of current and continuing interest: assessment centers, the interview, biodata and the application form, and the prediction of proneness to theft among employment applicants.

There was the usual spate of validity studies, usually of single jobs by single predictors against single criteria. Above the mine run, Anderson & Roush (7) correlated both judgmental and output criteria against General Aptitude Test Battery (GATB) scores for 76 coil winders and found that the published strategies for GATB use were ineffective in differentiating between good and poor workers.

Corlett et al (57), on a very small sample, found the O'Connor Finger Dexterity Test and the Purdue Pegboard unreliable over time. Cory (58) found a Navy Maze Test superior to the Porteus Mazes for assessing Category IV personnel and significantly different regression lines for Black and non-Black Naval personnel.

A few positive findings were reported for typical performance measures. The Eysenck Personality Inventory seems to contribute to the prediction of pass/fail in pilot training (102). The Navy Vocational Interest Inventory, on the basis of retest scores for Navy enlisted men obtained as civilians 6 years later, showed reliability and validity paralleling that obtained for the Strong VIB (104). Schwab & Packard (152) report that job applicants, as compared with employees, did not actually seem to try to distort their responses on the Gordon Personal Profile and Personal Inventory, calling into question the applicability of distortion research to the actual employment situation.

Assessment Centers

The growth of assessment centers and the development of materials for assessment center use continued strongly over the period surveyed. Blumenfeld (28) describes the history and operation of assessment centers and discusses reasons for the research findings that show assessment center procedures are likely to yield higher validity than usual employment office procedures. Moses (119) describes the AT&T program, reporting a high degree of relationship between predictions made at an assessment center and subsequent progress in management, and also (120) an abbreviated Early Identification Assessment program designed to evaluate substantial numbers of short service employees. The results obtained are highly predictive of those yielded by the company's more extensive Personnel Assessment Center Program. The economies effected are considerable. Dodd (65) reported high correlations between assessment center predictions and later management progress at IBM, and Huck (98) compared the external (on-the-job measures) and internal (predictor to assessment ratings) validities in assessment centers. Prusa (138) discusses the problems of the assessor in the context of a more clinical approach than is found in American practice, and the kind of training likely to improve the assessor's accuracy. In a provocative and argumentative treatment of the assessment of lives, Dailey (62) attacks the ". . . old objective methods [that] have failed us morally and scientifically" and argues for a humanistic model involving a human encounter between two equals. Assessment would be based upon the natural history of the person. Assessment center managers and assessors could read the volume with profit, if only to learn more about ways of eliciting and understanding life history data.

The Interview

Interest in the interview has continued unabated, but it would be optimistic to conclude that significant advances have been made. Fear (74) published a revision of his 1958 volume on the evaluation interview. Notable particularly for the structure, directions, and guides for the interviewer, the techniques he advocates, if faithfully followed, will yield substantial data. His trait approach to analyzing applicants, however, and his profiles of traits and characteristics for a variety of industrial jobs seem to be based primarily on intuition and not particularly supported by data. The general excellence of technique could well be dissipated by unwarranted conclusions based upon a rather outmoded static trait analysis. Peskin (129) goes much further in emphasizing not data collection but complex inferences about personality dynamics that most interview research indicates is the least valid outcome of the interview process. Carlson et al (43) showed that selection interviews can be improved if they are carefully structured and interviewers are trained. Schuh (151) found that training can significantly affect the interviewer's perception of the applicant.

Corroborating a large number of earlier studies, a wide variety of factors were found to affect the interviewer's decision process. Baskett (23) found that the interviewer takes into account both cues as to the interviewee's competency and similarity of attitude between the interviewer and the interviewee; in an interview simulation, both tended to influence the interviewer's hiring recommendation and hiring salary offered. Hollmann (95) reexamined interviewer errors in processing negative and positive information. He concluded that while both negative and positive information is processed with equivalent accuracy, insufficient weight is placed on positive information. This conclusion is already well documented, although Hollmann criticizes methodological shortcomings of previous studies. The amount of job information available also influences interviewers' decisions, and particularly leads to higher inter-interviewer agreement. Langdale & Weitz (103) compared interrater reliability for interviewers who had an extensive job description with those who had only a job title. The former, presumably knowing what to look for in candidates, had far superior interrater reliability than the latter. Ledvinka (105) confirmed what a number of other studies have also shown: that there is an interaction between the race of the interviewer and the race of the interviewee. In this study, the reason given by black job seekers for leaving previous job was compared for black and white state employment service interviewers. Black interviewers elicited more reasons that involved rejection of the job by the worker or rejection of the worker by the employer than did white interviewers. Valenzi & Andrews (167) documented inter-interviewer disagreement in rating a group of 243 secretarial applicants for whom each of four interviewers received substantially a standard set of information cues. In part at least the rating differences could be attributed to differences in cue utilization. Wexley et al (173) reexamined the impact of contrast effects, and found them strongest when an average applicant was preceded by two highly qualified applicants or two low suitability applicants. It is overly simple, however, to generalize from the results of simulated interview situations with students to an actual personnel office operation. Given a set of open requisitions and line departments pressing for replacements, the pressure to fill jobs tends to be momentarily alleviated if a few obviously suitable people can be hired, but exacerbated if the office faces a string of obviously unsuitable candidates.

The employment interview is not only a data acquisition process. It is also an informational and public relations process, designed to influence suitable candidates to accept jobs. The interviewer and the interviewing organization can indeed take positive steps to achieve this end. Wanous (170) found that a realistic presentation of job content and job expectations contributes to survival in the organization. Ivancevich & Donnelly (101) found that reinforcement of a job offer by subsequent communication significantly reduced the rate at which college seniors rescinded job offer acceptances.

The interview continues to be the principal selection procedure used in business and industry. As the standards for use of more elaborate psychometric devices are raised by government regulation, it is likely that the role of the interview will increase even more. The *technology* of increasing interviewer effectiveness is reasonably well known—it involves both training and the imposition of structure via guides and rating scales—but there is little cause for optimism that precisely those organizations that give up on psychometric approaches to selection because the cost of validation is too high will be motivated to do much about improving their interview process either.

Biodata and Reference Checks

When Glennon, Albright & Owens published the *Catalog of Life History Items* (88), biodata, standardized and validated, seemed to give great promise for selection. The last 3 years, however, saw little published on the use of biodata in employment selection. One possible index of dwindling interest was the experience of the authors of the *Catalog*, who invited reports of validation studies of the items: not one study has been received. Asher (17) expresses reservations about the possibility of improving the biographical item. Roach (142) reported a substantial loss in predictive power of a previously cross-validated weighted applicant blank for predicting tenure of clerical employees, attributing the loss in efficiency to changes in labor market conditions, manpower needs, and personnel policies. Federal and state guidelines on testing also raise questions about biodata. In the first place, it may be difficult to establish job-relatedness for many items frequently used; in the second, the problem of adverse impact for minority group applicants may seriously reduce the usefulness of many items which appear to be culture-specific.

In a somewhat related kind of selection device, Carroll & Nash (44, 122) report on a forced-choice format reference check for clerical hires, which, after correction for the effects of five moderator variables (sex, longevity, job congruity, nationality, and race) yielded validities for the best subsets of items of .64 and .56 against a supervisory performance rating criterion. The reference check does seem to be a device for which the forced-choice technique is particularly appropriate.

The Detection of Proneness to Theft

In business and industries in which employees have largely unsupervised responsibility for money or merchandise (e.g. armored truck drivers, vending machine and bakery route drivers, grocery clerks, department store personnel), employee theft can be a serious source of loss or "shrinkage." Where security needs are high, many employers screen employment applicants by means of a polygraph ("lie detector") interview, but an increasing number of states have banned the pre-employment use of the polygraph. The *Reid Report* (140) is a paper and pencil test based upon the notion that if the questions are asked properly, applicants will accurately reveal their attitudes toward honesty and their own defalcations, if any. A series of studies by Ash (11, 12, 14) led to an instrument validated ($r = .6$) against verified theft history. Using a moderate cutoff score, a base-rate expectancy of dishonest employee behavior of 40 percent is reduced to 15 percent among those selected. In a somewhat related area, Weiler & Weinstein (171) demonstrated significant differences in interview behavior as between qualified persons (honest performers) and unqualified persons (dishonest performers). The old Hartshorne & May findings that honesty is situation specific may be due for qualification or revision.

CONCLUSIONS

Federal and state regulation has become a permanent aspect of personnel selection and placement, and litigation over allegedly discriminatory selection procedures is predictably going to increase. Several results seem likely. First, small organizations unable or unwilling to establish the validity of tests they use will give up the uncritical off-the-shelf use of tests—indeed, this trend is documented in several unpublished surveys. Second, the development of selection procedures on an industry-wide basis, combining small organizations and taking advantage of the economies of scale to apply advanced statistical techniques and assemble large samples, will come increasingly to the fore. This process may be noted currently in the banking industry, in the bus transportation industry, in police patrolman selection, and in national boards for professional accreditation. Third, painful though the medicine seems to be to some, legal pressure seems to be bringing to professional practice the teachings of the science in respect to standards for selection and placement.

Although there is a small continuous flow of literature on "systems approaches" to selection, the reviewers find little evidence that systems rhetoric will be translated into useful practice in the near future. We are more likely to see proliferation and application of alternatives to the old standby paper-and-pencil multiple choice instrument, such as Job Element examining, man-job matching, job-derived work sample and performance testing, and structured exercises like those now in use in assessment centers. We also expect that the assessment center itself, as a locus and procedure for assembling selection data, will be more widely replicated.

Above all, however, we do not believe that the next review will find any greater increment of change than we have over the last—and that was small. As for the longer view, the perspective of the last half century commands cautious optimism for small improvements over the next half century. But the mind of man runneth not that far.

502   ASH & KROEKER

Literature Cited

1. Abrahams, N. M., Alf, E. 1972. Pratfalls in moderator research. *J. Appl. Psychol.* 56:245–51
2. Ibid. Reply to Dunnette's Comments on Abrahams' & Alf's "Pratfalls in Moderator Research," 257–61
3. *Alabama Black Lawyers vs Board of Commissioners of the Alabama State Bar* 1972. U.S. District Court Middle District of Alabama, Northern Division. Civil Action No. 3809–N
4. *Allen vs City of Mobile* 1971. U.S. District Court Southern District, Alabama. 331 Fed. Suppl. 1134
5. American Psychological Association 1966. *Standards for Educational and Psychological Tests and Manuals.* Washington, D.C.: APA
6. American Psychological Association, American Educational Research Association, National Council on Measurement in Education 1974. *Standards for Educational and Psychological Tests.* Washington, D.C.: APA
7. Anderson, H. E., Roush, S. L. 1973. Relationships among ratings, production, efficiency, and the General Aptitude Test Battery in an industrial setting. *J. Appl. Psychol.* 58:77–82
8. *Armstead vs Starkville Municipal Separate School District* 1972. 4 FEP 864
9. *Arrington vs Massachusetts Bay Transportation Authority* 1969. 206 Fed. Suppl. 1355
10. Arvey, R. D., Mussio, S. J. 1973. Determining the existence of unfair test discrimination for female clerical workers. *Personnel Psychol.* 26:559–68
11. Ash, P. 1970. The validation of an instrument to predict the likelihood of employee theft. *Proc. 78th Ann. Conv. APA.* 579–80
12. Ash, P. 1971. Screening employment applicants for attitudes toward theft. *J. Appl. Psychol.* 55:161–64
13. Ash, P. 1971. *Guide for Selection and Placement of Employees.* Chicago: Midwest. Ind. Manage. Assoc.
14. Ash, P. 1973. Attitudes of work applicants toward theft. *Proc. 17th Int. Conv. Appl. Psychol.*, 590–91. Liege, Belgium: Editest
15. Ash, P. 1973. Reading difficulty of merit system tests. *Proc. 81st Ann. Conv. APA*, 49–50
16. Ash, P., Taylor, N., Hoel, L. 1973. The University Civil Service System of Illinois: updating a merit system. *Public Personnel Manage.* 2:456–61
17. Asher, J. J. 1972. The biographical item: can it be improved? *Personnel Psychol.* 25:251–69
18. Astin, A. W. 1972. A manpower placement system for APA. *Am. Psychol.* 27:479–81
19. Astin, H. S., Suniewick, N., Dweck, S. 1971. *Women: A Bibliography on Their Education and Careers.* Washington, D.C.: Human Services Press
20. Baehr, M. 1973. *The validation of a selection test battery for transit operators.* Mass.–MTD–8 Contract No. DOT–UT–289. Univ. Chicago, Ind. Relat. Center
21. *Baker vs Columbus Municipal Separate School District* 1971. 329 Fed. Suppl. 702
22. Bartlett, C. J., O'Leary, B. 1969. A differential prediction model to moderate the effects of heterogeneous groups in personnel selection and classification. *Personnel Psychol.* 22:1–19
23. Baskett, G. B. 1973. Interview decisions as determined by competency and attitude similarity. *J. Appl. Psychol.* 57:343–45
24. Bass, A. R. 1971. Personnel selection and evaluation. In *Management of the Urban Crisis*, ed. S. E. Seashore, R. J. McNeill. New York: Free Press
25. Bass, A. R., Turner, J. N. 1973. Ethnic group differences in relationships among criteria of job performance. *J. Appl. Psychol.* 57:101–9
26. Biddle, R. E. 1974. *Discrimination— What does it mean?* Chicago: Int. Personnel Manage. Assoc.
27. Bloxom, B. 1972. Alternative approaches to factorial invariance. *Psychometrika* 4:425–40
28. Blumenfeld, W. S. 1971. Early identification of managerial potential by means of assessment centers. *Atl. Econ. Rev.* 21(12):35–38
29. Boehm, V. B. 1972. Negro-White differences in validity of employment and training selection procedures. *J.*

Appl. Psychol. 56:33–39

30. Boyd, J. L., Shimberg, B. 1971. *Handbook of Performance Testing.* Princeton, N.J.: Educ. Test. Serv.

31. Bray, D. W., Moses, J. L. 1972. Personnel selection. *Ann. Rev. Psychol.* 23:545–76

32. *Bridgeport Guardians vs Bridgeport Civil Service Commission* 1972. U.S. District Court of Connecticut, Civil Action No. B–457

33. *Brief for the Executive Committee of the Division of Industrial and Organizational Psychology, APA as amicus curiae* 1972. Submitted in U.S.A. vs Georgia Power, U.S. Court of Appeals, 5th Circuit, No. 71–3447

34. Bryson, R. 1972. Shortening tests: Effects of method used, length, and internal consistency on correlation with total score. *Proc. Ann. Conv. APA* 7:7–8

35. Buros, I. K., Ed. 1972. *The Seventh Mental Measurements Yearbook,* Vol. 1 and 2. Highland Park, N.J.: Gryphon

36. Byham, W. C., Spitzer, M. E. 1971. Personnel testing: the law and its implications. *Personnel* Sept.-Oct.: 8–19

37. Byham, W. C., Spitzer, M. E. 1971. *The Law and Personnel Testing.* New York: Am. Manage. Assoc.

38. California State Fair Employment Practice Commission 1972. *The California Fair Employment Practice Commission Guidelines on Employee Selection.* San Francisco: Calif. State FEP Comm.

39. Campbell, B. E. 1960. Readability of written tests. *Public Personnel Rev.* 21:121–26

40. Campbell, J. T. 1973. Tests are valid for minority groups too. *Public Personnel Manage.* 2:70–73

41. Campbell, J. P., Dunnette, M. D., Arvey, R., Hellervik, L. V. 1973. The development and evaluation of behaviorally based rating scales. *J. Appl. Psychol.* 57:15–22

42. Campion, J. E. 1972. Work sampling for personnel selection. *J. Appl. Psychol.* 56:40–44

43. Carlson, R. E., Thayer, P. W., Mayfield, E. C., Peterson, D. A. 1971. Improvements in the selection interview. *Personnel J.* 50:268–75

44. Carroll, S. J., Nash, A. N. 1972. Effectiveness of a forced-choice reference check. *Personnel Admin.* 35:42–46

45. *Carter vs Gallagher* 1971. U.S. 8th Circuit Court of Appeals. 3 CCH Employment Pract. Decis. 8205

46. *Castro vs Beecher* 1972. 334 Fed. Suppl. 930

47. *Chance vs New York City Board of Examiners and Board of Education* 1972. 4 FEP 596

48. Civil Rights Act of July 2, 1964, P.L. 88–352, 42 U.S.C., 1964 Ed., effective July 2, 1965, as amended March 24, 1972, P.L. 92–261, 86 Stat. 103, Equal Employment Opportunities Act of 1972

49. Cleary, T. A. 1968. Test bias: Prediction of grades of Negro and White students in integrated colleges. *J. Educ. Meas.* 5:115–24

50. Cleff, S. H. 1972. *Matching People, Jobs, and Training.* Princeton, N.J.: Behav. Syst.

51. *Coffey vs Braddy* 1971. U.S. District Court, Florida, Northern District

52. Cole, N. S. 1972. *Bias in Selection.* ACT Res. Rep. 51

53. Conger, A. J. 1969. An analysis of Ghiselli's moderator variable. *Psychol. Rep.* 25:519–27

54. Conger, A. J., Jackson, D. N. 1972. Suppression variables, prediction, and the interpretation of psychological relationships. *Educ. Psychol. Meas.* 32: 579–99

55. Conger, A. J., Lipshitz, R. 1973. Measures of reliability for profiles and test batteries. *Psychometrika* 38:411–27

56. Cooper, G., Sobol, R. S. 1969. Seniority and testing under fair employment laws: A general approach to objective hiring and promotion. *Harvard Law Rev.* 82:1598–1677

57. Corlett, E. N., Salvendy, G., Seymour, W. D. 1971. Selecting operators for five manual tasks: a study of the O'Connor Finger Dexterity Test and the Purdue Pegboard. *Occup. Psychol.* 45:57–65

58. Cory, C. H. 1971. A comparison of the Porteus and Navy maze tests. *U.S. Naval Personnel and Train. Res. Lab. Bull. No. STB* 71–11

59. Cravens, D. W., Woodruff, R. B. 1973. An approach for determining criteria

of sales performance. *J. Appl. Psychol.* 57:242–47

60. Crooks, L. A., Ed. 1972. *An Investigation of Sources of Bias in the Prediction of Job Performance: A Six-Year Study.* Princeton, N.J.: Educ. Test. Serv.

61. Cureton, E. E. et al 1973. Length of test and standard error of measurement. *Educ. Psychol. Meas.* 33:63–68

62. Dailey, C. A. 1971. *Assessment of Lives.* San Francisco: Jossey-Bass

63. *Decision of the Supreme Court of the United States in the Case of Willis S. Griggs vs Duke Power Company* 1971. Bur. Nat. Aff. Daily Labor Rep.

64. *Discrimination in public employment: summary of recent and pending cases,* July 1972. New York: Nat. Employment Law Proj.

65. Dodd, W. E. 1971. Summary of IBM assessment validations. Symp. Validity of Assessment Centers. *79th Ann. Conv. APA*

66. *Douglas vs Hampton* 1973. On appeal from the District Court, District of Columbia, to the Circuit Court of Appeals of D.C.; No. 72–1376

67. DuBois, P. H. 1970. *A History of Psychological Testing.* Boston: Allyn & Bacon

68. Dunnette, M. D. 1972. Comments on Abrahams' & Alf's Pratfalls in Moderator Research. *J. Appl. Psychol.* 56:252–56

69. Einhorn, H. J., Bass, A. R. 1971. Methodological considerations relevant to discrimination in employment testing. *Psychol. Bull.* 75:261–69

70. Elshout, J. J., Roe, R. A. 1973. Restriction of range in the population. *Educ. Psychol. Meas.* 33:53–62

71. *Emeryville Citizens for Better Government vs Neary* 1971. U.S. District Court, Northern District, Col. Civil Action No. 71–940–WTS

72. Employment discrimination and Title VII of the Civil Rights Act of 1964. 1971. *Harvard Law Rev.* 84:1109–1316

73. *Espinosa et al vs Committee of Bar Examiners of the State Bar of California* 1972. San Francisco: Supreme Court of the State of California 22928

74. Fear, R. A. *The Evaluation Interview.* New York: McGraw-Hill

75. Fidell, L. S. 1970. Empirical verification of sex discrimination in hiring

practices in psychology. *Am. Psychol.* 25:1094–98

76. Fine, S. A., Wiley, W. W. 1971. *An Introduction to Functional Job Analysis.* Washington, D.C.: Upjohn Inst.

77. Fleishman, E. A., Bass, A. R. 1974. *Studies in Personnel and Industrial Psychology.* Homewood, Ill.: Dorsey. 3rd ed.

78. Fleishman, E. A., Stephenson, R. W. 1970. Development of a taxonomy of human performance: A review of the third year's progress. *Am. Inst. Res. Tech. Progr. Rep.* 3:1–68

79. Forbes, F. W., Cottle, W. C. 1953. New method for determining readability of standardized tests. *J. Appl. Psychol.* 37:185–90

80. Fossum, J. A. 1973. An application of techniques to shorten tests and increase validity. *J. Appl. Psychol.* 57:90–92

81. *Fowler vs Schwartzwalder* 1971. 5EDP 8062

82. Gael, S., Grant, D. L. 1972. Employment test validation for minority and non-minority telephone company service representatives. *J. Appl. Psychol.* 56:135–39

83. Ghiselli, E. E. 1966. *The Validity of Occupational Aptitude Tests.* New York: Wiley

84. Ghiselli, E. E. 1972. Comment on the use of moderator variables. *J. Appl. Psychol.* 56:270

85. Ghiselli, E. E. 1973. The validity of occupational aptitude tests. *Personnel Psychol.* 26:461–77

86. Ghiselli, E. E. 1974. Some perspectives for industrial psychology. *Am. Psychol.* 29:80–87

87. Gleason, T. C., Staelin, R. 1973. Improving the metric quality of questionnaire data. *Psychometrika* 38:393–410

88. Glennon, J. R., Albright, L. E., Owens, W. A. 1966. *A Catalog of Life History Items.* Greeneville, N.C.: Creativity Inst. Richardson Found.

89. Gordon, G. G. 1973. Letter to the Editor inre test validity. *Ind.-Organ. Psychol.* 11(1):15–18

90. Grant, D. L., Bray, D. W. 1970. Validation of employment tests for telephone company installers and repair occupations. *J. Appl. Psychol.* 54:7–14

91. Gross, A. L. 1973. Prediction in future samples studied in terms of gain from

selection. *Psychometrika* 38:151-72
92. Guidelines on Employee Selection Procedures 1970. *Fed. Regist.* 35: 12333-36
93. Hoffman, J. P. 1972. *Readability: The measurement of reading difficulty levels of Pennsylvania State Civil Service Commission written tests and test-related materials.* Harrisburg: Pennsylvania State Civil Serv. Comm.
94. Holdsworth, R. F. 1971. Mathematical models and selection decisions. *Occup. Psychol.* 45:99-109
95. Hollmann, T. D. 1972. Employment interviewers' errors in processing positive and negative information. *J. Appl. Psychol.* 56:130-34
96. Holmen, M. G., Docter, R. 1972. *Educational and Psychological Testing.* New York: Russell Sage Found.
97. Howell, M. A. 1971. Combining the ipsative and normative approaches in selection validation. *Educ. Psychol. Meas.* 31:931-33
98. Huck, J. R. 1973. Assessment centers: a review of external and internal validities. *Personnel Psychol.* 26: 191-212
99. Humphreys, L. G. 1973. Statistical definitions of test validity for minority groups. *J. Appl. Psychol.* 58:1-4
100. Inskeep, G. C. 1970. Statistically guided employee selection: An approach to the labor turnover problem. *Personnel J.* 49:15-24
101. Ivancevich, J. M., Donnelly, J. H. 1971. Job offer acceptance behavior and reinforcement. *J. Appl. Psychol.* 55:119-22
102. Jessup, G., Jessup, H. 1971. Validity of the Eysenck Personality Inventory in pilot selection. *Occup. Psychol.* 45: 111-23
103. Langdale, J. A., Weitz, J. 1973. Estimating the influence of job information on interviewer agreement. *J. Appl. Psychol.* 57:23-27
104. Lau, A. W., Abrahams, N. M. 1972. Predictive validity of vocational interests within non-professional occupations. *J. Appl. Psychol.* 56:181-83
105. Ledvinka, J. 1973. Race of employment interviewer and reasons given by black job seekers for leaving their jobs. *J. Appl. Psychol.* 58:362-64
106. *Lee et al vs Kuykendall et al* 1972. U.S. District Court for the Eastern District of Virginia, Richmond Division. Civil

Action No. 505-72-R
107. Lefkowitz, J. 1972. Differential validity: ethnic group as a moderator in predicting tenure. *Personnel Psychol.* 25:223-40
108. Lennon, R. T. 1956. Assumptions underlying the use of content validity. *Educ. Psychol. Meas.* 16:294-304
109. Lent, R. H., Aurbach, H. A., Levin, L. S. 1971. Predictors, criteria and significant results. *Personnel Psychol.* 24: 519-33
110. Linn, R. L., Rock, D. A., Cleary, T. A. 1972. Sequential testing for dichotomous decisions. *Educ. Psychol. Meas.* 32:85-96
111. Lissitz, R. W., Henschke-Mason, C. 1972. The selection of independent variables and prior probabilities as a factor influencing the accuracy of classifying individuals to existing groups. *Multivar. Behav. Res.* 7:489-97
112. Love, R. E. 1972. Getting your first job: A view from the bottom. *Am. Psychol.* 27:425-30
113. McCormick, E. J. 1959. Application of job analysis to indirect validity. *Personnel Psychol.* 12:402-12
114. McCormick, E. J. 1971. Application of a structured job analysis procedure. *Proc. 79th Ann. Conv. APA* 501-2
115. McCormick, E. J., Jeanneret, P. R., Mecham, R. C. 1972. A study of job characteristics and job dimensions as based on the Position Analysis Questionnaire (PAQ). *J. Appl. Psychol.* 56:347-68
116. McCornack, R. L. 1970. A comparison of three predictor selection techniques in multiple regression. *Psychometrika* 35:257-71
117. McLaughlin, G. H. 1969. Smog grading—a new readability formula. *J. Reading* 12:639-46
118. Melbin, M. J. 1973. Employment Report: Proposed federal guidelines on hiring could have far-reaching impact. *Nat. J. Rep.* 5(39):1429-34
119. Moses, J. L. 1972. Assessment center performance and management progress. *Stud. Personnel Psychol.* 4:7-12
120. Moses, J. L. 1973. The development of an assessment center for the early identification of supervisory potential. *Personnel Psychol.* 26:569-80
121. Mussio, S. J., Smith, M. K. 1973. *Con-*

tent Validity: A Procedural Manual. Chicago: Int. Personnel Manage. Assoc.

122. Nash, A. N., Carroll, S. J. 1970. Improving the validity of a forced-choice reference check with selected rater and job moderators. *Proc. 78th Ann. Conv. APA* 5(Pt. 2):577–78

123. O'Connor, A. G. 1971. The application of biostatistical methodology to personnel classification and turnover. *Diss. Abstr. Int.* 31:5687–88

124. Office of Federal Contract Compliance 1968. Validation of employment tests by contractors and subcontractors subject to the provisions of executive order 11246. *Fed. Regist.* 33:14392–94

125. Office of Federal Contract Compliance 1974. Employee testing and other selection procedures. *Fed. Regist.* 39: 2094–96

126. O'Leary, B. S., Farr, J. L., Bartlett, C. J. 1970. *Ethnic group membership as a moderator of job performance.* Tech. Rep. No. 1, Contract No. N00014–68–C–0341. Silver Spring, Md.: Am. Inst. Res.

127. *Perry vs Sell* 1973. U.S. District Court for the Northern District of Georgia, Atlanta Division. Civil Action No. 17688

128. Peskin, D. B. 1971. *The Building Blocks of EEO.* New York: World Publ.

129. Peskin, D. B. 1971. *Human Behavior and Employment Interviewing.* New York: Am. Manage. Assoc.

130. Petersen, G., Bryant, L. 1973. Eliminating sex discrimination: who must act? *Personnel J.* 51(8):587–91

131. Prien, E. P., Ronan, W. W. 1971. Job analysis: a review of research findings. *Personnel Psychol.* 24:371–96

132. Primoff, E. S. 1957. The J-coefficient approach to jobs and tests. *Personnel Psychol.* 10:34–40

133. Ibid 1959. Empirical validations of the J-coefficient. 12:413–18

134. Primoff, E. S. 1971. *Summary of job-element principles: Preparing a job-element standard.* Washington, D.C.: U.S. Civil Serv. Comm.

135. Primoff, E. S. 1972. *The job-element procedure in relation to employment procedures for the disadvantaged.* Washington, D.C.: U.S. Civil Serv. Comm.

136. Primoff, E. S. 1973. *Introduction to J-coefficient analysis.* Project Nos. 6B531A, 6B532A. Personnel Res. Develop. Center. Washington, D.C.: U.S. Civil Serv. Comm.

137. Primoff, E. S. 1973. *How to prepare and conduct job-element examinations.* Project No. 6B531A. Personnel Res. Develop. Center. Washington, D.C.: U.S. Civil Serv. Comm.

138. Prusa, J. 1971. The danger of subjective faults in assessments of employees. *Psychol. Ekon. Praxi* 6(2):65–71

139. Ramirez, D. A., Lotero, R. J. 1973. *Job analysis for personnel selection.* Sacramento: California State Personnel Board

140. Reid, J. E. 1967. *The Reid Report.* Chicago: Reid

141. Richardson, K., Spears, D., 1972. *Race and Intelligence: The Fallacies Behind the Race-IQ Controversy.* Baltimore: Penguin Books

142. Roach, D. E. 1971. Double cross-validation of a weighted application blank over time. *J. Appl. Psychol.* 55:157–60

143. Rock, D. A., Barone, J. L., Boldt, R. F. 1972. A two-stage decision approach to the selection problem. *Brit. J. Math. Statist. Psychol.* 25:274–82

144. Rosen, B., Jerdee, T. H. 1974. Sex stereotyping in the executive suite. *Harvard Bus. Rev.* 52(2):45–58

145. Rosenbaum, B. L. 1973. Attitude toward invasion of privacy in the personnel selection process and job applicant demographic and personality characteristics. *J. Appl. Psychol.* 58: 333–38

146. Rossi, A. S. 1970. Job discrimination and what women can do about it. *Atlantic* 225(3):99–102

147. Sands, W. A. 1973. Method for evaluating alternative recruiting selection strategies: The caper model. *J. Appl. Psychol.* 57:222–27

148. Schmidt, F. L., Berner, J. G., Hunter, J. E. 1973. Racial differences in validity of employment tests: reality or illusion? *J. Appl. Psychol.* 58:5–9

149. Schmidt, F. L., Hoffman, B. 1973. Empirical comparison of three methods of assessing utility of a selection device. *J. Ind. Organ. Psychol.* 1:13

150. Schmidt, F. L., Hunter, J. E. 1974. Racial and ethnic bias in tests: Divergent

implications of two definitions of test bias. *Am. Psychol.* 29:1–8

151. Schuh, A. J. 1971. Effects of employment interviewing training on perceptions of a job applicant. *Diss. Abstr. Int.* 32(5–B):3051

152. Schwab, D. P., Packard, G. L. 1973. Response distortion on the Gordon Personal Inventory and Gordon Personal Profile in a selection context: Some implications for predicting employee tenure. *J. Appl. Psychol.* 58: 372–74

153. Shapiro, H. D. 1973. Women on the line, men at the switchboard. *NY Times Mag.* May 20, 1973:26ff

154. Sledr, J. 1970. System of psychological employee selection. *Psychol. Ekon. Praxi* 4:218–24

155. Smith, J., Nieedzwiedz, E., Davis, M., Kniesner, C. 1973. *Handbook of Job. Proficiency Criteria.* Columbus: Ohio Dep. State Personnel

156. Smith, R. D. 1968. Heuristic simulation of psychological decision processes. *J. Appl. Psychol.* 52:325–30

157. Smolinsky, H. J. 1972. Psychological testing and selection procedures. *Personnel J.* 51:283–84

158. Taylor, V. R. 1971. *Test validity in public personnel selection.* Public Employment Pract. Bull. No. 2. Chicago: Public Personnel Assoc.

159. Tenopyr, M. L. 1972. *Selected references on employee selection with emphasis on testing the disadvantaged.* Washington, D.C.: U.S. Civil Serv. Comm.

160. Thomas, R. R. 1971. The omnipotence of work samples: a closer look. *Vocat. Eval. Work Adjust. Bull.* 4(4):10–12

161. Thorndike, R. L. 1971. Concepts of culture fairness. *J. Educ. Meas.* 8:63–70

162. Tyler, L. E. 1971. *Tests and measurements.* Englewood Cliffs, N.J.: Prentice-Hall. 2nd ed.

163. U.S. Civil Service Commission 1972. Examining, testing, standards, and employment practices. *Fed. Regist.* 37:112

163a. U.S. Civil Service Commission, June 1974. New exam. *Admin. Alert* 4 (12):2

164. U.S. Department of Labor 1972. *Handbook for Analyzing Jobs.* Washington, D.C.: GPO

165. U.S. Equal Employment Opportunity Coordinating Council 1973. *Uniform Guidelines on Employee Selection Procedures.* (Discussion draft, August 23, 1973.) Washington, D.C.: Bur. Nat. Aff. No. 859, 9/7/73

166. *U.S.A. vs Georgia Power Company* 1973. Civil No. 71–3447. U.S. Court of Appeals, Fifth Circuit

167. Valenzi, E., Andrews, I. R. 1973. Individual differences in the decision process of employment interviews. *J. Appl. Psychol.* 58:49–53

168. Velicer, W. F. 1972. Comment on the general inapplicability of Ghiselli's moderator system for two predictors. *J. Appl. Psychol.* 56:262–65

169. Ibid. The moderator variable viewed as heterogeneous regression, 266–69

170. Wanous, J. P. 1973. Effects of a realistic job preview on job acceptance, job attitudes, and job survival. *J. Appl. Psychol.* 58:327–31

171. Weiler, J., Weinstein, E. 1972. Honesty, fabrication, and the enhancement of credibility. *Sociometry* 35:316–31

172. Wekley, R. N., Yukl, G. A., Kovacs, S. Z., Sanders, R. E. 1972. Importance of contrast effects in employment interviews. *J. Appl. Psychol.* 56:45–48

173. Werts, C. E., Linn, R. L. 1972. Corrections for attenuation. *Educ. Psychol. Meas.* 32:117–27

174. Winicky, F. 1968. Selection as a process of human adjustment in work. *Arq. Bras. Psicotec.* 20:73–79

175. Wisconsin State 1972. *Selection oriented job analysis procedures. A selection system analysis and development report.* Milwaukee: State of Wis. Bur. Personnel

176. Zedeck, S. 1971. Identification of moderator variables by discriminant analysis in a multipredictable group validation model. *J. Appl. Psychol.* 55:364–71

177. Zedeck, S. 1971. Problems with the use of moderator variables. *Psychol. Bull.* 76:295–310

INDIVIDUAL PSYCHOTHERAPY AND BEHAVIOR THERAPY

§ 242

Allen E. Bergin[1]

Brigham Young University, Provo, Utah 84602

Richard M. Suinn

Colorado State University, Fort Collins, Colorado 80521

This review completes a three-part series in the *Annual Review of Psychology* under the new design for intervention in psychopathology. The first in this series appeared in 1973 under the heading Social and Community Interventions, and the second appeared in 1974 entitled Intervention Techniques: Small Groups. The present review on individual psychotherapy covers 1971 through 1973 and is the responsibility of Bergin. The material on behavior therapy covers 1970 through 1973 and is the responsibility of Suinn.

STATUS OF ACTIVITY IN THE FIELD

Previous reviewers have noted the marked increase in publications focusing on behavior therapy, and clearly this movement has an identity and an energy level in a class by itself. For this reason, it seemed appropriate in this review to devote about half of the space to an account of behavior therapy research, with the remainder being devoted to research on all other forms of individual therapy. If one takes as a standard the broad spectrum journals such as *The Journal of Abnormal Psychology* and *The Journal of Consulting and Clinical Psychology*, or the major psychiatric journals, the frequency of journal articles in these two broad areas is about equal.

OUTCOME

In outcome studies, more attention is being paid to specifying the nature of therapeutic ingredients as they relate to changes in specific problems or symptoms.

[1] The authors are indebted to the following persons who helped in a massive enterprise: Glenn Brasington, Philip Berghausen, Diana Berghausen, Jane Bever, Lori Banta, Sharee Bunker, John Collins, Davilyn Dalton, James Holley, Lois Huebner, Stephen Klein, Pam Knight, Joanne Moran, Paul Russell. This project was supported in part by a Research Division Faculty Research Fellowship, Brigham Young University.

509

In keeping with this trend, there has been a maturing of comparative studies which contrast two or more techniques and which may also consider commonalities in divergent approaches to treatment.

Comparative Studies

THE TEMPLE STUDY   Conducted by Sloane et al (316), this is probably the best comparative outcome study done to date. It involved more than 90 outpatients seen at the Temple University Health Sciences Center who were typical clinic outpatients generally similar to those described by Wolpe as "complex neurotic states." They were assigned to behavior therapy or to short-term analytically oriented psychotherapy or to a minimal treatment waiting list group. The groups receiving each treatment were matched with respect to sex and severity of symptoms but otherwise were randomly assigned. The three behavior therapists and the three analysts were well trained and highly experienced. Pretesting and posttesting utilized standard psychological tests, the target symptoms technique, a standardized interview, reports by informants who had known the patients for an average of 12 years, and ratings by the therapist, the client, and an independent assessor. In addition, tape recordings were taken of each fifth interview for the purpose of describing typical behaviors of the therapists.

At the 4-month posttesting, all three groups, including the wait list group, had significantly improved on target symptoms, but the behavior therapy (BT) and psychoanalytic therapy (PT) groups had improved significantly more than the wait (W) group. There were, however, no differences between behavior therapy and psychoanalytic therapy on any of the target symptoms as rated by an independent assessor whose knowledge of the design was kept as blind as possible. On estimates of more general functioning such as at work and in social situations, the groups also improved but did not differ from each other in amount of improvement. In rating global outcome, the independent assessor rated 80% of the BT and the PT groups as improved, whereas only 48% of the W group was improved. On general adjustment, 93% of the BT group and 77% of the PT and W groups were rated as significantly improved. All three groups were found to have maintained their improvement after one year. The general trend was for improvement to continue and for the patients in the wait group gradually to approach or equal the therapy groups. This suggests that the main effect of therapy was to accelerate change rather than to produce more change than occurs without therapy in these cases. Comparative change between BT and PT varied across different criteria with a slight trend favoring BT. There was generally an absence of deterioration effects, which is predictable in light of the competence of the therapists.

The analyses of tape recordings indicated striking similarities and differences between these two small groups of therapists. The behavior therapists were more active and directive and talked more. The two groups were equal on warmth, but the behavior therapists received higher ratings on empathy and congruence as measured by the Truax scales. Interestingly, the therapists did not differ in frequency of interpretations. Also of considerable interest was the fact that the Truax scores were unrelated to outcome, a more and more common finding which is discussed later in this review.

The psychotherapists had better outcomes with patients who were less disturbed, whereas the behavior therapists did equally well with all levels of disturbance. In addition, they tended to do particularly well with the more extroverted cases and those scoring higher on the MA, HY, and PD scales of the MMPI. This greater versatility for behavior therapy may have less to do with the BT techniques than it does with the fact that behavior therapists seemed to be more flexible than the psychotherapists and used a wider variety of techniques including psychoanalytic, client-centered, and rational-emotive ones. This may explain why the behavior therapists can handle a broader range of cases effectively. This study will undoubtedly become a landmark reference in the field and will be analyzed and debated for a long time. It is likely to be compared frequently to the Paul study (267) but is clearly superior in the sense of involving clinical cases representing a number of syndromes and treatment by experts in a natural setting.

THE DI LORETO STUDY   Di Loreto (80) compared systematic desensitization, Ellis' rational therapy, and Roger's client-centered therapy. The study involved 100 college student volunteers who reported high interpersonal anxiety and a desire for treatment. Twenty were assigned to each treatment group and an equal number to a placebo therapy group and a no-contact group, with approximately half of the subjects being introverts and half extroverts. All groups except the no-contact group were seen for 11 hours of therapy in group sessions consisting of five persons per group. The therapists were advanced graduate students who had experience in and commitment to each of the three main orientations. Evaluation included a multiple test battery and behavior observation ratings.

All three types of therapy were consistently superior to the control groups in outcome. Systematic desensitization was equally effective with introverts and extroverts, while the other treatments tended to be more effective with introverts. Although the study included elaborate experimental controls and 72 pages of statistical analyses, the results are somewhat limited by the nature of the subjects and the therapists. In addition, commentators representing the three schools of therapy each criticized the way in which their own therapy was conducted.

This study, however, does support the findings of the Temple study in that major differences in outcome as a result of different techniques were not evident. Since the phenomena and processes involved were somewhat closer to the "real thing" than in the Paul study, this adds further weight to the notion that the Paul results were not relevant to real-life problems.

OTHER COMPARATIVE STUDIES   Luborsky's (205) definitive review of more than 100 comparative studies reveals little or no difference in the effects of a wide variety of therapy techniques and emphasizes the common components in them. Roback (293), in an overlapping review, concludes that there are no significant differences between insight therapy and behavior therapy outcomes. Allen (5) examined the comparative effectiveness of desensitization and "study counseling" techniques in reducing test anxiety and increasing academic performance. The techniques were not different in outcome and were not better than a placebo. Patterson, Levene & Breger (266) compared outcomes of psychoanalytic and behavioral methods as taught to mental health trainees and found no differences between therapies at 3 months follow-up. A subsequent report (188) indicated similar results with a slight trend in favor of behavior therapy.

PSYCHOTHERAPY VERSUS BEHAVIOR THERAPY   The foregoing accounts suggest that the supposed major differences between the behavioral and traditional insight therapies are not as great as was once believed, either in outcome or process. This is particularly true for the broad cross-section of typical outpatients and is probably less true with respect to circumscribed disorders, such as special kinds of phobias, sexual disorders, etc. The earlier zeal in favor of behavior therapy with a broad class of neuroses was probably based upon misleading studies with minimally disturbed volunteers.

Behavioral methods are loaded with affective and cognitive variables of the same kind that dominate other therapies, and the esoteric techniques employed by behavioral therapists are not always crucial in producing positive outcomes. It is interesting that when asked what helped them the most, the patients in the Temple study identified the interpersonal characteristics of the therapists. Such a view is strongly supported in a separate study by Ryan & Gizynski (300). Marmor (217) provides a sophisticated analysis of the differences and commonalities between the therapies, along with a penetrating critique of the weaknesses in the behavioral position. He believes that BT makes excessive claims and is based upon many of the elements of traditional psychotherapy.

Despite obvious successes, behavior therapy is not yet a cure-all, as is indicated by Lazarus' account of where behavior therapists take their troubles (182). Of 20 behavior therapists surveyed who were in personal therapy for themselves, 10 were in psychoanalytic therapy, 5 in Gestalt therapy, 3 in bioenergetics, 4 in existential therapy, 1 in group dynamics, and not one in behavior therapy! In explaining their choices, different therapists made the following remarks: "I have decided to give the opposition a fair try." "My therapist is a beautiful human being and that means more to me than his theoretical orientation." "Let's face it, if you can afford it in terms of time and money, psychoanalysis is still the treatment of choice" (182, p. 349).

Outcomes with Specific Techniques and Patients

THE MENNINGER STUDY   Summarizing the Menninger study over the 20-year period since its inception in 1954 and the publications of results in recent years is a difficult task. Among the reports that have been published, two recent ones are of particular interest (Kernberg et al 164; Voth & Orth 349). The study included 42 adult outpatients and inpatients. The objective of the project was to investigate the relationship of personality change to patient, treatment, and situational variables.

The patients were seen in either psychoanalysis or psychoanalytically oriented psychotherapy by experienced therapists. Those in analysis were seen for an average of 835 hours and those treated by psychotherapy for 289 hours. Improvement in life adjustment appeared to occur on a number of concrete indicators such as work status and social functioning, although a number did not seem to improve on these criteria and some seemed to be worse. On the Health-Sickness Rating Scale, which was devised specifically for this study, the majority of patients improved although there was no difference in improvement between those in psychoanalysis and those in analytic psychotherapy. The absolute amount of change from pre- to posttesting was apparently significant, though ordinary outcome data are not provided. Voth & Orth (349) provide evidence of a number of failures to produce therapeutic improvement and also inadequate attempts to prevent further deterioration.

This naturalistic study provides an enormous number of correlations. These indicate that: a high level of initial ego strength is correlated with positive change regardless of type of therapy, whether psychoanalysis, expressive psychotherapy, expressive-supportive psychotherapy, or only supportive psychotherapy. The feature of ego strength most predictive of outcome was the quality of interpersonal relationships. While high ego strength provides good prognosis for all types of treatment, psychoanalysis appears to produce the most improvement in such cases. Patients with low ego strength, when treated by therapists with high skill, improved significantly more when focus on the transference was high. Also, patients with ego weakness improve better when a special treatment is provided, namely supportive-expressive treatment. Patients with a low quality of interpersonal relationships tended to do poorly regardless of type of therapy. Patients with severe ego weakness did better under an expressive approach which focused on the here and now of the transference and structuring of their life outside of treatment. Another significant finding was that the initial characteristics of the environment had no significant value as predictors of outcome. With respect to therapist skill it was found that highly skilled therapists succeed regardless of type of therapy, whereas the less skilled therapists do better with expressive therapy, perhaps because expressive therapy implies a standardized technique and does not require as much flexibility and involvement by the therapist as supportive therapy. The study also indicated that motivation for change and psychological mindedness are not necessary prerequisites for analytically oriented therapy and that the "preparation" of the patient can be achieved within the early stages of treatment.

A summary of the Kernberg (162) report has been reprinted in the *International Journal of Psychiatry* with critiques by Malan (212), Greenson (122), and May (224), and a reply by Kernberg (163). Criticisms of the study include: the fact of a highly selected patient population which biases outcome in favor of the therapy; the testing of an enormous number of hypotheses on a small number of patients; the strong reliance upon factor analyses for deducing variables for study which has been criticized by some observers as a "garbage-in and garbage-out process"; the fact that the ratings of therapist skill were not independent of knowledge of the therapists and their outcomes; and the fact that it is difficult to draw any strong conclusions about the general effectiveness of the treatment in light of the absence of an experimental design which includes control groups, etc. Over all, the study is commendable in its adherence to the clinical phenomena and its adaptation of clinical judgments to the needs of research. The correlation data have implications at least for the practice of psychoanalysis and tend to support the notion that appropriate transference resolution enhances outcome. The results, however, are not generally dramatic and cannot be shown to be better than the results of placebo therapy or other therapies; therefore, the findings of this project are interesting but have not yet been demonstrated to have a profundity commensurate with the enormous investment of time, energy, and funds over a 20-year period.

THE MALAN STUDIES   Malan (213) and colleagues at the Tavistock Clinic in London have conducted a series of outcome studies of psychoanalytically oriented therapy focusing upon assessing change via dynamic criteria which depend upon the skilled judgments of experienced clinicians. As in the Menninger study, the thesis is that meaningful results having implications for practice can only be obtained by remaining close to the complexity of live therapy and judging changes from a clear theoretical and clinical perspective. In this manner, criteria of positive change can be individually established for each case and then ratings can be made on a simple scale of improvement.

Their results indicate that both psychoanalysis and brief psychoanalytic therapy can be highly effective for a small minority of patients, although the characteristics of these specific cases is not yet entirely clear except for the importance of motivation for insight. Perhaps the most important finding, and one that has been replicated, is that the frequency with which the therapist makes transference-parent interpretations (but not other transference interpretations) is positively correlated with outcome. This holds even for brief therapy, as it did for supportive therapy in the Menninger study. Together the two studies provide renewed support for the importance of transference and its resolution in personality change, but it is still unclear when or with whom this is especially effective since many patients definitely improve without going through this process.

Evidence of the latter is shown by careful analyses of dynamically sound changes in untreated cases and in persons seen for a single interview. The value of the psychodynamic assessment criteria is seen in the fact that 69% of untreated cases appear to have improved on traditional symptomatic criteria, whereas, when examined in terms of dynamic assessment, only 26% had improved—a valuable lesson for Professor Eysenck here!

THE ROGERS-TRUAX-CARKHUFF THERAPIST FACILITATIVE CONDITIONS   One of the most popular areas of research continues to be the analysis of empathy, warmth, and therapist genuineness or congruence and other therapist behaviors as they relate to process and outcome. In recent years, a number of studies have induced skepticism concerning the potency of these variables except in highly specific, client-centered type conditions. Among recently completed studies, two indicate positive support for the notion of a relationship between empathy and outcome (256, 348). Several others failed to replicate this type of finding, including the study done at Temple and a major study (248) done on 30 patients with experienced therapists. Similar findings have been obtained by Kurtz & Grummon (174), Winborn & Rowe (364), and apparently Di Loreto (80), although his content analysis does not precisely fit the paradigm in question. It could be that a number of the negative findings on empathy etc, are due to the fact that the therapists being studied were not employing a strictly client-centered technique and thus the Truax-type scales were not applicable even though the original claim was that these variables cut across schools. Perhaps these conditions are vital to positive change, or are at least correlated with it, but are not being measured appropriately. For example, in a number of studies showing no relationship between tape-rated empathy and outcome there were quite significant correlations between *patient perceived empathy* and outcome, usually as measured by the Barrett-Lennard Relationship Inventory.

Many critical questions concerning the nature of these therapeutic conditions, as rated by the currently popular scales, have been raised by Chinsky & Rappaport (62), who carried on a debate with Truax (282, 346). They show a number of psychometric defects in the nature of the scales and question the validity of the outcome studies. They seem to have gotten the better of the argument despite some support of Truax's[2] position by Bozarth & Krauft (51). Mintz & Luborsky (247), in their major process-outcome study, measured a large variety of therapist behaviors and in a factor analysis found a first factor which they entitled "optimal empathic relationship." This variable included warmth, empathy, skill, relaxed style, spontaneity, sensitivity, and perceptiveness. Other factors included "directive mode," "patient health-distress," and "interpretive mode with receptive patient." In analyzing 4 min segments as opposed to whole sessions, they discovered similar variables with much overlap in correlation except for the empathy variable, indicating that judgments of therapist empathy based on brief segments *cannot* be generalized to whole sessions! This finding is given strong support by Gurman's study (126) in which three high-facilitative and three low-facilitative therapists were found to be extremely variable in empathy etc, both within hours and between hours. These findings may invalidate much of this program of research. Interestingly, Bachrach, Mintz & Luborsky (12) found that the Truax empathy scale correlated nearly perfectly with two other empathy scales, including Raskin's. Since the Raskin scale is easier to rate and is more relevant to a wide range of empathy, perhaps it should be used more widely.

One of the most stunning reports in this area has been provided by Mitchell et al (249) in a study of 75 expert therapists with 120 clients. Generally there was no

---

[2] We note here with sadness the regrettable and untimely death of Dr. Truax in December 1973.

relationship of empathy or warmth and outcome, even when the most and least changed clients were selected. The findings indicate that between 32 and 71% improved, depending on the criterion.

OUTCOMES OF OTHER METHODS   New therapy methods continue to be invented and evaluated, and some older methods that have received little evaluation are beginning to be tested more systematically. Trexler & Karst (345) tested rational-emotive therapy versus placebo and no-treatment effects on public speaking anxiety in 33 students in a public speaking class. Like most studies of outcome with a single technique, there was at least modest support for the effects of the therapy on some criteria compared with the control groups, but there was no comparison with any other form of therapy. The problems were mild and changes were more evident on an irrational beliefs test and self-rating of confidence as a public speaker than on a behavioral check list or an anxiety scale. Fransella (100) adapted George Kelly's theory and technique to the therapy of 20 adult stutterers and found that a majority improved, with 10 out of 16 tested at termination having reduced their dysfluencies by 50%. Of those contacted at follow-up, about half had continued to improve.

In an intriguing application of therapy to Harlow's neurotic monkeys, Suomi, Harlow & McKinney (340) provided young monkey psychiatrists for the disturbed ones. These monkey therapists engaged in clinging and play behavior with the isolate monkeys who had been separated from their mothers and were 6 months of age at the time of treatment. At 1 year the isolates had greatly improved, and at 2 years there was virtually complete recovery in monkeys whose defects were considered irreversible. The authors and inventors of "monkey psychiatry" offer the following thought: "In conclusion, we are all aware of the existence of some therapists who seem inhuman. We find it refreshing to report the discovery of nonhumans who can be therapists" (340, p. 932).

Other studies of interest include a well-advertised but artifact-ridden attempt to evaluate primal therapy (155); an extensive review (317) of outcome in brief psychotherapies; and a review (125) of the use of nonprofessionals as therapeutic agents.

Feighner (94) attempted to evaluate the Russian method of using electrosleep therapy to treat psychiatric disorders. Although about one third of the patients treated appeared to improve, nearly all relapsed within a month, and four of the more depressed patients became significantly worse.

STUDIES OF THERAPEUTIC CHANGE IN SCHIZOPHRENIA   Outcome studies with schizophrenics continue to show mixed results (see 85, 102, 253). Much of the evidence seems to be on the negative side, but an exception is the study by Karon & Vandebos (156), who found a significant effect of individual psychoanalytically oriented therapy at termination and at follow-up 2 years later. They also found that patients of experienced therapists did better in the long run.

An interesting study that has stimulated some controversy was done by Rosenhan (295) and colleagues. Eight sane people gained secret admission to 12 hospitals of diverse quality and orientation. All reported to the admitting person that they had heard voices and then, while falsifying their identities, gave accurate personal case histories that were not seriously pathological in any way. All were admitted and immediately after admission stopped simulating any symptoms and attempted to prove they were sane. All were eventually released but with a diagnosis of "schizophrenia in remission." Rosenhan appears to think that this is exceptional, but it seems to be a perfectly natural diagnosis for people who have reported having hallucinations.

In a related study, staff members were warned that during a 3-month period one or more pseudopatients would attempt to be admitted. During this period 193 patients were admitted but no pseudopatient actually tried to get in and 41 patients were believed, with high confidence by at least one staff member, to be a pseudopatient and 19 were suspected by two independent evaluators. Rosenhan presents this as evidence that is is impossible to distinguish the sane from the insane, yet the small, reliable error rate of 10% could well be an artifact of the instructions which gave the staff a set to watch for simulating. It may be that Rosenhan is correct in declaring that "the mentally ill are society's lepers," but it is hard to believe that his provocative and overstated study provides unique evidence of this. One has the feeling that his attack on hospital staffs is not new and that what is new is not true.

Persisting Issues

The question of whether therapy has any effect continues to provoke strong opinions. Rachman's book on *The Effects of Psychotherapy* (276) and a digest thereof (279) reassert the claims of Eysenck regarding (*a*) the ineffectiveness of psychoanalysis and other traditional psychotherapies; (*b*) a two-thirds spontaneous remission rate for neuroses; and (*c*) the superiority of behavioral methods of treatment. Some support is given to Truax and Carkhuff's idea of utilizing Rogerian therapist behavior as reinforcers. In addition, Rachman attacks evidence for lower spontaneous remission rates and for improvement and deterioration effects presented by Bergin, Truax, and others, viewing these findings as threats to the antipsychotherapy, probehavior therapy position. May (223) also criticizes the evidence for deterioration effects.

DETERIORATION VERSUS IMPROVEMENT   Reviews of this same literature have been produced by Malan (211) and Frank (99), both of whom conclude that the cumulative weight of evidence for deterioration (and the opposite improvement effects) is substantial despite the fact that individual studies may be open to criticism. Additional evidence appeared in a truly monumental study of encounter groups by Lieberman, Yalom & Miles (191), in which 10 to 19% of a large number of participants were considered to be worse as a result of therapy, depending upon the criteria used, and this was significantly greater than any "spontaneous" negative changes occurring among controls. Positive changes resulting from these brief but intense methods were not as great as usually occur in individual psychotherapy nor did they last as long. Using a cumulative change index, the authors estimate that 1/3 changed positively, 1/3 did not change, and 1/3 manifested negative effects, if dropping out is counted as negative. Gurman's (127) thorough review of marital therapy outcome revealed 5 to 17% deterioration in three studies and none in 8 others. Across a total of 15 studies, he found an improvement rate of 66%. The most striking new data are presented in a definitive report by Ricks (289), who studied the adult status of several disturbed adolescent boys who had been seen by two therapists in a major child guidance center. While the long-term outcomes of these two therapists was not different for less disturbed clients, there were striking differences in their therapeutic styles and outcomes with the more disturbed boys. The more successful therapist was labeled "Supershrink" by one of the boys, and Ricks retains this term in describing his techniques versus those of therapist B (whom we might call "Pseudoshrink"), most of whose cases became schizophrenic.

The weight of evidence and the views of reviewers (31, 99, 127, 211, 347) support the notion of significant improvement and deterioration effects in psychotherapy, with improvement rates averaging about 67% and deterioration rates about 10%. However, these averages obscure wide variations in figures. It should be noted here that deterioration resulting from behavior therapies has not been reported, but generally it has not been looked for.

SPONTANEOUS REMISSION   Malan (211), in his thorough and scholarly review of outcome research over the past 20 years, agreed with Bergin (31) that the Eysenck-Rachman position on spontaneous remission is weak, that Eysenck's own figures do not add up to a two-thirds spontaneous change rate, and that true rates are probably much lower than this. However, he describes Bergin's alternative figure of 30% as insecurely based and calls for properly controlled studies of the natural course of neurosis, a reasonable opinion in light of the quality of much of the evidence. Subotnik (333) reviews the relevant studies and concludes—supported by his own study (334)—that spontaneous remission is small or nonexistent (see also 191). Following Eysenck's mathematical formula for spontaneous remission, Gurman (127) noted that the rate for marital therapy should be 16% after 17.5 weeks, which was the average length of treatment, whereas the improvement rate for treated cases was 66%—quite a difference! Indeed, applying Eysenck's own formula to most controlled outcome studies shows similarly dramatic differences between experimentals and controls, which proves the opposite of what he and Rachman claim. Therapy rarely lasts 2 years, which is the amount of time the formula requires to reach a 67% improvement rate.

This recalls the fact, however, that in numerous studies large differences between treated and untreated cases at termination tend to wash out over long-term follow-up. Conceivably Frank is correct in suggesting that in many cases the effect of therapy is to accelerate or intensify change rather than to create greater absolute change than would eventually occur through "natural" healing processes. The Hopkins group (189) have found this for the second time in another long-term follow-up study. This process of accelerating change may also account for the few cases where behavior therapy outcome appears better than that of other therapies, though this potential for making equal change in shorter time (i.e. efficiency) should not be ignored.

GENERAL OUTCOME ANALYSES   Luborsky et al (203), in a thorough and penetrating review of 166 outcome studies, evaluated the factors that correlate with positive change. They found that most prognostic studies deal with patient factors. Initially sicker patients do not improve as much as the initially healthier. Schizoid trends were especially negative prognostic indicators. Motivation, anxiety, educational and social assets, and experiencing levels in early sessions all appeared as strong correlates of outcome. Therapist correlates included experience level, attitudes and interests, empathy, and similarity of patient and therapist. Technique factors included number of sessions, but not type of therapy. Unfortunately, nearly all of the change criteria in these studies were dominated by therapist ratings; thus the predictions are of mainly one kind of change and a particularly suspect one at that. Eysenck (89) criticized this paper and, repeating his mathematical formula, claimed that the changes studied by Luborsky et al were not shown to have anything to do with psychotherapy. Luborsky (201) provided an apt reply, to which we might add that those 166 studies reveal far more change per unit time following treatment than Eysenck's formula predicts for spontaneous changes. Eventually this dubious equation should be quietly buried.

The Shore & Massimo study (312) is now in its tenth year of follow-up, showing continued improvement in the treated group and continuing deterioration in most of the control cases. This study provides evidence that untreated delinquent boys tend to deteriorate much more than most neurotics, suggesting that amount of spontaneous deterioration is probably symptom specific. Rachman and Eysenck seem now to agree that spontaneous remission rates also must be symptom specific and that general rates are inappropriate, even though they do not carry the logic of this position through to its normal conclusion in their writings.

Several reviews evaluate further the general question of therapeutic effects and provide a number of stimulating suggestions (69, 173, 255, 307). In his comprehensive review, Malan (211) concludes that (a) the evidence for the effectiveness of psychotherapy is now relatively strong; (b) dynamic psychotherapy is effective in psychosomatic conditions; and (c) dynamic psychotherapy with the ordinary run of neuroses and character disorders is weak, except for a small percentage of apt clients who have strong motivation for insight and the ego strength with which to work through a strong transference relationship to successful resolution.

CRITERIA AND ASSESSMENT OF CHANGE   Outcome measurement continues to attract interest and defy clarity. Garfield, Prager & Bergin (108) reaffirm the difficulty in obtaining consensus across multiple criteria and also find further support for the notion that clients and therapists tend to rate outcome as better than observers or other more objective methods do. Fiske (97) and Luborsky (200) offer criticism and wisdom on these points and are responded to by Garfield, Prager &

Bergin (109). Berzins, Bednar & Severy (36) give a new perspective on this problem with an excellent study of 79 therapist-patient dyads evaluated on 22 measures. Their elaborate statistical treatment reveals that canonical correlations are more appropriate than factor analysis for analyzing the amount of intersource consensus in diverse measures of therapy outcome; and they show that higher agreement is obtained in this way. Mintz (245) conducted an ingenious study in which contrived cases were judged for amount of change by experts. Better prognosis patients were judged more improved even though the actual amount of change was equal across prognostic types. A subsequent experiment showed that judges value changes at higher (healthier) levels even though they are metrically smaller. Success ratings were thus influenced mainly by posttreatment level regardless of amount of change. He concludes that initially better individuals are rated as having improved more when global posttreatment outcome ratings are used; whereas the initially worse cases do better when gain scores are used, i.e. the more disturbed patients change more and the less disturbed end therapy at a healthier level, and judges value the latter more.

THERAPIST, CLIENT, AND PROCESS

Therapist Variables

THE A-B DIMENSION   Considerable activity persists on the A-B variable, but this area is plagued by ambiguities and poor studies, many of them doctoral dissertations employing analog designs. It seems increasingly likely that the A-B measures will go the way of others, such as the Fascism (F) scale developed during the authoritarian personality studies. These deceptively simple and easily scored scales attract investigators, and numerous studies are then published which later seem trivial or misleading when the real complexity of the phenomena under study becomes clear (50). Some investigators, however, are convinced that the dimension is a viable one. Berzins has produced some elegant studies, though he now has doubts about the variable. In an analog using undergraduates (84), A therapists responded with greater immediacy to schizoid statements and Bs responded similarly to neurotic statements. Studies of large numbers of professionals and nonprofessionals seem to support the idea of personality differences between As and Bs (35, 37). As score higher than Bs on inhibition, harmavoidance, and submissiveness and lower on sentience, dominance, openness and fun-loving. As tend also to score higher on feminine items and Bs higher on masculine ones. Berzins et al (39), applying the dimension to an actual treatment situation with 6 therapists and 57 clients in brief therapy with college students, found that Bs did better with neurotics than schizoids, while As unexpectedly did well with both patient types.

Bednar & Mobley (29) had experienced therapists rate working with schizophrenics and neurotics on a semantic differential and other scales. Differences between As' and Bs' ratings of these patients in terms of esteem, warmth, and liking were minimal or nonexistent. Beutler et al (40) found that As had higher empathy scores with schizophrenics than neurotics, but Bs' empathy did not differ for these different patients. No differences were noted on warmth and genuineness.

THE TRUAX AND CARKHUFF MEASURES   These methods have been discussed in the section on outcome. Empathy, warmth, etc appear to be trainable and learnable provided that a modicum of talent for interpersonal relating already exists. It is clearer now that these variables are not as prepotent as once believed; but their presence and influence is ubiquitous, even showing up strongly in behavior therapies.

OTHER VARIABLES   Henry, Sims & Spray (140) have produced the second volume of their comprehensive study of nearly 4000 practicing therapists in New York, Chicago, and Los Angeles. The authors present an endless array of data on the backgrounds, beliefs, and behaviors of this select group. Many will be interested in the fact that, on the average, therapists' sexual behavior (as self-reported) is neither precocious nor extreme. Another unexpected finding is that two thirds of the therapists refer to their colleagues in terms of function and orientation rather than profession (psychoanalyst, psychiatrist, clinical psychologist, or social worker). When rating each others' professions in terms of character styles, clinical psychologists are seen as aggressive, competitive, and overly intellectual; psychiatrists are viewed as rigid and authoritarian; and social workers are described as people-oriented and passive. When listing professions in terms of positive and negative traits, analysts are seen most positively and psychiatrists most negatively in terms of proportion of plus and minus traits. Clinical psychologists, however, are rated as having the largest absolute number of negative traits. Clinical psychologists are most negative toward psychiatrists and most positive toward analysts; whereas analysts are most negative toward clinical psychologists and seem to feel most threatened by them. In terms of love, therefore, the analysts and social workers seem to come off best.

Of 3400 therapists responding, 71% considered themselves to have some form of psychoanalytic orientation as their dominant mode, with only 13% primarily group or community oriented. Behavior therapy preference was virtually nonexistent. These data, of course, reflect one of the main defects of the report, namely, that the opinions were gathered in the middle 1960s and are probably unrepresentative of current views and practices.

Client Characteristics and Process and Outcome

Prager & Garfield (273) found little or no relationship between a variety of initial client measures and a variety of outcome indices. Critiquing this and other studies, Miller & Gross (241) argue that the relationship of initial disturbance to amount of change is curvilinear; thus, studies showing a positive relationship may have been sampled from a different portion of the disturbance distribution than studies showing a negative or zero relationship. Heilbrun (134) found that briefing clients on what to expect regarding counselor directiveness versus nondirectiveness yielded higher client satisfaction. Auerbach, Luborsky & Johnson (9) rated 47 patients on 31 variables and found quality of outcome related to (*a*) general emotional health, (*b*) intellectual achievement, (*c*) acute depression, (*d*) attractiveness, and (*e*) interviewer's global estimate of change; however, the correlations were low (.27 to .37). Rickers-Ovsiankina et al (288) found client expectations of therapy to diverge markedly from those of therapists; and Berzins & Herron (38) provide a factor analysis of therapist expectations of client role behaviors. Wilkins (360), in a hard-hitting critique of expectancy studies, asserts that expectancy is a poorly defined construct and has not been proved to influence outcome.

Additional valuable data on client characteristics is provided in the second edition of Eysenck's *Handbook of Abnormal Psychology* (90), which deals extensively with issues of classification, definition, and measurement important in establishing criteria of change.

Race, Class, and Sex

RACE   Client and therapist race has become a prominent topic of recent research, with most studies focused on black and white participants. Banks (18) found that same race client-therapist pairs yielded the highest rapport ratings and degree of self-exploration in initial interviews. Empathy levels of therapists, however, were more strongly related to client ratings of rapport than racial similarity. Cross-race pairing seemed to work better with a white therapist and black client than vice versa. Bryson & Cody (53) obtained very similar results.

W. E. Gardner (106) found that black students rated counselor's facilitative conditions as higher when race was the same, but Cimbolic (63) failed to find such a result. Williams (361) found client racial differences to be unrelated to attitude toward psychotherapy, but blacks disclosed less than whites during interviews, regardless of therapist race. Krebs (172) found no evidence of negative effects of a white hospital staff on black patients compared with whites. Similarly, Winston, Pardes & Papernik (366) found that black inpatients did as well or better than white inpatients with white therapists. L. H. Gardner (105) provides an overview of this general issue.

CLASS   Goldstein's (118) psychotherapy for the poor is one of the most elaborate and empirically rigorous attempts to adapt therapy methods to the needs of less privileged clients. He adapts the language and methods to their style, leaning heavily upon modeling, role playing, and other behavioral techniques. He has assembled an impressive array of tapes and instructions for developing interpersonal skills among these clients and also provides an outline of a para-professional training program. Mayer & Timms (228) found that working class clients preferred therapists with better interpersonal skills and a capacity to intervene directly. They disliked the more aloof, nondirective, insight-oriented types. Strupp & Bloxom (331) have developed an effective role-induction film for preparing lower class patients for group psychotherapy. Warren & Rice (352) and Lorion (196) also provide suggestions for improving methods with these clients, while Lerner & Fiske (187) show that poor prognosis for lower class clients has more to do with therapist attitudes than client attributes. Also, Lerner (186) provides a penetrating critique of therapy in the ghetto, along with substantial statistical evidence that white therapists can have significant effects on lower class blacks and severely disturbed clients.

SEX   Sex differences in outcome have not usually been found in previous years, but some investigators feel that many former studies can and should be reexamined in terms of sex role dimensions. Heilbrun's studies (133, 135) focused on undergraduate females and found that girls were more likely to defect from therapy with males to whom they had disclosed more. Riess (291) found that patients remain longer with female therapists and that female/female dyads continue treatment longer than male/male dyads, though the majority of patients prefer or request male therapists.

Process Studies

In his forward to Kiesler's (165) unique book summarizing and analyzing all of the important process analysis systems in psychotherapy research, Strupp asks: ". . . If the therapeutic force is somehow encoded in the messages, where shall we look for it?" Reading Kiesler's treatise is certainly a good place to begin the search, since each system and a critique of the research done on it is included. Regrettably, many short-lived efforts abound in this field, and process analysts are still attempting to capture new "essential" ingredients of therapy.

Matarazzo & Wiens (221) provide an excellent overview of one venerable program of research on speech interaction in dyads. Much of the data gathered since the early studies in 1954 focus on formal properties such as utterance durations, frequencies, latencies, interruptions, proportions of therapist-client talk, etc; but more recent work reveals some relationships between formal speech units and content variables. The latter is a valuable trend that needs extension into the meaningful content so prevalent in therapy interviews. Siegman & Pope (314) similarly summarize and update their long series of studies and the work of others on dyadic communication in interviews, and continue to add rigorous data (272) to this cumulative effort.

The prominent series of studies on the classic Rogerian conditions has been expanded to include a wide spectrum of presumably facilitative dimensions such as immediacy, concreteness, intimacy, confrontation. Carkhuff (56) summarizes some of this work and extends it into many areas of human need, focusing especially on the provocative idea that training clients in these therapist skills is a preferred mode of treating disorders and social deficiencies.

In a variety of process studies, Mintz et al (246) found therapists, patients, and observers able to attain moderate agreement regarding "goodness" of sessions on the Orlinsky-Howard instrument; Griest, Klein & Van Cura (123) demonstrated the value of a computerized diagnostic interview that even psychotic and suicidal patients can respond to; Lauver et al (178) show that clients can directly modify counselor speech and silence behavior; Packwood & Parker (265) reveal new methods for measuring therapist reinforcement and persuasiveness; McCarron & Appel (230) and McCarron (229) show relationships between verbal and autonomic responses during therapy sessions; Lassen (177) shows the effect of physical distance (personal space) on client openness and facility of communication (better at 6 feet); Hekmat (137) shows that reflections are better reinforcers than interpretations in a quasitherapy interview; Luborsky et al (204) provide a method for quantifying transference; and Luborsky (202) reports a careful study of momentary forgetting in psychotherapy.

CHILD THERAPY

Elaborate research programs on child psychotherapy are still not the norm, and one tends to find more data on behavioral treatments with children, perhaps because such studies are easier to do and the simplicity and manipulative nature of behavior therapies make them more readily adaptable to children. Davids (73), for example, documents improved effectiveness with psychotic children after switching from psychotherapy to behavior therapy. He also presents evidence for the effectiveness of paraprofessional college students as therapeutic models for underachieving adolescents. Miller, Barrett & Hampe (242), however, found no differences between psychotherapy and desensitization with nonpsychotic, phobic children, though both therapies were better than a control group.

Rosenthal & Levine (296) showed that brief therapy can be as effective as longer therapy for selected cases but they do not define which ones. Wright, Truax & Mitchell (371) found that therapist facilitative conditions were difficult to rate reliably in play therapy due to too much nonverbal interaction, but Siegel (313) obtained high reliabilities under similar circumstances. Schopler et al (304) found autistic children to respond better to a structured than an unstructured therapy. McConville, Brian & Purohit (231) devised a new approach to classifying children's disorders that may improve clarity and the ability to measure change. Jacob, Magnussen & Kemler (148) provide data on the long-term course of children's disorders that have been minimally or maximally treated, and show the relevance of these observations to the spontaneous remission and deterioration controversies.

Finally, Klein (167–169) has assembled comprehensive and very useful bibliographies on this subject matter totaling 1667 references through 1972, including international items and dissertations.

ISSUES AND INNOVATIONS IN METHODOLOGY

Perhaps the most important methodological trend is toward designing research that is close to the clinical phenomena while also providing objectivity and quantification not present in traditional case histories. This has been the thrust of the Menninger study which (a) produced the Health-Sickness Rating Scale, (b) applied the paired comparisons method to clinical judgments, and (c) provided the first utilization of multidimensional scalogram analysis to psychotherapy (294, 310).

Perhaps the most widespread version of this trend is the development of sophisticated single-case methodologies. Such approaches have the advantage of providing results that are most readily applicable to practice and reveal more clearly the causes of changes. Many of these methods derive from behavior therapy experiments but they have wide relevance and applicability. Gottman & Leiblum (121), Gottman (120), and Barlow & Hersen (22) provide some of the most interesting and exciting possibilities for this type of research. Additional paradigms and examples are provided by Leitenberg (185), Shontz (311), and Bergin & Strupp (32). May (225) also presents mathematical models for monitoring patterns of change over time along with further suggestions for the design of outcome assessments (226, 227). Weissman et al (357) suggest ways of quantifying the dosage and quality of psychotherapy so that inputs across cases or techniques may be equated.

Generally, the new suggestions for methodologies are most encouraging, and if followed, should yield doctoral dissertations and programatic research studies of much greater practical significance than heretofore. Some of the important trends in research and in where the likely payoffs may exist have been discussed in detail by Bergin & Strupp (32) and more than two dozen prominent researchers during an elaborate study of the status of the field and the feasibility of establishing large, collaborative studies.

BROAD SPECTRUM TREATISES

Prominent among the broad overviews of the literature and theoretical suggestions that have been published recently are the second edition of Frank's (99) important interpretation of psychotherapy phenomena; Strupp's (329) collection of his papers and summations on clinical, research, and theoretical issues; the Aldine Annuals on practice and research which presumably select the best articles for each year (216, 220); and the Bergin-Strupp (32) synthesis of the literature.

Strupp continues to develop incisive theoretical interpretations of the basic ingredients in therapeutic change (328, 330); Holt & Peterfreund (146) have initiated an important new series relating psychoanalysis and contemporary science; and Mahrer & Pearson (210) have collected creative contributions to psychotherapy with extensive commentaries by prominent workers in the field.

In general, this review has arrived at the surprising conclusion that evidence favoring behavior therapy (especially desensitization with complex cases) and the Rogerian conditions has declined while the empirical status of psychoanalytic therapy has improved. Differential effectiveness of techniques is not well established. Also, neither old nor new style groups have been shown to be superior to individual therapy. On the other hand, psychotherapies of all kinds are much more clearly established now as superior to untreated and placebo controls, though this difference in outcome appears to decline with time. This small batch of facts is of considerable import and is likely to stimulate new developments in theory and in technique experimentation.

BEHAVIOR THERAPY

The field of behavior therapy has continued to mushroom since it was reviewed by Krasner (171) in the *Annual Review of Psychology* (1971). Some attempt will be made here at a representative sampling since the field has reached such prominence, but priorities will be given to some areas because of space limitations.

Operant Conditioning

The operant approach involves the systematic use of positive consequences to shape desired behaviors. As in the past, research on this topic has continued to be among the top two in terms of sheer quantity. An enormous amount of writing involves the application of operant conditioning to a variety of clinical problems. Among the problem behaviors examined have been anorexia nervosa (41), assertive or prosocial behaviors (132), compulsions (222), incontinence (166), hysterical blindness (152), mutism (262), obesity (326), phobias (141), psychotic behaviors (131), and self-help behaviors (96, 193). Some of the procedures applied to phobias are interesting inasmuch as they offer an alternative to desensitization. Barlow et al (21) used social approval to reinforce approach behavior to a snake, and discovered the procedure to be more effective in increasing such behavior but no different from desensitization in reducing GSR measured anxiety. Shaping was found facilitated by therapist presence or by modeling. Other studies provide further insights into the use of reinforcement to deal with problem behaviors. Browning (52) discovered that a reinforcement program failed with autistic children because the learned behaviors did not generalize to new cues outside of the institution. Ravensborg (285) concluded that chronic schizophrenics increased social awareness behaviors only with the combined reinforcement of money and praise and not with praise alone. Lovaas, Litrownik & Mann (197) demonstrated that self-stimulation in autistic children is reinforcing. In a related sense, the question of what might constitute a reinforcer for autistic children was involved in a study by Steeves, Martin & Pear (323), in which they discovered that time-out itself might be a type of reinforcer for some cases.

There appears to be increasing use of paraprofessionals to conduct operant programs in clinic settings (129). Kass, Silvers & Abrams (157) utilized patients themselves, who specified one another's target behaviors and established rewards and penalties for behavioral change. Similarly, Nelson, Worell & Polsgrove (260) wrote contracts involving disturbed children as behavioral change agents for one another. These contingency contracts clearly specified the consequences of concrete behaviors for both behavioral agent and target child paired together through the contract. Paraprofessionals are not always able to conduct programs well without receiving some payoffs themselves. Thus hospital aides showed substantial changes in their use of contingency work with patients when reinforcers were also distributed to the aides themselves (158).

The use of token systems of reinforcement has become a technique in itself. Pomerleau, Bobrove & Harris (271) describe specific issues related to the establishment of a token economy ward, with attention to costs, fines, incomes. Johnson, Katz & Gelfand (150) add an important aspect to the literature in describing a rationale and training procedure for undergraduate behavior technicians. Some evidences of the success of token programs continue to be reported. Henderson & Scoles (139) report that patients from a token ward had a shorter average length of hospitalization. Hersen et al (144) recommend the use of reinforcement techniques in hospital wards to prevent young psychiatric patients from slipping into chronic hospitalization. Along with these continuing signs of successful intervention, more studies have appeared that attend to problems in implementing token programs. Allen & Magaro (4) criticize the indiscriminate establishment of token programs without attention to which types of patients would respond most favorably. They argue that some patients will emit the desired target responses even without reinforcement, some will not participate even for reinforcement, while others will participate only when tokens can be earned. They conclude that "the token economy has the most impact upon this last group" (4, p. 316).

Hall & Baker (128) summarize several potential sources of failure in token economy programs: the inability of the ward staff in some hospitals to deny acceptance of a patient with poor prognosis for success on a token system; the unwillingness of some token economy staff to use the system appropriately to shape behaviors; the low morale created if the token ward director fails to spend adequate time in supervising the ward's progress; poor support from hospital administrators in preventing turnover of ward staff; and the interference of family members in influencing patients towards relapse. Kazdin (160) adds other possible reasons for failure of a patient to respond to token systems, such as the inadequacy of back-up reinforcers, the availability of other behaviors which the patient can show to obtain reinforcement from other sources, the absence of the target behavior in the repertoire of the patient, or the conflict between ward reinforcement and peer reinforcement. Atthowe (8) adds his concern for better planning based upon more individualized program design and less reliance on mechanical interventions. Winckler (365) offers specific insights deriving from economic theory regarding the better control of reinforcers.

Desensitization

Desensitization involves breaking a stimulus-response association through the development of an incompatible response to the same stimulus. Typically the client is exposed systematically to anxiety hierarchy cues, with the incompatible response being mainly relaxation. Research on desensitization continues to appear at a high rate in the literature as it has in the past. One apparent new trend seems to be in the journals now accepting such studies. In the past, operant conditioning research seemed to be more attractive than desensitization studies to journals other than those which specialized in behavior therapy, but lately desensitization reports are appearing with greater frequency in nearly all clinical journals.

As might be expected, desensitization continues to be applied toward the treatment of phobias or specific anxieties. Reports on the treatment of fear of snakes has received such attention as to precipitate minor controversy over the heuristic value of the topic (23). A new contender for researchers' interest seems to be test anxiety. Test anxiety is being investigated as much for being a clinical problem needing resolution as for being a focus for examining the variables affecting desensitization outcomes (68, 81, 101, 250, 275). Other than such direct fears, a review of the literature does uncover some other applications of desensitization. Rimm et al (292) reduced inappropriate feelings of anger through the application of desensitization. Schnurer, Rubin & Roy (302) found increases in caloric intake in a case of anorexia nervosa treated through desensitization. Handwashing compulsions were successfully treated by Rackensperger & Feinberg (281). Depression and fatigue seemed to lift as a result of desensitization for assertiveness by Schrauger & Katkin (305). In cases where homosexuality was linked to a fear of women, heterosexual behaviors were increased following desensitization therapy by LoPiccolo (195). Marzagao (219) analyzed a case of kleptomania as involving the maintenance of such behavior through anxiety reduction; desensitization was substituted as a means of coping with anxiety, after which the stealing diminished. An anxious patient with psychotic auditory hallucinations was substantially helped in a study by Slade (315). A combination of desensitization and covert sensitization was a superior approach to reduce smoking in studies by Wagner & Bragg (350).

The delivery of desensitization treatment through automated or semiautomated procedures seems to be useful. Baker, Cohen & Saunders (13) compared therapist-directed desensitization with tape recorded treatment and found equivalent effects. Cotler (67) ran four therapist present and four tape recorded treatment groups and discovered that approach behaviors to the feared animals and subject estimates of anxiety were similar for all treatment groups. Donner (81) reported on a 5 month follow-up of automated desensitization for test anxiety and found that treatment effects were not only maintained but further gains were made during the period without symptom substitution. Therapist presence did appear to have an effect in improvement of grades. Spinelli (320) found that therapist presence or the opportunity for a relationship had no effect on symptom reduction, but did affect client satisfaction with the service. A somewhat dissenting note appears in the study of Paul & Trimble (268) in which physiological measures were compared for live relaxation training versus taped training. Taped training was found inferior except on self-report measures. From these basically promising beginnings, further methods for reducing the role of the therapist have been attempted. Beck (28) and Mann (214) utilized video tapes for the treatment of test anxiety. Denholtz (79) encouraged the use of audio tapes recorded during live treatment sessions for clients to take home for further use. Clark (64) and Phillips (270) relied upon self-administered desensitization, typically through the help of self-instructional manuals. Goldfried (112) instructed clients in how to use desensitization principles; and Russell & Sipich (299) added training in how to cue off relaxation. Lutker, Tasto & Jorgensen (206) had subjects memorize their individualized hierarchies from index cards to eliminate the necessity for the therapist to describe the scenes.

Other variations or emphases on technique variables in desensitization have been published. Suinn, Edie & Spinelli (337) massed treatment in a 2 hour time span, using only the highest anxiety hierarchy items and without use of anxiety signaling from the subjects. The success of this approach raised some questions regarding the necessity of hierarchies or repetition of lower scenes following signaling. Dua (83) examined massing effects using 12 hour, 5 day, and 15 day treatment periods and found that the two shorter term treatment periods were better than the 15 day procedure. The use of abbreviated hierarchies raises the question regarding the importance of such hierarchies. Mylar & Clement (258), dealing with public speaking anxiety, concluded that there was a low correlation between the number of hierarchy items completed and recovery. Further examination of the entire issues of anxiety hierarchies, the length of treatment, and the requirement of signaling seems desirable.

As desensitization therapy has become accepted as a mode of treatment, research has moved away from proving its worth and more towards methodological issues. One primary methodological criticism of previous research has been that related to expectancy, demand characteristics, or set. Simply, the concern is that desensitization has been shown to work, but because clients have been led to expect it would work. Thus it has been the suggestibility of the clients rather than the elements of counterconditioning which is responsible for the favorable outcomes. Lomont & Brock (194) discovered that all desensitization groups showed equivalent reduction in snake phobia regardless of whether they expected a favorable outcome or were given a rationale about the treatment. McGlynn (236) gave one group therapeutically favorable expectations, a second therapeutically unfavorable expectations, and a third instructions suggesting that the study did not involve therapy at all, and compared results against pseudotherapy and no-treatment groups. All desensitization groups showed behavioral improvements better than the two control groups. Moreover, the three treatment groups did not differ from one another, suggesting that level or nature of expectations are not influential variables. A study with conflicting findings was completed by Miller (244) using (a) a therapeutically favorable desensitization group; (b) a desensitization group with no instructional set; (c) a group with the set that the study involved imagery research rather than therapy; (d) a pseudotherapy group with favorable therapeutic instructions; and (e) a no-treatment group. Groups a and b showed greater behavioral changes than groups c, d, and e. A measure of awareness regarding the therapeutic nature of the research was found related to outcome. Miller concludes that therapeutically favorable instructions do not enhance desensitization efficacy, although misleading subjects so that they are unaware of the therapeutic intent of the procedures seems to reduce the effects of desensitization. Persley & Leventhal (269) developed groups differing on two factors: therapeutically favorable versus neutral set, and imagery paired or not paired with relaxation. Behavior approaches to a rat improved for all groups except the one involving a neutral set combined with imagery without relaxation. The therapeutically favorable instructions did not seem to substantially alter the level of fear reduction; this is consistent with the Miller results. On the other hand, imagery without relaxation was found effective when the subjects also had a therapeutically favorable set, suggesting that expectancy plays some role in behavioral change.

Another major issue raised in the literature involves the role of relaxation. One series of studies was concerned with whether relaxation was needed for desensitization; another series aimed at the effects of relaxation alone and without anxiety hierarchy imagery. Crowder & Thornton (70) had subjects imagine scenes without relaxation and discovered that this group made gains on a behavioral avoidance task equivalent to that of a standard desensitization group. Waters, McDonald & Koresko (353) also found no differences across groups in behavioral avoidance measures, but the standard desensitization group showed better improvement on subjective fear and some physiological measures. They concluded that relaxation played a limited role in desensitization. Agras et al (3) used subjects as their own control by doing a reversal type study. With a very small sample size, they found that therapeutic gains were generally maintained when relaxation was removed. Aponte & Aponte (6) attacked the issue in a slightly different fashion by rearranging the time of appearance of the relaxation responses. The standard desensitization group received the relaxation training prior to scene visualization, while the experimental group was provided with the anxiety imagery first and then trained in relaxation. Both groups fared equally well on test anxiety measures following treatment. Other researchers have worked with relaxation alone. Although earlier studies suggest that relaxation alone is less effective than desensitization, two recent ones concluded otherwise. Freeling & Shemberg (101) examined the relative contributions of relaxation alone, imagery alone, and relaxation plus imagery (standard desensitization). They found relaxation alone led to equal reductions on subjective measures of test anxiety compared to relaxation plus desensitization, with these two methods being superior to imagery alone. On the other hand, imagery was found to lead to substantial improvements on a behavioral task as compared to the other methods. Laxer & Walker (180) also studied test anxiety and concluded that relaxation alone was a successful approach.

A confounding variable which confuses attempts to clarify methodological problems such as that just reviewed has to do with criterion measures. Some of the inconsistencies across studies may well be related to differences in measures. Among the common means used to assess fear reduction are changes in self-estimations of subjective anxiety, physiological measures, or behavioral avoidance tasks. It is becoming clearer that these measures do not correlate well with one another. Ross & Proctor (298) reported a .41 correlation between subjective anxiety measures and performance on a behavior avoidance task. Mylar & Clement (258) found discrepant results regarding the effects of implosive therapy when subjective measures were compared with a behavioral measure. Wilson & Thomas (363) noted that favorable therapeutic instructions affected fear reduction as measured by subjective reports of anxiety, but not when measured by behavior avoidance tasks. Davidson & Hiebert (74) discovered a stressor film presented under varied conditions to have an effect on subjective anxiety but that the results differed with physiological measures. Riddick & Meyer (290) were able to use therapeutic instructions with a placebo pill to make it effective in reducing subjective anxiety but not physiological responses. Thus one need which faces future research is the need for standardization of criterion measures, and better understanding of the meaning of differing measures.

Aversive Conditioning

Aversive conditioning techniques typically rely upon aversive consequents as a means of modifying behaviors. Aversive procedures may involve escape learning, active avoidance learning, passive avoidance learning, or response contingent aversive stimulation (punishment) (198). A review of the literature quickly confirms that aversive treatment seems reserved for those behaviors considered to be deviant because of cultural factors or excesses. Thus, common target behaviors include excessive eating, habitual smoking, heavy consumption of alcohol, or sexually deviant activities. Indeed, Davison & Wilson (76) discovered in a survey that behavior therapists overwhelmingly select aversive therapy for homosexual problems. Over the period of this review, studies were found reporting on the treatment of eating problems (358), exhibitionism (325) and other sexual deviations (1), hallucinations (356), seizures (370), stuttering (72), and voyeurism (110). Some of the cases of deviancy were removed by a shame aversion technique. Serber (308) required the patients to perform their deviant behaviors in the presence of observers, emphasizing the embarrassing consequences of such revelation. Stevenson & Jones (325) increased the aversive experience through having staff directly discuss the patient and his deviancy. Self-administered shock was useful in reducing hallucinatory behaviors among schizophrenics to a greater degree than for a placebo group who had a shock box but received no shock (356), or a no-treatment group. However, hallucinations decreased for all groups, raising methodological questions about how the placebo influences the research.

A case report on self-induced seizures is one of the few that resulted in symptom substitution of sorts. Wright (370) eliminated self-induced seizures triggered by hand cues, but the mentally retarded client switched to eyeblinks to stimulate seizures. Another case of individual failure was reported by Kenny, Solyom & Solyom (161). Of five patients with obsessional thoughts, four showed reductions following aversive treatment. However, the remaining patient developed psychotic delusions. Some informative results were obtained by Daly & Frick (72) in understanding possible failures with stutterers. They discovered that shock administered when a stutterer expected to stutter failed to reduce stuttering; however, shock presented when stuttering occurred did lead to reduction. It may be that covert responses such as expectations are not necessarily anticipatory cues for stuttering.

A research on stridor emissions has added information to further evaluate variables involved in aversion control. Lebow, Gelfand & Dobson (184) experimented with a patient who emitted high pitched sounds by placing him on different schedules of aversive conditioning. During one experimental phase the patient was able to escape shock if he emitted less than 10 sounds within 10 seconds; in a second phase the patient escaped if less than 3 sounds were emitted in 10 seconds; in a third phase the patient was shocked after any emission. They discovered that a regular reinforcement schedule was inferior in controlling the behaviors. In addition, they noticed that the transition from one schedule to another tended to promote relapses in learning. Rosenthal (297) discovered that the application of aversive therapy based upon a traditional punishment paradigm failed with a pedophiliac. However, using aversive consequences based on a shaping paradigm was successful. The examination of data associated with prognosis is slowly reaching the literature. Evans (88) compared ten failures with ten successes in the aversive treatment of exhibitionism. Failures appeared related to frequency of masturbation, deviant fantasy, and length and frequency of exhibitionism prior to treatment; failure rate was not associated with marital status, age, educational level, frequency of masturbation or intercourse. MacCulloch, Birtles & Feldman (207) suggest that "weak-willed" and attention-seeking homosexuals are poor risks for anticipatory avoidance aversion therapy, while those with satisfactory prior heterosexual relations are good risks.

The treatment of excessive alcoholic consumption or smoking has received much attention. Based upon the relationship between blood alcohol concentration and drunken behavior, Lovibond & Caddy (199) trained patients to discriminate levels of concentration. Patients were shocked if their alcohol level went beyond .065%. Of 31 patients, 21 were able to learn to drink at the moderate level. Follow-up data appeared to show retention of the moderation. Sobell & Sobell (319) describe an intensive program for training moderation involving shock, identification of alternative behaviors, stimulus control, and video tape feedback. Patients treated through this program did substantially better than patients treated by traditional hospital treatment at discharge and 6 month follow-up. An important aspect of the research was the application of the program to investigate effects on two different target behaviors: drinking in moderation versus complete abstinence. Follow-up results indicate that patients trained in moderate drinking were as free from drunkenness as the patients trained in abstinence. Moreover, the moderate drinkers were able to participate in alcohol consumption for a larger percentage of days without excess than the patients trained in abstinence. These studies are encouraging in light of the previously held assumption that alcoholic excesses can only be dealt with by abstinence and not by controlled drinking.

The control of smoking has been notoriously resistant to change. Research has been frustrating when follow-up data are considered because of the relapse rate. Chapman, Smith & Layden (61), included therapist monitoring at follow-up periods as part of their program of shock and self-management training. They discovered that the subjects with 2 weeks of posttreatment follow-up meetings had a 75% relapse rate, while subjects with 11 weeks of follow-up had a 45% relapse rate. Schmahl, Lichtenstein & Harris (303) confirmed that different intervals of follow-up led to differential outcomes in abstinence. Their program involved aversive training with smoky air as well as high favorable expectancy instructions and social reinforcement. The expectancy factor may have been a component in the finding that a control group also showed gains. Some self-control approaches have been attempted, emphasizing covert variables. Berecz (30) used self-administered shock with one group, using the shock following imagined smoking, while another administered the shock following actual smoking. The results suggested that the covert imagery procedure was more effective for the heavy smoker, while both procedures were of value for the moderate smoker. Sex differences appeared to be present, with the results being inconclusive for female subjects. Such studies start to focus attention on covert stimuli as part of the prompts for behavioral excesses. Along this line, one final study might be mentioned briefly. Gaupp, Stern & Ratliff (110) directed the treatment of voyeurism towards words associated with the deviant behavior. Shock was administered to slides with voyeur-related words and aversion relief to slides associated with acceptable sexual behaviors. The success of this approach expands the selection of target behaviors to include semantic responses and is consistent with language behavior therapy (321) and semantic desensitization (136, 138).

Anxiety Induction Methods

FLOODING[3]   Flooding eliminates fears through forcing the patient to continuously experience anxiety in imagery or in reality. Although originally aimed at fear reduction, some recent applications have been made of flooding to obsessive-compulsive behaviors. For example, Baum & Poser (26) used the technique with a neurotic and a psychotic with success. Hodgson, Rachman & Marks (145) compared a flooding approach to others and found flooding plus modeling in vivo to be better than flooding alone, modeling alone, or relaxation alone with five obsessive-compulsives. These authors (280) added a unique concept to the literature through an appendix to their article describing patients within each group and reporting on treatment failures.

Some variations in the flooding method have been tried to improve on its usage. Dawley & Wenrich (77) designed high anxiety scenes to provide flooding to test anxious subjects in a group setting. Prochaska (275) selected the scenes on the basis of situation specific cues or psychodynamic cues. In the latter group, scenes were composed based upon the assumed dynamics of test anxiety. A third group was faced with scenes associated with general anxiety settings not related to test anxiety. Following tape recorded treatment, it was found that the use of flooding with either situational or psychodynamic cues was more effective in reducing test anxiety than the general anxiety approach, a placebo group, or a no-treatment group. However, the general anxiety group showed significant decreases in general anxiety as measured by a fear inventory. Stadter (322) examined the recommendation that encouraging clients to emit tense bodily movements during flooding

---

[3] A variety of terms have been used to refer to high intensity anxiety stimulation. *Flooding* tends to mean the evoking of high anxiety through real or imaginal stimuli, while *implosion* generally has meant the arousal through fantasy. In agreement with Marks (215), the term flooding will be used to refer generically to both techniques.

exposure would enhance the outcome. Results on rat phobics did not support the hypothesis; rather it was discovered that bodily movements plus using a toy rat to mimic scenes seemed helpful even without flooding arousal.

Further investigation of the variables influencing the outcome of flooding have revealed some interesting results. Stern & Marks (324) discovered that two hours of flooding reduced agoraphobia substantially more than four half-hour sessions. Heart rate and subjective anxiety decreased more over the second than the first hour of prolonged exposure. In a small sample of case studies, Boulougouris & Bassiakos (48) continue the discussion of prolonged implosion techniques as applied to obsessive-compulsive behaviors. Fantasy sessions lasted up to 50 min, and combined fantasy-practice sessions were run for up to 3 hours. Fazio (92) attempted to evaluate the reality-testing and supportive components of flooding separate from the anxiety induction aspect. One of the few double-blind experiments was carried through, with findings indicating the reality testing-supportive oriented treatment group subjects showed greater reductions in fear than the flooding subjects. Watson & Marks (355) compared flooding of fears expressed by the subjects (relevant) with flooding of fears irrelevant (because of being unlikely to occur, e.g. being eaten by a tiger). Both approaches led to similar reductions in the subjects' fears. However, the authors examined the data for information possibly associated with prognosis. They discovered that subjects showing high physiological reactivity at the start of treatment appeared to profit from flooding of relevant but did not profit from flooding of irrelevant scenes. High subjective anxiety subjects prior to therapy experience poor outcome with flooding of irrelevant scenes. On the other hand, subjects who reported high subjective anxiety during treatment sessions seemed to respond favorably to flooding of irrelevant scenes. A final study should be mentioned regarding the influence of expectancy on outcome. Borkovec (42) manipulated favorable therapy versus neutral nontherapy and false physiological feedback in snake phobic subjects. Results indicated that the subjects with positive expectations of improvement and false feedback showed significant reductions in avoidance measures, while the neutral plus false feedback subjects showed no effects.

The comparative effects of flooding and desensitization have received much attention because of the similarity of target behaviors treated. Mylar & Clement (258) found flooding to be equal to desensitization in the treatment of public speaking anxiety. DeMoor (78) reported the two approaches to be equivalent with snake phobia, although there was a nonsignificant trend for desensitization to be more stable at follow-up. Mealiea & Nawas (238) determined desensitization to be better than flooding, with flooding being no better than pseudotreatment on snake phobics. At follow-up desensitization continued to be the best, with flooding the worst. Hekmat (136) indicated that desensitization was better than pseudotherapy in the treatment of fear of rats. Flooding was not found to be effective. On test anxiety, Cornish & Dilley (65) found desensitization to be better when the criterion was a measure of debilitating anxiety. However, both approaches were equivalent on a physiological measure. Using grades, Smith & Nye (318) reported desensitization to be better in effecting change than flooding. Finally, Boulougouris, Marks & Marset (49) concluded that implosion was better for agoraphobia, while desensitization had better results with "specific phobias."

ANXIETY MANAGEMENT METHODS   Methods such as anxiety management training (AMT) and induced anxiety (IA) encourage clients to focus attention on anxiety arousal. However, unlike the implosion technique, the anxiety management approaches then train the clients in anxiety control. Anxiety management training is based upon the idea that anxiety can be viewed as a response as well as a stimulus. By increasing the stimulus properties and then associating the stimuli to responses incompatible to anxiety, the client learns to reduce the anxiety. Although AMT was originally designed to train coping behaviors in clients with "free-floating anxiety," early published studies were on specific anxieties. Suinn & Richardson (339) compared AMT-treated mathematics-anxious subjects with desensitization subjects and a no-problem control group. The AMT and desensitization groups both showed significant reductions in subjective anxiety, with anxiety levels reaching that of a no-problem group. Improvements in behavioral measures were also observed. Edie (86) and Nicoletti (261) studied the effects of AMT on free-floating anxiety and public speaking anxiety and discovered AMT to be beneficial when compared with no-treatment groups and no-problem control groups. Clinical observations suggested that some clients who were originally unable to specify the stimuli prompting anxiety responses were later able to identify such cues during AMT treatment. Goldfried (113) also used a method combining anxiety arousal followed by the use of relaxation as a self-control technique. Unlike AMT, Goldfried's method is a variant of desensitization and retains some of the desensitization procedures and concepts. His technique continues to rely upon the use of hierarchical scenes to prompt anxiety, although the scenes may be reduced to a single multithematic one. Whereas the AMT method was derived from a specific theoretical viewpoint and aimed at free-floating anxiety, Goldfried's variation of desensitization appears to have been developed for clinical rather than theoretical reasons. The variation overlaps enough with AMT as to be classifiable as an anxiety arousal method.

Whereas AMT stimulates anxiety arousal through directing clients to use imagery, recall of previous anxiety experiences, the induced anxiety method uses suggestion to bring forth unspecified feelings which are later shaped into affective reactions. The IA procedure also reinforces overt responses, utilizes inquiries about thoughts and feelings linked to affective states, and follows up with interpretation and discussion to promote understanding and integration. Korn, Ascough & Kleeneier (170) tested the hypothesis that IA actually aroused anxiety among subjects. Results confirm that IA led to change in state measures while not affecting trait measures. Burns & Ascough (55) basically confirmed the ability of IA to increase anxiety as measured by physiological instruments and when compared to relaxation suggestions. Bornstein & Sipprelle (47) applied IA to weight reduction. An IA group was compared with a relaxation-only group, a group receiving verbal reinforcement, and a wait list group. The IA group showed the maximum weight loss following treatment and on through a 3 and a 6 month follow-up.

Modeling

The presentation of a model is based upon the premise that behaviors may be altered through imitative learning. A variety of behaviors have been approached through modeling techniques, including moral judgments among delinquents (274, 301) and independence in neurotic and psychotic patients (117). A favored use of modeling is in the treatment of assertive behavior deficits. Unassertive psychiatric patients were trained to respond to five interpersonal conditions via models by Eisler, Hersen & Miller (87). A control group received practice in the five situations but no models to view. The model-trained patients showed significant improvement on five of eight components of assertiveness as compared to the control group and a no-treatment group. McFall & Twentyman (235) conducted a series of four experiments involving as many as 90 patients to determine the relative contributions of modeling, rehearsal, and coaching to assertive training. Behavior rehearsal seemed to be the most important variable in effecting change, with modeling adding little when combined with rehearsal. This held regardless of the media used: video versus audio only. Finally, overt and covert rehearsal appeared to be equally effective. Young, Rimm & Kennedy (373) examined the relative contribution of verbal reinforcement to the acquisition of assertive behavior. Using undergraduate women, they discovered modeling alone to significantly increase assertiveness as compared with pseudotherapy or no treatment. Reinforcement added to modeling did not appear to make a substantial contribution. Rathus (284) used video tapes with models discussing assertive behaviors and then displaying them. Subjects showed increase in assertive behaviors, but their social fears remained unchanged.

Studies have been aimed at determining the specific variables affecting the outcomes of modeling attempts. The characteristics of the model appear to have some effect. Doster & McAllister found that a high status model affected undergraduate subjects more than a peer model (82). Kazdin (159) attempted to reduce fears of snakes through the presenting of either a model who was "coping" (anxious in approach but eventually successful) or "mastering" (confident and at ease in successfully approaching the snake). Control groups included a no-model group and a no-treatment group. The modeling groups showed greater reductions in emotional arousal and anxiety ratings than the control groups. The coping model was more influential than the mastery model, suggesting the impact of model-to-client similarity. On the other hand, Bandura & Barab (17) discovered that subjects improved regardless of similarity to the model. They concluded that fear reduction for adults and children occurred for differing reasons. The mechanism associated with reduction via adult modeling was considered to be that of vicarious extinction, while the reduction via child modeling was viewed as involving motivational inducements. Jaffe & Carlson (149) had models who were calm receiving positive feedback, or anxious with positive feedback, or calm with negative feedback, or anxious with negative feedback. Test anxious subjects exposed to anxious models showed most improvement in grades, while viewing models with negative consequences seemed to lead to reductions in subjective anxiety. The authors question the validity of other researchers' reliance upon models in competent roles in treatment studies. Of final interest is the possible effect of sex differences. O'Sullivan, Gilner & Krinski (264) used male and female models to reduce snake phobia. Male subjects seemed to respond equally well to either sex models, doing better than males without modeling treatment. On the other hand, women students failed to show any gains throughout the study.

Rachman (278) concludes that modeling is facilitated by a combination of audio and visual presentations, repeated practice, prolonged exposure times, the use of multiple models, the use of multiple fear stimuli, the use of participant modeling, and the use of relaxation training. He summarizes Bandura's recommendations as involving the use of clear pretherapy instructions, repeated modeling, a progressive increase in the difficulty of modeled approaches, the use of a model similar to the observer, and the description by the model of progress. Bandura's comments regarding participatory modeling include the need for repeated practice, provision of guidance during practice, encouragement, the graduation of practice exercises, the use of feedback, the provision of favorable conditions during practice, and regular reinforcement.

Contact desensitization may be viewed as a form of participatory modeling. By this procedure, the therapist models the adaptive response, using graduated exposure to the feared object and physical assistance to aid the client in performing fear-eliciting behavior. A few studies deserve mention as attempts to identify the influence of specific variables on outcome. Lick & Bootzin (192) compared contact desensitization with a placebo group with a high expectation of success, a role-playing group asked to simulate change, and a no-treatment group. It was discovered that contact desensitization was clearly superior to the other groups, suggesting that expectancy or demand characteristics play minimal roles in this therapy procedure. Murphy & Bootzin (257) compared the use of active versus passive participation in contact desensitization. In an active mode, the child was encouraged to approach the feared snake; in the passive mode, the child had the snake brought nearer by the therapist while the child remained seated. Although stimuli were more fear eliciting in a passive mode, both procedures led to equivalent levels of fear reduction.

Other Techniques

COVERT METHODS   Covert reinforcement (COR) is based upon the assumption that mediational thought cues can serve to reinforce desired behaviors (58). Added to COR has been the related methods of covert negative reinforcement (59) and covert extinction (60). All of these methods aim at control over the presentation or removal of reinforcers through controlled fantasy. In covert sensitization, an undesirable response is eliminated through pairing fantasy of the action with aversive fantasy. Wisocki (367) used covert sensitization, covert reinforcement, and thought stopping to treat a heroin addict. Curtis & Presly (71) eliminated homosexual activities through covert sensitization, showing a reduction from a baseline of one homosexual encounter per week to none. Barlow et al (20) found covert sensitization successful in counteracting homosexual arousal to photographs despite instructions to achieve arousal. Foreyt & Hagen (98) demonstrated that overweight subjects reported decreased liking for favored foods following either covert sensitization or placebo treatment. Thus the influence of expectancy or demand characteristics is raised.

Coverant control methods are basically covert although the target behaviors for change are thoughts, fantasies, or imaginations themselves. COR and covert sensitization, on the other hand, deal with imaginations primarily as a means to alter overt behaviors. Johnson (151) and Todd (344) both used index cards with statements read by their clients, followed by a high frequency response as a reinforcer. Depressive states were reduced in both reports.

Self-management training is becoming a significant trend. The stress is on helping patients to help themselves. Self-control techniques are reviewed by Mahoney (208) and Meichenbaum (239). Self-monitoring is one such technique. McFall (233) discovered that recording resistances of the urge to smoke led to decreases in smoking, while self-monitoring of the actual frequency of smoking led to increases. Mahoney et al (209) found that continuous self-monitoring tended to maintain desired behaviors longer than intermittent self-monitoring. Gordon & Sachs concluded that "... having a S keep a daily record of his own smoking behavior is *the most active* ingredient of change ..." (italics added) (119, p. 12). Kanfer (153) suggests that self-monitoring should be viewed as involving self-reinforcement. A different perspective is provided by Logan (193), who views self-control itself as a drive or learned response which might be shaped.

ASSERTIVE TRAINING   Some of the literature has been covered in the prior section on modeling. Lazarus (183) criticizes researchers for overtraining in negative, aggressive responses in assertive training, while overlooking positive aspects. He also adds a conceptualization of assertion as involving the ability to say "no," the ability to ask for favors, the ability to express positive and negative feelings, and the ability to initiate or terminate conversations. Rathus (284) classifies assertive behaviors into nine categories, including: assertive talk, feeling talk, active disagreement, agreeing with compliments, and avoidance of justifying of opinions. Wolpe (368) through his "supervision transcripts" elaborates on training novice therapists in learning to give up control as patients learn greater assertiveness.

BEHAVIOR REHEARSAL   Behavior rehearsal employs the concept that emitting a response is a necessary step in its acquisition. When used therapeutically the rehearsal is typically achieved under controlled conditions. Hedquist & Weinhold (132) found a behavior rehearsal group to emit more assertive verbal responses than a placebo control group. McFall & Marston (234) found a nonsignificant tendency for behavior rehearsal with feedback to be better than without feedback, using an unobtrusive assertive test. Suinn (335) used visuomotor behavior rehearsal (rehearsal with controlled imagery) to help a doctoral student pass his examinations. Results involved behavioral change without reduction of anxiety. Suinn also employed visuomotor behavior rehearsal to enhance the performance of ski racers.

FEEDBACK This technique involves providing information to the subject regarding performance. Typically the feedback data are in the form of physiological information. Considerable controversy has arisen regarding the ability of false heart rate feedback to reduce fears. Borkovec (46) points to the variables of expectancy, level of fear, belief in the data, and pretesting demands as all affecting false feedback. In another light, Borkovec (43) also raises the possibility that subjects who perceive their autonomic cues accurately should be equally responsive to either desensitization or flooding therapies for fears. Inaccurate perceivers may be better candidates for flooding, while low autonomic reactors might be better for cognitive restructuring. Feedback has also been used as a direct training method for relaxation. Some form of biofeedback was used to treat pain or anxiety symptoms by Budzinski, Stoyva & Adler (54) and Raskin, Johnson & Rondestvedt (283).

MISCELLANEOUS A variety of interesting miscellaneous techniques have been reported. Marquis (218) changed sexual object choice through masturbatory fantasies. Moan & Heath (251) initiated heterosexual behavior in a homosexual through direct electrical septal stimulation. A fading technique interchanging male and female slides was used for treating homosexuality by Barlow & Agras (19) and McCrady (232). Suinn (338) used excitatory scenes to counter highway hypnosis, while tension headaches (342) and an LSD freakout (336) were controlled by relaxation training alone.

ASSESSMENT METHODS A number of approaches to facilitate behavioral assessment have been developed. These include: assertiveness scales (25, 103, 104, 284); homosexual arousal testing equipment (14); a sexual orientation measure (95); a school behavior check list (243); and imagery measures (286). A variety of instruments are also compared and discussed in the literature (34, 45, 124, 142, 306). Finally, several studies have reported on the Fear Survey Schedule (91, 179) or offered a factored version (24, 175, 240, 341, 343).

Reviews and Books

A number of valuable reviews have been published with conclusions relevant to either theory, practice, or research. Goldfried & Kent (114) discuss the predictive ability of behavioral versus traditional assessment. Davison & Wilson (75) report on research as it relates to desensitization theory and practice and also review fear reduction studies on animals as an experimental basis for desensitization (362). Wilkins (359) and Borkovec (44) both discuss the social and cognitive variables potentially involved in desensitization. Ayer (10), Morganstern (252), and Marks (215) cite the literature on flooding or implosion. Blanchard & Young (27) survey the effects of cardiac self-control studies. Rachman (278) discusses the applications of modeling. Carlson, Hersen & Eisler (57) examine trends in token economy programs. Berkowitz & Graziano (33) review the role of parents as behavioral change agents. Mahoney (208) offers recommendations regarding further research in self-control methods. Hersen, Eisler & Miller (143) summarize clinical work on assertive responses. Abramson (2) and Stunkard (332) discuss differing approaches to weight control. Hartmann (130) raises several issues within behavior modification methods with children. McNamara & MacDonough (237) comment on methodological problems facing general behavioral research. Atthowe (7) surveys a variety of contributions of behavioral techniques for intervention. Finally, Lanson & Benassi (176) offer some data on the availability of behavior modification training.

As the field of behavior therapy has expanded, so has the availability of books on the topic. This period has seen the publication of some truly important volumes aimed at scholarly overviews, such as the works of Kanfer & Phillips (154) and Yates (372), which fit in nicely with the previously published books of Bandura (15) and Franks (93). Some materials emphasizing clinical technique are also now available including the slightly expanded second edition of Wolpe's (369) book, Lazarus' writing on broad spectrum therapy (181), Watson & Tharp's unique self-modification book (354), Stuart & Davis' on control of obesity (327), Gelfand & Hartmann's on child behavior modification (111), and Liberman's (190), and Goldfried & Sprafkin's (116) on behavioral analysis and therapy. Topics of special interest include the writings of Bandura (16) on aggression, Rickard (287) on programmatic approaches, Gardner (107) on mental retardation, O'Leary & O'Leary (263) on classroom management, Feldman & MacCulloch (95) on homosexuality, Shapiro et al (309) on biofeedback, and Goldfried & Merbaum (115) on self control. In addition to the directory of the Association for the Advancement of Behavior Therapy, there is also available a directory of behavioral therapists in the United States and Canada (254).

Critique and the Future

During one early phase of preparation of this review over a thousand files on published research had been formed. Such an impressive amount of literature must surely reflect major investments of research efforts by vast numbers of behaviorists. As we conclude this review, we are struck by both positive and negative feelings. On the favorable side, it is gratifying from a *clinical* viewpoint to see the wide usage of behavior therapy techniques and the apparent continuing success of such approaches. Somehow behavior therapy continues to have a positive impact on clients even amidst the theoretical ambiguities that still surround therapeutic methods and the controversies which continue to arise. On the unfavorable side, it is highly unsatisfying from an *experimental* viewpoint to note that the field still suffers from its share of poor research designs and inconclusive results. From a clinical sense, we seem to know how to intervene successfully; but from an experimental sense, we may not be able to specify precisely or conclusively the crucial variables involved in such intervention. Our salvation, of course, is that such a dilemma may be simply inherent in the field of therapy, whether it be behavior therapy or psychotherapy, for both suffer equally.

Several important methodological issues have become evident in the behavioral research. First, clarification is needed about the discrepancies observed among differing measures. For example, behavior avoidance measures of fears do not always correlate with subjective estimates or physiological data (290, 298). One explanation is that each measure reflects different components of fear responding. Thus an improved behavioral approach score but an unchanged subject anxiety score would mean that the client had learned new overt responses but has not yet altered affective responses or covert attitudinal responses. Overt behavior change may precede or follow, but it is independent of affective, attitudinal, or cognitive change. The case of the client mentioned earlier who learned to perform adaptively in spite of anxiety (335) is an example. Another explanation is that discrepancies reflect methodological flaws in research design or in measurement. A subject might successfully undertake an anxiety-eliciting act while remaining fearful because of the demand characteristics of the experiment (269). Given the lack of clarity and consistency in outcome measures, then it is difficult to interpret outcome studies on a treatment technique where different criterion measures are used. A second methodological issue is the great need for more research relying upon standardized measures. Even the Fear Survey Schedule now has so many forms that it is difficult to know whether there is comparability of data across studies using this instrument. A third issue is the fact that several extraneous variables appear to influence outcomes and thus demand better control. Client expectations seem to be important under some conditions with some measures and for some treatments. More detailed studies are needed to specify such interactions more precisely. In passing it might be stated that methods for manipulating expectancies differ across research. "High expectancy" sometimes refers to instructions that the procedure involves simply a form of therapy, while at other times it refers to instructions that the procedure has been found to lead to symptom reduction. A fourth problem concerns the effects of modeling. To what extent are token economy or other group setting studies effective because patients observe others?

With the growing data on attentional variables, a fifth serious question can be raised regarding the effects of self-report pretesting, base-line data gathering, or even the singling out of a chronic patient to receive a new treatment. Perhaps all of these promote change solely because of the observer-attention or self-attending features. Regarding self-monitoring to obtain base lines, Gordon & Sachs accuse " . . . researchers unaware of the reactive nature of self-monitoring of being guilty of failing to set a true base-line prior to specific treatment" (119, p. 14). Self-report measures may be influenced by the reinforcing value of self-monitoring (233, 244) or the observer reliability problem. Walter & Gilmore (351) found that even though a placebo treatment group of parents accurately described no change in their children, they still answered "Yes" to the question, "Has your child improved?" Therapists are often also observer-raters in their own research; as such, they too may be faulty observers because of bias and dissonance (147). The base-line phase of research suffers potentially from the reinforcing value of attention, but may also be a problem in that there may be alterations of behaviors due to change itself regardless as to the content of the change (184). Chronic patients who have been left as hopeless may change when suddenly faced with an "enriched" therapeutic environment provided by a therapist with a new technique to try. Another confounding variable occurs from the fact that such chronic patients are often the target of a variety of treatments in their histories, and it is difficult to determine whether change is related to the new treatment or the combined results of all the experiences.

On a more global scale, after methodological changes are instituted research endeavors need to refocus attention if the field is to benefit. Instead of continuing the comparisons of treatment methods to determine whether they are equally successful on the same problem, it is time to catalog which techniques are most efficient for each of a series of problems. Instead of studying the overall effects of a given technique on patients with a common problem, it is now time to isolate the variables involved in success or failure with that technique. Failures should not be filed away as information mitigating against further use of a technique. Most modern behavior therapy methods have received basic experimental support; it is important therefore to examine negative results as they might provide guidelines for making such therapy techniques more effective. One type of information so gained might be through reanalysis based upon further empirical data; shock applied to the covert cues prior to stuttering may be found to fail, but shock applied to the overt act of stuttering may be successful (72). Another approach to profit from failure might be reanalysis with better behavioral analyses; common reinforcers might not affect an autistic child because self-stimulation is in itself a powerful reinforcer, and a greater magnitude reinforcer is needed to alter such behavior (197).

Instead of combining patients with common overt symptoms, it is time to be more precise about behavioral antecedents which would require different inter-ventions. For homosexuals, anxiety-reduction techniques might be used where heterosexual anxiety is prominent and heterosexual skills already available in the patient's repertoire (195), while anticipatory avoidance, controlled fantasy, or fading procedures might be appropriate where deviant sex object preference is the predominating feature (95, 218). The interaction between patient behavioral characteristics and treatment modality can appear in another way. Patients with high frequency desirable responses may require tokens to *maintain* these re-sponses, while patients lacking such responses in their repertoire may first require reinforcers to shape or *initiate* such responses (4). Self-modification techniques may eventually prove to be more efficient with nonhospitalized clients who al-ready have self-control behaviors in their repertoire. For others, treatment might first be aimed at shaping self-control as a learned "drive" even before attempting to train the client in self-control techniques (193).

Instead of accepting previous explanations for problems, it is time to develop better behavioral theories. Some progress is being made in such areas as behavioral analyses of aggression (16), depression (66), self-injurious behavior (11), obsessions (277), and excessive drinking (259). In the area of behavioral deficits, it is time to develop more precise behavioral definitions of the target adaptive behaviors. As an example, step-by-step behavioral objectives or behavioral sequences have been defined for assertiveness (183, 284). More work is needed regarding such definitions of various adaptive behaviors, as well as integrating training in adaptive skills into treatment packages. Removal of anxiety may permit one client to then emit available adaptive responses, but another client may require training or rehearsal of such responses. Diagnostic and prognostic indices need to be better understood. The studies of Borkovec (43) and Watson & Marks (355) are tentative but promising along these lines.

Finally, it is time to extend research for longer follow-up periods instead of limiting reports to single posttesting. Relapses and failures of transfer of learning occur only too frequently for some approaches on some problems. Research might attend more to variables associated with preventing relapse and promote generalization such as overlearning, intermittent schedules of treatment, random cueing, lengthening of exposure times, multiple modeling, introduction of covert responses in behavioral chaining, imagery rehearsal for transfer, and training in principles of self-management.

Literature Cited

1. Abel, G. C., Levis, D. J., Clancy, J. 1970. Aversion therapy applied to taped sequences of deviant behavior in exhibitionism and other sexual deviations: a preliminary report. *J. Behav. Ther. Exp. Psychiat.* 1:59–66
2. Abramson, D. H. 1972. *Some neglected issues in behavior modification with children.* Presented at 6th Assoc. Advan. Behav. Ther. New York
3. Agras, W. S. et al 1971. Relaxation in systematic desensitization. *Arch. Gen. Psychiat.* 25:511–14
4. Allen, D. J., Magaro, P. A. 1971. Measures of change in token economy programs. *Behav. Res. Ther.* 9:311–18
5. Allen, G. J. 1971. Effectiveness of study counseling and desensitization in alleviating test anxiety in college students. *J. Abnorm. Psychol.* 77:282–89
6. Aponte, J. F., Aponte, C. E. 1971. Group preprogrammed systematic desensitization without the simultaneous presentation of aversive scenes with relaxation training. *Behav. Res. Ther.* 9:337–46
7. Atthowe, J. M. Jr. 1973. Behavior innovation and persistence. *Am. Psychol.* 28:34–41

8. Atthowe, J. M. Jr. 1973. Token economies come of age. *Behav. Ther.* 4:646–54
9. Auerbach, A. H., Luborsky, L., Johnson, M. 1972. Clinicians' predictions of outcome of psychotherapy: a trial of a prognostic index. *Am. J. Psychiat.* 128:830–35
10. Ayer, W. A. 1972. Implosive therapy: a review. *Psychother. Theory Res. Pract.* 9:242–50
11. Bachman, J. A. 1972. Self-injurious behavior: a behavioral analysis. *J. Abnorm. Psychol.* 80:211–24
12. Bachrach, H., Mintz, J., Luborsky, L. 1971. On rating empathy and other psychotherapy variables. *J. Consult. Clin. Psychol.* 36:445
13. Baker, B. L., Cohen, D. C., Saunders, J. T. 1973. Self-directed desensitization for acrophobia. *Behav. Res. Ther.* 11:79–89
14. Bancroft, J. 1971. The application of psychophysiological measures to the assessment and modification of sexual behavior. *Behav. Res. Ther.* 9:119–30
15. Bandura, A. 1969. *Principles of Behavior Modification.* New York: Holt, Rinehart & Winston. 677 pp.

16. Bandura, A. 1973. *Aggression: A Social Learning Analysis*. Englewood Cliffs: Prentice-Hall. 390 pp.

17. Bandura, A., Barab, P. G. 1973. Processes governing disinhibitory effects through symbolic modeling. *J. Abnorm. Psychol.* 82:7–9

18. Banks, W. M. 1972. The differential effects of race and social class in helping. *J. Clin. Psychol.* 28:90–92

19. Barlow, D. H., Agras, W. S. 1973. Fading to increase heterosexual responsiveness in homosexuality. *J. Appl. Behav. Anal.* 6:355–66

20. Barlow, D. H., Agras, W. S., Leitenberg, H., Callahan, E. J., Moore, R. C. 1972. The contribution of therapeutic instruction to covert sensitization. *Behav. Res. Ther.* 10:411–15

21. Barlow, D. H., Agras, W. S., Leitenberg, H., Wincze, J. P. 1970. An experimental analysis of the effectiveness of "shaping" in reducing maladaptive avoidance behavior: an analogue study. *Behav. Res. Ther.* 8:165–73

22. Barlow, D. H., Hersen, M. 1973. Single-case experimental designs. *Arch. Gen. Psychiat.* 29:319–25

23. Bates, H. D. 1970. Relevance of animal-avoidance analogue studies to the treatment of clinical phobias: a rejoinder to Cooper, Furst, and Bridges. *J. Abnorm. Psychol.* 75:12–14

24. Bates, H. D. 1971. Factorial structure and MMPI correlates of a fear survey schedule in a clinical population. *Behav. Res. Ther.* 9:355–60

25. Bates, H. D., Zimmerman, S. F. 1971. Toward the development of a screening scale for assertion training. *Psychol. Rep.* 28:99–107

26. Baum, M., Poser, E. G. 1971. Comparison of flooding procedures in animals and man. *Behav. Res. Ther.* 9:249–54

27. Blanchard, E. B., Young, L. B. 1973. Self-control of cardiac functioning: a promise as yet unfulfilled. *Psychol. Bull.* 79:145–63

28. Beck, T. K. H. 1972. Videotaped scenes for desensitization of test anxiety. *J. Behav. Ther. Exp. Psychiat.* 3:195–97

29. Bednar, R. L., Mobley, M. J. 1971. A-B therapist perceptions and preferences for schizophrenic and psychoneurotic clients. *J. Abnorm. Psychol.* 78:192–97

30. Berecz, J. 1972. Modification of smoking behavior through self-administered punishment of imagined behavior: a new approach to aversion therapy. *J. Consult. Clin. Psychol.* 38:244–50

31. Bergin, A. E. 1971. The evalutaion of therapeutic outcomes. In *Handbook of Psychotherapy and Behavior Change*, ed. A. E. Bergin, S. L. Garfield, 217–70. New York: Wiley. 957 pp.

32. Bergin, A. E., Strupp, H. H. 1972. *Changing Frontiers in the Science of Psychotherapy*. Chicago: Aldine. 468 pp.

33. Berkowitz, B. P., Graziano, A. M. 1972. Training parents as behavior therapists: A review. *Behav. Res. Ther.* 10:297–317

34. Bernstein, D. A., Nietzel, M. T. 1973. Procedural variations in behavioral avoidance tests. *J. Consult. Clin. Psychol.* 41:165–74

35. Berzins, J. I., Barnes, D. F., Cohen, D. I., Ross, W. F. 1971. Reappraisal of the A-B therapist "type" distinction in terms of the personality research form. *J. Consult. Clin. Psychol.* 36:360–69

36. Berzins, J. I., Bednar, R. L., Severy, L. J. 1974. The problem of intersource consensus in measuring therapeutic outcomes. *J. Abnorm. Psychol.* In press

37. Berzins, J. I., Dove, J. L. Ross, W. F. 1972. Cross-validational studies of the personality correlates of the A-B therapist "type" distinction among professionals and non-professionals. *J. Consult. Clin. Psychol.* 39:388–95

38. Berzins, J. I., Herron, E. W. 1971. Patient's role behaviors as seen by therapists: a factor-analytic study. *Psychother. Theory Res. Pract.* 8:127–30

39. Berzins, J. I., Ross, W. F., Friedman, W. H. 1972. A-B therapist distinction, patient diagnosis, and outcome of brief psychotherapy in a college clinic. *J. Consult. Clin. Psychol.* 38:321–37

40. Beutler, L. E., Johnson, D. T., Neville, C. W., Workman, S. N., Elkins, D. 1973. The A-B therapy type distinction, accurate empathy, nonpossessive warmth, and therapist genuineness in psychotherapy. *J. Abnorm. Psychol.* 82:273–77

41. Bianco, F. J. 1972. Rapid treatment of two cases of anorexia nervosa. *J. Behav. Ther. Exp. Psychiat.* 3:223–24

42. Borkovec, T. D. 1972. Effects of expectancy on the outcome of systematic desensitization and implosive treatments for analogue anxiety. *Behav. Ther.* 3:29-40

43. Ibid 1973. The effects of instructional suggestion and psychological cues on analogue fear. 4:185-92

44. Ibid. The role of expectancy and physiological feedback in fear research: a review with special reference to subject characteristics, 491-505

45. Borkovec, T. D., Craighead, W. E. 1971. The comparison of two methods of assessing fear and avoidance behavior. *Behav. Res. Ther.* 9:285-91

46. Borkovec, T. D., Glasgow, R. E. 1973. Boundary conditions of false heart-rate feedback effects on avoidance behavior: a resolution of discrepant results. *Behav. Res. Ther.* 11:171-77

47. Bornstein, P. H., Sipprelle, C. N. 1973. Group treatment of obesity by induced anxiety. *Behav. Res. Ther.* 11:339-41

48. Boulougouris, J. C., Bassiakos, L. 1973. Prolonged flooding in cases with obsessive-compulsive neurosis. *Behav. Res. Ther.* 11:227-31

49. Boulougouris, J. C., Marks, I. M., Marset, P. 1971. Superiority of flooding (implosion) to desensitization for reducing pathological fear. *Behav. Res. Ther.* 9:7-16

50. Bowden, C. I., Endicott, J., Spitzer, R. L. 1972. A-B therapist variable and psychotherapeutic outcome. *J. Nerv. Ment. Dis.* 154:276-86

51. Bozarth, J. D., Krauft, C. C. 1972. Accurate empathy ratings: some methodological considerations. *J. Clin. Psychol.* 28:407-10

52. Browning, R. M. 1971. Treatment effects of a total behavior modification program with five autistic children. *Behav. Res. Ther.* 9:319-27

53. Bryson, S., Cody, J. 1973. Relationships of race and level of understanding between counselor and client. *J. Couns. Psychol.* 10:495-98

54. Budzynski, T., Stoyva, J., Adler, C. 1970. Feedback-induced muscle relaxation: Application to tension headache. *J. Behav. Ther. Exp. Psychiat.* 1:205-11

55. Burns, J. M., Ascough, J. C. 1971. A psychophysiological comparison of two approaches to relaxation and anxiety induction. *Behav. Ther.* 2:170-76

56. Carkhuff, R. R. 1971. *The Development of Human Resources: Education, Psychology and Social Change.* New York: Holt, Rinehart & Winston. 422 pp.

57. Carlson, C. G., Hersen, M., Eisler, R. M. 1972. Token economy programs in the treatment of hospitalized adult psychiatric patients: current status and recent trends. *J. Nerv. Ment. Dis.* 155:192-204

58. Cautela, J. R. 1970. Covert reinforcement. *Behav. Ther.* 1:33-50

59. Cautela, J. R. 1970. Covert negative reinforcement. *J. Behav. Ther. Exp. Psychiat.* 1:273-78

60. Cautela, J. R. 1971. Covert extinction. *Behav. Ther.* 2:192-200

61. Chapman, R. F., Smith, J. W., Layden, R. A. 1971. Elimination of cigarette smoking by punishment and self-management training. *Behav. Res. Ther.* 9:255-64

62. Chinsky, J. M., Rappaport, J. 1970. Brief critique of the meaning and reliability of "accurate empathy" ratings. *Psychol. Bull.* 73:379-82

63. Cimbolic, P. 1972. Counselor race and experience effects on black clients. *J. Consult. Clin. Psychol.* 39:328-32

64. Clark, F. 1973. Self-administered desensitization. *Behav. Res. Ther.* 11:335-38

65. Cornish, R. D., Dilley, J. S. 1973. Comparison of three methods of reducing test anxiety: systematic desensitization, implosive therapy, and study counseling. *J. Couns. Psychol.* 20:499-503

66. Costello, C. G. 1972. Depression: loss of reinforcers or loss of reinforcer effectiveness? *Behav. Ther.* 3:240-47

67. Cotler, S. B. 1970. Sex differences and generalization of anxiety reduction with automated desensitization and minimal therapist interaction. *Behav. Res. Ther.* 8:273-85

68. Crighton, J., Jehu, D. 1969. Treatment of examination anxiety by systematic desensitization or psychotherapy in groups. *Behav. Res. Ther.* 7:245-48

69. Cristol, A. H. 1972. Studies of outcome in psychotherapy. *Comp. Psychiat.* 3:189-200

70. Crowder, J., Thornton, D. 1970. Effects

of systematic desensitization. Programmed fantasy and bibliotherapy on a specific fear. *Behav. Res. Ther.* 8:35–41

71. Curtis, R. H., Presly, A. S. 1972. The extinction of homosexual behavior by covert sensitization: a case study. *Behav. Res. Ther.* 10:81–83

72. Daly, D. A., Frick, J. V. 1970. The effects of punishing stuttering expectations and stuttering utterances: a comparative study. *Behav. Ther.* 1:228–39

73. Davids, A. 1972. *Abnormal Children and Youth: Therapy and Research.* New York: Wiley. 211 pp.

74. Davidson, P. O., Hiebert, S. F. 1971. Relaxation training, relaxation instruction, and repeated exposure to a stressor film. *J. Abnorm. Psychol.* 78:154–159

75. Davison, G. C., Wilson, G. T. 1973. Processes of fear-reduction in systematic desensitization: cognitive and social reinforcement factors in humans. *Behav. Ther.* 4:1–21

76. Ibid. Attitudes of behavior therapists towards homosexuality, 686–96

77. Dawley, H. H. Jr., Wenrich, W. W. 1973. Group implosive therapy in the treatment of test anxiety: a brief report. *Behav. Ther.* 4:261–63

78. DeMoor, W. 1970. Systematic desensitization versus prolonged high intensity stimulation (flooding). *J. Behav. Ther. Exp. Psychiat.* 1:45–52

79. Denholtz, M. 1970. The use of tape recordings between therapy sessions. *J. Behav. Ther. Exp. Psychiat.* 1:139–43

80. Di Loreto, A. O. 1971. *Comparative Psychotherapy: An Experimental Analysis.* Chicago: Aldine-Atherton. 315 pp.

81. Donner, L. 1970. Automated group desensitization—a follow-up report. *Behav. Res. Ther.* 8:241–48

82. Doster, J. A., McAllister, A. 1973. Effect of modeling and model status on verbal behavior in an interview. *J. Consult. Clin. Psychol.* 40:240–43

83. Dua, P. S. 1972. Group desensitization of a phobia with three massing procedures. *J. Couns. Psychol.* 19:125–29

84. Dublin, J. E., Berzins, J. I. 1972. A-B variable and reactions to nonimmediacy in neurotic and schizoid communications: a longitudinal analogue of psychotherapy. *J. Consult. Clin. Psychol.* 39:86–93

85. Dyrud, J. E., Holzman, P. S. 1973. The psychotherapy of schizophrenia: does it work? *Am. J. Psychiat.* 130:620–73

86. Edie, C. A. 1972. *Uses of AMT in treating trait anxiety.* PhD thesis. Colorado State Univ., Fort Collins. 158 pp.

87. Eisler, R. M., Hersen, M., Miller, P. M. 1973. Effects of modeling on components of assertive behavior. *J. Behav. Ther. Exp. Psychiat.* 4:1–6

88. Evans, D. R. 1970. Subjective variables and treatment effects in aversion therapy. *Behav. Res. Ther.* 8:147–52

89. Eysenck, H. J. 1972. Note on "factors influencing the outcome of psychotherapy." *Psychol. Bull.* 78:403–5

90. Eysenck, H. J., Ed. 1973. *Handbook of Abnormal Psychology.* San Diego: Knapp. 906 pp. 2nd ed.

91. Farley, F. H., Mealiea, W. L. Jr. 1971. Dissimulation and social desirability in the assessment of fears. *Behav. Ther.* 2:101–2

92. Fazio, A. F. 1970. Treatment of components in implosive therapy. *J. Abnorm. Psychol.* 76:211–19

93. Franks, C. M., Ed. 1969. *Behavior Therapy: Appraisal and Status.* New York: McGraw-Hill. 730 pp.

94. Feighner, J. P., Brown, S. L., Olivier, J. E. 1973. Electrosleep therapy. *J. Nerv. Ment. Dis.* 157:121–28

95. Feldman, M. P., MacCulloch, M. J. 1971. *Homosexual Behaviour: Therapy and Assessment.* Oxford: Pergamon. 288 pp.

96. Ferraro, D. P. 1973. Self-control of smoking: the amotivational syndrome. *J. Abnorm. Psychol.* 81:152–57

97. Fiske, D. W. 1971. The shaky evidence is slowly put together. *J. Consult. Clin. Psychol.* 37:314–15

98. Foreyt, J. P., Hagen, R. L. 1973. Covert sensitization: conditioning or suggestion. *J. Abnorm. Psychol.* 82:17–23

99. Frank, J. D. 1973. *Persuasion and Healing.* Baltimore: Johns Hopkins Univ. Press. 378 pp. 2nd ed.

100. Fransella, F. 1972. *Personal Change and Reconstruction: Research on Treatment of Stuttering.* New York:

Academic. 282 pp.

101. Freeling, N. W., Shemberg, K. M. 1970. The alleviation of test anxiety by systematic desensitization. *Behav. Res. Ther.* 8:293–99

102. Friedman, R. J., Gunderson, J. G., Feinsilver, D. B. 1973. The psychotherapy of schizophrenia; an NIMH program. *Am. J. Psychiat.* 130:674–76

103. Galassi, J. P., DeLo, J. S., Galassi, M. D., Bastien, S. 1973. The college self-expression scale: a measure of assertiveness. Personal communication

104. Gambrill, E. D., Richey, C. A. 1972. Assertive inventory. Personal communication

105. Gardner, L. H. 1971. The therapeutic relationship under varying conditions of race. *Psychother. Theory Res. Pract.* 8:78–87

106. Gardner, W. E. 1972. The differential effects of race, education, and experience in helping. *J. Clin. Psychol.* 28:87–89

107. Gardner, W. I. 1971. *Behavior Modification in Mental Retardation.* Chicago: Aldine. 339 pp.

108. Garfield, S. L., Prager, R. A., Bergin, A. E. 1971. Evaluation of outcome in psychotherapy. *J. Consult. Clin. Psychol.* 37:307–13

109. Ibid. Evaluating outcome in psychotherapy: a hardy perennial, 320–22

110. Gaupp, L. A., Stern, R. M., Ratliff, R. G. 1971. The use of aversion-relief procedures in the treatment of a case of voyeurism. *Behav. Ther.* 2:585–88

111. Gelfand, D. M., Hartmann, D. P. 1974. Child behavior modification techniques: a guide to analysis and treatment of problem behaviors. Personal communication

112. Goldfried, M. R. 1971. Systematic desensitization as training in self-control. *J. Consult. Clin. Psychol.* 37:228–34

113. Goldfried, M. R. 1973. Reduction of generalized anxiety through a variant of systematic desensitization. See Ref. 115, 297–304

114. Goldfried, M. R., Kent, R. N. 1972. Traditional versus behavior personality assessment: a comparison of methodological and theoretical assumptions. *Psychol. Bull.* 77:409–20

115. Goldfried, M. R., Merbaum, M. 1973. *Behavior Change Through Self-Control.* New York: Holt, Rinehart & Winston. 438 pp.

116. Goldfried, M., Sprafkin, J. 1973. Behavioral personality assessment. Personal communication

117. Goldstein, A. P. et al 1973. The use of modeling to increase independent behavior. *Behav. Res. Ther.* 11:31–42

118. Goldstein, A. P. 1973. *Structured Learning Therapy: Toward a Psychotherapy for the Poor.* New York: Academic. 421 pp.

119. Gordon, S. B., Sachs, L. B. 1973. Self-control with a covert aversive stimulus modification of smoking. Personal communication

120. Gottman, J. M. 1973. N-of-one and N-of-two research in psychotherapy. *Psychol. Bull.* 80:93–105

121. Gottman, J. M., Leiblum, S. R. 1974. *How to do Psychotherapy and How to Evaluate it.* New York: Holt, Rinehart & Winston. 184 pp.

122. Greenson, R. 1973. A critique of Kernberg's "summary and conclusions." *Int. J. Psychiat.* 11:91–94

123. Griest, J. H., Klein, M. H., Van Cura, L. J. 1973. A computer interview for psychiatric patient target symptoms. *Arch. Gen. Psychiat.* 29:247–53

124. Griffiths, R. D., Joy, M. 1971. The prediction of phobic behavior. *Behav. Res. Ther.* 9:109–18

125. Gruver, G. G. 1971. College students as therapeutic agents. *Psychol. Bull.* 76:111–27

126. Gurman, A. S. 1973. Instability of therapeutic conditions in psychotherapy. *J. Couns. Psychol.* 20:16–24

127. Gurman, A. S. 1973. The effects and effectiveness of marital therapy: a review of outcome. *Fam. Proc.* 12:145–70

128. Hall, J., Baker, R. 1973. Token economy systems: breakdown and control. *Behav. Res. Ther.* 11:253–63

129. Hartlage, L. C. 1970. Subprofessional therapists' use of reinforcement versus traditional psychotherapeutic techniques with schizophrenics. *J. Consult. Clin. Psychol.* 34:181–83

130. Hartmann, D. P. 1972. *Some neglected issues in behavior modification with*

children. Presented at 6th Assoc. Advan. Behav. Ther. New York

131. Haynes, S. N., Geddy, P. 1973. Suppression of psychotic hallucinations through time-out. *Behav. Ther.* 4:123–27

132. Hedquist, F. J., Weinhold, B. K. 1970. Behavioral group counseling with socially anxious and unassertive college students. *J. Couns. Psychol.* 17:237–42

133. Heilbrun, A. B. 1973. History of self-disclosure in females and early defection from psychotherapy. *J. Couns. Psychol.* 20:250–57

134. Heilbrun, A. B. 1972. Effects of briefing upon client satisfaction with the initial counseling contact. *J. Consult. Clin. Psychol.* 38:50–56

135. Heilbrun, A. B. 1971. Female preference for therapist interview style as a function of "client" and therapist social role variables. *J. Couns. Psychol.* 18:285–91

136. Hekmat, H. 1973. Systematic versus semantic desensitization and implosion therapy. *J. Consult. Clin. Psychol.* 40:202–9

137. Hekmat, H. 1971. Reinforcing values of interpretations and reflections in a quasi-therapeutic interview. *J. Abnorm. Psychol.* 77:25–31

138. Hekmat, H., Vanian, D. 1971. Behavior modification through covert semantic desensitization. *J. Consult. Clin. Psychol.* 36:248–51

139. Henderson, J. D., Scoles, P. E. 1970. Conditioning techniques in a community-based operant environment for psychotic men. *Behav. Ther.* 1:245–51

140. Henry, W. E., Sims, J. H., Spray, S. L. 1973. *Public and Private Lives of Psychotherapists.* San Francisco: Jossey-Bass. 272 pp.

141. Hersen, M. 1970. Behavior modification approach to a school phobia case. *J. Clin. Psychol.* 26:128–32

142. Hersen, M. 1973. Self-assessment of fear. *Behav. Ther.* 4:241–57

143. Hersen, M., Eisler, R. M., Miller, P. M. 1973. Development of assertive responses: clinical measurement and research consideration. *Behav. Res. Ther.* 11:505–21

144. Hersen, M., Eisler, R. M., Smith, B.,

145. Agras, W. 1972. A token reinforcement ward for young psychiatric patients. *Am. J. Psychiat.* 129:228–33

145. Hodgson, R., Rachman, S., Marks, I. M. 1972. The treatment of chronic-obsessive compulsive neurosis: follow-up and further findings. *Behav. Res. Ther.* 10:181–89

146. Holt, R. R., Peterfreund, E., Eds. 1972. *Psychoanalysis and Contemporary Science.* New York: Macmillan. 399 pp.

147. Innes, J. M. 1972. Dissonance reduction in the therapist and its relevance to aversion therapy. *Behav. Ther.* 3:441–43

148. Jacob, T., Magnussen, M. G., Kemler, W. M. 1972. A follow-up of treatment terminators and remainers with long-term and short-term symptom duration. *Psychother. Theory Res. Pract.* 9:139–42

149. Jaffe, P. G., Carlson, P. M. 1972. Modeling therapy for test anxiety: the role of model affect and consequences. *Behav. Res. Ther.* 10:329–39

150. Johnson, C. A., Katz, R. C., Gelfand, S. 1972. Undergraduates as behavioral technicians on an adult token economy ward. *Behav. Ther.* 3:589–92

151. Johnson, W. G. 1971. Some applications of Homme's coverant control therapy: two case reports. *Behav. Ther.* 2:240–48

152. Jones, W. L., Weststrate, H. C., Crawley, R. C. 1970. Behaviour therapy in a case of hysterical blindness. *Behav. Res. Ther.* 8:79–85

153. Kanfer, F. H. 1965. Perspectives in psychology XXIV: control of coverants, the operants of the mind. *Psychol. Rec.* 15:501–11

154. Kanfer, F. H., Phillips, J. S. 1970. *Learning Foundations of Behavior Therapy.* New York: Wiley. 642 pp.

155. Karle, W., Corriere, R., Hart, J. 1973. Psychophysiological changes in abreactive therapy—Study I: Primal therapy. *Psychother. Theory Res. Pract.* 10:117–22

156. Karon, B. P., Vandenbos, G. R. 1972. The consequences of psychotherapy for schizophrenic patients. *Psychother. Theory Res. Pract.* 9:111–19

157. Kass, D. J., Silvers, F. M., Abrams, G.

M. 1972. Behavioral group treatment of hysteria. *Arch. Gen. Psychiat.* 26:42–50

158. Katz, R. C., Johnson, C. A., Gelfand, S. 1972. Modifying the dispensing of reinforcers: some implications of behavior modification with hospitalized patients. *Behav. Ther.* 3:579–88

159. Kazdin, A. E. 1973. Covert modeling and the reduction of avoidance behavior. *J. Abnorm. Psychol.* 81:87–95

160. Kazdin, A. E. 1973. The failure of some patients to respond to token programs. *J. Behav. Ther. Exp. Psychiat.* 4:7–14

161. Kenny, F. T., Solyom, L., Solyom, C. 1973. Faradic disruption of obsessive ideation in the treatment of obsessive neurosis. *Behav. Ther.* 4:448–57

162. Kernberg, O. F. 1973. Summary and conclusions of "Psychotherapy and Psychoanalysis, Final report of the Menninger Foundation's Psychotherapy Research Project." *Int. J. Psychiat.* 11:62–77

163. Ibid. Author's reply, 95–103

164. Kernberg, O. F. et al 1972. Psychotherapy and psychoanalysis: Final report of the Menninger Foundation's psychotherapy research project. *Bull. Menninger Clin.* 36:1–276

165. Kiesler, D. J. 1973. *The Process of Psychotherapy: Empirical Foundations and Systems of Analysis.* Chicago: Aldine. 464 pp.

166. Kimmel, H. D., Kimmel, H. 1970. An instrumental conditioning method for the treatment of enuresis. *J. Behav. Ther. Exp. Psychiat.* 1:121–23

167. Klein, Z. E. 1971. *Research in the Child Psychiatric and Guidance Clinics: A Bibliography (1923–1970).* Dep. Psychiatry, Univ. Chicago

168. Klein, Z. E. 1973. *Research in the Child Psychiatric and Guidance Clinics: Supplementary Bibliography I (through 1971).* Dep. Psychiatry, Univ. Chicago

169. Klein, Z. E. 1973. *Research in the Child Psychiatric and Guidance Clinics: Supplementary Bibliography II (1972).* Dep. Psychiatry, Univ. Chicago

170. Korn, E. J., Ascough, J. C., Kleeneier, R. B. 1972. The effects of induced anxiety on state-trait measures of anxiety in high, middle, and low trait-anxious individuals. *Behav. Ther.* 3: 547–54

171. Krasner, L. 1971. Behavior therapy. *Ann. Rev. Psychol.* 22:483–532

172. Krebs, R. L. 1971. Some effects of a white institution on black psychiatric outpatients. *Am. J. Orthopsychiat.* 41:589–96

173. Kubie, L. S. 1973. The process of evaluation of therapy in psychiatry. *Arch. Gen. Psychiat.* 28:880–84

174. Kurtz, R. R., Grummon, D. L. 1972. Different approaches to the measurement of empathy and their relationship to therapy outcomes. *J. Consult. Clin. Psychol.* 39:106–15

175. Landy, F. J., Gaupp, L. A. 1971. A factor analysis of the fear survey schedule 111. *Behav. Res. Ther.* 9: 89–93

176. Lanson, R. N., Benassi V. A. 1973. Some data on the availability of behavior modification training. Personal communication

177. Lassen, C. L. 1973. Effect of proximity on anxiety and communication in the initial psychiatric interview. *J. Abnorm. Psychol.* 81:226–32

178. Lauver, P. J., Kelley, J. D., Frochle, T. C. 1971. Client reaction time and counselor verbal behavior in an interview setting. *J. Couns. Psychol.* 18:26–30

179. Lawlis, G. F. 1971. Response styles of a patient population on the fear survey schedule. *Behav. Res. Ther.* 9:95–102

180. Laxer, R. M., Walker, K. 1970. Counterconditioning versus relaxation in the desensitization of test anxiety. *J. Couns. Psychol.* 17:431–36

181. Lazarus, A. A. 1971. *Behavior Therapy and Beyond.* New York: McGraw-Hill. 306 pp.

182. Lazarus, A. A. 1971. Where do behavior therapists take their troubles? *Psychol. Rep.* 28:349–50

183. Lazarus, A. A. 1973. On assertive behavior: a brief note. *Behav. Ther.* 4:697–99

184. Lebow, M. D., Gelfand, S., Dobson, N. R. 1970. Aversive conditioning of a phenothiazine-induced respiratory stridor. *Behav. Ther.* 1:222–27

185. Leitenberg, H. 1973. The use of

single-case methodology in psychotherapy research. *J. Abnorm. Psychol.* 82:87–101

186. Lerner, B. A. 1972. *Therapy in the Ghetto: Political Impotence and Personal Disintegration.* Baltimore: Johns Hopkins Univ. Press. 222 pp.

187. Lerner, B. A., Fiske, D. W. 1973. Client attributes and the eye of the beholder. *J. Consult. Clin. Psychol.* 40:272–77

188. Levene, H., Breger, L., Patterson, V. 1972. A training and research program in brief psychotherapy. *Am. J. Psychother.* 26:90–100

189. Liberman, B. L. et al 1972. Patterns of change in psychoneurotic patients: a five-year follow-up investigation of the systematic preparation of patients for psychotherapy. *J. Consult. Clin. Psychol.* 38:36–41

190. Liberman, R. P. 1972. *A Guide to Behavioral Analysis and Therapy.* New York: Pergamon

191. Lieberman, M. A., Yalom, I. D., Miles, M. B. 1973. *Encounter Groups: First Facts.* New York: Basic Books. 495 pp.

192. Lick, J. R., Bootzin, R. R. 1970. Expectancy, demand characteristics, and contact desensitization in behavior change. *Behav. Ther.* 1:176–83

193. Logan, F. A. 1973. Self control as habit, drive and incentive. *J. Abnorm. Psychol.* 81:127–36

194. Lomont, J. F., Brock, L. 1971. Cognitive factors in systematic desensitization. *Behav. Res. Ther.* 9:187–95

195. LoPiccolo, J. 1971. Case study: systematic desensitization of homosexuality. *Behav. Ther.* 2:394–99

196. Lorion, R. P. 1973. Socioeconomic status and traditional treatment approaches reconsidered. *Psychol. Bull.* 79:263–70

197. Lovaas, O. I., Litrownik, A., Mann, R. 1971. Response latencies to auditory stimuli in autistic children engaged in self-stimulatory behavior. *Behav. Res. Ther.* 9:39–49

198. Lovibond, S. H. 1970. Aversive control of behavior. *Behav. Ther.* 1:80–91

199. Lovibond, S. H., Caddy, G. 1970. Discriminated aversive control in the modification of alcoholics' drinking behavior. *Behav. Ther.* 1:437–44

200. Luborsky, L. 1971. Perennial mystery of poor agreement among criteria for psychotherapy outcome. *J. Consult. Clin. Psychol.* 37:316–19

201. Luborsky, L. 1972. Another reply to Eysenck. *Psychol. Bull.* 78:406–8

202. Luborsky, L. 1973. Forgetting and remembering (momentary forgetting) during psychotherapy: a new sample. In *Psychoanalytic Research: Three Approaches to the Experimental Study of Subliminal Processes,* ed. M. Mayman, 29–55. New York: Int. Univ. Press. 135 pp.

203. Luborsky, L., Chandler, M., Auerbach, A. H., Cohen, J., Bachrach, H. M. 1971. Factors influencing the outcome of psychotherapy: a review of quantitative research. *Psychol. Bull.* 75: 145–85

204. Luborsky, L., Graff, H., Pulver, S., Curtis, H. 1973. A clinical-quantitative examination of consensus on the concept of transference. *Arch. Gen. Psychiat.* 29:69–75

205. Luborsky, Lester, Singer, B., Luborsky, Lise. 1974. *Comparative studies of psychotherapies: Is it true that "everybody has won and all must have prizes?"* Presented at Soc. Psychother. Res., Denver, Colo.

206. Lutker, E. R., Tasto, D. L., Jorgensen, G. 1972. A brief note on multi-hierarchy desensitization. *Behav. Ther.* 3:619–21

207. MacCulloch, M. J., Birtles, C. J., Feldman, M. P. 1971. Anticipatory avoidance learning for the treatment of homosexuality: recent developments and an automatic aversion therapy system. *Behav. Ther.* 2:151–69

208. Mahoney, M. J. 1972. Research issues in self-management. *Behav. Ther.* 3:45–63

209. Mahoney, M. J., Moore, B. S., Wade, T. C., Moura, N. G. M. 1973. Effects of continuous and intermittent self-monitoring on academic behavior. *J. Consult. Clin. Psychol.* 41:65–69

210. Mahrer, A. R., Pearson, L., Eds. 1971. *Creative Developments in Psychotherapy.* Cleveland: Case Western Reserve. 510 pp.

211. Malan, D. H. 1973. The outcome problem in psychotherapy research: A his-

torical review. *Arch. Gen. Psychiat.* 29:719-29

212. Malan, D. H. 1973. Science and psychotherapy. *Int. J. Psychiat.* 11:87-90

213. Malan, D. H. 1973. Therapeutic factors in analytically oriented brief psychotherapy. In *Support, Innovation, and Autonomy: Tavistock Clinic Golden Jubilee Papers,* ed. R. Gosling, 187-205. London: Tavistock. 303 pp.

214. Mann, J. 1972. Vicarious desensitization of test anxiety through observation of videotaped treatment. *J. Couns. Psychol.* 19:1-7

215. Marks, I. M. 1972. Perspectives on flooding. *Sem. Psychiat.* 4:129-38

216. Marks, I. M. et al, Eds. 1973. *Psychotherapy and Behavior Change 1972: An Aldine Annual on Practice and Research.* Chicago: Aldine

217. Marmor, J. 1971. Dynamic psychotherapy and behavior therapy: Are they irreconcilable? *Arch. Gen. Psychiat.* 24:22-28

218. Marquis, J. N. 1970. Orgasmic reconditioning: changing sexual object choice through controlling masturbation fantasies. *J. Behav. Ther. Exp. Psychiat.* 1:203-71

219. Marzagao, L. R. 1972. Systematic desensitization treatment of kleptomania. *J. Behav. Ther. Exp. Psychiat.* 3:327-28

220. Matarazzo, J. D. et al, Eds. 1972. *Psychotherapy 1971: An Aldine Annual.* Chicago: Aldine. 593 pp.

221. Matarazzo, J. D., Wiens, A. N. 1972. *The Interview: Research on its Anatomy and Structure.* Chicago: Aldine-Atherton. 183 pp.

222. Mather, M. D. 1970. The treatment of an obsessive-compulsive patient by discrimination learning and reinforcement of decision-making. *Behav. Res. Ther.* 8:315-18

223. May, P. R. A. 1971. For better or for worse? Psychotherapy and variance change: A critical review of the literature. *J. Nerv. Ment. Dis.* 152:185-92

224. May, P. R. A. 1973. Research in psychotherapy and psychoanalysis. *Int. J. Psychiat.* 11:78-86

225. May, P. R. A. 1973. Assessment of psychiatric outcome—III. Process analysis. *J. Psychiat. Res.* 10:31-42

226. May, P. R. A., Potepan, P., Yale, C., Dixon, W. J. 1972. Assessment of psychiatric outcome—II. Simple Simon analysis. *J. Psychiat. Res.* 9:285.

227. May, P. R. A., Yale, C., Dixon, W. J. 1972. Assessment of psychiatric outcome—I. Cross-section analysis. *J. Psychiat. Res.* 9:271

228. Mayer, J. E., Timms, N. 1970. *The Client Speaks: Working Class Impressions of Casework.* London: Routledge and Kegan Paul. 193 pp.

229. McCarron, L. J. 1973. Paralanguage and autonomic response patterns in psychotherapy. *Psychother. Theory Res. Pract.* 10:229-30

230. McCarron, L. J., Appel, V. H. 1971. Categories of therapist verbalizations and patient-therapist autonomic response. *J. Consult. Clin. Psychol.* 37:123-34

231. McConville, B. J., Brian, J., Purohit, A. P. 1973. Classifying confusion: A study of results of inpatient treatment in a multidisciplinary childrens' center. *Am. J. Orthopsychiat.* 43:411-17

232. McCrady, R. E. 1973. A forward-fading technique for increasing heterosexual responsiveness in male homosexuals. *J. Behav. Ther. Exp. Psychiat.* 4:257-61

233. McFall, R. M. 1970. Effects of self-monitoring on normal smoking behavior. *J. Consult. Clin. Psychol.* 35:135-42

234. McFall, R. M., Marston, A. R. 1970. An experimental investigation of behavior rehearsal in assertive training. *J. Abnorm. Psychol.* 76:293-303

235. McFall, R. M., Twentyman, C. T. 1973. Four experiments on the relative contributions of rehearsal, modeling, and coaching to assertion training. *J. Abnorm. Psychol.* 81:199-218

236. McGlynn, F. D. 1971. Experimental desensitization following three types of instructions. *Behav. Res. Ther.* 9:367-69

237. McNamara, J. R., MacDonough, T. S. 1972. Some methodological considerations in the design and implementation of behavior therapy research. *Behav. Ther.* 3:361-78

238. Mealiea, W. L. Jr., Nawas, M. M. 1971. The comparative effectiveness of

systematic desensitization and implosive therapy in the treatment of snake phobia. *J. Behav. Ther. Exp. Psychiat.* 2:85–94

239. Meichenbaum, D. H. 1971. *Cognitive factors in behavior modification: modifying what clients say to themselves.* Presented at 5th Assoc. Advan. Behav. Ther. Washington, D. C.

240. Merbaum, M., Stricker, G. 1972. Factor analytic study of male and female responses to the fear survey schedule. *J. Behav. Ther. Exp. Psychiat.* 3:87–90

241. Miller, J. O., Gross, S. J. 1973. Curvilinear trends in outcome research. *J. Consult. Clin. Psychol.* 41:242–44

242. Miller, L. C., Barrett, C. L., Hampe, E., Noble, H. 1972. Comparison of reciprocal inhibition, psychotherapy, and waiting list control for phobic children. *J. Abnorm. Psychol.* 79:269–79

243. Miller, L. C. 1972. School behavior check list: an inventory of deviant behavior for elementary school children. *J. Consult. Clin. Psychol.* 38:134–44

244. Miller, S. B. 1972. The contribution of therapeutic instructions to systematic desensitization. *Behav. Res. Ther.* 10:159–69

245. Mintz, J. 1972. What is "success" in psychotherapy? *J. Abnorm. Psychol.* 80:11–19

246. Mintz, J., Auerbach, A. H., Luborsky, L., Johnson, M. 1973. Patient's, therapist's, and observers' views of psychotherapy: A 'Rashomon' experience or a reasonable consensus. *Brit. J. Med. Psychol.* 46:83–89

247. Mintz, J., Luborsky, L. 1971. Segments vs. whole sessions: which is the better unit for psychotherapy process research? *J. Abnorm. Psychol.* 78:180–91

248. Mintz, J., Luborsky, L., Auerbach, A. H. 1971. Dimensions of psychotherapy: A factor-analytic study of ratings of psychotherapy sessions. *J. Consult. Clin. Psychol.* 36:106–20

249. Mitchell, K. M., Truax, C. B., Bozarth, J. D., Krauft, C. C. 1973. Antecedents to psychotherapeutic outcome. *NIMH Final Rep.—MH 12306*

250. Mitchell, K. R., Ingham, R. J. 1970. The effects of general anxiety on group desensitization of test anxiety. *Behav. Res. Ther.* 8:69–78

251. Moan, C. E., Heath, R. G. 1972. Septal stimulation for the initiation of heterosexual behavior in a homosexual male. *J. Behav. Ther. Exp. Psychiat.* 3:23–30

252. Morganstern, K. P. 1973. Implosive therapy and flooding procedures: a critical review. *Psychol. Bull* 79:318–34

253. Mosher, L. R. 1973. Current studies on schizophrenia. *Int. J. Psychoanal. Psychother.* 2:7–61

254. Moss, C. 1972. *Behavioral Therapists in U.S. and Canada.* Monticello, NY

255. Mullen, E. J., Dumpson, J. R., Eds. 1972. *Evaluation of Social Intervention.* San Francisco: Jossey-Bass. 267 pp.

256. Mullen, J., Abeles, N. 1971. Relationship of liking, empathy, and therapist's experience to outcome of therapy. *J. Couns. Psychol.* 18:39–43

257. Murphy, C. M., Bootzin, R. R. 1973. Active and passive participation in the contact desensitization of snake fear in children. *Behav. Ther.* 4:203–11

258. Mylar, J. L., Clement, P. W. 1972. Prediction and comparison of outcome in systematic desensitization and implosion. *Behav. Res. Ther.* 10:235–46

259. Nathan, P. E., O'Brien, J. S. 1971. An experimental analysis of the behavior of alcoholics and nonalcoholics during prolonged experimental drinking: a necessary precursor of behavior therapy? *Behav. Ther.* 2:455–76

260. Nelson, C. M., Worell, J., Polsgrove, L. 1973. Behaviorally disordered peers as behavioral managers. *Behav. Ther.* 4:270–76

261. Nicoletti, J. A. 1972. *Anxiety management training.* PhD thesis. Colorado State Univ., Fort Collins. 122 pp.

262. Nolan, J. D., Pence, C. 1970. Operant conditioning principles in the treatment of a selectively mute child. *J. Consult. Clin. Psychol.* 35:265–68

263. O'Leary, K. D., O'Leary, S. G. 1972. *Classroom Management: the Successful Use of Behavior Modification.* New York: Pergamon. 664 pp.

264. O'Sullivan, M., Gilner, F. H., Krinski, R. 1973. The influence of sex of experimenter on modeling in the reduction of fear. *Behav. Ther.* 4:535–42

265. Packwood, W. J., Parker, C. A. 1973. A method for rating counselor social

reinforcement and persuasion. *J. Couns. Psychol.* 20:38–43

266. Patterson, V., Levene, H., Breger, L. 1971. Treatment and training outcomes with two time limited therapies. *Arch. Gen. Psychiat.* 25:161–67

267. Paul, G. L. 1966. *Insight vs. Desensitization in Psychotherapy: An Experiment in Anxiety Reduction.* Stanford Univ. Press

268. Paul, G. L., Trimble, R. W. 1970. Recorded vs. "live" relaxation training and hypnotic suggestion: comparative effectiveness for reducing physiological arousal and inhibiting stress response. *Behav. Ther.* 1:283–302

269. Persley, G., Leventhal, D. B. 1972. The effects of therapeutically oriented instructions and of the pairing of anxiety imagery and relaxation in systematic desensitization. *Behav. Ther.* 3:417–24

270. Phillips, R. E., Johnson, G. D., Geyer, A. 1972. Self-administered systematic desensitization. *Behav. Res. Ther.* 10:93–96

271. Pomerleau, O. F., Bobrove, P. H., Harris, L. C. 1972. Some observations on a controlled social environment for psychiatric patients. *J. Behav. Ther. Exp. Psychiat.* 3:15–21

272. Pope, B., Siegman, A. W., Blass, T., Cheek, J. 1972. Some effects of discrepant role expectations of interviewer verbal behavior in the initial interview. *J. Consult. Clin. Psychol.* 39:501–7

273. Prager, R. A., Garfield, S. L. 1972. Client initial disturbance and outcome in psychotherapy. *J. Consult. Clin. Psychol.* 38:112–17

274. Prentice, N. M. 1972. The influence of live and symbolic modeling on promoting moral judgment of adolescent delinquents. *J. Abnorm. Psychol.* 80:157–61

275. Prochaska, J. O. 1971. Symptom and dynamic cues in the implosive treatment of test anxiety. *J. Abnorm. Psychol.* 77:133–42

276. Rachman, S. 1971. *The Effects of Psychotherapy.* Oxford: Pergamon. 186 pp.

277. Rachman, S. 1971. Obsessional ruminations. *Behav. Res. Ther.* 9:229–35

278. Rachman, S. 1972. Clinical applications of observational learning, imita-

tion, and modeling. *Behav. Ther.* 3:379–97

279. Rachman, S. 1973. The effects of psychotherapy. See Ref. 90, 805–61

280. Rachman, S., Hodgson, R., Marks, I. M. 1971. The treatment of chronic obsessive-compulsive neurosis. *Behav. Res. Ther.* 9:237–47

281. Rackensperger, W., Feinberg, A. M. 1972. Treatment of a severe handwashing compulsion by systematic desensitization: a case report. *J. Behav. Ther. Exp. Psychiat.* 3:123–27

282. Rappaport, J., Chinsky, J. M. 1972. Accurate empathy: Confusion of a construct. *Psychol. Bull.* 77:400–4

283. Raskin, M., Johnson, G., Rondestvedt, J. 1973. Chronic anxiety treated by feedback-induced muscle relaxation. *Arch. Gen. Psychiat.* 28:263–67

284. Rathus, S. A. 1973. Instigation of assertive behavior through videotape-mediated assertive models and directed practice. *Behav. Res. Ther.* 11:57–65

285. Ravensborg, M. R. 1972. An operant conditioning approach to increasing interpersonal awareness among chronic schizophrenics. *J. Clin. Psychol.* 28:411–13

286. Rehm, L. P. 1973. Relationships among measures of visual imagery. *Behav. Res. Ther.* 11:265–70

287. Rickard, H. C. 1971. *Behavioral Intervention in Human Problems.* New York: Pergamon. 422 pp.

288. Rickers-Ovsiankina, M. A., Berzins, J. I., Geller, J. D., Rogers, G. W. III. 1971. Patients' role-expectancies in psychotherapy: A theoretical and measurement approach. *Psychother. Theory Res. Pract.* 8:124–26

289. Ricks, D. F. 1974. Supershrink: Methods of a therapist judged successful on the basis of adult outcomes of adolescent patients. In *Life History Research in Psychopathology,* ed. D. F. Ricks, M. Roff, A. Thomas, 3:275–97. Minneapolis: Univ. Minnesota

290. Riddick, C., Meyer, R. G. 1973. The efficacy of automated relaxation training with response contingent feedback. *Behav. Ther.* 4:331–37

291. Riess, B. F. 1973. Some causes and correlates of psychotherapy termination: A study of 500 cases. *Int. Ment.*

Health Res. Newslett. 15:4–7

292. Rimm, D. C., deGroot, J. C., Boord, P., Heiman, J., Dillow, P. V. 1971. Systematic desensitization of an anger response. *Behav. Res. Ther.* 9:273–80

293. Roback, H. B. 1971. The comparative influence of insight and non-insight psychotherapies on therapeutic outcome: A review of the experimental literature. *Psychother. Theory Res. Pract.* 8:23–25

294. Romney, A. K., Shepard, R. N., Nerlove, S. B., Eds. 1972. *Multidimensional Scaling, Vol. 2.* New York: Seminar

295. Rosenhan, D. L. 1973. On being sane in insane places. *Science* 179:250–58

296. Rosenthal, A. J., Levine, S. V. 1971. Brief psychotherapy with children: Process of therapy. *Am. J. Psychiat.* 128:141–46

297. Rosenthal, T. L. 1974. Response-contingent versus fixed punishment in aversion conditioning of pedophilia: a case study. *J. Nerv. Ment. Dis.* In press

298. Ross, S. M., Proctor, S. 1973. Frequency and duration of hierarchy item exposure in a systematic desensitization analogue. *Behav. Res. Ther.* 11:303–12

299. Russell, R. K., Sipich, J. F. 1973. Cue controlled relaxation in the treatment of test anxiety. *J. Behav. Ther. Exp. Psychiat.* 4:47–49

300. Ryan, V. L., Gizynski, M. N. 1971. Behavior therapy in retrospect: Patients' feelings about their behavior therapies. *J. Consult. Clin. Psychol.* 37:1–9

301. Sarason, I. G., Ganzer, V. J. 1973. Modeling and group discussion in the rehabilitation of juvenile delinquents. *J. Couns. Psychol.* 20:442–49

302. Schnurer, A. T., Rubin, R. R., Roy, A. 1973. Systematic desensitization of anorexia nervosa seen as a weight problem. *J. Behav. Ther. Exp. Psychiat.* 4:149–53

303. Schmahl, D. P., Lichtenstein, E., Harris, D. E. 1972. Successful treatment of habitual smokers with warm, smoky air and rapid smoking. *J. Consult. Clin. Psychol.* 38:105–11

304. Schopler, E., Brehm, S. S., Kinsbourne, M., Reichler, R. J. 1971. Effect of treatment structure on development in autistic children. *Arch. Gen. Psychiat.* 24:415–21

305. Schrauger, J. S., Katkin, E. S. 1970. Case report: the use of nonspecific underlying motivational factors in the systematic desensitization of specific marital and interpersonal fears. *J. Abnorm. Psychol.* 75:221–26

306. Schroeder, H., Craine, L. 1971. Relationships among measures of fear and anxiety for snake phobics. *J. Consult. Clin. Psychol.* 36:443

307. Schwartz, C. C., Myers, J. K., Astrachan, B. M. 1973. The outcome study in psychiatric evaluation research. *Arch. Gen. Psychiat.* 29:98–102

308. Serber, M. 1970. Shame aversion therapy. *J. Behav. Ther. Exp. Psychiat.* 1:213–15

309. Shapiro, D. et al 1972. *Biofeedback and Self-Control.* Chicago: Aldine. 534 pp.

310. Shepard, R. N., Romney, A. K., Nerlove, S. B., Eds. 1972. *Multidimensional Scaling, Vol. 1: Theory.* New York: Seminar

311. Shontz, F. C. 1972. Individuality in evaluations of treatment effectiveness. *J. Couns. Psychol.* 19:76–80

312. Shore, M. F., Massimo, J. L. 1973. After ten years: A follow-up study of comprehensive vocationally oriented psychotherapy. *Am. J. Orthopsychiat.* 43:128–32

313. Siegel, C. L. F. 1972. Changes in play therapy behaviors over time as a function of differing levels of therapist-offered conditions. *J. Clin. Psychol.* 28:235–36

314. Siegman, A. W., Pope, B., Eds. 1972. *Studies in Dyadic Communication.* New York: Pergamon. 336 pp.

315. Slade, P. D. 1972. The effects of systematic desensitization on auditory hallucinations. *Behav. Res. Ther.* 10:85–91

316. Sloane, R. B. et al 1974. *Short-term analytically oriented psychotherapy vs. behavior therapy.* Cambridge, Mass.: Harvard. In press

317. Small, L. 1971. *The Briefer Psychotherapies.* New York: Bruner/Mazel. 262 pp.

318. Smith, R. E., Nye, S. L. 1973. A comparison of implosion therapy and systematic desensitization in the treatment of test anxiety. *J. Consult. Clin. Psychol.* 41:37–42

319. Sobell, M. B., Sobell, L. C. 1973. Indi-

vidualized behavior therapy for alcoholics. *Behav. Ther.* 4:49–72

320. Spinelli, P. R. 1972. *Therapist presence and desensitization.* PhD dissertation. Colorado State Univ., Fort Collins. 152 pp.

321. Staats, A. 1972. Language behavior therapy: a derivative of social behaviorism. *Behav. Ther.* 3:165–92

322. Stadter, M. 1973. In vivo facilitation as a variable in the effectiveness of taped flooding. *Behav. Res. Ther.* 11:239–41

323. Steeves, J. M., Martin, G. L., Pear, J. J. 1970. Self-imposed time-out by autistic children during an operant training program. *Behav. Ther.* 1:371–81

324. Stern, R., Marks, I. 1973. Brief and prolonged flooding: a comparison in agoraphobic patients. *Arch. Gen. Psychiat.* 28:270–76

325. Stevenson, J., Jones, I. H. 1972. Behavior therapy technique for exhibitionism: a preliminary report. *Arch. Gen. Psychiat.* 27:839–41

326. Stuart, R. B. 1971. A three-dimensional program for the treatment of obesity. *Behav. Res. Ther.* 9:177–86

327. Stuart, R. B., Davis, B. 1972. *Slim Chance in a Fat World.* Champaign: Research Press. 245 pp.

328. Strupp, H. H. 1972. On the technology of psychotherapy. *Arch. Gen. Psychiat.* 26:270–78

329. Strupp, H. H. 1973. *Psychotherapy: Clinical, Research, and Theoretical Issues.* New York: Aronson. 816 pp.

330. Strupp, H. H. 1973. On the basic ingredients of psychotherapy. *J. Consult. Clin. Psychol.* 41:1–8

331. Strupp, H. H., Bloxom, A. L. 1973. Preparing lower class patients for group psychotherapy: Development and evaluation of a role-induction film. *J. Consult. Clin. Psychol.* 41:373–84

332. Stunkard, A. 1972. New therapies for the eating disorders: behavior modification of obesity and anorexia nervosa. *Arch. Gen. Psychiat.* 26:391–98

333. Subotnik, L. 1972. Spontaneous remission: fact or artifact? *Psychol. Bull.* 77:32–48

334. Subotnik, L. 1972. "Spontaneous remission" of deviant MMPI profiles among college students. *J. Consult. Clin. Psychol.* 38:191–201

335. Suinn, R. M. 1972. Behavior rehearsal training for ski racers. *Behav. Ther.* 3:19–20

336. Suinn, R. M., Brittain, J. 1970. The termination of an LSD "freak-out" through the use of relaxation. *J. Clin. Psychol.* 26:126–27

337. Suinn, R. M., Edie, C. A., Spinelli, P. R. 1970. Accelerated massed desensitization: innovation in short-term treatment. *Behav. Ther.* 1:303–11

338. Suinn, R. M., Richardson, F. 1970. Behavior therapy in an unusual case of highway hypnosis. *J. Behav. Ther. Exp. Psychiat.* 1:175–76

339. Suinn, R. M., Richardson, F. 1971. Anxiety management training: a nonspecific behavior therapy program for anxiety control. *Behav. Ther.* 2:498–510

340. Suomi, S. J., Harlow, H. F., McKinney, W. T. 1972. Monkey psychiatrists. *Am. J. Psychiat.* 128:927–32

341. Tasto, D. L., Hickson, R., Rubin, S. E. 1971. Scaled profile analysis of fear survey schedule factors. *Behav. Ther.* 2:543–49

342. Tasto, D. L., Hinkle, J. E. 1973. Muscle relaxation treatment for tension headaches. *Behav. Res. Ther.* 11:347–49

343. Tasto, D. L., Suinn, R. M. 1972. Fear schedule changes on total and factor scores due to nontreatment effects. *Behav. Ther.* 3:275–78

344. Todd, F. J. 1972. Coverant control of self-evaluative responses in the treatment of depression: a new use for an old principle. *Behav. Ther.* 3:91–94

345. Trexler, L. D., Karst, T. O. 1972. Rational-emotive therapy, placebo, and no-treatment effects on public-speaking anxiety. *J. Abnorm. Psychol.* 79:60–67

346. Truax, C. B. 1972. The meaning and reliability of accurate empathy ratings. *Psychol. Bull.* 77:397–99

347. Truax, C. B., Mitchell, K. M. 1971. Research on certain therapist interpersonal skills in relation to process and outcome. See Ref. 31, 299–344

348. Truax, C. B., Wittmer, J. 1971. The effects of therapist focus on patient anxiety source and the interaction with therapist level of accurate empathy. *J. Clin. Psychol.* 27:297–99

349. Voth, H. M., Orth, M. H. 1973. *Psychotherapy and the Role of the Envi-*

ronment. New York: Behavioral. 354 pp.

350. Wagner, M. K., Bragg, R. A. 1970. Comparing behavior modification approaches to habit decrement smoking. *J. Consult. Clin. Psychol.* 34:258–63

351. Walter, H. I., Gilmore, S. K. 1973. Placebo versus social learning effects in parent training procedures designed to alter the behavior of aggressive boys. *Behav. Ther.* 4:361–77

352. Warren, N. C., Rice, L. N. 1972. Structuring and stabilizing of psychotherapy for low prognosis clients. *J. Consult. Clin. Psychol.* 39:173–81

353. Waters, W. F., McDonald, D. G., Koresko, R. L. 1972. Psychophysiological responses during analogue systematic desensitization and nonrelaxation control procedures. *Behav. Res. Ther.* 10:381–93

354. Watson, D. L., Tharp, R. G. 1972. *Self-Directed Behavior: Self-Modification for Personal Adjustment.* Monterey: Brooks/Cole. 264 pp.

355. Watson, J. P., Marks, I. M. 1971. Relevant and irrelevant fear in flooding—a crossover study of phobic patients. *Behav. Ther.* 2:275–93

356. Weingaertner, A. H. 1971. Self-administered aversive stimulation with hallucinating hospitalized schizophrenics. *J. Consult. Clin. Psychol.* 36:422–29

357. Weissman, M. M., Prusoff, B. A., Paykel, E. S. 1972. Checklist quantification of a psychological therapy: Pilot studies of reliability and utility. *J. Nerv. Ment. Dis.* 154:125–36

358. Wijesinghe, B. 1973. Massed electrical aversion treatment of compulsive eating. *J. Behav. Ther. Exp. Psychiat.* 4:133–35

359. Wilkins, W. 1971. Desensitization: social and cognitive factors underlying the effectiveness of Wolpe's procedure. *Psychol. Bull.* 76:311–17

360. Wilkins, W. 1973. Expectancy of therapeutic gain: An empirical and conceptual critique. *J. Consult. Clin.*

Psychol. 46:69–77

361. Williams, K. J. 1973. Race and social class as factors in the orientation toward psychotherapy. *J. Couns. Psychol.* 20:312–16

362. Wilson, G. T., Davison, G. C. 1971. Processes of fear reduction in systematic desensitization: animal studies. *Psychol. Bull.* 76:1–14

363. Wilson, G. T., Thomas, M. G. W. 1973. Self- versus drug-produced relaxation and the effects of instructional set in standardized systematic desensitization. *Behav. Res. Ther.* 11:279–88

364. Winborn, B. B., Rowe, W. 1972. Self-actualization and the communication of facilitative conditions—a replication. *J. Couns. Psychol.* 19:26–29

365. Winkler, R. C. 1972. A theory of equilibrium in token economies. *J. Abnorm. Psychol.* 79:169–73

366. Winston, A., Pardes, H., Papernik, D. S. 1972. Inpatient treatment of blacks and whites. *Arch. Gen. Psychiat.* 26:405–9

367. Wisocki, P. A. 1973. The successful treatment of a heroin addict by covert conditioning techniques. *J. Behav. Ther. Exp. Psychiat.* 4:55–61

368. Wolpe, J. 1972. Supervision transcripts II: problems of a novice. *J. Behav. Ther. Exp. Psychiat.* 3:199–203

369. Wolpe, J. 1973. *The Practice of Behavior Therapy.* New York: Pergamon. 318 pp.

370. Wright, L. 1973. Aversive conditioning of self-induced seizures. *Behav. Ther.* 4:712–13

371. Wright, L., Truax, C. B., Mitchell, K. M. 1972. Reliability of process ratings of psychotherapy with children. *J. Clin. Psychol.* 28:232–34

372. Yates, A. J. 1970. *Behavior Therapy.* New York: Wiley. 445 pp.

373. Young, E. R., Rimm, D. C., Kennedy, T. D. 1973. An experimental investigaion of modeling and verbal reinforcement in the modification of assertive behavior. *Behav. Res. Ther.* 11:317–19

PRIMARY PREVENTION §243

Marc Kessler and George W. Albee[1]

Department of Psychology, University of Vermont

Burlington, Vermont 05401

A quick glance at articles published over the years in the *Annual Review of Psychology* shows that many authors start out with disclaimers about the possibility of completing the task in the space assigned them by the editors. We are in this tradition. The editors asked for a chapter on Prevention of Mental Disorders. The review was to be accomplished in 25 pages (or less). Obviously, an impossible task. Preventive efforts have been divided by Caplan (71) into three separate major areas: primary prevention, secondary prevention, and tertiary prevention. As in conventional medicine, primary prevention is the steps taken to prevent the occurrence of a disease, secondary prevention is early treatment of the disease once it has occurred, and tertiary prevention is the attempt to minimize the long-term effects of the disease.

Recognizing the impossibility of the task of reviewing this tripartite field, and with the agreement of the editors, this chapter will be limited to an examination of primary prevention. Even here the literature is so enormous and amorphous as to defy adequate coverage. Our reading for a year leads us to the conclusion that practically every effort aimed at improved child rearing, increasing effective communication, building inner control and self-esteem, reducing stress and pollution etc—in short, everything aimed at improving the human condition, at making life more fulfilling and meaningful—may be considered to be part of primary prevention of mental or emotional disturbance. Legislators, social reformers, radicals, conservatives, and practically everyone else, propose solutions to human ills. The law requiring seat belts in automobiles which must be fastened before the car can function will clearly reduce the incidence of brain damage in thousands of people in the course of a year. Enforcing lower speed limits during the energy shortage has reduced the number of accidents and auto fatalities. Clearly this is primary prevention of emotional distress in persons not injured and in families of nonvictims.

The plan of this chapter is to provide a few guideposts through the maze of the

---

[1] We wish to thank J. Greene, M. Solan, I. Turcot, and L. Weiger for their valuable assistance.

557

vast literature on prevention. We start with definitions, or preconceptions, that people in the field bring to the area. Then we will examine some of the important models of the conditions that have been the targets for primary prevention. We will go on to discuss epidemiology and some of the social conflicts that may be generated by action programs. We will attempt to point out where efforts at primary prevention are being made and what the future may hold. Through all of this we will try to show the difficulties for scientific study inherent in the field, and we will make some attempts at clarifying the research problems.

The field of primary prevention is analogous in many ways to the great Oke-fenokee Swamp. Attractive from a distance and especially from the air, it lures the unwary into quagmires, into uncharted and impenetrable byways. There are islands of solid ground, sections of rare beauty, unexpected dangers, and violent inhabitants. If one explores, and survives, the area becomes compelling, even addictive. Meanwhile, the rest of the outside world goes on unconcerned and unaware. As we undertook the task of exploring this vast area we became more and more conscious of its size and of its undisciplined nature and the vagueness of the existing maps. Like many explorers we became a little crazy, somewhat monomaniacal. After this heady experience we still remain enchanted, although not overanxious to make the same trip again soon. This analogy, too, soon fails to represent reality. When reading through the literature on prevention we kept thinking of Raimy's (270) definition of psychotherapy as an "Unidentified technique applied to unspecified problems with unpredictable outcomes", ... for which long and rigorous training is required (p. 3). In comparison with the field of primary prevention the field of psychotherapy is tough-minded and exact! Wherever we looked, whatever we read or heard, there were unexplored or unresearched hypotheses about primary prevention.

What is meant by primary prevention in the field of behavioral disorders? Most authors in this area have wrestled with attempts at definition, interspersed with more or less optimistic hopes for the future of primary preventive efforts (11, 28, 29, 33, 43, 45, 51, 73, 79, 86, 92, 94, 97, 106, 112, 124, 131, 134, 137, 140, 143, 151, 176, 177, 188, 201, 205, 206, 213, 215, 219, 220, 244, 262, 273, 274, 282, 283, 293, 294, 301, 303, 325, 329, 341, 342, 358, 368, 371.) While Caplan (e.g. 69, 72) has written much recently to advance his own model of primary prevention, the mental hygiene movement has been around for a much longer period of time than he, getting a tremendous impetus in the early part of this century (e.g. 43, 75). We are still experiencing a backlash against the extravagant claims of the "mental hygiene movement" started by Clifford Beers and others early in the century. This movement promised to eliminate most forms of mental and emotional distress through education—education of parents, education of children, teaching sound mental health principles to teachers, clergymen, and other significant influencers (99, 203, 211).

Currently there are several varying usages of the term primary prevention. A sampling of the terminology used in the literature may give an indication of the lack of consistency in the field. Wagenfeld (344) sees primary prevention as taking two basic forms: (*a*) intervention in life crises of individuals, and (b) altering the balance of physical, social, cultural, and psychosocial forces in the community. This is close to Caplan's position (e.g. 70). He says the primary prevention of mental disorders has a long-term goal of assuring continually adequate physical, psychosocial, and sociocultural supplies, which both enable the individual to avoid stress and which increase the individual's capacity to withstand future stress. Definitions of primary prevention sometimes tend to be quite general. For example, Zax & Cowen (374) say that virtually all that is done to improve the lot of humans should be included. Or the definition can be very abstract. Roberts (283) lists three actions as preventive: (a) the removal of the noxious agent; (b) strengthening of the host to increase its resistance to noxious agents; or (c) preventing contact between the agent and the host. Bower (54) defines primary prevention as getting children through our health, family, and school institutions "smelling like a rose." Bower (51) has outlined a detailed action-oriented framework for accomplishing primary prevention. Without attempting to deal fully with his fairly complex model, we note that he believes primary prevention can be accomplished through medical, social, and psychological actions which must occur during prenatal, perinatal, and later periods of life in those areas of the normal social milieu like the school, and in employment settings, and by professionals (such as clergy, police, teachers) in institutions affecting people in trouble. He gives many examples of normal emotional hazards for which effective knowledge of preventive intervention exists and could be brought to bear. In his context primary prevention programs are "aimed at persons not yet separated from the general population and, hopefully, an intervention specific enough to be operationally defined and measured" (51, p. 837).

Given the large number of definitions of primary prevention, we were tempted to follow a suggestion of Wagenfeld (344). He suggested a return to the terminology everyone used before Caplan confused matters—namely to discuss prevention, treatment, and rehabilitation. Prevention here means the prevention of the occurrence of mental disorders; treatment means intervention after the onset of the disorder; and rehabilitation means trying to reverse the damage and to rebuild the systems that have been disrupted by the disorder. Primary prevention is generally applied to groups or made available to everyone. It can be anything which prevents the occurrence of disorder. (Our conflict is that we gag on the word treatment as reflecting an inappropriate medical model.)

Problems of ideology often enter into attempts at defining primary prevention. There are political, social, and ethical implications when things are done to large groups (211). Elaine Cumming (98) divides mental health preventive efforts into two main strategies: (*a*) finding out what causes mental illness, then removing or preventing the cause, using malaria as her example; and (*b*) discovering the characteristics of immune or resistant populations and then making everyone else resemble them. She was quite aware of the ideological problems that might be involved in mental health preventive efforts. She quotes Bleuler who, in talking about prevention of schizophrenia, said "the avoidance of masturbation, of disappointments in love, of strains or frights, are recommendations which can be made with a clear conscience, because these are things to be avoided in all circumstances." (98, p. 3). Not everyone today would agree.

The platforms of political parties, the writings of political theorists from Lenin and Mao, to Lincoln and Ghandi, to DeGaulle and Buckley, all claim as their major goal the improvement of the human condition, the creation of environments that will reduce or eliminate human misery and emotional distress for large groups of people and for future generations. The writings of the utopians from Plato to Skinner promise a more rational, orderly, and satisfying life for all, or nearly all. Philosophers, theologians, economists, and humanists have in common with politicians, environmentalists, and liberationists the goal of a better and more satisfying tomorrow. Few have any published data!

During the past year we found ourselves constantly writing references and ideas on scraps of paper and emptying our pockets each day of notes on the primary prevention relevance of childrens' group homes, titanium paint, parent-effectiveness-training, consciousness raising, Zoom, Sesame Street, the guaranteed annual wage, legalized abortion, school integration, limits on international cartels, unpolished rice, free prenatal clinics, antipollution laws, a yoghurt and vegetable diet, free VD clinics, and a host of other topics. Nearly everything, it appears, has implications for primary prevention, for reducing emotional disturbance, for strengthening and fostering mental health. And anyway, as Bleuler said, they are good things in themselves.

MODELS OF DISTURBANCE

Our problem then is to review a vast literature having to do with the prevention of conditions which are not clearly defined, which vary in rate enormously as a function of community tolerance for deviance, which change frequences with changing social conditions, and which may not even exist as identifiable individual defects.

What order can we bring into the bewildering variety of efforts at primary prevention? A number of alternative approaches is available:

1. We could adopt a *developmental scheme*, examining efforts aimed at different developmental stages—efforts at genetic counseling (e.g. 229), marriage counseling (332), pregnancy planning (88, 182), prenatal care (290), good obstetrical care, parental assistance and guidance (38, 80, 175, 181), well-baby clinics and early identification and intervention (e.g. 53, 97, 272), preschool programs and enrichment programs (e.g. 14, 236, 318), foster home and group home care (87), early school intervention and mental hygiene programs in the schools (e.g. 8, 13, 14, 50, 55, 93, 94, 336, 337, 346, 356, 378), sex education and human relations groups, the variety of crisis programs available (e.g. 16, 122, 154, 189, 223, 224, 309), and so on through the life span (15, 44, 152, 157, 159, 242, 339, 347) to the plethora of proposed support programs for the aged.

2. Or we could adopt a more usual scheme which separates the field into broad areas of preventive special focus: (*a*) preventing organic dificulties which cause

emotional distress such as untreated syphilis, lead poisoning, endocrinological malfunctioning, brain injury etc; (b) attending to the psychodynamic problems which could be prevented through "mental hygiene education" of parents, teachers etc; and (c) dealing with social problems which affect large numbers and which can only be prevented through efforts at changing the larger social environment. Sanford (301) gives a clear and concise overview of this particular logical division of effort (63).

3. Or we could examine the separate mental "diseases" or conditions which are to be prevented with reference to programs designed specifically for each: schizophrenia (32, 171, 291, 292), alcoholism (261), manic depressive disorder (87, 316), existential neurosis (222), juvenile delinquency (134, 135, 266, 286), addiction to drugs (39, 145, 316), mental deficiency (84, 156, 195, 267, 312), etc.

4. Or we could argue that the prevention of mental "illness" or emotional distress is just a disguised form of the old medical model—that we are really distracted by the conventional wisdom of our time, and that we should focus on the development of competence, or achievement, self-actualization, and on positive mental health (e.g. 173).

Unwilling to adopt one of these models, and without space to consider them all, we will simply draw a rough map of the swamp as we see it—pointing to quagmires, putting in danger signs, and leaving much as terra-incognita in the hope that other explorers will be tempted by the lure of the unknown and mysterious.

In any discussion of the field of primary prevention of disorders it early becomes imperative to define reliably the disorders that we are striving to prevent. Programs of prevention in our area also talk about the development of positive effects, about fostering "mental health" (173). Similar questions of definition can be asked about these conditions we are attempting to foster. If we cannot define mental illness reliably, how can we prevent it? (62, 355). If there is no such thing as mental illness, if there are only problems in living (334), then it may be foolish to talk about prevention in the usual sense. If there are such "things" as emotional distresses and behavioral disturbances which have antecedent causes, then our task is not meaningless at all. But before we become optimistic we must consider the ethical problems of trying to prevent "problems in living."

If mental disorders are primarily organic (279, 280, 313), if they are caused by a discoverable physical defect, the strategy for reducing the number of mentally disordered people then involves public health efforts of the sort that have been so successful in reducing the incidence of other widespread diseases (112, 113, 206, 221). If we are concerned only with prevention of the conditions which fit the diagnostic nomenclature of the *Diagnostic and Statistical Manual No. 2* (10), persons who have been labeled schizophrenic, or neurotic, or brain damaged, then the problem, while still enormous, is of a particular order of magnitude. But if we define as emotionally disturbed those additional people who are prejudiced against other people because of their religion, age, or sex, then the number of disturbed people grows dramatically and the dimensions of the effort at prevention grow apace (1, 5-7).

Bower (51) cautions us:

A common conception of prevention often obfuscates thinking and action, namely, that little can be accomplished short of major social overhaul. Prevention of mental and emotional disorders is seen as the exclusive result of the abolition of injustice, discrimination, economic insecurity, poverty, slums, and illness. To seek less is to attempt to fell a giant sequoia with a toy axe (p. 833).

Different behavioral models have led to the choice of different areas of investigation. The organicists frequently look at the molecular level for their explanations of behavior. Research has established the effects of genetic factors (103, 160, 295), nutritional factors (240), damage to the various parts and levels of the central nervous system, and other organic conditions which have measurable subsequent behavioral consequences (88, 248).

There can be no socially oriented prevention without the acceptance of psychological determinism. Psychological determinism holds that all behavior is caused by antecedent interpersonal conditions and events. The scientific problem is to identify the antecedent—consequent pattern of relationships in order to be able to explain, predict, and control events (192, 225, 276, 288, 289).

Many psychologists have focused on more molar events, particularly the experiences called conditioning and learning (e.g. 259). There is no question but that human behavior is changed and modified as a consequence of experience. Sometimes both of these approaches are brought together into interactional studies. For example, there seem to be critical periods in the maturation of the human organism when exposure to particular learning experiences has most definite and the strongest effects (see 306 for bibliography). When the organism is ready it can learn, but no amount of practice before this time has much effect, and practice subsequent to the critical period (306) has lesser effect. Proponents of the "psychogenic hypothesis" have argued that the most critical period for the learning of emotional reactions is during infancy and early childhood. This hypothesis suggests that the formation of adult personality is very largely the consequence of the emotional conditions during these early formative critical periods. This observation is both obvious to most clinicians and difficult to prove scientifically. Clinicians tend to accept it unquestioningly, as a result of their experience, and scientists tend to question it because it is unsubstantiated by unambiguous research findings (179, 247, 280, 372).

Not all investigators accept the psychogenic hypothesis. For example, Rimland (280) says "I predict that research will ultimately show psychosocial influences to have minor—if any—relevance in causing the limited disorders called 'neuroses' and even less relevance in causing severe disorders known as psychoses" (p. 704). Hebb (155) supports this position, "there are no data to prove that . . . there is a class of 'functional' mental illness that is produced by emotional disturbance alone." Frank (125) concluded that no factors of parent-child interaction could be found to be unique in any diagnostic groups, nor to distinguish these groups from controls (p. 191).

Much of this iconoclasm will sound strange to clinicians with the social-developmental-dynamic orientation. Every graduate student in psychology has been exposed to the "classic" works of people like Spitz (331), Goldfarb (138, 139), and Bowlby (58). The message transmitted by these different investigators has to do with the importance of early experiences of "mothering," of the affectional ties between infant and caregiver, and of the terribly damaging later consequences of inconsistency, of placing infants in institutions and other settings where their affectional needs were not satisfied. Recently a widely quoted study by Heston (158) presented another side of the picture. Heston found that when infants who had been born to schizophrenic mothers were placed for adoption within a matter of days after birth, their subsequent rate for schizophrenia was considerably greater than the rate for a control group born to nonschizophrenic but emotionally disturbed mothers in the same institutions. Both kinds of studies have been criticized for methodological deficits and both must be viewed with some caution because, as is so often the case, the respective investigators believed they would find the results they did.

It should be noted that critics of the psychogenic hypothesis do not say that childhood experiences do not cause later problems; rather they say that the relationship has not been proved. One has the feeling that they believe that organic explanations ultimately will be sufficient. If this were really true, our task would be easy, for it is in the complex area of social, cultural, and familial causation that we have our greatest confusion and complexity. In order to substantiate the "psychogenic hypothesis" it would be necessary to demonstrate with a high order of reliability a clear relationship between specific and objectively identifiable early forms of emotionally distressing experiences and subsequent behavioral disturbances. It would also be useful to show that most persons whose early experiences were free of such disturbances developed into normal adults. It would also be desirable to show that persons with exceptionally warm and supportive early experiences were, as a group, relatively successful and creative in addition to being free of pathological symptoms. Because of the enormously complicated problems of stretching a research effort over the long years between the possible cause and the later effects, clear relationships are difficult to establish with scientific precision. This difficulty is even greater than in other areas of prevention in medical epidemiology, because of the problems of definition described above.

There are a few longitudinal studies of humans, and many with animals, which seem to support conventional clinical observations. Thus, for example, Bayley (25) reports strong negative association between maternal hostility during the early years of the child's life and measured intelligence more than 30 years later, and positive association between ratings of maternal affection during the early years and intelligence in middle age (26). There are other studies which deal with various psychological and social factors in the development of mental disturbances which are relevant to the psychogenic hypothesis (20, 66, 102, 104, 119, 125, 126, 141, 161, 165, 166, 169, 170, 191, 232, 246, 251, 260, 275, 286, 306, 326, 353).

The major strategies of primary prevention depend for their relevance and effectiveness on the truth of this proposition—that early happenings have later consequences, especially that emotional damage to the child is reflected in its adult disturbance. There is no argument in the organic area. Organic damage is the easiest to measure. Thus lead poisoning from the ingestion of lead paint, for example, produces measurable changes in the blood and damage to the brain, with long-term consequences for the child's ability to learn and to behave normally (214). German measles during the first 3 months of pregnancy can produce irreversible retardation in the child. Chromosomal anomalies can lead to Down's Syndrome and to other structural mental diseases. Blood changes, chromosomal anomalies, disturbed reflexes etc are all objective and measurable in the infant and young child. They usually are associated with conditions that bring the infant or young child to a medical setting where records are made and observations are quantified and stored (250, 251). Later investigators can go back and find these objective records and correlate them with current problems.

The situation gets much more complicated when we search for relationships between social experiences during early life and later behavior. These relationships are more dificult to establish because of the more difficult problem of measurement. In the case of psychological influences—social experiences and events—no such permanent records are likely to have been made. The ambivalent alternation of affection and rejection by the mother, the child's experience of being left frequently with a negligent baby sitter, the effects of the sudden withdrawal of love and attention at the time of arrival of a new sibling—where are these events recorded, and how are they retrieved? Three recent volumes on life history research in psychopathology go a long way toward summarizing the scattered evidence of these and related relationships (276, 288, 289).

Yet much of our clinical experience suggests the powerful long-term effects of damaging emotional experiences which have occurred early in the life of individuals. Almost inevitably the evidence is less reliable than the evidence for organic factors. In the absence of well-documented longitudinal studies with follow-up observations, we must rely on retrospective studies with all of the methodological problems they entail.

The psychogenic hypothesis seems often to elicit strong feelings of opposition from those hardnosed scientists who like to deal only with "facts" and objective measurements. The evening that Freud announced to the Viennese Neurological Society that all adult neuroses, in his experience, could be traced to early sexual trauma the reaction of his audience was either skeptical or hostile (178). Audience reaction continues to reflect these feelings. As evidence of the weakness of the psychogenic hypothesis the organicists point to the fact that some children from the most emotionally deprived and difficult backgrounds often grow up to be apparently well-adjusted and well-balanced adults. It is interesting in this respect to note the fact that only one person in 20 with untreated syphilis develops the mental illness we call general paresis. This low rate in no way invalidates the certainty of organic connection between syphilis and paresis.

Clearly, the "psychogenic hypothesis" held by a majority of present-day clinicians seems to have had its primary origin in the work of Freud. Everyone who has studied Freud's work is familiar with his attempts at relating adult disturbance to childhood experience. Yet Lemkau (204), making a careful search of all Freud's writings, including writing to a number of Freudian scholars, searching for some indication of Freud's specific ideas on prophylaxis, concluded that Freud made no specific mention of the subject.

Lemkau (204) does attempt to summarize Freud's work as it relates to primary prevention with propositions such as the following: All behavior is caused and causes may be modified in such a way that undesirable behavior is avoided; emotional reactions follow a maturational process which is orderly and predictable, and to some extent controllable; while human development involves stress, and excessive stress is unfortunate, consequences could be prevented by the control of excessive stress; personality is markedly influenced by emotional relationships particularly with parents; and finally, cultural factors have significant effects on the individual's adjustment. While Freud never examined the specific implications of these relationships for prevention, a great many persons influenced by his work have attempted to apply these principles in the area of prevention (301).

Sanford (301) discusses those followers of Freud, especially his daughter, Anna Freud, who have been interested in the application of psychoanalytic knowledge to prevention. The coincidence of social cataclysms, the Russian Revolution, the Great Depression, with the development of analytic theory, resulted in a school of socially oriented analysts. The most notable instigator of psychological and social theories relevant to prevention was Alfred Adler. Adler (3) argued for the development through education of social responsibility (also see Ansbacher & Ansbacher 12).

But psychodynamic theories are not the only source of the psychogenic hypothesis. Darwin (see 75) had shattered the illusion of the fixity of the species, advancing the idea of the modifiability of every species including the human. Clifford Beers wrote his book in 1908, and the mental hygiene movement sprung out of the ready *zeitgeist*. William James and Adolf Meyer were influenced by Beers, influenced him in turn, and helped spread the idea that "mental disease" could be prevented if the human environment was improved.

Bloom (43) quotes Meyer as follows: "Communities have to learn what they produce in the way of mental problems and waste of human opportunities, and with such knowledge they will rise from mere charity and mere mending, or hasty propaganda, to well balanced early care, prevention and general gain of health" (p. 1).

The point is that efforts at primary prevention must stress the temporal order of social cause and effect. If an effect is to be prevented, experiences that precede the phenomenon must somehow be controlled in order to prevent its occurrence. In the field of mental health, one of the major clinical hypotheses involves the long-term effect of infant's and child's experiences on adult personality and the causation of personality disturbance. If the evidence is accepted that certain experiences in early childhood have positive or negative effects on adult functioning, then efforts at prevention should attempt to maximize the early positive experiences and minimize or eliminate the negative experiences. Evidence supporting these relationships, we believe, is so voluminous as to defy summarization.

Both in infrahuman and human subjects careful research studies have demonstrated the power of early positive and negative experience on adult experience
(note the earlier references).

Important sources of documentation of the "psychogenic hypothesis" have
come from both human and controlled animal laboratory studies (e.g. 61, 192, 199,
335, etc). The work of Harlow (153) is well known in this context. Severe and
pathological adult behavior follows from the absence of adequate mothering of
monkey infants; lack of love is permanently damaging without the restorative
effect of peer group play. Such laboratory studies are difficult to duplicate in the
human arena. One of the most convincing was the observation of Skeels
(321–323), who documented the remarkable and dramatic improvement in a
group of very young children who were labeled retarded and who made dramatic
and unexpected intellectual and emotional progress when "adopted" by a group
of older retarded girls in an institution in Iowa. Most of these children, Skeels
showed, reached a normal level of intelligence and on being placed in adoptive
families grew up to be normal healthy emotionally stable adults in contrast to
those left in institutions.

The important point is that unless the "psychogenic hypothesis" is an accurate
reflection of the true state of affairs there is no basis for efforts at primary
prevention which focus on the social and emotional experiences of children. To
argue that the nature and quality of early experience has little effect on the
development of adult personality, and especially disturbed personality, would
make unnecessary all of the elaborate attempts at protecting infants and young
children from psychological damage. Orphanages and foundling homes have
been replaced by more carefully designed systems of foster home placement of
children. Attention to the psychological and emotional needs of children is based
on repeated clinical reports of the damage done by cold and impersonal handling
(e.g. 57, 331).

On the other hand, if we do accept the psychogenic hypothesis, then efforts at
primary prevention, in addition to being concerned with prevention of organic
and physical damage, must also be directed at the social and emotional experience
of children. This latter effort will lead social scientists directly into social and
political action in the attempt to shape social conditions in ways that directly or
indirectly affect the security and emotional responses of parents and children.

Both approaches to primary prevention (preventing or eliminating organic
damage due to defective genes, disease, toxins, and accidents, and prevention of
damaging emotional experiences) ultimately lead to some interference with individual freedom. In the extreme, primary preventive efforts might be expected to
lead eventually to social control of child bearing, with licenses issued only to
persons genetically sound, to prenatal tests which could result in therapeutic
abortions, to sperm banks and ova banks etc (33). Similarly, efforts at primary
prevention could ultimately lead especially to nursery and child rearing institutions where the negative effects of emotionally immature parents could be
avoided.

Perhaps the most compelling reason for continuing the efforts of prevention, given a lack of coherent understanding of what it is that we are really trying to prevent, is cited in Bloom's paper on the medieval miasma theory (41). Miasma theory held that soil polluted with waste products of any kind gave off a miasma into the air which caused many major diseases. Bloom goes on to say that current theories of prevention may appear to be patterned after the model first proposed by the miasmatists. In spite of the groundless basis for miasma as cause, the attempts of the sanitarians did have the effect of reducing the rate of infectious diseases. Perhaps in our current attempts at social overhaul, sweeping clean with a wide broom will be efficacious only because we may inadvertently hit the appropriate dirt.

EPIDEMIOLOGY AND ECOLOGY

It is public health dogma that no widespread human disease is ever brought under control by the treatment of afflicted individuals. Smallpox was not conquered by treating smallpox patients; neither was treatment of the individual the answer to typhoid fever, nor polio, nor measles. Every plague afflicting humankind has been controlled when discovery of the cause led to taking effective steps to remove it. This process is primary prevention. We vaccinate all children and adults so that they will not contract smallpox. We give children polio viruses that have been killed or attenuated for the same reason, and we give them measles vaccine, and we put fluorides into their drinking water to prevent dental caries.

There are at least two approaches to establish the research base for preventive efforts in mental health. The first is the attempt to study the possible biological, psychological, and sociological factors in the origins of disorders discussed above under the headings of biogenesis and psychogenesis. A second is the attempt to study the pattern of distribution of disturbances in the population: epidemiology.

According to Gruenberg (149), epidemiology "includes a study of the factors that determine the patterns of disease occurrence and how the factors can be modified to eliminate the disease from the population." He goes on to say:

> Epidemiological analysis follows a fairly simple pattern. A factor, f, is suspected of playing a role in the production of a disease, d; populations having much more f are examined to see if they have more d than populations having little f; through inferences based on all relevant knowledge and on theories derived from clinical familiarity with the disease, the investigators obtain a picture of the chain of circumstances that leads to the occurrence of the disease; finally, crucial links in the chain are attacked experimentally. The relationships are often highly indirect and highly complicated but this general strategy has succeeded in bringing many animal and plant diseases under control (149, p. 2).

Obviously this approach to the study of mental disorders has its problems. One is the absence of any objective means of identifying the presence of the "disease." It is relatively easy to study the epidemiology of diabetes, or bone fractures, or murder, because each provides objective data to be counted. The effectiveness of a prevention program can be measured by looking at changes in rates. But if we have no reliable way of identifying the phenomenon, the problem of measuring change becomes insurmountable (105, 114, 115). Mental illness usually involves a social judgment about behavior, a social decision to call the behavior deviant or sick. Barbara Wooten (367) has discussed this problem at some length. She says:

> . . . anti-social behavior is the precipitating factor that leads to mental treatment. But at the same time the fact of the illness is itself inferred from this behavior: indeed it is almost true to say that the illness is the behavior for which it is also the excuse. But any disease, the morbidity of which is established only by the social failure that it involves, must rank as fundamentally different from those with which the symptoms are independent of social norms.

Obviously the rate of mental conditions is not only a function of the frequency of the "pathological" behavior, but also of the community's tolerance for the behavior. Thus, San Francisco has been called "the tolerant city" because much wider ranges of deviant behavior are tolerated by the citizenry. This would tend to decrease the rate of reported disturbance there in comparison with what the rate might be in other cities, except perhaps that the tolerance may also serve to attract a wider range and larger number of deviant persons to the more tolerant environment.

Primary prevention may demand various kinds of social action to reduce the subsequent rate of disturbance. Paradoxically, and perhaps only in the case of mental disorders, increasing community toleration also has the effect of reducing the rates. Sexual behavior which is forbidden by law in certain states or countries, and which leads to severe penalties if discovered, may well be tolerated in other states or countries. Where homosexuality was once punished as a monstrous deviation it now has been decriminalized in parts of the world if occurring between consenting adults. A newly formed Association of Gay Psychologists is working to increase public understanding and tolerance of this sexual choice. A recent vote of the American Psychiatric Association has removed homosexuality as a disease entity from the diagnostic and statistical manual. (This is a fascinating use of democracy rather than science in the description and definition of "disease.") Similar changes in attitudes have occurred toward consumption of pornography, and the result is a change in reported rates of consumption independent of a change in the actual rate of the behavior.

Obviously then one way to reduce the rate of mental disorders in the population would be to change the definition of what constitutes mental disorder. We could either sharply limit the use of the term "mental illness" to the most obviously and seriously disturbed people, or we could broaden the definition to include mild disturbances to which everyone is subjected (268). Either change would have immediate effects on rates and would be reflected in our epidemiological studies. Inasmuch as public attitudes about mental disorder tend to be more tolerant (S. Starr in 177) than the views of the experts, it is possible to manipulate data on rates by manipulating the groups that make the definition. It is possible to manipulate opinions about mental illness through various kinds of instruction, information, and personal contact (110, 241, 249). The extensive literature concerning both public attitudes and professional attitudes has been reviewed recently by Judith Rabkin (268).

Reviewing the earlier literature on the epidemiology of mental illness, Plunkett & Gordon (263) suggested that its value is more potential than actual. Sources of data were examined by them and found wanting. The inability of the field of psychiatry to develop a meaningful and reliable classification system was identified as a major problem. Plunkett and Gordon set forth a preliminary research plan for well-controlled field experiments to identify and codify causal factors in such problems as suicide, alcoholism, postpartum psychoses, and psychosomatic disturbances. Because each of these conditions offers some hope for objective, reliable identification, their distribution in the population might be measured as a first step toward discovering causal factors. But these authors, both experienced epidemiologists, were less than sanguine about our chances for the meaningful study of the other so-called mental illnesses.

In any attempt to assess the success of efforts at primary prevention, one is faced with examining programs that are aimed at conditions of uncertain identification, and of unknown distribution, in an area where objectivity is lacking or may be unobtainable (e.g. 115, 116).

In spite of the difficulties involved in the epidemiological approach in this area, a number of studies have been conducted. Gruenberg (149, 150), Hollingshead & Redlich (162), Langner and Srole (197–199, 333), Leighton (200), Pasamanick (257), Zusman (381) have all reported epidemiological data on general populations. An excellent review and critique of problems in this field is by Miller & Mishler (232).

Epidemiology has also been applied to more specialized populations such as elementary school children (83, 127, 133), native Americans on reservations (315, 316), and of course to many specific disorders. An excellent example of the latter is the work of Calahan (65) on alcoholics.

One of the earliest epidemiological studies of mental disturbances and mental retardation was the "Jarvis Report," the *Report of the Commission on Lunacy and Idiocy in Massachusetts, 1855* (174). In this classic study Jarvis was convinced by his data of the intimate relationship between pauperism and insanity. Clearly there were more insane persons among the poor, and especially among those who were paupers. One hundred years later Ryan (297) reported high rates of untreated or neglected disturbance among the poor. Multiproblem families, together with the children of the poor, and the elderly had the highest rates of disturbance. Most of the recent epidemiological research reports the same finding (e.g. 104, 126, 162, 167–170, 228, 232, 277, 348, 370).

The critical problem is "attribution of cause." Does poverty cause in a direct or indirect way the high rate of mental disturbance among the poor? Does poverty cause high rates of crime, alcoholism, drug addiction, and related indices of social pathology? Or perhaps both poverty and various forms of pathological behavior might be due to some common underlying defect. Jarvis (and more recent conservatives) hold the latter view. Jarvis saw poverty as "An inward principle, enrooted deeply within the man, and running through all his elements . . . and hence we find that, among those whom the world calls poor, there is less vital force, a lower tone of life, more ill health, more weakness, more early death, a diminished longevity. There is also less self respect, more idiocy and insanity and more crime than in the independent." These "diseases" of poverty and lunacy were traceable to an "imperfectly organized brain and feeble mental constitution" (114, pp. 45, 52–56). It is instructive to remember that the foreign insane paupers whom Jarvis considered defective were the immigrant Irish, whose descendants have long since disappeared into middle class respectability and whose rates of mental disturbance have dropped dramatically in the intervening century. It is instructive also to note that each succeeding wave of immigrants to the inner city—the Scandinavians, the eastern European Jews, the southern Italians, and most recently the Chicanos, Puerto Ricans, and Blacks—have taken their place among the Class Five poor and have shown high rates of social pathology during the time that they occupy the low rung on the social ladder. It seems reasonable to argue that if both poverty and a high rate of social pathology were due to some common defect, genetic or constitutional, the rates for these groups would not decline precipitously as they achieve economic security. Such evidence is difficult to document statistically, but circumstantially at least we would argue that the predominant weight of evidence supports the position that poverty causes social disability rather than both being due to some inherent common defect (298, 299).

Much of this literature has been reviewed recently by Elizabeth Taylor Vance (343). She reviews the widespread efforts in conceptualizing the dimension *social competence—social disability* which she sees as the major continuum for a wide variety of syndromes such as process schizophrenia, antisocial behavior, and cognitive deficit. In her thorough review she suggests that "there is much evidence to suggest that the extrinsic conditions in contemporary life that seem most conducive to the development of syndromes of social disability converge in the environmental correlates of urban poverty. Social disability would appear to be a dynamic and organic outcome of such conditions" (p. 508).

The clear implication is that individual therapy will be helpless to break the cycle. Rather "the traditional activities of the clinician must be modified in the direction of greater involvement in the developmental, environmental and social context of the individual. On the other hand, an intimate knowledge and conceptualization of human behavior and development should guide the shaping of community psychology activity" (p. 508).

In this regard, primary prevention of mental disorders is frequently claimed as "belonging" to community psychology, a new applied specialty field.

Many persons date the beginning of community psychology with the Boston (Swampscott) Conference of 1965 (34). There a group of persons dissatisfied with the traditional and reactive role of clinical psychology invented or appropriated the term "community psychology" to designate a new specialty more interested in prevention than in psychotherapy and rehabilitation. Community psychology deals with social systems, programmed interventions, and the planning of environments. It aims at enhancing human competency and adheres to an ecological rather than a psychoanalytic model.

Cowen (92), in his *Annual Review* article on community psychology in 1973, suggested that attempts at splitting review articles in this field into (*a*) intervention in psychopathology, and (*b*) prevention of mental disorders, leads to all kinds of conceptual difficulties. He suggested that eventually community intervention chapters might begin to fuse with prevention chapters. He searched for all the articles in the *Community Mental Health Journal* that dealt with "prevention," "preventing," or "prevent," and he was frustrated to find that only some 3 percent dealt with these topics. In his search of the *Coordinate Index Reference Guide to Community Mental Health* (136) he found only 2 percent of the references classified under "primary prevention." He came to the disheartening conclusion that the social-community intervention area has largely ignored primary prevention and has failed to develop a research base.

Ecological variables recently have come to be seen as possible contributing factors in the development of mental disorder (63, 107, 108, 128). Epidemiologists have long appreciated the complexity of ecological systems producing health and disease. Their insights are applicable to some rather serious mental disturbances which may not be diseases at all but conditions which are a result of complex ecological systems. A characteristic of an ecological system is that disturbance in one place and time may set off a complex chain of events which leads to consequences only dimly and distantly perceived. Thus the spraying of orchards in Minnesota with biocides may affect the oyster beds in Louisiana, with long-range consequences to the health of children eating oysters from these beds. Many years later a senator from Louisiana may die of a coronary, partly because of damage done by her childhood eating habits and food intake. But the chain is not so simple and direct. The prosperity of the Minnesota apple growers may have stimulated the production of beef in Iowa, making pork cheaper in Louisiana during the young adulthood of the coronary victim ... etc, etc. Similar complex chains certainly exist in the mental health field so that we should not be surprised to discover that only relatively modest research efforts have been made, and great controversy and disagreement exist, to tease out cause and effect relationships. Three recent volumes on life history research examine some of these research questions (276, 288, 289; see also 59, 60).

In the complex "web of causation" is entangled a swarm of effects. Thus married persons in general have a smaller chance of developing a mental disturbance than single persons. Elderly persons who are living with a spouse have a strikingly lower rate of hospitalization for mental conditions than solitary elderly folk (172). Children from intact families have lower rates than children from broken homes (254–256, 286). Even more complex societal variables enter into the web of causation. Persons living in preindustrial societies reportedly are rarely affected with manic depressive psychosis (235, 360), nor are they subject to the classical Victorian neruoses that Freud spent his life studying. The sexually repressed Victorians, on the other hand, developed high rates of depression and symptom neurosis when as children they were taught to inhibit sexual thoughts, feelings, and behavior in order to struggle upward into the middle class, taking either the route of education or capital accumulation. In the old industrial societies like England and the United States the symptom neuroses are declining in frequency, but there is a dramatic rise in existential anxiety and the existential neurosis (Who am I? What is the purpose of my existence? What does it all mean?)

Actually a number of social changes that have been adopted without consideration of their ultimate benefits in preventing mental disturbance may prove to have significant mental health implications. The discovery and widespread use of controlled methods of contraception should reduce the number of unwanted children. As these children often experience rejection and, as a consequence, emotional deprivation leading to later behavioral disturbances, their number being reduced should reduce disturbance rates. The widespread use of compulsory seat belts in automobiles, and the development of other safety devices including padded dashboards and inflation devices, should reduce significantly the number of injuries to the brain suffered in auto accidents, with the resulting prevention of mental disorders associated with laceration and trauma to the brain. Reducing the amount of carbon monoxide and lead in the air breathed by children in our cities should also have the effect of reducing the amount of cellular damage to the central nervous system and its consequences.

One recent review (76) of ecological stress examined a whole range of genuine environmental stresses—such as radiation, laser beams, insecticides, noise pollution, air pollution, temperature extremes, driving problems, overcrowding, etc (31, 36, 85, 194, 245, 359, 362). These all have been shown to affect mental health in some way, and therefore their distribution and control should concern those in primary prevention.

We do not know enough yet about all the possible effects of these and other contaminants, but the evidence that does exist suggests unfortunate behavioral consequences on animals and children. Unhappily, Dubos (107–109) has pointed out that the worst of the environment pollution contaminants are still to come. He cites English studies which demonstrate an apparently permanent malfunctioning of children reared under high pollution conditions.

While psychologists have been interested in the study of stress for many years, the last decade has seen an increased concern with an ecological approach which examines the complexities of interacting factors in the environment inducing stress in the individual and thereby affecting mental health (141). Primary prevention in the mental health field ordinarily connotes prevention of psychological problems. But a voluminous body of evidence also indicates that the stresses of complex societies lead to disorders labeled *psychosomatic*. For example, a spate of recent books examines the relationship between life stress and coronary heart disease. The literature on stress inducing hypertension, duodenal ulcers, and other physical symptoms is enormous and obviously beyond the space limits of this chapter (see 87, 117, 230, 253, 269, 357, 364, 374).

The new approach to the contribution of environmental factors on the development of mental disorders opens yet another alleyway in the maze of factors that must be studied and accounted for in attempting to organize the field of primary prevention. For those interested in pursuing further studies we can suggest the references cited above, as well as the National Institute of Mental Health's *Bib-*

liography: Epidemiology of Mental Disorders: 1966–1968 (381), which lists some 170 titles concerning the design and implementation of studies, over 500 articles on the etiology of mental disease, close to 400 on rates, and about 250 on the characteristics of "diseased populations." (See also 60, 101, 141, 361.)

PRIMARY PREVENTION PROGRAMS

The social-developmental psychological hypotheses concerning the origins of mental disorders has led to many programs and proposals that have as their focus either broad or specific disorders. These programs range all the way from the general education programs of the mental hygiene movement that started with the work of Adolf Meyer and Clifford Beers to more specific programs of early intervention cited, for example, by Bower, Rolf, Zax & Cowen, Kelly, Garmezy, etc (56, 130, 185, 291, 338, 376).

The question that we must address briefly is how primary preventive efforts are to take place. Knowing as much or as little as we do, what is to be done? The National Association for Mental Health (238) has prepared one of the most specific blueprints for action in primary prevention. It gives actual steps to be taken by citizens' groups in their community to achieve the goal of the prevention of later emotional disturbance. The NAMH proposal focuses specifically on prenatal and perinatal conditions as areas where definite action should be taken. The time from conception to 6 months after birth was chosen as the action period. Among the actions recommended are prenatal and perinatal care affecting the expecting mother and the developing fetus, ways of coping with life crisis situations affecting the mother particularly, the development of better parenting skills, the modification of the social system which may be expected to be a source of stress if unmodified (welfare, medical care, day care etc), and the insurance of adequate medical care for mother and infant following birth.

There is no dearth of other suggestions concerning how primary preventive programs should be carried out (202, 226, 338). Caplan (73), for example, discusses those preventive programs which focus on strengthening physical and social resources: efforts to prevent prematurity; to provide appropriate nutrition to children with a genetic metabolic defect such as phenylketonuria; requiring iodized salt in areas where iodine supplies may be inadequate; prevention of psychosis due to pellagra; action to prevent lead poisoning in slum children; opportunities for cognitive enrichment for preschool children through the educational system. Caplan goes on to examine other psychosocial resources and suggests that efforts should be directed to the maintenance of a healthy family environment; to special intervention at the illness, hospitalization, or death of the mother; provision of homemaker services when needed; provision of in-hospital care by the mother when the child is hospitalized. He also suggests the application of crisis intervention as a preventive effort, as well as education of caregivers, mental health consultation, personal preparation for healthy crisis coping through education and anticipatory guidance (see also, 24, 30, 68, 217, 369, 371).

Bloom (43) suggested three action tactics: crisis intervention; anticipatory guidance, including, for example, meetings between clergymen and engaged parish-ioners, between social workers and groups of new parents; and consultation. Eisenberg (111) called for preventive programs to include: family planning, good health care and decent housing, adequate unemployment compensation and job training for displaced workers, case work service to minimize family breakdown, effective substitute care for homeless children, enriched school programs, recrea-tional facilities, vocational training, and other services.

The National Institute of Mental Health (239, 241, 243, 244) has proposed a program of mental health prevention which is educational rather than clinical in conception, with a goal to increase the individual's capacity for improving the quality of his life. It calls for use of a developmental approach, including efforts to improve early child development and to increase parental competence, then focusing on mental health aspects of public school education and on adolescence. It also considers special needs of high risk groups including high risk pregnancies with better prenatal care. Socialization training, development of competence, and improved self-esteem are included in the plan.

Kelly (184, 185) talks of three types of therapeutic programs: (a) the clinical approach focuses on changes in individuals or small groups which radiates its effects to others as one of the indirect results of the services offered; (b) systematic changes in organizations are aimed at helping the organizations deal with future crises; (c) community organization techniques focused on mobilizing community resources for community action. Kelly gives examples of each of these approaches.

Poser (265) suggests an approach to prevention based on the principles of learning. He suggests that mechanisms involving remedial learning techniques such as desensitization, flooding, and aversive conditioning be used to immunize subjects against later encounters with crisis. He suggests that primary prevention might best be achieved by the deliberate exposure of susceptible high risk individ-uals to learning experiences that are spontaneously encountered by most normal individuals.

Smith (327) suggests that a real attempt should be made to identify those inevitable crisis or life stress events viewed as critical to the mental health of individuals. Then we should help or teach the individuals to deal effectively with those crises. Early intervention at the school or preschool level is really geared toward the prevention of disorders which occur later in life: 10, 15, even 20 years after the time of the intervention. Evaluative programs should engage in such long-term follow-up in order to ascertain the effectiveness of the program study. Unfortunately, this kind of long-term follow-up has not been characteristic of most studies in the mental health field. Exceptions are the Berkeley Growth Studies (25, 26), Project Talent, and the studies cited in Rolf et al (276, 288, 289). Future preventive approaches to mental disorder must provide the necessary long-term funding for follow-up measures.

The above are just a sample of the discussion in the literature of general strategies for the prevention of mental disorders. What about more specific pro-grams? We will mention some representative current approaches to the prevention of mental disorders, without attempting to evaluate the adequacy of these ap-proaches.

PROGRAMS

The aim of preventive techniques in social planning is to use the social system to strengthen adaptive behaviors. Preventive approaches have been attempting to use major components of the social system, including the family, the schools, the world of work, and the community.

There have been a number of fairly specific targets for preventive efforts. For example, the family has been a focus, including attempts at parental education, early family intervention as preschool intellectual training (e.g. 21, 47, 78, 80, 120, 272, 284, 319, 320), work on training parents as therapists (e.g. 305), programs in the school (49, 52, 90, 91, 93, 94, 96, 97, 144, 304), programs in compensatory education such as the Headstart Program and the special programs for low income and minority groups (81, 82, 86, 90, 181, 189, 258, 278, 304, 381), and for the community (2, 9, 27, 35, 118, 121, 148, 164, 183, 189, 190, 212, 218, 237, 264, 281, 311, 328, 349, 352, 354).

One major focus for attempts at intervention and prevention is at an early age with children. This area has been given special attention in the recent past. Both the Group for the Advancement of Psychiatry (147) and the Joint Commission on the Mental Health of Children (176) have focused on this important area and have pointed to the serious lack of mental health programs, not only primary but secondary and tertiary programs as well, for children. There are a number of programs aimed at children (4, 17, 37, 40, 61, 74, 129, 142, 175, 181, 193, 272, 307, 317, 318, 340, 345, 351). Bolman reviews a number of these current programs (46).

The important role of the school in the prevention of mental disorders, and the promotion of competence, has been discussed for a number of years (61, 163, 176, 177). There is a growing number of programs in school settings to develop the competencies of school children and to prevent the educational and learning difficulties that can lead to further emotional and social maladjustment. It is noteworthy to emphasize that some of these programs are not, in the main, geared towards the prevention or amelioration of emotional disorders. They are in many instances geared toward the development of competence in the individuals. Many authors feel these are interdependent (13, 72, 89–97, 132, 144, 180, 216, 300, 373, 375, 376).

Bolman has reviewed programs for the family, and general programs (47, 48). Other program reports include those by Rees (271), Robertson (284), Ryan (296), the Skeels and Skodak studies (321–324), and that by Slobin (325). There is some question about whether crisis intervention and suicide prevention is primary or secondary prevention. Rather than go into a detailed review of these areas we list a number of references for those who are interested in this approach to preventive intervention (18, 19, 100, 122, 154, 189, 208–210, 223, 233, 285, 309, 310, 314, 315, 350, 363).

A major question to be addressed concerns the efficacy of primary preventive programs. Do they work? Much has been written about the evaluation of primary preventive efforts (42, 123, 130, 207, 231, 234, 252, 287, 288, 291, 308), and these references should be consulted for detailed information concerning evaluation research. The work of Campbell & Stanley (67) stands out as one of the definitive works in the field of evaluative research. It takes into account the realistic constraints that are found in doing action-oriented research in a number of fields, and its guidance is quite applicable to the field of primary prevention.[2]

SUMMARY AND CONCLUSIONS

Primary prevention in many areas may require social and political changes to improve the "quality of life" (302). Bower and others suggest that a lack of progress in the area of prevention may be traced to specific social resistances to the changes that would be required to actually make a difference. A major source of resistance is to the idea that real prevention must make major social system changes. It is true that many observers of our social pathology argue that patchwork solutions will not do, and that the whole structure of our polluted, industrialized, overpopulated, overenergized, overcrowded sexist and racist society breeds such massive human injustice and distress that the only hope for prevention is for major social reorganization. To prevent mental and emotional disorders, it is argued, we must abolish such injustices as unemployment, bad housing, social discrimination, personal insecurity, and poverty. As a consequence of the threat all of this holds to the status quo, the Establishment does little to encourage or support efforts at primary prevention in the social sphere because it believes, with some justification, that it would be funding programs aimed at a major redistribution of its power. Money is generally available for biomedical research on the search for the individual defect, but social programs are more often suspect (6, 186, 187).

A second force operating to resist efforts at primary prevention, for example, is our societal commitment to privacy and to personal freedom of choice, "the right and privilege of each person, and family, in a free society to mind his own business and have others mind theirs" (51). Even such relatively simple matters as the fluoridization of the water supply, and the requirement of vaccination against polio and smallpox—clear as is the research evidence which supports these practices—elicit widespread resistance and public debate. To urge even more drastic invasions of privacy, to propose the more emotion-laden kinds of intervention believed by many to have profound preventive implications for mental health, is to call out even more violent resistance. Sex education, growth groups, consciousness raising, parent effectiveness training, day-care, etc are programs that make many members of our society tremble with anger (64).

---

[2] Since completing this chapter, we have seen additional reviews of the field of primary prevention which cover the subject, or parts of it, in much greater detail than we have been able to do in the space available to us. The interested reader is referred to these publications:

(a) R. F. Muñoz and J. G. Kelly. The prevention of mental disorders. *Programmed Learning Aid Series*, ed. C. Cofer. Richard Irwin Co. In press.

(b) J. Monahan 1974. The prevention of violence. In *Community Mental Health and the Criminal Justice System*, ed. J. Monahan. New York: Pergamon.

(c) A. Binder, J. Monahan and M. Newkirk. Diversion from the juvenile justice system and the prevention of delinquency (same publication).

Society is ambivalent enough about requiring people whose behavior is already disturbed to undergo compulsory therapeutic procedures. Profound philosophic questions are involved in programs like behavioral modification aimed at improving the mental functioning. But society is highly ambivalent about utilizing some of these same techniques to intervene in the lives of individuals, especially children, who have not yet shown any kind of behavioral disturbance. Even when the approach is to prevent the development of later antisocial behaviors, as the implications in the work of the Gluecks (134, 135), for example, there is a great deal of concern over the rights of individuals to be let alone.

We assume that both childhood experiences and societal rules are important determinants of later behavioral adjustment or disturbance. It has been noted that two of the most important activities engaged in by members of our society legally require no training or demonstrated ability—that of governing and that of raising children—and that any laws proposed in either area would be quickly rejected as a serious curtailment of freedom.

The explanatory models we use to account for mental disorder have profound implication for choosing our strategies for primary prevention. Most true diseases can be brought under control with relatively little disturbance to the existing social order. These are the familiar public health methods. The requirement of vaccination against smallpox implies some degree of coercion, the treatment of public water supplies with antibacterial agents to prevent disease, and with fluorides to prevent tooth decay, are public health measures adopted without the individual consent of the people affected. Most rational observers would agree that such preventive measures involve little threat to the social order. It is when we get to efforts at preventing mental disorder and emotional distress that real ethical problems begin to appear. To get really involved in primary prevention of emotional disturbance often suggests social and political change quite far removed from the conventional conservatism characteristic of middle class professionals. Here is another interesting paradox. Those persons most likely to understand the relationship between social problems like poverty, unemployment, discrimination, and prejudice, and resulting high rates of mental disorder and distress, are members of the professions who work most closely with these "mental cases." Yet members of professions, in large measure because of the nature of their professional training, are selected to be relatively conscience laden upwardly mobile politically conservative-to-liberal, but certainly not revolutionary, social change agents. In addition, they tend to be the most informed and therefore the most logical ones to be concerned about individuals' rights. Too often they remain silent.

We can say with Bloom (41) that the most compelling reason for continuing efforts at prevention is suggested by the success of the miasmatists. Cleaning up the waste turned out to be the way to prevent disease. While elements of the theory were wrong the results were right.

It is tempting to search for a simple formula to cover all of the complexities of environmental stress in causing disruptive behavior and emotional problems. It is tempting to suggest an extension to the human environment of Lord Acton's (23) dictum: "Power tends to corrupt—absolute power corrupts absolutely." Everywhere we looked, every social research study we examined suggested that major sources of human stress and distress generally involve some form of excessive power. The pollutants of a power-consuming industrial society; the exploitation of the weak by the powerful; the overdependence of the automotive culture on powerful engines—power-consuming symbols of potency; the degradation of the environment with the debris of a comfort-loving impulse-yielding society; the power struggle between the rich consuming nations and the exploited third world; the angry retaliation of the impoverished and the exploited; on a more personal level the exploitation of women by men, of children by adults, of the elderly by a youth-worshiping society—it is enough to suggest the hypothesis that a dramatic reduction and control of power might improve the mental health of people. It is a tempting oversimplification, an hypothesis we will not propose seriously, but one that we recommend for quiet contemplation. We have found it particularly satisfying under relaxed environmental conditions—in a rowboat on a quiet Vermont lake on a sleepy summer day just before the fish begin to bite.

Literature Cited

1. Abell, P., McNeil, E., Powell, B. 1973. Prejudice and the helping relationship: One method for increasing awareness. *Am. J. Orthopsychiat.* 43:254
2. Aberle, D. F. 1950. Introducing preventive psychiatry into a community. *Hum. Organ.* 9:5–9
3. Adler, A. 1930. *The Education of Children.* New York: Greenberg
4. Ahmad, M., Simmons, E. 1972. A comprehensive child guidance service (an initial survey of North Wales Child Guidance Clinics). *Acta Paedopsychiat.* 39:92–98
5. Albee, G. W. 1969. Emerging concepts of mental illness and models of treatment: The psychological point of view. *Am. J. Psychiat.* 125:870–76
6. Albee, G. W. 1969. Who shall be served? *Prof. Psychol.* 1:4–7
7. Albee, G. W. 1970. The uncertain future of clinical psychology. *Am. Psychol.* 25:1071–80
8. Allinsmith, W., Goethals, G. W. 1962. *The Role of Schools in Mental Health.* New York: Basic Books
9. Altrocchi, J., Eisdorfer, C. 1970. Apprentice-collaborator field training in community psychology: The Halifax County program. In *Community Psychology: Perspectives in Training and Research,* ed. I. Iscoe, C. D. Spielberger. New York: Appleton-Century-Crofts
10. American Psychiatric Association

1968. *Diagnostic and Statistical Manual of Mental Disorders.* Washington, D.C.: APA
11. American Public Health Association, Program Area Committee on Mental Health 1962. *Mental Disorders: A Guide to Control Methods.* New York: Am. Public Health Assoc.
12. Ansbacher, H. L., Ansbacher, R. R., Eds. 1956. *The Individual Psychology of Alfred Adler.* New York: Basic Books
13. Anthony, E. J. 1971. Primary prevention with school children. See Ref. 22, 131–58
14. Arnold, R., Perlman, M., McQueeney, D., Gordan, D. 1973. Nature of mental health consultation to preschool problems. *Am. J. Orthopsychiat.* 43:220
15. Ashman, G. R., Dowles, W. E., Ron, W. D., Agranoff, B. 1963. Case finding and interviewing methods for a preventive occupational psychiatry programme. *Proc. 3rd World Conf. Psychiat.* Toronto Univ. Toronto Press
16. Augenbaum, R. J., Augenbaum, F. D. 1967. Brief intervention as a preventive force in disorders of early childhood. *Am. J. Orthopsychiat.* 37:697–702
17. Baer, C. J. 1958. The school progress and adjustment of underage and overage students. *J. Educ. Psychol.* 49:17–19
18. Bagley, C. 1968. Evaluation of a suicide prevention scheme by an ecological method. *Soc. Sci. Med.* 2:1–14

19. Bagley, C. 1971. An evaluation of agencies concerned with the prevention of suicidal behaviors. *Life Threatening Behav.* 1:33–50

20. Bandura, A., Walters, R. H. 1963. *Social Learning and Personality Development.* New York: Holt, Rinehart & Winston

21. Bard, M., Berkowitz, B. 1967. Training police as specialists in family crisis intervention: a community psychology action program. *Community Ment. Health J.* 3:315–17

22. Barten, H. H., Bellak, L., Eds. 1972. *Progress in Community Mental Health,* Vol. 2. New York: Grune & Stratton

23. Bartlett, J. 1955. *Familiar Quotations; a Collection of Passages, Phrases, and Proverbs Traced to Their Sources, in Ancient and Modern Literature,* 663. Boston: Little, Brown. 13th ed.

24. Barton, D., Abram, H. S. 1971. Preventive psychiatry in the general hospital. *Compr. Psychiat.* 12:330–36

25. Bayley, N. 1968. Behavioral correlates of mental growth: birth to 36 years. *Am. Psychol.* 23:1–17

26. Bayley, N., Shaefer, E. S. 1964. *Correlation of Maternal and Child Behaviors with the Development of Mental Abilities,* 29:97. Monogr. Soc. Res. Child Develop.

27. Becker, R. E. 1972. The organization and management of community mental health services. *Community Ment. Health J.* 8:292

28. Beier, E. G. 1969. Preventive measures in mental health area: some theoretical considerations on justification and a fantasy about the future. In *Future of Psychotherapy,* ed. C. Frederich. Boston: Little, Brown

29. Beiser, M. 1968. Primary prevention of mental illness: general vs. specific approaches. See Ref. 282, 84–91

30. Belknap, I. 1965. *Human Problems of State Mental Health Hospital.* New York: McGraw Hill

31. Bell, G., MacGreevey, P. 1969. *Behavior and Environment: A Bibliography of Social Activities in Urban Space.* Univ. Pittsburgh Dep. Urban Aff.

32. Bellak, L., Ed. 1958. *Schizophrenia: A Review of the Syndrome.* New York: Logos

33. Bellak, L. 1964. *Handbook of Com-*munity *Psychiatry and Community Mental Health.* New York: Grune & Stratton

34. Bennett, C. C. et al, Eds. 1966. *Community Psychology: A Report of the Boston Conference on the Education of Psychologists for Community Mental Health.* Boston Univ. Press

35. Bennett, W. H. 1972. *Community Mental Health Services Based on Established Health Unit Offices.* Pilot project report from the Muskoka-Parry Sound Health Unit. Ontario Ministry of Health Meeting with Medical Officers of Health, Toronto

36. Beranek, L. L. 1966. Noise. *Sci. Am.* 215:66–76

37. Berlin, I. N. 1972. Prevention of mental and emotional disorders of childhood. See Ref. 366, 1088–1109

38. Berlin, I. N., Berlin, R. 1973. Parents' role in education as primary prevention. *Am. J. Orthopsychiat.* 43:221

39. Bernstein, A., Epstein, L. J., Lennard, H. R., Ransom, D. C. 1972. The prevention of drug abuse. See Ref. 137, 439–47

40. Birch, H. G., Gussow, J. D. 1970. *Disadvantaged Children: Health, Nutrition and School Failure.* New York: Harcourt

41. Bloom, B. L. 1965. The "medical model", miasma theory, and community mental health. *Community Ment. Health J.* 1:333–38

42. Bloom, B. L. 1968. The evaluation of primary prevention programs. See Ref. 281, 117–35

43. Bloom, B. L. 1971. Strategies for the prevention of mental disorders. See Ref. 293, 1–20

44. Bloom, B. L. 1971. A university freshman preventive intervention program: report of a pilot project. *J. Consult. Clin. Psychol.* 37:235–42

45. Blostein, S. 1969. Prevention in mental health: selected annotated bibliography. *Can. Ment. Health* 17, Suppl.

46. Bolman, W. M. 1967. An outline of preventive psychiatric programs for children. *Arch. Gen. Psychiat.* 17:5–8

47. Bolman, W. M. 1968. Preventive psychiatry for the family: theory approaches and programs. *Am. J. Psychiat.* 125:458–72

48. Bolman, W. M., Westman, J. C. 1967.

Prevention of mental disorder: an overview of current programs. *Am. J. Psychiat.* 123:1058–68

49. Bower, E. M. 1961. Primary prevention in a school setting. See Ref. 69, 353–77

50. Bower, E. M. 1964. The modification, mediation and utilization of stress during the school years. *Am. J. Orthopsychiat.* 34:667–74

51. Bower, E. M. 1965. Primary prevention of mental and emotional disorders. A conceptual framework and action possibilities. See Ref. 196, 1–9

52. Bower, E. M. 1967. Preventive services for children. In *Preventive Services in Mental Health Programs*, ed. B. L. Bloom, Dorothy P. Buck. Boulder, Colo.: Wiche

53. Bower, E. M. 1969. *Early Identification of Emotionally Handicapped Children in School.* Springfield, Ill.: Thomas

54. Bower, E. M. 1969. Slicing the mystique of prevention with Occam's razor. *Am. J. Public Health* 59:478–84

55. Bower, E. M. 1972. K.I.S.S. and Kids: A mandate for prevention. *Am. J. Orthopsychiat.* 42:556–65

56. Bower, E. M. 1963. Primary prevention of mental and emotional disorders. *Am. J. Orthopsychiat.* 33:832–48

57. Bower, E. M., Shellhamer, T. A., Dailey, J. M. 1960. School characteristics of male adolescents who later became schizophrenic. *Am. J. Orthopsychiat.* 30:712–29

58. Bowlby, J., Ainsworth, M. 1964. *Maternal Care and Mental Health.* World Health Organization. Geneva: Penguin

59. Brown, G. W., Harris, T. O., Peto, J. 1973. Life events and psychiatric disorders. Part 2: nature of causal link. *Psychol. Med.* 3:159–76

60. Brown, G. W., Sklair, F., Harris, T. O., Birley, J. L. T. 1973. Life events and psychiatric disorders. Part 1: some methodological issues. *Psychol. Med.* 3:74–87

61. Brownbridge, R., Van Vleet, P., Eds. 1969. *Investment in Prevention: The Prevention of Learning and Behavior Problems in Young Children.* San Francisco: Pace I.D. Center

62. Buell, B. 1969. Is Prevention Possible?

Lindemann Memorial Lecture, Nat. Conf. Soc. Welfare. New York: Community Res. Assoc.

63. Byers, R. K. 1959. Lead poisoning: review of the literature and report on 45 cases. *Pediatrics* 23:585–603

64. Cain, A. 1967. The perils of prevention. *Am. J. Orthopsychiat.* 37:640–42

65. Cahalan, D. 1970. *Problem Drinkers.* San Francisco: Jossey-Bass

66. Calhoun, J. B. 1962. Population density and social pathology. *Sci. Am.* 206:139

67. Campbell, D. T., Stanley, J. C. 1966. *Experimental and Quasi-Experimental Designs for Research.* Chicago: Rand McNally

68. Caplan, G. 1959. Practical steps for the family physician in the prevention of emotional disorders. *J. Am. Med. Assoc.* 170:1497–1506

69. Caplan, G. 1961. *Prevention of Mental Disorders in Children.* New York: Basic Books

70. Caplan, G. 1963. Opportunities for school psychologists in the primary prevention of mental disorders in children. *Ment. Hyg.* 47:525–39

71. Caplan, G. 1964. *Principles of Preventive Psychiatry.* New York: Basic Books

72. Caplan, G. 1964. The role of pediatricians in community mental health (with particular reference to primary prevention of mental disorders in children). See Ref. 33, 287–99

73. Caplan, G., Grunebaum, H. 1967. Perspectives on primary prevention: a review. *Arch. Gen. Psychiat.* 17:331–46

74. Caplan, G., Lebovici, S., Eds. 1969. *Adolescence: Psychosocial Perspectives.* New York: Basic Books

75. Caplan, R. 1969. *Psychiatry in the Community in 19th Century America.* New York: Basic Books

76. Carson, D. H., Driver, B. L. 1966. A summary of an ecological approach to environmental stress. *Am. Behav. Sci.* 10:8–11

77. Carter, J. W., Ed. 1968. *Research Contributions From Psychology to Community Mental Health.* New York: Behavioral Publ.

78. Cary, A., Reveal, M. 1967. Prevention and detection of emotional distur-

bances in preschool children. *Am. J. Orthopsychiat.* 37:719

79. Chalke, F. C. R., Day, J. J., Eds. 1968. *Primary Prevention of Psychiatric Disorders.* Univ. Toronto Press

80. Charny, I. 1972. Parental intervention with one another on behalf of their child: a breakthrough tool in preventing emotional disturbance. *J. Contemp. Psychother.* 5:19

81. Christmas, J. J. 1969. Sociopsychiatric rehabilitation in a black urban ghetto. 1. Conflicts, issues and directions. *Am. J. Orthopsychiat.* 39:651–61

82. Christmas, J. J. 1972. Philosophy and practice of socio-psychiatric rehabilitation in economically deprived areas. See Ref. 22, 159–74

83. Clarfield, S. 1973. An analysis of referral problems and their relation to intervention goals in a school based preventive mental health program. *Diss. Abstr. Int.* 33:6072

84. Clarke, A. D. B. 1973. Prevention of subculture subnormality: problems and prospects. *Brit. J. Subnorm.* 19: 7–20

85. Cohen, A. 1968. *Noise and Psychological State.* Nat. Center for Urban Ind. Health, U.S. Public Health Serv., Cincinnati, Ohio

86. Cohen, R. E. 1972. Principles of preventive mental health programs for ethnic minority populations: the acculturation of Puerto Ricans to the United States. *Am. J. Psychiat.* 128: 1529–33

87. Coleman, J. C., Broen, W. E. 1972. *Abnormal Psychology and Modern Life.* Glenview, Ill.: Scott Foresman. 4th ed.

88. Colman, A. D., Colman, L. L. 1971. *Pregnancy—The Psychological Experience.* New York: Heider & Heider

89. Committee on Preventive Psychiatry of the Group for the Advancement of Psychiatry 1951. *Promotion of Mental Health in the Primary and Secondary Schools: An Evaluation of Four Projects.* Topeka, Kans.: G.A.P.

90. Cowen, E. L. 1967. Emergent approaches to mental health problems. An overview and directions for future work. See Ref. 96, 389–455

91. Cowen, E. L. 1969. Mothers in the classroom. *Psychol. Today* 2:36–39

92. Cowen, E. L. 1973. Social and community interventions. *Ann. Rev. Psychol.* 24:423–72

93. Cowen, E. L. et al 1963. A preventive mental health program in the school setting: description and evaluation. *J. Psychol.* 56:307–56

94. Cowen, E. L., Dorr, D., Izzo, L. D., Madonia, A., Trost, M. A. 1971. The primary mental health project: a new way to conceptualize and deliver school mental health service. *Psychol. Sch.* 8:216–25

95. Cowen, E. L., Dorr, D., Trost, M. A., Izzo, L. D. 1972. A follow-up study of maladapting school children seen by non-professionals. *J. Consult. Psychol.* 36:235–38

96. Cowen, E. L., Gardner, E. A., Zax, M., Eds. 1967. *Emergent Approaches to Mental Health Problems.* New York: Appleton-Century-Crofts

97. Cowen, E. L., Zax, M. 1968. Early detection and prevention of emotional disorder: conceptualization and programs. See Ref. 77, 46–59

98. Cumming, E. 1968. Unsolved problems of prevention. *Can. Ment. Health* Suppl. 56

99. Davis, J. A. 1963. *Education for Positive Mental Health.* Rep. 88 Nat. Opin. Res. Center, Univ. Chicago Press

100. Decker, J. B., Stubblebine, J. M. 1972. Crisis intervention and prevention of psychiatric disability: a follow-up study. *Am. J. Psychiat.* 129:725–29

101. Defense Documentation Center 1970. *Environmental Effects on Behavior: A Report Bibliography.* Alexandria, Va.: Def. Doc. Center

102. Deutsch, M., Katz, I., Jensen, A. R., Eds. 1968. *Social Class, Race and Psychological Development.* New York: Holt, Rinehart & Winston

103. Dobzhansky, T. 1972. Genetics and the diversity of behavior. *Am. Psychol.* 27:523–30

104. Dohrenwend, B. P., Dohrenwend, B. S. 1969. *Social Status and Psychological Disorder.* New York: Wiley

105. Dohrenwend, B. P., Egri, G., Mendelsohn, F. S. 1971. Psychiatric disorder in general populations: a study of the

problem of clinical judgment. *Am. J. Psychiat.* 127:1304–12

106. Dorr, D. 1972. An ounce of prevention. *Ment. Hyg.* 56:25

107. Dubos, R. 1968. Environmental determinants of human life. In *Environmental Influences*, ed. D. C. Glass. New York: Russell Sage Found.

108. Dubos, R. 1968. *So Human an Animal.* New York: Scribner

109. Dubos, R. 1970. We can't buy our way out. *Psychol. Today* 3:20, 22, 86–87

110. Edwards, J. E., Penick, E. C., Suway, B. 1973. Evaluating the use of television in community mental health education. *Hosp. Community Psychiat.* 24:711

111. Eisenberg, L. 1962. Possibilities for a preventive psychiatry. *Pediatrics* 30:815–28

112. Eisenberg, L. 1962. Preventive psychiatry. *Ann. Rev. Med.* 13:343–60

113. Eisenberg, L. 1963. Preventive psychiatry—if not now, when. *World Ment. Health* 19:48–64

114. Elkind, H. B. 1927. The epidemiology of mental disease. *Am. J. Psychiat.* 6:623

115. Elkind, H. B. 1938. Is there an epidemiology of mental disease? *Am. J. Public Health* 28:245

116. Emerson, H. 1969. Epidemiology a possible resource in preventing mental disease. In *Mental Health*, ed. F. R. Moulton. Am. Assoc. Advan. Sci.

117. Engel, G. L., Adler, R. 1967. Psychological factors in organic disease. *Ment. Health Progr. Rep.* U.S. Dep. H.E.W. 1–23

118. Epps, R. et al 1965. *A Community Concern.* Springfield, Ill.: Thomas

119. Eysenck, H. J., Rachman, S. 1965. *The Causes and Cures of Neurosis.* London: Routledge & Kegan Paul

120. Fabian, A. 1972. The disturbed child in the ghetto day care center: the role of the psychiatric consultant. *J. Am. Acad. Child Psychiat.* 11:467

121. Fairweather, G. 1967. *Methods for Experimental Social Intervention.* New York: Wiley

122. Farbern, N. 1969. *Bibliography on Suicide and Suicide Prevention.* Public Health Ser. Publ. 1979. Washington D.C.: Supt. Documents. 203 pp.

123. Flanagan, J. C. 1971. Evaluation and validation of research data in primary prevention. *Am. J. Orthopsychiat.* 41:117–23

124. Foley, A. R., Gorham, C. S. W. 1973. Toward a new philosophy of care: perspectives on prevention. *Community Ment. Health J.* 9:99–107

125. Frank, G. H. 1965. The role of the family in the development of psychopathology. *Psychol. Bull.* 64:191–205

126. Fried, M. 1964. *Social Problems and Psychopathology.* Group for the Advancement of Psychiatry. Symp. 10:403–46

127. Fuller, G., Friedrich, D. 1973. Predicting potential school problems. *Percept. Mot. Skills* 37:453

128. Galle, O. R., Groue, W. R., McPherson, J. M. 1972. Population density and pathology: what are the relations for man? *Science* 176:23–30

129. Garber, N. 1973. Pediatric child psychiatry collaboration in a health maintenance organization. *Am. J. Psychiat.* 130:1227

130. Garmezy, N. 1971. Vulnerability research and the issue of primary prevention. *Am. J. Orthopsychiat.* 41:101–16

131. Glidewell, J. C. 1971. *Issues in Community Psychology and Preventive Mental Health.* New York: Behavioral Publ.

132. Glidewell, J. C., Gildea, M. C. L., Kaufman, M. K. 1973. The preventive and therapeutic effects of the school mental health programs. *Am. J. Community Psychol.* 1:295–329

133. Glidewell, J. C., Swallow, C. S. 1969. *The Prevalence of Maladjustment in Elementary Schools: A Report Prepared for the Joint Commission on the Mental Health of Children.* Univ. Chicago Press

134. Glueck, S., Glueck, E. T. 1952. *Delinquents in the Making: Paths to Prevention.* New York: Harper

135. Glueck, S., Glueck, E. 1962. *Family Environment and Delinquency.* Boston: Houghton Mifflin

136. Golann, S. E., Ed. 1969. *Coordinate Index Reference Guide to Community Mental Health.* New York: Behavioral Publ.

137. Golann, S. E., Eisdorfer, C. 1972. *Handbook of Community Mental Health*. New York: Appleton-Century-Crofts

138. Goldfarb, H. 1943. The effects of early institutional care on adolescent personality. *Child Develop.* 14:213-23

139. Goldfarb, H. 1945. Effects of psychological deprivation in infancy and subsequent stimulation. *Am. J. Psychiat.* 102:18-33

140. Goslin, D., Ed. 1969. *Handbook of Socialization Theory and Research*. New York: Rand McNally

141. Green, C. S. 1969. *Psychological Stress and Mental Dysfunction*. Chicago: Crerar Library

142. Greenberg, J. 1973. Differential prediction of reading failure at the first grade level: the goal, prevention. *Am. J. Orthopsychiat.* 43:223

143. Greenblatt, M. et al 1963. *The Prevention of Hospitalization*. New York: Grune & Stratton

144. Griffin, C. L., Reinhorz, H. Z. 1969. Prevention of the 'failure syndrome' in the primary grades: implications for intervention. *Am. J. Public Health* 59:2029-34

145. Grinspoon, L. 1971. *Marihuana Reconsidered*. Cambridge, Mass.: Harvard Univ. Press

146. Group for the Advancement of Psychiatry 1953. *Psychopathological Disorders in Childhood: Theoretical Considerations and a Proposed Classification*. New York: G.A.P. Rep. 62

147. Group for the Advancement of Psychiatry 1970. *Crisis in Child Mental Health: A Critical Assessment*. G.A.P. Rep. 82

148. Group for the Advancement of Psychiatry 1968. *The Dimensions of Community Psychiatry*. New York: G.A.P. Rep. 69, Vol. 6

149. Gruenberg, E. M. 1954. The epidemiology of mental disease. *Sci. Am.* 190:38-42

150. Gruenberg, E. M. 1957. Epidemiology of mental disorders. *Milbank Mem. Fund Quarter.* 35:107-26

151. Gruenberg, E. M. 1959. The prevention of mental disorders. *J. Chron. Dis.* 9:187-98

152. Gump, L. R. 1973. The application of primary preventive mental health principles to the college community. *Community Ment. Health J.* 9:133

153. Harlow, H. F., Harlow, M. 1966. Learning to love. *Am. Sci.* 54:244-72

154. Haughton, A. 1968. Suicide prevention program in the U.S.: an overview. *Bull. Suicidology* 7:25-29

155. Hebb, D. D. 1949. *Organization of Behavior*. New York: Wiley

156. Heber, R., Stevens, H. A., Eds. 1964. *Mental Retardation: Review of Research*. Univ. Chicago Press

157. Herzberg, F. 1966. *Work and the Nature of Man*. Cleveland: World Publ. Co.

158. Heston, L. L. 1966. Psychiatric disorders in foster home reared children of schizophrenic mothers. *Brit. J. Psychiat.* 112:819-25

159. Hilleboe, H. E. 1972. Preventing future shock: healthy development in the 60's and imperatives for the 70's. Eleventh Bronfman Lecture. *Am. J. Public Health* 62:136-45

160. Hirsch, J., Hostetter, R. C. Behavior genetics. In *Foundations of Abnormal Psychology*, ed. P. London, D. Rosenhan. New York: Holt, Rinehart & Winston

161. Hoffman, M., Hoffman, L. 1964. *Review of Child Development Research*, Vol. I. New York: Russell Sage Found.

162. Hollingshead, A. B., Redlich, F. C. 1968. *Social Class and Mental Illness*. New York: Wiley

163. Hollister, W. 1966. Issues for school mental health. *N.C. J. Ment. Health* 2:42

164. Hornstein, H. A., Bunker, B. B., Burke, W. W., Glindes, M., Lewicki, R. J., Eds. 1973. *Social Intervention: A Behavioral Science Approach*. New York: Free Press

165. Hunt, J. McV. 1961. *Intelligence and Experience*. New York: Ronald

166. Hunt, J. McV. 1968. Toward the prevention of incompetence. See ref. 77, 19-45

167. Hunt, J. McV. 1970. Poverty versus equality of opportunity. In *Psychological Factors in Poverty*, ed. V. L. Allen. Chicago: Markham

168. Hunter, R. C. A., Rassell, J. A., Goldberg, B., Kral, V. A., Lamberti, A.

1968. Primary prevention of specific disorders: neurotic states; suicide; brain damage and retardation, in genetic psychiatry; delinquency. See Ref. 282, 98–110

169. Hurley, R. 1969. *Poverty and Mental Health: A Causal Relationship.* New York: Random House

170. Huttman, E. D. 1971. *Public Housing: The Negative Psychological Effects on Family Living.* Presented at Am. Orthopsychiat. Assoc. 48th Ann. Meet.

171. Jackson, D. D. 1960. *The Etiology of Schizophrenia.* New York: Basic Books

172. Jaco, E. G. 1960. *The Social Epidemiology of Mental Disorders.* New York: Russell Sage Found.

173. Jahoda, M. 1958. *Current Concepts of Positive Mental Health; A Report to the Staff Director, Jack R. Ewalt.* New York: Basic Books

174. Jarvis Report 1855. *The Report of the Commission on Lunacy and Idiocy in Massachusetts.* Cambridge: Harvard Univ. Press, 1971

175. Johnson, D. L. et al. The Houston Parent-Child Development Center: A Parent Education Program for Mexican-American Families. Mimeo: Univ. Houston

176. Joint Commission on the Mental Health of Children 1970. *Crisis in Child Mental Health: Challenge for the Seventies.* Hagerstown: Harper & Row

177. Joint Commission on Mental Illness and Health 1961. *Action for Mental Health.* New York: Basic Books

178. Jones, E. 1953. *Life and Works of Sigmund Freud,* Vols. 1, 2, 3. New York: Basic Books

179. Kagan, J. 1968. Personality development. In *Foundations of Abnormal Psychology,* ed. P. London, D. Rosenhan, 117–73. New York: Holt, Rinehart & Winston.

180. Kantor, M. B., Gildea, M. C. L., Glidewell, J. C. 1969. Preventive and therapeutic efforts of maternal attitude change in the school setting. *Am. J. Public Health* 59:490–502

181. Karnes, M. B., Studley, W. M., Wright, W. R., Hodgins, A. S. 1968. An approach for working with mothers of disadvantaged pre-school children. *Merrill-Palmer Quart. Behav. Develop.* 14:174–84

182. Kawi, A. A., Pasamanick, B. 1959. Associations of factors of pregnancy with development of reading disorders in childhood. *Soc. Reading Disord. Child Develop.* Yellow Springs, Ohio

183. Kellam, S. G., Schiff, S. K. 1966. The Woodlawn mental health center; a community mental health model. *Soc. Serv. Rev.* 40:255–63

184. Kelly, J. G. Towards an ecological conception of preventive interventions. See ref. 77, 76–99

185. Kelly, J. G. 1970. The quest for valid preventive interventions. In *Current Topics in Clinical and Community Psychology,* Vol. 2, ed. C. D. Spielberger. New York: Academic

186. Keniston, K. 1973. How community mental health stamped out the riots, 1968–1978. In *Community Mental Health: Social Action and Reaction,* ed. B. Denner, R. H. Price. New York: Holt, Rinehart & Winston

187. Kennedy, J. F. 1965. *Message From the President of the United States Relative to Mental Illness and Mental Retardation.* House Doc. No. 58, 88th Congress 1st session. Washington, D.C.: G.P.O.

188. Kiesler, F. 1965. Programming for prevention. *N.C. J. Ment. Health* 1:3–17

189. Kiev, A. 1972. New directions for suicide prevention centers. *Life Threatening Behav.* 2:189–93

190. Kirk, E. W. 1973. Group practice of psychology: A community model. *Diss. Abstr. Int.* 33:3310

191. Kirk, S., Weiner, B., Eds. 1963. *Behavioral Research on Exceptional Children.* Washington, D.C.: Counc. Except. Childr.

192. Kohlberg, L., LaCross, J., Ricks, D. 1972. The predictability of adult mental health from childhood behavior. See ref. 366, 1217–84

193. Kraft, I. 1964. Preventing mental ill health in early childhood. *Ment. Hyg.* 48:414–23

194. Kryter, K. D. 1966. Psychological reactions to aircraft noise. *Science* 151:1346–55

195. Kuman, B. H. 1968. *Mental Retarda-*

tion: Some Recent Developments in the Study of Causes and Social Effects of this Problem. New York: Pergamon

196. Lambert, N. M., Ed. 1965. *The Protection and Promotion of Mental Health in Schools,* 1–9. Bethesda, Md.: U.S. Dep. H.E.W., P.H.S. Publ. 1226

197. Langner, T. S., Herson, J. H., Greene, E. T., Jameson, J. D., Goff, J. 1970. Children of the city: affluence, poverty, and mental health. In *Psychological Factors in Poverty,* ed. V. L. Allen. Chicago: Markham

198. Langner, T. S., Michael, S. T. 1963. *Life Stress and Mental Health.* New York: Macmillan

199. Langner, T. S., Michael, S. T. 1963. *Life Stress and Mental Health: II. The Midtown Manhattan Study.* New York: Free Press

200. Leighton, A. H. 1959. *My Name is Legion, Stirling County Study,* Vol. 1. New York: Basic Books

201. Leighton, A. H. 1967. Some notes on preventive psychiatry. *Can. Psychiat. Assoc. J.* 12:43N52

202. Lemert, E. M. 1967. *Human Deviance, Social Problems and Social Control.* Englewood Cliffs, N.J.: Prentice-Hall

203. Lemkau, P. V. 1955. *Mental Hygiene in Public Health.* New York: McGraw-Hill

204. Lemkau, P. V. 1956. Freud and prophylaxis. *Bull. NY Acad. Med.* 32:887–93

205. Lemkau, P. V. 1966. Prospects for the prevention of mental illness. *Ment. Hyg.* 53:172–79

206. Lemkau, P. V. 1968. Prevention in psychiatry. *Brit. J. Soc. Psychiat.* 2: 127–33

207. LeRiche, W. H. 1968. Preventive programmes in mental diseases: their evaluation. See ref. 282, 69–83

208. Lester, D. 1971. The evaluation of suicide prevention centers. *Int. Behav. Sci.* 3:40–47

209. Lester, D. 1972. The myth of suicide prevention. *Compr. Psychiat.* 13:555–60

210. Lester, D. 1972. The prevention of homicide. *Crisis Interven.* 4:105

211. Levine, M., Levine, A. 1970. *A Social History of the Helping Services.* New York: Appleton-Century-Crofts

212. L'Hote, M. 1971. On an experience of primary prevention in a community service. *Psychiat. l'Enfant* 14:283

213. Linderman, E. 1964. Current concept of prevention in mental health. See ref. 330

214. Lin-Fu, J. S. 1967. *Lead Poisoning in Children.* U.S. Dep. H.E.W., Child. Bur. Publ. No. 452. Washington, D.C.: Supt. Doc.

215. Lombroso, C. 1911. *Crime: Its Causes and Remedies.* Boston: Little Brown

216. Long, B. E. 1970. Behavioral science for elementary school pupils. *Elem. Sch. J.* 70:253–60

217. Luban-Plozza, B. 1972. Preventive medical and psychosocial aspects of family practice. *Psychiat. Med.* 3:327

218. Lubchansky, I. L. 1972. Social psychiatry: contents and form of an experience. *Acta Psiquiat. Psicol. Am. Lat.* 18:154

219. Malmquist, C. P. 1960. Preventive psychiatry—present status and future. *Minn. Med.* 42:333–43

220. Ibid. Preventive psychiatry—present status and future. 43:237–43

221. Martin, J. P. 1972. Conquest of general paresis. *Brit. Med. J.* 3:159–60

222. Maslow, A. H. 1962. *Toward a Psychology of Being.* Princeton: Van Nostrand

223. McGee, R. 1972. Evaluation of crisis intervention programs and personnel: a summary and critique. *Life Threatening Behav.* 2:168–82

224. McKerracher, D. G., Griffin, J. D., Szyrynski, V. 1968. Some methods of primary prevention: the general medical practitioner: public education and school procedures: crisis theory and preventive interaction. See ref. 282, 145–68

225. Mellsop, G. W. 1972. Psychiatric patients seen as children and adults: childhood predictions of adult illness. *J. Child. Psychol. Psychiat.* 13:91–101

226. *Mental Disorders: A Guide to Control Methods* 1962. New York: Am. Public Health Assoc. 132 pp.

227. Meyers, J. K., Bean, L. C. 1968. *A Decade Later: A Follow-up of Social Class and Mental Illness.* New York: Wiley

228. Meyers, J. K., Roberts, B. H. 1959.

Family and Class Dynamics in Mental Illness. New York: Wiley

229. Mikhelios, M., Stene, J. 1970. Genetic counseling in Down's Syndrome. *Hum. Genet.* 20:457

230. Milgram, S. 1970. The experience of living in cities. *Science* 167:1461–68

231. Miller, K. S. 1970. Research training in community mental health. In *Community Psychology: Perspectives in Training and Research*, ed. I. Iscoe, C. D. Spielberger. 215–24 New York: Appleton-Century-Crofts

232. Miller, S. M., Mishler, E. G. 1959. Social class, mental illness and American psychiatry: an expository review. *Milbank Mem. Fund. Quart.* 37:174–99

233. Murphy, G. E. 1972. Clinical identification of suicidal risk. *Arch. Gen. Psychiat.* 27:356–59

234. Murphy, G. E. 1960. Prevention of mental disorder: some research suggestions. *J. Hillside Hosp.* 9:146

235. Murphy, H. B. M., Wittkower, E. D., Chance, N. A. 1967. Crosscultural inquiry into the symptomatology of depression: a preliminary report. *Int. J. Psychiat.* 3:6–15

236. Murphy, L. B., Chandler, C. A. 1972. Building foundations for strength in the preschool years: preventing developmental disturbances. See ref. 137, 303–30

237. Nangeroni, A. 1968. Social action in preventive psychiatry. *Can. Ment. Health* 15:19–24

238. National Association for Mental Health 1973. *Primary Prevention of Mental Disorders in Prenatal and Perinatal Periods—Action Guidelines*, 1–25

239. National Institutes of Health 1968. Report of meeting on primary prevention, Dec. 12–13

240. National Institutes of Health 1970. *The Effects of Diet and Nutrition on Learning.* Bethesda, Md: N.I.H.

241. National Institutes of Health 1970. *Promoting Mental Health.* Report of the Primary Prevention Panel to the Director, N.I.M.H.

242. National Institutes of Mental Health 1965. *A Selected Bibliography on Occupational Mental Health.* Rockville, Md.: Nat. Clearinghouse Ment. Health Inform. Public Health Serv. Publ. 1338

243. National Institutes of Mental Health 1968. *The Protection and Promotion of Mental Health In Schools.* Ment. Health Monogr. 5

244. National Institutes of Mental Health 1969. *Consultation in Mental Health and Related Fields: A Reference Guide.* Public Health Serv. Publ. 1920

245. National Research Council, Committee on Biologic Effects of Atmospheric Pollutants 1972. *Lead: Airborne in Perspective.* Washington, D.C.: Nat. Acad. Sci.

246. Newman, M. B., San Martino, M. 1973. The child and the seriously disturbed parent: treatment issues. *J. Am. Acad. Child Psychiat.* 12:162–81

247. Newton, G., Levine, S., Eds. 1968. *Early Experience and Behavior.* Springfield, Ill.: Thomas

248. Noyes, A., Kolb, L. C. 1968. *Modern Clinical Psychiatry.* Philadelphia: Saunders. 7th ed.

249. Ohio Department of Mental Health and Mental Retardation, Columbus, 1973. Gold Award: Television as a tool in primary prevention. *Hosp. Community Psychiat.* 24:691

250. Ojemann, R. H., Ed. 1959. *Four Basic Aspects of Preventive Psychiatry.* Rep. 1st Inst. Prev. Psychiat. Univ. Iowa Press

251. Ojemann, R. H., Ed. 1959. *Recent Contributions of Biological and Psychosocial Investigations to Preventive Psychiatry.* Pro. 2nd Inst. Prev. Psychiat. Univ. Iowa Press

252. Ojemann, R. H. 1961. *Recent Research Looking Toward Preventive Intervention.* Iowa City: Univ. of Iowa

253. Ojemann, R. H., Ed. 1963. *Recent Research on Creative Approaches to Environmental Stress.* Pro. 4th Inst. Prev. Psychiat. Univ. Iowa Press

254. O'Neal, P., Robins, L. N. 1958. The relation of childhood behavior problems to adult psychiatric status: a 30 year follow up of 150 subjects. *Am. J. Psychiat.* 114:961–69

255. Ibid. Childhood patterns predictive of adult schizophrenia: a 30 year follow up. 115:385–91

256. O'Neal, P., Robins, L. N. 1968. Relations of childhood behavior problems to adult psychiatric status. In *Chil-*

dren's Behavior Disorders, ed. H. C. Quay. Princeton: Van Nostrand

257. Pasamanick, B., Ed. 1959. *Epidemiology of Mental Disorders*. Washington, D.C.: Am. Ass. Advan. Sci.

258. Peck, H. B., Kaplan, S. R., Roman, M. 1966. Prevention, treatment and social action: a strategy of intervention in a disadvantaged urban area. *Am. J. Orthopsychiat.* 36:57–69

259. Phillips, L. 1967. The competence criterion for mental health programs. *Community Ment. Health J.* 3:73–76

260. Phillips, L., Zigler, E. 1961. Social competence: the action-thought parameter and vicariousness in normal and pathological behaviors. *J. Abnorm. Soc. Psychol.* 63:137–46

261. Plaut, T. F. A. 1972. Prevention of alcoholism. See ref. 137, 421–38

262. Plog, C. S., Edgerton, W. B., Ed. 1969. *Changing Perspectives in Mental Illness.* New York: Holt, Rinehart & Winston

263. Plunkett, R. J., Gordon, J. E. 1960. *Epidemiology and Mental Illness.* New York: Basic Books

264. Poorkaj, H., Boccelman, C. 1973. The impact of community volunteers on delinquency prevention. *Sociol. Soc. Res.* 57:335

265. Poser, E. G. 1970. Toward a theory of behavioral prophylaxis. *J. Behav. Ther. Exp. Psychiat.* 1:39–45

266. Powers, E., Witmer, H. 1951. *An Experiment in the Prevention of Delinquency.* New York: Columbia Univ. Press

267. President's Task Force on Mentally Handicapped 1970. *President's Task Force, Action Against Mental Disability.* Washington, D.C.: GPO

268. Rabkin, J. 1972. Opinions about mental illness: review of the literature. *Psychol. Bull.* 77:153–71

269. Rahe, R. H., Holmes, T. H. 1966. Life crisis and major health change. *Psychosom. Med.* 28:774

270. Raimy, V. 1950. *Training in Clinical Psychology.* New York: Prentice Hall

271. Rees, S. C., Doan, H. McK. 1973. An evaluation of a pilot treatment for infants and mothers (Mimeo). West End Creche, Toronto, Canada

272. Reid, H., Brown, E., Hansen, Y.,

Sperber, Z. 1973. Preventive interventions for the very young: an infant consultation service interweaves service, training and research. *Am. J. Orthopsychiat.* 43:246

273. Reiff, R. 1966. Mental health manpower and institutional change. *Am. Psychol.* 21:540–48

274. Reiff, R. 1967. Mental Health manpower and institutional change. See ref. 96, 74–88

275. Ribble, M. 1943. *Rights of Infants.* New York: Columbia Univ. Press

276. Ricks, D. F., Thomas, A., Roff, M. 1974. *Life History Research in Psychopathology*, Vol. 3. Minneapolis: Univ. Minnesota Press

277. Riessman, F., Cohen, J., Perl, A., Eds. 1964. *Mental Health of the Poor.* New York: Free Press

278. Riessman, F., Hallowitz, E. 1967. The neighborhood service center; an innovation in preventive psychiatry. *Am. J. Psychiat.* 123:1408–12

279. Rimland, B. 1964. *Infantile Autism.* New York: Appleton-Century-Crofts

280. Rimland, B. 1969. Psychogenesis versus biogenesis: the issues and the evidence. See ref. 262, 702–35

281. Roberts, L. M., Greenfield, N. S., Miller, M. H., Eds. 1968. *Comprehensive Mental Health.* Madison: Univ. Wisconsin Press

282. Roberts, C. A. 1968. *Primary Prevention of Psychiatric Disorders*: Clarence Hincks Mem. Lect. 1967. Univ. Toronto Press

283. Roberts, C. A. 1970. Psychiatric and mental health consultation. *Can. J. Public Health* 51:17–24

284. Robertson, B. 1968. Primary prevention: a pilot project. *Can. Ment. Health* 15:20–22

285. Robins, E., Murphy, G. E., Wilkinson, R. H., Gassner, S., Kayes, J. 1959. Some clinical consideration in the prevention of suicide based on a study of 134 successful suicides. *Am. J. Public Health* 49:888–99

286. Robins, L. N. 1966. *Deviant Children Grown Up.* Baltimore: Williams & Wilkins

287. Roen, S. R. 1971. Evaluative research and community mental health. In *Handbook of Psychotherapy and Be-*

havior Change: An Empirical Analysis, ed. A. E. Bergin, S. L. Garfield 776–811. New York: Wiley

288. Roff, M., Ricks, D. F., Eds. 1970. *Life History Research in Psychopathology*. Minneapolis: Univ. Minnesota Press

289. Roff, M., Robins, L. N., Pollack, M. 1972. *Life History Research in Psychopathology*, Vol. 2. Minneapolis: Univ. Minnesota Press

290. Rogers, M. E. et al 1966. Prenatal and perinatal factors in the development of childhood behavior disorders. *Acta Psychiat. Neurol. Scand.* Suppl. 102

291. Rolf, J. E., Harig, P. T. 1974. Etiological research in schizophrenia and the rationale for primary intervention. *Am. J. Orthopsychiat.* 44:538–84

292. Romano, J., Ed. 1968. *Origins of Schizophrenia*. Amsterdam: Excerpta Med. Found.

293. Rosenblum, G., Ed. 1971. *Issues in Community Psychology and Preventive Mental Health*. New York: Behavioral Publ.

294. Rosenblum, G. 1972. Mental health retools for the 70's. *Mass. J. Ment. Health* 2:5

295. Rosenthal, D., Kety, S. S., Eds. 1968. *The Transmission of Schizophrenia*. Elmsford, NLYL: Pergamon

296. Ryan, W. 1967. Preventive services in the social context: power, pathology and prevention. In *Preventive Services in Mental Health Programs, Proceedings of a Mental Health Institute, Salt Lake City*, 49–60. Boulder, Colo.: W.I.C.H.E.

297. Ryan, W. 1969. *Distress in the City*. Cleveland: Case Western Reserve Univ. Press

298. Ryan, W. 1971. *Blaming the Victim*. New York: Random House

299. Ryan, W. 1971. Emotional disorder as a social problem: implications for mental health programs. *J. Orthopsychiat.* 41:638–45

300. Sandler, I. N. 1972. Characteristics of women working as child aides in a school-based preventive mental health program. *J. Consult. Clin. Psychol.* 39:56

301. Sanford, N. 1965. The prevention of mental illness. See ref. 365, 1378–1400

302. Sanford, N. 1972. Is the concept of prevention necessary or useful? See ref. 137, 461–71

303. Sarason, I. G. 1972. *Abnormal Psychology*. New York: Appleton-Century-Crofts

304. Sarason, S. B., Levine, M., Goldenberg, I. I., Cherlin, D. L., Bennett, E. M. 1966. *Psychology in Community Settings*. New York: Wiley

305. Scarr-Salapatek, S. 1971. Race, social class and I.Q. *Science* 174:1285–95

306. Schecter, M. D. 1970. Prevention in psychiatry: problems and prospects. *Child Psychiat. Hum. Develop.* 1:68–82

307. Schulhofer, E. 1973. Short term preparations of children for separation, divorce, and remarriage of parents. *Am. J. Orthopsychiat.* 43:248

308. Schuman, L. M. 1963. Research methodology and potential in community health and preventive medicine. *Ann. NY Acad. Sci.* 107:557–69

309. Schwartz, S. L. 1971. A review of crisis intervention programs. *Psychiat. Quart.* 45:498–508

310. Seiden, R. 1972. Suicide and public health: a brief appraisal. *Life Threatening Behav.* 2:99

311. Selig, A. L. 1973. Prevention of mental illness and community organization. A review and annotated bibliography. *J. Suppl. Abstr. Serv.* MS 369

312. Sergovich, F. R. 1967. Cytogenetic practise in a mental retardation clinic. *Can. Psychiat. Assoc. J.* 12:35

313. Sheldon, W. H., Stevens, S. S. 1942. *The Varieties of Temperament: A Psychology of Constitutional Differences*. New York: Harper

314. Shneidman, E. S. 1972. Prevention of suicide: A challenge for community science. See ref. 137, 449–60

315. Shore, J. H., Bopp, J. F., Waller, T. R., Dawes, J. W. 1972. A suicide prevention center on an Indian reservation. *Am. J. Psychiat.* 128:1086–91

316. Shore, J. H., Kinzie, J. D., Hampton, J. L., Pattison, E. M. 1973. Psychiatric epidemiology of an Indian village. *Psychiatry* 36:70–81

317. Shrier, D., Lourman, S. 1973. Psychiatric consultation at a day care center. *Am. J. Orthopsychiat.* 43:394

318. Shure, M., Spivack, G., Gordon, R. 1972. Problem solving thinking: A

preventive mental health program for preschool children. *Reading World* 11:259

319. Signell, K. A. 1972. Kindergarten entry: A preventive approach to community mental health. *Community Ment. Health J.* 8:60–70

320. Silver, A. A., Hagin, R. A. 1972. Profile of a first grade: A basis for preventive psychiatry. *J. Am. Acad. Child Psychiat.* 11:645–74

321. Skeels, H. M. 1965. Effect of adoption of children from institutions. *Children* 12:33–34

322. Skeels, H. M. 1966. Adult status of children with contrasting early life experiences. *Monogr. Soc. Res. Child Develop.* 31:1–65

323. Skeels, H. M. 1967. Headstart on Headstart: 30 year evaluation. *5th Annual Distinguished Lectures in Special Education: Summer Session 1966.* Los Angeles: U.S.C. Sch. Educ.

324. Skodak, M., Skeels, H. M. 1949. A final follow-up study of 100 adopted children. *J. Gen. Psychol.* 75:85–125

325. Slobin, M. S. 1972. A resource center for primary prevention in mental health. Cleveland State Univ. Dep. Psychol. (mimeo)

326. Smith, M. B. 1968. Competence and socialization. In *Socialization and Society*, ed. J. A. Clausen. New York: Little, Brown

327. Smith, W. G. 1971. Critical life-events and prevention strategies in mental health. *Arch. Gen. Psychiat.* 25:103–9

328. Sobey, F. 1970. *Nonprofessional Revolution in Mental Health.* New York: Columbia Univ. Press

329. Soddy, K., Ahrenfeldt, R. H. 1967. *Mental Health and Contemporary Thought*, Vol. 2. London: Tavistock

330. Spiegel, A., Ed. 1964. *The Mental Health Role of Settlement and Community Centers.* NIMH Tech. Assistance Proj.

331. Spitz, R. 1946. Anaclitic depression: An inquiry into the genesis of psychiatric conditions in early childhood. *Psychoanal. Study Child* 2:313–42

332. Spoon, D., Southwick, J. 1972. Promoting mental health through family life education. *Family Coordinator*, 279–86

333. Srole, L., Langner, T. S., Michael, S. T., Opler, M. K., Rennie, T. A. C. 1962. *Mental Health in the Metropolis: The Midtown Manhattan Study*, Vol. 1. New York: McGraw-Hill

334. Szasz, T. 1961. *The Myth of Mental Illness.* New York: Hoeber-Harper

335. Szurek, S. 1969. *Antisocial Child: His Family and His Community.* Palo Alto, Calif.: Science & Behavior Books

336. Trost, M. A. 1968. The child aide mental health program. *Ment. Health in Classroom* 7

337. Trost, M. A. 1968. The preventive role of social work in a school setting. *Child Welfare* 47:397–404, 425

338. Treisman, M. 1969. Mind, body and behavior: Control systems and their disturbances. In *Theory and Research in Abnormal Psychology.* ed. P. London, D. Rosenhan. New York: Holt, Rinehart & Winston

339. Tureen, L., Wortman, M. 1965. A program sponsored by a labor union, for treatment and prevention of psychiatric conditions. *Am. J. Orthopsychiat.* 35:594

340. Udry, J. R., Morris, N. M. 1971. A spoonful of sugar helps the medicine go down. *Am. J. Public Health* 61:776–85

341. VanAntwerp, M. 1970. Primary prevention: A challenge to mental health associations. *Ment. Hyg.* 54:453–56

342. VanAntwerp, M. 1971. The route to primary prevention. *Community Ment. Health J.* 7:193

343. Vance, E. T. 1963. Social disability. *Am. Psychol.* 28:498–511

344. Wagenfeld, M. O. 1972. The primary prevention of mental illness. *J. Health Soc. Behav.* 13:195–203

345. Walder, W. M., Cohen, S. I., Daston, P. G. 1967. *Teaching parents and others principles of behavior control for modifying the behavior of children.* Rep. to U.S. Off. Educ., Washington, D.C.

346. Walker, L. 1973. The school psychologist as a preventive mental health consultant. *Diss. Abstr. Int.* 33:5024

347. Waxer, P., White, R. 1973. Introducing psychological consultation to a university community. *Can. Psychol.* 14:256

348. Weinberg, A. A. 1967. Mental illhealth, consequent to migration and

loneliness, and its prevention. *Psychother. Psychosom.* 15:69

349. Weinberg, S. K. 1967. Part VIII: Prevention of disordered behavior and mental health, "Community Psychiatry." *The Sociology of Mental Disorders.* Chicago: Aldine

350. Weiner, S. 1969. Effectiveness of a suicide prevention program. *Ment. Hyg.* 53:357

351. Wellington, J. 1973. Mothers' day out: Description of a program for the psychologist consultant to parents and their pre-school children. *Proc. 81st Ann. Conv. APA* 8:963

352. W.I.C.H.E. 1967. *Preventive Services in Mental Health Programs.* Proc. Ment. Health Inst., Boulder, Colo.

353. White, R. W. 1959. Motivation reconsidered: The concept of competence. *Psychol. Rev.* 66:297–333

354. Whitlock, G. 1973. *Preventive Psychology and the Church.* Westminster Press

355. Whittington, H. G. 1967. *Is Prevention of Mental Illness Possible?* Chicago: Florence Crittenton Assoc. Am.

356. Wiener, G., Andrews, S. R., Blumenthal, J., Rabinowitz, M. 1973. *New Orleans Parent Child Development Center* (mimeo)

357. Wilkinson, R. 1969. Some factors influencing the effect of environmental stressors upon performance. *Psychol. Bull.* 72:260–72

358. Williams, R. D., Ed. 1962. *The Prevention of Disability in Mental Disorders.* Washington, D.C.: U.S. Dep. HEW Publ. 924

359. Wilner, D. M., Walkley, R. P., Pinkerton, T. C., Tayback, M. 1962. *The Housing Environment and Family Life: A Longitudinal Study of the Effects of Housing on Morbidity and Mental Health.* Baltimore: Johns Hopkins

360. Wittkower, E. D., Fried, S. 1958. Some problems of transcultural psychiatry. *Int. J. Soc. Psychiat.* 3:245–52

361. Wohlwill, J. F. 1970. The emerging discipline of environmental psychology. *Am. Psychol.* 25:303–12

362. Wohlwill, J. F., Carson, D. H. 1972. Environment and behavioral science: Retrospect and prospect. In *Environment and the Social Sciences: Perspec-* *tives and Applications,* ed. J. F. Wohlwill, D. H. Carson. Washington, D.C.: APA

363. Wold, C. 1973. A two year follow up of suicide prevention center patients. *Life Threatening Behav.* 3:171

364. Wolff, H. S. 1950. Life stress and bodily disease: A formulation. In *Proceedings of the Association for Research in Nervous and Mental Disease,* Vol. 29. Baltimore: Williams & Wilkins

365. Wolman, B., Ed. 1965. *Handbook of Clinical Psychology.* New York: McGraw-Hill

366. Wolman, B., Ed. 1972. *Manual of Child Psychopathology.* New York: McGraw-Hill

367. Wooten, B. 1959. *Social Science and Social Pathology.* London: Allen & Unwin

368. World Health Organization Technical Report Series 9. Mental Health: Report of the First Session of the Expert Committee. Geneva: WHO

369. World Health Organization Technical Report Series 134. The psychiatric hospital as a center for preventive work in mental health: Fifth Report of the Expert Committee on Mental Health. Geneva: WHO

370. World Health Organization Technical Report Series 185. Epidemiology of Mental Disorders: Eighth Report of the Expert Committee on Mental Health. Geneva: WHO

371. Wortiz, S. B. 1968. General topics. *Year Book of Neurology, Psychiatry and Neurosurgery.* Chicago: Year Book Med. Publ.

372. Yarrow, L. S. 1961. Maternal deprivation: Toward an empirical and conceptual re-evaluation. *Psychol. Bull.* 58:459

373. Zax, M. 1966. A teacher-aide program for preventing emotional disturbance in primary grade school children. *Ment. Hyg.* 50:406–14

374. Zax, M., Cowen, E. L. 1972. *Abnormal Psychology: Changing Conceptions.* New York: Holt, Rinehart & Winston

375. Zax, M., Cowen, E. L. Early identification and prevention of emotional disturbance in a public school. See ref. 96, 331–51

376. Zax, M., Cowen, E. L. 1969. Research on early detection and prevention of emotional dysfunction in young school children. In *Current Topics in Clinical and Community Psychology*, ed. C. D. Spielberger, Vol 1. New York: Academic

377. Zax, M., Specter, G. A. 1974. *An Introduction to Community Psychology*. New York: Wiley

378. Ibid. Primary prevention in the schools, 147–72

379. Zubin, J., Freyhan, F. A. 1968. Social psychiatry. *Proc. 57th Ann. Meet. APA* New York City. New York: Grune & Stratton

380. Zusman, J., Davidson, D. L. 1974. Practical aspects of mental health consultation. *Contemp. Psychol.* 19:114

381. Zusman, J., Hannon, V., Locke, B. Z., Geller, M. 1970. *Bibliography: Epidemiology of Mental Disorders: 1966–1968*. NIMH, NCHMHI Publ. 5030

ASSESSMENT OF SCHIZOPHRENIA §244

Rue L. Cromwell

Department of Psychiatry, University of Rochester School of Medicine and Dentistry
Rochester, New York 14642

This review is a highly selective coverage of literature. Its purpose is to give a historical perspective in order to illustrate how early issues in the concept of schizophrenia have a direct bearing on contemporary problems of investigation and how, in spite of it all, some promising pathways may be present which can lead us out of this current problem wilderness in schizophrenia research.

The concept of schizophrenia as we know it today was developed by Kraepelin in 1896 and called dementia praecox. Considering forms of insanity already described by other clinicians, he defined dementia praecox as a group of disorders of psychosis which were characterized by early onset and progressive deterioration. "Dementia praecox is the name provisionally applied to a large group of cases which are characterized . . . by mental deterioration in varying grades" (21, p. 219).

Kraepelin was criticized for his concept primarily on four grounds. First, progressive deterioration did not always occur; that is, some patients had remissions. Therefore, it was not always dementia. Second, the onset was not always early, i.e. during puberty and adolescence; therefore, it was not always praecox. Third, instead of defining a disorder by the custom of clinical manifestations, Kraepelin defined it in terms of the course of the disease. Fourth, the subclasses of dementia praecox were not mutually exclusive and did not lend themselves to reliable subdiagnosis.

Kraepelin, besides being a sensitive clinician and lucid writer of modern psychiatry, was gifted with a flexibility in his thinking. He spent his remaining professional years after 1896 sorting out the clinical data and valid criticisms and trying to modify and improve the clinical groupings. Of particular interest are the positions he arrived at in regard to deterioration, remission, early onset, defining symptoms, and subclassification, considered in light of current knowledge.

Even before Kraepelin's writings were translated into English, it was clear that he acknowledged that progressive deterioration did not occur in all cases. ". . . whether the process is always the same is by no means certain. Dementia fortunately does not occur in all cases, but it is so prominent a feature that the name dementia praecox is best retained until the symptom group is better understood" (21, p. 219).

Regarding remission, Kraepelin, like Bleuler (11) in his 1911 work, recognized that the personality of the remitted patient was characteristically modified from its premorbid state. Thus these cases of insanity could seldom be described as completely cured.

Writing a decade before the beginning of modern developments in the philosophy of science, Kraepelin was not cognizant of the pitfalls of using deterioration or incurability as part of the definition of a disorder. A clinician in Kraepelin's day would designate a patient dementia praecox if insane, if the insanity fit no other diagnostic type, and if the onset was early. Strictly speaking, a final diagnosis could not be confirmed until the patient had expired with no evidence of remission. Any adequate diagnostic system today would separate diagnosis from prognosis. The diagnosis would be evaluated for its useful prognostic statements but would not be governed by them.

By the time of Bleuler, it was also acknowledged by Kraepelin that not all cases had early onset, such as in puberty or adolescence. Current epidemiological data (44) indicate that the mean age of onset and first hospitalization for schizophrenia, although not during adolescence, is nevertheless distinctively earlier than that for the remainder of hospitalized mental disorders taken as a group. The peak age of first admission for schizophrenia falls between 25 and 40 years. After that the frequency tapers off. For nonschizophrenic first admissions, the disorders related to aging are so prevalent that the frequency curve continues to rise with increasing age. Thus Kraepelin is found to be accurate in a relative sense—or else modern diagnosticians have simply learned it is unacceptable to label a first-admitted older person as schizophrenic.

Regarding the lack of a defining clinical syndrome, Kraepelin did not depart from his scientifically careful position. Dementia praecox for him was an arbitrary generic grouping of poorly understood psychotic disorders. It was not a clinical syndrome or entity. He was willing to admit that variations and exceptions occurred which did not fit his arbitrary schema.

Kraepelin changed his scheme of subclassifications. In his published lectures 8 years later (41), "katatonia" was excluded and considered separately from the disorders of dementia praecox. In Bleuler's (11) text of 1911, he appeared to have overlooked this change and responded only to the 1896 version of Kraepelin's nosology.

The tenuous advances in knowledge since Kraepelin's time allow us to see his views as still valid on several counts. He hesitated to posit a clinical entity. Once posited by his successors, it still has not attained a standard of scientific certitude. He put emphasis on the formal aspects (or course) of the disorder rather than the clinical manifestations. Indeed, our current knowledge tells us that premorbid adjustment, speed of onset, and readmission history have proved useful. Clinical symptoms, on the other hand, are of less value because they are inextricably confounded with the nonpathological factors of personality, socioeconomic status, and level of cognitive functioning.

Still another view of Kraepelin is of increasing importance. This view concerns the response to the momentarily presented stimulus. "Ordinary external impressions are correctly apprehended, the patients being able to recognize their environments and to comprehend most of what takes place about them. Yet accurate tests show that very brief stimuli are not well apprehended" (21, p. 222). Recent evidence indicates much is to be understood about schizophrenia in the few seconds and fractions of seconds following such a stimulus. A major focus of this chapter will be on this promising aspect in the assessment of schizophrenia.

Bleuler (11), whose 1911 text on schizophrenia was not published in English until 1950, rejected Kraepelin's agnostic view. He declared that dementia praecox had sufficient common characteristics to be a clinical entity. He renamed the disorder schizophrenia to avoid troublesome connotations in dementia praecox. He recognized the multiplicity of the disorder as did Kraepelin, but he proceeded to point out the primary symptoms common to all groups of schizophrenics. Disorders of associations, affect, ambivalence, and sometimes autism were included.

> By the presence of the symptom complex so selected and defined (by Kraepelin) the great group of dementia praecox is characterized as a unit . . . A closer examination shows that, in fact, all these cases have much in common, that they are clearly marked off from other types of mental disease (11, p. 3).
>
> . . . Thus, we are left with no alternative but to give the disease a new name . . . schizophrenia . . . For the sake of convenience I use the word in the singular although it is apparent that the group includes several diseases (11, p. 8).

In his declaration, Bleuler presented a substantive clinical point of view which was readily adopted by other clinicians. However, an apparent contradiction was initiated which continues to the current day in text books of psychiatry. After recognizing that schizophrenia is a group of disorders, its description is then elaborated as if it were a single clinical entity. To this day there is no firm evidence by which to say that the subclassifications of schizophrenia—either the Kraepelinian subclassification or its later modifications—represent separate disorders or whether they represent separate personalities or cognitive styles onto which a single disorder has been afflicted. We do not yet know if Bleuler's common clinical entity position is the mistake of the century which has misdirected the understanding of schizophrenia or whether he was six decades or more ahead of his time.

Misguided or not, the door was open for psychologists and psychiatrists to deal in assessment problems with more sophisticated and complex clinical content. Rather than the simplistic procedure to identify a dementia praecox, described earlier, the clinician was now expected to gain from clinical data a more detailed understanding of associations, affect, ambivalence, and bizarre behavior.

It should be noted that this new emphasis on clinical assessment evolved from the fact that Bleuler stood between two giants of his day: Kraepelin with his nosology; Freud with his analysis of intrapsychic phenomena. Bleuler wished to build an effective rapproachement between the two. In doing so, the focus upon associations of distinct and idiosyncratic nature was relevant to both Kraepelin's psychosis classification and Freud's theory and treatment approach. Bleuler drew upon the work of Semon to elaborate the intrapsychic role of associations:

> In following Semon, Bleuler distinguished (that) associations are formed as a result of our experiences. They integrate themselves into clusters which under certain conditions can be evoked and be integrated with other clusters. In order to serve our cognitive adaptation, the associations must lend themselves to becoming ordered, 'streamlined,' and hierarchically organized; that is, they must become goal-directed (69).

Jung, a colleague of Bleuler, developed the word association test as an assessment tool. However, it was not until the 1960s, when Bannister and his co-workers (4–7) employed the Kelly Rep Test (39), that progress was made in describing this interplay of schizophrenic associative clusters.

The rapprochement attempted by Bleuler was not well received by Freud. Freud, while welcoming disciples, did not feel disposed to have his ideas "rapproched." Consequently, Freud concluded Bleuler was a victim of his own third primary symptom: ambivalence (69).

History from 1911 to 1957

A brief comment may be made about what happened in work on assessment of schizophrenia between 1911 and 1957. The work by Rorschach and later by Shakow represented significant steps. The work on subclassification of schizophrenia and later on the process-reactive (premorbid adjustment) concept are worthy of note.

Rorschach developed and published in 1911 an inkblot test as a tool to diagnose psychopathology. This tool, for several decades an important diagnostic device, was a ready victim of abuse by the stupid and ignorant. The stupid accepted and propagated its clinical interpretations regardless of their validity. The ignorant rejected its validity out of hand without exerting the effort to learn which indices had evidence of experimental and clinical validity and which ones did not. While not to be reviewed here, the use of this instrument in assessing schizophrenia may be summarized in certain respects: 1. Schizophrenics, and others such as retardates, psychopaths, and brain damaged, showed poor form quality. 2. Schizophrenics gave "sick" content of dead, deceased, and impaired creatures. 3. The frequency of creatures being acted upon rather than taking action was high. 4. Peculiar (idiosyncratic) associations and displays of affect occurred. 5. Boundary problems, especially the preserving of body boundary integrity, occurred. 6. Once identified as schizophrenic, a patient's Erlebnistypus (movement vs color and shading balance) was useful in predicting the type of symptoms, e.g. hallucinations vs delusions. For the past the Rorschach perhaps served its greatest purpose in providing an entree for the clinical psychologist into the institutional storehouses to study psychopathology. For the future, the Rorschach, now becoming less used, will probably have made its greatest contribution by pointing the way to pertinent visual information processing phenomena which can better be studied in a well-controlled perceptual laboratory.

Shakow and his group at Worcester State Hospital played a significant role in introducing experimental psychological techniques into the clinical study of psychopathology. Looking for the simplest levels of behavior where the schizophrenic deficit appears, Shakow and his group found chronic schizophrenics to be normal in automatized (repetitive) motor response, sensory acuity, motor reflexes, and steadiness tasks. However, a breakdown occurred in speed of initiating a fast reaction to a predesignated stimulus. In effect, the apprehension of the briefly presented stimulus, mentioned by Kraepelin, had come back into study. Rodnick & Shakow (57) identified conditions under which schizophrenic groups were slower than normals without exception (i.e. without overlap in their distributions). Later these differences became better understood in relation to the length of preparatory intervals (between warning and imperative stimuli) and the unusually potent influence in schizophrenics of the preparatory interval in the immediately preceding reaction time trial (79).

As a number of perceptual and motor tasks were examined by Shakow and his group, one disappointing type of finding occurred and recurred. Regardless of the cognitive or attentional task given, schizophrenics tended to perform more poorly and more variably than normals. This was disappointing to clinical investigators because it precluded the attractive possibility of explaining schizophrenia in terms of a single kind of performance deficit. The Shakow attentional set deficit notion, and later the inhibition interpretation offered by Zubin (81), represented the major ways by which to explain schizophrenic behavior.

Among scholars of schizophrenia, Shakow's experimental behavioral studies did not reach a level of popularity which was in proportion to their scientific merit. One possible reason was that they were conducted during a time when the exquisitely phrased psychodynamic interpretation had a greater appeal than cold numbers and statistical inference. Also, reductionistic thinking made biochemical hypotheses seem more real and relevant than millisecond latencies in a simple task. Another reason may be that to this day no schizophrenic has been arrested, held in jail, or committed to a mental hospital for having a slow reaction time, a strong crossover effect between regular and irregular series, or any of the other phenomena which were studied. Only the saying and doing of crazy things caused such consequences. Perhaps the time had not yet come when the typical clinical scientist could see the connection between millisecond differences in response and the infrequent but blatant characteristics of madness.

Attempts continued during this period to sort out and improve the Kraepelinian subclassifications of schizophrenia. Elaborations were made in the *Diagnostic and Statistical Manual* of the American Psychiatric Association (1). Factor analysis of ward and interview behavior were conducted by Wittenborn (75) and Lorr, O'Connor & Stafford (43). No dramatic consequence has come as a result of this line of work. Perhaps it is because neither the clinical psychiatrists nor the factor analysts kept in mind that diagnoses, like other scientific constructs, must be developed in close relation to the variables with which they are supposed to be related, i.e. in this case prognosis and, if possible, treatment indications and etiology. In the extreme case, a classification system could be developed from data of schizophrenics' arithmetic competence or some other equally irrelevant variable. To scrutinize clinically or to factor analyze the behaviors seen often in schizophrenia does not mean an adequate classification system can be built from such an endeavor.

Many steps were made in clarifying the process-reactive construct in schizophrenia during this period. Following Langfeld, Wittman (76) developed the Elgin Scale to measure it. Independently, Phillips (55), a member of the Worcester group who was studying indices to predict successful response to shock therapy, published the scale of premorbid adjustment which came to be viewed as conceptually equivalent to the process-reactive measure. In 1956 a classic study by Farina & Webb (24) revealed that regardless of shock or other hospital treatment good premorbid schizophrenics had better prognosis than poor premorbid schizophrenics. Since that time the process-reactive dimension has generally been recognized as the one best single indicator of prognosis in schizophrenia. This dramatic finding, while very important to current research in schizophrenia, was also observed two centuries before Kraepelin. Willis appeared to be aware of it in *The London Practice of Physick* in 1685:

> (Madness) rais'd on a sudden from some solemn evident cause, as from a vehement passion, is much safer than invading by degrees.

> ... It is a common observation, that men born of parents that are sometimes wont to be mad, will be obnoxious to the same disease; and that often they have lived prudently and soberly above thirty or forty years, yet afterward without any occasion or evident cause will fall mad (74).

A Turning Point: Visual Size Estimation Assessment

In 1957 a major milestone quietly occurred in the history of assessment in schizophrenia. Jesse Harris, a graduate student doing a dissertation (34) with Garmezy at Duke University, was pursuing a Bruner-Postman-based hypothesis that affective evaluative response would influence visual size estimation. Schizophrenics, it was felt, in particular would be influenced in evaluating size of threatening and nonthreatening mother-child interaction scenes. The hypothesis was tested with acute (i.e. early hospitalized) schizophrenics and normals, and no differences were revealed. The scale of premorbid adjustment, adopted by Rodnick and Garmezy from Phillips at Worcester, was applied to the schizophrenic subject sample. In an earlier Duke dissertation by Bleke this scale had been discovered to be useful in accounting for schizophrenic subject variance. The result with Harris' data was something which had never previously occurred in the history of schizophrenia research. The two schizophrenic groups classified in terms of premorbid history fell in opposite directions in size estimation level from the normal control group. Good premorbid schizophrenics tended to underestimate and poor premorbid schizophrenics tended to overestimate visual stimulus size. Normals did not differ significantly from veridicality.

What did these results mean? Premorbid adjustment had already been identified as a prognostic index relevant to schizophrenia. Was this an indication of two different types of schizophrenia with opposing abnormalities in perceptual behavior? Was it an indication that the singular disorder of schizophrenia affects the perception of people with different cognitive styles differently—such people also differing in ability to get out of the hospital and readjust? The certain and immediate outcome was that the article based on the dissertaion was accepted for publication (34) and was greatly ignored for a number of years.

Silverman and Venables: Homogeneous Subgrouping

In 1964 another milestone occurred. In two independent review articles, Silverman (66) and Venables (72) pointed to the importance of having all schizophrenics under research study classified in terms of three dimensions: (a) premorbid adjustment (process-reactive); (b) paranoid vs nonparanoid symptomatology; and (c) chronicity (length of hospitalization). This was a major but not complete step in the direction away from considering the Kraepelinian classification system to be first and foremost. Only the paranoid-nonparanoid distinction was retained. The evidence from numerous research studies had made it clear that the great variability in schizophrenic behavior was reduced if homogeneous subgrouping (or covariance) was carried out with these three dimensions.

The manner in which Silverman arrived at these conclusions regarding subclassification is of interest. A new emphasis upon scanning characteristics of schizophrenics was developed. Being a graduate student at the University of Michigan and studying for qualifying examinations, Silverman had read the Harris article and was intrigued by its unusual findings. He also discovered the early child development research on centration and decentration by Piaget, which related eye movement of young children to visual size estimation. Likewise, he read the work by Gardner and his Menninger colleagues on cognitive styles. In his integration of this material, Silverman concluded that Harris' data could be explained on the basis of scanning and eye movement differences between good vs poor premorbid schizophrenics. The former, Silverman proposed, had frequent eye movements consequent to a cognitive style of extensive scanning; the latter, by contrast, had fewer eye movements consequent to minimal scanning. Silverman's formulation suggested that paranoid and nonparanoid schizophrenics should also differ in size estimation level, and his own research proved this true (65). Silverman's fellow students were impressed by this integration of ideas, not only because of the insight it illustrated but also because Silverman stood on a table in the student study room as he first described it.

A number of questions were left unanswered by the new formulations of 1964.[1] Thus the heuristic implications were formidable. The case made by Venables and Silverman regarding the importance of the three variables was based primarily upon studies which took only one or at most two of the variables into consideration at a time. No study had taken all three into consideration. No study had compared

---

[1] While biochemical studies will not be reviewed here, it is worth pointing out that most of them have not taken advantage of the 1964 formulations. Hopefully, the advancement of biochemical understandings would profit from these principles also.

the process-reactive and paranoid-nonparanoid dimensions at the same time. No one had looked at scanning in psychotic children. No one had thoroughly studied eye movement in schizophrenics; only inferences had been made about it from size estimations.

Subsequent studies indicated that among acute schizophrenics (hospitalized less than 3 years) good vs poor premorbid adjustment and paranoid vs nonparanoid symptomatology were indeed significant and independent (i.e. noninteracting) factors influencing size estimation (20). Thus Silverman's (66) formulation was supported. No size estimation effect was found in disturbed acting-out and with-drawn-psychotic children, except the already established Piaget age relationship for children in general. That is, size overestimation decreased with increasing age (20). The phenomenon seen in adult schizophrenics does not seem to be present in children. When eye movement on the standard stimulus was restricted to 100 msec (a time which would preclude multiple information-search eye movements on the stimulus target), the same pronounced differences in size estimation between acute process nonparanoids and reactive paranoids were displayed (50). Thus eye movement, while remaining as a possible operant, could not be viewed as the sole factor which mediates this size estimation abnormality among adult schizophrenics.

So the embarrassing situation faced by Harris was back again: a fascinating phenomenon was being observed when people showed pictures to patients, but no one had an adequate way to explain it.

Stimulus Redundancy Formulation

A tentative explanation called "stimulus redundancy" was developed (15) on the basis of theoretical observations by Pribram & Melges (56) in neurophysiology. Essentially the formulation held that rates of processing of external stimulus information are determined not only by the availability of such information but also by controls within organisms. These controls can reduce or shut down the external input to produce a condition of stimulus sameness (high stimulus redundancy). On the other hand, the processing can be set at a high rate (low stimulus redundancy). Rate of processing was proposed to affect the way visual size is estimated: high rate, low size; low rate, high size, for any given element processed; or stated differently, low redundancy, low size; high redundancy, high size. From this formulation, two ways appear available to influence size estimation, one primarily environmental and one primarily organismic. For size under-estimation, choose (*a*) a highly varied and/or changing field and/or (*b*) a subject who processes at a fast rate. For size overestimation, choose (*a*) a simple field or ganzfeld (stimulus-free surrounding) with a limited number of unchanging visual elements and/or (*b*) a subject who processes at a low rate. Eye movement would have an effect so long as the shifting of images to the retina would allow information processing rate to vary.

If such a formulation were to have value, its predictability should be tested in a situation different from one on which supporting data was already available. Kar (38; see also 16), considering the Müller-Lyer illusion, noted that the processing of information from the arrowheads and tails in this illusion figure obstructed the accurate size matching of the arrow shafts. Thus it was reasoned that increasing the nonrelevant processing would increase the illusion. This was done by adding distracting figures and words to the background on the illusion card. Acute reactive paranoid schizophrenics, alleged to be high rate processors, were expected to have increased illusion, while acute process nonparanoids were expected to have less illusion. Results gave partial support to the predictions. The background distraction, as predicted, greatly increased the illusion for all groups. The reactive paranoids, as predicted, displayed much greater illusion errors than the normals and the process nonparanoid schizophrenics. The latter two groups, contrary to prediction, did not differ. The final clencher came, however, when Kar asked subjects after the experiment to recall all the distracting elements they could remember. Reactive paranoids recalled more than normal controls; normal controls recalled more than process nonparanoids. These results on incidental recall were clearly in line with the predictions. From this study some promise was offered that the redundancy formulation might be useful.

Clinical features and other research results were then related to the redundancy formulation (16). The high redundancy schizophrenics tended to have a gradual onset of psychosis, were consequently hospitalized from loss of family or community supports rather than from sudden psychotic symptoms, were more often nonparanoid (28), were the victims of soft signs of organic brain damage (36) with increasing chronicity (71), were tolerant of stimulus deprivation but unable to tolerate high stimulus bombardment (49), tended to profit from phenothiazine therapy (27, 29), had a more stable course of illness without clear-cut remissions or enhanced floridity of psychosis, and had generally poor prognosis (24). The low redundancy schizophrenics tended to have a sudden onset of psychosis, were blatant in symptoms especially during the early (acute) stage, were prone often to remission and/or episodic relapses, were averse to stimulus deprivation, were not prone to profit from phenothiazines, and had a good prognosis for spontaneous recovery.

Key questions remained: Does the redundancy dimension have anything to do with schizophrenia? Do the different processing rates result from schizophrenia? Do the rates reflect different disorders, or the same disorder at different temporal points during the progression of the illness or at different severity levels? Or are these processing differences a matter of cognitive style or other factors onto which a disorder has been imposed? No evidence now exists which will answer these questions conclusively.

One type of evidence which suggests that high and low redundancy schizophrenics are different disorders comes from biological data. As already indicated, good premorbids do not profit from phenothiazine therapy, but poor premorbids do (27, 29). Kety et al (40), in comparing adopted acute (good premorbid, quick onset), chronic (poor premorbid, slow onset), and borderline (poor premorbid, slow onset) schizophrenics found evidence of the disorder in only the biological (not adoptive) relatives of only the chronic and borderline (but not acute) schizophrenics. Thus transmission of schizophrenia was associated with only poor premorbid, slow onset patients. These findings suggest that only the high redundancy disorder is susceptible to biological transmission. A cloud of doubt was placed over the argument that good premorbid schizophrenia is merely a less severe version of process psychosis. From these data the borderline condition would seem to be the less severe form of process schizophrenia. On the other hand, these exciting data are still susceptible to alternative interpretations. That which is biologically transmitted may not be a direct etiological factor of high redundancy schizophrenia. It may be the transmission of one or more biologic inferiorities which add to life stress. If so, the genetic transmission of sporadic shortcomings, like deviant family communication (77) on the nonbiologic level, may summate to increase the probability of breakdown.

European diagnostic practices suggest a difference between high and low redundancy patients. Diagnosis of schizophrenia there is greatly restricted to what would be described here as high redundancy schizophrenia. Several sources (45; Lennart Kaij, personal communication; S. S. Kety, personal communication) make it clear that European, especially Scandinavian, definitions of schizophrenia tend to restrict or even exclude what Americans refer to as reactive (good premorbid) schizophrenia. Evidence of a clear precipitating event, marked affective[2] or confusional symptoms upon admission, and quick onset would be basis for ruling out a schizophrenia diagnosis in Sweden. Patients with good premorbid adjustment would be called schizophrenic retrospectively only if they continued a steady course of psychosis without remissions or episodes. In the United States-United Kingdom study (32), Zubin's group conducted an intensive survey of these diagnostic differences. Consequently, European readers should be reminded that findings and observations reported here conform to the broader, less exclusive American definition of schizophrenia.

All readers should be warned that some of the ambiguities of research findings may be directly attributable to these differences in diagnostic practice. Bleuler's suggestion that schizophrenia be treated as a reliable clinical entity has yet to be proved successful.

Following the European diagnostic tradition, phenothiazines tend to be given primarily to those indicated by research as most likely to profit from them. Those who fail to meet the European definition of schizophrenia but still are psychotic often receive antidepressant drugs or lithium but not phenothiazines. Yet in this country the distinction is almost always ignored by clinicians. As a consequence we are in a golden age of research, which may not continue into the next decade. Process and reactive schizophrenics may be compared with little or no fear that they differ in kind or level of drugs in their clinical treatment.

Recent work by Zigler and his co-workers supports an argument that high vs low redundancy is related to level and style of cognitive functioning independently of schizophrenia. Zigler was puzzled by the fact that Johannsen et al (35) had

---

[2] Recent schizophrenia high risk studies have made it clear that schizophrenic females with offspring have abundant affective symptoms even though they may be designated on other grounds as process schizophrenics.

reported an independence between premorbid adjustment and paranoid symptomatology, while Goldstein, Held & Cromwell (28) reported two separate studies in which a particular relationship existed. According to the latter, good premorbids may be either paranoid or nonparanoid, but poor premorbids almost always tended to be nonparanoid. Sanes & Zigler (61) obtained data which supported the Johannsen et al interpretation of no relationship. The present reviewer (see 61) offered the interpretation that the differences in results may derive from cognitive differences in the VA and state hospital populations, the former being somewhat higher because of having passed a mental and intelligence examination in order to get into military service. Johannsen et al and Sanes & Zigler had studied VA populations, and Goldstein et al had studied state hospital populations.

Zigler & Levine (80), therefore, conducted an investigation in both types of hospitals and found, in accordance with past results, that the VA population fit the conclusions of Johannsen et al (35) and the state hospital population fit the conclusions by Goldstein et al (28). Eisenthal, Harford & Solomon (23) failed to find such differences between private and state hospitals but observed that the base rate for diagnosing paranoid vs nonparanoid schizophrenia varied greatly from hospital to hospital. While 39% to 40% of schizophrenics in their and the Johannsen et al data were diagnosed paranoid, 59% in the Sanes & Zigler data and only 27% in the Goldstein et al data were diagnosed paranoid. Thus the base rate for paranoid status as well as social competence was different among the different hospital populations. The resulting effect on the relationship of premorbid adjustment and paranoid symptomatology may be viewed with at least two interpretations: cognitive level and admission evaluation differences.

The first interpretation has the following logic. Schizophrenics classified as paranoid have by definition delusions as their prominent symptoms. Delusions are false ideas. To have a false idea requires the capacity to have ideas. Ideas require cognitive ability. Cognitive ability is higher in VA and higher socioeconomic populations. Therefore, such populations show a greater incidence of paranoid symptoms, but on this stratum the relationship between paranoid symptoms and premorbid adjustment does not necessarily covary. On the lower stratum of state hospital populations, the poor premorbid and nonparanoid characteristics would frequently concur.

The second interpretation has the following logic. In better staffed, private, or training hospitals clinicians will more often spend a longer time examining and listening to a patient upon his admission. The longer a person (even this author) is listened to, the greater the likelihood that he will reveal a false idea. Once he has revealed a false idea, the likelihood is greater that a patient will be diagnosed paranoid schizophrenic. Thus the staffing structure of the hospital may influence the ratio of diagnosed paranoid vs nonparanoid schizophrenics. So the inarticulate and unattended poor premorbid patients in an understaffed state hospital are more likely to be diagnosed with a nonparanoid classification.

Finally, Zigler & Levine (80) studied the symptoms of turning away from others, against others, or against self. They found that the poor premorbids (those with low social competence) tended to turn away from others (consistent with a nonparanoid interpretation). Good premorbids (those with high social competence) took one of two directions. Either they had symptoms of turning against others (consistent with a paranoid interpretation) or against self (consistent with a depressive or schizoaffective interpretation). This pattern of symptoms presents an additional explanation of why Goldstein et al (28) found poor premorbids were almost always nonparanoid, while good premorbids tended to be either paranoid or nonparanoid. The good premorbid nonparanoids were apparently the ones with depressive or other affective components in their disorder.

The results of Zigler and his colleagues are sobering (disappointing, if you will) to the clinical scientist trying to sort out the etiology of schizophrenia. They suggest that clinical symptoms (delusions, affect, redundancy level) may be telling us more about the cognitive level of the individual than about the mental disorder. Perhaps it is not surprising, therefore, that recent research (70) has found clinical symptoms of limited value in predicting outcome in schizophrenia.

Arousal

Of what relevance is arousal to the redundancy concept, i.e. to the high and low rate of processing in schizophrenia? If any relationship exists at all, it is that the low rate processors (high redundancy schizophrenics) are higher in arousal. However, the findings do not seem to fit together into one neat conceptual picture, perhaps because arousal may mean different things when measured differently, and because the concept of schizophrenia is elusive. Before moving on to recent research which does fit into an exciting conceptual picture, it behooves this author to face some of the issues of arousal and schizophrenia and to do so with humility.

Mednick (47) offered a theory that acute schizophrenics became hyperaroused through a cyclic pattern of increasing fear response and increasing stimulus generalization. Chronic schizophrenics, on the other hand, were proposed to have low levels of arousal, possibly even lower than normals. This formulation accounted for overinclusive behavior in acute schizophrenics and a withdrawn quality in chronic schizophrenics.

Venables (72) reviewed literature which proposed acute schizophrenics to have a broad focus of attention and chronic schizophrenics a narrow focus of attention. These results were interpreted in a direction reverse to Mednick's formulation (47). That is, the acute schizophrenic was interpreted to be low in arousal and lacking the power to block out irrelevant peripheral stimuli in order to attend to the task. The chronic schizophrenic was interpreted as having high arousal and from that the power to channel attention narrowly.

The research since that time has done some damage to the earlier positions of both Mednick (47) and Venables (72). Both have revised their formulations on the basis of their own and other data. Most research since their initial formulations has supported the notion that chronic schizophrenics are higher in arousal than acutes and normals, thus supporting Venables. The possibility that acute schizophrenics are lower than normals in arousal is in no way confirmed. Also, the relationship of arousal to broad versus narrow attention in the simple sense offered by Venables has lacked support.

The major areas of focus on arousal-related research more recently have concerned the GSR responsivity, GSR response recovery time, EEG power density variations, EEG alpha blocking latency and blocking characteristics, evoked response, and contingent negative variation.

When schizophrenics were described in one research study (78) as highly responsive in GSR amplitudes and in another study as low in responsivity (10), Gruzelier & Venables (31) took note of this discrepancy and proceeded to identify groups of schizophrenic "responders" and "non-responders." The non-responders are deficient in two-flash threshold performance as compared to "responders" and normal subjects. Heart rate differences were also shown. However, contrary to what might have been expected, no findings have indicated a relationship between this GSR-responder dichotomy and the major variables related to the redundancy classification, i.e. paranoid symptomatology and premorbid adjustment during the acute phase of illness.

Mednick (48), in his study of offspring of process schizophrenic parents, found GSR recovery time following a specific response to be the most important autonomic discrimination between children who later suffered mental breakdowns and those who did not. The ones susceptible to breakdown had quicker GSR recovery. Following up on this finding, Ax & Bamford (3) found that chronic schizophrenics also had faster GSR recovery than normals. Mednick interpreted fast recovery to mean that the individual has such a quick avoidance response to a fear-producing situation that the avoidance response never has a chance to extinguish. A slow recovery to a new baseline, i.e. continued responsiveness to the fear-producing stimuli, would allow time for extinction, i.e. for competing responses to replace the "fear-then-quick-avoidance" response.

An alternative, and not entirely contradictory, interpretation to the Mednick reinforcement-learning one is that the continued elevation of the GSR prior to recovery may be a correlate of the amount of information processing of the stimulus event at that instant. If the schizophrenic, presumably in high redundancy mode, "shuts down" his information processing activity, then he would have less registry and less subsequent trace from the stimulus event. He would be likely to respond, as Shakow (63) described, to a later presentation of the same stimulus as if it were brand new. Consistent with this notion, Edelberg (22) has reported fast GSR recovery time to be associated with poor habituation, another characteristic of schizophrenic subjects.[3]

Recent research on EEG has fairly consistently been interpreted to indicate schizophrenics are high in arousal. Goldstein & Sugermann (26), finding

[3] During a visit with E. Rodnick at UCLA in 1972, I was discussing Mednick's and Ax's new findings, and my interpretation of what they might mean, when Rodnick pulled from his shelf the dissertation of Carl F. Frost (25) which he supervised at Clark University in 1948. It contained charts and data analyses demonstrating the faster GSR recoveries of the schizophrenic subjects. Thus the findings described above do not represent the first time that fast GSR recovery phenomenon was observed in schizophrenics. Nor was it the first time I have been humbled by the vast personal experience and knowledge of people such as Rodnick, Shakow, and Zubin.

schizophrenics to be less variable over time in EEG power density, interpreted such patients to have a hyperregulated, hyperaroused system which did not allow fluctuations as a function of the incoming stimuli. Cromwell & Held (18) found reactive schizophrenics, ordinarily as slow or slower than normals in motor reaction time, to have a significantly faster alpha blocking latency than normals in response to a reaction time stimulus presented during alpha rhythms. Process schizophrenics could not be tested because insufficient alpha was shown. These findings were also interpreted to indicate high arousal in reactive schizophrenics and either higher arousal or a noisy brain in process schizophrenics. The oftheld interpretation that schizophrenics are slow in motor reaction time simply because they are not motivated to the task is difficult to reconcile with the short alpha blocking latency findings. Nideffer et al (52) studied alpha percent time in reactive schizophrenics and normals with eyes open and closed. They found the well-known differential probability of less alpha with eyes open (and more alpha with eyes closed) to be significantly greater in schizophrenics than in normals. They also found schizophrenics better in reaction time with eyes closed than open and normals better in reaction time with eyes open than closed. These results were also interpreted in terms of a greater arousal in reactive schizophrenics as regards visual sensitivity.

Research on visual evoked response (13) has led to the identification of patterns of augmenting and reducing in an early component of the averaged wave. Augmenters tend to have increasing amplitude of the wave component with increasing light intensity; reducers show less amplitude at high light intensities. While this finding appeared to have implications for both arousal and redundancy, Schechter & Buchsbaum's (62) subsequent research has indicated that this effect is greatly influenced by instructions and attentional set given to the subject. Meanwhile, Asarnow (2) has found the "reducing" tendency to be highly related to digit symbol deficit, a well-known psychoneurological soft sign of organic brain damage. Also, while schizophrenics tend in general to be greater augmenters than normals, those without a family history of schizophrenia tend toward the "reducing" tendency more than schizophrenics with a family history of schizophrenia.

As indicated previously, the conclusions which can be drawn about arousal in schizophrenics are tenuous. Some data indicate that schizophrenics, acute and chronic, are high in arousal. However, one should be cautious, if not resistant, in generalizing from one arousal measure to another, or in assuming arousal is a monolithic construct. It would also appear that the measurement of arousal, whether singular or plural, is often overriden by other factors. At least one of these factors is probably the redundancy level. In other words, both extremely high-rate and low-rate processing of external stimulus information occurs during high arousal in schizophrenics.

Predicting When Pathology Will or Will Not Occur

A most beneficial trend in recent research has been away from schizophrenic-normal comparisons. An increase has occurred in the number of studies to predict when schizophrenics will or will not manifest their pathology. Schizophrenics have long been noted for displaying normal behavior most of the time and showing their pathological behavior only on rare critical occasions (33). Nideffer & Cromwell (51) illustrated this fact by examining choice reaction times of chronic good and poor premorbid schizophrenics and normal subjects. Looking into a dark box with two pinpoints of light, subjects lifted the left forefinger from a key if the left light went out and the right forefinger from a key if the left light went out. Trials were plotted as a trade-off function between speech and accuracy. As expected, the faster, the less accurate; the slower, the more accurate. Poor premorbids, usually slower than good premorbids, were surprisingly faster than the goods and were equal to normals, perhaps because all peripheral visual stimulation was removed. Normals had an unusually straight line function of accuracy as a function of speed. Schizophrenics, however, especially the good premorbid patients, had a trade-off function which bent at the slow end as a result of a large group of trials which were both very slow and inaccurate. Thus two schizophrenic deficits were described. One was a general slowness in reaction time at all levels of accuracy, which was shown only by the good premorbids. The other was a "high-redundancy" or "out-of-contact" slowness, where schizophrenics were not only slow but were inaccurate at a response speed level where accuracy should be optimal. Since the latter deficit occurs only on some trials and not on others, an important unanswered question concerns the trial-to-trial determinants which are related to this sporadic deficit.

THE WATERLOO STUDIES   What are the conditions which will cause a schizophrenic to act schizophrenic, and what conditions will produce essentially normal behavior? Steffy, his students, and co-workers at the University of Waterloo have perhaps made the greatest recent impact on this question. Their strategy, like that of Shakow's group, has been to study reaction time, the simplest level of response in which schizophrenic pathology occurs.

As a preface for these Waterloo studies, some of the major reaction time findings of the Shakow group will be summarized. Schizophrenics were found to be slower than normals in simple reaction time. Also, they were found to have greater intrasubject and intersubject variability than normals (64). The preparatory interval (PI; time between warning and imperative stimulus) was found to be an important source of variance. When PIs of different lengths are presented in regular series (e.g. a series of 3-sec PIs, then 1-sec PIs, then 7-sec PIs), the results are different from when they are presented in irregular series (random order of PI length from trial to trial). Regularity means a degree of certainty about what PI is coming next. Normals tend to utilize the information provided by regularity and to perform faster than when PIs are irregular. Many schizophrenics, however, show a crossover effect which normals do not show. With trials of short PIs a regular series yields faster reaction times than an irregular series. A reversal occurs with PIs longer than approximately 5 sec. That is, when the series is regular and the PI is long, schizophrenics perform more poorly than if it were an irregular series. Why should certainty of information impair schizophrenics? The mystery of this phenomenon had been reduced when Zahn, Rosenthal & Shakow (79) identified the PPI-PI relationship. The PI on the immediately previous trial (the PPI) was found to have a great influence on the subsequent trial. When the PPI was greater than the PI (i.e. when a long PI was followed by a short one), the reaction time was slower. When the PPI was less than the PI (a short PI followed by a long one), the reaction time on the latter was relatively faster. Schizophrenics were found to have this PPI "overdetermination" more than normals. This helped explain the crossover phenomenon in schizophrenics. In an irregular series, a long PI would have a high probability of being preceded by a shorter PI, and vice versa. Thus the curve of reaction time as a function of PI in the irregular series would be affected in a direction consistent with the crossover effect.

The "catcher," however, was this: The role of the PPI in accounting for the crossover effect was marred by one additional finding. While PPI < PI gave better performance than PPI > PI, the PPI = PI combination was shown to yield the best performance of all (54). This fact should override the PPI-PI inequality effect and still give the advantage to a regular series at all levels of schizophrenic reaction time performance. Why do the crossover data directly contradict this expectation? Steffy was the first to see the importance of this question.

To grapple with the question, Bellissimo & Steffy (9) introduced a series of four regular PI trials within a long irregular series. A striking thing happened when this procedure was conducted with process schizophrenics. In the interpolated regular trials, relatively independent of length of PI, the reaction time at first improved and then became progressively worse. The immediate improvement was what had been observed in the PPI = PI effect (53). The subsequent deterioration had never before been identified. With short PIs the immediate improvement was more pronounced. Thus two different contradictory factors seemed to be operating: an immediate facilitation from the certainty information, then a deterioration resulting from repetition, all within a four-trial span. Bellissimo & Steffy interpreted this progressive deterioration from trial to trial as a redundancy-related deficit. It was as if an event had occurred (the discovery of regularity after a prolonged irregular series) which caused the window shades to come down on the attentional focus of the process schizophrenic so that the outside world would be less and less adequately responded to. Since schizophrenics are usually unable to describe any change in the PIs in the Bellissimo-Steffy paradigm, it would appear that change of response takes place on a level of information processing which is not always linked to verbal awareness. Alas, this finding also accounted for the existence and extent of the mysterious and paradoxical crossover effect.

The crossover and redundancy-related deficit were then subjected by Steffy's group to several systematic investigations. The crossover had been shown in the original study (9) not to occur in reactive schizophrenics or normals. How durable was it, however, in process schizophrenics? As a first step, Steffy[4] conducted a study in which schizophrenic reaction time was lowered by a combination of preliminary training and positive urging and support from the examiner. Dramatically, another important finding emerged. While schizophrenic reaction time went down into normal limits through the positive urging, the crossover remained.

---

[4] Unpublished research.

Thus the crossover effect, like anticipatory responses with long PIs (53), is a more enduring and distinctive descriptor of process schizophrenia than is slow reaction time.

The durability of the crossover effect was then tested in a different way. Bellissimo & Steffy (8) examined different PPI-PI relationships in the interpolated paradigm. Their purpose was to seek some condition where the paradoxical effect might disappear, but they failed to do so. In one condition, where the antecedent irregular trials had a range of short PIs and the interpolated regular set were longer in PI length, the latter regular series produced slower reaction times at all PI levels tested. In other words, uncertainty gave better performance in schizophrenics in short as well as long regular PIs.

Finally, Kaplan (37) found a way to "cure" the crossover in process schizophrenics. After a pretesting to determine the presence and extent of the crossover, one group of subjects was given training on length-of-line judgments, then on length-of-PI judgments. After subjects reached a criterion in their training on the temporal discriminations, they were then posttested. The crossover disappeared. In a control group of schizophrenics where the training involved recognizing shapes, the crossover remained. After these initial findings, Kaplan extended his investigation by comparing four groups of process schizophrenics in obstruction of the crossover effect. Essentially the findings confirmed and extended the previous study in showing that the pretraining (i.e. the increasing of certainty in PI information) could obstruct the crossover effect. In addition, instructions that PI was going to be "same" or different" during posttest trials contributed additively to the crossover obstruction. The remarkable observations, however, were first that three of the four groups showed return of the crossover in immediate posttesting. Second, when the group with the most powerful anticrossover interventions was retested a month later, the crossover returned in three of eight subjects. Both the lasting effects of the obstructions in some and the resilience of crossover in others was demonstrated.

Along with testing the durability of the crossover effect, another study was conducted which magnified it. If the crossover results from interference with the maintenance of set, then it should become greater with longer intervals between trials. Longer intervals would allow more opportunity for interference to take place. On the other hand, if the crossover phenomenon results from an accumulated inhibitory factor which dissipates with the passage of time (e.g. defensive or reactive inhibition), then the crossover should become greater with shorter intertrial intervals. Steffy & Galbraith (67) examined crossover in process schizophrenics with 2 and 7 sec intertrial intervals. The crossover was distinctly greater with 2 sec between trials. No difference in mean reaction time accompanied the difference in amount of crossover. These findings suggested that the phenomenon being studied could not be explained by set factors.

If a stimulus condition so mild as a change in PI format could precipitate a momentary high redundancy condition, as shown by Bellissimo & Steffy (9), could other mild but novel stimuli do the same thing? And if they could, what time is required for the process schizophrenic to recover? Steffy & Galbraith (68) addressed themselves to these questions by introducing an unexpected border of Xs around the visual ready signal on a display scope and flashing a brief unexpected dim light in the dark testing room when a visual warning signal initiated the PI. Trials with this gentle intrusion were compared with those of the same PI length which had no such intrusion. Normals showed no effect from the intrusion. Reactive schizophrenics showed a slowing when PI was only 1 sec. When the PI was longer, complete recovery occurred. Within the context of these two comparison groups an extraordinary effect was again shown in the process schizophrenics. For them, the intrusion brought about a slowing which followed a specific pattern throughout the 1 to 9 sec range of PIs. As might be expected, the deficit was greatest after a PI of only 1 sec, and then it became less. At PIs of 5 and 7 sec, the deficit was minimal. Then at 9 sec the performance was again debilitated. This shifting of the debilitation, being greatest at 1 and 3 sec, recovering at 5 and 7 sec, and recurring at 9 sec, was correlated with the Elgin scale measure (76) of degree (severity) of the process disorder. At the 1 sec PI, the more the process score, the slower the reaction time. As the PI delay became 5 and 7 sec, the correlation became negative; the more the process, the shorter the reaction time. Then with a PI of 9 sec, the correlation was back in the positive direction. The findings just described were then replicated in a second sample of 16 process schizophrenic subjects.[5] Thus some confidence may be attached to these unique findings.

For the first time in history the length of the deficit following mild intrusive stimulation was traced. While the deficit would not be expected over minutes or hours, a momentary deficit in the order of seconds does exist. Is the momentary deficit cyclic in nature? Or does the process schizophrenic overrespond to the distraction in the immediate short PI range and then, in an attempt to dampen his responsivity, does he "over-damp?" That is, after reaching a state of optimal performance, does he then become underresponsive? If so, the early deficit observed would result from overresponsivity to distracting stimuli, and the late deficit would result from underresponsivity to relevant stimuli. Whatever the explanation, the greater the Elgin process score, the greater the phasic shift.

While the "mild intrusion" study just described was being done, Green (30) became interested in the capacity of schizophrenics to handle stimuli at higher intensity levels. Rosenbaum, Mackavey & Grisell (58) had shown schizophrenics to improve in reaction time with high intensity stimulation, yet Steffy & Galbraith (68) were finding the disabling effect. Green examined the effects of (a) pulses of loud and soft tones delivered just prior to the reaction time task and (b) different intensities of imperative stimulus tone. In accord with the more subtle stimulation given by Steffy & Galbraith, Green found that the preliminary irrelevant stimulation of greater loudness produced a slowing of reaction time. However, in line with Rosenbaum et al, increased intensity of the imperative stimulus tone short-

---

[5] One of the lessons learned by recent schizophrenia researchers is that the small Ns with replication is wisely chosen practice. Careful subject classification is so important and the availability of subjects within any subclass is so limited that the attempt to collect a large N will often either strain the criteria for careful subject selection or the resources of research subjects available. Replication becomes important to compensate for the small sample size.

ened the reaction time. Again, as in the other Waterloo studies reported, the effect occurred only in process schizophrenics. Repeated testing from one-half to one day later revealed no trace of the effects of the preliminary disrupting stimulation. In fact, recovery was beginning to occur from the prestimulation by the time 25 reaction time trials had been administered. Green repeated the experiment with bright versus dim light flahses for the preliminary disrupting stimulation, and he obtained the same results as with the tones.

THE HEART RATE STUDIES   The heart rate interpretation by Lacey (42) suggests itself as relevant to the redundancy formulation in schizophrenia. Heart rate deceleration, being associated with orientation, possibly could be viewed as low redundancy (high-rate processing). Heart rate acceleration, being associated with either fear or tuning out of external stimuli, could be associated with high redundancy (low rate processing). If so, heart rate should have some relationship to the redundancy-related deficits in schizophrenia.

Bradley (12), another student in Steffy's Waterloo group, examined heart rate changes occurring in process schizophrenics and normals during the preparatory interval in a reaction time task. A PI of 6 sec in a regular series was compared with a PI of the same length in an irregular series. Normal subjects, as reported by Obrist and co-workers (54), show a deceleration in heart rate during the PI. Bradley found this deceleration to occur in normals for both the regular and irregular series. In process schizophrenics a striking phenomenon occurred. In the irregular series, a detectable deceleration was apparent throughout the 6 sec. In the regular series, however, the heart rate oscillated in a marked acceleration-deceleration pattern. As expected, in normals the deceleration and the regular series were associated with faster reaction times. The irregular series were associated with slower reaction times. For the process schizophrenics the heart rate deceleration and irregular series were associated with faster reaction times, and the acceleration-deceleration pattern and regular series were associated with slower reaction times.

These results support the notion that heart rate indeed is a mediating or correlating factor of stimulus redundancy. More important, the results suggest the possibility that the moment-to-moment changes in redundancy-related deficit may be predicted on the basis of heart rate. Why heart rate? No one knows. Independent of the studies of regular versus irregular series, schizophrenics have been shown to become slower and normals faster in reaction time when they are given relevant information about the task (e.g. 19). One possible interpretation, suggested also by Kaplan (37), is that process schizophrenics feel distressed when they are called upon to respond adequately, and increased information only heightens the feeling of being "on the carpet." Heart rate may therefore accelerate momentarily because of the fear of having to deal with relevant information. Heart rate deceleration may result from bodily processes slowing down so that biologic conditions are optimal for processing information. If this interpretation is correct, a change in redundancy level could change heart rate, but a change in heart rate would not necessarily change redundancy level.

Warner (73), in a masters thesis supervised by Broekema at the University of Wisconsin, studied heart rate acceleration and deceleration during the presentation of a standard stimulus in a size estimation task. Acute good premorbid paranoid schizophrenics, poor premorbid nonparanoid schizophrenics, and alcoholic control subjects were included in the study. The study confirmed earlier results (20, 50) that size overestimation occurred in the poor premorbid nonparanoids and underestimation occurred in the good premorbid paranoids. As expected, heart rate deceleration during the presentation of the standard stimulus was associated with size underestimation in schizophrenics. However, the same degree of deceleration was associated with veridical estimation in the alcoholics. While the alcoholics showed consistent cardiac deceleration, the decelerative response was very small in the schizophrenic group. A greater correlation was obtained between heart rate acceleration and size overestimation in the schizophrenics. Again, the acceleration present in the alcoholics' heart beats was not associated with size overestimation.

McCormick (46), in a doctoral dissertation supervised by Broekema, studied the same variables as Warner (73) as a part of a larger study. In this study even in the alcoholics the size overestimation responses were associated with cardiac acceleration and size underestimation responses were associated with cardiac deceleration. Groupwise, the size estimation results were consistent with previous findings: paranoids underestimated; nonparanoids overestimated; and alcoholics averaged out to no difference from veridicality. However, the decelerative response was this time more pronounced in the schizophrenics. Greater cardiac deceleration in the paranoids was associated with size underestimation, as expected. A new finding was that greater cardiac deceleration in the nonparanoids was associated with size overestimation. This finding, as compared to the Warner data, places new interest on the subject and stimulus parameter differences which occurred between the Warner and McCormick studies. Warner tested schizophrenics on phenothiazine drugs; McCormick tested schizophrenics immediately on admission who were verified to be on no drugs. Warner examined heart rate during 10-sec exposure times of the standard size estimation stimuli; McCormick examined heart rate during only a 6-sec standard stimulus presentation. These differences in parameters leave the reader with some provocative hypotheses: (a) phenothiazines may influence the accelerative and decelerative response limbs of the heart rate orienting response, especially in process schizophrenics; (b) the cardiac acceleration, found by Warner to be associated with size overestimation in poor premorbid nonparanoids, may occur primarily after the 6-sec standard stimulus presentation as given by McCormick. If so, this would conform to the interpretation of the Steffy & Galbraith results (68) that an optimal orienting period around 5 sec is followed by "damping" around 9 sec following stimulus onset.

Since 1964, the subclassification approach to schizophrenia has been the most useful tool available to control and account for the great variance in schizophrenic behavior. With the constitution of extreme groups in the Warner (73) study, this proposition still holds true. That is, the subject classification (reactive paranoid, process nonparanoid) accounts for more of the variance in size estimation than does heart rate acceleration and much more than heart rate deceleration. However, perhaps the door is now being opened to an era where the prediction of schizophrenic pathology (and nonpathology) can soon be done better by the monitoring of concurrent organismic variables than by the use of subtypes to predict group differences.

SCHIZOPHRENIC LANGUAGE   As mentioned earlier, the skeptic may still ask: "What does all of this have to do with schizophrenia? You can fiddle around with these miniscule variables for ages, but they may bear no relationship or use in what we recognize as the schizophrenia in schizophrenics." Stated differently, schizophrenics do not get arrested or hospitalized for size estimation error or heart rate change any more than they do for slow reaction time and crossover. Indeed, no evidence yet exists that these variables have anything to do with etiology or intervention in schizophrenia. A recent study of schizophrenic language, however, suggests that some rapprochement of the laboratory and clinical aspects may soon be possible.

Cohen, Nachmani & Rosenberg (14) have reported a study in which the probability of schizophrenic language was influenced through the manipulation of briefly presented stimuli. The study was stimulated by a self-editing theory of schizophrenic language (59). According to this theory, people select appropriate words for their referential communication by examining the element to which they are referring, developing an association to that element from their own response repertory, and comparing the association to irrelevant elements. If the association is appropriate to relevant and not to irrelevant elements, it is emitted as part of the communication; if the association is inappropriate to distinguish the relevant from irrelevant elements, the association is rejected. In the latter case, a new association of lower dominance is called forth, and the cycle is repeated. The theory holds that the difficulty in schizophrenic language is in the inability to reject an inappropriate association, once elicited, in order to recycle and search for a more appropriate one.

Cohen et al (14) used a referential discrimination paradigm with color discs to examine the self-editing formulation. Two or more color discs were shown, one designated as the target. The subjects were instructed to read into a tape recorder a description of the designated disc so that a listener could pick it out. When the hues on the color discs are widely separated, the dominant association usually discriminates adequately and minimal self-editing is necessary. Under these conditions normal and nonparanoid patient responses were found to be indistinguishable in communication accuracy, reaction time, and utterance length. For example, when a green and a blue disc were shown and the blue disc was the target, both normals and schizophrenics gave responses such as "blue," "the bluer," "the blue one," etc.

When the color distinction was more difficult, such as with two very close shades of pinkish salmon, then a situation was created where the most dominant association, such as "pink" or "salmon," was inappropriate. It had to be edited out in order to allow a "second take." Although both groups increased the number of

spoken words during a difficult discrimination, normals showed evidence of having rejected their initial associations, made finer distinctions, and then emitted an
appropriate association. For example:

> "My God, this is hard. They are both about the same except this one might be a little
> redder."

> "Both are salmon-colored. This one, however, has more pink."

By contrast, the schizophrenics, after making the initial dominant association (and
possibly discovering the difficulty of the situation), were generally unable to reject
it, go back to process more information, and select an appropriate discriminative
association. For example:

> "A fish swims. You call it a salmon. You cook it. You put it in a can. You open a can.
> You look at it in this color. Salmon fish."

> "This is the color of a shit-ass bowl of salmon. Mix it with mayonnaise. Then it gets
> tasty. Leave it alone and puke all over the fuckin' place. Puke fish."

Cohen et al (14) interpreted these results as supporting a perseverative-chaining
model of schizophrenic language. Emphasis was put on inability to disattend (17)
from immediate (60) stimuli. The relevance of these results to the redundancy
hypothesis may also be interpreted. Once the schizophrenic fails to edit, he not
only begins perseverative chaining, but he also ceases to process the relevant
discriminative information. It is as if once he discovers his dominant association
does not meet the task demand, he "pulls the window shades down" on the outside
world and starts associating to his own associations. As might be expected from the
redundancy formulation, Cohen et al reported that these findings might not be
obtainable from paranoid (low redundancy) schizophrenics. One cannot help but
wonder whether these circumstances which produce schizophrenic language are
related to the size estimation, reaction time, illusion, and heart rate findings
previously discussed.

Conclusion

In this chapter a number of schizophrenia-related deficits have been described.
Each one followed what Kraepelin referred to as a "briefly presented stimulus."
While the time relationships differ, it would appear that schizophrenic deficit may
well be studied and better understood during the few seconds and fractions of
seconds which follow carefully constructed novel, ambiguous, decision-demand-
ing, or otherwise difficult stimuli. Reaction time, size estimation, illusion, GSR,
heart rate, and language are some of the behaviors affected.

Various milestones in the history of assessment of schizophrenia, some beneficial and some not, have been described briefly. The past decade has shown how
effective but fairly crude subclassifications of schizophrenia have added to our
understanding. A new era of schizophrenia research may be starting. We may now

begin identifying mechanisms by which behavior from one instance to another in the same patient, as well as differences between patients, may be predicted.

Perhaps the great tragedy in the study of schizophrenia in the past eight decades has been that the interview to study clinically manifest symptoms has been the major tool. In this chapter we have seen how these manifest symptoms are influenced and obscured by the cognitive style, social competence, and preexisting personality of the individual. We have seen that premorbid history rather than clinically manifest symptoms is more relevant for predicting outcome of hospitalization and drug treatment. Advances in understanding etiology may also require that we turn away from our preoccupation with these clinically manifest symptoms, from our preoccupation with the necessity of interview and projective techniques. The observation and concern with coughing is clinically relevant in deciding that a person needs relief from respiratory misery; however, the classification and factor analysis of coughs does not permit an understanding of the etiology of a respiratory infection, its definitive treatment, or its prognosis. While schizophrenia is unlikely to be explained by this model, the disorder has indeed been susceptible to such a misguided orientation of study. The laboratory measures of reaction time and other factors on a more molecular level of behavior have often been dismissed as not clinically relevant. The time has come to accept the fact that what is clinically relevant may not be etiologically relevant.

The clinically manifest symptoms will remain relevant and important in judging whether an individual will disturb other people with his madness, will be able to cope, will adapt to his community supports. The more subtle manifestations of the illness, such as have been reviewed here, may be what is crucial for purposes of differential treatment, prognosis, and etiology of the disorder.

Once schizophrenia is more completely assessed in these subtle deficits, then the concept may change. Rather than Bleuler's notion of a clinical entity, some people having it and some not, we may shift our concerns to specific mechanisms which are diffusely present to some degree among the well functioning segment of the population. These mechanisms, which may indicate risk for showing the more socially disturbing features, may be at some degree of disorder from time to time in all of us.

Literature Cited

1. American Psychiatric Association 1952. *Diagnostic and Statistical Manual of Mental Disorders.* Washington, D.C.
2. Asarnow, R. 1973. *Information processing in schizophrenics with and without a family history of schizophrenia.* Ann Arbor, Mich.: Wayne State Univ. Microfilms
3. Ax, A. F., Bamford, J. L. 1970. The GSR recovery limb in chronic schizophrenia. *Psychophysiology* 7:145–47

4. Bannister, D. 1960. Conceptual structure in thought disordered schizophrenics. *J. Ment. Sci.* 106:1230–49
5. Ibid 1962. The nature and measurement of schizophrenic thought disorder. 108:825–42
6. Bannister, D., Fransella, F. 1966. A grid test of schizophrenic thought disorder. *Brit. J. Soc. Clin. Psychol.* 5:96–102
7. Bannister, D., Salmon, P. 1966. Schizophrenic thought disorder: specific or

diffuse? *Brit. J. Med. Psychol.* 39: 215–19

8. Bellissimo, A., Steffy, R. A. 1974. Contextual influences on crossover in the reaction time performance of schizophrenics. *J. Abnorm. Psychol.* In press

9. Bellissimo, A., Steffy, R. A. 1972. Redundancy-associated deficit in schizophrenic reaction time performance. *J. Abnorm. Psychol.* 80:229–307

10. Bernstein, A. S. 1970. Phasic electrodermal orienting response in chronic schizophrenics: II. Response to auditory signals of varying intensity. *J. Abnorm. Psychol.* 75:146–56

11. Bleuler, E. 1911. *Dementia Praecox oder die Gruppe der Schizophrenien.* Leipzig: Deuticke. Transl. J. Zinkin 1950. *Dementia Praecox or the Group of Schizophrenias.* New York: Int. Univ. Press

12. Bradley, I. 1975. *Reaction time as a function of heart rate in process schizophrenic and normal subjects.* PhD thesis. Univ. Waterloo, Ontario

13. Buchsbaum, M., Silverman, J. 1968. Stimulus intensity control and the cortical evoked response. *Psychosom. Med.* 30:12–22

14. Cohen, B. D., Nachmani, G., Rosenberg, S. 1974. Referent communication disturbances in acute schizophrenia. *J. Abnorm. Psychol.* 83:1–13

15. Cromwell, R. L. 1968. Stimulus redundancy and schizophrenia. *J. Nerv. Ment. Dis.* 146:360–75

16. Cromwell, R. L. 1972. Strategies for studying schizophrenic behavior. *Psychopharmacologia* 24:121–46

17. Cromwell, R. L., Dokecki, P. A. 1968. Schizophrenic language: a disattention interpretation. In *Developments in Applied Psycholinguistics Research,* ed. S. Rosenberg, J. K. Koplin, 209–60. New York: Macmillan

18. Cromwell, R. L., Held, J. M. 1969. Alpha blocking latency and reaction time in schizophrenics and normals. *Percept. Mot. Skills* 29:195–201

19. Cromwell, R. L., Rosenthal, D., Shakow, D., Zahn, T. P. 1961. Reaction time, locus of control, choice behavior, and descriptions of parental behavior in schizophrenic and normal subjects. *J. Pers.* 29:363–79

20. Davis, D. W., Cromwell, R. L., Held, J. M. 1967. Size estimation in emotionally disturbed children and schizophrenic adults. *J. Abnorm. Psychol.* 72: 395–401

21. Diefendorf, A. R. 1923. *Clinical Psychiatry: A Textbook for Students and Physicians Abstracted and Adapted from the Seventh German Edition (1896) of Kraepelin's "Lehrbuch der Psychiatrie."* New York: Macmillan

22. Edelberg, R. 1970. The information content of the recovery limb of the electrodermal response. *Psychophysiology* 6:527–39

23. Eisenthal, S., Harford, T., Solomon, L. 1972. Premorbid adjustment, paranoid-nonparanoid status, and chronicity in schizophrenic patients. *J. Nerv. Ment. Dis.* 155:227–31

24. Farina, A., Webb, W. W. 1956. Premorbid adjustment and recovery. *J. Nerv. Ment. Dis.* 124:612–13

25. Frost, C. F. 1948. *The relationship between the verbal and galvanic skin response to the Rorschach Test for schizophrenic and normal subjects.* PhD thesis. Clark Univ., Worcester, Mass.

26. Goldstein, L., Sugermann, A. A. 1969. EEG correlates in psychopathology. In *Neurobiological Aspects of Psychopathology,* ed. J. Zubin, C. Shagass 25:1–20. New York: Grune & Stratton

27. Goldstein, M. J. 1973. *Premorbid adjustment and paranoid status as significant variations in schizophrenia research.* Presented at APA meet. Montreal

28. Goldstein, M. J., Held, J. M., Cromwell, R. L. 1968. Premorbid adjustment and paranoid-nonparanoid status in schizophrenia. *Psychol. Bull.* 70: 382–86

29. Goldstein, M. J., Judd, L. L., Rodnick, E. H., LaPolla, A. 1969. Psychophysiological and behavioral effects of phenothiazine administration in acute schizophrenics as a function of premorbid status. *J. Psychiat. Res.* 6:271–87

30. Green, A. A. 1974. *Effects of signal intensity, prestimulation, and time controls upon simple reaction time in process schizophrenic patients.* PhD thesis. Univ. Waterloo, Ontario

31. Gruzelier, J. H., Venables, P. H. 1971.

Two-flash thresholds, heart rate, skin temperature, and blood pressure in schizophrenics with and without skin conductance orienting responses. Presented to Brit. Psychol. Soc. London

32. Gurland, B. J., Fleiss, J. L., Cooper, J. E. 1969. Cross-national study of diagnosis of mental disorders. Am. J. Psychiat. 125 suppl.

33. Harmatz, M. G., Mandelsohn, R., Glassman, M. L. 1973. Behavioral observation in the study of schizophrenia. Presented at APA meet. Montreal

34. Harris, J. G. 1957. Size estimation of pictures as a function of thematic content for schizophrenic and normal subjects. J. Pers. 25:651–71

35. Johannsen, W. J., Friedman, S. H., Leitschuh, T. H., Ammons, H. A. 1963. A study of certain schizophrenic dimensions and their relationship to double alternate learning. J. Consult. Psychol. 27:375–82

36. Kantor, R. R., Winder, C. L. 1959. The process-reactive continuum: a theoretical proposal. J. Nerv. Ment. Dis. 129:429–34

37. Kaplan, R. D. 1974. The crossover phenomenon: Three studies of the effect of training and information on process schizophrenic reaction time. PhD thesis. Univ. Waterloo, Ontario, Canada

38. Kar, B. C. 1967. Müller-Lyer illusion in schizophrenics as a function of field distraction and exposure time. MA thesis. George Peabody Coll. Teach., Nashville, Tenn.

39. Kelly, G. A. 1955. The Psychology of Personal Constructs. New York: Norton. 2 vols.

40. Kety, S. S., Rosenthal, D., Wender, P. H., Schulsinger, F. 1968. The types and prevalence of mental illness in the biological and adoptive families of adopted schizophrenics. In The Transmission of Schizophrenia, ed. D. Rosenthal, S. S. Kety, 345–62. London: Pergamon

41. Kraepelin, E. 1968. Lectures on Clinical Psychiatry. Revised version of 1904 edition by T. Johnstone. New York: Hafner

42. Lacey, J. I. 1958. Psychophysiological approaches to the evaluation of psychotherapeutic process and outcome. In Conference on Research in Psychotherapy, ed. E. A. Rubinstein, M. B. Parloff, 1:160–208. Proc. Conf. Washington, D.C.: Nat. Publ. Co.

43. Lorr, M., O'Connor, J. P., Stafford, J. W. 1961. The Psychotic Reaction Profile: An Inventory of Patient Behavior for Use by Hospital Personnel. Beverly Hills, Calif.: Western Psychol. Serv.

44. Malmquist, A., Orr, W. F., Cromwell, R. L. 1974. Admissions and readmissions to Tennessee State Hospitals. Tenn. J. Med. In press

45. Malmquist, A., Orr, W. F., Cromwell, R. L. 1974. Prognostic outcome in schizophrenia. Am. J. Psychiat. In press

46. McCormick, W. K. 1974. Cardiac rate and size estimation in schizophrenic and normal subjects. MA thesis. Univ. Wisconsin, Madison

47. Mednick, S. A. 1958. A learning theory approach to research in schizophrenia. Psychol. Bull. 55:316–27

48. Mednick, S. A. 1967. The children of schizophrenias: Serious difficulties in current research methodologies which suggest the use of the "high-risk group" method. In The Origins of Schizophrenia, ed. J. Romano. Amsterdam: Excerpta Med. Found.

49. Mehl, M., Cromwell, R. L. 1969. The effect of brief sensory deprivation and sensory stimulation on the cognitive functioning of chronic schizophrenics. J. Nerv. Ment. Dis. 148:586–96

50. Neale, J. M., Cromwell, R. L. 1968. Size estimation in schizophrenics as a function of stimulus presentation time. J. Abnorm. Psychol. 73:44–48

51. Nideffer, R. M., Cromwell, R. L. 1972. Sensitivity and response factors in the choice reaction times of good and poor premorbid schizophrenic and normal subjects. Proc. Am. Psychol. Assoc. 331–32

52. Nideffer, R. M., Deckner, C. W., Cromwell, R. L., Cash, T. F. 1971. The relationship of alpha activity to attentional sets in schizophrenia. J. Nerv. Ment. Dis. 152:346–53

53. Nideffer, R. M., Neale, J. M., Kopfstein, J. H., Cromwell, R. L. 1971. The effect of previous preparatory intervals

upon anticipatory responses in reaction time of schizophrenic and non-schizophrenic patients. *J. Nerv. Ment. Dis.* 153:360–54

54. Obrist, P. A., Howard, J. L., Sutterer, J. R., Sterling-Hennis, H., Murrell, D. J. 1969. Cardiac changes during a simple reaction time task: a developmental study. Presented at meet. Soc. Psychophysiol. Res. Monterey, Calif.

55. Phillips, L. 1953. Case history data and prognosis in schizophrenia. *J. Nerv. Ment. Dis.* 117:515–25

56. Pribram, K. H., Melges, F. T. 1969. Psychophysiological basis of emotion. In *Handbook of Clinical Neurology*, ed. P. Vinkin, G. W. Bruyn, 3:316–42. Amsterdam: North Holland

57. Rodnick, E. H., Shakow, D. 1940. Set in the schizophrenic as measured by a composite reaction time index. *Am. J. Psychiat.* 97:214–25

58. Rosenbaum, G., Mackavey, W. R., Grisell, J. L. 1957. Effects of biological and social motivation on schizophrenic reaction time. *J. Abnorm. Soc. Psychol.* 54:364–68

59. Rosenberg, S., Cohen, B. D. 1964. Speakers' and listeners' processes in a word communication task. *Science* 145:1201–3

60. Salzinger, K. 1971. The immediacy hypothesis and schizophrenia. In *The Future of Time; Man's Temporal Environment*, ed. H. M. Yaker, H. Osmond, F. Cheek. New York: Doubleday

61. Sanes, J., Zigler, E. 1971. Premorbid social competence in schizophrenia. *J. Abnorm. Psychol.* 78:140–44

62. Schechter, G., Buchsbaum, M. 1973. The effects of attention, stimulus intensity, and individual differences on the average evoked response. *Psychophysiology* 10:392–400

63. Shakow, D. 1962. Segmental set. *Arch. Gen. Psychiat.* 6:1–17

64. Shakow, D. 1963. Psychological deficit in schizophrenia. *Behav. Sci.* 8:275–305

65. Silverman, J. 1964. Scanning control mechanism and "cognitive filtering" in paranoid and nonparanoid schizo-phrenia. *J. Consult. Psychol.* 28:385–93

66. Silverman, J. 1964. The problem of attention in research and theory in schizophrenia. *Psychol. Rev.* 71:357–79

67. Steffy, R. A., Galbraith, K. 1974. A comparison of segmental set and inhibitory deficit explanations of the crossover pattern in process schizo-phrenic reaction time. *J. Abnorm. Psychol.* In press

68. Steffy, R. A., Galbraith, K. 1975. Time-linked impairment in schizophrenic reaction time performance. *J. Abnorm. Psychol.* In press

69. Stierlin, H. 1967. Bleuler's concept of schizophrenia: a confusing heritage. *Am. J. Psychiat.* 123:996–1001

70. Strauss, J. S., Carpenter, W. T. Jr. 1972. Prediction of outcome in schizophrenia. *Arch. Gen. Psychiat.* 27:739–46

71. Tyrell, D. J., Struve, F. A., Schwartz, M. L. 1965. A methodological consideration in the performance of process and reactive schizophrenics on a test for organic brain pathology. *J. Clin. Psychol.* 21:254–56

72. Venables, P. H. 1964. Input dysfunction in schizophrenia. In *Progress in Experimental Personality Research*, ed. B. A. Maher, 1:1–42. New York: Academic

73. Warner, D. E. 1973. Cardiac rate responses in two groups of schizophrenics during the performance of a size estimation task. MA thesis. Univ. Wisconsin, Madison

74. Wender, P. H. 1963. Dementia praecox: the development of the concept. *Am. J. Psychiat.* 119:1143–51

75. Wittenborn, J. R. 1951. Symptom patterns in a group of mental hospital patients. *J. Consult. Psychol.* 15:290–302

76. Wittman, P. 1941. Scale for measuring prognosis in schizophrenic patients. *Elgin State Hosp. Pap.* 4:20–33

77. Wynne, L. C. 1967. Family transactions and schizophrenia: II. Conceptual considerations for a research strategy. In *The Origins of Schizophrenia*, ed. J. Romano, 165–78. Amsterdam: Excerpta Med. Found.

78. Zahn, T. P., Rosenthal, D., Lawlor, W. G. 1968. Electrodermal and heart rate

orienting reactions in chronic schizophrenia. *J. Psychiat. Res.* 6:117–34

79. Zahn, T. P., Rosenthal, D., Shakow, D. 1963. Effects of irregular preparatory intervals in reaction time in schizophrenia. *J. Abnorm. Soc. Psychol.* 67:44–52

80. Zigler, E., Levine, J. 1973. Premorbid adjustment and paranoid-nonparanoid status in schizophrenia: a further investigation. *J. Abnorm. Psychol.* 82: 189–99

81. Zubin, J. 1975. Problem of attention in schizophrenia. In *Experimental Approaches to Psychopathology*, ed. M. Kietzman, S. Sutton, J. Zubin. New York: Academic. In press

BIOMETRIC APPROACH TO PSYCHOPATHOLOGY:

§245

Abnormal and Clinical Psychology— Statistical, Epidemiological, and Diagnostic Approaches

Joseph Zubin, Kurt Salzinger, Joseph L. Fleiss,
Barry Gurland, Robert L. Spitzer, Jean Endicott, and
Samuel Sutton

Biometrics Research Unit, New York State Department of Mental Hygiene
New York, N.Y. 10032

FOREWORD

Joseph Zubin

This review consists not of the contribution of a single author, but of several of the staff members of the Biometrics Research Unit (BRU) of the New York State Department of Mental Hygiene. Since we believe that such fields as abnormal and clinical psychology can no longer be reviewed adequately by one worker, this review may mark a turning point in future reviews of similar fields. The BRU was established in 1956 with the mandate to provide an objective assessment of the behavior of mentally disordered individuals with the view of improving diagnosis, prognosis, and evaluation of outcome of mental disorders, as well as promoting investigations into etiology and prevention. This chapter reviews some of the accomplishments of this endeavor on the part of the BRU staff, as well as by similar staffs and research workers elsewhere.

This review has been limited to the following sections:

1. Behavioral Analysis—Kurt Salzinger
2. The Measurement and Classification of Depression—Joseph L. Fleiss
3. Psychiatric Epidemiology—Barry Gurland

621

4. Attempts to Improve Psychiatric Diagnosis—Robert L. Spitzer and Jean Endicott
5. A Psychophysiological Approach to Psychopathology—Samuel Sutton

My task is to introduce this survey and then to conclude it with an integration summary.

Introduction

The field of abnormal and clinical psychology, which at one time was a relatively homogeneous entity, has separated into two distinct and only slightly overlapping disciplines, with the clinical wing far surpassing the abnormal in number of adherents and applications. Abnormal psychology can still be regarded as the basic experimentally oriented part of the endeavor, while clinical psychology may be viewed as the applied field largely invested in treatment and application (292). The apparent impotence of the standard clinical tests in prognosis (280, 295), their low reliability, their lack of value as independent instruments in diagnosis, and their dependence for validity on the criterion provided by the clinical interview, has forced BRU into abandoning the use of routine clinical tests in research on diagnosis and prognosis and evaluation of treatment. Instead we turned our attention to the clinical interview itself—our ultimate criterion of psychopathology—and developed a series of systematic structured interviews which have proved to be reliable and valid (247, 252, 253, 255, 256). The interview techniques have served as a basis for making cross-national comparisons, as described in the section by Gurland; as a basis for computer diagnosis, as described in the section by Spitzer & Endicott; as a basis for developing a newer anatomy of psychopathology in the form of dimensions of psychopathology, as described in the section by Fleiss.

With one leg up on the problem of diagnosis, we then turned our attention to the problem of more direct examination of the behavior of the patient. Following in the footsteps of general learning theory, Salzinger in his section applies the behavioral analysis approach pioneered by Kanfer and Saslow to the salient features of psychopathological behavior exhibited by the patient. Sutton, on the other hand, makes a more atomistic analysis of the laboratory-elicited behavior of the patient in his physiological, sensory, perceptual, psychomotor, and conceptual responses. To elicit these responses he applied the framework of the Mendeleev-like table of Burdock, Sutton & Zubin (19), in which the following types of stimuli are applied: idling state (when no stimulus is applied); energy stimulus (when some relationship exists between intensity and response, e.g. shorter latency for more intense stimuli); and signal stimuli (in which the response bears little relationship to the stimulus intensity but is related to the signal value of the stimulus based on either prior experience or wired-in propensities). In his section he develops the rationale for utilizing the paradigm of the Mendeleev-like table, offers certain research strategies to overcome the "orneriness" of mental patients, and demonstrates their use in differential diagnosis.

Up to this point we have dealt mostly with the description of abnormal behavior. Description, however, is not enough, for it never cured a disorder, nor has it of its own accord yielded any insight into the nature of the disorder. To go deeper we must appeal to etiology, even though our knowledge of etiology is skimpy, if not entirely lacking. To make up for our ignorance we must resort to "as if" causes in the form of scientific models. However, mere postulation of models is also not enough; we must proceed further to draw from them inferred hypotheses and test them in the crucible of observation and experimentation. This part of our endeavor is still in its preliminary stages, and we shall deal with it in the summary at the end of this chapter.

1. BEHAVIORAL ANALYSIS

Kurt Salzinger[1]

Spurred on by the fact that psychiatric diagnosis continues to suffer the pains of low reliability and validity, behaviorally oriented therapists have started to codify their own kind of behavioral analysis. This analysis has been applied to both kinds of behavior therapies: that based on the classical or respondent conditioning paradigm and that based on the instrumental or operant conditioning paradigm. This is not to say that in practice one kind of conditioning occurs without the other. On the contrary, the two always co-occur (212). What differentiates the therapies is the focus of the therapist. It determines the kind of behavioral analysis engaged in and, therefore, also the kind of assessment procedure used.

The main business of the therapist following the respondent paradigm is the identification of the stimuli that act as conditional stimuli (CS) for the patient's current state. When using desensitization, the therapist must, according to Wolpe's (286) original formulation, also establish a hierarchy of aversiveness of stimuli in order to be able to present the CSs in an increasing order of anxiety productiveness.

The operant conditioner, on the other hand, has the task of identifying the discriminative stimuli (S^D) in the reinforcement contingency ($S^D \ldots R \rightarrow S^R$) that precede the undesirable or desirable behavior (R), and those reinforcing stimuli (primary S^Rs and conditioned S^rs) that follow them; in addition, the operant conditioner must estimate the strength of those behaviors examined within the reinforcement contingency.

Distinctive Features of Behavioral Analysis

Behavioral analysis focuses on those aspects of the individual and his environment that can be directly used in therapy. Respondent conditioning emphasizes the autonomic responses, while the operant paradigm emphasizes the behavior of the patient that directly engages the external environment. Behavioral analysis is functional, not topographical. More important than the presence of a fear are the conditions (the particular CSs) that elicit the fear (respondent conditioning). More

[1] The author is also affiliated with the Polytechnic Institute of New York.

The writing of this paper was supported in part by NIMH Grant Number 1 R01 MH 22890–01 and 02.

important than the individual's fighting behavior are the conditions under which it takes place, namely when, where, and to what effect (operant conditioning). Behavioral analysis classifies behaviors rather than people. This is not to say, however, that behavior therapists restrict their work to the analysis of single behaviors. They take into account all relevant behaviors. For example, if such therapists discover that a particular individual is currently reinforced for undesirable behavior, they determine in addition what reasonable behavior the individual has in his repertory; then, if it is thought advisable, that person can be retrained to emit the reasonable behavior to obtain the positive reinforcers earlier obtained by undesirable behavior.

Finally, while diagnosis is supposed to shed light on the cause of disorders (actually it rarely does so for psychiatric disorders), the relationship of behavioral analysis to the cause of the disorder is relatively unimportant. More significant than how the behavior started is what is maintaining it. In some cases this amounts to knowing the cause, but not usually. On the other hand, behavior analysts do assume that most types of behavioral abnormalities are produced through one of the learning paradigms. Even though some particular physical insult may be vitally involved in a particular abnormality, the interaction of that physical insult with the conditioning paradigms is held responsible for the current abnormal behavior (see 213 for this kind of explanation of the immediacy hypothesis and schizophrenic behavior).

The Behavior-Analytic View of Testing

Goldfried & Kent (76) and Mischel (159) explain that test responses are regarded as *signs* of behavior by the traditional approach and as *samples* of behavior by the behavior theory approach. Basically, behavior analysts prefer direct observation of the individuals in the actual situation, but they accept the creation of an experimental analog situation, including role playing and the use of self-report techniques. In the better assessment programs, the patient is taught how to observe his or her own behavior in an objective manner; unfortunately, more often than should be true, self-report is obtained through the clinical interview, which is beset by the artifacts of influence on the part of the interviewer (217–219).

The traditional approach to testing also carries along with it the assumption that the test responses reveal behavior patterns invariant with respect to the situations in which they occur. However, as long ago as 1928, Hartshorne & May (92) showed that the behavior of individuals depends in large part on the situation (the reinforcement contingency). Behavior is flexible in that it varies with environmental stimuli. Only the most extreme abnormality would produce the kind of invariance of behavior that traditional tests demand for their validity.

The use of self-report is often found to be a poor substitute for behavioral observation. One study (88, 216) focused on the relationship between communicability (behaviorally defined) and amount of contact in a group of people. Objectively observed amount of contact was the best predictor of communicability; self-reported contact was predictive only when considering presence vs absence; and self-estimated degree of closeness was not predictive to a significant degree. If these are the findings with respect to amount of social contact, how much greater must be the problem of estimating behaviors more vaguely specified, such as anxiety. Tests used to obtain self-report need to be behavioral, specific, and close in time to the occurrence of the behavior in question.

Behavioral Analysis and Environmental Psychology

Although the reinforcement contingency deals directly with the environment and its effect on behavior (see 220 for a review of this subject with respect to the measurement of abnormal behavior), a separate field of environmental psychology has sprung up in recent years. Its discoveries might well contribute to a behavioral analysis with its methods of objectively describing the "personality" of environments (97, 161, 162). The environment has been described by such dimensions as ecology, organization structure, personality of milieu inhabitants, behavior settings, reinforcement properties of the environment, and psychosocial characteristics. Although only one of the dimensions is conceptualized in terms of behavior theory, behavior theory provides the mechanism through which the dimensions no doubt influence people's behavior. The more important point here, however, is that the behavior analyst trying to assess the viability of programs of reinforcement or extinction should obtain accurate knowledge about the environment in which the patient resides.

Behavioral Analysis of Traditionally Categorized Disorders

Dollard & Miller (47) provided an early extensive treatment of neurosis in terms of behavior theory. Their analysis, unfortunately, accepted as fact too many of the concepts of psychoanalytic theory. More recently, Salzinger (214) showed how a number of learning paradigms could produce known entities of abnormal behavior such as delusions, depression, and psychophysiological reactions. Because of the recent increase in interest in the depression syndrome, it might be useful to note two new behavioral analyses of depression (55, 160).

Methods of Behavioral Analysis Related to the Classical Conditioning Model

The basic approach to assessment for Wolpe's behavior therapy and some of its variants consists of the classical psychological procedures, namely the paper-and-pencil test. Wolpe (286) led the way by using the Willoughby Personality Schedule, a test for neuroticism or unadaptive anxiety reactions. The patient responds to such questions as, "Do you get stage fright?" Other questions deal with daydreams, being easily discouraged, feeling miserable, feeling inferior, and being unable to make up one's mind. In addition, Wolpe (287) uses the Bernreuter (9) Self-sufficiency Questionnaire primarily to assess the degree to which the patient is able to carry out instructions with regard to self-assertion. He also suggested the use of the Maudsley Personality Inventory. Finally, Wolpe (287) uses the Fear Survey Schedule, which is quite popular in respondent conditioning behavior therapy. This test (288) lists situations that might provoke fear in the patient. The patient indicates degree of disturbance on a five point scale, ranging from "not at all" to "very much." The 1969 version lists 87 situations, including noise of vacuum cleaners, falling, sirens, failure, sick people, receiving an injection, birds, lightning, doctors, people with deformities, dirt, and a lull in conversation.

The fear-survey schedules used by Wolpe and others have been fully reviewed by Hersen (94) and by Wolff & Merrens (285). Tasto & Hickson (268) standardized and scaled a 122-item Fear Survey Schedule (FSS). They administered it to a group of 132 male and 107 female undergraduate students at a large university. Standardization of a test presents the therapist with an objective criterion for determining when the fear has been reduced to the level that characterizes most of the population. Standardization on a college population, however, is questionable in terms of how representative it is of the population at large. In a later paper, Tasto, Hickson & Rubin (269) performed a profile analysis for the five factors earlier derived by Rubin et al (210). These factors and their corroboration by profile analysis give some empirical basis for gauging the generalization to be expected from the treatment of one problem to that of another. In 1972, Tasto & Suinn (270) administered the same test twice within a 10-week period and found generally high correlations, but not uniformly so, for all factors. More troublesome were the significant decreases in the factor scores from the first to the second test administration. As the authors point out, this "natural" decrease would definitely have to be taken into account when estimating the effectiveness of therapeutic intervention by this test.

Hersen (94) presents additional results on the fear survey schedules. Female subjects, whether undergraduates or patients in inpatient or outpatient therapy situations, have higher fear scores than male counterparts. It is not clear whether this difference is to be ascribed to differences in fears, to the selection of items of the test, or to the difference in tendency to admit to having fears. Normals have the smallest number of fears, neurotics the next larger, and psychotics the largest. Reliability of the fear survey was very high on a split-half basis but not as high on a test-retest basis. Furthermore, schizophrenic subjects showed a significantly lower reliability than normals on a snake fear (.53 as opposed to .79 for normals).

Although the modification of self-assertive responses consists of the conditioning of operant behavior, Wolpe has used it as part of the inhibitory mechanism in his reconditioning paradigm, and therefore we shall deal with it here. Rathus (202), inspired by the ever greater use of assertiveness training, devised a schedule of 30 items for its measurement. Both test-retest reliability and split-half reliability correlations were above .77. With respect to validity, Rathus had the testers choose a group of people they knew well and whom they could rate on a 17-item rating scale. Intercorrelation of the ratings with the subjects' responses about themselves yielded a series of positive values, indicating that subjects who appeared to be assertive to friends revealed themselves to be so by their own responses on the self-assertiveness scale. Furthermore, the degree of assertiveness shown by subjects' stories correlated positively ($r = .70$) to their scores on the assertiveness scale.

It is not surprising that at least some behavior therapists were not satisfied with behavioral diagnoses on the basis of paper-and-pencil tests (69). Rutner & Pear

(211) devised a behavioral measure of the avoidance of a feared object by measuring the length of time a subject is willing to observe a rat pressing a lever on a food reinforcement contingency. This length-of-observation measure distinguished high from low phobic subjects as determined by how close they were willing to approach a rat in a cage. Craighead (41) related the proximity of a subject to a snake to verbal self-report of fear and to level of physiological arousal. The closer the subject was able to approach the snake, the less the physiological arousal measure and the greater the subjective fear measure. Unfortunately, the magnitudes of the correlations were not high. With respect to sexual problems, however, specific physiological measures, such as those of penile volume (4, 285), are more directly relevant.

Methods of Behavioral Analysis Related to the Operant Conditioning Model

Behavioral analysis is an intrinsic aspect of operant conditioning. Goldiamond (77) instructed his clients in behavior theory; then he told them to think of their own problems as an experiment in which they are trying to modify the probability of a particular class of behavior.

The single most significant effort in the area of behavior analysis stems from Kanfer & Saslow (101), along with a later revision by the same authors (102). They present the following outline for eliciting information: 1. Analysis of the problem situation—is the behavior excessive or deficient? Under this category the therapist also looks for the patient's behavioral assets. 2. Clarification of the problem situation—people involved in the behaviors and the consequences of the behaviors. 3. A motivational analysis—a listing of the reinforcers, positive and negative, now impinging on the patient, those that could be used for therapy later, and those that might change if therapy is successful. 4. Developmental analysis—patient's biological equipment and sociocultural background which may limit behavior, as, for example, a limp or blindness, poor education, or different language background. These factors and characteristic behaviors at different times of life are investigated. 5. Analysis of self-control—inadequate or excessive. 6. Analysis of social relationships—the patient's social networks reveal who can help and who is hindering the patient. 7. Analysis of the social-cultural-physical environment—comparison of the patient's behavior to that expected by someone of that social background. Kanfer & Saslow explain that the information to be collected for this type of analysis need not all be garnered from the usual patient interview but, on the contrary, ought to be obtained by talking to significant others in the patient's life, by watching him or her in interaction with those significant others, by observing that patient at work and at play, by interviewing people who might know about the patient, and also by employing paper-and-pencil tests and specific laboratory techniques as they are called for.

In their book, Kanfer & Phillips (100) successfully relate the particular problems a patient might have (as ascertained from the above analysis) to the techniques of therapy that should be used, such as extinction and conditioning of competing responses.

Storrow (260) has devised various check lists for his behavior analysis. The

Personal Data Form, filled out by the patient, has questions such as: "What persons, situations, activities, etc seem to set these symptoms off or make them worse?" (p. 219). He completes the Psychiatric Case Study form on the basis of the Personal Data Form, a physical examination, information from relatives and the patient in the interview, and psychological testing. Although he calls the behaviors he wishes to modify symptoms, he views them as the dependent variables to be modified, rather than the epiphenomena of the medical model. The final part of his form notes his decision of what to change in the patient and by what method. Another variation on the Kanfer-Saslow behavioral analysis is the work by Stuart (261), in which forms are used following the $S^D \ldots R \to S^R$ paradigm. He categorizes what we have called S^Ds into four classes: 1. instructional stimuli; 2. discriminative stimuli (which Stuart restricts to mean an offer of positive reinforcement for a response); 3. potentiating variables which insure that the reinforcer is effective, (for example, by depriving an individual of those things that will be given later as reinforcers); 4. facilitating stimuli (tools such as books if the subject is expected to read). Pomeranz & Goldfried (186) presented another variant of this basic kind of outline. Finally, Carter & Thomas (24) presented 27 categories of "problems in communication" in marital couples. These are for the most part operationally defined and consist of overtalk, fast talk, quiet talk, affective talk, abusive talk, opinion deficit, and topic avoidance, among others.

A very important aspect of behavioral analysis is the use of observation by trained personnel, by the patient, or by a significant other. In many studies it has been shown that the act of observation by interested parties, whether the patient or significant others, increases self-control. In view of the frequent deficit in such self-control initially, it is perhaps not surprising that behavior should improve merely because it has been observed in an objective manner. Salzinger, Feldman & Portnoy (215) trained parents to use a form to record their observations of the behavior of their children by noting the children's responses, their time of occurrence, the people present at that time, the occasion on which the behavior occurred, and the events that followed that behavior. Typical results showed that the observations were too vague at first, but with shaping through discussion of the recorded observations, the parents became more specific. At that point the parents' behavior also changed, and occasionally the behavior of the target child improved before any special program was enacted. Apparently the requirement to record what was happening made the parent hesitate long enough at the time of such behaviors as tantrums so as not to reinforce them. In some cases a behavioral change is easy to record objectively, as in the case of weight loss. In most others, unfortunately, despite the therapist's best intentions, the only measure available is the less easily verifiable patient-recorded behavior. Simkins (234) reported on the lack of data concerning reliability of such records. Electronic devices (227) might eventually yield indices of validity for such observations.

One more type of assessment ought to be mentioned. In 1967, Cautela & Kastenbaum (25) devised a reinforcement survey schedule on which subjects may indicate the extent to which certain items give them "joy or other pleasurable feeling." Examples are: eating, beverages, nude men, nude women, reading, singing, skin diving, and being praised by the boss for having completed a job well done. Thorndike & Kleinknecht (272) found that test-retest reliability over 5 weeks ranged from .40 to .91 for various clusters of reinforcers. It is suggested that at least some of the clusters are sufficiently reliable for therapy research.

Conclusion

There are now a number of methods of behavioral analysis available. They include the usual techniques for obtaining information in the area of clinical psychology. They differ in the main from the older techniques in being more focused and in requiring fewer assumptions about the meaning of the responses obtained. Much more work needs to be done, however, before we can say that we have well-standardized methods of doing behavioral analysis. What we have so far are some specific tests and some general outlines of inquiry.

2. THE MEASUREMENT AND CLASSIFICATION OF DEPRESSION

Joseph L. Fleiss[2]

After long neglect at the expense of research in schizophrenia, research in depression resumed actively in the early and middle 1960s. The research has been on many fronts: biochemical (224), epidemiological (131, 233), genetic (181), and clinical. Even though the unit of analysis in these research endeavors is invariably the individual depressed patient, the results are meant to be applied to depressives in general. This means that in each of these kinds of research, evaluation methods must be applied to measure a subject's degree of depression (in order to screen out nondepressives as not suitable for study, to describe one's resulting sample, or to measure change), and to classify him into one of a number of diagnostic categories (in order to ascertain which kinds of patients one's results apply to, and to communicate one's results to others).

This review will be restricted to methods that have been employed to measure and classify depression. Attention will be limited as far as possible to so-called unipolar depression, i.e. depression as the primary current complaint with no previous episodes of mania or hypomania. Research into the distinction between unipolar depression and bipolar depression (i.e. manic-depressive illness) has been reviewed elsewhere (2, 283), as has been research into the etiology and treatment of depression (39, 258). Some of the signs and symptoms used to characterize depression are, in addition to a depressed mood, a loss of interest in usual activities, an inability to concentrate, psychomotor retardation or agitation, suicidal thinking, weight loss, and feelings of hopelessness.

[2] The author is also affiliated with the Division of Biostatistics, Columbia University, New York City.

The preparation of this review was supported in part by grant MH 23964 from the National Institute of Mental Health. Criticisms provided by Drs. David Dunner and Frank Stallone of the Department of Internal Medicine, Dr. Jean Endicott of Biometrics Research, and Dr. Alexander Glassman of the Department of Biological Psychiatry (all at the New York State Psychiatric Institute) are gratefully acknowledged.

The Measurement of Depression

RATING SCALES   Rating scales most frequently employed for measuring depression are of three kinds: self-report questionnaires to be completed by the subject; scales to be filled out by a professional after interviewing and observing the subject; and scales to be completed by a nurse or attendant on the basis of naturalistic ward observations.

Self-report scales for depression have been developed by Beck et al (6), Pilowsky & Spalding (184), Rockliff (206), the Wakefield Hospital group (241), and Zung (296). The major advantage to relying on the subject to rate his own condition is the saving of professional time. Self-report scales are thus economical sources of data for large-scale surveys. They have been shown to be sensitive in assessing a patient's degree of recovery from a depressive episode (190, 198), but not in estimating the severity of an acute episode experienced by a psychiatric inpatient (190). Their usefulness may be greater with outpatients and private patients.

One disadvantage to self-report scales is that some subjects may be unable to understand the intent of the questions. Because of denial or deliberate falsification, the severity of depression is frequently underestimated by the subject himself (178, 206, 275). In addition, many newly admitted inpatients are too acutely ill even to complete a short questionnaire within a few days of admission (250).

An alternative procedure for measuring depression is a clinical interview of the subject, followed by or coincident with the completion of a rating scale. Scales for depression to be administered by clinicians or other professionals after an interview have been developed by Hamilton (86), Pilowsky and his colleagues (184), and Zung (298). Wechsler et al (277) developed a scale which relies on both sources, the patient's self-report as well as a professional's judgments.

Spitzer & Endicott (248) have indicated how the interview is superior to other methods of data collection in psychopathology. They point out, however, that differences among interviewers in the topics they cover and in how they phrase their questions, and differences for the same interviewer in how he interacts with different subjects, can greatly affect the final ratings. Thus sizable proportions of the variance in scores from rating scales based on an interview may be associated with differences among interviewers rather than differences among subjects (58).

In order to reduce this extraneous variation, structure may be imposed on the interview by specifying for the interviewer the order of topics to be covered, the questions to be asked, or even the probes to be put to the subject. Only Zung's later scale (298), among those specifically designed for depression, seems to incorporate a structured interview.

The self-report and interviewer-completed scales cited above limit the measurement of depression to that currently being experienced by a subject, and are thus useful for sample description and for establishing baselines in the study of change. They do not cover previous episodes or other aspects of psychiatric history. As pointed out by increasing numbers of investigators (3, 54, 205), however, history is at least as important as current state for describing depression when one's purpose is classification. Only one scale, a structured interview procedure developed by Spitzer & Endicott (249), appears to exist for covering thoroughly both current and past aspects of depression. The scale also has sections for manic and schizophrenic behavior.

Ratings made by nurses or other ward personnel of patients' overt behavior provide a useful adjunct to ratings based on an interview (18, 198, 199). They may even reveal patterns of behavior that are not picked up by other rating methods. Raskin and his colleagues (200, 201), for example, found a factor of excitement in nurses' ratings of the ward behavior of depressed patients which was not present in either self-report or interview-based ratings. The nurses may have noted either transitory manic states or periods of extreme agitation that neither the patients nor the interviewers were aware of.

A limitation on naturalistic observations of ward behavior is that they may be applied only to hospitalized patients and not to outpatients or nonpatients in the community. In addition, ward personnel may be insensitive to aspects of psychopathology (e.g. emotional withdrawal) which are revealed by the other sources of ratings (199).

Each source of information—the patient himself, the interviewer, and the nurse—provides data about various aspects of depression, but these data are often in conflict. The multitrait-multimethod studies of Raskin and his colleagues (199–201) represent an attempt to dovetail these observations into a coherent portrait of depression.

Although most of the scales cited above are intended to describe the depression currently experienced by psychiatric patients, some were designed for use with nonpatients (296, 298), and at least one was especially designed for describing course of illness (18). Before selecting a scale, therefore, the investigator must specify the kinds of subjects he intends to study, who is to make the ratings, and whether the data are to be analyzed cross-sectionally or longitudinally.

SLEEP DISTURBANCE IN DEPRESSION   A stereotype characterizes the place of sleep disturbance in depression. Neurotic depressives are supposed to experience difficulty in falling asleep, whereas psychotic depressives are supposed to experience early morning wakening. See below for a review of the distinction between neurotic and psychotic depression. A number of studies (85, 117, 209) have confirmed this classic picture. In a review of six studies contrasting the symptoms of neurotic and psychotic depression, Costello (38) found that early morning wakening was one of only two signs agreed upon by at least four of the studies as characterizing psychotic depression.

Other studies (22, 40, 150, 153), however, have failed to confirm this stereotype. A major source of discrepancy between studies is a reliance on different kinds of information. Some studies have relied on the patient's own recollection of the quality of his sleep (22, 85, 117), and others have relied on the observations made by nurses throughout the night (40, 150). The latter kind of study has tended to be negative, reporting small if any differences between neurotic and psychotic depressives.

Two other studies (168, 185) have relied on both the patient and the nurse as sources of data, but their results disagree. One (168) reported good agreement between nurses' observations and patients' reports of the quality of sleep, and the other (185) that patients tend to report their sleep to be poorer than nurses perceive it. Weiss and his colleagues (278) found that neither nurses nor patients were able to agree well with information provided by electroencephalographic studies.

The definitive description of the patterns of sleep disturbance in depression will only come from all-night EEG studies. Kales & Berger (99) reviewed the relatively small number of such studies performed through 1969. Their review suggests that neurotic and psychotic depressives have similar patterns of sleep disturbance, with the disturbances perhaps being more severe in the psychotic than in the neurotic group.

RATER PERCEPTIONS   Even if structure is imposed on the clinical interview, which is the most important source of information about depression, extraneous variation will remain due to differences in how raters perceive what the subject reports and how he behaves (58). In one study (184), for example, ratings of depressed patients made by medical students relatively unsophisticated in psychopathology correlated much more strongly with patients' self-reports ($r = .91$) than did ratings made by either experienced psychologists ($r = .40$) or psychiatrists ($r = .36$). The higher correlation achieved by the students may be attributed either to their being less influenced than the professionals by theoretical formulations, or to their naively accepting as fact, without further probing, whatever the patients reported.

Reliance on standardized and structured procedures for assessing depression assures a reduction in, although not an elimination of, both bias (which might result in spurious differences) and unreliability (which might obscure real differences) (108). Such reductions are especially likely in the context of a single study, for the raters can be trained in the comparable use of such procedures.

The theoretical background of the rater is known, however, to affect strongly how he perceives and rates depressive symptoms (38, 51, 107, 108, 156, 179). No amount of standardization and structuring, therefore, will guarantee comparability across studies if the personnel employed in each perceive these symptoms differently.

The Classification of Depression

RELIABILITY OF DIAGNOSIS   The major diagnostic subdivisions of the unipolar depressive disorders are neurotic depression, psychotic depression, and involutional melancholia (1, 74). On the basis of evidence reviewed by Zubin (291), as well as more recent data (37), one must conclude that the routine diagnosis of depression is grossly unreliable.

In the original reports, data on diagnostic agreement were presented as simple proportions of agreement, uncorrected for the degree of agreement expected by chance alone. Because chance-expected agreement varies across studies as a function of the base rates with which the diagnoses are made, the uncorrected proportions are not comparable. A statistic, kappa, has been developed for measuring how well two (32) or more (59) judges agree beyond the level predicted by chance.

Values of kappa less than or equal to zero imply that agreement is no better than that predicted by chance, and values greater than zero imply that agreement is better than that predicted by chance. Kappa assumes its maximum value of $+1$ only when agreement is perfect, and is interpretable as an intraclass correlation coefficient (61, 127).

Three studies (7, 37, 221) report sufficient data on the reliability of the diagnosis of depression to permit the calculation of kappa. For neurotic depression, kappa varies from .10 to .47; for psychotic depression, from .19 to .30; and for involutional melancholia, from .21 to .38. When the subcategories are combined into the single diagnosis of depression, the resulting mean value of kappa is only in the neighborhood of .30.

Serious cross-national differences exist in the criteria for diagnosing depression (37, 110, 230), with British psychiatrists tending to diagnose depressive disorders relatively more frequently than American psychiatrists. Equally serious are the biases against diagnosing depression in lower class patients in general (131) and blacks in particular (98, 144, 235). When blacks and whites are assessed by means of standardized procedures, the difference in the prevalence rate of depression all but vanishes (236, 273, 297).

A study of New York hospital psychiatrists (83) revealed that they were sensitive to the depression exhibited by some of their patients, but were reluctant to bring this sensitivity to bear in making their diagnoses. A sample of patients was identified on the basis of a standardized interview conducted by independent investigators as suffering from severe depression, but with no signs of schizophrenia. These patients were treated with antidepressive therapy by the hospital psychiatrists significantly more frequently than were other kinds of patients, but were nevertheless more frequently diagnosed schizophrenic than depressive.

The inability of clinicians to agree well on the diagnosis of depression, the systematic bias against diagnosing depression in certain kinds of patients, and the tendency among American psychiatrists to underdiagnose depression must be borne in mind as major reasons for disagreements among the studies to be reviewed below.

THE DICHOTOMY BETWEEN NEUROTIC AND PSYCHOTIC DEPRESSION   Of the three major subdivisions of the unipolar depressive disorders, involutional melancholia stands out as apparently not meriting status as a separate diagnostic entity. With the trivial exception of age, few differences of practical magnitude in etiology, clinical characteristics, or outcome have been reported between involutional and other depressives (2, 43, 106, 155).

The validity of separating the other two subdivisions, neurotic depression and psychotic depression, however, has been the subject of intensive research and debate. An alternative dichotomy, reactive versus endogenous depression, overlaps the neurotic-psychotic dichotomy to such an extent (5) that neurotic depression and reactive depression are virtually synonymous, as are psychotic depression and endogenous depression.

Reactive or neurotic depression is presumedly characterized by the existence of a precipitating event, anxiety in the clinical picture, difficulty in falling asleep, and poor premorbid adjustment. Endogenous or psychotic depression is presumedly characterized by the absence of a precipitating event, retardation, early morning wakening, and a history of previous depressive episodes. Personality variables appear not to be useful in distinguishing between the two types (68), nor perhaps is the existence of life-changing events prior to the onset of illness (271).

Some investigators have either suggested (105, 154, 156) or reported data which suggest (116, 174) that psychotic or endogenous depression is a tightly organized syndrome representing a well-defined illness, whereas neurotic depression is a term applied to a heterogeneous collection of signs and symptoms frequently found together with other neurotic features, personality disturbances, and hysteria.

The validity of this view has been brought into question by Costello's review (38) of six studies (22, 87, 117, 208, 209, plus an unpublished report) which factorially separated features of neurotic from features of psychotic depression. He found that the studies tended to agree on the variables loading on the factor for neurotic depression, but did not agree on the variables loading on the factor for psychotic depression. Only psychomotor retardation was reported by all six studies as a symptom loading high on psychotic depression. Early morning wakening was cited as an important feature by four studies, and all other features were cited by three or fewer studies.

The overwhelming importance of retardation in distinguishing between different kinds of depressed patients has been confirmed by other studies (62, 170). It is crucial, however, that psychomotor retardation be measured separately from flat affect (62), something not possible with all rating scales (142, 256).

In addition to the studies reviewed by Costello (38), others (104, 116) have found that ratings of depressed patients factor either into a bipolar factor, with features of the two kinds of depression loading on opposite ends, or into two factors, one defined by signs of neurotic and the other by signs of psychotic depression. The inference frequently drawn from such results has been to confirm the validity of the diagnostic separation between neurotic and psychotic depression. Such an inference is erroneous, for factor analysis is not by itself informative about the existence of types (51, 108, 120, 163, 207).

One criticism leveled at the studies reporting bipolar factors has been that bipolarity may result from raters' perceiving the two kinds of depression as distinct, and thus tending to rate patients as exhibiting either signs appropriate to one type or signs appropriate to the other, but rarely signs appropriate to both (51, 107, 156). When factor analyses have been applied to ratings made by professionals not committed to the dichotomy between the two kinds of depression, neither bipolar factors nor separate factors for neurotic and psychotic depression have been found (148, 165, 199).

More germane to the validation of a typology than the results of factor analyses is an examination for clustering or multimodality of the frequency distributions of patients on quantitative variables (87, 163). Increasing numbers of investigators have been examining and reporting distributions of both factor scores and discriminant function scores best distinguishing neurotic depressives from psychotic depressives, but the results have been contradictory. Some studies have reported bimodality (22, 53, 73, 222), others have reported unimodality (105, 106, 111, 170, 179, 207, 271, 294), and yet others have reported equivocal results (104, 116). The same biases which give rise to bipolar factors may give rise to bimodal distributions, and such biases may explain some of the positive findings of bimodality.

Another reason—a statistical one—may account for some of the negative and equivocal results. Multimodality is not a necessary condition for the existence of subtypes. Unless two underlying distributions are well separated or are present in nearly equal proportions, their mixture will result in a unimodal but skewed distribution (67). It is therefore inappropriate to examine a frequency distribution only visually, or to apply only goodness-of-fit tests for normality. A more powerful but more complicated procedure is to test whether a mixture of normal distributions fits a given distribution significantly better than does a single normal distribution (60, 284). If the factor or discriminant function scores are weighted sums of sufficiently many variables, the model of underlying normality becomes tenable by the central limit theorem (60).

NUMERICAL TYPOLOGIES OF DEPRESSION   Rather than looking for modes in a frequency distribution as evidence for the existence of types, other investigators (80, 173, 174, 182, 183) have applied methods of numerical taxonomy (70, 141, 163) to cluster depressed patients directly into homogeneous subgroups. Although some of these numerical typologies have been validated by demonstrations that members of different types respond differentially to treatment (96, 175) or perform differentially on other tests (176, 184), the results must be suspect because of deficiencies in most clustering methods (50, 63, 67), especially their tendency to yield artifactual types. Thus the demonstration of differential response to treatment may be little more than a demonstration of a correlation between response to treatment and one or more of the variables (e.g. retardation) most important in effecting the apparent separation between patients (60, 170).

One of the apparently more promising typologies of depression is that derived by Paykel (174). He found four types, one corresponding to psychotic depression and the others representing subdivisions of neurotic depression. A major difficulty in interpreting these types is that Paykel's sample of depressives was selected from different sources: outpatient clinics, emergency services, day care centers, and the wards of mental hospitals. The importance has been recognized of the effects of social and cultural variables on the type of treatment patients seek (121) and on the patterns of psychopathology they present (103, 131). It was hardly surprising, therefore, that differences in the patterns of depression were found among patients from the various sources of Paykel's sample (120, 177), and therefore that his four types overlapped considerably with the sources of his sample (176). One cannot tell, therefore, whether his typology is one of depressed patients or of facilities treating depressed patients.

Aside from the defect in Paykel's sample selection, his work represents a paradigm for future research. Standardized observations of mental state and history should be made by professionals not committed to any theoretical model of depression, and should be used according to specified rules (205) to select subjects whose primary disorder is depression.

The resulting data should be subjected to the most powerful analytic methods available. The Friedman-Rubin clustering method (70), the one used by Paykel (174), seems to be one of the best available. Within any study, however, one's sample of diagnosed depressives must be derived from one source only (e.g. public mental hospitals or a probability sample of a community) rather than from many sources. It is better to describe one particular kind of depressed patient precisely than to describe many kinds of depressed patients ambiguously.

3. PSYCHIATRIC EPIDEMIOLOGY

Barry Gurland

The generally healthy state of psychiatric epidemiology is evidenced by the tone of the review papers that have recently appeared on this subject (34, 36, 81, 123), by the scientific rigor of the papers in the international conference in Aberdeen (90), and by the appearance of the first textbook devoted exclusively to this topic (35).

The Symposium on Psychiatric Epidemiology, held at Aberdeen University in July 1969, was the first of its kind in nearly a decade and produced almost 20 papers of high standard, published as a volume in 1970 (90). Gruenberg (81), looking back to the pioneering Milbank Memorial Fund meeting on psychiatric epidemiology in 1949, and forward to developments in the near future, concludes that "the epidemiology of mental disorders has become an established category of research in the related scientific disciplines," and he regards it as now inappropriate, for epidemiological purposes, to view mental disorder in isolation rather than as one of the consequences of a variety of conditions, since the latter view provides a more useful unifying theme. Thus, in a wry compliment to the Aberdeen proceedings, he sees no further necessity for such meetings. Although that may be true for substantive studies, the methodological problems of assessing mental disorder seem sufficiently peculiar to this class of disorders to warrant its delineation as a special field for some time to come.

Among the major recent advances in the methodology of psychiatric epidemiology has been progress towards the development of reliable and valid measures for assessing psychopathology in different national or cultural groups and across language barriers; for recording the interaction between patients and treatment services by means of case registers or record linkages; and for assessing forces in the biological or cultural milieu which might show associations with psychopathology.

As a measure of psychopathology, psychiatric diagnosis has been much improved by the use of semistructured mental state interviews to standardize the scope and style of collecting information for diagnosis and to allow an analysis and synthesis of the discrete items of psychopathology which relate to diagnosis; and by the use of glossaries to aid in the definition of diagnostic labels. The use of such standard diagnoses and diagnostically oriented symptom analysis for epidemiological purposes has been demonstrated by the US-UK Diagnostic Project in a study of recent admissions to public mental hospitals in London and New York (37, 84). Diagnoses and symptom ratings made by the project's research psychiatrists were shown to be cross-nationally reliable, whereas the routine diagnoses by hospital psychiatrists were based on different though overlapping criteria in the two cities. The New York hospital psychiatrists had a much wider concept of schizophrenia compared to their London colleagues so that the hospital statistics gave a misleading picture of the relative distribution of diagnostic groups in the two cities.

Unfortunately there is no evidence as yet that semistructured interview techniques and glossaries of diagnostic terms have done much to improve the reliability of *routine* hospital diagnoses which are potentially the backbone of epidemiological work based on admission records or case registers, Kendell (109) found that there was no appreciable change in the specification of diagnostic labels by psychiatrists in English mental hospitals after the promulgation of an official glossary for diagnostic categories in the mental disorders section of the International Classification of Diseases.

This is not to beg the question of whether psychiatric diagnosis is necessarily the best reference point for epidemiological work. Some general population studies rely on inventories of symptoms which, though highly associated with psychiatric impairment, are not intended to cover the wide range of symptoms essential to the diagnostic process. However, when contrasting results are found between surveys based on diagnosis or diagnostic constellations of symptoms and those based on single symptom rates alone, then the most serious questions arise about the relative usefulness of these contrasting measures of psychopathology for the particular purpose of that survey. Examples of such a contrast may be found in studies on the age distribution of depression where diagnostic surveys show the well-known bell-shaped curve of prevalence between 20 years and 60 years of age, while surveys based on symptom counts may show an age-prevalence curve resembling an inverted bell (71, 226). In terms of the purposes of psychiatric epidemiology (which have been described as serving the interests of public health efforts, clinical recognition of treatable cases, and research work into the etiology of psychopathology) it might seem that both diagnostic and symptom orientations are worth exploring, as well as other factors in case definition. Clearly a key area in epidemiological work is the identification of the intervening variables between symptoms and clinical diagnosis in a nonpatient population.

Dohrenwend et al (44) have directed their attention to what they consider as the "central unsolved problem of psychiatric epidemiology—the problem of how to conceptualize and measure psychiatric disorder independently of treatment status." They collected data by means of two different interview techniques, one a mental state interview with open-ended questions and the assignment of responses to defined categories by rater judgment, and the other a screening interview for psychiatric impairment with prescribed response alternatives presented to the respondent. The interviews were conducted by psychiatrists on psychiatric patients, community leaders, and a probability sample of five ethnic groups in a community. The investigators found, *inter alia*, that relations between judged disorder, ethnic status, and class status varied with the type of research interview and whether judgments were made face to face or by "blind" review of the protocols. Community subjects were judged to be more ill on the basis of protocol review than at face-to-face interview, and this discordance was greatest for community leaders. The weighing of positive strengths that are observed in a face-to-face situation but not recorded is postulated as contributing to the discordance between interviewer-reviewer ratings of psychiatric disorder.

Assessment Across Racial Boundaries

The study cited above is a fine example of scientific carefulness and restraint in that the methodology is being painstakingly worked out before the substantive goal is tackled (in this instance, the relationship between social class and psychiatric disorder). This is not always the case. Often the substantive cart is put before the methodological horse, or methodological contributions are the result of secondary analyses of data collected for some other purpose. Thus it is not surprising that there have been many unconvincing statements and theoretical inferences in the literature about the differences between ethnic or racial groups in the frequency and forms of mental disorder. For example, it has been claimed that blacks, compared with whites, less often suffer from depressive disorders and more often suffer from schizophrenia; when depressed, the blacks are less likely to show guilt or suicidal trends and more likely to complain of somatic symptoms; and when schizophrenic they are more likely to show hallucinations. However, as Simon et al (236) remarked, "a major drawback to almost all the studies [until recently] is that, for data on psychopathology or diagnosis, they relied on hospital statistics, on the patients' hospital records, or, in the few instances in which ' patients were actually interviewed, on the psychiatrists' clinical impression."

Several recent papers have greatly improved the methodology in the assessment of psychopathology across racial boundaries. Simon et al (236) reanalyzed data from the US-UK Diagnostic Project in which semistructured mental state interviews were carried out by research psychiatrists on recently admitted patients in public mental hospitals in London and New York. When the type and degree of psychopathology was controlled, a bias was revealed in the *hospital* diagnosis towards schizophrenic rather than depressive disorder in blacks compared to whites. When the *research* diagnosis was controlled there were no significant interracial differences in symptomatology among schizophrenics, but the black depressives reported significantly more anxiety, somatic complaints, and irritability than did the white depressives.

Tonks et al (273) reanalyzed data from a study on depressed inpatients and outpatients in New Haven, all of whom received semistructured mental state interviews and a diagnosis of depressive disorder from a research psychiatrist. Significant interracial differences were found for several symptoms, but were much reduced when social class was controlled, and all but vanished when patients were matched for severity of illness; only the symptom of feeling helpless remained significantly different between the races (being more frequent in whites than blacks). As a whole, the black group was less severely depressed than the white group, possibly because the black patients tended to seek treatment earlier in the course of their disorder than did the whites.

Liss et al (140) and Welner et al (279) examined patients who had been admitted to a private hospital in St. Louis, Missouri. One hundred and nine of these patients were followed up and given a semistructured mental state interview an average of 3 years later. Blacks, compared to whites, were found significantly more often to show delusions (of reference, bodily change, and grandeur) and hallucinations (both auditory and visual). These differences were regarded as characteristic of the racial groups rather than as diagnostic factors, partly because symptoms and diagnosis were more highly correlated in whites than in blacks.

Leff (129) has provided a closely argued hypothesis that as cultures develop the members of the culture learn to express emotional states in a more differentiated form. Primitive expression of a limited variety of somatic experiences grows into sophisticated references to a wide range of emotional states based upon learning of the different social contexts in which the somatic experience can occur. He suggests that possibly this progression of emotional differentiation parallels the development of individual as opposed to group identity. In support of his basic hypothesis, Leff reanalyzed data from the International Pilot Study of Schizophrenia (289), in which a semistructured mental state interview was used for psychiatric evaluation in five "developed" and four "developing" countries, in each case in the appropriate indigenous language. The emotions of anxiety, depression, and irritability showed generally higher correlations (i.e. less differentiation) among patients within developing than within developed countries. Leff also reanalyzed data from the US-UK Diagnostic Project (New York sample) to show that among public mental hospital admissions blacks showed less differentiation than whites even when the patients were matched for social class. In a further data analysis, based on the reliability trials in the IPSS study, Leff (130) showed that his previous findings on the differentiation of emotional states were probably not an artifact of differences in the rating behavior of psychiatrists from developing and from developed countries.

It would appear that advances in method are enabling statements and theories on interracial differences in psychopathology to become more precise but no less challenging or conflicting than previously. It remains unclear whether conflicts between different studies result, on the one hand, from differences in methods of data collection, in rater bias, selection of the samples (e.g. in the referral mechanisms for becoming a patient), diagnostic criteria, or, on the other hand, from cultural differences between the samples. However, an important product of this work has been to underline the importance of semistructured interviewing and strict criteria for diagnosis as a means of reducing diagnostic errors in black patients, particularly with regard to detecting affective disorders.

Effects of Language on Assessment

The study of the relationship between race and psychopathology often confounds the effects of language and culture. By way of contrast, the studies of Marcos et al (146, 147) demonstrate the care required in experimental design to enable the isolation of the effects of interview language on the evaluation of psychopathology. These investigators prerecorded on audiotape the questions in a mental state interview and replayed the tapes to ten bilingual psychiatric inpatients with a hospital diagnosis of schizophrenia. Half the initial interviews were in Spanish and half in English, with a crossover design for a second interview within 24 hours. The patients' responses were videotaped and rated by English and by Spanish speaking psychiatrists. Higher levels of pathology were rated from the English than from the Spanish interview, even in those patients who had higher vocabulary scores in English than in Spanish. In a subsequent study, bilingual raters reviewed the videotapes and directly compared Spanish and English responses to the same questions. They noted several possible reasons for the higher scores in the English than in the Spanish interview, including frank contradictions (i.e. admits to pathology in English but not Spanish interview), increased tenseness and uncommunicativeness in English, downgrading of somatic complaints by Spanish psychiatrists because of high frequency in the Spanish culture, and the infracontent structure of the patients' speech in English resembling the features of depression (slowness, pauses, etc). However, having said all that, the authors attempt to resolve the conflict between their results and those of some previous workers by speculating on the interaction between language and the social context of the interview. Even this most careful study, because of its limited scope, leaves the generality of its findings in great uncertainty.

Assuming that the psychopathology shown by a patient varies with the language in which he expresses his symptoms, there arises the question of whether the patient is more or less "sick" in one or the other language. Careful discussions of the different concepts and components of sickness have recently been given by Wing et al (281) and Mechanic (151). However, for the purposes of this review it is important to emphasize that the interview assessment is at best only a predictor of the patient's behavior under the usual circumstances of his life, of his response to treatment, of his future progress, and possibly of the etiology of his disorder. These would seem to be the appropriate criteria to which we must ultimately refer in establishing the relative value or validity of cross-cultural variations in symptoms.

Fortunately, there now exist translations from English into various foreign languages for most of the well-established techniques for reliably assessing psychopathology. For instance, the Present State Examination has been translated into Chinese, Czech, Danish, Hindi, Russian, Spanish, and Yoruba (289); the Psychiatric Status Schedule has been translated into Polish, Spanish, Italian, Hebrew, and Flemish (R. L. Spitzer & J. Endicott, personal communication, 1974). For the most part comparability between the different language versions has been established by independent "back-translation." An example of a carefully designed and organized multilingual study is the International Collaborative Study on the Efficacy of Loxapine, involving the use of English, French, and German versions of the Structured Clinical Interview (18a) for the assessment of psychopathology at initial and follow-up interviews. Such studies may contribute much to the identification of the predictive equivalence of symptoms between language groups. A comprehensive account of the problems and provisional solutions in cross-national social-psychological research is provided in a recent book by Manaster & Havighurst (145).

Cross-Cultural Assessments

Despite the many difficulties in assessing psychopathology cross-culturally, some solid ground is evident in that the symptom profiles of certain diagnostic categories may be remarkably similar between different national, racial, and cultural groups. From this solid ground suggestions have been made for standardizing diagnoses by nominating a limited set of symptoms to define a group of patients whose diagnosis seems to meet with universal agreement, or by utilizing statistical techniques for reliably replicating the classification achieved by clinical diagnosis.

Carpenter et al (23), reporting on data from the International Pilot Study of Schizophrenia collected by psychiatrists from centers in the nine participating countries, propose the use of 12 signs and symptoms of psychopathology as an operational definition of schizophrenia. In this study, 1202 patients recently hospitalized with evidence of psychosis were examined with a semistructured mental state interview and given a diagnosis according to the International Classification of Diseases. The wide range of items in the interview schedule were winnowed out by analysis of variance to find the strongest discriminators between cases diagnosed schizophrenia and those given some other diagnosis. These discriminators were then subjected to a stepwide discriminant function analysis using the distinction between schizophrenia and other diagnoses as the criterion. Twelve symptoms or signs were thus selected for differential diagnosis. The more of these symptoms that were present, the more likely was the case to be diagnosed schizophrenia. Taking into account both the initial and the replication samples, the presence of four or more of these symptoms identified correctly over 90% of the diagnosed schizophrenics and included less than 40% of the cases receiving other diagnoses. The corresponding figures for the presence of six or more symptoms was about 65% correctly and 5% incorrectly predicted to be schizophrenic. These promising results invite further work to establish whether or not the key items can be reliably rated by other research groups; whether the group of schizophrenics accurately identified in this way are more or less useful for research or clinical purposes than other groups of schizophrenics (e.g. for predicting outcome, treatment response, biological indices, genetic findings, and associations with possibly etiological factors); and whether nonschizophrenics can be similarly accurately identified for control groups in schizophrenia research.

Use of Case Registers

If cross-sectional epidemiological studies are difficult enough, an even more complex and difficult task is the collection of data on a given population over time.

This aspect of epidemiology is vital for the description of the long-term course of mental disorder, for chronicling utilization of services, for assessing incidence rates, for studying differences between generations (successive cohorts), and for relating etiological factors to consequences remote in time. Case registers and cohort studies are being used with growing sophistication for such longitudinal epidemiological inquiries.

Richman (204) has recently reviewed the use of case registers of psychiatric care in epidemiological research. He defined case registers as "systems whereby records from a specified set of psychiatric facilities are collected for individual persons from a defined population and accumulated over time," and noted that the usefulness of the register increased with the duration of its existence. As of now there are several case registers in English-speaking countries which have been in operation over a decade, including those in Aberdeen, Scotland; Dutchess County and Rochester in New York; and Camberwell, London. However, many registers have been born and abandoned in the past 15 years, largely because of their expense and because the effort sunk into data collection was not matched by an equal devotion to data analysis and practical utilization of the results. It is therefore particularly encouraging that Wing and his colleagues (281) have demonstrated the rich potential of a register in a volume which reports the use of the Camberwell Psychiatric Register between 1964–71 for monitoring and planning the introduction of a community psychiatric service. Wing emphasizes that this register is a scientific instrument "to measure the extent and type of current use of services, to facilitate the examination of patterns of contact over time, to monitor changes accidentally or deliberately introduced, to allow estimation of future trends, to indicate researchable issues and to act as a sampling frame for more intensive studies."

Gruenberg (81) draws attention to the importance of "population laboratories" enabling longitudinal studies on cohorts of births, relating the course of the pregnancy to the child's mental development. He refers to the birth registers or cohort studies in Birmingham, Newcastle, Cardiff, and Aberdeen.

Although the Scandinavian countries have long since shown the value of a national network of records on mental health statistics, similar enterprise has been relatively recent in the United States and the United Kingdom. In the United States, Kramer, Chief of the Biometry Branch, National Institute of Mental Health, and his colleagues have organized and analyzed the national statistics on admission rates to mental hospitals and other relevant inpatient and outpatient facilities for the purpose, among others, of applying epidemiological methods to the planning and evaluation of community mental health programs. Their recent work has emphasized the importance of taking household size and composition into account in identifying groups at high risk for requiring psychiatric treatment (123); of age variation in the pattern of use of various types of psychiatric facilities (124); and of the need for improving the completeness and comparability of case findings and diagnostic and record keeping systems within and between countries. In the United Kingdom, the Department of Health and Social Security collates certain information, including diagnosis, on every case admitted to public psychiatric hospitals in England and Wales. In view of the relatively uniform and high standard of diagnosis in these hospitals, these data have proved very useful for epidemiological inquiry as exemplified by the age distribution studies of Hare et al (89), Spicer et al (243), and McDonald (149).

Biological or Cultural Milieu

One side of the coin in psychiatric epidemiological research is the assessment of psychopathology so that its distribution in time and space may be plotted. The other side of the coin is the assessment of factors that might be associated with this distribution.

Studies on family history, on genetic markers, and on associated disorders (e.g. alcoholism) have advanced knowledge on the etiology of manic-depressive disorders (157, 282). Refinement of indices for biological aging (14, 139) is making it possible to reexamine biological concomitants of age variation in the distribution of depression and dementia.

The assessment of the cultural milieu has reached a stage of sophistication at which substantive examination of the interaction between the ecological niche and psychopathology is possible. The concept of life events and their change has proved a powerful approach to isolating one of the pathogenic influences in the environment.

The pioneering work of Holmes, Wolff, Rahe, and their co-workers in establishing the association between stress associated with life events and illness, and the great volume of related work that followed, has led in the last few years to intensive study of the types and timing of life changes that are particularly likely to precede the onset of various psychiatric disorders (16, 46, 180) and to community surveys aimed at examining the relationship between the distribution of measures of psychiatric symptoms or disorders and of life events across various demographic groups (167, 274a).

Although this area of measurement is replete with methodological pitfalls (17), consistency in social consensus on the degree of change in given life events across cultures (191) makes a measure of life events a possible tool for cross-cultural and cross-national research.

4. ATTEMPTS TO IMPROVE PSYCHIATRIC DIAGNOSIS

Robert L. Spitzer and Jean Endicott[3]

Computerized Diagnosis

The limitations of the clinical method for arriving at a psychiatric diagnosis, particularly the low reliability generally associated with routine clinical diagnosis, have led many investigators to explore the potential of computers for integrating the clinical observations into standard psychiatric diagnoses. Although some

[3] Both authors are also affiliated with the Department of Psychiatry, College of Physicians and Surgeons, Columbia University, New York City.

efforts have been made to develop programs in which the patient interacts directly with the computer via a console, the inherent limitations of this approach have led most investigators in this area to employ models in which the basic observations of signs and symptoms are still made by clinicians. These are the clinical observations which are then introduced into a computer for summarization into a diagnosis.

There are several advantages to this kind of computer-generated diagnosis. First of all, there is the value of the computer's necessarily perfect reliability in the sense that, given the same data, the computer program will always yield the same diagnosis. Secondly, the computer program can utilize rules developed from a larger and more diverse sample of actual patients than any single clinician can command. In addition, the rules by which a computer assigns a diagnosis are explicit and public. Finally, empirically based rules constitute at least potential advances in our scientific understanding of the complex relationship between symptom characteristics and diagnosis.

The most frequently employed models for computer diagnosis are either discriminant function .or Bayes classification (11, 57, 171, 192, 240). Both of these models are empirically derived from data on patients for whom there are available clinical diagnoses. The data is usually psychiatric symptomatology, but may include demographic and historical information. These two statistical methods are used to develop optimal classification rules for the particular sample to which they were originally applied, the "developmental" sample. The derived rules are then applied to classify new cases. The major limitation of these models is the requirement of a very large sample size. Even with sample sizes in the thousands, which are rarely available, a very limited number of categories can be employed. A second limitation is the lack of generalizability of the rules to samples which differ greatly from the developmental sample.

The Bayes method has been applied to psychiatric classification by Birnbaum & Maxwell (11), Overall & Gorham (171), and Smith (240). The discriminant function method has been used by Rao & Slater (193), Melrose, Stroebel & Glueck (152), and Sletten, Altman & Ulett (237). Sletten and his group have applied this method to five hospitals in the Missouri automated record keeping system and developed a method for classifying patients into one of 12 diagnostic groups. The overall agreement between computer classification and clinical diagnosis was sufficiently high for them to make the system operational in the Missouri Standard System of Psychiatry used in Missouri state hospitals.

An alternative to the statistical models is the logical decision tree approach developed by Spitzer & Endicott (245, 246, 251). In this approach, which emulates the clinical differential diagnostic procedure, the computer program consists of a sequence of questions. The answer to each question is either "true" or "false" and rules out one or more diagnoses and determines which question is to be examined next. Some questions may ascertain the presence of a single critical sign or symptom, others whether a numerical score is in a certain range, and yet others whether a complex pattern of both signs and symptoms is present. The logical decision tree approach has the advantage of being independent of any specific body of data although, of course, not of accumulated clinical and research experience. For this reason the method can be used with different psychiatric populations, since it is not designed to be optimal for a particular population of psychiatric patients.

The two statistical models and the logical decision tree model have been compared on the same data base (64). The logical decision tree model performed as well as the two statistical models (in terms of agreement with clinical diagnosis) on a large cross-validation sample which was similar to the developmental sample. The logical decision tree method performed better than the two statistical approaches on a sample drawn from a totally new population.

The logical decision tree approach has been employed in three programs of increasing complexity: DIAGNO, DIAGNO II, and DIAGNO III by Spitzer & Endicott. The validity issue has been studied primarily by examining the agreement between the computer diagnoses and the diagnoses of expert clinicians, since the purpose of the program was to simulate expert clinical practice. When the computer and the clinician were limited to the same information (from research protocols of psychiatric ratings), the agreement between the computer and clinical diagnosis was as good as that between the diagnoses of pairs of clinicians (245, 246). However, in a study in which the clinicians had direct access to the patient or a narrative case record, the agreement between the clinicians exceeded agreement between the computer and the clinicians. The output of these programs has been judged to have sufficient validity for use in various research projects for describing samples of subjects, selecting subjects for experiments, in epidemiological and cross-cultural studies, and investigating problems in classification.

Dissatisfaction with the treatment relevance of standard diagnoses has led some investigators to employ computers to develop treatment-relevant typologies rather than to simulate the practices of expert clinicians using the standard nomenclature (93, 119, 172, 238). Each of these programs has been shown to have some value in predicting which patient will respond best to a limited number of drugs in samples similar to those used to develop the program. The general utility of such programs across samples of patients who differ from the samples from which the programs were derived has yet to be demonstrated.

In so far as the computer is used to simulate expert clinical practice in making a standard psychiatric diagnosis, the major constraints on further developments in computerized diagnosis appear to lie in limitations in the standard nomenclature itself. Although improvements in the raw data and the computer algorithms may lead to some improvement in computer diagnosis using the current ambiguous criteria, a quantum jump in the validity of computer diagnosis is dependent upon improvements in the system itself.

Specified Criteria for Psychiatric Diagnosis

In the usual diagnostic manual, such as the American Psychiatric Association's *Diagnostic and Statistical Manual* (DSM-II), diagnostic stereotypes are described under each category. The task of the diagnostician then becomes one of selecting the diagnostic category in which the stereotype most closely resembles the characteristics of the patient being diagnosed. In addition, the standard nomenclature includes many categories for which there is little validity evidence in terms of discriminability from other conditions, long-term follow-up studies, specific treatment response, typical course, and elevated familial incidence.

The Renard hospital group in St. Louis (54) has developed a diagnostic system which limits itself to those conditions for which it believes there is good research

Table 1   Specified criteria for major depressive illness (A through E required)

A. Dysphoric mood characterized by symptoms such as the following: depressed, sad, blue, hopeless, down in the dumps, empty, "don't care," irritable, fearful, worried. The dysphoric mood must be prominent and relatively persistent but not necessarily the most dominant symptom.

B. At least 5 of the following symptoms for definite and 4 for probable (for past episodes because of memory difficulty, the criteria are 4 and 3 symptoms):
   1. Poor appetite or weight loss (2 lbs. a week or 10 lbs. or more a year when not dieting) or increased appetite or weight gain.
   2. Sleep difficulty or sleeping too much.
   3. Loss of energy, fatigability, or tiredness.
   4. Psychomotor agitation or retardation (but not mere subjective feeling of restlessness or being slowed down).
   5. Loss of interest in usual activities, or decrease in sexual drive, (do not include if limited to a period when delusional or hallucinating).
   6. Feelings of self-reproach or excessive or inappropriate guilt (either may be delusional).
   7. Complaints of or evidence of diminished ability to think or concentrate, such as slow thinking or mixed-up thoughts (do not include if associated with obvious thought disorder).
   8. Recurrent thoughts of death or suicide, including thoughts of wishing to be dead.

C. Depressive features of illness lasting at least 2 weeks.

D. Sought help from someone during the dysphoric period or had impaired functioning socially with family, at home, or at work.

E. None of the following which suggests schizophrenia is present:
   1. Delusions of control or thought broadcasting of any duration if definitely present.
   2. Hallucinations throughout the day for several days, or intermittently throughout a 1 month period unless content is clearly related to lowered or elevated self-esteem.
   3. Auditory hallucinations in which either a voice keeps up a running commentary on the patient's behavior as it occurs, or 2 or more voices converse with each other (of any duration as long as definitely present).
   4. At some time during the period of illness had delusions or hallucinations for more than 1 month in the absence of prominent affective (manic or depressive) symptoms (although typical depressive delusions, such as delusions of guilt, sin, poverty, nihilism, or self-deprecation or hallucinations of similar content are permitted).
   5. Preoccupation with a delusion or hallucination to the relative exclusion of other symptoms or concerns (other than delusions of guilt, sin, poverty, nihilism, or self-deprecation or hallucinations with similar content).
   6. Definite instances of schizophrenic thought disorder.

evidence for the validity of the conditions as diagnostic entities. The system provides for explicit criteria which are in the form of sets of items, a specified number of which are necessary or sufficient to make the diagnosis. A consequence of this approach is the recognition of the need for an "undiagnosed psychiatric disorder" category for the patients who do not meet any of the specified disorders, yet exhibit significant psychopathology.

Spitzer, Endicott, and Robins (personal communication, 1974), as part of a collaborative study of the psychobiology of depression, have expanded the Renard system to include other categories and have modified and refined the specified criteria in an effort to improve reliability. An example of the criteria for one category, Major Depressive Illness, is shown in Table 1.

The reliability of these diagnostic criteria has been evaluated based on both interviews of patients and case records. The reliabilities obtained with 104 newly admitted psychiatric inpatients from four participating facilities were generally considerably higher than those reported in other diagnostic reliability studies (254). The study of case records used 120 patients from the New York State Psychiatric Institute and permitted a comparison between the reliabilities obtained when research assistants used the specified criteria and when a different set of experienced clinicians used the official nomenclature of the American Psychiatric Association. The results of the case record study are shown in Table 2,

Table 2   Kappa coefficients of agreement for major diagnosis on 120 case records

Diagnostic category	Kappa using specified criteria	Kappa using DSM-II criteria
Major groupings		
Affective	.70	.48
Schizophrenia	.84	.48
Other	.74	.61
Specific Categories		
Nonaffective schizophrenia	.70	.49
Schizoaffective schizophrenia	.24	.37
Manic illness	.76	.37
Major depressive illness[a]	.66	.25
Minor depressive illness[b]	.56	.07
Alcoholism	.66	—[c]
Drug dependence	1.00	—[c]
Obsessive-compulsive	.65	.42
Anxiety neurosis	.52	.06
Phobic neurosis	.66	.32
Borderline psychosis	.20	
Undiagnosed	.59	

[a] Considered equivalent to any psychotic affective illness in DSM-II.
[b] Considered equivalent to Neurotic Depression in DSM-II.
[c] Neither of the raters used this category.

using a measure of agreement called kappa, which indexes agreement for nominal categories corrected for chance agreement (244). Not only are virtually all of the reliabilities higher for the research assistants using the specified criteria, but the values obtained are higher than those ever reported in diagnostic studies of heterogeneous samples of patients.

To further increase the reliability of this set of diagnoses, an instrument has been developed by Spitzer and Endicott, called the Schedule for Affective Disorders and Schizophrenia (SADS). The SADS has a structured interview and a set of rating scales to enable a clinician to collect the information necessary to make the diagnostic distinctions provided in the list of diagnostic criteria. In addition, a computer program will be developed which will use the specified diagnostic decision rules to classify patients on the basis of the individual items. It is quite clear that one way of increasing reliability of diagnoses is to provide more specific criteria for each diagnostic category.

5. A PSYCHOPHYSIOLOGICAL APPROACH TO PSYCHOPATHOLOGY

Samuel Sutton

The rationale for applying an experimental approach to mental disorders derives in part from the need for objectifying and measuring the observations of the clinician on the characteristics and behavior of patients and, more deeply, from the hope of finding some kind of indicator of difference in central nervous system functioning that might define a group of patients. The concern of this section is primarily with the latter aim. In remarking some time ago on the subtlety and complexity of the etiological factors in mental illness, as well as on the kinds of artifact which may arise in biochemical research involving the analysis of body fluids and tissues, Kety (112) noted that it would be highly desirable if some clues as to what should be looked for could be supplied to the biochemist from other fields—not least of all, psychology.

It might seem paradoxical that one would turn to psychological rather than physiological responses when one's primary goal is to obtain some reflection of central nervous system functioning. However, to the extent that the physiological variables are sensitive to the psychological state of the subject (263), no advance is made merely by moving from the psychological to the physiological level. Thus it is true that schizophrenic patients may be shown to have unusual evoked potential waveforms to stimuli whose identity they did not know in advance (133). However, from the point of view of providing *etiological* clues, such findings may be viewed as redundant support of available psychological data, e.g. reaction time, which have shown that the response of schizophrenic patients to the condition of uncertainty is different from that of normal subjects (266). Both the physiological and psychological data share a common problem of validity. In neither case do we know whether the difference between groups is in the way they respond to uncertainty, or whether other differences between groups, such as the level of attention or motivation, determine the findings. The problem of validity can be solved at the psychological level by eliminating or controlling the effect of extraneous psychological processes on the behavior on which the experimenter is focused. Only then might the obtaining of physiological correlates of deviant performance be illuminating with respect to etiological questions.

The fundamental difficulty in the interpretation of findings arises from the fact that patient groups almost universally perform more poorly than normals. But it is the sources of the poor performance that are unclear. It may in fact be true that the patient has a deficit in information processing, or in perceptual sensitivity, or in psychomotor function. However, the poor performance may have nothing directly to do with these functions and may arise for quite different reasons. The patient may be less cooperative or less attentive. He may be concerned with his troubles, may be preoccupied with his hallucinations, and may care very little about this apparently meaningless task we put before him. Given the disturbed state of the patient, the complexities of the task may be too much for him. Paradoxically we may obtain erroneous results because the patient is too motivated, too anxious, and too concerned with the results of his performance, and as is well known, a very high degree of anxiety and motivation often lead to poor performance. The problem in obtaining valid data in these situations is in a sense not logically different from the problems of controlling for "faking" or malingering which has been most often raised in relation to responses to questionnaires (228).

Several strategies have been developed for coping with some of these problems and obtaining more valid indicators of central nervous system differences. These will now be presented (98a, 264).

Simplicity of the Task

Simple reaction time can be used to reflect fairly subtle discriminations between stimuli (242, 257). The subject's task is only to lift his finger as rapidly as possible when one of several stimuli is presented. No discrimination is required in this procedure. Nevertheless, a finding of differences in reaction time to different stimuli inescapably leads to the inference that the nervous system is capable of appreciating the differences among them. The advantage in such a strategy is that the same stimuli presented as a discrimination may for whatever reason prove to be too difficult or too subtle a task for certain groups of patients. This would lead to the usual uninterpretable "poorer" performance.

However, the reaction time of schizophrenic patients, and to some extent of most hospitalized psychotic patients, is generally slower than normals to all stimuli. This brings into play a second strategy.

Own-Control Design

The rationale of the own-control approach is based on the hope that confounding or trivial factors enter equally into the two or more measures being compared. This would presumably permit the ruling out of confounding factors by the use of difference scores or some other maneuver. While this can be a powerful tool, it can also lead to serious misinterpretations. For example, if the measures being used involve tasks of different degrees of difficulty, then it is possible that the level of difficulty can interact with differences between groups in motivation or attention. Performance on the difficult task may be more severely handicapped by low motivation than performance on the easy task; thus a difference between groups in motivational level would make performance on the easy task an inappropriate correction factor for comparison of groups on the more difficult task. Furthermore, this process of correcting for performance at one level by performance at another level has a number of other pitfalls, and one cannot with impunity take difference scores or use even covariance analysis indiscriminately in all cases (66, 264).

Patients and normals must be tested on identical experimental conditions to avoid bringing range effects into play (187). Furthermore, care must be used to randomize experimental conditions, by trial if possible, so that subjects cannot assume different attitudes to various experimental conditions, e.g. the attitude that "this is a challenging condition I will try harder"; or "this is a very difficult condition, I give up on this one"; or "this is an easy condition, I don't have to try so hard"; and so on. Even with all these provisos, a series of sequential experiments may be necessary to establish the interpretation of a particular finding (188). For example, Sutton & Zubin (266) reported that schizophrenic patients have longer reaction time than normals when the immediately preceding trial is in a different sensory modality than when the immediately preceding trial is in the same sensory modality, even though the stimulus of the previous trial occurs as long as several seconds earlier. This appears to imply a difference in bias or expectancy or segmental set on the part of the patients. However, in a subsequent experiment it was shown that the greater crossmodal retardation continues to be found in such patients even when the subject is told prior to each trial what the sensory modality of the stimulus will be (275a).

Controlling the Criterion Variable

Signal detection theorists (79) have been able to demonstrate that they can obtain two independent measures in threshold situations: one is a measure of sensitivity called d'; and the other is a measure of criterion[4] called β. The basic advance consists of the fact that it can be demonstrated both logically and experimentally that these two measures can be obtained independently of each other. This is an important step forward since many patients tend to be more cautious than normals. It is indeed this cautiousness which accounts for the earlier reports that schizophrenic patients were less sensitive in their ability to detect flicker. What Clark, Brown & Rutschmann (28) have shown is that, rather than being less sensitive, the patients appear to have a need for seeing definite flicker before they are willing to say that the light is flickering. With classical psychophysical methods such a bias yields an apparently poorer sensitivity. When measures of sensitivity

---

[4] Beta is the term more commonly used to refer to the signal detection measure of criterion. Actually, what is usually computed from hits and false alarm rates is L_x. For the difference between L_x and β, see Swets, Tanner & Birdsall (267).

are obtained which are independent of the criterion variable, there is no difference between schizophrenic patients and normals in sensitivity to the rate at which light and darkness must alternate before flicker is detected. The pioneering papers by Clark and his colleagues (27, 28, 31) have cut the underpinnings from a great deal of research comparing the sensitivity of patients and normals which was done by classical psychophysical techniques. If the difference in performance is in fact due to the criterion variable, then it is the criterion variable and not sensitivity which requires further study.

Several other investigators have since reported that the use of signal detection methods yields a finding of no differences between groups. Milner et al (158) found no differences in either d' or β for the detection of auditory tones in noise by obsessional and nonobsessional patients. However, in one experimental condition which permitted the subjects to ask for repeat observations of the signal before making a decision, it was found that obsessional patients asked for repeats more than four times as often. Clark & Rubin (30) found that while the constant stimulus method showed that the psychiatric patients (who were older) had poorer thermal sensitivity than the normals, a signal detection theory analysis of the same data showed no differences in d', but rather differences in the criterion variable. The psychiatric patients were more conservative.

Not all use of signal detection methods has led to negative results with respect to sensitivity differences between psychiatric or retarded groups and normals. Korzh & Vaytkyavichyus (122) found differences between schizophrenic patients and normals in alpha suppression and electromyographic responses to auditory stimuli presented in a signal detection task. Kuechler & Dodwell (128) found that while normals increased their d' for the detection of a tone in noise under the stress of electric shock, neurotic and schizophrenic patients showed a decrement in d' under these conditions. Boissonneault et al (13) found d' differences in the resolution of paired flashes only under a high exercise-induced activation level—but not under moderate or low activation levels—between extroverts with a high neuroticism score and extroverts with a low neuroticism score. Suboski (262) found signal detection theory of use in the analysis of results of published experiments which investigated classical discrimination conditioning in relation to ratings on manifest anxiety.

In a comparison of retarded and normal adults, Bernstein & Day (10) found differences between groups in size constancy with both classical and signal detection psychophysical methods. In the Price & Eriksen (189) study of size constancy, differences were found between nonparanoid schizophrenic patients, paranoid schizophrenic patients, and normal controls with the signal detection measure, despite the findings of *no* differences with the classical psychophysical measures. When criterion is uncontrolled, no real inference about sensitivity can be made; therefore, we should not be surprised by whatever permutation of positive and negative results we obtain with classical psychophysical and detection theory methods.

In psychiatric illness, differences between groups in the criterion variable are more often than not viewed as an artifact which interferes with the evaluation of differences in sensitivity. Signal detection methods, however, have also been applied where the primary goal of the study was to look for criterion differences between groups, rather than for sensitivity differences. In one study, Carney (21) found no differences between delusional and nondelusional schizophrenic patients in their response to the use of monetary payoff to manipulate the criterion level. The assessment of the effects of aging presents a contrast to the assessment of psychiatric illness. While investigators of aging are also concerned with the evaluation of sensitivity, the hypothesis that criterion differences such as conservativeness or cautiousness are associated with aging has been of particular interest to investigators. Craik (42) reviewed the evidence from his own earlier study as well as the available literature which used signal detection methods. While support was found for high βs (greater cautiousness) to be positively associated with age, there were also negative and contradictory findings. Evidently the nature of the task enters as a factor in determining whether or not a relationship with age will be found as well as the direction of the relationship (29, 30, 78, 203).

The evaluation of the effects of drugs on performance in both normal subjects and patient groups raises many of the same difficulties that comparison of normal and patient groups raises. Here, too, the problem which arises is whether the drug has affected the subject's sensitivity, his criterion, his attention level, his motivation, etc. An increasing number of drug studies using signal detection theory methods in an attempt to disentangle some of these effects are beginning to appear (48, 49, 82, 143, 164, 194–197, 225, 290).

Problems of comparing patient groups with normals are by no means all solved by the use of signal detection methods. Thus Rappaport et al (196), who used signal detection methods, discounted a finding of poorer sensitivity in nonparanoid schizophrenic patients than normals when they found that at still lower stimulus intensities where the discrimination is more difficult, the same patients were no less sensitive than the normals. They argue that such contradictory findings reflect the fact that signal detection methods cannot cope with the variable attention level characteristic of certain patient groups. However, strictly speaking, they did not use a signal detection format since a "no" response was defined as a failure to make a response (48).

Accuracy Indicators

While the subject's response in the "yes-no" or one-interval signal detection format is a forced choice in that the subject must make a decision, other forced-choice designs have different properties. Thus in the three-interval forced choice, the subject must in each trial decide whether the stimulus was in the first, second, or third observation interval. Such a procedure differs from the one-interval detection theory procedure in two important ways. First, it provides the subject with a comparison in each trial—namely, the observation interval in which the stimulus was present compared with the two observation intervals in which the stimulus was not present. Second, the subject is in effect being forced to respond "present" following each trial, eliminating the usual avenue for expressing cautiousness or laxness of criterion. Thus the three-interval forced-choice procedure is criterion free; criterion in the usual sense does not enter nor can it be measured. But it should be noted that it is not free of response bias. The subject may not distribute his responses equally among the three observation intervals (although the stimuli are equally distributed). When this occurs, it can be corrected for by examining the hit rate separately for each interval, thus correcting for the subject's response bias. In a spatial forced choice, Calfee (20) showed that subjects did not utilize the end positions and the center positions in the same way. This was a short-term memory task and subjects remembered stimuli in the end positions better than stimuli in the center positions. As a result, when they were uncertain they more often picked center positions. This bias was the same for retarded as for normal children.

As with signal detection methods, few investigators are using forced-choice methods to compare groups. Emmerich & Levine (48) found that schizophrenic patients had less sensitive auditory thresholds than normals. Bruder et al[5] found that only patients with affective psychoses had less sensitive auditory thresholds than normals. The sensitivity of schizophrenic patients was found to be within the normal range. Hare (91) found that psychopathic criminals were less sensitive in detecting electric shock than nonpsychopathic criminals.

Broen & Nakamura (15) compared the auditory sensitivity of acute paranoid and chronic nonparanoid schizophrenic patients under distraction and no distraction. They found no difference under the no-distraction condition, but under distraction the sensitivity of the chronic nonparanoid patients deteriorated while that of the acute paranoid patients did not. Neale et al (169) found that there were no differences in the ability of normals, good premorbid paranoid schizophrenic patients, and poor premorbid nonparanoid schizophrenic patients to identify whether a tachistoscopically displayed letter was a T or an F. However, when the signal letters were imbedded in an 8 letter matrix, both schizophrenic groups performed more poorly than the normals. Stilson & Kopell (259) compared normals, nonschizophrenic, and schizophrenic patients in their ability to identify geometrical figures against a background of visual noise as opposed to no visual noise. All forced-choice thresholds were elevated by visual noise; the schizophrenic thresholds were most elevated, the nonschizophrenic patients were intermediate, and the normals were least elevated. Smith (239) reported that chronic schizophrenic patients showed an impairment in short-term memory when compared with nonschizophrenic patients. Also see Shallice & Warrington (229) for a study of short-term memory in a case of conduction aphasia.

Walker & Birch (276) had schizophrenic and nonschizophrenic children between ages 7–11 select from three visual dot patterns the one which best matched an auditorily presented temporal pattern. Schizophrenic children at each age made fewer correct matches.

---

[5] G. E. Bruder, S. Sutton, H. Babkoff, B. J. Gurland, A. Yozawitz, J. L. Fleiss & M. L. Kietzman. Auditory signal detectability and facilitation of simple reaction time in psychiatric patients and nonpatients. Unpublished manuscript.

Better Patient Performance

While the use of forced-choice methodology controls the criterion problem very well and also gives us a safeguard against falsely attributing to patients a better performance than they can actually accomplish, it does not solve the fundamental problem. One can argue very persuasively that the patients who have poorer thresholds than normals were simply less attentive or less motivated than normals. Presumably, according to this argument, had the patients been in a state which permitted them to be fully attentive and cooperative they might have obtained just as good thresholds as the normals. There is only one satisfactory answer to this argument. If we could demonstrate in a particular task that patients were able to perform better than normals, it would then not be possible to attribute the better performance for that task to poorer attention and cooperation on the part of the patients. There are so far only a few instances of reported better performance on the part of patients.

Bruder et al (see footnote[5]) presented randomly either a single click which was 25 dB above each subject's absolute threshold, or the 25 dB click followed 15 msec later by a click which was 10 dB above the subject's absolute threshold. The subject lifted his finger from a key as rapidly as possible in response to the presentation of either stimulus package. They found that reaction time of normal subjects to the paired clicks was only very slightly faster than reaction time to the 25 dB click by itself. However, for patients with affective psychoses, reaction time to the paired clicks was much faster than reaction time to the 25 dB click by itself. Here then is evidence that these patients were benefiting more from the presence of the 10 dB click than were the normals. The patients with affective psychoses were more "sensitive" to the presence of the 10 dB click and in that sense were performing better.

Collins (33) presented an even more convincing case of better performance. There were two 2 msec flashes of light, which in one stimulus package were separated by 2 msec giving a total duration of 6 msec, and in another stimulus package were separated by 0 msec—that is, a continuous 4 msec flash of light. The two stimulus packages had the same total amount of light energy; however, the energy was distributed differently over time. As is known from Bloch's Law, if the total stimulus duration of both packages is shorter than a value known as critical duration, then the level of response to these two packages of light will be identical. If, however, one of the stimulus packages exceeds critical duration for the class of response under consideration, then the level of response to the two equal-energy packages will be different. These two stimulus packages were presented in random sequence, and subjects lifted their finger as rapidly as possible whichever stimulus package appeared. For normals and nonschizophrenic psychiatric patients no reaction time differences were found between the two stimulus packages. However, schizophrenic patients showed significantly longer reaction times to the 6 msec package of light than to the 4 msec package of light. From this it is inferred that for schizophrenics, critical duration is shorter than 6 msec. Presumably, for this group some portion of the 6 msec package is not fully integrated. It therefore contains less effective energy and reaction time is longer.

These experimenters (33, 264) make no claim that a shorter critical duration is biologically "better" than a longer critical duration—in fact, the reverse may well be true. But whichever is functionally more advantageous, the schizophrenics in this design make a discrimination, in the sense of different reaction time to the two packages, which normals are unable to make. (The two stimulus packages are also perceptually identical for normals;[6] comparable perceptual studies are not available for patients.) It would be difficult to attribute such a group difference to defective attention or cooperation on the part of the patient group.

Two studies of behavior at a much more complex level report findings which may also be interpretable as better performance by patients. Goldfarb & Braunstein (75) reported that the speech of schizophrenic children is less disturbed than the speech of normal children by a delay in auditory feedback while speaking. Levine et al (132) reported a similar finding for schizophrenic adults. However, an earlier study in schizophrenic adults by Sutton et al (265) reported negative results.

Iterative Procedures

All the above strategies are addressed to the design of the tasks that the subjects perform. However, there is at least as serious a problem in defining the independent variable, namely the group to which each subject belongs. For the definition of patient groups, there is the problem of the lack of objectivity of the criteria and the lack of agreement among clinicians. Less well recognized is the fact that a "normal" population may often contain a significant proportion which is far from normal. For the classification of both patients and normals, the use of standardized rating scales which have good reliability is a distinct advantage. Kriegel (126) reported that in her samples only half of the hospital-diagnosed schizophrenics were diagnosed schizophrenic by rating scale procedures. Even more surprising is the fact that only half her normals, recruited through the usual channels, were diagnosed as normal by the rating scale procedures. When her group comparisons were confined to the "pure" schizophrenics and the "pure" normals, not only were the reported differences in crossmodal retardation larger, but also intragroup variability was found to be smaller. Along similar lines, in the Collins study (33), it was those schizophrenics who rated high in "speech disorganization" who demonstrated shorter critical duration. By similar post hoc analyses, Satterfield (223) showed that it was depressives with a family history of mental illness who were most different from normals in their evoked potential waveforms.

Because such findings are post hoc discoveries, they must be subjected to replication before being accepted. Sutton (264) has argued that it is through such a series of sequential experiments that the experimental psychologist may make the

---

[6] M. L. Kietzman, R. Rutschmann & E. Shapiro. Visual temporal integration: A comparison of discrimination and reaction time to pairs of suprathreshold flashes. Unpublished manuscript.

greatest contribution toward the "purification" of groups and thus to the problems of diagnosis and etiology. A series of sequential experiments permits the utilization of an "iterative" strategy. For example, after replication of the initial finding with respect to critical duration, the measure of critical duration can then be used as the independent variable in selecting subjects to see whether it is only schizophrenic "speech disorganization" that is associated with shorter critical duration. Other objective, physiological, and clinical techniques can then be brought to bear in the attempt to define and describe subpopulations of patients who by other procedures are inseparable from poorly defined larger categories.

ACKNOWLEDGMENTS

The author is indebted to Dr. W. Crawford Clark for advice and consultation. Preparation of the manuscript was in part supported by grant MH–18422 from the National Institute of Mental Health, United States Public Health Service, and by a project grant from the New York State Department of Mental Hygiene.

SUMMARY AND CONCLUSIONS

Joseph Zubin

With the tools described in the prior sections we can proceed to examine some of the scientific models that have been proposed for the etiology of the mental disorders.

Descriptive Model

In the descriptive area we have made considerable progress in demonstrating that systematic structured interviews of high reliability can be successfully applied to answering such questions as (*a*) whether more schizophrenic than affective disorders are admitted to the hospitals in London than in New York (see p. 637); (*b*) whether diagnoses arrived at by computers are comparable in reliability to those arrived at by clinicians (see section by Spitzer & Endicott); (*c*) whether patients who differ from their peers in the processing of information in the central nervous system show any characteristic difference in their psychopathology (see pp. 654–55); and (*d*) whether different treatments affect psychopathology differentially (95).

In addition to the quantitative approaches some notable progress has also been made in the historical documentation of qualitative description of psychopathological phenomena. Thus Sir Aubrey Lewis (134–136), one of the collaborators on the bilateral studies of diagnoses in the United States and the United Kingdom has traced the varying phenomenological description of the terms of anxiety, paranoia, and endogenous-exogenous historically and indicated their clinical significance in each period, including their present connotations. He has similarly described the development of the diagnostic schemas (137). Fleiss (62), on the other hand, with the help of his clinical colleagues has succeeded in developing a dimensional analysis of psychopathology based on the results of systematic interviews which yields measures of anxiety separated from depression, and of flatness of affect separated from retardation. These separations were rarely achieved before in the factor analytic literature, and only a combination of clinical acumen supported by factor analytic flair succeeded in purifying these factors. They have already demonstrated their usefulness in separating clinically based categories of patients.

The diagnostic categories themselves have been subjected to reliability investigation. Thus, in an examination by the US-UK project of a sample of American patients whose interviews were tape-recorded, a second rater reviewed the tapes and applied a second diagnosis (65). The overall agreement as measured by kappa for the primary diagnosis given by each diagnostician was .51; the agreement coefficients for schizophrenia and for affective psychosis were both .59. When secondary diagnoses were considered, the value of kappa rose to .64 for overall agreement, to .91 for schizophrenia, and to .68 for affective disorders.

A second estimate of reliability was obtained by noting the distribution of diagnoses made by the New York team on 96 American patients whom they interviewed and by the London team on 49 American patients whom they interviewed. Since these two groups of patients were unselected and could be regarded as a random sample of the total, the remarkable degree of agreement in the distribution of diagnoses attests to their high degree of reliability. It still remains an open question whether the diagnoses made by the state hospital clinicians in the United States and the corresponding area hospital clinicians in London differed because of differences in sensitivity to the presence of schizophrenic vs affective psychopathology or because of preference in style of diagnosis. Accepting the project diagnosis as the correct diagnosis, the signal detection theory method was applied to determining whether the two groups of clinicians differed in sensitivity or in criterion. The difference in sensitivity turned out to be very small, but significant differences in the criterion—a greater readiness to apply the label of schizophrenia in the United States than in the United Kingdom—were noted. Apparently American psychiatrists are as sensitive as the English psychiatrists to the presence of psychopathology of the schizophrenic and affective type, but the greater readiness of the Americans to apply the schizophrenic label and the greater readiness of the British to apply the affective label produced the observed difference in national statistics (W. C. Clark, personal communication, 1974).

Perhaps one of the most striking recent developments in the use of these interviews is the 9-country investigation of schizophrenia in centers throughout the world (289). Through a variety of statistical procedures, 12 items from the systematic structured interview (Present State Examination) were found characterizing the group of patients who were given the label of schizophrenia in these 9 centers. In a replicated study, the presence of 8 or more positive symptoms out of the 12 identified about one-fifth of the schizophrenics (four-fifths false negatives) but not a single nonschizophrenic scored that high. Adopting a more lenient cutoff point at a score of 6 or more, two-thirds of the schizophrenics are correctly identified (only one-third false negatives) and only 5% of the nonschizophrenics (false positives) fall into the net. It must be remembered, however, that the psychiatrists making these diagnoses, though indigenous to their own particular cultures, were all trained in the West and were viewing the patients through a Western-tinted screen. Nevertheless, the presence of similar groups of patients across this wide cultural spectrum would argue for the ubiquity of schizophrenia and presents a quandry for those who regard the diagnostic nomenclature as a myth. The items forming the 12 point scale included: 1. absence of waking early, depressed facies and elation, which represent affective components unfavorable to a diagnosis of schizophrenia; 2. presence of delusions (widespread, bizarre, nihilistic, and thoughts aloud); 3. disturbance of communication (incoherent speech, poor rapport, and unreliable information); and 4. poor insight and restricted affect.

Etiological Models

The etiological models that have been proposed for the mental disorders range from field-theory.based models, imbedded in the ecological niche that the person occupies, to atomistic (biological) models of the genetic variety. Leaning towards the ecological model but containing also biological elements are two psychologically based models—the developmental model and learning theory model—while the two physiologically based models—the internal environment model and the brain function model—lean more in the direction of the atomistic approach.

This composite review has dealt with the learning theory model in the section by Salzinger and with the neurophysiological model in the section by Sutton. We shall not deal with these further, but instead will devote some attention to the ecological, developmental, genetic, and internal environment models.

The ecological model for the etiology of mental disorders assumes that their cause is to be sought in the stressors affecting the ecological niche which the person occupies. A full taxonomy of the parameters of the ecological niche and the stress they produce is not yet available, but such factors as low socioeconomic status have been implicated either as causes or as effects of mental disorder. A current investigation by the Dohrenwends (45) may throw light on this question. Assuming that old American stock who are now found in the low socioeconomic strata have gravitated there because of their lack of capacity to rise with the upward mobility thrust of the general population, they would tend to have higher rates of mental disorder than the newly arrived immigrants who contain a large proportion of capable people in their midst who have not yet had the opportunity to rise. On the other hand, if we assume that the stressful environment is the cause of mental disorder, we would expect the newly arrived immigrants who have risen to the higher levels to have more mental disorder than their peers of the old American stock who have not had to struggle to rise.

Perhaps the most striking evidence for the possible role of the ecological model comes from H. B. M. Murphy (166), who has found that whenever ethnic groups containing both Protestant and Catholic subgroups are compared by religious subdivisions for first admission rates for schizophrenia, the Catholic subgroup invariably has the higher rate. Whether this is attributable to Catholic upbringing or whether some artifact such as greater utilization of hospitals is the basis for this finding is not yet determined.

With regard to the developmental model, Garmezy (72) has recently reviewed the entire field. Among the most vocal proponents of the role of the developmental model, especially with regard to family structure, is Lidz (138). He makes a good case for the degree of warping that may occur in families of the deviant type, but unfortunately provides no normal control groups for contrast. The dire role that family interaction plays in the development of schizophrenia has recently been deflated by Manfred Bleuler's long-term study of 208 schizophrenic probands and their families (12). It is interesting to note that Manfred Bleuler, who grew up at the Bürgholzli Hospital, found no help in diagnosis or in understanding his patients from the Rorschach technique which was administered to all the probands and their relatives. One of the more striking findings in the developmental model is the lack of intimacy which characterizes the adolescent friendship pattern of preschizophrenics (125). Another set of findings are the poorer scores on a visual reasoning factor, on a social conformity factor, and on an impulse control factor achieved by a group of Project Talent subjects at the time they took the tests in 1960, and who subsequently were hospitalized for mental disorder (8).

The genetic model is spreading from the field of schizophrenia into other diagnostic categories such as depression (56), neurosis (231), and even criminality (274). The introduction of the study of adoptees for contrasting biological (genetic) and environmental (rearing) factors has demonstrated the strength with which the genetic component will make itself felt independently of rearing, but this victory of the geneticists has been gained at some sacrifice. The inheritance of schizophrenia, though undeniable, is no longer specific, but lies along a continuum spreading from genotypes whose phenotype is quite normal to those who are schizoid and to the more severely afflicted (114). One of the most interesting contributions of the introduction of the adoptee studies is the finding that the slow reaction time exhibited by schizophrenics might be due to rearing rather than to genetics.[7]

Genetics has also demonstrated its importance in the field of affective disorders. Although the earlier twin and family studies had stressed the importance of genetics in the transmission of manic-depressive psychosis, the mechanisms involved were not known until the recent findings concerning linkage with markers on the X chromosome—color blindness and Xg blood group—in the families of bipolar depressives. The most recent findings in the genetic area were reported at the recent symposium by the American Psychopathological Association (56).

The internal environment model, which has been in the doldrums for awhile, is again in the forefront of scientific promise (113). The early work on the internal environment model proved disappointing because it dealt with peripheral blood flow and metabolic correlates in the brain. Furthermore, it was focused on discovering some unique toxic substance not present in normals. It was not until central synaptic mechanisms became the focus of attention that progress became apparent. Furthermore, the search for uniquely novel substances gave way to searching for inappropriate interconnections or interactions between chemically normal

---

[7] J. L. Van Dyke, D. Rosenthal & P. V. Rasmussen. Schizophrenia: effects of inheritance and rearing on reaction time. Unpublished manuscript.

components of the brain. Now at least three hypotheses seem promising. The first is the transmethylation hypothesis, which stipulates that the accumulation of methylated hallucinogenic substances underlies schizophrenic behavior. The second hypothesis postulates that the disturbance in central catecholamine synapses underlies the vulnerability in schizophrenia and is based on the similarity to schizophrenia noted in the toxic psychosis induced by amphetamine. Apparently release of dopamine in the brain is the culprit. The third hypothesis postulates that monoamine oxidase which is markedly reduced in the platelets of schizophrenics may serve as a marker for schizophrenia (113).

Can these various scientific models be integrated in some way? If we could squeeze out the essence of the six models into a goblet, we would find that the common element in all of these models is the production of some kind of vulnerability in the mental patients. When they are subjected to sufficient stressful situations in life, this vulnerability produces an episode of illness. We know that depressive or manic episodes are time limited; that schizophrenic episodes are also time limited remains to be demonstrated, since some schizophrenics appear to remain ill indefinitely. From our prognostic literature we know that good premorbids improve while poor premorbids do not. If we make the assumption that both good and poor premorbids have time-limited episodes from which they recover, it is possible to explain the paradox. Both good and poor premorbids return to their premorbid level when the episode is finished. The good premorbids recover and return to their premorbid status in life, but the poor premorbids, even when the episode is over, still cannot cope. We are not even sure that the episode is finished; furthermore, because of their high vulnerability, they are catapulted into another episode soon after the first is ended. The problem facing clinical research is how to improve the poor premorbids so that they will be able to cope with life's exigencies when an episode ends. Perhaps an investigation of good premorbids who fail and of poor premorbids who succeed may hold the key to the solution (293).[8]

Literature Cited

1. American Psychiatric Association. 1968. *Diagnostic and Statistical Manual of the Mental Disorders*. Washington, D.C. 2nd ed.
2. Angst, J., Perris, C. 1972. The nosology of endogenous depression. Comparison of the results of two studies. *Int. J. Ment. Health* 1:145–58
3. Baker, M., Dorzab, J., Winokur, G., Cadoret, R. J. 1971. Depressive disease: Classification and clinical characteristics. *Compr. Psychiat.* 12:354–65
4. Bancroft, J. 1973. The application of psychophysiological measures to the assessment of modification of sexual behaviour. In *Annual Review of Behavior Therapy: Theory and Practice*, ed. C. M. Franks, G. T. Wilson, 447–63. New York: Brunner/Mazel
5. Beck, A. T. 1967. *Depression: Causes and Treatment*. Philadelphia: Univ. Pennsylvania Press
6. Beck, A. T., Ward, C. H., Mendelson, M., Mock, J. E., Erbaugh, J. K. 1961. An inventory for measuring depression. *Arch. Gen. Psychiat.* 4:561–71

[8] For other recent literature not reviewed by this author but highly recommended by colleagues, see (26, 52, 118, 232).

7. Beck, A. T., Ward, C. H., Mendelson, M., Mock, J. E., Erbaugh, J. K. 1962. Reliability of psychiatric diagnosis: 2. A study of consistency of clinical judgments and ratings. *Am. J. Psychiat.* 119:351–57

8. Bergenn, V. W. 1972. *The relationship of adolescent test performance to subsequent psychiatric deviance.* DEd thesis. Columbia Univ., New York City. 97 pp.

9. Bernreuter, R. G. 1933. The measurement of self sufficiency. *J. Abnorm. Soc. Psychol.* 28:291–300

10. Bernstein, I. H., Day, R. M. 1971. Size constancy in mental retardates and normals: a signal-detectability analysis. *J. Abnorm. Psychol.* 78:177–79

11. Birnbaum, A., Maxwell, A. E. 1960. Classification procedures based on Bayes' formula. *Appl. Statist.* 9:152–69

12. Bleuler, M. 1972. *Die schizophrenen Geistesstörungen im lichte langjähriger kranken-und Familiengeschicten* (The Schizophrenic Mental Disturbances in the Light of the Long Term Patient and Family Histories). New York: Intercontinental Med. Book Corp. 666 pp.

13. Boissonneault, D. R., Dorosh, M. E., Tong, J. E. 1970. The effect of induced heart rate change and neuroticism on the resolution of temporally paired flashes. *Psychophysiology* 7:465–74

14. Bourliere, F. 1970. *The Assessment of Biological Age in Man.* Public Health Papers No. 37. Geneva: WHO

15. Broen, W. E., Nakamura, C. Y. 1972. Reduced range of sensory sensitivity in chronic nonparanoid schizophrenics. *J. Abnorm. Psychol.* 79:106–11

16. Brown, G. W. 1972. Life events and psychiatric illness: Some thoughts on methodology and causality. *J. Psychosom. Res.* 16:311–20

17. Brown, G. W., Sklair, F., Harris, T., Birley, J. L. T. 1973. Life events and psychiatric disorders: Part 1. Some methodological issues. *Psychol. Med.* 3:74–87

18. Bunney, W. E., Hamburg, D. A. 1963. Methods for reliable longitudinal observation of behavior. *Arch. Gen. Psychiat.* 9:280–94

18a. Burdock, E. I. 1974. *Methodology of collaborative international studies in psychopharmacology.* Presented at meet. Int. Congr. Int. Coll. Neuropsychopharmacol. Paris

19. Burdock, E. I., Sutton, S., Zubin, J. 1958. Personality and psychopathology. *J. Abnorm. Soc. Psychol.* 56: 18–30

20. Calfee, R. C. 1970. Short-term recognition memory in children. *Child Develop.* 41:145–61

21. Carney, D. J. 1969. *Signal detection performance of delusional and nondelusional schizophrenics.* PhD thesis. Univ. Rochester, Rochester, NY. 91 pp.

22. Carney, M. W. P., Roth, M., Garside, R. F. 1965. The diagnosis of depressive syndromes and the prediction of E.C. T. response. *Brit. J. Psychiat.* 111: 659–74

23. Carpenter, W. Jr., Strauss, J., Bartko, J. 1973. Flexible system for the diagnosis of schizophrenia: Report from the WHO International Pilot Study of Schizophrenia. *Science* 182:1275–78

24. Carter, R. D., Thomas, E. J. 1973. Modification of problematic marital communication using corrective feedback and instruction. *Behav. Ther.* 4:100–9

25. Cautela, J. R., Kastenbaum, R. 1967. A reinforcement survey schedule for use in therapy, training, and research. *Psychol. Rep.* 20:1115–30

26. Chapman, L. J., Chapman, J. P. 1973. *Disordered Thought in Schizophrenia.* New York: Appleton-Century-Crofts. 359 pp.

27. Clark, W. C. 1966. The psyche in psychophysics: A sensory-decision theory analysis of the effect of instructions on flicker sensitivity and response bias. *Psychol. Bull.* 65:358–66

28. Clark, W. C., Brown, J. C., Rutschmann, J. 1967. Flicker sensitivity and response bias in psychiatric patients and normal subjects. *J. Abnorm. Psychol.* 72:35–42

29. Clark, W. C., Mehl, L. 1971. Thermal pain: A sensory decision theory analysis of the effect of age and sex on d', various response criteria, and 50% pain threshold. *J. Abnorm. Psychol.* 78: 202–12

30. Clark, W. C., Rubin, L. H. 1969. Signal detection theory analysis of threshold

differences in psychiatric patients and normal controls. *Proc. 77th Ann. Conv. APA* 4:3–4

31. Clark, W. C., Rutschmann, J., Link, R., Brown, J. C. 1963. Comparison of flicker-fusion thresholds obtained by the methods of forced-choice and limits on psychiatric patients. *Percept. Mot. Skills* 16:19–30

32. Cohen, J. 1960. A coefficient of agreement for nominal scales. *Educ. Psychol. Meas.* 20:37–46

33. Collins, P. J. 1972. *Reaction time measure of visual temporal integration in schizophrenic patients, other psychiatric patients, and normal subjects.* PhD thesis. Columbia Univ., New York City. 140 pp.

34. Cooper, B. 1973. Epidemiological psychiatry (editorial). *Psychol. Med.* 3:401–4

35. Cooper, B., Morgan, H. 1973. *Epidemiological Psychiatry.* Springfield, Ill.: Thomas

36. Cooper, B., Shepherd, M. 1973. Epidemiology and abnormal psychology. See Ref. 52, 34–66

37. Cooper, J. E. et al 1972. *Psychiatric Diagnosis in New York and London: A Comparative Study of Mental Hospital Admissions.* Maudsley Monogr. No. 20. London: Oxford Univ. Press. 152 pp.

38. Costello, C. G., Ed. 1970. Classification and psychopathology. See Ref. 38a, 1–26

38a. Costello, C. G., Ed. 1970. *Symptoms of Psychopathology: A Handbook.* New York: Wiley

39. Costello, C. G., Belton, G. P. 1970. Depression: Treatment. See Ref. 38a, 201–15

40. Costello, C. G., Selby, M. M. 1965. Sleep patterns in reactive and endogenous depression. *Brit. J. Psychiat.* 111:497–501

41. Craighead, W. E. 1973. The assessment of avoidance responses on the Levis Phobic Test Apparatus. *Behav. Ther.* 4:235–40

42. Craik, F. I. M. 1969. Applications of signal detection theory to studies of ageing. In *Decision Making and Age,* ed. A. T. Welford, J. E. Birren, 147–57. New York: Karger. 166 pp.

43. Daly, R. J., Cochrane, C. M. 1968.

Affective disorder taxonomies in middle aged females. *Brit. J. Psychiat.* 114:1295–97

44. Dohrenwend, B. P., Chin-Shong, E. T., Egri, G., Mendelsohn, F. S., Stokes, J. 1970. Psychiatric disorders in contrasting class and ethnic groups. See Ref. 90, 157–202

45. Dohrenwend, B. P., Dohrenwend, B. S. 1969. *Social Status and Psychological Disorder.* New York: Wiley. 207 pp.

46. Dohrenwend, B. S. 1973. Life events as stressors: A methodological inquiry. *J. Health Soc. Behav.* 14:167–75

47. Dollard, J., Miller, N. E. 1950. *Personality and Psychotherapy.* New York: McGraw-Hill

48. Emmerich, D. S., Levine, F. M. 1973. Phenothiazine dosage levels and auditory signal detection in schizophrenia. *Science* 179:405–6

49. Evans, T. R. 1969. Differential effects of dexamphetamine and phenidylate on auditory detection. *Psychon. Sci.* 17:139–40

50. Everitt, B. S. 1972. Cluster analysis: A brief discussion of some of the problems. *Brit. J. Psychiat.* 120:143–45

51. Eysenck, H. J. 1970. The classification of depressive illnesses. *Brit. J. Psychiat.* 117:241–50

52. Eysenck, H. J., Ed. 1973. *Handbook of Abnormal Psychology.* San Diego: Knapp. 906 pp. 2nd ed.

53. Fahy, T. J., Brandon, S., Garside, R. F. 1969. Clinical syndromes in a sample of depressed patients: A general practice material. *Proc. Roy. Soc. Med.* 62:331–35

54. Feighner, J. P. et al 1972. Diagnostic criteria for use in psychiatric research. *Arch. Gen. Psychiat.* 26:57–63

55. Ferster, C. B. 1973. A functional analysis of depression. *Am. Psychol.* 28: 857–70

55a. Fieve, R. R., Ed. 1971. *Depression in the 1970's: Modern Theory and Research.* The Hague: Excerpta Medica

56. Fieve, R. R., Brill, H., Rosenthal, D., Eds. 1975. *Genetic Research in Psychiatry.* Baltimore: Johns Hopkins Univ. Press. In press

57. Fisher. R. A. 1936. The use of multiple measurements in taxonomic problems. *Ann. Eugen.* 7:179–88

58. Fleiss, J. L. 1970. Estimating the reliability of interview data. *Psychometrika* 35:143–62

59. Fleiss, J. L. 1971. Measuring nominal scale agreement among many raters. *Psychol. Bull.* 76:378–82

60. Fleiss, J. L. 1972. Classification of the depressive disorders by numerical typology. *J. Psychiat. Res.* 9:141–53

61. Fleiss, J. L., Cohen, J. 1973. The equivalence of weighted kappa and the intraclass correlation coefficient as measures of reliability. *Educ. Psychol. Meas.* 33:613–19

62. Fleiss, J. L., Gurland, B. J., Cooper, J. E. 1971. Some contributions to the measurement of psychopathology. *Brit. J. Psychiat.* 119:647–56

63. Fleiss, J. L., Lawlor, W., Platman, S. R., Fieve, R. R. 1971. On the use of inverted factor analysis for generating typologies. *J. Abnorm. Psychol.* 77: 127–32

64. Fleiss, J. L., Spitzer, R. L., Cohen, J., Endicott, J. 1972. Three computer diagnosis methods compared. *Arch. Gen. Psychiat.* 27:643–49

65. Fleiss, J. L., Spitzer, R. L., Endicott, J., Cohen, J. 1972. Quantification of agreement in multiple psychiatric diagnosis. *Arch. Gen. Psychiat.* 26:168–71

66. Fleiss, J. L., Tanur, J. M. 1973. The analysis of covariance in psychopathology. See Ref. 88a, 509–28

67. Fleiss, J. L., Zubin, J. 1969. On the methods and theory of clustering. *Multivar. Behav. Res.* 4:235–50

68. Forbes, A. R. 1972. Some differences between neurotic and psychotic depressives. *Brit. J. Soc. Clin. Psychol.* 11:270–75

69. Franks, C. M., Ed. 1969. *Behavior Therapy: Appraisal and Status.* New York: McGraw-Hill

69a. Freedman, A. M., Kaplan, H. I., Sadock, B. J., Eds. 1975. *Comprehensive Textbook of Psychiatry.* Baltimore: Williams & Wilkins. 2nd ed. In press

70. Friedman, H. P., Rubin, J. 1967. On some invariant criteria for grouping data. *J. Am. Statist. Assoc.* 62:1159–78

71. Gaitz, C., Scott, J. 1972. Age and the measurement of mental health. *J. Health Soc. Behav.* 13:55–67

72. Garmezy, N., Streitman, S. 1974. Children at risk: The search for the antecedents of schizophrenia. Part I. conceptual models and research methods. *Schizophrenia Bull.* No. 8:14–90

73. Garside, R. F., Kay, D. W. K., Wilson, I. C., Deaton, I. D., Roth, M. 1971. Depressive syndromes and the classification of patients. *Psychol. Med.* 1:333–38

74. General Register Office 1968. *A Glossary of Mental Disorders.* Studies on medical and population subjects No. 22. London: H. M. Sta. Off.

75. Goldfarb, W., Braunstein, P. 1958. Reactions to delayed auditory feedback in schizophrenic children. In *Psychopathology of Communication,* ed. P. H. Hoch, J. Zubin, 49–63. New York: Grune & Stratton. 305 pp.

76. Goldfried, M. R., Kent, R. N. 1972. Traditional versus behavioral personality assessment: A comparison of methodological and theoretical assumptions. *Psychol. Bull.* 77:409–20

77. Goldiamond, I. 1965. Self-control procedures in personal behavior problems. *Psychol. Rep.* 17:851–68

78. Gordon, S. K., Clark, W. C. 1974. Application of signal detection theory to prose recall and recognition in elderly and young adults. *J. Gerontol.* 29: 64–72

79. Green, D. M., Swets, J. A. 1966. *Signal Detection Theory and Psychophysics.* New York: Wiley. 445 pp.

80. Grinker, R. R., Miller, J., Sabshin, M., Nunn, R., Nunnally, J. C. 1961. *The Phenomena of Depressions.* New York: Hoeber

81. Gruenberg, E. 1973. Progress in psychiatric epidemiology. *Psychiat. Quart.* 47:1–11

82. Gruzelier, J. H., Corballis, M. C. 1970. Effects of instructions and drug administration on temporal resolution of paired flashes. *Quart. J. Exp. Psychol.* 22:115–24

83. Gurland, B. J. et al 1972. The mislabeling of depressed patients in New York state hospitals. See Ref. 294a, 17–28

84. Gurland, B. J., Sharpe, L., Simon, R., Kuriansky, J., Stiller, P. 1972. On the use of psychiatric diagnosis for comparing psychiatric populations. *Psy-*

chiat. Quart. 46:461–73
85. Haider, I. 1972. Disturbance of sleep pattern in depression. *Pakistani Med. Forum* 7:7–14
86. Hamilton, M. 1960. A rating scale for depression. *J. Neurol. Neurosurg. Psychiat.* 23:56–62
87. Hamilton, M., White, J. M. 1959. Clinical syndromes in depressive states. *J. Ment. Sci.* 105:985–98
88. Hammer, M., Polgar, S. K., Salzinger, K. 1969. Speech predictability and social contact patterns in an informal group. *Hum. Organ.* 28:235–42
88a. Hammer, M., Salzinger, K., Sutton, S., Eds. 1973. *Psychopathology: Contributions from the Social, Behavioral, and Biological Sciences.* New York: Wiley. 588 pp.
89. Hare, E., Price, J., Slater, E. 1971. The age-distribution of schizophrenia and neurosis: Findings in a national sample. *Brit. J. Psychiat.* 119:445–48
90. Hare, E., Wing, J., Eds. 1970. *Psychiatric Epidemiology: An International Symposium.* London: Oxford Univ. Press. 379 pp.
91. Hare, R. D. 1968. Detection threshold for electric shock in psychopaths. *J. Abnorm. Psychol.* 73:268–72
92. Hartshorne, H., May, M. A. 1928. *Studies in the Nature of Character.* Vol. I. *Studies in Deceit.* New York: Macmillan
93. Hedberg, D., Houck, J., Glueck, B. 1970. *Tranylcypromine-Trifluoperazine combination in the treatment of schizophrenia.* Presented at Ann. Meet. Am. Psychiat. Assoc.
94. Hersen, M. 1973 Self-assessment of fear. *Behav. Ther.* 4:241–57
95. Herz, M. I., Endicott, J., Spitzer, R. L., Mesnikoff, A. 1971. Day versus inpatient hospitalization: a controlled study. *Am. J. Psychiat.* 127:1371–82
96. Hollister, L. E. et al 1967. Drug therapy of depression: Amitriptyline, perphenazine and their combination in different syndromes. *Arch. Gen. Psychiat.* 17:486–93
97. Insel, P. M., Moos, R. H. 1974. Psychological environments: Expanding the scope of human ecology. *Am. Psychol.* 29:179–88
98. Jaco, G. 1960. *Social Epidemiology of Mental Disorders.* New York: Russell Sage Found.
98a. Jenness, D., Kietzman, M. L., Zubin, J. 1975. Cognition and perception. See Ref. 69a.
99. Kales, A., Berger, R. J. 1970. Psychopathology of sleep. See Ref. 38a, 418–47
100. Kanfer, F. H., Phillips, J. S. 1970. *Learning Foundations of Behavior Therapy.* New York: Wiley
101. Kanfer, F. H., Saslow, G. 1965. Behavioral diagnosis. *Arch. Gen. Psychiat.* 12:529–38
102. Kanfer, F. H., Saslow, G. 1969. Behavioral diagnosis. See Ref. 69, 417–44
103. Katz, M. M. 1971. The classification of depression: Normal, clinical and ethnocultural variations. See Ref. 55a, 31–40
104. Kay, D. W. K., Garside, R. F., Beamish, P., Roy, J. R. 1969. Endogenous and neurotic syndromes of depression: A factor analytic study of 104 cases. Clinical features. *Brit. J. Psychiat.* 115:377–88
105. Kear-Colwell, J. J. 1972. A taxonomy of depressive phenomena and its relationship to the reactive endogenous dichotomy. *Brit. J. Psychiat.* 121: 665–71
106. Kendell, R. E. 1968. *The Classification of Depressive Illnesses.* London: Oxford Univ. Press
107. Kendell, R. E. 1968. An important source of bias affecting ratings made by psychiatrists. *J. Psychiat. Res.* 6:135–41
108. Kendell, R. E. 1969. The classification of depressive illness: The uses and limitations of multivariate analysis. *Psychiat. Neurol. Neurochir.* 72: 207–16
109. Kendell, R. E. 1973. The influence of the 1968 glossary on the diagnoses of English psychiatrists. *Brit. J. Psychiat.* 123:527–30
110. Kendell, R. E. et al 1970. The diagnostic criteria of American and British psychiatrists. *Arch. Gen. Psychiat.* 25:123–30
111. Kendell, R. E., Gourlay, J. 1970. The clinical distinction between psychotic and neurotic depressions. *Brit. J. Psychiat.* 117:257–66
112. Kety, S. S. 1959. Biochemical theories

of schizophrenia. II. *Science* 129: 1590–96

113. Kety, S. S. 1975. Progress toward an understanding of the biological substrates of schizophrenia. See Ref. 56

114. Kety, S. S., Rosenthal, D., Wender, P. H., Schulsinger, F., Jacobsen, B. 1975. Mental illness in the biological and adoptive families of adopted individuals who have become schizophrenic: A preliminary report based upon psychiatric interviews. See Ref. 56

115. Kietzman, M. L., Sutton, S., Zubin, J., Eds. 1975. *Experimental Approaches to Psychopathology*. New York: Academic. In press

116. Kiloh, L. G., Andrews, G., Neilson, M., Bianchi, G. N. 1972. The relationship of the syndromes called endogenous and neurotic depression. *Brit. J. Psychiat.* 121:183–96

117. Kiloh, L. G., Garside, R. F. 1963. The independence of neurotic depression and endogenous depression. *Brit. J. Psychiat.* 109:451–63

118. Klein, D. F., Davis, J. M. 1969. *Diagnosis and Drug Treatment of Psychiatric Disorders*. Baltimore: Williams & Wilkins. 480 pp.

119. Klein, D. F., Honigfeld, G., Feldman, S. 1972. Predictions of drug effect in personality disorders. *J. Nat. Assoc. Priv. Psychiat. Hosp.* 4:11–25

120. Klerman, G. L. 1972. Clinical research in depression. See Ref. 294a, 165–93

121. Klerman, G. L., Paykel, E. S. 1970. Depressive pattern, social background, and hospitalization. *J. Nerv. Ment. Dis.* 150:466–78

122. Korzh, N. N., Vaytkyavichyus, G. G. 1972. The mechanism of sensory processes in signal detection by schizophrenics. *Zh. Nevropatol. Psikhiatr.* 72:1689–94

123. Kramer, M. 1970. Problems in psychiatric epidemiology. *Proc. Roy. Soc. Med.* 63:553–62

124. Kramer, M., Taube, C., Redick, R. 1973. Patterns of use of psychiatric facilities by the aged: Past, present and future. In *The Psychology of Adult Development and Aging*, ed. C. Eisdorfer, M. P. Lawton. Washington, D.C.: Am. Psychol. Assoc.

125. Kreisman, D. 1970. Social interaction

and intimacy in preschizophrenic adolescence. In *The Psychopathology of Adolescence*, ed. J. Zubin, A. M. Freedman, 299–318. New York: Grune & Stratton. 342 pp.

126. Kriegel, J. 1967. *Reaction time in schizophrenics and normals as a function of stimulus uncertainty, guessing, and modality shift*. PhD thesis. Columbia Univ., New York City. 123 pp.

127. Krippendorff, K. 1970. Bivariate agreement coefficients for reliability of data. In *Sociological Methodology 1970*, ed. E. T. Borgatta, 139–50. San Francisco: Jossey-Bass

128. Kuechler, H. A., Dodwell, P. C. 1968. Auditory signal detectability as a function of pre-experimental shock. *Quart. J. Exp. Psychol.* 20:305–8

129. Leff, J. 1973. Culture and the differentiation of emotional states. *Brit. J. Psychiat.* 123:299–306

130. Leff, J. Transcultural influences on psychiatrists' rating of verbally expressed emotion.

131. Lehmann, H. E. 1971. Epidemiology of depressive disorders. See Ref. 55a, 21–30

132. Levine, F. M., Pomeranz, D., Toscano, P. 1974. *Non-attending as an adaptive response in chronic schizophrenic patients on a delayed auditory feedback task*. Presented at East. Psychol. Assoc. Philadelphia

133. Levit, R. A., Sutton, S., Zubin, J. 1973. Evoked potential correlates of information processing in psychiatric patients. *Psychol. Med.* 3:487–94

134. Lewis, A. 1967. Problems presented by the ambiguous word "anxiety" as used in psychopathology. *Israel Ann. Psychiat.* 5:105–21

135. Lewis, A. 1970. Paranoia and paranoid: a historical perspective. *Psychol. Med.* 1:2–12

136. Ibid 1971. "Endogenous" and "exogenous": a useful dichotomy? 1:191–96

137. Lewis, A. 1972. Classification and diagnosis in psychiatry: a historical note. See Ref. 37, 1–5

138. Lidz, T. 1973. *Family studies and a theory of schizophrenia*. Presented as Stanley R. Dean Award Lecture, Am. Coll. Psychiat., New Orleans

139. Lipton, M. 1972. *Age differentiation in*

depression: Biochemical aspects. Presented at meet. Gerontol. Soc. San Juan

140. Liss, J., Welner, A., Robins, E., Richardson, M. 1973. Psychiatric symptoms in white and black inpatients. I: Record study. *Compr. Psychiat.* 14: 475–81

141. Lorr, M. 1966. *Explorations in Typing Psychotics.* New York: Pergamon

142. Lorr, M., Klett, C. J., McNair, D. M., Lasky, J. J. 1962. *Inpatient Multidimensional Psychiatric Scale: Manual.* Palo Alto: Consult. Psychol. Press

143. Mackworth, J. 1965. The effect of amphetamine on the detectability of signals in a vigilance task. *Can. J. Psychol.* 19:104–10

144. Malzberg, B. 1963. Mental disorders in the U.S. In *Encyclopedia of Mental Health,* ed. A. Deutsch, H. Fishman, 3:1051–66. New York: Watts

145. Manaster, G., Havighurst, R. 1972. *Cross-National Research: Social-Psychological Methods and Problems.* New York: Houghton Mifflin

146. Marcos, L., Alpert, M., Urcuyo, L., Kesselman, M. 1973. The effect of interview language on the evaluation of psychopathology in Spanish-American schizophrenic patients. *Am. J. Psychiat.* 130(5):549–53

147. Marcos, L., Urcuyo, L., Kesselman, M., Alpert, M. 1973. The language barrier in evaluating Spanish-American patients. *Arch. Gen. Psychiat.* 29:655–59

148. McConaghy, N., Joffe, A. D., Murphy, B. 1967. The independence of neurotic and endogenous depression. *Brit. J. Psychiat.* 113:479–84

149. McDonald, C. 1973. An age-specific analysis of the neuroses. *Brit. J. Psychiat.* 122:477–80

150. McGhie, A. 1966. The subjective assessment of sleep patterns in psychiatric illness. *Brit. J. Med. Psychol.* 39:221–30

151. Mechanic, D. 1969. *Mental Health and Social Policy.* Englewood Cliffs, N.J.: Prentice-Hall

152. Melrose, J. P., Stroebel, C., Glueck, B. 1970. Diagnosis of psychopathology using stepwise multiple discriminant analysis. *Compr. Psychiat.* 11:43–50

153. Mendels, J. 1965. Electroconvulsive therapy and depression: The prognostic significance of clinical factors. *Brit. J. Psychiat.* 111:675–81

154. Ibid 1968. Depression: The distinction between syndrome and symptom. 114: 1549–54

155. Mendels, J. 1970. *Concepts of Depression.* New York: Wiley

156. Mendels, J., Cochrane, C. 1968. The nosology of depression: The endogenous-reactive concept. *Am. J. Psychiat.* (May suppl.) 124:1–11

157. Mendlewicz, J., Fieve, R., Rainer, J., Fleiss, J. 1972. Manic-depressive illness: a comparative study of patients with and without a family history. *Brit. J. Psychiat.* 120:523–30

158. Milner, A. D., Beech, H. R., Walker, V. J. 1971. Decision processes and obsessional behavior. *Brit. J. Soc. Clin. Psychol.* 10:88–99

159. Mischel, W. 1971. *Introduction to Personality.* New York: Holt, Rinehart & Winston

160. Moos, G. R., Boren, J. J. 1972. Depression as a model for behavioral analysis. *Compr. Psychiat.* 13:581–90

161. Moos, R. H. 1973. Conceptualizations of human environments. *Am. Psychol.* 28:652–65

162. Moos, R. H., Insel, P. M., Eds. 1974. *Issues in Social Ecology: Human Milieus.* Palo Alto, Calif.: National Press

163. Moran, P. A. P. 1966. The establishment of a psychiatric syndrome. *Brit. J. Psychiat.* 112:1165–71

164. Moskowitz, H., DePry, D. 1968. Differential effect of alcohol on auditory vigilance and divided-attention tasks. *Quart. J. Stud. Alcohol* 29:54–63

165. Mowbray, R. M. 1972. The Hamilton rating scale for depression: A factor analysis. *Psychol. Med.* 2:272–80

166. Murphy, H. B. M. 1968. Sociocultural factors in schizophrenia: a compromise theory. In *Social Psychiatry,* ed. J. Zubin, F. Freyhan, 74–92. New York: Grune & Stratton. 382 pp.

167. Myers, J., Lindenthal, J., Pepper, M. 1971. Life events and psychiatric impairment. *J. Nerv. Ment. Dis.* 152:149–57

168. Naylor, G. J., Le Poidevin, D. 1972. Sleep patterns in depressive states.

Brit. J. Med. Psychol. 45:171-76
169. Neale, J. M., McIntyre, C. W., Fox, R., Cromwell, R. L. 1969. Span of apprehension in acute schizophrenia. *J. Abnorm. Psychol.* 74:593-96
170. Noble, P., Lader, M. 1972. A physiological comparison of "endogenous" and "reactive" depression. *Brit. J. Psychiat.* 120:541-42
171. Overall, J. E., Gorham, D. R. 1963. A pattern probability model for the classification of psychiatric patients. *Behav. Sci.* 8:108-16
172. Overall, J. E., Henry, B. W., Markett, J., Emken, R. 1972. Decisions about drug therapy. 1. Prescriptions for adult psychiatric outpatients. *Arch. Gen. Psychiat.* 26:140-45
173. Overall, J. E., Hollister, L. E., Johnson, M., Pennington, V. 1966. Nosology of depression and differential response to drugs. *J. Am. Med. Assoc.* 195:946-48
174. Paykel, E. S. 1971. Classification of depressed patients: A cluster analysis derived grouping. *Brit. J. Psychiat.* 118:275-88
175. Ibid 1972. Depressive typologies and response to amitriptyline. 120:147-56
176. Paykel, E. S. 1972. Correlates of a depressive typology. *Arch. Gen. Psychiat.* 27:203-10
177. Paykel, E. S., Klerman, G. L., Prusoff, B. A. 1970. Treatment setting and clinical depression. *Arch. Gen. Psychiat.* 22:11-21
178. Paykel, E. S., Prusoff, B. A. 1973. Response set and observer set in the assessment of depressed patients. *Psychol. Med.* 3:209-16
179. Paykel, E. S., Prusoff, B. A., Klerman, G. L. 1971. The endogenous-neurotic continuum in depression: Rater independence and factor distributions. *J. Psychiat. Res.* 8:73-90
180. Paykel, E., Prusoff, B. A., Uhlenhuth, E. 1971. Scaling of life events. *Arch. Gen. Psychiat.* 25:340-47
181. Perris, C. 1968. Genetic transmission of depressive psychoses. *Acta Psychiat. Scand. Suppl.* 203:45-52
182. Pilowsky, I., Boulton, D. M. 1970. Development of a questionnaire-based decision rule for classifying depressed patients. *Brit. J. Psychiat.* 116:647-50
183. Pilowsky, I., Levine, S., Boulton, D. M.

1969. The classification of depression by numerical taxonomy. *Brit. J. Psychiat.* 115:937-45
184. Pilowsky, I., Spalding, D. 1972. A method for measuring depression: Validity studies on a depression questionnaire. *Brit. J. Psychiat.* 121:411-16
185. Platman, S. R., Fieve, R. R. 1970. Sleep in depression and mania. *Brit. J. Psychiat.* 116:219-20
186. Pomeranz, D. M., Goldfried, M. R. 1970. An intake report outline for behavior modification. *Psychol. Rep.* 26:447-50
187. Poulton, E. C. 1973. Unwanted range effects from using within-subject experimental designs. *Psychol. Bull.* 80:113-21
188. Price, R. H. 1966. Signal-detection methods in personality and perception. *Psychol. Bull.* 66:55-62
189. Price, R. H., Eriksen, C. W. 1966. Size constancy in schizophrenia: a reanalysis. *J. Abnorm. Psychol.* 71:155-60
190. Prusoff, B. A., Klerman, G. L., Paykel, E. S. 1972. Concordance between clinical assessments and patients' self report in depression. *Arch. Gen. Psychiat.* 26:546-52
191. Rahe, R. 1969. Multi-cultural correlations of life change scaling: America, Japan, Denmark and Sweden. *J. Psychosom. Res.* 13:191-95
192. Rao, C. R. 1948. The utilization of multiple measurements in problems of biological classification. *J. Roy. Statist. Soc. B* 10:159-93
193. Rao, C. R., Slater, P. 1949. Multivariate analysis applied to differences between neurotic groups. *Brit. J. Psychol.* (Statist. sec.) 2:17-29
194. Rappaport, M., Hopkins, H. K. 1969. Drug effects on auditory attention in paranoid and nonparanoid schizophrenics. *J. Nerv. Ment. Dis.* 148:597-605
195. Rappaport, M., Hopkins, H. K. 1971. Signal detection and chlorpromazine. *Hum. Factors* 13:387-90
196. Rappaport, M., Hopkins, H. K., Silverman, J., Hall, K. 1972. Auditory signal detection in schizophrenics. *Psychopharmacologia* 24:6-28
197. Rappaport, M., Silverman, J., Hopkins, H. K., Hall, K. 1971. Phenothia-

zine effects on auditory signal detection in paranoid and nonparanoid schizophrenics. *Science* 174:723-25

198. Raskin, A. 1971. Drugs and depression subtypes. See Ref. 55a, 87-95

199. Raskin, A., McKeon, J. J. 1971. Super factors of psychopathology in hospitalized depressed patient. *J. Psychiat. Res.* 9:11-19

200. Raskin, A., Schulterbrandt, J., Reatig, N., McKeon, J. J. 1969. Replication of factors of psychopathology in interview, ward behavior and self-report ratings of hospitalized depressives. *J. Nerv. Ment. Dis.* 148:87-98

201. Raskin, A., Schulterbrandt, J., Reatig, N., Rice, C. E. 1967. Factors of psychopathology in interview, ward behavior, and self-report ratings of hospitalized depressives. *J. Consult. Psychol.* 31:270-78

202. Rathus, S. A. 1973. A 30-item schedule for assessing assertive behavior. *Behav. Ther.* 4:398-406

203. Rees, J. N., Botwinick, J. 1971. Detection and decision factors in auditory behavior of the elderly. *J. Gerontol.* 26:133-36

204. Richman, A. 1970. The use of case-registers of psychiatric care in epidemiological research of mental disorders. See Ref. 90, 257-72

205. Robins, E., Munoz, R. A., Martin, S., Gentry, K. A. 1972. Primary and secondary affective disorders. See Ref. 294a, 33-45

206. Rockliff, B. W. 1969. A brief self-rating questionnaire for depression. *Psychosomatics* 10:236-43

207. Rosenthal, S. H. 1967. Neurotic and endogenous depressions: A sceptical view. *Brit. J. Psychiat.* 113:1154-55

208. Rosenthal, S. H., Gudeman, J. E. 1967. The endogenous depressive pattern: An empirical investigation. *Arch. Gen. Psychiat.* 16:241-49

209. Rosenthal, S. H., Klerman, G. L. 1966. Content and consistency in the endogenous depressive pattern. *Brit. J. Psychiat.* 112:471-84

210. Rubin, S. E., Lawlis, G. F., Tasto, D. L., Namenek, T. 1969. Factor analysis of the 122-item fear survey schedule. *Behav. Res. Ther.* 7:381-86

211. Rutner, I. T., Pear, J. J. 1972. An observational methodology for investigating phobic behavior: Preliminary report. *Behav. Ther.* 3:437-40

212. Salzinger, K. 1969. The place of operant conditioning of verbal behavior in psychotherapy. See Ref. 69, 375-95

213. Salzinger, K. 1973. *Schizophrenia: Behavioral Aspects.* New York: Wiley

214. Salzinger, K. 1975. Behavior theory models of abnormal behavior. See Ref. 114a, 213-44

215. Salzinger, K., Feldman, R. S., Portnoy, S. 1970. Training parents of brain-injured children in the use of operant conditioning procedures. *Behav. Ther.* 1:4-32

216. Salzinger, K., Hammer, M., Portnoy, S., Polgar, S. K. 1970. Verbal behaviour and social distance. *Lang. Speech* 13:25-37

217. Salzinger, K., Pisoni, S. 1958. Reinforcement of affect responses of schizophrenics during the clinical interview. *J. Abnorm. Soc. Psychol.* 57:84-90

218. Ibid 1960. Reinforcement of verbal affect responses of normal subjects during the interview. 60:127-30

219. Ibid 1961. Some parameters of the conditioning of verbal affect responses in schizophrenic subjects. 63:511-16

220. Salzinger, K., Salzinger, S. 1973. Behavior theory for the study of psychopathology. See Ref. 88a, 111-25

221. Sandifer, M. G., Pettus, C., Quade, D. 1964. A study of psychiatric diagnosis. *J. Nerv. Ment. Dis.* 139:350-56

222. Sandifer, M. G., Wilson, I. C., Green, L. 1966. The two-type thesis of depressive disorders. *Am. J. Psychiat.* 123: 93-97

223. Satterfield, J. H. 1972. Auditory evoked cortical response studies in depressed patients and normal control subjects. In *Recent Advances in the Psychobiology of the Depressive Illnesses*, ed. T. A. Williams, M. M. Katz, J. A. Shield Jr., 87-98. Washington, D.C.:GPO. 389 pp.

224. Schildkraut, J. J. 1972. Neuropharmacological studies of mood disorders. See Ref. 294a, 65-84

225. Schneider, E. W., Carpenter, J. A.

1973. The influence of ethanol on auditory signal detection. *Quart. J. Stud. Alcohol.* 231:357–70

226. Schwab, J., Holzer, C., Warheit, G. 1973. Depressive symptomatology and age. *Psychosomatics* 14:135–41

227. Schwitzgebel, R. L., Schwitzgebel, R. K., Eds. 1973. *Psychotechnology: Electronic Control of Mind and Behavior.* New York: Holt, Rinehart & Winston

228. Shackleton, V. J., Fletcher, C. A. 1973. Psychiatric patients: motivation in an assessment situation: implications arising from recent work. *Bull. Brit. Psychol. Soc.* 26:17–23

229. Shallice, T., Warrington, E. K. 1970. Independent functioning of verbal memory stores: A neuropsychological study. *Quart. J. Exp. Psychol.* 22:261–73

230. Sharpe, L. et al 1974. Comparisons of American, Canadian and British psychiatrists in their diagnostic concepts. *Can. Psychiat. Assoc. J.* 19:235–45

231. Shields, J. 1973. Heredity and psychological abnormality. See Ref. 52, 540–603

232. Siegler, M., Osmond, H. 1966. Models of madness. *Brit. J. Psychiat.*, 112:1193–1203

233. Silverman, C. 1968. *The Epidemiology of Depression.* Baltimore: Johns Hopkins Press

234. Simkins, L. 1971. The reliability of self-recorded behaviors. *Behav. Ther.* 2:83–87

235. Simon, R. I. 1963. Involution psychosis in Negroes. *Arch. Gen. Psychiat.* 13:148–54

236. Simon, R. J., Fleiss, J. L., Gurland, B. J., Stiller, P. R., Sharpe, L. 1973. Depression and schizophrenia in hospitalized black and white mental patients. *Arch. Gen. Psychiat.* 28:509–12

237. Sletten, I., Altman, H., Ulett, G. 1971. Routine diagnosis by computer, *Am. J. Psychiat.* 127:1147–52

238. Sletten, I., Osborn, R., Cho, D., Altman, H. 1971. Agreement on specificity of psychotropic drugs. *Curr. Ther. Res.* 13:292–97

239. Smith, E. E. 1969. Short-term memory impairment in chronic schizophrenics.

Can. J. Psychol. 23:114–26

240. Smith, W. G. 1966. A model for psychiatric diagnosis. *Arch. Gen. Psychiat.* 14:521–29

241. Snaith, R. P., Ahmed, S. N., Mehta, S., Hamilton, M. 1971. Assessment of the severity of primary depressive illness: Wakefield self-assessment depression inventory. *Psychol. Med.* 1:143–49

242. Snodgrass, J. G. 1975. Psychophysics. In *Contemporary Experimental Psychology*, Vol. 2, ed. S. Reynolds, B. Scharf. Glenview, Ill.: Scott Foresman. In press

243. Spicer, C., Hare, E., Slater, E. 1973. Neurotic and psychotic forms of depressive illness: Evidence from age-incidence in a national sample. *Brit. J. Psychiat.* 123:535–41

244. Spitzer, R. L., Cohen, J., Fleiss, J. L., Endicott, J. 1967. Quantification of agreement in psychiatric diagnosis: A new approach. *Arch. Gen. Psychiat.* 17:83–87

245. Spitzer, R. L., Endicott, J. 1968. DIAGNO: A computer program for psychiatric diagnosis utilizing the differential diagnostic procedure. *Arch. Gen. Psychiat.* 18:746–56

246. Spitzer, R. L., Endicott, J. 1969. DIAGNO II: Further developments in a computer program for psychiatric diagnosis. *Am. J. Psychiat.* 125 suppl.:12–21

247. Spitzer, R. L., Endicott, J. 1971. An integrated group of forms for automated psychiatric case records: progress report. *Arch. Gen. Psychiat.* 24:448–53

248. Spitzer, R. L., Endicott, J. 1973. The value of the interview for the evaluation of psychopathology. See Ref. 88a, 397–408

249. Spitzer, R. L., Endicott, J. 1973. *Schedule for Affective Disorders and Schizophrenia.* Biometrics Res., NY State Dep. Ment. Hyg.

250. Spitzer, R. L., Endicott, J. 1975. Psychiatric rating scales in the evaluation of psychiatric treatment. See Ref. 69a

251. Spitzer, R. L., Endicott, J. 1974. Can the computer assist clinicians in psychiatric diagnosis? *Am. J. Psychiat.* 131:523–30

252. Spitzer, R. L., Endicott, J., Fleiss, J. L. 1967. Instruments and recording forms for evaluating psychiatric status and history: rationale, method of development, and description. *Compr. Psychiat.* 8:321–43

253. Spitzer, R. L., Endicott, J., Fleiss, J. L., Cohen, J. 1970. The psychiatric status schedule: a technique for evaluating psychopathology and impairment in role functioning. *Arch. Gen. Psychiat.* 23:41–55

254. Spitzer, R. L., Fleiss, J. L. 1974. A reanalysis of the reliability of psychiatric diagnosis. *Brit. J. Psychiat.* In press

255. Spitzer, R. L., Fleiss, J. L., Burdock, E. I., Hardesty, A. 1964. The mental status schedule: rationale, reliability, and validity. *Compr. Psychiat.* 5:384–95

256. Spitzer, R. L., Fleiss, J. L., Endicott, J., Cohen, J. 1967. Mental status schedule: Properties of factor-analytically derived scales. *Arch. Gen. Psychiat.* 16:479–93

257. Steinman, A. R. 1944. Reaction time to change compared with other psychophysical methods. *Arch. Psychol.* 292

258. Stern, J. A., McClure, J. N., Costello, C. G. 1970. Depression: Assessment and aetiology. See Ref. 38a, 169–200

259. Stilson, D. W., Kopell, B. S. 1964. The recognition of visual signals in the presence of visual noise by psychiatric patients. *J. Nerv. Ment. Dis.* 139: 209–21

260. Storrow, H. A. 1967. *Introduction to Scientific Psychiatry: A Behavioristic Approach to Diagnosis and Treatment.* New York: Appleton-Century-Crofts

261. Stuart, R. B. 1970. *Trick or Treatment: How and When Psychotherapy Fails.* Champaign, Ill.: Res. Press

262. Suboski, M. D. 1967. The analysis of classical discrimination conditioning experiments. *Psychol. Bull.* 68:235–42

263. Sutton, S. 1969. The specification of psychological variables in an average evoked potential experiment. In *Average Evoked Potentials—Methods, Results, and Evaluations*, ed. E. Donchin, D. B. Lindsley, 237–62. Washington, D.C.: GPO. 400 pp.

264. Sutton, S. 1973. Fact and artifact in the psychology of schizophrenia. See Ref. 88a, 197–213

265. Sutton, S., Roehrig, W. C., Kramer, J. 1964. Delayed auditory feedback of speech in schizophrenics and normals. *Ann. NY Acad. Sci.* 105:832–44

266. Sutton, S., Zubin, J. 1965. Effect of sequence on reaction time in schizophrenia. In *Behavior, Aging and the Nervous System*, ed. A. T. Welford, J. E. Birren, 562–97. Springfield, Ill.: Thomas. 637 pp.

267. Swets, J. S., Tanner, W. P., Birdsall, T. G. 1961. Decision processes in perception. *Psychol. Rev.* 68:301–40

268. Tasto, D. L., Hickson, R. 1970. Standardization and scaling of the 122-item fear survey schedule. *Behav. Ther.* 1:473–84

269. Tasto, D. L., Hickson, R., Rubin, S. E. 1971. Scaled profile analysis of fear survey schedule factors. *Behav. Ther.* 2:543–49

270. Tasto, D. L., Suinn, R. M. 1972. Fear survey schedule changes on total and factor scores due to nontreatment effects. *Behav. Ther.* 3:275–78

271. Thomson, K. C., Hendrie, H. C. 1972. Environmental stress in primary depressive illness. *Arch. Gen. Psychiat.* 26:130–32

272. Thorndike, R. M., Kleinknecht, R. A. 1974. Reliability of homogeneous scales of reinforcers: A cluster analysis of the reinforcement survey schedule. *Behav. Ther.* In press

273. Tonks, C. M., Paykel, E. S., Klerman, G. L. 1970. Clinical depression among Negroes. *Am. J. Psychiat.* 127:329–34

274. Trasler, G. 1973. Criminal behavior. See Ref. 52, 67–96

274a. Uhlenhuth, E., Lipman, R., Balter, M., Stern, M. 1975. Symptom, intensity, and life stress in the city. *Arch. Gen. Psychiat.* In press

275. Vath, R., Miranda, M., Becker, J., Gibson, S. 1972. Attempted validation of a pragmatic classification of depression. *Psychol. Rep.* 30:287–90

275a. Waldbaum, J. L. (Kriegel), Sutton, S., Kerr, J. 1975. Shift of sensory modality and reaction time in schizophrenia. See Ref. 115, 167–76

276. Walker, H. A., Birch, H. G. 1970. Neurointegrative deficiency in schizophrenic children. *J. Nerv. Ment. Dis.* 151:104–13

277. Wechsler, H., Grosser, G. H., Busfield, B. L. 1963. The depression rating scale. *Arch. Gen. Psychiat.* 9:334–43
278. Weiss, B. L., McPartland, R. J., Kupfer, D. J. 1973. Once more: The inaccuracy of non-EEG estimations of sleep. *Am. J. Psychiat.* 130:1282–85
279. Welner, A., Liss, J., Robins, E. 1973. Psychiatric symptoms in white and black inpatients. II: Follow-up study. *Compr. Psychiat.* 14:483–88
280. Windle, C. 1952. Psychological tests in psychopathological prognosis. *Psychol. Bull.* 49:452–82
281. Wing, J., Hailey, A., Eds. 1972. *Evaluating a Community Psychiatric Service: The Camberwell Register 1964–71.* London: Oxford Univ. Press
282. Winokur, G. 1971. The genetics of manic-depressive illness. See Ref. 55a, 47–54
283. Winokur, G., Clayton, P. J., Reich, T. 1969. *Manic-Depressive Illness.* St. Louis: Mosby
284. Wolfe, J. H. 1970. Pattern clustering by multivariate mixture analysis. *Multivar..Behav. Res.* 5:329–50
285. Wolff, W. T., Merrens, M. R. 1974. Behavioral assessment: A review of clinical methods. *J. Pers. Assess.* 38:3–16
286. Wolpe, J. 1958. *Psychotherapy by Reciprocal Inhibition.* Stanford Univ. Press
287. Wolpe, J. 1969. *The Practice of Behavior Therapy.* New York: Pergamon
288. Wolpe, J., Lang, P. J. 1964. A fear survey schedule for use in behavior therapy. *Behav. Res. Ther.* 2:27–30
289. World Health Organization 1973. *The International Pilot Study of Schizophrenia,* Vol. 1. Geneva: WHO. 427 pp.

290. Zeidenberg, P., Clark, W. C., Jaffe, J., Anderson, S. W., Chin, S., Malitz, S. 1973. Effect of oral administration of Δ^9 tetrahydrocannabinol on memory, speech, and perception of thermal stimulation: results with four normal human volunteer subjects. Preliminary report. *Compr. Psychiat.* 14:549–56
291. Zubin, J. 1967. Classification of the behavior disorders. *Ann. Rev. Psychol.* 18:373–406
292. Zubin, J. 1969. Contributions of experimental and abnormal psychology to clinical psychology. *Int. Rev. Appl. Psychol.* 18:65–77
293. Zubin, J. 1974. *A biometric approach to diagnosis and evaluation of therapeutic intervention in schizophrenia.* Presented as Stanley R. Dean Award Lecture, Am. Coll. Psychiat. Key Biscayne
294. Zubin, J., Fleiss, J. L. 1971. Current biometric approaches to depression. See Ref. 55a, 7–19
294a. Zubin, J., Freyhan, F. A., Eds. 1972. *Disorders of Mood.* Baltimore: Johns Hopkins Press
295. Zubin, J., Windle, C. 1954. Psychological prognosis of outcome in the mental disorders. *J. Abnorm. Soc. Psychol.* 49:272–81
296. Zung, W. W. K. 1965. A self-rating depression scale. *Arch. Gen. Psychiat.* 12:63–70
297. Zung, W. W. K. 1971. Depression in the normal adult population. *Psychosomatics* 12:164–67
298. Zung, W. W. K. 1972. The depression status inventory: An adjunct to the self-rating depression scale. *J. Clin. Psychol.* 28:539–43

AUTHOR INDEX

673

SUBJECT INDEX

Cornell JDK
see Tests and scales
Corticosterone
rhythms
entrainment of, 142
in seasonal cycle studies
in sparrows, 153
Counseling, 337-50
and client behavior
process research in,
348
confrontation and self-
exploration
studies of effectiveness,
342-43
empathy
and other therapist-offered
conditions, 338-40
evaluation of psychotherapy,
345-47
human helping skills
training in, 343-44
interaction between counsel-
or and client
study of, 338-39
prevention of mental dis-
orders
role in, 560
role-theory in, 340
selection of counselors, 344-
50
criterion problem, 345-
47
relationship as intermediate outcome, 347-50
self-disclosure
studies of effectiveness,
340-42
and student development,
337-61
therapeutic systems
diversity of opinion, 348
therapist training theories,
347-50
training innovators
listing of, 343
Covert reinforcement
as behavior therapy, 537-
38
Creative functioning
and masculinity-femininity,
3
Creativity
and cognitive style
study of, 80
and hypnosis
study of, 24
and hypnotic responsiveness,
27-28
and personality
and Jungian thought, 397
sex differences in, 104-6
Crime
as drug addiction indicator,
47
Criminality
genetic model of, 659

Crisis intervention
in preventing mental dis-
orders, 573, 575
Cross-cultural studies
of balance theory, 433
of mother-infant interac-
tions, 121-22
on perception of pictorial
materials, 272
of personality
proposal for, 397
in Ponzo effect, 268-69
psychopathology assess-
ments, 636-41
in reasoning, 192
Cross-national studies
diagnosis
in mental disorders, 637
differences in depression
diagnosis, 633
of sex-role socialization,
402-3
Cross-racial bias
in facial recognition, 279
Cross-sectional studies
of adult personality structure, 81-82
of student development, 351-
53
Cryptarithmetic
and problem solving processes, 177
Cultural differences
in color naming
theory of, 269-70
Cultural factors
and failure of children,
100
in family interaction, 121-
22
in prosocial behavior, 116
Culture
effects on mental disorder
assessment, 640-41
and emotional expression,
408
and personality
and psychoanalytic theory,
397
subjective
and attitude research,
416
Cyclazocine
in addiction treatment, 59
Cyclic adenosine monophosphate (cAMP)
neuronal plasticity, 381-82

D

Dating couples
and fear of success
studies of, 7
Deaf
language and cognition in
relation of, 100
language studies

verbal mediation, 194
Death
attitudes of aged toward,
83
cerebral
EEG and ER as measures
of, 246
prediction of
in adult development studies,
70-71
Deception and suspicion
as methodological issues
in attitude experiments,
420-21
Decision-making
and dissonance studies,
425
Decrement models
in adult development studies,
66-68
Defensiveness
in personnel attitudes
and motivation, 469
Depression
behavioral analysis of, 543,
625
characteristic symptoms of,
629
classification of, 632-36
neurotic-psychotic dichotomy, 633-35
numerical typologies of,
635-36
reliability of diagnosis,
632-33
criteria for diagnosis
table of, 646-47
cross-racial assessment of,
638-39
and fatigue
desensitization in treating,
528
genetic model of, 659
measurement of, 630-32
rater perception, 632
rating scales, 630-31
sleep disturbance in, 631-
32
measurement and classification of, 629-36
Desensitization
behavior therapy
role in, 527-31
compared with flooding,
35
compared with other therapies
in Di Loreto study, 511
in counselor training, 344
definition of, 527
reviews applying to, 539
Deterioration vs improvement
in various therapies, 517-
Determinism
in expectancy theory, 461-
62
Deuterium oxide
effects on biological rhythms,

419-20
Extroversion
and personality
role of biology in, 403-5
Eye contact
and personality
biological role in, 405-7
Eysenck Personality Inventory
see Tests and scales

F

Facial expressions
and emotion, 408-9
Factor-analytic studies
of adult personality in age,
81
Family
guidance
role in preventing mental
disorders, 560
interaction
in social and personality
development, 121-23
programs
preventing mental disorders,
575
of schizophrenic
role of, 659
sex-role socialization
role in, 2, 402
Family structure
in social and personality
development
birth order, 124-25
fatherless families, 123-
24
parent-child interaction,
122-23
parent-infant interaction,
121-22
Fantasy
in behavior therapy, 537
goal-directed
in hypnosis, 23
involvement
and hypnosis, 19-20
Fatherhood
and sex roles, 2
Fear of success (FOS)
in women, 6-7
Fear Survey Schedule
see Tests and scales
Federal Service Entrance
Examination
see Tests and scales
Feedback
as behavior therapy, 539
Female psychosexual development
biosocial theory of, 2
Freudian theory of
criticism of, 8-13
Field dependence
related to disengagement
and personality, 80
and Rod-and-frame test

measured by, 274-75
Finances
effect of
on college attendance, 359-
60
Flexion reflex
neurophysiology of, 368-
69
Flooding or implosion
compared with desensitization, 534-35
reviews of, 539
Focusing
role in concept attainment
and problem solving, 182-
84
Follicle stimulating hormone
(FSH)
in seasonal cycle studies,
153, 155
Free recall
in memory, 300-1, 314,
316-18
Frequency
distributions
of depressed patients, 635
modulation
auditory pathways for,
212
Freud
criticism of sexual theory,
8-13
Frigidity
treatment of, 9-10
Functional age
in adult development studies,
70

G

Galvanic skin response
age differences in, 78
in schizophrenic arousal,
605
Gambling
and aging
study of, 82
General Aptitude Test Battery
see Tests and scales
Generational change
in adult development studies,
72-73
Genetics
in aggression, 403
counseling
in mental disorder prevention, 560
effects
of mental disorders, 562
factors
in schizophrenia transmission, 601-2
and intelligence levels, 102-
3
Gestalt theory
in low pitch theory,
215

in thinking research, 173-
75
Goal setting
and management by objectives
in personnel research,
465-68
Goal theory
and expectancy theory
relationship between, 467-
68
Gonadotropins
cyclic release of
in rats, 160
Gordon Personal Profile and
Personal Inventory
see Tests and scales
Graduate Record Examination
(GRE)
see Tests and scales
Graeco-Latin Square
in problem solving, 178
Graphic skills
developmental studies of,
109
Group
pressures on employees,
475
social psychology of
and attitude research,
416
Group Therapist Orientation
Scale
see Tests and scales
Guatemalan children
aggression and popularity,
118

H

Habituation
in infants
methodological improve-
ments in, 109
in information processing,
243-44
invertebrate studies, 369-
74
behavioral, 370
locus of plastic changes,
372-73
neural circuits and escape
responses, 371-72
peripheral mechanisms,
370-71
as neurophysiological function, 368-74
in schizophrenics, 605
synaptic change during
mechanism of, 373-74
vertebrate studies, 368-69
Hallucinations
aversive conditioning in,
531
as hypnotic phenomena, 31-
32
psychotic auditory
and behavior therapy, 528

see Tests and scales
Wechsler's Adult Intelligence
    Scales
    see Tests and scales
Willoughby Personality
    Schedule
    see Tests and scales
Witkins' field dependence-
    independence
    see Tests and scales
Women
    achievement motivation in,
        1, 5-8
    emotional development in
        effect of father absence on,
        124
    fear of success in, 6-7
    feminine development

biosocial theory of, 2
hypnosis and creativity, 27
low income
    in student development
        studies, 360
personality studies of, 81
personnel testing
    and civil rights, 491-92
psychology of
    introduction, 1-2
    selected topics, 1-13
and psychotherapy, 8-13
and self-disclosure in
    therapy, 341
sex roles
    psychological studies of,
        2-5
sex-typed behavior in

encouragement of, 106
therapy substitutes for, 9
Wonderlic
    see Tests and scales
Word Fluency
    and aging studies, 73
WWII army General Classi-
    fication Test
    see Tests and scales

Z

Zambian infants
    in spatial ability studies,
        121-22
Zinacanteco Indians
    mother-infant interaction
        studies, 121

CUMULATIVE INDEXES

CONTRIBUTING AUTHORS VOLUMES 22-26

CHAPTER TITLES VOLUMES 22-26